Lecture Notes in Computer Science 8681

Commenced Publication in 1973
Founding and Former Series Editors:
Gerhard Goos, Juris Hartmanis, and Jan van Leeuwen

Stefan Wermter   Cornelius Weber
Wlodzislaw Duch   Timo Honkela
Petia Koprinkova-Hristova   Sven Magg
Günther Palm   Alessandro E.P. Villa (Eds.)

Artificial Neural Networks and Machine Learning – ICANN 2014

24th International Conference
on Artificial Neural Networks
Hamburg, Germany, September 15-19, 2014
Proceedings

 Springer

Volume Editors

Stefan Wermter
Cornelius Weber
Sven Magg
University of Hamburg, Hamburg, Germany
E-mail: {wermter, weber, magg}@informatik.uni-hamburg.de

Wlodzislaw Duch
Nicolaus Copernicus University, Torun, Poland
E-mail: wduch@is.umk.pl

Timo Honkela
University of Helsinki, Helsinki, Finland
E-mail: timo.honkela@helsinki.fi

Petia Koprinkova-Hristova
Bulgarian Academy of Sciences, Sofia, Bulgaria
E-mail: pkoprinkova@bas.bg

Günther Palm
University of Ulm, Ulm, Germany
E-mail: guenther.palm@uni-ulm.de

Alessandro E.P. Villa
University of Lausanne, Lausanne, Switzerland
E-mail: alessandro.villa@unil.ch

ISSN 0302-9743   e-ISSN 1611-3349
ISBN 978-3-319-11178-0   ISBN 978-3-319-11179-7 (eBook)
DOI 10.1007/978-3-319-11179-7
Springer Cham Heidelberg New York Dordrecht London

Library of Congress Control Number: 2014947446

LNCS Sublibrary: SL 1 – Theoretical Computer Science and General Issues

Typesetting: Camera-ready by author, data conversion by Scientific Publishing Services, Chennai, India

Printed on acid-free paper

Springer is part of Springer Science+Business Media (www.springer.com)

Preface

The International Conference on Artificial Neural Networks (ICANN) is the annual flagship conference of the European Neural Network Society (ENNS). Its wide scope in neural networks ranges from machine learning algorithms to models of real nervous systems. ICANN aims at bringing together researchers from different research fields, such as computer science, neuroscience, cognitive science, and engineering. Further aims are to address new challenges, share solutions, and discuss future research directions toward developing more intelligent artificial systems and increasing our understanding of neural and cognitive processes in the brain.

The ICANN series of conferences was initiated in 1991 and soon became the major European conference in its field, with experts coming from several continents. The 24th ICANN was held during 15–19 September 2014 at the University of Hamburg. The hosts were the University of Hamburg and its Knowledge Technology Institute (http://www.informatik.uni-hamburg.de/WTM/).

The conference attracted contributions from among the most internationally established researchers in the neural network community. The six keynote speakers in 2014 covered a wide spectrum: Christopher M. Bishop, expert in machine learning; Jun Tani, expert in recurrent neural networks; Paul F.M.J. Verschure, expert in autonomous systems; Yann LeCun, expert in neural vision; Barbara Hammer, expert in computational intelligence; Kevin N. Gurney, expert in computational neuroscience. We also acknowledge support from the Körber Foundation for a special session on "Human-Machine Interaction".

A total of 173 papers was submitted to the ICANN 2014 conference. A large Program Committee, including accepted authors from recent ICANN conferences, performed altogether 744 reviews, delivering an average of 4.3 reviews per paper. This helped to obtain a reliable evaluation score for each paper, which was computed by the Springer Online Conference Service (OCS) by av- 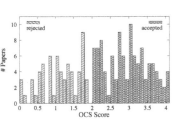 eraging the reviewers' ratings and taking into account the reviewers' confidences. Papers were sorted with respect to their scores (see figure) and 108 papers with a score of 2.0 or higher were accepted. Furthermore, the multiple professional reviews delivered valuable feedback to all authors.

The conference program featured 24 sessions, which contained 3 talks each, and which were arranged in 2 parallel tracks. There were 2 poster sessions with 33 posters and 2 live demonstrations of research results. Talks and posters were categorized into topical areas, providing the titles for the conference sessions and for the chapters in this proceedings volume. Chapters are ordered roughly in chronological order of the conference sessions.

Liangxiao Jiang   Wuhan, China
Jenia Jitsev   Köln, Germany
Vacius Jusas   Kaunas, Lithuania
Ryotaro Kamimura   Tokyo, Japan
Juho Kannala   Oulu, Finland
Iakov Karandashev   Moscow, Russia
Juha Karhunen   Espoo, Finland
Nikola Kasabov   Auckland, New Zealand
Enkelejda Kasneci   Tübingen, Germany
Gjergji Kasneci   Potsdam, Germany
Yohannes Kassahun   Bremen, Germany
Naimul Mefraz Khan   Toronto, Canada
Abbas Khosravi   Melbourne, Australia
DaeEun Kim   Seoul, South Korea
Edson Kitani   Sao Paulo, Brazil
Katsunori Kitano   Shiga, Japan
Jyri Kivinen   Edinburgh, UK
Jens Kleesiek   Heidelberg, Germany
Tibor Kmet   Nitra, Slovakia
Mario Koeppen   Kawazu, Japan
Denis Kolev   Lancaster, Russia
Stefanos Kollias   Athens, Greece
Ekaterina Komendantskaya   Dundee, UK
Peter König   Osnabrück, Germany
Petia Koprinkova-Hristova Sofia, Bulgaria
Irena Koprinska   Sydney, Australia
Pavel Kromer   Ostrava, Czech Republic
Vera Kurkova   Prague, Czech Republic
Giancarlo La Camera   New York, USA
Jong-Seok Lee   Yonsei University, South Korea
Grégoire Lefebvre   Orange Labs, France
Diego Liberati   Milano, Italy
Aristidis Likas   Ioannina, Greece
Priscila Lima   Rio de Janeiro, Brazil
Alejandro Linares-Barranco Seville, Spain
Jindong Liu   London, UK
Oliver Lomp   Bochum, Germany
Matthew Luciw   Lugano, Switzerland
Marcin Luckner   Warsaw, Poland
Jörg Lücke   Oldenburg, Germany
Teresa Ludermir   Recife, Brazil
Zhiyuan Luo   London, UK
Jesus M. Lopez   Valencia, Spain

Table of Contents

Competitive Learning and Self-Organisation

Clustering and Classification

Trees and Graphs

Human-Machine Interaction

Deep Networks

Theory

Optimization

Layered Networks

Reinforcement Learning and Action

Vision

Detection and Recognition

Invariances and Shape Recovery

Attention and Pose Estimation

Supervised Learning

Ensembles

Regression

Classification

Dynamical Models and Time Series

Neuroscience

Cortical Models

Line Attractors and Neural Fields

Spiking and Single Cell Models

Applications

Users and Social Technologies

Technical Systems

Demonstrations

Dynamic Cortex Memory:
Enhancing Recurrent Neural Networks
for Gradient-Based Sequence Learning

Sebastian Otte[1], Marcus Liwicki[2], and Andreas Zell[1]

[1] Cognitive Systems Group, University of Tübingen, Tübingen, Germany
[2] German Research Center for Artificial Intelligence, Kaiserslautern, Germany

Abstract. In this paper a novel recurrent neural network (RNN) model for gradient-based sequence learning is introduced. The presented dynamic cortex memory (DCM) is an extension of the well-known long short term memory (LSTM) model. The main innovation of the DCM is the enhancement of the inner interplay of the gates and the error carousel due to several new and trainable connections. These connections enable a direct signal transfer from the gates to one another. With this novel enhancement the networks are able to converge faster during training with back-propagation through time (BPTT) than LSTM under the same training conditions. Furthermore, DCMs yield better generalization results than LSTMs. This behaviour is shown for different supervised problem scenarios, including storing precise values, adding and learning a context-sensitive grammar.

Keywords: Dynamic Cortex Memory (DCM), Recurrent Neural Networks (RNN), Neural Networks, Long Short Term Memory (LSTM).

1 Introduction

Almost two decades ago, Hochreiter et al. [6] introduced the long short term memory (LSTM) as a novel learning architecture to solve hard long time lag problems, such as, context-sensitive grammars. The key idea of that work was the introduction of multiplicative units, which simulate a behavior of *gates* to set, read, and reset [2] the internal state of the *memory cell*. The internal state is provided by self-connected linear cell referred as *constant error carousel* (CEC). LSTM networks have been successfully applied to various tasks, such as speech [4] and handwriting recognition [5], optical character recognition [10] or OCT based lung tumor detection [9].

While in the original work some connections between the gates existed (though not in the same structured manner as proposed in this paper), they have been removed by later work because of training issues [3]. Note that earlier LSTM variants were trained using a truncated gradient, while it is more common today to use the full gradient computed with *back-propagation through time* (BPTT). However, we think that there is a great potential of speeding up the training and

S. Wermter et al. (Eds.): ICANN 2014, LNCS 8681, pp. 1–8, 2014.

improving the generalization abilities of the LSTM if specific gate connections are available.

The main contribution of this paper is to investigate the importance of the gate connections and propose a novel LSTM structure called *dynamic cortex memory* (DCM). The DCM contains connections between all the three gates and therefore enable a collaborative learning. We show that these networks are able to train faster and generalize better than traditional LSTM networks on diverse problems. Our experiments include precise value storing, adding and learning a context-sensitive grammar.

Noteworthy, the importance of the connections has also been investigated recently in [1], where the whole structure of the network evolves during training. The authors of [1] have shown that in their experiments the mutated structures work better for formal language experiments than the common LSTM structure. We have rerun the experiments and experienced similar results when using the standard training parameters (see Section 3.3). However, a simple change of the training parameters lead to significantly better generalization abilities. Thus, LSTM and DCM generalize perfectly for such problems.

2   Dynamic Cortex Memory

During LSTM training the gates learn to handle the inner state, i.e, to write, forget, and read it. Hereby, the gates may — at least partially — learn redundant information. This might lead to long training times as similar behavior should be learned at several gates.

The main motivation of our work is the idea enabling the gates to share information, such that they can learn commonly important patterns collectively and, due to the relief of learning effort, particularly important patterns earlier and, perhaps, even better. The DCM model bases on LSTM and establishes an inter gate communication infrastructure by adding new and trainable connections. In particular, a circular connection pattern connecting the gates with one another (which we call *cortex*) and a self recurrent connection for each of the gates (that can be seen as a very local *gate state*) are added. An illustration of our DCM model is presented in Fig. 1.

2.1   Forward Pass

In the following the equations for the forward pass of a single DCM block D are given. D may contain multiple CECs indexed by c. We assume that the neural network consists of an input layer I, a recurrent hidden layer H (containing D), and an output layer K. All layers are fully connected. Further, v_j denotes the input, φ_j the activation function and x_j the activation of a unit j. f_c gives the input squashing function and g_c the output squashing function of a particular inner cell c. Note that the order of the equations given of the forward pass, as well as of the backward pass in the next section is essential to correctly compute the activations and the gradient respectively. Let all x_j^t and s_c^t at time $t = 0$ be defined as 0.

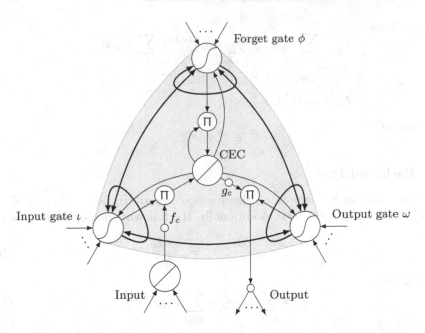

Fig. 1. Illustration of the Dynamic Cortex Memory. Like in the LSTM model one or more CECs are surrounded by three gating neurons. Each gate is linked with each other gate in both directions (cortex) and has a self-recurrent connection (gate state).

Input Gate:

$$v_\iota^t = \sum_{i \in I} w_{i\iota} x_i^t + \sum_{h \in H} w_{h\iota} x_h^{t-1} + \sum_{c \in D} w_{c\iota} s_c^{t-1}$$
$$+ w_{\iota\iota} x_\iota^{t-1} + w_{\phi\iota} x_\phi^{t-1} + w_{\omega\iota} x_\omega^{t-1} \tag{1}$$
$$x_\iota^t = \varphi_\iota(v_\iota^t) \tag{2}$$

Forget Gate:

$$v_\phi^t = \sum_{i \in I} w_{i\phi} x_i^t + \sum_{h \in H} w_{h\phi} x_h^{t-1} + \sum_{c \in D} w_{c\phi} s_c^{t-1}$$
$$+ w_{\iota\phi} x_\iota^t + w_{\phi\phi} x_\phi^{t-1} + w_{\omega\phi} x_\omega^{t-1} \tag{3}$$
$$x_\phi^t = \varphi_\phi(v_\phi^t) \tag{4}$$

Cell Input:

$$v_c^t = \sum_{i \in I} w_{ic} x_i^t + \sum_{h \in H} w_{hc} x_h^{t-1} \tag{5}$$

Cell State:

$$s_c^t = x_\iota^t f_c(v_c^t) + x_\phi^t s_c^{t-1} \tag{6}$$

Output Gates:

$$v_\omega^t = \sum_{i \in I} w_{i\omega} x_i^t + \sum_{h \in H} w_{h\omega} x_h^{t-1} + \sum_{c \in D} w_{c\omega} s_c^{t-1}$$

$$+ w_{\iota\omega} x_\iota^t + w_{\phi\omega} x_\phi^t + w_{\omega\omega} x_\omega^{t-1} \tag{7}$$

$$x_\omega^t = \varphi_\omega(v_\omega^t) \tag{8}$$

Cell Output:

$$x_c^t = x_\omega^t g_c(s_c^t) \tag{9}$$

2.2 Backward Pass

Here the equation for computing the gradient are given. Let further all δ_j^t, ϵ_c^t and ζ_c^t at time $t = T + 1$ be 0. Additionally, the following helper definitions are used.

$$\epsilon_c^t =_{\text{def}} \frac{\partial E}{\partial x_c^t}, \quad \zeta_c^t =_{\text{def}} \frac{\partial E}{\partial s_c^t}. \tag{10}$$

Cell Output:

$$\epsilon_c^t = \sum_{k \in K} w_{ck} \delta_k^t + \sum_{h \in H} w_{ch} \delta_h^{t+1} \tag{11}$$

Output Gate:

$$\delta_\omega^t = \varphi_\omega'(v_\omega^t) \left[\sum_{c \in D} \sigma_c(s_c^t) \epsilon_c^t + w_{\omega\iota} \delta_\iota^{t+1} + w_{\omega\phi} \delta_\phi^{t+1} + w_{\omega\omega} \delta_\omega^{t+1} \right] \tag{12}$$

Cell State:

$$\zeta_c^t = x_\omega^t g_c'(s_c^t) \epsilon_c^t + x_\phi^{t+1} \zeta_c^{t+1} + w_{c\iota} \delta_\iota^{t+1} + w_{c\phi} \delta_\phi^{t+1} + w_{c\omega} \delta_\omega^t \tag{13}$$

Cell Input:

$$\delta_c^t = x_\iota^t f_c'(v_c^t) \zeta_c^t \tag{14}$$

Forget Gate:

$$\delta_\phi^t = \varphi_\phi'(v_\phi^t) \left[\sum_{c \in D} s_c^{t-1} \zeta_c^t + w_{\phi\iota} \delta_\iota^{t+1} + w_{\phi\phi} \delta_\phi^{t+1} + w_{\phi\omega} \delta_\omega^t \right] \tag{15}$$

Input Gate:

$$\delta_\iota^t = \varphi_\iota'(v_\iota^t) \left[\sum_{c \in D} \varphi_c(v_c^t) \zeta_c^t + w_{\iota\iota} \delta_\iota^{t+1} + w_{\iota\phi} \delta_\phi^t + w_{\iota\omega} \delta_\omega^t \right] \tag{16}$$

3   Experiments

In this section DCMs are compared with LSTMs on three different sequential problems with long term dependencies. In order to provide a fair comparison our general proceeding for the experiments was to first look for a training configuration that works well for the LSTM and then use exactly the same configuration for the DCM.

3.1   Storing

In this relatively simple experiment the task is just to learn memorizing a value at a marked position within a sequence and keep the value until the end of the sequence. Note, that just keeping a constant value for several time steps ($>$ 10) and reproducing it precisely afterwards is difficult for classical RNNs.

A training sample is generated as follows. Given a sequence over $\mathbb{R}^2$ of length $T/2 + rand(T/2)$, whereby the components of a vector at a certain time step t are denoted with u_1^t and u_2^t. All u_1^t are randomly chosen from $[0, 1]$. One sequence index t' is randomly selected and the value of $u_2^{t'}$ is set to 1, while all other u_2^t with $t \neq t'$ are 0. The target value of the sequence is then $u_1^{t'}$.

The tested architectures are in particular a standard LSTM, a DCM, a DCM with no cortex and a DCM with no gate state. Each consists of two input units, only one self-recurrent hidden block and one non-linear output unit. The training was performed with gradient descent and momentum term, whereby the gradient was computed with BPTT using 6,000 training samples generated with $T = 60$ and 200 epochs.

Fig. 2 depicts the typical training behavior of all four architectures for the given learning problem. The corresponding generalization results are given in Table 1. By adding the gate states (DCM with no cortex) the network behaves turbulent in the very early phase of the training. But afterwards, it converges slightly faster than the LSTM. However, despite the lower final training error,

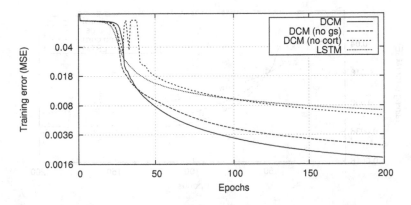

Fig. 2. Training convergence of different memory cell architectures for storing

Table 1. Generalization results for the storing experiment

Network	Training error	Generalization results		
		$T = 60$	$T = 100$	$T = 1,000$
LSTM	0.007	99.3 %	96.4 %	67.4 %
DCM (no cort)	0.006	99.6 %	95.6 %	60.0 %
DCM (no gs)	0.003	100 %	100 %	72 %
DCM	0.002	100 %	100 %	72.2 %

the generalization for $T = 100$ and $T = 1,000$ is inferior. The DCM with no gate states performs significantly better here. On the one hand, the error converges much faster, which results in a clearly lower final error. On the other hand, the generalization is superior. Finally, the proposed DCM performs best. An interesting aspect here is, that there is apparently a synergy effect between both types of new connections.

3.2 Adding

This experiment is similar to the previous one but more difficult. Each RNN has to learn not only to store one value, but to add two values and to store the result. The presented formulation is a slightly modified variant of that in [7]. Samples are also sequences over $\mathbb{R}^2$ of length $T/2 + rand(T/2)$ with all u_1^t randomly chosen from $[0, 1]$. Two indices are randomly selected, t_1 within the first 10 time steps and t_2 within the first $T/2$ time steps. $u_2^{t_1}$ and $u_2^{t_2}$ are set to 1, all other are 0. The target value of the sequence is then $(u_1^{t_1} + u_1^{t_2})/2$.

The convergence (see Fig. 3) and the generalization results (see Tab. 2) provide a very similar situation as in the previous experiment. It should be mentioned that the improvement is not caused by the higher general neural capacity of the DCM. We have performed experiments with LSTM having more blocks which did not lead to this improvement, neither for storing nor for adding.

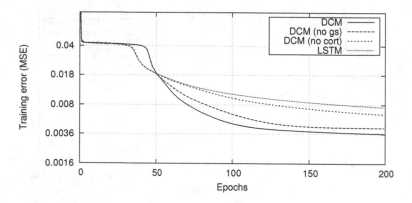

Fig. 3. Training convergence of different memory cell architectures for adding

Table 2. Generalization results for the adding experiment

Network	Training error	Generalization results		
		$T = 60$	$T = 100$	$T = 1000$
LSTM	0.008	96.6 %	96.6 %	52.2 %
DCM (no cort)	0.006	97.6 %	97.5 %	22.0 %
DCM (no gs)	0.004	99.2 %	99.7 %	63.1 %
DCM	0.003	98.9 %	99.7 %	80.0 %

3.3   Context Sensitive Language

Often performed benchmarks for LSTMs are context-free or context-sensitive grammars, because they are usually hard to be learned by classical RNNs. In this prediction experiment the context-sensitive language $\{a^n b^n c^n\}$ is learned. Hereby, the training setup is similar to that in [1]. We trained on samples with only $n \in \{0, \ldots, 5\}$, with a learning rate of 0.01 and momentum of 0.99. Two architectures were tested: an LSTM and a DCM, both with 4 input units, 3 hidden blocks and 4 non-linear output units. A sample ($n = 3$) looks as follows.

$$
\begin{array}{lcccccccccc}
\text{Input:} & S & a & a & a & b & b & b & c & c & c \\
\text{Target:} & \#, a & a, b & a, b & a, b & b & b & c & c & c & \#
\end{array}
$$

In contrast to the first two experiments, the lowest final error does not necessarily lead to the best generalization but to over-fitting. In fact, the entire training procedure is less stable and less reproducible, which might be reinforced due to the high learning rate. The results presented in Fig. 4 are averaged over 10 runs in which the error really converged (every 5-10th run led to convergence, whereas the DCM tended to converge more often).

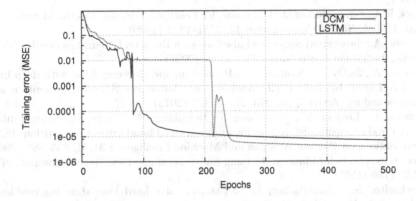

Fig. 4. Training convergence of learning the language $\{a^n b^n c^n\}$

Both architectures are enabled to process samples with $n > 1,000,000$ (a sequences length of more than $3,000,000$) or even bigger n correctly. We would like to emphasize that for this particular problem with such small n for training, a maximum value of $n = 100$ for testing was reported in the literature [1]. Furthermore, LSTM were only known being able to handle sequences with roughly $10,000$ time steps [3]. Noteworthy, the better generalization behavior could also be an effect of the implementation (we used the JANNLab framework [8], see http://www.jannlab.de). On average, the LSTM achieved correct predictions for $n = 213,004$, whereas the DCM could generalize up to $n = 314,580$.

4   Conclusion

In this work the dynamic cortex memory (DCM), which is an extension of the long short term memory (LSTM), was initially presented. Due to several novel trainable connections, namely connections from each gate to each other gate (in both directions) and a self-recurrent connection for each gate, the gates are enabled to share information directly and, thus, learn collectively. This results in a better convergence as well as in better generalization behavior for different sequence learning problems. An interesting observation was also, that these two additional connection schemes provide a synergy effect. Besides, we showed that DCMs just as LSTMs are able to generalize correctly over millions of time steps, which is, as far as we know, for the first time reported in the literature.

Next, we plan to investigate the DCM in more detail and study its performance on some real-world problems.

References

1. Bayer, J., Wierstra, D., Togelius, J., Schmidhuber, J.: Evolving memory cell structures for sequence learning. In: Alippi, C., Polycarpou, M., Panayiotou, C., Ellinas, G. (eds.) ICANN 2009, Part II. LNCS, vol. 5769, pp. 755–764. Springer, Heidelberg (2009)
2. Gers, F.A., Schmidhuber, J., Cummins, F.: Learning to forget: Continual prediction with LSTM. Neural Computation 12, 2451–2471 (1999)
3. Graves, A.: Supervised Sequence Labelling with Recurrent Neural Networks. Ph.D. thesis, Technische Universitaet Muenchen (2008)
4. Graves, A., Jaitly, N., Mohamed, A.R.: Hybrid speech recognition with deep bidirectional lstm. In: 2013 IEEE Workshop on Automatic Speech Recognition and Understanding (ASRU), pp. 273–278. IEEE (2013)
5. Graves, A., Liwicki, M., Fernández, S., Bertolami, R., Bunke, H., Schmidhuber, J.: A novel connectionist system for unconstrained handwriting recognition. IEEE Transactions on Pattern Analysis and Machine Intelligence 31(5), 855–868 (2009)
6. Hochreiter, S., Schmidhuber, J.: Long Short-Term memory. Neural Comput. 9(8), 1735–1780 (1997)
7. Hochreiter, S., Schmidhuber, J.: LSTM can solve hard long time lag problems. Advances in Neural Information Processing Systems 9, 473–479 (1997)
8. Otte, S., Krechel, D., Liwicki, M.: JANNLab neural network framework for java. In: MLDM 2013, pp. 39–46. Ibai-Publishing, New York (2013)
9. Otte, S., Otte, C., Schlaefer, A., Wittig, L., Hüttmann, G., Drömann, D., Zell, A.: A-Scan based lung tumor tissue classification with bidirectional long short term memory networks. In: 2013 IEEE International Workshop on Machine Learning for Signal Processing, MLSP (2013)
10. Ul-Hasan, A., Breuel, T.M.: Can we build language-independent OCR using LSTM networks? In: Proceedings of the 4th International Workshop on Multilingual OCR, p. 9. ACM (2013)

Learning and Recognition of Multiple Fluctuating Temporal Patterns Using S-CTRNN

Shingo Murata[1], Hiroaki Arie[2], Tetsuya Ogata[2],
Jun Tani[3], and Shigeki Sugano[1]

[1] Department of Modern Mechanical Engineering,
Waseda University, Tokyo, Japan
[2] Department of Intermedia Art and Science,
Waseda University, Tokyo, Japan
[3] Department of Electrical Engineering,
Korea Advanced Institute of Science and Technology,
Daejeon, Republic of Korea

Abstract. In the present study, we demonstrate the learning and recognition capabilities of our recently proposed recurrent neural network (RNN) model called stochastic continuous-time RNN (S-CTRNN). S-CTRNN can learn to predict not only the mean but also the variance of the next state of the learning targets. The network parameters consisting of weights, biases, and initial states of context neurons are optimized through maximum likelihood estimation (MLE) using the gradient descent method. First, we clarify the essential difference between the learning capabilities of conventional CTRNN and S-CTRNN by analyzing the results of a numerical experiment in which multiple fluctuating temporal patterns were used as training data, where the variance of the Gaussian noise varied among the patterns. Furthermore, we also show that the trained S-CTRNN can recognize given fluctuating patterns by inferring the initial states that can reproduce the patterns through the same MLE scheme as that used for network training.

Keywords: recurrent neural network, S-CTRNN, variance estimation.

1 Introduction

Recurrent neural networks (RNNs) are known to be powerful tools for learning to predict various types of temporal sequences. RNN-based models have been applied, for example, in the learning of symbolic sequences [1–3], continuous spatiotemporal patterns [4–6], and perceptual sequences of robots [7–9]. However, one problem with RNN-based models is their inability to extract stochastic properties hidden in fluctuating temporal sequences in a set of training data because of the network characteristics of deterministic prediction. Another problem with RNN-based models is that if each training pattern includes noise with a different variance, effective prediction learning cannot be implemented. This can be a substantial problem because the learning of fluctuating patterns with larger

S. Wermter et al. (Eds.): ICANN 2014, LNCS 8681, pp. 9–16, 2014.

noise variance can corrupt the learning of patterns with smaller noise variance, which can make the entire learning process unstable. In order to avoid such situations, prediction errors should be uniformly scaled among training patterns before back-propagation through time (BPTT) [10] in the prediction learning process.

Recently, Namikawa and colleagues [11,12] proposed a novel continuous-time RNN (CTRNN) called stochastic CTRNN (S-CTRNN) that has the ability to predict not only the mean but also the variance of the next state of the learning targets. The predicted variance works as an inverse weighting factor for the prediction error because the error is divided by the variance in the likelihood function used for prediction learning. Furthermore, Murata et al. [12] demonstrated that S-CTRNN can learn to correctly predict time-varying mean and variance values through maximum likelihood estimation (MLE) using the gradient descent method. They also demonstrated an S-CTRNN that was able to learn to reproduce 12 fluctuating Lissajous curves with multiple constant values for the noise variance.

In the present study, first we demonstrate the learning results for a conventional CTRNN in which the abovementioned 12 fluctuating Lissajous curves were reused as training data. Note that the learning results for an S-CTRNN have already been published in [12]. This study revisits the results for S-CTRNN and compares them with the learning results for CTRNN in order to clarify the essential differences in learning capabilities between conventional CTRNN and S-CTRNN. In addition, the present paper presents the results of an additional experiment on the recognition of fluctuating temporal patterns using the trained S-CTRNN in order to demonstrate the recognition capabilities of the network, and provides an analysis of a self-organized initial state space of the S-CTRNN that seems to contribute to both its learning and recognition capabilities.

2   Neural Network Model

In this section, we briefly introduce the generation, training, and recognition methods for S-CTRNN. Please refer to [12] for details.

2.1   Generation Method

S-CTRNN consists of input, context, output, and variance layers. The internal state of the i-th neuron at time step $1 \leq t$ ($u_{t,i}$) for each layer, with the exception of the input layer, is updated in accordance with

$$
u_{t,i} = \begin{cases} \left(1 - \dfrac{1}{\tau_i}\right) u_{t-1,i} + \dfrac{1}{\tau_i} \left(\displaystyle\sum_{j \in I_I} w_{ij} x_{t,j} + \sum_{j \in I_C} w_{ij} c_{t-1,j} + b_i \right) & (i \in I_C), \\ \displaystyle\sum_{j \in I_C} w_{ij} c_{t,j} + b_i \quad (i \in I_O \cup I_V), \end{cases}
$$

$$(1)$$

where I_I, I_C, I_O, and I_V are the neuron index sets for the input, context, output, and variance layers, respectively; τ_i is the time constant of the i-th context neuron; $w_{i,j}$ is the weight of the connection from the j-th to the i-th neuron; $c_{t,j}$ is the activation value of the j-th context neuron at time step t; $x_{t,j}$ is the j-th input at time step t; and b_i is the bias of the i-th neuron. In network training, externally provided values are used as the input state. This generation method is known as open-loop generation. The generation method in which the network outputs, with added Gaussian noise corresponding to the predicted variance, are fed into the input-layer is known as closed-loop generation.

The activation values of a context neuron ($c_{t,i}$), an output neuron ($y_{t,i}$), and a variance neuron ($v_{t,i}$) are calculated by using the following respective activation functions:

$$c_{t,i} = \tanh(u_{t,i}) \qquad (i \in I_C), \qquad (2)$$

$$y_{t,i} = \tanh(u_{t,i}) \qquad (i \in I_O), \qquad (3)$$

$$v_{t,i} = \exp(u_{t,i}) \qquad (i \in I_V). \qquad (4)$$

2.2 Training Method

S-CTRNN is trained through MLE using the gradient descent method. Let $X_I = (\boldsymbol{x}_t)_{t=1}^T$ be a fluctuating input sequence and $\hat{Y}_O = (\hat{\boldsymbol{y}}_t)_{t=1}^T$ be a fluctuating ideal output (training) sequence, where T is the length of the sequence. Here, if the dimensions of the input and output layers are the same, the ideal value $\hat{\boldsymbol{y}}_t$ is equal to the next input value $\boldsymbol{x}_{t+1}$. The network training is defined as the problem to optimize, given a data set $D = (X_I, \hat{Y}_O)$, the network parameters $\boldsymbol{\theta}$ consisting of weights $\boldsymbol{w}$, biases $\boldsymbol{b}$, and an initial internal state of the context neurons $\boldsymbol{u}_0$. When $(\boldsymbol{x}_{t'})_{t'=1}^t$ is given, the probability density for the i-th ideal value $\hat{y}_{t,i}$ at time step t in the training sequence is defined by

$$p(\hat{y}_{t,i} \mid (\boldsymbol{x}_{t'})_{t'=1}^t, \boldsymbol{\theta}) = \frac{1}{\sqrt{2\pi v_{t,i}}} \exp\left(-\frac{(y_{t,i} - \hat{y}_{t,i})^2}{2v_{t,i}}\right), \qquad (5)$$

where $y_{t,i}$ and $v_{t,i}$ are the mean (output) and the variance predicted by the network. This equation is derived with the assumption that the observable fluctuating sequence is embedded into additive Gaussian noise. The likelihood function parameterized by $\boldsymbol{\theta}$, which is maximized using the gradient descent method with a momentum term, can be obtained by multiplying Eq. (5) for each dimension and each time step of the training sequence. Note that when we fix the value of the variance, e.g., $v_{t,i} = 1$, the training of an S-CTRNN with MLE is equivalent or reduced to the training of a CTRNN with minimum mean square error estimation.

If multiple sequences are given as a set of training data, these sequences can be embedded into the initial state space of the context neurons by optimizing the respective initial states for the corresponding sequences. The other parameters, such as the weights and the biases, are common for all sequences. The likelihood function for all sequences can be obtained by multiplying the likelihood functions for all sequences. After optimization of the network parameters θ, the network can autonomously reproduce multiple trained fluctuating temporal sequences in the form of mean and variance values with the closed-loop generation method by setting the corresponding initial states of the context neurons.

2.3   Recognition Method

The recognition of given sequences can be defined as the process of inferring the initial states that can reproduce the sequences with closed-loop generation. Although all parameters (including the weights and biases, which are common for all sequences, and the initial states, which are different for each sequence) are optimized during the training process, only the initial states are optimized during the recognition process.

3   Numerical Experiment

3.1   Training Sequences

The task for the CTRNN and the S-CTRNN was learning to predict the temporal developments of 12 fluctuating two-dimensional Lissajous curves with a sequence length $T = 1000$. These fluctuating curves were obtained by adding Gaussian noise $\epsilon(\{\hat{\sigma}_i^{(s)}\}^2)$ with variance $\{\hat{\sigma}_i^{(s)}\}^2$ to each clean Lissajous curve, where $i \in \{1, 2\}$ represents the axis of two-dimensional training data space. In the present study, the value of the variance $\{\hat{\sigma}_i^{(s)}\}^2$ corresponded to the s-th sequence $\{\hat{\sigma}_1^{(s)} = \hat{\sigma}_2^{(s)} = 0.01 \ (s \in \{1, 5, 9\}), \ 0.03 \ (s \in \{2, 6, 10\}), \ 0.05 \ (s \in \{3, 7, 11\}), \ 0.07 \ (s \in \{4, 8, 12\})\}$. Figure 1(a) shows the training data in two-dimensional space. Details about the data are provided in [12].

3.2   Network Training

We trained both the CTRNN and the S-CTRNN with the same parameter setting for 500,000 training steps to embed all 12 patterns as multiple attractors into the networks, where the number and time constant of context neurons were $N_C = 60$ and $\tau = 2$, respectively. Through the training process, the network parameters (weights, biases, and initial states of the context neurons) were optimized by the MLE scheme introduced above. As mentioned in Sec. 2.2, to train the CTRNN, we set the variance of an S-CTRNN to $v_{t,i} = 1$, which transformed it into a CTRNN. After training, we evaluated whether the trained networks were able to reproduce all the trained patterns by using the respective optimized initial state for each network.

3.3   Generation Results

Figure 1 shows the 12 training patterns $(\hat{y}_{t,1}^{(s)}, \hat{y}_{t,2}^{(s)})$ and the corresponding prediction results $(y_{t,1}^{(s)}, y_{t,2}^{(s)})$ generated by the CTRNN and by the S-CTRNN, where

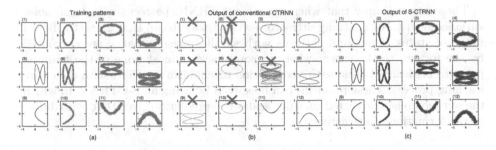

Fig. 1. Phase plots of (a) training patterns, (b) output generated by the CTRNN, and (c) output generated by the S-CTRNN. In each row in (a), the noise variance increases from left to right ($\{\hat{\sigma}^{(s)}\}^2 = 0.0001, 0.0009, 0.0025, 0.0049$). The red crosses in (b) mark cases of failure.

Gaussian noise with the variance predicted by the network was added to the output generated by the S-CTRNN.

Upon comparison of the phase plots of the training patterns in Fig. 1(a) and the corresponding outputs of the conventional CTRNN in Fig. 1(b), it is clear that the CTRNN failed to generate some patterns whose noise variance was small. For example, we can observe the three patterns with the smallest noise variance (1, 5, 9) are corrupted by the three patterns with the largest noise variance (4, 12, 8). The network also failed to reproduce the stochastic properties of the training patterns. In contrast, the S-CTRNN correctly reproduces the fluctuating Lissajous curves (Fig. 1(c)).

Figure 2 shows the results for other CTRNNs in which different randomly chosen values were used for parameter initialization before network training. Figure 2 shows three different cases of learning failure. In (a), patterns with smaller noise variance were corrupted by patterns with larger noise variance, in the same manner as in Fig. 1(b). In (b), untrained attractors appeared (such as (1, 2)), and in (c), almost none of the training patterns were learned.

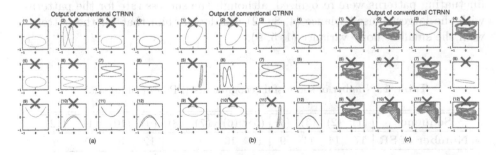

Fig. 2. Phase plots of output generated by CTRNNs initialized with different random values. The format of each panel is the same as that of Fig. 1(b).

These results imply that when we use a CTRNN, patterns with large noise variance tend to form strong attractors with a wide basin that attract a board range of states. Therefore, patterns with smaller noise variance are corrupted by the former, to the extent where in some cases almost none of the training patterns are learned because this corruption mechanism interferes with the entire learning process. These problems can be solved by using an S-CTRNN, in which the autonomously predicted variance scales the prediction error that contributes to the formation of attractors.

3.4   Recognition Results

In a recognition experiment, we evaluated whether the trained S-CTRNN was able to infer the initial states of the context neurons given multiple temporal patterns. Although all parameters (including the weights, biases, and initial states) were updated 500,000 times during network training, the initial states were updated only 300 times, with the remaining parameters fixed during the recognition process. In the experiment, the search for initial states using the gradient descent method sometimes falls to a local minimum. Therefore, we tested 20 different sets of randomly chosen values for the initial state for each sequence.

In order to evaluate the recognition error, we computed the following mean square error (MSE) for each sequence s:

$$E^{(s)} = \frac{1}{2Td} \sum_{t=1}^{T} \sum_{i=1}^{d} (y_{t,i}^{(s)} - \hat{y}_{t,i}^{(s)})^2, \tag{6}$$

where $y_{t,i}^{(s)}$ and $\hat{y}_{t,i}^{(s)}$ are the output value of the network and the ideal value in the training data corresponding to the s-th sequence, respectively. $T = 1000$ and $d = 2$ are the length and dimension of each sequence, respectively. As a criterion for the success or failure of recognition, we set the upper bound of MSE for successful recognition to $(3\hat{\sigma}^{(s)})^2/2$ with respect to the noise variance of each trained pattern.

Table 1 shows the total number of successful recognitions out of 20 trials. All fluctuating patterns were recognized, although the success rate for the patterns with the largest noise variance (4, 8, 12) was lower than that for the patterns with the smallest noise variance (1, 5, 9).

Table 1. Number of successful recognitions (SR) out of 20 trials

Sequence	(1)	(2)	(3)	(4)	(5)	(6)	(7)	(8)	(9)	(10)	(11)	(12)
Number of SR	17	14	11	9	11	16	9	1	12	16	9	9

3.5   Initial State Space Analysis

We visualized the 60-dimensional initial state space of the context neurons, which was self-organized during the learning process, by applying principal component analysis (PCA) in the space. Figure 3 shows the compressed initial state space defined by the first and second principal components, where we can see four clusters based on the noise variance of the training patterns. This analysis result implies that the self-organized initial state space, which represents the variance prediction mechanism, is essential to the ability of the S-CTRNN to both learn and recognize multiple fluctuating temporal patterns.

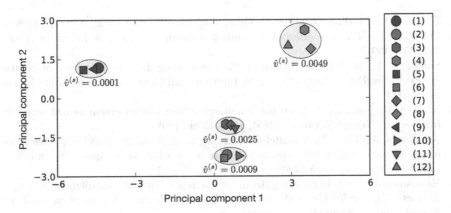

Fig. 3. Initial state space of the context neurons. The dimensionality of the space was reduced from 60 to 2 by PCA. Four clusters based on the noise variance of the training patterns can be observed.

4   Summary and Conclusion

In this study, we clarified the difference in learning capabilities between the conventional CTRNN and the recently proposed S-CTRNN. We demonstrated that the CTRNN was unable to learn to generate fluctuating Lissajous curves with different magnitudes of noise variance because the learning of patterns with larger noise variance interfered with the learning of patterns with smaller noise variance. In contrast, the S-CTRNN was able to reproduce learned patterns as well as to recognize given fluctuating patterns by inferring the initial states of the context neurons. Analyzing the initial state space revealed isolated clusters based on the noise variance of the training patterns. The variance prediction mechanism represented in the initial state space enabled the learning, reproduction, and recognition of multiple fluctuating temporal patterns. Future work will focus on more practical applications, where S-CTRNNs will be applied to human motion prediction and recognition tasks or multiple-action sequence learning tasks for robots.

Acknowledgement. This work was supported in part by the "Information Environment and Humans," JST PRESTO; Grant-in-Aid for Scientific Research on Innovative Areas "Constructive Developmental Science" (24119003), MEXT; Grant for Excellent Graduate Schools, MEXT; Grant-in-Aid for Scientific Research (S) (25220005), JSPS; "Fundamental Study for Intelligent Machine to Coexist with Nature," Research Institute for Science and Engineering, Waseda University, Japan; and the Industrial Strategic Technology Development Program, MKE, Korea (10044009).

References

1. Elman, J.L.: Finding Structure in Time. Cognitive Science 14(2), 179–211 (1990)
2. Pollack, J.B.: The induction of dynamical recognizers. Machine Learning 7(2-3), 227–252 (1991)
3. Sutskever, I., Martens, J., Hinton, G.E.: Generating Text with Recurrent Neural Networks. In: Proceedings of the 28th International Conference on Machine Learning (2011)
4. Kimura, M., Nakano, R.: Learning dynamical systems by recurrent neural networks from orbits. Neural Networks 11(9), 1589–1599 (1998)
5. Namikawa, J., Tani, J.: A model for learning to segment temporal sequences, utilizing a mixture of RNN experts together with adaptive variance. Neural Networks 21(10), 1466–1475 (2008)
6. Namikawa, J., Tani, J.: Building Recurrent Neural Networks to Implement Multiple Attractor Dynamics Using the Gradient Descent Method. Advances in Artificial Neural Systems 2009(14), 1–11 (2009)
7. Tani, J.: Model-based learning for mobile robot navigation from the dynamical systems perspective. IEEE Transactions on Systems, Man, and Cybernetics 26(3), 421–436 (1996)
8. Ito, M., Noda, K., Hoshino, Y., Tani, J.: Dynamic and interactive generation of object handling behaviors by a small humanoid robot using a dynamic neural network model. Neural Networks 19(3), 323–337 (2006)
9. Yamashita, Y., Tani, J.: Emergence of functional hierarchy in a multiple timescale neural network model: A humanoid robot experiment. PLoS Computational Biology 4(11), e1000220(2008)
10. Rumelhart, D.E., Hinton, G.E., Williams, R.J.: Learning Internal Representations by Error Propagation. In: Rumelhart, D.E., McClelland, D. (eds.) Parallel Distributed Processing: Explorations in the Microstructure of Cognition, pp. 318–362. MIT Press, Cambridge (1986)
11. Namikawa, J., Nishimoto, R., Arie, H., Tani, J.: Synthetic approach to understanding meta-level cognition of predictability in generating cooperative behavior. In: Advances in Cognitive Neurodynamics (III) Proceedings of the Third International Conference on Cognitive Neurodynamics 2011 (2013)
12. Murata, S., Namikawa, J., Arie, H., Sugano, S., Tani, J.: Learning to Reproduce Fluctuating Time Series by Inferring Their Time-Dependent Stochastic Properties: Application in Robot Learning Via Tutoring. IEEE Transactions on Autonomous Mental Development 5(4), 298–310 (2013)

Regularized Recurrent Neural Networks for Data Efficient Dual-Task Learning

Sigurd Spieckermann[1,2], Siegmund Düll[1,3],
Steffen Udluft[1], and Thomas Runkler[1,2]

[1] Siemens Corporate Technology, Learning Systems
Otto-Hahn-Ring 6 – 81739 Munich, Germany
[2] Technical University of Munich, Department of Informatics
Boltzmannstr. 3 – 85748 Garching, Germany
[3] Berlin University of Technology, Machine Learning
Franklinstr. 28-29 – 10587 Berlin, Germany

Abstract. We introduce a regularization technique to improve system identification for dual-task learning with recurrent neural networks. In particular, the method is introduced using the Factored Tensor Recurrent Neural Networks first presented in [1]. Our goal is to identify a dynamical system with few available observations by augmenting them with data from a sufficiently observed similar system. In our previous work, we discovered that the model accuracy degrades whenever little data of the system of interest is available. The presented regularization term in this work allows to significantly reduce the model error thereby improving the exploitation of knowledge of the well observed system. This scenario is crucial in many real world applications, where data efficiency plays an important role. We motivate the problem setting and our regularized dual-task learning approach by industrial use cases, e.g. gas or wind turbine modeling for optimization and monitoring. Then, we formalize the problem and describe our regularization term by which the learning objective of the Factored Tensor Recurrent Neural Network is extended. Finally, we demonstrate its effectiveness on the cart-pole and mountain car benchmarks.

Keywords: multi-task learning, recurrent neural networks, factored tensor recurrent neural networks, system identification, dynamical systems, regularization.

1 Introduction

Consider a complex technical system, e.g. a gas or wind turbine, for which a model of the dynamics is needed to perform tasks such as condition monitoring or model based control [2]. Analytical models explicitly incorporate the technical understanding of domain experts about the system of interest, but they may be expensive to build and may not be able to capture the full complexity of a particular real system. Data driven methods, such as recurrent neural networks [3],

S. Wermter et al. (Eds.): ICANN 2014, LNCS 8681, pp. 17–24, 2014.

alleviate some of the difficulties with analytical models by learning the actual dynamics of a system from observations [4], but this approach often requires large amounts of data which is a scarce resource in many real-world applications. For instance, the dynamics of an industrial plant may change due to maintenance or upgrades invalidating the previously optimized model. However, an accurate model is desired as soon as possible after recommissioning the plant and only few data are available after the modifications. Hence, data efficient procedures utilizing all available data are crucial. The fact that the overall plant is still the same, and thus no fundamental change of the general structure and complexity of the dynamics is expected, suggests to exploit information collected prior to modifications.

In this paper, we extend our work presented in [1] in which we used Factored Tensor Recurrent Neural Networks (FTRNN) in a dual-task learning setting to identify a system with few available observations (the system of interest) by augmenting the data with plenty observations from a similar system (the reference system). The FTRNN model consists of cross-system and system specific parameters which are disentangled by discriminating the two systems. Thus, the joint model shares knowledge among the systems while yet being able to identify the peculiarities of each individual one. We showed its effectiveness on the cart-pole benchmark observing superior performance compared to other considered methods for most data ratios. However, the performance degraded for the largest data ratio which we attributed to overfitting and incomplete information about the system of interest. Therefore, we now propose a regularization term to penalize dissimilarities between the system specific parameters of the system of interest and the reference system and demonstrate its effectiveness on the cart-pole and mountain car benchmarks.

2   Problem Definition

Consider a set $I := \{1, 2\}$ of similar fully observable deterministic dynamical systems. Let S denote the state space, A the action space, and $f \colon I \times S \times A \to S$ the state transition function which describes the evolution of the states for subsequent observations in fixed time intervals τ. Then, the dynamical system is defined by the tuple (S, A, f).

Let $D = \bigcup_{i \in I} D_i$ denote a data set consisting of $|D|$ observations $(i, s, a, s') \in D_i$ drawn at random from a probability distribution $\mathcal{D}$. Each observation describes the transition from state $s \in S$ to state $s' \in S$ of system $i \in I$ in consequence of the momentum and the effect of action $a \in A$.

Let $H \subseteq \{h \mid h \colon I \times S \times A \to S\}$ denote the space of hypotheses, which approximate the state transition function f. Within this space, $h^* \in H$ is the best approximation of f, i.e. the optimal hypothesis of f. The prediction error of a hypothesis between a predicted successor state $\hat{s}' = h(i, s, a)$ and the true successor state s' is expressed by an error metric $\mathcal{L} \colon S \times S \to \mathbb{R}_{\geq 0}$. The expectation of this error metric, i.e. $\varepsilon(h) := \mathbb{E}_{(i,s,a,s') \sim \mathcal{D}}[\mathcal{L}(h(i, s, a), s')]$ where $\mathbb{E}$ denotes the expectation operator, is minimized by the optimal hypothesis h^*, hence, $h^* =$

$\arg\min_h \varepsilon(h)$. The data distribution $\mathcal{D}$ is generally unknown though. Therefore, an approximation $\hat{h}$ of the optimal hypothesis is sought for through minimization of the empirical error $\hat{\varepsilon}_D(h) := \frac{1}{|D|} \sum_{(i,s,a,s')\in D} \mathcal{L}(h(i,s,a),s')$ for a hypothesis h on a data set D. For a parameterized hypothesis $h_\theta(i,s,a)$ with the parameters θ, the empirically determined optimal hypothesis is $\hat{h}_\theta = \arg\min_\theta \hat{\varepsilon}_D(h_\theta)$.

Let h_i^* be the optimal hypothesis of the dynamics of system i within H. For a sufficient number of observations $|D_1|$, the empirically optimal hypothesis $\hat{h}_1$ is close to the truly optimal hypothesis h_1^* within H. In contrast, given $|D_2|$ is insufficient, $\hat{h}_2$ has a significantly higher model error than h_2^*. In this paper, we assess a regularization technique applied to the FTRNN hypothesis [1] to yield better parameters for the hypothesis $\hat{h}_2$ by augmenting the data D_2 by auxiliary data D_1 given sufficient similarity of the two systems.

3   System Identification with the FTRNN

Let $W_{vu} \in \mathbb{R}^{n_v \times n_u}$ denote the weight matrix from layer u to layer v, $b_v \in \mathbb{R}^{n_v}$ is the bias vector of layer v and $\sigma(\cdot)$ is an elementwise nonlinear function, e.g. $\tanh(\cdot)$. For system identification with RNNs, the sequence of successor states $s_2, ..., s_{T+1}$ is predicted given the initial state s_1 and a trajectory of actions $a_1, ..., a_T$ for $T \in \mathbb{N}_{\geq 2}$ time steps. Each example is represented as a tuple $(s_1, a_1, ..., s_T, a_T, s_{T+1})$. The loss function is typically chosen as the the mean squared error (MSE) between the predicted and the true successor state sequence, i.e. $\mathcal{L}(\hat{s}_2, ..., \hat{s}_{T+1}, s_2, ..., s_{T+1}) = \frac{1}{2} \sum_{t=1}^{T} \|s_{t+1} - \hat{s}_{t+1}\|_2^2$.

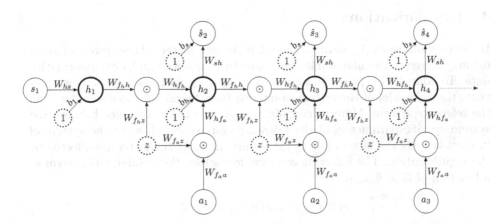

Fig. 1. A graphical representation of the FTRNN architecture. The dotted nodes indicate identical nodes which are replicated for convenience. The nodes having the $\odot$-symbol in their centers are "multiplication nodes", i.e. the input vectors of the nodes are multiplied component-wise. The standard nodes imply the summation of all input vector. Bold bordered nodes indicate the use of an activation function, e.g. $\tanh(\cdot)$.

The Factored Tensor Recurrent Neural Network (FTRNN) extends the Tensor Recurrent Neural Network (TRNN) as denoted in [5]. The TRNN uses third-order tensors W_{vuz} where each slice $W_{vuz}z$, $z \in \{e_1, ..., e_{|I|}\}$, is the weight matrix associated with a particular system. This way, the linear transformations of multiple systems are independent within the joint model. In our considered application, it seems conclusive that some transformations share a common overall structure and there are merely certain aspects that make them different from one another. On top of that, full tensors introduce many additional parameters per system harming data efficiency.

The same conclusions were drawn by Taylor et. al. [6] and Sutskever et. al. [5] in the context of modeling motion style from images with Restricted Boltzmann Machines and character-level language modeling with recurrent neural networks. They proposed to use the factored representation of a parameter tensor of the form

$$W_{vuz}z \approx W_{vf} \operatorname{diag}(W_{fz}z)W_{fu} \tag{1}$$

which, in our case, yields the FTRNN equations

$$h_1 = \sigma_h(W_{hs}s_1 + b_1) \tag{2a}$$

$$h_{t+1} = \sigma_h\big(W_{hf_a} \operatorname{diag}(W_{f_a z}z)W_{f_a a}a_t + \tag{2b}$$
$$W_{hf_h} \operatorname{diag}(W_{f_h z}z)W_{f_h h}h_t + b_h\big)$$

$$\hat{s}_{t+1} = W_{sh}h_{t+1} + b_s \tag{2c}$$

with the cross-system parameters $\theta_{\text{cross}} = \{W_{hs}, W_{hf_a}, W_{f_a a}, W_{hf_h}, W_{f_h h}, b_1, b_h\}$ and the system specific parameters $\theta_{\text{specific}} = \{W_{f_a z}, W_{f_h z}\}$. Figure 1 depicts a graphical representation of the FTRNN architecture.

4 Regularization

In our previous work [1], we discovered that the parameters of the system of interest may converge to unfavorable values due to insufficient and/or uninformative data. To address this problem, we now present a regularization term which prevents the submodel of the system of interest from becoming too dissimilar from the reference system. More specifically, we penalize the ℓ_2 distance between the system specific parameters of the reference system and those of the system of interest keeping the latter close to the former, i.e. only the latter are affected by the regularization. The following equation formalizes the regularization term as a function of $W \in \theta_{\text{specific}}$

$$r(W) = \|\operatorname{const}(W)e_1 - We_2\|_2^2 \tag{3}$$

where $\operatorname{const}(\cdot)$ is a function whose argument is made constant with respect to differentiation, i.e. $\frac{\partial \operatorname{const}(W)}{\partial W} = 0$. The error function, minimized with respect to $\theta = \theta_{\text{cross}} \cup \theta_{\text{specific}}$, is given by

$$E(\theta; \lambda_a, \lambda_h) = \varepsilon_D(h_{\text{FTRNN}, \theta}) + \lambda_a r(W_{f_a z}) + \lambda_h r(W_{f_h z}). \tag{4}$$

There are two reasons for constraining the effect of the regularization to the system of interest. First, the parameters of the reference system are well determined by the data. Hence, there is no need to exploit information from another system. In fact, the little and possibly incomplete information about the system of interest might even corrupt the parameters of the reference system. Second, the cross-system parameters adjust according to the dual-task learning objective which is the minimization of equation 4. Since the data of the system of interest are considered insufficient and likely incomplete, minimizing the prediction error on the training data is likely to generalize poorly for this system. Thus, not only the system specific parameters of the system of interest but also the cross-system parameters may adjust unfavorably. By constraining the parameters of the system of interest to remain similar to those of the reference system, the cross-system parameters are less likely to be affected by incomplete information about the system of interest.

5 Experiments

We empirically assessed the effectiveness of our regularization technique on the cart-pole [7] and mountain car [8] benchmarks. To be consistent with our previous work [1], we used the same settings for the cart-pole for training and evaluation and show the performance graph of the FTRNN that we obtained in the paper. All experiments were implemented using Theano [9]. The parameters were learned using Hessian-Free optimization with structural damping [10,11].

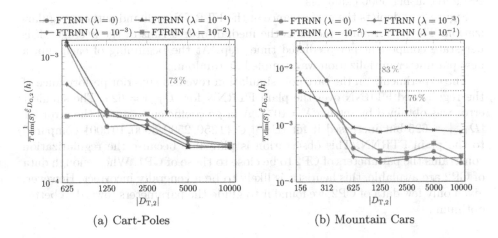

(a) Cart-Poles   (b) Mountain Cars

Fig. 2. Experimental results: the average MSE per state component per time step of the predicted and the true successor state sequence is plotted against the varying training set size of {CP,MC}2 for $|D_{T,1}| = 10\,000$ training examples of {CP,MC}1

5.1   Cart-Poles

The cart-pole simulation consists of a pole hinged to a cart which moves on a one-dimensional track. The control objective, as state in [8], is to balance the pole by moving the cart accordingly. The state of the cart-pole is described by the position and velocity of the cart, and the angle and angular velocity of the pole, i.e. $(x, \dot{x}, \alpha, \dot{\alpha})$. To obtain a more natural state representation for learning, we use the (co)sine components of the pole angle. The cart is moved by applying an external force $a \in [-1, 1]$.

Sequences of 1000 actions $a \sim \mathcal{U}(-1, 1)$ were applied to the cart-pole every $\tau = 0.02\,$s for which the resulting state transitions were observed. After completing a sequence, the simulations was reset to its initial. We observed two different cart-poles whose configurations varied in terms of the pole length l_{pole} and pole mass m_{pole}. We configured the two cart-poles by setting $l_{\text{pole}} \in \{0.5, 1.0\}$ and $m_{\text{pole}} = 0.1 l_{\text{pole}}$. For cart-pole 1 (CP1), we created a training data set with 10 000 and a validation data set with 5000 examples. For cart-pole 2 (CP2), we created various training data sets sized $\{10\,000, 5000, ..., 625\}$ and validation data sets sized $\{5000, 2500, ..., 312\}$. During training, we concatenated the two training and validation data sets and upsampled the data of CP2 to be equal in size with those of CP1. To test the performance of our models, we further created a generalization data set for CP2 sized 30 000. The FTRNN was configured using $n_h = n_{f_h} = 10$, $n_{f_a} = 2$ and $T = 10$. The regularization strength was set to $\lambda = \lambda_a = \lambda_h \in \{10^{-4}, 10^{-3}, 10^{-2}\}$. We set the maximum number of parameter updates to 10 000. The number of CG iterations per update was limited to 150. The gradient was computed using the full training set and the curvature was estimated using 5000 examples.

Figure 2(a) depicts the performance of the FTRNN with and without regularization. The performance metric is the median of five runs of the average MSE per state component per predicted time step. At the beginning of each run, a new parameter initialization was sampled at random.

The experiments on the cart-pole simulation revealed superior performance of the regularized FTRNN over the plain FTRNN for $|D_{\text{T},2}| = 625$. The smallest error was obtained by setting $\lambda = 10^{-2}$. A large coefficient reduced the error for $|D_{\text{T},2}| = 625$ but increased it for $|D_{\text{T},2}| \in \{1250, 2500, 5000, 10\,000\}$ compared to the plain FTRNN. This observation is plausible because the regularization constrains the parameters of CP2 to be close to those of CP1. When enough data of CP2 are available, this heuristic is likely to be a generally incorrect. However, given only few data of CP2, we found it to guide the parameters towards a better optimum.

5.2   Mountain Cars

The mountain car simulation consists of a valley an underpowered car whose control objective, as stated in [8], is to drive up the hill. The state is described by the position and velocity of the car, i.e. $(x, \dot{x})$, $x \in [-1.2, 0.6]$ and $\dot{x} \in [-0.07, 0.07]$. The acceleration $a \in \{-1, 0, 1\}$ of the car defines the action space which we converted to a continuous-valued variable, i.e. $a \in [-1, 1]$, in order to make the simulation more realistic.

Sequences of 500 actions $(a_1, ..., a_{500})$, computed by the equations

$$a_0 = 0 \tag{5a}$$
$$\tilde{a}_t \sim \mathcal{U}(-1, 1) \tag{5b}$$
$$a_t = \max(-1, \min(1, a_{t-1} + \tilde{a}_t)), \tag{5c}$$

were applied to the mountain car. After completing a sequence, the simulation was reset to its initial state. We observed two mountain cars whose configurations differed in terms of the gravity $g \in \{0.0005, 0.0009\}$. For mountain car 1 (MC1), we created a training data set with 10 000 and a validation data set with 5000 examples. For mountain car 2 (MC2), we created various training data sets sized $\{10\,000, 5000, ..., 156\}$ and validation data sets sized $\{5000, 2500, ..., 78\}$. During training, we concatenated the two training and validation data sets and upsampled the data of MC2 to be equal in size with those of MC1. To test the performance of our models, we further created a generalization data set for MC2 sized 100 000. The FTRNN was configured using $n_h = n_{f_h} = 10$, $n_{f_a} = 2$ and $T = 10$. The regularization strength was set to $\lambda = \lambda_a = \lambda_h \in \{10^{-3}, 10^{-2}, 10^{-1}\}$. We set the maximum number of parameter updates to 5000. The number of CG iterations per update was limited to 100. The gradient was computed using the full training set and the curvature was estimated using 10 000 examples.

Figure 2(b) depicts the performance of the FTRNN with and without regularization. The performance metric is the average MSE per state component per predicted time step of the best model among five runs, determined by the validation set error. At the beginning of each run, a new parameter initialization was sampled at random.

The experiments on the mountain car simulation revealed superior performance of the regularized FTRNN over the plain FTRNN for $|D_{T,2}| \in \{312, 156\}$. Given $|D_{T,2}| = 312$ and for $\lambda = 10^{-3}$, we observed a relative error reduction of approximately 76 % compared to the plain FTRNN. For $|D_{T,2}| = 156$ and $\lambda = 10^{-2}$, the regularization yielded a relative improvement of approximately 83 %. Similar to what we observed in the cart-pole experiments, the regularization reduced the error for $|D_{T,2}| \in \{312, 156\}$ but tended to increase it for $|D_{T,2}| \in \{625, 1250, ..., 10\,000\}$.

6   Conclusion

We presented a regularization technique for the Factored Tensor Recurrent Neural Network (FTRNN) to learn the dynamics of an insufficiently observed system by exploiting the similarity to a well observed system in a dual-task learning approach. The FTRNN disentangles cross-system properties from peculiarities enabling to share knowledge efficiently among the systems. In previous work, we discovered that the parameters of the system of interest can converge to unfavorable values when information is insufficient. In this paper, we addressed this problem through regularization which penalizes dissimilarities between the system specific parameters of the system of interest and the reference system. We demonstrated the effectiveness of this approach on the cart-pole and mountain car benchmarks achieving significantly lower errors using the regularized FTRNN compared to the plain FTRNN.

Current and future work includes investigating the effect of noisy observation functions and adapting the method for partially observable systems along the lines of the work presented in [12] in order to eventually apply this method to real world systems.

References

1. Spieckermann, S., Düll, S., Udluft, S., Hentschel, A., Runkler, T.: Exploiting similarity in system identification tasks with recurrent neural networks. In: European Symposium on Artificial Neural Networks, ESANN, pp. 473–478 (2014)
2. Schäfer, A.M., Udluft, S., Zimmermann, H.G.: The recurrent control neural network. In: European Symposium on Artificial Neural Networks, ESANN, pp. 319–324 (2007)
3. Bailer-Jones, C.A.L., MacKay, D.J.C., Withers, P.J.: A recurrent neural network for modelling dynamical systems. Network: Computation in Neural Systems 9(4), 531–547 (1998)
4. Schäfer, A.M., Schneegass, D., Sterzing, V., Udluft, S.: A neural reinforcement learning approach to gas turbine control. In: Proceedings of the International Joint Conference on Neural Networks, pp. 1691–1696 (August 2007)
5. Sutskever, I., Martens, J., Hinton, G.E.: Generating text with recurrent neural networks. In: Proceedings of the 28th International Conference on Machine Learning, pp. 1017–1024 (2011)
6. Taylor, G.W., Hinton, G.E.: Factored conditional restricted boltzmann machines for modeling motion style. In: Proceedings of the 26th International Conference on Machine Learning, pp. 1025–1032 (2009)
7. Florian, R.V.: Correct equations for the dynamics of the cart-pole system. Center for Cognitive and Neural Studies (Coneural), Romania (2007)
8. Sutton, R.S., Barto, A.G.: Reinforcement Learning: An Introduction, vol. 1. Cambridge University Press (1998)
9. Bergstra, J., Breuleux, O., Bastien, F., Lamblin, P., Pascanu, R., Desjardins, G., Turian, J., Warde-Farley, D., Bengio, Y.: Theano: a CPU and GPU math expression compiler. In: Proceedings of the Python for Scientific Computing Conference (SciPy). Oral Presentation (2010)
10. Martens, J., Sutskever, I.: Learning recurrent neural networks with Hessian-Free Optimization. In: Proceedings of the 28th International Conference on Machine Learning, pp. 1033–1040 (2011)
11. Martens, J., Sutskever, I.: Training deep and recurrent networks with Hessian-Free Optimization. In: Montavon, G., Orr, G.B., Müller, K.-R. (eds.) NN: Tricks of the Trade, 2nd edn. LNCS, vol. 7700, pp. 479–535. Springer, Heidelberg (2012)
12. Düll, S., Hans, A., Udluft, S.: The markov decision process extraction network. In: European Symposium on Artificial Neural Networks, ESANN (2010)

On-line Training of ESN and IP Tuning Effect

Petia Koprinkova-Hristova

IICT, Bulgarian Academy of Sciences,
Acad. G. Bonchev str. bl.25A,
Sofia 1113, Bulgaria
pkoprinkova@bas.bg

Abstract. In the present paper we investigate influence of IP tuning of Echo state network (ESN) reservoir on the overall behavior of the on-line trained adaptive critic network. The experiments were done using Adaptive Critic Design (ACD) scheme with on-line trainable ESN critic for real time control of a mobile laboratory robot. Comparison of behavior of ESN critics trained with and without IP tuning showed that IP algorithm improved critic behavior significantly. It was observed that IP tuning prevents uncontrolled increase of reservoir output weights during on-line training.

Keywords: Echo state network, RNN stability, IP training of reservoir, on-line training, Recursive Least Squares.

1   Introduction

Nowadays applications of neural networks to real-time control of complex dynamical systems require fast and stable trainable recurrent neural network (RNN) structures. Such a structure named "Echo state network" (ESN) [2, 3, 8] has recently been proposed. It incorporates a dynamic recurrent reservoir with randomly generated connections and easily trainable output neurons. There are no universal recipes for reservoir generation [8]. The usual recommendation for achieving the so called "echo state property" that has to guarantee reservoir stability is to generate the reservoir weight matrix with spectral radius below one. However as it was mentioned in many works [8] this condition will not guarantee ESN stable behavior in general. Another way to obtain stable behavior of the reservoir is to use a bias term [2, 9] that will move the operating point of the system in the desired direction. This approach is based on average entropy maximization at the ESN output. Another direction of work, also aimed at maximization of information transmission trough the ESN (equivalent to its output entropy maximization), is called "intrinsic plasticity" (IP) [10, 11]. However all the works on IP reported that reservoir spectral radius increases thus causing danger to corrupt stability of the ESN.

RNN stability was theoretically investigated in [1]. The authors proved that addition of a bias term to the neural activation functions can improve the system stability. These results correspond very well to what was done in practice by the IP method [10, 11]. In fact maximization of entropy could be related to an increase of the ESN reservoir stability since it is well known that any stable stationary state has a local maximum of

S. Wermter et al. (Eds.): ICANN 2014, LNCS 8681, pp. 25–32, 2014.

entropy [4]. In our investigations we observed much more stable behavior of IP pre-trained reservoirs in comparison to randomly generated ones [5]. In [6] we proved that IP training squeezes the neurons nonlinearity sectors thus stabilizing even initially unstable reservoirs.

In the present paper our aim was to investigate the effect of IP tuning of reservoirs in real-time applications. The experiments was done using Adaptive Critic Design (ACD) scheme [7] with on-line trainable ESN critic for real time control of a mobile laboratory robot. Comparison of ESN critic behavior trained with and without IP tuning of reservoir showed that IP algorithm improved critic behavior significantly. It was observed that IP tuning prevents uncontrolled increase of reservoir output weights during on-line training.

2   IP Tuning of ESN Reservoir

ESNs are a kind of recurrent neural networks that arise from so called "reservoir computing approaches" [8]. Their dynamics is describes as follows:

$$r(k) = f^{res}\left(W^{in}in(k) + W^{res}r(k-1)\right)$$
$$out(k) = f^{out}\left(W^{out}[in(k) \quad r(k)]\right) \tag{1}$$

Here, $in(k)$ is a vector of network inputs, $r(k)$ a vector of the reservoir neuron states; f^{out} is usually the identity function, W^{out} is a trainable $n_{out} \times (n_{in} + n_r)$ matrix (here n_{out}, n_{in} and n_r are the dimensions of the corresponding vectors out, in and r); W^{in} and W^{res} are $n_r \times n_{in}$ and $n_r \times n_r$ matrices that are randomly generated and are not trainable. The neurons in the reservoir have a simple sigmoid output function f^{res} that is usually hyperbolic tangent.

Although the initial idea of the reservoir approach was to use randomly generated connections, it appears that some adjustment of reservoir with respect to its operating conditions is necessary. A recently proposed approach for this aim called Intrinsic Plasticity (IP) is defined in [10, 11]. This algorithm adds two additional adjustable parameters into the reservoir neurons non-linearity as follows:

$$r(k) = f^{res}\left(diag(a)\left(W^{in}in(k) + W^{res}r(k-1)\right) + b\right) \tag{2}$$

Here a is vector containing the gain terms and b – vector containing the biases of each reservoir neuron. Both vectors have size equal to the reservoir size. The core of IP improvement consists of adjusting the gain and bias terms so as to achieve desired distributions of the reservoir output. This is done by minimization of the Kullback-Leibler divergence as a measure for the difference between the actual and the desired distribution of reservoir neuron outputs r. In the case of hyperbolic tangent non-linearity the proper target distribution that maximizes the information at the reservoir output according to [10] has to be the Gaussian one.

Although there were some concerns about influence of IP tuning on the reservoir stability, our previous investigations showed that IP improvement can stabilize even generated as unstable reservoirs [6].

3   On-line Training of ESN Critic for ACD Control Scheme

3.1   "Learning from Experience" Approach

Reinforcement learning (RL) aroused as a training method of artificial neural networks "by experience", rather than "by examples" in attempt to mimic animal behavior that explains Pavlovian conditioning. Nowadays it is also recognized as an approximation of Bellman's dynamic programming method. Hence the developments during last thirty years led to a group of RL approaches commonly called Adaptive Dynamic Programming (ADP). One of these approaches named Adaptive critic design (ACD) was adopted in our model of agent-environment interactions.

The common optimization task is defined as follows: for a given discrete dynamical system:

$$S(k+1) = F(S(k), c(k)), \quad k = 0,1,2,\ldots,N-1 \tag{3}$$

find such control policy $\{c(0), c(2), \ldots c(N-1)\}$ that maximizes (minimizes) given utility function:

$$U(k) = G(S(k), c(k)), \quad k = 0,1,2,\ldots,N-1 \tag{4}$$

along all the time instants k. Here $S(k)$ denotes current system state and $c(k)$ – currently applied action. Dynamic programming method proposes the following decision of that optimization task: maximize (minimize) the discounted sum of the utility function:

$$J(S(k), c(k)) = \sum_{t=0}^{N} \gamma^t U(S(k+t), c(k+t)) \tag{5}$$

by solving N maximization (minimization) sub-tasks backwards starting from the final time instant to the initial one. Unfortunately the calculation complexity in this case increases dramatically with increase of system dimension.

Created to overcome the "curse of dimensionality", Adaptive Critic Design (ACD), which basic scheme is shown on Fig. 1, proposes approximation of Bellman's equation using some non-linear dependence (usually a neural network model) $J(S(k), c(k)) \approx J_{NN}(k)$. This approximation model is called "adaptive critic" or briefly critic. Obtaining such model allows to solve the optimization task in forward manner by maximizing (minimizing) currently predicted discounted sum of future utilities J. Adjustment of the action network (dashed lines on Fig. 1) is done by a gradient method using critic network to calculate derivatives of J with respect to actions applied to the plant.

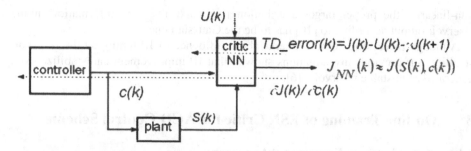

Fig. 1. Adaptive Critic Design scheme

In [5] algorithm for on-line training of ESN adaptive critic is described in details and initial results from its application for real time control of a mobile laboratory robot were demonstrated.

3.2   On-line Training of ESN Critic

The usual approach to train ESN is to collect training data off-line and then to solve a matrix equality with respect to output weights so as to obtain their proper values with single iteration [8]. In the case of on-line training authors of [8] proposed to use Recursive Least Squares (RLS) algorithm. Application of this algorithm proposed in a free software by these authors showed however uncontrolled increase of output weights [5]. This led to the need of normalization of these weights that however influenced training accuracy.

In [5, 6] we observed that application of IP tuning to adjust ESN reservoir before its on-line training improved the achieved results significantly and output weights didn't increase dramatically. Here we demonstrate the results obtained using IP tuning simultaneously with RLS on-line training of ESN critic during real time ACD control of a mobile laboratory robot. The utility function is aimed at obstacle avoidance based on information received from the robot infrared sensors. More detailed explanation of definition of utility function and control low calculations are given in our previous work [5].

4   Results and Discussion

During the real-time training we started with $\gamma=0$. Then after achievement of predefined error of the ESN critic predictions, we started to increase γ gradually up to 0.9. Robot path during real time learning is shown in Fig. 2. Fig. 3 shows training history of ESN critic (in the case of IP tuning in combination with RLS) together with increase of parameter γ from zero up to 0.9. It is observed that with increase of γ above zero critic starts to predict changes in utility function earlier thus allowing the robot to take proper actions on time.

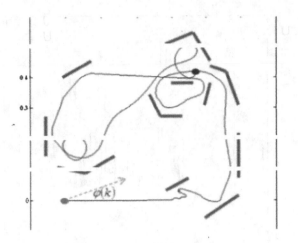

Fig. 2. Robot path during on-line training of ESN critic. Red lines represent the obstacles that must be avoided. Blue line is robot trajectory during on-line control and learning.

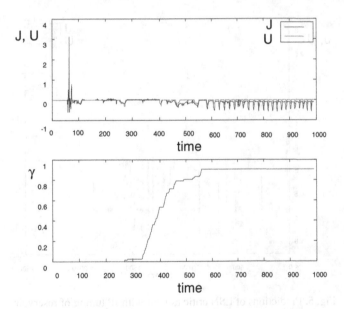

Fig. 3. ESN predictions (J) in comparison with utility function (U) during the all training course in parallel with time varying parameter γ

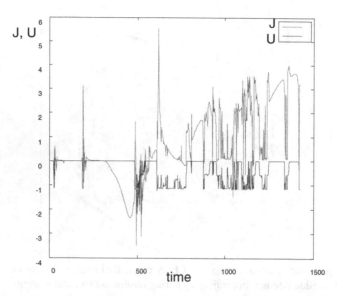

Fig. 4. Predictions of ESN critic trained without IP tuning of reservoir

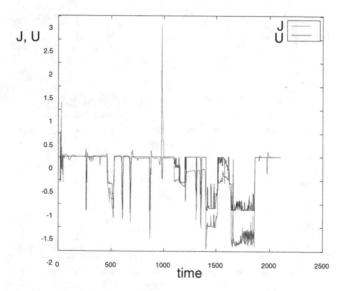

Fig. 5. Predictions of ESN critic trained with IP tuning of reservoir

Next we investigated the predictions of ESN critic in comparison with utility function in the case when IP tuning is not involved (Fig. 4) and in combined IP-RLS training (Fig. 5). It was observed that after some time critic predictions deteriorate significantly without IP improvement of reservoir while in the second case critic demonstrated stable behavior during all course of real time control of the robot.

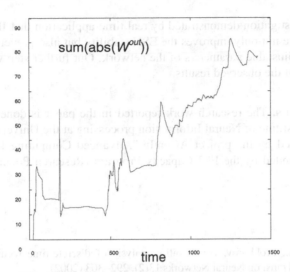

Fig. 6. Sum of reservoir weights without IP tuning

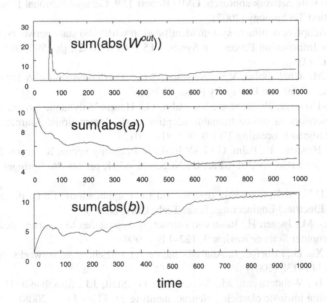

Fig. 7. Sum of weights, gain and bias terms without IP tuning of reservoir

Figures 6 and 7 represent changes with time of the sums of absolute values of ESN output weights without (Fig. 6) and with IP tuning (Fig. 7). In addition on Fig. 7 are shown changes in gain and bias terms. From these results we conclude that IP tuning prevents uncontrolled increase of all adjustable parameters during on-line training of ESN reservoir.

5   Conclusions

The present investigation demonstrated by real time application that IP tuning of reservoir in real time not only improves the ESN stability but also prevents uncontrolled increase of all adjustable parameters of the network. Our further step will be theoretical explanation of the observed results.

Acknowledgments. The research work reported in the paper is done during DAAD scholarship at Institute of Neural Information processing at the University of Ulm and is partly supported by the project AComIn "Advanced Computing for Innovation", grant 316087, funded by the FP7 Capacity Program (Research Potential of Convergence Regions).

References

1. Barabanov, N., Prokhorov, D.: Stability analysis of discrete-time recurrent neural networks. IEEE Trans. on Neural Networks 13(2), 292–303 (2002)
2. Jaeger, H.: Tutorial on training recurrent neural networks, covering BPPT, RTRL, EKF and the echo state network approach. GMD Report 159, German National Research Center for Information Technology (2002)
3. Jaeger, H.: Adaptive nonlinear system identification with echo state networks. In: Advances in Neural Information Processing Systems 15 (NIPS 2002), pp. 593–600. MIT Press, Cambridge (2003)
4. Haddad, W.M., Chellaboina, V.S., Nersesov, S.G.: Thermodynamics: A Dynamical System Approach. Princeton University Press (2005)
5. Koprinkova-Hristova, P., Oubbati, M., Palm, G.: Heuristic dynamic programming using echo state network as online trainable adaptive critic. International Journal of Adaptive Control and Signal Processing 27(10), 902–914 (2013)
6. Koprinkova-Hristova, P., Palm, G.: ESN Intrinsic Plasticity versus Reservoir Stability. In: Honkela, T. (ed.) ICANN 2011, Part I. LNCS, vol. 6791, pp. 69–76. Springer, Heidelberg (2011)
7. Prokhorov, D.V.: Adaptive critic designs and their applications. Ph.D. dissertation. Department of Electrical Engineering, Texas Tech. Univ. (1997)
8. Lukosevicius, M., Jaeger, H.: Reservoir computing approaches to recurrent neural network training. Computer Science Review 3, 127–149 (2009)
9. Ozturk, M., Xu, D., Principe, J.: Analysis and design of Echo state networks. Neural Computation 19, 111–138 (2007)
10. Schrauwen, B., Wandermann, M., Verstraeten, D., Steil, J.J., Stroobandt, D.: Improving reservoirs using intrinsic plasticity. Neurocomputing 71, 1159–1171 (2008)
11. Steil, J.J.: Online reservoir adaptation by intrinsic plasticity for back-propagation-decoleration and echo state learning. Neural Networks 20, 353–364 (2007)

An Incremental Approach to Language Acquisition: Thematic Role Assignment with Echo State Networks

Xavier Hinaut and Stefan Wermter

University of Hamburg, Department Informatics, Knowledge Technology, WTM
22527 Hamburg, Germany
{hinaut,wermter}@informatik.uni-hamburg.de

Abstract. In previous research a model for thematic role assignment (θRARes) was proposed, using the Reservoir Computing paradigm. This language comprehension model consisted of a recurrent neural network (RNN) with fixed random connections which models distributed processing in the prefrontal cortex, and an output layer which models the striatum. In contrast to this previous batch learning method, in this paper we explored a more biological learning mechanism. A new version of the model (i-θRARes) was developed that permitted incremental learning, at each time step. Learning was based on a stochastic gradient descent method. We report here results showing that this incremental version was successfully able to learn a corpus of complex grammatical constructions, reinforcing the neurocognitive plausibility of the model from a language acquisition perspective.

Keywords: reservoir computing, recurrent neural network, language acquisition, incremental learning, anytime processing, grammar acquisition.

1 Introduction

How do humans link the form of a sentence and its meaning? Here we propose a general approach to understand how language can be acquired based on a simple and generic neural architecture, namely recurrent neural networks. This approach provides a robust and scalable way of language processing for robotic architectures (Hinaut et al., 2014). The proposed model is not embodied, but it has many requirements to be included in a more global embodied architecture as it uses a generic architecture that is not hand-crafted for a particular task, but can be used for a broad range of applications (see Lukoševičius et al. 2009 for a review).

Mapping the surface form onto the meaning (or deep structure) of a sentence is not an easy task since simply associating words to specific actions or objects is not sufficient to take into account the expressive content of sentences in language. For instance given the two sentences "The cat scratched the dog" and "The dog was scratched by the cat" which have the same meaning but a different focus or point of view, how could a purely word-based system extract the exact meaning of the sentence? How could an infant determine who is doing the action (the *agent*) and who

S. Wermter et al. (Eds.): ICANN 2014, LNCS 8681, pp. 33–40, 2014.
© Springer International Publishing Switzerland 2014

endures the action (the *object* or *patient*)? As simple as this example is, relying only on the semantic (i.e. content) words, and their order in the sentence, will not permit to reliably distinguish the *agent* from the *object*.

To begin to answer this question, we consider the notion of grammatical construction as the mapping between a sentence's form and its meaning (Goldberg 2003). Goldberg defines constructions as "stored pairings of form and function, including morphemes, words, idioms, partially lexically filled and fully general linguistic patterns". Constructions are an intermediate level of meaning between the smaller constituents of a sentence (grammatical markers or words) and the full sentence itself.

How could one use grammatical constructions to solve this thematic role task for different surface forms? According to the cue competition hypothesis of Bates et al. (1982) the identification of distinct grammatical structures is based on a combination of cues including grammatical (i.e. function) words, grammatical morphemes, word order and prosody. Thus the mapping between a given sentence and its meaning can rely on the order of words, and particularly on the pattern of function words and markers (Dominey et al. 2003). As we will see in section 3, this is the assumption made in the model in order to bind the sentence surface to its meaning.

Typical grammatical constructions could be used to achieve thematic role assignment, that is answering the question "Who did what to whom". This corresponds to filling in the different slots, the roles, of a basic event structure that could be expressed in a predicate form like *predicate(agent, direct object, indirect object* or *recipient)*. Different recurrent neural models have been used to process sentences, namely Recursive SOM (Farkas et al. 2008) and ESN (Tong et al. 2007). In contrast, the θRARes model processes grammatical constructions, not sentences, thus it permits putting the emphasis on the exploration of complex sentence structures.

2   Previous Work

Previously, it was demonstrated that a recurrent neural network, based on the reservoir computing approach, could learn grammatical constructions by mapping a sentence structure to thematic roles (Dominey et al. 2006; Hinaut et al. 2013). This sentence structure could be thought of as a "sentence category" where content words – or semantic words – are replaced by "slots" that could be filled by any noun or verb according to the position in the sentence structure.

The model processed categories (i.e. abstractions) of sentences called "grammatical constructions". In (Hinaut et al. 2013), the Thematic Role Assignment Reservoir (θRARes) model was able to (1) process the majority of the given grammatical constructions in English correctly, even if not learned before, demonstrating generalization capabilities, and (2) to make online predictions while processing a grammatical construction. Moreover, the model provided insights on how language could be processed in the brain. Hinaut et al. were able to show that for less frequent inputs an important shift in output predictions occurred. It was proposed that this could be a potential explanation for human electrophysiological data, like event-related potentials (e.g. P600) that occur when processing unusual sentences (Hinaut et al. 2013).

This language model was successfully used in the iCub humanoid robot platform. Naïve users could teach the robot basic language capabilities through interaction with the robot (Hinaut et al., 2014).

A very similar model of prefrontal cortex was used to model abstract motor sequence processing, and was able to represent categorical information inside the reservoir (Hinaut et al. 2011), thus reinforcing the plausibility of a common generic area used for both abstract motor sequence processing and syntactic processing.

3   Material and Methods

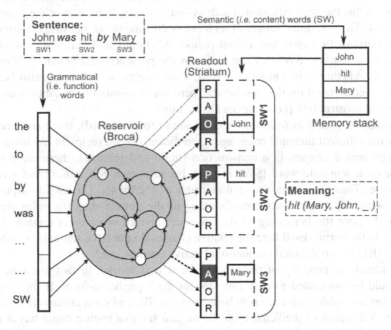

Fig. 1. Thematic Role Assignment Reservoir model (θRARes). All the process from the input sentence (top left) to output predicate-form meaning (middle right) is displayed. Semantic words (SWs) are extracted from the input sentence, in order to transform the sentence into grammatical construction before giving it as input to the reservoir (one word at a time). The output meaning is expressed as the following: predicate(agent, object, recipient). Dashed connections (between reservoir and readout) are the only ones modified during learning. The schema is the same for the incremental version (i-θRARes). Inspired from (Hinaut et al. 2013).

3.1   The Neural Language Model

The core part of the θRARes model is an Echo State Network (Jaeger et al. 2004). It is a recurrent neural network with sparse, random and fixed connectivity: in this paper we will refer to this core part as the "reservoir". Only the weights from the reservoir to the readout (thematic role layer) are learned. Input and reservoir weights are generated randomly. In the previous model, weights were set by linear regression in batch form. Please refer to (Hinaut et al. 2013) for a more detailed description.

3.2   Input and Output Coding

The localist input at each time step t is coded as a symbolic vector, with all values except one set to zero. The only non-zero input (i.e. equal to 1) is the current word. At each time step a word is presented (*i.e.* activation time=1). The input vector dimension is 13. This corresponds to 10 for grammatical words or markers '-ed', '-ing', '-s', 'by', 'is', 'it', 'that', 'the', 'to', 'was', 1 for SW, 1 for the comma and 1 for the period. One can see that the verb inflexions (such as '-ed', '-s', '-ing') are part of the grammatical markers. The maximum length of an input is 20 time steps, because constructions has at maximum 19 words and a final period. All nouns and verbs are coded by a common input marker 'SW' that just indicates the presence of a Semantic Word, independently whether it is a noun or a verb. Thus one could not distinguish between nouns and verbs based on the raw input. There are maximum 6 semantic words per grammatical construction (i.e. sentence abstraction).

The output is coded as follows: for each noun (content word), there are 4 readout units for the different thematic roles: agent, predicate, object, recipient. As there could be at maximum 2 clauses in a construction (main and relative), there are 8 output units for each semantic word (SW) in total, because each SW could have a role in each clause. Thus the output vector dimension is 4*2*6=48. The target output is as the following: all output units corresponding to the correct thematic roles are activated, at 1, since the beginning of the sentence, and all other units remain at zero. Note that in the corpus used here the relative clauses do not have semantic words with recipient (R) role, so the total number of effective outputs is 42.

One interesting property of the output is that it is sparse. In fact semantic word (SW) could be associated to only one slot for each predicate-form. If the output is represented as a table with each row being a given SW and each column is an atomic role (e.g. A-2: agent of predicate-form 2), we can see that each column has at maximum one unit activated because one atomic role corresponds to none or to only one SW.

We used the same error measures as in Hinaut et al. (2013): the *meaning* error is the average number of correct thematic roles, averaged over all constructions; and the *sentence* error is the average of sentences/constructions fully recognized (*i.e.* the percentage of sentences that are fully understood). The latter is a very strict measure.

3.3   Incremental Learning

We want to extend the neurocognitive plausibility of this reservoir language model approach by using a simple incremental learning algorithm based on stochastic gradient descent, namely the Least Mean Square (LMS) algorithm. We used only the information available at a given time step t in order to modify the weights. During the learning phase, the error between the model output and the desired output is computed. The error is used to modify the weights (from the reservoir to the read-out layer) for the last 2 time steps of each construction (i.e. during the last word and the final period). Thus the output weights are modified only at the end of the sentence, when enough information has been processed to establish the thematic roles. The error made by the output units is defined as follows:

$$\text{err}(t+1) = \mathbf{W}_{out}(t) . \mathbf{v}(t+1)' - \mathbf{d}(t+1) \tag{1}$$

with v(t) the reservoir state at time t, d(t) the desired activity at time t, $\mathbf{W}_{out}(t)$ the output weight matrix at time t. $\mathbf{x}'$ indicates the transpose of vector $\mathbf{x}$. During training the weights are updated as follows:

$$\mathbf{W}_{out}(t+1) = \mathbf{W}_{out}(t) - \text{eta} * \text{err}(t+1).\mathbf{v}(t+1)' \tag{2}$$

with eta the learning rate, and with Wout(0)=0. We found that a learning rate of 10-3 permitted to obtain reasonable results. Note that the output activity at time step t+1 is computed with the previous error value. The output activity of the readout units is as follows:

$$\text{out}(t+1) = \mathbf{W}_{out}(t).\mathbf{v}(t+1)' \tag{3}$$

3.4   Corpus and Reservoir Parameters

The corpus was first used in Hinaut et al. (2012). The full corpus can be found in the supplementary materials of Hinaut et al. (2013). It contains 462 English grammatical constructions with their corresponding predicate-meaning. Constructions could have zero or one relative clause (e.g. "The boy *that hit the cat* ate the apple."), which corresponds to one level of nesting. Each construction thus could have 1 or 2 verbs, and a total of 6 semantic words, of which 2 belong to the core part of the relative clause, and 1 belongs to both the main and relative clauses. This corpus was generated in order to have all the possible constructions combining 6 semantic words in all the possible orders. Given the following notation A: agent, P: predicate, O: object, R: recipient, and m or r denotes the main or relative resp., here are examples of semantic word order with their corresponding constructions:

- m(AP), r(): "The giraffe walk -s ."
- m(AOP), r(): "By the beaver the fish was cut -ed ."
- m(APRO), r(): "The dog give -s to the mouse the cat ."
- m(APO), r(AP): "The beaver that think -s cut -s the fish ."
- m(PA), r(AP): "Walk -ing was the giraffe that think -s ."
- m(PARO), r(OAP): "Give -ed by the dog to the mouse that the guy kiss -s was the cat ."

Semantic Word (SW) markers were replaced by words so that human readers could understand them, there are shown in italic. Note that this corpus includes unlikely word orders, so is more difficult to learn than other generated corpora for a given number of semantic words. On the contrary, the sentence structures generated in (Miikkulainen, 1996) are much more regular.

The parameters of the reservoir were the following: units in the ESN: 500 ; spectral radius: 6; input scaling: 2.75; time constant: 6; input connectivity: 10%; reservoir connectivity: 20%; activation time (i.e. number of time steps during which each word was presented): 1; activation function of ESN units: hyperbolic tangent (tanh).

4 Results

The error measures obtained by 10-fold cross-validation (CV) for 4 reservoir instances of 500 units each during 1000 epochs of training are the following: 17.6% (±0.8) for the meaning error, and 86.5% (±1.5) for the sentence error. Better results could be obtained by increasing the number of units; for 4 instances with 1000 units during 500 epochs: 15.6% (±0.8) for the meaning error, and 81.9% (±2.9) for the sentence error. With 1000 units, even better results could be obtained with more epochs (<70% for the sentence error for 5000 epochs for instance).

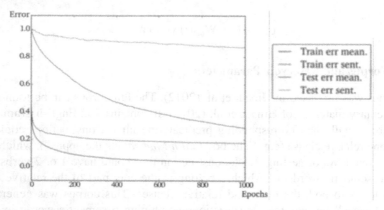

Fig. 2. Meaning and sentence errors over 1000 epochs of training for the i-θRARes model, obtained with a 10-fold CV for a reservoir instance. Number of neurons: 500. The minimum error values are: error meaning: train 3.3%, test 17.5%; error sentence: train 28.7%, test 87.0%.

In Figure 2 we can see an example of the decay of both meaning and sentence errors across training epochs. In Figure 3 a subset of output (readout) units for the construction 244 can be seen. Even if the weights are modified only at the end of the sentence during learning, spontaneous representation emerges after learning.

5 Discussion

It was shown in Hinaut et al. (2013) that forcing the network to decide (about a thematic role) as soon as possible, by considering the activity during the whole sentence to learn the weights, enables the output units to represent the on-going pseudo-probabilities of the current parse of the grammatical construction. This means that even before the network has enough input information to assign the role for each semantic word, the target output is already used to compute the current error.

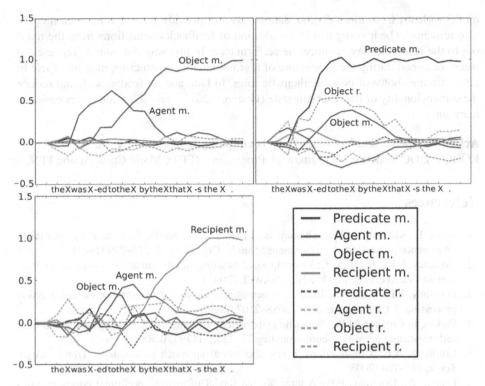

Fig. 3. Subset of output units for the construction 244: "The *cat* was *give* -ed to the *mouse* by the *dog* that *kiss* -s the *girl* ." after only 500 epochs of training. Output units for the first three semantic words (SW) are shown (top left, top right, bottom left resp.). On the x-axis we can see the corresponding input words at each time step. The output activity becomes active since the beginning of the construction. All possible thematic roles for each SW are shown for both possible clauses: main (m.) and relative (r.).

Here, only the last two time steps are used to learn the weights. Nevertheless, a spontaneous output representation seems to emerges during the sentence processing. This spontaneous activity seems different for different reservoir instances. It remains to be explored what kind of information is embedded in this representation, and if an average of the activities over several reservoir instances might produce pseudo-probabilities even without target forcing since the beginning of the sentence. This spontaneous output representation is an interesting property to understand how such on-going information on the current parse might be represented in the human brain.

Direct comparison with performances obtained in Hinaut et al. (2013) is not possible here due to the important number of epochs and reservoir units needed. But it is already very interesting that generalization works with a simple incremental algorithm (LMS) using a complex corpus. Performance could also be improved using an activation time (i.e. number of time steps during which a word is presented) greater than 1 and by using a corpus with redundancies (e.g. small variations of grammatical constructions by adding adjectives; see Hinaut et al. (2013)). This would enable the model to learn from more diverse data points and provide a more robust learning. It also remains to be investigated if the addition of feedback connections from the readout to the reservoir may enhance the performance. In this way the output "representations" obtained during the processing of a grammatical construction may be of use to constrain the choice of possible thematic roles. In fact, adding feedback should reduce the dimensionality of the reservoir state (Hoerzer, 2012), providing attractors easier to learn on.

Acknowlegment. This research has been partly supported by the EU 235065 ROBOT-DOC from the 7th Framework Programme (FP7), Marie Curie Action ITN.

References

1. Bates, E., McNew, S., MacWhinney, B., Devescovi, A., Smith, S.: Functional constraints on sentence processing: A cross-linguistic study. Cognition 11, 245–299 (1982)
2. Dominey, P.F., Voegtlin, T.: Learning word meaning and grammatical constructions from narrated video events. In: Proc HLT-NAACL (2003)
3. Dominey, P.F., Hoen, M., Inui, T.: A neurolinguistic model of grammatical construction processing. J. Cogn. Neurosci. 18, 2088–2107 (2006)
4. Farkas, I., Crocker, M.W.: Syntactic systematicity in sentence processing with a recurrent self-organizing network. Neurocomputing 71, 1172–1179 (2008)
5. Goldberg, A.E.: Constructions: a new theoretical approach to language. Trends. Cogn. Sci. 7, 219–224 (2003)
6. Hinaut, X., Dominey, P.F.: A three-layered model of primate prefrontal cortex encodes identity and abstract categorical structure of behavioral sequences. J. Physiol. - Paris 105, 16–24 (2011)
7. Hinaut, X., Dominey, P.F.: On-Line Processing of Grammatical Structure Using Reservoir Computing. In: Villa, A.E.P., Duch, W., Érdi, P., Masulli, F., Palm, G. (eds.) ICANN 2012, Part I. LNCS, vol. 7552, pp. 596–603. Springer, Heidelberg (2012)
8. Hinaut, X., Dominey, P.F.: Real-Time Parallel Processing of Grammatical Structure in the Fronto-Striatal System: A Recurrent Network Simulation Study Using Reservoir Computing. PloS ONE 8(2), e52946 (2013)
9. Hinaut, X., Petit, M., Pointeau, G., Dominey, P.F.: Exploring the Acquisition and Production of Grammatical Constructions Through Human-Robot Interaction with Echo State Networks. Front. Neurorobot. 8, 16 (2014)
10. Hoerzer, G.M., Legenstein, R., Maass, W.: Emergence of complex computational structures from chaotic neural networks through reward-modulated Hebbian learning. Cereb Cortex, Advance online publication (November 11, 2012) (retrieved)
11. Jaeger, H., Haas, H.: Harnessing nonlinearity: Predicting chaotic systems and saving energy in wireless communication. Science 304, 78–80 (2004)
12. Lukoševičius, M., Jaeger, H.: Reservoir computing approaches to recurrent neural network training. Comput. Sci. Rev. 3, 127–149 (2009)
13. Miikkulainen, R.: Subsymbolic case-role analysis of sentences with embedded clauses. Cognitive Sci. 20, 47–73 (1996)
14. Tong, M.H., Bickett, A.D., Christiansen, E.M., Cottrell, G.W.: Learning grammatical structure with Echo State Networks. Neural Networks 20, 424–432 (2007)

Memory Capacity of Input-Driven Echo State Networks at the Edge of Chaos

Peter Barančok and Igor Farkaš

Faculty of Mathematics, Physics and Informatics
Comenius University in Bratislava, Slovakia
farkas@fmph.uniba.sk

Abstract. Reservoir computing provides a promising approach to efficient training of recurrent neural networks, by exploiting the computational properties of the reservoir structure. Various approaches, ranging from suitable initialization to reservoir optimization by training have been proposed. In this paper we take a closer look at short-term memory capacity, introduced by Jaeger in case of echo state networks. Memory capacity has recently been investigated with respect to criticality, the so called edge of chaos, when the network switches from a stable regime to an unstable dynamic regime. We calculate memory capacity of the networks for various input data sets, both random and structured, and show how the data distribution affects the network performance. We also investigate the effect of reservoir sparsity in this context.

Keywords: echo state network, memory capacity, edge of chaos.

1 Introduction

The reservoir computing (RC) paradigm [9] has turned out to be a computationally efficient approach for online computing in spatiotemporal tasks, compared to classical recurrent networks suffering from complicated training and slow convergence. RC utilizes appropriate initialization of the input and recurrent part (reservoir) of the network, and only the memoryless output part (readout) of the network is trained (in supervised way). More recently, research has also focused on various ways how to optimize the reservoir properties. Numerous methods for unsupervised, semi-supervised or supervised optimization methods have been investigated, see e.g. [9] for a comprehensive survey. In addition, it has been shown that the computational capabilities of reservoir networks are maximized when the recurrent layer is close to the border between a stable (ordered) and an unstable (chaotic) dynamics regime, the so called *edge of chaos*, or criticality [8]. Furthermore, the phase transition between ordered and chaotic network behavior for the binary (spiking) circuits has been shown to be much sharper than that of analog circuits [12]. In RC, various quantitative measures for assessing the network information processing have been proposed. One of the indicators is memory capacity (MC), introduced and defined by Jaeger [6], as the ability to reconstruct the past input signal from the immediate state of the

S. Wermter et al. (Eds.): ICANN 2014, LNCS 8681, pp. 41–48, 2014.

system. For instance, MC is increased when the reservoir dynamics are enriched by spreading the eigenvalues of the recurrent weight matrix over a disk [10], or can become very robust against noise by reservoir orthogonalization [15]. These results for discrete networks also served as inspiration for reservoir optimization in continuous-time networks [4]. In this paper, we take a closer look at MC in the edge of chaos in case of (discrete-time analog) echo state networks (ESNs) [7] with respect to input data distribution. We calculate MC of the networks for various input data sets, both random and structured, and show how the statistical properties of data affect network performance. We also test the effect of reservoir sparsity. Somewhat related research was made in [14], where the memory (not MC) and the nonlinearity (of the reservoir) were analyzed as a function of input scaling and spectral radius of ESNs. Some authors have taken a principled approach by introducing an ESN with minimal complexity and estimating its MC on a number of widely used benchmark time series [11].

In our simulations, we consider an ESN with a single input. Hence, the activation of reservoir units is updated according to $\mathbf{x}(t) = \mathbf{f}(\mathbf{W}\mathbf{x}(t-1) + \mathbf{w}^{\text{in}}u(t))$, where $\mathbf{f} = (f_1, ... f_N)$ are internal unit's activation functions (typically a sigmoid or $tanh$ function; we used the latter). $\mathbf{W}$ is a matrix of reservoir connections, $\mathbf{w}^{\text{in}}$ is a vector of input weights and $u(t)$ is the (single) input. We considered linear outputs (readout), so the network output is computed as $\mathbf{y}(t) = \mathbf{W}^{\text{out}}\mathbf{x}(t)$ and output weights can be computed offline via linear regression.

2   Estimating the Criticality in Input-Driven ESN

The common way how to determine whether a dynamical system has ordered or chaotic dynamics, is to look at the average sensitivity to perturbations of the initial conditions [1,3]. If the system is in ordered state, small differences in the initial conditions of two otherwise equal systems should eventually vanish. In chaotic state, they will persist and amplify. A measure for the exponential divergence of two trajectories of a dynamical system in state space with very small initial separation is the (characteristic) Lyapunov exponent (LE). LE is defined as $\lambda = \lim_{l \to \infty} \ln(\gamma_l/\gamma_0)/l$, where γ_0 is the initial distance between the perturbed and the unperturbed trajectory (given by their state vectors), γ_l is the distance between the two state vectors at time l. Ordered state occurs for $\lambda < 0$, whereas $\lambda > 0$ implies chaotic state. Hence, a phase transition occurs at $\lambda \approx 0$ (the critical point, or the edge of chaos). Since λ is an asymptotic quantity, it has to be estimated for most dynamical systems. Following [2], we adopt here the method described in [13, chap. 5.6]. Two equal networks are simulated for a sufficiently large number of steps, in order to eliminate transient random initialization effects. Then we proceed as follows:

1. Add a small perturbation ϵ into a unit of one network. This separates the state of the perturbed network $\mathbf{x}^p(0)$ from the state of the unperturbed network $\mathbf{x}^u(0)$ by an amount γ_0. We used $\epsilon = 10^{-12}$ as appropriate [13].[1]

---

[1] The perturbation should be as small as possible, but still large enough so that its influence will be measurable with limited numerical precision on a computer.

2. Run the simulation one step and record the resulting state difference (in Euclidean norm) for this l-th step $\gamma_l = \|\mathbf{x}^u(l) - \mathbf{x}^p(l)\|$.
3. Reset $\mathbf{x}^p(l)$ to $\mathbf{x}^u(l) + (\gamma_0/\gamma_l)(\mathbf{x}^p(l) - \mathbf{x}^u(l))$, which keeps the two trajectories close to each other in order to avoid numerical overflows.

As performed in [13] and [2], γ_l is added to a running average and steps 2 and 3 are performed repeatedly until the average converges. We repeat these steps for a total of $l_{max} = 500$ times and then average the logarithm of the distances along the trajectory as $\lambda_n = \langle \ln(\gamma_l/\gamma_0) \rangle$. For each tested reservoir with N units, we calculate N different λ_n values, choosing a different reservoir unit to be perturbed each time. The average of these values is (for the simulated network) then taken as a final estimate of LE (for that network), i.e. $\lambda \approx \langle \lambda_n \rangle$.

3   Memory Capacity of ESN

To evaluate the short-term memory capacity of the networks, we computed the k-delay memory capacity (MC_k) introduced and derived in [6] as

$$MC_k = \frac{cov^2(u(t-k), y_k(t))}{\sigma^2(u(t)) \, \sigma^2(y_k(t))} \tag{1}$$

where $u(t-k)$ is a k-step delayed input, $y_k(t) = \tilde{u}(t-k)$ is its reconstruction at the network output (using linear readout), cov denotes covariance (of the two time series) and σ^2 means variance. So the concept of memory is based on network's ability to retrieve the past information (for various k) from the reservoir using the linear combinations of internal unit activations. Hence, the vector of reconstructed past inputs (from the training set, concatenated in the matrix $\mathbf{U}$) was computed using the output weight matrix $\mathbf{W}^{out} = \mathbf{U}\mathbf{X}^+$, where $\mathbf{X}^+$ denotes the pseudoinverse matrix of concatenated state vectors. The overall short-term memory capacity is approximated as $MC = \sum_{k=1}^{k_{max}} MC_k$. We used $k_{max} = 100$. Jaeger [6] experimented with memory capacity of linear ESNs, driven by i.i.d. scalar inputs and his main result was that $MC \leq N$.

4   Experiments

We experimented with ESNs driven by various types of time series (stochastic and structured) and calculated the MC as a function of LE. The networks had $N = 150$ reservoir units.[2] As in [2], we used ESNs whose reservoir weights were drawn from a normal distribution with zero mean and variance σ^2. We systematically changed σ between simulations such that $\log \sigma$ varied within the interval $[-1.5; -0.5]$, increasing in steps of 0.1. A more fine-grained resolution was used close to the edge of chaos, between $[-1.2; -0.9]$. Here, we increased $\log \sigma$ in steps of 0.02. For each σ we generated 50 instances of ESN (that slighly differed in their estimated LE). For all networks, LE was estimated as described

---

[2] We chose this size in order to be able to verify some results presented in [2].

in Section 2. Input weights were drawn uniformly from the interval $[-0.1; 0.1]$. In case of stochastic sequences (uniform data), we looked at the effect of the following parameters on MC: (a) interval shift (given by its mean), (b) interval length, and (c) sparsity of the reservoir. In case of structured data, we evaluated MC for various data sets (mostly chaotic).

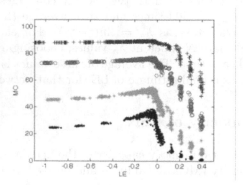

Fig. 1. Effect of random data interval shift on memory capacity, as a function of the Lyapunov exponent. From bottom to top: [-1;4], [0;5], [2;7], [5;10]. Larger random values lead to higher MC that does not clearly peak at the edge of chaos.

Uniform Data. We generated 7000 data points for this time series, discarded the first 1000 points to get rid of transients, another set of 1000 was used for calculating $\mathbf{W}^{\text{out}}$ and the remaining subset was used for calculating MC (this resulted in 1000:1000:5000 split). The effect of interval shift is shown in Figure 1. In the figure, each symbol corresponds to one instance of ESN, characterized by its LE and MC values.[3] It can be seen that larger input values lead to higher MC. Interestingly, for $\lambda > 0$, MC drops gradually (and not sharply, as in some cases of structured input data shown below). The results are symmetric with respect to zero, so e.g. the range $[-10; -5]$ leads to the same result as $[5; 10]$. This is due to the symmetry of the *tanh* activation function (which preserves the stability assumptions behind the spectral radius scaling).

Next, the effect of the interval size for zero-mean i.i.d. data is shown in Figure 2 which reveals that the range does matter but only at the edge of chaos. For smaller intervals, MC reaches the maximum of around 45, as opposed to 30 in the case of the larger interval. The explanation can probably be sought in the properties of *tanh* activation function which saturates at argument values ± 3.

It is to be noted that these results hold for *tanh* activation function. Comparison with a unipolar sigmoid $f(z) = 1/(1 + \exp(-z))$, which is also used in ESNs, reveals much different MC profiles (not shown here due to lack of space). For various input data intervals (as those used in Figure 1), MC was observed to

---

[3] For each considered σ, the instances of ESN can (slightly) differ in terms of their λ and MC estimates. Also, two ESN instances with the same λ can differ in their MC.

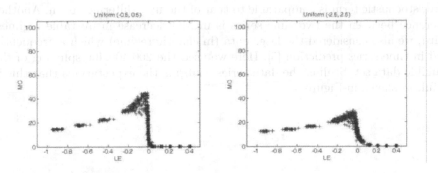

Fig. 2. Effect of random data interval size on memory capacity. It can be observed that the smaller range leads to higher MC, especially at the edge of chaos.

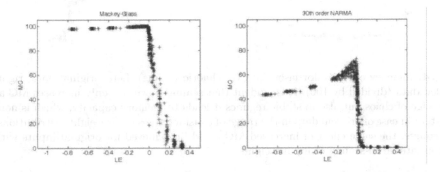

Fig. 3. Memory capacity for structured input data: Mackey–Glass data leads to well-preserved memory in stable configurations, as opposed to drops in case of the NARMA dataset

remain approximately constant (ranging from 25 to 85), shifted towards stable regimes, i.e. without configurations operating at the edge of chaos.

Structured Data. First, we used the well-known Mackey–Glass series, computed by integrating the system $du/dt = 0.2u(t-\tau)/(1+u(t-\tau)^{10}) - 0.1u(t)$, where with $\tau = 17$ we get a slightly chaotic behavior. We had available 1200 generated data points, split in the 200:500:500 ratio.

Second, following [2], we modeled a 30th order nonlinear autoregressive moving average (NARMA) system, generated by the equation $u(t+1) = 0.2\,u(t) + 0.004\,u(t)\sum_{i=0}^{29} u(t-i) + 1.5\,z(t-29)z(t) + 0.001$, where the input $z(t)$ has uniform distribution from [0;0.5]. For this data set, we use the same size as described for uniform data (7000 points in total). Results for MC in case of these two data sets are shown in Figure 3. In case of Mackey-Glass data, at the edge of chaos, the effect is minimal, so the networks preserve a very good MC also for more ordered configurations. In case of NARMA data set, MC does increase towards the edge of chaos. Actually, the MC profile for NARMA looks very similar to the case of iid. data set in the interval [0;0.5], the reason being that NARMA can still be viewed as inherently a stochastic (filtered) system because the effect of the third, stochastic term is comparable to that of the first (filtering) term. Another difference between the two time series is in MC decrease in unstable regimes. Third, we also considered the laser data (in chaotic regime) which is frequently used in time-series prediction [5]. Here we used the 200:400:400 splitting of the available data set. Scaling the data series confirms the expectations that this is useful, as shown in Figure 4.

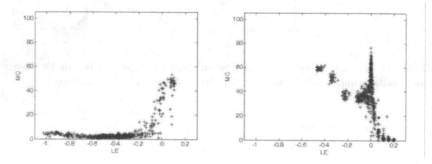

Fig. 4. Memory capacity for laser data (in chaotic regime). Left: original data, right: scaled data (divided by 100). It is evident that scaling down not only increases MC at the edge of chaos but also in stable regimes it leads to memory capacity, which is non-existent in case of original data in the range of considered reservoir weight distributions. Of course, the same effect of increased MC could be achieved for original inputs with apropriate down-scaling of input weights.

Reservoir Sparsity. Last but not least, we investigated the effect of reservoir sparsity on memory capacity. MC for various sparse reservoirs are shown in Figure 5. The sparsity values were selected (from the interval 10-100% with a step 10%) to highlight the differences. It is observed that more significant changes appear for very sparse reservoirs. Consistently with previous findings [7], the maximum MC is not affected by sparsity, so in all cases the critical networks have similar memory capacity. What changes, however, is that the sparser connectivity pushes the networks toward more stable regimes (with shorter memory span), as shown by shifting the clowd of points to the left. Hence, it has the tendency to stabilize the reservoirs.

The second comparison, related to sparsity, relates to one ESN with full connectivity (i.e. with N^2 connections in the reservoir) and another network with the same number of connections but only 20% connectivity, which can be achieved with approximately $N = 335$. It is interesting to see in Figure 6 that sparsity leads to higher MC at the edge of chaos. As shown in Figure 5, sparsity does not affect the MC profile, so the network with $N = 335$ units in the reservoir performs better simply because it is larger, so it can store more inofrmation. On the other hand, sparsity pushes the network configurations to stable regimes, as shown by the shifted cloud of points to the left. In all simulations, it was observed that the values of MC were well below the theoretical limit ($N = 150$), including the edge of chaos.

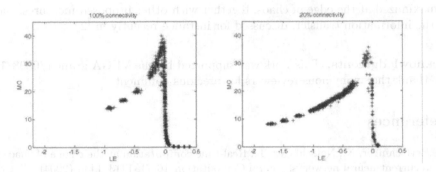

Fig. 5. Memory capacity for random data, for reservoirs with full connectivity (left) and 20% connectivity (right). Significant changes in MC profile appear at sparse connectivity below 50%.

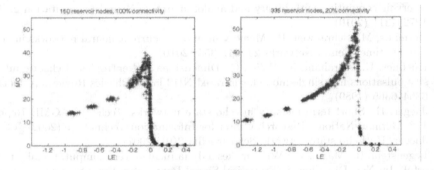

Fig. 6. Memory capacity for two networks with the same number of reservoir connections. The difference in MC in favour of sparse network occurs at the edge of chaos.

5 Conclusion

We focused on memory capacity of echo state networks (with *tanh* activation function) at the edge of chaos, and its dependence on input data statistics and reservoir properties, because these issues have not been sufficiently dealt with in the literature. The observations can be summarized as follows: For uniformly distributed input data, the interval shift matters, such that higher values lead to higher MC. Similarly, the smaller interval range seems to increase MC at the edge of chaos. In case of structured data, the results vary depending on data properties. Chaotic Mackey–Glass time series leads to very high MC but the edge of chaos plays no role, whereas for NARMA data the MC behaves similarly to uniform data (as explained in the text). In case of chaotic laser data, the data scaling confirms a desirable effect of increased MC, consistently with observations on uniform data. Last but not least, reservoir sparsity appears to affect MC, not only by increasing the memory at the edge of chaos, but also by shifting the network configuration towards more stable regimes (with negative Lyapunov exponents). Taken together, memory capacity is a crucial network property that is maximized at the edge of chaos, together with other proposed measures, such as the information transfer, discussed for instance recently in [2].

Acknowledgments. This work was supported by the VEGA grant 1/0898/14. We thank the anonymous reviewers for precious comments.

References

1. Bertschinger, N., Natschläger, T.: Real-time computation at the edge a of chaos in recurrent neural networks. Neural Computation 16(7), 1413–1436 (2004)
2. Boedecker, J., Obst, O., Lizier, J., Mayer, N., Asada, M.: Information processing in echo state networks at the edge of chaos. Theory in Biosciences 131, 205–213 (2012)
3. Büsing, L., Schrauwen, B., Legenstein, R.: Connectivity, dynamics, and memory in reservoir computing with binary and analog neurons. Neural Computation 22(5), 1272–1311 (2010)
4. Hermans, M., Schrauwen, B.: Memory in linear recurrent neural networks in continuous time. Neural Networks 23, 341–355 (2010)
5. Huebner, U., Abraham, N., Weiss, C.: Dimensions and entropies of chaotic intensity pulsations in a single-mode far-infrared NH3 laser. Physics Reviews A 40(11), 6354–6365 (1989)
6. Jaeger, H.: Short term memory in echo state networks. Tech. Rep. GMD Report 152, German National Research Center for Information Technology (2002)
7. Jaeger, H.: Echo state network. Scholarpedia 2(9) (2007)
8. Legenstein, R., Maass, W.: What makes a dynamical system computationally powerful? In: New Directions in Statistical Signal Processing: From Systems to Brain, pp. 127–154. MIT Press (2007)
9. Lukosevicius, M., Jaeger, H.: Reservoir computing approaches to recurrent neural network training. Computer Science Review 3(3), 127–149 (2009)
10. Ozturk, M., Xu, C., Principe, J.: Analysis and design of echo state networks. Neural Computation 19, 111–138 (2006)
11. Rodan, A., Tiňo, P.: Minimum complexity echo state network. IEEE Transaction on Neural Networks 21(1), 131–144 (2011)
12. Schrauwen, B., Buesing, L., Legenstein, R.: On computational power and the order-chaos phase transition in reservoir computing. In: Advances in Neural Information Processing Systems, pp. 1425–1432 (2009)
13. Sprott, J.: Chaos and Time-Series Analysis. Oxford University Press (2003)
14. Verstraeten, D., Dambre, J., Dutoit, X., Schrauwen, B.: Memory versus nonlinearity in reservoirs. In: International Joint Conference on Neural Networks, pp. 1–8 (2010)
15. White, O., Lee, D., Sompolinsky, H.: Short-term memory in orthogonal neural networks. Physical Review Letters 92(14), 148102 (2004)

Adaptive Critical Reservoirs with Power Law Forgetting of Unexpected Input Sequences

Norbert Michael Mayer

Dept. of Electrical Engineering and
Advanced Institute of Manufacturing with High-tech Innovations (AIM-HI),
Nat'l. Chung Cheng University,
University Rd. 168, Min-Hsiung, Chia-Yi, Taiwan
nmmayer@gmail.com
http://www.crudescientists.org

Abstract. The echo-state condition names an upper limit for the hidden layer connectivity in recurrent neural networks. If the network is below this limit there is an injective, continuous mapping from the recent input history to the internal state of the network. Above the network becomes chaotic, the dependence on the initial state of the network may never be washed out. I focus on the biological relevance of echo state networks with a critical connectivity strength at the separation line between these two conditions and discuss some related biological findings, i.e. there is evidence that the neural connectivity in cortical slices is tuned to a critical level. In addition, I propose a model that makes use of a special learning mechanism within the recurrent layer and the input connectivity. Results show that after adaptation indeed traces of single unexpected events stay for a longer time period than exponential in the network.

1 Introduction

Stability of a dynamical system is usually described in terms of the eigenvalues of the Jacobian, which clearly can identify a system as asymptotically stable or unstable. In the simplest scalar case one might consider a system with a fix-point at $x = 0$ and a dynamics like

$$\dot{x} = \alpha x + \beta x^2 + \gamma x^3 \dots \tag{1}$$

Here near the fix-point, one has only to consider the sign of the scalar value α in order to predict the future of the dynamic, whether it converges ($\alpha < 0$) to the fix-point or it diverges from it ($\alpha > 0$). However, for a narrow class of systems the linear term vanishes ($\alpha = 0$). If for example the parameter α is a function of a system parameter one may interpret the moment when α changes its sign a phase transition of the dynamical system. For this reason the case of α being 0 might be considered critical in that sense that in the environment of this point the dynamical properties of the system change rapidly if one assumes relatively small variations of α. In the critical regime the dynamical system

S. Wermter et al. (Eds.): ICANN 2014, LNCS 8681, pp. 49–56, 2014.

shows different properties than non-critical systems. One significant difference is that the correlation lengths and also convergence/divergence of the system is according to a power law [1] instead of exponential. More general, in critical states power law properties in the dynamic variables and statistics can appear. For example, in brain slices of rats, electrode measurements revealed such kind of statistics in spontaneous activity cascade lengths ('avalanches')[1]. As a working hypothesis of this contribution I assume that indeed networks in the brain are dynamical systems in a critical regime.

If the working hypothesis is true this is an interesting feature which rises the question of the information theoretic purpose of such an phenomenology even more if one accounts for the fact such a tuning requires a rather sophisticated control mechanism[2].

In this paper a reservoir computing approach (for an overview over some recent developments see [3]) is presented where a critical dynamics is arranged around the expected input, .i.e. if the network is fed with the expected input it forgets any unexpected input in a power law fashion.

One can interpret some recent experiments [4] as a hint that at least with respect to untrained stimuli some cortical areas can be interpreted as a kind of reservoir computing. In the scope of this work I am going to introduce a neural networks approach that bases on Echo-State-Networks (ESNs). The ESN is a reservoir approach that bases on sigmoid neurons. For my very basic considerations it turned out to be sufficient and can be easily tuned into a critical regime in the sense of this paper. In the context of the present approach most important are those approaches that relate to critical ESNs [5–7]. The learning approach is specifically designed in that way that the network learns to anticipate the input i.e. to predict it. The predicted input is then subtract from the initial signal. This damping could also be labeled as balancing the network; a term which has been coined earlier [8] in the context of chaotic dynamics of integrate and fire neurons.

The purpose of this mechanism is to prevent predictable information to enter the network, and produce activity in the recurrent layer. The intention is rather to let only the un-predicted input pass into the recurrent layer and stay there for further processing.

In the following section I introduce the Echo-State paradigm and how it can be tuned into the critical state. I then discuss the role and implementation of the anticipation/balancing part of the algorithm. A result section follows. I conclude the work with as discussion in which I turn towards the potential information theoretic benefit of my model.

2   Model

The model is based on Jäger's ESN approach [9, 10]. The model consists of an input, recurrent layer and finally an output layer is possible (though not

---

[1] Power law means that the time series behave as t^a, where a is constant and t represents the time.

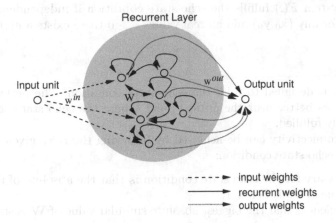

Fig. 1. ESN scheme: The initial ESN approach choses input and recurrent connectivity randomly, although it has to obey the echo state condition. Learning is only applied to the output layer. What is "optimal" connectiviy with regard to the other layers and some certain input statistics is still subject to an ongoing debate to which this work would like to contribute.

explicitly introduced in the scope of this paper, see fig. 1). ESNs are composed of sigmoid neurons, the update rule is:

$$\mathbf{x}_{lin,t} = \mathbf{W}\mathbf{x}_{t-1} + \mathbf{w}^{in}\mathbf{u}_t \tag{2}$$

$$\mathbf{x}_t = \sigma\left(\mathbf{x}_{lin,t}\right) \tag{3}$$

where the vectors $\mathbf{u}_t$,$\mathbf{x}_t$, $\mathbf{o}_t$, are the input and the neurons of the hidden layer and output layer respectively, and $\mathbf{w}^{in}$, $\mathbf{W}$ are the matrices of the respective synaptic weight factors. Different from the Jäger approach the following sigmoid function was used:

$$\sigma(x) = 0.5x - 0.25\,sin(2x) \tag{4}$$

It has to be noted that the maximal derivative $\sigma'(x)$ is 1 at $-\pi$ and π, while Jägers model's sigmoid $(tanh)$ this point is at 0.

Necessary for the performance of the ESN network is that the echo state condition is fulfilled:

Echo-State Condition: Consider a time-discrete recursive function $\mathbf{x}_{t+1} = F(\mathbf{x}_t, \mathbf{u}_t)$ that is defined at least on a compact sub-area of the vector-space

$\mathbf{x} \in R^n$. and where $\mathbf{x}_t$ are to be interpreted as internal states and $\mathbf{u}_t$ is some external input sequence, i.e. the stimulus.

The definition of the echo-state condition is the following: Assume an infinite stimulus sequence: $\bar{\mathbf{u}}^\infty = \mathbf{u}_0, \mathbf{u}_1, \dots$ and two random initial internal states of the system $\mathbf{x}_0$ and $\mathbf{y}_0$. To both initial states $\mathbf{x}_0$ and $\mathbf{y}_0$ the sequences $\bar{\mathbf{x}}^\infty = \mathbf{x}_0, \mathbf{x}_1, \dots$ and $\bar{\mathbf{y}}^\infty = \mathbf{y}_0, \mathbf{y}_1, \dots$ can be assigned.

$$\mathbf{x}_{t+1} = F(\mathbf{x}_t, \mathbf{u}_t) \tag{5}$$

$$\mathbf{y}_{t+1} = F(\mathbf{y}_t, \mathbf{u}_t) \tag{6}$$

Then the system $F(.)$ fulfills the echo-state condition if independent from the set $\mathbf{u}_t$ and for any $(\mathbf{x}_0, \mathbf{y}_0)$ and all real values $\epsilon > 0$ there exists a $\delta(\epsilon)$ for which

$$d(\mathbf{x}_t, \mathbf{y}_t) \leq \epsilon \tag{7}$$

for all $t \geq \delta$.

The ESN is designed to fulfil the echo-state condition. The performance of ESNs becomes better near the critical point where the echo state condition is just narrowly fulfilled.

Critical connectivity can be achieved by following the rules given by Jäger's rule for the echo state condition:

- C1 Necessary for the echo state condition is that the absolute of the biggest eigenvalue of $\mathbf{W}$ is below 1.
- C2 Sufficient is that the biggest absolute singular value of $\mathbf{W}$ is smaller than one[2].

The network becomes critical somewhere in the range between this two conditions. In the case of normal matrices for the recurrent connectivity $\mathbf{W}$, i.e. matrices that fulfill:

$$\mathbf{W}^T \mathbf{W} = \mathbf{W} \mathbf{W}^T, \tag{8}$$

both conditions are either true or false at the same time. These matrices have the same biggest absolute singular value and absolute eigenvalue[3]. Thus, in this case the critical value can be estimated easily. Several prominent types of matrices are normal: Symmetric, orthogonal, permutation, and –what I use here– real skew-symmetric (aka. anti-symmetric). So, for the present model always the two constraints

- C3 anti-symmetric $\mathbf{W}$,
- C4 largest absolute eigenvalue/singular value set to 1,

are enforced. The advantage of this setting is that the limit of the echo state condition is exactly reached, when

$$\mathbf{x}_{lin,t} = [\pm\frac{\pi}{2}, \pm\frac{\pi}{2}, \pm\frac{\pi}{2} \ldots]. \tag{9}$$

This results in 2^N different possible states for the total network, where N is the number of the hidden neurons, whereas the initial model of Jäger ($\sigma(x) = tanh(x)$) at most only has one such possible state, that is:

$$\mathbf{x}_{lin,t} = [0, 0, 0 \ldots], \tag{10}$$

which makes information transfer within a critical network in the critical state impossible.

---

[2] A closer sufficient condition has been found in[11, 12]. It is slightly better than the one outlined here, but still leaves a gap to the necessary condition for general matrices.

[3] For a proof refer online on Wikipedia under singular value decomposition: Relation to eigenvalue decomposition.

2.1   Learning Anticipation in the Hidden Layer

Several learning rules for the hidden layer have been proposed. Main focus has always been the idea that an information theoretic measure is applicable[7, 13]. In the present approach it is intended to follow the idea to anticipate the input, which also has been tried in different ways previously [14, 5] For the present contribution I propose the minimization of the cost function

$$E(\mathbf{W}, \mathbf{w}^{in}) = \sum_i < cos(\mathbf{x}_{lin,t,i})^2 >_t, \qquad (11)$$

where $\mathbf{x}_{lin,t,i}$ is the ith component of $\mathbf{x}_{lin,t}$ (see eq.(2)). The cost function becomes minimal if $\mathbf{x}_{lin,t,i} = \pi(n+1/2)$, where n is an integer number. Since initial $\mathbf{W}$ and $\mathbf{w}^{in}$ are chosen to be small, practically only $\pm\pi/2$ are reachable. Note that $\mathbf{x}_{lin,t}$ contains also input to the system at the time t. Thus, the optimization includes an 'anticipation' of the input, i.e. some input is expected and already counted in order to come close to $\pm\pi/2$ for each neuron. The optimization is done on both $\mathbf{W}$ and $\mathbf{w}^{in}$ by gradient descent

$$\Delta\mathbf{W} = -\epsilon\frac{\partial E}{\partial \mathbf{W}} \qquad (12)$$

$$\Delta\mathbf{w}^{in} = -\epsilon\frac{\partial E}{\partial \mathbf{w}^{in}},$$

where E is the cost-function of eq. (11). In each iteration after adaptation the conditions C3 and C4 are enforced by reassigning $\mathbf{W}$:

$$\mathbf{W} \leftarrow \mathbf{W} - \mathbf{W}^T$$
$$\mathbf{W} \leftarrow \mathbf{W}/max(abs(eigval(\mathbf{W}))). \qquad (13)$$

3   Simulation Results

3.1   Reduced Model

The first experiment was done with a model of 5 neurons, input was one neuron alternating 1 and -1. In this case the learning algorithm for the hidden layer converges rapidly ($\approx$ 5000 iterations with a learning rate of 0.01). In Fig. 2 the left graph depicts the linear response of each neuron during the learning process. One can see that the learning follows the intended effect, i.e. the linear responses become more and more accurately whole number multitudes of $\pi/2$. Then 2 identical copies of the network are created. As a second step, after the learning process an unexpected input is presented to one of these networks. The internal state of both networks is then in each iteration compared by means of a metrical 'measure, in analogue fashion as in Eq. (7)[4]. Results are depicted in Fig. 3. The results indicate that the reduced model shows the echo state property, however the decay is not exponential but a power law. Therefor for a very long time period traces of the single unexpected event can be found in the network.

---

[4] The applied metric was $d = \sum_i abs(x_i - y_i)$, where x and y are the respective states of both networks.

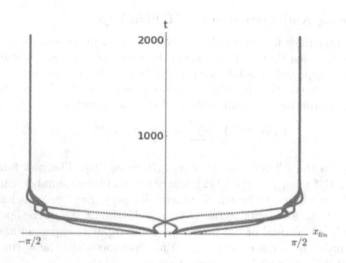

Fig. 2. Linear response of a network during the learning process

3.2   Preliminary Tests

Some tests have been undertaken for some non-trivial tasks, in particular the reservoir was tested as a likelihood machine as in [15]. Only for a few conditions the trained reservoirs could really show better capabilities so far. The reason may be that the cost function so far does not converge very good to 0 during training for the more complicated input statistics, which is different from the setting outlined in the previous section. One reason can be that the learning usually gets caught in a local minimal state, here a change of the design of the cost could provide a solution.

4   Discussion

Different from machine learning human memory works often in that way that one can remember events better if these events were unexpected. Moreover, this seems to be useful paradigm of memory compression since it helps to avoid unnecessary redundancy in a recurrent stochastic or neural model. Although the human memory system is by far more complex mechanisms similar to those that are outlined here may underly short-term memory. Also, human memory does not work from the first day – an effect known as childhood amnesia[16] – , it seems rather that before the onset of memory a little child has early experiences that are not stored in the memory in that way that they can be memorized. Rather it seems plausible to assume that these early experience's form a framework of expectations of what happens during normal life, only the deviations from these expectations are stored and stay as re-iterable memories.

Another aspect is a glance to possibilities that arise from reservoir computing that are tuned into a critical state. To the best knowledge of the author, no

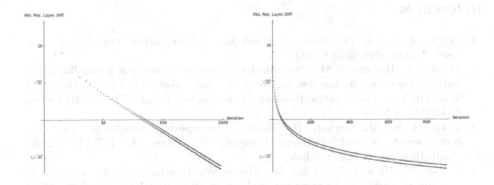

Fig. 3. Left: Double log plot of the reduced model. The x-axis depicts time (iterations) the y-axis the difference measure between the undisturbed network with the network that received one unexpected input at one iteration. Right: Log-lin plot fo the same data. One can see that the decay is proportional to t^{-a} which results in a straight line in the double log plot.

other approaches have been published. The result here is that the tuning into the critical state makes sense in order to keep old memories for a long period of time if no new memories make the forgetting necessary.

Moreover most related technical methods share the property that earlier collected information is lost exponentially as a function of time, even if there is only a finite amount of information contained in an infinite time series. It would be very good if an algorithm could be derived that combines a kind of data compression with the properties of Markov chains or similar approaches.

At the present algorithm the performance is still improvable. However, it is a RNN that has a slower forgetting property than exponential. Since the capacity of the RNN is constant, some kind of primitive data compression is obviously achieved.

Finally, one result of this work is to show up a possible functional connection between two phenomena that have been either seen in experiments or for other reasons postulated as mechanisms in neuronal tissue: dynamic balancing of neuronal activity and tuning the connectivity into a critical state. Although, this approach so far had a completely biological context it may be interesting to discuss in the following some aspects of the technical information processing.

Recently interesting approaches concerned proposed the connectivity as a result of self-organized criticality (e.g. [17]).

Acknowledgement. NSC (Nation Science Council) in Taiwan provided the budget for our project - project number : NSC 101-2221-E-194-038- and NSC 101-2221-E-758 -001-.

References

1. Beggs, J., Plenz, D.: Neuronal avalanches in neocortical curcuits. J. Neurosci. 24(22), 5216–5229 (2004)
2. Levina, A., Herrmann, M.: Dynamical synapses give rise to a power-law distribution of neuronal avalanches. In: Weiss, Y., Schoellkopf, B., Patt, J. (eds.) Advances in Neural Information Processing Systems, vol. 18, pp. 771–778. MIT Press, Cambridge (2006)
3. Lukoševičius, M., Jaeger, H.: Reservoir computing approaches to recurrent neural network training. Comput. Sci. Rev. 3, 127–149 (2009), doi:10.1016/j.cosrev.2009.03.005.
4. Nikolić, D., Häusler, S., Singer, W., Maass, W.: Distributed fading memory for stimulus properties in the primary visual cortex. PLoS Biol 7(12), e1000260 (2009), doi:10.1371/journal.pbio.1000260.
5. Hajnal, M.A., Lőrincz, A.: Critical echo state networks. In: Kollias, S.D., Stafylopatis, A., Duch, W., Oja, E. (eds.) ICANN 2006. Part I. NCS, vol. 4131, pp. 658–667. Springer, Heidelberg (2006)
6. Boedecker, J., Obst, O., Lizier, J., Mayer, N., Asada, M.: Information processing in echo state networks at the edge of chaos. Theory in Biosciences 131, 205–213 (2012)
7. Obst, O., Boedecker, J.: Guided self-organization of input-driven recurrent neural networks. In: Guided Self-Organization, pp. 319–340 (2014)
8. van Vreeswick, C., Sompolinsky, H.: Chaotic balanced state in a model of cortical circuits. Neural Computation 10, 1321–1371 (1998)
9. Jaeger, H.: The 'echo state' approach to analysing and training recurrent neural networks. In: GMD Report 148, GMD German National Research Insitute for Computer Science (2001),
   http://www.gmd.de/People/Herbert.Jaeger/Publications.html
10. Jaeger, H.: Adaptive nonlinear system identification with echo state networks. In: Becker, S., Thrun, S., Obermayer, K. (eds.) Advances in Neural Information Processing Systems 15 (NIPS 2002). MIT Press, Cambridge (2003)
11. Buechner, M., Young, P.: A Tighter Bound for the Echo State Property. IEEE Transaction on Neural Networks 17(3), 820–824 (2006)
12. Yildiz, I.B., Jaeger, H., Kiebel, S.J.: Re-visiting the echo state property. Neural Networks 35, 1–20 (2012)
13. Steil, J.: Online stability of backpropagation-decorrelation recurrent learning. Neurocomputing 69(79), 642–650 (2006),
   http://dx.doi.org/10.1016/j.neucom.2005.12.012
14. Mayer, N.M., Browne, M.: Self-prediction in echo state networks. In: Proceedings of The First International Workshop on Biological Inspired Approaches to Advanced Information Technology (BioAdIt 2004), Lausanne (2004)
15. Mayer, N.M., Obst, O., Yu-Chen, C.: Time series causality inference using echo state networks. In: Vigneron, V., Zarzoso, V., Moreau, E., Gribonval, R., Vincent, E. (eds.) LVA/ICA 2010. LNCS, vol. 6365, pp. 279–286. Springer, Heidelberg (2010)
16. Herbert, J.S., Pascalis, O.: Memory development. In: Slator, A., Lewis, M., eds.: Introduction to Infant Development. Oxford University Press (2007)
17. Uhlig, M., Levina, A., Geisel, T., Herrmann, J.M.: Critical dynamics in associative memory networks. Front Comput. Neurosci. 7(87) (2013)

Interactive Evolving Recurrent Neural Networks Are Super-Turing Universal

Jérémie Cabessa[1,2] and Alessandro E.P. Villa[2]

[1] Laboratory of Mathematical Economics (LEMMA),
University of Paris 2 – Panthéon-Assas,
4 Rue Blaise Desgoffe,
75006 Paris, France
[2] Neuroheuristic Research Group,
Department of Information Systems,
University of Lausanne,
1015 Lausanne, Switzerland

Abstract. Understanding the dynamical and computational capabilities of neural models represents an issue of central importance. In this context, recent results show that interactive evolving recurrent neural networks are super-Turing, irrespective of whether their synaptic weights are rational or real. We extend these results by showing that interactive evolving recurrent neural networks are not only super-Turing, but also capable of simulating any other possible interactive deterministic system. In this sense, interactive evolving recurrent neural networks represents a super-Turing universal model of computation, irrespective of whether their synaptic weights are rational or real.

Keywords: evolving recurrent neural networks, neural computation, interactive computation, analog computation, Turing machines with advice, super-Turing.

1 Introduction

Understanding the dynamical and computational capabilities of neural models represents an issue of central importance. In this context, much interest has been focused on comparing the computational capabilities of diverse theoretical neural models to those of abstract computing devices, see [9,17,8,11,10,13,14,12,2] as well as [15]. As a consequence, the computational power of neural networks has been shown to be intimately related to the nature of their synaptic weights and activation functions, and capable to range from finite state automata up to super-Turing capabilities.

In this global line of thinking, the computational capabilities of neural models have generally been characterised with respect to the classical computational framework introduced by Turing [16]. But this approach is inherently restrictive, and has nowadays been argued to "no longer fully corresponds to the current notion of computing in modern systems" [21], especially when it refers to bio-inspired complex information processing systems [18,21]. Indeed, in the brain (or

S. Wermter et al. (Eds.): ICANN 2014, LNCS 8681, pp. 57–64, 2014.

in organic life in general), information is rather processed in an interactive way, where previous experience must affect the perception of future inputs, and where older memories may themselves change with response to new inputs. Accordingly, the computational power of recurrent neural networks should rather be conceived from the perspective of *interactive computation* [22,7,20].

In this context, the capabilities of neural networks involved in an interactive computational paradigm have recently been studied [3,1,4,5]. It was proven that interactive static rational- and real-weighted recurrent neural networks are Turing equivalent and super-Turing, respectively [3,4], and that interactive evolving recurrent neural networks are super-Turing, irrespective of whether their synaptic weights are rational or real [1,5].

The present paper extends these results by showing that interactive evolving recurrent neural networks are not only super-Turing, but also capable of simulating any other possible interactive deterministic system. In this sense, interactive evolving recurrent neural networks represents a universal super-Turing model of computation, irrespective of whether their synaptic weights are modelled by rational or real numbers.

2   Preliminaries

Given some finite alphabet Σ, we let Σ^*, Σ^+, Σ^n, and Σ^ω denote respectively the sets of finite words, non-empty finite words, finite words of length n, and infinite words, all of them over alphabet Σ. Let also $\Sigma^{\leq\omega} = \Sigma^* \cup \Sigma^\omega$ be the set of all possible words (finite or infinite) over Σ. The empty word is denoted λ.

For any $x \in \Sigma^{\leq\omega}$, the *length* of x is denoted by $|x|$ and corresponds to the number of letters contained in x. If x is non-empty, we let $x(i)$ denote the $(i+1)$-th letter of x, for any $0 \leq i < |x|$. The prefix $x(0)\cdots x(i)$ of x is denoted by $x[0{:}i]$, for any $0 \leq i < |x|$. For any $x \in \Sigma^*$ and $y \in \Sigma^{\leq\omega}$, the fact that x is a *prefix* (resp. *strict prefix*) of y is denoted by $x \subseteq y$ (resp. $x \subsetneq y$). If $x \subseteq y$, we let $y - x = y(|x|)\cdots y(|y|-1)$ be the *suffix* of y that is not common to x (if $x = y$, then $y - x = \lambda$). Moreover, the *concatenation* of x and y is denoted by $x \cdot y$ or sometimes simply by xy. The word x^n consists of n copies of x concatenated together, with the convention that $x^0 = \lambda$.

Given some sequence of finite words $\{x_i : i \in \mathbb{N}\}$ such that $x_i \subseteq x_{i+1}$ for all $i \geq 0$, one defines the *limit* of the x_i's, denoted by $\lim_{i\geq 0} x_i$, as the unique finite or infinite word which is ultimately approached by the sequence of growing prefixes $\{x_i : i \geq 0\}$. Formally, if the sequence $\{x_i : i \in \mathbb{N}\}$ is eventually constant, i.e. there exists an index $i_0 \in \mathbb{N}$ such that $x_j = x_{i_0}$ for all $j \geq i_0$, then $\lim_{i\geq 0} x_i = x_{i_0}$, meaning that $\lim_{i\geq 0} x_i$ corresponds to the smallest finite word containing each word of $\{x_i : i \in \mathbb{N}\}$ as a finite prefix; if the sequence $\{x_i : i \in \mathbb{N}\}$ is not eventually constant, then $\lim_{i\geq 0} x_i$ corresponds to the unique infinite word containing each word of $\{x_i : i \in \mathbb{N}\}$ as a finite prefix.

Besides, a function $f : \Sigma^* \to \Sigma^*$ is called *monotone* if the relation $x \subseteq y$ implies $f(x) \subseteq f(y)$, for all $x, y \in \Sigma^*$. Any function $\varphi : \Sigma^\omega \to \Sigma^{\leq\omega}$ mapping infinite words to finite or infinite words will be referred to as an *ω-translation*.

Note that any monotone function $f : \{0,1\}^* \to \{0,1\}^*$ induces "in the limit" an ω-translation $f_\omega : \{0,1\}^\omega \to \{0,1\}^{\leq \omega}$ defined by $f_\omega(x) = \lim_{i \geq 0} f(x[0{:}i])$ for all $x \in \{0,1\}^\omega$. The monotonicity of f ensures that the value $f_\omega(x)$ is well-defined for all $x \in \{0,1\}^\omega$. In words, the value $f_\omega(x)$ corresponds to the finite or infinite word ultimately approached by the sequence of growing prefixes $\{f(x[0{:}i]) : i \geq 0\}$. Finally, an ω-translation $\psi : \{0,1\}^\omega \to \{0,1\}^{\leq \omega}$ will be called *continuous* if there exists a monotone function $f : \{0,1\}^* \to \{0,1\}^*$ such that $f_\omega = \psi$.

3   Interactive Computation

The general interactive computational paradigm consists of a step by step exchange of information between a system and its environment. In order to capture the unpredictability of next inputs at any time step, the dynamically generated input streams need to be modelled by potentially infinite sequences of symbols (the case of finite sequences of symbols would necessarily reduce to the classical computational framework) [22,7,21].

Throughout this paper, we consider a basic interactive computational scenario where, at every time step, the environment sends a non-empty input bit to the system (full environment activity condition), the system next updates its current state accordingly, and then either produces a corresponding output bit, or remains silent for a while to express the need of some internal computational phase before outputting a new bit, or remains silent forever to express the fact that it has died [20]. Consequently, after infinitely many time steps, the system will have received an infinite sequence of consecutive input bits s and translated it into a corresponding finite or infinite sequence of not necessarily consecutive (non-λ) output bits o_s. Note that when the system is deterministic, the output stream o_s associated to the input stream s is necessarily unique.

Accordingly, any interactive deterministic system S realises an ω-translation $\varphi_S : \{0,1\}^\omega \to \{0,1\}^{\leq \omega}$ defined by $\varphi_S(s) = o_s$, for every $s \in \{0,1\}^\omega$. An ω-translation ψ is then called *interactively computable* iff there exists an interactive deterministic system S such that $\varphi_S = \psi$. Note that in this definition, we do absolutely not require for the system S to be driven by a Turing program nor to contain any computable component of whatever kind. We simply require that S is deterministic and performs ω-translations in conformity with our interactive paradigm described above.

Van Leeuwen and Widermann introduced the concepts of an *interactive Turing machine* (I-TM) and an *interactive Turing machine with advice* (I-TM/A) as relevant extensions of their classical counterparts to the context of interactive computation. Interactive Turing machines with advice were shown to be strictly more powerful than interactive Turing machines (without advice) [18,19], and computationally equivalent to several other non-uniform models of interactive computation, like sequences of interactive finite automata, site machines, web Turing machines [18], and more recently to interactive analog neural networks and interactive evolving neural networks [3,5].

4   Interactive Evolving Recurrent Neural Networks

An *evolving recurrent neural network* (Ev-RNN) consists of a synchronous network of neurons (or processors) related together in a general architecture. The network contains N internal neurons $(x_i)_{i=1}^{N}$, M parallel input cells $(u_i)_{i=1}^{M}$, and P designated output neurons among the N. The dynamics of the network is computed as follows: given the activation values of the internal and input neurons $(x_j)_{j=1}^{N}$ and $(u_j)_{j=1}^{M}$ at time t, the activation value of each neuron x_i at time $t+1$ is updated by the following equation

$$x_i(t+1) = \sigma \left(\sum_{j=1}^{N} a_{ij}(t) \cdot x_j(t) + \sum_{j=1}^{M} b_{ij}(t) \cdot u_j(t) + c_i(t) \right) \qquad (1)$$

for $i = 1, \ldots, N$, where all $a_{ij}(t)$, $b_{ij}(t)$, and $c_i(t)$ are *time dependent* values describing the evolving weighted synaptic connections and weighted bias of the network, and σ is the classical saturated-linear activation function defined by $\sigma(x) = 0$ if $x < 0$, $\sigma(x) = x$ if $0 \leq x \leq 1$, and $\sigma(x) = 1$ if $x > 1$.

An *interactive evolving recurrent neural network* (I-Ev-RNN) $\mathcal{N}$ consists of an Ev-RNN provided with a single binary input cell u as well as two binary output cells: a data cell y_d and a validation cell y_v. Any infinite *input stream* $s = s(0)s(1)s(2)\cdots \in \{0,1\}^{\omega}$ transmitted to the input cell u induces via Equation (1) a corresponding pair of infinite streams $(y_d(0)y_d(1)y_d(2)\cdots, y_v(0)y_v(1)y_v(2)\cdots)$ $\in \{0,1\}^{\omega} \times \{0,1\}^{\omega}$. The *output stream* of $\mathcal{N}$ according to input s is then given by the finite or infinite subsequence o_s of successive data bits that occur simultaneously with positive validation bits, namely $o_s = \langle y_d(i) : i \in \mathbb{N}$ and $y_v(i) = 1 \rangle \in \{0,1\}^{\leq \omega}$. Hence, any I-Ev-RNN $\mathcal{N}$ naturally induces an ω-translation $\varphi_{\mathcal{N}} : \{0,1\}^{\omega} \rightarrow \{0,1\}^{\leq \omega}$ defined by $\varphi_{\mathcal{N}}(s) = o_s$, for each $s \in \{0,1\}^{\omega}$. An ω-translation $\psi : \{0,1\}^{\omega} \rightarrow \{0,1\}^{\leq \omega}$ is said to be *realisable* by some I-Ev-RNN iff there exists some I-Ev-RNN $\mathcal{N}$ such that $\varphi_{\mathcal{N}} = \psi$.

Throughout this paper, two models of interactive evolving recurrent neural networks are considered according to whether their underlying synaptic weights are confined to the class of rational or real numbers. Rational- and real-weighted interactive evolving recurrent neural network will be dented by I-Ev-RNN[$\mathbb{Q}$] and I-Ev-RNN[$\mathbb{R}$], respectively. Note that since rational numbers are included in real numbers, every I-Ev-RNN[$\mathbb{Q}$] is also a particular I-Ev-RNN[$\mathbb{R}$] by definition.

5   The Super-Turing Universal Computational Power of Interactive Evolving Recurrent Neural Networks

In a previous paper [5], we proved that interactive evolving recurrent neural networks were computationally equivalent to interactive Turing machines with advice, hence capable of a super-Turing computational power. Here, we extend this result by showing that interactive evolving recurrent neural networks are *super-Turing universal*, in the sense of being capable to realise any possible interactively computable ω-translation. Formally, for any possible interactively computable ω-translation ψ, there exists some I-Ev-RNN $\mathcal{N}$ such that $\varphi_\mathcal{N} = \psi$. Equivalently, for any interactive deterministic system $\mathcal{S}$, there exists some I-Ev-RNN $\mathcal{N}$ such that $\varphi_\mathcal{N} = \varphi_\mathcal{S}$. In words, any interactive deterministic system can be simulated by some interactive evolving recurrent neural networks.

Theorem 1. *Interactive evolving recurrent neural networks are super-Turing universal, irrespective of whether their synaptic weights are rational or real.*

Proof. We prove the result in two steps. Firstly, we show that any interactively computable ω-translation is continuous. Secondly, we prove that any continuous ω-translation is realisable by some I-Ev-RNN[$\mathbb{Q}$]. Consequently, for any interactively computable ω-translation ψ, there exists some I-Ev-RNN[$\mathbb{Q}$] $\mathcal{N}$ such that $\varphi_\mathcal{N} = \psi$, meaning that I-Ev-RNN[$\mathbb{Q}$]s are super-Turing universal. Finally, if I-Ev-RNN[$\mathbb{Q}$]s are super-Turing universal, then so are I-Ev-RNN[$\mathbb{R}$]s, since I-Ev-RNN[$\mathbb{R}$]s are more powerful than I-Ev-RNN[$\mathbb{Q}$]s. We now give the proofs of steps 1 and 2.

Step 1: Let ψ be some interactively computable ω-translation. Then by definition, there exists an interactive deterministic system $\mathcal{S}$ such that $\varphi_\mathcal{S} = \psi$. Now, consider the function $f : \{0,1\}^* \to \{0,1\}^*$ which maps every finite word u to the unique corresponding finite word produced by $\mathcal{S}$ after exactly $|u|$ steps of computation over input stream u provided bit by bit. The deterministic nature of $\mathcal{S}$ ensures that the finite word $f(u)$ is unique, and thus that f is well-defined.

We show that f is monotone. Suppose that $u \subseteq v$. It follow that $v = u \cdot (v - u)$. Hence, according to our interactive paradigm, the output strings produced by $\mathcal{S}$ after $|v|$ time steps of computation over input stream v, namely $f(v)$, simply consists of the output string produced after $|u|$ time steps of computation over input u, namely $f(u)$, followed by the output string produced after $|v - u|$ time steps of computation over input $v - u$. Consequently, $f(u) \subseteq f(v)$.

We now prove that the ω-translation $\varphi_\mathcal{S}$ performed by $\mathcal{S}$ satisfies $\varphi_\mathcal{S} = f_\omega$. Towards this purpose, given some infinite input stream $s \in \{0,1\}^\omega$, we consider in turn the two possible cases where either $\varphi_\mathcal{S}(s) \in \{0,1\}^\omega$ or $\varphi_\mathcal{S}(s) \in \{0,1\}^*$.

Firstly, suppose that $\varphi_\mathcal{S}(s) \in \{0,1\}^\omega$. According to our interactive scenario, $f(s[0{:}i])$ is a prefix of $\varphi_\mathcal{S}(s)$, for all $i \geq 0$. Moreover, since $\varphi_\mathcal{S}(s) \in \{0,1\}^\omega$, the sequence of partial output strings produced by $\mathcal{S}$ on input s after i time steps of computation cannot be eventually constant, i.e. $\lim_{i \to \infty} |f(s[0{:}i])| = \infty$. Hence, the two properties $f(s[0{:}i]) \subseteq \varphi_\mathcal{S}(s) \in \{0,1\}^\omega$ for all $i \geq 0$ and $\lim_{i \to \infty} |f(s[0{:}i])| = \infty$ ensure that $\varphi_\mathcal{S}(s)$ is the unique infinite word containing each word of $\{f(s[0{:}i]) : i \geq 0\}$ as a finite prefix, which is to say by definition that $\varphi_\mathcal{S}(s) = \lim_{i \geq 0} f(s[0{:}i]) = f_\omega(s)$.

Secondly, suppose that $\varphi_\mathcal{S}(s) \in \{0,1\}^*$. Once again, one has that $f(s[0{:}i])$ is a prefix of $\varphi_\mathcal{S}(s)$, for all $i \geq 0$. Moreover, since $\varphi_\mathcal{S}(s) \in \{0,1\}^*$, the sequence of partial output strings produced by $\mathcal{S}$ on input s after i time steps of computation must become stationary from some time step j onwards, i.e. $\lim_{i \to \infty} |f(s[0{:}i])| < \infty$. Hence, the entire finite output stream $\varphi_\mathcal{S}(s)$ must necessarily have been produced after a finite amount of time, and thus $\varphi_\mathcal{S}(s) \in \{f(s[0{:}i]) : i \geq 0\}$. Consequently, the three properties $f(s[0{:}i]) \subseteq \varphi_\mathcal{S}(s) \in \{0,1\}^*$ for all $i \geq 0$, $\lim_{i \to \infty} |f(s[0{:}i])| < \infty$, and $\varphi_\mathcal{S}(s) \in \{f(s[0{:}i]) : i \geq 0\}$ ensure that $\varphi_\mathcal{S}(s)$ is the smallest finite word that contains each word of $\{f(s[0:i]) : i \geq 0\}$ as a finite prefix, which is to say by definition that $\varphi_S(s) = \lim_{i \geq 0} f(s[0:i]) = f_\omega(s)$. Consequently, $\varphi_S(s) = f_\omega(s)$ for any $s \in \{0,1\}^\omega$, meaning that $\varphi_S = f_\omega$.

We proved that f is a monotone function such that $\varphi_S = f_\omega$. Hence, φ_S is continuous. Since $\varphi_S = \psi$, it follows that ψ is also continuous.

Step 2: Let ψ be a continuous ω-translation. Then there exists some monotone function $f : \{0,1\}^* \to \{0,1\}^*$ such that $f_\omega = \psi$. We begin by encoding all possible values of f into successive distinct rational numbers. For any $n > 0$, let $w_{n,1}, \ldots, w_{n,2^n}$ be the lexicographical enumeration of $\{0,1\}^n$, and let $w_n \in \{0,1,2\}^*$ be the finite word given by $w_n = 2 \cdot f(w_{n,1}) \cdot 2 \cdot f(w_{n,2}) \cdot 2 \cdots 2 \cdot f(w_{n,2^n}) \cdot 2$. Then, consider the rational encoding q_n of the word w_n given by $q_n = \sum_{i=1}^{|w_n|} \frac{2 \cdot w_n(i)+1}{6^i}$. Note that for all $n > 0$, one has $q_n \in]0,1[$ and $q_n \neq q_{n+1}$, since $w_n \neq w_{n+1}$. Moreover, it can be shown that w_n can be decoded from q_n by some Turing machine, or equivalently, by some rational recurrent neural network [13,14].

Now, consider Procedure 1 below. Note that its only non-recursive instruction is "wait for next value q_{i+1} to come". We show that there exists some I-Ev-RNN[$\mathbb{Q}$] $\mathcal{N}$ that performs Procedure 1. The network $\mathcal{N}$ consists of one evolving and one non-evolving rational sub-network connected together. The evolving rational-weighted part of $\mathcal{N}$ is made up of a single processor x_e receiving a background activity of evolving intensity $c_e(t)$. The synaptic weight $c_e(t)$ takes the successive values $q_1, q_2, q_3, \ldots$, by switching from value q_k to q_{k+1} after every N_k time steps, for some large enough $N_k > 0$ to be described. The non-evolving rational-weighted part of $\mathcal{N}$ is designed in order to perform the successive recursive steps of Procedure 1 every time neuron x_e receives some new activation value q_k [14]. For each $k > 0$, the time interval N_k is chosen large enough in order for $\mathcal{N}$ to be able to perform all such successive steps before the apparition of the next value q_{k+1}. Moreover, the network $\mathcal{N}$ outputs the current pair $(v - u, 1^{|v-u|})$ bit by bit every time it reaches up the instructions "$p_s \leftarrow p_s \cdot (v - u)$" and "$q_s \leftarrow q_s \cdot 1^{|v-u|}$", and it keeps outputting pairs of bits $(0,0)$s meanwhile.

Procedure 1.

Infinite input stream $s = s(0)s(1)s(2) \cdots \in \{0,1\}^\omega$ provided bit by bit
$i \leftarrow 0$; $u \leftarrow \lambda$; $v \leftarrow \lambda$; $p_s \leftarrow \lambda$; $q_s \leftarrow \lambda$;
loop
    Wait for next value q_{i+1} to come;   Decode $f(s[0:i])$ from q_{i+1}; $v \leftarrow f(s[0:i])$;
    if $u \subsetneq v$ **then**
        $p_s \leftarrow p_s \cdot (v - u)$; $q_s \leftarrow q_s \cdot 1^{|v-u|}$;
    else
        $p_s \leftarrow p_s \cdot 0$; $q_s \leftarrow q_s \cdot 0$;
    end if
    $i \leftarrow i + 1$; $u \leftarrow v$;
    end loop

It remains to prove that $\varphi_{\mathcal{N}} = \psi$. Note that, for any input stream $s \in \{0,1\}^\omega$, the finite word that has been output by $\mathcal{N}$ at the end of each instruction "output $v - u$ bit by bit" corresponds precisely to the finite word $f(s[0:i])$ currently stored in the variable v. Hence, after infinitely many time steps, the finite or infinite word $\varphi_{\mathcal{N}}(s)$ output by $\mathcal{N}$ contains all words of $\{f(x[0:i]) : i \geq 0\}$ as a finite prefix. Moreover, if $\varphi_{\mathcal{N}}(s)$ is finite, its value necessarily corresponds to some current content of the variable v, i.e to some finite word $f(s[0:j])$, for some $j \geq 0$. Hence, irrespective of whether $\varphi_{\mathcal{N}}(s)$ is finite or infinite, one always has $\varphi_{\mathcal{N}}(s) = \lim_{i \geq 0} f(x[0:i]) = f_\omega(s)$, for any $s \in \{0,1\}^\omega$. Therefore, $\varphi_{\mathcal{N}} = f_\omega = \psi$, meaning that ψ is realised by $\mathcal{N}$. □

By putting together previous Theorem 1 and Theorem 1 of [5], one obtains the following complete characterisation of the computational power of interactive evolving recurrent neural networks.

Theorem 2. *Let $\psi : \{0,1\}^\omega \to \{0,1\}^{\leq \omega}$ be an ω-translation. The following conditions are equivalent:*
1. *ψ is interactively computable;*
2. *ψ is realisable by some I-Ev-RNN[$\mathbb{Q}$];*
3. *ψ is realisable by some I-Ev-RNN[$\mathbb{R}$];*
4. *ψ is realisable by some I-TM/A;*
5. *ψ is continuous.*

Proof. The equivalences between 2, 3, 4, and 5 are proven in [5]. The implication $1 \Rightarrow 2$ is stated in Theorem 1, and the implication $2 \Rightarrow 1$ holds by definition. □

6 Discussion

Interactive evolving neural networks (I-Ev-RNNs) are computationally equivalent to interactive machines with advice (I-TM/As), hence capable of super-Turing potentialities, irrespective of whether their synaptic weights are rational or real [5]. They are also capable of simulating any other possible interactive deterministic system. In this sense, I-Ev-RNNs and I-TM/As represent two equivalent super-Turing universal models of computation.

These results can be understood as follows: similarly to the classical context, where every possible partial function from integers to integers can be computed by some Turing machine with oracle [16], in the interactive context, every possible ω-translation performed in an interactive way can be computed by some interactive Turing machine with advice, or equivalently, by some interactive evolving recurrent neural network. These results support the extension of the Church-Turing Thesis to the context of interactive computation stated by van Leeuwen and Wiedermann [19]: "Any (non-uniform interactive) computation can be described in terms of interactive Turing machines with advice."

The question of the possible achievement of such super-Turing capabilities by real biological neural networks remains beyond the scope of this paper. We refer to Copeland's extensive work for deeper philosophical considerations about hypercomputation in general [6].

References

1. Cabessa, J.: Interactive evolving recurrent neural networks are super-Turing. In: ICAART 2012, pp. 328–333. SciTePress (2012)
2. Cabessa, J., Siegelmann, H.T.: Evolving recurrent neural networks are super-turing. In: IJCNN 2011, pp. 3200–3206. IEEE (2011)
3. Cabessa, J., Siegelmann, H.T.: The computational power of interactive recurrent neural networks. Neural Computation 24(4), 996–1019 (2012)
4. Cabessa, J., Villa, A.E.P.: The expressive power of analog recurrent neural networks on infinite input streams. Theor. Comput. Sci. 436, 23–34 (2012)
5. Cabessa, J., Villa, A.E.P.: The super-turing computational power of interactive evolving recurrent neural networks. In: Mladenov, V., Koprinkova-Hristova, P., Palm, G., Villa, A.E.P., Appollini, B., Kasabov, N. (eds.) ICANN 2013. LNCS, vol. 8131, pp. 58–65. Springer, Heidelberg (2013)
6. Copeland, B.J.: Hypercomputation. Minds Mach. 12(4), 461–502 (2002)
7. Goldin, D., Wegner, P.: Principles of interactive computation. In: Goldin, D., Smolka, S.A., Wegner, P. (eds.) Interactive Computation, pp. 25–37. Springer (2006)
8. Kleene, S.C.: Representation of events in nerve nets and finite automata. In: Shannon, C., McCarthy, J. (eds.) Automata Studies, pp. 3–41. Princeton University Press (1956)
9. McCulloch, W.S., Pitts, W.: A logical calculus of the ideas immanent in nervous activity. Bulletin of Mathematical Biophysic 5, 115–133 (1943)
10. Minsky, M.L.: Computation: finite and infinite machines. Prentice-Hall, Inc. (1967)
11. von Neumann, J.: The computer and the brain. Yale University Press (1958)
12. Siegelmann, H.T.: Neural networks and analog computation: beyond the Turing limit. Birkhauser Boston Inc. (1999)
13. Siegelmann, H.T., Sontag, E.D.: Analog computation via neural networks. Theor. Comput. Sci. 131(2), 331–360 (1994)
14. Siegelmann, H.T., Sontag, E.D.: On the computational power of neural nets. J. Comput. Syst. Sci. 50(1), 132–150 (1995)
15. Síma, J., Orponen, P.: General-purpose computation with neural networks: A survey of complexity theoretic results. Neural Comput. 15(12), 2727–2778 (2003)
16. Turing, A.M.: On computable numbers, with an application to the Entscheidungsproblem. Proc. London Math. Soc. 2(42), 230–265 (1936)
17. Turing, A.M.: Intelligent machinery. Technical report, National Physical Laboratory, Teddington, UK (1948)
18. van Leeuwen, J., Wiedermann, J.: Beyond the Turing limit: Evolving interactive systems. In: Pacholski, L., Ružička, P. (eds.) SOFSEM 2001. LNCS, vol. 2234, pp. 90–109. Springer, Heidelberg (2001)
19. van Leeuwen, J., Wiedermann, J.: The Turing machine paradigm in contemporary computing. In: Engquist, B., Schmid, W. (eds.) Mathematics Unlimited - 2001 and Beyond, pp. 1139–1155. Springer (2001)
20. van Leeuwen, J., Wiedermann, J.: A theory of interactive computation. In: Goldin, D., Smolka, S.A., Wegner, P. (eds.) Interactive Computation, pp. 119–142. Springer (2006)
21. Wiedermann, J., van Leeuwen, J.: How we think of computing today. In: Beckmann, A., Dimitracopoulos, C., Löwe, B. (eds.) CiE 2008. LNCS, vol. 5028, pp. 579–593. Springer, Heidelberg (2008)
22. Wegner, P.: Interactive foundations of computing. Theor. Comput. Sci. 192, 315–351 (1998)

Attractor Metadynamics
in Adapting Neural Networks

Claudius Gros, Mathias Linkerhand, and Valentin Walther

Institute for Theoretical Physics, Goethe University Frankfurt, Germany
{gros07,linkerhand,walther}@itp.uni-frankfurt.de
http://itp.uni-frankfurt.de/~gros

Abstract. Slow adaption processes, like synaptic and intrinsic plasticity, abound in the brain and shape the landscape for the neural dynamics occurring on substantially faster timescales. At any given time the network is characterized by a set of internal parameters, which are adapting continuously, albeit slowly. This set of parameters defines the number and the location of the respective adiabatic attractors. The slow evolution of network parameters hence induces an evolving attractor landscape, a process which we term attractor metadynamics. We study the nature of the metadynamics of the attractor landscape for several continuous-time autonomous model networks. We find both first- and second-order changes in the location of adiabatic attractors and argue that the study of the continuously evolving attractor landscape constitutes a powerful tool for understanding the overall development of the neural dynamics.

Keywords: adiabatic attractors, attractor metadynamics, neural networks, adaption, homeostasis.

1 Fast Neural Dynamics vs. Slow Adaption Processes

Complex dynamical systems are often characterized by a variety of timescales and the brain is no exception here [1,2]. It has been observed that the neural dynamics is contingent, for time scales ranging from hundreds of milliseconds to minutes, on the underlying anatomical network structure in distinct ways [3]. This relation between anatomy and the timescale characterizing neural activity is present even for autonomous systems, viz in the absence of external stimuli. It has been proposed, complementarily, that certain temporal aspects of the brain activity may reflect the multitude of timescales present in the environment [4], and could be induced through adaptive processes [5].

The neurons in the brain are faced with the problem, in a related perspective, of maintaining long-term functional stability on both the single neuron level, as well as on the level of network activities, in view of the fact that the constituents of the molecular and biochemical machinery, such as ion channel proteins and synaptic receptors, have lifetimes ranging only from minutes to weeks [6]. This situation results in the need to regulate homeostatically both the inter-neural synaptic strength [7], and the intra-neural parameters, the latter process termed intrinsic plasticity [8,9].

S. Wermter et al. (Eds.): ICANN 2014, LNCS 8681, pp. 65–72, 2014.

Homeostatic mechanisms in the brain can be regarded as part of the generic control problem of the overall brain dynamics [10], with the adaption of neural parameters being necessary to achieve certain targets [11]. Here we study the consequences of ongoing slow adaption for the time evolution of the landscape of adiabatic attractors, viz of the attractors of the dynamical system obtained by temporarily freezing the adaption process. We find that the locus of the instantaneous attracting state guides the overall time evolution and that the study of the attractor metadynamics, which find to be possibly both continuous and discontinuous, constitutes a powerful tool for the study of evolving neural networks.

2   Adapting Continuous-Time Recurrent Neural Networks

We consider continuous-time neural networks [12,13], defined by

$$\dot{x}_i = -\Gamma x_i + \sum_j w_{ij} y_j, \qquad y_i = \frac{1}{1 + e^{a_i(b_i - x_i)}} \, . \qquad (1)$$

One may consider either the firing rates $y_i = y_i(t)$ as the primary dynamical variables or, equivalently, the corresponding membrane potentials $x_i = x_i(t)$, with the sigmoidal $g(z) = 1/(1 + \exp(z))$ constituting the standard non-linear input-output relation for a single neuron. One denotes a_i the gain (slope) of the sigmoidal and b_i the respective threshold. Here $\Gamma > 0$ sets the relaxation rate for the membrane potentials x_i and the w_{ij} are the inter-neural synaptic weights.

One speaks of intrinsic adaption when the internal parameters of an individual neuron adapt slowly over time [14,15]. In our case the bias a_i and threshold b_i. This kind of internal adaption is necessary for keeping the output $y_i(t) \in [0, 1]$ within the desired dynamical range, viz within the working regime of the dynamical system. Anatomical constraints such as the limited availability of energy are imposed on the long-term firing statistics of each neuron. On a functional level, the firing patterns are expected to encode maximal information. This distribution of maximal information is at the same time the least biased or 'noncomittal' with respect to the constraints [16] and it is obtained by maximizing Shannon's information entropy. Given a certain mean μ, here the mean target firing rate [2], the desired output distribution is an exponential,

$$p_\lambda(y) \propto e^{\lambda y}, \qquad \mu = \int dy \, y \, p(y) \, , \qquad (2)$$

for the neural model (1), with λ being the respective Langrange multiplier. The distance of a time series of data, like the neural firing rate $y_i(t)$ for a given neuron i, relative to this target distribution function $p_\lambda(y)$ is captured by the Kullback-Leibler divergence K_i [2]

$$K_i = \int dy \, p_i(y) \log\left(\frac{p_i(y)}{p_\lambda(y)}\right), \qquad p_i(y) = \lim_{T \to \infty} \int_0^T \delta(y - y_i(t - \tau)) \frac{d\tau}{T} \, , \qquad (3)$$

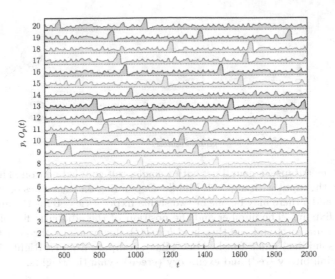

Fig. 1. A network with $N = 1000$ neurons and $N_p = 20$ encoded attractor states, see Eq. (5). The neurons adapt, trying to optimized the relative information content (3) of their respective activities. Shown are vertically displaced, as a function of time t, time lines of the overlaps $O_p(t) \in [0, 1]$, see Eq. (6). Notice, that the polyhomeostatic adaption (4) leads to transient-state dynamics, one attractor relict ξ^p after the other is transiently visited by the state of network activities, as evident by the bumps in the respective time lines.

where $p_i(y)$ is the time-averaged distribution of $y_i(t)$. One can now optimize the adaption by minimizing (3) with respect to the intrinsic parameters a_i and b_i and one obtains [17,18]

$$
\begin{aligned}
\dot{a}_i &= \epsilon_a \big(1/a_i + (x_i - b_i)\theta \big) \\
\dot{b}_i &= \epsilon_b (-a_i)\theta, \qquad\qquad \theta = 1 - 2y_i + \lambda\,(1 - y_i)\,y_i
\end{aligned}
\tag{4}
$$

with ϵ_a and ϵ_b being adaption rates for the gain a_i and the threshold b_i respectively. In effect, the system is given an entire distribution function $p_\lambda(y)$ as an adaption target. The adaption rules (4) hence generalize the principle of homeostasis, which deals with regulating a single scalar quantity, and have been denoted polyhomeostatic optimization [19].

3   Transient State Dynamics

A convenient way to construct networks with a predefined set $\xi^p = (\xi_1^p, \xi_2^p, ..)$ of attracting states, with $p = 1, .., N_p$, is by selecting the synaptic weights as [20]

$$
w_{ij} \propto \sum_p \big(\xi_i^p - \bar{\xi}_i \big)\big(\xi_j^p - \bar{\xi}_j \big) ,
\tag{5}
$$

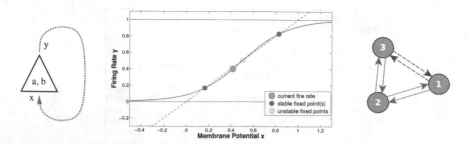

Fig. 2. Left: The autapse, a neural net with a single, self-coupled neuron. The output is directly fed to the input with $w_{11} = 1$. Middle: Depending on the values of the intrinsic parameters a and b there may be one or two stable fixpoints $\dot{x} = 0$ for the autapse, and one unstable fixpoint. The number and the position of the adiabatic fixpoints change when the gain $a = a(t)$ and the threshold $b = b(t)$ slowly adapt through (4). Shown are $y(x)$ (red solid line) and x (dashed black line), compare Eq. (1). Right: A three-site network with inhibitory (red) and excitatory (green) synaptic weights.

where $\bar{\xi}_j$ is a local activity, averaged over all encoded patterns ξ^p. With the Hopfield encoding (5) one can hence construct attractor networks having point attractors close to the patterns ξ^p, with a given, predefined average activity level $\bar{\xi}^p = \sum_i \xi_i^p / N$, where N is the number of neurons in the network.

As a first application we study a network of $N = 1000$ neurons with the synaptic weights selected using the Hopfield encoding (5) and $N_p = 20$ random binary patterns $\xi^p = (\xi_1^p, .., \xi_N^p)$ drawn from an uniform distribution. We define with

$$O_p(t) = \frac{\sum_i \xi_i^p y_i}{||\xi^p|| \, ||y||}, \qquad ||z|| \equiv \sqrt{\sum_i z_i^2} \qquad (6)$$

the overlap between the current state $y(t) = (y_1(t), .., y_N(t))$ and a given stored attractor state ξ^p, in terms of the respective normalized scalar product.

In Fig. 1 we show a typical simulation result for the overlaps $O_p(t) \in [0, 1]$, with the individual time lines being shown vertically displaced and color-coded. The parameters used for the simulation are $\Gamma = 1$, $\epsilon_a = 0.1$, $\epsilon_b = 0.01$ and $\bar{\xi}^p = 0.2$, $\mu = 0.2$. Alternative values for the adaption rates $\epsilon_{a,b}$ lead qualitatively to similar behaviors, whenever the adaption process is substantially slower than the neural dynamics (1). One observes two distinct features.

– For $\epsilon_a = \epsilon_b = 0$ the dynamics would eventually settle into a steady state close to one of the stored patterns ξ^p. The dynamical activity is, on the other hand, continuous and autonomously ongoing when intrinsic adaption is present, as evident from Fig. 1. This is due to the fact that the system tries to achieve exponentially distributed firing-rate distributions. Without adaption the individual $p_i(y)$ would be simple δ-functions in any fixpoint state and this would lead to a very high and therefore sub-optimal Kullback-Leibler divergence (3).

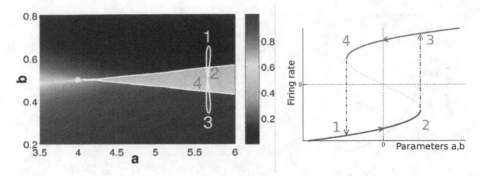

Fig. 3. Left: Phase diagram of the autapse, as illustrated in Fig. 2. The activity $y \in [0,1]$ of the fixpoint is color-coded, for fixed gains a and thresholds b of the sigmoidal, see Eq. (1), when only a single stable fixpoint is present. The greenish area within the two white lines denotes the phase space containing two stable fixpoints. The thick white line is the limiting cycle for polyhomeostatically adapting intrinsic parameters $(a(t), b(t))$, compare Eq. (4). Right: The firing rate of the adiabatic fixpoint (stable/unstable: thick/dashed lines) as function of the intrinsic parameters. The arrows and numbers indicate the section of the hysteresis loop in the landscape of adiabatic fixpoints corresponding to the equally labeled sections of the limiting cycle of $(a(t), b(t))$ shown in the left panel.

- The overlaps $O_p(t)$ are, most of the time, relatively small with temporally well defined characteristic bumps corresponding to dynamical states $y(t)$ approaching closely one of the initially stored patterns ξ^p. This type of dynamics has been termed transient-state [21] and latching [22] dynamics and may be used for semantic learning in autonomously active neural networks [23,24].

The inclusion of intrinsic adaption hence destroys all previously present attracting states. When the adaption process is slow and hence weak, with the actual values for the adaption rates ϵ_a and ϵ_b not being relevant, the system will however still notice the remains of the original point attractors and slow down when close by. The resulting type of network has been termed attractor relict network [23].

4   Discontinuous Attractor Metadynamics

A complete listing of all attracting states and the study of their respective time evolution is cumbersome for a large network like the one of Fig. 1. For an in-depth study we have selected two small model systems, we start with a single, self-coupled neuron, the autapse, as illustrated in Fig. 2 (left).

The fixpoint condition is $x = y(x)$, for $\Gamma = 1 = w_{11}$, and it is depicted in Fig. 2 (middle). Depending on the location of the turning point b of the sigmoidal and on its steepness a, there may be either one or two stable fixpoints, the respective

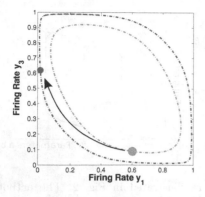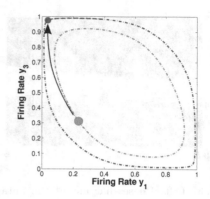

Fig. 4. For the three site network illustrated in Fig. 2 (right), the time evolution of the firing rates $(y_1(t), y_3(t))$. The green line is the trajectory of the final limiting cycle and the red line of the single adiabatic attractor present in the system. The black arrows illustrate the instantaneous flow, attracting the current dynamical state (green filled circles) to the current position of the adiabatic attractor (red filled circles). The right panel follows in time shortly after the left panel.

phase diagram is presented in Fig. 3 (left). Additionally an unstable fixpoint may be present (central region).

The actual values $(a(t), b(t))$ of the intrinsic parameters polyhomeostatically adapt via (4), an example of an actual state is included in Fig. 2 (middle) and the final limiting cycle in Fig. 3 (left). The internal parameters settle, after an initial transient, in a region of phase space crossing two first-order phase transitions at which the number of attractors changes from $1 \leftrightarrow 2 \leftrightarrow 1$, resulting in a hysteresis loop for the adiabatic attractor landscape, compare Fig. 3 (right).

In the limit of long times the internal parameters, as given by the white elongated eight-shaped loop in Fig. 3 (left), stay for finite time intervals in the regions of the phase diagram characterized by a single fixpoint (top/bottom : blue/red). The limiting cycle of the adaption trajectory hence overshoots the hysteresis loop characterized by the vertical transitions illustrated in Fig. 3 (right).

The dynamics is relatively slow on the hysteresis branches $1 \rightarrow 2$ and $3 \rightarrow 4$ and becomes very fast when the local adiabatic fixpoints vanishes. At this point the system is forced to rapidly evolve towards the opposite branch of the hysteresis loop, an example of self-organized slow-fast dynamics.

5   Continuous Attractor Metadynamics

As a second model system we consider the three-site network depicted in Fig. 2 (right), with $w_{12} = w_{21} = 1 = w_{32} = w_{23}$ and $w_{31} = w_{13} = -1$. At first sight one may expect an attractor metadynamics equivalent to the one of the autapse, since the three-site net also has two possible attracting states (y_1^*, y_2^*, y_3^*), with either y_2^* and y_1^* large and y_3^* small, or with y_2^* and y_3^* large and y_1^* small.

There is indeed a region in phase space for which these two fixpoints coexist [25], but the system adapts the six internal parameters $a_i(t)$ and $b_i(t)$ such that a single adiabatic fixpoint remains, which morphs continuously under the influence of the polyhomeostatic adaption (4).

In Fig. 4 we present the resulting limiting cycle of the full dynamics projected onto the (y_1, y_3) plane (the activity of y_2 is intermediate and only weakly changing). One observes that the adiabatic fixpoint moves on a continuous trajectory, an adiabatic limiting cycle. This behavior contrasts with the time evolution of the attractor landscape observed for the autapse, as presented in Fig. 3 (right), which is characterized by a discontinuous hysteresis loop.

The adiabatic fixpoint approaches $(y_1^* \approx 1, y_3^* \approx 0)$ and $(y_1^* \approx 0, y_3^* \approx 1)$ repeatedly, as evident in Fig. 4. The corresponding phase space trajectory then slows down, as one can observe when plotting the actual time evolution, an example of transient-state dynamics.

6   Carrot and Donkey Dynamics

In the metaphor of the donkey trying to reach the carrot it carries itself, the animal will never reach its target. The case of self-generated attractor metadynamics studied here is analogous. The current dynamical state is attracted by the nearest adiabatic attractor, but the systems itself morphs the attractor continuously when the trajectory tries to close in. The locus of the attractor evolves, either continuously or discontinuously, and the trajectory is then attracted by the adiabatic fixpoint at its new locus.

This feature allows to characterize decision processes in the brain and in model task problems dynamically [26,27], and choice options can be extracted in terms of corresponding adiabatic fixpoints. Here we studied autonomous systems, starting from attractor networks, with the aim to obtain a first overview regarding the possible types of self-generated attractor metadynamics.

Acknowledgments. The authors would like to thank Peter Hirschfeld for illuminating suggestions.

References

1. Izhikevich, E.M.: Dynamical systems in neuroscience. The MIT press (2007)
2. Gros, C.: Complex and adaptive dynamical systems: A primer. Springer (2013)
3. Honey, C.J., Kötter, R., Breakspear, M., Sporns, O.: Network structure of cerebral cortex shapes functional connectivity on multiple time scales. Proceedings of the National Academy of Sciences 104(24), 10240–10245 (2007)
4. Kiebel, S.J., Daunizeau, J., Friston, K.J.: A hierarchy of time-scales and the brain. PLoS Computational Biology 4(11), e1000209 (2008)
5. Ulanovsky, N., Las, L., Farkas, D., Nelken, I.: Multiple time scales of adaptation in auditory cortex neurons. The Journal of Neuroscience 24(46), 10440–10453 (2004)
6. Marder, E., Goaillard, J.M.: Variability, compensation and homeostasis in neuron and network function. Nature Reviews Neuroscience 7(7), 563–574 (2006)

7. Turrigiano, G.G., Nelson, S.B.: Homeostatic plasticity in the developing nervous system. Nature Reviews Neuroscience 5(2), 97–107 (2004)
8. Daoudal, G., Debanne, D.: Long-term plasticity of intrinsic excitability: learning rules and mechanisms. Learning & Memory 10(6), 456–465 (2003)
9. Echegoyen, J., Neu, A., Graber, K.D., Soltesz, I.: Homeostatic plasticity studied using in vivo hippocampal activity-blockade: synaptic scaling, intrinsic plasticity and age-dependence. PloS one 2(8), e700 (2007)
10. O'Leary, T., Wyllie, D.J.: Neuronal homeostasis: time for a change? The Journal of Physiology 589(20), 4811–4826 (2011)
11. Ge, S., Hang, C.C., Lee, T.H., Zhang, T.: Stable adaptive neural network control. Springer Publishing Company, Incorporated (2010)
12. Beer, R.D.: On the dynamics of small continuous-time recurrent neural networks. Adaptive Behavior 3(4), 469–509 (1995)
13. Beer, R.D., Gallagher, J.C.: Evolving dynamical neural networks for adaptive behavior. Adaptive Behavior 1(1), 91–122 (1992)
14. Triesch, J.: A gradient rule for the plasticity of a neuron's intrinsic excitability. In: Duch, W., Kacprzyk, J., Oja, E., Zadrożny, S. (eds.) ICANN 2005. LNCS, vol. 3696, pp. 65–70. Springer, Heidelberg (2005)
15. Marković, D., Gros, C.: Intrinsic adaptation in autonomous recurrent neural networks. Neural Computation 24(2), 523–540 (2012)
16. Jaynes, E.T.: Information theory and statistical mechanics. Physical Review 106(4), 620 (1957)
17. Linkerhand, M., Gros, C.: Self-organized stochastic tipping in slow-fast dynamical systems. Mathematics and Mechanics of Complex Systems 1(2), 129–147 (2013)
18. Steil, J.J.: Online reservoir adaptation by intrinsic plasticity for backpropagation–decorrelation and echo state learning. Neural Networks 20(3), 353–364 (2007)
19. Markovic, D., Gros, C.: Self-Organized Chaos through Polyhomeostatic Optimization. Physical Review Letters 105(6) (August 2010)
20. Hopfield, J.J.: Neural networks and physical systems with emergent collective computational abilities. Proceedings of the National Academy of Sciences 79(8), 2554–2558 (1982)
21. Gros, C.: Neural networks with transient state dynamics. New Journal of Physics 9(4), 109 (2007)
22. Russo, E., Namboodiri, V.M., Treves, A., Kropff, E.: Free association transitions in models of cortical latching dynamics. New Journal of Physics 10(1), 15008 (2008)
23. Gros, C.: Cognitive computation with autonomously active neural networks: An emerging field. Cognitive Computation 1(1), 77–90 (2009)
24. Gros, C., Kaczor, G.: Semantic learning in autonomously active recurrent neural networks. Logic Journal of IGPL 18(5), 686–704 (2010)
25. Linkerhand, M., Gros, C.: Generating functionals for autonomous latching dynamics in attractor relict networks. Scientific Reports 3 (2013)
26. Beer, R.D.: Dynamical approaches to cognitive science. Trends in Cognitive Sciences 4(3), 91–99 (2000)
27. Deco, G., Rolls, E.T., Romo, R.: Synaptic dynamics and decision making. Proceedings of the National Academy of Sciences 107(16), 7545–7549 (2010)

Basic Feature Quantities of Digital Spike Maps

Hiroki Yamaoka, Narutoshi Horimoto, and Toshimichi Saito

Hosei University, Koganei, Tokyo 184-8584, Japan
tsaito@hosei.ac.jp

Abstract. The digital spike-phase map is a simple digital dynamical system that can generate various spike-trains. In order to approach systematic analysis of the steady and transient states, four basic feature quantities are presented. Using the quantities, we analyze an example based on the bifurcating neuron with triangular base signal and consider basic four cases of the spike-train dynamics.

Keywords: digital spike-trains, spiking neurons, dynamical systems.

1 Introduction

The digital spike-phase map (DPM) is a simple digital dynamical system on a set of lattice points. Depending on parameters and initial value, the DPM can generate a variety of periodic/transient spike-trains (PSTs/TSTs). The PSTs and TSTs represent steady and transient states, respectively. Motivations for studying the DPM are many and include the following three points [1]-[4]. First, a computer-aided exact analysis is possible because the DPM is digital. The analysis results can contribute to develop study of various digital dynamical systems such as cellular automata and dynamic binary neural networks [5]-[7]. Second, the variety of PSTs is useful in spike-based applications such as signal processing, communication, modeling and neural prosthesis [6]-[12]. Third, analysis of the TSTs are basic to control stability and transient phenomena of the reconfigurable spike-train generators [12].

In order to approach systematic analysis of the DPM dynamics, this paper presents four basic feature quantities. For the steady states, we present the number of co-existing PSTs (#PST) and the maximum period of the PSTs (P_{max}). #PST and P_{max} can characterize variation and complexity of the PSTs, respectively. For the transient states, we present the concentricity of TSTs (C_t) and the maximum transient step of the TSTs (T_{max}). C_t and T_{max} can characterize the domain of attraction and complexity of TSTs, respectively. The C_t is an improved version of that in [3] [4] and is based on the concentricity of state transition in random neural networks [13].

Using these quantities, we analyze an example of the DPM based on a piecewise linear analog spike-phase map (APM) of a bifurcating neuron (BN [14] [15]) with triangular base signal. Although the APM exhibits either chaos [16] or fixed point (the dynamics is simple), the DPM can exhibit a variety of PSTs/TSTs. Performing numerical experiments, we consider four basic cases of the dynamics

S. Wermter et al. (Eds.): ICANN 2014, LNCS 8681, pp. 73–80, 2014.

including very complex steady states. Note that Refs. [1]-[4] do not use (P_{max}, T_{max}) and have not considered the four basic cases and complex steady states.

2   Digital Spike-Phase Map

The DPM is a mapping from a set of lattice points to itself as shown in Fig. 1.

$$\theta_{n+1} = f(\theta_n), \ f : L_0 \to L_0 \equiv \{l_0, l_1, \cdots l_{N-1}\}, \ l_i \equiv \frac{i}{N}, \ i = 0 \sim N - 1 \quad (1)$$

where θ_n is the n-th digital spike-phase. Iteration of f generates the sequence of phases θ_n. Since each of N lattice points has one image, the DPM has N^N variations. Applying the normalized period 1, we define the spike-train:

$$Y(\tau) = \begin{cases} 1 & \text{for } \tau = \tau_n \\ 0 & \text{for } \tau \neq \tau_n \end{cases} \ \tau_n = \theta_n + n \in L_n \equiv \{l_0 + n, \cdots, l_{N-1} + n\} \quad (2)$$

where τ_n is the n-th digital spike position and $n = 0, 1, 2, \cdots$. The spike-train is represented by the spike-position that appears ones per unit interval L_n. The DPM can output various spike-trains. We give basic definitions.

Definition 1: A point $p \in L_0$ is said to be a periodic point (PEP) with period k if $p = f^k(p)$ and $f(p)$ to $f^k(p)$ are all different where f^k is the k-fold composition of f. The PEP with period 1 is referred to as a fixed point. A sequence of the PEPs, $\{p, f(p), \cdots, f^{k-1}(p)\}$, is said to be a periodic orbit (PEO) with period k.

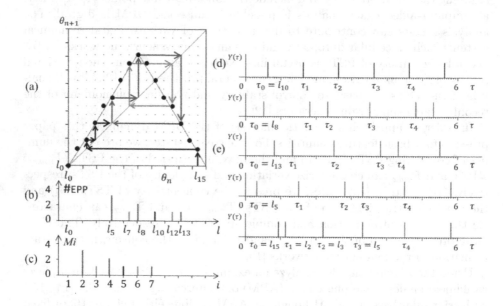

Fig. 1. Digital spike-phase map (DPM). (a) PEOs and EPP, (b)&(c) Distribution of EPPs (M_i), (d) PST of fixed point, (e) PSTs and TST of PEO with period 3.

Since one PEP corresponds to an initial spike position of a PST, one PEP with period k corresponds to one PST with period k and one PEO with period k corresponds to k PSTs. Since the domain of the DPM consists of a finite number of lattice points, the steady state is a PST. The DPM cannot output chaotic spike-train. In Fig 1(a), the DPM has one PEO with period 3, one PEO with period 2 and two fixed points. The PEO with period 3 corresponds to three PSTs as shown in Fig 1(e). This DPM has 7 PSTs in total and exhibits either PST depending on the initial value.

Definition 2: A point $q \in L_0$ is said to be an eventually periodic point (EPP) with step k if the q is not a PEP but falls into some PEP p after k steps: $f^k(q) = p$.

An EPP corresponds to an initial spike-position that gives a TST to a PST. In Fig. 1, the lattice point l_{15} is an EPP that falls into the PEP with period 3 after three steps ($k = 3$). The EPP characterizes transient phenomenon and the domain of attraction to the PST. Note that #PEP + #EPP = N. A simple calculation algorithm of PEPs and EPPs can be found in [2].

3   Four Basic Feature Quantities

In order to approach systematic analysis of the DPM, we introduce four basic feature quantities. The first quantity is the number of co-existing PSTs. It can characterize variation of the steady states.

$$\text{\#PST} = \#\{\text{PEPs of } f\}, \quad 1 \leq \text{\#PST} \leq N \tag{3}$$

The DPM must have at least one PST hence the minimum value is 1. Since PEP and EPP of f are equivalent to PST and TST, we mainly use PST and TST in this section. The maximum value is N in which case all the lattice points are fixed points. The second quantity is the maximum period of the PSTs. It can characterize the complexity of the PSTs.

$$P_{max} = \max\{\text{Periods of PSTs}\}, \quad 1 \leq P_{max} \leq N \tag{4}$$

The minimum value $P_{max} = 1$ means that the DPM has fixed points only. The maximum value $P_{max} = N$ means the the DPM exhibits a maximum length sequence. In Fig. 1, the DPM has 7 PSTs and the maximum period is 3: #PST=7 and P_{max}=3. #PST and P_{max} characterize the steady state.

In order to define the third quantity, let M_i be the number of TSTs that fall into the i-th PST where $i = 1 \sim N_p$ and N_p is the number of the PSTs. The third quantity is the concentricity of TSTs given from the distribution of M_i.

$$C_t = \frac{1}{N-1} \sum_{i=1}^{N_p} M_i^2, \quad 0 \leq C_t \leq N-1 \tag{5}$$

$C_t = 0$ means that the DPM does not have EPP. $C_t = N - 1$ means that the DPM has only one fixed point and all the other $(N - 1)$ points are EPPs that fall into the fixed point. C_t is based on the concentricity of state transition in random neural networks [13]. C_t can characterize the domain of attraction to PSTs. Figure 1 (c) illustrates distribution of M_i that gives $C_t = (0^1 + 3^2 + 1^1 + 2^2 + 1^1 + 1^1 + 1^1)/15 = \frac{17}{15}$. The fourth quantity is the maximum transient steps of TSTs. It can characterize complexity of the TSTs.

$$T_{max} = \max\{\text{Steps of TSTs (EPPs)}\}, \quad 1 \le T_{max} \le N - 1 \qquad (6)$$

where existence of the EPP is assumed. $T_{max} = N - 1$ means that the DPM has only one fixed point and there exists some EPP that falls into the fixed point after visiting all the other points. In Fig. 1(a), l_{15} falls into a PEP with period 3 after three steps: $T_{max}=3$. C_t and T_{max} characterize the transient states. Note that, in our previous papers [1]-[4], P_{max} and T_{max} are not used and definition of C_t is different.

4   Digital Spike-Phase Map Based on Bifurcating Neuron

Although there exist various examples of DPMs, we consider one example based on the bifurcating neuron (BN). The BN is a simple switched dynamical system inspired by spiking neurons. Repeating integrate-and-fire behavior between the constant threshold and periodic base signal $b(\tau)$, the BN output a spike-train as shown in Fig. 2. Let τ_n denote the n-th analog spike position and let $\theta_n = \tau_n$ mod 1 be the n-th analog spike phase. The dynamics is governed by the analog spike-phase map (APM):

$$\theta_{n+1} = \theta_n + 1 - b(\theta_n) \bmod 1 \equiv g(\theta_n) \qquad (7)$$

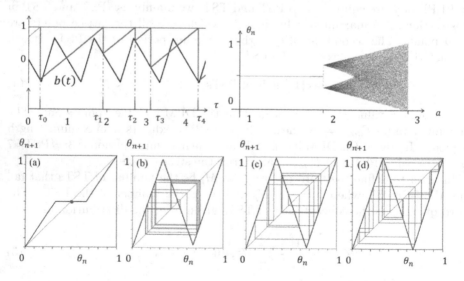

Fig. 2. Bifurcating neuron with triangular base signal and APM. (a) Stable fixed point for $a = 1.5$, (b) chaos for $a = 2.896$, (c) chaos for $a = 2.97$, (d) chaos for $a = 3.0$.

where $\theta_n \in [0,1)$ and $|b(\tau)| < 1$ for all τ. The BN can output spike-trains depending on the shape of $b(\tau)$. We use a triangular base signal:

$$b(\tau) = \begin{cases} -(a-1)\tau & \text{for } -d \leq \tau < d \\ \beta(\tau - 0.5) & \text{for } d \leq \tau < 1-d \end{cases}, \quad b(\tau) = b(\tau + 1) \qquad (8)$$

where $0 < d < 0.5$, $1 \leq a < 1/d$ and $\beta \equiv 2d(a-1)/(1-2d)$. Substituting Eq. (8) into Eq. (7), we obtain piecewise linear APMs as shown in Fig. 2. For simplicity, we select $1 \leq a < 3$ as a control parameter and fix $d = 1/3$ ($\beta \equiv 2(a-1)$). This APM exhibits stable fixed point for $1 \leq a < 2$ and chaos for $2 < a < 3$: the dynamics is simple. Discretizing the APM onto a set of N lattice points (L_0), we obtain the DPM:

$$\theta_{n+1} = \frac{1}{N}\text{INT}(Ng(\theta_n) + 0.5) \equiv f(\theta_n) \qquad (9)$$

where $\theta_n \in L_0$ and $\text{INT}(X)$ means the integer part of X. This is a concrete example of the DPM defined in Eq.(1). Note that our purpose is analysis of dynamics of this DPM itself. We do not regard the DPM as an approximate system

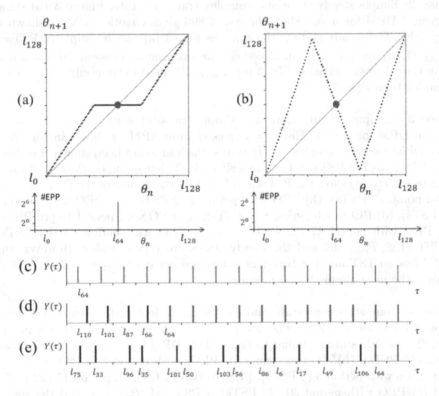

Fig. 3. DPMs of simple steady states. (a) DPM for $a = 1.5$ (#PST=2, $P_{max} = 1$, $C_t = \frac{126^2}{127}$, $T_{max} = 9$). (b) DPM for $a = 2.896$ (#PST=2, $P_{max} = 1$, $C_t = \frac{126^2}{127}$, $T_{max} = 23$). (c) PST for fixed point l_{64}. (d) TST for $a = 1.5$. (e) TST for $a = 2.896$.

of the APM as is in our previous papers [1]-[4]. The DPM in Eq. (9) is characterized by two parameters N and a. Although the dynamics of APM in Fig. 2 is simple, the DPM can exhibit extremely complex phenomena as N and/or a vary. Systematic analysis of the phenomena is extremely hard. For simplicity, we fix $N = 128$ and consider four basic cases of the DPM using the four feature quantities.

Case 1: Simple steady state and simple transient state. Figure 3 (a) shows a typical example of DPM for $a = 1.5$. APM for $a = 1.5$ has one stable fixed point as shown in Fig. 2(a). This DPM has two fixed points l_1 and l_{64}. The fixed point corresponds to a simple PST with period 1 as shown in Fig. 3 (c). That is, #PST=2, $P_{max} = 1$ and the steady state is simple. Excepts for the two fixed points, all the points are EPPs. All the EPPs fall into one fixed point l_{64} and the concentricity of EPPs is very large: $M_1 = 0$, $M_2 = 126$ and $C_t = \frac{126^2}{127} \simeq 125$, where $M_2 = 126$ means that 126 EPPs fall into one fixed point l_{64}. However, the maximum transient step is short as suggested in Fig. 3 (d): $T_{max}=9$ and the transient state is simple.

Case 2: Simple steady state and complex transient state. Figure 3 (b) shows a typical DPM for $a = 2.896$. The $a = 2.896$ gives chaotic APM as shown in Fig. 2(b). The steady state is the same as Fig. 3 (a) and is simple (#PST=2, $P_{max}=1$, $C_t = \frac{126^2}{127} \simeq 125$). However, the maximum transient step is longer than Case 1 as suggested in Fig. 3 (e): $T_{max}=23$ and the transient state is more complex than Case 1.

Case 3: Complex steady state and simple transient state. Figure 4 shows a typical DPM for $a = 3$. The $a = 3$ gives chaotic APM as shown in Fig. 2(d). This DPM has very complex steady states which have not been shown elsewhere. The DPM has 128 PSTs and exhibits either PST depending on the initial value. Figure 4 (a) to (g) show the PEOs and Fig. 4 (i) show some of the PSTs: (a) two fixed points (2 PSTs), (b) PEO with period 2 (2 PSTs), (c) PEO with period 4 (4 PSTs), (d) PEO with period 8 (8 PSTs), (e) PEO with period 16 (16 PSTs), (f) PEO with period 32 (32 PSTs) and (g) PEO with period 64 (64 PSTs). #PST=128, $P_{max}=64$ and the steady states are very complex. However, this DPM has no TST and the transient state does not exist ($C_t = 0$, $T_{max}=N/A$). This is the most simple transient state.

Case 4: Complex steady state and complex transient state. Figure 5 shows a typical DPM for $a = 2.97$. The $a = 2.97$ gives chaotic APM as shown in Fig. 2(c). The steady state is similar to Fig. 4. This DPM has 54 PSTs: (a) two fixed points (2 PSTs), (b)&(f) two symmetric PEOs with period 2 (4 PSTs), (c)&(g) two PEOs with period 3 (6 PSTs), (d)&(h) two PEOs with period 11 (22 PSTs) and (e) PEO with period 20 (20 PSTs). #PST=54, $P_{max}=20$ and the steady states are very complex. This DPM has 74 TSTs: $C_t = \frac{198}{127} \simeq 1.56$ and $T_{max}=15$. The transient states are also complex.

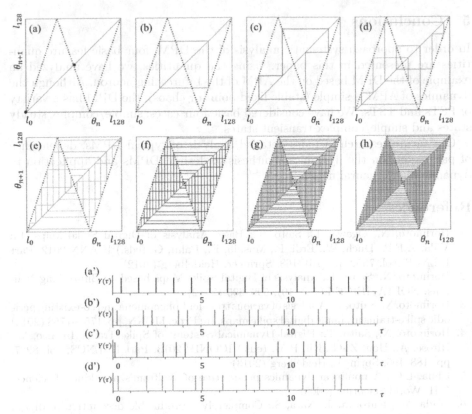

Fig. 4. DPM for $a = 3$ (#PST=128, $P_{max} = 64$, $C_t = 0$, $T_{max} = 0$). (a) two fixed points, (b) PEO with period 2, (c) period 4, (d) period 8, (e) period 16, (f) period 32, (g) period 64, (h) overlapped drawing of all the PEOs, (a') to (d') PST with period 1, period 2, period 4 and period 8.

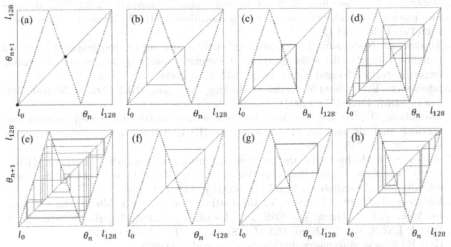

Fig. 5. DPM for $a = 2.97$ (#PST=54, $P_{max} = 20$, $C_t = \frac{198}{127} \simeq 1.56$, $T_{max} = 15$). (a) two fixed points, (b)&(f) period 2, (e)&(g) period-3, (d)&(h) period-11, (e) period-20.

5   Conclusions

In order to approach systematic analysis of the DPM, four basic feature quantities are presented in this paper. Using the quantities, we have analyzed an example of the DPM based on the APM of the bifurcating neuron. Although the dynamics of APM is simple (stable fixed point or chaos), the DPM has a variety of PSTs and TSTs. We have considered basic four cases: simple/complex steady states and simple/complex transient states.

Our future research includes detailed analysis of typical DPMs, dependence of parameters on the dynamics, synthesis of desired DPMs and application to dynamic digital neural networks.

References

1. Horimoto, N., Ogawa, T., Saito, T.: Basic Analysis of Digital Spike Maps. In: Villa, A.E.P., Duch, W., Érdi, P., Masulli, F., Palm, G. (eds.) ICANN 2012, Part I. LNCS, vol. 7552, pp. 161–168. Springer, Heidelberg (2012)
2. Horimoto, N., Saito, T.: Analysis of Digital Spike Maps based on Bifurcating Neurons. NOLTA, IEICE E95-N(10), 596–605 (2012)
3. Horimoto, N., Saito, T.: Analysis of various transient phenomena and co-existing periodic spike-trains in simple digital spike maps. In: Proc. IJCNN, pp. 1751–1758 (2013)
4. Horimoto, N., Saito, T.: Digital Dynamical Systems of Spike-Trains. In: Lee, M., Hirose, A., Hou, Z.-G., Kil, R.M. (eds.) ICONIP 2013, Part II. LNCS, vol. 8227, pp. 188–195. Springer, Heidelberg (2013)
5. Chua, L.O.: A nonlinear dynamics perspective of Wolfram's new kind of science, I, II. World Scientific (2005)
6. Wada, W., Kuroiwa, J., Nara, S.: Completely reproducible description of digital sound data with cellular automata. Physics Letters A 306, 110–115 (2002)
7. Kouzuki, R., Saito, T.: Learning of simple dynamic binary neural networks. IEICE Trans. Fundamentals E96-A(8), 1775–1782 (2013)
8. Campbell, S.R., Wang, D., Jayaprakash, C.: Synchrony and desynchrony in integrate-and-fire oscillators. Neural Computation 11, 1595–1619 (1999)
9. Rulkov, N.F., Sushchik, M.M., Tsimring, L.S., Volkovskii, A.R.: Digital communication using chaotic-pulse-position modulation. IEEE Trans. Circuits Systs. I 48(12), 1436–1444 (2001)
10. Torikai, H., Nishigami, T.: An artificial chaotic spiking neuron inspired by spiral ganglion cell: Parallel spike encoding, theoretical analysis, and electronic circuit implementation. Neural Networks 22, 664–673 (2009)
11. Izhikevich, E.M.: Simple Model of Spiking Neurons. IEEE Trans. Neural Networks 14(6), 1569–1572 (2003)
12. Matsubara, T., Torikai, H.: Asynchronous cellular automaton-based neuron: theoretical analysis and on-FPGA learning. IEEE Trans. Neiral Netw. Learning Systs. 24, 736–748 (2013)
13. Amari, S.: A Method of Statistical Neurodynamics. Kybernetik 14, 201–215 (1974)
14. Perez, R., Glass, L.: Bistability, period doubling bifurcations and chaos in a periodically forced oscillator. Phys. Lett. 90A(9), 441–443 (1982)
15. Kirikawa, S., Ogawa, T., Saito, T.: Bifurcating Neurons with Filtered Base Signals. In: Villa, A.E.P., Duch, W., Érdi, P., Masulli, F., Palm, G. (eds.) ICANN 2012, Part I. LNCS, vol. 7552, pp. 153–160. Springer, Heidelberg (2012)
16. Ott, E.: Chaos in dynamical systems, Cambridge (1993)

Discriminative Fast Soft Competitive Learning

Frank-Michael Schleif

University of Birmingham, School of Computer Science,
Edgbaston, B15 2TT Birmingham, UK

Abstract. Proximity matrices like kernels or dissimilarity matrices provide non-standard data representations common in the life science domain. Here we extend fast soft competitive learning to a discriminative and vector labeled learning algorithm for proximity data. It provides a more stable and consistent integration of label information in the cost function solely based on a give proximity matrix without the need of an explicit vector space. The algorithm has linear computational and memory requirements and performs favorable to traditional techniques.

1 Introduction

The amount of digital data doubles roughly every 20 months often given by non-vectorial data formats such as XML, graph structures, sequence data or others. Such data is getting more and more frequent, leading to large proximity data sets. Classical cluster methods, like k-means process Euclidean data only. Also kernel approaches like kernel-k-means or kernel soft competitive learning (KSCL) [1] are often limited, due to the lack of a valid kernel. More recently indefinite kernel techniques were proposed [2] but often with high complexity or by optimizing an aligned kernel matrix.

A further efficient alternative is given by dissimilarity learners like the relational soft competitive learning [3] (R-SCL), a clustering algorithm for arbitrary dissimilarity data. R-SCL is an extension of soft-competitive learning (SCL) [4]. It replaces the Euclidean distance function of a data point $\mathbf{v}$ to a cluster representant or prototype $\mathbf{w}$ by an implicit representation which refers to the dissimilarity matrix $D \in \mathbb{R}^{N \times N}$ only with N as the number of samples and $d_{ij} = |\mathbf{v}_i - \mathbf{v}_j|^2$ denotes the underlying dissimilarities induced by an arbitrary symmetric bilinear form. While standard R-SCL has squared complexity a linear cost algorithm can be obtained by using the Nyström approximation [5].

In [6] the author has shown that arbitrary proximity matrices can be used by the R-SCL algorithm by integrating simple transformation rules in the original formulation. The obtained fast soft competitive learning algorithm (FSCL) is an effective approach to analyze large proximity datasets for *unsupervised* problems. Often the given data may also contain partial or full label information and especially in the life science domain those labels may be probabilistic in contrast to crisp labels. Considering such data sets, standard supervised or even semi-supervised learning algorithm are not applicable in general. To apply a standard support vector classifier (SVM) we would need to defuzzify the labels making them crisp which in general can degenerate accuracy.

Here we extend batch FSCL to take this label information into account, leading to a new formulation of FSCL called supervised FSCL (S-FSCL) which is a discriminative

S. Wermter et al. (Eds.): ICANN 2014, LNCS 8681, pp. 81–88, 2014.

clustering approach. In contrast to the former approaches also partial labeling is permitted and even more important the labels need not to be crisp such that probabilistic or fuzzy labeled data can be analyzed.

In section 2 we briefly review related work on proximity learning focusing on discriminative clustering approaches. We present the supervised fast soft competitive learning in section 3 and summarize the results of our empirical studies in section 4.

2   Related Work

Clustering analysis has found a wide range of application [7] and with the advent of large proximity data sets also proximity clustering has been studied by different authors, e.g. in the line of large scale kernel clustering [8] and relational or dissimilarity clustering [3]. The availability of label information may help to improve current cluster approaches by guiding the optimization process. This is also interesting if data are only partially labeled or fuzzy labeled and fully supervised approaches are inaccessible or semi-supervised techniques are limited e.g. to two class scenarios [9].

In the last years different clustering approaches were proposed using partial label information, some of them also supported fuzzy-labeled data. In [10] an online SCL clustering approach was coupled with an additive label error term in the cost function to allow for fuzzy-labeled data [11], but this approach is sensitive to the balancing parameter in the cost function. In [12] this *online* approach was changed to a product based label-error leading to a more stable behavior. Both former approaches were found to be efficient but do not scale well to larger problems and consider vectorial datasets only. A batch SCL clustering method using the additive label error was proposed in [13] motivating also a relevance learning strategy for vectorial data, but also this approach is sensitive to the parameters. More recently also an *online* supervised Learning Vector Quantizer for multivariate class labels[1] was proposed in [14] which was found to be very efficient and which we will use as our baseline method. Other recent methods to incorporate label information for kernel clustering were proposed e.g. in [15] and for vectorial data in [16]. All these approaches focus either on vectorial data or do not scale to larger problems. Although some of the methods are online, and theoretically of linear complexity, the repetitive calculation of distances for high dimensional data and the used gradient descent learning makes them slow in practice whereas batch methods are known for quick convergence. Our proposal is a *batch* approach for fuzzy labeled data which is efficient for larger scale proximity matrices. Hence it keeps a lot of flexibility regarding the data encoding, e.g. by a dedicated kernel or distance function.

To address large scale problem in proximity clustering a multitude of contributions have been made in the last years e.g. by means of core set clustering [17], the Nyström approximation [8, 6] or patch learning approaches [18]. We will use a Nyström strategy as given in [6]. Subsequently, we will briefly introduce soft competitive learning as the basic method for multiple related approaches [13, 10–12, 6] mentioned above followed by the derivation of a (semi-)supervised extension of FSCL.

---

[1] Not to mix-up with multi labels, where an object can fully belong to multiple classes.

2.1 Soft Competitive Learning

In contrast to regular k-means, soft competitive learning (SCL) [4] extends the quantization error to incorporate data induced neighborhood cooperation: $E_{\text{SCL}} := \sum_{ij} h_\sigma(r_{ij}) d(\mathbf{v}_i, \mathbf{w}_j)$ where $h_\sigma(t) = \exp(-t/\sigma)$ exponentially scales the neighborhood range, and r_{ij} denotes the rank of prototype $\mathbf{w}_j$ with respect to $\mathbf{v}_i$, i.e. the number of prototypes $\mathbf{w}_k$ with $k \neq j$ which are closer to $\mathbf{v}_i$ as measured by the Euclidean distance d. SCL optimizes the prior cost function E_{SCL} by means of a stochastic gradient descent, annealing the neighborhood range σ during training such that, in the limit, the standard quantization error is approximated [4]. The iterative adaptation rule is $\mathbf{w}_j := \mathbf{w}_j + \eta \cdot h_\sigma(r_{ij})(\mathbf{v}_i - \mathbf{w}_j)$ where η denotes the learning rate. There exists a faster (euclidean) batch optimization scheme as introduced in [19] which optimizes prototype locations and assignments as:

$$\mathbf{w_j} := \sum_i h_\sigma(r_{ij})\mathbf{v}_i / \sum_i h_\sigma(r_{ij}) \tag{1}$$

with r_{ij} based on $d(\mathbf{v}_i, \mathbf{w}_j)$. The online kernelized SCL was proposed in [1], replacing the original distance calculation by a kernel expansion and a batch version was implicitly proposed in the FSCL [6].

2.2 Relational Soft Competitive Learning

Relational soft competitive learning (R-SCL) as introduced in [3] assumes that a symmetric dissimilarity matrix D with entries d_{ij} describing pairwise dissimilarities of data is available. In principle, it is very similar to KSCL. There are two differences: R-SCL is based on dissimilarities rather than similarities, and it solves the resulting cost function using a *batch* optimization with quadratic convergence as compared to a stochastic gradient descent.

As shown in [20], there always exists a so-called pseudo-Euclidean embedding of a given set of points characterized by pairwise symmetric dissimilarities by means of a mapping Φ, i.e. a real vector space and a symmetric bilinear form (with probably negative eigenvalues) such that the dissimilarities are obtained by means of this bilinear form. As before, prototypes are restricted to convex combinations $\mathbf{w}_j = \sum_l \alpha_{jl}\Phi(\mathbf{v}_l)$ with $\sum_l \alpha_{jl} = 1$ Dissimilarities are computed as:

$$d(\Phi(\mathbf{v}_i), \mathbf{w}_j) = [D^t \alpha_j]_i - \frac{1}{2} \cdot \alpha_j^t D\alpha_j \tag{2}$$

where $[\cdot]_i$ refers to component i of the vector. This allows a direct transfer of batch SCL to general dissimilarities by the following iterations derived from (1)

$$\alpha_{jl} := h_\sigma(r_{jl}) / \sum_l h_\sigma(r_{jl}) \tag{3}$$

with r_{jl} based on $d(\Phi(\mathbf{v}_j), \mathbf{w}_l)$. This algorithm is soft competitive learning in pseudo Euclidean space for every symmetric dissimilarity matrix D. If negative eigenvalues are present convergence is not always guaranteed, but observed in general[3].

3 Supervised Fast Soft Competitive Learning

Let Y be the label matrix of the training points with entries $\mathbf{y}_i \in \mathbb{R}^C$ and C the number of classes. For each $\mathbf{y}_i$ we expect entries $y_{ic} \in [0,1]$ and $\sum_{c=1}^{C} y_{ic} = 1$. Further we introduce a vector label $\mathbf{l}_j$ for each prototype $\mathbf{w}_j$ following the same constraints.

To integrate supervised information in the FSCL approach we extend the original distance calculation[2] by a multiplicative error term similar as suggested for online, vectorial SCL in [12].

Former approaches using an additive or multiplicative label error were found to be sensitive to the used weighting or offset parameter to rescale the different error contributions. This problem is addressed subsequently by application of the softmax function on the individual distance errors and the label error of each data point such that both error functions provide values in a range $[0,1]$. In this way we avoid additional control parameters and obtain a stable learning behavior[3].

Accordingly the original distance function Eq. (2) is adapted to:

$$d((\Phi(\mathbf{v}_i), \mathbf{y}_i), (\mathbf{w}_j, \mathbf{l}_j)) = 1 - \underbrace{(f(d(\Phi(\mathbf{v}_i), \mathbf{w}_j)) \cdot f(d^*(\mathbf{y}_i, \mathbf{l}_j)))}_{(s)} \tag{4}$$

with f being a softmax function and d^* the squared Euclidean distance. If only partial label information is given we can just ignore the label part in Eq 4. The *initial* label $\mathbf{l}_j$ of the prototypes are determined by post labeling and are updated as:

$$\mathbf{l}_j^* = \alpha_j \cdot Y \tag{5}$$

being the mean label of all data points weighted by the contribution of each point to this prototype. It should be noted that the distance in Eq. (4) is always non-negative and symmetric but may be non-metric as easily shown by counter examples, this however is not a severe problem for the underlying R-SCL as discussed in [3]. For test data points the distance calculation remains unchanged following the winner takes all scheme. The formulation given in Eq. (4) can be interpreted as the probability that a data point was generated by a Gaussian distribution centered on the prototype under the condition of similar labeling of the data point and the prototype. The obtained similarity (s) is subsequently mapped back into a dissimilarity by $1 - (s)$ to keep the distance interpretation of the remaining optimization function.

To address the problem of large input proximity matrices we use the Nyström approximation [21, 22]. The practical idea is to select m landmark indices and the corresponding rows and columns from the matrix S to obtain the landmark matrix $S_{m,m}$. The original gram matrix S can then be approximated as $\tilde{S} = S_{N,m} S_{m,m}^{-1} S_{m,N}$ which is of complexity $\mathcal{O}(m^3 N)$ instead of $\mathcal{O}(N^2)$, i.e. it is linear if the approximation quality m is fixed. In [22] it was shown that the same strategy can also be applied to symmetric dissimilarity matrices. For R-SCL, this yields the approximation of the distance computation (2)

---

[2] Either based on a kernel expansion or on a dissimilarity expansion, as shown e.g in Eq. (2).
[3] The softmax parameter σ is fixed to $\sigma = 1$ and is insensitive with respect to the data, assuming that the data representation is reasonable expressive. It can be subsumed by the given distance if we assume σ to be equal for each prototype.

$$d(\mathbf{v_i}, \mathbf{w_j})^2 \approx [D_{N,m}(D_{m,m}^{-1}(D_{m,N}\alpha_j))]_i - \frac{1}{2} \cdot (\alpha_j^t D_{N,m}) \cdot (D_{m,m}^{-1}(D_{m,N}\alpha_j))$$

which is $\mathcal{O}(m^3 N)$. Again, the approximation is exact if the number of samples m is chosen according to the rank of D. For similarity data we transform the similarity matrix S to a dissimilarity matrix D using Equations from [20].

$$d(\mathbf{v_i}, \mathbf{v_j})^2 = s(\mathbf{v_i}, \mathbf{v_i}) + s(\mathbf{v_j}, \mathbf{v_j}) - 2s(\mathbf{v_i}, \mathbf{v_j}) \qquad (6)$$

which can be coupled with the Nyström approximation, avoiding the full calculation of the matrix S [22]. S-FSCL is a wrapper around a modified R-SCL using the distance function Eq. (4) followed by a subsequent update of the prototype labels using Eq. (5) details on the implementation of the original R-SCL are given in [3]. The runtime-complexity of S-FSCL is dominated by the distance calculations with $\mathcal{O}(m^3 N)$. R-SCL and hence S-FSCL shows fast convergence (see [3]) due to the batch approach. The memory complexity is dominated by the $m \times N$ dis-/similarity matrix and is $\mathcal{O}(mN)$.

4 Experiments

We compare the efficiency of supervised fast SCL (S-FSCL) with its unsupervised fast SCL (FSCL) and the online Robust Soft-LVQ for multivariate (MRSLVQ) labels as proposed in [14], for very large data sets we use the core vector machine (CVM) [23]. Initially we show the usefulness of the introduced supervision concept and the effectiveness of the batch approach by use of the classical checkerboard data set. The data form a 5×5 checkerboard with each cluster consisting of 200 Gaussian distributed points, so we have $N = 5000$ points. To represent the data we use an rbf kernel which is approximated in the FSCL method by a Nyström approximation with $N/10$ landmarks. We use 2 prototypes which is theoretically sufficient to represent the checkerboard data in a supervised learning task. We apply the supervised FSCL and the unsupervised FSCL and obtain prototype assignments as shown in Figure 1. For both methods the prototypes are finally located in the center of the data. The supervised FSCL achieves an accuracy of 95.12%, whereas the unsupervised FSCL got 52.96%. For this test data the supervised information is clearly needed to achieve a good classification result since the data distribution is not sufficient to estimate the prototype labels. To get a fair comparison the *only* difference between the supervised and unsupervised FSCL is the distance function as discussed before with respect to Eq. (4).

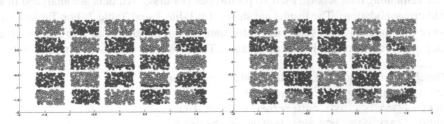

Fig. 1. Checkerboard data (left) supervised FSCL, (right) unsupervised FSCL. The predicted label is given by color (gray shade) and the true label by the shape of the objects.

Table 1. Results of the fuzzy labeled data with mean and standard deviation of the test error

	FSCL	S-FSCL	MRSLVQ
Checkerboard (rbf)	44.14 ± 3.51	0.52 ± 3.77	$\mathbf{0.40 \pm 0.05}$
Plant-Tissue (rbf)	42.76 ± 1.19	$\mathbf{32.23 \pm 1.00}$	37.62 ± 2.13
Remote-Sensing (euclidean)	40.86 ± 0.94	$\mathbf{39.95 \pm 1.09}$	44.27 ± 1.61

In the further experiments we used fuzzy labeled data sets, all represented by means of dissimilarity matrices using either the Euclidean distance or an underlying rbf kernel so all data are metric but as already shown in [6] more generic data formats can be used. All data matrices have been approximated with a constant number of 100 randomly chosen landmarks. (1) *Plant tissue data*: The data are 4418 points of 22 dimensional image features in 11 classes of a serial transverse section of barley grains taken from [24]. The different tissue regions are hard to discriminate such that for a substantial part of this datasets items are labeled by fuzzy labels. (2) *Remote sensing data*: is a multi-spectral LANDSAT TM satellite image of the Colorado area taken from [25] with 6 different spectral bands. There are 14 labels describing different vegetation types and geological formations. The size of the original image is 1907×1784 pixels[4]. Fuzzy labels were obtained by a downsampling of this data set to 12650 points where the original image was cut to 1840×1760 pixel. The fuzzy labels were derived from the histograms of the averaged pixel areas.

For comparison to other alternative methods we also analyze different medium scale standard datasets using either a linear kernel or a defacto parameter-free extreme learning machine (elm) kernel [26] compared with a core vector machine classifier [23]. The MNIST data[5] contains $70000, 719$-dimensional binary images from 10 digit classes. We used a neural kernel $k(\mathbf{v_i}, \mathbf{v_j}) = \tanh(a v_i^\top v_j + b)$ with $a = 0.0045$ and $b = 0.11$ acc. to [8]. The USPS[6] contains $11000, 256$-dimensional character feature vectors from 10 classes analyzed by a parameter free elm kernel. The SPAM database[7], contains $4601, 57$-dimensional feature vectors, processed by a linear kernel. All matrices have been Nyström approximated and converted to a distance matrix at linear costs[22].

The model complexity for (supervised) FSCL and MRSLVQ has to be determined in advance, although one prototype per class if often sufficient it is beneficial to spend some extra prototypes to address potential sub-populations. Unused prototypes are removed either during learning (FSCL) or in the final model (MRSLVQ). For the Plant-Tissue data we use 2 prototypes per class, for the Checkerboard data 1 per class and for the remaining data sets we used 10 prototypes per class. All data are analyzed in a 5-fold crossvalidation. The results are shown in Table 1 and Table 2. For Table 1 we observe that the additional supervised information is in general helpful to improve the model with respect to the classification task[8]. The proposed approach is in parts better

---

[4] Thereby 9 pixel have an unknown label and have been removed.
[5] http://yann.lecun.com/exdb/mnist/
[6] http://www.cs.nyu.edu/~roweis/data.html
[7] http://archive.ics.uci.edu/ml/datasets
[8] The effect is obviously less severe if the data distribution follows the labeling very closely as e.g. for the remote sensing data, where also an unsupervised clustering gives similar results.

Table 2. Test set error (mean/std) of medium to large scale standard data set

	FSCL	S-FSCL	CVM
MNIST	**20.83 ± 1.05**	22.16 ± 7.61	40.04 ± 3.54
USPS	15.62 ± 1.01	**14.33 ± 1.10**	18.77 ± 1.01
SPAM	17.26 ± 1.79	**12.06 ± 1.20**	27.67 ± 1.08

or competitive to the MRSLVQ but substantially faster under practical settings due to the batch strategy, avoiding repetitive calculations of distance or gradients as needed in MRSLVQ. The general runtime for S-FSCL for a single model is in the range of seconds whereas the MRSLVQ is most often slower by two magnitudes. In Table 2 we observe again that the supervision is in general helpful although often the effect is not so substantial. The results in Table 2 are again quite good compared to a CVM result. Due to the pre-calculation of the approximated kernel the actual model calculation can be done within seconds to minutes. Note that e.g. for the SPAM database fuzzy labels are not given but likely to observe in practical applications because multiple users will consider almost identical emails as spam or non-spam. Hence, the S-FSCL model would be more appropriate in these cases than the crisp CVM approach.

5 Conclusions

Here we proposed a *supervised* version of the batch FSCL algorithm. The algorithm permits the usage of fuzzy labeled input data by means of a dissimilarity matrix representation. The given dissimilarity data can be of large scale due to the underlying Nyström approximation such that data with multiple 1000 points can be handled easily. The obtained supervised clustering approach provides probabilistic class assignments and was found to be quite robust and achieved better or competitive results to alternative approaches. Using the suggested transformation and Eq. (6) also kernel representation are available. In this way S-FSCL can be used for a wide range of problem settings. Considering the very limited and restricted amount of classifiers for fuzzy labeled data the FSCL is an effective solver for medium to large scale problems in this line. In future work we will focus on further improvements for very large scale problems using e.g. random approximation strategies as suggested in [27] and analyze the efficiency for practical problems with unsafe label information in the life sciences.

Acknowledgment. Marie Curie Intra-European Fellowship (IEF): FP7-PEOPLE-2012-IEF (FP7-327791-ProMoS) is greatly acknowledged.

References

1. Qin, A.K., Suganthan, P.N.: Kernel neural gas algorithms with application to cluster analysis. In: ICPR, vol. 4, pp. 617–620 (2004)
2. Pekalska, E., Haasdonk, B.: Kernel discriminant analysis for positive definite and indefinite kernels. IEEE TPAMI 31(6), 1017–1032 (2009)
3. Hammer, B., Hasenfuss, A.: Topographic mapping of large dissimilarity datasets. Neural Computation 22(9), 2229–2284 (2010)
4. Martinetz, T., Berkovich, S., Schulten, K.: Neural Gas Network for Vector Quantization and its Application to Time-Series Prediction. IEEE TNN 4(4), 558–569 (1993)

5. Gisbrecht, A., Mokbel, B., Schleif, F.-M., Zhu, X., Hammer, B.: Linear time relational prototype based learning. Journal of Neural Systems 22(5) (2012)
6. Schleif, F.-M., Zhu, X., Gisbrecht, A., Hammer, B.: Fast approximated relational and kernel clustering. In: Proc. of ICPR 2012, pp. 1229–1232. IEEE (2012)
7. Jain, A.K.: Data clustering: 50 years beyond K-means. Pat. Rec. Let. 31, 651–666 (2010)
8. Chitta, R., et al.: Approximate kernel k-means: solution to large scale kernel clustering. In: Apté, C. (ed.) KDD, pp. 895–903. ACM (2011)
9. Zhu, X., Goldberg, A.B.: Introduction to semi-supervised learning. Synthesis Lectures on Artif. Intell. and Machine Learning 3(1), 1–130 (2009)
10. Villmann, T., Hammer, B., Schleif, F.-M., Geweniger, T., Herrmann, W.: Fuzzy classification by fuzzy labeled neural gas. Neural Netw. 19(6-7), 772–779 (2006)
11. Villmann, T., Schleif, F.-M., Hammer, B., Kostrzewa, M.: Exploration of mass-spectrometric data in clinical proteomics using learning vector quantization methods. Briefings in Bioinformatics 9(2), 129–143 (2008)
12. Kästner, M., Villmann, T.: Fuzzy supervised self-organizing map for semi-supervised vector quantization. In: Rutkowski, L., Korytkowski, M., Scherer, R., Tadeusiewicz, R., Zadeh, L.A., Zurada, J.M. (eds.) ICAISC 2012, Part I. LNCS, vol. 7267, pp. 256–265. Springer, Heidelberg (2012)
13. Hammer, B., Hasenfuss, A., Schleif, F.-M., Villmann, T.: Supervised batch neural gas. In: Schwenker, F., Marinai, S. (eds.) ANNPR 2006. LNCS (LNAI), vol. 4087, pp. 33–45. Springer, Heidelberg (2006)
14. Schneider, P., Geweniger, T., Schleif, F.-M., Biehl, M., Villmann, T.: Multivariate class labeling in robust soft LVQ. In: Proc. of ESANN 2011, pp. 17–22 (2011)
15. Finley, T., Joachims, T.: Supervised clustering with support vector machines. In: De Raedt, L. (ed.) ICML, vol. 119, pp. 217–224. ACM (2005)
16. Arandjelovic, O.: Discriminative k-means clustering. In: IJCNN, pp. 1–7 (2013)
17. Badoiu, M., Har-Peled, S., Indyk, P.: Approximate clustering via core-sets. In: STOC, pp. 250–257 (2002)
18. Alex, N., Hasenfuss, A., Hammer, B.: Patch clustering for massive data sets. Neurocomputing 72(7-9), 1455–1469 (2009)
19. Cottrell, M., Hammer, B., Hasenfuss, A., Villmann, T.: Batch and median neural gas. Neural Networks 19, 762–771 (2006)
20. Pekalska, E., Duin, R.: The dissimilarity representation for pattern recognition. World Scientific (2005)
21. Williams, C., Seeger, M.: Using the nyström method to speed up kernel machines. In: Leen, T.K. (ed.) NIPS, pp. 682–688. MIT Press (2000)
22. Schleif, F.-M., Gisbrecht, A.: Data analysis of (non-)metric proximities at linear costs. In: Hancock, E., Pelillo, M. (eds.) SIMBAD 2013. LNCS, vol. 7953, pp. 59–74. Springer, Heidelberg (2013)
23. Tsang, I., Kocsor, A., Kwok, J.: Simpler core vector machines with enclosing balls. In: Proc. of the 24th Int. Conf. on Machine Learning (ICML 2007), pp. 911–918 (2007)
24. Brüß, C., Bollenbeck, F., Schleif, F.-M., et al.: Fuzzy image segmentation with fuzzy labelled neural gas. In: Proc. of ESANN 2006, pp. 563–569 (2006)
25. Schleif, F.-M., Ongyerth, F.-M., Villmann, T.: Supervised data analysis and reliability estimation for spectral data. Neuro Comp. 72(16-18), 3590–3601 (2009)
26. Frénay, B., Verleysen, M.: Parameter-insensitive kernel in extreme learning for non-linear support vector regression. Neuro Comp. 74(16), 2526–2531 (2011)
27. Schleif, F.-M.: Proximity learning for non-standard big data. In: Proceedings of ESANN 2014, pp. 359–364 (2014)

Human Action Recognition with Hierarchical Growing Neural Gas Learning

German Ignacio Parisi, Cornelius Weber, and Stefan Wermter

University of Hamburg, Department of Computer Science,
Vogt-Koelln-Strasse 30, 22527 Hamburg, Germany
{parisi,weber,wermter}@informatik.uni-hamburg.de
http://www.informatik.uni-hamburg.de/WTM/

Abstract. We propose a novel biologically inspired framework for the recognition of human full-body actions. First, we extract body pose and motion features from depth map sequences. We then cluster pose-motion cues with a two-stream hierarchical architecture based on growing neural gas (GNG). Multi-cue trajectories are finally combined to provide prototypical action dynamics in the joint feature space. We extend the unsupervised GNG with two labelling functions for classifying clustered trajectories. Noisy samples are automatically detected and removed from the training and the testing set. Experiments on a set of 10 human actions show that the use of multi-cue learning leads to substantially increased recognition accuracy over the single-cue approach and the learning of joint pose-motion vectors.

Keywords: human action recognition, growing neural gas, motion clustering, assistive system.

1 Introduction

Recently, there has been a significant increase of research on ambient intelligence for the recognition of human activity in indoor environments [1]. In this context, the classification of human actions has proven to be a challenging task to accomplish with an artificial system, where the prompt recognition of potentially risky situations can represent a key issue. In the last four years, the prominent use of low-cost depth sensing devices such as the Kinect sensor led to a great number of vision-based applications using depth information instead of, or in combination with, color [2]. These methods generally extract and process motion from depth map sequences in terms of spatiotemporal patterns. Despite the reduced computational cost of processing depth maps instead of RGB pixel matrices, the robust recognition of articulated human actions remains an enticing milestone, also for machine learning and neural network-based approaches [3,4,11].

A promising scheme to tackle such a demanding task is the application of biological principles derived from the human visual system and its outperforming ability to process visual information. Studies in neurophysiology suggest a highly flexible and adaptive biological system for processing visual cues at multiple levels for motion and action perception [5]. In fact, computational implementations

S. Wermter et al. (Eds.): ICANN 2014, LNCS 8681, pp. 89–96, 2014.

of simplified biological models have shown motivating results on the recognition of dynamic pose-motion patterns [6]. In the biological visual system, dynamic scenes are analyzed in parallel by two separate channels [5]. The ventral channel processes shape features while the dorsal channel recognizes location and motion properties in terms of optic-flow patterns. Both channels are composed by hierarchies that extrapolate visual features with increasing complexity of representation. Specific areas of the visual system are composed of topographically arranged structures that organize according to the distribution of the inputs [13]. Input-driven self-organization allows to learn representations with an unsupervised scheme by adaptively obtaining the feature subspace. Under this assumption, the use of self-organizing maps (SOM) [7] has shown to be a plausible and efficient model for clustering visual patterns in terms of multi-dimensional flow vectors. With the use of extended models of hierarchical self-organization it is possible to obtain progressively generalized representations of sensory inputs and learn inherent spatiotemporal dependencies. While depth data-driven techniques currently represent a well-established approach for action recognition, the combination of the above-mentioned bio-inspired approach with this emerging sensory trend has not yet extensively developed.

In this work, we propose a novel learning framework for recognizing human full-body actor-independent actions. We first extract pose and motion features from depth map video sequences and then cluster actions in terms of prototypical pose-motion trajectories. Multi-cue samples from matching frames are processed separately by a two-stream hierarchical architecture based on growing neural gas (GNG) [8]. The GNG is an unsupervised incremental clustering algorithm extended from the SOM and the neural gas (NG) [9], able to dynamically change its topological structure to better represent the input space. Clustered trajectories from the parallel streams are combined to provide joint action dynamics. We process the samples under the assumption that action recognition is selective for temporal order [5]. Therefore, positive recognition of an action occurs only when trajectory samples are activated in the correct temporal order. In order to assign labels to clustered trajectories, we extend the GNG with two offline labelling functions. Noisy samples are automatically detected and removed from the training and the testing set to increase recognition accuracy. We present and discuss experimental results on a data set of 10 articulated actions.

2   Pose-Motion Estimation

The first step in the proposed framework constitutes the extraction of human body features from the visual scene. The use of skeleton model-based techniques for tracking action features in terms of a set of joints and limbs has shown good results, especially for approaches using depth maps [4]. On the other hand, joints are often subject to occlusion during the execution of actions. This may lead to significantly decreased reliability of estimated joints and subsequent tracking inaccuracies. In our approach, we estimate spatiotemporal properties for representing actor-independent actions based on the estimation of body centroids

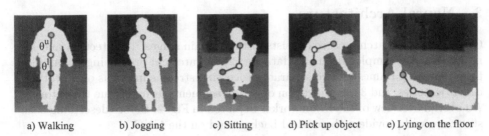

a) Walking   b) Jogging   c) Sitting   d) Pick up object   e) Lying on the floor

Fig. 1. Full-body representation for pose-motion extraction. We estimate three centroids C_1 (green), C_1 (yellow) and C_1 (blue) for upper, middle and lower body respectively. We compute the segment slopes (θ^u and θ^l) to describe the posture with the overall orientations of the upper and lower body.

that describe pose-motion features. This technique extrapolates significant action characteristics while maintaining a low-dimensional feature space and increasing tracking robustness for situations of partial occlusions. In [11], we proposed a simpler model to track a spatially extended body with two centroids and a global body orientation. The centroids were estimated as the centers of mass that follow the distribution of the main body masses on each posture.

We now extend our previous model to describe more accurately articulated actions by considering three body centroids (Fig. 1): C_1 for upper body with respect to the shoulders and the torso; C_2 for middle body with respect to the torso and the hips; and C_3 for lower body with respect to the hips and the knees. Each centroid is represented as a point sequence of real-world coordinates $C = (x, y, z)$. We then estimate upper and lower orientations θ^u and θ^l given by the slope angles of the segments $\overline{C_1 C_2}$ and $\overline{C_2 C_3}$ respectively. As seen in Fig. 1, θ^u and θ^l describe the overall body pose as the orientation of the torso and the legs, which allows to capture significant pose configurations in actions such as walking, sitting, picking up and lying down. We calculate the body velocity S_i as the difference in pixels of the centroid C_1 between two consecutive frames i and $i-1$. The upper centroid was selected based on the consideration that the orientation of the torso is the most characteristic reference during the execution of a full-body action [4]. We then estimate horizontal speed h_i and vertical speed v_i as in [11]. For each action frame i we obtain a pose-motion vector:

$$F_i = (\theta_i^u, \theta_i^l, h_i, v_i). \tag{1}$$

Each action A_j will be composed of a set of sequentially ordered pose-motion vectors $A_j := \{(F_i, l_j) : i \in [1..n], l_j \in L\}$, where l_j is the action label, L is the set of class labels, and n is the number of training vectors for the action j. This representation describes spatiotemporal properties of actions in terms of length-invariant patterns, particularly suitable for feeding into a neural network.

3   Neural Architecture

Our GNG-based architecture consists of three main stages: 1) detection and removal of noisy samples from the data set; 2) hierarchical processing of samples from matching frames by two separate processing streams in terms of prototypical trajectories; and 3) classification of action segments as multi-cue trajectories. An overall overview of the framework is depicted in Fig. 2. Before describing each stage, we will provide a theoretical background on the GNG.

3.1   The Growing Neural Gas

Neural network approaches inspired by biological self-organization such as self-organizing maps (SOM) [7] and neural gas (NG) [9] have been successfully applied to a great number of learning tasks. Their advantage lies in their ability to learn the important topological relations of the input space without supervision. Both methods use the vector quantization technique in which the neurons (nodes) represent codebook vectors that encode a submanifold of the input space. The number of nodes in the SOM and the NG is fixed beforehand and cannot be changed over time. The growing neural gas (GNG) proposed by Fritzke [8] represents an incremental extension of these two networks. The GNG algorithm has the ability to create connections between existing nodes and to add new nodes in order to effectively map the topology of the input data distribution.

A growing network starts with a set N of two nodes at random positions w_a and w_b in the input space. At each iteration, the algorithm is given an input signal ξ according to the input distribution $P(\xi)$. The closest unit s_1 and the second closest unit s_2 of ξ in N are found and if the connection (s_1, s_2) does not exist, it is created. The local error of s_1 is updated by $\Delta E_{s_1} = \|\xi - w_{s_1}\|^2$ and w_{s_1} is moved towards ξ by a fraction ϵ_b. The weight of all the topological neighbors of s_1 are also moved towards ξ by a fraction ϵ_n. If the number of given inputs is a multiple of a parameter λ, a new node is inserted halfway between those two nodes that have maximum accumulated error. A connection-age-based mechanism leads to nodes being removed if rarely used. The algorithm stops when a criterion is met, i.e. some performance measure or network size. For the complete training algorithm see [8].

3.2   GNG-Based Noise Detection

Pose-motion vectors F (Eq. 1) are susceptible to tracking errors due to occlusion or systematic sensor errors, which may introduce noise in terms of values highly detached from the dominating point clouds. We consider inconsistent changes in body velocity to be caused by tracking errors rather than actual motion. Therefore, we remove noisy motion samples to create smoother inter-frame transitions. First, the network G^N is trained using only the motion samples from F. Second, the training motion samples are processed again to obtain the set of errors E from the trained network, which contains the distance from the closest unit $d(s_1)$ for each motion sample. We then calculate the empirically defined threshold that

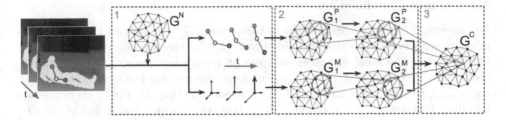

Fig. 2. Three-stage framework for the GNG-based processing of pose-motion samples: 1) detection and removal of sample noise; 2) hierarchical processing of pose-motion trajectories in two parallel streams; 3) classification of multi-cue trajectories

considers the distribution of the samples as $th = 2\sigma(E)\sqrt{\mu(E)}$, where $\sigma(E)$ is the standard deviation of E and $\mu(E)$ is its mean. For each motion sample, if $d(s_1) > th$, then the sample is considered to be noisy and its associated vector F_i is removed from the training set. We then obtain a new denoised training set from which we create two distinct sets with sequentially ordered pose and motion features, formally defined as $P = \{(\theta^u, \theta^l)\}$ and $M = \{(h, v)\}$ respectively.

3.3 Hierarchical Learning

The second stage is composed of a two-stream hierarchy for processing pose-motion cues separately. Each stream consists of two GNG networks that process prototypical samples under the assumption that recognition is selective for temporal order [5]. Therefore, sequence selectivity results from the use of node trajectories to describe spatiotemporal action segments.

We first train the networks G_1^P and G_1^M with the denoised training sets P and M respectively. After this training phase, chains of codebook nodes for training samples produce time varying trajectories on each network. For a given trained network G and a training set X, we define the set of labelled trajectories as:

$$T(G, X) := \{(s(x_{i-1}), s(x_i), l(x_i)) : l(x_i) = l(x_{i-1}), i \in [2..n(X)]\}, \quad (2)$$

where the function $s(x)$ returns the closest node s_1 of sample x in G, $l(x) \in L$ returns the label of x, and $n(X)$ is the number of samples in X. We compute the sets $T(G_1^P, P)$ and $T(G_1^M, M)$, for convenience denoted as T^P and T^M, and use them as input for the networks G_2^P and G_2^M respectively. This step produces a mapping with temporally ordered prototypes from consecutive samples. We now couple the outputs from both networks to create a set of multi-cue trajectories:

$$\Omega := \{(T(G_2^P, T_k^P), T(G_2^M, T_k^M), l_j) : k \in [2..g]\}, \quad (3)$$

where g is the number of elements in T^P and T^M and $l_j \in L$ is the label associated with the multi-cue trajectory. We finally feed the set of pairs into G^C and process Ω again to obtain the set with the mapping of codebook nodes corresponding to multi-cue pairs from consecutive trajectories.

3.4   Action Classification

For assigning labels to clustered trajectories with G^C, we extend the GNG algorithm with two offline labelling functions: one for the training phase and one for predicting the label of unseen samples at recognition time. These labelling techniques are considered to be offline since we assume that the labelled training pairs (ω, l_j) with $\omega \in \Omega$ and $l_j \in L$ are stored in F (Eq. 1). First, we define a labelling function $l : N \to L$ where N is the set of nodes and L is the set of class labels. According to the minimal-distance strategy [14], the sample $\omega_k \in \Omega$ adopts the label l_j of the closest $\omega \in \Omega$:

$$l(\omega_k) = l_j = l(\arg\min_{\omega \in \Omega} \|\omega_i - \omega\|^2). \tag{4}$$

At recognition time, our goal is to classify unseen samples as pose-motion trajectory prototypes (Eq. 4). Therefore, we define a prediction function $\varphi : \Omega \to L$ inspired by a single-linkage strategy [14] in which a new sample ω_{new} is labelled with l_j associated to the node n that minimizes the distance to this new sample:

$$\varphi(\omega_{new}) = \arg\min_{l_j}(\arg\min_{n \in N(l_j)} \|n - \omega_{new}\|^2). \tag{5}$$

The adopted labelling techniques have shown to achieve best classification accuracy among other offline labelling strategies [14].

4   Results and Discussion

We collected a data set of 10 actions performed by 13 different actors with a normal physical condition. To avoid biased execution, the actors had not been explained how to perform the actions. The data set contained the following periodic actions (PA) and goal-oriented actions (GA):

- PA: Standing, walking, jogging, sitting, lying down, crawling (10 minutes each);
- GA: Pick up object, jump, fall down, stand up (60 repetitions each).

For the data collection we monitored people in a home-like environment with a Kinect sensor installed 1,30 meters above the ground. Depth maps were sampled with a VGA resolution of 640x480, an operation range from 0.8 to 3.5 meters and a constant frame rate of 30Hz. To reduce sensor noise, we sampled the median value of the last 3 estimated points. Body centroids were estimated from depth map sequences based on the tracking skeleton model provided by OpenNI. Action labels were manually annotated from ground truth of sequence frames. We divided the data equally into training set and testing set: 30 sequences of 10 seconds for each periodic action and 30 repetitions for each goal-oriented action.

  We used the following GNG training parameters: learning step sizes $\epsilon_b = 0.05$, $\epsilon_n = 0.005$, node insertion interval $\lambda = 350$, error reduction constant $\alpha = 0.5$, and error reduction factor $d = 0.995$ (see [8] for details). Maximum network size and the number of iterations varied for each GNG and were experimentally adjusted based on the network performance for different input distributions.

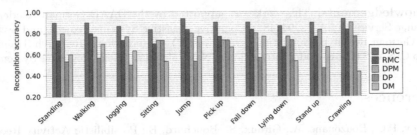

Fig. 3. Evaluation on recognition accuracy under 5 different processing conditions: Denoised multi-cue (*DMC*), denoised pose-motion vector (*DPM*), raw multi-cue (*RMC*), denoised pose-only (*DP*), and denoised motion-only (*DM*)

We evaluated the recognition accuracy of the framework under 5 different processing conditions: denoised multi-cue (DMC) and raw multi-cue (RMC) samples, denoised "pose only" (DP) and denoised "motion only" (DM) samples, and joint pose-motion vectors (DPM) as defined in Eq. 1 processed by a single stream. As seen in Fig. 3, the use of denoised multi-cue trajectory prototypes obtains the best average recognition result (89%). The removal of noise from the data sets increases average recognition accuracy by 13%. The DMC approach exhibits average improvements over DP and DM of 28% and 26% respectively.

Our results also show that DMC exhibits increased accuracy over the learning of joint pose-motion vectors (DPM) by 10%. This is partly due to the fact that the DPM approach forces the early convergence of the networks in the joint pose-motion space, while DMC and RMC learn a sparse representation of disjoint pose-motion prototypes that are subsequently combined to provide joint action dynamics. The reported results for actor-independent action recognition were obtained with low latency providing real-time characteristics.

5   Conclusion and Future Work

We presented a novel learning framework for the robust recognition of human full-body actions from pose-motion cues. Multi-cue trajectories from matching frames were processed separately by a hierarchical GNG-based architecture. This approach captures correlations between pose and motion prototypes to provide joint action dynamics. Experiments on a data set of 10 actions have shown that the proposed multi-cue strategy increases recognition accuracy over a single-cue approach and joint pose-motion vectors.

While the use of multi-cue learning has previously shown compelling results for robust action recognition [3,10,12], this approach is also supported by neural evidence. Therefore, the obtained results motivate further work in two directions. First, the evaluation of our framework on a wider number of actions and more complex pose-motion characteristics, e.g. including arm movements and hand gestures. Second, an extended neural architecture based on a more biologically plausible model of the visual system.

Acknowledgements. This work was supported by the DAAD German Academic Exchange Service (Kz:A/13/94748) - Cognitive Assistive Systems Project, and by the DFG German Research Foundation (grant #1247) - International Research Training Group CINACS (Cross-modal Interaction in Natural and Artificial Cognitive Systems).

References

1. Roy, P.C., Bouzouane, A., Giroux, S., Bouchard, B.: Possibilistic Activity Recognition in Smart Homes for Cognitively Impaired People. Applied Artificial Intelligence: An International Journal 25, 883–926 (2011)
2. Suarez, J., Murphy, R.: Hand Gesture Recognition with Depth Images: A review. In: IEEE Int. Symposium on Robot and Human Interactive Communication, France, pp. 411–417 (2012)
3. Xu, R., Agarwal, P., Kumar, S., Krovi, V.N., Corso, J.J.: Combining Skeletal Pose with Local Motion for Human Activity Recognition. In: Perales, F.J., Fisher, R.B., Moeslund, T.B. (eds.) AMDO 2012. LNCS, vol. 7378, pp. 114–123. Springer, Heidelberg (2012)
4. Papadopoulos, G.T., Axenopoulos, A., Daras, P.: Real-Time Skeleton-Tracking-Based Human Action Recognition Using Kinect Data. In: Gurrin, C., Hopfgartner, F., Hurst, W., Johansen, H., Lee, H., O'Connor, N. (eds.) MMM 2014, Part I. LNCS, vol. 8325, pp. 473–483. Springer, Heidelberg (2014)
5. Giese, M.A., Poggio, T.: Neural Mechanisms for the Recognition of Biological Movements. Nature Reviews Neuroscience 4, 179–192 (2003)
6. Escobar, M.-J., Kornprobst, P.: Action Recognition with a Bioinspired Feedforward Motion Processing Model: The Richness of Center-Surround Interactions. In: Forsyth, D., Torr, P., Zisserman, A. (eds.) ECCV 2008, Part IV. LNCS, vol. 5305, pp. 186–199. Springer, Heidelberg (2008)
7. Kohonen, T.: Self-organizing Maps. Series in Information Sciences, vol. 30. Springer, Heidelberg (1995)
8. Fritzke, B.: A Growing Neural Gas Network Learns Topologies. In: Advances in Neural Information Processing Systems, vol. 7, pp. 625–632. MIT Press (1995)
9. Martinetz, T., Schluten, K.: A "neural-gas" network learns topologies. In: Artificial Neural Networks, pp. 397–402. Elsevier (1991)
10. Jiang, Z., Lin, Z., Davis, L.S.: Recognizing Human Actions by Learning and Matching Shape-Motion Prototype Trees. IEEE Transactions on Pattern Analysis and Machine Intelligence 31(3), 533–547 (2012)
11. Parisi, G.I., Wermter, S.: Hierarchical SOM-based Detection of Novel Behavior for 3D Human Tracking. In: IEEE Int. Joint Conf. on Neural Networks (IJCNN), USA, pp. 1380–1387 (2013)
12. Parisi, G.I., Barros, P., Wermter, S.: FINGeR: Framework for Interactive Neural-based Gesture Recognition. In: European Symposium of Artificial Neural Networks (ESANN), Belgium, pp. 443–447 (2014)
13. Miikkulainen, R., Bednar, J.A., Choe, Y., Sirosh, J.: Computational Maps in the Visual Cortex. Springer, New York (2005)
14. Beyer, O., Cimiano, P.: Online Labelling Strategies for Growing Neural Gas. In: Yin, H., Wang, W., Rayward-Smith, V. (eds.) IDEAL 2011. LNCS, vol. 6936, pp. 76–83. Springer, Heidelberg (2011)

Real-Time Anomaly Detection
with a Growing Neural Gas

Nicolai Waniek, Simon Bremer, and Jörg Conradt

Technische Universität München, Neuroscientific System Theory,
Karlstraße 45, 80333 München, Germany
{nicolai.waniek,simon.bremer,conradt}@tum.de
http://www.nst.ei.tum.de

Abstract. We present a novel system for vision based anomaly detection in real-time environments. Our system uses an event-based vision sensor consisting of asynchronously operating pixels that is inspired by the human retina. Each pixel reports events of illumination changes, are processed in a purely event-based tracker that pursues edges of events in the input stream. The tracker estimates are used to determine whether the input events originate from anomalous or regular data. We distinguish between the two cases with a Growing Neural Gas (GNG), which is modified to suite our event-based processing pipeline. While learning of the GNG is supervised and performed offline, the detection is carried out online. We evaluate our system by inspection of fast-spinning cogwheels. Our system achieves faster than real-time speed on commodity hardware and generalizes well to other cases. The results of this paper can be applied both to technical implementations where high speed but little processing power is required, and for further investigations into event-based algorithms.

Keywords: event-based vision, growing neural gas, real-time anomaly detection, event-based tracking.

1   Introduction

Detecting anomalies in visual data is a common task in computer vision. For instance, detecting malformed objects in a production line is usually automated using a dedicated inspection setup. However, most of the scenarios involve static images at a low frame rate or only slowly moving targets. This leaves enough time to process the visual input data before the next frame arrives.

Solving anomaly detection tasks in real-time environments with quickly moving objects is more intricate, though. Usually, huge amounts of data need to be acquired by expensive high-speed equipment and subsequently processed by significant amounts of processing hardware. This is not only expensive in terms of the equipment which needs to be acquired, but also with respect to maintenance, running, and power consumption costs. In addition, the size of the required cameras and especially of the processing pipeline usually constrains such systems to

S. Wermter et al. (Eds.): ICANN 2014, LNCS 8681, pp. 97–104, 2014.

a permanent location. These restrictions prohibit the use of anomaly detection systems in small environments or when mobility is required.

We present a new approach to visual anomaly detection for real-time environments using a neurobiologically inspired event-based vision sensor. Such a sensor emits small packets of information (events) on a per pixel basis. Each event carries only little information about the perceived environment but allows for a more efficient design of algorithms [7]. In addition, the small size of the sensor and limited amount of processing power which is required allows the utilization in constrained environments.

The remainder of this paper is outlined as follows: first we will give a coarse description of the whole system. Then we will detail each of the different modules and the computations which are performed. Finally we evaluate our system, given the task to detect malformed cog-wheels, e.g. cog-wheels with completely missing or broken cogs, while the wheel is spinning at a very high speed.

2   Event-Based Anomaly Detection

We propose a novel system which uses an event-based Dynamic Vision Sensor (eDVS, [4]) for real-time visual anomaly detection. The system is made of different building blocks which are depicted in Figure 1. Input data from the eDVS will be presented to a tracking unit which identifies unique edges in the input data. The tracker unit will give rise to a feature vector which is forwarded to a Growing Neural Gas (GNG, [5,6]). Using the GNG which was previously trained on normal data, we are able able to discern whether the feature vector presents an anomaly or not. Each of these blocks will be described separately in the following sections.

Fig. 1. Building blocks of the anomaly detection system

2.1   Event-Based Vision

The eDVS provides single pixel events $e_m, e_{m+1}, \cdots \in \mathcal{P}$ for an array of 128×128 asynchronously operating pixels. $\mathcal{P} = [0, 127]^2$ denotes the range of possible pixel locations. Each pixel measures illumination changes and emits an event as soon as an individual threshold is reached. Thus, the sensor transmits a stream of events which forms a sparse representation of changes in the environment. High transfer rates allow event rates of multiple 100K events to be transmitted per second. Due to a per-pixel bias, the sensor reaches a dynamic range of over 120dB. Besides its location, each event discloses polarity information and a time stamp. Figure 2 shows a picture of an eDVS as well as a visualization of event data of a waving hand.

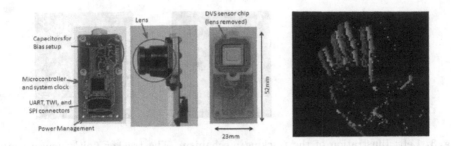

Fig. 2. Left: picture of the event-based Dynamic Vision Sensor (eDVS). Right: Visualization of 0.1s integrated event data of a moving hand in front of the eDVS. Red pixels correspond to events which change polarity from light to dark (off-events), green pixels are events which change from dark to light (on-events).

2.2 Tracking

Single events yield only little information about the stimuli which produced them. However, integrating many events in order to reason about the stimuli neglects the benefits of event based computation as well as it introduces unwanted memory consumption and temporal delays. To avoid the integration of events, we devised a tracking module which operates on single events and creates and updates individual tracking units.

Tracking units are spawned at locations where a huge number of events originate and destroyed where they disappear. Such event sources and sinks can be selected either manually or automatically. The number of tracking units is variable and denoted as $\mathcal{K}$.

Each tracker unit $t_1, \ldots, t_\mathcal{K}$ consists of a certain number $\mathcal{N}$ of connected neurons $\tau_1^{(r)}, \ldots, \tau_\mathcal{N}^{(r)} \in \mathcal{P}$. The subscript denotes the neuron index, the superscript (r) the tracker unit index. The number $\mathcal{N}$ depends on the object that should be tracked and is 2 in our case of tracking simple edges of cog-wheels.

The neurons' update mechanics are inspired by the attraction dynamics of Self-Organizing Maps (SOM) during their learning phase [3]. Similar to a SOM, the first step of the tracking algorithm is selecting the neuron $\tau_j^{(r)}$ which is closest to an event e_k with respect to the Euclidean distance. Given an event e_k, $\tau_j^{(r)}$ will be updated according to

$$\tau_j^{(r)} = \tau_j^{(r)} + \nu \cdot \delta, \tag{1}$$

where $\nu = e_k - \tau_j^{(r)}$ is the directional vector to which τ_j is pulled and $\delta = \min\left(\frac{\eta}{d^2}, \delta_{max}\right)$ is the attraction strength. η is a learning rate and δ_{max} sets a maximal attraction strength.

Subsequently, all other neurons $\tau_i^{(r)}, i \neq j$ in the relevant tracker unit t_r will be updated. This differs from a regular SOM in the way that the direction of the update is the same as for updating $\tau_j^{(r)}$. The reasoning for this change is that we

Fig. 3. Left: Illustration of the tracking mechanism. The tracker unit's neurons are pulled along the direction of the closest neuron to the event. (see text for details). Middle: three valid tracker units and one outlier tracker unit (blue circles) latch to off-events of edges of the teeth of a cog-wheel. Right: The same scenario as in the middle, but with artificial noise. Still, the tracker units only track cog-wheel edges. Curiously the same outlier tracker unit was spawned.

expect edges to move coherently into one direction and not towards a singular point. Thus, the update to $\tau_i^{(r)}$ can be stated as

$$\tau_i^{(r)} = \tau_i^{(r)} + \nu \cdot \delta \cdot G(d_i), \tag{2}$$

where G is the Gaussian function and d_i the distance between $\tau_i^{(r)}$ and e_k. We used the parameters $\eta = 3.0, \sigma = 3.0$, and $\delta_{max} = 0.3$ in all our computations. The update process and example tracker units for noiseless and noisy input are shown in Figure 3.

We evaluated our tracker implementation and found it to be robust even with a noise to signal ratio of 97% (data not shown). Note that the algorithm holds for more complex scenarios where the number of neurons per tracker unit is not limited to 2.

2.3 Feature Description

After an event e_k was tracked and the corresponding tracker unit t_r has adjusted to its new position, a preliminary feature vector $\hat{\xi}_i$ will be created. Each $\hat{\xi}_i$ is defined as $\hat{\xi}_i = (x, y, s, \theta, \sigma, t, d)$, where x, y define the tracker unit's position in the 2D input space $\mathcal{P}$, s the speed, θ the orientation, σ the unit's size, t the time relative to the spawn time of the tracker unit and d the distance to the next tracker unit. Finally, each dimension of $\hat{\xi}_i$ is normalized to be within $[-1, 1]$. This yields the final feature vector $\xi_i \in \mathbb{R}^7$ for event e_k and tracker unit t_r.

2.4 Growing Neural Gas for Vector Representation

A Growing Neural Gas (GNG) is a network of neurons which grows over time [5,6]. Such networks learn a representation of input data and spawn new neurons as soon as the internal representation significantly mismatches the input. They were successfully applied to a variety of tasks, e.g. representing object knowledge given visual input [1].

The feature vectors $\xi_i, \xi_{i+1}, \dots$ will form one or more point clouds in the corresponding multidimensional feature vector space. Shape, size and density of these accumulations may differ and may not be known in advance of applying the setup to a specific use case. We thus used a Growing Neural Network (GNG) to learn a generalized representation of input vectors in a fully supervised manner. This avoids having to worry about the precise structure of the space of feature vectors for different tasks.

Learning Phase. We adapted the learning method described in [2] to suite our requirements. Each neuron $n_j, j \in \mathcal{M}$ not only stores its corresponding position p_j in the feature vector space and its set of edges, but also an accumulated error value ε_j. This error measure is initialized to 0 when n_j is created. In addition, edges between two neurons n_j and n_l have an age $a_{j,l}$ which is initialized to 0. The GNG is initially started with $\mathcal{M} = 2$ neurons and grows over time.

For each feature vector ξ_i that we present to the GNG during the learning phase, we select the two closest neurons s_1 and s_2. The error ε_{s_1} will be updated according to

$$\varepsilon_{s_1} = \varepsilon_{s_1} + \|p_{s_1} - \xi_i\|^2, \tag{3}$$

whereas the errors ε_i of all other neurons $n_i \neq s_1$ are decayed exponentially according to $\varepsilon_i = \varepsilon_i \cdot d$ with $d = 0.95$.

Likewise, the position p_{s_1} is updated by

$$p_{s_1} = p_{s_1} + \epsilon_b \cdot (\xi_i - p_{s_1}), \tag{4}$$

while all other positions $p_i \neq p_{s_1}$ are relocated according to

$$p_i = p_i + \epsilon_n \cdot (\xi_i - p_i), \tag{5}$$

with $\epsilon_b = 0.2$ and $\epsilon_n = 0.01$.

After all positions are updated, we set $a_{s_1,s_2} := 0$ if an edge exists between s_1 and s_2. If not, we create a new edge with age 0. Next up we remove all edges between all neurons $n_i, n_j, i \neq j$ which have an age $a_{i,j} > a_{max} = 20$. Neurons that hold an in-degree of 0 after this step will be pruned as well.

The final step of the algorithm creates a new neuron every $\lambda = 100$ iterations as long as the maximum number $\mathcal{M}_{max} = 200$ is not reached. Note that we chose this number arbitrarily. We create a new neuron n_p by selecting neuron n_q with the highest accumulated overall error ε_q and insert the new neuron n_p exactly between n_q and n_f. n_f is selected according to

$$f = \operatorname*{argmax}_{j \in \mathcal{M}} (\varepsilon_j : \exists \text{ edge between } n_j, n_p). \tag{6}$$

Finally the errors of n_q, n_f, and n_r are updated according to $\varepsilon_q = \varepsilon_q \cdot \alpha, \varepsilon_f = \varepsilon_f \cdot \alpha$, and $\varepsilon_r = \varepsilon_q$, with $\alpha = 0.5$.

The learning phase of the GNG takes only a couple of minutes on commodity hardware for a recorded event stream of several minutes.

Evaluation Phase. Remember that ultimately our system needs to evaluate a continuous stream of events online. To achieve this goal we need to compare novel event data to the offline-learned representation of the GNG on a per-event basis. Thus, each of the tracker units contributes with an error measure to an overall instantaneous input quality as long as the unit is alive.

For any event e_k we determine the best matching tracker unit t_r and its corresponding feature vector ξ_i as described above. Thereupon we compute the distance ε_i between ξ_i and the closest neuron s_1 of the previously trained GNG.

The value ε_i gives a measure about how surprising a specific event is. For instance, an ε_i value which is near zero will be not surprising as the GNG learned to represent the corresponding ξ_i. However, larger error values would indicate a very high level of surprise, as the distance between ξ_i and anything previously learned is significant.

As mentioned above, each tracker unit contributes with some error ε_i as long as it is alive. Nevertheless, we expect the input data to be noisy. Consequently we do not simply store ε_i along its tracker unit t_r but filter the error exponentially and update the filtered error measure ε_i^f according to

$$\varepsilon_i^f = (1 - \gamma) \cdot \varepsilon_i^f + \gamma \cdot \varepsilon_i, \tag{7}$$

where $\gamma = 0.04$ in all our computations.

We expect that the instantaneous error distribution of all ε_i^f follows a unimodal distribution for normal data. Contrary, we expect deviations from a unimodal distribution as soon as anomalies are introduced in the input data.

2.5   Recording and Evaluation Setup

We evaluated our system with spinning cog-wheels in front of an event-based vision sensor (eDVS). The cog-wheels, each about 5 cm in diameter, were mounted on a DC motor 20 cm apart from the sensor and partially occluded. The motor speed was set to about 10 cycles per second and was limited by the sensor's USART-USB connection. This connection has an upper transmission limit of 4 MBit/s. Higher DC motor speeds would induce higher event rates than could be transmitted.

We recorded multiple sets of differently shaped cog-wheels to train the GNG with. Each data set consists of one cog-wheel spinning at a high speed, being recorded with the eDVS for a few minutes. The evaluation was carried out with data sets which were not used during the learning phase.

3   Results and Discussion

After the Growing Neural Gas (GNG) successfully learned to represent data without any anomalies, we evaluated the system performance with novel data sets and online evaluations. These new data sets contained flawless cog-wheels as well as cog-wheels with deformed, broken or missing teeth.

Category	Average	Min	Max	Samples
flawless	0.0132010	0.0113580	0.0167701	112
broken tooth	0.0577727	0.0313477	0.2536080	22
deformed tooth	0.0348418	0.0311630	0.0404653	11
missing tooth	0.0455668	0.0404988	0.0525160	22

Fig. 4. Statistical summary of the evaluation. Average, Min and Max values are the error values reported by our system after presenting a complete data sets.

Given a huge number of samples with regular cog-wheels, we found that the system never reports any error value above 0.03. On the other hand, as soon as events from deformed or broken cog-wheels are inbound the error value rises above and beyond $\Gamma = 0.03$. We therefore conclude that our system has to notify about any input as soon as an error value above Γ is detected.

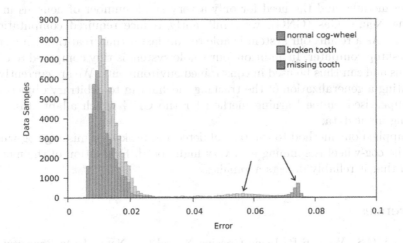

Fig. 5. Histogram of the instantaneous error distributions for different cog-wheels. Green is the error for a flawless cog-wheel, blue shows the distribution for a cog-wheel with one broken tooth, and red shows the distribution for a cog-wheel with one tooth completely missing. Note that there were no errors reported above 0.03 for the flawless cog-wheel. Data samples tells how many events were already presented to the detection system. Values higher than 0.01 are not shown.

Figure 4 shows more details of these evaluations. Especially interesting is that the maximal error value for broken teeth lays above the maximal error value of missing teeth. We understand that feature vectors for broken or malformed teeth may be distinct in more than only one dimension (e.g. time, speed, *and* position). Feature vectors for missing teeth exhibit this anomaly only in fewer dimension, namely the distance between two tracking units. Another interesting point is that the error values for deformed teeth are more similar to missing teeth. We assume that the tracker units are not able to properly latch to deformed teeth. Consequently, a deformed tooth would be considered a missing tooth.

Further inspection of the instantaneous error distributions confirmed our prediction of Section 2.4. Figure 5 shows stereotypical distributions for three different cog-wheels after presenting a certain number of events to the system. Whereas the distribution of the flawless cog-wheel follows a uni-modal distribution, the distributions for the two other shown cases follows a bi-modal distribution. Note that the values presented in Figure 5 differ from Figure 4. The table presents values averaged over whole data sets whereas the figure displays instantaneous error distributions at one specific point in time for only one data set.

4   Conclusion

We demonstrated a novel method for detecting anomalies in a real-time environment. Due to the sparse nature of the event stream, our purely event-based tracking module, and the need for only a very small number of neurons in the Growing Neural Gas (GNG), we significantly reduce required computational resources. As a result, our system is able to run faster than real-time on a standard desktop computer. In addition, our whole system is tiny compared to other solutions and can thus be used in constrained environments. We are currently investigating a generalization of the tracking mechanism to arbitrary objects and an unsupervised online learning method for the GNG which adapts to slowly changing input data.

We applied our method to the task of detecting broken or missing cog-wheels while the cog-wheel is spinning at a very high speed. Evaluation of the method showed that it reliably detects anomalies.

References

1. Donatti, G.S., Wrtz, R.P.: Using Growing Neural Gas Networks to Represent Visual Object Knowledge. In: 2009 21st IEEE International Conference on Tools with Artificial Intelligence, pp. 54–58 (2009)
2. Fritzke, B.: A growing neural gas network learns topologies. In: Advances in Neural Information Processing Systems, vol. 7, pp. 625–632. MIT Press (1995)
3. Kohonen, T.: Self-Organizing Maps, 3rd edn. Springer, Heidelberg (2000)
4. Lichtsteiner, P., Posch, C., Delbruck, T.: A 128× 128 120 db 15 μs latency asynchronous temporal contrast vision sensor. IEEE Journal of Solid State Circuits 43, 566–576 (2007)
5. Martinetz, T., Schulten, K.J.: A "neural-gas" network learns topologies. In: Artificial Neural Networks, pp. 397–402. North-Holland, Amsterdam (1991)
6. Martinetz, T., Schulten, K.J.: Topology representing networks. Neural Networks 7, 507–522 (1994)
7. Weikersdorfer, D., Hoffmann, R., Conradt, J.: Simultaneous Localization and Mapping for Event-Based Vision Systems. In: Chen, M., Leibe, B., Neumann, B. (eds.) ICVS 2013. LNCS, vol. 7963, pp. 133–142. Springer, Heidelberg (2013)

Classification with Reject Option Using the Self-Organizing Map

Ricardo Sousa[1,*], Ajalmar R. da Rocha Neto[3,*],
Jaime S. Cardoso[4], and Guilherme A. Barreto[2]

[1] INEB – Instituto de Engenharia Biomédica, Universidade Porto, Portugal
[2] Departamento Engenharia de Teleinformática, Universidade Federal do Ceará (UFC), Brazil
[3] Departamento de Telemática, Instituto Federal do Ceará (IFCE), Brazil
[4] INESC Porto, FEUP, Universidade Porto, Portugal

Abstract. Reject option is a technique used to improve classifier's reliability in decision support systems. It consists on withholding the automatic classification of an item, if the decision is considered not sufficiently reliable. The rejected item is then handled by a different classifier or by a human expert. The vast majority of the works on this issue have been concerned with implementing a reject option by endowing a supervised learning scheme (e.g., Multilayer Perceptron, Learning Vector Quantization or Support Vector Machines) with a reject mechanism. In this paper we introduce variants of the Self-Organizing Map (SOM), originally an unsupervised learning scheme, to act as supervised classifiers with reject option, and compare their performances with that of the MLP classifier.

Keywords: Self-Organizing Maps, Reject Option, Robust Classification, Prototype-based Classifiers, Neuron Labeling.

1 Introduction

The field of machine learning has been evolving at a very fast pace, being mostly motivated and pushed forward by increasingly challenging real world applications. For instance, in credit scoring modeling, models are developed to determine how likely applicants are to default with their repayments. Previous repayment history is used to determine whether a customer should be classified into a 'good' or a 'bad' category [1].

Notwithstanding, real world problems still pose challenges which may not be solvable satisfactorily by the existing learning methodologies used by automatic decision support systems [2], leading to many incorrect predictions. However, there are situations in which the decision should be postponed, giving the support system the opportunity to identify critical items for posterior revision, instead of trying to automatically classify every and each item. In such cases, the system automates only those decisions

---

* This work was partially supported through Program CNPq/Universidade do Porto/590008/2009-9 and conducted when Ricardo Sousa was in internship at Universidade Federal do Ceará, Brazil. This work was also partially funded by Fundação para a Ciência e a Tecnologia (FCT) - Portugal through project PTDC/SAU-ENB/114951/2009 and by FEDER funds through the Programa Operacional Factores de Competitividade - COMPETE in the framework of the project PEst-C/SAU/LA0002/2013. First and second authors contributed equally to this article.

S. Wermter et al. (Eds.): ICANN 2014, LNCS 8681, pp. 105–112, 2014.
© Springer International Publishing Switzerland 2014

which can be reliably predicted, letting the critical ones for a human expert to analyze. Therefore, the development of binary classifiers with a third output class, usually called the *reject class*, is attractive. This approach is known as classification with reject option [3, 4] or soft decision making [5]. Roughly speaking, reject option comprises a set of techniques aiming at improving the classification reliability in decision support systems, being originally formalized in the context of statistical pattern recognition in [4], under the minimum risk theory. Basically, it consists in withholding the automatic classification of an item, if the decision is considered not sufficiently reliable. Rejected patterns can then be handled by a different classifier, or manually by a human. Recently, this paradigm was tailored to obtain efficient learning models [6].

In this paper we develop two novel variants of the SOM network to act as supervised classifiers with reject option, and compare their performances with that of the MLP classifier. To the best of our knowledge, this is the first time such approach is developed for the self-organizing map or similar neural networks. Computational simulations conducted in this study shows the robustness for our proposal.

2   Basics of Classification with Reject Option

As mentioned before, in possession of a "complex" dataset (e.g. from a medical diagnosis problem), every classifier is bound to misclassify some data samples. For that, we assume that the problem (and hence, the data) involves only two classes, say $\{\mathcal{C}_{-1}, \mathcal{C}_{+1}\}$, but the classifier must be able to output a third one, the reject class $\{\mathcal{C}_{-1}, \mathcal{C}_{\text{Reject}}, \mathcal{C}_{+1}\}$. Assuming that the input information is represented by an n-dimensional real vector $\mathbf{x} = [x_1 \ x_2 \ \cdots \ x_n]^T \in \mathbb{R}^n$, the design of classifiers with reject option can be systematized in three different approaches for the binary problem[1]:

Method 1: It involves the design of a single, standard binary classifier. If the classifier provides some approximation to the a posteriori class probabilities, $\mathbb{P}(\mathcal{C}_k | \mathbf{x})$, $k = 1, 2, ..., K$, then a pattern is rejected if the largest value among the K posterior probabilities is lower than a given threshold, say β ($0 \le \beta \le 1$);

Method 2: The design of two, *independent*, classifiers. A first classifier is trained to output $\mathcal{C}_{-1}$ only when the probability of $\mathcal{C}_{-1}$ is high and a second classifier trained to output $\mathcal{C}_{+1}$ only when the probability of $\mathcal{C}_{+1}$ is high. When both classifiers agree on the decision, the corresponding class is outputted. Otherwise, in case of disagreement, the reject class is the chosen one;

Method 3: The design of a single classifier with embedded reject option; that is, the classifier is trained following optimality criteria that automatically take into account the costs of misclassification and rejection in their loss functions, leading to the design of algorithms specifically built for this kind of problem.

In this paper we will introduce two SOM-based strategies for the classification with reject option paradigm under Methods 1 and 2.

3   The Self-Organizing Map

The Self-Organizing Map (SOM) [8] is one of the most popular neural network architectures. It belongs to the category of unsupervised competitive learning algorithms and

---

[1] Please consider reading [7] for further information.

it is usually designed to build an ordered representation of spatial proximity among vectors of an unlabeled data set. The neurons in the SOM are put together in an output layer, $\mathcal{A}$, in one-, two- or even three-dimensional arrays. Each neuron $j \in \mathcal{A}$, $j = 1, 2, \ldots, q$, has a weight vector $\mathbf{w}_j \in \mathbb{R}^d$ with the same dimension of the input vector $\mathbf{x} \in \mathbb{R}^d$. The network weights are trained according to a competitive-cooperative learning scheme in which the weight vectors of a winning neuron (also called, the best-matching unit – BMU) and its neighbors in the output array are updated after the presentation of an input vector (see [9, 10]).

3.1 SOM for Supervised Classification

In order to use the SOM for supervised classification, modifications are necessary in its original learning algorithm. There are many ways to do that (see [11] and references therein), but in the present paper we will resort to two well-known strategies.

Strategy 1: The first strategy involves a post-training neuron labeling. SOM is trained in the usual unsupervised way and once done the whole training data is presented to the SOM in order to find the winning neuron for each pattern vector. The labelling of the winning neuron is conducted according to the majority voting basis, for instance. Two undesirable situations may occur: (*i*) ambiguity or (*ii*) dead neurons. In these cases, the neuron could be pruned (i.e. disregarded) from the map, or even be tagged with a "rejection class" label. In this paper, we extend Strategy 1 in order to allow the SOM network to handle pattern classification problems with reject option. For this purpose, we follow a more systematic and principled approach based on Chow's concept of rejection cost [4], instead of simply tagging ambiguous or dead neurons with "rejection class" labels.

Strategy 2: The second strategy, usually called the *self-supervised SOM* training scheme, is the one used by Kohonen for the neural phonetic typewriter [12]. According to this strategy, the SOM is made supervised by adding class information to each input pattern vector. Specifically, the input vectors $\mathbf{x}(n)$ are now formed of two parts, $\mathbf{x}_p(n)$ and $\mathbf{x}_l(n)$, where $\mathbf{x}_p(n)$ is the pattern vector itself, while $\mathbf{x}_l(n)$ is the corresponding class label of $\mathbf{x}_p(n)$. During training, these vectors are concatenated to build augmented vectors $\mathbf{x}(n) = [\mathbf{x}_p(n)\ \mathbf{x}_l(n)]^T$ which are used as inputs to the SOM. The corresponding augmented weight vectors, $\mathbf{w}_j(n) = [\mathbf{w}_j^p(n)\ \mathbf{w}_j^l(n)]^T$, are adjusted as in the usual SOM training procedure.

4 Incorporating Reject Option into the SOM: Two Proposals

Before proceeding with the description of the two proposals, it is worth exposing the main reasons that led to the choice of the SOM for supervised classification with rejection option instead of other prototype-based classifiers. Firstly, it has been verified that the use of a neighborhood function makes the SOM less sensitive to weight initialization [13] and accelerates its convergence [14] when compared with other prototype-based classifiers, such as the LVQ. Once trained, one can also take advantage of the SOM's density matching and topology-preserving properties to extract rules from a trained SOM network [15] in order to permit further analysis of the results towards better decision making. In particular, the density matching and topology-preserving properties will be used by both proposals to be described in order to estimate $\mathbb{P}(\mathbf{x}|\mathcal{C}_k)$ (or

$\mathbb{P}(\mathcal{C}_k|\mathbf{x})$) using the distribution of SOM's weight vectors. An optimal threshold value has to be determined in order to re-tag some of the weight vectors with the rejection class label. In this paper we will also provide techniques to obtaining suitable estimates of the likelihood function $\mathbb{P}(\mathbf{x}|\mathcal{C}_k)$ or the posterior probability $\mathbb{P}(\mathbf{x}|\mathcal{C}_k)$. As a final remark, it is worth mentioning that the design methodologies of the classifiers proposed in this work, Reject Option SOM with 1 map for Classification (ROSOM-1C) and Reject Option SOM with 2 maps for Classification (ROSOM-2C), are general enough in the sense that they can be used to develop pattern classifiers with reject option using, in principle, any topology-preserving prototype-based neural networks, such as the Growing Neural Gas (GNG) [16] and the Parameterless SOM (PLSOM) [17] algorithms.

4.1 SOM with Reject Option Using One Classifier

Initially, the ROSOM-1C requires post-training neuron labeling via Strategy 1, as described in Section 3.1. Additional steps are included in order to change the labels of some neurons to *rejection class*. The main idea behind the proposal of the ROSOM-1C approach relies exactly on developing formal techniques to assign the rejection class label to a given neuron. In greater detail, the design of the ROSOM-1C requires the following steps.

▷ **STEP 1:** For a given data set, a number of training realizations are carried out using a single SOM network in order to find the best number of neurons and suitable map dimensions. For this purpose, the conventional unsupervised SOM training is adopted.

▷ **STEP 2:** Present the training data once again and label the prototypes $\mathbf{w}_j$, $j = 1, ..., q$, according to the mode of the class labels of the patterns mapped to them. No weight adjustments are carried out at this step.

▷ **STEP 3:** Based on the SOM's ability to approximate the input data density, we approximate $\mathbb{P}(\mathbf{x}|\mathcal{C}_k)$ with $\mathbb{P}(\mathbf{w}_j|\mathcal{C}_k, \mathbf{x})$, for $j = 1, ..., q$ and $k = 1, ..., K$. In the end of this Section, we describe two techniques to compute $\mathbb{P}(\mathbf{w}_j|\mathcal{C}_k, \mathbf{x})$ based on standard statistical techniques, namely, Parzen Windows and Gaussian Mixture Models.

▷ **STEP 4:** Finding an optimum value for the rejection threshold β requires the minimization of the empirical risk as proposed in [4]:

$$\widehat{R} = w_r R + E \tag{1}$$

where R and E are, respectively, the ratio of rejected and misclassified patterns (computed using validation data), while w_r is the rejection cost (whose value must be specified in advance by the user).

▷ **STEP 5:** Re-label the prototypes as belonging to the rejection class if $\max_k \{\mathbb{P}(\mathcal{C}_k)\mathbb{P}(\mathbf{w}_i|\mathcal{C}_k, \mathbf{x})\} < \beta$ verifies.

On the Estimation of $\mathbb{P}(w_j|\mathcal{C}_k, x)$: The first approach to be used to compute SOM-based estimates of $\mathbb{P}(\mathbf{w}_j|\mathcal{C}_k)$ is through the Parzen windows nonparametric method. The estimation is usually performed by some kernel function, usually a Gaussian, averaged by the number of points belonging to a given class. Another approach that can also be used to estimate $\mathbb{P}(\mathbf{w}_j|\mathcal{C}_k, \mathbf{x})$ based on the distribution of weight vectors of the SOM is the Gaussian Mixture Models (GMM) [18–20]. In this paper we follow the approach developed by [19], which is implemented in the SOM toolbox[2].

---

[2] Available for download at http://www.cis.hut.fi/somtoolbox/

Neuron Re-labeling Based on Gini Index: For the application of the decision rule in **STEP 5**, one has to store all the values of the posterior probabilities estimates $\mathbb{P}(\mathcal{C}_k|\mathbf{w}_j,\mathbf{x}) \propto \mathbb{P}(\mathcal{C}_k)\mathbb{P}(\mathbf{w}_j|\mathcal{C}_k,\mathbf{x})$ for each neuron j. The quantity $\mathbb{P}(\mathcal{C}_k|\mathbf{w}_j,\mathbf{x})$ express the probability of an instance that has fallen within the Voronoi cell of neuron j to belong to class $\mathcal{C}_k$. By means of concepts borrowed from information theory, it is possible to merge all the probabilities $\mathbb{P}(\mathcal{C}_k|\mathbf{w}_j,\mathbf{x})$, $k = 1,...,K$, associated with a given neuron, into a single quantity to be called *cell impurity*.

4.2   SOM with Reject Option Using Two Classifiers

In comparison to the ROSOM-1C, the individual SOM networks that comprise the ROSOM-2C have an extra feature: the ability to control the preference for patterns of a given class by the inclusion of cost parameter w_r into the learning rules of the individual networks. In other words, one individual network is trained to become specialized, say, on class $\mathcal{C}_{-1}$, while the other is trained to become specialized on class $\mathcal{C}_{+1}$.

By allowing one of the networks to have preference for (i.e. to be biased toward) the patterns of class C_{+1}, while the other has preference for the patterns of class C_{-1}, makes the decision rule of ROSOM-2C more reliable. More reliable in the sense that a pattern is classified only when the outputs of both network coincides, otherwise the pattern is rejected. The design of the ROSOM-2C requires the following steps.

▷ **STEP 1:** Choose a rejection cost w_r.
▷ **STEP 2:** Train two SOM networks following the self-supervised SOM training scheme describe in Section 3.1.

2.1) Train the first SOM network, henceforth named SOM-1 classifier, to become specialized on the class $\mathcal{C}_{-1}$. For that, we replace the standard SOM learning rule with Equation (2).

$$\mathbf{w}_j(n+1) = \mathbf{w}_j(n) + \begin{cases} \eta(n)h(i,j;n)[\mathbf{x}(n) - \mathbf{w}_j(n)]w_r, & \text{if } \text{class}(\mathbf{x}(n)) = \mathcal{C}_{+1} \\ \eta(n)h(i,j;n)[\mathbf{x}(n) - \mathbf{w}_j(n)](1-w_r), & \text{if } \text{class}(\mathbf{x}(n)) = \mathcal{C}_{-1}. \end{cases}$$
(2)

2.2) Train the second SOM network, henceforth named SOM-2 classifier, to become specialized on the class $\mathcal{C}_{+1}$. For that, we replace the standard SOM learning rule with Equation (3).

$$\mathbf{w}_j(n+1) = \mathbf{w}_j(n) + \begin{cases} \eta(n)h(i,j;n)[\mathbf{x}(n) - \mathbf{w}_j(n)](1-w_r), & \text{if } \text{class}(\mathbf{x}(n)) = \mathcal{C}_{+1} \\ \eta(n)h(i,j;n)[\mathbf{x}(n) - \mathbf{w}_j(n)]w_r, & \text{if } \text{class}(\mathbf{x}(n)) = \mathcal{C}_{-1}. \end{cases}$$
(3)

▷ **STEP 3, 4 and 5:** The same as the ones described for the ROSOM-1C classifier. The Gini coefficient approach can also be used to re-label the prototypes of the ROSOM-2C classifier.

A final remark is necessary here. Extension of the ROSOM-2C approach to multiclass problems is straightforward. For this, one should adopt a One-Against-One strategy, which is commonly used to extend SVM binary classifiers to multiclass problem. In this case the algorithm would be the following: For K classes, construct $K(K-1)/2$ ROSOM-2C classifiers. Each classifier discriminates between two classes. A new incoming pattern is assigned using each classifier in turn and a majority vote taken. In case of ambiguity of the majority vote, with no clear decision for some patterns, the pattern is rejected.

5 Experimental Study and Discussion

The performance of the classification methods were assessed over two datasets: One synthetic dataset was generated as in [7, 21] (syntheticI) and a real-world dataset. The real-world data set represents the discrimination of normal subjects from those with a pathology on the vertebral column (VC). This database, also publicly available on the UCI machine learning repository, contains information about 310 patients obtained from sagittal panoramic radiographies of the vertebral column described by 6 different biomechanical features. See [22] for more detail on this data set.

In the experiments, we used the SOM toolbox for implementing the ROSOM-1C and ROSOM-2C classifiers and the Matlab^{TM} Neural Networks toolbox for MLP-based classifiers. For fair performance comparison, we have instantiated the same rejection option strategies used for the SOM-based classifiers into the MLP-based classifiers, giving rise to the MLP-1C and MLP-2C classifiers. For the SOM-based classifiers we used a two-dimensional map with a hexagonal neighborhood structure and a Gaussian neighborhood function. A 5-fold cross validation was conducted to find the best number of neurons and the initial radius size for the neighborhood function. Our search considered a squared map spanning 5×5 to 25×25 neurons. The learning phase stopped after 200 epochs. A similar search was conducted for the MLP-based classifiers to find the best number of neurons that composed the network: 5 to 20 neurons with one hidden layer, a single output neuron, and logistic sigmoid as activation function for all neurons. We defined a maximum number of 15 epochs as the stopping criterion in order to avoid overfitting. The resilient back-propagation training algorithm was used.

It is important to point out that, in the absence of further insights about the problem at our disposal (other than the data itself), we cannot select only one value for w_r, since its selection is intrinsically application-dependent. Thus, we started by running the classifiers spanning three values for w_r in Equation (1): 0.04, 0.24 and 0.44[3]. As mentioned the w_r value is directly related to how many patterns an expert is willing to reject. To assess the stability of the proposed approaches the experiments were repeated 50 times by averaging the results. The performance of our methods are plotted on an Accuracy-Reject (A-R) curve where each point break in the curves corresponds to a given w_r value.

By analyzing the performance on an A-R curve one can easily read the performance achieved by a given method and how much it was rejected for a given w_r: the highest the curve, the better the performance is. For example, for the A-R curves shown in Fig. 1, the ROSOM-1C using the Parzen and Gini coefficient approaches achieved the best overall results. We can also see that the performances of all ROSOM-2C variants and the MLP-2C were equivalent. For the VC dataset, the A-R curves in Fig. 1 (second row) indicate that the ROSOM-1C/Gini achieved the best overall performance. Also in the same Figure, we see that all the ROSOM-2C variants performed better than the MLP-2C. It is worth mentioning that to verify that the performances of the SOM-based and MLP-based classifiers are equivalent is *not* a bad thing for the SOM-based classifiers. On the

---

[3] Values of w_r higher than 0.5 are equivalent to random guesses.

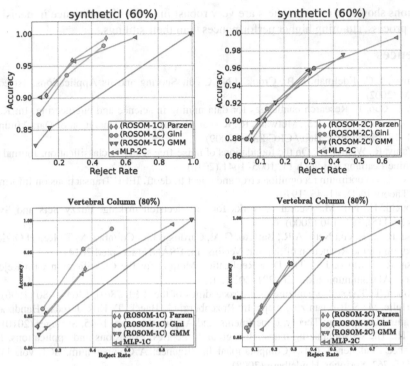

Fig. 1. The A-R curves for the SyntheticI dataset using 60% of training data (first row); and, VC dataset using 80% of training data (second row)

contrary, it is a good thing. Let us recall that the SOM is being adapted to work as a supervised classifier, since it is originally an unsupervised learning algorithm. But even so, the proposed SOM-based approaches achieved very competitive results in comparison with the MLP-based approaches. For all datasets the ROSOM-1C/GMM achieved in average the worst results. However, the ROSOM-2C/GMM achieved competitive results in comparison with the other approaches based on two classifiers. Such behavior can be partly explained by the fact that the proposed modified learning rules in (2) and (3) provide additional improvement over the raw estimates of the posterior probabilities in the performances of the ROSOM-2C classifier. As a general conclusion, although neither the Parzen windows nor the Gini coefficient approaches outperformed one another over all datasets, Parzen and Gini attained better performances than the MLP-based counterparts. Future experiments will be conducted in a larger set of datasets.

6 Conclusions

In this paper we presented two SOM-based pattern classifiers that incorporate the rejection class option: (a) ROSOM-1C, encompassing a single SOM network trained in the usual unsupervised way; and (b) ROSOM-2C, requiring two SOMs which are trained in the self-supervised learning scheme. For both proposals we analysed the advantages on using existing estimates for the likelihood function or the posterior probability tailored for the rejection problem. For ROSOM-2C a new learning rule was proposed. The simulations show that our classifiers are very robust in terms of confidence in decision making process, attaining higher performances than their siblings.

References

1. Thomas, L.C., Edelman, D.B., Crook, J.N.: Credit Scoring and Its Applications, 1st edn. SIAM (2002)
2. Han, J., Gao, J.: Research challenges for data mining in science and engineering. In: Kargupta, H., Han, J., Yu, P.S., Motwani, R., Kumar, V. (eds.) Next Generation of Data Mining, pp. 1–18. Chapman & Hall / CRC Press (2009)
3. El-Yaniv, R., Wiener, Y.: On the foundations of noise-free selective classification. Journal of Machine Learning Research 11, 1605–1641 (2010)
4. Chow, C.: On optimum recognition error and reject tradeoff. IEEE Transactions on Information Theory 16(1), 41–46 (1970)
5. Ishibuchi, H., Nii, M.: Neural networks for soft decision making. Fuzzy Sets and Systems 34(115), 121–140 (2000)
6. Sousa, R., da Rocha Neto, A.R., Barreto, G.A., Cardoso, J.S., Coimbra, M.T.: Reject Option Paradigm for the Reduction of Support Vectors. In: ESANN (accepted 2014)
7. Sousa, R., Cardoso, J.S.: The Data Replication Method for the Classification with Reject Option. AI Communications 26, 281–302 (2013)
8. Kohonen, T.: The self-organizing map. Proceedings of the IEEE 78(9), 1464–1480 (1990)
9. van Hulle, M.: Self-organizing maps. In: Rozenberg, G., Baeck, T., Kok, J. (eds.) Handbook of Natural Computing: Theory, Experiments, and Applications, pp. 1–45. Springer (2010)
10. Yin, H.: The self-organizing maps: Background, theories, extensions and applications. In: Jain, L.C., Fulcher, J. (eds.) Computational Intelligence: A Compendium. SCI, vol. 115, pp. 715–762. Springer, Heidelberg (2008)
11. Mattos, C.L.C., Barreto, G.A.: ARTIE and MUSCLE models: building ensemble classifiers from fuzzy ART and SOM networks. Neural Computing & Applications (2012)
12. Kohonen, T.: The 'neural' phonetic typewriter. Computer 21(3), 11–22 (1988)
13. Kohonen, T.: Self-Organizing Maps, 3rd edn. Springer (2001)
14. de Bodt, E., Cottrell, M., Letremy, P., Verleysen, M.: On the use of self-organizing maps to accelerate vector quantization. Neurocomputing 56, 187–203 (2004)
15. Malone, J., McGarry, K., Wermter, S., Bowerman, C.: Data mining using rule extraction from Kohonen self-organising maps. Neural Computing and Applications 15, 9–17 (2005)
16. Fritzke, B.: A growing neural gas network learns topologies. In: Advances in Neural Information Processing Systems, vol. 7, pp. 625–632. MIT Press, Cambridge (1995)
17. Berglund, E., Sitte, J.: Parameterless self-organizing map algorithm. IEEE Transactions on Neural Networks 17(2), 305–316 (2006)
18. Yin, H., Allinson, N.M.: Self-organizing mixture networks for probability density estimation. IEEE Transactions on Neural Networks 12(2), 405–411 (2001)
19. Alhoniemi, E., Himberg, J., Vesanto, J.: Probabilistic measures for responses of self-organizing map units. In: International ICSC Congress on Computational Intelligence Methods and Applications CIMA, pp. 286–290. ICSC Academic Press (1999)
20. Holmström, L., Hämäläinen, A.: The self-organizing reduced kernel density estimator. In: Proceedings of the 1993 IEEE International Conference on Neural Networks (ICNN 1993), pp. 417–421 (1993)
21. Cardoso, J.S., da Costa, J.F.P.: Learning to classify ordinal data: the data replication method. Journal of Machine Learning Research 8, 1393–1429 (2007)
22. da Rocha Neto, A.R., Sousa, R., de Barreto, G.A., Cardoso, J.S.: Diagnostic of pathology on the vertebral column with embedded reject option. In: Vitrià, J., Sanches, J.M., Hernández, M. (eds.) IbPRIA 2011. LNCS, vol. 6669, pp. 588–595. Springer, Heidelberg (2011)

A Non-parametric Maximum Entropy Clustering

Hideitsu Hino[1] and Noboru Murata[2]

[1] University of Tsukuba, 1-1-1 Tennoudai, Tsukuba, Ibaraki 305-8573, Japan
[2] Waseda University, 3-4-1 Ohkubo, Shinjuku-ku, Tokyo, 169-8555, Japan

Abstract. Clustering is a fundamental tool for exploratory data analysis. Information theoretic clustering is based on the optimization of information theoretic quantities such as entropy and mutual information. Recently, since these quantities can be estimated in non-parametric manner, non-parametric information theoretic clustering gains much attention. Assuming the dataset is sampled from a certain cluster, and assigning different sampling weights depending on the clusters, the cluster conditional information theoretic quantities are estimated. In this paper, a simple clustering algorithm is proposed based on the principle of maximum entropy. The algorithm is experimentally shown to be comparable to or outperform conventional non-parametric clustering methods.

Keywords: Information Theoretic Clustering, Non-parametric, Likelihood and Entropy estimator.

1 Introduction

As an approach for extracting intrinsic structures of the given data without prior knowledge, clustering is widely used and intensively studied [1]. Among many approaches for clustering, the k-means algorithm [2] is widely used. However, k-means is based on strong assumptions on data distribution, and its applicability and effectiveness are quite limited. Since clustering is mainly used for exploratory data analysis, methods with flexibility and without prior knowledge for the given data are preferable. A seminal work on the development of flexible clustering based on the kernel trick is spectral clustering [3], which shows state-of-the-art performance for many problems.

Information theoretic clustering (ITC; [4]) is actively studied in machine learning and data mining as another direction of flexible clustering. Let X be a random variable for the observed data. Let Y be a random variable for cluster assignment which takes value in a set $\mathcal{Y} = \{1, \ldots, K\}$, where we suppose there are K possible clusters. Then, typical ITC algorithms find the cluster assignment which maximizes the mutual information between X and Y. For realizing ITC, non-parametric estimators for information theoretic quantities such as entropy and mutual information are indispensable. Recently, based on a non-parametric estimator for Shannon's differential entropy, an information theoretic clustering method called NIC (Non-parametric Information theoretic Clustering; [5]) is proposed. On the other hand, instead of dealing with cluster conditional entropy, information maximization approach formalizes the clustering problem as

S. Wermter et al. (Eds.): ICANN 2014, LNCS 8681, pp. 113–120, 2014.

unsupervised learning of a conditional probabilistic model. In this approach, the cluster posterior probability $p(Y|X)$ is learnt so that "information" between feature vector X and class label Y is maximized [6].

There has been considerable research on initialization and parameter selection for clustering algorithms. As an initialization problem for the classical k-means algorithm, it is experimentally shown that recently proposed k-means++ method [7] offers favorable results. For spectral clustering, a self-tuning spectral clustering algorithm which automatically determines the kernel width parameter and the number of clusters is proposed in [8]. In the framework of ITC, an information maximization clustering algorithm with an automatic parameter selection method is proposed in [9]. As another line of non-parametric ITC, a method based on minimum spanning tree-based entropy estimation is proposed [10].

Recently, a family of non-parametric estimators for information theoretic quantities using a dataset with *sampling weights* are proposed in [11]. In this paper, a simple non-parametric clustering algorithm based on the estimator for negative log likelihood is proposed.

The rest of this paper is organized as follows. In Sec. 2, we establish notations and introduce non-parametric estimators for negative log likelihood and entropy. In Sec. 3, we propose a non-parametric clustering algorithm, and Sec. 4 shows experimental results. The last section offers concluding remarks.

2   Preliminary

Firstly, we introduce important notions for developing an information theoretic clustering algorithm. Then, we introduce non-parametric likelihood and entropy estimators taking the sampling weights into account.

2.1   Notations

Let $\mathcal{D} = \{x_i\}_{i=1}^n, x_i \in \mathbb{R}^r$ be a set of r-dimensional observations. We assume that we are given a distance function $d(x_i, x_j)$ for each pair $x_i, x_j \in \mathcal{D}$, and the number of clusters K. In this paper, we divide a set of data $\mathcal{D}$ into clusters, and each datum x_i is associated with a set of *membership* levels m_i^k, $k = 1, \ldots, K$, which indicates the strength of the association between the datum x_i and a cluster k. We suppose that membership m_i^k is normalized to satisfy $\sum_{k=1}^K m_i^k = 1$, $m_i^k \geq 0$, and we identify this membership as the conditional probability $P(Y = k|X = x_i)$. We hereafter omit X and Y and write $P(k|x_i) = P(Y = k|X = x_i)$ when there is no confusion. Let

$$M = \begin{pmatrix} m_1^1 & \cdots & m_1^K \\ \vdots & \ddots & \vdots \\ m_n^1 & \cdots & m_n^K \end{pmatrix} \in \mathbb{R}^{n \times K} \qquad (1)$$

be a *membership matrix*, where its rows correspond to data indices and columns correspond to cluster indices. We define the empirical probability of x_i

conditioned by k as

$$w_i^k = p(x_i|k) = \frac{P(k|x_i)p(x_i)}{P(k)}. \tag{2}$$

The vector $\boldsymbol{w}^k = (w_1^k, \ldots, w_n^k)$ is the sampling probability of the dataset $\mathcal{D} = \{x_i\}_{i=1}^n$ under the assumption that the data belong to the k-th cluster k. Using the empirical distribution $p(x_i) = 1/n$,

$$P(k) = \sum_{i=1}^n P(k|x_i)p(x_i) = \sum_{i=1}^n p(x_i)m_i^k = \mathrm{E}_X[m_i^k] = \frac{\sum_{i=1}^n m_i^k}{n}, \tag{3}$$

then $w_i^k = p(x_i|k) = m_i^k / \sum_{j=1}^n m_j^k$.

2.2   Estimator for Negative Log Likelihood

The Negative Log Likelihood (NLL) of the observation x is defined as

$$l(x) = -\log p(x), \tag{4}$$

where $p(x)$ is the probability density function of the random variable X, and x is regarded as a realization of X. One of the widely used estimators for information theoretic quantities is a family of k-nearest neighbor (k-NN) based methods [12], which is also reformulated as *quantile*-based methods and extended to *weighted observations* [11]. A set of weighted observation is defined as

$$D_{\boldsymbol{w}} = \{\mathcal{D}, \boldsymbol{w}\}, \quad \sum_{i=1}^n w_i = 1, \ w_i \geq 0, \tag{5}$$

where the elements w_i of the weight vector $\boldsymbol{w} = (w_1, \ldots, w_n)^\top$ is the sampling probability for the datum x_i. Given the weighted dataset $D_{\boldsymbol{w}}$, the empirical average for a function $G(x)$ is defined as $\mathrm{E}_{D_{\boldsymbol{w}}}[G(X)] = \sum_{i=1}^n w_i G(x_i)$. A point x which is the subject of NLL estimation is called an *inspection point*. Sorting the points $x_i \in \mathcal{D}$ in ascending order of the distance $d(x, x_i)$, we denote the index of the i-th nearest point to x by $(i)_x$. The *quantile* of $x_{(i)_x}$ with respect to x is defined by $\sum_{j=1}^i w_{(j)_x}$. Conversely, when an inspection point x and a quantile $\alpha \in [0,1]$ are specified, the point $x_{\iota(\alpha)_x} \in \mathcal{D}$ where $\iota(\alpha)_x = \arg\max_k \sum_{j=1}^k w_{(j)_x} \leq \alpha$, is called the *$\alpha$-quantile point*. For the sake of notational simplicity, we omit the subscript x for $(i)_x$ henceforth. We write $d_x(\alpha; \boldsymbol{w}) = d(x, x_{\iota(\alpha)_x})$ to explicitly show the dependence of the weight $\boldsymbol{w}$ for the distance. For a given weighted dataset $D_{\boldsymbol{w}}$, the *α-quantile negative log-likelihood estimator*

$$l(x) \simeq l_\alpha(x; D_{\boldsymbol{w}}) = \log c_r - \log \alpha + r \log d_x(\alpha; \boldsymbol{w}) \tag{6}$$

for an inspection point x is proposed in [11]. Here c_r is the volume of the unit ball in an r-dimensional space defined as $c_r = \frac{\pi^{r/2}}{\Gamma(1+r/2)}$. In this paper, the notation $S \simeq E$ indicates that E is the estimate of a statistics S. Since entropy is defined by average of NLL, we obtain the α-quantile entropy estimator for weighted data as the empirical average of the α-quantile NLL estimator:

$$H(X) \simeq H_\alpha(D_w) = \mathbb{E}_{D_w}[l_\alpha(X; D_w)] = \log c_r - \log \alpha + r \sum_{i=1}^{n} w_i \log d_{x_i}(\alpha; w).$$

3   A Non-parametric Information Theoretic Clustering

Let $D_w^k = \{D, w^k\}$ be the weighted dataset, where $w^k = (w_1^k, \ldots, w_n^k) \in \mathbb{R}^n$. Consider the entropy of joint distribution (X, Y):

$$H(X, Y) = -\sum_{i=1}^{n}\sum_{k=1}^{K} P(k|x_i)p(x_i) \log P(k|x_i)p(x_i)$$

$$= -\sum_{i=1}^{n} p(x_i) \log p(x_i) - \sum_{i=1}^{n}\sum_{k=1}^{K} m_i^k p(x_i) \log m_i^k.$$

Assuming the unconditional sampling probability $p(x_i)$ for each $x_i \in \mathcal{D}$ are equal to $1/n$, we obtain an entropy of (X, Y) as a function of M where distribution of X is set to a uniform distribution:

$$H_{X \sim U}(M) = -\sum_{i=1}^{n}\sum_{k=1}^{K} p(x_i, k) \log p(x_i, k) = \log n - \frac{1}{n}\sum_{i=1}^{n}\sum_{k=1}^{K} m_i^k \log m_i^k.$$

When estimating the probability distribution, we should select that distribution which leaves us the largest remaining uncertainty (i.e., the maximum entropy) consistent with given constraints. Following the principle of information theoretic clustering, we consider to minimize the cluster conditional entropy for obtaining a good cluster assignment while maximizing the entropy of cluster assignment in order to restrict too much flexibility inherent in non-parametric modeling. Introducing a balancing parameter $\lambda > 0$, we define the objective function to be maximized with respect to M:

$$J(M, \lambda) = \lambda H_{X \sim U}(M) - H(X|Y) = \lambda H(M) - \sum_{k=1}^{K} P(k)H(X|Y = k)$$

$$\simeq \lambda\left\{\log n - \frac{1}{n}\sum_{i=1}^{n}\sum_{K=1}^{K} m_i^k \log m_i^k\right\} - \sum_{k=1}^{K} P(k)H_\alpha(D_{w^k})$$

$$\propto -\frac{\lambda}{n}\sum_{i=1}^{n}\sum_{k=1}^{K} m_i^k \log m_i^k$$

$$- \sum_{k=1}^{K} \frac{\sum_{j=1}^{n} m_j^k}{n}\left(\log c_r/\alpha + r\sum_{i=1}^{n} \frac{m_i^k}{\sum_{j=1}^{n} m_j^k} \log d_{x_i}(\alpha; w^k)\right)$$

Algorithm 1. Non-parametric Maximum Entropy Clustering algorithm

input: a dataset $\mathcal{D} = \{x_i\}_{i=1,\ldots,n}$, number of clusters K, and stopping criteria.
initialize: choose an initial membership $m_i^k(0), i = 1,\ldots,n, \ k = 1,\ldots,K$. Set
iteration counter $t \leftarrow 0$, an initial quantile $\alpha_0 = 0.9$.
while : stopping criterion not met, **do**
    update memberships $m_i^k = P(k|x_i)$ by Eq. (8)
    $\alpha \leftarrow \max\{0.01, \alpha * 0.9\}$ ▷ update α
    $t \leftarrow t + 1$
end while
output: optimized membership matrix M, and predicted cluster assignments $\{y_i\}_{i=1}^n$
where

$$y_i = \underset{k \in \{1,\ldots,K\}}{\arg\max} \ P(k|x_i) = \underset{k \in \{1,\ldots,K\}}{\arg\max} \ m_i^k, \quad i = 1,\ldots,n. \tag{9}$$

$$\propto -\frac{\lambda}{n} \sum_{i=1}^n \sum_{k=1}^K m_i^k \log m_i^k - \frac{r}{n} \sum_{k=1}^K \sum_{i=1}^n m_i^k \log d_{x_i}(\alpha; \boldsymbol{w}^k).$$

We fix the weight vectors $\boldsymbol{w}^k$ appear in $d_{x_i}(\alpha; \boldsymbol{w}^k)$ to the weight vectors obtained
by the previous update of the algorithm, and minimize

$$Q(M) = \sum_{i=1}^n \sum_{k=1}^K m_i^k \log m_i^k + \frac{r}{\lambda} \sum_{i=1}^n \sum_{k=1}^K m_i^k \log d_{x_i}(\alpha; \boldsymbol{w}^k(t)) \tag{7}$$

with respect to M. Solving this minimization problem, under constraint $\sum_{k=1}^K m_i^k$
$= 1$, by the method of Lagrange multiplier leads an update rule for m_i^k as

$$m_i^k \leftarrow \frac{d_{x_i}^{-r/\lambda}(\alpha; \boldsymbol{w}^k(t))}{\sum_{l=1}^K d_{x_i}^{-r/\lambda}(\alpha; \boldsymbol{w}^l(t))}. \tag{8}$$

The value of λ controls *fuzziness* of the cluster assignment. For the sake of
simplicity, we fixed $\lambda = 1$ in all of experiments in this paper.

We iterate the membership updating procedure shown in Eq. (8) until certain
stopping criteria are satisfied. For the α-quantile estimator, we need to fix the
value $\alpha \in (0, 1]$. There are several possibilities for determining the value α.
Although elaborately designed methods could find an appropriate α value, we
introduce a simple and computationally efficient way for the problem of the
selection of α value, which is proven to work well in our experiments. Since α
controls the locality around inspection points, we gradually decrease α in the
iteration of the algorithm. In particular, we update α as $\alpha \leftarrow \min\{0.01, \alpha * 0.8\}$.
In this paper, we stopped the iteration when the maximum of the element-
wise absolute difference between $M(t + 1)$ and $M(t)$ becomes less than 10^{-5} or
the number of iteration reaches $m = 30$. The proposed clustering procedure is
summarized in Algorithm 1.

The outcome of the proposed algorithm depends on the initial membership.
For determining the initial membership, we utilize the initial K points obtained

by the k-means++ algorithm [7]. Let $x^k, \ldots, x^K \in \mathcal{D}$ be the K medoids of the clusters found by k-means++. Then, we define the initial weight $w_i^k(0)$ as

$$w_i^k(0) = \frac{\exp\left(-\frac{d(x_i, x^k)^2}{\sigma^2}\right)}{\sum_{j=1}^n \exp\left(-\frac{d(x_j, x^k)^2}{\sigma^2}\right)}, \quad i = 1, \ldots, n. \tag{10}$$

Then, we obtain the initial membership matrix by $m_i^k(0) = w_i^k(0)/\sum_{k=1}^K w_i^k(0)$. The bandwidth of the Gaussian kernel σ^2 should be taken large enough so as not to the initial membership completely determine the cluster assignments. For that purpose, we suggest to use the maximum distance between points in the given data as $\sigma = \max_{i,j=1,\ldots,n} d(x_i, x_j)$.

4   Experimental Result

We perform a set of comparative experiments of the proposed and several conventional clustering algorithms. The clustering algorithms compared to the proposed algorithm are k-means++ (kmpp [7]), NIC [5], SMIC [9], and the Self-Tuning Spectral Clustering (STSC [8]). The k-means++ algorithm is regarded as a baseline method, while all of the other methods offer state-of-the-art performance in the literatures. NIC and SMIC are representatives of information theoretic clustering algorithms, and STSC is a representative of versatile non-parametric clustering algorithms. We note that to avoid implementation bias, we use softwares released by the authors of the original methods for these three methods. As for NIC, the number of restarting is set to 10, and for SMIC, the number of candidate kernel parameters are 10. Both settings are default values in the provided softwares. For quantitatively evaluating the clustering performance, we adopt the Arabie's adjusted Rand index calculated by using the ground truth cluster labels, which is recommended by [13]. The closer to 1 the value, the more similarity between the obtained and the ground truth partitions.

We show the datasets adopted for evaluation. The numbers of samples shown below are that used in each trial in 10-fold cross validation. All of these datasets are obtained from UCI machine learning repository.

1. **USPS**: hand written digits ($K = 10$, $n = 5000$, $r = 256$)
2. **seeds**: varieties of wheat seeds ($K = 3$, $n = 189$, $r = 7$)
3. **segmentation**: image segmentation ($K = 7, n = 2079$, $r = 19$)
4. **yeast**: yeast cellular localization ($K = 9$, $n = 1333$, $r = 8$)
5. **wine**: wine cultivars categorization ($K = 3$, $n = 160$, $r = 13$)
6. **libras_movement**: hand gesture categorization ($K = 15$, $n = 324$, $r = 90$)

We show box plots of the adjusted Rand index in Fig. 1. From the experimental results shown, we see that the proposed clustering algorithm outperforms other methods in many datasets. Particularly, it shows salient advantages in **segmentation** and **wine** datasets. On the other hand, ITC methods including the proposed method do not perform well for **yeast** data.

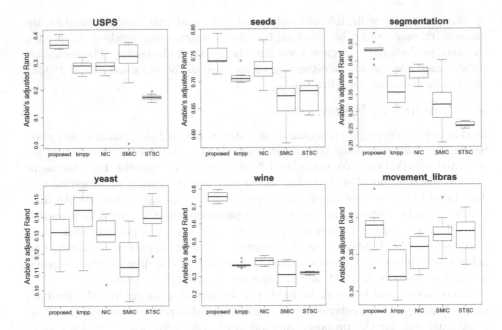

Fig. 1. Experimental results for six different real-world datasets. Values of the performance index for five different clustering methods are plotted.

4.1 Out of Sample Problem and Posterior Cluster Distribution

Finally, we show a preliminary result of the use of the propose method for estimating a posterior cluster distibution. The proposed method can obtain a model for estimating the membership probability $P(k|x_{new})$ to a new input point x_{new} by $P(k|x_{new}) = d_{x_{new}}^{-r}(\alpha; \boldsymbol{w}^k)/\sum_{l=1}^{K} d_{x_{new}}^{-r}(\alpha; \boldsymbol{w}^l)$. Figure 2 shows membership probability for whole of the input space. For plotting these figures, we estimated the membership probabilities at 2-dimensional grid points using the optimized membership matrices M obtained by clustering the given points (depicted by $\bigcirc$ and $\triangle$). This kind of non-linear separation of clusters can not be achieved

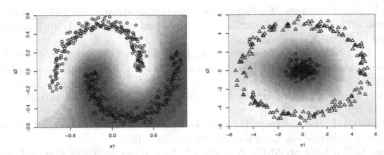

Fig. 2. Mapping of cluster memberships $P(k|x)$ obtained by the proposed method for two toy problems

by conventional less flexible clustering methods, and this kind of membership probability map cannot be obtained by standard clustering methods without a concrete probabilistic interpretation like the spectral clustering. These characteristic motivates us for investigating further use of the obtained model $P(k|x)$ for classification and visualization.

5   Concluding Remarks

In this paper, we proposed a maximum entropy and regularization based clustering algorithm using the recently developed NLL and entropy estimators for weighted observations. We considered "soft" cluster assignment, i.e., the membership distribution of each datum to clusters was the target to be estimated. The notable characteristics of the proposed clustering algorithm are its high performance in clustering accuracy and its parameter-free nature. The proposed algorithm is evaluated by real-world datasets, and shown to perform well. Most of conventional ITC utilize biased or alternative Shannon entropy estimators to achieve scalability. We conjecture that the favorable performance of the proposed method stems from the fact that it relies on accurate NLL estimator.

There are several issues to be further investigated. Particularly, the analysis on the convergence property of the proposed algorithm remains to be done. Computational cost for the proposed method is of order $O(n^2 \log n)$, which should be improved to make the proposed method applicable to large scale datasets.

References

1. Jain, A.K., et al.: Data clustering: A review. ACM Computing Surveys 31(3), 264–323 (1999)
2. McLachlan, G.J., Basford, K.E.: Mixture Models: Inference and Applications to Clustering. Marcel Dekker, New York (1988)
3. Ng, A.Y., et al.: On spectral clustering: Analysis and an algorithm. In: NIPS (2001)
4. Gokcay, E., Principe, J.C.: Information theoretic clustering. IEEE Trans. Pattern Anal. Mach. Intell. 24(2), 158–171 (2002)
5. Faivishevsky, L., Goldberger, J.: A Nonparametric Information Theoretic Clustering Algorithm. In: ICML (2010)
6. Gomes, R., et al.: Discriminative clustering by regularized information maximization. In: NIPS, pp. 775–783 (2010)
7. Arthur, D., Vassilvitskii, S.: K-means++: the advantages of careful seeding. In: SODA (2007)
8. Zelnik-Manor, L., Perona, P.: Self-tuning spectral clustering. In: NIPS (2005)
9. Sugiyama, M., et al.: On information-maximization clustering: Tuning parameter selection and analytic solution. In: ICML (2011)
10. Müller, A.C., Nowozin, S., Lampert, C.H.: Information Theoretic Clustering Using Minimum Spanning Trees. In: Pinz, A., Pock, T., Bischof, H., Leberl, F. (eds.) DAGM and OAGM 2012. LNCS, vol. 7476, pp. 205–215. Springer, Heidelberg (2012)
11. Hino, H., Murata, N.: Information estimators for weighted observations. Neural Networks 46, 260–275 (2013)
12. Kozachenko, L.F., Leonenko, N.N.: Sample estimate of entropy of a random vector. Problems of Information Transmission 23, 95–101 (1987)
13. Milligan, G.W., Cooper, M.C.: A study of the comparability of external criteria for hierarchical cluster analysis. Multivariate Behavioral Research (1986)

Instance Selection Using Two Phase Collaborative Neighbor Representation*

Fadi Dornaika[1,2] and I. Kamal Aldine[1]

[1] University of the Basque Country EHU/UPV, San Sebastian, Spain
[2] IKERBASQUE, Basque Foundation for Science, Bilbao, Spain

Abstract. Finding relevant instances in databases has always been a challenging task. Recently a new method, called *Sparse Modeling Representative Selection* (SMRS) has been proposed in this area and is based on data self-representation. SMRS estimates a matrix of coefficients by minimizing a reconstruction error and a regularization term on these coefficients using the $L_{1,q}$ matrix norm. In this paper, we propose another alternative of coding based on a two stage Collaborative Neighbor Representation in which a non-dense matrix of coefficients is estimated without invoking any explicit sparse coding. Experiments are conducted on summarizing a video movie and on summarizing training face datasets used for face recognition. These experiments showed that the proposed method can outperform the state-of-the art methods.

Keywords: Instance selection, collaborative neighbor representation, video summarization, classification.

1 Introduction

Finding a subset of a set of data points, known as representatives or exemplars, that can effectively describe the entire dataset, is a very important issue in the analysis of scientific data, with a lot of application in machine learning, data recovery, signal processing, image processing, etc. The representatives can summarize datasets of images, videos, texts or Web documents. Finding a small number of examples which replaces the learning database has two main advantages: (i) reducing the memory space needed to store data and (ii) improving the computation time of classification algorithms. For example, the method of nearest neighbors (NN) is more efficient [1] when comparing test samples to the K representatives rather than to all the N training samples, with generally $K \ll N$.

The problem of finding representative data has been well studied in the literature [2–7]. Depending on the information that must be preserved by representatives, the algorithms used in this area can be divided into two categories. The first category finds representatives from data contained in one or several subspaces of reduced dimensionality [4–9]. The algorithm *Rank Revealing QR*

* This work was supported by the projects EHU13/40 and S-PR13UN007.

S. Wermter et al. (Eds.): ICANN 2014, LNCS 8681, pp. 121–128, 2014.

($RRQR$) [5, 8] tries to select a few data points through finding a permutation of the data which gives the best conditioned submatrix. *Greedy* and *Randomized* algorithms have also been proposed in order to find a subset of columns in a reduced rank matrix [4, 7].

The second group of algorithms finds representatives assuming there is a natural grouping of data collection based on an appropriate measure of similarity between pairs of data points [3, 10, 11]. Accordingly, these algorithms generally work on the similarity/dissimilarity between data points to be grouped. The *Kmedoids* algorithm, which can be considered as a variant of *Kmeans* [12], supposes that the data are located around several centers of classes, called medoids, which are selected from the data. Another algorithm based on the similarity/dissimilarity of data points is the *AP* (*Affinity propagation*) [3, 11]. This algorithm tries to find representatives from the similarities between pairs of data points by using a message passing algorithm. Although AP has suboptimal properties and can find approximate solutions, it does not require any initialization (like Kmeans and Kmedoids) and has shown good performance in problems such as unsupervised image categorization [13].

Recently a new method, called *Sparse Modeling Representative Selection* (SMRS) [6] has been proposed in this area and is based on setting every data sample as a linear combination of the whole dataset. The computation of the combination coefficients has been solved by optimizing a criterion formed by two terms: the least square error of data self-representation, and (ii) a regularization term set to the $L_{1,q}$ norm of the coefficient matrix. The instances are selected according to the norm of the estimated matrix rows where a row reflects the relevance of a given instance in the whole reconstruction. In this paper, we propose a Two phase Collaborative Neighbor Representation for estimating the coefficient matrix needed for instance selection. Our proposed scheme implicitly takes into account the locality and similarity among samples. Furthermore, our proposed scheme aims to compute a non-dense coefficient matrix. These two properties can lead to a better estimation of the coefficient matrix than that obtained with SMRS.

This paper is structured as follows: in Section 2, we provide a brief review of the Sparse Modeling Representative Selection. In Section 3, we describe our proposed two phase Collaborative Neighbor Representation. The experimental results are presented in Section 4. Section 5 concludes the paper.

2 Review of SMRS

Consider a set of data points in $\mathbb{R}^m$ arranged as the columns of the data matrix $\mathbf{Y} = [\mathbf{y}_1, \dots, \mathbf{y}_N]$. The key idea proposed by [6] is to set the coding dictionary to the original collection data $\mathbf{Y}$. This lead to the self-representativeness of data samples. The basic assumption is that every data sample can be set to a linear combination of the dataset. Mathematically, this assumption can be written as $\mathbf{y}_i = \mathbf{Y}\,\mathbf{b}_i$ where $\mathbf{b}_i$ is a vector of coefficients. The N equations, associated with the N samples, can be encapsulated in one single matrix equation:

$$Y = YB$$

where $\mathbf{B} = [\mathbf{b}_1, \ldots, \mathbf{b}_N]$. One likes to minimize the following criterion using some constraints on the coefficients:

$$\sum_{i=1}^{N} \|\mathbf{y}_i - \mathbf{Y}\,\mathbf{b}_i\|^2 = \|\mathbf{Y} - \mathbf{Y}\mathbf{B}\|_F^2$$

The SMRS method [6] proposes to solve the matrix $\mathbf{B}$ by imposing some regularization on the unknown coefficients. Thus, the matrix $\mathbf{B}$ is estimated by minimizing the following criterion:

$$\mathbf{B} = \arg\min_{\mathbf{B}} \left(\frac{1}{2}\|\mathbf{Y} - \mathbf{Y}\mathbf{B}\|^2 + \lambda\,\|\mathbf{B}\|_{1,q} \right) \quad s.t. \quad \mathbf{1}^T\mathbf{B} = \mathbf{1}^T \qquad (1)$$

The criterion has two terms. The first term is the Least square error associated with the self-representativeness of data. The second term is set to the $L_{1,q}$ norm of the matrix $\mathbf{B}$, i.e., $\|\mathbf{B}\|_{1,q} = \sum_j [|B_{(j,1)}|^q + \ldots + |B_{(j,N)}|^q]^{\frac{1}{q}}$. Thus, if $q = 2$, the regularization term is the sum of L_2 norm of the rows of $\mathbf{B}$.

Similar to other dimensionality reduction methods, the affine constraint $\mathbf{1}^T\mathbf{B} = \mathbf{1}^T$ makes the selection of representatives to be invariant with respect to a global translation of the data. The optimization of (1) can be carried out using the Alternating Direction Method of Multipliers (ADMM) technique.

The framework for this selection is summarized in Algorithm 1. It should be noticed that in supervised learning context the same framework of SMRS can be applied on each class separately in order to retrieve the most representative examples in each class.

Data: Dataset $\mathbf{Y} = [\mathbf{y}_1, \ldots, \mathbf{y}_N]$ and the desired number of representatives K
Result: Set of representatives $\{\mathbf{y}_1^*, \ldots, \mathbf{y}_K^*\}$

- Calculate the coding coefficients $\mathbf{B}$ using
$\mathbf{B} = \arg\min_{\mathbf{B}} \left(\frac{1}{2}\|\mathbf{Y} - \mathbf{Y}\mathbf{B}\|^2 + \lambda\,\|\mathbf{B}\|_{1,q} \right) s.t. \mathbf{1}^T\mathbf{B} = \mathbf{1}^T$;
- Compute the L_2 norms of the rows of $\mathbf{B}$ as $l_j = \|\mathbf{B}(j,:)\|, j = 1, \ldots, N$;
- Select the K samples that correspond to the largest K norms $\{\mathbf{y}_1^*, \ldots, \mathbf{y}_K^*\}$;
- $\mathbf{Y}_s = [\mathbf{y}_1^*, \ldots, \mathbf{y}_K^*]$;

Algorithm 1. Representative selection using SMRS.

---

3 Proposed Two Phase CNR-Based Instance Selection

In this section we propose a different methodology for constructing the matrix of coefficients. Our proposed scheme retrieves the coefficient matrix $\mathbf{B}$ from the data matrix $\mathbf{Y}$ using two phase Collaborative Neighbor Representation (CNR). By adopting our coding scheme both implicit similarity among samples and sparsity are imposed. This leads to a better estimation of the coefficient matrix than that obtained with SMRS. In this section, we first describe the one stage estimation, and then we describe the stage estimation scheme.

One Phase CNR. Collaborative Neighbor Representation or locality constrained coding is essentially a least square coding in which the regularization
term contains individual weights [14]. Let $\mathbf{y}$ be the vector to be coded using $\mathbf{Y}$
as a dictionary. In our work, $\mathbf{y}$ will be one sample $\mathbf{y}_i$ and the dictionary will be
the original data matrix from which the sample $\mathbf{y}_i$ is removed. For the sake of
presentation simplicity, we present the principle using $\mathbf{Y}$ as a dictionary and $\mathbf{y}$
as the sample to be coded. CNR coding estimates the vector of coefficients, $\mathbf{b}$,
by minimizing the following criterion:

$$\mathbf{b} = \arg\min_{\mathbf{b}} \frac{1}{2} \left(\|\mathbf{y} - \mathbf{Yb}\|_2^2 + \sigma \sum_{j=1}^{N} w_j^2 b_j^2 + \lambda \|\mathbf{b}\|^2 \right) \ s.t. \mathbf{1}^T \mathbf{b} = 1 \quad (2)$$

where λ and σ are two small positive scalars, and w_j^2 is a positive weight associated with the coefficient b_j (or equivalently the sample $\mathbf{y}_j$). The solution to (2)
will reconstruct the input signal $\mathbf{y}$ by a combination of the space spanned by $\mathbf{Y}$.
In (2), the second term is the weighted regularized term. The linear constraint
on the $\mathbf{b}$ can be included in the reconstruction error by appending the vector $\mathbf{y}$
and the matrix $\mathbf{Y}$ by 1 and $[1, \ldots, 1, 1]$, respectively. For the sake of simplicity,
in the sequel, we will omit the linear constraint. The weights w_j are usually set
to the Euclidean distance such that $w_j^2 = \|\mathbf{y} - \mathbf{y}_j\|^2$. Let $\mathbf{W}$ denote a diagonal
matrix formed by $W_{jj} = w_j = \|\mathbf{y} - \mathbf{y}_j\|$.

The one phase CNR estimates the coefficient vector $\mathbf{b}$ by minimizing:

$$\mathbf{b} = \arg\min_{\mathbf{b}} \frac{1}{2} \left(\|\mathbf{y} - \mathbf{Yb}\|_2^2 + \sigma \|\mathbf{W b}\|^2 + \lambda \|\mathbf{b}\|^2 \right) \quad (3)$$

After some algebraic manipulation, we get the solution to (3):

$$\mathbf{b} = \left(\mathbf{Y}^T \mathbf{Y} + \sigma \mathbf{W} + \lambda \mathbf{I} \right)^{-1} \mathbf{Y}^T \mathbf{y} \quad (4)$$

where $\mathbf{I}$ is the identity matrix.

The columns of the matrix of coefficient $\mathbf{B} = (\mathbf{b}_1, \ldots, \mathbf{b}_N)$ are estimated using
Eq. (4). For estimating the ith column vector $\mathbf{b}_i$, $\mathbf{y}$ is set to the sample $\mathbf{y}_i$ and
the dictionary $\mathbf{Y}$ is set to $[\mathbf{y}_1, \ldots, \mathbf{y}_{i-1}, \mathbf{y}_{i+1}, \ldots, \mathbf{y}_N]$. The diagonal elements of
$\mathbf{B}$ are set to zero.

Two Phase CNR. In this scheme, every column vector of coefficients, $\mathbf{b}_i$, is
estimated in two consecutive stages. In the first stage, this vector is given by Eq.
(4). In the second stage, we invoke another coding in which only a small dictionary is used. This dictionary is formed by the most relevant samples selected
according to the sample contribution. Let us assume that the vector $\mathbf{b}$ is estimated using Eq. (4). In order to detect the most similar or relevant samples in
the original dictionary, we will use the concept of contribution. The contribution
of a given sample $\mathbf{y}_j$ (the jth column in the original dictionary) in constructing
the test sample $\mathbf{y}$ is $b_j \mathbf{y}_j$. In order to evaluate the contribution of the samples
$\mathbf{y}_j$ in representing the test sample, the following equation can be used.

$$e_j = \|\mathbf{y} - b_j \mathbf{y}_j\|^2 \quad (5)$$

A small e_j means a large contribution. Based on this fact, we can estimate an automatic threshold given by the mean, $\overline{e_j}$, of all contributions $e_j, j = 1, \ldots, N$. Let Th denotes this threshold (i.e., $Th = \overline{e_j}$). We form another dictionary $\mathbf{Y}_{sel}$ formed by all $\mathbf{y}_j$ whose contribution is large enough. In other words, we only keep the samples that satisfy $e_j < Th$.

Let $\mathbf{Y}_{sel}$ be the data matrix formed by the selected examples (the ones whose contribution is greater than the chosen threshold). Then, the vector $\mathbf{b}'$ associated with the selected examples will be solved using a formula similar to (4):

$$\mathbf{b}' = \left(\mathbf{Y}_{sel}^T \mathbf{Y}_{sel} + \sigma \, \mathbf{W}_{sel} + \lambda \mathbf{I} \right)^{-1} \mathbf{Y}_{sel}^T \mathbf{y} \tag{6}$$

The original N-vector $\mathbf{b}$ is set as follows. A non-selected sample $\mathbf{y}_j$ will have $b_j = 0$ and a selected one will have the corresponding coefficient in the vector $\mathbf{b}'$ estimated by (6).

Finally, each column vector in $\mathbf{B} = (\mathbf{b}_1, \ldots, \mathbf{b}_N)$ is estimated using the two phases described above (i.e., Eqs. (4) and (6)). The matrix $\mathbf{B}$ obtained by the two phase CNR is sparser than the one obtained with the one phase CNR since the columns contain a lot of zeros due to the introduced filtering scheme.

4   Experimental Results

In this section, we evaluate the performance of the proposed algorithm for finding representatives of real datasets on two illustrative problems: video summarization (qualitative evaluation) and face recognition (quantitative evaluation). Firstly, we demonstrate the applicability of our proposed algorithm for summarizing videos. Secondly, we evaluate the performance of our method as well as other algorithms for finding representatives that are used for face classification.

Video Summarization. We consider a video sequence of a tennis match, the total duration of this video is 59 seconds. It contains 1331 frames. The video consists of several shots depicting several series of activities. Figure 1 illustrates 30 random images from that video. The goal is to summarize these 30 images by only 9 frames.

We used two different methods: the SMRS and the proposed Two phase CNR. The results are illustrated in Figure 1 where the selected images were shown in red boxes. The above video consists of a sequence of first and last stroke between two tennis players, after that there are sequences of a player who wins the point, the audience applauded, the player who lost the point and a sequence of a player ready to play the other point. With our proposed scheme, we get 3 representatives in the sequence between the first and last shot which consists of several activities. In addition, for sequences which consist of two or three activities, we obtain 1-2 representatives. The most representative images were corresponding to different activities and scenes of the video. One can also observe that redundancies of data were considerably reduced since the court and players got 3 representatives from 21 original frames.

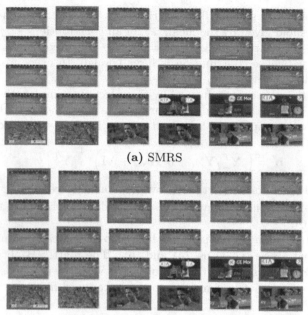

(a) SMRS

(b) Proposed method

Fig. 1. Frames of a tennis match video, which consists of multiple shots, and the automatically computed representatives using the SMRS method **(a)** and the proposed method **(b)**. Depending on the activities in each shot of the video and on the method used, we obtained one or a few representatives for that shot.

Face Recognition. We considered two public face datasets, which are characterized by a large variation in face appearance: **Extended Yale - part B**[1] (1774 images, 28 subjects), and **PIE**[2] (a subset is used: 1926 images, 68 subjects).

We now evaluate the performance of our method as well as other algorithms for selecting representatives that are used for classification. For training data in each class of a dataset, we find the representatives and use them as a reduced training dataset to perform classification. Ideally, if the representatives are informative enough about the original data, the classification performance using the representatives should be close to the performance using all the training data. Therefore, representatives not only summarize a dataset and reduce the data storage requirements, but also can be effectively used for tasks such as recognition and clustering.

Table 1 illustrates the recognition performance on the Extended Yale B face dateset after the selection of 12 representatives of the 51 training samples in each class. The number of test images is 8 images per class. The results correspond to an average over 10 random train/test splits. The classifiers used are the Nearest Neighbor, Sparse Representation Classifier (SRC), and Support Vector Machines

---

[1] http://vision.ucsd.edu/~leekc/ExtYaleDatabase/ExtYaleB.html

[2] http://www.ri.cmu.edu/projects/project_418.html

Table 1. Classification Results on the Extended Yale B face database using 12 representatives of the 51 training samples in each class. The selection methods used are: RAND, K-medoids, SMRS, One phase CNR, Two Phase CNR, and All data.

Selection method \ Classifier	1-NN	SRC	SVM
Rand	63.1	83.4	83.7
K-medoids	67.1	87.6	90.9
SMRS	68.6	89.1	92.4
One phase CNR	71.3	86.4	86.4
Two Phase CNR	**72.1**	**90.0**	**92.7**
All data	86.1	96.3	98.8

Table 2. Classification Results on the PIE face database using 7 representatives of the 22 training samples in each class.

Selection method \ Classifier	1-NN	SRC	SVM
Rand	32.1	54.6	54.2
K-medoids	38.5	**63.1**	62.8
SMRS	27.7	50.6	53.6
One phase CNR	32.4	52.1	51.4
Two phase CNR	**38.7**	59.4	**62.9**
All data	62.3	83.2	87.4

(SVM). As can be seen, the proposed Two Phase CNR has provided the best performance for the three classifiers used. Table 2 illustrates the recognition performance on the PIE face dateset after the selection of 7 representatives of the 22 training samples in each class. The number of test images is 6 images per class. The results correspond to an average over 10 random splits.

5 Conclusion

We proposed a Two phase Collaborative Neighbor Representation for finding a subset of the data points in a dataset as the representatives. We compare our proposed algorithm with several standard methods used in the domain: Kmedoids, simple random selection of training data (Rand), and the recent method SMRS. Experimental results on three widely used public face databases and a video movie are presented to demonstrate the efficacy of the proposed approach. Future work will investigate efficient schemes for large datasets (e.g., above 10K of samples). Moreover, it will investigate the automatic estimation of the number of representatives.

References

1. Garcia, S., Derrac, J., Cano, R., Herrera, F.: Prototype selection for nearest neighbor classification: Taxonomy and empirical study. IEEE Transactions on Pattern Analysis and Machine Intelligence 34(3), 417–435 (2012)

2. Gu, M., Eisenstat, S.: Efficient algorithms for computing a strong rankrevealing qr factorization. SIAM Journal on Scientific Computing 17, 848–869 (1996)
3. Frey, B., Dueck, D.: Clustering by passing messages between data points. Science Magazine 315, 972–976 (2007)
4. Tropp, J.: Column subset selection, matrix factorization and eigenvalue optimization. In: Proc. of ACM-SIAM Symposium on Discrete Algorithms (SODA), pp. 978–986 (January 2009)
5. Boutsidis, C., Mahoney, M., Drineas, P.: An improved approximation algorithm for the column subset selection problem. In: Proc. of ACM-SIAM Symposium on Discrete Algorithms (SODA), pp. 968–977 (January 2009)
6. Elhamifar, E., Sapiro, G., Vidal, R.: See all by looking at a few: Sparse modeling for finding representative objects. In: Proc. of IEEE Conference on Computer Vision and Pattern Recognition, pp. 1600–1607 (June 2012)
7. Bien, J., Xu, Y., Mahoney, M.: CUR from a sparse optimization viewpoint. In: Advances in Neural Information Processing Systems, pp. 217–225 (December 2010)
8. Chan, T.: Rank revealing qr factorizations. Linear Algebra and its Applications 88–89, 67–82 (1987)
9. Esser, E., Moller, M., Osher, S., Sapiro, G., Xin, J.: A convex model for nonnegative matrix factorization and dimensionality reduction on physical space. IEEE Transactions on Image Processing 21(7), 3239–3252 (2012)
10. Charikar, M., Guha, S., Tardos, A., Shmoys, D.: A constant-factor approximation algorithm for the k-median problem. Journal of Computer System Sciences 65(1), 129–149 (2002)
11. Givoni, I., Chung, C., Frey, B.: Hierarchical affinity propagation. In: Conference on Uncertainty in Artificial Intelligence (July 2011)
12. Duda, R., Hart, P., Stork, D.: Pattern Classification. Wiley-Interscience (2004)
13. Dueck, D., Frey, B.: Non-metric affinity propagation for unsupervised image categorization. In: Proc. of International Conference in Computer Vision, pp. 1–8 (October 2007)
14. Waqas, J., Yi, Z., Zhang, L.: Collaborative neighbor representation based classification using l_2-minimization approach. Pattern Recognition Letters 34(2), 201–208 (2013)

Global Metric Learning by Gradient Descent

Jens Hocke and Thomas Martinetz

University of Lübeck - Institute for Neuro- and Bioinformatics
Ratzeburger Allee 160, 23538 Lübeck, Germany
hocke@inb.uni-luebeck.de

Abstract. The k-NN classifier can be very competitive if an appropriate distance measure is used. It is often used in applications because the classification decisions are easy to interpret. Here, we demonstrate how to find a good Mahalanobis distance for k-NN classification by a simple gradient descent without any constraints. The cost term uses global distances and unlike other methods there is a soft transition in the influence of data points. It is evaluated and compared to other metric learning and feature weighting methods on datasets from the UCI repository, where the described gradient method also shows a high robustness. In the comparison the advantages of global approaches are demonstrated.

Keywords: Metric Learning, Feature Weighting, k-Nearest-Neighbors, Neighborhood Component Analysis, Large Margin Nearest Neighbor Classification, Relief.

1 Introduction

In many pattern recognition problems, we have datasets with statistical regularities that can be used as prior knowledge. For example, there may be measurements from different domains, which makes the relative scaling of the dimensions in the given dataset arbitrary. Also often the data from different classes lie on submanifolds. If some class labels are available for the data, this information can be captured by a distance metric. This prior knowledge can be used to improve the performance of clustering [13], learning vector quantization [6], or k-Nearest-Neighbor (k-NN) classification [4]. We will focus here on the broadly used k-NN classifier [1]. That often allows competitive non-linear classification, even though it is very simple.

The k-NN classifier labels unknown data points to the most frequently occurring label of the k closest points. Which points are the closest, depends on the distance measure used. A standard choice is the Euclidean distance. However, to increase the probability of correct classification, it might be advantageous to adapt the metric to the data. Very popular for this purpose is the Mahalanobis distance

$$d(\boldsymbol{x}_i, \boldsymbol{x}_j) = \sqrt{(\boldsymbol{x}_i - \boldsymbol{x}_j)^T M (\boldsymbol{x}_i - \boldsymbol{x}_j)}, \tag{1}$$

S. Wermter et al. (Eds.): ICANN 2014, LNCS 8681, pp. 129–135, 2014.

where M is a positive semidefinite matrix to be learned. Instead of adapting a distance measure, a matrix W can be learned, that projects the data to a more suitable space. The distance in that space is

$$d(\boldsymbol{x}_i, \boldsymbol{x}_j) = \|W\boldsymbol{x}_i - W\boldsymbol{x}_j\| = \|\boldsymbol{x}_i - \boldsymbol{x}_j\|_W. \qquad (2)$$

This is equivalent to the Mahalanobis distance with $M = WW^\top$. However, W does not need to be positive semidefinite.

The well known metric learning methods either optimize W or M. Probabilistic Global Distance Metric Learning (PGDM) by Xing et al. [13] maximizes interclass distances, while keeping intraclass distances below some threshold. Neighborhood Component Analysis (NCA) [4] as well as Large Margin Nearest Neighbors (LMNN) [11,12] try to free a neighborhood around every data point from differently labeled data points.

Related to metric learning is feature weighting. Here only the data dimensions are rescaled. This is equivalent to optimizing only the diagonal elements of M or W. All other elements are set to zero. Methods designed specifically for this task are Relief [8], Simba [3] and MDM [7]. Relief and Simba both use the closest same and differently labeled data points for optimization, while MDM uses the globally largest distances for same labeled data and the shortest distances for differently labeled data.

In the following we describe a gradient method to find W and evaluate it using UCI datasets [2] in both metric learning and feature weighting tasks.

2   Global Metric Learning

Our goal is to find a matrix $W = (\boldsymbol{w}_1, \ldots, \boldsymbol{w}_n) \in \mathbb{R}^{n \times m}$ that projects data points $\boldsymbol{x}_i \in \mathbb{R}^n$ with a given label y_i to a m dimensional space, where the k-NN classification performance is improved. This becomes more likely when for every data point the same labeled points (intraclass) are close together and the differently labeled data points (interclass) are far away. To achieve this we will use a cost function consisting of two parts weighted by a parameter α. The first part of the cost function punishes small distances of pairs from the set of interclass tuples $\mathcal{D} = \{(\boldsymbol{x}_i, \boldsymbol{x}_j) : y_i \neq y_j\}$. If the distance one is reached, the cost will become zero due to a cutoff. We chose a squared cost term to penalize close interclass pairs significantly more than far apart pairs and to make a smooth transition at the cutoff. In Figure 1 the squared error term is compared to a linear term, where the gradient is constant and also not continuous at the cutoff. The second part punishes large distances of intraclass tuples from the set $\mathcal{S} = \{(\boldsymbol{x}_i, \boldsymbol{x}_j) : y_i = y_j\}$. We use the distance measure $\|\boldsymbol{x}_i - \boldsymbol{x}_j\|_W = \sqrt{(\boldsymbol{x}_i - \boldsymbol{x}_j)^\top WW^\top (\boldsymbol{x}_i - \boldsymbol{x}_j)}$ in the cost function

$$E(W) = \alpha \sum_{(i,j) \in \mathcal{D}} \left(1 - \min\left(\|\boldsymbol{x}_i - \boldsymbol{x}_j\|_W, 1\right)\right)^2 + (1 - \alpha) \sum_{(i,j) \in \mathcal{S}} \|\boldsymbol{x}_i - \boldsymbol{x}_j\|_W^2. \qquad (3)$$

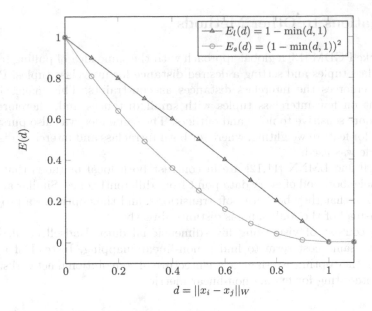

Fig. 1. Interclass cost function comparison. The linear function $E_l(d)$ has a constant gradient. Therefore, all interclass pairs influence the projection matrix W equally. For the non-linear function $E_s(d)$, close by pairs have a larger influence due to their steeper gradient compared to the far apart pairs. In addition, the non-linear function is continuously differentiable at the cutoff at $d = 1$.

The gradient for any weight vector $\boldsymbol{w}_k$ is given by

$$\frac{\partial E(W)}{\partial \boldsymbol{w}_k} = -2\alpha \sum_{(i,j)\in\mathcal{D}} \frac{(1 - \min(\|\boldsymbol{x}_i - \boldsymbol{x}_j\|_W, 1))}{\|\boldsymbol{x}_i - \boldsymbol{x}_j\|_W} \left(\boldsymbol{w}_k^\top (\boldsymbol{x}_i - \boldsymbol{x}_j)\right)(\boldsymbol{x}_i - \boldsymbol{x}_j)$$

$$+ 2(1 - \alpha) \sum_{(i,j)\in\mathcal{S}} \left(\boldsymbol{w}_k^\top (\boldsymbol{x}_i - \boldsymbol{x}_j)\right)(\boldsymbol{x}_i - \boldsymbol{x}_j). \tag{4}$$

Due to this purely cost function driven design without any hard constraints, there is always a trade off between minimizing and maximizing distances influenced by many tuples. There is a soft transition between tuples close to their desired distance with little influence and tuples far from their desired distance with large influence. All intraclass tuples are taken into account, making this a global approach with a Gaussian prior on the intraclass distances. Due to this property we coin this approach *Global Metric Learning* (GML).

There are of course many optimizers available, that will find good solutions. We use stochastic gradient descent (SGD), because it works fast in case of redundant data. To avoid the need to select a learning rate, we applied variance-based SGD [10,9].

3   Relations to Other Methods

GML is like PGDM [13] a global approach with the same idea of pulling together all intraclass tuples and setting a desired distance for interclass tuples. PGDM, however, enforces the interclass distances as constraints. This makes PGDM dependent on few interclass tuples with small distances and, therefore, may make it more sensitive to noise and outliers. The same idea was also pursued by MDM [7] for feature weighting, where for both intraclass and interclass distances a hard rule was used.

NCA [4] and LMNN [11,12] are in contrast both local methods that try to free the neighborhood of every data point from differently ones. Similar are NCA and GML in that they both use soft transitions, and they optimize a projection matrix instead of the Mahalanobis distance directly.

In the context of visualizing high-dimensional data, Hadsell et al. [5] use almost the same cost term to find a non-linear mapping. Instead of a linear transform, they optimize a siamese architecture of convolutional networks, which may be interesting for finding non-linear metrics.

4   Experiments

For evaluation we used datasets from the UCI repository described in Table 1. The datasets were split into 50% training data and 50% test data. 10 different splits were generated for each dataset. To compare our method to LMNN, NCA and PGDM, we determined the k-NN classification error rates with $k = 3$. The metrics were learned on the training sets and used by k-NN while testing. As a reference the Euclidean metric was also tested.

Table 1. Description of the UCI datasets

Name	Samples	Dimensions	Classes
Iris	150	4	3
Wine	178	13	3
Breast Cancer	683	10	2
Pima Diabetes	768	8	2
Balance Scale	625	4	3
Parkinsons	195	22	2
Seeds	210	7	3

Our method has only the weighting parameter, which we set to $\alpha = 0.9$ to emphasize the interclass distances. The optimal α depends on the data distributions, and it may be beneficial to tune it for every dataset, e.g. by cross-validation. However, this is out of the scope of this work. The weighting parameter of LMNN was set according to the authors advise to $\alpha = 0.5$. NCA and PGDM are parameter free.

In Table 2 the 3-NN classification error rates after metric learning without preprocessing the data are shown, followed by the standard deviation in parentheses. We can see that GML performs well on all datasets. In three cases it is slightly outperformed by PGDM, and only on the Balance Scale data set it is significantly outperformed by NCA. In the three cases where GML is the best, it is by far the best. NCA is the worst on all other data sets and improves the classification performance only marginally or even deteriorates it compared to the standard Euclidean distance.

Table 2. Classification results after metric learning. There was no preprocessing applied to the data sets. The error rates are given in percent followed by the STD in parentheses. The best results are marked in bold face and the worst in italic.

	LMNN	NCA	PGDM	GML	Euclidean
Iris	3.07(1.89)	*4.13(1.93)*	**2.27(1.99)**	2.53(1.72)	3.33(1.81)
Wine	5.22(2.03)	*29.78(5.87)*	5.89(3.67)	**2.89(1.75)**	31.00(4.52)
Breast Cancer	3.80(0.57)	*39.71(2.24)*	**3.60(0.44)**	3.68(0.68)	39.68(2.21)
Pima Diabetes	29.14(2.33)	*31.12(1.94)*	**27.19(1.34)**	27.89(1.74)	30.78(1.99)
Balance Scale	*15.50(1.95)*	**7.60(2.87)**	10.00(1.14)	9.33(1.31)	21.73(1.36)
Parkinsons	14.18(2.90)	*17.24(2.47)*	16.63(3.57)	**10.10(4.04)**	16.73(2.46)
Seeds	6.95(2.88)	*7.71(1.76)*	6.86(2.14)	**4.10(1.19)**	11.33(2.64)

When preprocessing is done by scaling each dimension such that the data distribution has variance one, the results for some methods change dramatically. This is shown in Table 3. While all other methods benefit clearly from the preprocessing, there are only small changes in the results of GML and PGDM. In fact, due to the global cost function, there should be no change at all. However, the stochastic gradient descent may not find the exact optimum in case of GML, and also the small changes in PGDM seem to be due to convergence issues. GML still achieves the best results in three cases, and in the other four cases is never much worse the best one. Note, that for all methods except for GML, there is always one dataset where it performs significantly worse than all the others (the worst results are marked in *italic*).

Table 3. Classification results after metric learning on preprocessed data. The dimensions of the datasets were normalized to variance one.

	LMNN	NCA	PGDM	GML	Euclidean
Iris	2.80(1.93)	*3.20(2.10)*	**2.27(1.99)**	**2.27(1.89)**	3.60(1.55)
Wine	3.00(2.10)	5.67(1.85)	*5.89(3.67)*	**2.67(1.67)**	5.67(1.52)
Breast Cancer	3.65(0.57)	*4.71(0.71)*	**3.60(0.44)**	3.83(0.76)	3.74(0.76)
Pima Diabetes	27.97(1.33)	*29.69(1.77)*	**27.19(1.34)**	27.92(1.76)	27.84(1.93)
Balance Scale	*14.41(1.90)*	**6.71(1.72)**	10.03(1.25)	9.74(1.08)	18.95(0.85)
Parkinsons	**9.49(2.26)**	10.71(2.86)	*15.10(3.36)*	10.71(3.13)	10.00(3.22)
Seeds	6.67(2.06)	7.43(1.33)	*6.86(2.14)*	**4.29(1.63)**	8.29(2.50)

We also tested the feature weighting performance of GML. In Table 4 the results for preprocessed datasets are listed. The experimental set up and the preprocessing is the same as for metric learning, however, GML was only used to optimize the diagonal elements of W, leaving the off diagonal elements to zero. For comparison the feature weighting methods MDM, Relief, and Simba were used. Also in this feature weighting scenario GML performs well compared to the other methods and is again the best in three out seven cases. Of course, for feature weighting there is the same effect as observed for metric learning: Global methods are robust to the initial scaling, while local methods are effected heavily. Because the best results for the local methods were obtained in the preprocessed setting, we only show those.

Table 4. Results for feature weighting. In a preprocessing step the dimensions of the datasets were normalized to variance one.

	MDM	Relief	Simba	GML	Euclidean
Iris	**2.93(1.97)**	3.20(2.10)	**2.93(1.51)**	*3.33(2.01)*	3.60(1.55)
Wine	4.00(2.23)	*4.22(2.39)*	4.00(2.11)	**2.67(2.11)**	5.67(1.52)
Breast Cancer	**3.54(0.67)**	4.06(1.02)	*4.12(0.71)*	4.06(0.79)	3.74(0.76)
Pima Diabetes	*28.49(1.87)*	**27.16(1.43)**	27.86(2.04)	28.26(1.64)	27.84(1.93)
Balance Scale	**18.95(0.85)**	19.17(1.31)	19.23(1.24)	*21.31(2.00)*	19.23(0.95)
Parkinsons	10.00(4.13)	9.18(2.50)	*10.82(3.73)*	**8.78(3.01)**	10.00(3.22)
Seeds	8.29(3.56)	9.62(3.06)	*10.19(3.39)*	**7.33(2.50)**	8.29(2.50)

Interestingly, when the metric learning and the feature weighting results are compared (Tables 3 and 4), most error rates are quite close, showing that often a proper scaling of the dimensions is most important for good classification. Only for the Balance Scale and the Seeds datasets there are significant improvements when using the more powerful metric learning. Scaling only the original dimensions has the advantage that the dimensions are not mixed, which makes it easier to interpret the results, e.g. relevant dimensions.

5   Conclusion

We showed that an optimized similarity metric can easily be obtained by gradient descent. Two weighted cost terms represent the inter- and intraclass distances. Optimizing their sum yields a trade off between both. All intraclass pairs are taken into account, making this a global approach which is independent of the initial scaling. By optimizing a projection matrix instead of the Mahalanobis distance, we avoid to introduce a constraint to enforce the optimized matrix to be positive semidefinite. While GML is not always the best method on the datasets we used, it was the best method most often (together with PGDM), and it never performed much worse than the others. In this sense it was the most robust method, at least on the datasets we used for comparison.

References

1. Cover, T., Hart, P.: Nearest neighbor pattern classification. IEEE Transactions on Information Theory 13(1), 21–27 (1967)
2. Frank, A., Asuncion, A.: UCI machine learning repository (2010), http://archive.ics.uci.edu/ml
3. Gilad-Bachrach, R., Navot, A., Tishby, N.: Margin based feature selection - theory and algorithms. In: Proceedings of the Twenty-first International Conference on Machine Learning, ICML 2004, pp. 43–50. ACM, New York (2004)
4. Goldberger, J., Roweis, S.T., Hinton, G.E., Salakhutdinov, R.: Neighbourhood components analysis. In: NIPS (2004)
5. Hadsell, R., Chopra, S., LeCun, Y.: Dimensionality reduction by learning an invariant mapping. In: 2006 IEEE Computer Society Conference on Computer Vision and Pattern Recognition, vol. 2, pp. 1735–1742. IEEE (2006)
6. Hammer, B., Villmann, T.: Generalized relevance learning vector quantization. Neural Networks 15(8), 1059–1068 (2002)
7. Hocke, J., Martinetz, T.: Feature Weighting by Maximum Distance Minimization. In: Mladenov, V., Koprinkova-Hristova, P., Palm, G., Villa, A.E.P., Appollini, B., Kasabov, N. (eds.) ICANN 2013. LNCS, vol. 8131, pp. 420–425. Springer, Heidelberg (2013)
8. Kira, K., Rendell, L.A.: A practical approach to feature selection. In: Proceedings of the Ninth International Workshop on Machine Learning, pp. 249–256 (1992)
9. Schaul, T., LeCun, Y.: Adaptive learning rates and parallelization for stochastic, sparse, non-smooth gradients. CoRR abs/1301.3764 (2013)
10. Schaul, T., Zhang, S., LeCun, Y.: No More Pesky Learning Rates. In: ICML, vol. (3), pp. 343–351 (2013)
11. Weinberger, K., Blitzer, J., Saul, L.: Distance metric learning for large margin nearest neighbor classification. In: Advances in Neural Information Processing Systems, vol. 19. MIT Press, Cambridge (2006)
12. Weinberger, K.Q., Saul, L.K.: Distance metric learning for large margin nearest neighbor classification. J. Mach. Learn. Res. 10, 207–244 (2009)
13. Xing, E.P., Ng, A.Y., Jordan, M.I., Russell, S.: Distance metric learning, with application to clustering with side-information. Advances in Neural Information Processing Systems 15, 505–512 (2002)

Leaving Local Optima in Unsupervised Kernel Regression

Daniel Lückehe[1] and Oliver Kramer[2]

[1] Department of Geoinformation, Jade University of Applied Sciences,
Oldenburg, Germany
daniel.lueckehe@uni-oldenburg.de
[2] Department of Computing Science, University of Oldenburg, Oldenburg, Germany
oliver.kramer@uni-oldenburg.de

Abstract. Embedding high-dimensional patterns in low-dimensional latent spaces is a challenging task. In this paper, we introduce re-sampling strategies to leave local optima in the data space reconstruction error (DSRE) minimization process of unsupervised kernel regression (UKR). For this sake, we concentrate on a hybrid UKR variant that combines iterative solution construction with gradient descent based optimization. Patterns with high reconstruction errors are removed from the manifold and re-sampled based on Gaussian sampling. Re-sampling variants consider different pattern reconstruction errors, varying numbers of re-sampled patterns, and termination conditions. The re-sampling process with UKR can also improve ISOMAP embeddings. Experiments on typical benchmark data sets illustrate the capabilities of strategies for leaving optima.

1 Introduction

As the dimensionality of patterns in machine learning is steadily increasing, methods have to be developed that reduce them effectively. In dimensionality reduction, we seek for a low-dimensional representation of high-dimensional patterns, which conserves their distances and neighborhoods, see Lee and Verleysen [6] and Hastie *et al.* [2].

In this work, we focus on re-sampling strategies for UKR to leave local optimal in a gradient descent based optimization process. Results of an UKR embedding are evaluated w. r. t. the DSRE. If DSRE and regression model are derivable, an initial low-dimensional latent space solution can be optimized with gradient descent like proposed by Klanke and Ritter [4]. An approach by Kramer [5] constructs the low-dimensional latent space iteratively using a nearest neighbors regression model. In this paper, we combine the iterative solution construction with the Broyden-Fletcher-Goldfarb-Shanno (BFGS) [8] algorithm. It turns out that the optimization process easily gets stuck in local optima. To overcome getting stuck, we propose and analyze various re-sampling strategies. This paper is structured as follows. Section 2 presents the foundations of unsupervised kernel regression. Section 3 introduces re-sampling strategies that improve the

S. Wermter et al. (Eds.): ICANN 2014, LNCS 8681, pp. 137–144, 2014.

embedding optimization process. An application of the re-sampling strategies to ISOMAP manifolds is presented in Section 4. Conclusions are drawn in Section 5.

2 Unsupervised Kernel Regression

In UKR low-dimensional patterns $\mathbf{X} = [\mathbf{x}_i]_{i=1}^N$ from a latent space $\mathbb{R}^q$ are projected to high-dimensional data space $\mathbb{R}^d$ using a regression model $f : \mathbb{R}^q \to \mathbb{R}^d$. We define $\mathbf{f} : \mathbb{R}^{q \times N} \to \mathbb{R}^{d \times N}$ to map from the latent matrix $\mathbf{X}$ to the data space pattern-wise. The more similar the projection $\mathbf{f}(\mathbf{X})$ is to the high-dimensional pattern matrix $\mathbf{Y} = [\mathbf{y}_i]_{i=1}^N$, the better is the solution w.r.t. the DSRE, which is defined as:

$$R(\mathbf{f}(\mathbf{X}), \mathbf{Y}) = \|\mathbf{f}(\mathbf{X}) - \mathbf{Y}\|_F^2 \tag{1}$$

with Frobenius norm $\| \cdot \|_F$. For a single embedding $\mathbf{x}_i = [\mathbf{X}]_i$ and its corresponding high-dimensional pattern $\mathbf{y}_i = [\mathbf{Y}]_i$, we define the single pattern reconstruction error (SPRE):

$$r(f(\mathbf{x}_i), \mathbf{y}_i) = \|f(\mathbf{x}_i) - \mathbf{y}_i\|_2^2. \tag{2}$$

Leave-one-out cross-validation ensures that for prediction of $\mathbf{x}_i$ the regression model is not affected by the embedding $\mathbf{x}_i$ itself. In this paper, we use the Nadaraya-Watson estimator [7] as regression model f defined as follows:

$$f(\mathbf{x}_i) = \sum_{j=1}^N \mathbf{y}_j \cdot \frac{\mathbf{K}_h(\mathbf{x}_i - \mathbf{x}_j)}{\sum_{k=1}^N \mathbf{K}_h(\mathbf{x}_i - \mathbf{x}_k)} \tag{3}$$

with Gaussian kernel function $\mathbf{K}(\mathbf{x}_i) = (2\pi)^{-1} \cdot e^{-(\mathbf{x}_i^2/2)}$. Like Kramer [5] proposed for unsupervised nearest neighbors (UNN), the latent space will be created iteratively by using Gaussian sampling. The first pattern $\mathbf{y}_1$ is usually embedded at the origin $\overline{\mathbf{X}} = [\mathbf{0}]$. If $1 \leq n < N$ patterns $\overline{\mathbf{Y}}$ have been embedded $\overline{\mathbf{X}}$, pattern $\mathbf{y}_i$ is embedded by creating κ candidate positions:

$$\mathbf{x}_i \sim \mathcal{N}\left(\mathbf{x}_j, \|\mathbf{y}_i - \mathbf{y}_j\|_2^2\right) \text{ with } j = \arg \min_{\mathbf{y}_j = [\overline{\mathbf{Y}}]_j} \|\mathbf{y}_i - \mathbf{y}_j\|_2^2, \tag{4}$$

$\mathbf{x}_j = [\overline{\mathbf{X}}]_j, \mathbf{y}_j = [\overline{\mathbf{Y}}]_j$ and the latent position leading to the lowest SPRE is chosen. Because we use Nadaraya-Watson estimator as regression modell and iterative embedding this approach is called itUKR. For the Gaussian kernel function, the bandwidth is set to $h = 0.675 \cdot \delta$, while δ is the average distance between patterns in the training set, i.e. $\delta = \frac{1}{N-1} \cdot \sum_{i=1}^{N-1} \|\mathbf{y}_i - \mathbf{y}_{i+1}\|_2^2$.

For the gradient descent based optimization process, we use BFGS, which employs the gradient:

$$\nabla R(\mathbf{f}(\mathbf{X}), \mathbf{Y}) = \begin{pmatrix} \frac{\partial R(\mathbf{f}(\mathbf{X}), \mathbf{Y})}{\partial x_{11}} & \cdots & \frac{\partial R(\mathbf{f}(\mathbf{X}), \mathbf{Y})}{\partial x_{n1}} \\ \cdots & \cdots & \cdots \\ \frac{\partial R(\mathbf{f}(\mathbf{X}), \mathbf{Y})}{\partial x_{1m}} & \cdots & \frac{\partial R(\mathbf{f}(\mathbf{X}), \mathbf{Y})}{\partial x_{nm}} \end{pmatrix} \tag{5}$$

and the derivation of the DSRE:

$$\frac{\partial R(\mathbf{f}(\mathbf{X}), \mathbf{Y})}{\partial x_{nm}} = \sum_{i=1}^{N} \left\| -2 \cdot (\mathbf{y}_i - f(\mathbf{x}_i)) \cdot \left(\frac{\partial f(\mathbf{x}_i)}{\partial x_{nm}} \right) \right\|_2 \qquad (6)$$

For the derivation of the Nadaraya-Watson estimator and kernel functions, we also refer to Klanke and Ritter [4].

3 Re-sampling

When optimizing unsupervised regression models with gradient descent based methods, the search may get stuck because of multiple local optima in the DSRE space. Local optima may also be induced in the iterative solution construction process.

3.1 Analysis of Latent Space Structure

Structures of latent spaces depend on the regression methods that have been employed for the embedding process. In this section, we analyze the 2-dimensional latent space ($q = 2$) created by itUKR embedding the two digits '1','3' from the *Digits* data set [3], which comprises handwritten digits. In the following, we plot the DSRE induced in a latent space with $N = 100$ points when embedding a single pattern $\mathbf{y}_i$, see Figure 1. Blue parts represent areas with low, red parts areas with high DSRE. It can be observed that when embedding a single pattern, the DSRE does not suffer from many local optima and is comparatively simple structured, an observation that justifies the application of gradient descent based methods. However, there are situations, when two or more local optima exist, see Figure 1(c). Further, the DSRE space becomes more complex, when embedding larger sets of patterns at once.

To illustrate, how the DSRE improves using BFGS, we create a latent space $q = 2$ with itUKR and optimize the DSRE until the optimization process

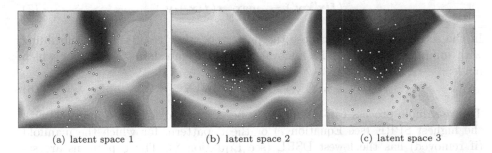

| (a) latent space 1 | (b) latent space 2 | (c) latent space 3 |

Fig. 1. The DSRE space induced when embedding a single pattern $\mathbf{y}_i$ in a $q = 2$-dimensional latent space can have different characteristics: (a)+(b) simple DSRE space with one local optimum, (c) two local optima

runs into a local optimum, see Table 1. Algorithm 1 shows the pseudocode of the employed gradient descent based optimization process. In this experiment, $N = 100$ patterns with $d = 64$ from the *Digits* data set (even digits) were used. The experiment, which is called *even numbers experiment* in the following, is run 100 times and shows mean values and standard deviations. We can observe that further BFGS steps improve the DSRE and reduce the standard deviations.

Table 1. DSRE of even Digits with various repetitions of BFGS

rep.	DSRE	rep.	DSRE
0	2060.7 ± 50.2	5	1815.7 ± 33.2
1	1964.2 ± 55.4	...	
3	1865.2 ± 39.0	opt.	1735.5 ± 25.0

Algorithm 1. BFGS optimization

Require: X, R, f, h
1: Err $\leftarrow R(\mathbf{f}(\mathbf{X}), \mathbf{Y})$, lastErr $\leftarrow$ Err $+ 1$, $\mathbf{X'} \leftarrow \mathbf{X}$
2: **while** Err $<$ lastErr **do**
3:    $\mathbf{X} \leftarrow \mathbf{X'}$, lastErr $\leftarrow$ Err
4:    $\mathbf{X'} \leftarrow$ BFGS($\mathbf{X}$)
5:    Err $\leftarrow R(\mathbf{f}(\mathbf{X'}), \mathbf{Y})$
6: **end while**
7: **return** Err, $\mathbf{X'}$

The BFGS optimization process runs into local optima after 15 repetition in average. In the following section, we introduce a new re-sampling procedure to improve the optimization process.

3.2 Re-sampling Process

The re-sampling process introduced in the following should improve the latent space structure w.r.t. DSRE. Re-sampling is a two-step process. In the first step, the BFGS optimization is conducted until no improvement of the DSRE is achieved. In the second step, latent points $\mathbf{x'}$ with a comparatively high error are chosen and re-embedded. For this re-embedding, we employ the Gaussian sampling that is used for the iterative solution construction process, see Equation 4. The process is repeated until no improvement can be achieved. Two variants of the re-sampling procedure concern the error measure that determines, which patterns are re-sampled. In the first variant, we choose the latent point $\mathbf{x'}$ with the largest SPRE for which holds:

$$r(f(\mathbf{x'}), \mathbf{y'}) = \max_{i=1,\ldots,N} r(f(\mathbf{x}_i), \mathbf{y}_i) \tag{7}$$

In the second variant, we choose the pattern $\mathbf{x'}$ that results in an embedding with minimal DSRE after its removal[1] from the embedding $\mathbf{X}$, i.e., for which holds:

$$R(\mathbf{f}(\mathbf{X}_{-\mathbf{x'}}), \mathbf{Y}_{-\mathbf{y'}}) =^{\bullet} \min_{i=1,\ldots,N} R(\mathbf{f}(\mathbf{X}_{-\mathbf{x}_i}), \mathbf{Y}_{-\mathbf{y}_i}) \tag{8}$$

The re-sample process can alternatively be conducted for the ζ patterns with the highest SPRE (see Equation 7) or the ζ pattern, for which the manifold (if removed) has the lowest DSRE (see Equation 8). The ζ patterns are sequentially re-sampled until ξ sequential iterations no improvement is observed.

---

[1] We use the notation $\mathbf{X}_{-\mathbf{x}}$ for a latent space $\mathbf{X}$, from which the point $\mathbf{x}$ has been removed.

Table 2. DSRE of even Digits with re-sampling and small settings for ζ employing SRE and DSRE as re-sampling quality measure

mode	$\zeta = 1$	$\zeta = 2$	$\zeta = 3$	$\zeta = 4$	$\zeta = 5$
SPRE	1698.7 ± 24.3	1693.3 ± 21.4	1690.8 ± 23.8	1684.4 ± 18.6	1681.6 ± 17.8
DSRE	1709.0 ± 29.2	1694.7 ± 25.0	1687.8 ± 20.5	1682.2 ± 20.2	1681.0 ± 20.2

Algorithm 2. Re-sampling

Require: $\mathbf{X}$, R, f, h, ζ
1: $\mathbf{X}' \leftarrow$ Choose ζ different $\mathbf{x}'$ (Eq. 7, 8)
2: **for all** $\mathbf{x}'_i \in \mathbf{X}'$ **do**
3:     Remove $\mathbf{x}'_i$ for $\mathbf{X}$
4:     Re-embed $\mathbf{x}'_i$ by Gaussian Sampling (Eq. 4)
5: **end for**
6: **return** $\mathbf{X}$

Algorithm 2 shows the re-sampling method in pseudocode, while Algorithm 3 illustrates the whole re-sampling optimization process. For the following experimental analysis of these re-sampling strategies, we use the settings of the *even numbers experiment*. Table 2 shows the results for small values of ζ. First, we can observe that the re-sampling process significantly improves the quality of the embeddings, i.e., we observe an improvement from $R(\cdot) = 1735.5 \pm 25.0$, see Table 1, to $R(\cdot) = 1681.6 \pm 17.8$ for $\zeta = 5$. No significant difference can be observed between re-sampling of patterns based on the SPRE or the DSRE. To reduce the runtime, we recommend to use the SPRE, which will be used in the remainder of this paper. The tendency can be observed that the DSRE is improved for increasing ζ. This observation becomes clearer, if one has a closer look at the re-sampled patterns. For example, the following sequence of patterns in a re-sampling process using DSRE with $\zeta = 1$ has been observed: $\mathbf{x}_1, \mathbf{x}_2, \mathbf{x}_3, \mathbf{x}_4, \mathbf{x}_4, \mathbf{x}_5, \mathbf{x}_4$. The repeated selection of pattern $\mathbf{x}_4$ shows that the re-sampling process gets stuck in a repeated loop. To avoid this, we increase the number of simultaneously chosen patterns to $\zeta = 3$, where we can still observe repetitions, e.g., in the following sequence $[\mathbf{x}_1, \mathbf{x}_2, \mathbf{x}_3], [\mathbf{x}_4, \mathbf{x}_1, \mathbf{x}_5], [\mathbf{x}_6, \mathbf{x}_1, \mathbf{x}_3], [\mathbf{x}_7, \mathbf{x}_1, \mathbf{x}_3], [\mathbf{x}_7, \mathbf{x}_1, \mathbf{x}_3]$.

As a consequence, we increase ζ to settings up to $\zeta = N$. Table 3 shows an experiment on the same data set with the same experimental settings for an increasing ζ, which clearly shows that the DSRE is decreasing with increasing ζ. Also the corresponding standard deviation is decreasing significantly.

Algorithm 3. Re-sampling optimization process

Require: $\mathbf{Y}$, manifold method M, R, f, h, ζ, ξ
1: $\mathbf{X} = M(\mathbf{Y})$
2: lastErr $\leftarrow R(f(\mathbf{X}), \mathbf{Y})$, $i \leftarrow 0$
3: **while** $i < \xi$ **do**
4:     Err, $\mathbf{X}' \leftarrow$ BFGS optimization$(\mathbf{X}, R, f, h)$
5:     **if** Err $<$ lastErr **then**
6:         $i \leftarrow -1$, lastErr $\leftarrow$ Err, $\mathbf{X}^* = \mathbf{X}'$
7:     **end if**
8:     $i \leftarrow i + 1$
9:     $\mathbf{X} \leftarrow$ re-sampling$(\mathbf{X}', R, f, h, \zeta)$
10: **end while**
11: **return** $\mathbf{X}^*$

Table 3. DSRE of even Digits with re-sampling, large ζ employing the SPRE

$\zeta = 10$	$\zeta = 20$	$\zeta = 30$	$\zeta = 50$	$\zeta = 70$	$\zeta = 100$
1674.9 ± 19.9	1663.6 ± 16.4	1655.5 ± 14.7	1652.8 ± 13.5	1648.8 ± 13.3	1647.5 ± 10.6

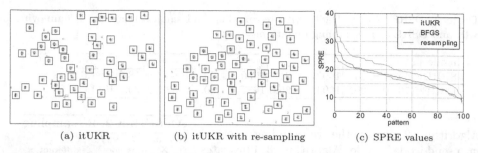

(a) itUKR   (b) itUKR with re-sampling   (c) SPRE values

Fig. 2. Visualization of embeddings generated with (a) itUKR and (b) itUKR with re-sampling, and a comparison of sorted SPRE values after optimization

A comparison between the embedding of $N = 100$ even digits with itUKR, see Figure 2(a), to the corresponding embedding optimized with re-sampling, see Figure 2(b), shows that the embeddings are significantly improved. Neighborhoods are more defined, i.e., patterns with different labels are clearly separated, while similar patterns lie closer together. Further, latent points are more uniformly distributed. Figure 2(c) shows a comparison of the SPRE values for itUKR (red), itUKR with BFGS optimization (blue), and itUKR with re-sampling process (green). Patterns are sorted decreasingly w. r. t. their SPRE. The SPRE of itUKR with re-sampling achieves the lowest SPRE values in the complete manifold.

In the last experiments, the re-sampling process was terminated, when no improvement is achieved in two successive iterations. Here, we analyze the variant to termine the optimization process, if no improvement could be observed in ξ successive iterations. Table 4 shows results. Based on the previous experiments, we choose the settings $\zeta = 30$ and $\zeta = 100$.

Table 4. DSRE of even Digits with varying termination condition

ζ	$\xi = 1$	$\xi = 2$	$\xi = 3$	$\xi = 4$	$\xi = 5$
30	1655.5 ± 14.7	1649.8 ± 14.2	1649.3 ± 12.6	1646.1 ± 12.6	1644.9 ± 11.8
100	1647.5 ± 10.6	1645.4 ± 9.6	1645.0 ± 10.7	1643.7 ± 10.5	1642.5 ± 9.6

With increasing ξ, the DSRE can be reduced, in case of $\zeta = 30$, the standard deviation could also be decreased.

4   Re-sampling for Isometric Mapping

In this section, we introduce the re-sampling process for isometric mapping (ISOMAP) [10] and compare the methods on three test data sets. For this sake, we have to determine a proper choice for the bandwidth parameter h of the Gaussian kernel function. According to Silverman's rule-of-thumb [9], we choose $h = \hat{\sigma} \cdot c \cdot N^{-0.2}$ with $c = 1.06$ for a Gaussian kernel density function. Table 5 shows an experimental comparison of itUKR and ISOMAP with various optimization variants and three different neighborhood sizes K on the data sets

Table 5. Comparison of itUKR and ISOMAP with various optimization strategies on the data sets *Digits*, *Iris* and *Gaussian blobs*

method	opt.	Digits K	ζ	DSRE	Iris K	ζ	DSRE	Gaussian blobs K	ζ	DSRE
it-UKR	none	-	-	2060.7 ± 50.2	-	-	61.30 ± 2.37	-	-	350.74 ± 44.05
	grad.	-	-	1735.5 ± 25.0	-	-	36.06 ± 2.50	-	-	316.70 ± 6.41
	res.	-	30	1649.8 ± 14.2	-	60	29.79 ± 0.73	-	15	314.18 ± 0.77
	res.	-	100	**1645.4 ± 9.6**	-	100	30.17 ± 0.71	-	30	312.91 ± 0.28
ISO-MAP	none	5	-	2714.5 ± 0.0	5	-	73.94 ± 0.00	5	-	893.31 ± 0.00
	none	20	-	2418.5 ± 0.0	20	-	70.70 ± 0.00	10	-	317.85 ± 0.00
	none	50	-	2224.9 ± 0.0	50	-	64.94 ± 0.00	25	-	316.42 ± 0.00
	grad.	50	-	1752.7 ± 0.0	50	-	32.28 ± 0.00	25	-	316.42 ± 0.00
	res.	50	30	1698.4 ± 11.9	50	60	**28.29 ± 0.39**	25	15	313.46 ± 0.22
	res.	50	100	1725.5 ± 17.9	50	100	28.82 ± 0.28	25	30	**312.65 ± 0.37**

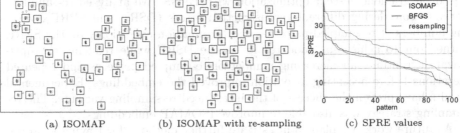

(a) ISOMAP   (b) ISOMAP with re-sampling   (c) SPRE values

Fig. 3. Visualization of embeddings generated with (a) ISOMAP and (b) ISOMAP with re-sampling, and a comparison of sorted SPRE values after optimization

Digits, *Iris* [1], and *Gaussian blobs* with $\xi = 2$. On the *Digits* data set, we can observe an improvement of the DSRE via re-sampling for itUKR, while the standard deviation is decreasing, i.e., local optima can be left and more similar optimal solutions are reached in different runs. For ISOMAP on Digits re-sampling achieves a significant improvement, but too large ζ can deteriorate result. The reason is probably that not the same regression method is employed for the embedding process as for the re-sampling strategy. On the *Iris* data set, re-sampling also leads to improvements and to a leaving of local optima. For itUKR the standard deviation is decreased, which is also a hint that less optimization runs get stuck in local optima. On the *Gaussian blobs* data set with only $N = 30$ patterns, 3 centers and $d = 100$, post-optimization with BFGS optimization does not improve the embeddings for ISOMAP, but with re-sampling. In case of itUKR, BFGS optimization and re-sampling can both improve the embeddings. In particular, re-sampling significantly reduces the standard deviation, i.e., the optimum is reached in most runs. The overall best result on *Digits* is achieved by itUKR with re-sampling and on *Iris* and *Gaussian blobs* by ISOMAP with re-sampling.

Again, a visualization of the computed embeddings is presented. Figure 3(a) shows the $q = 2$-dimensional latent space generated by ISOMAP for the *even numbers experiment*. The optimized manifold generated by ISOMAP with re-sampling, see Figure 3(b), again shows that the latent points are more uniformly distributed in latent space, which is again reflected by a lower DSRE. The distribution of SPRE values, see Figure 3(c), shows the superiority of the optimized ISOMAP variants in comparison to standard ISOMAP, while the re-sampling ISOMAP variant is slightly better than ISOMAP with BFGS.

5   Conclusions

Optimizing UKR manifolds is a difficult undertaking. In this work, we introduced re-sampling strategies that select latent points with comparatively large reconstruction errors for leaving local optima in the optimization process. These points are re-embedded by Gaussian sampling and a hybrid optimization procedure based on gradient descent optimization with BFGS. We analyzed re-sampling variants considering different reconstruction errors (DSRE and SPRE), varying numbers of re-sampled patterns, and termination conditions. As the SPRE turned out to achieve as good results as the DSRE while reducing the optimization runtime, an increasing number of re-sampled patterns and repeated iterations before accepting a solution improved the embeddings. Experimental results have proven the success of the introduced re-sampling variants. The re-sampling strategy was also able to improve ISOMAP embeddings.

As future work, we plan to investigate further methods for leaving local optima in optimization of UKR embeddings and other dimensionality reduction methods. First promising results have been achieved by repeatedly resizing the whole latent space.

References

1. Bache, K., Lichman, M.: UCI machine learning repository (2013)
2. Hastie, T., Tibshirani, R., Friedman, J.: The Elements of Statistical Learning. Springer, Berlin (2009)
3. Hull, J.: A database for handwritten text recognition research. IEEE PAMI 5(16), 550–554 (1994)
4. Klanke, S., Ritter, H.: Variants of unsupervised kernel regression: General cost functions. Neurocomputing 70(7-9), 1289–1303 (2007)
5. Kramer, O.: Dimensionality reduction by unsupervised k-nearest neighbor regression. In: International Conference on Machine Learning and Applications (ICMLA), pp. 275–278 (2011)
6. Lee, J.A., Verleysen, M.: Nonlinear Dimensionality Reduction. Springer (2007)
7. Nadaraya, E.: On estimating regression. Theory of Probability and Its Application 10, 186–190 (1964)
8. Nocedal, J., Wright, S.J.: Numerical Optimization. Springer (2000)
9. Silverman, B.W.: Density Estimation for Statistics and Data Analysis. Monographs on Statistics and Applied Probability, vol. 26. Chapman and Hall, London (1986)
10. Tenenbaum, J.B., Silva, V.D., Langford, J.C.: A global geometric framework for nonlinear dimensionality reduction. Science 290, 2319–2323 (2000)

An Algorithm for Directed Graph Estimation

Hideitsu Hino[1], Atsushi Noda[2], Masami Tatsuno[3], Shotaro Akaho[4],
and Noboru Murata[2]

[1] University of Tsukuba, 1-1-1 Tennoudai, Tsukuba, Ibaraki 305–8573, Japan
[2] Waseda University, 3-4-1 Ohkubo, Shinjuku-ku, Tokyo 169–8555, Japan
[3] University of Lethbridge, Lethbridge, AB, T1K 3M4, Canada
[4] National Institute of Advanced Industrial Science and Technology,
1-1-1 Umezono, Tsukuba, Ibaraki 305-8568, Japan

Abstract. A problem of estimating the intrinsic graph structure from
observed data is considered. The observed data in this study is a matrix
with elements representing *dependency* between nodes in the graph. Each
element of the observed matrix represents, for example, co-occurrence of
events at two nodes, or correlation of variables corresponding to two
nodes. The dependency does not represent direct connections and includes influences of various paths, and spurious correlations make the
estimation of direct connection difficult. To alleviate this difficulty, digraph Laplacian is used for characterizing a graph. A generative model
of an observed matrix is proposed, and a parameter estimation algorithm for the model is also proposed. The proposed method is capable of
dealing with directed graphs, while conventional graph structure estimation methods from an observed matrix are only applicable to undirected
graphs. Experimental result shows that the proposed algorithm is able
to identify the intrinsic graph structure.

Keywords: digraph Laplacian, directed graph, graph estimation.

1   Introduction

A graph is a mathematical structure that represents relationship between data,
and has a lot of applications [1,2]. A graph is composed of nodes and edges,
where a connection between a pair of nodes is expressed by an edge. For example, neural networks can be regarded as a graph in which nodes correspond
to nerve cells (neurons) and edges correspond to direct connectivity between
neurons. If coincident multi-neuronal firings are observed, correlations between
these observed neurons are stronger than others. However, these neurons may
not be connected directly, and the observed coincident firings may be a result of
influences from other neurons. This effect is called the pseudo-correlation and it
is problematic in data analysis.

There are two major graph estimation problems. One is a problem of estimating importance of nodes when connectivities of whole edges are known, e.g. web
pages ranking problem such as PageRank [3]. The other is a problem of estimating edges based on certain statistics, which represent dependency between nodes,

S. Wermter et al. (Eds.): ICANN 2014, LNCS 8681, pp. 145–152, 2014.

e.g., cell-signaling data analysis [4]. We deal with the latter problem in this paper. There are many kinds of statistics for representing relationship between nodes, and hereafter we collectively refer to these statistics as *dependency*.

In graph structure estimation, it is typically assumed that a set of observed data is generated from a multivariate Gaussian distribution. Then, the inverse covariance matrix is regarded as the intensity of direct connections between nodes, and estimated under a certain sparseness assumption to capture a few intrinsic connections between nodes. This formulation is referred to as the Sparse Inverse Covariance Selection (SICS [5]). In this framework, given the empirical covariance matrix T and a sparsity controlling parameter, the objective is to minimize the ℓ_1 regularized negative log-likelihood of a Gaussian distribution. However, SICS methods cannot be used for estimating asymmetric graph structures, and it is difficult to optimize the number of edges of the estimated graph.

In this paper, based on the random walk model on graphs, we propose a method that can extract only important *directed* connections in graphs. The number of edges in a graph is decided by maximum likelihood estimation. The proposed method is experimentally shown to find meaningful graph structure using an electrophysiological data.

2   Problem Setting

We consider a problem of estimating the intrinsic graph connectivity when a certain kind of dependency between nodes are observed with noise. Let V be a set of nodes $\{1, \ldots, n\}$, and E be a set of edges $(i, j), i, j \in V$ from node i to j. Let Θ be a *connectivity matrix* with $[\Theta]_{ij} = \theta_{ij}$, $i \neq j$, which represents the connection intensity between nodes i and j, and θ_{ij} can be zero if there is no edge from i to j. Note that $\theta_{ij} \neq \theta_{ji}$ in general. We assume Θ does not include self-loops hence diagonal elements $[\Theta]_{ii}$ are always set to 0.

Since we cannot observe Θ directly, we introduce another parameter which represents not edge connections but dependent relations between nodes. Let Ξ be a *dependency matrix* with $[\Xi]_{ij} = \xi_{ij}$, $i \neq j$, which can be represented as

$$\xi_{ij} = c_i + c_{ij}\theta_{ij} + \sum_{k \in V} c_{ij}^k \theta_{ik}\theta_{kj} + \sum_{k,l \in V} c_{ij}^{kl} \theta_{ik}\theta_{kl}\theta_{lj} + \cdots, \text{ for } i \neq j, \quad (1)$$

where $c_i, c_{ij}, c_{ij}^k, c_{ij}^{kl} \ldots$ are attenuation coefficients. The first term of Eq. (1) represents external inputs, which is included to improve the expressiveness of the model. The second term represents direct information propagation between nodes i and j, while the third term represents information propagation via one intermediate node k and so on. In more general form, the relationship of intrinsic graph connectivity Θ and dependency between nodes Ξ is modeled by a function

$$f : \mathbb{R}^{n \times n} \ni \Theta \mapsto f(\Theta) = \Xi \in \mathbb{R}^{n \times n}. \quad (2)$$

As a concrete model of f, we introduce the random walk on graphs, which is characterized by the digraph Laplacian introduced in Sec. 3. An algorithm for estimating the connectivity Θ and model parameters is derived in Sec. 4.

3   Models of Graph Structure and Observed Data

We propose to use the exponential map as the function f in Eq. (2) because of both theoretical and computational simplicity. In this section, we explain digraph Laplacian [6] for considering the exponential map of directed graphs. We then explain the random walk model for information transition on a graph, which is characterized by the digraph Laplacian.

3.1   Digraph Laplacian and Random Walk on Graph

We assume the connectivity matrix Θ as

$$[\Theta]_{ij} = \theta_{ij} = \begin{cases} 1 & \text{there is an edge from } i \text{ to } j \text{ and } i \neq j, \\ 0 & \text{otherwise.} \end{cases} \quad (3)$$

A digraph Laplacian L is defined as a function of Θ as

$$[L(\Theta)]_{ij} = \begin{cases} \sum_{k \in V} \theta_{ik} & i = j, \\ -\theta_{ij} & i \neq j. \end{cases} \quad (4)$$

Let $\beta \in \mathbb{R}_+$ be the transition tendency between connected nodes in unit time. The i, j element of the transition probability matrix in a short interval $1/\tau$ is written as

$$\left[I_n - \frac{\beta}{\tau} L(\Theta) \right]_{ij} = \begin{cases} 1 - \frac{\beta}{\tau} \sum_{k \in V} \theta_{ik} & i = j, \\ \frac{\beta}{\tau} \theta_{ij} & i \neq j, \end{cases} \quad (5)$$

where I_n is the $n \times n$ unit matrix. Note that $(I_n - \beta L(\Theta)/\tau)\mathbf{1} = \mathbf{1}$ holds. The element $[I_n - \beta L(\Theta)/\tau]_{ij}$ is the transition probability from node i to j in the interval $1/\tau$, and $[I_n - \beta L(\Theta)/\tau]_{ii}$ is the probability that a random walker remains in node i. Since $[I_n - \beta L(\Theta)/\tau]_{ii}$ is a probability, β should satisfy τ/d, where $d = \max_{i,k} \sum_{k \in V} \theta_{ik}$. By considering the continuous time limit of the random walk, we define the transition probability in unit time as

$$\lim_{\tau \to \infty} \left(I_n - \frac{\beta L(\Theta)}{\tau} \right)^{\tau} = e^{-\beta L(\Theta)}. \quad (6)$$

In summary, the digraph Laplacian $L(\Theta)$ characterizes a random walk on a directed graph, and $[e^{-\beta L(\Theta)}]_{ij}$ is regarded as the probability that the walker starting from the node i stays at the node j after unit time.

3.2   Observed Data Model

In this section, we introduce a generative model of the observed data using the exponential map defined in Eq. (6). In our model, $[\Xi]_{ij} = \xi_{ij}$ is composed of *intrinsic connectivity* $\theta_{ij}, i, j \in V$ modeled by a function f in Eq. (2). Since we assumed that there are no self-loop, ξ_{ii} are not calculated using Eq. (1). Here we assume that the dependency Ξ is observed as $t_{ij} = \xi_{ij} + \varepsilon$, where ε represents a noise term. Specifically, we consider $t_{ij} \in \mathbb{R}$ is an estimate of $\xi_{ij}, i \neq j$, and T is an $n \times n$ matrix with the ij element t_{ij}. For the sake of simplify, we assume t_{ij} are samples

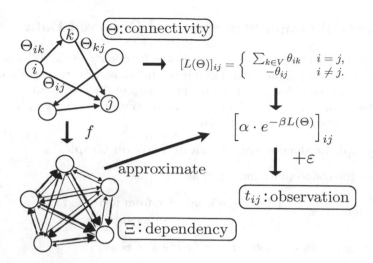

Fig. 1. Relationship between variables. The dependency matrix Ξ is obtained by mapping the connectivity matrix Θ. The quantity $T = (t_{ij})$ is the observed dependency $\Xi = (\xi_{ij})$ with noise ε.

from Gaussian distributions with means ξ_{ij}. The probability density function of observed data t_{ij} is written as $p(t_{ij}; \xi_{ij}) = \frac{1}{\sqrt{2\pi\sigma^2}}\exp\left\{-\frac{1}{2\sigma^2}(t_{ij} - \xi_{ij})^2\right\}$, where σ^2 is a common variance. The joint distribution of the observed data T can be expressed as $p(T; \Xi) = \prod_{i \neq j} p(t_{ij}; \xi_{ij})$. We observe only the dependency Ξ with noises, though we can estimate connectivity Θ by the algorithm proposed in the next section. Figure 1 shows that the digraph Laplacian $L(\Theta)$ is calculated from the intrinsic connectivity Θ. On the other hand, the intrinsic connectivity leads dependency Ξ via a function f. We approximate Ξ using the random walk, and we assume a matrix T is observed as Ξ contaminated by additive noises.

With a multiplicative factor $\alpha \in \mathbb{R}_+$ for $e^{-\beta L(\Theta)}$ in Eq. (6), the random walk on a graph is equivalent to a polynomial transformation model in Eq. (1) and by a Taylor series expantion, we obtain

$$\alpha e^{-\beta L(\Theta)} = \alpha \cdot \left(I_n - \beta L(\Theta) + \frac{\beta^2 L(\Theta)^2}{2!} - \frac{\beta^3 L(\Theta)^3}{3!} + \cdots \right). \quad (7)$$

The off-diagonal element of $\alpha e^{-\beta L(\Theta)}$, i.e., $\left[\alpha e^{-\beta L(\Theta)}\right]_{ij}$ is written as

$$\alpha \cdot \left\{ \beta\theta_{ij} + \frac{\beta^2}{2!}\left(\sum_{k \in V} \theta_{ik}\theta_{kj} - \theta_{ij}\sum_{k \in V}\theta_{ik} - \theta_{ij}\sum_{k \in V}\theta_{jk} \right) + \cdots \right\} \quad (8)$$

$$= \alpha \left(\beta - \frac{\beta}{2!}\sum_{k \in V}(\theta_{ik} + \theta_{jk}) + \cdots \right)\theta_{ij} + \alpha\left(\frac{\beta^2}{2!} + \cdots \right)\sum_{k \in V}\theta_{ik}\theta_{kj} + \cdots. \quad (9)$$

Equation (9) corresponds to Eq. (1), i.e.

$$\Xi = f(\Theta | \alpha, \beta) = \alpha e^{-\beta L(\Theta)}, \quad (10)$$

where we extended the function f to have additional parameters in the random walk in Eq. (7). We note that diagonal elements of Ξ are not defined in Eq. (1), but calculated via Eq. (10). Since $\xi_{ij} = [\alpha e^{-\beta L(\Theta)}]_{ij}$ by Eq. (10),

$$t_{ij} = \xi_{ij} + \varepsilon = \left[\alpha e^{-\beta L(\Theta)}\right]_{ij} + \varepsilon, \quad \varepsilon \sim \mathcal{N}(0, \sigma^2). \tag{11}$$

The rationales behind the generative model defined by Eq. (11) are wide use of random walk for graph, and feasibility of parameter estimation at least for graphs with small number of nodes. We have to calculate the inverse function of f in Eq. (2) to estimate a graph structure Θ. Since f is modeled by the exponential map $\alpha e^{-\beta L(\Theta)}$, we only have to calculate $\log \Xi$ by using fixed α and β.

4   Algorithm for Estimating Graph Structure

In this section, we propose an algorithm for estimating parameters α, β and Θ for the proposed model in Eq. (11) from an observed matrix T. This procedure is summarized in Algorithm 1. Since we assume observation noises are Gaussian, we consider the objective function as the sum of squared residuals

$$J(\alpha, \beta, \Theta) = \sum_{i,j \in V, i \neq j} \left(t_{ij} - \left[\alpha e^{-\beta L(\Theta)}\right]_{ij}\right)^2, \tag{12}$$

and estimate α, β and Θ that minimize Eq. (12). If $\Xi = \alpha e^{-\beta L(\Theta)}$, the ij element of the logarithm of Ξ is

$$[\log \Xi]_{ij} = [\log(\alpha I) - \beta L(\Theta)]_{ij} = \begin{cases} \log \alpha - \beta \sum_{k \in V} \theta_{ik} & i = j, \\ \beta \theta_{ij} & i \neq j. \end{cases} \tag{13}$$

We can estimate Θ as

$$[\hat{\Theta}]_{ij} = \hat{\theta}_{ij} = \frac{[\log \Xi]_{ij}}{\beta}, \text{ for } i \neq j. \tag{14}$$

We note that diagonal elements of Ξ are not defined and we have to estimate $[\Xi]_{ii}$ while updating parameters α, β and Θ using the following iterative algorithm. First, we initialize Ξ as $\Xi = T + rI_n$, $r > 0$, where r is chosen so as to $\det \Xi \neq 0$. In our preliminary experiments, we saw that the value of r did not affect the result. For the sake of simplicity, we set $r = 1$ henceforth. Next, for fixed α and β, we calculate an approximation of the matrix logarithm using the Jordan normal form of Ξ to obtain $\hat{\Theta}$ [7] . Let ζ_m be the m-th largest value of $|[\log \Xi]_{ij}|$, for $i \neq j$. Then, we choose m most likely connected edges by the following thresholding operation:

$$[\hat{\Theta}]'_{ij} = \hat{\theta}'_{ij} = \begin{cases} 1 & |[\log \Xi]_{ij}| \geq \zeta_m \text{ and } i \neq j \\ 0 & \text{otherwise.} \end{cases} \tag{15}$$

Algorithm 1. Proposed algorithm for graph structure estimation

---

input observed data $T \in \mathbb{R}^{n \times n}, [T]_{ii} = 0, i = 1, \cdots, n$
initialize $\Xi = T + I_n$
for $m = 1$ to $n(n-1)$ **do**
    while not convergence **do**
$$[\hat{\Theta}]'_{ij} = \hat{\theta}'_{ij} = \begin{cases} 1 & |[\log \Xi]_{ij}| \geq \zeta_m \text{ and } i \neq j \\ 0 & \text{otherwise.} \end{cases}$$
                                              ▷ Estimate Θ^m from $[\log \Xi]_{ij}$
$$(\alpha^m, \beta^m) = \arg\min_{\alpha, \beta} J(\alpha, \beta, \Theta^m)$$
                                               ▷ Estimate α^m and β^m
$$\Xi = T + \text{diag}\left(\alpha^m \cdot e^{-\beta^m L(\Theta^m)}\right)$$
                                               ▷ Update diagonal elements of Ξ
    end while
end for
$$\hat{m} = \arg\min_{m \in \{1, 2, \cdots, n(n-1)\}} J(\alpha^m, \beta^m, \Theta^m) \quad \text{▷ Select } \hat{m} \text{ which minimizes the objective } J$$
return $\Theta^{\hat{m}}$

We estimate α and β that minimize the objective function in Eq. (12) with $\hat{\Theta}'$ as $(\hat{\alpha}, \hat{\beta}) = \arg\min_{\alpha, \beta} J(\alpha, \beta, \hat{\Theta}')$. We used Nelder-Mead method [8] for optimizing α and β. We update diagonal elements of Ξ by

$$\Xi = T + \text{diag}\left(\hat{\alpha} e^{-\hat{\beta} L(\hat{\Theta}')}\right). \tag{16}$$

For a fixed m, we repeat this procedures until convergence. We denote the estimates obtained by these procedures as α^m, β^m and Θ^m.

We repeat the above updating procedure. During the repetition, the number of maximum possible edges m is incremented by 1 starting from $m = 1$. After we obtain a set of estimates $S = \{(\alpha^m, \beta^m, \Theta^m)\}_{m=1}^{n(n-1)}$, we select $\hat{m}$ as

$$\hat{m} = \arg\min_{m \in \{1, 2, \cdots, n(n-1)\}} J(\alpha^m, \beta^m, \Theta^m), \tag{17}$$

and obtain the estimate $\Theta^{\hat{m}}$, the estimate of the intrinsic connectivity.

5　Experiments

Firstly, we explain the data used for showing the effectiveness of the proposed directed graph estimation algorithm.

Multi-unit activities (MUAs) of the rat medial prefrontal cortex (3.2 mm anterior and 1.3 mm lateral (left) to bregma) were recorded continuously over 25 hours by chronically implanted tetrodes (See [9] for details). A recording session consisted of three epochs where the rat was allowed to behave freely throughout the recording; 12 hours of the first free-running epoch (pre-task), 1 hour of novel experience epoch (task), and 12 hours of the second free-running epoch (post-task). The MUAs were bandpass filtered between 600 Hz and 6 kHz and spike waveforms were recorded at 32 kHz whenever the signal exceeded a predetermined threshold. The peak of the spike waveform was considered the timing of spikes and those from 32 isolated single units were saved in 0.1 ms resolution. It means that we consider graphs with 32 nodes corresponding to the 32 neurons, and for each node, we have a point process indicating the timing of spikes. Brain states (wake and sleep) were identified by monitoring behavior of the rat.

We divide the each time series data corresponding to node i into windows of size $\tau = 3$ ms. For each windows indicated by an index q, we defined a $\{0,1\}$-valued variable

$$R_i(q) = \begin{cases} 1 & \text{there is at least a firing within the window,} \\ 0 & \text{otherwise.} \end{cases} \tag{18}$$

Then, for every pairs of $(i,j), i \neq j = 1,\ldots,32$, we estimated the conditional probabilities $P(R_j(q+1) = 1|R_i(q) = 1)$ and $P(R_j(q+1) = 1|R_i(q) = 0)$ by counting the cases. Using these conditional probabilities, we define the $(i,j), i \neq j = 1,\ldots,32$ element of observation matrix T as

$$[T]_{ij} = P(R_j(q+1) = 1|R_i(q) = 1) - P(R_j(q+1) = 1|R_i(q) = 0). \tag{19}$$

By its construction, the ij element of the matrix T is considered as how firing of the i-the neuron at the previous time window affects that of the j-the neuron at the current time window. We generated an observation matrix T using spike timing data corresponding to five sleep periods in pre-task and show the union of edges of five graphs in Fig. 2(a). Figure 2(b) is a graph corresponding to the period in during task, and Fig. 2(c) is the union of five graphs estimated using spike timing data corresponding to five sleep periods in post-task. Pre- and post-task sleep periods are within one hour from the during task period. Comparing Figs. 2(a) and (b), and (b) and (c), we see the increase of the number of edges,

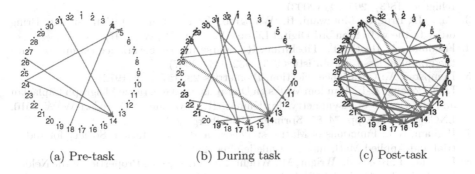

(a) Pre-task	(b) During task	(c) Post-task

Fig. 2. Estimated graphs in (a)pre-, (b)during, and (c)post-task. It is seen a drastic change in the pattern of edges in (a) and (b). Edges in common with the pre-task graph are drawn in dashed arrows. In (c), edges arose during the task and are kept connected after the task are drawn in bold arrows.

which can be attributed to the effect of the task. As shown by bold arrows of Fig. 2 (c), there are some directed edges appear during the task and remaining connected after the task. Also, as shown by dashed arrows, there are certain edges in common with pre- and post-task period, which are regarded to be irrelevant to the task. Structural changes in neural networks can be captured by the proposed method, and we expect it serves as a useful method for analysing the neural state and behaviour in electrophysiological studies.

6   Conclusion

In this paper, we proposed a method for estimating graph structures using dependency between nodes. Since only intrinsic connectivity of a graph is important in many cases, we simply represented a graph structure using an adjacency matrix, and modeled dependency between nodes using a probability matrix of transition on a graph characterized by a digraph Laplacian. In contrast to conventional approaches to graph structure estimation, the proposed method is applicable to estimate asymmetric graphs. As shown in the real-world experiment, it is able to capture an asymmetric structure.

When we apply the proposed method to graph structure estimation, the most important thing is how to define the observed matrix T characterizing the dependency of nodes. Further investigation will be needed for defining the observed matrix. The propose algorithm includes calculation of matrix logarithm, which prohibits application of the proposed method to large scale graph analysis. Improving computational efficiency is another direction of our future work.

References

1. Bunke, H., Riesen, K.: Recent advances in graph-based pattern recognition with applications in document analysis. Pattern Recognition 44(5), 1057–1067 (2011)
2. Conte, D., Foggia, P., Sansone, C., Vento, M.: Thirty years of graph matching in pattern recognition. International Journal of Pattern Recognition and Artificial Intelligence 18(3), 265–298 (2003)
3. Page, L., Brin, S., Motowani, R., Winograd, T.: PageRank citation ranking: Bring order to the web. Stanford Digital Library Working Paper (1997)
4. Friedman, J., Hastie, T., Tibshirani, R.: Sparse inverse covariance estimation with the graphical lasso. Biostatistics 9(3), 432–441 (2007)
5. Dempster, A.: Covariance selection. Biometrics 28, 157–175 (1972)
6. Li, Y., Zhang, Z.-L.: Random Walks on Digraphs, the Generalized Digraph Laplacian and the Degree of Asymmetry. In: Kumar, R., Sivakumar, D. (eds.) WAW 2010. LNCS, vol. 6516, pp. 74–85. Springer, Heidelberg (2010)
7. Higham, N.J.: Functions of Matrices: Theory and Computation. Society for Industrial and Applied Mathematics, Philadelphia (2008)
8. Lagarias, J., Reeds, J., Wright, M., Wright, P.: Convergence Properties of the Nelder-Mead Simplex Method in Low Dimensions. SIAM Journal on Optimization 9(1), 112–147 (1998)
9. Tatsuno, M., Lipa, P., McNaughton, B.L.: Methodological considerations on the use of template matching to study long-lasting memory trace replay. Journal of Neuroscience 26(42), 10727–10742 (2006)

Merging Strategy for Local Model Networks Based on the Lolimot Algorithm

Torsten Fischer and Oliver Nelles

University Siegen, Department of Mechanical Engineering,
Paul-Bonatz-Strasse 9-11, 57068 Siegen, Germany
{torsten.fischer,oliver.nelles}@uni-siegen.de
http://www.mb.uni-siegen.de/mrt

Abstract. In this paper an extension of the established training algorithm for nonlinear system identification called LOLIMOT is presented [9]. It is a heuristic tree-construction method that trains a local linear neuro-fuzzy network. Due to its very simple partitioning strategy, LOLIMOT is a fast and robust modeling approach, but has a limited flexibility. Therefore a new merging approach for regression tasks is presented, that can rearrange the local model structure in the input space, without harming the global model complexity.

1 Introduction

The experimental model design, called identification, has become increasingly important as an active research area during the recent years. In the field of identification neural networks and fuzzy systems are common methods. A structure based on these ideas are local linear neuro-fuzzy models. The well-known incremental tree-construction algorithm called LOLIMOT (**LO**cal **LI**near **MO**del **T**ree) [9,11] trains such a local model network. The algorithm introduced in this paper tries to increase the flexibility of this algorithm. Therefore a "merging" step is added to the training strategy, which enables the method to replace two similar, adjoined local models by one single model. In combination with the splitting procedure of the standard LOLIMOT the new approach achieves the ability to rearrange the validity regions of the local models within one complexity level.

2 Local Model Networks

The general principle of a local model network is shown in Fig. 1, see [9]. In a local model network every neuron consists of two parts. The first one is a local model LM_i, that describes the process behavior in a certain local area $\hat{y}_i$. The second part is called validity function Φ_i. These validity functions defines the local area where the corresponding local model is valid. Therefore the model output $\hat{y}$ with p inputs $\underline{u} = [u_1, u_2, \ldots, u_p]^T$ is a superposition of M weighted local models, respectively M neurons. In terms of fuzzy logic Fig. 1 can be interpreted as M fuzzy rules. The validity functions Φ_i represent the rule premises and the local

S. Wermter et al. (Eds.): ICANN 2014, LNCS 8681, pp. 153–160, 2014.

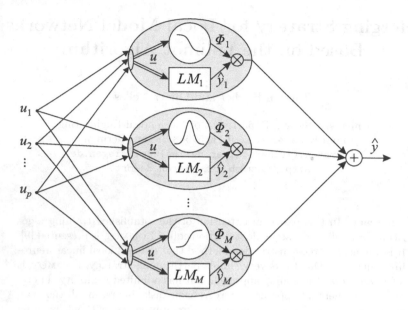

Fig. 1. Local model network (LMN): The outputs $\hat{y}_i$ of the local models (LM_i) are weighted by their validity functions Φ_i and sum up

model $\hat{y}_i$ are the associated rule consequents. To generate a smooth transition between the local model the validity function are smooth functions between 0 and 1. A reasonable interpretation of local model networks demands the use of validity functions that form a *partition of unity*. Thus, everywhere in the input space the contributions of all local models sum up to 100%. In general, the local model structure can be chosen arbitrarily. However, choosing a linearly parameterized model class, like polynomials, leads to a better result, if the their parameters are estimated from data. Besides the possibilities of transferring parts

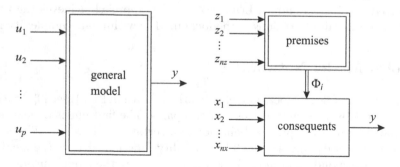

Fig. 2. The input vector $\underline{u}$ assigned to the nonlinear premise ($\underline{z}$) and/or the linear consequent ($\underline{x}$) input space

of mature linear theory to the nonlinear world, local linear models seem to represent a good trade-off between the required number of local models and the complexity of the local models themselves. One of the great advantages of local model networks is that different input spaces for the validity functions and the local models can be chosen. In the fuzzy interpretation this means that the rule premises (IF) can operate on (partly) other variables than the rule consequents (THEN). Using independent input spaces the illustrated superposition in Fig. 1 leads to Eq. 1.

$$\hat{y} = \sum_{i=1}^{M} \hat{y}_i(\underline{x})\Phi_i(\underline{z}) . \tag{1}$$

Here the vector $\underline{z}$ is spanning the premise input space and the vector $\underline{x}$ is spanning the consequent input space, see Fig. 2. This feature enables the user to incorporate prior knowledge or gain information about the nonlinearity of the black-box model.

3 LOLIMOT

LOLIMOT stands for **LO**cal **LI**near **MO**del **T**ree. It is an incremental tree-construction algorithm, that trains a local model network by adding one new model in each iteration, see [9,11]. Choosing a reasonable partition of the premise input space is the most challenging part. It uses a heuristic search to avoid a time-consuming nonlinear optimization. Other algorithms like CART [2] or the ones from [7,12] also follows this strategy. LOLIMOT partitions the input space using axis-orthogonal splitting functions, which results in a structure of hyper rectangles. Here, the so called membership functions are orthogonal Gaussians. The center of each Gaussian is the center of the corresponding rectangle and its standard derivation is proportional to the size of this rectangle. These Gaussians are normalized in order to ensure a partition of unity, similar to a NRBF network. The trained net uses linear (more precise *affine*) models as rule conclusions. Their parameters can be easily estimated by a local least squares methods, if the validity functions are determined once. A local estimation approach is used due to the lower computational effort [9]. A typical partitioning done over the first four iterations of LOLIMOT is shown in Fig. 3. In each step the currently worst local model is divided and two new local models are estimated. The best split according to a quality criterion is finally chosen. Step by step the training algorithm follows the nonlinear process behavior until one of the user termination criterions is reached. Because of the flat structure the number of the local models and size of their validity areas are good indicators for the characteristics of the process and the model is easy to interpret. The regularization effect of the local estimation of the parameters and the use of the Akaike information criterion (AIC) for model complexity selection reliably avoid overfitting [3,9].

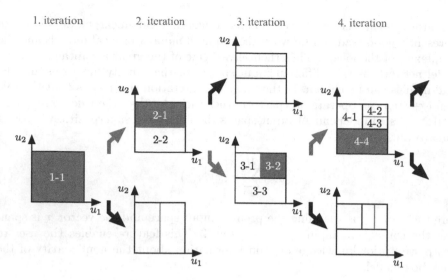

Fig. 3. Four typical iterations of the training algorithm LOLIMOT. In each step one new local model is added by deviding the currently worst local model.

4   LOLIMOT with Merging

Because the complexity of the global model increases moderately and the computational effort for each iteration is low, the LOLIMOT method can in general be used to train models for high-dimensional data sets. Avoiding a nonlinear optimization by a heuristic search, the algorithm is fast and easy to interpret but inflexible. Other algorithms like HILOMOT (**HI**erachical **LO**cal **MO**del **T**ree) [10] or product space clustering algorithms like Gustafson-Kessel [6] try to overcome this drawback by splitting the premise input space arbitrarily. Another problem is the greedy splitting strategy. During the training procedure some of the formerly made divisions may become suboptimal or even superfluous. By pruning these kind of splits, this drawback could be remedied. Research done in [9] shows that pruning leads to no essential improvement of the performance of the LOLIMOT-Algorithm. Another idea to overcome both drawbacks is merging similar local models. It leads to a higher flexibility without needing a computational expensive optimization. Research done in [4,5,8] shows the potential of the approach for a grid partitioned local model network and for a Gustafson-Kessel algorithm. The idea is to combine some validity functions into one area within the premise input space, if it leads to an improvement with respect to the used quality criterion. This merging step is added after the split. Figure 4 takes the best split of the the third and fourth iteration shown in Fig. 3 to illustrate the potential of merging. It allows the creation of very complex validity areas for each of the local models.

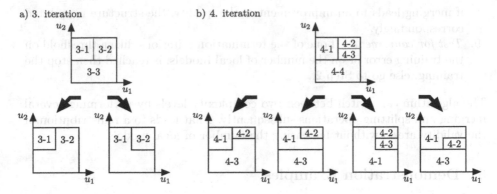

Fig. 4. Here the possible merging results are shown for (a) the third iteration and (b) the fourth iteration in Fig. 3. The algorithm does no simple pruning. A very complex area consisting of several Gaussians are possible for each local model, by combining any neighbored validity regions.

The LOLIMOT Algorithm with Merging

1. *Start with initial model:* Construct the validity functions for the initial input space partitioning and estimate the local model parameters. If no input space partitioning is available a priori then start with one single local model for the whole input space.
2. *Find Worst local model:* Calculate the local loss function for each local model and find the worst performing local model.
3. *Check all divisions:* Divide the worst local model orthogonally in each of the p dimensions of the z-space and estimate two new local models. Calculate the loss function for each global model structure.
4. *Find best devision:* Chose the best of the p splits according to the used quality criterion and update the structure.
5. *Find all possible merging partners:* Only adjoint Gaussians of the neighbored validity regions are allowed to be merged. This restriction guarantees that the local characteristic of each local model and its region remains. Therefore a good interpretability of the local model structure is ensured.
6. *Check all merging partners:* Combine each of them by summing up their validity functions: $\Phi(z)_{ij} = \Phi(z)_i + \Phi(z)_j$. Note that is does not matter whether the normalized or unnormalized Gaussians are added, because the sum of all Gaussians in the denominator used for normalization is equal. Estimate local models for the new validity areas and calculate the loss function for each global model structure.
7. *Find best merging result:* Select the best of the merging possibilities with respect to the used quality criterion.
8. *Test for improvement:* Only global models of the same complexity can be compared in a meaningful way. Therefore the merged model structures must be compared to the model structure before the best orthogonal split. Only

if merging leads to an improvement of the quality, the structure is updated correspondingly.

9. *Test for convergence:* If one of the termination criterions, like a threshold on the training error or on the number of local models, is reached then stop the training, else go to Step 2.

The algorithm can switch between two complexity levels by performing several merging and splitting operations subsequently. That leads to a redistribution of the validity areas, without increasing the number of local models.

5   Demonstration Examples

To illustrate the potential of the new approach a 2-dimensional Gaussian with the center $\underline{c} = [c_1, c_2] = [0.5, 0.5]$ and the standard deviation $\sigma = 0.125$, see Eq. 2, and the well known auto mpg data set for regression, see [1], are examined. For both regression examples a modeling with and without merging is done. All inputs $\underline{u}$ are used for the premise and consequent input space. Therefore the used model structure is an universal approximator [9].

$$y = \exp\left(-\frac{\left((u_1 - c_1)^2 + (u_2 - c_2)^2\right)}{2 \cdot \sigma}\right). \tag{2}$$

The loss function used to calculate the error values is the NRMSE (normalized root mean squared error). To guarantee comparable results for the Gaussian both methods train a global model with the same data set containing a 15 x 15 grid in the input space. A Gaussian white noise with standard deviation of 0.01 is added to the output. For testing, a noiseless data set with 200 uniformly distributed samples is used. The termination criterion is a training error of less than 15 %. The partitions are shown in Fig. 5. The standard LOLIMOT generates 14 local models to reach a training error of 13.4 % and a test error of 13.1 %. The new approach with merging achieves an identical training error of 13.4 % and a test error of 13.5 % with 7 local models. The extended algorithm needs half the local models to fulfill the demanded performance. The function quickly tends to zero with increasing distance to its center. Therefore the outer areas of the input space are actually flat. LOLIMOT captures this characteristic by 8 local models with similar parameters. The merging approach only needs one single local model to cover the flat area. Its partitioning illustrates the advantage of multiple Gaussians describing a validity area of one single local model. Merging possibly decreases the training error without increasing the number of local model. For a reasonable comparison of the performance on the auto mpg data set, it is divided into training (85%) and test data (15%). The test data is deterministically chosen to avoid extrapolation. Both algorithms train their LMN until all local models are locked, which is specified by an insufficient amount of data points for further splitting. The standard LOLIMOT reaches a training error of 24.82% and a test error of 32.45% within 25 iterations. The merging approach

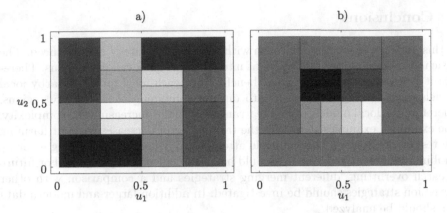

Fig. 5. Partitioning of the 2-dimensional Gaussian a) for the standard LOLIMOT and b) for LOLIMOT with merging. The different shades of grey signify different local models and thier validity areas. Each rectagular indicates one Gaussian.

needs one local model less to achieve a training error of 23.74% and a test error of 30.25%, which is a slightly better result. In Fig. 6 the training error is plotted over the model complexity to illustrate the behavior of the merging strategy for both examples. By switching back and forth between complexity levels in each iteration, a rearrangement of the validity areas is possible, as long as the loss function decreases. As the examples illustrate, the presented algorithm has the ability to reach an equal approximation quality within a smaller complexity level or achieves a lower error within the same complexity level.

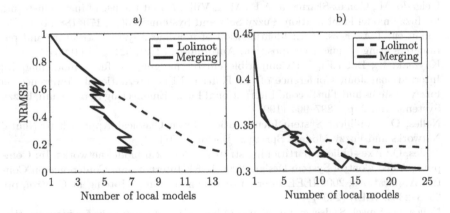

Fig. 6. NRMSE progression of the test error plotted over the number of local models for both examples: a) Gaussian and b) auto mpg data set. The merging approach shows the typical zig-zagging.

6 Conclusions

In this article a LOLIMOT approach with a merging strategy is introduced. The basic idea is combining the Gaussians into more complex validity regions. Therefore it is possible to gain a higher benefit from each local model. Nearby local models can be merged together into one by combining their validity regions. Therefore the local models can be rearranged, without increasing the complexity. The examined examples show that the training error decreases without harming the test error. However, the multiple attempts to decrease the training error by combining different local models, could harm the out-of-sample error. For future research overfitting, different merging strategies and a comparison with other regression strategies should be investigated. In addition larger and modern data sets should be analyzed.

References

1. Bache, K., Lichman, M.: UCI machine learning repository (2013)
2. Breiman, L., Stone, C.J., Friedman, J.H., Olshen, R.: Classification and Regression Trees. Chapman and Hall, Boca Raton (1984)
3. Burnham, K.P., Anderson, D.R.: Model Selection and Multimodel Inference: A Practical Information-Theoretic Approach. Springer, New York (2002)
4. Gasso, K., Mourot, G., Ragot, J.: Structure identification in multiple model representation: Elimination and merging of local models. In: Proceedings of the 40th IEEE Conference on Decision and Control, vol. 3, pp. 2992–2997 (2001)
5. Gasso, K., Mourot, G., Ragot, J.: Structure identification of multiple models with output error local models. In: Proceedings of 15th IFAC World Congress on Automatic Control, vol. M, pp. 151–156 (2002)
6. Delgado, M., Gómez-Skarmeta, A.F.: M.A. Villa. About the use of fuzzy clustering for fuzzy model identification. Fuzzy Sets and Systems 106(2), 179–188 (1999)
7. Johansen, T.A., Foss, B.A.: Identification of non-linear system structure and parameters using regime decomposition. Automatica 31(2), 321–326 (1995)
8. Kaymak, U., Babuska, R.: Compatible cluster merging for fuzzy modelling. In: International Joint Conference of the Fourth IEEE International Conference on Fuzzy Systems and The Second International Fuzzy Engineering Symposium, Fuzzy Systems, vol. 2, pp. 897–904 (1995)
9. Nelles, O.: Nonlinear System Identification: From Classical Approach to Neural Networks and Fuzzy Models. Springer, Berlin (2001)
10. Nelles, O.: Axes-oblique partitioning strategies for local model networks. In: Computer Aided Control System Design, 2006 IEEE International Conference on Control Applications, 2006 IEEE International Symposium on Intelligent Control, pp. 2378–2383. IEEE (2006)
11. Nelles, O., Sinsel, S., Isermann, R.: Local basis function networks for identification of a turbocharger. In: Control 1996, UKACC International Conference on (Conf. Publ. No. 427), vol. 1, pp. 7–12 (1996)
12. Sugeno, M., Kang, G.T.: Structure identification of fuzzy model. Fuzzy Sets and Systems 28(1), 15–33 (1988)

Factor Graph Inference Engine
on the SpiNNaker Neural Computing System

Indar Sugiarto and Jörg Conradt

Neuroscientific System Theory, Fakultät für Elektro- und Informationstechnik,
Technische Universität München, Germany
{indar.sugiarto,conradt}@tum.de

Abstract. This paper presents a novel method for implementing Factor Graphs in a SpiNNaker neural computing system. The SpiNNaker system provides resources for fine-grained parallelism, designed for implementing a distributed computing system. We present a framework which utilizes available SpiNNaker resources to implement a discrete Factor Graph: a powerful graphical model for probabilistic inference. Our framework allows mapping and routing a Factor Graph on the SpiNNaker hardware using SpiNNaker's event-based communication system. An example application of the proposed framework in a real-world robotics scenario is given and the result shows that the framework can handle computation of 26.14 MFLOPS only in 30.5ms. We demonstrate that the framework easily extends for larger Factor Graph networks in a bigger SpiN-Naker system, which makes it suitable for complex and challenging computational intelligence tasks.

Keywords: parallel distributed system, SpiNNaker, Factor Graph.

1   Introduction

A Factor Graph (FG) is a graphical model quite popular for probabilistic inferences. It is designed to complement already existing models such as Bayesian Network and Markov Random Field and it provides convenient mechanism to transform between those models [1] [2]. In probabilistic perspective, an FG is an appropriate model to represent factorization of joint as well as conditional probability. The standard FG is regarded as a bipartite graph since it is composed of two different types of node: variable nodes and factor nodes. To perform an exact inference on an FG (i.e. computing marginal probability), one usually uses belief propagation mechanism through message passing algorithm. FG is a powerful tool for probabilistic inference in many machine learning and signal processing applications [3].

The SpiNNaker (Spiking Neural Network Architecture) system is a distributed computing system designed to simulate spiking neural networks [4]. It is developed by the Advanced Processor Technologies Research Group (APT) at University of Manchester (UK). The SpiNNaker system is composed of many SpiNNaker chips in a torus network, which allows simulation of thousands of artificial neurons in real time.

S. Wermter et al. (Eds.): ICANN 2014, LNCS 8681, pp. 161–168, 2014.

Each chip is a multi-core system, consisting of 18 ARM968-based cores and also several internetworking elements and supporting modules. Comparing with the usage of a standard PC (or even a mainframe) for simulating spiking neural networks, the SpiNNaker system has several benefits such as smaller size and low power consumption. Hence it is a very promising platform for application in mobile robot.

This inference mechanism can be used to create control applications in robotics. Here we use our previous work on kinematic control of a mobile robot using FG as an example case for our new framework [8]. In an FG, each variable can represent a belief about a specific robot state and they exchange information by sending messages to each other for updating the overall belief. In this work, we implement an FG on a SpiNNaker system and demonstrate its promising performance especially when comparing its implementation on a standard computer (PC), as we belief that conventional PCs are particularly poor matched to instantiate such graphical networks. This paper will not describe in detail the FG performance for robot kinematic control since it has been presented in [8]; rather, we focus on the development of the embedded FG framework. Our contribution in this research is the SpiNNaker-FG framework. This SpiNNaker-FG framework is comparable to "PACMAN" [6], which is the framework for emulating spiking neural networks on a SpiNNaker hardware, in the sense that it provides mapping and configuration functionalities to FG-based applications implemented on a SpiNNaker system.

2   Design and Specifications

2.1   Design Consideration

Deploying a program on a dedicated hardware, especially the one with intrinsic parallelism, requires different treatments and explicit consideration [9][10]. The same challenge is also valid for our SpiNNaker-FG framework. Here we develop our framework with the following criteria.

- **Scalability** The framework should be able to work with a variable number of chips, allowing us to resize the networks.
- **Flexibility** The framework should be flexible enough to be reconfigured for many general purpose applications without too much modification in the framework.
- **Cross-boundary** The framework should be able to connect the separated elements of the factor graph seamlessly.

In the following sub-sections we will describe in more detail how we achieve such criteria in our proposed framework.

2.2   SpiNNaker Infrastructure

The SpiNNaker chip contains interconnected microcontrollers (ARM968) with a specific routing mechanism. This routing mechanism involves several modules inside the chip and a special look-up table which is maintained by a Packet Router. The key feature of this chip lays on this specialty; by properly configuring the Packet Router, the developer can create an efficient massively distributed computing system [5].

There are several communication protocols available for an application program. In this work, two of them will be used for developing the embedded FG: the neural event multicast (MC) and the SpiNNaker Datagram Protocol (SDP). The MC packets will be used for transferring "messages" between nodes and SDP packets will be used for communication between the FG in the SpiNNaker system and the host PC.

There are four elements that need to be specified in advance when implementing an FG on a SpiNNaker system: the SpiNNaker cores which handle the nodes (variable or factor nodes), the routing mechanism which transfers messages from node to node, the memory layout for vectors such as messages and local functions, and the converting mechanism between real-valued data to/from discrete probabilistic representation. In this work, we use a spiNN-3 board which consists of four SpiNNaker chips and develop the mapping and routing framework (we called it SpiNNaker-FG).

2.3   SpiNNaker-FG Building Block

There are two important aspects of an FG that require distributed computation. The first is the state distribution of input/output values and the second is sum-product computation of the message passing algorithm.

Neurons Population Mapping

In this work, following our previous work, we use population coding principle to discretize the input/output values [7]. For this discretization, the chip "0,0" (see Fig 1b, box colored in green) will be used. The rest of the chips will be used for distributing nodes and sum-product computing engine (see Fig 1b, boxes colored in pink).

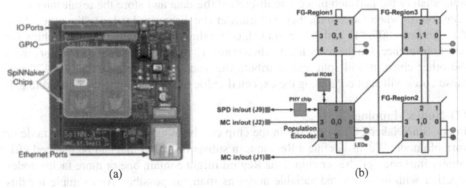

(a)   (b)

Fig. 1. The SpiNN-3 board (a) and its chips layout[1] (b). The chip "0,0" is chosen for population encoder since it has a direct Ethernet connection to the external system.

In the theory of population coding, a group of homogenous neurons will generate spikes in synchrony and produce a certain distribution specific for input stimuli.

---

[1] Adapted from "AppNote 1 – SpiNN-3 Development Board" by the SpiNNaker Group.

Although the SpiNNaker system is originally designed to emulate spiking neurons, but we don't use this emulation mechanism since we are not interested in neuron-by-neuron spike generation. Instead, our SpiNNaker-FG will only use SpiNNaker abundant resources to implement population coding principles over a fully connected homogenous networks as described in [7]. Fig 2 shows how the population coding with Gaussian response is mapped into SpiNNaker cores.

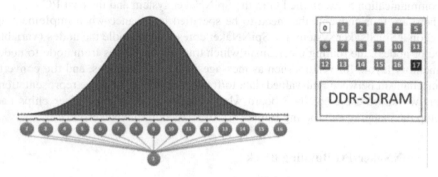

Fig. 2. Mapping neurons population into SpiNNaker cores in one chip (note: the white and the black cores is reserved for SpiNNaker kernel)

The mapping shown in Fig. 2 uses 15 cores and those cores are controlled by core "1" which also behaves as an I/O port for sending and receiving data to/from external devices (e.g. a robot or host PC) via SDP. Core "0" and "17" are used by the SpiN-Naker kernel for monitoring; both cores cannot be used by any application program.

When data comes from the external device, core "1" will distribute the data to the other cores (except to core "0" and "17") as MC packets and those cores will start immediately the partition process to discretize the data and store the result internally. Later on (or when requested), they will transfer the discretized value to the other chips through links "0", "1" and "2" in chip "0,0" so that it can be used by those chips for an FG inference. On the other hand, when core "1" receives a message (a vector) from the other chips, it will split and distribute the vector value to core "2" to "17" and those cores will start computing the expected value using mechanism explained in [7].

FG-Nodes Mapping

In our SpiNNaker-FG, every core in the chip can be assigned as either factor node or variable node. We also define a Region as a subset of an FG that can be mapped efficiently into one SpiNNaker chip. This Region might contain one or more factor nodes together with its associated variable nodes as many as possible. An example for this Region splitting is shown in Fig 3. The constraint of this design is that all associated variable nodes should reside in the same chip with its associated factor node as much as possible. The reasons is that we want to minimize the traffic overhead of "messages" in the Region and also for load balancing between cores. We also envision further improvement for this load distribution for our future work (see section 4).

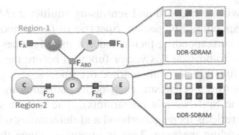

Fig. 3. Mapping Regions into SpiNNaker chips. The color illustrates node-core mapping.

In Region-1 in Fig. 3, the factor F_A and F_B only occupy one core each since these factors are essentially inputs for node A and node B in the case that node A and node B are observed. These factors also don't have a vector value but only '1' as its local function. However, the factor F_{ABD} occupies 10 cores since it is the only factor in the region which has a vast computation process of (2) due to its link to the three nodes. Also, the factor F_A and F_B could be assigned with the task of communication with the chip "0,0" (see Fig. 1b) to get the input as well as sending the message out to the chip "0,0" before sending it to the external system (e.g. the robot). The only computation that might be performed by A and B is the marginalization, hence we assign each node with only two cores. If the application doesn't require marginalization in node A and B, they can use only one core each. The local function of F_{ABD} will be stored in the internal SDRAM.

In Region-2, the node C and D also occupies two cores each since they might need to compute its marginal (however, if they don't, then they can be reduced to only one core each and assign the remaining cores to the more "busy" nodes). The node D, the factor F_{CD} and the factor F_{DE}, each occupy four cores since they compute messages product intensively. Same as in Region-1, the local function of F_{CD} and F_{DE} will be stored in the internal SDRAM of the chip. In the case of node D, it can be accessed in the following way. If Region-1 is placed on the chip "0,1" and Region-2 is placed on the chip "1,0" (see Fig. 1b), then the routing table for the output of F_{ABD} towards node D can be assigned with link "1" of the chip "0,1" and, correspondingly, the routing table for the input of node D from F_{ABD} must be assigned with link "4" of the chip.

2.4   Mapping and Routing Factor Graph in the SpiNNaker

An FG is a bipartite graph and it has two types of node: variable nodes and factor nodes. With this bipartite nature, using FG for inference in a message passing mechanism means that there will be two types of message: variable to factor node message (as expressed in (1)) and factor to variable node message (as expressed in (2)).

$$b(X_i) = \prod_{ne(X_i)} \mu_{f(X_i) \to X_i}(X_i) \tag{1}$$

$$b_F(X_F) = f_F(X_F) \prod_{ne(F)} \mu_{X_i \to f(X_i)}(X_i) \tag{2}$$

Those messages will be encoded and sent using multicast (MC) mechanism as the payload of the corresponding MC packet. Specific to factor nodes: the f_F in (2) is the local function of the corresponding factor node. It usually takes form as a vector in a discrete FG. We have to provide this vector function before the FG executes its inference and this vector function normally learned off-line.

Regarding this routing mechanism, each node maintains its table and registers it only once (due to the SpiNNaker's constraints). The node also has its own input-output matrix which reflects its neighborhood and determines which node has sent the message or has a pending message. This is important since the node computes the outgoing message only when all neighboring nodes have sent their messages.

3   Example Application

As the test case of our new SpiNNaker-FG, we use the scenario from our previous work [8]. In this example, an FG model for kinematic control of an omnidirectional mobile robot is developed. The task is to compute the correct robot command given the desired translational and rotational velocities. The model has been trained using data from a camera tracking system which provides the absolute pose of the robot. This example shall be viewed as a proof of concept which demonstrates a small subset of the features from our proposed SpiNNaker-FG framework.

The robot (see Fig 4a.) has three wheels and the complete FG model of the robot will involve at least 12 nodes. As explained in [8], the model is broken down into three similar networks and the kinematics model for each wheel is shown in Fig 4b. This also gives benefits such that it makes easier to fit the model into three Regions. The models are then implemented in the chip "0,1" for wheel-1, in the chip "1,0" for wheel-2, and in the chip "1,1" for wheel-3 (see Fig 1b).

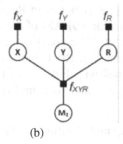

(a)   (b)

Fig. 4. Omnidirectional mobile robot which is used as a model. (b) The kinematics model for each wheel of the robot in (a) as one Region in FG.

We use maximum likelihood estimation (MLE) for training the network (e.g. updating the factor f_{XYR}). After the training has been completed, the vector value of the factor f_{XYR} is sent into the SpiNNaker system via SDP mechanism. To evaluate the performance of our embedded FG, we send the desired velocities of the robot (represented as factors f_X, f_Y and f_R in Fig. 4b) and observe the computed motor command by the model (represented as node M_2, which reflects the motor command for the second wheel of robot in Fig. 4a). We measure the time needed to complete one such inference to see how effective the proposed parallelism strategy is. The result is shown in Table 1.

Table 1. Execution time for a single run of inference

Number of States in a Node	15	30	45	60
Time (ms)	12.6	17.4	23.2	30.5

Although it is obvious that the number of node's states linearly influences the execution time, it is interesting to note that for the highest number of the states in the scenario, the system just needs 30.5ms to complete one full inference computation. Using 60 states, actually the system computes 26.14 MFLOPS for one complete cycle (from the discretization until the final message decoding); a very fast computation, especially when regarding the core speed which is only 150MHz and without any dedicated floating point unit. As a comparison, our previous work which uses standard PC with processor Intel i5 3.30GHz and memory 16GB DDR3 running at 1.3GHz, takes 5ms to complete one full inference computation. Also, the SpiNNaker-FG offers two additional important advantages:

1. The SpiNNaker version consumes much lower energy than the PC implementation.
2. If we increase the problem size such that Fig 4b is replicated three times using the remaining chips in the SpiNNaker board, for this particular example, the execution time in Table 1 remains the same; while in a PC, it needs three times.

These advantages show that our SpiNNaker-FG framework has very promising features for future real robotics applications.

4   Result and Discussion

This paper describes a new implementation strategy of a Factor Graph on a SpiNNaker neural computing system. In this work, we explore one possible configuration of a SpiNNaker chip as a Region. We fit the Region with arbitrary nodes and split the CPU cores accordingly. Another possible configuration which can increase the computational efficiency is by introducing a generic Region which only contains smaller number of nodes (e.g. three variable nodes and one factor node). This is similar with the idea of binary DAG used in [10]. For example, the network in Fig 4b can be decomposed into the network shown in Fig 5a. Although it will introduce hidden nodes which need to be learned beforehand, the sum-product algorithm will run faster due to smaller number of items to be processed by the algorithm. This is preferable for future implementation using a bigger SpiNNaker system.

Currently, we are also targeting the SpiNN-4 board which has 48 SpiNNaker chips (see Fig 5b). At this stage, we are still developing an application test case for which we can demonstrate the applicability of our SpiNNaker-FG framework in the more complex scenario using that massive SpiNNaker system. Also as an extension of the framework, we will be using our SpiNNaker interface board [9] so that we can use the SpiNNaker system in real time robotics control as a standalone application.

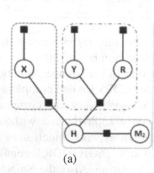
(a)

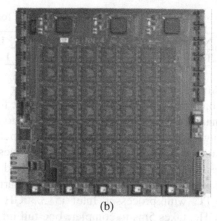
(b)

Fig. 5. (a) Decomposing network in Fig 4b into three Regions for better computational efficiency. (b) A Bigger SpiNNaker board which can be used for larger FG networks.

References

1. Kschischang, F.R., Frey, B.J., Loeliger, H.-A.: Factor Graphs and the Sum-Product Algorithm. IEEE Transactions on Information Theory 47(2), 498–519 (2001)
2. Frey, B.J.: Extending Factor Graphs so as to Unify Directed and Undirected Graphical Models. In: Proc. The 19th Conference on Uncertainty in Artificial Intelligence (2003)
3. Abbeel, P., Koller, D., Andrew, Y.N.: Learning Factor Graphs in Polynomial Time & Sample Complexity. In: Proc. the 21th Conference on Uncertainty in Artificial Intelligence, UAI 2005 (2005)
4. Khan, M., Lester, D., Plana, L.A., Rast, A., Jin, X., Painkras, E., Furber, S.B.: SpiNNaker: Mapping Neural Networks onto a Massively-Parallel Chip Multiprocessor. In: Proc. IEEE International Joint Conference on Neural Networks (IJCNN), pp. 2849–2856 (2008)
5. Plana, L.A., Bainbridge, J., Furber, S., Salisbury, S., Shi, Y., Wu, J.: An on-Chip and Inter-Chip Communications Network for the SpiNNaker Massively-Parallel Neural Net Simulator. In: Proc. 2nd ACM/IEEE NoCS, pp. 215–216. IEEE (2008)
6. Galluppi, F., Davies, S., Rast, A., Sharp, T., Plana, L.A., Furber, S.: A Hierarchical Configuration System for a Massively Parallel Neural Hardware Platform. In: Proc. 9th Conference of Computing Frontiers, pp. 183–192. ACM, New York (2012)
7. Sugiarto, I., Maier, P., Conradt, J.: Reasoning with discrete factor graph. In: Proc. International Conference on Robotics, Biomimetics, Intelligent Computational Systems 2013 (Robionetics), Yogyakarta, Indonesia (2013)
8. Sugiarto, I., Conradt, J.: Discrete belief propagation network using population coding and factor graph for kinematic control of a mobile robot. In: Proc. International Conference on Computational Intelligence and Cybernetics 2013 (Cyberneticscom 2013), Indonesia,
9. Denk, C., Llobet-Blandino, F., Galluppi, F., Plana, L., Furber, S., Conradt, J.: Real-Time Interface Board for Closed-Loop Robotic Tasks on the SpiNNaker Neural Computing System. In: Proc. International Conference on Artificial Neural Networks (ICANN), Sofia, Bulgaria, pp. 467–474 (2013)
10. Lin, M., Lebedev, I., Wawrzynek, J.: High-Throughput Bayesian Computing Machine with Reconfigurable Hardware. In: Proc. The 18th Annual ACM/SIGDA International Symposium on Field Programmable Gate Arrays (FPGA 210), Monterey, USA, pp. 73–82 (2010)

High-Dimensional Binary Pattern Classification
by Scalar Neural Network Tree

Vladimir Kryzhanovsky[1], Magomed Malsagov[1], Juan Antonio Clares Tomas[2],
and Irina Zhelavskaya[3]

[1] Scientific Research Institute for System Analysis, Russian Academy of Sciences, Russia
{Vladimir.Krizhanovsky,Magomed.Malsagov}@gmail.com
[2] Institute of Secondary Education: IES SANJE, Alcantarilla, Murcia, Spain
juanantonio.clares@murciaeduca.es
[3] Skolkovo Institute of Science and Technology, Moscow, Russia
irina.zhelavskaya@skolkovotech.ru

Abstract. The paper offers an algorithm (SNN-tree) that extends the binary tree
search algorithm so that it can deal with distorted input vectors. Perceptrons are
the tree nodes. The algorithm features an iterative solution search and stopping
criterion. Unlike the SNN-tree algorithm, popular methods (LSH, k-d tree,
BBF-tree, spill-tree) stop working as the dimensionality of the space grows
($N > 1000$). With such high dimensionality, our algorithm works 7 times faster
than the exhaustive search algorithm.

Keywords: Nearest neighbor searching, perceptron, search tree, hierarchical
classifier, multi-class classification.

1 Introduction

The paper considers the problem of nearest-neighbor search in a high-dimensionality
($N > 1000$) configuration space. The components of reference vectors take either +1
or -1 equiprobably, so the vectors are the same distance apart from each other and
distributed evenly. We measure the distance between two points with the Hamming
distance. In this case popular algorithms become either unreliable or computationally
infeasible.

We have investigated the following algorithms: k-dimensional trees (k-d trees) [1],
spill-trees [2], LSH (Locality-sensitive Hashing) [3]. We have found that the number
of computations with k-d trees for $N > 100$ is one or two orders of magnitude greater
than that of the exhaustive search (BBF-trees (best bin first) [4] were used). As dimensionality N grows, the error probability of the LSH algorithm approximates unit.
In the event when the working point coincides with a reference, the spill-tree algorithm works faster than the exhaustive search (by an order of magnitude), but slower
than the binary tree by approximately five orders of magnitude. The paper examines
the case when the distance between query point and reference one is greater than

S. Wermter et al. (Eds.): ICANN 2014, LNCS 8681, pp. 169–176, 2014.

0.1*N*. In these conditions the spill-tree algorithm is slower than the exhaustive search and thus its use makes no sense.

We offer a tree-like algorithm with perceptrons at tree nodes. Going down the tree is accompanied with the narrowing of the search area. The tree-walk continues until the stop criterion is satisfied. The algorithm is faster than the exhaustive search, even with growing dimensionality it still works faster (for example, with $N = 2048$, it is 7.5 times faster).

2   Problem Statement

The algorithm we offer tackles the following problem. Let there be M binary N-dimensional patterns:

$$\mathbf{X}_\mu \in R^N,\; x_{\mu i} = \{\pm 1\},\; \mu \in [1; M].$$

(1)

A binary vector $\mathbf{X}$ is an input of the system. It is necessary to find any reference vector $\mathbf{X}_\mu$ belonging to a predefined vicinity of input vector $\mathbf{X}$. In mathematical terms the condition looks like:

$$\forall \mathbf{X}_\mu : \mathbf{X}\mathbf{X}_\mu \ge (1 - 2b_{max})N,$$

(2)

where $b_{max} \in [0; 0.5)$ is a predefined constant that determines the size of the vicinity.

We will show below that from a statistical point of view the algorithm solves a more complex problem: it can find a pattern that is closest to an input vector. The Hemming distance is used to determine the closeness of vectors.

In this paper we consider the case when reference vectors are bipolar vectors generated in a random fashion. Generated independently of one another, the components of the reference vectors take +1 or -1 with equal probability (density coding).

3   The Point of the Algorithm

The idea of the algorithm is that the search area becomes consecutively smaller. In the beginning the whole set of patterns is divided into two nonoverlapping subsets. A subset that may contain an input vector is picked using the procedure described below. The subset is divided into another two nonoverlapping subsets, and a subset that may contain the input vector is chosen again. The procedure continues until each subset consists of a single pattern. Then the input vector is associated with one of the remaining patterns using the same procedure.

The division of the space into subsets and search for a set containing a particular vector can be quickly done by a simple perceptron with a "winner takes all" decision rule. Each set is controlled by a perceptron trained with the use of patterns of corresponding subset. Each output of the root perceptron points to a tree node of the next level. The perceptron of the descendant node is trained on a subset of patterns corresponding to one output of the root perceptron. The descent down a particular branch of the tree brings us to a pattern that can be regarded as a solution. At each stage of the descent we pick a branch that corresponds to the perceptron output with the highest signal. It is important to note that the same vector $\mathbf{X}$ is passed to each node rather than the result of work of the preceding-node perceptron.

4   The Process of Learning

Each node of the tree is trained independently on its own subset of reference points. A root perceptron of the tree is trained on all M patterns. Each descendent of a root node is trained on $M/2$ patterns. The nodes of the i-th layer are trained on $M/2^{i-1}$ patterns, $i = 1, 2, \ldots k; k = \log_2 M$ is the number of layers in the tree.

All nodes have the same structure – a single-layer perceptron [5] that has N input bipolar neurons and 2 output neurons each of which takes one of the three values $y_i \in \{-1, 0, +1\}$, $i = 1, 2$.

Let us consider the operation of one node using a root element as an example (all nodes are identical to each other). The Hebb rule is used to train the perceptron:

$$\hat{\mathbf{W}} = \sum_{\mu=1}^{M} \mathbf{Y}_\mu \mathbf{X}_\mu^T, \tag{3}$$

where $\hat{\mathbf{W}}$ is a $2 \times N$-matrix of synaptic coefficients, and $\mathbf{Y}_\mu$ is a two-dimensional vector that defines the required response of the perceptron to the μ-th reference vector $\mathbf{X}_\mu$. $\mathbf{Y}_\mu$ may take one of the following combinations: (-1,0), (+1,0), (0,-1), and (0,+1). If the first component of $\mathbf{Y}_\mu$ is nonzero, the reference vector $\mathbf{X}_\mu$ is assigned to the left branch. Otherwise, it is assigned to the right branch. Since the patterns are generated randomly (and therefore distributed evenly), the way they are divided into subsets is not important. So, when training the tree, the set of patterns is always divided into two equal portions corresponding to the left and right branches of the tree, so that the four possible values of $\mathbf{Y}_\mu$ should be distributed evenly among all patterns, i.e.

$$\sum_{\mu=1}^{M} \mathbf{Y}_\mu = 0.$$

The perceptron works in the following way. The signal on output neurons is first calculated:

$$\mathbf{h} = \hat{\mathbf{W}} \mathbf{X}. \tag{4}$$

Then the "winner takes all" criterion is used: a component of vector $\mathbf{h}$ with the largest absolute value is determined. If it is the first component, the reference vector should be sought for in the left branch, otherwise in the right branch.

The number of operations needed to train the whole tree is

$$\Theta = 2MN \log_2 M \ . \tag{5}$$

5   The Search Algorithm

Before we start describing the search algorithm, we should introduce a few notions concerning the algorithm.

Pool of losers. When vector X is presented to a perceptron, it produces certain signals at the outputs. An output that gives the largest signal is regarded as a winner, the others as losers. The pool of losers keeps the amplitude of the output-loser and the location of the corresponding node.

Pool of responses. After the algorithm comes to a solution (tree leaf), the number of a pattern associated with the leaf and the amplitude of the output signal of a perceptron corresponding to the solution are stored in the pool of responses. So each pattern has its leaf in the tree.

Search stopping criterion. If the algorithm comes to a tree leaf and the signal amplitude becomes greater than a threshold value, the search stops. It means that condition (2) holds.

Location of a node is a unique identifier of the node.

Descending the tree is going down from one node to another until the leaf is reached. The branching algorithm is as follows:

1. The input neurons of a perceptron associated with a current tree node are initiated by input vector **X**. Output signals of the perceptron h_L and h_R are calculated.
2. The output with a higher signal and the descendent node related to this output (descendent-winner) are determined. The signal amplitude of the loser output and location of the corresponding descendent-node are stored in the pool of losers.
3. If we reach a tree leaf, we go to step 5, otherwise to step 4.
4. Steps 1 to 4 are repeated for the descendent-winner.
5. The result is put in the pool of responses. At this point the branching algorithm stops.

Now we can formulate our algorithm. Process of descending different tree branches is repeated until the stopping criterion is met. The stages of the algorithm can be described as follows:

1. We descend the tree from the root node to a leaf. The pool of losers and pool of responses are filled in during the process.
2. We check the stopping criterion (2) for the leaf, i.e. we check if the scalar product of vector **X** and the pattern related to the leaf is greater than a predefined threshold. If the criterion is met, we go to step 4, otherwise to step 3.
3. If the criterion fails, we pick a node with the highest signal amplitude from the pool of losers and repeat steps 1 to 3 starting the descend from this node now.
4. We pick a pattern with the highest signal amplitude in the pool of responses, and regard it as a solution.

6   Example of the Algorithm Operation

Let us exemplify the operation of the algorithm. Figure 1 shows a step-by-step illustration of the algorithm for a tree built around eight patterns $(M = 8)$. Step 1: the tree root (node 0) receives input vector $\mathbf{X}$. The root perceptron generates signals h_L and h_R at its outputs. Let $|h_L| > |h_R|$, then h_R and the location of the descendant-node connected to the right output (node 2) are placed in the pool of losers. Step 2: vector $\mathbf{X}$ is fed to the node-winner (node 1). A winning node is determined again and the loser is put in the pool (e.g. h_{LL} and node 3). Step 3: after reaching leaves, we put patterns ($\mathbf{X}_3$ and $\mathbf{X}_4$) associated with the leaves and signal amplitudes $h_{LRL} = \mathbf{X}\mathbf{X}_3$ and $h_{LRR} = \mathbf{X}\mathbf{X}_4$ in the pool of responses. Then we find if the patterns meet criterion (2). In our case the criterion is not met, and the algorithm continues. Step 4: if neither pattern gives the solution, we pick the highest-signal node from the pool of losers (e.g. node 2 with signal h_R). Step 5: now the descent starts from this node (node 2) and goes on until we reach the leaves, the pool of losers taking new elements and pair $(h_R; 2)$ leaving the pool of losers. Here $|h_{RLL}| > |h_{RLR}|$ and $(1 - 2b_{\max})N < |h_{RLR}|$, i.e. criterion (2) is true for pattern $\mathbf{X}_6$. The pattern becomes the winner and the algorithm stops. If the criterion never works during the operation of the algorithm, the pattern from the pool of responses that has the highest signal amplitude is regarded as winner.

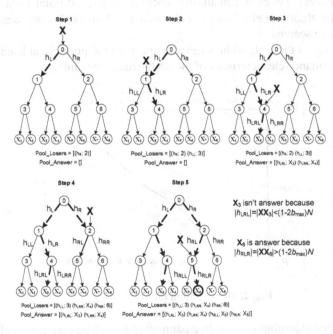

Fig. 1. An example of the algorithm operation

7   Results of Modeling

This section consists of two parts. First, we will discuss how the popular algorithms such as kd-tree (BBF-tree), spill-tree and LSH can tackle the problem. Then we will come to the results of the work of the proposed perceptron tree.

Our aim was to develop an algorithm capable of dealing with high-dimensional vectors, given the query point is the Hemming distance away from the nearest reference and the distance is greater than $0.1N$.

The recognition failure probability of the LSH algorithm grows quickly to 90% with the dimensionality and net load (the number of stored reference points). As long as the network loading is low $(M/N < 2)$, the LSH algorithm copes quite well with the problem (the error probability is nearly zero); however, it takes 80-100 times more computations than the exhaustive search. With higher loading the algorithm begins finding the solution 2-4 times faster than the exhaustive search does; yet the failure probability exceeds the acceptable value $(P_{err} < 1/M)$.

When $N > 100$, the kd-tree algorithm (specifically, a modification of the BBF-tree) works tens of times slower than the exhaustive search, so its use under the given conditions makes no sense.

When the request point is a reference point, the spill-tree algorithm demonstrates good results: it surpasses the exhaustive search in operation rate (the superiority grows with dimensionality and net loading, e.g. with $N = 2048$ and $M = 0.1N$-$4N$ it is 1.5-30 times faster). Yet even a small difference of the request point from a reference one impairs the algorithm efficiency – it shows a 1.5-2 times slowdown as compared to the exhaustive search.

It is clear that all these algorithms cannot cope with the problem at hand. So we go on to the performance characteristics of the SNN-tree algorithm.

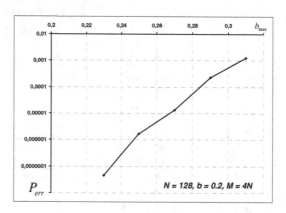

Fig. 2. The algorithm failure probability

The SNN-tree algorithm has one free parameter b_{max}. The parameter defines a distance range around a reference point, within which the query point can be located for the algorithm to recognize it (i.e. $b \le b_{max}$). Here b is an actual distance between the request point and the nearest reference. If $b > b_{max}$, criterion (2) never works and all tree branches have to be walked, i.e. the algorithm turns into exhaustive search with the number of scalar products twice as many. Malfunction of criterion (2) exponentially becomes less probable with decreasing b_{max}. So, it is not reasonable to increase b_{max} too much. Particularly, if the number of changed bits in input vectors are known to be less than 20%, it makes sense to set $b_{max} = 0.2$. Indeed, looking at Figure 2, we see that a small decrease of b_{max} (from 0.31 to 0.29) results in the chances of the algorithm malfunction falling by more than an order of magnitude. If we set $b_{max} = 0.2$, it becomes almost impossible to measure the algorithm failure probability experimentally (it would take a few months to compute it).

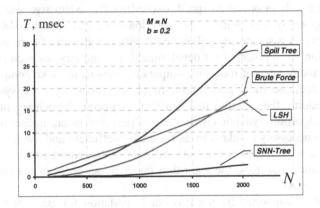

Fig. 3. Algorithms search time

Now let us evaluate the efficiency of the algorithm. The computational complexity of the SNN-tree grows slower with dimensionality than it does with other algorithms (Fig.3). It results in the SNN-tree proving to be the only functional algorithm at high dimensionality $\left(N = 10^5\right)$. In our experiment the error probability of the algorithm is not greater than 10^{-4} at $N = 128$ and approach zero with increasing dimensionality.

The attentive reader may note that the root node bears most of the load. For example, in the above-mentioned experiments the load of the root perceptron is much greater than $0.14N$ (the maximum load allowing the use of the Hebb rule). One may ask how well it actually works. The answer: it works badly – the chances that the root node picks a right branch are 57%. Yet, even such small advantage in favor of the right decision is enough to get the effective work of the whole tree because the reliability of the nodes grows exponentially as we descend the tree. This allows us to make the answer more exact step by step, and additional iterations can always correct the result in the case of the wrong choice.

8   Conclusion

The paper considers the problem of nearest-neighbor search in a high-dimensional configuration space. The use of most popular methods (kd-tree, spill-tree, BBF-tree, LSH) proved to be inefficient in this case. The equidistance of reference points between each other leads to the following conclusions:

- First, the principle of locality underlying the LSH algorithm, is violated, which results in the error probability increasing abruptly.
- Second, reference points are the Hemming distance of $0.5N$ away from each other. The sphere of such radius holds a half of available bins (with which the kd-tree algorithm operates), which finally leads to the necessity to try all reference points.

We have offered a tree-like algorithm that solves the given problem statistically. The algorithm excels in operation speed, exceeding the exhaustive search algorithm by up to 7 times on average (with the network load of 0.25 and $N = 2048$, $b = 0.2$, the gain is 22 times). This superiority will increase with the growth of dimensionality.

The algorithm has a potential for development. Preliminary research promises that an increase of the number of root-node outputs permits us to make computations less complex and decrease the algorithm malfunction probability. The system can be improved by adding the criterion that can stop erroneous branching. In the current version of the algorithm synaptic coefficients of perceptrons are integer numbers. For that reason it is necessary to take 4 bytes for each coefficient and use integer arithmetic. Going to binary synaptic coefficients will lessen the requirement for RAM by an order of magnitude and make the algorithm faster by an order of magnitude (due to use of bit operations).

The research is supported by the Russian Foundation for Basic Research (grant 12-07-00295 and 13-01-00504).

References

1. Friedman, J.H., Bentley, J.L., Finkel, R.A.: An algorithm for finding best matches in logarithmic expected time. ACM Transactions on Mathematical Software 3, 209–226 (1977)
2. Liu, T., Moore, A.W., Gray, A., Yang, K.: An Investigation of Practical Approximate Nearest Neighbor Algorithms. In: Proceeding of the Conference on Neural Information Processing Systems (2004)
3. Indyk, P., Motwani, R.: Approximate nearest neighbors: Towards removing the curse of dimensionality. In: Proc. 30th STOC, pp. 604–613 (1998)
4. Beis, J.S., Lowe, D.G.: Shape Indexing Using Approximate Nearest-Neighbour Search in High-Dimensional Spaces. In: Proceedings of IEEE Computer Society Conference on Computer Vision and Pattern Recognition, pp. 1000–1006 (1997)
5. Kryzhanovsky, B., Kryzhanovsky, V., Litinskii, L.: Machine Learning in Vector Models of Neural Networks. In: Koronacki, J., Raś, Z.W., Wierzchoń, S.T., Kacprzyk, J. (eds.) Advances in Machine Learning II. SCI, vol. 263, pp. 427–443. Springer, Heidelberg (2010)

Human Activity Recognition on Smartphones with Awareness of Basic Activities and Postural Transitions

Jorge-Luis Reyes-Ortiz[1,2,*], Luca Oneto[1], Alessandro Ghio[1], Albert Samá[2],
Davide Anguita[1], and Xavier Parra[2]

[1] DITEN – University of Genoa, Via Opera Pia 11A, Genova, 16145, Italy
{Luca.Oneto,Alessandro.Ghio,Davide.Anguita}@unige.it
[2] CETpD - Universitat Politècnica de Catalunya, Vilanova i la Geltrú 08800, Spain
Jorge.Luis.Reyes@estudiant.upc.edu, {Albert.Sama,Xavier.Parra}@upc.edu

Abstract. Postural Transitions (PTs) are transitory movements that describe the change of state from one static posture to another. In several Human Activity Recognition (HAR) systems, these transitions cannot be disregarded due to their noticeable incidence with respect to the duration of other Basic Activities (BAs). In this work, we propose an online smartphone-based HAR system which deals with the occurrence of postural transitions. If treated properly, the system accuracy improves by avoiding fluctuations in the classifier. The method consists of concurrently exploiting Support Vector Machines (SVMs) and temporal filters of activity probability estimations within a limited time window. We present the benefits of this approach through experiments over a HAR dataset which has been updated with PTs and made publicly available. We also show the new approach performs better than a previous baseline system, where PTs were not taken into account.

Keywords: Human Activity Recognition, Smartphones, Postural Transitions, Support Vector Machines, Temporal Filtering.

1 Introduction

Human Activity Recognition is nowadays an active research field which aims to understand human behavior through the interpretation of sensory information gathered from people and the environment they live in: this enables context-awareness, which allows emergence of more interactive and cognitive environments [7,4]. One of the mechanisms to obtain user-related activity information is through wearable sensors. With them, attributes for describing motion, location and physiological signals can be easily and directly collected from the user. However, sometimes they have the disadvantage being obtrusive and restrict

---

* This work was supported in part by the Erasmus Mundus Joint Doctorate in Interactive and Cognitive Environments, which is funded by the EACEA Agency of the European Commission under EMJD ICE FPA n 2010-0012.

S. Wermter et al. (Eds.): ICANN 2014, LNCS 8681, pp. 177–185, 2014.

user's movement. For this reason, the use of smartphones for wearable sensing is a interesting alternative that brings significant advantages: *a.)* These devices are already provided with embedded motion sensors (e.g. accelerometer, gyroscope, magnetometer, GPS, etc) that can be used for activity detection, and *b.)* People are nowadays familiarized and more comfortable with smartphones because they continuously interact with these devices throughout the day. These two aspects, combined with their computing characteristics and the possibility of collecting and distributing data, make them a exploitable tool for HAR.

In this work we present a novel smartphone-based online HAR system for the classification of activities, which takes into consideration the impact of PTs in the system performance. Most of the HAR approaches ignore transitions between activities because their occurrence is quite low and duration with respect to other activities is shorter [9]. Nevertheless, this assumption is application-dependent and does not apply in cases where various tasks need to be performed in a short time, such as in the development of monitoring systems for patients during reha-bilitation practices. In general, when PTs occur, an online system can manifest fluctuations in the classification as these states are unspecified and therefore re-duce its performance. To overcome this problem, we propose a method based on a multiclass Support Vector Machine (SVM) that performs activity probability estimations for each activity. Then, these estimations are interpreted as activity probability signals when combined with the predictions of previous samples, and finally they are heuristically filtered in order to improve classification accuracy during PTs. The proposed method is benchmarked against previous propositions (e.g. [1]). However, though various HAR datasets have been publicly distributed [13,14,5], only few publicly available HAR datasets include smartphone iner-tial data: therefore, in this paper, the authors contribute by introducing a HAR dataset for research purposes built from the recordings of people performing BAs and also PTs that occur in between them.

2 The HAR Dataset with Postural Transitions

PTs are events with a limited duration. They are characterized by start and end times which usually vary slightly from one person to another. Also, these events are bounded between other two activities and correspond to the transition pe-riod between them. Conversely, BAs, such as *standing* and *walking*, can prolong indefinitely. Data collection for these two types of activity is also different: PTs need to be executed repeatedly to get separate samples; instead, BAs are contin-uous, thus allow many (window) samples to be taken from a single test, limited only by its time extent.

This section contains a detailed description of the HAR dataset. In [1], we pre-sented a publicly available dataset ($\mathcal{D}_0$) for the classification of activities using data gathered from the smartphone inertial sensors, which was made available on the Internet [3]. We have updated this original approach in order to include PTs. The experiment was planned in order to contain six BAs: three static pos-tures (*standing, sitting, lying*) and three ambulation activities (*walking, walking downstairs and walking upstairs*). Moreover, it was arranged with the intention of having also available all the possible PTs that occur between the three existing static postures. These are: *stand-to-sit, sit-to-stand, sit-to-lie, lie-to-sit, stand-to-lie*, and *lie-to-stand*. We collected signals from the device's embedded triaxial accelerometer and gyroscope at a proper frequency to capture human body motion [7]. Signals were then synchronized with the experiment videos in order to use them as the ground-truth for manual labeling. Finally, the dataset was randomly partitioned into two groups (70% for training and 30% for testing purposes).

The updated dataset[1], from now on referred as $\mathcal{D}_1$, provides some relevant information regarding the duration of activities. By repeating twice each PT, the patients involved in the dataset creation allowed to derive a total of 60 labels for each PT, comprising a non-negligible 9% of the entire recorded time of the experimental data. In particular, PTs have an average duration of 3.73s $\pm$ 1.17 seconds, though this duration varies on each type of PT. We also found that inverse transitions such as *lie-to-sit* and *sit-to-lie* have different average durations. Moreover, some PTs can be described as the sequence of other two (e.g. *stand-to-lie* combines *stand-to-sit* and *sit-to-lie* PTs), as it can be observed on the experiment videos. In the particular case of *sit-to-stand* and *stand-to-sit* PTs, our finding matches the measurements of the average duration of these transitions performed by healthy patients in [10].

On the other hand, we found that the execution of the rest of activities (BAs) took longer times (17.3s $\pm$ 5.7 in average). This finding is important given that, in general, the execution time of activities in real life takes longer than PTs which have nearly-fixed duration. As a consequence, this helps us to define the heuristic rules to filter PTs in the proposed recognition system.

3   The Method

The entire recognition algorithm is composed of three modules. The first one (MOD1) comprises data acquisition and signal conditioning from the inertial sensors to obtain the features that characterize each activity sample. These features become the input of the prediction module (MOD2), *SVM with probability estimates*, where they are evaluated and, from each sample, the probabilities of belonging to each of the 6 BAs are estimated. These probabilities are then joined in the last module (MOD3) along with the predictions of previous activity window samples and processed by means of temporal filtering. This is achieved by applying a set of defined heuristic filters aiming to avoid fluctuations in the classification of BAs. These filters also introduce the *unknown activity* (UA) class when BA probabilities are marginal. Lastly, probabilities are used to define the most likely activity at a given time t. This is combined with further pruning of the discrete output through filtering using a rule-based approach. Algorithm 1 depicts the whole recognition process and its main modules are described as follows.

MOD1 takes as input the triaxial linear acceleration $a_{raw}(t)$ and angular velocity $\omega_{raw}(t)$ time signals. Signal conditioning consists of first applying noise

---

[1] The dataset is currently available at http://har.smartlab.ws.

Algorithm 1. HAR Method

Require: a: Triaxial linear acceleration, ω: Triaxial angular velocity, g: Gravity, $H_1(\cdot)$: Noise reduction transfer function, $H_2(\cdot)$: Body acceleration transfer function, $\phi(\cdot)$: Feature extraction function, T: Windows size, d: Number of classes, n: Buffer length, B: Buffer of probability vectors $B \in \mathbb{R}^{d \times n}$, B': Filtered buffer of probability vectors, z: Buffer of discrete activity predictions $z \in \mathbb{R}^n$, $\Phi(\cdot)$: Probability filtering function, $\Psi(\cdot)$: Discrete filtering function

function $(a(t), g(t), \omega(t)) = \texttt{ProcessInertialSignals}(a_{raw}(t), \omega_{raw}(t))$

$\quad a_{total}(t) = H_1(a_{raw}(t))$,   // Noise Filtering

$\quad \omega(t) = H_1(\omega_{raw}(t))$, $a(t) = H_2(a_{total}(t))$ // Body acceleration Extraction

$\quad g(t) = a_{total}(t) - a(t)$ // Gravity extraction

end

function $\alpha = \texttt{OnlinePrediction}(t, a(t), g(t), \omega(t), B, z)$

$\quad A = \{a(t')\}$, $G = \{g(t')\}$, $\Omega = \{\omega(t')\}$, $t' \in [t - T, \ldots, t]$ // Window sampling

$\quad x = \phi(A, G, \Omega)$ // Feature Extraction and Normalization

$\quad p = []$

$\quad$**for** $c \in \{1, \ldots, d\}$ **do**   // Multiclass SVM

$\quad\quad p = \left[p \mid 1 / \left(1 + e^{\left[\Gamma^c \left(w_c^T x + b_c \right) + \Delta^c \right]} \right) \right]$ // FFP with probability estimation

$\quad$**end**

$\quad B = \{ p^T \mid B(1 : end - 1, :) \}$ // Append probability vector

$\quad B' = \Phi(B)$ // Activity probability filtering

$\quad \hat{\theta}_{MAP} = \arg \max_{c \in [1, \ldots, d]} b'_{(n-1, c)}$ // MAP

$\quad z = \{ \hat{\theta}_{MAP} \mid z(1 : end - 1) \}$ // Append last activity prediction

$\quad \alpha = \Psi(z)$ // Discrete filtering and activity estimation

end

reduction filters (with transfer function is represented by $H_1()$). After that, clean triaxial acceleration $a_{total}(t)$ and angular velocity $\omega(t)$ signals are obtained. The acceleration signal is further processed and separated into body motion acceleration $a(t)$ and gravity $g(t)$. A detailed description of this module is described in [1].

The signal conditioning process is continuously executed over the inertial signals as represented in the *ProcessInertialSignals*() function in Algorithm 1. In addition, the *OnlinePrediction*() function is in charge of the recognition of activities and it is periodically executed to obtain and classify window samples (A, G, Ω) from the filtered inertial signals. Its periodicity satisfies the sliding-windows criteria: a time span of 2.56s and 50% overlap between them. Features are extracted from these window samples through measures in the time and frequency domain (represented by the function $\phi()$). They provide a collection of 561 informative features which has been selected based on previous works in the literature [1].

MOD2 consists of a set of 6 One-Vs-All (OVA) binary SVMs [6,12] which characterize each of the one studied activities. This algorithm is comprehensively described in [2]. In particular, if we consider a dataset composed of l patterns of pairs (x_i, y_i) $i \in \{1, \ldots, l\}$, $x_i \in \mathbb{R}^m$, and $y_i = \{\pm 1\}$, a binary SVM model can be identified by solving a Convex Constrained Quadratic Programming (CCQP) minimization problem:

$$\min_{\alpha} \frac{1}{2} \alpha^T Q \alpha - \mathbf{1}^T \alpha \qquad \text{s.t.} \quad \mathbf{0} \leq \alpha \leq C \quad y^T \alpha = 0 \qquad (1)$$

where the C hyperparameter is the regularization term and the matrix $Q \in \mathbb{R}^{l \times l}$ is defined such that $q_{ij} = y_i y_j x_i^T x_j$. The prediction of new patterns can be achieved with the SVM Feed Forward Phase (FFP) given by $f(x) = \sum_{i=1}^{l} y_i \alpha_i x_i^T x_j + b =$

$\boldsymbol{w}^T\boldsymbol{x} + b$, where the bias term b is obtained with the method proposed in [8]. As, in this case, we are dealing with a multiclass problem, for each binary classifier we have to compute probability estimates $p_c(\boldsymbol{x})$ which represent how likely is for a new sample pattern to be classified as a given class. For a given number of classes d and a test sample $\boldsymbol{x}$, the probability output of each SVM ($p_c(\boldsymbol{x}) \ \forall \, c \in [1, ..., d]$) is compared against the others to find the class c^* with the Maximum A–Posteriori Probability (MAP). Assuming that all the classes have the same a priori distribution then: $c^* = \arg\max_c p_c(\boldsymbol{x})$. The probability estimation method we employ was proposed by Platt in [11] and uses the predicted FFP output of the training set and its ground-truth label to fit a sigmoid function of the form: $p(\boldsymbol{x}) = \left(1 + e^{(\Gamma f(\boldsymbol{x}) + \Delta)}\right)^{-1}$, where Γ and Δ are the function parameters which optimal values can be found using the error minimization function:

$$\arg\min_{\Gamma, \Delta} \sum_{i=1}^{l} y_i \log p(\boldsymbol{x}_i) + (1 - y_i) \log(1 - p(\boldsymbol{x}_i)) \qquad (2)$$

The last module (MOD3) is composed of a series of filtering processes. The standard SVM classifier produces only a discrete output that indicates the class that best represents a test input (window sample). Moreover, this classifier is a static method which only depends on its input $\boldsymbol{x}$ and is not affected, for instance, by other factors such as previous samples or how probable the other activities are while running the FFP. Considering that in real world situations activities can be described as a sequence of correlated events, we take advantage of the SVM with probability estimates in a more extensive way. Indeed, the SVM probability predictions for all the activities $\boldsymbol{p} = \{p_1, \ldots, p_d\}$ can be interpreted as an activity probability signal in time when combined with the predicted output from previous samples. This assumption can improve the recognition system as we can exploit signal processing techniques, such as filtering, to make the overall classification performance more robust. We take into account aspects such as the interrelationship within activities and the fact that only one activity happens at a time (e.g. including transitions, which is one of our areas of interest). We have developed a set of heuristic filters to improve the probabilistic output of the SVM using temporal information from each prediction and its neighboring samples. This process is divided in two parts: *Probability Filtering*, which directly handles the probability signals, and *Discrete filtering* that further filters the activity output after the discretization of probabilities into activities.

For the first part, the implemented filters are a rule-based approach that uses as input the matrix of probability vectors B whose columns are the SVM predictions of the last n overlapped windows. The largest filter requires $n_{max} = 5$, which is equivalent to a prediction delay of 5.12s. They use probability thresholds to define whether a class is considered active (e.g. $p_c > threshold$) or to condition the filtering of an activity based on the value of other classes. $B' = \Phi(B)$ represents the application of the probability filters over the activity sequence. Two types of probability filters were used: the *Transition Filter* is aimed to remove peaks and transients of dynamic activities when they appear amongst static ones. This is applied to PTs as they exhibit a spiky behavior and usually take a short time (from

2 to 3 seconds): therefore this filter measures the length of the activation of these dynamic signals for a number of overlapping windows (maximum 3). The *Smoothing Filter* targets, on the other hand, the probability signals during the occurrence of BAs. It helps to stabilize signal fluctuations when their probability values are greater than a threshold (0.2) within the activity sequence. This is aimed to make evident, in a sequence of window samples, small differences between activities with high interclass misclassification e.g. *standing* and *sitting* or *walking* and *walking upstairs*. Oscillations are smoothed using a linear interpolation.

The second part (Discrete Filtering) defines the most likely activity for each window sample $\hat{\theta}_{MAP}$. This is done using MAP over the probability vector $b'_{(n-1,:)}$ of the filtered activity sequence matrix B'. It selects one of the classes as the predicted activity. However, sometimes it happens that all the probability values are low. This indicates that none of the classes seems to be representative of the current activity. For this, we have defined a minimum activity threshold which is used to label samples as undefined (UA) when none of the classes reaches this value. This is particularly useful when PTs occur as they are not learned by the SVM model. But in general, this approach can be beneficial in real life situations when the HAR system is used while activities outside the studied set occur. These will not be categorized as any of learned activities, instead the system will show that an unknown event has occurred. This filter removes sporadic activities that appear for a short time and are unlikely to happen for only a single window sample. It also includes cases when the UA is detected and its contiguous activities belong to the same class. The filter allows to relabel them as their neighbors. As a consequence, the final predicted activity is the result of this discrete filter $\alpha = \Psi(z)$, where z in the buffer containing the last 3 predicted activities $\hat{\theta}_i$.

4   Experimental Results and Discussions

To evaluate the error of the approach at runtime, some new considerations are required given that PTs are taken into account. The system is expected to avoid fluctuations or activity misclassifications during the occurrence of PTs, either by detecting a UA or by preserving the class of the activities adjacent to each PT. Therefore, in Table 1 we propose a new error assessment method for PTs and BAs. Notice that it considers all the possible activity combinations. Moreover, the selected metric also penalizes unwanted conditions in BAs such as the appearance of the UA class in the classification as these activities are learned in the SVM and should be correctly classified. To evaluate the performance of the new algorithm, we took the original offline HAR system presented in [1] as a reference point which is similar to the proposed method without temporal

Table 1. Classification error assessment. A = Activity, U = Unknown.

Basic Activities			Postural Transitions		
Ground-Truth	Prediction	Evaluation	Ground-Truth	Prediction	Evaluation
A1 - A1 - A1	A1 - A1 - A1	Correct	A1 - PT - A2	A1 - A1∨A2 - A2	Correct
A1 - A1 - A1	A1 - A2 - A1	Incorrect	A1 - PT - A2	A1 - A3 - A2	Incorrect
A1 - A1 - A1	A1 - UA - A1	Incorrect	A1 - PT - A2	A1 - UA - A2	Correct

activity filtering ($\Phi(\cdot)$ and $\Psi(\cdot)$). First of all, we learned the original dataset ($\mathcal{D}_0$) which only considered the 6 BAs and achieved a system error of 3.59%. Then, we applied the same procedure with the updated dataset ($\mathcal{D}_1$), the one with the labeled postural transitions, obtaining an error of 7.72%. This showed an increase of the system error by 4.13% percentage points mainly due to the misclassifications that occurred in PTs. This finding show how the first offline approach fails to work online when it is under a large number of transitory events such as PTs, that in the dataset cover nearly 9% of the data. Although this is a rather small portion, it is influential in the overall system performance.

Henceforth, we separately considered the effect of PTs and BAs in the system and work only with $\mathcal{D}_1$. Table 2 presents the the accumulated error of the HAR approach including intermediate stages of the processing. In this way, it is possible to have an idea how the different stages of the algorithm are progressively affecting the overall classification accuracy. The three stages are: No filtering or just the SVM output ($-$), Probability Filtering (Φ), and Discrete filtering (Φ, Ψ). Every row represents the stages of the algorithm and the columns the type of activity (BAs, PTs and Combined). From the table, it can be also noticed that the error without filtering is the highest achieved (7.72%). As we decompose this, we can also see that this is mainly due to a large error of 41.34% when classifying PTs. BAs instead remain much lower with a 4.46%. We can also observe that the temporal activity filters widely improve the classification of PTs reaching a minimum error of 5.77%. BAs instead improve only slightly after filtering. The final error achieved was 3.34% which is even lower that what we had obtained with offline approach and the dataset that did not take into account PTs.

In Table 2 we can find the confusion matrices of the system classification before ($\mathcal{C}_1$) and after ($\mathcal{C}_2$) activity temporal filters. For clarity, in the column of predictions of PTs we find true positives even if PTs are not predicted by the SVM: this is because we have relabeled as PT the samples correctly predicted based on the error metric we defined in Table 1 (e.g. predicted as UA or as an adjacent BA). In this way we make the confusion matrix still informative and preserve in its diagonal the correct classifications. Moreover, notice that $\mathcal{C}_2$ is not squared. The number of classes of the ground truth (7 rows: 6 BAs + 1 PT class which combines the 6 available PTs) differs from the number of predicted outputs where the UA was added. In this last column, we allocate the correct predictions of UA during PTs so they do not appear as misclassifications outside the diagonal. In these matrices it is also evident the effects of filtering in the system. For example, the number of false negatives for the PT class in $\mathcal{C}_1$ is quite large but reduced after temporal

Table 2. System error based on filtering stage, type of activity and confusion matrices before and after filtering

Filters	BAs	PTs	Overall
–	4.46%	41.34%	7.72%
Φ	3.45%	18.24%	4.76%
Φ, Ψ	3.10%	5.77%	3.34%

Filters Activity	$\mathcal{C}_1$: – WK	WU	WD	SI	ST	LD	PT	$\mathcal{C}_2$: $\Phi(\cdot), \Psi(\cdot)$ WK	WU	WD	SI	ST	LD	PT	UA
WK	542	0	3	1	0	0	0	545	0	0	0	0	0	0	1
WU	32	523	2	0	2	0	0	28	514	1	0	1	0	0	15
WD	3	4	498	0	4	0	0	0	0	505	0	3	0	0	1
SI	0	4	0	481	71	1	0	0	0	0	504	52	0	0	1
ST	3	3	0	18	588	0	0	0	1	0	1	610	0	0	0
LD	0	0	0	0	0	604	0	0	0	0	0	0	604	0	0
PT	12	101	1	18	4	0	193	0	10	0	9	0	0	310	0

filtering, in particular for the dynamic activities (e.g. in *walking upstairs*), which provide most of these misclassifications. It is also worth noting the reduction of interclass misclassifications between similar activities such as in the static postures *sitting* and *standing*, and also between *walking* and *walking upstairs*. Even the false negatives of the *standing* class produced by *sitting* misclassifications are nearly zero; however, the opposite case still preserves some errors.

References

1. Anguita, D., Ghio, A., Oneto, L., Parra, X., Reyes-Ortiz, J.L.: A public domain dataset for human activity recognition using smartphones. In: European Symposium on Artificial Neural Networks (2013)
2. Anguita, D., Ghio, A., Oneto, L., Parra, X., Reyes-Ortiz, J.L.: Energy Efficient Smartphone-Based Activity Recognition using Fixed-Point Arithmetic. Journal of Universal Computer Science 19, 1295–1314 (2013)
3. Bache, K., Lichman, M.: UCI machine learning repository (2013), http://archive.ics.uci.edu/ml
4. Bao, L., Intille, S.S.: Activity recognition from user-annotated acceleration data. In: Ferscha, A., Mattern, F. (eds.) PERVASIVE 2004. LNCS, vol. 3001, pp. 1–17. Springer, Heidelberg (2004)
5. Dernbach, S., Das, B., Krishnan, N., Thomas, B., Cook, D.: Simple and complex activity recognition through smart phones. In: International Conference on Intelligent Environments (2012)
6. Hsu, C.-W., Lin, C.-J.: A comparison of methods for multiclass support vector machines. EEE Transactions on Neural Networks 13, 415–425 (2002)
7. Karantonis, D.M., Narayanan, M.R., Mathie, M., Lovell, N.H., Celler, B.G.: Implementation of a real-time human movement classifier using a triaxial accelerometer for ambulatory monitoring. IEEE Transactions on Information Technology in Biomedicine 10, 156–167 (2006)
8. Keerthi, S.S., Shevade, S.K., Bhattacharyya, C., Murthy, K.R.K.: Improvements to platt's smo algorithm for svm classifier design. Neural Computation 13, 637–649 (2001)
9. Lara, O., Labrador, M.: A survey on human activity recognition using wearable sensors. IEEE Communications Surveys Tutorials 1, 1–18 (2012)
10. Najafi, B., Aminian, K., Loew, F., Blanc, Y., Robert, P.A.: Measurement of stand-sit and sit-stand transitions using a miniature gyroscope and its application in fall risk evaluation in the elderly. IEEE Transactions on Biomedical Engineering 49, 843–851 (2002)
11. Platt, J.C.: Probabilistic outputs for support vector machines and comparisons to regularized likelihood methods. In: Advances in Large Margin Classifiers (1999)
12. Rifkin, R., Klautau, A.: In defense of one-vs-all classification. Journal of Machine Learning Research 5, 101–141 (2004)
13. Roggen, D., Calatroni, A., Rossi, M., Holleczek, T., Förster, K., Tröster, G., Lukowicz, P., Bannach, D., Pirkl, G., Ferscha, A.: Collecting complex activity data sets in highly rich networked sensor environments. In: International Conference on Networked Sensing Systems 2010 (2010)
14. Tapia, E.M., Intille, S.S., Lopez, L., Larson, K.: The design of a portable kit of wireless sensors for naturalistic data collection. In: Fishkin, K.P., Schiele, B., Nixon, P., Quigley, A. (eds.) PERVASIVE 2006. LNCS, vol. 3968, pp. 117–134. Springer, Heidelberg (2006)

sNN-LDS: Spatio-temporal Non-negative Sparse Coding for Human Action Recognition

Thomas Guthier[1], Adrian Šošić[2], Volker Willert[1], and Julian Eggert[3]

[1] Control Theory and Robotics, TU Darmstadt, Landgraf-Georg Strasse 4, Darmstadt, Germany
[2] Signal Processing Group, TU Darmstadt, Merckstrasse 25, Darmstadt, Germany
[3] Honda Research Institute Europe, Carl-Legien Strasse 30, Offenbach, Germany

Abstract. Current state-of-the-art approaches for visual human action recognition focus on complex local spatio-temporal descriptors, while the spatio-temporal relations between the descriptors are discarded. These bag-of-features (BOF) based methods come with the disadvantage of limited descriptive power, because class-specific mid- and large-scale spatio-temporal information, such as body pose sequences, cannot be represented. To overcome this restriction, we propose sparse non-negative linear dynamical systems (sNN-LDS) as a dynamic, parts-based, spatio-temporal representation of local descriptors. We provide novel learning rules based on sparse non-negative matrix factorization (sNMF) to simultaneously learn both the parts as well as their transitions. On the challenging UCF-Sports dataset our sNN-LDS combined with simple local features is competitive with state-of-the-art BOF-SVM methods.

1 Introduction

Visual human action recognition is a vivid research topic where the goal is to classify various actions performed by humans in a video. Actions consist of temporal sequences of body poses; and single poses, such as standing, can be part of more than one action class, *e.g.* golfing or kicking. To robustly separate different action classes it is thus useful to encode the temporal relations in addition to static pose information.

Human actions are restricted by the human body structure, which reduces the space of possible poses significantly. However, human actions can vary in speed, intensity and individual performance, alongside with additional variations, such as different view points, scales and occlusions. Current approaches combine the ideas of local spatio-temporal histogram descriptors with *bag-of-features* (BOF) and *support vector machine* (SVM) classifiers [10,11,13,14]. Here, the spatio-temporal information is encoded in the local descriptors, which are typically restricted to 3D cubes around salient key points [13] or dense trajectories [14]. Each action video is then represented by its descriptors mapped onto a *codebook* that can be pre-learned *e.g.* with k-means clustering, sparse coding [3,11] or non-negative matrix factorization [4,5,10]. The main downside of the BOF-methods is that the spatio-temporal relations between the local descriptors are discarded. Consequently, all topological information as well as temporal relations between the descriptors are lost for the classification. Due to the local nature of the descriptors it is thus not possible to describe action specific body poses as an entity and subsequently, it is not possible to explicitly describe pose-sequences either.

S. Wermter et al. (Eds.): ICANN 2014, LNCS 8681, pp. 185–192, 2014.
© Springer International Publishing Switzerland 2014

In related work, *e.g.* [17] the inter-descriptor spatio-temporal relations are described by designed and locally bound contextual features. A similar approach, *i.e.* using designed relations, is proposed in [16].

Unlike the related approaches we do not hand design, but *learn* the spatio-temporal relations between the local descriptors and represent them as *sparse non-negative linear dynamical systems* (sNN-LDS). The local descriptors are grouped into a pooling block structure, similar to the complex cells of feed-forward-neural-networks. The spatial relations between the descriptors are thus encoded by their relative positions in the pooling block grid. The sNN-LDS models the input consisting of all descriptors of the grid by a linear superposition of local prototypical parts while the temporal relations between consecutive video frames are captured by the dynamics of the sNN-LDS.

In contrast to other learning algorithms, *e.g.* fused lasso [18] or [15], in our method both, the transition matrix $\mathcal{K}$, that defines the model dynamics, and the observation matrix $\mathcal{W}$, which consists of prototypical parts, are learned. We use fast and simple update rules based on *sparse non-negative matrix factorization* (sNMF) [8,9]. The algorithm can either be interpreted as incorporating non-negativity and sparsity constraints into high-dimensional linear dynamical systems or as an extension of sNMF with a novel transition component that models the temporal relations between the activations. The sparse and parts-based properties give rise to models that are more robust than holistic or designed models. Compared to classic BOF approaches, which make use of high-dimensional spatio-temporal relations *inside* a space-time-volume, we propose large scale spatial and temporal relations *between* simple low-dimensional local descriptors.

Next, we introduce the central part of our approach, the sNN-LDS algorithm. Thereafter, we describe our classification system for human action recognition based on the sNN-LDS and provide benchmark results on the Weizmann [1] and UCF-Sports datasets [2].

2   Sparse Non-negative Linear Dynamical System (sNN-LDS)

Desired properties of a learned model are: a) the ability to *explain the given data* and b) that it should *generalize to new data* while staying *class-specific*. This can be realized by *learning and representing* all relevant variations in one global model. In order to obtain such a representation we choose a dynamic, generative, linear and parts-based approach, because local parts tend to generalize better than holistic models, while the assumption of an underlying generative process guarantees the entire input to be represented. We achieve parts-basedness by combining the ideas of *sparse coding* [3] and *non-negative matrix factorization* (NMF) [5]. Non-negativity ensures that components can only be added, while sparsity prefers as few components as necessary, meaning that from the set of possible solutions those with few but meaningful parts are favoured. The temporal relations are modeled by the transitions between the activations of the parts.

2.1   sNN-LDS Model

A sNN-LDS is a generative model with non-negativity constraints on all model parameters that uses sparse activations for the encoding of the input. The model is depicted

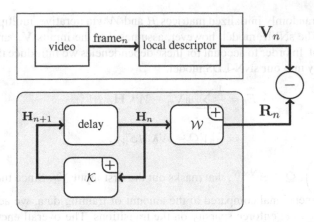

Fig. 1. The sNN-LDS (blue) works as a generative model whose internal state $\mathbf{H}_n$ is adapted so that the model output $\mathbf{R}_n$ resembles the observed descriptors $\mathbf{V}_n$

in Fig. 1. Given a set $\mathcal{V} \in \mathbb{R}^{X \times N}$ of input signals $\mathbf{V}_n \in \mathbb{R}^X$ ($X :=$ input dimension, $N :=$ number of inputs) the corresponding observation model or reconstruction $\mathbf{R}_n$ is given by a weighted sum of normalized basis vectors $\bar{\mathcal{W}} \in \mathbb{R}^{X \times J}$ ($J :=$ number of basis vectors), with $\bar{\mathbf{W}}_j = \frac{\mathbf{W}_j}{\|\mathbf{W}_j\|_2}$,

$$\mathbf{V}_n \approx \mathbf{R}_n = \sum_j h_{jn} \bar{\mathbf{W}}_j, \tag{1}$$

$$v_{xn}, h_{jn}, w_{xj} \geq 0, \quad \forall n \in [1, N], x \in [1, X], j \in [1, J]. \tag{2}$$

The weight or activation matrix $\mathcal{H} \in \mathbb{R}^{J \times N}$ consists of activation vectors $\mathbf{H}_n$. The system dynamics are represented by a non-negative linear transition model $\mathcal{K} \in \mathbb{R}^{J \times J}$ that encodes the relations between the activation vectors $\mathbf{H}_n$ and $\mathbf{H}_{n+1}$ of all consecutive inputs $\mathbf{V}_n$ and $\mathbf{V}_{n+1}$. The predicted activations are

$$\hat{h}_{jn} = \sum_l k_{jl} h_{ln-1}, \quad \forall n \in [2, N], j \in [1, J], \tag{3}$$

$$\hat{\mathcal{H}} = \mathcal{K}\mathcal{H}\mathcal{S}, \tag{4}$$

$$k_{jl} \geq 0, \quad \forall j \in [1, J], l \in [1, J], \tag{5}$$

with the shift matrix $\mathcal{S} = \begin{pmatrix} 0 & \mathcal{I} \\ 0 & 0 \end{pmatrix}, \mathcal{S} \in \mathbb{R}^{N \times N}$.

2.2 Learning the sNN-LDS Model

Our learning method is motivated by the sNMF learning algorithm. Here, the unknown model parameters $\mathcal{W}$ and $\mathcal{H}$ are learned by minimizing the reconstruction energy

$$E_r = \frac{1}{2}\|\mathcal{V} - \bar{\mathcal{W}}\mathcal{H}\|_F^2 + \lambda_H \|\mathcal{H}\|_1 \tag{6}$$

with respect to randomly initialized matrices $\mathcal{H}$ and $\mathcal{W}$ via iterative, multiplicative gradient descent. The sNMF model, however, assumes that the inputs $\mathbf{V}_n$ are conditionally independent. In order to account for these dependencies we introduce the following transition energy into our sNN-LDS model.

$$E_t = \frac{1}{2}\sum_{n=2} \|\mathbf{V}_n - \bar{\mathcal{W}}\mathcal{K}\mathbf{H}_{n-1}\|_2^2, \tag{7}$$

$$= \frac{1}{2}\|\mathcal{V}\mathcal{Q} - \bar{\mathcal{W}}\mathcal{K}\mathcal{H}\mathcal{S}\|_F^2, \tag{8}$$

with $\mathcal{Q} = \begin{pmatrix} 0 & 0 \\ 0 & \mathcal{I} \end{pmatrix}$, $\mathcal{Q} \in \mathbb{R}^{N \times N}$, that masks out the first input $\mathbf{V}_1$. Since the activations may be high-dimensional compared to the amount of training data, we add a regularization parameter, *i.e.* enforce sparsity on the transitions. The overall energy function of the sNN-LDS then becomes

$$E = \frac{1}{2}\|\mathcal{V} - \bar{\mathcal{W}}\mathcal{H}\|_F^2 + \frac{1}{2}\|\mathcal{V}\mathcal{Q} - \bar{\mathcal{W}}\mathcal{K}\mathcal{H}\mathcal{S}\|_F^2 \tag{9}$$
$$+ \lambda_H\|\mathcal{H}\|_1 + \lambda_{KS}\|\mathcal{K}\|_1.$$

Following the concept of sNMF, the unknown model parameters $\mathcal{W}$ and $\mathcal{K}$ as well as the activations $\mathcal{H}$ of the sNN-LDS are learned by minimizing the energy function (9) with respect to randomly initialized matrices $\mathcal{W}$, $\mathcal{K}$ and $\mathcal{H}$ via iterative, multiplicative gradient descent. The update rules are

$$\mathcal{H} \to \mathcal{H} \circ \frac{(\nabla_{\mathcal{H}}E)^-}{(\nabla_{\mathcal{H}}E)^+}, \tag{10}$$

$$\mathcal{W} \to \mathcal{W} \circ \frac{(\nabla_{\mathcal{W}}E)^-}{(\nabla_{\mathcal{W}}E)^+}, \tag{11}$$

$$\mathcal{K} \to \mathcal{K} \circ \frac{(\nabla_{\mathcal{K}}E)^-}{(\nabla_{\mathcal{K}}E)^+}, \tag{12}$$

where the positive and negative gradient components, including the inner derivative of the normalized basis vectors [9], are given as

$$(\nabla_{\mathcal{H}}E)^+ = \bar{\mathcal{W}}^\top\bar{\mathcal{W}}\mathcal{H} + \mathcal{K}^\top\bar{\mathcal{W}}^\top\bar{\mathcal{W}}\mathcal{K}\mathcal{H}\mathcal{S}\mathcal{S}^\top + \lambda_H, \tag{13}$$

$$(\nabla_{\mathcal{H}}E)^- = \bar{\mathcal{W}}^\top\mathcal{V} + \mathcal{K}^\top\bar{\mathcal{W}}^\top\mathcal{V}\mathcal{S}^\top, \tag{14}$$

$$(\nabla_{\bar{\mathcal{W}}}E)^+ = \bar{\mathcal{W}}\mathcal{H}\mathcal{H}^\top + \bar{\mathcal{W}}\mathcal{K}\mathcal{H}\mathcal{S}\mathcal{S}^\top\mathcal{H}^\top\mathcal{K}^\top, \tag{15}$$

$$(\nabla_{\bar{\mathcal{W}}}E)^- = \mathcal{V}\mathcal{H}^\top + \mathcal{V}\mathcal{Q}\mathcal{S}^\top\mathcal{H}^\top\mathcal{K}^\top, \tag{16}$$

$$(\nabla_{\mathcal{W}}E)^+ = (\nabla_{\bar{\mathcal{W}}}E)^+ + \bar{\mathcal{W}}\bar{\mathcal{W}}^\top(\nabla_{\bar{\mathcal{W}}}E)^-, \tag{17}$$

$$(\nabla_{\mathcal{W}}E)^- = (\nabla_{\bar{\mathcal{W}}}E)^- + \bar{\mathcal{W}}\bar{\mathcal{W}}^\top(\nabla_{\bar{\mathcal{W}}}E)^+, \tag{18}$$

$$(\nabla_{\mathcal{K}}E)^+ = \bar{\mathcal{W}}^\top\bar{\mathcal{W}}\mathcal{K}\mathcal{H}\mathcal{S}\mathcal{S}^\top\mathcal{H}^\top + \lambda_{KS}, \tag{19}$$

$$(\nabla_{\mathcal{K}}E)^- = \bar{\mathcal{W}}^\top\mathcal{V}\mathcal{Q}\mathcal{S}^\top\mathcal{H}^\top. \tag{20}$$

Throughout all experiments the input is normalized using the max-norm and the regularization parameters are set to $\lambda_H = 0.1$ and $\lambda_{KS} = 0.2$.

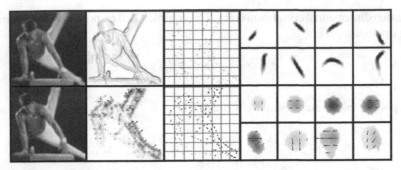

Fig. 2. Gradient and optical flow descriptors. Upper row from left to right: input image $\mathbf{I}_n$, gradient amplitude $\mathbf{V}_n^{(g)}$, simple cell response $\mathbf{S}_n^{(g)}$ with pooling cell structure and the eight learned gradient patterns $\mathcal{W}^{(g)}$ (scaled by factor 4). Lower row from left to right: input image $\mathbf{I}_{n+1}$, optical flow $\mathbf{V}_n^{(f)}$, simple cell response $\mathbf{S}_n^{(f)}$ with pooling cell structure and the eight learned optical flow patterns $\mathcal{W}^{(f)}$ (scaled by factor 4).

3   System Outline

In the following we explain how the sNN-LDS is included in our human action recognition algorithm. Similar to a BOF approach our algorithm consists of four components: 1.) Figure centric dense sampling, 2.) Calculation of local descriptors, 3.) Mapping local descriptors onto a sNN-LDS model and 4.) Frame-wise classification of the activations.

3.1   Figure Centric Dense Sampling

For each frame we cut out a window around the person whose action we want to classify and rescale it to a reference size of 128×128 pixels, resulting in a *figure centric* representation.[1] In this window we perform a dense sampling with 50% overlapping pooling blocks, each having a spatial resolution of 32×32 pixels which leads to $7 \cdot 7 = 49$ blocks. For all blocks we calculate low level features of gradient amplitudes and optical flow fields estimated using the algorithm described in [12].

3.2   Local Descriptors

For each pair of input images $\mathbf{I}_n$ and $\mathbf{I}_{n+1}$ the local descriptors are biologically inspired simple cell/complex cell descriptors of the gradient amplitude $\mathbf{V}_n^{(g)}$ and the optical flow field $\mathbf{V}_n^{(f)}$. To this end, a set of eight basic patterns is learned using the unsupervised learning algorithm described in [7]. The patterns and the simple cell responses are shown in Fig. 2. The simple cell response $s_{dn}^{(g)}, d \in [1, ..., 8]$ of the gradient patterns $\mathbf{W}_d^{(g)}$ for the input $\mathbf{V}_n^{(g)}$ is given by

$$s_{dn}^{(g)} = \mathrm{corr}_2(\mathbf{V}_n^{(g)}, \mathbf{W}_d^{(g)}), \tag{21}$$

---

[1] This step is currently performed manually but could be automized by a robust motion detector, *e.g.* [6], in future work.

with the two dimensional correlation corr$_2$. The complex cell response is an overlapping pooling operation

$$\hat{c}_{dn}^{(g)}(\mathbf{x}) = \sum_{\mathbf{y} \in A(\mathbf{x})} \mathbf{s}_{dn}^{(g)}(\mathbf{y}), \tag{22}$$

and the pooled values are subsequently binarized

$$c_{dn}^{(g)}(\mathbf{x}) = 1, \quad \text{if} \quad \hat{c}_{dn}^{(g)}(\mathbf{x}) > 0.2, \tag{23}$$

$$c_{dn}^{(g)}(\mathbf{x}) = 0, \quad \text{else.} \tag{24}$$

The same procedure is performed for the optical flow patterns. For each of the 49 blocks we get a local descriptor that contains the complex cell responses for all 16 basic patterns. The final dimension of the descriptor grid $\mathbf{V}_n$ is $D = 49 \cdot 16 = 784$ for each image. An input image $\mathbf{I}_n$ is therefore described by its local descriptor grid $\mathbf{V}_n \in \mathbb{R}^D$ and the spatial relations between the local descriptors are captured by the relative positions of the pooling blocks.

3.3   Learning the sNN-LDS

We combine the local descriptors of a batch of videos to create the input matrix $\mathcal{V}$, for which the parameters $\mathcal{W}$, $\mathcal{K}$ and $\mathcal{H}$ of a sNN-LDS are learned using the update rules in eq. (10), (11) and (12). After the model parameters are learned, $\mathcal{W}$ and $\mathcal{K}$ are fixed. For each new video, the activations $\mathcal{H}$ are calculated using eq. (10).

3.4   Frame-Wise Classification

Each frame $\mathbf{V}_n$ of an input video $\mathcal{V}$ is represented by the corresponding activation vector $\mathbf{H}_n$, which defines the current state of the sNN-LDS. Our sNN-LDS can thus be considered as a *codebook* for which the basis vectors $\mathcal{W}$ and the corresponding transitions $\mathcal{K}$ define the prototypical words, while the activations $\mathbf{H}_n$ represent the presence of the words in the current frame.

The feature vectors of the training videos and the mirrored version of the training videos are then used to train a soft-margin multiclass SVM with radial basis function kernels and class-weights that account for unbalanced training sets. All classification parameters are learned by 5-fold cross-validation on the training data. The classification of the test data is performed per frame and the video result is thereafter the weighted classification result of all its frames. The weighting factor for each frame and class is provided by the SVM classifier.

4   Classification Results

We evaluate how the sNN-LDS perform in leave-one-out experiments on the challenging 9-class UCF-Sports dataset and the 10-class Weizmann dataset. On the UCF-Sports dataset sequences of the same action, *e.g.* kicking, include karate kicks as well as soccer

Table 1. Classification results for leave-one-out experiments

	sNMF		sNN-LDS		Related Work		
J	50	100	50	100	[6]	[14]	[19]
Weizmann	0.98	0.99	0.99	**1.00**	**1.00**	-	-
UCF-Sports	0.88	0.87	0.90	**0.92**	-	0.89	0.90

kicks which differ strongly in their movements. The evaluation focuses on two aspects: First, the influence of the transition matrix $\mathcal{K}$, *i.e.* the difference between sNMF and sNN-LDS. Second, we compare the classification results for two different numbers of basis vectors J.

Table 1 shows the results for the different experiments on the UCF-Sports and Weizmann dataset. The sNN-LDS slighty outperforms the sNMF on the Weizmann datasets and by 2% on the UCF-Sports datasets, which shows that modeling the temporal relations improves the classification performance. Increasing the number of basis vectors J from 50 to 100 improves the results, but not as significantly as adding the temporal relations. Our algorithm outperforms the state-of-the-art algorithm proposed in [14]. However, as discussed in [19], we would expect their results to be competitive with ours when applied to the same figure-centric representation.

5   Summary and Discussion

We show that our generative sNN-LDS, which explicitly represents the spatio-temporal relations between the local descriptors, is a highly discriminative dynamical model that is well suited for, yet not restricted to, human action recognition. Due to its non-negative representation, learning rules from sNMF can be adapted to simultaneously learn all model parameters of the sNN-LDS.

Our experiments on the UCF-Sports dataset raise the following question: Are the large scale spatio-temporal relations *between* the local descriptors more important than complex spatio-temporal relation *inside* a local descriptor?

The sNN-LDS system slightly outperforms the BOF methods [14,19] by 2% even though the dimensionality of their highly sophisticated trajectory-descriptors [14] is as high as 396, while our local descriptors have only 16 dimensions. In addition, the dimensionality of our sNN-LDS is significantly smaller than the codebooks learned with k-means in *e.g.* [14,19], which typically consist of 4000 clusters, while we use only 100 basis vectors. Hence, we assume that the descriptive power of the sNN-LDS must come from the spatial and temporal relations between the simple local descriptors.

References

1. Blank, M., Gorelick, L., Shechtman, E., Irani, M., Basri, R.: Actions as Space-Time Shapes. In: IEEE Int. Conf. on Computer Vision, ICCV (2005)
2. Rodriguez, M.D., Ahmed, J., Shah, M.: Action MACH: A Spatio-temporal Maximum Average Correlation Height Filter for Action Recognition. In: IEEE Conf. on Computer Vision and Pattern Recognition, CVPR (2008)

3. Olshausen, B., Field, D.J.: Emergence of simple-cell receptive field properties by learning a sparse code for natural images. Nature 381, 607–609 (1996)
4. Paatero, P., Tapper, U.: Positive matrix factorization: A non-negative factor model with optimal utilization of error estimates of data values. Environmetrics 5(2), 111–126 (1994)
5. Lee, D.D., Seung, S.: Learning the parts of objects by non-negative matrix factorization. Nature 401, 788–791 (1999)
6. Tian, Y., Sukthankar, R., Shah, M.: Spatiotemporal Deformable Part Models for Action Detection. In: Int. Conf. on Computer Vision and Pattern Recognition, CVPR (2013)
7. Guthier, T., Eggert, J., Willert, V.: Unsupervised learning of motion patterns. In: European Symposium on Artificial Neural Networks, ESANN (2012)
8. Hoyer, P.O.: Non-negative sparse coding. IEEE Neural Networks for Signal Processing (2002)
9. Eggert, J., Koerner, E.: Sparse coding and NMF. In: IEEE Int. Joint Conf. on Neural Networks (IJCNN), vol. 4, pp. 2529–2533 (2004)
10. Amiri, S.M., Nasiopoulos, P., Leung, V.: Non-negative sparse coding for human action recognition. In: IEEE Int. Conf. on Image Processing, ICIP (2012)
11. Guha, T., Ward, R.K.: Learning sparse representations for human action recognition. IEEE Transactions on Pattern Analysis and Machine Intelligence 34(8), 1576–1588 (2012)
12. Guthier, T., Willert, V., Schnall, A., Kreuter, K., Eggert, J.: Non-negative sparse coding for motion extraction. In: IEEE Int. Joint Conf. on Neural Networks, IJCNN (2013)
13. Wang, H., Ullah, M.M., Klaser, A., Laptev, I., Schmid, C.: Evaluation of local spatio-temporal features for action recognition. In: British Machine Vision Conference, BMVC (2009)
14. Wang, H., Klaser, A., Schmid, C., Liu, C.L.: Dense trajectories and motion boundary descriptors for action recognition. International Journal of Computer Vision, 1–20 (2013)
15. Lakshminarayanan, B., Raich, R.: Non-negative matrix factorization for parameter estimation in hidden markov models. In: IEEE Int. Workshop on Machine Learning for Signal Processing, MLSP (2010)
16. Bilinski, P., Bremond, F.: Contextual statistics of space-time ordered features for human action recognition. In: IEEE Int. Conf. on Advanced Video and Signal-Based Surveillance (AVSS), pp. 228–233 (2012)
17. Wang, J., Chen, Z., Wu, Y.: Action recognition with multiscale spatio-temporal contexts. In: IEEE Conf. on Computer Vision and Pattern Recognition (CVPR), pp. 3185–3192 (2011)
18. Tibshirani, R., Saunders, M., Rosset, S., Zhu, J., Kneight, K.: Sparsity and smoothness via the fused lasso. Journal of the Royal Statistical Society: Series B (Statistical Methodology), 91–108 (2005)
19. Klaser, A., Marszałek, M., Laptev, I., Schmid, C., et al.: Will person detection help bag-of-features action recognition (2010)

Interactive Language Understanding with Multiple Timescale Recurrent Neural Networks

Stefan Heinrich and Stefan Wermter

University of Hamburg, Department of Informatics, Knowledge Technology
Vogt-Kölln-Straße 30, 22527 Hamburg, Germany
{heinrich,wermter}@informatik.uni-hamburg.de
http://www.informatik.uni-hamburg.de/WTM/

Abstract. Natural language processing in the human brain is complex and dynamic. Models for understanding, how the brain's architecture acquires language, need to take into account the temporal dynamics of verbal utterances as well as of action and visual embodied perception. We propose an architecture based on three Multiple Timescale Recurrent Neural Networks (MTRNNs) interlinked in a cell assembly that learns verbal utterances grounded in dynamic proprioceptive and visual information. Results show that the architecture is able to describe novel dynamic actions with correct novel utterances, and they also indicate that multi-modal integration allows for a disambiguation of concepts.

Keywords: Actions, Embodied, MTRNN, Language Acquisition.

1 Introduction

Natural language is the cognitive capability that clearly distinguishes humans from other living beings but is by far not yet understood. Methods in neuroscience to examine processes of natural language in the brain have evolved, but are mostly restricted to non-invasive external measurements. As a direct consequence, we have limited knowledge of the characteristics of natural language in terms of connectivity, plasticity, and temporal dynamics. On the other hand, we are able to build up analogies in neuro-robotic agents that are grounded in real world scenarios to study plausible characteristics [6,19].

Traditional generativist's theories for explaining language acquisition often fail to explain 'the how', because they leave out the evident involvement of modal embodiment and situated context, for example the close relation of language processing and motor action [3,12,15]. Recent constructivist's hypotheses aim to capture these characteristics, e.g. by grounding higher order symbols in action primitives and action primitives in sensory-motor experience [6,17,18]. Although these models help to understand how concepts can be bound to sensation, they are limited by the assumption of having a built-in lexicon of items on word level, not capturing the complex temporal dynamics in language.

In a recent study Hinoshita et al. claim that an "appropriate architecture is sufficient" for the emergence of language [11]. They state that information processing on different timescales in a *Multiple Timescale Recurrent Neural Network*

S. Wermter et al. (Eds.): ICANN 2014, LNCS 8681, pp. 193–200, 2014.

(MTRNN) can lead to the acquisition of language in a self-organised way. In our previous study we followed up on this approach and showed that a hierarchical structure with timescales and the embodiment of language in perception are important aspects of an appropriate architecture for language [9]. We demonstrated that our extended MTRNN is capable of generalisation in terms of describing novel perceived scenes with correct novel verbal utterances.

In this paper we scale up our architecture to multi-modal processing of proprioceptive and visual embodied perception, where information for all modalities is processed in similar recurrent network structures and are integrated in a cell assembly. We show that the architecture can generalise well for producing novel verbal utterances for novel dynamic visual and motor stimuli. Additionally, we analyse how embodied perception is processed and abstracted and how concepts for the respective scenes are formed in the cell assembly.

2   Multi-modal MTRNNs Model

In our approach we employ an MTRNN to process verbal utterances over time, extended by an MTRNN to process motor proprioception, an MTRNN to process visual perception, linked by a cell assembly of fully connected neurons that process and represent the concepts of the information [5]. Refining our previous extended MTRNN model [9], we aim at capturing the hierarchical structure found for action processes in the cortex [2] and account for cortical cell assemblies that interlink concepts in language, action, and perception [15]. In Fig. 1 we provide an overview of our proposed new architecture.

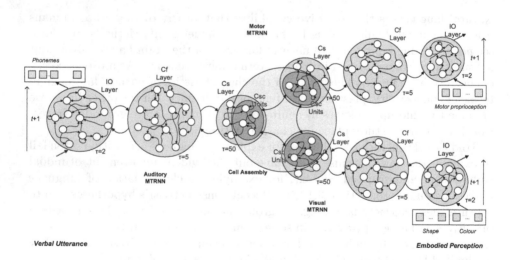

Fig. 1. Architecture of the multi-modal MTRNN model, consisting of MTRNNs for auditory, proprioceptive, and visual information processing as well as a cell assembly for representing and processing the concepts. A sequence of phonemes (utterance) is produced over time, based on sequences of embodied multi-modal perception.

The MTRNNs are each composed by an Input- and Output layer (IO) and two context layers called Context fast (Cf) and Context slow (Cs) [20]. Compared to other RNNs, the specific characteristic of an MTRNN is the full connectivity of neurons to all neurons of the same and of adjacent layers, and the mechanism of processing information with increasing timescales τ. The cell assembly interconnects these networks and integrates information processed over time.

Training

During training of the system, verbal utterances are presented together with sequences of the proprioceptive and visual stimuli of an action sequence. For the production of utterances, the auditory MTRNN self-organises the weights and also the internal states of some of the neurons in the Cs layer (denoted *Context Controlling units* (Csc)). In parallel, the motor MTRNN and the visual MTRNN self-organise the weights and also the internal states of the Csc units for the processing of an incoming perception. The important difference is that the auditory MTRNN self-organises towards the *initial* internal states of the Csc (start of utterance), while the motor MTRNN and the visual MTRNN self-organise towards the *final* internal states of the Csc (end of perception). Finally, the activity of the Csc units of all MTRNNs get associated in the cell assembly.

For the training of the auditory MTRNN we employ an adaptive mechanism, which is a variant of the *real-time backpropagation through time* (RTBPTT) algorithm [8]. Since we aim at an abstraction from the perception to concepts we modify the partial derivatives for the internal state z at time step t of neurons $i \in I_{all} = I_{IO} \cup I_{Cf} \cup I_{Cs}$ for the proprioceptive and visual MTRNN as follows:

$$\frac{\partial E}{\partial z_{t,i}} = \begin{cases} (1 - \psi) \, f'(y_{t,i}) \, (y_{t,i} - f(c_{T,i} + b_i)) & \text{iff } i \in I_{Csc} \wedge t = T \\ f'(y_{t,i}) \sum_{k \in I_{all}} \frac{w_{k,i}}{\tau_k} \frac{\partial E}{\partial z_{t+1,k}} + \left(1 - \frac{1}{\tau_i}\right) \frac{\partial E}{\partial z_{t+1,i}} & \text{otherwise} \end{cases},$$

$$(1)$$

where f and f' denote an arbitrary differentiable transfer function and its derivative respectively, b and w are the biases and weights, y denotes the neurons output, and $c_{T,i}$ are internal states at the final time step T of the Csc units $i \in I_{Csc} \subset I_{Cs}$. Here, we also introduce a very small *self-organisation-forcing* constant ψ that allows the final internal states $c_{T,i}$ of the Csc units to adapt upon the data, although they actually serve as a target for shaping the weights of the network. Accordingly, the final internal states $c_{T,i}$ of the Csc units define the abstraction of the input data and are also updated as follows:

$$c_{T,i}^{n+1} = c_{T,i} + \psi \zeta_i \frac{\partial E}{\partial c_{T,i}} = c_{T,i} + \psi \zeta_i \frac{1}{\tau_i} \frac{\partial E}{\partial z_{T,i}} \quad \text{iff } i \in I_{Csc} \quad , \qquad (2)$$

where ζ_i denotes the learning rates for the changes. Further formal descriptions of the MTRNN can be found in the work of Yamashita and Tani [20]. In our study we specify the timescale parameters as depicted in Fig. 1 based on previous studies [1,20] and our experiences [10]. The associations of the Csc units are trained with the conventional delta rule.

Generation

With a trained network the generation of novel verbal utterances from proprioception and visual input can be tested. The final Csc values of the respective MTRNNs are abstracted from the input sequences and associated with initial Csc values of the auditory MTRNN. These values in turn initiate the generation of a phoneme sequence.

3   Scenario

To understand and to approach a plausible architecture for the emergence of language, we believe it is crucial to ground the analysis in raw real world perception [7]. We therefore base the scenario in the interaction of a human teacher with a robotic learner that is supposed to acquire and ground language in embodied and situated experience. In particular a humanoid robot, NAO, should learn verbal utterances for manipulation actions of various objects to be able to describe novel actions with correct novel verbal utterances (Fig. 2c for an overview).

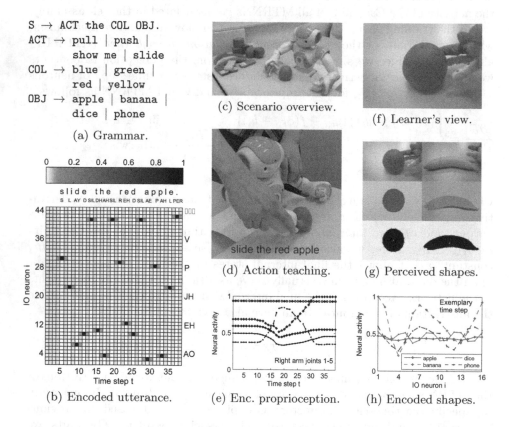

Fig. 2. Representations and scenario of language learning in human-robot interaction

For a given scene the teacher guides the robot's arm in an interaction with a coloured object and describes the action verbally, e.g. "SLIDE THE RED APPLE". Later, the robot should be able to describe a new interaction composed of motor movements and visual experience that it may have seen before with a verbal utterance, e.g. "SHOW ME THE YELLOW APPLE".

The scenario should be controllable in terms of combinatorial complexity and mechanical feasibility for the robot, but at the same time allow for valuable analysis. For this reason we limit the corpus of verbal utterances to a small grammar as summarised in Fig 2a. We use unambiguous utterances for four different actions that can be performed differently by the NAO and four different objects with similar mass but different shapes, each in four different colours.

To obtain a biologically-inspired auditory representation, we transform every sentence from the grammar to a phonetic utterance based on the ARPAbet with additional signs for pauses and intonation of propositions, exclamations, and questions: $\Sigma = \{$'AA', ..., 'ZH'$\} \cap \{$'SIL', 'PER', 'EXM', 'QUM'$\}$, $|\Sigma| = 44$. In the next step we encode the utterance $u = (p_1, \ldots, p_l)$ into neural activation over time, where the occurrence of a phoneme p_k is represented by a spike-like neural activity of a specific neuron i at relative time step r with some activity spreading backwards in time (rising phase) and some activity spreading forward in time (falling phase), represented as a Gaussian. A detailed description of the encoding and the used parameters can be found in [10] and [11]. The ideal neural activation for an encoded sample utterance is presented in Fig. 2b.

To gather and encode the proprioception of a corresponding action, we guide the NAO's right arm and directly measure the joint angles of five joints with a sampling rate of 20 frames per second and scale the values to $[0,1]$, based on the minimal and maximal joint positions (see Fig. 2d). Having an encoding on the joint angle level is biologically plausible, because the (human) brain merges information from joint receptors, muscle spindles, and tendon organs into a similar proprioception representation in the S1 area [4]. Fig. 2e shows the encoded proprioception for an exemplary action.

For the visual perception we aim at capturing a representation that is biologically plausible but on a level of abstraction of shapes as found in the *posterior infero-temporal* (PIT)/V4 area [14]. Specifically, we obtain the objects shape in NAO's field of view and capture 16 points around the object from which we determine the distance to the objects centre of mass divided by the area of the object, and scale to $[0, 1]$ for all shapes (see [10] for details). The measured shape features are invariant to rotation and scaling and capture the shape persistently over time. Additionally, we obtain the shape's colour by determining the average red, green, and blue values within the object's shape. With this method we encode the perception into a sequence of equal sampling rate and length compared to the proprioception sequence. Fig. 2f–h show the NAO's view, respective object perception, and representative differences in the encoding of the objects.

Generating novel utterances from a trained system by presenting new interactions only depends on the calculation time needed for the pre-processing and encoding, and can be done in real time. No additional training is needed.

4   Analysis

To learn from the model's characteristics we are interested in the generalisation capabilities and the information pattern that emerges in the cell assembly. We recorded the 64 different interactions four times each with the same verbal utterance and arm starting position but with slightly varying movements and object placements to collect a data set. We divided the data 50:50 into training and test set (all variants of a specific interaction are either in the training or in the test set only) and trained ten randomly initialised systems. We repeated this process ten times with different distributions of data in training and test set to arrive at 100 runs for analysis. The MTRNNs were parametrised as follows: the auditory MTRNN consisted of $|I_{Cf}| = 80$ and $|I_{Cs}| = 23$ neurons; the motor and visual MTRNNs were set up each with $|I_{Cf}| = 40$ and $|I_{Cs}| = 23$ neurons. The number of IO neurons in all three MTRNNs were based on the representations for utterances, proprioception, and visual perception and set to 44, 5, and 19 respectively, while the number of Csc units was set to $|I_{Csc}| = \lceil |I_{Cs}|/2 \rceil$. We initialised all weights in the interval $[-0.025, 0.025]$ as well as the initial Csc in the intervals $[-0.01, 0.01]$ (auditory MTRNN) and $[-1.0, 1.0]$ (motor and visual MTRNNs) and set the feedback rate $\varphi = 0.1$ for the auditory MTRNN as well as the self-organisation rate $\psi = 0.001$ for the motor and visual MTRNN.

Generalisation of Novel Interactions

The results of the experiment show that the system is able to generalise: We obtained an F_1-score of 0.984 on the training and 0.476 on the test set for the best network. Although training is hard and we rarely obtained perfect but not over-fitted systems on the training data, we observed a high precision (small number of false positives) with a lower to medial recall (not exact production of desired positives) on the test data. The errors made in production were mostly minor substitution errors (single wrong phonemes) and only rarely word errors. Also, we learned that the timescale values were not crucial, but that ideal sizes of the Cf and Cs layers depend on the complexity of the problem (compare [10]).

Using a self-organisation mechanism on the final initial Csc values for the motor and visual MTRNNs caused good abstraction from the perception for the described scenario and ψ value. We learned: to avoid that the cell assembly part does not converge well and produces activity for the auditory MTRNN leading to production of erroneous utterances (false positives or incomplete utterances) up to arbitrary phoneme babbling, the ψ should not be very small. To avoid that the MTRNNs contribute different patterns for the same interactions to the auditory MTRNN, due to premature convergence to the final Csc values, without appropriately self-organising the weights, the ψ should not be very large.

Self-organisation in the Cell Assembly

Across all experiments we observed diverse patterns in the internal states of the Csc units, but always found similar patterns in the respective modality for similar utterances or perceptions. A *principal component analysis* (PCA) on the

Csc values revealed that these patterns are not very distinct for motor movements but most distinct for visual perceptions (compare Fig. 3). However, different shapes have slightly different affordances for the same 'type' of movements (e.g. different wrist angles for sliding the banana or sliding the apple), which indicates that the cell assembly integrates the perception of the different shapes and the variances of the movements into a more distinct meaning for the auditory Csc.

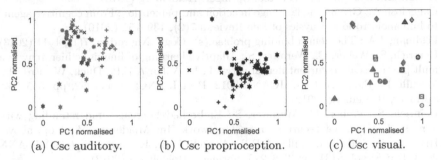

(a) Csc auditory.   (b) Csc proprioception.   (c) Csc visual.

Fig. 3. Internal state values of the Csc units for the initial (auditory) and final time step (motor and visual) reduced from $|I_{Csc}|$ to two dimensions (PC1 and PC2) and normalised. Different shapes/movements and colours are shown with different coloured markers. For Csc auditory the distinction between shapes has been omitted for clarity.

5   Conclusion

To learn the brain's architectural characteristics for language acquisition, we believe, it is crucial to enable an agent to a) acquire concepts from temporally dynamic and raw sensory input and b) base information processing on hierarchical abstraction and integration of all modalities. Neuroscientists suggested that temporal dynamics can be explained by synfire chains [16], however this level of detail would hinder an analysis to learn the key characteristics on cortex level and the models would be hard to test due to the complexity. Even with our RNN architecture, which consists of similar components for different modalities, training is very complex, due to a vast parameter space and a very deep network structure. This challenge is similar to deep NNs and ongoing research [13].

Our architecture reveals the importance of the suggested characteristics and shows that verbal utterances can be learned and grounded in dynamic multi-modal perception of actions, and can produce novel utterances for novel actions. The integration of multi-modal perceptions on concept level leads to a representation that disambiguates the meaning for proprioceptive and visual perceptions.

Acknowledgments. The authors would like to thank S. Magg and C. Weber for critical and inspiring discussions as well as G. Parisi and F. v. Stosch for support with the robot interaction data acquisition.

References

1. Alnajjar, F., Yamashita, Y., Tani, J.: The hierarchical and functional connectivity of higher-order cognitive mechanisms: neurorobotic model to investigate the stability and flexibility of working memory. Front. Neurorobotics 7(2), 13 (2013)

2. Badre, D., Kayser, A.S., D'Esposito, M.: Frontal cortex and the discovery of abstract action rules. Neuron. 66(2), 315–326 (2010)
3. Barsalou, L.W.: Grounded cognition. Annu. Rev. Psychol. 59, 617–645 (2008)
4. Bear, M.F., Connors, B.W., Paradiso, M.A.: Neuroscience: Exploring the Brain, 3rd edn. Lippincott Williams & Wilkins (2006)
5. Braitenberg, V.: Cell assemblies in the cerebral cortex. In: Theoretical Approaches to Complex Systems, pp. 171–188. Springer, Heidelberg (1978)
6. Cangelosi, A.: Grounding language in action and perception: From cognitive agents to humanoid robots. Physics of Life Reviews 7(2), 139–151 (2010)
7. Feldman, J.A.: The neural binding problem(s). Cogn. Neurodyn. 7(1), 1–11 (2013)
8. Heinrich, S., Weber, C., Wermter, S.: Adaptive learning of linguistic hierarchy in a multiple timescale recurrent neural network. In: Villa, A.E.P., Duch, W., Érdi, P., Masulli, F., Palm, G. (eds.) ICANN 2012, Part I. LNCS, vol. 7552, pp. 555–562. Springer, Heidelberg (2012)
9. Heinrich, S., Weber, C., Wermter, S.: Embodied language understanding with a multiple timescale recurrent neural network. In: Mladenov, V., Koprinkova-Hristova, P., Palm, G., Villa, A.E.P., Appollini, B., Kasabov, N. (eds.) ICANN 2013. LNCS, vol. 8131, pp. 216–223. Springer, Heidelberg (2013)
10. Heinrich, S., Magg, S., Wermter, S.: Analysing the multiple timescale recurrent neural network for embodied language understanding. In: Koprinkova-Hristova, P.D., Mladenov, V.M., Kasabov, N.K. (eds.) Artificial Neural Networks - Methods and Applications in Bio-/Neuroinformatics. SSBN, vol. 4, p. 26. Springer, Heidelberg (in press, 2014)
11. Hinoshita, W., Arie, H., Tani, J., Okuno, H.G., Ogata, T.: Emergence of hierarchical structure mirroring linguistic composition in a recurrent neural network. Neural Networks 24(4), 311–320 (2011)
12. Hoffmann, T., Trousdale, G. (eds.): The Oxford handbook of construction grammar. Oxford Univ. Press (2013)
13. Larochelle, H., Bengio, Y., Bengio, J., Lamblin, P.: Exploring strategies for training deep neural networks. The Journal of Machine Learning Research 10, 1–40 (2009)
14. Orban, G.A.: Higher order visual processing in macaque extrastriate cortex. Physiological Reviews 88(1), 59–89 (2008)
15. Pulvermüller, F., Moseley, R.L., Egorova, N., Shebani, Z., Boulenger, V.: Motor cognitionmotor semantics: Action perception theory of cognition and communication. Neuropsychologia, 28 (2013) (in press)
16. Pulvermüller, F., Shtyrov, Y.: Spatiotemporal signatures of large-scale synfire chains for speech processing as revealed by MEG. Cereb. Cortex 19(1), 79–88 (2009)
17. Roy, D., Mukherjee, N.: Towards situated speech understanding: Visual context priming of language models. Computer Speech and Language 19, 227–248 (2005)
18. Stramandinoli, F., Marocco, D., Cangelosi, A.: The grounding of higher order concepts in action and language: A cognitive robotics model. Neural Networks 32, 165–173 (2012)
19. Wermter, S., Page, M., Knowles, M., Gallese, V., Pulvermüller, F., Taylor, J.G.: Multimodal communication in animals, humans and robots: An introduction to perspectives in brain-inspired informatics. Neural Networks 22(2), 111–115 (2009)
20. Yamashita, Y., Tani, J.: Emergence of functional hierarchy in a multiple timescale neural network model: A humanoid robot experiment. PLoS Computational Biology 4(11), e1000220 (2008)

A Neural Dynamic Architecture Resolves Phrases about Spatial Relations in Visual Scenes

Mathis Richter*, Jonas Lins, Sebastian Schneegans, and Gregor Schöner

Institut für Neuroinformatik, Ruhr-Universität Bochum, 44870 Bochum, Germany
{mathis.richter,jonas.lins,sebastian.schneegans,
gregor.schoener}@ini.rub.de
http://www.ini.rub.de

Abstract. How spatial language, important to both cognitive science and robotics, is mapped to real-world scenes by neural processes is not understood. We present an autonomous neural dynamics that achieves this mapping flexibly. Neural activation fields represent and spatially transform perceptual information. An architecture of dynamic nodes interacts with these perceptual fields to instantiate categorical concepts. Discrete time processing steps emerge from instabilities of the time-continuous neural dynamics and are organized sequentially by these nodes. These steps include the attentional selection of individual objects in a scene, mapping locations to an object-centered reference frame, and evaluating matches to relational spatial terms. The architecture can respond to queries specified by setting the state of discrete nodes. It autonomously generates a response based on visual input about a scene.

Keywords: spatial language, sequence generation, autonomy, neural dynamics, Dynamic Field Theory.

1 Introduction

Spatial language helps point people to objects in the world. For instance, in Fig. 1 the kaki fruit can be singled out by asking "What kind of fruit is to the right of the lime?", while referring to its orange color would not have been sufficient. A relational spatial phrase like this consists of a target (the orange kaki), a reference (the green lime), and a relational term (to the right). Humans employ a series of processing steps when interpreting such a phrase [7] that include binding each object to its role, centering the reference frame on the reference object, mapping the relational term onto this frame, and assessing the match of the target object with the spatial term. These processes have been addressed in both psychological (e.g., [3]) and robotic contexts (e.g., [4]). Roboticists tend to use ad-hoc algorithms to organize the perceptual processing, while psychologists have

---

* The authors gratefully acknowledge the financial support of the European Union Seventh Framework Programme FP7-ICT-2009-6 under Grant Agreement no. 270247—NeuralDynamics.

S. Wermter et al. (Eds.): ICANN 2014, LNCS 8681, pp. 201–208, 2014.

Fig. 1. Visual scenario affording the use of spatial language

typically invoked concepts of information processing. A neural process account for how flexible spatial language may tie to perception is lacking to date.

The first challenge for such a neural approach is that spatial language involves two types of representation. A relational phrase consists of a set of amodal, discrete symbols, signifying reference object, target object, and the relational term. The referent of such a phrase, say the pair of objects in a visual scene, is provided in a modal, subsymbolic format. Resolving a spatial phrase consists of establishing a coherent mapping between these two types of representations. We address this challenge using Dynamic Field Theory (DFT) [12] in which neural population activity is described by activation fields, defined over metric feature dimensions, that evolve continuously in time through a neural dynamics. In DFT, modal representations are captured as dynamic neural fields, while amodal, categorical representations are modeled by activation nodes, that share the same neural dynamics. The shared dynamics and mutual coupling enable integrating modal and amodal representations.

People use spatial language flexibly, in that they are able to (1) direct their attention to an object guided by a relational phrase, (2) generate a relational phrase to describe a visual scene, and (3) answer questions about spatial relations between objects in a visual scene. These tasks differ in how much information is already provided in the phrase and how much must be extracted from the sensory representation. Achieving this flexibility is a second challenge for a neural account. This requires that the elementary processing steps must be recombined depending on the context. We address this problem by exploiting an analogy with a DFT-based approach to the autonomous generation of behavioral sequences [11,10]. In that approach, a neural representation of an *intention* activates the neural processes that execute the intention. A *condition of satisfaction* detects predicted changes in activation states that indicate that the processing steps have been successfully completed. A *condition of dissatisfaction* indicates failure to do so. Bifurcations of the neural dynamics create these events and trigger the transition to the next processing step.

We build on an earlier DFT model of spatial language [6] that provided the key processes for resolving spatial phrases, including the attentional selection of target and reference objects and the transformation of target locations into a frame centered on the reference object. The processing sequence was externally controlled in that earlier model, while we will demonstrate the emergence of the discrete steps from continuous neural dynamics here. The resulting neural architecture is able

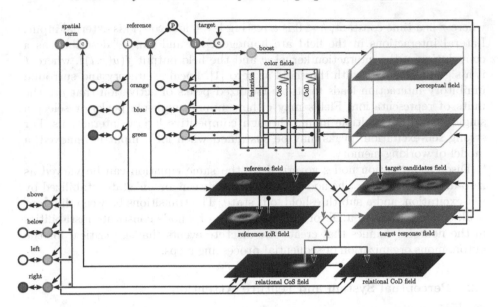

Fig. 2. Overview of the architecture, showing the activation state when answering the question "What is to the right of the green object?" on the scene in Fig. 1. On the right, dynamic fields are shown as color-coded activation patterns (blue for lowest, red for highest activation). On the left, dynamic nodes are denoted as circles with activation levels indicated by fill color opacity. The three-dimensional perceptual field is shown as slices through the activation pattern for the colors orange and green. Excitatory synaptic connections are denoted by arrows, inhibitory connections by lines ending in circles. Arrows marked with stars are patterned connections that encode concepts.

to autonomously resolve relational phrases and answer questions about real visual scenes.

2   Methods

The DFT architecture shown in Fig. 2 can be viewed as one integrated dynamical system, that combines coupled dynamics fields (DFs) supporting perception with coupled dynamic nodes that instantiate concepts and organize sequential processing.

2.1   Dynamic Fields and Dynamic Nodes

DFs can be thought of as a temporally and spatially continuous form of neural networks. Activation fields, $u(x,t)$, over a continuous feature dimension x (e.g., hue or spatial position) evolve over time t according to

$$\tau \dot{u}(x,t) = -u(x,t) + h + S(x,t) + \int f(u(x',t))\, w(x-x')\, dx',$$

where τ is a time constant, $h < 0$ is a resting level, and $S(x, t)$ is external input. Lateral interactions in the field are homogeneous and can be described as a convolution of the interaction kernel w and the field output $f(u(x, t))$, where f is a sigmoid function with threshold at zero [1]. Local excitatory and surround inhibitory interaction leads to stable localized peaks of activation that are the units of representation. Fields may either support multiple peaks or select a single peak from multiple inputs through competitive lateral interactions. For strong self-excitation, peaks may be sustained when local input is removed, a model of working memory.

Discrete activation nodes governed by the same equation can be viewed as zero-dimensional DFs. The nodes can switch between an 'on' state, stabilized by self-excitation, and a sub-threshold 'off' state. The transitions between different peak configurations in a DF or different states of a node constitute instabilities in the neural dynamics that create the discrete events that are critical for the autonomous organization of sequential processing steps.

2.2 Perceptual System and Feature Attention

The *perceptual field* (top right in Fig. 2) represents the current visual scene as a distribution of salient colors. Activation along two spatial and one color (hue) dimension is driven by input from a camera image. The perceptual field is coupled to three color fields (top middle in Fig. 2): In the *color intention field*, input from color nodes (explained below) induces a peak at the currently relevant hue value. That peak projects to the perceptual field where it enables peaks to form at locations in the scene that match this color. At the same time, it pre-activates the corresponding color value in the *color condition-of-satisfaction (CoS) field* and suppresses that value in the *color condition-of-dissatisfaction (CoD) field*. These two fields receive excitatory input also from the perceptual field. A match of the two inputs leads to a peak in the CoS field, a mismatch to a peak in the CoD field.

2.3 Representing Spatial Relations

The *reference field* holds the location of a single reference object, the *target candidates field* holds the locations of one or more potential targets. Both fields are defined over the two-dimensional space of the camera image and receive input from the perceptual field. The reference field drives the *reference inhibition-of-return (IoR) field*, in which all locations that have previously been selected are stored, sending back inhibition to the reference field.

The outputs of the target and reference field are combined in a coordinate transformation (blue diamond in Fig. 2), to determine the relative position of the target candidates with respect to the selected reference object. Neurally, this can be realized using a four-dimensional DF [6], but for performance reasons we use a convolution here. The result is fed into a pair of *relational fields*, organized as one CoS and one CoD field. In these fields, the match of the transformed locations with the relational term is evaluated based on a spatial template for that term that is provided to the two fields as additional input. The input is excitatory for the relational CoS field to detect a match and inhibitory for the relational CoD field to detect a mismatch. An inhibitory projection from the CoS to the CoD field ensures that only the CoS field forms a peak if both matching and mismatching target candidates are present. From the relational CoS field, a reverse transformation back into image coordinates (green diamond in Fig. 2) projects to the *target response field* using the stored location of the reference object.

2.4   Processing Spatial Phrases

Dynamic nodes represent concepts, here colors and spatial terms, in an amodal form. These concepts can fill different roles in a relational spatial expression, namely target object, reference object, and spatial relation. To realize role-filler binding, we employ conjunctive coding, such that a copy of each concept representation exists for every role it can take (e.g., 'target: red' and 'reference: red'). Each concept-role conjunction is represented by one pair of nodes, a *production node* and a *memory node* (purple and blue circles in Fig. 2). Reciprocal patterned connections between the production nodes and the perceptual feature spaces of different fields instantiate concepts. The connection weights encoding these concepts are handcoded here but should eventually be learned using neurally realistic methods. When the production nodes are activated, they induce specific activation patterns in the color intention field or the relational CoS and CoD fields. The memory nodes, coupled bidirectionally to their corresponding production nodes, remain active by self-excitation to encode a relational phrase while it is processed.

Production nodes are excited by their memory nodes, but become fully active only when receiving input from an additional set of nodes that control the sequential processing of a phrase. These nodes are organized in pairs of an *intention* and a *CoS* node (green and red circles in Fig. 2), with one such pair for each of the three roles in a relational phrase. The intention node for a specific role projects to all its production nodes and provides homogeneous input to fields associated with that role (e.g., the reference field). The corresponding CoS node in turn receives input from these fields and from the intention node. It is turned on when activation peaks form in the fields while the matching intention node is active. On activation, a CoS node suppresses its intention node. Which intention nodes can be active simultaneously is controlled by *precondition constraints* (black circles) which suppress the intention node of one role until the CoS node of another role becomes active.

3   Results

We illustrate the core functionality of the architecture by showing the dynamic processes that unfold when answering the question "What is to the right of the green object?" about the scene shown in Fig. 1. To simplify the visual object recognition, the scene consists of uniformly colored objects on a white background. We implemented and simulated the architecture in real time using *cedar* [8], an open source library for DFT.

The question is encoded by activating specific memory nodes, here 'reference: green' and 'spatial term: right of'. Since the question asks for information about the target object, we enable the architecture to provide homogeneous input to the perceptual field and the target production nodes when the intention node for the target object becomes active. We will now follow along Fig. 3, which shows how the activation patterns of the architecture evolve over time.

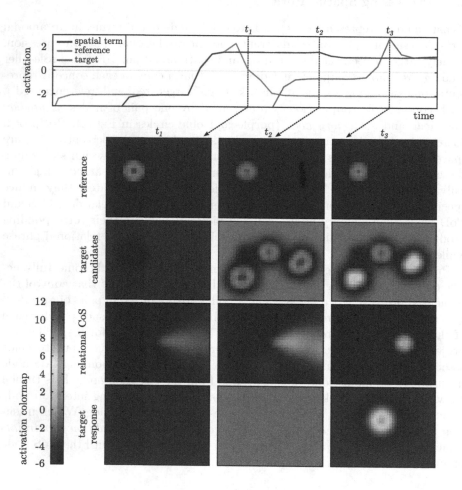

Fig. 3. Evolution of activation patterns for answering a question about the scene in Fig. 1. On top we show continuous activation time courses for the production nodes 'reference: green', 'target: orange', and 'spatial term: right of'. On the bottom, we show activation snapshots at three time steps for relevant fields using a color code (see colorbar; the threshold is at zero).

We initiate the processing by giving a task input that activates all intention nodes as well as the precondition node. The architecture works autonomously from this point on. The intention nodes for reference and spatial term become active, while the one for target is inhibited by the precondition node. The reference intention node boosts the reference field while the spatial term intention node boosts the relational CoS and CoD fields. Additionally, both intention nodes homogeneously boost their associated production nodes, activating those nodes that receive input from their respective memory nodes (i.e., 'reference: green' and 'spatial term: right of'). This can be seen by the green and blue curves rising above the treshold in Fig. 3. The production node for reference induces a peak at the color green in the color intention field. This brings green objects into the attentional foreground, forming a peak in the perceptual field at the location of the lime. That position is projected to the reference field, which is visible at time t_1 in Fig. 3. At the same time, the production node for the spatial term 'right of' projects activation into the relational CoS and CoD fields.

Having represented the position of the green lime in the reference field, the reference CoS node is activated, which deactivates the precondition node. This in turn enables the target intention node to become active, boosting the perceptual field and bringing all available objects into the target candidates field (in this field, the reference object is suppressed; see snapshot at t_2 in Fig. 3). The snapshot of the relational CoS field at the same time shows slightly elevated activation levels at the spatially transformed locations for the target candidates. One of the target candidates—the orange kaki to the right of the green lime— overlaps with the spatial template. This overlap leads to a peak in the relational CoS field, which is projected back to the image space in the target response field and from there into the perceptual field, highlighting the final target object (see snapshots of the target response and target candidates field at t_3 in Fig. 3). As a response to the question "What is to the right of the green object?", the architecture activates the production and memory node 'target: orange'.

4 Discussion

We have shown how autonomous processing of relational phrases can be achieved in a neural architecture. In particular, we have demonstrated how the architecture can identify target objects in a visual scene whose location is only indirectly specified via a reference object and a relational term. Due to lack of space we could only hint at further capabilities of the architecture. They emerge from its structure in a way analogous to the detailed example shown here. The architecture is, for instance, able to select a relational term as a response to a question and ground a complete relational phrase in perceptual representations.

We can extend the architecture to include other feature dimensions beyond color (e.g., shape), by adding one set of feature fields (i.e., perceptual, intention, CoS, and CoD fields) for each dimension.[1]

---

[1] Note, however, that this does not address the neurally plausible extraction of features from visual scenes, which is beyond the scope of the architecture.

Combining dynamic nodes and neural fields, the architecture connects to theoretical strands that stress the modal nature of mental processes [2] as well as to traditional, amodal views on cognition [9]. The architecture has the potential to generalize to non-spatial and abstract problems. This is based on evidence [5] suggesting a pervasive role of spatial representation in reasoning. With the current architecture, we have provided a first step toward connecting these ideas and thereby grounding mechanisms of higher cognition in neural reality.

References

1. Amari, S.I.: Dynamics of pattern formation in lateral-inhibition type neural fields. Biological Cybernetics 27(2), 77–87 (1977)
2. Barsalou, L.W.: Perceptual symbol systems. Behavioral and Brain Sciences 22(04), 577–660 (1999)
3. Carlson, L.A., Logan, G.D.: Attention and spatial language. In: Itti, L., Rees, G., Tsotsos, J.K. (eds.) Neurobiology of Attention, ch. 54, pp. 330–336. Elsevier Academic Press (2005)
4. Guadarrama, S., Riano, L., Golland, D., Gohring, D., Jia, Y., Klein, D., Abbeel, P., Darrell, T.: Grounding spatial relations for human-robot interaction. In: IEEE/RSJ International Conference on Intelligent Robots and Systems (2013)
5. Knauff, M.: Space to reason: A spatial theory of human thought. MIT Press, Cambridge (2013)
6. Lipinski, J., Schneegans, S., Sandamirskaya, Y., Spencer, J.P., Schöner, G.: A neurobehavioral model of flexible spatial language behaviors. Journal of Experimental Psychology. Learning, Memory, and Cognition 38(6) (2012)
7. Logan, G.D., Sadler, D.D.: A computational analysis of the apprehension of spatial relations. In: Bloom, P., Peterson, M., Nadel, L., Garrett, M. (eds.) Language and Space, ch. 13, pp. 493–529. MIT Press, Cambridge (1996)
8. Lomp, O., Zibner, S.K.U., Richter, M., Rañó, I., Schöner, G.: A software framework for cognition, embodiment, dynamics, and autonomy in robotics: cedar. In: Mladenov, V., Koprinkova-Hristova, P., Palm, G., Villa, A.E.P., Appollini, B., Kasabov, N. (eds.) ICANN 2013. LNCS, vol. 8131, pp. 475–482. Springer, Heidelberg (2013)
9. Pylyshyn, Z.W.: The imagery debate: Analogue media versus tacit knowledge. Psychological Review 88, 16–45 (1981)
10. Richter, M., Sandamirskaya, Y., Schöner, G.: A robotic architecture for action selection and behavioral organization inspired by human cognition. In: IEEE/RSJ International Conference on Intelligent Robots and Systems, pp. 2457–2464 (2012)
11. Sandamirskaya, Y., Schöner, G.: An embodied account of serial order: How instabilities drive sequence generation. Neural Networks 23(10), 1164–1179 (2010)
12. Schneegans, S., Schöner, G.: Dynamic field theory as a framework for understanding embodied cognition. In: Calvo, P., Gomila, T. (eds.) Handbook of Cognitive Science: An Embodied Approach. Perspectives on Cognitive Science, pp. 241–271. Elsevier (2008)

Chinese Image Character Recognition Using DNN and Machine Simulated Training Samples

Jinfeng Bai, Zhineng Chen, Bailan Feng, and Bo Xu*

Interactive Digital Media Technology Research Center,
Institute of Automation, Chinese Academy of Sciences, Beijing 100190, China
{jinfeng.bai,zhineng.chen,bailan.feng,xubo}@ia.ac.cn

Abstract. Inspired by the success of deep neural network (DNN) models in solving challenging visual problems, this paper studies the task of Chinese Image Character Recognition (ChnICR) by leveraging DNN model and huge machine simulated training samples. To generate the samples, clean machine born Chinese characters are extracted and are plus with common variations of image characters such as changes in size, font, boldness, shift and complex backgrounds, which in total produces over 28 million character images, covering the vast majority of occurrences of Chinese character in real life images. Based on these samples, a DNN training procedure is employed to learn the appropriate Chinese character recognizer, where the width and depth of DNN, and the volume of samples are empirically discussed. Parallel to this, a holistic Chinese image text recognition system is developed. Encouraging experimental results on text from 13 TV channels demonstrate the effectiveness of the learned recognizer, from which significant performance gains are observed compared to the baseline system.

Keywords: Chinese Image Character Recognition, Deep Neural Network, Image Text, Video Text.

1 Introduction

Image character recognition (ICR) aims to automatically recognize characters appearing in an image including scene characters and superimposed characters. It is an important yet very challenging task in the field of optical character recognition (OCR) and highly desirable for many real-world applications, such as image understanding and video summarization [1]. ICR is also quite different with two other classical tasks, namely document character recognition and handwriting character recognition, in OCR. ICR focuses on recognizing machine simulated characters appearing in natural scenes. In one hand, characters are usually composed of different locations, sizes, fonts, boldness, etc., and always are mixed with complex background. On the other hand, document character recognition focuses on recognizing characters appearing in scanned documental

* The work was supported by National Nature Science Foundation of China(grant No.61202326, No.61303175).

S. Wermter et al. (Eds.): ICANN 2014, LNCS 8681, pp. 209–216, 2014.

images, and handwriting character recognition focuses on recognizing handwritten characters. Both tasks are different from that of ICR.

ICR is a language-dependent task. Over the years many techniques and benchmark systems have been developed for different languages, especially for English [5]. Chinese image character recognition (ChnICR) also received intensive attention. However, it is cumbersome to directly apply existing English ICR systems to ChnICR, as the task of ChnICR is fundamentally different from that in English, which has only dozens of characters (or say categories) to be recognized. There are more than 10,000 Chinese characters in total, in which 3,755 ones are of GB2312-1 (a Chinese national standard character set). Generally, a practical ChnICR system should recognize at least the 3,755 characters.

Building a visual recognition system with thousands of categories is nevertheless a very challenging task. It usually suffers from some common drawbacks, e.g., the performance decreases when the number of categories to be recognized increase, being difficult and expensive to collect large high-quality training samples. As for the task of ChnICR, the recent advancement of DNN model in solving challenging visual problems [7–9] shows that it might be an appropriate choice for investigating this task. Training a good DNN model for ChnICR generally requires a large number of samples that covers thousands of Chinese characters and most variants of these characters in real life images. However, there is no publicly available large dataset for Chinese Image Characters so far. The scarcity of high-quality Chinese character samples seems to be the major concern. Moreover, it is also almost impossible to manually create diverse training samples for thousands of Chinese characters. Methods that are capable of generating large auto-labeled character samples for DNN training are highly demanded.

Motivated by the reasons above, this paper studies the problem of ChnICR by leveraging DNN model and huge machine simulated training samples. Specifically, we propose a scheme to automatically generate huge training data using clean machine born characters plus with variations commonly seen in character images, including variants in size, font, boldness, shift and complex backgrounds. By taking into account these variations, our scheme constructs totally over 28 million Chinese character samples, and based on which, a DNN training procedure is employed to learn the appropriate DNN structure for ChnICR. where the width and depth of DNN, and the volume of samples are empirically discussed. To speed up the training on tens of millions of samples, the training is performed on GPUs, which finishes the training procedure in dozens of hours to several days, two orders of magnitude faster than its CPU counterpart.

We evaluate performance of the learned recognizer in both ChnICR and Chinese image text recognition context, i.e., recognizing text lines each corresponding to a sentence of multiple characters. For ICR, the recognizer achieves a recognition accuracy of 0.852 on average. For Chinese image text recognition, a holistic Chinese text image recognition system consisting of image text over-segmentation, ChnICR and beam search determination is developed. Experimental results on text from 13 TV channels demonstrate the effectiveness of the system. Significant performance gains are observed compared to ABBYY

FineReader [6], which is used as the baseline system at 11th [3, 4], 12th [5] the Robust Reading Competition respectively. In summary, the contributions of our work are as follow:

- We propose a practical scheme to automatically generate huge character samples by combining clean machine born characters and variations commonly seen in character images. Our work provides a valuable attempt in exploiting computers to generate high-quality data.
- We apply the DNN model to investigate the problem of ChnICR, in which the width and depth of DNN, and the volume of samples are empirically discussed. Our work provides useful guidelines in using DNN model to solve visual recognition problems with thousands of categories. Additionally, to our knowledge, this is the first work of applying DNN model to ChnICR.
- We develop a holistic Chinese text image recognition system to evaluate the performance of the learned recognizer in real life Chinese image text recognition. Experimental results show the proposed system performs significantly better than the widely used ABBYY FineReader system.

2   The Detail of ChnICR

In this part, the proposed scheme of generating training samples without labeling will be depicted in detail firstly. Then, every generated sample will be normalized to 32×32 pixels and a 512-d feature vector composed of 8 direction gradient histograms is extracted based on normalized image subsequently. At last, multi-layer perceptions with different width and depth are trained and analyzed, on top of which the character recognizer is determined.

2.1   Training Sample Generation

The training samples are generated as follows. Firstly, 4,120 characters are selected as the vocabulary, which include 3,755 standard Chinese characters from GB2312-1, 245 extensional Chinese characters, 94 printable Ascii symbols and 26 punctuation symbols. The extensional characters and punctuation symbols are selected according to their frequencies on a 2GB news corpus. Secondly, we extract clean machine born 8-bit grayscale Chinese characters of 11 fonts, 5 sizes and 3 degrees of boldness. By doing this, each Chinese character is associated with 165 different representations. Note that the value of background pixel of the clean machine born characters is all zero, such that we can easily extract the exactly contour of each representation. Thirdly, the foreground pixels (extracted based on the contour) of each representation are given a randomly shift θ, where the value of θ is drawn from a uniform distribution in [-4, 4]. The shift is repeated 6 times. As a result, the number of representations associated with a character rise to 990. Fourthly, the foreground pixels of each of the 990 representations are embedded into a randomly generated complex background. To implement this process, we download a large set of grayscale images and videos from the

Internet in advance. For each embedding, a candidate background patch is randomly cropped from a randomly selected grayscale image, the pixel variance level of the patch is evaluated and discarded if it is low (corresponding to little texture circumstance). Once a satisfactory patch is selected, it is combined with the current representation. This combination also is repeated 7 times for each representation. Therefore, 6,930 training samples are generated for each Chinese character, and totally, there are 28,551,600 samples generated. The configuration details of the proposed scheme is summarized in Fig. 1, in which some typical samples are also showed for illustration. As can be seen, the constructed samples constitute a rich representation set that are very likely to cover most of occurrences of Chinese character in real life images.

Constitution	Variations	Descriptions
Size	5	$16 \times 16,\ 20 \times 20,\ 24 \times 24,\ 28 \times 28,\ 32 \times 32$
Font	11	Song, KaiShu, LiShu, Hei, FangSong, ...
Boldness	3	Font Weight: 200, 400, 700
Shift	6	Drawn from a uniform distribution [-4, 4]
Background	7	Cropped from natural image
Example		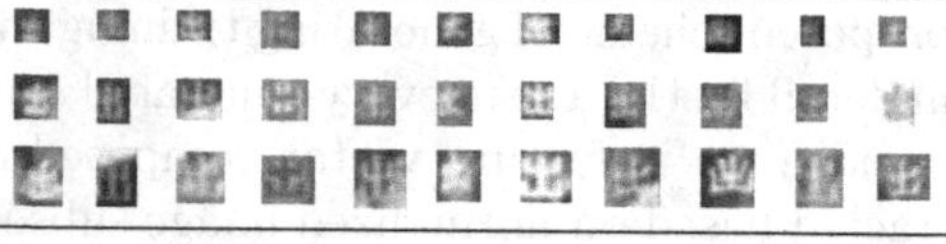

Fig. 1. The configuration of proposed scheme of generating training data

2.2 Feature Extraction

Three steps are employed to extract features for the over 28 million samples. Firstly, the bi-moment normalization proposed by [10] is adopted to normalize the character images to size 32×32. This size almost maintains all important information of Chinese characters and can be processed very fast. Secondly, local gradient direction histogram features, which are proved to be effective in differentiating Chinese characters [11], are extracted. Specifically, gradient directions map of each normalized character image is calculated by using sobel operators, then the map is evenly split into 64 patches of size 4×4. Based on this partition, 8 directions gradient histogram are calculated patch by patch and are concatenated to a 512-d feature vector, which forms the input of the subsequently DNN.

2.3 Structure of DNN

DNN is a multi-layer perception with multiple hidden layers. Usually, the first layer is the input layer and the last layer is the output layer, in which the number of neurons is equal to the feature dimension and number of categories, respectively. The mid-layers are hidden layers, of which the number of layers and the number of neurons in each layer could be specified manually. The terms *deep* and *wide* in DNN means that the network has many hidden layers and there are many neurons in each hidden layer. In practical systems, the number of hidden layers is often 5, 6 or more and each hidden layer consists of hidden units with a few thousands (e.g. 4,096). The output of each neuron is transformed by a non-linear function. As a deep and wide neural network, training large DNN models on traditional CPU requires several weeks to even months. Fortunately, fast parallel neural net code for graphics cards (GPUs) has facilitated this difficulty and could drastically reduce the training time to dozens of hours to several days.

Here, we choose sigmoid function as the activation function of all hidden neurons, and softmax function as the activation function of output layer neurons. The input layer has 512 neurons, corresponding to the 512-d feature vector, while the output layer has 4,120 neurons corresponding to the 4,120 Chinese characters. Initial weights are drawn from a uniform random distribution in the range [-0.1; 0.1] and initial biases are drawn from a uniform random distribution in the range [-4.1; -3.9]. We use the standard back-propagation algorithm to train the network, and employ the conditional decayed learning rate schedule, which learns at a fixed rate until the accuracy on cross-validation set fails to improve by more than 0.5% between two epochs. Then, DNN continues to halve the learning rate at each epoch until the CV accuracy again fails to improve by more than a predetermined minimum, at which point the algorithm terminates. The initial learn rate and the batch size are empirically set to 0.032 and 512. Finally, the trained character recognizer is a 6-layer DNN with hidden neurons 4096-4096-4096-4096, which achieves the best performance in the width and depth analysis detained in Section 3.1.

2.4   The Chinese Image Text Recognition System

We also develop a holistic ChnICR system to evaluate performance of the learned recognizer in Chinese image text recognition context. The proposed system consists of three components: image text over-segmentation, ChnICR and beam search determination. In the first component, an over-segmentation based on a vertical projection of the binarized image for generating potential splitting points is performed. Based on this, a graph is built on account of geometry information of splitting points, and the learned recognizer (i.e., the character recognition component) is applied to every cropped image defined by two connected vertexes. Then, from start vertex step by step all the way to end vertex, a dynamical process of building and pruning the lattice is performed. At each step, every recognition result is estimated by a 3-gram language model according to different histories. Along with this, a beam search by maximizing the objective function defined on the linear combination of recognition score and language model score is performed to find the best path. The characters corresponding to arches in the best path are thus the recognition results. Details of the proposed system are elaborated in [2].

3   Experiments and Results Analysis

3.1   Dataset

We conduct experiments on a real TV dataset, which is composed of 6.5 hours videos collected from 13 Chinese TV Channels (30 minutes each channel). In order to fully evaluate the character and text recognition performance, we have manually labeled these videos including position and content of each line and character in the corresponding keyframes, totally obtaining 1,131 test lines and 12,700 characters respectively. Fig. 3 shows some typical samples of this dataset. We can observe that characters from different TV channels are of various sizes, colors, fonts, pitches and distortions.

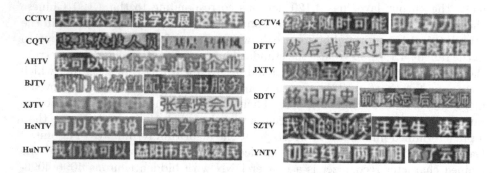

Fig. 2. Examples from different TV news

3.2   Sensibilities of Width, Depth and Volume of Learning Data

In order to address the challenging task of ChnICR, different volume of training data and models are tested and analyzed in detail based on the testing character set depicted before. Table 1 lists the training time, testing speed (frames per second) and recognition accuracy of cross-validation set (ten percent of training data) and test set based on one hidden layer with 4096 neurons when different sizes of training data is used. From Table 1, we can observe that the larger proportion of data is used for training, the higher recognition accuracy is obtained either in develop-set or real test dataset, which confirms the importance of our proposed training data generation scheme for deep neural network optimization. Table 2 and Table 3 investigate the influence of depth and width of the model on the condition that all the training data are used. From the tables, we can see that, on one hand, model network with the deeper and wider structure can gain a higher recognition accuracy as well. But on the other hand, we can also observe that the improvement is getting narrowing when the depth and width increases. Although the test set never used in the training process, with the improvement of performance on cross-validation set, recognition accuracy of test set is improved too. And so we can conclude that the proposed scheme of constructing training data using clean machine-born character is feasible and effective.

Note that, all the experiments are run on NVIDIA GeForce GTX 690, and time consumption increases dramatically even with GPU when the network is wide and deep. Hence, the model having 4 hidden layer with 4096 neurons for each is chosen as the character recognizer for ChnICR considering the performance and efficiency.

Table 1. Comparison of volume of training data

Proportion of used	Train Time	CV Accuracy	Test Speed	Test Accuracy
0.28M (1%)	0.86 h	20.34%	136.7 F/s	43.97%
2.8M (10%)	8.20 h	51.18%	136.7 F/s	69.97%
28M (100%)	90.60 h	62.61%	136.7 F/s	80.39%

Table 2. Comparison of width of network (3 layer used)

#Neurons	Train Time	CV Accuracy	Test Speed	Test Accuracy
1024	48.70 h	49.03%	181.8 F/s	76.54%
2048	68.16 h	56.81%	164.3 F/s	79.28%
4096	90.60 h	62.61%	136.7 F/s	80.39%

Table 3. Comparison of depth of network (4096 neurons used)

#Layers	Train Time	CV Accuracy	Test Speed	Test Accuracy
3	90.60 h	62.61%	136.7 F/s	80.39%
4	146.3 h	66.11%	107.2 F/s	82.19%
5	155.2 h	71.70%	87.80 F/s	84.07%
6	192.5 h	73.88%	74.10 F/s	85.21%

3.3 Character Image Text Recognition

For comparison, we test all the text lines using the ABBYY FineReader 10.0 [6]. As commercial OCR system, ABBYY supports simplified Chinese character recognition and thus can serve as the baseline system for ChnICR. Text recognition accuracy of both systems is listed in Table 4. It can be found that when image text lines have clean background and high resolution, both systems could achieve a high performance, such as in DFTV. But when applied to complex background and low resolution image text, our system is more robust than AB-BYY (e.g., CCTV1, AHTV). The average recognition accuracy of both system is 85.44% and 53.59% respectively. There is an enhancement of 59.4% relatively. Since our scheme directly recognizes image in grayscale space and only machine simulated data is used to train the recognizer, it is independent of data and more reliable over different kinds of image text.

Table 4. Configuration and String Accuracy

Channels	#Lines	#Chars	ABBYY[8]	Proposed	Channels	#Lines	#Chars	ABBYY[8]	Proposed
CCTV1	97	1026	48.43%	91.91%	CCTV4	83	817	50.80%	93.39%
CQTV	132	1093	22.87%	82.25%	DFTV	204	2009	89.60%	93.53%
AHTV	84	788	38.32%	86.80%	JXTV	41	369	17.89%	64.77%
BJTV	137	1359	31.79%	68.43%	SDTV	93	1022	38.36%	86.69%
XJTV	100	904	49.78%	73.86%	SZTV	44	403	26.55%	76.18%
HeNTV	126	1172	80.63%	95.73%	YNTV	59	557	44.70%	84.02%
HuNTV	111	1181	76.38%	90.09%	Total	1311	12700	53.59%	85.45%

4   Conclusion

In this paper, we research on the problem of ChnICR by leveraging DNN and huge machine simulated samples. Our contributions are threefold. Firstly, a scheme is proposed to construct huge auto-labeled training samples for over 4,000 Chinese characters. The scheme successfully avoids the time consuming and bored human label process. Secondly, the sensibilities of width, depth of DNN and the volume of training data with respect to the recognition performance are empirically evaluated, and based on this an appropriate Chinese character recognizer is determined. Thirdly, a Chinese text image recognition system is built on top of the learned recognizer, which performs much better than the baseline system. In future, we are interested in learning more effective DNN models, as well as testing the proposed recognizer in more kinds of image text.

References

1. Lew, et al.: Content-based multimedia information retrieval: State of the art and challenges. TOMCCAP 02(1), 1–19 (2006)
2. Bai, J., et al.: 'Chinese image text recognition on grayscale pixels. In: ICASSP (2014)
3. Karatzas, et al.: Icdar 2011 robust reading competition - challenge 1: Reading text in born-digital images (web and email). In: ICDAR, pp. 1485–1490 (2011)
4. Shahab, et al.: Icdar 2011 robust reading competition challenge 2: Reading text in scene images. In: ICDAR, pp. 1491–1496 (2011)
5. Karatzas: Icdar 2013 robust reading competition. In: ICDAR, pp. 1484–1493 (2013)
6. ABBYY Finereader 9.0, http://www.abbyy.com
7. Cireşan, et al.: Flexible, high performance convolutional neural networks for image classification. In: IJCAI 2011, pp. 1237–1242. AAAI Press (2011)
8. Krizhevsky, A., et al.: Imagenet classification with deep convolutional neural networks. In: Advances in Neural Information Processing Systems (2012)
9. Ciresan, et al.: Multi-column deep neural networks for image classification. In: CVPR, pp. 3642–3649 (2012)
10. Liu, C.-L., et al.: Handwritten chinese character recognition: Alternatives to non-linear normalization. In: ICDAR, vol. 3, pp. 524–528 (2003)
11. Liu, C.-L.: Normalization-cooperated gradient feature extraction for handwritten character recognition. TPAMI 29(8), 1465–1469 (2007)

Polyphonic Music Generation by Modeling Temporal Dependencies Using a RNN-DBN

Kratarth Goel, Raunaq Vohra, and J.K. Sahoo

Birla Institute of Technology and Science, Pilani
Goa, India
{kratarthgoel,ronvohra}@gmail.com, jksahoo@goa.bits-pilani.ac.in

Abstract. In this paper, we propose a generic technique to model temporal dependencies and sequences using a combination of a recurrent neural network and a Deep Belief Network. Our technique, RNN-DBN, is an amalgamation of the memory state of the RNN that allows it to provide temporal information and a multi-layer DBN that helps in high level representation of the data. This makes RNN-DBNs ideal for sequence generation. Further, the use of a DBN in conjunction with the RNN makes this model capable of significantly more complex data representation than a Restricted Boltzmann Machine (RBM). We apply this technique to the task of polyphonic music generation.

Keywords: Deep architectures, recurrent neural networks, music generation, creative machine learning, Deep Belief Networks, generative models.

1 Introduction

Creative machine learning, or using machine learning techniques to impart human-like creativity to machines, is an extremely relevant research area today. Generative models form the basis of creative learning, and for this reason, a high level of sophistication is required from these models. Also, identifying features in the subjective fields of art, literature and music is an arduous task, which is only made more difficult when more elaborate learning is desired. Deep architectures, therefore, present themselves as an ideal framework for generative models, as they are inherently stochastic and support increasingly complex representations with each added layer. Recurrent neural networks (RNNs) have also used with great success as regards generative models, particularly handwriting generation, where they have been used to achieve the current state-of-the-art results. The internal feedback or memory state of these neural networks is what makes them a suitable technique for sequence generation in tasks like polyphonic music composition.

There have been many attempts to generate polyphonic music in the past. Matic *et al.* [1] used neural networks and cellular automata to generate melodies. However, this is dependent on a feature set based on emotions and further requires specialized knowledge of musical theory. A similar situation is observed

S. Wermter et al. (Eds.): ICANN 2014, LNCS 8681, pp. 217–224, 2014.

with the work done by Maeda and Kajihara [2], who used genetic algorithms for music generation. Elman networks with chaotic inspiration were used by [3] to compose music. While RNNs are an excellent technique to model sequences, they used chaotic inspiration as an external input instead of real stochasticity to compose original music. A Deep Belief Network with a sliding window mechanism to create jazz melodies was proposed by [4]. However, due to lack of temporal information, there were many instances of repeated notes and pitches. This problem was solved by Boulanger-Lewandowski *et al.* [5] who used RNN-RBMs that facilitated retention of temporal dependencies, for polyphonic music generation and obtained promising results. We propose a generic technique which is a combination of a RNN and a Deep Belief Network for sequence generation, and apply it to automatic music composition. Our technique, the RNN-DBN, effectively combines the superior sequence modeling capabilities of a RNN with the high level data modeling that a DBN enables to produce rich, complex melodies which do not feature significant repetition. Moreover, the composition of these melodies does not require any feature selection from the input data. This model is presented as a generic technique, *i. e.* it does not make any assumptions about the nature of the data. We apply our technique to a variety of datasets and have achieved excellent results which are on par with the current state-of-the-art.

The rest of this paper is organized as follows: Section 2 discusses various deep and neural network architectures that serve as the motivation for our technique, described in Section 3. We demonstrate the application of RNN-DBNs to the task of polyphonic music generation in Section 4 and present our results. Section 5 discusses possible future work regarding our technique and concludes the paper.

2   Preliminaries

2.1   Restricted Boltzmann Machines

Restricted Boltzmann machines (RBMs) are energy based models with their energy function $E(v, h)$ defined as:

$$E(v, h) = -b'v - c'h - h'Wv \tag{1}$$

W represents the weights connecting hidden (h) and visible (v) units and b, c are the biases of the visible and hidden layers respectively.

This translates directly to the following free energy formula:

$$\mathcal{F}(v) = -b'v - \sum_i \log \sum_{h_i} e^{h_i(c_i + W_i v)}. \tag{2}$$

Because of the specific structure of RBMs, visible and hidden units are conditionally independent given one another. Using this property, we can write:

$$p(h|v) = \prod_i p(h_i|v) \tag{3}$$

$$p(v|h) = \prod_j p(v_j|h). \tag{4}$$

Samples can be obtained from a RBM by performing block Gibbs sampling, where visible units are sampled simultaneously given fixed values of the hidden units. Similarly, hidden units are sampled simultaneously given the visible unit values. A single step in the Markov chain is thus taken as follows,

$$h^{(n+1)} = \sigma(W'v^{(n)} + c)$$
$$v^{(n+1)} = \sigma(Wh^{(n+1)} + b), \tag{5}$$

σ represents the sigmoid function acting on the activations of the $(n + 1)^{th}$ hidden and visible units. Several algorithms have been devised for RBMs in order to efficiently sample from $p(v, h)$ during the learning process, the most effective being the well-known contrastive divergence (CD-k) algorithm [6].

In the commonly studied case of using binary units (where v_j and $h_i \in \{0, 1\}$), we obtain, from Eqn. 4, a probabilistic version of the activation function:

$$P(h_i = 1|v) = \sigma(c_i + W_i v)$$
$$P(v_j = 1|h) = \sigma(b_j + W'_j h) \tag{6}$$

The free energy of an RBM with binary units thus further simplifies to:

$$\mathcal{F}(v) = -b'v - \sum_i \log(1 + e^{(c_i + W_i v)}). \tag{7}$$

We obtain the following log-likelihood gradients for an RBM with binary units:

$$-\frac{\partial \log p(v)}{\partial W_{ij}} = E_v[p(h_i|v) \cdot v_j] - v_j^{(i)} \cdot \sigma(W_i \cdot v^{(i)} + c_i)$$

$$-\frac{\partial \log p(v)}{\partial c_i} = E_v[p(h_i|v)] - \sigma(W_i \cdot v^{(i)}) \tag{8}$$

$$-\frac{\partial \log p(v)}{\partial b_j} = E_v[p(v_j|h)] - v_j^{(i)}$$

$\sigma(x) = (1 + e^{-x})^{-1}$ is the element-wise logistic sigmoid function.

2.2   Recurrent Neural Network

Recurrent neural networks (RNNs) are a particular family of neural networks where the network contains one or more feedback connections, so that activation of a cluster of neurons can flow in a loop. This property allows for the network to effectively model time series data and learn sequences. An interesting property of RNNs is that they can be modeled as feedforward neural networks by unfolding them over time. RNNs can be trained using the Backpropagation Through Time (BPTT) technique. If a network training sequence starts at a time instant t_0

and ends at time t_1 (thus, $t_1 - t_0$ is the entire sequence length), the total cost function is simply the sum over the standard error function $E_{sse/ce}$ at each time step, which is the sum of the deviations of all target signals from the corresponding activations computed by the network. Thus, for a training set of numerous sequences, the total error E_{total} is the sum of the errors of all individual sequences:

$$E_{total} = \sum_{t=t_0}^{t_1} E_{sse/ce}(t) \tag{9}$$

and the gradient descent weight update contributions for each time step are given by,

$$\Delta w_{ij} = -\eta \frac{\partial E_{total}(t_0, t_1)}{\partial w_{ij}} = \sum_{t=t_0}^{t_1} \frac{\partial E_{sse/ce}(t)}{\partial w_{ij}} \tag{10}$$

The partial derivatives of each component $\frac{\partial E_{sse/ce}}{\partial w_{ij}}$ now have contributions from multiple instances of each weight $w_{ij} \in \{W_{v^{(t-1)}h^{(t-1)}}, W_{(h^{t-1})h^{(t)}}\}$ and are dependent on the inputs and hidden unit activations at previous time instants. The errors now must be back-propagated through time as well as through the network.

2.3   Deep Belief Network

RBMs can be stacked and trained greedily to form *Deep Belief Networks* (DBNs). DBNs are graphical models which learn to extract a deep hierarchical representation of the training data [7]. They model the joint distribution between observed vector $\mathbf{x}$ and the ℓ hidden layers h^k as follows:

$$P(\mathbf{x}, h^1, \ldots, h^\ell) = \left(\prod_{k=0}^{\ell-2} P(h^k | h^{k+1}) \right) P(h^{\ell-1}, h^\ell) \tag{11}$$

$\mathbf{x} = h^0$, $P(h^{k-1} | h^k)$ is a conditional distribution for the visible units conditioned on the hidden units of the RBM at level k, and $P(h^{\ell-1}, h^\ell)$ is the visible-hidden joint distribution in the top-level RBM.

The principle of greedy layer-wise unsupervised training can be applied to DBNs with RBMs as the building blocks for each layer [8]. We begin by training the first layer as an RBM that models the raw input $x = h^{(0)}$ as its visible layer. Using that first layer, we obtain a representation of the input that will be used as data for the second layer. Two common solutions exist here, and the representation can be chosen as the mean activations $p(h^{(1)} = 1 | h^{(0)})$ or samples of $p(h^{(1)} | h^{(0)})$. Then we train the second layer as an RBM, taking the transformed data (samples or mean activations) as training examples (for the visible layer of that RBM). In the same vein, we can continue adding as many hidden layers as required, while each time propagating upward either samples or mean values.

2.4 Recurrent Temporal Restricted Boltzmann Machine

The Recurrent Temporal Restricted Boltzmann Machine (RTRBM) [9] is a sequence of conditional RBMs (one at each time instant) whose parameters $\{b_v^t, b_h^t, W^t\}$ are time-dependent and depend on the sequence history at time t, denoted by $A(t) = \{v^{(\tau)}, u^{(\tau)} | \tau < t\}$, where $u^{(t)}$ is the mean-field value of $h(t)$, as seen in [5]. The RTRBM is formally defined by its joint probability distribution,

$$P(v^{(t)}, h(t)) = \prod_{t=1}^{T} P(v^{(t)}, h^{(t)} | A^{(t)}) \tag{12}$$

$P(v^{(t)}, h^{(t)} | A^{(t)})$ is the joint probability of the tth RBM whose parameters are defined below, from Eqn. 13 and Eqn. 14. While all the parameters of the RBMs may usually depend on the previous time instants, we will consider the case where only the biases depend on $u^{(t-1)}$.

$$b_h^{(t)} = b_h + W_{uh} u^{(t-1)} \tag{13}$$

$$b_v^{(t)} = b_v + W_{uv} u^{(t-1)} \tag{14}$$

The RTRBM has six parameters, $\{W, b_v, b_h, W_{uv}, W_{uh}, u^{(0)}\}$, the more general scenario is derived in similar fashion. While the hidden units $h^{(t)}$ are binary during inference and sample generation, it is the *mean-field* value $u^{(t)}$ that is transmitted to its successors (Eqn. 15). This important distinction makes exact inference of the $u^{(t)}$ easy and improves the efficiency of training[9].

$$u^{(t)} = \sigma(W_{vh} v^{(t)} + b_h^{(t)}) = \sigma(W_{vh} v^{(t)} + W_{uh} u^{(t-1)} + b_h) \tag{15}$$

Observe that Eqn. 15 is exactly the defining equation of a RNN (defined in Section 4) with hidden units $u^{(t)}$.

3 RNN-DBN

The RTRBM can be thought of as a sequence of conditional RBMs whose parameters are the output of a deterministic RNN [5], with the constraint that the hidden units must describe the conditional distributions and convey temporal information for sequence generation. The use of a single RBM layer greatly constricts the expressive power of the model as a whole. This constraint can be lifted by combining a full RNN having distinct hidden units $u^{(t)}$ with a RTRBM graphical model, replacing the RBM structure with the much more powerful model of a DBN. We call this model the RNN-DBN.

In general, the parameters of the RNN-DBN with 2 hidden layers for the second hidden layer are made to depend only on $u^{(t-1)}$ given by Eqn. 13 and Eqn. 14 along with,

$$b_{h_2}^{(t)} = b_{h_2} + W_{uh_2} u^{(t-1)} \tag{16}$$

The joint probability distribution of the RNN-DBN is also given by Eqn. 12, but with $u^{(t)}$ defined arbitrarily, as given by Eqn. 17. For simplicity, we consider the RNN-DBN parameters to be $\{W_{vh^{(t)}}, b_v^{(t)}, b_{h_1}^{(t)}, b_{h_2}^{(t)}\}$ for a 2 hidden layer RNN-DBN (shown in Fig. 1), i.e. only the biases are variable, and a single-layer RNN, whose hidden units $u^{(t)}$ are only connected to their direct predecessor $u^{(t-1)}$ and to $v^{(t)}$ by the relation,

$$u^{(t)} = \sigma(W_{vu}v^{(t)} + W_{uu}h^{(t-1)} + b_u). \tag{17}$$

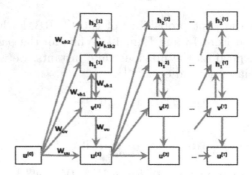

Fig. 1. A RNN-DBN with 2 hidden layers

The DBN portion of the RNN-DBN is otherwise exactly the same as any general DBN. This gives the two hidden layer RNN-DBN a total of twelve parameters - $\{W_{vh_1}, W_{h_1h_2}, b_v, b_{h_1}, b_{h_2}, W_{uv}, W_{uh_1}, W_{uh_2}, u^{(0)}, W_{vu}, W_{uu}, b_u\}$.

The training algorithm is based on the following general scheme:

1. Propagate the current values of the hidden units $u^{(t)}$ in the RNN portion of the graph using Eqn.17.
2. Calculate the DBN parameters that depend on the $u^{(t)}$ (Eqn. 13, 14 and 16) by greedily training layer-by-layer of the DBN, each layer as an RBM (Train the first layer as an RBM that models the raw input as its visible layer and use that first layer to obtain a representation of the input that will be used as data for the second layer and so on).
3. Use CD-k to estimate the log-likelihood gradient (Eqn. 8) with respect to W, b_v and b_h for each RBM composing the DBN.
4. Repeat steps 2 and 3 for each layer of the DBN.
5. Propagate the estimated gradient with respect to $b_v^{(t)}, b_h^{(t)}$ and $b_{h_2}^{(t)}$ backward through time (BPTT) [10] to obtain the estimated gradient with respect to the RNN, for the RNN-DBN with 2 hidden layers.

Table 1. Log-likelihood (LL) for various musical models in the polyphonic music generation task

Model	JSB Chorales (LL)	MuseData (LL)	Nottingham (LL)	Piano-Midi.de (LL)
Random	-61.00	-61.00	-61.00	-61.00
RBM	-7.43	-9.56	-5.25	-10.17
NADE	-7.19	-10.06	-5.48	-10.28
Note N-Gram	-10.26	-7.91	-4.54	-7.50
RNN-RBM	-7.27	-9.31	-4.72	-9.89
RNN[1] (HF)	-8.58	-7.19	-3.89	-7.66
RTRBM[1]	-6.35	-6.35	-2.62	-7.36
RNN-RBM[1]	-6.27	-6.01	-2.39	-7.09
RNN-NADE[1]	-5.83	-6.74	-2.91	-7.48
RNN-NADE[1] (HF)	-5.56	-5.60	-2.31	-7.05
RNN-DBN	**-5.68**	**-6.28**	**-2.54**	**-7.15**

4 Implementation and Results

We demonstrate our technique by applying it to the task of polyphonic music generation. We used a RNN-DBN with 2 hidden DBN layers - each having 150 binary units - and 150 binary units in the RNN layer. The visible layer has 88 binary units, corresponding to the full range of the piano from A0 to C8. We implemented our technique on four datasets - *JSB Chorales* , *MuseData*[2], *Nottingham*[3] and *Piano-midi.de*. None of the preprocessing techniques mentioned in [5] have been applied to the data, and only raw data has been given as input to the RNN-DBN. We evaluate our models qualitatively by generating sample sequences and quantitatively by using the *log-likelihood* (LL) as a performance measure. Results are presented in Table 1 (a more comprehensive list can be found in [5]).

The results indicate that our technique is comparable with the current state-of-the-art. We believe that the difference in performance between our technique and the current best can be attributed to lack of preprocessing. For instance, transposing the sequences in a common tonality (*e.g.* C major/minor) and normalizing the tempo in beats (quarternotes) per minute as preprocessing can have the most effect on the generative quality of the model. It also helps to have as pretraining, the initialization the $W_{vh_1}, W_{h_1h_2}, b_v, b_{h_1}, b_{h_2}$ parameters with independent RBMs with fully shuffled frames i.e. $W_{uh_1} = W_{uh_2} = W_{uv} = W_{uu} = W_{vu} = 0$). Initializing the $W_{uv}, W_{uu}, W_{vu}, b_u$ parameters of the RNN with the auxiliary cross-entropy objective via either stochastic gradient descent (SGD) or,

---

[1] These marked results are obtained after various preprocessing, pretraining methods and optimization techniques described in the last paragraph of this section.

[2] http://www.musedata.org

[3] ifdo.ca/~seymour/nottingham/nottingham.html

preferably, Hessian-free (HF) optimization and subsequently finetuning significantly helps the density estimation and prediction performance of RNNs which would otherwise perform worse than simpler Multilayer Perceptrons [5]. Optimization techniques like gradient clipping, Nesterov momentum and the use of NADE for conditional density estimation also improve results.

5   Conclusions and Future Work

We have proposed a generic technique called *Recurrent Neural Network-Deep Belief Network* (RNN-DBN) for modeling sequences with generative models and have demonstrated its successful application to polyphonic music generation. We used four datasets for evaluating our technique and have obtained results on par with the current state-of-the-art. We are currently working on improving the results this paper, by exploring various pretraining and optimization techniques. We are also looking at showcasing the versatility of our technique by applying it to different problem statements.

References

1. Matic, I., Oliveira, A., Cardoso, A.: Automatic melody generation using neural networks and cellular automata. In: 2012 11th Symposium on Neural Network Applications in Electrical Engineering (NEUREL), pp. 89–94 (September 2012)
2. Maeda, Y., Kajihara, Y.: Rhythm generation method for automatic musical composition using genetic algorithm. In: 2010 IEEE International Conference on Fuzzy Systems (FUZZ), pp. 1–7 (July 2010)
3. Coca, A., Romero, R., Zhao, L.: Generation of composed musical structures through recurrent neural networks based on chaotic inspiration. In: The 2011 International Joint Conference on Neural Networks (IJCNN), pp. 3220–3226 (July 2011)
4. Bickerman, G., Bosley, S., Swire, P., Keller, R.: Learning to create jazz melodies using deep belief nets. In: First International Conference on Computational Creativity (2010)
5. Boulanger-Lewandowski, N., Bengio, Y., Vincent, P.: Modeling temporal dependencies in high-dimensional sequences: Application to polyphonic music generation and transcription. In: ICML. icml.cc / Omnipress (2012)
6. Hinton, G.E.: Training products of experts by minimizing contrastive divergence. Neural Computation 14(8), 1771–1800 (2002)
7. Hinton, G.E., Osindero, S.: A fast learning algorithm for deep belief nets. Neural Computation 18, 2006 (2006)
8. Bengio, Y.: Learning deep architectures for ai. Foundations and Trends in Machine Learning 2(1), 1–127 (2009)
9. Sutskever, I., Hinton, G.E., Taylor, G.W.: The recurrent temporal restricted boltzmann machine. In: NIPS, pp. 1601–1608 (2008)
10. Rumelhart, D., Hinton, G., Williams, R.: Learning representations by backpropagating errors. Nature 323(6088), 533–536 (1986)

On Improving the Classification Capability of Reservoir Computing for Arabic Speech Recognition

Abdulrahman Alalshekmubarak and Leslie S. Smith

Dept. of Computing Science, University of Stirling,
Stirling FK9 4LA, UK
{aal,lss}@cs.stir.ac.uk

Abstract. Designing noise-resilient systems is a major challenge in the field of automated speech recognition (ASR). These systems are crucial for real-world applications where high levels of noise tend to be present. We introduce a noise robust system based on Echo State Networks and Extreme Kernel machines which we call ESNEKM. To evaluate the performance of the proposed system, we used our recently released public Arabic speech dataset and the well-known spoken Arabic digits (SAD) dataset. Different feature extraction methods considered in this study include mel-frequency cepstral coefficients (MFCCs), perceptual linear prediction (PLP) and RASTA- perceptual linear prediction. These extracted features were fed to the ESNEKM and the result compared with a baseline hidden Markov model (HMM), so that nine models were compared in total. ESNEKM models outperformed HMM models under all the feature extraction methods, noise levels, and noise types. The best performance was obtained by the model that combined RASTA-PLP with ESNEKM.

Keywords: Reservoir computing, Speech recognition, PLP, MFCC, RASTA-PLP, Speech corpus, Arabic language.

1 Introduction

Speech communication is one of the most distinguishing capabilities of humans. Indeed the ability to conduct a conversation was introduced in the early days of computation as a measurement of intelligence in the well-known Turing test. Automatic speech recognition (ASR), mapping the acoustic signal into a string of words, forms the first part in such an intelligent system. A major challenge in the field of automated speech recognition (ASR) lies in designing noise-resilient systems. These systems are crucial for real-world applications where high levels of noise are often present. In this paper, we introduce a noise robust system based on Echo State Networks (ESN)[1] and the Extreme Kernel Machine (EKM)[2] which we call ESNEKM to improve the performance of ESN in the presence of noise. The proposed model maintains the main attractions of ESN, being very fast to train and able to handle multi-class classification problems. The paper

S. Wermter et al. (Eds.): ICANN 2014, LNCS 8681, pp. 225–232, 2014.

is organised as follows. A brief review of ESN and EKM is presented in the section 2. The proposed system is introduced in section 3, and section 4 contains a detailed report of our experiments to ensure the reproducibility of our results. We discuss our results in section 5, and present our conclusions in section 6.

2 Background

2.1 Reservoir Computing

Reservoir Computing is an emerging field that offers a novel approach to training Recurrent Neural Networks. Originally proposed in 2002, its popularity has grown rapidly due to the simplicity of its implementation and its robust performance [3]. RC contains several techniques that derived from different backgrounds. However, all of them share the main idea of RC: random initialisation of the weights of the recurrent nodes and only learning weights in the output layer which implements a simple readout function. The two major approaches under the umbrella of RC are the Echo State Network (ESN) and the Liquid State Machine (LSM).

Echo State Network. ESN was introduced by Jaeger in 2001 [1] and has been applied in different real world applications where it proved to achieve a superior performance, or similar, compared to the state of the art algorithms. This success lead to a wide acceptance of this technique in the field and encouraged researchers to conduct studies that aim to explore the fundamental properties and behaviour nature of ESN that lie behind its performance. Another, rather more empirical effort has also been made to investigate the applicability of ESN on new and more challenging real world problems and to conduct extensive comparisons among the state of the art techniques [4]. The ESN model is characterised in the following way. First, $\mathbf{W^{in}}$, which is an m by n matrix (where m is the size of the input vector and n is the size of the reservoir), is initialised randomly. Second, $\mathbf{W^{res}}$, which is an n by n matrix, is initialised randomly as well and scaled to obtain the desirable dynamics. Another important component of this model is the fading memory (forgetting) parameter α, which plays a major role in controlling the memory capacity of the reservoir. The model update equations are as follows[5]:

$$\bar{x}(t) = f(\mathbf{W^{in}}[1; u(t)] + \mathbf{W^{res}}x(t-1)) \tag{1}$$

$$x(t) = (1 - \alpha)x(t-1) + \alpha\bar{x}(t) \tag{2}$$

where $x(t)$ is the reservoir's state at time t, $u(t)$ is the input signal at time t and f is a nonlinear transfer function: commonly logistic or tanh is applied. The response of the reservoir is dynamic and the class labels of training are used to train a simple linear read-out function by learning the weights of the output layer $\mathbf{W^{out}}$. This is typically accomplished by applying the pseudo-inverse equations:

$$\mathbf{W^{out}} = (\mathbf{X^T X})^{-1}\mathbf{X^T Y} \tag{3}$$

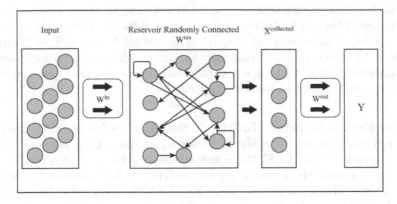

Fig. 1. The structure of the ESN and readout system. On the left, the input signal is fed into the reservoir network through the fixed weights $\mathbf{W}^{in}$. The reservoir network recodes these, and the output from the network is read out using the readout network on the right $\mathbf{W}^{out}$, which uses the the learned weights.

2.2 Extreme Learning Machine (ELM)

The ELM was proposed as an efficient model to train the single-hidden layer feedforward networks (SLFNs) by Huang in 2004 [6]. The basic concept is similar to reservoir computing in that both approaches map the input to a higher dimensional space using random weights and only learn the weights of the output layer. The main difference is that ELM, unlike RC, does not use recurrent nodes, which prevents it from modelling dynamic systems. ELM has been applied successfully in many real-world conditions in a variety of fields [7] [8].

Instead of using a relatively small number of nodes in the hidden layer and applying a powerful optimisation technique such as back-propagation, which suffers from several well-known issues (e.g. local minima, sensitivity to initialisation weights, implementation complexity, tendency to over-fit, long training time), ELM uses a very large number of nodes, typically more than 1,000 and only uses a simple read-out function at the output layer. Despite the use of this large number of nodes, ELM offers superior generalisation performance, which can be explained by the random weights applied on the learning and testing samples. This means the mapping mechanism is not based on the learning dataset. ELM can be described mathematically as follows [2]:

$$f_L(x) = \sum_{n=1}^{L} \beta_i h_i(x) = \mathbf{h}(\mathbf{x})\boldsymbol{\beta} \qquad (4)$$

where $\boldsymbol{\beta} = [\beta_1, ..., \beta_L]^T$ is the output learned weights by the simple linear readout function and $\mathbf{h}(\mathbf{x}) = [h(x)_1, ..., h(x)_L]^T$ is calculated by mapping the input vector by the random initialised weights. A variety of nonlinear functions may be chosen in the mapping layer: commonly, logistic or tanh is applied.

Researchers have demonstrated that ELM offers superior, or similar, performance to LS-SVMs and SVMs but trains more rapidly [2]. This, and the limited number of hyper-parameters that need to be selected, encouraged Huang to argue that ELM can promote real-time learning without human intervention. The main limitation of ELM is its inability to handle dynamic systems, which prevents its use in many real-world applications.

Extreme Kernel Machine (EKM). In the EKM version of ELM, the input vector x is not mapped to a higher dimensional space by a random matrix, but by a kernel. Similar to SVMs, a kernel is applied here, which means users do not have to know the actual mapping function. It is important to state the differences in applying the kernel among EKM, SVMs and LS-SVMs. SVMs and LS-SVMs are binary classifiers whereeas EKM is not, which allows it to deal with multi-label tasks efficiently. The main equation of EKM used to estimate the decision function from a training dataset is as follows [2]:

$$f(x) = h(x)\mathbf{H}^T(\frac{\mathbf{I}}{C} + \mathbf{H}\mathbf{H}^T)^{-1}\mathbf{T} \tag{5}$$

$$= \begin{bmatrix} K(x, x_1) \\ \vdots \\ K(x, x_N) \end{bmatrix}^T \left(\frac{\mathbf{I}}{C} + \Omega_{ELM}\right)^{-1}\mathbf{T}$$

where $\Omega_{ELM_{i,j}} = K(x_i, x_j)$ and C is the regularisation parameter. As can be seen from the previous brief mathematical description, users do not need to specify the number of nodes used in the mapping layer. As in EKM, the length of the mapping function is the number of training samples. In other words, in EKM, the size of the mapping layer cannot exceed the number of training samples. However, this is not guaranteed in ELM.

3   Proposed System

The proposed model aims to improve the classification capability of the ESN by applying the EKM classifier on the output layer instead of the linear classifier used in the conventional approach. We have found few attempts in the literature [9][10] to overcome the limitation of the linear readout function and replace it with a nonlinear classifier. The added training time (or the binary nature of some classifiers such as SVMs) makes this impractical for many tasks, specifically for multi-label tasks with a relatively large number of classes. However, using EKM yields the benefits of using the nonlinear function while maintaining a single-shot convex solution that can handle multi-label tasks even when the number of labels is large. This is important not only from the efficiency aspect but also from reproducibility: many nonlinear classifiers such as multilayer perceptron are sensitive to their initial weights. In addition, we have found that dividing the signal into subparts and separately feeding these subparts to the reservoir improves the performance, particularly in the presence of noise. The proposed model is summarised in the following steps:

1. Divide the signal into subparts (in our experiments, we have found two parts is adequate).
2. Process these subparts by randomly initialising the reservoir and store the reservoir responses.
3. Train EKM classifier using reservoir responses (after normalisation) and the teaching signal (label).

4 Experiments

4.1 Datasets

Spoken Arabic Digits. Spoken Arabic Digits (SAD) is the only publicly accessible Arabic speech corpus. It is published in a processed format (as MFCCs) which prevents the development of novel feature extraction methods and comparison between them. It contains the Arabic digits 0- 9, with each digit spoken 10 times by 88 native speakers, 44 males and 44 females. Thus, it contains 8800 samples which are divided as follows: 6600 instances for training and 2200 instances for testing.

Arabic Speech Corpus for Isolated Words. The development of an Arabic speech corpus for isolated words has been conducted at the Department of Management Information Systems, King Faisal University. It contains about 10000 utterances of 20 words spoken by 50 native male Arabic speakers. The corpus has been made freely accessible for non-commercial use in the raw format (.wav files) and other formats to allow researchers to apply different feature extraction methods. The corpus has been recorded with a 44100 Hz sampling rate and 16-bit resolution, as well as two channels-stereo mode.

4.2 Feature Extraction and Noise Addition

In the SAD dataset, we used the processed MFCC features. It is not possible to compare different feature extraction methods or evaluate the performance of the proposed model in the presence of different types of noise. However, in the Arabic Speech Corpus for Isolated Words, dataset a variety of feature extraction methods have been considered, namely MFCCs, perceptual linear prediction (PLP) and RASTA-perceptual linear prediction. In addition, white noise and babble noise have been added to the test set in three levels of noise: 30 db, 20 db, 10 db.

4.3 Hyperparameters Optimisation

A validation set is used to optimise the hyperparameters of each model. This validation set is extracted from the training in the SAD set, and we report the result on the unseen test set. The optimisation has been carried out on the clean dataset only, meaning that all of these models have not been exposed to noisy data in the optimisation phase or in the training phase. In the ESN and ESNEKM we suggest fixing the size of the reservoir to a relatively small number, while optimising the rest of parameters reduces the required time to select the hyperparameters.

5   Results and Discussions

The results on the SAD, summarised in table 1, show the superior performance of the proposed system compared to the systems found in the literature. To account for the stochastic behaviour of ESN, we repeated the experiments ten times and report the mean and standard deviation. In this dataset (no noise added), the performance of ESN and ESNEKM is relatively similar; however, ESNEKM is more stable as can be seen from the value of its standard deviation.

Table 1. The results obtained by the proposed system , ESN and from the compared studies

System	Result
TM (Nacereddine Hammami et al, 2010) [11]	93.10%
CHMM (Nacereddine Hammami et al 2012) [12]	94.09%
LoGID (Paulo R. Cavalin et al,2012)[13]	95.99%
ESN(This work)	99.06% (0.23)
ESNEKM(This work)	99.16% (0.12)

Table 2 shows the results for the Arabic Speech Corpus for Isolated Words. In the absence of noise, ESN and ESNEKM were examined under all the considered feature extraction approaches, and approximately all of them provide a similar performance when fed to ESNEKM. This result does not hold true in the noisy sets as PLP-RASTA provides a superior performance regardless of the type or the level of noise. As in the previous experiment, ESNEKM provides much more stable results and outperforms the baseline model in all the sets. The best results on the clean and the noisy sets are achieved when combining PLP-RASTA with ESNEKM.

In our experiments ESNEKM provides a better performance compared to ESN even if the reservoir size is relatively small (100 nodes). However, there are some limitations related to the proposed system, and the added complexity in the output layer of the network (resulting from replacing the linear readout function with a nonlinear function) can be seen as the major issue. This issue includes the selection of the kernel and optimising its parameters. In addition, the testing time depends on the training size. Unlike support vector machines (SVM), the solution in EKM is not sparse.

Table 2. The results obtained by the proposed system, ESN and a baseline hidden Markov model (HMM). In ESN and ESNEKM, we report the means and the standard deviations over ten runs.

Dataset		Feature Extraction	HMM	ESN	ESNEKM
Clean		MFCCs	97.65%	98.97%(0.15)	99.59%(0.05)
		PLP	98.45%	99.16%(0.11)	99.31%(0.09)
		RASTA-PLP	98.8 %	99.38%(0.11)	99.69%(0.06)
White Noise	30 db	MFCCs	96.4%	98.03%(0.21)	99.05%(0.13)
		PLP	91.3%	90.13%(0.36)	97.59%(0.17)
		RASTA-PLP	98.1%	99.04%(0.11)	99.59%(0.06)
	20 db	MFCCs	85.29%	94.91%(0.37)	94.82%(0.30)
		PLP	51.13%	56.07%(6.66)	75.39%(0.97)
		RASTA-PLP	96.05%	97.32% (0.33)	98.41%(0.07)
	10 db	MFCCs	45.67%	77.19%(2.12)	79.50%(0.85)
		PLP	12.06%	19.83%(3.83)	35.35%(1.96)
		RASTA-PLP	81.99%	87.48%(1.47)	90.29%(0.53)
Babble Noise	30 db	MFCCs	95.85%	97.23 %(0.29)	99.35 %(0.18)
		PLP	97.05%	97.87%(0.36)	99.02%(0.06)
		RASTA-PLP	98.65%	99.22%(0.19)	99.65%(0.06)
	20 db	MFCCs	78.49%	89.72%(0.87)	94.41%(0.34)
		PLP	86.64%	89.47% (2.43)	96.64%(0.22)
		RASTA-PLP	96.75%	97.18%(0.42)	98.30%(0.14)
	10 db	MFCCs	31.77%	64.12%(2.31)	65.48%(0.86)
		PLP	54.23%	56.23%(4.82)	81.23%(0.32)
		RASTA-PLP	85.14%	85.45%(8.6)	90.76%(0.44)

6   Conclusions

A novel speech recognition model based on RC and EKM which we call ES-NEKM was proposed, and was evaluated on a newly developed corpus and the well-known spoken Arabic digits (SAD). Different feature extraction methods considered in this study include mel-frequency cepstral coefficients (MFCCs), perceptual linear prediction (PLP) and RASTA-perceptual linear prediction. The result was compared with a baseline hidden Markov model (HMM), so that nine models were compared in total. These models were trained on clean data and then tested on unseen data with different levels and types of noise. ESNEKM models outperformed HMM models under all the feature extraction methods, noise levels, and noise types. The best performance was obtained by the model that combined RASTA-PLP with ESNEKM. Future work will include an investigation of the system usability in Arabic continuous speech and the possible use of a language model.

References

1. Jaeger, H.: The "echo state" approach to analysing and training recurrent neural networks-with an erratum note. Tecnical report GMD report 148 (2001)
2. Huang, G.B., Zhou, H., Ding, X., Zhang, R.: Extreme learning machine for regression and multiclass classification. IEEE Transactions on Systems, Man, and Cybernetics, Part B: Cybernetics 42, 513–529 (2012)
3. Verstraeten, D.: Reservoir computing: computation with dynamical systems. Electronics and Information Systems, Gent. Ghent University (2009)
4. Lukoševičius, M., Jaeger, H., Schrauwen, B.: Reservoir computing trends. KI-Künstliche Intelligenz, 1–7 (2012)
5. Lukoševičius, M.: A practical guide to applying echo state networks. Neural Networks: Tricks of the Trade, 659–686 (2012)
6. Huang, G.B., Zhu, Q.Y., Siew, C.K.: Extreme learning machine: A new learning scheme of feedforward neural networks. In: Proceedings of the 2004 IEEE International Joint Conference on Neural Networks, vol. 2, pp. 985–990. IEEE (2004)
7. Huang, G.B., Zhu, Q.Y., Siew, C.K.: Extreme learning machine: theory and applications. Neurocomputing 70, 489–501 (2006)
8. Huang, G.B., Wang, D.H., Lan, Y.: Extreme learning machines: a survey. International Journal of Machine Learning and Cybernetics 2, 107–122 (2011)
9. Triefenbach, F., Martens, J.P.: Can non-linear readout nodes enhance the performance of reservoir-based speech recognizers? In: 2011 First International Conference on Informatics and Computational Intelligence (ICI), pp. 262–267 (2011)
10. Alalshekmubarak, A., Smith, L.S.: A novel approach combining recurrent neural network and support vector machines for time series classification. In: 2013 9th International Conference on Innovations in Information Technology (IIT), pp. 42–47 (2013)
11. Hammami, N., Bedda, M.: Improved tree model for arabic speech recognition. In: 2010 3rd IEEE International Conference on Computer Science and Information Technology (ICCSIT), vol. 5, pp. 521–526 (2010)
12. Hammami, N., Bedda, M., Nadir, F.: The second-order derivatives of mfcc for improving spoken arabic digits recognition using tree distributions approximation model and hmms. In: 2012 International Conference on Communications and Information Technology (ICCIT), pp. 1–5 (2012)
13. Cavalin, P.R., Sabourin, R., Suen, C.Y.: Logid: An adaptive framework combining local and global incremental learning for dynamic selection of ensembles of hmms. Pattern Recognition 45, 3544–3556 (2012)

Neural Network Based Data Fusion for Hand Pose Recognition with Multiple ToF Sensors

Thomas Kopinski[1], Alexander Gepperth[2], Stefan Geisler[1],
and Uwe Handmann[1]

[1] University of Applied Sciences Bottrop, Computer Science Institute,
Postfach 100755, 45407 Mühlheim, Germany
[2] ENSTA ParisTech- UIIS Lab,
828 Blvd des Maréchaux, 91120 Palaiseau, France

Abstract. We present a study on 3D based hand pose recognition using a new generation of low-cost time-of-flight(ToF) sensors intended for outdoor use in automotive human-machine interaction. As signal quality is impaired compared to Kinect-type sensors, we study several ways to improve performance when a large number of gesture classes is involved. We investigate the performance of different 3D descriptors, as well as the fusion of two ToF sensor streams. By basing a data fusion strategy on the fact that multilayer perceptrons can produce normalized confidences individually for each class, and similarly by designing information-theoretic online measures for assessing confidences of decisions, we show that appropriately chosen fusion strategies can improve overall performance to a very satisfactory level. Real-time capability is retained as the used 3D descriptors, the fusion strategy as well as the online confidence measures are computationally efficient.

1 Introduction

As "intelligent" devices enter more and more areas of everyday life, the issue of man-machine interaction becomes ever more important. As interaction should be easy and natural for the user and also not require a high cognitive load, non-verbal means of interaction such as hand gestures will play a decisive role in this field of research. With the advent of low-cost Kinect-type 3D sensors, and more recently of low-cost ToF sensors (400-500€) that can be applied in outdoor scenarios, the use of point clouds seems a very logical choice. This presents challenges to machine learning approaches as the data dimensionality and sensor noise are high, as well as the number of interesting gesture categories. In this article, we confine ourself to optimize the categorization of static hand gestures (denoted "poses"), and investigate whether the addition of a second ToF sensor, viewing the hand from a different angle, may improve categorization performance if an appropriate fusion is performed. As the sensors we use are very cheap, this is not a barrier to wide-spread deployment in mass products. We will first discuss the related work relevant for our research (Sec. 2) and then go on to describe the sensors and the used database in Sec. 3. Subsequently, in Sec. 4 we will

S. Wermter et al. (Eds.): ICANN 2014, LNCS 8681, pp. 233–240, 2014.

give an account of the used different holistic point cloud descriptors and explain the meaning of the parameter variations we will test. The key questions we will investigate in Sec. 5 concern the proper **choice of parametrized descriptors**, furthermore the **added value of a second ToF sensor**, and lastly the issue of **efficient neural network based fusion strategies**. In Sec. 6, the obtained results will be discussed in the light of these questions.

2   Related Work

Depth sensors allow for an easy and robust solution for recognizing hand poses as they can easily deal with tasks as segmentation of the hand/arm from the body by simple thresholding as described in [1]. Several surveys have made use of this feature with various approaches to segmentation. Moreover it is possible to make use of the depth information to distinguish between ambiguous hand postures [2]. Nevertheless, it has not been possible to achieve satisfactory results utilizing only a single depth sensor. Either the range of application was limited or the performance results were dissatisfying. Usually a good performance result was achieved with a very limited pose set or if designed for a specific application [3]. ToF-Sensors - although working at stereo-frame rate - generally suffer from a low resolution which of course makes it difficult to extract proper features. Improved results can be achieved when fusing Stereo Cameras with Depth Sensors, e.g. in [4]. In [5] a single ToF-Sensor is used to detect hand postures with the Viewpoint Feature Histogram.

Various approaches make use of the Kinect's ability to extract depth data and RGB data simultaneously [6]. However this approach relies heavily on finding hand pixels in order to be able to segment the hand correctly. Moreover, approaches utilising the Kinect sensor will always suffer from changing lighting conditions which in our case is no drawback as ToF-sensors show robust results in such situations. [7] also make use of the Kinect sensor's ability to acquire RGB and depth data simultaneously albeit using a hand model as a basis for hand pose detection. Nevertheless this algorithm also relies on finding skin-colored pixels to allow for segmentation in 2D and 3D as well as tracking the hand.

Beneath the technology development research is conducted on how to design intuitive user interfaces. Bailly et al. investigate and compare different menu techniques in [8]. Wilson and Benko developed a system with several projectors and depth cameras named LightSpace [9].

In-car scenarios have been developed for several years as the the driver can keep his hands close to the steering wheel while being able to focus on the surrounding environment. Pointing capabilities could be interesting to control content in the head-up displays. A good overview is given in [10].

Such scenarios demand robust data extraction techniques which is provided by the aforementioned ToF-sensor. Our approach shows that it is possible to achieve satisfactory results relying solely on depth data when detecting various hand poses. In merging information from a second depth sensor we are able to boost our results significantly while always retaining the applicability under various lighting conditions - one of the greatest advantages of ToF-sensors compared to e.g. the frequently used Kinect sensor.

3   Database

The data was recorded using two ToF-Sensors (Figure 1 and 2) of type Cam-board nano which provides depth images of resolution 165x120px with a frame rate of 90fps. The illumination wavelength is 850nm which makes the cameras applicable in various light conditions whilst maintaining robustness versus day-light interferences. Since the ToF-principle works by measuring the time the emitted light needs to travel from the sensor to an object and back pixel-wise the light is modulated by a frequency of 30MHz in order to be able to distinguish it from interferences. In a multi-sensor setup however this may lead to a distor-tion of measurements since both sensors have the same modulation frequency. To avoid such measurement errors, the data was recorded by taking alternating snapshots from each sensor. As can be seen in Figure 1 the cameras are mounted in a fixed position at a distance of approx 49.5cm and a perpendicular angle from the recorded object. This allows for a recording of the database such that the hand can be placed in an equal distance of about 35cm from each camera to the centroid of the resulting point cloud dataset and therefore each camera can also be calibrated to its needs. For the current experiments, focus has been put on the recognition of static hand gestures which are contrasted to dynamic hand gestures. Each set of poses was recorded with a variation of the hand posture in terms of translation and rotation of the hand and fingers. This results in an alphabet of ten hand poses: *point*, *fist*, *grip*, *L*, *stop* and counting from 1-5 (cf. Figure 2). For each pose, a set of 2000 point clouds was recorded for each cam-era. Since we recorded hand poses from four different persons independently, this yields a dataset of 160.000 samples. Additionally, we rotated one camera by 60° towards the other camera and recorded the same set now from an angle of 30° and compared the results to each other resulting in another dataset of 160.000 point clouds. The database is randomly split into two parts of equal size for training and evaluation purposes.

Fig. 1. The current setup for 90°

Fig. 2. The hand pose database

4 Point Cloud Descriptors

All used global descriptors were calculated using methods of the publicly available Point Cloud Library (PCL).

4.1 The ESF-Descriptor

The ESF-Descriptor (Ensemble of Shape Function) [11] is a global descriptor which does not rely on the calculation of the normals. First, 20000 points are sub-sampled from the input point cloud. Then, the algorithm repeatedly samples three points, from which four simple measures are calculated, which are discretized and used for histogram calculation.

4.2 The VFH-Descriptor

The VFH-Descriptor(Viewpoint Feature Histogram) [12] is a global descriptor partially based on the local FPFH (Fast Point Feature Histogram)[13] descriptor. It uses normal information, taking into consideration the view angle between the origin of the source and each point's normal. It furthermore includes the SPFH (Simplified Point Feature Histogram) for the centroid of the cloud, as well as a histogram of distances of the points in the cloud to the centroid. When calculating the VFHs for the various hand poses we have to take into consideration the influence of the normals on the results. In the described case the search parameter r guides the influence of the surrounding for the calculation of the normal. Choosing a small r can result in low descriptive power while a large r results in high computational load. We empirically chose a value of $r = 5cm$ and denote the resulting descriptor VFH5.

4.3 Neural Network Classification and Fusion

With M cameras, N descriptors will be produced per frame (here: M=N) according to the methods described above. We use a multilayer perceptron (MLP) network[14] to implement the multi-class decision, which is either based on the the concatenation of all N descriptors ("early fusion"), or on each descriptor individually, with a subsequent combination of results ("late fusion"). The MLP training algorithm is "RProp"[14], with standard hyperparameters $\eta^+ = 1.2$, $\eta^- = 0.6$, $\Delta_0 = 0.1$, $\Delta_{\min} = 10^{-10}$ and $\Delta_{\max} = 5$. Network topology is NK-150-10 (hidden layers are fixed to 1[14], hidden layer sizes from 10-500 were tested), K indicating the method-dependent descriptor size, and N the number of cameras, here $N = 2$. Us usual, activation functions are sigmoid throughout the network. MLP classifiers have 10 output neurons (one per gesture class) with activities o_i. Thus, the final classification decision is obtained by taking the class of the neuron with the highest output. However, we do not necessarily wish for every classification to be taken seriously, and we define several confidence measures $\text{conf}(\{o_i\})$ to this effect. Final decisions are thus taken in the following way:

$$\text{class} = \begin{cases} \text{argmax}_i o_i & \text{if } \text{conf}(\{o_i\}) > \theta_{\text{conf}} \\ \text{no decision} & \text{else} \end{cases}$$

We test three ad hoc confidence measures, which perform a mapping from $\mathbb{R}^{10} \to \mathbb{R}$: "confOfMax", "diffMeasure" and "varianceMeasure". Each of these measures is derived from the idea of approximating an entropy calculation, based on the information-theoretic idea that low entropy means high information content. The precise definitions are as follows:

$$\text{confOfMax}(\{o_i\}) = \max o_i$$
$$\text{diffMeasure}(\{o_i\}) = \max_i o_i - \max_i^2 o_i$$
$$\text{varianceMeasure}(\{o_i\}) = \frac{1}{N} \sum_i (o_i - E(\{o_i\}))^2 \tag{1}$$

where $\max_i^2 o_i$ indicates the second-strongest maximum over the neural outputs. For performing late fusion, that is, obtaining two independent classifications o_i^1, o_i^2 based on each camera's features, we simply calculate the arithmetic mean of both output vectors: $o_i^F = 0.5(o_i^1 + o_i^2)$. This intrinsically takes into account the variance in each response, as an output distribution strongly peaked on one class will dominate a flat (or less peaked) distribution. The resulting output distribution o_i^F can then be subjected to the decision rule of Eqn. (1).

5   Experiments

We implement a multilayer perceptron (MLP) as described in Sec. 4.3 using the freely available OpenCV library[15] and its C++ interface[1]. Each experiment is performed 10 times with different initial conditions for the MLP, and the best result is retained. In these experiments, we systematically evaluate the influence of different confidence measures("confOfMax","diffMeasure" or "varianceMeasure", see Sec. 4.3) on the fusion strategy ("add", see Sec. 4.3) while measuring the performance of the first camera, the second camera as well as an "early fusion" or a "late fusion" of the two cameras. In order to test the influence of different 3D descriptors, we perform an identical evaluation except that the VFH5 point cloud descriptors is replaced by ESF. Additionally, we perform the same evaluation on an analogous database using the VFH5 descriptor where the angle between ToF sensors is 90 deg. Results are evaluated by default according to whether one among the S strongest output neurons coincides with the true class of a point cloud ("S-peak measure"). Unless explicitly states, we use $S = 1$. Results are given in Fig. 3. Several important aspects may be perceived: first of all, fusion strongly improves

---

[1] The code and data for all experiments is available under
www.gepperth.net/alexander/downloads/2014_icann.tar.gz

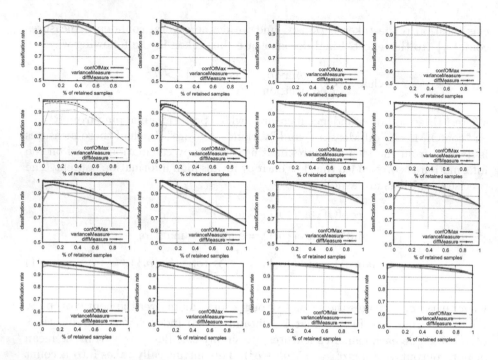

Fig. 3. Experimental results. First row: VFH5 descriptor, 30 degree between cameras. Second row: VFH5, 90 degrees between cameras. Third row: ESF descriptor, 30 degrees between cameras. Last row: Same as third row, only classification errors evaluated using the two-peak measure, see text. In all rows, the order of diagrams is, from left to right: 1,2) first/second sensor 3) late fusion 4) early fusion. Individual plots show the effects of varying confidence thresholds on classification accuracies for several possible online confidence measures. We do not show the method-dependent confidence thresholds but rather the acceptance rates which vary if thresholds are varied. At the far right of each diagram, we recover the classification performance obtained when not rejecting anything, naturally leading to reduced performance.

results in comparison to any single sensor, w.r.t. to the efficiency of sample rejection but also in absolute terms when no samples are rejected, corresponding to the intersection of the graphs with the right boundary of the coordinate system. Secondly, early fusion has slightly superior performance than late fusion but the difference is marginal, potentially giving a preference to late fusion due to reduced computational complexity. Lastly, the different confidence measure are consistently ranked throughout all experiments, with the "diffMeasure" being the best-performing one, closely followed by "confOfMax". This is encouraging as especially confOfMax is computationally very lightweight, again favoring real-time execution. Thirdly, the angle between cameras does not seem to play a crucial role even though individual camera results differ considerably. Here, the beneficial aspects of fusion can be clearly demonstrated. And lastly, the ESF descriptor seems to perform slightly better than VFH5, which might lead us to prefer this descriptor as it is computationally simpler and requires constant execution time regardless of point cloud size. An interesting observation is that the two-peak measure enormously improves classification rates in all conditions. This is very useful for an application, especially for temporal filtering, as the behaviour of the second-strongest output can obviously also provide valuable information about the true pose class.

Training times are around 10min per single experiment, which outperforms an equivalent SVM-based (Support Vector Machine) "one-versus-all" implementation by a large margin. Average execution times vary between 1-5 Hz depending of the use of the descriptor (ESF: 0.2s/0.2s for 30/90 deg. between cameras, VFH5: 0.4s/0.9s) whereas NN execution time is $< 0.005s$. On average the point clouds contain 1300-1600 points, depending on the angle between cameras and the distance of the recorded hand to each camera.

6   Discussion and Outlook

Analyzing the results in the light of the key research questions formulated in Sec. 1, we can state that, first of all, fusion with data from a second ToF sensor improves results tremendously in all investigated conditions, camera setups and point cloud descriptors. Interestingly, late fusion performs globally just as well as early fusion, which is important as it has the potential to be much more computationally efficient. However, even when considering individual ToF sensors, the computation of confidence measures from output activity distributions is of tremendous impact as well. Confidence can be efficiently extracted at execution time (no need to see the class labels for this) and used to avoid classification decisions when they are likely to be incorrect anyway. We tested a number of information-theoretically motivated measures and luckily the most efficient measures seem to perform best. Concerning the influence of the used 3D descriptors: the ESF descriptor yields best performance with or without fusion. As this descriptor does not require normals computation and has approximately constant scaling behavior w.r.t. point cloud size, it is the most appropriate choice for real-time applications in the targeted automotive domain.

Summarizing, we have presented an adaptive data fusion approach for multiple ToF sensors adressing the generic task of 3D point cloud categorization in a multi-class setting. The fact of using a neural network for this purpose is of high advantage (besides very favorable database size scaling and multi-class issues) as the ensemble of normalized output confidences contains valuable information as well that can be efficiently exploited at runtime to improve results. Neural network learning furthermore removes the need for precise multi-sensor calibration as long as only categorization is targetted. Further work will include an implementation of this system in a true automotive setting, extensive performance evaluations, and possibly a fusion with a visual sensor as well.

References

1. Oprisescu, S., Rasche, C., Su, B.: Automatic static hand gesture recognition using tof cameras. In: 2012 Proceedings of the 20th European Signal Processing Conference (EUSIPCO), pp. 2748–2751. IEEE (2012)

2. Kollorz, E., Penne, J., Hornegger, J., Barke, A.: Gesture recognition with a time-of-flight camera. International Journal of Intelligent Systems Technologies and Applications 5(3), 334–343 (2008)
3. Soutschek, S., Penne, J., Hornegger, J., Kornhuber, J.: 3-d gesture-based scene navigation in medical imaging applications using time-of-flight cameras. In: IEEE Computer Society Conference on Computer Vision and Pattern Recognition Workshops, CVPRW 2008, pp. 1–6. IEEE (2008)
4. Wen, Y., Hu, C., Yu, G., Wang, C.: A robust method of detecting hand gestures using depth sensors. In: 2012 IEEE International Workshop on Haptic Audio Visual Environments and Games (HAVE), pp. 72–77. IEEE (2012)
5. Kapuscinski, T., Oszust, M., Wysocki, M.: Hand gesture recognition using time-of-flight camera and viewpoint feature histogram. In: Korbicz, J., Kowal, M. (eds.) Intelligent Systems in Technical and Medical Diagnostics. AISC, vol. 230, pp. 403–414. Springer, Heidelberg (2013)
6. Tang, M.: Recognizing hand gestures with Microsoft's kinect (2011), http://www.stanford.edu/class/ee368/Project_11/Reports/ Tang_Hand_Gesture_Recognition.pdf
7. Oikonomidis, I., Kyriazis, N., Argyros, A.A.: Efficient model-based 3d tracking of hand articulations using kinect. In: BMVC, pp. 1–11 (2011)
8. Bailly, G., Walter, R., Müller, J., Ning, T., Lecolinet, E.: Comparing free hand menu techniques for distant displays using linear, marking and finger-count menus. In: Campos, P., Graham, N., Jorge, J., Nunes, N., Palanque, P., Winckler, M. (eds.) INTERACT 2011, Part II. LNCS, vol. 6947, pp. 248–262. Springer, Heidelberg (2011)
9. Wilson, A.D., Benko, H.: Combining multiple depth cameras and projectors for interactions on, above and between surfaces. In: Proceedings of the 23nd Annual ACM Symposium on User Interface Software and Technology, pp. 273–282. ACM (2010)
10. Pickering, C.A., Burnham, K.J., Richardson, M.J.: A research study of hand gesture recognition technologies and applications for human vehicle interaction. In: 3rd Conf. on Automotive Electronics, Citeseer (2007)
11. Wohlkinger, W., Vincze, M.: Ensemble of shape functions for 3d object classification. In: 2011 IEEE International Conference on Robotics and Biomimetics (ROBIO), pp. 2987–2992. IEEE (2011)
12. Rusu, R.B., Bradski, G., Thibaux, R., Hsu, J.: Fast 3d recognition and pose using the viewpoint feature histogram. In: 2010 IEEE/RSJ International Conference on Intelligent Robots and Systems (IROS), pp. 2155–2162. IEEE (2010)
13. Rusu, R.B., Blodow, N., Beetz, M.: Fast point feature histograms (fpfh) for 3d registration. In: IEEE International Conference on Robotics and Automation, ICRA 2009, pp. 3212–3217. IEEE (2009)
14. Haykin, S.: Neural networks: a comprehensive foundation. Prentice Hall (1999)
15. Bradski, G., Kaehler, A.: Learning OpenCV: Computer vision with the OpenCV library. O'Reilly Media, Incorporated (2008)

Sparse Single-Hidden Layer Feedforward Network for Mapping Natural Language Questions to SQL Queries

Issam Hadj Laradji, Lahouari Ghouti, Faisal Saleh, and Musab A. AlTurki

Department of Information and Computer Science,
King Fahd University of Petroleum and Minerals, Dhahran 3126, Saudi Arabia
issam.laradji@gmail.com, {lahouari,musab}@kfupm.edu.sa,
faisal86@icloud.com

Abstract. Mapping natural language (NL) statements into SQL queries allows users to interact with systems through everyday language. Semantic parsing has seen a growing interest over the past decades. In this paper, we extend single hidden layer feedforward network (SLFN) by adding the Kullback-Liebler (KL) divergence parameter to its objective function. We refer to this algorithm as Sparse SLFN (S-SLFN) which can learn whether an SQL query answers a particular NL question. With Bag of Words (BoW) representing the questions and the queries, the algorithm, by enforcing sparsity, is meant to retain robust features representing informative relationships and structure of the data. Experimental results show that S-SLFN outperforms SLFN and other algorithms for the GeoQueries dataset by a respectable margin.

Keywords: Single-hidden Layer Feedforward Network (SLFN), Sparsity, Semantic Parsing.

1 Introduction

Powerful consumer handheld devices became increasingly dominant over the past years, underscoring the need to simplify complex tasks for users not well-acquainted with technology. One such task is to retrieve data records corresponding to the user's query. To simplify the task is to allow users to ask for information in everyday language. Therefore, a system should be able to map the received natural language (NL) statement into SQL queries to fetch the right records.

Some early methods for semantic parsing adopted formal rules for mapping NL statements to machine instructions. Jones et al. [1] developed tree transducers for the mapping, with a variational Bayesian inference algorithm providing elegant solutions to the problem. Further, Jones et al. [2] presented an approach that makes use of synchronous context free graph grammars. It constructs an intermediate graph-structured meaning representation, which, with the application of synchronous hyperedge replacement grammars, can be translated into either its respective machine instruction or natural language statement.

S. Wermter et al. (Eds.): ICANN 2014, LNCS 8681, pp. 241–248, 2014.
© Springer International Publishing Switzerland 2014

Other learning algorithms employing probability functions have emerged as well. Poon and Domingos [3] developed a deep network whose inputs represent the dependency trees of given sentences, and whose hidden features represent clusters of meaning expressions, realizing a novel unsupervised approach to semantic parsing. Involving Support Vector Machines, Giordani and Moschitti [4] provided an interesting perspective to semantic parsing by constructing custom kernels and applying them to datasets containing NL statements with their matching SQL statements.

The work in this paper is inspired by the unsupervised feature extraction algorithm, Sparse Auto-encoders (SAE) [5]. From image pixels, SAE would extract new robust features representing interesting structural information of the pixels, meant to hold essential information of the image. However, when facing datasets containing only few question-SQL matching pairs, the features extracted from learning to reconstruct them would not likely be robust.

Classifiers, on the other hand, can leverage samples of non-matching question-query pair representing the combined features of questions and their non-matching queries, to efficiently construct the decision function. Furthermore, what advantages SAE has in extracting features can be added to single-hidden layer feedforward networks (SLFN). Therefore, we developed a sparse SLFN containing the Kullback-Liebler (KL) divergence parameter in its objective function. By injecting sparsity, the hidden layer would learn robust hidden features representing superior structural information that would otherwise foster correct mapping of natural language (NL) statements to their respective SQL queries.

While the first step of the approach involves Bag of Words (BoW) extraction of terms and their occurrences as features, KL divergence ensures that the relationships between these features developed in the hidden layer are informative by discarding those that do not contribute much in building the decision function.

Results on the GeoQueries showed that S-SLFN outperformed single hidden layer feedforward network [6], Logistic Regression [7], and Support Vector Machines [8], by at least 2% AUC. The process involves the classifier training on the training dataset - containing the correct and incorrect pairs of NL statement and SQL query - and then predicting the SQL queries closest in answering the NL statements in the testing set.

The remainder of the paper is organized as follows. Section 2 provides technical background; section 3 presents the proposed approach; section 4 explains the experimentation results and analysis; section 5 concludes the paper.

2   Technical Background

2.1   Single-Hidden Layer Feedforward Neural Network

Assume a single hidden layer feedforward network SLFN with L hidden neurons and n training samples. Consider a matrix $X \in R^n \times R^m$ defining the input vectors as $\{x_i | x_i \in R^m\}$ for $i = 0, 1, ..., n$ where m is the number of input features representing a vector x_i, the bias vectors $b_1 \in R^L$ and $b_2 \in R$, and the target vector $Y \in R^n$ defined as y_i for $i = 1, 2, ..., n$ where y_i is the respective output of

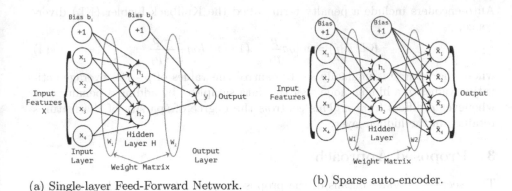

(a) Single-layer Feed-Forward Network.   (b) Sparse auto-encoder.

Fig. 1. Neural Networks

x_i. Let us also consider the matrices $W_1 \in R^m \times R^L$, and $W_2 \in R^L$ representing the outgoing weights of the input layer and the hidden layer, respectively. Then, the output of SLFN is,

$$f(x) = W_2 \, g(X \cdot W_1 + b_1) + b_2 \qquad (1)$$

where $g(x) : R \rightarrow R$ is the activation function (e.g. sigmoid and hyperbolic tanh).

The objective function set as cross-entropy is defined as follows,

$$J(W, b; x, y) = -f(x) \ln y - (1 - f(x)) \ln(1 - y) \qquad (2)$$

Taking the gradient of eq. (2) with respect to the parameters would allow updating the parameters as follows,

$$W_i := W_i - \alpha \left[\frac{1}{n} \Delta W_i \right]$$

$$b_i := b_i - \alpha \left[\frac{1}{n} \Delta b_i \right] \qquad (3)$$

where α is the learning rate, ΔW_i is the weight change in terms of the objective function derivative with respect to weight i, and Δb_i is the bias change in terms of the objective function derivative with respect to the bias unit i. An SLFN network is shown in Fig. 1 (a).

2.2 Sparse Auto-encoders

Illustrated in Fig. 1 (b), Sparse Auto-encoders aim to extract a robust representation - retained in the hidden layer - of the data by learning to reconstruct the input features. In addition to the objective function defined for SLFN, Sparse

Auto-encoders include a penalty term called the Kullback-Liebler (KL) divergence,

$$KL(p||\hat{p}) = p \, log \frac{p}{\hat{p}_j} + (1-p) \, log \frac{1-p}{1-\hat{p}_j} \tag{4}$$

where the value ρ is manually set to control the values of $\hat{\rho}$ - the average activation values of a hidden node over the data samples - by adding a penalty cost whenever $\hat{\rho}$ differs from ρ. This controls the degree of sparsity of the features retained in the hidden layer.

3   Proposed Approach

This section provides details of the proposed approach, whose scheme is illustrated in Fig. 2.

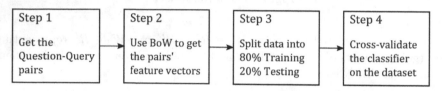

Fig. 2. Flow diagram of proposed procedure

3.1   Feature Representation

Given a set of samples $(x_i, y_i), i = 1, 2, ..., N$ where $x \in \mathbb{R}^{(n+m)}$ and $y_i = \{0, 1\}$, n and m are the number of features representing question q_i and SQL query s_i, respectively. For q_i and s_i that match, $y_i = 1$; otherwise, $y_i = 0$. We say q_i matches s_i when s_i returns results relevant to q_i. It is worth noting that for datasets containing no non-matching question-query pairs (negative sample), by the Cartesian product, we create negative samples by concatenating the feature vector of each question with each wrong query.

These features are extracted using Bag of Words (BoW) [9], where for each unique term, except for the stop words - like 'a', and 'the', the number of occurrences are counted and given in the feature vector.

To illustrate this, given feature vectors representing q_i and s_i, as in Fig. 3. We join the feature vectors together to form the question-query pair qs_i.

The benefit of BoW lies in their ability to compactly, and effectively summarize the features defining the statements.

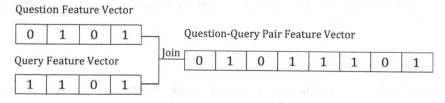

Fig. 3. Joining the feature vectors to form the question-query pair

3.2   Sparse Single-Layer Feed-Forward Network

We developed a Sparse Single-layer Feed-Forward Network (S-SLFN) that extends SLFN by adding the sparsity term - Kullback-Liebler (KL) divergence - to the objective function given in eq. (2). The term works by discouraging redundant and uninformative hidden activations. In other words, on training, the algorithm discards hidden activations whose penalty cost, determined by KL, supersedes their contributions to constructing the decision boundary. To put this under mathematical formulation, the modified objective function is the combination of $J(W, b; x, y)$ in eq. (2) and $KL(p||\hat{p})$ in eq. (4), which is,

$$J_{Sparse}(W, b) = J(W, b; x, y) + KL(p||\hat{p}) \tag{5}$$

The value for ρ is set arbitrarily. ρ penalizes the objective function when the average hidden activation values of a hidden node over the data samples - given as $\hat{\rho}$ - is different from ρ. The Kullback-Liebler (KL) divergence measures the distance between the two distributions, ρ and $\hat{\rho}$. It is asymmetric in the sense that a $\hat{\rho}$ larger than ρ is penalized with higher cost than if it were smaller, even when the difference is equal. This provides a favorable outcome, as having lower penalty for smaller $\hat{\rho}$ would serve the main objective of the algorithm: to extract a sparse set of hidden features.

Since the meaning of a phrase is not necessarily reflected by the meaning of the individual constituent words, the sparsity term would provide more information about a statement than word occurrences. It allows for the extraction of robust features describing the essence of a statement while eliminating possibly noisy information from redundant words.

4   Experimentation

4.1   Experimental Setup

We ran the experiments in a machine with 3.6 GHz quad-core CPU and 32 GB RAM operating a 64-bit Windows 7. For a fair, reliable assessment, we split the data into 80% training set and 20% testing set in a stratified manner. As such, both sets have the same ratio of positive samples to negative samples. We repeated the cross-validation five times and took the average of their scores, based on the metric Area Under the Receiver Operating Characteristic (ROC) curve (AUC). The reason for such metric is that, the datasets are imbalanced, as they contain negative samples (non-matching question-SQL query pairs) that highly outnumber matching pairs. After all, AUC is a popular metric for imbalanced datasets [10].

For the benchmark, we evaluated the following algorithms with the described settings (unless specified otherwise),

1. Logistic Regression with stochastic gradient descent and iterations till convergence.

2. Three different Support Vector Machines (SVM): SVM with linear kernel, SVM with polynomial kernel of degree 3, and SVM with Radial Basis Function (RBF) kernel.
3. Single-hidden layer feedforward neural network (SLFN) with 25 hidden neurons, stochastic gradient descent and iterations till convergence
4. Sparse (SLFN) with 25 hidden neurons, stochastic gradient descent, iterations till convergence, and ρ set to 0.12 for GeoQueries, and 0.1 for RestQueries.

While the choice of ρ is subjective, we found that these values has lead to better results than otherwise.

For each question-query pair from the testing set, the classifier outputs the probability that the pair matches. The AUC metric then evaluates the performance of the computed probabilities.

4.2 Experimental Design

We evaluated the learning algorithms on two datasets: GeoQueries[1] and RestQueries[1]. Table 1 reports the statistics of the two datasets including the number of samples, and the number of extracted BoW features. It is noteworthy to mention that, while the original datasets contained only positive samples (matching pairs), by the Cartesian product explained in section 3.1, we introduced a large number of negative samples to help classifiers develop robust decision functions.

Table 1. Generated dataset statistics

Dataset	Questions	Queries	Positive samples	Negative samples	BoW features
GeoQueries	149	80	164	11756	89
RestQueries	126	77	852	8850	21

Below we show an example of a matching question-query pair from the GeoQueries dataset.

– **Question:** what is the capital of the state with the largest population?
– **Query:**   select   distinct   state.capital   from   state   where state.population=(select max(state.population) from state)
– **Extracted BoW terms:** what, capital, state, largest, population, select, distinct, capital, max

The feature vector representing the question-query pair above will contain '1's in the indices corresponding to the extracted BoW terms and '0' s for the rest of the BoW terms. The construction of this feature vector is explained in section 3.1.

---

[1] Available at: http://disi.unitn.it/~agiordani/corpora.htm

4.3   Results and Analysis

We trained the algorithms on the GeoQuery dataset to evaluate the hypothesis that S-SLFN achieves the better performance. Table 2 shows that S-SLFN has indeed topped the benchmark with a solid improvement of 2% over the next best achieving algorithm - SVM with RBF kernel.

This suggests that the Kullback-Liebler (KL) divergence term retained better features of the training samples, whereas SLFN and SVM retained weaker features that are possibly redundant and uninformative.

Finally, testing the algorithms on the RestQuery dataset have shown another favorable achievement of S-SLFN. As illustrated in Table 2, while S-SLFN did not see a vast improvement over SLFN, it still maintained its first position as the best performing classifier.

Why S-SLFN did not improve much over SLFN can be attributed to the fact that only few BoW features are extracted from RestQueries dataset (Table 1). Because of the limited number of hidden features that can be extracted from the dataset, S-SLFN and SLFN would more or less retain similar features.

Table 2. Comparison between algorithms using the AUC performance metric

Algorithm	GeoQueries	RestQueries
Logistic Regression (LR)	0.84 ± 0.019	0.80 ± 0.015
SVM with Linear Kernel	0.71 ± 0.035	0.47 ± 0.076
SVM with polynomial kernel	0.80 ± 0.026	0.54 ± 0.032
SVM with RBF kernel	0.91 ± 0.021	0.49 ± 0.086
Single-layer Feed-Forward Network (SLFN)	0.89 ± 0.038	0.82 ± 0.010
Sparse SLFN (S-SLFN)	$\mathbf{0.93} \pm 0.020$	$\mathbf{0.83} \pm 0.009$

For RestQueries, each SVM achieved low, yet highly unstable AUC results - as illustrated by the high standard deviation given in Table 2, unlike Logistic Regression, SLFN and S-SLFN. This suggests that SVM is not efficient for RestQueries' type of data, as SVM labeled almost all samples as non-matching pairs, favoring the majority class (negative samples) over the minority (positive samples).

5   Conclusion

We developed a sparse single-hidden feedforward network, a supervised learning algorithm for semantic parsing, specifically for mapping Natural language questions to formal SQL queries. The Kullback-Liebler (KL) divergence parameter in the objective function allows for learning robust features for the hidden layer.

Experimental results have justified the efficacy of S-SLFN over the standard SLFN when the number of BoW is large. For future work, it would be interesting to apply S-SLFN for other problems under semantic parsing, and for online (real-time) mapping of natural questions to SQL queries.

Acknowledgment. The authors would like to thank King Fahd University of Petroleum and Minerals (KFUPM) for supporting this work.

References

1. Jones, B.K., Johnson, M., Goldwater, S.: Semantic parsing with bayesian tree transducers. In: Proceedings of the 50th Annual Meeting of the Association for Computational Linguistics: Long Papers, vol. 1, pp. 488–496. Association for Computational Linguistics (2012)
2. Jones, B., Andreas, J., Bauer, D., Hermann, K.M., Knight, K.: Semantics-based machine translation with hyperedge replacement grammars. In: COLING, pp. 1359–1376 (2012)
3. Poon, H., Domingos, P.: Deep learning for semantic parsing
4. Giordani, A., Moschitti, A.: Semantic mapping between natural language questions and sql queries via syntactic pairing. In: Horacek, H., Métais, E., Muñoz, R., Wolska, M. (eds.) NLDB 2009. LNCS, vol. 5723, pp. 207–221. Springer, Heidelberg (2010)
5. Ng, A.: Sparse autoencoder
6. Sanger, T.D.: Optimal unsupervised learning in a single-layer linear feedforward neural network. Neural Networks 2(6), 459–473 (1989)
7. Hosmer Jr., D.W., Lemeshow, S., Sturdivant, R.X.: Applied logistic regression. Wiley. com (2013)
8. Hearst, M.A., Dumais, S., Osman, E., Platt, J., Scholkopf, B.: Support vector machines. IEEE Intelligent Systems and their Applications 13(4), 18–28 (1998)
9. Wallach, H.M.: Topic modeling: beyond bag-of-words. In: Proceedings of the 23rd International Conference on Machine Learning, pp. 977–984. ACM (2006)
10. He, H., Garcia, E.A.: Learning from imbalanced data. IEEE Transactions on Knowledge and Data Engineering 21(9), 1263–1284 (2009)

Towards Context-Dependence Eye Movements Prediction in Smart Meeting Rooms

Redwan Abdo A. Mohammed, Lars Schwabe, and Oliver Staadt

University of Rostock, Institute of Computer Science, Rostock, Germany
{redwan.mohammed,lars.schwabe,oliver.staadt}@uni-rostock.de

Abstract. Being able to predict gaze locations, as compared to only measuring them, is desirable in many systems such as the design of web pages and commercials adaptive user interfaces, interactive visualization, or attention management systems. However, accurately predicting eye movements remains a challenging problem. In this paper, we present the results of experimental study to improve the prediction of saliency maps in smart meeting rooms. More specifically, we investigate meeting scenarios in terms of their context-dependence saliency based on different image features. We have recorded the center of gaze of users in meeting rooms in different scenarios (giving a talk, listening). We then used a data-driven approach to find out which features are important in each scenario. We found that the predictions differ according to the type of features we selected. Most interestingly, we found that models trained on face features perform better than the models trained on other features in the giving a talk scenario, but in the listening scenario the models trained on competing saliency features from Itti and Koch perform better than the models trained on another features. This finding points towards including context information about the scene and situation into the computation of saliency maps as important towards developing models of eye movements, which operate well under natural conditions such as those encountered in ubiquitous computing settings.

1 Introduction

Understanding the behaviors that are exhibited during human interaction are important. Among these behaviors, gaze represents one of the essential cues. Unfortunately, even though eye movements can now be accurately *measured* with remote sensors, properly *predicting* eye movements is still a challenging task, in particular for more natural scenarios such as those encountered in ubiquitous computing [1]. Prediction, as compared to only to only measuring eye movements, is important for realizing proactive environments. There has been much development of technology-oriented tools to make meetings more effective, for example browsing elements of interest within a recorded meeting [2] or the use of tools that allowed parallel access to shared objects [3] or create abstractive summaries [4]. Considering the social aspects of meetings requires the analysis of different communication cues, for examples, recognizing meeting activities cues [5] and recognition of roles in meetings [6].

S. Wermter et al. (Eds.): ICANN 2014, LNCS 8681, pp. 249–256, 2014.
© Springer International Publishing Switzerland 2014

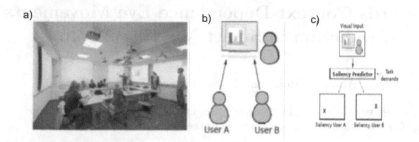

Fig. 1. Application scenario for using saliency maps in smart environments. **a)** A typical scenario in the smart meeting room of the MuSAMA GRK (see musama.de). **b)** First abstraction with a speaker in front of a presentation screen and two users looking at that screen. **c)** Illustration of how to use a saliency predictor, which computes a saliency map, in such a setting: Users A and B have approximately the same visual input, but depending on their task demands, different locations in their visual field are rendered as most salient (red crosses).

Models of saliency have been used to predict fixation locations. Most models of saliency [7,8] are biologically inspired and based on a bottom-up computational model which does *not* take into account contextual factors or the goal of a user in a visual task. Multiple low-level visual features such as intensity, color, orientation, texture and motion are extracted from the image at multiple scales. Then, a saliency map is computed for each of the features and combined in a linear or non-linear fashion into a master saliency map that represents the saliency of each pixel. This idea of saliency maps was used in other studies, where it was extended and further developed. For example, Mahadevan and Vasconcelos [9] proposed a discriminant formulation of center-surround saliency for static images. One can view their work as a normative approach, because they first formulate the saliency map computation as a problem, and then derive their algorithm as the solution to this problem. This shows that the concept of saliency maps is still very fruitful and can guide research in predicting eye movements. These saliency-based models are all based on low-level image features. Even though the computational models were quite successful in the sense of predicting saliency maps, the models have limited use because they frequently do not match actual human saccades from eye-tracking data [10]. Therefore, a data-driven approach was recently conducted, which uses a linear support vector machine (SVM) as the classifier and various visual features as inputs [10]. It was shown that combining all features produces the best eye fixation predictions. However, it is known for a long time that task-demands affect the patterns of eye movements [11], but neither saliency models nor the data-driven approach take that into account.

Figure 1 illustrates how saliency maps can be used within a so-called smart lab (Figure 1a): Various sensors may extract the gaze direction of users in a room. But even if the gaze direction is similar, as for user A and B (Figure 1b), the saliency maps can still differ due to different task demands. For example, while user A aims at following the presentation, user B's task might be to spot spelling mistakes in slides, which shall make different visual field locations salient. Moreover, saliency maps yield richer information than just gaze direction, because they label the whole visual field of a user. This is valuable information for estimating the internal states of users such as in, for example, intention recognition, to adapt visual interfaces, or to place important information.

In this paper, we present the results of experimental study to improve the prediction of saliency maps in smart meeting rooms. More specifically, we investigate meeting scenarios in terms of their context-dependence saliency based on different image features. We used data-driven approach to derive models that describe the features that play a role in these scenarios. We found that the prediction differs according to the type of features we selected. Most interestingly, we found that models trained on the face features perform better than models trained on other features in the "giving a talk -speaker- " scenario, but in the listening scenario the models trained on competing saliency features from Itti and Koch perform better than models trained on other features. The investigation of context in analyzing group interactions is a prominent approach, as the same nonverbal behavior can have a different interpretation depending on the context. For eye movement prediction, the task context (what are the people or the group doing) affect the gaze of people. The knowledge of these contexts can improve the gaze prediction. However, here we go beyond that by investigating which features are important in each circumstance in meeting scenarios (giving a talk and listening) in term of predicting eye movements. Thus, we hypothesize that saliency maps respecting this will ultimately outperform saliency maps computed only on the basis of 2D pixel images.

This paper is organized as follows: First, we describe the material and methods including the eye tracking experiment (Sec. 2.2) and the features we extracted from our dataset (Sec. 2.3). Then, we present the results of our analysis, we first compare the predictions for the individual features in both scenarios (giving a talk and listening) and then we present the results from features combined (Sec. 3).

2 Material and Methods

2.1 Measuring Gaze Locations

An iView X HED 4 Eye Tracking System (SMI) was used to record eye position. The gaze positions is reported with a sampling rate of 50 Hz and a reported accuracy of 0.5°-1°. We used the default lens (3.6 mm) for the scene camera which provides a viewing angle of 31 horizontally and 22 vertically. The eye tracker' scene camera has a resolution 752 × 480.

2.2 Eye Tracking Experiment

We collected a database of eye tracking data in a meeting room in two scenarios (giving a talk vs. listening) in which three people were involved, each of them is supposed to make a presentation. At the beginning of the meeting the three participants enter the room, one of them goes to the stage to give a talk for four minutes where he was wearing a head mounted eye tracker and the other go to their respective seat. After the presentation is over, the presenter repeats his talk without wearing the eye tracker but one of the audience was wearing the head mounted eye tracker. The same procedure was repeated for the other participants. During these meetings, people had natural behaviors. We generate a saliency map of the locations fixated by the viewer in each frame. Also, we convolve a Gaussian filter across the user's fixation locations in order to obtain a continuous saliency map of an image from the eye tracking data of a user.

2.3   Features of Luminance Image

For each image frame in the dataset, we compute a number of low-, mid- and high- level features for every pixel of the image and used these to train our model similar to [10] . We used the local energy of the steerable pyramid subbands (S-Features) in four orientations and three scales [12]. We also include features used in the Torralba saliency model (T-Saliency)[13]. In addition to, the intensity, orientation and color contrast channels as calculated by Itti and Koch saliency method [7]. Also, we used a horizon line detector from mid-level gist features, because most objects rest on the surface, besides a feature which indicates the distance to the center for each pixel. Furthermore, we used the Viola Jones face detector [14] to find how humans fixated so consistently on people and faces in meeting.

2.4   Classifiers for Predicting Gaze Locations

Opposed to previous computational models that combine a set of biologically plausible filters together to estimate saliency maps, we use a learning approach to train a classifier directly from human eye tracking data. We use a linear Support Vector Machine (SVM) to find out which features are informative. We used models with linear kernels because it performed well for our specific task. We divided our set of images into training images and testing images in order to train and test our model. From each image we chose 200 positively labeled pixels randomly from the top 40% salient locations of the human ground truth saliency map and 200 negatively labeled pixels from the bottom 60% salient locations. In order to have zero mean and unit variance we normalized the features of our training set and used the same normalization parameters to normalize our test data. For each image in our dataset, we predict the saliency per pixel using a particular trained model. The continuous saliency map, which indicates how salient each pixel is, represented by the the values of $w^T x + b$ (where w and b are learned parameters and x refers to the feature vector). Then we threshold this saliency map at 40% percent of the image for binary saliency maps.

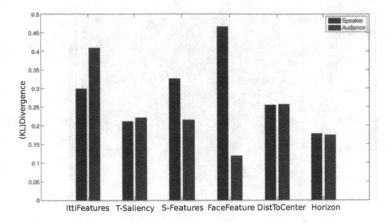

Fig. 2. The KL divergence describing the performance of different SVMs models trained on a set of features individually in two scenarios (speaker vs. audience), averaged over all subjects

2.5 Error Measure

The Kullback–Leibler (KL) divergence was used to measure the distance between distributions of saliency values at human vs. random eye positions. Let $ti = 1 \cdots N$ be N human eye positions in the experimental session. For a saliency model, Estimated Saliency Map is sampled at the human saccade $X_{i,Human}$ and at a random point $X_{i,random}$. First the saliency magnitude at the sampled locations is then normalized to the range [0,1]. Then histogram of these values in q=10 bins across all eye positions is then calculated. $\Pr(X_{Human}(i))$ and $\Pr(X_{random}(i))$ are the fraction of points in bin i for salient and random points. Finally the difference between these histograms was measured using KL divergence:

$$KL\left(X_{Human}; X_{random}\right) = \sum_{i}^{q} \Pr\left(X_{Human}\left(i\right)\right) \log\left(\frac{\Pr\left(X_{Human}\left(i\right)\right)}{\Pr\left(X_{random}\left(i\right)\right)}\right). \quad (1)$$

Models that can better predict human fixations show higher KL divergence. Since observers typically gaze towards a minority of regions with the highest model responses while avoiding the majority of regions with low model responses.

3   Results : Gaze Location Prediction in Meeting Scenarios (Giving a Talk vs. Listening)

We measured the performance of saliency models using KL divergence (see Section 2.5). The results of the performance of different features models averaged over all testing frames are shown in Figure 2. For each frame we predict the saliency per pixel using a specific trained model. We can see that the prediction

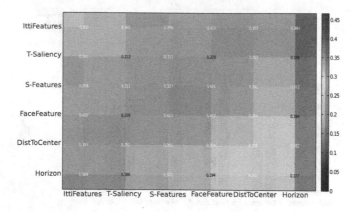

Fig. 3. The KL divergence matrix describing the performance of different SVMs models trained on a set of features individually and pairs of features combined together, in the "giving a talk-speaker-" scenario, averaged over all subjects

differ according to the type of features we selected in both scenarios (giving a talk and listening scenarios) (see Figure 2), also the context dependence shows up: In the listening scenario, models trained on competing saliency features from Itti and Koch perform better than the models trained on other features (i.e. only S-Features, face features,...) (see Figure 2 red bars). This is not a surprise but expected, because the presentation slides may contain many colored figures, images or text which are more important for the audience. In the giving a talk scenario, models trained on the face features perform better than the models trained on other single features (i.e. Itti features or S-Features,...) (see Figure 2 blue bars). This may be due to the fact that in the giving talk scenario the speaker intends to look on faces to indicate whom they address and secure the listeners attention.

Interestingly the model trained on Itti and face features combined outperforms models trained on other features combined in both scenarios (see Figures 3 and 4 for speakers and audience scenarios). This may be due to, while listeners turn their gaze toward speakers to show their attentiveness and find suitable time windows to interact, speakers also find that time windows to gaze his / her presentation slides.

Finally, the overall summary of our analysis is shown in Figures 3 and 4. We can see the KL divergence matrices describing the performances of different SVMs models averaged over all testing images in the "giving a talk-speaker-" scenario (Fig.3) and "listening -audience-" scenario (Fig. 4). The KL divergence matrices are symmetric with respect to the main diagonal. The main diagonals show the performance of SVMs models trained on individual features. The lower/upper triangular parts of the matrices show the performance for SVMs models trained on pairs of features combined.

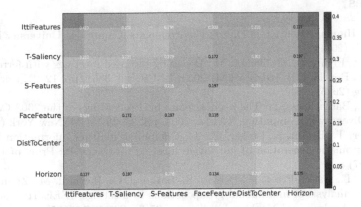

Fig. 4. The KL divergence matrix describing the performances of different SVMs models trained on a set of features individually and pairs of features combined together, in the "listening -audience-" scenario, averaged over all subjects

4   Conclusion

We have examined the prediction of eye movements in meeting scenarios using different low, middle and high-level visual features. We trained a linear SVM to find out which features are descriptive in different scenarios. We found that the prediction differs according to the type of features we selected. Most interestingly, we found that models trained on the face features perform better than models trained on other features in the "giving a talk" scenario, but in the listening scenario the models trained on competing saliency features from Itti and Koch performs better than models trained on other features. This finding points towards including context information about the scene and situation into the computation of saliency maps as important towards developing models of eye movements, which operate well under natural conditions such as those encountered in ubiquitous computing settings. Our results suggest that context dependent saliency maps could become an integral part of any user model in ubiquitous computing settings, where users are experiencing a much richer visual environment than in the desktop computing settings.

Our work is an important step towards building generative models for recognition of gaze in meetings, which explicitly take the context information into account and, most importantly, we suggest that a new series of analyses can even empirically measure the corresponding prior probabilities over latent variables in such models.

Acknowledgments. This work was supported by the DFG GRK 1424 MuSAMA. We would also like to thank the anonymous reviewers for their valuable comments and suggestions.

References

1. Roda, C.: Human Attention in Digital Environments. Cambridge University Press, Cambridge (2011)
2. Wellner, P., Flynn, M., Guillemot, M.: Browsing recorded meetings with ferret. In: Bengio, S., Bourlard, H. (eds.) MLMI 2004. LNCS, vol. 3361, pp. 12–21. Springer, Heidelberg (2005)
3. Ellis, C.S., Barthelmess, P.: The neem dream. In: Proceedings of the 2003 Conference on Diversity in Computing, TAPIA 2003, pp. 23–29. ACM, New York (2003)
4. Kleinbauer, T., Becker, S., Becker, T.: T.: Combining multiple information layers for the automatic generation of indicative meeting abstracts. In: Proc. of ENLG 2007 (2007)
5. McCowan, L., Gatica-Perez, D., Bengio, S., Lathoud, G., Barnard, M., Zhang, D.: Automatic analysis of multimodal group actions in meetings. IEEE Transactions on Pattern Analysis and Machine Intelligence 27(3), 305–317 (2005)
6. Favre, S., Salamin, H., Vinciarelli, A., Hakkani Tür, D., Garg, N.P.: Role recognition for meeting participants: an approach based on lexical information and social network analysis. In: ACM International Conference on Multimedia (October 2008)
7. Itti, L., Koch, C., Niebur, E.: A model of saliency-based visual attention for rapid scene analysis. IEEE Transactions on Pattern Analysis and Machine Intelligence 20(11), 1254–1259 (1998)
8. Mahadevan, V., Vasconcelos, N.: Spatiotemporal saliency in dynamic scenes. IEEE Trans. Pattern Anal. Mach. Intell. 32(1), 171–177 (2010)
9. Gao, D., Vasconcelos, N.: Discriminant saliency for visual recognition from cluttered scenes. In: NIPS (2004)
10. Judd, T., Ehinger, K., Durand, F., Torralba, A.: Learning to predict where humans look. In: ICCV (2009)
11. Yarbus, A.: Eye-movements and vision. Plenum Press, New York (1967)
12. Simoncelli, E.P., Freeman, W.T.: The steerable pyramid: A flexible architecture for multi-scale derivative computation. In: IEEE Intl Conf. on Image Processing, pp. 444–447. IEEE Signal Processing Society (1995)
13. Torralba, A.: Modeling global scene factors in attention. JOSA - A 20, 1407–1418 (2003)
14. Viola, P., Jones, M.J.: Robust real-time face detection. Int. J. Comput. Vision 57(2), 137–154 (2004)

Variational EM Learning of DSBNs
with Conditional Deep Boltzmann Machines

Xing Zhang and Siwei Lyu

Computer Science Department
State University of New York, Albany, USA

Abstract. Variational EM (VEM) is an efficient parameter learning scheme for sigmoid belief networks with many layers of latent variables. The choice of the inference model that forms the variational lower bound of the log likelihood is critical in VEM learning. The mean field approximations and wake-sleep algorithm use simple models that are computationally efficient, but may be poor approximations to the true posterior densities when the latent variables have strong mutual dependencies. In this paper, we describe a variational EM learning method of DSBNs with a new inference model known as the *conditional deep Boltzmann machine* (cDBM), which is an *undirected* graphical model capable of representing complex dependencies among latent variables. We show that this algorithm does not require the computation of the intractable partition function in the undirected cDBM model, and can be accelerated with contrastive learning. Performances of the proposed method are evaluated and compar ed on handwritten digit data.

A deep sigmoid belief network (DSBN) is a generative probabilistic model that has many latent variables organized in a hierarchy, with lower layers corresponding to basic features and upper layers representing more "abstract" concepts [7], Fig.1(a). DSBNs provide great flexibility in modeling complex dependencies of the "hidden" causes that generate data [1]. However, both maximum likelihood and expectation-maximization (EM) [4] learning become difficult for a densely connected DSBNs with many layers of latent variables, mainly because the *posteriors*, i.e., the conditional distribution of the latent variables given data, are usually complicated and prohibit efficient computation [13].

In variational EM learning (VEM) [12], the intractable posterior distribution of DSBN is approximated with a computationally efficient *inference model*, and learning becomes an iterative optimization with regards to a variational lower bound of the (log) likelihood formed using the inference model. For any legitimate inference model, the VEM algorithm has a guaranteed convergence to a local maximum of the variational lower bound. Good choices of the inference model can lead to learning results close to that using maximum likelihood, and thus critical for the effectiveness of VEM learning. In this paper, we describe a VEM learning method for DSBNs using *conditional deep Boltzmann machine* (cDBM), which is an *undirected* graphical model capable of representing complex dependencies among latent variables. We first briefly review the gradient ascent

S. Wermter et al. (Eds.): ICANN 2014, LNCS 8681, pp. 257–264, 2014.

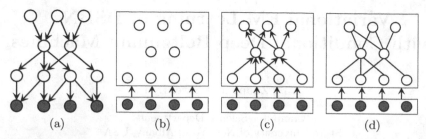

Fig. 1. (a) Structures for a DSBN. Shaded nodes indicate visible variables and empty nodes indicate latent variables. **(b)-(d)** The structures of different inference models used in VEM learning of the DBN in (a), with **(b)** the mean field approximation, **(c)** the HM, and **(d)** the conditional deep Boltzmann machine. The surrounding box and up-directing arrows in (b)-(d) denote that the visible variables can have complete connections to all latent variables.

optimization in the VEM learning of DBSNs [10], and then describe a particular gradient based VEM learning using cDBM as inference model. We show that this algorithm does not require the computation of the potentially intractable partition function in the undirected cDBM model, and can be further accelerated with contrastive learning. Performances of these methods are evaluated and compared on learning model parameters of DSBNs for handwritten digit data.

1   VEM Learning DSBNs

A DSBN [11] is a probabilistic graphical model of binary variables that corresponds to a directed acyclic graph, whose nodes can be organized into non-overlapping layers with an order so that all edges are directed from one layer to the next layer. For a DSBN with $L + 1$ layers of $n_0, \cdots, n_L$ variables each, we denote $\mathbf{h}_k$, $k = 0, 1, \cdots, L$, as the vectorized ensemble of binary variables in the kth layer, with all edges directed from $\mathbf{h}_k$ to $\mathbf{h}_{k-1}$ for $k = 1, \cdots, L$. As a hierarchical latent variable model, in a DSBN, variables in the bottom layer that have no descendants correspond to observed data, while all other layers are latent variables. We specify $\mathbf{v} = \mathbf{h}_0$ as the bottom layer observed variables and $\mathbf{h}_L$ as the topmost latent layer. When we do not intend to distinguish individual layers of the latent variables, we denote $\mathbf{h}_1, \cdots, \mathbf{h}_L$ collectively as $\mathbf{h}$. The graphical structure of a DSBN implies that the joint density it represents has factorization: $p(\mathbf{v}, \mathbf{h}; \Theta) = \prod_{j=1}^{n_0} p(v_j | \mathbf{h}_1) \prod_{k=1}^{L-1} \prod_{j=1}^{n_k} p(h_{kj} | \mathbf{h}_{k+1}) \prod_{j=1}^{n_L} p(h_{Lj})$, with each of the contributing distributions specified as:

- $p(v_j = 1 | \mathbf{h}_1) = \sigma(\mathbf{b}_{0j}^T \mathbf{h}_1 + c_{0j})$, for $j = 1, \cdots, n_0$,
- $p(h_{kj} = 1 | \mathbf{h}_{k+1}) = \sigma(\mathbf{b}_{k+1,j}^T \mathbf{h}_{k+1} + c_{k,j})$, for $j = 1, \cdots, n_k$, $k = 1, \cdots, L-1$,
- $p(h_{Lj} = 1) = \sigma(c_{L+1,j})$, for $j = 1, \cdots, n_L$,

where $\sigma(x) = 1/(1 + e^{-x})$ is the sigmoid function, and $\mathbf{b}_{j,k} \in R^{n_k}, c_{k,j} \in R$ are model parameters collectively represented by Θ. The graphical structure of an example of the DSBN is shown in Fig.1(a). Evaluating the log joint density and its gradient with regards to the model parameters are simple efficient computations when one has access to the values of all variables of each layer [11].

Furthermore, the mutual independence of the latent variables of one layer given their parents in the above layer suggests that unbiased samples from the joint model can be generated with one top-down swipe of the model [11].

Learning a DSBN is to estimate the model parameter Θ according to some optimization criterion. In the *maximum likelihood* learning, we find Θ that induces the marginal density $p(\mathbf{v}; \Theta) = \sum_{\mathbf{h}} p(\mathbf{v}, \mathbf{h}; \Theta)$ that maximizes the log likelihood of the observed variable $\mathbf{v}$ under its density $q_0(\mathbf{v})^1$, $\mathcal{L}(\Theta) = \sum_{\mathbf{v}} q_0(\mathbf{v}) \log p(\mathbf{v}; \Theta)$. As direct maximizing the log likelihood involves a summation over all possible states of every latent variables, which is computationally intractable for large models, a more efficient method is the expectation-maximization (EM) learning [4], where starting from an initial value, we keep updating

$$\Theta_{t+1} \leftarrow \arg\max_{\Theta} \sum_{\mathbf{v}} q_0(\mathbf{v}) \sum_{\mathbf{h}} p(\mathbf{h}|\mathbf{v}; \Theta_t) \log p(\mathbf{v}, \mathbf{h}; \Theta)$$

until learning converges to a local maximum of $\mathcal{L}(\Theta)$. However, the "explain away" phenomenon [13], i.e., the latent variables can become highly *dependent* given the visible data even though they may be independent in the generative model, makes either direct computation or Monte-Carlo approximation of the EM step still difficult. A more flexible approach is the *variational EM* (VEM) method [12], where we use an *inference model* $q(\mathbf{h}|\mathbf{v}; \Phi)$ with parameter Φ to form

$$\begin{aligned} \mathcal{F}(\Theta, \Phi) &= \sum_{\mathbf{v}} q_0(\mathbf{v}) \sum_{\mathbf{h}} q(\mathbf{h}|\mathbf{v}; \Phi) \log \left(\frac{p(\mathbf{v}, \mathbf{h}; \Theta)}{q(\mathbf{h}|\mathbf{v}; \Phi)} \right) \\ &= \mathcal{L}(\Theta) - \sum_{\mathbf{v}} q_0(\mathbf{v}) D_{\mathrm{KL}} \left(q(\mathbf{h}|\mathbf{v}; \Phi) \| p(\mathbf{h}|\mathbf{v}; \Theta) \right). \end{aligned}$$

where $D_{\mathrm{KL}} \left(q(\mathbf{h}|\mathbf{v}; \Phi) \| p(\mathbf{h}|\mathbf{v}; \Theta) \right) \geq 0$ is the Kulback-Leibler (KL) divergence between $q(\mathbf{h}|\mathbf{v}; \Theta)$ and $p(\mathbf{h}|\mathbf{v}; \Phi)$ [2]. As $\forall \Theta, \Phi$ we have $\mathcal{F}(\Theta, \Phi) \leq \mathcal{L}(\Theta)$, $\mathcal{F}(\Theta, \Phi)$ is always a lower-bound of the log likelihood, and the difference is the *variational gap*. The variational gap is non-zero except in the case when a specific choice of Φ makes $q(\mathbf{h}|\mathbf{v}; \Phi)$ equal to the true posterior, $p(\mathbf{h}|\mathbf{v}; \Theta)$. VEM learning then proceeds as coordinate optimization, which starts with initial values for Θ and Φ, and alternates between the optimization of Θ and Φ, as $\Theta_{t+1} \leftarrow \arg\max_{\Theta} \mathcal{F}(\Theta, \Phi_t)$ and $\Phi_{t+1} \leftarrow \arg\max_{\Phi} \mathcal{F}(\Theta_{t+1}, \Phi)$, until it reaches a local maximum of $\mathcal{F}(\Theta, \Phi)$. As $\mathcal{F}(\Theta, \Phi)$ bounds $\mathcal{L}(\Phi)$ from below, each VEM iteration will not reduce the log likelihood below this lower bound, but the non-decremental update of log likelihood is not guaranteed.

Following the VEM updates, we can update the parameters of the DSBN and the inference mode, Θ and Φ, using the gradients $\mathcal{F}(\Theta, \Phi)$, as:

$$\Theta_{t+1} \leftarrow \Theta_t - \eta_t \left. \frac{\partial \mathcal{F}(\Theta, \Phi_t)}{\partial \Theta} \right|_{\Theta=\Theta_t} \quad \text{and} \quad \Phi_{t+1} \leftarrow \Phi_t - \eta_t \left. \frac{\partial \mathcal{F}(\Theta_t, \Phi)}{\partial \Phi} \right|_{\Phi=\Phi_t},$$

where η_t are corresponding step sizes that, if properly chosen, guarantee the convergence of the overall algorithm. Using the definition of $\mathcal{F}(\Theta, \Phi)$, we can compute the two gradients as

$$\frac{\partial \mathcal{F}}{\partial \Theta} = \sum_{\mathbf{v}} q_0(\mathbf{v}) \sum_{\mathbf{h}} q(\mathbf{h}|\mathbf{v}; \Phi) \frac{\partial}{\partial \Theta} \log p(\mathbf{v}, \mathbf{h}; \Theta), \tag{1}$$

$$\frac{\partial \mathcal{F}}{\partial \Phi} = \sum_{\mathbf{v}} q_0(\mathbf{v}) \sum_{\mathbf{h}} q(\mathbf{h}|\mathbf{v}; \Phi) \left[\frac{\partial}{\partial \Phi} \log q(\mathbf{h}|\mathbf{v}; \Phi) \right] \log \frac{p(\mathbf{v}, \mathbf{h}; \Theta)}{q(\mathbf{h}|\mathbf{v}; \Phi)}. \tag{2}$$

---

[1] With a set of samples $\{\underline{\mathbf{v}}_1, \cdots, \underline{\mathbf{v}}_n\}$, $q_0(\mathbf{v})$ represents the empirical distribution from the samples and the empirical log likelihood is $\sum_{i=1}^{n} \log p(\underline{\mathbf{v}}_i; \Theta)$.

Derivation of Eq.(2) are provided in a longer version of the paper due to space limit. In summary, to compute Eq.(1) and Eq.(2) three basic computation steps are required:

- (i) computing $\log p(\mathbf{v}, \mathbf{h}; \Theta)$ and $\frac{\partial}{\partial \Theta} \log p(\mathbf{v}, \mathbf{h}; \Theta)$,
- (ii) computing $\log q(\mathbf{h}|\mathbf{v}; \Phi)$ and $\frac{\partial}{\partial \Phi} \log q(\mathbf{h}|\mathbf{v}; \Phi)$,
- (iii) sampling from density $q(\mathbf{h}|\mathbf{v}; \Phi)$.

Both Eq.(1) and Eq.(2) are in the form of expectations of some functions of $\mathbf{v}$ and $\mathbf{h}$ with regards to the joint density $q_0(\mathbf{v})q(\mathbf{h}|\mathbf{v}; \Phi)$. However, directly evaluating these expectations is usually hard, for that we may not have direct access to $q_0(\mathbf{v})$ and the analytical form of $q(\mathbf{h}|\mathbf{v}; \Phi)$ may still be too complicated to directly work with. As such, it is a natural idea to approximate these expectations using Monte-Carlo method, by sampling from $q_0(\mathbf{v})q(\mathbf{h}|\mathbf{v}; \Phi)$, and compute the average of the function evaluations over these samples. With sufficient number of data, these averages are good approximation to the true expectation. However, the variance of the estimation based on Eq.(2) could be very large and making the estimation practically unusable. To alleviate this problem, several variance reduction measures have been described in a recent work [10], which are also adopted in this work.

2   VEM with Conditional Deep Boltzmann Machine

The inference model $q(\mathbf{h}|\mathbf{v}; \Phi)$ is key to the efficiency and efficacy of the VEM learning. On one hand, the inference model should be "similar" to the true posterior density, $p(\mathbf{h}|\mathbf{v}; \Theta)$, so that at convergence the variational gap is small and the bias due to the use of a "wrong" posterior model is minimal. On the other hand, the chosen model has also to be significantly simpler than the true posterior density so the overall computation will be tractable.

In the *mean field approximation* learning of sigmoid networks, factorial models (i.e., with fully independent components) [15] or mixture of factorial models [8] are used as inference models, Fig.1 (b). The computation based on such models is simple and efficient, but as there is only weak or no dependency among the latent variables, they may be poor approximations to the true posterior densities when the DBN has many latent variables.

The HM (HM) [6] is another framework of VEM learning for DSBNs. In the wake-sleep algorithm, the inference model is another "bottom-up" DSBN, which has exactly the same structure as the generative DBN, but have all edges pointing to the opposite directions[2], as shown in Fig.1(c). Specifically, the inference model in an HM is $q(\mathbf{h}|\mathbf{v}; \Phi) = \prod_{k=1}^{L-1} \prod_{j=1}^{n_{k+1}} p(h_{k+1,j}|\mathbf{h}_k, \mathbf{v}) \prod_{j=1}^{n_1} p(h_{1j}|\mathbf{v})$, where with simple computations, $p(h_{k+1,j} = 1|\mathbf{h}_k, \mathbf{v}) = \sigma(\mathbf{f}_{k+1,j}^T \mathbf{h}_k + \mathbf{g}_{k+1,j}^T \mathbf{v} + r_{k+1,j})$, and $p(h_{1j} = 1|\mathbf{v}) = \sigma(\mathbf{g}_{1,j}^T \mathbf{v} + r_{1,j})$, with $\sigma(\cdot)$ being the sigmoid function and Φ denotes all parameters $(\mathbf{f}_{k,j}, \mathbf{g}_{k,j}, r_{k,j})$ collec tively. The bottom-up DSBN inference model in the wake-sleep algorithm has clear computational advantages: it is easy

---

[2] Here, the model is more generalized than the original work in [6], as the visible variables can have full connections to all latent variables.

to sample from and it can model latent variable dependencies across different layers. However, it is still restricted as latent variables of the same layer are independent given their parents in the layer directly below, and thus cannot model the "explain away" behavior of the true posterior density.

Other more sophisticated inference models have been proposed to better capture the dependencies in posteriors. For instance, the work [3] includes dangling units and recurrent connections to HM, and similarly the work in [10] introduce horizontal connection within each layer of the inference model. However, these new inference models loses the symmetric topology of the inference model as in HM with either new nodes or new connections.

Here, we introduce a more effective inference model that we called the *conditional deep Boltzmann machine* (cDBM) [14]. Formally, a cDBM corresponds to a density as:

$$q(\mathbf{h}|\mathbf{v};\varPhi) = \frac{1}{Z(\mathbf{v},\varPhi)} \exp\left(-E(\mathbf{v},\mathbf{h};\varPhi)\right), \tag{3}$$

where $E(\mathbf{v},\mathbf{h};\varPhi) = \sum_{k=1}^{L-1} \mathbf{h}_k^T B_k \mathbf{h}_{k+1} - \sum_{k=1}^{L} \mathbf{h}_k^T C_k \mathbf{v}$ is the *energy function*, and $Z(\mathbf{v};\varPhi)$ is the *partition function* that assures $q(\mathbf{h}|\mathbf{v};\varPhi)$ normalizes to one. As usual, we use $\varPhi$ to represent all the model parameters ($B_k \in R^{n_k \times n_{k+1}}, C_k \in R^{n_k \times n_0}$). Note that the derivatives of the energy function with regards to the model parameters, $\frac{\partial E(\mathbf{v},\mathbf{h};\varPhi)}{\partial B_k} = \mathbf{h}_{k+1}\mathbf{h}_k^T$ and $\frac{\partial E(\mathbf{v},\mathbf{h};\varPhi)}{\partial C_k} = \mathbf{h}_k\mathbf{v}^T$, are simple local computations. The corresponding graphical structure of a cDBM for the latent variables is an *undirected* graph, where each node corresponds to a latent variable, and they are connected with edges as in the DSBN whose parameters are to be learned, except that these edges have no directions, see Fig.1 (d) for an example. The graphical structure in cDBM implies that latent variables of the same layer are independent given their neighbors in the layer directly below, and except for those at the topmost layer, those in the layer directly above. Unlike the directed inference model for HMs, latent variables of the same layer are generally dependent given the visible variables and other latent variables of layers below, because they are still connected through undirected edges across the layers above. Such complex dependency structures can be used to represent the "explain away" behavior of the true posterior density.

To use cDBM for VEM learning of DSBNs, we need efficient operations to draw samples from $q(\mathbf{h}|\mathbf{v};\varPhi)$ and to evaluate $\log q(\mathbf{h}|\mathbf{v};\varPhi)$ and $\frac{\partial}{\partial \varPhi}\log q(\mathbf{h}|\mathbf{v};\varPhi)$. In doing so, we need to resolve two challenges. First, there is no one-swipe direct sampling procedure for cDBM as the undirected graph provides no intrinsic order for the latent variables. But its hierarchical structure suggests a much efficient *block Gibbs sampling* procedure [14]. In the VEM learning, the block Gibbs sampling is further accelerated by alternatively sampling from variables in all even layers conditioned on the values of variables in all odd layers and vice versa (a step lends itself to simple parallelization). We can accelerate the computation of Eq.(1) and Eq.(2) using *contrastive update* [5], where we update the gradients using averages of samples obtained by running the block Gibbs sampler for only a finite number of steps.

The second problem lies in the computation of the partition function in the cDBM model, $Z(\mathbf{v};\varPhi) = \sum_{\mathbf{h}} \exp\left(-E(\mathbf{v},\mathbf{h};\varPhi)\right)$, which is intractable for large

	EM	WS HM	VEM HM	cDBM (RND)	cDBM (HM)
time (sec)	3,673	37	262	468	342
# of epochs	58	21	10	17	11
log var gap	-13.2	2.4	1.3	-3.5	-2.8
diff log likelihood	100.8	41.4	59.8	59.2	61.7

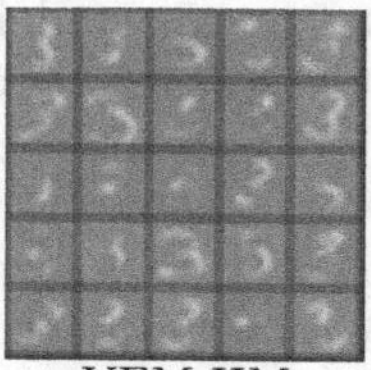

VEM-HM 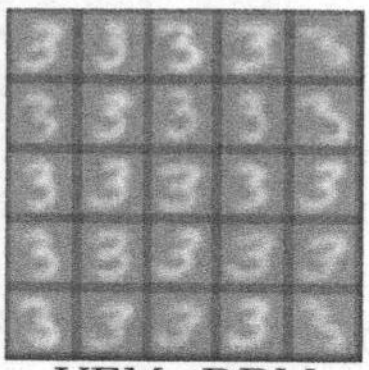   VEM-cDBM

Fig. 2. (left) Learning performance comparison of different methods. **(right)** Samples from DSBNs learned with the VEM-HM algorithm and the algorithm of this work.

models. We show here that the partition function can be removed from Eq.(2) after some manipulations, as

$$\frac{\partial \mathcal{F}}{\partial \Phi} = \sum_{\mathbf{v}} q_0(\mathbf{v}) \left\langle \frac{\partial E(\mathbf{v},\mathbf{h};\Phi)}{\partial \Phi} \right\rangle_q \langle \phi(\mathbf{v},\mathbf{h};\Phi) \rangle_q - \sum_{\mathbf{v}} q_0(\mathbf{v}) \left\langle \frac{\partial E(\mathbf{v},\mathbf{h};\Phi)}{\partial \Phi} \phi(\mathbf{v},\mathbf{h};\Phi) \right\rangle_q \quad (4)$$

where $\langle \cdot \rangle_q$ denote expectation w.r.t. distribution q and

$$\phi(\mathbf{v},\mathbf{h};\Phi) = \log p(\mathbf{v},\mathbf{h};\Theta) + E(\mathbf{h},\mathbf{v};\Phi).$$

Due to space limit, the detailed derivation of Eq.(4) is provided in a longer version of this work. Eq.(4) shows that $\frac{\partial \mathcal{F}(\Theta,\Phi)}{\partial \Phi}$ is computed as the difference between the product of the means of $\frac{\partial E(\mathbf{v},\mathbf{h};\Phi)}{\partial \Phi}$ and $\phi(\mathbf{v},\mathbf{h};\Phi)$ with regards to the joint density of $q_0(\mathbf{v})q(\mathbf{h}|\mathbf{v};\Phi)$, and the mean of their product. Also, we only need to evaluate $\frac{\partial E(\mathbf{v},\mathbf{h};\Phi)}{\partial \Phi}$ and $\phi(\mathbf{v},\mathbf{h};\Phi)$, which are simple and efficient for the setting of VEM learning DSBN with cDBM as the inference model.

To obtain initial values better than random for the VEM learning using cDBM, we run the gradient based VEM learning using HM for an efficient pre-training. After the pre-training converges, we use the learned parameters of the wake-sleep algorithm to initialize those of the DSBN and the cDBM inference model. Specifically, for the latter, the parameters of the wake-sleep algorithm inference model are "symmetrized" to be used in the undirected cDBM model. With the obtained samples, we evaluate Eq.(1) and Eq.(2) and update the gradients using the averages. The whole algorithm stops when the gradient update has a norm smaller than a pre-set threshold.

3   Experiments

We perform experiment based on the down-sampled grayscale images from the *MNIST Handwritten Digits* data set [9]. We model the 16×16 images with a DSBN with three latent layers, with 16, 16 and 64 components, for each layer starting from the top, and a visible layer with 256 components, where we represent the grayscale intensities normalized between [0,1] as probabilities. We randomly chose 300 images as training data for all the methods being studied. Based on the training data, we compare several different parameter learning methods for this model, including the actual EM algorithm, the wake-sleep algorithm with HM as inference model (WS HM) [6], the gradient based VEM using

HM as inference model (VEM HM) [10], and gradient based VEM learning with cDBM inference model described in this work (VEM cDBM). For VEM learning with cDBM inference model, we also consider two variants in implementations as random i nitial values (RND) and using VEM-HM for initial values (HM).

Because of the relatively low parameter dimensionality of the model we studied, we can compute the exact log likelihood, as well as the EM learning using Gibbs sampling with the true posteriors by brute-force. All learning algorithms start with the same set of randomly chosen initial values for parameters. We separate the 300 training data into 10 mini-batches [7], and update parameters using gradient descent. All gradient updates start with an initial step size $\eta = 0.1$, which is gradually reduced as the number of epochs increases. We found in our experiments that the variance reduction measures of [10] is effective but not sufficient to stabilize the learning process. Due to this, in the experiment we use a relative large number of samples to update variational parameters (10, 000). This reduces the overall running time but improve the fin al learning performance.

Table 2 summarizes the running efficiency and learning efficacy based on the averages of 10 running of the learning algorithms (for the wake-sleep learning, we only count convergence cases). We compare the overall time to converge and the total number of epochs for convergence. We use the logarithm of the variational gap at convergence to measure the closeness of the inference model to the true posterior density, and the difference between log likelihood at convergence and that for the initial values. We also show samples from DSBN learned with the weak-sleep algorithm and the algorithm of this work.

There are several points worth pointing out. First, note that the wake-sleep learning is efficient, there is a relatively large variational gap at convergence. This does not come as a surprise, as in the wake-sleep algorithm to avoid the high variance in Eq.(2), a different objective function is updated for the variational parameter, and this may "undo" the improvement of the true VEM lower bound in the wake phase. Second, VEM learning of HM converges in fewer iterations, yet its variational gap is significantly bigger than the cDBM based VEM learning, reflecting the advantage of the more complex structure of cDBM in approximating the true posterior. On the other hand, using the former to initialize the latter typically ends with improved performances. Finally, we saw an improved performance with increased number of contrastive sampling steps, but this typically comes with a price of increased running time.

4   Conclusion

In this paper, we introduce a variational EM learning of DBNs based on the conditional deep Boltzmann machine (cDBM) inference model, which can better model complex dependencies among latent variables such as "explain away". We describe a contrastive block Gibbs sampling based implementation of the variational EM learning using cDBM that does not rely on the partition function. Performances of this method is evaluated and compared with existing methods on learning model parameters for handwritten digit data.

There are several directions that we would like to extend this work. Recently, a greedy layer-wise training of DBN has been shown effective in learning parameters layer by layer [7]. It is thus of interest to combine this algorithm with the VEM learning methods described in this paper for better learning performance. Second, the variational EM learning scheme may be extended to the learning of other types of latent variable models, for instance, a general Boltzmann machine with partially visible data. Furthermore, the current algorithm still suffers from the high variance concomitant with the use of sampling average approximations in evaluating Eq.(4), and we need to investigate more effective variance reduction methods. Finally, we are currently working on applying these new learning methods to large data sets for practical problems in computer vision and other data modeling tasks.

Acknowledgement. We thank the anonymous reviewers for their constructive comments. This work is partially supported by the U.S. National Science Foundation Grant no. IIS-0953373.

References

1. Bengio, Y., LeCun, Y.: Scaling learning algorithms towards ai. In: Bottou, L., Chapelle, O., DeCoste, D., Weston, J. (eds.) Large-Scale Kernel Machines. MIT Press (2007)
2. Cover, T., Thomas, J.: Elements of Information Theory, 2nd edn. Wiley-Interscience (2006)
3. Dayan, P., Hinton, G.E.: Varieties of helmholtz machines. Neural Networks 9, 1385–1403 (1996)
4. Dempster, A., Laird, N., Rubin, D.: Maximum likelihood from incomplete data via the em algorithm. Journal of the Royal Statistical Society, Series B 39, 1–38 (1977)
5. Hinton, G.E.: Training products of experts by minimizing contrastive divergence. Neural Computation 14, 1771–1800 (2002)
6. Hinton, G.E., Dayan, P., Frey, B.J., Neal, R.: The wake-sleep algorithm for unsupervised neural networks. Science 268, 1158–1161 (1995)
7. Hinton, G.E., Osindero, S., Teh, Y.: A fast learning algorithm for deep belief nets. Neural Computation 18(10), 1527–1554 (2006)
8. Jaakkola, T., Jordan, M.: Improving the mean field approximation via the use of mixture distributions. In: Jordan, M.I. (ed.) Learning in Graphical Models. MIT Press (1998)
9. LeCun, Y., Bottou, L., Bengio, Y., Haffner, P.: Gradient-based learning applied to document recognition. Proceedings of the IEEE 86(11), 2278–2324 (1998)
10. Mnih, A., Gregor, K.: Neural variational inference and learning in belief networks. arXiv:1402.0030v1 (cs.LG) (January 2014)
11. Neal, R.M.: Connectionist learning of belief networks. Artificial Intelligence 56, 71–113 (1992)
12. Neal, R.M., Hinton, G.E.: A view of the em algorithm that justifies incremental, sparse, and other variants. In: Learning in Graphical Models, pp. 355–368. Kluwer Academic Publishers (1998)
13. Pearl, J.: Probabilistic Reasoning in Intelligent Systems. Morgan-Kaufmann (1988)
14. Salakhutdinov, R., Hinton, G.E.: Deep boltzmann machines. In: AISTATS (2009)
15. Saul, L.K., Jaakkola, T., Jordan, M.I.: Mean field theory for sigmoid belief networks. Journal of Artificial Intelligence Research 4, 61–76 (1996)

Improving Deep Neural Network Performance by Reusing Features Trained with Transductive Transference

Chetak Kandaswamy[1,2], Luís M. Silva[1,3], Luís A. Alexandre[4],
Jorge M. Santos[1,5], and Joaquim Marques de Sá[1,6]

[1] Instituto de Engenharia Biomédica (INEB), Porto, Portugal
[2] Dep. de Engenharia Electronica e de Computadores at FEUP, Porto, Portugal
chetak.kand@gmail.com
[3] Dep. de Matemática at Universidade de Aveiro, Portugal
lmas@ua.pt
[4] Universidade da Beira Interior and Instituto de Telecomunicações,
Covilhã, Portugal
lfbaa@di.ubi.pt
[5] Dep. de Matemática at Instituto Superior de Engenharia do Instituto Politécnico
do Porto, Portugal
[6] Dep. de Engenharia Electronica e de Computadores at FEUP, Porto, Portugal

Abstract. Transfer Learning is a paradigm in machine learning to solve a target problem by reusing the learning with minor modifications from a different but related source problem. In this paper we propose a novel feature transference approach, especially when the source and the target problems are drawn from different distributions. We use deep neural networks to transfer either low or middle or higher-layer features for a machine trained in either unsupervised or supervised way. Applying this feature transference approach on Convolutional Neural Network and Stacked Denoising Autoencoder on four different datasets, we achieve lower classification error rate with significant reduction in computation time with lower-layer features trained in supervised way and higher-layer features trained in unsupervised way for classifying images of uppercase and lowercase letters dataset.

Keywords: Feature Transference, Deep Neural Network.

1 Introduction

Machine learning can be broadly classified into Transductive or Inductive approach. In transductive learning, the objective is to learn from observed, specific (training) instances to specific (test) instances drawn from same distributions. In contrast, induction is to learn from observed training instances, a set of assumptions about the true distribution of the test cases (general rules). Transductive is preferable to inductive [1] since, induction requires solving a more general

S. Wermter et al. (Eds.): ICANN 2014, LNCS 8681, pp. 265–272, 2014.

problem (assumptions about the true distribution) before solving a more specific problem. This distinction is most interesting in cases where the predictions of the transductive model are not achievable by any inductive model.

Transfer Learning attempts to train a machine to solve a source problem and reuse it with minor modifications to solve a different but related target problem without having to train the machine from scratch. Thus transfer in transductive approach, a machine is trained on a specific problem to solve another specific problem, where the target problem distributions are not necessarily related to the source problem.

Deep Transfer Learning (DTL) is an alternative to transfer learning with shallow architectures [2]. The advantage of DTL is that it offers a far greater flexibility in extracting high-level features and transferring it from a source to a target problem, and unlike the classical approach, it is not affected by experts bias [2]. Despite the vast body of literature on the subject, there are still many contentious issues regarding avoiding negative transfer from source to target problems, especially when the source and target distributions are from different distributions. In this paper, we only consider transfer learning problems where the source and target distributions are different. Specially, in the case of negative transference from the source problem.

2   Deep Neural Network

We use state-of-the-art deep learning methods (see [3], [4]) that learn high-level features from large datasets and measure the classification performance of images.

Given an input space X, with a certain probability distribution $P(X)$, we draw a design data set $X_{ds} = \{\mathbf{x}_1, \ldots, \mathbf{x}_{n_{ds}}\}$ which may be accompanied by a set of labels $Y = \{1, 2, \ldots, c\}$ with c distinct class labels. We define a classification problem as any function $g(\mathbf{x}) : X \to Y$ that maps n_{ds} instances of $\mathbf{x} \in X$ to labels. Thus, the classifier attempts to learn features (or filters), represented as a vector w^j of optimal weights and biases. For a classifier with k number of layers, the features w^j are represented as a set of vectors of each layer, i.e., $\mathbf{w} = (w^1, \ldots, w^k)$. We use error rate ε and computation time t to measure the classifier performance to predict on a test set $X_{ts} = \{\mathbf{x}_1, \ldots, \mathbf{x}_{n_{ts}}\}$ with n_{ts} unlabeled instances drawn from the same distribution $P(X)$.

2.1   Stacked Denoising Autoencoder (SDA)

An autoencoder is a simple neural network with one hidden layer designed to reconstruct its own input, having, for that reason, an equal number of input and output neurons (tied weights). The reconstruction accuracy is obtained by minimizing the average reconstruction error between the original and the reconstructed instances. A denoising autoencoder is a variant of the autoencoder where now a corrupted version of the input is used to reconstruct the original instances. A SDA is made up of stacking multiple denoising autoencoder one on top of another. The training of SDA [3] comprises of two stages: an unsupervised pre-training stage followed by a supervised fine-tuning stage (see [5, Section 6.2]).

In the unsupervised pre-training stage $pretrain(\mathbf{w})$, the weights w^j of each hidden layer are trained in unsupervised way until the reconstruction cost of that layer reaches global minimum. Then we repeat the pre-training until the kth hidden layer is completely pre-trained to obtain unsupervised features $U(\mathbf{w})$.

In the supervised fine-tuning stage $finetune(\mathbf{w}, \mathbf{c})$, a logistic regression layer with c neurons is added to the top of the pre-trained machine. Then, the entire classifier is trained (fine-tuned) using both X_{ds} and Y_{ds} in order to minimize a cross-entropy loss function [6] measuring the error between the classifier's predictions and the correct labels to obtain supervised features $S(\mathbf{w})$.

2.2 Convolutional Neural Network (CNN)

CNN [4] is a deep neural network whose convolutional layers alternate with subsampling layers. CNN is better explained in two stages. The alternating convolutional and subsampling stage and the classification stage. The convolution layer convolute the input with set of filters like Gabor filters or trained filters producing feature maps. These feature maps are further reduced by subsampling. Then the supervised feature $S(w^k)$ or kernels of the top convolution filters and subsampling are fed to classification stage. Then we fine-tune the filters, $finetune(\mathbf{w}, \mathbf{c})$ with labeled source data to obtain supervised features $S(\mathbf{w})$.

In this paper the term "Baseline approach" to refer to either a SDA or a CNN machine trained on a target problem with no transference from the source problem (trained from scratch).

3   Transfer Learning Method

Traditionally, the goal of the transfer learning is to transfer the learning (knowledge) from a input space X_S of source-problem S to one or more target-problems T, or distributions to efficiently develop an effective hypothesis for a new task, problem, or distribution [7]. In this framework of transfer learning, we address transfer learning problems, where the source and target problems are from different distributions and also the source Y_S and target Y_T labels may be equal or different. Thus, we address two important cases of transfer learning problems:

1. The distributions are different $P_S(X) \neq P_T(X)$ and the labels are equal $Y_S = Y_T$.
2. The distributions are different $P_S(X) \neq P_T(X)$ and the labels are not equal $Y_S \neq Y_T$.

Under such hypothesis, our goal is to obtain an accurate classification for target-problem instances by exploiting labeled training instances drawn from the source-problem. We use two types of feature transference: 1) unsupervised feature transference (UFT) only for SDA model, and 2) supervised layer based feature transference (SLFT) for both SDA and CNN model

Table 1. Lists SLFT, UFT and Baseline Approach

Approaches	Transference	Target problem
FT	$S(\mathbf{w}_S) \Rightarrow \mathbf{w}_T$	$finetune\,(\mathbf{w}_T, \mathbf{c}_T)$
L1+L2+L3	$S(w_S^1, w_S^2, w_S^3) \Rightarrow w_T^1, w_T^2, w_T^3$	$finetune\,(\mathbf{c}_T)$
L1+L3	$S(w_S^1, w_S^3) \Rightarrow w_T^1, w_T^3$	$finetune\,(w_T^2, \mathbf{c}_T)$
L2+L3	$S(w_S^2, w_S^3) \Rightarrow w_T^2, w_T^3$	$finetune\,(w_T^1, \mathbf{c}_T)$
L1+L2	$S(w_S^1, w_S^2) \Rightarrow w_T^1, w_T^2$	$finetune\,(w_T^3, \mathbf{c}_T)$
L3	$S(w_S^3) \Rightarrow w_T^3$	$finetune\,(w_T^1, {w_T}^3, \mathbf{c}_T)$
L2	$S(w_S^2) \Rightarrow w_T^2$	$finetune\,(w_T^1, w_T^3, \mathbf{c}_T)$
L1	$S(w_S^1) \Rightarrow w_T^1$	$finetune\,(w_T^2, w_T^3, \mathbf{c}_T)$
UFT	$U(\mathbf{w}_S) \Rightarrow \mathbf{w}_T$	$finetune\,(\mathbf{w}_T, \mathbf{c}_T)$
Baseline	-	$finetune\,(pretrain(\mathbf{w}_T), \mathbf{c}_T)$

In the *Unsupervised Feature Transference* (UFT) approach we transfer the unsupervised features of the SDA model from the source to the target problem, that is, $U(\mathbf{w}_S) \Rightarrow \mathbf{w}_T$ as shown in Table 1. Once the features are transferred to the target problem, we add a logistic regression layer for the target Y_T with labels c_T on top of the transferred machine. We fine-tune this entire classifier $finetune(\mathbf{w}_T, c_T)$ as a multi-layer perceptron using back-propagation.

In the Supervised Layer Based Feature Transference (SLFT), lets consider the case of **L1** approach as listed in Table 1, we transfer $S(w_S^1) \Rightarrow w_T^1$ features from source to target problem. Then the rest of hidden and logistic regression layer of the target network is randomly initialized. Finally, we fine-tune the whole target network except w_T^1 feature set of the target network, $finetune\,(w_T^2, w_T^3, \mathbf{c}_T)$. Similarly, we can transfer the first and second layer features, that is, $S(w_S^1, w_S^2) \Rightarrow w_T^1, w_T^2$, listed as the **L1+L2** approach in Table 1. In the case of the **FT** approach we reuse the fully trained supervised features $S(\mathbf{w}_S) \Rightarrow \mathbf{w}_T$ of the source problem and then fine-tune again the entire classifier $S\,(\mathbf{w}_T, \mathbf{c}_T)$ for the target problem. In the case of $Y_S \neq Y_T$ transfer setting the FT approach cannot reuse the logistic regression layer. Thus the logistic regression layer is randomly initialized for the target problem.

4   Experiments and Results

In this work we used MNIST[1], MADbase[2] and Chars74k[3] [8] image datasets. The original Chars74k were split into two smaller datasets: *lowercase* with the a-to-z lowercase letters and *uppercase* with the A-to-Z uppercase letters. Then resized it to 28×28 pixels from original 128×128 pixels image. In our experiments we use Latin handwritten digits, Arabic handwritten digits, Lowercase synthetic letters and Uppercase synthetic letters datasets as shown in Table 2.

We performed all our experiments on a computer with i7-377 (3.50GHz) 16GB RAM using Theano [9] a GPU compatible machine learning library on a GTX

---

[1] http://yann.lecun.com/exdb/mnist/
[2] http://datacenter.aucegypt.edu/shazeem/
[3] We acknowledge Microsoft Research India for Chars74k dataset.

Table 2. Dataset characteristics, Average classification test error (%) ($\bar{\varepsilon}$), Average training times (seconds) ($\bar{t}$) with GTX 770 obtained for SDA and CNN baseline approach

Data set	Labels			Instances			SDA		CNN	
Distribution	Y	c	Train	Valid	Test		$\bar{\varepsilon}$	$\bar{t}$	$\bar{\varepsilon}$	$\bar{t}$
Latin P_L	0-to-9 Y_{09}	10	50,000	10,000	10,000		1.61±0.19	10698	0.93±0.06	1418
Arabic P_A	•-to-9 $Y_{•9}$	10	50,000	10,000	10,000		1.37±0.07	8051	0.96±0.06	1209
Lowercase P_{LC}	a-to-z Y_{az}	26	13,208	6,604	6,604		4.95±0.16	2997	3.65±0.12	445
Uppercase P_{UC}	A-to-Z Y_{AZ}	26	13,208	6,604	6,604		5.01±0.27	2567	3.42±0.10	444

770 GPU. The GPU parallel processing allows training both CNN's and SDA's deep neural networks with millions of neural connection faster than traditional CPUs. Each of these experiments are repeated 10 times to increase the confidence level of the results. The hyper parameters for CNN used kernel filter size of [20, 50] and max training epochs of 200. The learning rate of 0.1 is set with batch training of 500. The hyper parameters for SDA used pre-training and fine-tuning learning rates of 0.001 and 0.1, respectively. The stopping criteria for pre-training was fixed to 40 epochs; stopping criteria for fine-tuning was set to a maximum of 1000 epochs. The number of neurons in the three hidden layers and one output layer has a pyramidal structure with [576, 400, 256, c] neurons.

In the following experiments we compare baseline (BL) and transfer learning (TL) approach classification error ε using $X_{ts.target}$ dataset, for different amounts of instances per class, n_{ds}/c. We followed the procedure shown in Algorithm 1.

In step 1 of the experimental procedure, $X_{ds.source}$ for each n_{ds} samples were randomly picked from a set of different amounts of design samples per class [100, 250, 500, 1000, 1320, 2500, 5000]. Then in each of this iteration; step (a) we run the baseline approach from Algorithm 1, step (b) we build $X_{ds.target}$ by randomly picking n_{ts} samples, where $n_{ts} = n_{ds}$. Finally, in step (c), we apply the various layer based feature transference approaches as listed in Table 1.

Algorithm 1. Experimental procedure.

Given design sets $X_{ds.source}$, $X_{ds.target}$ and test set $X_{ts.source}$, $X_{ts.target}$,

For each *dataset* such that $(X_{ds}, X_{ts}) \in$ (Latin, Arabic, Lowercase, Uppercase)

1. For each n_{ds} such that $\frac{n_{ds}}{c} \in [100, 250, 500, 1000, 1320, 2500, 5000]$,
   (a) Run the baseline approach;
   (b) Obtain $X_{ds.target}$ by randomly picking n_{ds} samples from $X_{ds.target.full}$;
   (c) For each *TL* approach such that $L \in [L1, L1 + L2, ...]$ from Table 1,
       i. Fix L^{th} layer of the network trained on $X_{ds.source}$;
       ii. Retrain the network using $X_{ds.target}$ except the Lth layers;
       iii. Test the network using $X_{ts.target}$, obtaining classification error ε.

Table 3. Average classification test error (%) ($\bar{\varepsilon}$) obtained for different n_{ds}/c for SLFT approach on CNN model

Approaches	$X_{ds.upper}$ reuse $X_{ds.latin}$		$X_{ds.lower}$ reuse $X_{ds.latin}$	
Source:	Latin		Latin	
Target:	Uppercase		Lowercase	
$n_{ds.source}/c$:	1320	5000	1320	5000
L1+L2+L3	5.96±0.13	5.32±0.18	6.13±0.13	5.63±0.15
L1+L3	4.49±0.14	4.24±0.10	4.75±0.13	4.57±0.09
L1+L2	3.61±0.12	**3.39±0.12**	3.83±0.06	**3.63±0.13**
L3	4.30±0.13	4.20±0.16	4.62±0.18	4.61±0.14
L2	3.54±0.14	3.43±0.06	3.72±0.11	3.58±0.15
L1	3.43±0.11	**3.35±0.09**	**3.64±0.06**	**3.56±0.11**
BL	**3.42±0.10**	3.42±0.10	3.65±0.12	3.65±0.12

4.1 Results for Transductive Transfer: From Digits to Letters

Classifying images of lowercase from a-to-z by reusing supervised features of digits from 0-to-9. We train a CNN to solve Latin digits (specific source problem) and reuse it to solve a lowercase letters (different but related target problem) without having to train it from scratch.

Using Latin as source problem and either Lowercase or Uppercase letters as target problem. Table 3 presents the average classification error rate for SLFT approach on CNN model by applying Algorithm 1. We observe both **L1** and **L1+L2** approach performs better than the baseline approach for $n_{ds}/c = 5000$. In case of $n_{ds}/c = 1320$ we observe only **L1** approach performs better than the baseline approach. Reusing all three layers: L1+L2+L3 has degraded performs as the complete supervised features are well tuned for the source problem and training only the logistic regression layer has no improvement. Table 4 provides the summary of classification results for both CNN and SDA models.

Table 4. Summary: Average classification test error (%) ($\bar{\varepsilon}$), Average training times (seconds) ($\bar{t}$) by reusing Latin at $n_{ds}/c = 1320$

Approaches		Lowercase		Uppercase	
		$\bar{\varepsilon}$	$\bar{t}$	$\bar{\varepsilon}$	$\bar{t}$
SDA	BL	4.95±0.16	2997	5.01±0.27	2567
SDA	SLFT: L1	4.72±0.17	2261	4.72±0.18	2515
SDA	UFT	4.67±0.38	1148	4.65±0.19	1498
SDA	SLFT: FT	**4.57±0.08**	1020	**4.58±0.19**	1180
CNN	SLFT: L1+L2	3.83±0.06	196	3.61±0.12	197
CNN	BL	3.65±0.12	445	**3.42±0.10**	444
CNN	SLFT: L1	**3.64±0.06**	292	3.43±0.11	293

4.2   Transference from Arabic Digits to Latin Digits and Vice-Versa

Utilizing previous conclusion that reusing L1 and L1+L2 perform better other approaches. We performed similar experiment with Latin and Arabic digits and also reverse the role of source and target datasets. To study the effect of negative transference, for example, *digit 0* in latin is represented as **0** where as *digit 5* in arabic is written as **0**. These labels may lead to negative transference during supervised learning. We observe SLFT L1 and L1+L2 approaches performs better than baseline approach as shown in Fig 1 and Fig 2.

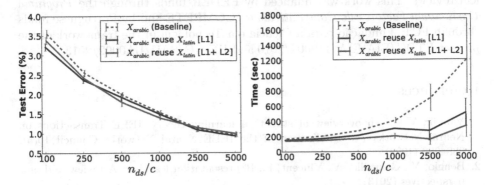

Fig. 1. Classification results on MAHDBase (Arabic digits) for SLFT: L1 and L1+L2 approach, for different numbers n_{ds}/c. **Left:** Average classification test error rate. **Right:** Average time taken for classification.

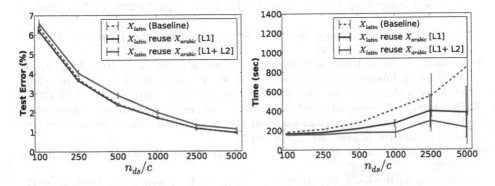

Fig. 2. Classification results on MNIST (Latin digits) for SLFT: L1 and L1+L2 approach, for different numbers n_{ds}/c. **Left:** Average classification test error rate. **Right:** Average time taken for classification.

5   Conclusions

We proposed a layer based feature transference approach that supports standard neural networks like CNN and SDA for solving transductive transfer learning problems. By transferring either low or high layer features on machines trained either unsupervised or supervised way. Using this approach we achieved performance improvement with significant reduction in computation time and also decreased classification error rate. We achieved significant performance by transferring learning from source to target problem, by using lower-layer features trained in supervised fashion in case of CNN's and unsupervised features trained in case of SDA's.

Acknowledgements. The authors would like to thank Dr Jaime S. Cardoso, Universidade do Porto, Dr Telmo Amaral and Dr Ricardo Sousa for their critical reviews. This work was financed by FEDER funds through the *Programa Operacional Factores de Competitividade* COMPETE and by Portuguese funds through FCT Fundação para a Ciência e a Tecnologia in the framework of the project PTDC/EIA-EIA/119004/2010 and PEst-C/SAU/LA0002/2013.

References

1. Vapnik, V.N.: An overview of statistical learning theory. IEEE Transactions on Neural Networks / a Publication of the IEEE Neural Networks Council 10(5), 988–999 (1999)
2. Bengio, Y., Courville, A., Vincent, P.: Representation learning: A review and new perspectives (2013)
3. Vincent, P., Larochelle, H., Lajoie, I., Bengio, Y., Manzagol, P.A.: Stacked denoising autoencoders: Learning useful representations in a deep network with a local denoising criterion. J. Mach. Learn. Res. 11, 3371–3408 (2010); Cited by 0083
4. LeCun, Y., Bottou, L., Bengio, Y., Haffner, P.: Gradient-based learning applied to document recognition. Proceedings of the IEEE 86(11), 2278–2324 (1998); Cited by 2008
5. Bengio, Y.: Learning deep architectures for AI. Foundations and Trends in Machine Learning 2(1), 1–127 (2009)
6. Amaral, T., Silva, L.M., Alexandre, L.A., Kandaswamy, C., Santos, J.M., de Sá, J.M.: Using different cost functions to train stacked auto-encoders. In: Proceedings of the 12th Mexican International Conference on Artificial Intelligence. IEEE (2013)
7. Bruzzone, L., Marconcini, M.: Domain adaptation problems: A dasvm classification technique and a circular validation strategy. IEEE Transactions on Pattern Analysis and Machine Intelligence 32(5), 770–787 (2010)
8. de Campos, T., Babu, B.R., Varma, M.: Character recognition in natural images (2009)
9. Bergstra, J., Breuleux, O., Bastien, F., Lamblin, P., Pascanu, R., Desjardins, G., Turian, J., Warde-Farley, D., Bengio, Y.: Theano: a CPU and GPU math expression compiler. In: Proceedings of the Python for Scientific Computing Conference (SciPy), vol. 4 (2010)

From Maxout to Channel-Out: Encoding Information on Sparse Pathways

Qi Wang and Joseph JaJa

Department of Electrical and Computer Engineering,
University of Maryland Institute of Advanced Computer Studies
University of Maryland, College Park, MD, USA
{qwang37,joseph}@umiacs.umd.edu

Abstract. Motivated by an important insight from neural science that "functionality is determined by pathway", we propose a new deep network framework, called "channel-out network", which encodes information on sparse pathways. We argue that the recent success of maxout networks can also be explained by its ability of encoding information on sparse pathways, while channel-out network does not only select pathways at training time but also at inference time. From a mathematical perspective, channel-out networks can represent a wider class of piecewise continuous functions, thereby endowing the network with more expressive power than that of maxout networks. We test our channel-out networks on several well-known image classification benchmarks, achieving new state-of-the-art performances on CIFAR-100 and STL-10.

Keywords: deep networks, pathway selection, sparse pathway encoding, channel-out.

1 Introduction

Many recent works on deep learning have focused on ways to regularize network behavior to avoid over-fitting. Dropout [1] has been widely accepted as an effective way for deep network regularization. Dropout was initially proposed to avoid co-adaptation of feature detectors, but it turns out it can also be regarded as an efficient ensemble model. The maxout network [2] is a newly proposed micro architecture of deep networks, which works well with the dropout technique. It sets the state-of-the-art performance on many popular image classification datasets. In retrospect, both methods follow the same approach: they restrict updates triggered by a training sample to affect only a sparse sub-graph of the network.

In this paper we provide a new insight into a possible reason for the success of maxout, namely that it partially takes advantage of what we call "sparse pathway encoding", a much more robust way of encoding categorical information than encoding by magnitudes. In sparse pathway encoding, the pathway selection itself carries significant amount of the categorical information. With a carefully designed scheme, the network can extract pattern-specific pathways during

S. Wermter et al. (Eds.): ICANN 2014, LNCS 8681, pp. 273–280, 2014.
© Springer International Publishing Switzerland 2014

training time and recognize the correct pathway at inference time. Guided by this principle, we propose a new type of network architectures called "channel-out networks". We run experiments with channel-out networks using several image classification benchmarks, showing competitive performances compared with state-of-the-art results. The channel-out network sets new state-of-the-art performance on two image classification datasets that are on the "harder" end of the spectrum - CIFAR-100 and STL-10 - demonstrating its potential to encode large amounts of information with higher level of complexity.

2   Review of Maxout Networks

The maxout network [2] is a recently proposed architecture that is significantly different from traditional networks in its activation style: the activation does not take a normal single-input-single-output form, but instead the maximum of several linear outputs. In [2], its advantage over normal differentiable activation functions (such as tanh) was attributed to its better approximation to exact model averaging, and the advantage over rectified linear (Relu) activation function was attributed to easier optimization at training time. Here we propose another insight of the power of the maxout network. The idea is motivated by a well-established principle in neural science: It is not the shape of the signal but the pathway along which the signal flows that determines the functionality of information processing [3]. The maxout node activates only one of the candidate input pathways, and the gradient is back-propagated only through that selected pathway, which means the information imposed by the training sample is encoded in a controlled sparse way. We call this behavior as "sparse pathway encoding". Note that although Relu networks also use sparse sub-networks, the pathway selection is less structured than that in maxout networks, which might be the reason that Relu networks are more vulnerable to over-fitting.

Although maxout networks encodes information sparsely, it does not infer sparsely. When doing inference every weight parameter effectively participates in computation. Since the power of deep networks lies in the hierarchical feature structure, it is worthwhile to think about whether the sparse pathway encoding can also be arranged in a hierarchical way. In this paper we made our first attempt along this line by proposing a new network architecture called "channel-out network", which is able to make active pathway selections at inference time.

3   The Channel-Out Network

A channel-out network is characterized by channel-out groups (Figure 1). At the end of a typical linear layer (e.g. fully connected or convolutional layer), output nodes are arranged into groups, and for each group a special channel selection function is performed to decide which channel opens for further information flow. Only the activation of the selected channels are passed through, other channels are blocked off. When gradient is back-propagated through the channel-out layer, it only passes through the open channels selected during forward propagation.

Formally, we define a scalar/vector-valued channel selection function $\mathbf{f}(a_1, a_2, ..., a_k)$ which takes as input a vector of length k and outputs an index set of length l ($l < k$). Elements of the index set are selected from the domain $\{1, 2, ..., k\}$:

$$f_s(a_1, a_2, ..., a_k) \in \{1, 2, ..., k\}$$
$$s \ from \ 1 \ to \ l$$
$$\forall s \neq t, f_s(\cdot) \not\equiv f_t(\cdot)$$

Then with an input vector (typically the previous layer output) $\mathbf{a} = (a_1, a_2, ..., a_k) \in \mathcal{R}^k$, a channel-out group implements the following activation functions:

$$h_i = \mathbf{I}_{\{i \in \mathbf{f}(a_1, a_2, ..., a_k)\}} a_i \tag{1}$$

where $\mathbf{I}(\cdot)$ is the indicator function, i indexes the candidates in the channel-out group, a_i is the ith candidate input, and h_i is the output (Figure 1). There are many possible choices of the channel selection function $f(\cdot)$. To ensure good performance, we require that the channel selection function possesses the following properties:

- The function must be piece-wise constant, and the piece-wise constant regions should not be too small. Intuitively, the function has to be "regular enough" to ensure robustness against the noise in the data.
- The pre-image size of each possible index output must be of almost the same size. In other words, each channel in the channel-out group should be equally likely to be selected as we process the training examples (so that the information capacity of the network is uniformly utilized).
- The computation cost for evaluating the function must be as low as possible.

Some examples of good channel selection functions are: $\arg\max(\cdot)$, $\arg\min(\cdot)$, $\arg\text{median}(\cdot)$, indices of the l largest candidates, and the absolute-max $\arg\max(|\cdot|)$. The test results reported in this paper all used the $\arg\max(\cdot)$ function.

Figure 2 compares a channel-out network with a maxout network. We can see that a channel-out network can actively select the pathway at a higher layer while maxout can't.

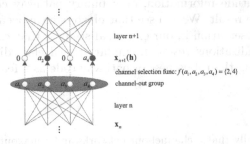

Fig. 1. Operation performed by a channel-out group

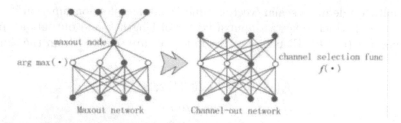

Fig. 2. Difference between maxout and channel-out: A maxout node is attached to a set of FIXED output links, resulting in same output pathway for different input pathways; A channel-out group is connected to a set of different output links, resulting in distinct output pathways

A side effect of enabling the network to do active pathway selection is the potential saving on computation power. As a concrete example, suppose all channel-out groups in a network are of size k and the channel selection function output is scalar. Consider a layer that's not the input or the output layer, with input dimension of m and output dimension of n. In forward propagation, since only m/k of the inputs are active, we can take advantage of index recording to reduce the computational cost to $1/k$ compared with a maxout layer of same size[1]. In back propagation, since both input and output active nodes are sparse, the computation can be reduced to $1/k^2$ of a full matrix computation. Maxout can also take advantage of sparsity of outputs to get $1/k$ computation reduction in back propagation, therefore channel-out training can be k times faster in back propagation also. Note that a channel-out layer and a maxout layer of same size (number of parameters) means that the number of channel-out groups of the channel-out layer is $1/k$ of the number of maxout nodes in the maxout layer.

To confirm that pathway encoding is indeed important in pattern recognition, we record the pathway selections of a well-trained channel-out model (with $\max(\cdot)$ channel selection function) using the CIFAR-10 dataset. For ease of visualization and analysis, we set the size of channel-out groups to 2, so that we can use binary codes to represent the pathway selection. To better visualize the space of pathway patterns, we perform PCA analysis on the pathway pattern vectors and project them into the three dimensional space. Note that here we have dropped the magnitude information, only binary pathway coding is retained. Figures 3 shows the result. We can see that clusters have been well formed. Another interesting observation in our empirical study is that channel-out models with different initializations result in similar spatial class distributions in 3D PCA space, implying the robustness of pathway code as a feature.

---

[1] We found empirically that a channel-out networks and a maxout network with similar number of parameters will perform similarly in practice, so the premise for comparison is valid.

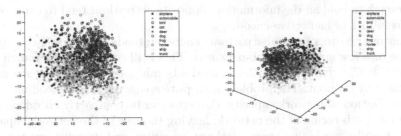

Fig. 3. 3D visualization of the pathway pattern: channel-out

4 Analysis of the Channel-Out Network

In this section we give an intuitive explanation about why sparse pathway encoding works well in practice, especially when combined with dropout.

Recall that dropout, with each presentation of a training sample, samples a sub-network and encodes the information revealed by the training sample onto this sub-network. Since the sampling of data and sub-networks are independent processes, in a statistical sense the information provided by each training sample will eventually be "squeezed" into each of these sub-networks (third row of Figure 4). The advantage of such scheme, as has been pointed out in various papers [1,4,5], is that the same piece of information is encoded into many different representations, adding to the robustness at inference time. The side-effect, which has not been highlighted before, is that encoding conflicting pieces of information densely into sub-networks with small capacities causes interference problem. Data samples of different patterns (classes) attempt to build different, maybe highly conflicting network representations. When the sub-network is not

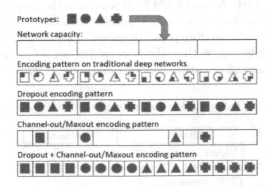

Fig. 4. Information encoding patterns. Each bin in the network capacity box represents a certain size sub-network. Dropout tends to encode all patterns to each capacity bin, resulting in efficient use of network capacity but high level of interference; Sparse pathway methods tend to encode each pattern to a specific sparse sub-network, resulting in least interference but waste of network capacity; The best approach is the combination of the two schemes.

large enough to hold all the information, opposite activations tend to cancel each other, resulting in ineffective encoding.

In contrast to dropout, sparse pathway encoding tends to encode each pattern onto one or a few specialized sub-networks. This is illustrated in the fourth row of Figure 4. Clearly, sparse pathway methods mitigate the interference problem caused by dropout. The problem with pure sparse pathway encoding is the under-utilization of network capacity. Patterns can be compactly encoded on to a small local sub-region of the network, leaving the rest of the network capacity unused. Finally, combining sparse pathway encoding and dropout can take advantage of the strengths of both methods to generate more efficient and accurate information encoding: the whole network will get used due to random sampling by dropout, while individual patterns are still compactly encoded onto certain local sub-networks, so that interference across patterns is much less severe. This is illustrated in the last row of Figure 4.

5   Benchmark Results

In this section we show the performance of the channel-out network on several image classification benchmarks. Our implementation is built on top of the efficient convolution CUDA kernels developed by Alex Krizhevsky [6].

5.1   CIFAR-10 [6]

The network used for CIFAR-10 experiment consists of 3 convolutional channel-out layers, followed by a fully connected channel-out layer, and then the softmax layer. The best model has 64-192-192 filters for the corresponding convolutional layers, and 1210 nodes in the fully connected layer. Dropout regularization is applied. No data augmentation is used.

The result along with the best CIFAR-10 results in the literature are shown in Table 1 (These are results with no data augmentation. Best results in [5] are with data augmentation and therefore is not included in this table). The channel-out network performs a bit worse than the state-of-the-art set by maxout network, but is better than any of the other previous methods as far as we know.

Table 1. Best methods on CIFAR-10

Method	Precision
Maxout+Dropout [2]	88.32%
Channel-out+Dropout	**86.80 ± 0.31%**
CNN+Spearmint [7]	85.02%
Stochastic Pooling [8]	84.87%

5.2   CIFAR-100 [6]

The CIFAR-100 dataset is similar to CIFAR-10, but with 100 classes. The channel-out network tuned for CIFAR-100 has similar achitecture as that for

CIFAR-10. Images are pre-whitened and when presented to the network each time, they are horizontally flipped with probability 0.5. The test set precision was 63.41%, improving the current state-of-the-art by nearly 2 percentage points. Table 2 shows the best results on CIFAR-100.

Table 2. Best methods on CIFAR-100

Method	Precision
Channel-out+Dropout	**63.41 ± 0.53%**
Maxout+Dropout [2]	61.43%
Stochastic Pooling [8]	57.49%
Learned Pooling [9]	56.29%

Motivated by the better performance on CIFAR-100 over CIFAR-10, we performed another experiment to test the assumption that channel-out networks might be better at encoding more variant patterns. We extract 10, 20, 50, 100 classes from the original dataset to form 4 classification tasks. We train a channel-out and a maxout network with similar number of parameters for each of the four tasks. We can see from Table 3 that channel-out performs better on tasks with more classes. We used smaller networks in this experiment for quick test.

Table 3. Comparison of channel-out and maxout on 4 tasks of different difficult levels: channel-out does better on tasks with more classes

No. of classes	10	20	50	100
Channel-out+Dropout	72.62%	**65.03%**	**53.95%**	**57.44%**
Maxout+Dropout	**75.80%**	61.97%	51.32%	53.57%

5.3   STL-10 [10]

STL-10 is also a 10-class small images dataset, but with more variant patterns and background clutters than CIFAR-10. The network constructed is similar to that for CIFAR-10. Whitening and flipping are applied to data. Our method improves the current state-of-the-art by 5%, as is shown in Table 4.

Table 4. Best methods on STL-10

Method	Precision
Channel-out+Dropout	**69.5 ± 0.40 %**
Hierarchical Matching Pursuit [11]	64.5%
Discriminative Learning of SPN [12]	62.3%

6   Conclusions

We have introduced the concept of sparse pathway encoding and argued that this can be a robust and efficient way for encoding categorical information in a deep network. Using sparse pathway encoding, the interference between conflicting patterns is mitigated, and therefore when combined with dropout, the network can utilize the network capacity in a more effective way. Along this direction we have proposed a novel class of deep networks, the channel-out networks. Our experiments show that channel-out networks perform very well on image classification tasks, especially for the harder tasks with more complex patterns.

Acknowledgements. Upon finishing this work, we found that a recent work from the IDSIA lab [13] proposed a similar model as the max($\cdot$) version of the channel-out network. Our work was independently developed, and provides a different perspective to explain its success - "sparse pathway encoding", which we believe to be a promising general direction that future research should pay attention to. New and state-of-the-art results are also important contributions of this paper. The main experiments in [13] were on different data sets so we did not compare their results with ours in this paper.

References

1. Hinton, G.E., Srivastava, N., Krizhevsky, A., Sutskever, I., Salakhutdinov, R.R.: Improving neural networks by preventing co-adaptation of feature detectors. arXiv preprint arXiv:1207.0580 (2012)
2. Goodfellow, I.J., Warde-Farley, D., Mirza, M., Courville, A., Bengio, Y.: Maxout networks. arXiv preprint arXiv:1302.4389 (2013)
3. Kandel, E.R., Schwartz, J.H., Jessell, T.M., et al.: Principles of neural science, vol. 4. McGraw-Hill, New York (2000)
4. Srivastava, N.: Improving neural networks with dropout. PhD thesis, University of Toronto (2013)
5. Wan, L., Zeiler, M., Zhang, S., Cun, Y.L., Fergus, R.: Regularization of neural networks using dropconnect. In: Proceedings of the 30th International Conference on Machine Learning (ICML 2013), pp. 1058–1066 (2013)
6. Krizhevsky, A., Sutskever, I., Hinton, G.: ImageNet classification with deep convolutional neural networks. In: Advances in Neural Information Processing Systems 25, pp. 1106–1114 (2012)
7. Snoek, J., Larochelle, H., Adams, R.P.: Practical Bayesian optimization of machine learning algorithms. arXiv preprint arXiv:1206.2944 (2012)
8. Zeiler, M.D., Fergus, R.: Stochastic pooling for regularization of deep convolutional neural networks. arXiv preprint arXiv:1301.3557 (2013)
9. Malinowski, M., Fritz, M.: Learning smooth pooling regions for visual recognition. In: British Machine Vision Conference (2013)
10. Coates, A., Ng, A.Y., Lee, H.: An analysis of single-layer networks in unsupervised feature learning. In: International Conference on Artificial Intelligence and Statistics, pp. 215–223 (2011)
11. Bo, L., Ren, X., Fox, D.: Unsupervised feature learning for rgb-d based object recognition. ISER (June 2012)
12. Gens, R., Domingos, P.: Discriminative learning of sum-product networks. In: Advances in Neural Information Processing Systems, pp. 3248–3256 (2012)
13. Srivastava, R.K., Masci, J., Kazerounian, S., Gomez, F., Schmidhuber, J.: Compete to compute. technical report (2013)

Minimizing Computation
in Convolutional Neural Networks

.

Jason Cong and Bingjun Xiao

Computer Science Department,
University of California,
Los Angeles, CA 90095, USA
{cong,xiao}@cs.ucla.edu

Abstract. Convolutional Neural Networks (CNNs) have been successfully used for many computer vision applications. It would be beneficial to these applications if the computational workload of CNNs could be reduced. In this work we analyze the linear algebraic properties of CNNs and propose an algorithmic modification to reduce their computational workload. An up to a 47% reduction can be achieved without any change in the image recognition results or the addition of any hardware accelerators.

1 Introduction

Biologically inspired convolutional neural networks (CNNs) have achieved good success in computer vision applications, e.g., the recognition of handwritten digits [7, 10], and the detection of faces [2, 8]. In the 2012 ImageNet contest [1], a CNN-based approach named SuperVision [6] outperformed all the other traditional image recognition algorithms. On one hand, CNNs keep the advantage of artificial neural networks which use a massive network of neurons and synapses to automatically extract features from data. On the other hand, CNNs further customize their synapse topologies for computer vision applications to exploit the feature locality in image data.

The success of CNNs promises wide use for many future platforms to recognize images, e.g., micro-robots, portable devices, and image search engines in data centers. It will be beneficial to improve the implementation of the CNN algorithm to reduce computational cost. One direction is to improve the CNN algorithm using hardware accelerators, e.g., GPUs and field-programmable gate arrays (FPGAs) [3,5,9]. Another orthogonal direction is to reduce the theoretical number of basic operations needed in the CNN computation from the algorithmic aspect, as will be discussed in this work. Here, we first reveal the linear algebraic properties in the CNN computation, and based on these properties, we propose an efficient algorithm that can be applied to generic CNN architectures to reduce the computational workload without any penalty on the image recognition quality or hardware cost.

2 Background

2.1 Algorithm Review of CNNs

Convolutional neural networks (CNNs) were extended from artificial neural networks (ANNs) and customized for computer vision [7]. An example of a CNN is given in

S. Wermter et al. (Eds.): ICANN 2014, LNCS 8681, pp. 281–290, 2014.

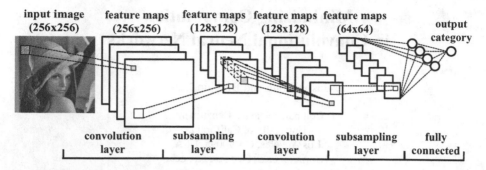

Fig. 1. An example of a convolutional neural network

Fig. 1. As shown in this figure, the intermediate results in a CNN are different sets of feature maps. The main working principle of a CNN is to gradually extract local features from feature maps of higher resolutions, and then to combine these features into more abstract feature maps of lower resolutions. This is realized by the two alternating types of layers in a CNN: convolution layers and subsampling layers. The last few layers in the CNN still use fully connected ANN classifiers to produce the abstracted classification results. The detailed computation patterns of different layers in the CNN are described as below:

Convolution Layer. In this layer, features, such as edges, corners, and crossings, are extracted from the input feature maps via different convolution kernels, and are combined into more abstract output feature maps. Assume there are Q input feature maps and R output feature maps, and the feature map size is $M \times N$. Also assume the convolution kernel size is $K \times L$. Then the computation in the convolution layer can be represented in a nested-loop description, as shown in Fig. 2. The array X contains the input feature maps, and the array Y contains the output feature maps which are initialized to zeros. The array W contains the weights in the convolution kernels. To regularize the computation pattern, we do not explicitly add the network bias to the output feature maps. Instead, we put a dummy input feature map of all 1's in array X and put the bias on the weights associated with this dummy input map in array W. The computational workload in the convolution layer is in the order of $O(R \cdot Q \cdot M \cdot N \cdot K \cdot L)$.

```
for (r=0; r<R; r++)              //output feature map
  for (q=0; q<Q; q++)            //input feature map
    for (m=0; m<M; m++)          //row in feature map
      for (n=0; n<N; n++)        //column in feature map
        for (k=0; k<K; k++)      //row in convolution kerenel
          for (l=0; l<L; l++)    //column in convolution kernel
            Y[r][m][n]+=W[r][q][k][l]*X[q][m+k][n+l];
```

Fig. 2. Example loop-nest representing the computation in a convolution layer of a CNN

Subsampling Layer. The purpose of this layer is to achieve spatial invariance by reducing the resolution of feature maps. In the example of Fig. 1, each feature map is scaled down by a subsample factor 2 × 2. The computational workload in this layer is in the order of $O(Q \cdot M \cdot N)$, which is much smaller than that in the convolution layer.

At the output of each layer, an activation function is further applied to each pixel in the feature maps to mimic the neuron activation.

2.2 Architecture of Real-Life CNN

The architecture of a real-life CNN that was used in the 2012 ImageNet contest [6] is shown in Fig. 3. It consists of eight layers. The first layer contains three 224 × 224 input images that are obtained from the original 256 × 256 image via data augmentation. The 1,000 neurons in the last layer report the likelihoods of the 1,000 categories that the input image might belong to. Layer 2 contains 96 feature maps, and each feature map is sized 55 × 55. They are partitioned into two sets, each containing 48 feature maps, so as to fit into two GPUs used in [6]. The other layers also follow notations similar to Fig. 3. Note that the convolution layer and the subsampling layer are merged together in Layers 1, 2, 3, and 6 of this architecture. There are no subsampling layers but only convolution layers in the other layers. The convolution kernel size is 11 in Layer 1, 5 in Layer 2, and 3 in the other layers. The default subsample factor is 2, except for a factor of 4 in Layer 1. The subsampling operations are not trainable in this architecture, but the function max is applied to the 2 × 2 or 4 × 4 pixel windows in each feature map, and is marked as max pooling in Fig. 3. The activation function is simplified to the Rectified Linear Unit (ReLU) function, $\max(0, x)$, as discussed in [6]. In Layer 2, 4, and 5, to avoid the inter-GPU communication, the features extracted from the two partitioned sets of input feature maps are not combined together at the output. The design choice of removing this combination is made by trial and error, and proves effective in [6].

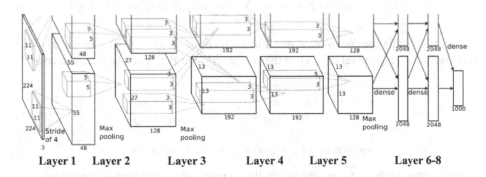

Fig. 3. A real-life CNN that was used in the 2012 ImageNet contest [6]

2.3 Runtime Breakdown of Real-Life CNN

To better understand the time-consuming part of the process of image recognition via a CNN, we reimplement the CNN in Fig. 3 in a single-thread CPU so that the workload can be measured by runtime. A breakdown of runtime is given in Table 1. We see that the runtime is dominated by the convolution layers. The main focus of this work is to optimize the computation in the convolution layers.

Table 1. Breakdown of CNN runtime in the recognition of 256 images

	Convolution Layer	Subsampling Layer	ReLU Activation	Fully Connected ANN
Layer 1	364s	720s	1.83s	-
Layer 2	1728s	416s	1.19s	-
Layer 3	5710s	147s	0.42s	-
Layer 4	2564s	-	0.42s	-
Layer 5	2652s	-	0.27s	-
Layer 6	-	29s	0.12	8.60s
Layer 7	-	-	0.12s	5.63s
Layer 8	-	-	0.03s	1.78s
Total	13018s	1313s	4.41s	16.0s
Breakdown	90.7%	9.15%	0.03%	0.11%

3 Properties of CNN Computation

3.1 Another View of CNN Computation

In this section we offer another view of the CNN computation in Fig. 2 that enables optimization of the computational workload. First denote the Q input feature maps as $x_1, x_2, ...x_Q$, and the R output feature maps as $y_1, y_2, ..., y_R$. Also denote the $R \times Q$ convolution kernels (each sized $K \times L$) as w_{rq} where $r = 1, 2, ..., R$ and $q = 1, 2, ..., Q$. We further denote the convolution operation between a kernel w_{rq} and a feature map x_q as

$$w_{rq} * x_q = z, \text{ where } z(m,n) = \sum_{k=0}^{K-1} \sum_{l=0}^{L-1} w_{rq}(k,l) x_q(m+k, n+l). \tag{1}$$

Here z represents the convolution result in the form of an $M \times N$ image, and $z(m, n)$ represents an image pixel in z. Then the computation in Fig. 2 can be represented as

$$\begin{aligned}
y_1 &= w_{11} * x_1 + w_{12} * x_2 + \cdots + w_{1Q} * x_Q \\
y_2 &= w_{21} * x_1 + w_{22} * x_2 + \cdots + w_{2Q} * x_Q \\
y_3 &= w_{31} * x_1 + w_{32} * x_2 + \cdots + w_{3Q} * x_Q \\
&\cdots \\
y_R &= w_{R1} * x_1 + w_{R2} * x_2 + \cdots + w_{RQ} * x_Q
\end{aligned} \tag{2}$$

If we reorganize these x_q, y_r and w_{rq} in the form of column vectors and matrices

$$\vec{x} = \begin{pmatrix} x_1 \\ x_2 \\ \vdots \\ x_Q \end{pmatrix}, \quad \vec{y} = \begin{pmatrix} y_1 \\ y_2 \\ \vdots \\ y_R \end{pmatrix}, \quad W = \begin{pmatrix} w_{11} & w_{12} & \cdots & w_{1Q} \\ w_{21} & w_{22} & \cdots & w_{2Q} \\ \vdots & \vdots & \ddots & \vdots \\ w_{R1} & w_{R2} & \cdots & w_{RQ} \end{pmatrix},$$

then the computation in Eq. (2) can be redefined as a special matrix/vector multiplication

$$\vec{y} = W \times \vec{x}.$$

Each element in the left operand W is a convolution kernel. Each element in the right operand $\vec{x}$ is an input feature map. Each element in the result $\vec{y}$ is an output feature map. The element-wise multiplication is redefined as the convolution between a kernel w_{rq} and a feature map x_q in Eq. (1). If a web server provider receives a batch of P images to recognize, we will have $\vec{x}_1, \vec{x}_2, \cdots, \vec{x}_P$ as parallel inputs, and $\vec{y}_1, \vec{y}_2, \cdots, \vec{y}_P$ as parallel outputs. Their computation can be merged as

$$(\vec{y}_1, \vec{y}_2, \cdots, \vec{y}_P) = (W \times \vec{x}_1, W \times \vec{x}_2, \cdots, W \times \vec{x}_P) = W \times (\vec{x}_1, \vec{x}_2, \cdots, \vec{x}_P).$$

This can be further simplified to a matrix multiplication

$$Y = W \times X,$$

where

$$X = (\vec{x}_1, \vec{x}_2, \cdots, \vec{x}_P), \ Y = (\vec{y}_1, \vec{y}_2, \cdots, \vec{y}_P).$$

Both the left operand X and the result Y are matrices of feature maps. This matrix multiplication representation provides a new view of the computation in convolution layers of CNNs. We name this representation Convolutional Matrix Multiplication (Convolutional MM).

3.2 Enabling New Optimization Opportunities

We can optimize the computation of Convolutional MM by revisiting techniques that have been built for normal matrix multiplication (Normal MM). For example, we can use the classical Strassen algorithm [11] to reduce the computational workload. In each recursion of matrix partitioning, the Strassen algorithm can reduce the number of multiplications by 1/8, but it incurs many extra additions. Note that in Normal MM, the element-wise multiplication is a multiplication between two numbers, while in our Convolutional MM, the element-wise multiplication is redefined as the convolution between a kernel and a feature map, which has a sufficiently high complexity to make the extra additions negligible. Our Convolutional MM is expected to experience more benefits from the Strassen algorithm than the Normal MM; this will be discussed in Section 4.

3.3 Properties of Convolutional MM

Before we go through any optimization, we first identify the properties of our Convolutional MM. If the addition of two convolution kernel matrices $W1$ and $W2$ of the same size are intuitively defined as the additions of all the pairs of weights at the same positions, i.e.,

$$W1 + W2 = W3, \text{ where } w3_{rq}(k, l) = w1_{rq}(k, l) + w2_{rq}(k, l),$$

combined with the linearity of the operation defined in Eq. (1), we have

$$(W1 + W2) \times X = W1 \times X + W2 \times X. \tag{3}$$

Similarly, if the addition of two feature map matrices $X1$ and $X2$ of the same size are intuitively defined as additions of all the pairs of pixels at the same positions, we have

$$W \times (X1 + X2) = W \times X1 + W \times X2. \tag{4}$$

4 Computation Optimization

In this section we show how to extend the Strassen algorithm [11] from Normal MM to reduce the computational workload of our Convolutional MM. We start from

$$Y = W \times X,$$

where the number of elements in both rows and columns of Y, W, X is assumed to be even. We partition W, X and Y into equally sized block matrices

$$W = \begin{pmatrix} W_{1,1} & W_{1,2} \\ W_{2,1} & W_{2,2} \end{pmatrix}, \ X = \begin{pmatrix} X_{1,1} & X_{1,2} \\ X_{2,1} & X_{2,2} \end{pmatrix}, \ Y = \begin{pmatrix} Y_{1,1} & Y_{1,2} \\ Y_{2,1} & Y_{2,2} \end{pmatrix}.$$

Then we have

$$
\begin{aligned}
Y_{1,1} &= W_{1,1} \times X_{1,1} + W_{1,2} \times X_{2,1} \\
Y_{1,2} &= W_{1,1} \times X_{1,2} + W_{1,2} \times X_{2,2} \\
Y_{2,1} &= W_{2,1} \times X_{1,1} + W_{2,2} \times X_{2,1} \\
Y_{2,2} &= W_{2,1} \times X_{1,2} + W_{2,2} \times X_{2,2}
\end{aligned}
\tag{5}
$$

Here, we still need 8 multiplications, the same number that we need in matrix multiplication before partitioning. We define new matrices

$$
\begin{aligned}
M_1 &:= (W_{1,1} + W_{2,2}) \times (X_{1,1} + X_{2,2}) \\
M_2 &:= (W_{2,1} + W_{2,2}) \times X_{1,1} \\
M_3 &:= W_{1,1} \times (X_{1,2} - X_{2,2}) \\
M_4 &:= W_{2,2} \times (X_{2,1} - X_{1,1}) \\
M_5 &:= (W_{1,1} + W_{1,2}) \times X_{2,2} \\
M_6 &:= (W_{2,1} - W_{1,1}) \times (X_{1,1} + X_{1,2}) \\
M_7 &:= (W_{1,2} - W_{2,2}) \times (X_{2,1} + X_{2,2})
\end{aligned}
\tag{6}
$$

Followed by the properties in Eq. (3) and Eq. (4), we can compute the result of the matrix multiplication from the 7 multiplications in Eq. (6) as follows:

$$
\begin{aligned}
Y_{1,1} &= M_1 + M_4 - M_5 + M_7 \\
Y_{1,2} &= M_3 + M_5 \\
Y_{2,1} &= M_2 + M_4 \\
Y_{2,2} &= M_1 - M_2 + M_3 + M_6.
\end{aligned}
$$

Here, we reduce the number of the redefined multiplications from 8 to 7 without changing the computation results. We can iterate this matrix partitioning process recursively until the submatrices degenerate into basic elements, i.e., separate convolution kernels and feature maps in our Convolutional MM. We can see that each recursion will reduce the number of multiplications by 1/8, but will incur 18 additions on the submatrices. In the Normal MM, all the elements are numbers, and either multiplications or additions are performed between these numbers. The overhead of 18 additions could completely eliminate the benefits brought by the multiplication savings in normal MMs. In our Convolutional MM, however, the element-wise multiplication is redefined as the convolution between a kernel and a feature map in Eq. (1). Suppose the convolution

Table 2. The FLOPS comparison of different operations in the Normal MM and our Convolutional MM

	element-wise addition	element-wise multiplication
the Normal MM	1	1
our Convolutional MM	$K \cdot L$ or $M \cdot N$	$2K \cdot L \cdot M \cdot N$

kernel size is $K \times L$, and the feature map size is $M \times N$. As shown in Table 2, the number of FLOPS (floating-point operations) in an element-wise multiplication will be $2K \cdot L \cdot M \cdot N$, which is much larger than either $K \cdot L$ FLOPS in a kernel addition or $M \cdot N$ FLOPS in a feature map addition. This makes the reduction of the number of multiplications very meaningful to our Convolutional MM.

5   Experimental Results

A comparison of our Convolutional MM with the Normal MM in terms of the savings of GFLOPS by the Strassen algorithm is shown in Fig. 4. We use the convolution kernel size 5×5 and the feature map size 55×55 in Layer 2 of Fig. 3, and sweep different square sizes for matrices W, X, Y in this experiment. We see that for the Normal MM, the Strassen algorithm may not bring benefits, but could lead to a >100% overhead, especially when the matrix size is small. In [4], even if the nested loops in Fig. 2 are unrolled and the computation is represented in a Normal MM to make the Strassen algorithm applicable, the Strassen algorithm still cannot bring too many benefits. But if the computation is represented in our Convolutional MM, much greater benefits can be achieved due to the redefined granularities of matrix elements and element-wise multiplications.

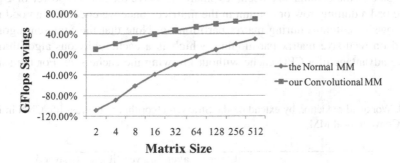

Fig. 4. Comparison of our Convolutional MM with the Normal MM in terms of the savings of GFLOPS by the Strassen algorithm

A sensitivity study on the convolution kernel size and the feature map size is provided in Fig. 5. Here we fix the matrix size to 256. As shown in Fig. 5(a), the convolution kernel size has a high impact on GFLOPS savings. This matches the analysis that the

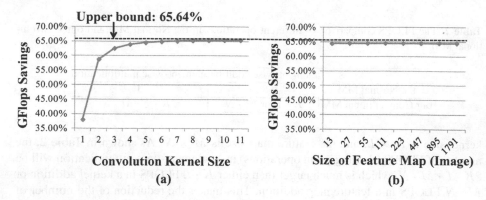

Fig. 5. A sensitivity study on convolution kernel size and feature map size

FLOPS difference between the element-wise multiplication and the element-wise addition of our Convolutional MM is proportional to the kernel size (assume the feature map size is much larger than the kernel size). Since the matrix size is limited to 256, there could be at most 8 recursions of the Strassen algorithm, which imposes an upper bound of $1 - (7/8)^8 = 65.64\%$ on the GFLOPS savings. Fig. 5(a) shows that we approach this upper bound as the convolution kernel size increases. The GFLOPS savings are invariant with the increase of the feature map size, as shown in Fig. 5(b), since the computational workloads of both the element-wise multiplication and addition will increase.

We reimplement the real-life CNN in Fig. 3 and apply the Strassen algorithm to reduce the computational workload. Experimental results are listed in Table 3. As shown in this table, no matrices are square, and no matrices have sizes equal to the power of 2. To deal with the non-square matrices, we stop matrix partitioning once either the row size or the column size becomes small. To solve the not-the-power-of-2 problem, we pad a dummy row or column in the matrices once we encounter an odd number of rows or columns during matrix partitioning. Note that the Strassen algorithm is based on recursive matrix partitioning, which is a cache-oblivious algorithm that can take advantage of a CPU cache without knowing the cache size. For the sake of

Table 3. Workload reduction by extending the Strassen algorithm to the real-life CNN in Fig. 3 via our Convolutional MM

		Layer 1	Layer 2	Layer 3	Layer 4	Layer 5
Matrix Parameters	Q	3	48	256	192	192
	R	96	128	384	192	128
	K, L	11	5	3	3	3
	M, N	224	55	27	13	13
Runtime	original	364s	865s	5710s	1282s	1326s
	our optimization	433s	864s	3863s	683s	998s
	savings	-18%	27%	32%	47%	24%

fairness, we also implement the baseline matrix multiplication in a cache-oblivious algorithm in Eq. (5). The hardware platform is a Xeon server with CPUs running at 2GHz. We limit the number of threads initialized by our Convolutional MM computation to 1 since we are measuring the reduction of total workloads by the runtime. Table 3 shows that we can get up to a 47% savings in certain convolution layers. Note that this gain is achieved without any change in image recognition results or the addition of any hardware accelerators.

6   Conclusion

In this work the computation in the convolution layers of a CNN is expressed in a new representation — Convolutional Matrix Multiplication (Convolutional MM). This representation helps identify the linear algebraic properties of the CNN computation, and enables extension of state-of-art algorithms that have been built for Normal Matrix Multiplication (Normal MM) to CNNs for computational workload reduction. This kind reduction does not change any image recognition results, and does not require any extra hardware accelerators. We use the Strassen algorithm as an example to show the necessary algorithmic extension from Normal MM to our Convolutional MM, and to show the extra benefits that can be gained by this Convolutional MM. Our methodology is verified on a real-life CNN. Experimental results show that we can reduce the computation by up to 47%. More well-studied algorithms on linear algebra can be further extended to our Convolutional MM to optimize the CNN computation.

Acknowledgements. This research is supported by the NSF Expedition in Computing Award CCF-0926127 and by C-FAR (one of six centers of STARnet, an SRC program sponsored by MARCO and DARPA).

References

1. ImageNet Contest (2012),
   http://www.image-net.org/challenges/LSVRC/2012/index
2. Behnke, S.: Hierarchical Neural Networks for Image Interpretation. LNCS, vol. 2766. Springer, Heidelberg (2003)
3. Chakradhar, S., Sankaradas, M., Jakkula, V., Cadambi, S.: A dynamically configurable co-processor for convolutional neural networks. In: International Symposium on Computer Architecture, p. 247 (2010)
4. Chellapilla, K., Puri, S., Simard, P.: High Performance Convolutional Neural Networks for Document Processing. In: International Workshop on Frontiers in Handwriting Recognition (2006)
5. Farabet, C., Poulet, C., Han, J.Y., LeCun, Y.: CNP: An FPGA-based processor for Convolutional Networks. In: International Conference on Field Programmable Logic and Applications, vol. 1, pp. 32–37 (August 2009)
6. Krizhevsky, A., Sutskever, I., Hinton, G.E.: ImageNet Classification with Deep Convolutional Neural Networks. In: Proceedings of Neural Information and Processing Systems, pp. 1–9 (2012)

7. Lecun, Y., Bottou, L., Bengio, Y., Haffner, P.: Gradient-based learning applied to document recognition. Proceedings of the IEEE 86, 2278–2324 (1998)
8. Osadchy, M., Yann, L.C., Matthew, L.M.: Synergistic Face Detection and Pose Estimation with Energy-Based Models. Journal of Machine Learning Research 8, 1197–1215 (2007)
9. Peemen, M., Setio, A.A.A., Mesman, B., Corporaal, H.: Memory-centric accelerator design for Convolutional Neural Networks. In: International Conference on Computer Design, pp. 13–19 (October 2013)
10. Simard, P., Steinkraus, D., Platt, J.: Best practices for convolutional neural networks applied to visual document analysis. In: International Conference on Document Analysis and Recognition (ICDAR), vol. 1, pp. 958–963 (2003)
11. Strassen, V.: Gaussian elimination is not optimal. Numerische Mathematik 13(4), 354–356 (1969)

One-Shot Learning with Feedback
for Multi-layered Convolutional Network

Kunihiko Fukushima

Fuzzy Logic Systems Institute,
680-41 Kawazu, Iizuka, Fukuoka 820-0067, Japan
fukushima@m.ieice.org
http://www4.ocn.ne.jp/~fuku_k/index-e.html

Abstract. This paper proposes an improved add-if-silent rule, which is
suited for training intermediate layers of a multi-layered convolutional
network, such as a neocognitron. By the add-if-silent rule, a new cell is
generated if all postsynaptic cells are silent. The generated cell learns the
activity of the presynaptic cells in one-shot, and its input connections will
never be modified afterward. To use this learning rule for a convolutional
network, it is required to decide at which retinotopic location this rule is
to be applied. In the conventional add-if-silent rule, we chose the location
where the activity of presynaptic cells is the largest. In the proposed new
learning rule, a negative feedback is introduced from postsynaptic cells
to presynaptic cells, and a new cell is generated at the location where
the presynaptic activity fails to be suppressed by the feedback. We apply
this learning rule to a neocognitron for hand-written digit recognition,
and demonstrate the decrease in the recognition error.

Keywords: add-if-silent, one-shot learning, negative feedback, neocognitron, convolutional network, pattern recognition.

1 Introduction

Multi-layered neural networks show a large power for robust recognition of visual
patterns. Training intermediate stages of a multi-layered network, however, is a
difficult problem, because it is not easy to know intuitively the desired response
of cells of intermediate layers. Various methods have been proposed for training
intermediate layers of a multi-layered network. Among them, deep learning has
become popular recently [1].

Add-if-silent is another promising learning rule, by which a new cell is generated if all postsynaptic cells are silent in spite of non-silent presynaptic cells [2].
The generated cell learns the activity of the presynaptic cells in one-shot, by
adjusting its input connections to be proportional to the activity of the presynaptic cells. Once a cell is generated, its input connections will never be modified
afterward. Hence the training process is very simple, and does not require time-
consuming calculation such as the gradient descent process.

This paper proposes an improved add-if-silent rule, and uses it for training
intermediate layers of the neocognitron. The neocognitron is a multi-layered

S. Wermter et al. (Eds.): ICANN 2014, LNCS 8681, pp. 291–298, 2014.

convolutional neural network for visual pattern recognition [3,4]. To use the add-if-silent rule for a convolutional network, it is required to decide at which retinotopic location in a layer this rule is to be applied. In the conventional add-if-silent rule, we chose the location where the activity of presynaptic cells is the largest in the layer. To determine the location, in the proposed new learning rule, the activity of the presynaptic cells is suppressed by negative feedback signals from postsynaptic cells. The strength of the negative feedback signals from a postsynaptic cell are proportional to the input connections to the cell. A new cell is generated at the retinotopic location where the presynaptic activity fails to be suppressed by the feedback.

We apply this learning rule to a neocognitron for hand-written digit recognition, and demonstrate the decrease in the recognition error rate.

2   Neocognitron

2.1   Network Architecture

The neocognitron [3] consists of layers of S-cells, which resemble simple cells in the visual cortex, and layers of C-cells, which resemble complex cells. As shown in Fig. 1, these layers of S-cells and C-cells are arranged alternately in a hierarchical manner. In the figure, U_{Sl}, for example, indicates the layer of S-cells of the lth stage. Although the number of stages can be much larger, we choose here a three-staged network to simplify discussions and computer simulation.

Each layer of the network is divided into a number of sub-layers, called *cell-planes*, depending on the feature to which cells respond preferentially. A cell-plane is a group of cells that are arranged retinotopically and share the same set of input connections. All cells in a cell-plane have receptive fields of an identical characteristic, but the locations of the receptive fields differ from cell to cell.

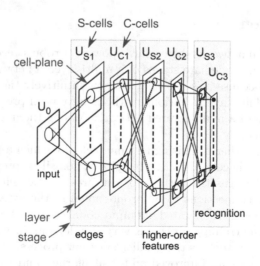

Fig. 1. The architecture of the neocognitron

The stimulus pattern is presented to the input layer, U_0. An S-cell of U_{S1} responds selectively to an edge of a particular orientation. The contours of the input image are decomposed into edges of every orientation in U_{S1}.

The input connections to S-cells, except in layer U_{S1}, are variable and are modified through learning. After having finished learning, S-cells come to work as feature-extracting cells. In a higher stage, they extract more global features.

In each stage of the network, the output of layer U_{Sl} is fed to layer U_{Cl}. Except the highest stage, U_{Cl} has the same number of cell-planes as U_{Sl} does, and there is a one-to-one correspondence between cell-planes of the two layers. Each C-cell has fixed excitatory connections from a group of S-cells of the corresponding cell-plane. Through these connections, each C-cell averages (by L2-pooling) the responses of S-cells whose receptive field locations are slightly deviated.

2.2 S-cell

As illustrated by Fig. 2(a), each S-cell of layer U_{Sl} ($l \geq 2$) receives excitatory signals directly from a group of C-cells, which are cells of the preceding layer U_{Cl-1}. It also receives an inhibitory signal, which works in a subtractive manner, through a V-cell, which accompanies the S-cell. The V-cell receives fixed excitatory connections from the same group of C-cells as does the S-cell.

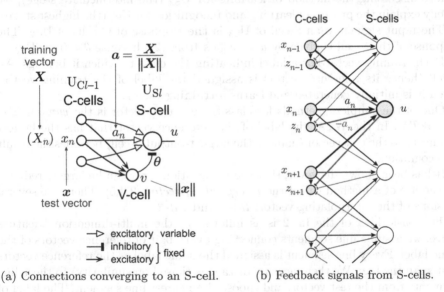

(a) Connections converging to an S-cell.   (b) Feedback signals from S-cells.

Fig. 2. Connections feed-forward to and feedback from an S-cell

Let a_n be the strength of the excitatory connection to an S-cell from the nth C-cell, whose output is x_n. Let θ be the strength of the inhibitory connection from the V-cell ($0 \leq \theta < 1$). The output u of the S-cell is given by

$$u = \frac{1}{1-\theta} \cdot \varphi \left[\sum_n a_n x_n - \theta v \right] \tag{1}$$

where $\varphi[\ ]$ is a rectified linear function defined by $\varphi[x] = \max(x, 0)$.

We now use vector notation $\boldsymbol{x} = (x_1, \cdots, x_n, \cdots)$ to represent the input signal to the S-cell, namely, the response of presynaptic C-cells. We sometimes call $\boldsymbol{x}$ the test vector. Connection $\boldsymbol{a}$ is given by $\boldsymbol{a} = \boldsymbol{X}/\|\boldsymbol{X}\|$, where $\boldsymbol{X} = (X_1, \cdots, X_n, \cdots)$ is the training vector (or a linear combination of training vectors) that the S-cell has learned. The response of the V-cell is equal to the norm of vector $\boldsymbol{x}$. Namely, $v = \|\boldsymbol{x}\|$. Then, (1) reduces to

$$u = \|\boldsymbol{x}\| \cdot \frac{\varphi[s - \theta]}{1 - \theta} \qquad \text{where} \qquad s = \frac{(\boldsymbol{X}, \boldsymbol{x})}{\|\boldsymbol{X}\| \cdot \|\boldsymbol{x}\|} \qquad (2)$$

In the multi-dimensional feature space, s shows a kind of similarity between $\boldsymbol{X}$ and $\boldsymbol{x}$, which is defined by the normalized inner product of $\boldsymbol{X}$ and $\boldsymbol{x}$. If similarity s is larger than θ, the S-cell yields a non-zero response [4]. Thus θ determines the threshold of the S-cell. We call $\boldsymbol{X}$ the reference vector of the S-cell. It represents the preferred (optimal) feature of the S-cell.

2.3   Interpolating-Vector for the Highest Stage

Before discussing the method of learning for U_{S2} (the intermediate stage), we briefly explain the process of learning and recognition for U_{S3} (the highest stage).

The input signals to an S-cell of U_{S3} is the response of C-cells of U_{C2}. The response of the S-cell is given by $u = \|\boldsymbol{x}\| \cdot s$ from (2), because $\theta = 0$ for U_{S3}.

Each training vector has a label indicating the class to which it belongs. An S-cell (hence its reference vector) is assigned the label of the training vector, when it is initially generated and learns a training vector.

One of the simplest methods for classifying a test vector is the *winner-take-all (WTA)*. In the WTA, the label of the reference vector that has the largest similarity to the test vector (namely, the largest-output S-cell) becomes the result of recognition.

It has been shown, however, that the recognition error can be largely reduced by the use of a method called the *interpolating-vector* [2,4,5]. There are several versions of the interpolating-vector: *Int-2* and *Int-3*.

The basic idea of the Int-2 is as follows. In the multi-dimensional feature space, we assume line segments connecting every pair of reference vectors of the same label. Every line segment is assigned the same label as the reference vectors that span the line. We then measure distances (based on similarity) to these line segments from the test vector, and choose the nearest line segment. The label of the nearest line segment shows the result of pattern recognition.

In the Int-3, we assume plane segments spanned by every trio of reference vectors of the same label. Although we use plane segments instead of line segments, the rest of the process is the same as for the Int-2.

The interpolating-vector is used also for the learning. Every time a training vector $\boldsymbol{x}$ is presented during learning, we try to classify it using the Int-2 or Int-3. If the result of classification is wrong, or if the similarity to the nearest line or plane segment is smaller than a certain threshold θ_3, a new S-cell (namely, a new reference vector) is generated. The training vector x is adopted as the reference vector of the generated S-cell, which is assigned the label of the class name. If the result of classification is correct, the two (Int-2) or three (Int-3) reference vectors, that span the nearest line or plane segment, learn the training vector by adjusting their values toward the training vector.

3 Add-if-Silent with Feedback

3.1 Conventional Add-if-Silent Rule

Here we first explain the conventional add-if-silent rule, which is used for training S-cells of the intermediate layer, U_{S2} [4,2]. During learning, training patterns from a training set are presented one by one to the input layer U_0, and the response of layer U_{C1} works as a training stimulus for U_{S2}.

If all postsynaptic S-cells are silent for a training stimulus, a new S-cell is generated and added to the layer. The strength of the input connections of the generated S-cell is determined to be proportional to the response of the presynaptic C-cells. The learning is done in one-shot: once an S-cell is generated and added to the network, the input connections to the S-cell do not change any more. This means that the learning by the add-if-silent is a process of choosing reference vectors from the large set of training vectors.

Since the minimum distance between reference vectors is determined by the threshold of S-cells, reference vectors of generated S-cells come to distribute uniformly in the multi-dimensional feature space after presentation of a high enough number of training vectors.

If the threshold of S-cells during recognition is kept to the same value as in the learning, however, S-cells behave like grandmother cells. Namely, each test vector elicits a response from only one (or a small number of) S-cell. This is not desirable for robust recognition of deformed patterns. To make these S-cells respond in such a way that the input pattern be represented by a population coding, we use *dual threshold* for S-cells [2]. During the recognition phase, after having finished the learning, the threshold of S-cells is set to a lower value than the threshold for the learning.

The reason why a good recognition rate can be obtained with a simple algorithm of the add-if-silent can be explained as follows. The final classification of input patterns is not made by an intermediate layer, but by the highest stage of the network. The role of the intermediate layer is to represent an input pattern accurately, not by the response of a single cell, but by the population coding. In the case of population coding, best-fitting of individual cells to training stimuli is not necessarily important. It is enough if the input stimulus can be accurately represented by the response of the population of the whole cells.

To apply the add-if-silent rule to a neocognitron, a slight modification is required because the neocognitron is a multi-layered convolutional network. Each layer of the neocognitron consists of a number of cell-planes. In a cell-plane, all cells are arranged retinotopically, and share the same set of input connections. This condition of shared connections has to be kept even during learning.

In the neocognitron, generation of a new S-cell means a generation of a new cell-plane. To keep the condition of shared connections, all S-cells in the generated cell-plane are organized so as to have the same input connections as the added S-cell.

Suppose a training pattern is presented to the input layer U_0. Here, the response of the C-cells of U_{C1} works as the training stimulus for U_{S2}. If all S-cells of U_{S2}, whose receptive fields are located in a certain small area, are silent in spite of non-zero training stimulus, a new S-cell is generated and is added to the network. The newly added S-cell learns this training stimulus. If there are a number of retinotopic locations where presynaptic C-cells are not silent, we choose the locations sequentially from the place where the activity of presynaptic C-cells is the largest.

After the generation of the new cell-plane, if there still remains any area in which all postsynaptic S-cells are silent in spite of non-zero training stimulus, the same process of generating a cell-plane is repeated until the whole area is covered by non-silent S-cells. After that, we proceed to the presentation of the next training pattern.

3.2   Add-if-Silent with Feedback

As explained above, to use the add-if-silent rule for the neocognitron, it is required to decide the retinotopic location at which the rule is to be applied. In the conventional add-if-silent rule, we choose the location where the activity of presynaptic C-cells is the largest in U_{C1}.

We propose a new method for choosing the location. In the proposed learning rule, the activity of the presynaptic cells is suppressed by negative feedback signals from postsynaptic cells. The negative feedback signals from a postsynaptic cell are proportional to the product of the strength of the input connections and the response of the postsynaptic cell. A new cell is generated at the retinotopic location where the suppressed activity of the presynaptic cells, instead of the unsuppressed activity, is the largest.

Fig. 2(b) illustrates this situation. Let the feedback signal from the postsynaptic S-cell to the nth presynaptic C-cell be $y_n = a_n u$. Then, from (2)

$$y = a\,u = \frac{X}{\|X\|} \cdot u = \frac{X}{\|X\|} \cdot \|x\| \cdot \frac{\varphi[s - \theta]}{1 - \theta} \tag{3}$$

The suppressed activity of the nth presynaptic cell is given by $z_n = \varphi[x_n - y_n]$. If $x = X$, we have $s = 1$ and then $y = X$. This means that, if the feature of the stimulus vector x is correctly extracted by the postsynaptic S-cell, we have $z_n = 0$. On the other hand, if a feature fails to be extracted correctly by the S-cell, z_n takes a large value.

Actually, there are a number of postsynaptic S-cells, and feedback signals come, not only from a single S-cell, but from all postsynaptic S-cells. If z_n is large, it means that the stimulus feature centered at location n has not been extracted correctly by any of the S-cells yet.

We then choose the retinotopic locations sequentially from the place at which $\sum z_n$ is the largest, where the sum is taken for all cells that have the same retinotopic location, and generate a new S-cell to extract the feature located there. Incidentally, in the conventional add-if-silent rule, $\sum x_n$ is used instead of $\sum z_n$. It should be noted here that z is used only for determining the retinotopic location where the add-if-silent rule is to be applied, and that the reference vector of the generated S-cell is set to be proportional, not to z, but to x.

4   Computer Simulation

To demonstrate the abilities of the new add-if-silent rule with feedback, we apply it to layer U_{S2} (the intermediate stage of the neocognitron). With computer simulation, we test how the recognition error is improved by the new rule.

The performance of the network is affected, not only by the method of learning for U_{S2}, but also by the method of learning and recognition for U_{S3} (the highest stage). We then compare the performance of the new and the conventional rule for U_{S2}, under various conditions of learning and recognition for U_{S3}.

For the simulation, we mainly use handwritten digits (free writing) randomly sampled from the ETL1 database [6]. Incidentally, the ETL1 is a large database of segmented handwritten digits written by about 1,400 different writers (namely, about 14,000 digits).

In Fig. 3, three curves with thick lines show the case of add-if-silent with feedback, and three curves with thin lines show the case of add-if-silent without feedback (namely, conventional add-if-silent). Among them, blue solid lines show the result where the Int-3 is used for U_{S3}. Similarly, red dashed lines show the result with Int-2, and the brown dotted lines show the result with WTA.

Under each condition, we repeated the simulation seven times and averaged the result. In each run of the simulation, we used a training set of 3,000 patterns (300 patterns for each digit) and a test set of 5,000 unlearned patterns randomly sampled from the ETL1 database. The average of seven runs is plotted, and the error bar, which is drawn only for the thick lines, shows the standard deviation.

Each of the six curves of Fig. 3 shows how the recognition error and the number of generated reference vectors K_{S3} change under different values of θ_3, which is the threshold used for the learning with the interpolating-vector. A higher value of θ_3 usually reduces the recognition error but increases K_{S3}. In each curve, the error rate is plotted as the ordinate against K_{S3} as the abscissa. Since the computational cost for learning and recognition increases with the increase of K_{S3}, we can say that the performance of the network is better if we can have a smaller recognition error with a smaller K_{S3}.

Comparing curves of thick lines (add-if-silent with feedback) with those of thin lines (add-if-silent without feedback), we can conclude that the feedback in the learning by the add-if-silent for the intermediate stage almost always improves the performance of the network, regardless of the method of learning and recognition used for the highest stage (especially when K_{S3} is small).

We also tested the performance of the neocognitron for recognizing handwritten digits of the MNIST database [7]. We used the training set of full 60,000

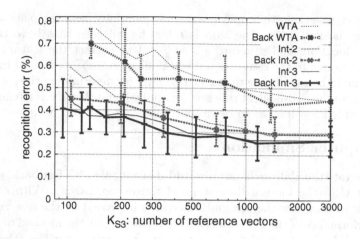

Fig. 3. Comparison between the conventional add-if-silent (thin lines) and the add-if-silent with feedback (thick lines) for layer U_{S2} in the intermediate stage. Each curve shows the recognition error vs. the number of generated reference vectors K_{S3}, under different θ_3 for the highest stage U_{S3}. Back: add-if-silent with feedback for U_{S2}.

images, and the test set of 10,000 images to measure the recognition error. When we used the add-if-silent with feedback, the recognition error was 0.73% by the Int-3. When we used the conventional add-if-silent rule (without feedback), the recognition error was 0.80% by the Int-3.

References

1. Hinton, G.E., Osindero, S., Teh, Y.: A Fast Learning Algorithm for Deep Belief Nets. Neural Computation 18, 1527–1554 (2006)
2. Fukushima, K.: Training Multi-layered Neural Network Neocognitron. Neural Networks 40, 18–31 (2013)
3. Fukushima, K.: Neocognitron: A Self-organizing Neural Network Model for a Mechanism of Pattern Recognition Unaffected by Shift in Position. Biol. Cybernetics 36(4), 193–202 (1980)
4. Fukushima, K.: Artificial Vision by Multi-layered Neural Networks: Neocognitron and its Advances. Neural Networks 37, 103–119 (2013)
5. Fukushima, K.: Interpolating Vectors for Robust Pattern Recognition. Neural Networks 20(8), 904–916 (2007)
6. ETL1 database, http://projects.itri.aist.go.jp/etlcdb/
7. MNIST database, http://yann.lecun.com/exdb/mnist/

Row-Action Projections
for Nonnegative Matrix Factorization

Rafał Zdunek

Department of Electronics, Wroclaw University of Technology,
Wybrzeze Wyspianskiego 27, 50-370 Wroclaw, Poland

Abstract. Nonnegative Matrix Factorization (NMF) is more and more
frequently used for analyzing large-scale nonnegative data, where the
number of samples and/or the number of observed variables is large. In
the paper, we discuss two applications of the row-action projections in
the context of learning latent factors from large-scale data. First, we show
that they can be efficiently used for improving the on-line learning in dynamic NMF. Next, they can also considerably reduce the computational
complexity of the optimization algorithms used for factor learning from
strongly redundant data. The experiments demonstrate high efficiency
of the proposed methods.

Keywords: NMF, Kaczmarz method, On-line NMF, Row-action projections, Feature extraction.

1 Introduction

Recent advances in the development of information technologies have led to a
considerably increase in the amount of high-dimensional massive data that needs
to be analyzed and interpreted. Nonnegative Matrix Factorization (NMF) [1,2] is
a commonly-used static tool for dimensionality reduction of nonnegative small-
scale and medium-scale data. Processing of large-scale data or dynamic data
with NMF is still a challenging and open problem. To tackle this problem, several
computational strategies have been recently proposed in the literature.

When the data is large, i.e. both in the number of samples and observed
variables, and the aim is to extract a few feature vectors from the dataset,
the alternating minimization problems in NMF are highly over-determined. To
decrease the computational complexity, the optimization tasks can be partitioned
into some blocks, and then the computations can be arranged in parallel or
distributed modes [3–6]. The heavy computations can be also performed in the
cloud computing [7] using the MapReduce framework. Efficient algorithms for
factorizing large-scale multi-linear data in parallel can be found, e.g. in [8].

Another computational strategy assumes an approximate factorization, which
is a typical case in practice. Highly over-determined problems usually come from
huge redundancy. To alleviate the computational complexity of such problems,
the solution can be updated using only partial but most relevant information
extracted from an entire dataset. When the data is represented by a matrix, the

S. Wermter et al. (Eds.): ICANN 2014, LNCS 8681, pp. 299–306, 2014.

feature vectors in NMF can be updated using only the selected columns from the observation matrix but the encoding vectors with some subset of the rows. This concept was proposed in [2], and referred to as the Large-Scale NMF (LS-NMF). In this paper, we extend the LS-NMF by using a different computational strategy for updating the factors. Using the row-action projection technique, we can update the factors using a smaller subset of data than in the LS-NMF. Moreover, the sequential projections have a better numerical behavior for ill-conditioned least-squares problems than the batch projections.

When the number of samples is large whereas the other dimensions are relatively small, a good choice seems to be Online NMF (ONMF). This technique was proposed by Cao et al. [9] in the context of temporal data analysis and tracking latent factors from time-varying data streams. Another version of ONMF was proposed in [10] for document clustering. ONMF is also a key tool for analyzing long records of audio signals, especially for blind separation of real-time sources. An interesting property of ONMF is not only a considerable reduction in computational complexity both in time and memory but also a possibility of updating the feature vectors over the time. Applying NMF to magnitude spectrograms of audio signals, the feature vectors represent frequency profiles, common for the whole observed signals. ONMF gives us a possibility to extract time-varying frequency profiles that are most suitable for analyzing non-stationary stochastic signals. In this context, Lefevre et al. [11] proposed ONMF that minimizes the Itakura-Saito distance. ONMF can be also resolved with the geometry-based algorithms [12] or stochastic approximation algorithms [13].

In this paper, we also extend ONMF by using the row-action projection-based algorithms that are very fast and are known to be efficient in other applications. A good representative of the row-action technique is the Kaczmarz algorithm [14] that was proposed for solving an over-determined system of linear equations. Due to its row-action projections, it has already found numerous real-world applications, especially in tomographic image reconstruction [15, 16].

In the Kaczmarz algorithm, a whole unknown vector of a solution can be updated at one iterative step, using only one equation, i.e. one row of a system matrix. This property can be efficiently used for updating a whole set of feature vectors using only one sample at a given time instant. This rule motivates the usage of this algorithm both for ONMF and LS-NMF.

The paper is organized as follows: The row-action projections are discussed in Section 2. The application of the row-action projections to large-scale and on-line NMF is presented Section 3. The numerical experiments are described in Section 4. Finally, the conclusions are drawn in Section 5.

2   Row-Action Projections

Let us consider the Linear Least-Squares (LLS) problem: $\min_{\mathbf{x}} \|\boldsymbol{y}_t - \boldsymbol{A}\boldsymbol{x}_t\|_2^2$, where $\boldsymbol{A} = [a_{ij}] \in \mathbb{R}^{I \times J}$, $\boldsymbol{y}_t = [y_{it}] \in \mathbb{R}^I$, $\boldsymbol{x}_t = [x_{jt}] \in \mathbb{R}^J$ and $I \geq J$. Let $\underline{\boldsymbol{a}}_i \in \mathbb{R}^{1 \times J}$ denote the i-th row of the matrix $\boldsymbol{A}$. In a geometrical approach, $\underline{\boldsymbol{a}}_i$ determines a hyperplane in $\mathbb{R}^J$. Assuming $\underline{\boldsymbol{a}}_i \neq \boldsymbol{0}$, an orthogonal projection of any point $\boldsymbol{x}_t \in \mathbb{R}^J$ onto that hyperplane can be expressed by the linear mapping $P^{(i)} : \mathbb{R}^J \to \mathbb{R}^J$:

$$P^{(i)}(\boldsymbol{x}_t) = \boldsymbol{x}_t + \frac{y_{it} - \boldsymbol{a}_i \boldsymbol{x}_t}{\|\boldsymbol{a}_i\|_2^2} \boldsymbol{a}_i^T . \tag{1}$$

Let $P(\boldsymbol{x}_t) = P^{(I)} \circ \ldots \circ P^{(1)} \in \mathbb{R}^J$ be a composed mapping, and $\boldsymbol{x}_t^{(0)} \in \mathbb{R}^J$ be an initial guess. The Kaczmarz method [14] iteratively generates the sequence $\{\boldsymbol{x}_t^{(k)}\}$ for $k = 1, 2, \ldots$, by the following updating rule:

$$\boldsymbol{x}_t^{(k+1)} = P(\boldsymbol{x}_t^{(k)}). \tag{2}$$

Tanabe [17] proved that the sequence $\{\boldsymbol{x}_t^{(k)}\}$ converges and

$$\lim_{k \to \infty} \boldsymbol{x}_t^{(k)} = P_{N(A)}(\boldsymbol{x}_t^{(0)}) + \boldsymbol{x}_{LS}, \tag{3}$$

where $P_{N(A)}(\boldsymbol{x})$ is the projection of the point $\boldsymbol{x}$ onto the nullspace of $\boldsymbol{A}$, and $\boldsymbol{x}_{LS}$ is the minimal-norm least-squares solution. If the LSS problem is consistent, i.e. $\boldsymbol{y}_t \in R(\boldsymbol{A})$ (column space of $\boldsymbol{A}$), then the limit in (3) is its solution.

The composition $P(\boldsymbol{x}_t)$ can take different forms. It may be ordered in any random way. However, if the successive hyperplanes are selected to be as orthogonal as possible, the convergence is the fastest. Since this method updates a solution using only one hyperplane that corresponds to one row of the matrix $\boldsymbol{A}$ in each iterative step, it is called the row-action projection method. After sweeping all the rows, one full cycle is completed.

The original Kaczmarz method estimates an unconstrained solution vector given only one data vector. In the basic version of NMF, the aim is to simultaneously estimate a group of vectors, subject to nonnegativity constraints. To enforce a nonnegative solution, the following additional projection of $P^{(i)}(\boldsymbol{x}_t)$ onto the nonnegative orthant $\mathbb{R}_+^J$ can be imposed to (1): $P_+^{(i)}(\boldsymbol{x}_t) = \left[P^{(i)}(\boldsymbol{x}_t)\right]_+$, where $[\xi]_+ = \max\{0, \xi\}$. Thus $P_+(\boldsymbol{x}_t) = P_+^{(I)} \circ \ldots \circ P_+^{(1)} \in \mathbb{R}_+^J$, which is not equivalent to the projection $[P(\boldsymbol{x}_t)]_+$. The constrained Kaczmarz algorithm has been successfully applied to tomographic image reconstruction from limited-data [18]. Due to the series of constrained projections, it somehow resembles the Hierarchical Alternating Least-Squares (HALS) algorithm [2] that is commonly-used for solving NMF problems.

The estimation of several samples of a solution can be done in a sequential way or by vectorization. However, such approaches are usually computationally very expensive. To alleviate this problem, we propose an extended constrained Kaczmarz method for processing all multiple right-hand vectors simultaneously. Let $\boldsymbol{Y} = [\boldsymbol{y}_1, \ldots, \boldsymbol{y}_T] \in \mathbb{R}^{I \times T}$ and $\boldsymbol{X} = [\boldsymbol{x}_1, \ldots, \boldsymbol{x}_T] \in \mathbb{R}^{J \times T}$. The extended constrained Kaczmarz method for the system $\boldsymbol{AX} = \boldsymbol{Y}$ can be expressed by the following rule:

$$\boldsymbol{X}^{(k+1)} = \left[\boldsymbol{X}^{(k)} + \boldsymbol{a}_{i_k}^T \frac{\boldsymbol{y}_{i_k} - \boldsymbol{a}_{i_k} \boldsymbol{X}^{(k)}}{\|\boldsymbol{a}_{i_k}\|_2^2}\right]_+, \tag{4}$$

where $i_k \in \{1, \ldots, I\}$ is the index of the row selected in the k-th iterative step. Note that the computational cost of one iterative step in (4) is only $O(JT)$. Obviously, for one full cycle it amounts to be $O(IJT)$.

3   Nonnegative Matrix Factorization

The aim of NMF is to find such lower-rank nonnegative matrices $A = [a_{ij}] \in \mathbb{R}_+^{I \times J}$ and $X = [x_{jt}] \in \mathbb{R}_+^{J \times T}$ that $Y = [y_{it}] \cong AX \in \mathbb{R}_+^{I \times T}$, given the data matrix Y, the lower rank J, and possibly some prior knowledge on the matrices A or X. Usually: $J << \min\{I, T\}$.

3.1   Large-Scale NMF

To estimate the factors A and X, we assume the squared Euclidean distance $\Psi(A, X) = \frac{1}{2}\|Y - AX\|_F^2$ is minimized with the following alternating minimization strategy: **For** $s = 1, 2, \ldots,$ **do:**

$$X^{(s)} = \arg\min_{X \geq 0} \Psi(A^{(s-1)}, X), \tag{5}$$

$$A^{(s)} = \arg\min_{A \geq 0} \Psi(A, X^{(s)}). \tag{6}$$

To solve the problem (5), we need to find the solution to the system: $AX = Y$, which is highly over-determined if the number I is large. A similar case occurs for the problem (6), if T is large. The computational complexity for calculating the matrix $A^T Y$ is $O(IJT)$ but this might be too much if T and I are very large.

Applying the iterative formula (4) to the problem (5), the computational complexity is only $O(KJT)$, provided that K rows are selected in each cycle. Let $J \leq K << I$, $I^{(K)} = \{i_1, i_2, \ldots, i_K\}$ be a subset of K entries from the set $\{1, 2, \ldots, I\}$, and $A_{I^{(K)}} = [a_{I^{(K)}, *}] \in \mathbb{R}^{|I^{(K)}| \times J}$ be a submatrix created from A by selecting the rows with the indices $I^{(K)}$. If $\text{rank}(A_{I^{(K)}}) = J$, the minimal-norm least-squares solution to (5) is unique according to (3), since $N(A_{I^{(K)}}) = \emptyset$.

A choice of the set $I^{(K)}$ may have a significant impact on the convergence rate. If the rows of A are selected in such a way that $A_{I^{(K)}}^T A_{I^{(K)}} = I_J$, the exact solution is obtained after one full cycle. However, this condition rarely takes place in practice. Moreover, the selection of K rows from I that are nearly orthogonal is time-consuming, especially as I is large. In the experiments, we assumed some heuristics, i.e. the set $I^{(K)}$ in each cycle is one K-elementary combination from the set $\{1, 2, \ldots, I\}$. In each cycle, a new random sample $I^{(K)}$ is drawn.

To estimate the matrix A from (6), the system $X^T A^T = Y^T$ is solved. We assume $J \leq K << T$, and the set $T^{(K)}$ is selected from $\{1, 2, \ldots, T\}$. Obviously, in each iterative cycle the condition $\text{rank}(X_{T^{(K)}}) = J$ should be satisfied. The selection of the indices $T^{(K)}$ is accomplished in a similar way.

3.2 On-line NMF

In ONMF we assume that at a given time instant we observe the sample $\boldsymbol{y}_t \in \mathbb{R}_+^I$ that represents I signals or realizations of I random variables. The samples $\{\boldsymbol{y}_t\}$ are gathered sequentially. The total number of recorded samples can be very large or even unlimited – we observe a slowly-time varying process. Let $\bar{\boldsymbol{Y}} = [\bar{\boldsymbol{y}}_1, \bar{\boldsymbol{y}}_2, \ldots, \bar{\boldsymbol{y}}_{t-1}] \in \mathbb{R}_+^{I \times (t-1)}$ contains a collection of the samples observed in the past. Let $\tilde{\boldsymbol{Y}} = [\bar{\boldsymbol{y}}_1, \ldots, \bar{\boldsymbol{y}}_{t-1}, \boldsymbol{y}_t] = [\bar{\boldsymbol{Y}}, \boldsymbol{y}_t]$. Under the assumption that the observed history is not very long, i.e. the number $(t-1)$ is rather small but $\min\{t-1, I\} >> J$, the matrix $\bar{\boldsymbol{Y}}$ can be readily factorized. Thus $\bar{\boldsymbol{Y}} = \boldsymbol{A}\bar{\boldsymbol{X}}$, where $\boldsymbol{A} \in \mathbb{R}_+^{I \times J}$ and $\bar{\boldsymbol{X}} \in \mathbb{R}_+^{J \times (t-1)}$. Given the sample $\boldsymbol{y}_t$, the encoding vector $\boldsymbol{x}_t$ can be obtained by solving the nonnegativity constrained least-squares problem:

$$\boldsymbol{x}_t = \arg\min_{\mathbf{x}} \frac{1}{2} \|\boldsymbol{y}_t - \boldsymbol{A}\boldsymbol{x}\|_2^2, \quad \text{s.t.} \quad \boldsymbol{x} \geq \mathbf{0}. \tag{7}$$

To accomplish this task, any constrained optimization method can be used but possibly with the lowest computational cost. Then: $\bar{\boldsymbol{X}} = [\bar{\boldsymbol{x}}_1, \ldots, \bar{\boldsymbol{x}}_{t-1}, \boldsymbol{x}_t] = [\bar{\boldsymbol{X}}, \boldsymbol{x}_t]$. The matrix $\boldsymbol{A}$ can be updated by solving the transposed system of linear equations:

$$\begin{bmatrix} \bar{\boldsymbol{X}}^T \\ \boldsymbol{x}_t^T \end{bmatrix} \boldsymbol{A}^T = \begin{bmatrix} \bar{\boldsymbol{Y}}^T \\ \boldsymbol{y}_t^T \end{bmatrix}. \tag{8}$$

Since the matrix $\boldsymbol{A}$ is sufficiently well estimated from the factorization of the matrix $\bar{\boldsymbol{Y}}$, it needs to be only slightly updated by the current sample, i.e. by the last row of the system in (8). This can be easily done using the Kaczmarz method. Thus:

$$\boldsymbol{A} \leftarrow \left[\boldsymbol{A} + \frac{\boldsymbol{y}_t - \boldsymbol{A}\boldsymbol{x}_t}{\|\boldsymbol{x}_t\|_2^2} \boldsymbol{x}_t^T \right]_+. \tag{9}$$

The computational complexity for the rule (9) is only $O(IJ)$. Given the sample $\boldsymbol{y}_{t+1}$, the updating process is repeated. According the rule (9) the matrix $\boldsymbol{A}$ is changing over the time.

4 Experiments

The experiments are carried out for the blind source separation problems. The entries of the original factors $\boldsymbol{A}$ and $\boldsymbol{X}$ are generated as follows: $\forall i, j : a_{ij} \sim \mathcal{U}(0,1)$ and $\forall j, t : x_{jt} \sim \max\{0, \check{x}_{jt}\}$, where $\check{x}_{jt} \sim \mathcal{N}(0,1)$. Thus, the matrix $\boldsymbol{A}$ is fully dense and the matrix $\boldsymbol{X}$ is sparse in 50 %.

The proposed algorithms are compared with respect to their performance and runtime with the following static NMF algorithms: the standard Lee-Seung algorithm [1] (denoted by the MUE acronym) for minimizing the Euclidean distance, HALS [2], and RASLS [19]. In LS-NMF, we set K to be equal to 10 % of the total number of rows/columns in a given problem. All the tested algorithms were initialized by the same random initializer generated from an uniform distribution. The iterative updates were terminated when $\frac{|r_{k-1}-r_k|}{r_0} <$ 10^{-5}, where $r_k = \frac{\|\boldsymbol{Y} - \boldsymbol{A}^{(k)}\boldsymbol{X}^{(k)}\|_F}{\|\boldsymbol{Y}\|_F}$ is the normalized residual error in the k-th alternating step. The performance of the NMF algorithms was evaluated with the Signal-to-Interference Ratio (SIR) [2, pp. 284–287] between the estimated signals and the true ones.

For testing the LS-NMF, which is presented in Section 3.1, we generated the synthetic dataset, assuming $I = T = 10^4$ and $J = 10$. Using the MUE, HALS and LS-NMF, we obtained the following SIRs : 21.3, 48.81 and 32.29 [dB] for estimating the matrix $\boldsymbol{A}$, and 23.43, 73.11 and 35.65 [dB] for the matrix $\boldsymbol{X}$, respectively. The runtime amounts to 870, 875.3 and 643.9 seconds.

The ONMF was tested using the following datasets: (A) $T = 10^3$, $I = 100$, $J = 10$; (B) $T = 10^5$, $I = 100$, $J = 10$; (C) $T = 10^6$, $I = 50$, $J = 10$. For the cases (B) and (C), the matrix $\bar{\boldsymbol{Y}}$ is created from the first 1 % of all the column vectors in $\boldsymbol{Y}$. The initial matrices $\boldsymbol{A}$ and $\bar{\boldsymbol{X}}$ were estimated using the HALS algorithm. The problem (7) is solved with the well-known Non-Negative Least-Squares (NNLS) algorithm [20] that is also used in the RASLS algorithm. The results presented in Fig. 1 are obtained for the dataset (A). It illustrates the mean-SIR behavior and the standard deviation (STD) for both factors versus time instants. Thus it shows a progressively updating process in ONMF versus sequential samples. The statistics, i.e. mean-SIR and STD, is calculated from 100 Monte Carlo samples at each time instant. In each MC run, an initializer

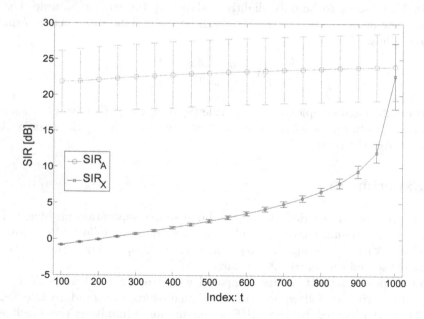

Fig. 1. Mean-SIR and STD (whiskers) for estimating both factors versus the time instant t in ONMF using the dataset (A): $T = 10^3$, $I = 100$ and $J = 10$

Table 1. Runtime [in seconds], mean-SIR [dB] and STDs (in parenthesis) for estimating the factors A and X from the datasets (B) and (C)

Algorithm	$T = 10^5$, $I = 100$, $J = 10$			$T = 10^6$, $I = 50$, $J = 10$		
	SIR_A	SIR_X	Time	SIR_A	SIR_X	Time
MUE	19.2 (3)	18.4 (2.8)	393 (115)	13.7 (3.8)	12.6 (3.6)	3030 (1021)
HALS	29 (2.1)	31.5 (3.3)	152.3 (27.7)	20.8 (4.2)	21.2 (5)	2063 (946)
RASLS	22.2 (2)	38.3 (4)	534 (132)	37.8 (7.2)	38.4 (6.9)	3347 (764)
ONMF	**64.7** (16.7)	**36.4** (2.1)	**116** (9.8)	28.1 (2.8)	24.9 (2)	**1204** (105)

is randomly selected. The SIRs, STDs, and runtime [in sec.], obtained for the datasets (B) and (C), are given in Table 1. Both datasets contain the signals observed in a long time window.

5   Conclusions

In this paper, we discuss a possibility of using the row-action projection technique for solving NMF problems. We applied the Kaczmarz algorithm both for LS-NMF and ONMF. The results demonstrate that our LS-NMF is somehow faster than all the tested algorithms. However, this is not a considerable improvement in runtime, since the Kaczmarz algorithm converges more slowly than the HALS algorithm. We also applied the Kaczmarz algorithm for online NMF. In this case, our ONMF significantly outperforms the other tested algorithms, especially in terms of the runtime. The SIRs obtained with ONMF are higher than with MUE and HALS. The RASLS sometimes gives better performance but it is justified by the fact that the RASLS uses some kind of regularization.

The proposed methods considerably improve the scalability of NMF algorithms by reducing time complexity and memory requirements. They can be used for analyzing a big data, especially for estimating slowly time-varying feature vectors from long training signals or streaming data. It might be useful for blind source separation of non-stationary signals, dynamic or adaptive learning.

References

1. Lee, D.D., Seung, H.S.: Learning the parts of objects by non-negative matrix factorization. Nature 401, 788–791 (1999)
2. Cichocki, A., Zdunek, R., Phan, A.H., Amari, S.I.: Nonnegative Matrix and Tensor Factorizations: Applications to Exploratory Multi-way Data Analysis and Blind Source Separation. Wiley and Sons (2009)
3. Dong, C., Zhao, H., Wang, W.: Parallel nonnegative matrix factorization algorithm on the distributed memory platform. International Journal of Parallel Programming 38, 117–137 (2010)
4. Wang, Q., Cao, Z., Xu, J., Li, H.: Group matrix factorization for scalable topic modeling. In: Proc. the 35th International ACM SIGIR Conference on Research and Development in Information Retrieval, SIGIR 2012, pp. 375–384. ACM Press, New York (2012)

5. Liu, C., Yang, H.C., Fan, J., He, L.W., Wang, Y.M.: Distributed nonnegative matrix factorization for web-scale dyadic data analysis on mapreduce. In: Proc. 19th International Conference on World Wide Web, WWW 2010, pp. 681–690. ACM, New York (2010)
6. Gemulla, R., Nijkamp, E., Haas, P.J., Sismanis, Y.: Large-scale matrix factorization with distributed stochastic gradient descent. In: Proc. the 17th ACM SIGKDD International Conference on Knowledge Discovery and Data Mining, KDD 2011, pp. 69–77. ACM, New York (2011)
7. Liao, R., Zhang, Y., Guan, J., Zhou, S.: CloudNMF: A mapreduce implementation of nonnegative matrix factorization for large-scale biological datasets. Genomics, Proteomics and Bioinformatics 12(1), 48–51 (2014)
8. Phan, A.H., Cichocki, A.: PARAFAC algorithms for large-scale problems. Neurocomputing 74(11), 1970–1984 (2011)
9. Cao, B., Shen, D., Sun, J.T., Wang, X., Yang, Q., Chen, Z.: Detect and track latent factors with online nonnegative matrix factorization. In: Proc. International Joint Conference on Artificial Intelligence (IJCAI), Hyderabad, India, pp. 2689–2694 (2007)
10. Wang, F., Tan, C., Konig, A.C., Li, P.: Efficient document clustering via online nonnegative matrix factorizations. In: Proc. 11-th SIAM Conference on Data Mining, pp. 908–919. SIAM / Omnipress (2011)
11. Lefevre, A., Bach, F., Févotte, C.: Online algorithms for nonnegative matrix factorization with the Itakura-Saito divergence. In: 2011 IEEE Workshop on Applications of Signal Processing to Audio and Acoustics (WASPAA), pp. 313–316. IEEE (2011)
12. Zhou, G., Yang, Z., Xie, S., Yang, J.M.: Online blind source separation using incremental nonnegative matrix factorization with volume constraint. IEEE Transactions on Neural Networks 22(4), 550–560 (2011)
13. Mairal, J., Bach, F., Ponce, J., Sapiro, G.: Online learning for matrix factorization and sparse coding. Journal of Machine Learning Research 11, 19–60 (2010)
14. Kaczmarz, S.: Angenaherte Auflosung von Systemen linearer Gleichungen. Bulletin de lAcademie Polonaise des Sciences et Lettres 35, 355–357 (1937)
15. Herman, G.T.: Image Reconstruction from Projections - The fundamentals of computerized tomography. Academic Press, New York (1980)
16. Popa, C., Zdunek, R.: Kaczmarz extended algorithm for tomographic image reconstruction from limited-data. Mathematics and Computers in Simulation 65(6), 579–598 (2004)
17. Tanabe, K.: Projection method for solving a singular system of linear equations and its applications. Numer. Math. 17, 203–214 (1971)
18. Popa, C., Zdunek, R.: On some constraining strategies in image reconstructions from projections. In: Proc. of 5th Workshop on Mathematical Modelling of Environmental and Life Sciences Problems, Constantza, Romania, Editura Academiei Romane (2006)
19. Zdunek, R.: Regularized nonnegative matrix factorization: Geometrical interpretation and application to spectral unmixing. International Journal of Applied Mathematics and Computer Science 24(2), 233–247 (2014)
20. Kim, H., Park, H.: Non-negative matrix factorization based on alternating nonnegativity constrained least squares and active set method. SIAM Journal in Matrix Analysis and Applications 30(2), 713–730 (2008)

Structure Perturbation Optimization for Hopfield-Type Neural Networks*

Gang Yang, Xirong Li**, Jieping Xu, and Qin Jin

Multimedia Computing Lab, School of Information,
Renmin University of China, Beijing 100872, China
{yanggang,xirong,xjieping,qjin}@ruc.edu.cn

Abstract. In this paper, we extract the core idea of state perturbation from *Hopfield-type* neural networks and define state perturbation formulas to describe the general way of optimization methods. Departing from the core idea and the formulas, we propose a novel optimization method related to neural network structure, named structure perturbation optimization. Our method can produce a structure transforming process to retrain *Hopfield-type* neural networks to get better problem-solving ability. Experiments validate that our method effectively helps *Hopfield-type* neural networks to escape from local minima and get superior solutions.

Keywords: stochastic noise, structure perturbation, Hopfield-type neural network, maximum clique problem.

1 Introduction

Neural networks could effectively solve combinatorial optimization problems in polynomial time. However, neural networks have a basic problem that they easily fall into local minima, and consequently produce suboptimal solutions. As a specific type of neural network, *Hopfield-type* neural networks (*HTNNs*) have already been applied in many applications including combinatorial optimization and pattern recognition [1]. Unfortunately, it has been observed that the local minima problem also exists in *HTNNs* [2]. To overcome the local minima problem, some methods were proposed to avoid algorithms falling into local minima or help them jump out of local minima. Several important methods should be remarked specially. Dynamics tunneling was proposed to drive away algorithms from local minima or plateau by executing another local or global searching [3]. The stochastic noise method was utilized widely to increase stochastic characteristic in algorithm searching [4], [11]. Chaotic dynamics is another important type of optimization method, which introduces chaotic attractors to increase

---

* This research was partially supported by the Fundamental Research Funds for the Central Universities, and the Research Funds of Renmin University of China (No. 14XNLQ01), and the grants from the Natural Science Foundation of China (No. 61303184).
** Corresponding author.

S. Wermter et al. (Eds.): ICANN 2014, LNCS 8681, pp. 307–314, 2014.

the probability of finding optimal solutions. Some typical improved algorithms embedded with the chaotic dynamics, such as transiently chaotic neural network (TCNN), chaotic simulated annealing (CSA) and chaotic maximum neural network (CMNN), are applied effectively in many practical fields [5], [6], [10]. Despite these good processes, the local minima problem remains unsolved. To the best of our knowledge, there is no general efficient method applied in the field to optimize *HTNNs*.

Existing optimization methods improve *HTNNs* by modifying their momentum functions to alter algorithm states [6]. However, because of the limitation of state modifications, the improvement is relatively limited. In this paper, we first define normal state formulas abstracted from existing *HTNNs*. The state formulas reveal a core state perturbation optimizing idea of these algorithms. Then, we propose the structure perturbation optimization (*SPO*) to help *HTNNs* jump out of local minima. Due to its wide adaptability, *SPO* is easy to be introduced into the existing *HTNNs*. Equipped with *SPO*, *HTNNs* have a higher opportunity to find better solutions in a more broad solution domain. Experiments on the maximum clique problem validate the effectiveness of *SPO*. The contributions of this paper are: (1) State perturbation formulas of *HTNNs* is defined to describe state optimizing process generally; (2) *SPO* containing structure perturbation characteristic provides a new point of view to optimize *HTNNs*, and possibly other neural networks.

The rest of the paper is organized as follows: We define in section 2 the general state perturbation formulas and explain the research background. In section 3, the *SPO* is proposed. In section 4, we introduce *SPO* into a *Hopfield* net and validate its performance on solving maximum clique problems. Finally, section 5 concludes the paper.

2   The State Perturbation Formulas

Hopfield-type neural networks (*HTNNs*) are fully connected recurrent networks. They can be implemented physically by interconnecting a set of resistors and amplifiers with symmetrical outputs and external bias current sources. In *HTNNs*, the state updating function is defined as follows [7]:

$$\tau_i \frac{du_i}{dt_t} = -\alpha_i u_i + \sum_{j=1}^{N} W_{ij} v_j + I_i, \ i = 1...N \tag{1}$$

But using Eq. 1, *HTNNs* get stuck into local minima easily although they sometimes find good solutions. To overcome the local minima problems to a certain extent, many optimization methods were presented. Among them, the transiently chaotic neural network (TCNN) is a typical effective algorithm, which introduces chaotic dynamics into *Hopfield* net to form superior problem solving ability. Besides TCNN, by introducing various complex dynamics, some other methods also produced effective improvements [4], [5], [6], [8]. Moreover, it is validated successfully that inner or outer dynamics favor the algorithm optimization. We

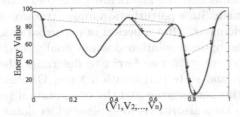

Fig. 1. The explanation of state perturbation. This is a schematic figure. Horizontal coordinate is the output vector, and vertical coordinate indicates the correlative problem energy value.

extract the core idea about the state updating function from *HTNNs*, and form a general expression to describe the optimization property as follows:

$$U(t+1) = G(WV(t) + P) \tag{2}$$

$$V(t+1) = F(U(t+1)) \tag{3}$$

where $V(t)$ represents the neuron output; $U(t)$ represents the neuron input; W is the synaptic connection reflecting the network weights; P is input bias of neuron forming variable inputting effects; G is the state function influencing the modification of neuron internal values; F is an activation function.

Previously, complex dynamics is a useful way to help *HTNNs* escape from local minima. Considering inner or outer complex dynamics, we define state perturbation formulas to describe the thought of complex dynamics optimization:

$$U(t+1) = G(W(V(t) + \Delta V'(t)) + P) \tag{4}$$

$$\Delta V'(t+1) = K(t)\Delta V'(t) \tag{5}$$

$$K(t+1) = \alpha K(t) \tag{6}$$

where $\Delta V'(t)$ is an additional complex dynamic; $K(t)$ is a damping factor for the additional complex dynamics; α is a coefficient constant affecting the descent of complex dynamics. According to different types of additional neuron dynamics, the state perturbation formulas mainly denote two types of optimization algorithms: stochastic dynamic algorithm and heuristic dynamic algorithm. Generally stochastic dynamic algorithms contain stochastic state perturbation, and heuristic dynamic algorithms contain heuristic state perturbation. A large number of algorithms have already utilized the characteristics of state perturbation to realize optimization [3], [4], [8], [10].

The state perturbation can be illustrated in Fig. 1 . Fig. 1 shows the evolution process of *HTNNs*, and it reveals a uniform optimization process further. The evolution process explains that the algorithm undergoes some iterations to explore the solution domain. State perturbation makes transformation mainly concentrate in neighbor domains. After a period of perturbations, the state reaches a valley bottom of the optimal solution domain finally. In *HTNNs* with state perturbations, there always exist two forces to determine the solution quality: gradient descent force and state perturbation force. Gradient descent force is responsible for algorithm convergence and the computation speed. State perturbation force not only drives algorithms to explore wider domains, but also helps algorithms jump out local minima. As illustrated in Eq.4-Eq.6, the algorithm is dominated by the state perturbation force in the beginning stage, so it could do wide searching in the whole domain. With the descent of the state perturbation force, which is affected by $K(t)$ and α, the gradient descent force controls the searching process gradually. Finally, the algorithm is saturated at those points in wide and deep solution spaces. Furthermore, it is well known that the points of optimal solutions have high probability to be located in deep and wide valleys of the solution space. Therefore, algorithms with state perturbation force and gradient descent force have larger opportunity to find optimal solutions.

3   The Novel Structure Perturbation Optimization

Previously, researchers mainly focused on exploring state perturbation to improve their algorithms. However, state perturbation has serious limitation on practical applications. Inspired by state perturbation formulas, a novel structure perturbation optimization (SPO) is proposed. By altering neuron connections gradually, SPO could help *HTNNs* jump out of local minima domain to improve their efficiency and capability. SPO are formulated as follows:

$$U(t+1) = G((W + \Delta W'(t'))V(t) + P) \tag{7}$$

$$\Delta W'(t'+1) = K(t)\Delta W'(t') \tag{8}$$

$$K(t+1) = (1-\beta)K(t) \tag{9}$$

where $\Delta W'(t')$ is the neuron connection variations corresponding to algorithm structure modifications; t' is the time slice; $K(t)$ is the damping factor affecting network structures; β is a coefficient constant. The connection intensity modifications revealed in SPO are defined as a structure perturbation. As shown in Eq.7-Eq.9, SPO can also be considered as weight fluctuations. In *HTNNs* and recurrent neural networks, the weight fluctuations are relative to the problem modifications or algorithm structure modifications. Eq. 8 and Eq. 9 show SPO contains a gradient descent process on the degree of weight, so *HTNNs* with SPO could get similar convergence finally and certainly.

Likewise, SPO has two types in detail: stochastic structure perturbation and heuristic structure perturbation. Stochastic structure perturbation modifies the algorithm structure randomly, which is like weight irregular modifications in

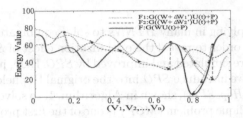

Fig. 2. The explanation of structure perturbation optimization. This is a schematic figure. The horizontal coordinate means the output vector, and the vertical coordinate indicates the correlative problem energy value. There are three different structure perturbations in this figure. F_1 is the initial structure, F_2 is one of the middle structure, and F is the final structure which is related to the original algorithm structure.

HTNNs. With the effect of stochastic structure perturbation, *HTNNs* embedded with *SPO* could alter the shape of solution domain, and transform a valley of local minima domain where the algorithm stuck in to be a peak where the algorithm can keep on converging. The structure perturbation vanishes finally, which can ensure that the gotten results are corresponding to feasible solutions. Similarly, heuristic structure perturbation could improve algorithm validity and efficiency by introducing heuristic strategies. Since heuristic strategy could produce oriented evolution, heuristic structure perturbation induces algorithms to achieve more efficient searching in a given solution domain.

SPO is illustrated in Fig. 2. In Fig. 2, the algorithm with *SPO* goes through several perturbation phases to find the optimal solution. Initially, the variant weights $\Delta W_1'$ are initiated to construct structure F_1. After many iterations denoted by t', the algorithm reaches a local minimum. Subsequently, the structure perturbation occurs and another algorithm structure F_2 is constructed. F_2 has a completely different structure to prompt the algorithm to jump out of the previous local minimum **vertically**. After t' iterations, the algorithm reaches saturated state again according to F_2 evolution process. Then, the perturbation process is repeated. Several perturbation epochs later, the structure perturbation controlled by β vanishes. Finally, the algorithm reduces to be a stable structure that is related to original problem structure. Since the original algorithm F is assured to get convergence, the improved algorithm is guaranteed to get convergence too. Therefore, *HTNNs* embedded with *SPO* are easy to form persistent valuable searching, and have larger probability to find the optimal solution.

Based on *SPO*, various optimizing algorithms could be constituted to solve different problems. For example, the simulated annealing algorithm with heuristic structure perturbation could produce gradient ascent effect at the steepest direction; the heuristic strategy of chaotic dynamics could form regular structure perturbation to build efficient chaotic algorithms. In practical applications, *SPO* can combine with resetting strategy to form powerful algorithms. So we believe *SPO* has wide range of application with good prospects.

4   Simulations

SPO is capable of applying in many *HTNNs* to solve combinatorial optimization problems (COPs). In order to reveal the optimization effect of *SPO*, several well-known algorithms were simulated and improved by *SPO*. Here, just to validate the fundamental theory, we introduce *SPO* into the original Hopfield net and form an improved algorithm (*Hop_SPO*), shown in Algorithm. 1, to solve maximum clique problem. Maximum clique problem (*MCP*) is one of the first problems which have been proven to be NP-complete. Maximum clique problem can be referenced in [9].

Algorithm 1. *Hop_SPO* for MCP.

1: Initialize algorithm parameters experimentally and input values at random.
2: **while** algorithm state does not reach balance under epoch threshold T_{limit} **do**
3:     **while** algorithm does not get short-term convergence or reach the max iteration **do**
4:         Run the algorithm with functions:

$$u_i(t+1) = ku_i(t) + \alpha\{\sum_j (w_{ij} + \Delta w'_{ij}(t'))v_j(t) + I\} \qquad (10)$$

$$v_i(t) = \frac{1}{1 + e^{-u_i(t)/\varepsilon}} \qquad (11)$$

5:         Calculate energy to judge convergence, and update weights according to Eq. 8 and Eq. 9;
6:     **end while**
7:     Reset weights according to *SPO* as $\Delta w'_{ij} = A' \, random(-1 \sim 1)$;
8:     Maintain the intermediate states, such as inputs, outputs and parameter values of previous state, to ensure the continuous process;
9: **end while**

In algorithm 1, the structure perturbation is initialized as $\Delta w'_{ij} = A' \, random$ $(-1 \sim 1)$, and A' is the amplitude of structure perturbation. And t' is time slice. In the inner loop, the algorithm structure will gradually transform to be the original algorithm structure, thus the algorithm could find a feasible solution related with the original problem. $\Delta w'_{ij}(t')$ only influences the medial states and drives the algorithm to escape from local minima. In every epoch, only the initial weights $\Delta w'_{ij}$ are reset, and other intermediate states such as outputs and inputs maintain their previous values. In *Hop_SPO*, *SPO* will force the algorithm to jump vertically out of local minima where the algorithm stuck in in previous epoch, and induce the algorithm to find optimal solutions gradually. As *SPO* just alters the algorithm structure and other algorithm elements preserve their original evolution process, that ensured *Hop_SPO* can get convergence ultimately.

We compared *Hop_SPO* with the original *Hopfield* net, TCNN and *Hopfield* with stochastic noises (*Hop_SN*) on four groups of problems in MCP data set. These algorithms were implemented using Matlab on a PC(Pentium Duo 2.2GHz, 4.0G RAM). In *Hop_SPO*, parameter β directly affects the convergent speed. Normally, β is set in domain (0.01~0.06). There are also existing some additional parameters in charge of the perturbation production. We fixed these parameters to investigate the effectiveness of the primary parameters. For MCP, the amplitude A' is always set to 1 experimentally, and the other parameters are set as the same as those in their original algorithms.

Table 1. The simulation results of *Hopfield*, *Hop_SN*, *Hop_SPO* and *TCNN* on *MCP*

Instance	Optimal Size	Hopfield		Hop_SN		Hop_SPO		TCNN	
		Average Size	Best Size	Average Size	Best Size	Average Size	Best Size	Average Size	Best Size
c125.9	34	30.3	33	32.1	34	34	**34**	27	33
C250.9	44	36.8	40	41.2	44	41.7	**44**	39.9	41
C500.9	57	46.4	49	49.3	51	52.9	**55**	48.8	51
brock200_2	12	7.5	8	10.1	11	10.2	**12**	10.2	11
brock200_4	17	13.6	14	13.9	15	14.6	**16**	14.3	16
brock400_2	29	19.3	22	21.9	23	23.6	**24**	21.3	23
Hamming6-2	32	30.2	32	32	32	32	**32**	32	32
Hamming6-4	4	4	4	4	4	4	**4**	4	4
Hamming8-2	128	121.8	128	128	**128**	128	**128**	128	128
P-hat300-1	8	7.2	8	7.1	8	8	**8**	8	8
P-hat300-2	25	23.7	25	24.5	**25**	25	**25**	22.2	24
P-hat300-3	36	32.4	33	32.9	34	33.3	**34**	34	34

Evidently, *SPO* is a basic optimizing way, so its performance and optimizing effect are able to be demonstrated by comparison between the improved algorithms and their original algorithms. Table. 1 shows the performance comparisons. Some best results in Table. 1 are marked in bold. From Table. 1, we can observe that *Hop_SPO* can find better or comparable results than *Hopfield net*, *TCNN* and *Hop_SN*. For instances of Hamming6-2, Hamming6-4, P-hat300-1 and P-hat300-3, *Hop_SN*, *Hop_SPO* and *TCNN* could find the same best solutions. For C500.9 and three brock_n_m instances, *Hop_SPO* could find better results than *Hopfield*, *Hop_SN* and *TCNN* on best solution aspect and average solution aspect. Furthermore, *Hop_SN* shows better solving ability than *Hopfield*. The comparison illustrates the performance of structure perturbation is better than state perturbation in this situation. Moreover, it also reveals *SPO* is an effective way to optimize the existing algorithms. Similarly, *TCNN* can be regarded as a special *Hopfield* net with both structure perturbation and state perturbation, thus *TCNN* also exhibits *SPO* superiority on optimizing algorithm aspect.

To show *SPO* effects, Fig. 3 displays the convergent process of *Hop_SPO* on C125_9 MCP instance. Fig. 3 illustrates *Hop_SPO* could find a near-optimal solution at the first epoch(about 170 iterations), and subsequently optimize

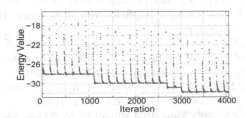

Fig. 3. The convergent process of the optimized *Hopfield* net with *SPO* on C125_9 MCP instance. The less the energy value is, the higher the solution quality will be. For showing the algorithm gradual evolution explicitly during many epoches, the convergence process is lengthened willfully with large T_{limit} value.

its solutions gradually. Since *Hop_SPO* maintained its previous epoch states, its solution quality could be optimized step by step. Finally, *Hop_SPO* found the optimal solution at about 3600 iterations. Actually, Fig. 3 shows a general process in applying *SPO*. And it reveals *SPO* is able to optimize solutions at proper direction. Furthermore, Fig. 3 illustrates the superiority of perturbation optimization method in structure optimization aspect.

5   Conclusion

In this paper, aimed to optimize *Hopfield-type* neural networks, a structure perturbation optimization method (*SPO*) is proposed. *SPO* is corresponding to the algorithm structure optimization, and exploits a new aspect to improve recurrent neural networks. Experiments validate *SPO* has superior optimization effect on *HTNNs*. Moreover, *SPO* displays widely flexible applicability on optimizing algorithms. Optimization algorithms could combine *SPO* to form their novel improved versions and increase their effectiveness further. Although some existing algorithms reveal more effective performance, those algorithms can still be further improved through combining with *SPO*.

References

1. Cheng, K., Lin, J., Mao, C.: The application of competitive Hopfield neural network to medical image segmentation. IEEE Trans. Med. Imag. 15, 560–567 (1996)
2. Van Den, D.E., Miller III, T.K.: Improving the Performance of the Hopfield-Tank Neural Network Through Normalization and Annealing. Biol. Cybern. 139, 129–139 (1989)
3. Singh, Y.: Dynamic Tunneling Based Regularization in Feedforward Neural Networks. Artificial Intell 131, 55–71 (2001)
4. Wang, L.P., Li, S., Tian, F.Y.: A Noisy Chaotic Neural Network for Solving Combinatorial Optimization Problems: Stochastic Chaotic Simulated Annealing. IEEE Trans. Syst. Man Cybern B Cybern. 34(5), 2119–2125 (2004)
5. He, Y.Y.: Chaotic Simulated Annealing with Decaying Chaotic Noise. IEEE Trans. Neural Netw. 13(6), 1526–1531 (2002)
6. Chen, S.S.: Chaotic simulated annealing by a neural network with a variable delay: design and application. IEEE Trans. Neural Netw. 22(10), 1557–1565 (2011)
7. Tatem, A.J., Lewis, H.G., Atkinson, P.M., Nixon, M.S.: Super-Resolution Land Cover Pattern Prediction Using a Hopfield Neural Network. Remote Sensing of Environment 79, 1–14 (2002)
8. Sun, M., Zhao, L., Cao, W., Xu, Y.Q., Dai, X.F., Wang, X.X.: Novel hysteretic noisy chaotic neural network for broadcast scheduling problems in packet radio networks. IEEE Trans. Neural Netw. 21(9), 1422–1433 (2010)
9. Yang, G., Yi, J.Y.: Dynamic characteristic of a multiple chaotic neural network and its application. Soft Comput. 17(5), 783–792 (2013)
10. Chen, L., Aihara, K.: Chaotic simulated annealing by a neural network model with transient chaos. Neural Networks 8(6), 915–930 (1995)
11. Karandashev, I., Kryzhanovsky, B.: The Mix-Matrix Method in the Problem of Binary Quadratic Optimization. In: Villa, A.E.P., Duch, W., Érdi, P., Masulli, F., Palm, G. (eds.) ICANN 2012, Part I. LNCS, vol. 7552, pp. 41–48. Springer, Heidelberg (2012)

Complex-Valued Multilayer Perceptron Search Utilizing Singular Regions of Complex-Valued Parameter Space

Seiya Satoh and Ryohei Nakano

Chubu University,
1200 Matsumoto-cho, Kasugai, 487-8501 Japan
tp13801-3493@sti.chubu.ac.jp, nakano@cs.chubu.ac.jp

Abstract. In the search space of a complex-valued multilayer perceptron having J hidden units, C-MLP(J), there exist flat areas called singular regions, as is the case with a real-valued MLP. The singular regions cause serious stagnation of learning, preventing usual search methods from finding an excellent solution. However, there exist descending paths from the regions since most points in the regions are saddles. This paper proposes a completely new learning method that does not avoid but makes good use of singular regions to stably and successively find excellent solutions commensurate with C-MLP(J). Our experiments showed the proposed method worked well.

Keywords: complex-valued multilayer perceptron, Wirtinger calculus, search method, singular region, reducibility mapping.

1 Introduction

Complex-valued neural networks have the attractive potential real-valued ones don't have [5]. For example, a complex-valued multilayer perceptron (C-MLP) can easily represent a function having attractive features such as periodicity and unboundedness, while a real-valued MLP is not easy to do so.

Among learning methods of complex-valued MLPs, complex back propagation (C-BP) [6,7] is basic and well-known. Recently a higher-order learning method has been proposed to get better performance [2]. Actually, our recent experiments showed complex Broyden-Fletcher-Goldfarb-Shanno (C-BFGS) found rather good solutions after many independent runs with different initial points.

Here we try to invent a completely new learning method which stably finds a series of excellent solutions for successive numbers of hidden units. Note that there exist flat subspaces called singular regions in the search space of a C-MLP [11], as is true with a real-valued MLP [4]. Singular regions have been avoided as far as possible [1] because they cause serious stagnation of learning; however, we think they can be utilized as excellent initial points for successive search. In this viewpoint, a method called SSF (Singularity Stairs Following) [9,13] was once proposed, which makes good use of singular regions to stably and successively find excellent solutions for real-valued MLPs.

S. Wermter et al. (Eds.): ICANN 2014, LNCS 8681, pp. 315–322, 2014.

This paper proposes a complex version of SSF, called Complex Singularity Stairs Following (C-SSF). C-SSF utilizes reducibility mapping [4,10], eigen vector descent [12], and complex BFGS, aiming to stably find excellent solutions in the complex search space. Our experiments showed that C-SSF worked well in fitting, model selection and generalization.

2   Background of C-SSF

Reducibility mapping and singular regions
Singular regions are generated using reducibility mapping. Here consider a complex-valued MLP with J hidden units, C-MLP(J), whose output is f_J.

$$f_J(x; \theta_J) = w_0 + \sum_{j=1}^{J} w_j z_j, \qquad z_j \equiv g(w_j^T x) \tag{1}$$

Here $\theta_J = \{w_0, w_j, \boldsymbol{w}_j, j = 1, \cdots, J\}$ is a parameter vector. Input $\boldsymbol{x}$, weights $\boldsymbol{w}_j$, w_j, output f_J, and teacher signal y are all complex. Given data $\{(\boldsymbol{x}^\mu, y^\mu), \mu = 1, \cdots, N\}$, we want to find θ_J minimizing the following error function.

$$E_J = \sum_{\mu=1}^{N} \delta^\mu \overline{\delta^\mu}, \qquad \delta^\mu \equiv f_J(\boldsymbol{x}^\mu; \theta_J) - y^\mu \tag{2}$$

Moreover, consider C-MLP($J-1$) whose output is $f_{J-1}(\boldsymbol{x}; \theta_{J-1}) = u_0 + \sum_{j=2}^{J} u_j v_j$, where $v_j \equiv g(u_j^T x)$. Here $\theta_{J-1} = \{u_0, u_j, \boldsymbol{u}_j, j = 2, \cdots, J\}$ is a parameter vector of C-MLP($J-1$), and let the optimal θ_{J-1} be $\widehat{\theta}_{J-1}$.

Sussmann [14] pointed out the uniqueness and reducibility of real-valued MLPs. Much the same uniqueness and reducibility hold for complex-valued MLPs [10]. Now consider three reducibility mappings [4,10] α, β, and γ; then, apply α, β, and γ to the optimal $\widehat{\theta}_{J-1}$ to get $\widehat{\Theta}_J^\alpha$, $\widehat{\Theta}_J^\beta$, and $\widehat{\Theta}_J^\gamma$ respectively.

$$\widehat{\theta}_{J-1} \xrightarrow{\alpha} \widehat{\Theta}_J^\alpha, \quad \widehat{\theta}_{J-1} \xrightarrow{\beta} \widehat{\Theta}_J^\beta, \quad \widehat{\theta}_{J-1} \xrightarrow{\gamma} \widehat{\Theta}_J^\gamma \tag{3}$$

$\widehat{\Theta}_J^\alpha \equiv \{\theta_J | w_0 = \widehat{u}_0, \ w_1 = 0, w_j = \widehat{u}_j, \boldsymbol{w}_j = \widehat{\boldsymbol{u}}_j, j = 2, ..., J\}$

$\widehat{\Theta}_J^\beta \equiv \{\theta_J | w_0 + w_1 g(w_{10}) = \widehat{u}_0, \boldsymbol{w}_1 = [w_{10}, 0, ..., 0]^T, w_j = \widehat{u}_j, \boldsymbol{w}_j = \widehat{\boldsymbol{u}}_j, j = 2, ..., J\}$

$\widehat{\Theta}_J^\gamma \equiv \{\theta_J | w_0 = \widehat{u}_0, w_1 + w_m = \widehat{u}_m, \boldsymbol{w}_1 = \boldsymbol{w}_m = \widehat{\boldsymbol{u}}_m,$
$\qquad w_j = \widehat{u}_j, \boldsymbol{w}_j = \widehat{\boldsymbol{u}}_j, j \in \{2, ..., J\} \setminus \{m\}\}$

From $\widehat{\Theta}_J^\alpha$, $\widehat{\Theta}_J^\beta$, and $\widehat{\Theta}_J^\gamma$, we have the following singular regions.
(1) The intersection of $\widehat{\Theta}_J^\alpha$ and $\widehat{\Theta}_J^\beta$ forms singular region $\widehat{\Theta}_J^{\alpha\beta}$, where only w_{10} is free: $w_0 = \widehat{u}_0$, $w_1 = 0$, $\boldsymbol{w}_1 = [w_{10}, 0, \cdots, 0]^T$, $w_j = \widehat{u}_j$, $\boldsymbol{w}_j = \widehat{\boldsymbol{u}}_j$, $j = 2, \cdots, J$.
(2) $\widehat{\Theta}_J^\gamma$ is a singular region, where the following holds: $w_1 + w_m = \widehat{u}_m$.

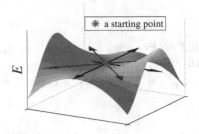

Fig. 1. Conceptual diagram of eigen vectors on a singular region

Starting from Singular Region

In the search space of C-MLP(J), C-SSF starts search from a point in the singular region of C-MLP(J). Since the gradient is zero all over the singular region, the gradient won't give us any information in which direction to go. Thus we employ eigen vector descent [12] whose conceptual diagram is shown in Fig. 1. Picking up each negative eigen value, two search routes start in the direction of its eigen vector and in the opposite direction.

Gradient and Hessian by Wirtinger Calculus

Since our objective function eq.(2) is not analytic under the standard complex calculus, we employ Wirtinger calculus [3] to get the gradient and Hessian.

Let E and $\boldsymbol{\theta}$ denote an error function and a parameter vector respectively. Parameters $\boldsymbol{\theta}$ ($= \boldsymbol{\theta}_x + i\,\boldsymbol{\theta}_y$) are used to form the complex variables $\boldsymbol{c} = [\boldsymbol{\theta}^T\ \overline{\boldsymbol{\theta}}^T]^T$ and the real variables $\boldsymbol{r} = [\boldsymbol{\theta}_x^T\ \boldsymbol{\theta}_y^T]^T$. Here $i = \sqrt{-1}$, $\overline{z}$ is the complex conjugate of z, $\boldsymbol{a}^T$ is the transpose of $\boldsymbol{a}$, and $\boldsymbol{A}^H \equiv \overline{\boldsymbol{A}}^T$. Then the complex Hessian $\boldsymbol{H}_c$ and the real Hessian $\boldsymbol{H}_r$ are defined respectively as below. Note that $\boldsymbol{H}_c$ is Hermitian and $\boldsymbol{H}_r$ is symmetric. We perform calculation using $\boldsymbol{r}$ representation since $\boldsymbol{r}$ is real.

$$\boldsymbol{H}_c = \frac{\partial^2 E}{\partial \overline{\boldsymbol{c}}\ \partial \overline{\boldsymbol{c}}^H}, \qquad \boldsymbol{H}_r = \frac{\partial^2 E}{\partial \boldsymbol{r}\ \partial \boldsymbol{r}^T} \tag{4}$$

3   C-SSF: Complex Singularity Stairs Following

The proposed method, a complex version of SSF [13], is explained. C-SSF starts search from C-MLP(J=1) and then gradually increases J one by one until J_{max}. When searching C-MLP(J), the method applies reducibility mapping to the optimum of C-MLP($J-1$) to get two kinds of singular regions $\widehat{\Theta}_J^{\alpha\beta}$ and $\widehat{\Theta}_J^{\gamma}$. When starting search from the singular region, the method employs eigen vector descent [12], which finds descending directions, and from then on employs complex BFGS. The general flow of C-SSF is given below. Let $w_0^{(J)}, w_j^{(J)}, \boldsymbol{w}_j^{(J)}$ denote parameters of C-MLP(J).

C-SSF Method:

1. Search for MLP(1):

   1.1 Set an initial point on $\widehat{\Theta}_J^{\alpha\beta}$: $w_0^{(1)} \leftarrow \bar{y}$, $w_1^{(1)} \leftarrow 0$, $\boldsymbol{w}_1^{(1)} \leftarrow [p, 0, \cdots, 0]^T$
   1.2 search_from_singular_region
   1.3 Store the best as $\widehat{w}_0^{(1)}$, $\widehat{w}_1^{(1)}$, and $\widehat{\boldsymbol{w}}_1^{(1)}$. Then, $J \leftarrow 2$.
2. **while** $J \leq J_{max}$ **do**
   2.1 Search from $\widehat{\Theta}_J^{\alpha\beta}$:

   2.1.1 Set an initial point on $\widehat{\Theta}_J^{\alpha\beta}$: $w_0^{(J)} \leftarrow \widehat{w}_0^{(J-1)}, w_1^{(J)} \leftarrow 0$,
   $\boldsymbol{w}_1^{(J)} \leftarrow [p, 0, \cdots, 0]^T, w_j^{(J)} \leftarrow \widehat{w}_{j-1}^{(J-1)}, \boldsymbol{w}_j \leftarrow \widehat{\boldsymbol{w}}_{j-1}^{(J-1)}, j=2,\cdots, J$
   2.1.2 search_from_singular_region
   2.2 Search from $\widehat{\Theta}_J^{\gamma}$:
   for $m = 1, \cdots, J-1$ **do**
   2.2.1 Set an initial point on $\widehat{\Theta}_J^{\gamma}$: $w_0^{(J)} \leftarrow \widehat{w}_0^{(J-1)}, w_1^{(J)} \leftarrow q \times \widehat{w}_m^{(J-1)}$,
   $w_{m+1}^{(J)} \leftarrow (1-q) \times \widehat{w}_m^{(J-1)}, \boldsymbol{w}_1^{(J)} \leftarrow \widehat{\boldsymbol{w}}_m^{(J-1)}, \boldsymbol{w}_{m+1}^{(J)} \leftarrow \widehat{\boldsymbol{w}}_m^{(J-1)}$,
   $w_j^{(J)} \leftarrow \widehat{w}_{j-1}^{(J-1)}, \boldsymbol{w}_j \leftarrow \widehat{\boldsymbol{w}}_{j-1}^{(J-1)}, j \in \{2, \cdots, J\} \setminus \{m+1\}$
   2.2.2 search_from_singular_region
   2.3 Get the best among all solutions obtained in step **2.1** and step **2.2**, and store it as $\widehat{w}_0^{(J)}, \widehat{w}_j^{(J)}, \widehat{\boldsymbol{w}}_j^{(J)}, j = 1, \cdots, J$. Then, $J \leftarrow J + 1$.

search_from_singular_region:

1. Calculate eigen values of the Hessian and get all negative ones and their eigen vectors.
2. **for** each negative eigen value whose eigen vector $\boldsymbol{u}$ **do**
   2.1 Perform line search in the direction of $\boldsymbol{u}$, start search using complex BFGS afterward, and keep the solution.
   2.2 Perform line search in the direction of $-\boldsymbol{u}$, start search using complex BFGS afterward, and keep the solution.

Here we give notes on the implementation used in our experiments. In the above, p in steps **1.1** and **2.1.1** is free and was set as -1, 0, and 1. Moreover, q in step **2.2.1** is also free and was set as 0.5, 1.0, and 1.5, which correspond to internal division, boundary, and external division respectively. In search_from_singular_region routine, the golden section search [8] was employed as a line search to find the suitable step length.

Now we claim the following, which will be evaluated in our experiments.
(1) The excellent solution of C-MLP(J) will be obtained one after another for $J=1,\cdots,J_{max}$. C-SSF guarantees that training error of C-MLP(J) is smaller than that of C-MLP($J-1$) since C-SSF descends in C-MLP(J) search space from the singular regions corresponding to the optimum of C-MLP($J-1$). The monotonic feature will be quite useful for model selection. However, such monotonic decrease of training error is not guaranteed for the existing methods.
(2) C-SSF runs without using random number, which means it always finds the same set of solutions.

4   Experiments

In a C-MLP an activation function plays an important role, and here we employed the following unbounded periodic function [6,7]. Here $h = h_x + ih_y$.

$$\sigma(h) = \frac{1}{1 + e^{-h}} = \frac{1 + e^{-h_x}\cos h_y + i\, e^{-h_x}\sin h_y}{1 + 2e^{-h_x}\cos h_y + e^{-2h_x}} \tag{5}$$

The proposed C-SSF was evaluated using two artificial data sets. The performance of C-SSF was compared with two existing methods: batch-type complex BP with line search (C-BP) and complex BFGS (C-BFGS). Real and imaginary parts of initial weights for existing methods were randomly selected from the range $[-1, 1]$. For each J each existing method was performed 100 times changing initial weights. Each run was terminated when the number of sweeps exceeded 10,000 or the step length got smaller than 10^{-16}.

Experiment Using Artificial Data 1

Artificial data 1 was generated using C-MLP having the following weights. Note that $J = 4$ and input x_5, x_6, x_7 are irrelevant.

$$[w_0, w_1, w_2, w_3, w_4] = [-4 + 3i, 2 - 2i, 3 - 2i, 3 + 5i, 0 - 5i], \tag{6}$$

$$[\boldsymbol{w}_1, \boldsymbol{w}_2, \boldsymbol{w}_3, \boldsymbol{w}_4] = \begin{bmatrix} 2+4i & 3+0i & -5+0i & 2-2i \\ 5-3i & -4-2i & -3-2i & -4-2i \\ 1+3i & 3-4i & 1+1i & -1-2i \\ 5+5i & -2-1i & 4-3i & -5+2i \\ -3-5i & 0-1i & 2-5i & 4-3i \\ 0+0i & 0+0i & 0+0i & 0+0i \\ 0+0i & 0+0i & 0+0i & 0+0i \\ 0+0i & 0+0i & 0+0i & 0+0i \end{bmatrix} \tag{7}$$

The real and imaginary parts of input x_k were randomly selected from the range $[0, 1]$. Teacher signal y^μ was generated by adding small Gaussian noise $\mathcal{N}(0,\ 0.01^2)$ to the output of C-MLP. The size of training data set was 500 ($N = 500$). The maximum number of hidden units was set to be 6 ($J_{max} = 6$).

To finish all learning, C-BP spent the longest CPU time 6 hr 11 min, which means the search easily got stuck in poor local minima. C-SSF required 27 min, three times longer than C-BFGS. In C-SSF, the numbers of search routes for J = 1,$\cdots$,6 were 27, 47, 92, 128, 180, and 234, which shows the number of search routes gets larger as J gets larger.

Figures 2 and 3 show minimum training error and the corresponding test error respectively. Test error was evaluated using test data set of 1,000 data points without noise, generated independently of training data. C-BP could hardly decrease training error and showed poor constant generalization. C-BFGS basically decreased training error as J got larger, but increased at $J = 5$. Test error of C-BFGS decreased in an up-and-down manner. C-SSF monotonically decreased training error and minimized test error at $J = 4$, which is correct.

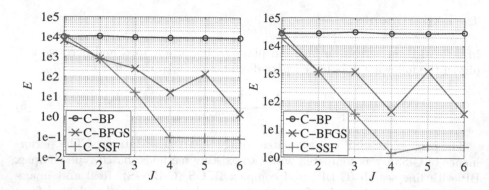

Fig. 2. Training error for artificial data 1   **Fig. 3.** Test error for artificial data 1

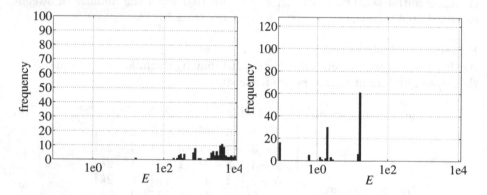

Fig. 4. Histogram of C-BFGS solutions **Fig. 5.** Histogram of C-SSF solutions for
for C-MLP(4)   C-MLP(4)

Figures 4 and 5 show histograms of C-MLP($J=4$) solutions obtained by C-BFGS and C-SSF respectively. We see C-BFGS found a good solution only once out of 100 runs, while C-SSF found much better solutions many times. Moreover, most solutions of C-BFGS are distributed in the poor range $[10^2, 10^4]$, while most solutions of C-SSF are located in the excellent range $[10^{-1}, 10^{1.2}]$.

Experiment Using Artificial Data 2
Artificial data 2 was generated using the following periodic function with changing amplitude. How flexibly C-MLP can represent periodicity was evaluated using three learning methods.

$$f(x) = (2e^{-10x} + e^x)\{\cos(30\pi x) + \sin(10\pi x)\} \tag{8}$$

The real part of input x^μ was randomly selected from the range $[0, 1]$, and the imaginary part was set zero. Teacher signal y^μ was generated by adding small Gaussian noise $\mathcal{N}(0, 0.01^2)$ to the output of the above function. The imaginary

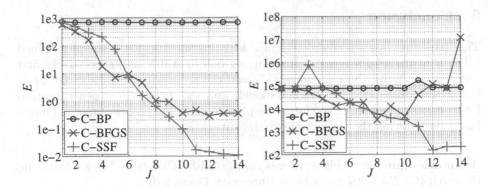

Fig. 6. Training error for artificial data 2   **Fig. 7.** Test error for artificial data 2

part of y^μ was set to be zero. The size of training data set was 200 ($N = 200$). The maximum number of hidden units was set to be 14 ($J_{max} = 14$).

To finish all learning, C-BP spent the longest 8 hr 1 min. C-SSF required 6 hr 55 min, 8.5 times longer than C-BFGS; C-SSF spent longer time for larger J since the number of search routes got larger. The numbers of search routes for J=1,...,14 were 12, 25, 39, 53, 65, 99, 170, 264, 287, 310, 529, 815, 918, and 949.

Figures 6 and 7 show minimum training error and the corresponding test error respectively. Test data set of 1,000 data points without noise was generated independently of training data. In test data the range of input x was expanded to [0, 3]; thus, the range [1, 3] was unknown for the trained C-MLP. Again C-BP could hardly decrease training error and showed poor constant generalization. C-BFGS basically decreased training error as J increased, but slightly increased at $J = 6, 11, 13$, and 14. Test error of C-BFGS was minimized at $J = 8$. C-SSF monotonically decreased training error and minimized test error at $J = 12$.

Figures 8, 9, and 10 show the output of the best model for each learning method. The best model means C-MLP(J) which minimizes test error; J=6 for C-BP, J=8 for C-BFGS, and J=12 for C-SSF. C-BP could hardly fit the periodic function for the range [0, 1] and showed very poor generalization for the range [1, 3]. C-BFGS nicely fitted the function in the range [0, 1.8], but the amplitude fitting got gradually deviated for $x > 1.8$. C-SSF very nicely fitted the function all over the range [0, 3] showing excellent generalization.

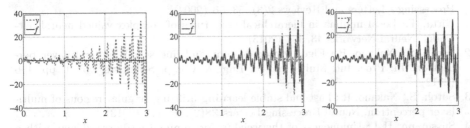

Fig. 8. Output of C-MLP(6) trained by C-BP   **Fig. 9.** Output of C-MLP(8) trained by C-BFGS   **Fig. 10.** Output of C-MLP (12) trained by C-SSF

5   Conclusion

This paper proposes a completely new learning method for a complex-valued MLP, that makes good use of singular regions to stably and successively find excellent solutions. Our experiments showed the proposed method showed excellent fitting, discovered the original model, and showed excellent generalization for a periodic function. In the future we plan to make the proposed method much faster by reducing the number of search routes.

Acknowledgments. This work was supported by Grants-in-Aid for Scientific Research (C) 25330294 and Chubu University Grant 24IS27A.

References

1. Amari, S.: Natural gradient works efficiently in learning. Neural Computation 10(2), 251–276 (1998)
2. Amin, M. F., Amin, M.I., Al-Nuaimi, A.Y.H., Murase, K.: Wirtinger calculus based gradient descent and Levenberg-Marquardt learning algorithms in complex-valued neural networks. In: Lu, B.-L., Zhang, L., Kwok, J. (eds.) ICONIP 2011, Part I. LNCS, vol. 7062, pp. 550–559. Springer, Heidelberg (2011)
3. Delgado, K.K.: The complex gradient operator and the CR-calculus. ECE275A-Lecture Supplement, Fall (2006)
4. Fukumizu, K., Amari, S.: Local minima and plateaus in hierarchical structure of multilayer perceptrons. Neural Networks 13(3), 317–327 (2000)
5. Hirose, A.: Complex-Valued Neural Networks, 2nd edn. SCI, vol. 400. Springer, Heidelberg (2012)
6. Kim, M.S., Guest, C.C.: Modification of backpropagation networks for complex-valued signal processing in frequency domain. In: Proc. IJCNN 1990, vol. 3, pp. 27–31 (1990)
7. Leung, H., Haykin, S.: The complex backpropagation algorithm. IEEE Trans. Signal Process. 39(9), 2101–2104 (1991)
8. Luenberger, D.G.: Linear and nonlinear programming. Addison-Wesley, Reading (1984)
9. Nakano, R., Satoh, S., Ohwaki, T.: Learning method utilizing singular region of multilayer perceptron. In: Proc. 3rd Int. Conf. on Neural Computation Theory and Applications, pp. 106–111 (2011)
10. Nitta, T.: Reducibility of the complex-valued neural network. Neural Information Processing - Letters and Reviews 2(3), 53–56 (2004)
11. Nitta, T.: Local minima in hierarchical structures of complex-valued neural networks. Neural Networks 43, 1–7 (2013)
12. Satoh, S., Nakano, R.: Eigen vector descent and line search for multilayer perceptron. In: Proc. Int. Multi-Conf. of Eng. & Comp. Scientists, vol. 1, pp. 1–6 (2012)
13. Satoh, S., Nakano, R.: Fast and stable learning utilizing singular regions of multilayer perceptron. Neural Processing Letters 38(2), 99–115 (2013)
14. Sussmann, H.J.: Uniqueness of the weights for minimal feedforward nets with a given input-output map. Neural Networks 5(4), 589–593 (1992)

Mix-Matrix Transformation Method
for Max-Cut Problem

Iakov Karandashev and Boris Kryzhanovsky

Scientific Research Institute for System Analysis of Russian Academy of Sciences,
Vavilova str. 44b.2, 119333 Moscow, Russia
{ya_rad_wsem,kryzhanov}@mail.ru

Abstract. One usually tries to raise the efficiency of optimization techniques by changing the dynamics of local optimization. In contrast to the above approach, we propose changing the surface of the problem rather than the dynamics of local search. The Mix-Matrix algorithm proposed by the authors previously [1] realizes such transformation and can be applied directly to a max-cut problem and successfully compete with other popular algorithms in this field such as CirCut and Scatter Search.

Keywords: Discrete optimization, mix-matrix, max-cut, quadratic binary minimization, combinatorial optimization.

1   Introduction

The max-cut problem is as follows: given a weighted undirected graph $G(V, W)$, it is necessary to find a partition of its vertexes V into two disjoint subsets V_1 and V_2, such that the sum of weights of edges whose end points belong to different subsets is largest, i.e.

$$\max_{V_1, V_2} \sum_{u \in V_1} \sum_{v \in V_2} w_{uv} \qquad (1)$$

Max-cut is an NP-complete problem, i.e. there is no polynomial algorithm for its solution in the general case.

It is known that some classes of graphs permit polynomial solutions, for example planar graphs, graphs not contractible to K_5 (the complete graph of five nodes), weakly bipartite graphs, graphs with negative edge weights, etc. This gives a reason to think that the problem for a two-dimensional spin grid where only closest neighbors can interact with non-repeating boundary conditions and the absence of external magnetic field amounts to the max-cut on a planar graph and is, therefore, polynomial-solvable. A two-dimensional grid with periodic boundary conditions is also polynomial-solvable if connections are of the form $\pm J$. The question is still open for Gaussian connections. Once we add an additional node connected to every vertex of the lattice (i.e. an external field to the system), the problem becomes NP-

S. Wermter et al. (Eds.): ICANN 2014, LNCS 8681, pp. 323–330, 2014.

complete for all sorts of interactions. The problem is NP-complete for a three-dimensional cubic grid even in the absence of an external field [2].

Algorithms of ε-approximation (i.e. polynomial algorithms yielding solutions that differ from the optimal cut by only ε) have been proposed to cope with NP-complete problems. An outstanding result in this field was demonstrated in paper [3]. It offers an algorithm that takes a polynomial time to solve a max-cut problem, the solution being not less than 0.878 the maximum cut magnitude, i.e. differing from the optimum by less than 13%. On the other hand, it follows from research [4] that on the assumption of $P \neq NP$ there is no polynomial algorithm that gives a provable solution whose value of the cut makes at least 98% of the optimum.

Research into ε-approximation algorithms has resulted in the discovery of methods that reduce max-cut problems to linear and semi-definite programming (so called LP and SDP relaxation). Widely used for finding upper and lower bounds in the branch and bound algorithm, the approach has made it possible to significantly narrow the exhaustive search and find exact solutions (not in the polynomial time, but within a satisfactory period) for a wider range of problems. Specifically, [2] describes an LP-relaxation-based algorithm allowing one to find the ground state for 2D and 3D Ising models with periodic boundary conditions and Gaussian connections for the dimensionality of up to several thousands, within minutes on an ordinary computer. Rendl et al. [5] and Wiegele [6] present SDP-relaxation methods for the max-cut problem permitting one to tackle more dense connection matrices than in 2D and 3D grids. However, the dimensionality of the problems with which this algorithm can cope decreases considerably as the density of non-zero matrix elements grows. Therefore, heuristic algorithms for such cases are especially called for.

Heuristic methods are used to deal with high-dimensionality problems and dense matrices. Local single-step search algorithms are the simplest and, therefore, most popular heuristic techniques.

1.1   Quadratic Optimization Problem and Hopfield Model

It is known that NP-complete problems can be reduced to one another in a polynomial number of steps. As an example of such reducibility, we consider the relationship between the max-cut problem, which we deal with here, and the quadratic binary optimization problem.

Introducing variables $s_i = +1$ for vertices belonging to one subset V_1 and $s_j = -1$ for vertices belonging to the other V_2, we get:

$$\sum_{u \in V_1} \sum_{v \in V_2} w_{uv} = \frac{1}{4} \sum_{i=1}^{N} \sum_{j=1}^{N} w_{ij} (1 - s_i s_j), \tag{2}$$

where N is the number of graph vertices. We see that the maximization of the cut comes down to the minimization of quadratic functional of binary variables built on the matrix $T_{ij} = -w_{ij} / 4$:

$$E(S) = -\sum_{i=1}^{N}\sum_{j=1}^{N} T_{ij} s_i s_j \qquad (3)$$

In this paper, we have chosen the asynchronous dynamics of the Hopfield model [7] as the elementary procedure of local minimization of the function given in Equation (3). The Hopfield model determines a system of N spins whose interactions are defined by the energy function $E(S)$. The standard (asynchronous) dynamics of minimization can be described as follows: we first compute the amplitude of a local field $h_i \sim -\partial E(S)/\partial s_i$ acting on a randomly picked i-th spin:

$$h_i = \sum_{j \neq i}^{N} T_{ij} s_j \qquad (4)$$

If the spin is directed along the field ($h_i s_i \geq 0$), its state does not change. If the spin is in an unstable state ($h_i s_i < 0$), it turns along the field taking state $s_i = \operatorname{sgn} h_i$. The operation is applied sequentially to all spins until the whole system converges to a stable state. Note that the state of only one spin changes at each point of time. This is the difference between the asynchronous and synchronous dynamics, the latter having all spins changed concurrently. The dynamics under consideration is no other than a descent down the energy surface $E(S)$, which is fully analogous to the coordinate-wise gradient descent in a continuous space. A decrease of energy at each flip of an unstable spin guarantees that the process described by the asynchronous dynamics brings the system into a stable lowest-energy state in a finite number of steps. Of course, the minimum we have found is most likely to be local while we meant to find the deepest (global) minimum of the function. A common method that can help in this event is the standard random search, which involves many repetitions of descents from different initial configurations.

Despite the simplicity of the algorithm, a descent from one random configuration requires roughly $O(N^2)$ operations for fully connected matrices (as in the Sherrington-Kirkpatrick model) or $O(N)$ for sparse matrices (as in the Edwards-Anderson model).

The number of local minima exponentially grows with N, therefore the probability of finding the global minimum falls exponentially. In spite of these difficulties, heuristic methods are widely used in binary optimization. Successful use of the Hopfield model for solving the salesman problem [8] started intensive research on similar techniques in other fields [11-23], e.g. graph theory [9], and neural-net optimization of image processing [10]. The reason for such a success is investigated in [14]: in random search the probability of finding a minimum grows with the depth of this minimum. Particularly, when a neural net is triggered at random, it is most likely to converge to a state corresponding to the global minimum [24-25]. The probability of the net converging to a minimum not as deep as the global one is slightly lower, while the probability of convergence to small-depth local minima is exponentially small. Such behavior of the net convergence probability means that the system is most likely to find one of sub-optimal solutions (a local minimum) if not the optimal solution (the global minimum).

One usually tries to raise the efficiency of random search by changing the dynamics of descent down the surface defined by function $E(S)$. A useful review of methods is given in papers [16-18]. In contrast to the above approach, in a previous paper [1], we proposed changing the surface of descent rather than the dynamics of descent. The goal of the surface transformation is to try to increase the radius of the attraction area of the global minimum (as well as other minima with depths comparable to the depth of the global one). The transformation of the surface we offer involves combining original matrix T with matrix T^2. By varying the combination of the matrices, we can control the depth of minima and their location in space to make the procedure of search of the global minimum work exponentially faster with N. This is the idea underlying the minimization algorithm we offered – Mix-Matrix (MM) algorithm.

Because the max-cut problem can be readily reduced to quadratic binary minimization, in this paper we apply the Mix-Matrix algorithm directly to the max-cut problem and compare its performance with the two well-known max-cut algorithms, namely CirCut and Scatter Search, on four benchmark test problems.

2   Mix-Matrix

In this Section, we briefly present the Mix-Matrix algorithm, introduced in [1]. The point of the method is transformation of the energy surface of the function in Equation (3). The surface is changed so that deep minima of the original function become even deeper. This enables an exponential growth of the probability of finding deep minima in random search.

A surface determined by quadratic form $E(S)$ can be transformed by only transforming the matrix on which it is built. Let us replace the matrix in Equation (3) by another matrix M, which we call mix-matrix:

$$M = \frac{1}{\sigma_T}(1-z)T + \frac{1}{\sigma_{2T}}zT^2, \tag{4}$$

where T^2 is the result of squaring matrix T followed by setting the main diagonal elements to zero, σ_T and σ_{2T} are mean square deviations of elements of matrices T and T^2, correspondingly. When parameter z changes from 0 to 1, matrix M is transformed from T to T^2. Correspondingly, the surface defined by the function $E(S)$ is transformed to a surface defined by the function $E_z(S)$:

$$E_z(S) = -\sum_{i=1}^{N}\sum_{j=1}^{N}M_{ij}s_i s_j, \tag{5}$$

As shown in [1], the transformation of the function leads to a considerable increase in the depth of the global minimum. The most deepening occurs at $z \approx 0.7$, and the probability of finding the global minimum grows exponentially with N. However, a minor shift of the minimum occurs in the process. In order to correct this shift, we offer the following two-stage minimization algorithm, called Mix-Matrix algorithm (MM):

1) in the first stage we start a descent from a random point down the surface $E_z(S)$ and find configuration $S_m^{(z)}$ corresponding to the minimum of function $E_z(S)$.

2) in the second stage we do corrections: we descend surface $E(S)$ from point $S_m^{(z)}$ down to the nearest minimum S_m of functional $E(S)$.

3   Results

We were interested to compare the efficiency of the Mix-Matrix (MM) algorithm with the most popular algorithms used for solving max-cut problems [27]. These are the Scatter-Search (SS) algorithm [28] and CirCut (CC) algorithm [29].

Alternative algorithms exist that could be included in the comparison, such as the Variable Neighbourhood Search (VNS) [30], or the Cut and Price method [31]. However, although VNS performs well (outperforming previous heuristic methods such as CirCut), it is very slow. Similarly, the Cut and Price method can optimally solve medium-sized instances, but this is limited to around n = 500 and so only applicable to the smallest 8x8x8 benchmarks.

[27] presents collections of max-cut problems and the results of testing these algorithms on these collections, a computer used in the tests being almost as powerful as ours (Intel 3.06 GHz processor). The comparison of the results is presented in Table 1. The first column holds the names of four test instances. The instances are of the type of 3D models with periodic (toroidal) boundary conditions. The first two problems feature Gaussian coupling T_{ij}, the other two $T_{ij} = \pm 1$. The dimensionality of the problems is $N = L \times L \times L$ with $L = 15$ and 8. The second and third columns carry the results: the objective value (i.e. the cut) and time in seconds given in [27] for Scatter Search and CirCut algorithms. The last column shows the average values of maximal cuts determined with the help of our MM-algorithm in 10^4 starts and the standard deviation of maximal cuts on several trials.

Table 1. Comparing the results of solving four max-cut instances by different algorithms. Note that higher is better for the ObjVal.

	Scatter Search (SS)		CirCut (CC)		Mix-Matrix (MM) z=0.7, 10^4 starts	
Problem	Obj Val	Time (sec)	Obj Val	Time (sec)	Obj Val	Time (sec)
g3-15	281 029 888	1023	268 519 648	788	$(2.73 \pm 0.004)*10^8$	8.8
g3-8	40 314 704	65	41 684 814	53	$(4.10 \pm 0.010)*10^7$	2.3
pm3-15-50	2 964	333	2 895	427	2 889.7 $\pm$ 4.6	8.9
pm3-8-50	442	48	454	38	451.9 $\pm$ 1.3	2.2

It is seen from the table that our algorithm produces a solution that is comparable to that generated by either of SS or CC, worse than any other by less than 3%, with both alternatives requiring between 20 and 100 times as long to find the solution. The best result was shown in solving the fourth problem (pm3-8) when our algorithm also found the solution 454 in some starts (the best solution produced by SS and CC).

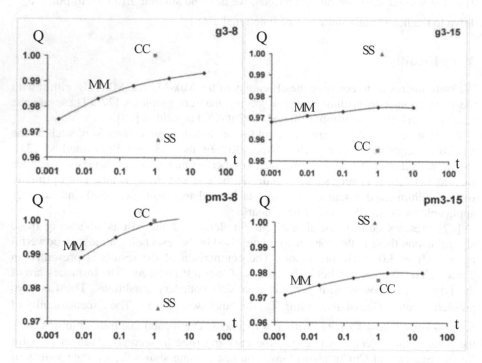

Fig. 1. Comparison of the results obtained by different algorithms for four test problems for different time of search by algorithm MM. On the X-axis is the relative time (logarithmic scale), the time used by CC being equal to 1. On the Y-axis is the relative quality of solution, the max of CC or SS being equal to 1.

As we see in Fig. 1, if we increase the time of computation, i.e. the number of starts, the quality of the solution found with MM will also increase. Moreover, when we increased the number of starts, we found the value of cut of 456 for the fourth problem (pm3-8), the value that was never found by other algorithm before.

Based on the obtained results, we can conclude that our algorithm MM finds solution of cut value:

$$Q_{MM} \geq 0.97 \cdot \max(Q_{CC}, Q_{SS}),$$

in a time that is two orders of magnitude shorter than that needed for the CC or SS algorithms.

4   Discussion and Conclusion

As we demonstrated in [1], the use of a mix-matrix in binary quadratic optimization problems brings about a transformation of the energy surface that results in deep minima growing noticeably deeper and shallow ones becoming still shallower or disappearing entirely. The transformation causes the attraction radius of a deep minimum to increase proportionally to its depth. As a consequence, the probability of finding this minimum grows exponentially with N. This resulted in the Mix-Matrix algorithm whose efficiency of finding the global minimum is much (exponentially with N) higher than the efficiency of the standard random-search algorithm.

As we showed here, the Mix-Matrix algorithm can be applied directly to the max-cut problem and successfully compete with other popular algorithms in this field. Comparing it with CirCut and Scatter Search algorithms showed that even at 10^4 starts (2 seconds for $N = 8^3$ and 8 seconds for $N = 15^3$) the MM algorithm proved to be as effective as either of the two, or worse but by no more than 3%, significant given the fact that the CirCut and Scatter Search algorithms take one or two orders of magnitude longer to produce the same result (see Table 1).

We would like to point out again that the mechanism of our algorithm is transformation of the energy surface of the functional rather than modification of the local search algorithm. This means that the Mix-Matrix algorithm can be improved considerably by changing the currently used asynchronous Hopfield dynamics by a more effective one.

Acknowledgments. The research was partially supported by RFBR grants No. 12-07-00295, No. 13-01-00504 and project 2.1 of the ONIT RAS.

References

1. Karandashev, I., Kryzhanovsky, B.: The Mix-Matrix Method in the Problem of Binary Quadratic Optimization. In: Villa, A.E.P., Duch, W., Érdi, P., Masulli, F., Palm, G. (eds.) ICANN 2012, Part I. LNCS, vol. 7552, pp. 41–48. Springer, Heidelberg (2012)
2. Liers, F., Junger, M., Reinelt, G., Rinaldi, G.: Computing Exact Ground States of Hard Ising Spin Glass Problems by Branch-and-Cut. In: New Optimization Algorithms in Physics, pp. 47–68. Wiley (2004)
3. Goemans, M.X., Williamson, D.P.: 878-approximation Algorithms for MAXCUT and MAX2SAT. In: ACM Symposium on Theory of Computing (STOC) (1994)
4. Bellare, M., Goldreich, O., Sudan, M.: Free bits, PCPs and nonapproximability-towards tight results. In: Proc. of 36th IEEE Symp. on Foundations of Computer Science, pp. 422–431 (1995)
5. Rendl, F., Rinaldi, G., Wiegele, A.: Solving Max-Cut to Optimality by Intersecting Semidefinite and Polyhedral Relaxations. Math. Programming 121(2), 307 (2010)
6. Wiegele, A.: Nonlinear Optimization Techniques Applied to Combinatorial Optimization Problems. Dissertation, i-x, pp. 1-131 (October 2006)
7. Hopfield, J.J.: Neural Networks and physical systems with emergent collective computational abilities. Proc. Nat. Acad. Sci. USA 79, 2554–2558 (1982)
8. Hopfield, J.J., Tank, D.W.: Neural computation of decisions in optimization problems. Biological Cybernetics 52, 141–152 (1985)

9. Fu, Y., Anderson, P.W.: Application of statistical mechanics to NP-complete problems in combinatorial optimization. Journal of Physics A 19, 1605–1620 (1986)
10. Poggio, T., Girosi, F.: Regularization algorithms for learning that are equivalent to multilayer networks. Science 247, 978–982 (1990)
11. Mulder, S., Wunsch II, D.: A Million City Traveling Salesman Problem Solution by Divide and Conquer Clustering and Adaptive Resonance Neural Networks. Neural Networks 16(5-6), 827–832 (2003)
12. Wu, F., Tam, P.K.S.: A neural network methodology of quadratic optimization. International Journal of Neural Systems 9(2), 87–93 (1999)
13. Pinkas, G., Dechter, R.: Improving Connectionist Energy Minimization. Journal of Artificial Intelligence Research 3(195), 23–48 (1995)
14. Kryzhanovsky, B.V., Magomedov, B.M., Mikaelyan, A.L.: A Relation Between the Depth of a Local Minimum and the Probability of Its Detection in the Generalized Hopfield Model. Doklady Mathematics 72(3), 986–990 (2005)
15. Kryzhanovsky, B.V., Magomedov, B.M.: Application of domain neural network to optimization tasks. In: Duch, W., Kacprzyk, J., Oja, E., Zadrożny, S. (eds.) ICANN 2005. LNCS, vol. 3697, pp. 397–403. Springer, Heidelberg (2005)
16. Hartmann, A.K., Rieger, H. (eds.): New Optimization Algorithms in Physics. Wiley-VCH, Berlin (2004)
17. Duch, W., Korczak, J.: Optimization and global minimization methods suitable for neural networks. KMK UMK Technical Report 1/99; Neural Computing Surveys (1998), http://www.is.umk.pl/~duch/cv/papall.html
18. Hartmann, A., Rieger, H.: Optimization Algorithms in Physics. Wiley-VCH, Berlin (2001)
19. Litinskii, L.B.: Eigenvalue problem approach to discrete minimization. In: Duch, W., Kacprzyk, J., Oja, E., Zadrożny, S. (eds.) ICANN 2005. LNCS, vol. 3697, pp. 405–410. Springer, Heidelberg (2005)
20. Smith, K.A.: Neural Networks for Combinatorial Optimization: A Review of More Than a Decade of Research. INFORMS Journal on Computing 11(1), 15–34 (1999)
21. Joya, G., Atencia, M., Sandoval, F.: Hopfield Neural Networks for Optimization: Study of the Different Dynamics. Neurocomputing 43(1-4), 219–237 (2002)
22. Litinskii, L.B., Magomedov, B.M.: Global Minimization of a Quadratic Functional: Neural Networks Approach. Pattern Recognition and Image Analysis 15(1), 80–82 (2005)
23. Boettecher, S.: Extremal Optimization for Sherrington-Kirkpatrick Spin Glasses. Eur. Phys. Journal B. 46, 501 (2005)
24. Kryzhanovsky, B.V., Magomedov, B.M., Fonarev, A.B.: On the Probability of Finding Local Minima in Optimization Problems. In: Proc. of Int. Joint Conf. on Neural Networks IJCNN 2006, pp. 5888–5892 (2006)
25. Kryzhanovsky, B.V., Kryzhanovsky, V.M.: The shape of a local minimum and the probability of its detection in random search. In: Filipe, J., Ferrier, J.-L., Andrade-Cetto, J. (eds.) Informatics in Control, Automation and Robotics. LNEE, vol. 24, pp. 51–61. Springer, Heidelberg (2009)
26. Houdayer, J., Martin, O.C.: Hierarchical approach for computing spin glass ground states. Phys. Rev. E 64, 56704 (2001)
27. http://www.optsicom.es/maxcut
28. Marti, R., Duarte, A., Laguna, M.: Advanced Scatter Search for the Max-Cut Problem. INFORMS Journal on Computing 01(21), 26–38 (2009)
29. Burer, S., Monteiro, R.D.C., Zhang, Y.: Rank-Two Relaxation Heuristics for Max-Cut and Other Binary Quadratic Programs. SIAM Journal on Optimization 12, 503–521 (2000)
30. Festa, P., Pardalos, P.M., Resende, M.G.C., Ribeiro, C.C.: Randomized heuristics for the max-cut problem. Optim. Methods Software 7, 1033–1058 (2002)
31. Krishnan, K., Mitchell, J.E.: A Semidefinite Programming Based Polyhedral Cut and Price Approach for the Maxcut Problem. Comput. Optim. Appl. 33(1), 51–71 (2006)

Complexity of Shallow Networks Representing Functions with Large Variations

Věra Kůrková[1] and Marcello Sanguineti[2]

[1] Institute of Computer Science, Academy of Sciences of the Czech Republic
Pod Vodárenskou věží 2, 18207 Prague, Czech Republic
vera@cs.cas.cz
[2] DIBRIS - University of Genoa
Via Opera Pia 13, 16145 Genova, Italy
marcello.sanguineti@unige.it

Abstract. Model complexities of networks representing multivariable functions is studied in terms of variational norms tailored to types of network units. It is shown that the size of the variational norm reflects both the number of hidden units and sizes of output weights. Lower bounds on growth of variational norms with increasing input dimension d are derived for Gaussian units and perceptrons. It is proven that variation of the d-dimensional parity with respect to Gaussian Support Vector Machines grows exponentially with d and for large values of d, almost any randomly-chosen Boolean function has variation with respect to perceptrons depending on d exponentially.

Keywords: One-hidden-layer networks, model complexity, representations of multivariable functions, perceptrons, Gaussian SVMs.

1 Introduction

A widely-used type of a neural-network architecture is the *one-hidden-layer network*. Typical computational units in the hidden layer are perceptrons, radial, and kernel units. Recently, one-hidden-layer networks have been called *shallow networks*, in contrast to *deep networks*, which contain more hidden layers (see, e.g., [1, 2]). A variety of learning algorithms for shallow networks have been developed and successfully applied (see, e.g., [3] and the references therein).

Shallow networks with many types of computational units are known to be universal approximators, i.e., they can approximate up to any desired accuracy all continuous functions or $\mathcal{L}^p$-functions on compact subsets of $\mathbb{R}^d$. In particular, the universal approximation property holds for one-hidden-layer networks with perceptrons having any non-polynomial activation function [4, 5] and with radial and kernel units satisfying mild conditions [6–8].

Available proofs of the universal approximation capability require potentially unlimited numbers of hidden units. Such numbers, which play the roles of *model complexities* of networks, are critical factors for practical implementations. Since typical neurocomputing applications deal with large numbers of variables, it

S. Wermter et al. (Eds.): ICANN 2014, LNCS 8681, pp. 331–338, 2014.

is particularly important to understand how quickly the model complexities of shallow networks grow with increasing input dimensions. Some estimates on rates of approximation of various classes of multivariable functions by networks with increasing numbers of hidden units were derived and employed to obtain estimates of model complexities (see, e.g., [9] and references therein).

On the other hand, limitations of computational capabilities of one-hidden-layer networks are less understood. Only few lower bounds on rates of approximations by such networks are known. Moreover, the bounds are mostly non-constructive and hold for types of computational units that are not commonly used [10, 11]. Also growth of sizes of weights is not well understood, although it was shown that in some cases, reasonable sizes of weights are more important for successful learning than bounds on the numbers of network units [12].

Recently, new learning algorithms that can be applied to deep networks were developed (see, e.g., [1, 2]). As training networks with more than one hidden layer involves complicated nonlinear optimization procedures, generally it is more difficult than training shallow ones. Hence, it is desirable to develop some theoretical background for characterization of tasks for which shallow networks require considerably larger numbers of units and/or sizes of weights than deep ones. Bengio et al. [13] suggested that a cause of large model complexities of shallow networks might be in the "amount of variations" of functions to be computed.

In this paper, we exploit the concept of *variational norm* from approximation theory as a measure of of variations of a function with respect to a type of computational units. We show that, besides playing a critical role in rates of approximation, the variational norm of a function with respect to a dictionary of computational units reflects both number of hidden units and sizes of the output weights in networks representing the function. For d-dimensional parities, we compare linear dependence on input dimension of their variational norms with respect to perceptrons with exponential growth of these norms with respect to dictionaries formed by Gaussian kernel units in Support Vector Machines. Our results show a seeming paradox: although almost any randomly-chosen Boolean function of d-variables has variation with respect to perceptrons depending on d exponentially, constructing such functions is difficult.

The paper is organized as follows. Section 2 contains basic concepts on shallow networks and dictionaries of computational units. Section 3 proposes a mathematical formalization of the concept of a "highly-varying function" in terms of variational norms and derives lower bounds on these norms for parities. Section 4 provides estimates of probabilistic measures of sets of functions with variations depending on d exponentially. Section 5 is a brief discussion.

2   Preliminaries

A widely-used network architecture is a *one-hidden-layer network with a single linear output*. Such a network with n hidden units computes input-output functions from the set

$$\operatorname{span}_n G := \left\{ \sum_{i=1}^{n} w_i g_i \,\middle|\, w_i \in \mathbb{R}, \, g_i \in G \right\},$$

where G, called *dictionary*, is a set of functions computable by a given type of units. In some literature, one-hidden-layer networks are called *shallow* networks.

We explore shallow networks with *perceptrons*, which compute functions of the form $\sigma(v \cdot . + b) : X \to \mathbb{R}$, where $\sigma : \mathbb{R} \to \mathbb{R}$ is an *activation function*. We denote by ϑ the *Heaviside activation function* defined as
$$\vartheta(t) := 0 \text{ for } t < 0 \quad \text{and} \quad \vartheta(t) := 1 \text{ for } t \geq 0$$
and by sgn the *signum activation function* $\text{sgn} : \mathbb{R} \to \{-1, 1\}$, defined as
$$\text{sgn}(t) := -1 \text{ for } t < 0 \quad \text{and sgn}(t) := 1 \quad \text{for } t \geq 0.$$
We denote by $H_d(X)$ the dictionary of functions on $X \subset \mathbb{R}^d$ computable by *Heaviside perceptrons*, i.e.,
$$H_d(X) := \{\vartheta(v \cdot . + b) : X \to \{0, 1\} \mid v \in \mathbb{R}^d, b \in \mathbb{R}\},$$
and by $P_d(X)$ the dictionary of functions on X computable by *signum perceptrons*, i.e.,
$$P_d(X) := \{\text{sgn}(v \cdot . + b) : X \to \{-1, 1\} \mid v \in \mathbb{R}^d, b \in \mathbb{R}\}.$$
We use the signum activation function as all units from $P_d(X)$ have the same norm $\sqrt{\text{card}\,X}$ and so are sometimes easier to work with. From point of view of model complexity, there is only a minor difference between dictionaries of signum and Heaviside perceptrons, as $\text{sgn}(t) = 2\vartheta(t) - 1$ and $\vartheta(t) = \frac{\text{sgn}(t)+1}{2}$.

For $X, U \subseteq \mathbb{R}^d$, we denote by $F_d^a(X, U)$ the dictionary of *Support-Vector-Machine (SVM) kernel units induced by the Gaussian kernel* with the width $1/a$ and centers in U, i.e.,
$$F_d^a(X, U) := \{e^{-a\|.-u\|^2} : X \to \mathbb{R} \mid u \in U\}.$$
When $X = U$, we write shortly $F_d^a(X)$. We denote
$$\mathcal{F}(X) := \{f \mid f : X \to \mathbb{R}\} \quad \text{and} \quad \mathcal{B}(X) := \{f \mid f : X \to \{-1, 1\}\}.$$
When $X \subset \mathbb{R}^d$ is finite, $\mathcal{F}(X)$ is isomorphic to the Euclidean space $\mathbb{R}^{\text{card}\,X}$. So, on $\mathcal{F}(X)$ we have the Euclidean inner product defined as $\langle f, g \rangle := \sum_{u \in X} f(u)g(u)$ and the Euclidean norm $\|f\| := \sqrt{\langle f, f \rangle}$. By $\cdot$ we denote the inner product on X, defined as $u \cdot v := \sum_{i=1}^d u_i v_i$.

Let $X \subset \bar{X} \subseteq \mathbb{R}$ and $G \subset \mathcal{F}(X)$ be obtained by restricting the functions from $\bar{G} \subset \mathcal{F}(\bar{X})$ to X. A lower bound on the number of units in a network from span G approximating $f \in \mathcal{F}(X)$ is also a lower bound on the number of units in a network from span $\bar{G}$ representing $\bar{f}$ such that $f = \bar{f}|_X$. Thus lower bounds for functions on finite subsets of $\mathbb{R}^d$, in particular on discretized cubes, e.g. $\{0, 1\}^d$, apply also to functions on infinite sets, e.g. $[0, 1]^d$.

Recall that all functions defined on finite subsets of $\mathbb{R}^d$ can be exactly represented by one-hidden-layer networks with sigmoidal perceptrons [14] or with Gaussian kernel units [15]. However, these two universality-type results assume that the number of network units is equal to $\text{card}\,X$.

3   Variation with Respect to a Dictionary

Bengio et al. [13] suggested that a cause of difficulties in representing functions by shallow networks of reasonable model complexities might be in "amounts of variations" of the functions. As an example of a class of functions having "high-variations", they considered parities on d-dimensional Boolean cubes $\{0, 1\}^d$.

They proved that a classification of points in $\{0,1\}^d$ according to their parities by SVM with Gaussian kernel units of any fixed width cannot be accomplished with less than $2^{d/2}$ units. The following theorem is a reformulation of [13, Theorem 2.4]. By $p^d : \{0,1\}^d \to \{-1,1\}$ we denote the d-*dimensional parity*, defined as $p^d(x) = 1$ if x has an even number of 1's and -1 otherwise. It is a special case of a generalized parity $p_u^d : \{0,1\}^d \to \{-1,1\}$, defined for every $u, x \in \{0,1\}^d$ as

$$p_u^d(x) := (-1)^{u \cdot x}.$$

So, $p^d = p_u^d$ where $u_i = 1$ for all $i = 1, \ldots, d$.

Theorem 1 (Bengio et al.). *Let d be a positive integer, $a > 0$, and $\{u_i \,|\, i = 1, \ldots, 2^d\}$ an ordering of the set $\{0,1\}^d$. If for some bias $b \in \mathbb{R}$ and weights $\{w_i \,|\, i = 1, \ldots, 2^d\} \subset \mathbb{R}$, $\mathrm{sgn}(\sum_{i=1}^{2^d} w_i e^{-a\|x - u_i\|^2} + b) = p(x)$ for all $x \in \{0,1\}^d$, then at least 2^{d-1} coefficients w_i are non-zero.*

Theorem 1 implies that if a function $f : \{0,1\}^d \to \mathbb{R}$ satisfies for some $b \in \mathbb{R}$ (i) $f(x) - b = p^d(x)$ for all $x \in \{0,1\}^d$ and (ii) $f \in \mathrm{span}_n F_d^a(\{0,1\}^d)$, then $n \geq 2^{d-1}$. So in this case, maximal generalization capability (maximal margin) is obtained at the expense of intractably large model complexity. On the other hand, it is known that parities can be computed by shallow networks with merely $d + 1$ Heaviside or signum perceptrons. Indeed, for all $x \in \{0,1\}^d$ we have

$$p_u^d(x) = (-1)^{x \cdot u} = \sum_{i=0}^{d} (-1)^i \vartheta(u \cdot x - i + 1/2). \tag{1}$$

The example of parities shows that the effect of high variations of a function on network complexity depends on a type of network units. In theory of approximation of functions by neural networks, the concept of *variation of a function with respect to a dictionary* has been studied. It was originally introduced by Barron [16] for Heaviside perceptrons as *variation with respect to half-spaces*. In Kůrková [17], this notion was extended to include general bounded sets of functions, in particular dictionaries of computational units. For a bounded subset G of a normed linear space $(\mathcal{X}, \|.\|_{\mathcal{X}})$, G-*variation (variation with respect to the set G)*, denoted by $\|.\|_G$, is defined as

$$\|f\|_G := \inf \{c \in \mathbb{R}_+ \mid f/c \in \mathrm{cl}_{\mathcal{X}} \, \mathrm{conv}\, (G \cup -G)\},$$

where $-G := \{-g \mid g \in G\}$, $\mathrm{cl}_{\mathcal{X}}$ denotes the closure with respect to the topology induced by the norm $\|\cdot\|_{\mathcal{X}}$, and conv denotes the convex hull. For properties of variation and its role in estimates of rates of approximation see [9, 18, 19] and the references therein.

The next proposition, which follows easily from the definition of G-variation, shows that $\|f\|_G$ reflects both the number of hidden units and the sizes of output weights in a shallow network with units from G representing f.

Proposition 1. *Let G be a bounded subset of a normed linear space $(\mathcal{X}, \|.\|)$, then for every $f \in \mathcal{X}$,* *(i)* $\|f\|_G \leq \left\{ \sum_{i=1}^k |w_i| \mid f = \sum_{i=1}^k w_i g_i , \, w_i \in \mathbb{R}, \, g_i \in G, k \in \mathbb{N} \right\};$

(ii) for G finite with card $G = k$,

$$\|f\|_G = \min \left\{ \sum_{i=1}^k |w_i| \mid f = \sum_{i=1}^k w_i g_i , \, w_i \in \mathbb{R}, \, g_i \in G \right\}.$$

Thus any representation of a function with large G-variation by a network with units from a dictionary G must have large number of units or the absolute values of some output weights must be large. By Proposition 1 and the equation (1), we get an upper bound $\|p_u^d\|_{H_d(\mathbb{R}^d)} \leq d+1$ on the variations of generalized parities with respect to Heaviside perceptrons. To estimate variations of p_u^d with respect to Gaussian SVMs on $\{0,1\}^d$, we use a lower bound on variational norm from [20] (see also [21]). By $G^\perp$ is denoted the *orthogonal complement of G*.

Theorem 2 ([20]). *Let* $(\mathcal{X}, \|.\|_{\mathcal{X}})$ *be a Hilbert space and G its bounded subset. Then for every* $f \in \mathcal{X} \setminus G^\perp$, *one has* $\|f\|_G \geq \frac{\|f\|^2}{\sup_{g \in G} |g \cdot f|}$.

The following theorem shows that the variations p^d and p_u^d with respect to the dictionary induced by Gaussian SVMs depend on d exponentially.

Theorem 3. *For every positive integer d and every* $a > 0$:
(i) $\|p^d\|_{F_d^a(\{0,1\}^d)} \geq 2^{d/2}$;

(ii) for every $u \in \{0,1\}^d$, $\|p_u^d\|_{F_d^a(\{0,1\}^d)} \geq \left(\frac{2}{(1+e^{-a})^2} \right)^{d/2}$.

Proof. By Theorem 2, $\|p_u^d\|_{F_d^a(\{0,1\}^d)} \geq \frac{\|p_u^d\|}{\sup_{g \in F_d^a(\{0,1\}^d)} |\langle p^d, g \rangle|}$.

(i) For the Gaussian g centered at $(0, \ldots, 0)$, we get $\langle p^d, g \rangle = \sum_{k=0}^d (-1)^k \binom{d}{k} e^{-ak}$. By the binomial formula we have $\sum_{k=0}^d (-1)^k \binom{d}{k} e^{-ak} = (1 - e^{-a})^d$. For the Gaussian centered at $x \in \{0,1\}^d$ such that $p^d(x) = 1$, we obtain the same value of the inner product with p^d by a suitable transformation of the co-ordinate system. When the Gaussian is centered at x with $p^d(x) = -1$, we get the same absolute value of the inner product by replacing p^d with $-p^d$ and by a transformation of the coordinate system. As $\|p^d\| = 2^{d/2}$, we have $\|p^d\|_{F_d^a(\{0,1\}^d)} \geq \frac{2^{d/2}}{(1-e^{-a})^d} \geq 2^{d/2}$.

(ii) For a generalized parity p_u^d and the Gaussian centered at $x \in \{0,1\}^d$, $|\langle p_u^d, g \rangle| = |\sum_{y \in \{0,1\}^d} -1^{u \cdot y} e^{-\|y-x\|}| \leq \sum_{k=0}^d \binom{d}{k} e^{-ak}$. Thus by the binomial formula $|\langle p_u^d, g \rangle| \leq (1 + e^{-a})^d$. So $\|p_u^d\|_{F_d^a(\{0,1\}^d)} \geq \frac{2^{d/2}}{(1+e^{-a})^d} = \left(\frac{2}{(1+e^{-a})^2} \right)^{d/2}$. □

Theorem 3 implies that the parity p^d is highly-varying with respect to the dictionary formed by Gaussian SVM units having any given width $1/a$. This lower bound confirms the conjecture of Bengio at al. [13] that a cause of large model complexities of networks representing functions are their high variations.

For a generalized parity p_u^d, the lower bound $\left(\frac{2}{(1+e^{-a})^2} \right)^{d/2}$ depends on the width $1/a$ of the Gaussian. For sufficiently flat Gaussians, whose widths $1/a$ satisfy $e^{-a} \leq \sqrt{2} - 1$, we have $\frac{2}{(1+e^{-a})^2} \geq 1$ and thus the lower bound from Theorem 3 grows exponentially with $d/2$.

4   Probability Distributions of Functions with Large Variations

We show that for "sufficiently small" dictionaries of functions from $\mathcal{B}(\{0,1\}^d)$, almost any randomly chosen function of the same norm as the norms of elements of the dictionary has variation depending on d exponentially. We estimates probability distribution of G-variations by exploiting the *Chernoff bound*.

Theorem 4 (Chernoff). *Let m be a positive integer, $Y_1, \ldots, Y_m$ independent uniformly distributed random variables with values in $\{-1,1\}$, and $\lambda > 0$. Then*

$$P\left(\left|\sum_{i=1}^m Y_i\right| \geq \lambda\right) \leq 2e^{-\frac{\lambda^2}{2m}}.$$

The following theorem estimates the probabilistic measures of sets of functions with large variations. For $f \in \mathcal{F}(X)$ with X finite, we denote $f^o := \frac{f}{\|f\|}$, where $\|.\|$ is induced by the Euclidean norm on $\mathbb{R}^{\text{card}\,X}$.

Theorem 5. *Let X be a finite set with $\text{card}\,X = m$, G a subset of $\mathcal{B}(X)$ with $\text{card}\,G = k$, μ a uniform probability measure on $\mathcal{B}(X)$, $\varepsilon \in (0,1)$, and $W_\varepsilon(G) := \{f \in \mathcal{B}(X) \mid \|f\|_G \geq \frac{1}{\varepsilon}\}$. Then $\mu(W_\varepsilon(G)) \geq 1 - 2k\,e^{-\frac{m\varepsilon^2}{2}}$.*

Proof. By Theorem 2, $W_\varepsilon(G)$ contains all $f \in \mathcal{B}(X)$ satisfying for all $g \in G$, $\langle f^o, g^o \rangle \leq \varepsilon$. Thus $W_\varepsilon(G)$ contains the complement of the set $\bigcup_{g \in G}\{f \in \mathcal{B}(X) \mid |\langle f^o, g^o \rangle| \geq \varepsilon\}$ and so $\mu(W_\varepsilon(G)) \geq 1 - \sum_{g \in G} \mu(\{h \in \mathcal{B}(X) \mid |\langle h^o, g^o \rangle| \geq \varepsilon\})$. We show that for every function $f \in \mathcal{B}(X)$, $P(|\langle h^o, f^o \rangle| \geq \varepsilon) \leq 2e^{-\frac{m\varepsilon^2}{2}}$.

First, we verify that this holds for the constant function f_1 defined for all $x \in X$ as $f_1(x) = 1$. Let $X = \{x_1, \ldots, x_m\}$. For every $h \in \mathcal{B}(X)$, we have $\langle h, f_1 \rangle = \sum_{i=1}^m h(x_i)$. By the Chernoff bound, $P(|\sum_{i=1}^m h(x_i)| \geq \lambda) \leq 2e^{-\frac{\lambda^2}{2m}}$. As for all $f \in \mathcal{B}(X)$, $\|f\| = \sqrt{m}$, setting $\varepsilon = \frac{\lambda}{m}$ we get $P(|\langle h^o, f_1^o \rangle| \geq \varepsilon) \leq 2e^{-\frac{\lambda^2}{2m}} = 2e^{-\frac{m\varepsilon^2}{2}}$. Any $f \in \mathcal{B}(X)$ can be obtained from f_1 by a finite sequence of sign-flips $F_x : \mathcal{B}(X) \to \mathcal{B}(X)$ defined as $F_x(f)(x) = -f(x)$ and $F_x(f)(y) = f(y)$ for all $y \neq x$. As the inner product is invariant under sign-flipping, for all $f \in \mathcal{B}(X)$, the probability distribution of inner products $\langle f^o, h^o \rangle$ on $\mathcal{B}(X)$ satisfies $P(|\langle f^o, h^o \rangle| \geq \varepsilon) \leq 2e^{-\frac{m\varepsilon^2}{2}}$. So in particular for every $g \in G$, $P(|\langle f^o, g^o \rangle| \geq \varepsilon) \leq 2e^{-\frac{m\varepsilon^2}{2}}$. Thus $\mu(W_\varepsilon(G)) \geq 1 - 2k\,e^{-\frac{m\varepsilon^2}{2}}$. $\qquad\square$

Theorem 5 can be applied to the dictionary $P_d(\{0,1\}^d)$ of signum perceptrons on $\{0,1\}^d$, which is relatively "small". Its size is the same as the cardinality of the set $H_d(\{0,1\}^d)$ of characteristic functions of half-spaces. An upper bound $\text{card}\,H_d(\{0,1\}^d) \leq 2^{d^2 - d\log_2 d + \mathcal{O}(d)}$ was derived by L. Schläfli [22] in 19th century. As $\text{card}\,P_d(\{0,1\}^d) = \text{card}\,H_d(\{0,1\}^d)$, we have $\text{card}\,P_d(\{0,1\}^d) \leq 2^{d^2}$.

Corollary 1. *Let d be a positive integer, μ a probability measure on $\mathcal{B}(\{0,1\}^d)$, $\varepsilon \in (0,1)$, and $W_\varepsilon(\mathcal{B}(\{0,1\}^d)) := \{f \in \mathcal{B}(\{0,1\}^d) \mid \|f\|_{P_d(\{0,1\}^d)} \geq \frac{1}{\varepsilon}\}$. Then*
$$\mu(W_\varepsilon(\mathcal{B}(\{0,1\}^d))) \geq 1 - 2^{d^2+1}\, e^{-\frac{2^d \varepsilon^2}{2}}.$$

For example setting $\varepsilon = 2^{-\frac{d-1}{4}}$, we obtain from Corollary 1 a lower bound $1 - 2^{d^2+1}e^{-2^{\frac{d-1}{2}}}$ on the probability that a function in $\mathcal{B}(\{0,1\}^d)$ has variation with respect to signum perceptrons greater than $2^{\frac{d-1}{4}}$. Although according to Corollary 1, $P_d(\{0,1\}^d)$-variations of most of the functions in $\mathcal{B}(\{0,1\}^d)$ depend on d exponentially, the only concrete example of such a function of which we are aware is the well-known function from theory of Boolean functions called "inner product mod 2" [23]. For a lower bound on its variation with respect to $P_d(\{0,1\}^d)$ see [20].

5   Discussion

Motivated by the conjecture of Bengio et al. [13] that representations of functions with high variations by shallow networks require "large" networks, we investigated the effect of variational norms of functions with respect to dictionaries of computational units to model complexities of networks representing the functions. We showed that for finite dictionaries, variational norms reflect both numbers of units and sizes of the output weights. It is analogous to theory of circuit complexity, where classes of functions defined by constraints on both numbers of gates and sizes of output weights have been investigated. In particular, the class $\widehat{LT_2}$ of depth-2 polynomial size threshold-gate circuits with weights being polynomially bounded integers plays an important role [23]. We derived an exponentially-increasing lower bounds on variational norms with respect to Gaussian SVMs and Heaviside perceptrons.

Acknowledgments. V.K. was partially supported by the grant COST LD13002 of the Ministry of Education of the Czech Republic and institutional support of the Institute of Computer Science RVO 67985807. M.S. was supported by the Gruppo Nazionale per l'Analisi Matematica, la Probabilità e le loro Applicazioni (GNAMPA) of the Istituto Nazionale di Alta Matematica (INdAM) and by the Progetto di Ricerca di Ateneo 2013 "Processing High-Dimensional data with Applications to Life Sciences", granted by the University of Genoa.

References

1. Bengio, Y.: Learning deep architectures for AI. Foundations and Trends in Machine Learning 2, 1–127 (2009)
2. Hinton, G.E., Osindero, S., Teh, Y.W.: A fast learning algorithm for deep belief nets. Neural Computation 18, 1527–1554 (2006)
3. Chow, T.W.S., Cho, S.Y.: Neural Networks and Computing: Learning Algorithms and Applications. World Scientific (2007)

4. Leshno, M., Lin, V.Y., Pinkus, A., Schocken, S.: Multilayer feedforward networks with a nonpolynomial activation function can approximate any function. Neural Networks 6, 861–867 (1993)
5. Pinkus, A.: Approximation theory of the MLP model in neural networks. Acta Numerica 8, 143–195 (1999)
6. Park, J., Sandberg, I.: Approximation and radial-basis-function networks. Neural Computation 5, 305–316 (1993)
7. Mhaskar, H.N.: Versatile Gaussian networks. In: Proc. of IEEE Workshop of Nonlinear Image Processing, pp. 70–73 (1995)
8. Kůrková, V.: Some comparisons of networks with radial and kernel units. In: Villa, A.E.P., Duch, W., Érdi, P., Masulli, F., Palm, G. (eds.) ICANN 2012, Part II. LNCS, vol. 7553, pp. 17–24. Springer, Heidelberg (2012)
9. Kainen, P.C., Kůrková, V., Sanguineti, M.: Dependence of computational models on input dimension: Tractability of approximation and optimization tasks. IEEE Transactions on Information Theory 58, 1203–1214 (2012)
10. Maiorov, V.: On best approximation by ridge functions. J. of Approximation Theory 99, 68–94 (1999)
11. Maiorov, V., Pinkus, A.: Lower bounds for approximation by MLP neural networks. Neurocomputing 25, 81–91 (1999)
12. Bartlett, P.L.: The sample complexity of pattern classification with neural networks: The size of the weights is more important than the size of the network. IEEE Trans. on Information Theory 44, 525–536 (1998)
13. Bengio, Y., Delalleau, O., Roux, N.L.: The curse of highly variable functions for local kernel machines. In: Advances in Neural Information Processing Systems 18, pp. 107–114. MIT Press (2006)
14. Ito, Y.: Finite mapping by neural networks and truth functions. Mathematical Scientist 17, 69–77 (1992)
15. Micchelli, C.A.: Interpolation of scattered data: Distance matrices and conditionally positive definite functions. Constructive Approximation 2, 11–22 (1986)
16. Barron, A.R.: Neural net approximation. In: Narendra, K. (ed.) Proc. 7th Yale Workshop on Adaptive and Learning Systems, pp. 69–72. Yale University Press (1992)
17. Kůrková, V.: Dimension-independent rates of approximation by neural networks. In: Warwick, K., Kárný, M. (eds.) Computer-Intensive Methods in Control and Signal Processing. The Curse of Dimensionality, pp. 261–270. Birkhäuser, Boston (1997)
18. Kůrková, V., Sanguineti, M.: Comparison of worst-case errors in linear and neural network approximation. IEEE Transactions on Information Theory 48, 264–275 (2002)
19. Gnecco, G., Sanguineti, M.: On a variational norm tailored to variable-basis approximation schemes. IEEE Trans. on Information Theory 57, 549–558 (2011)
20. Kůrková, V., Savický, P., Hlaváčková, K.: Representations and rates of approximation of real-valued Boolean functions by neural networks. Neural Networks 11, 651–659 (1998)
21. Kůrková, V.: Complexity estimates based on integral transforms induced by computational units. Neural Networks 33, 160–167 (2012)
22. Schläfli, L.: Theorie der vielfachen Kontinuität. Zürcher & Furrer, Zürich (1901)
23. Roychowdhury, V., Siu, K., Orlitsky, A.: Neural models and spectral methods. In: Roychowdhury, V., Siu, K., Orlitsky, A. (eds.) Theorertical Advances in Neural Computation and Learning, pp. 3–36. Kluwer Academic Publishers (1997)

Visualizing Hierarchical Representation in a Multilayered Restricted RBF Network

Pitoyo Hartono[1], Paul Hollensen[2], and Thomas Trappenberg[2]

[1] School of Engineering, Chukyo University, Nagoya, Japan
[2] School of Computer Science, Dalhousie University, Halifax, Canada

Abstract. In this study we propose a hierarchical neural network that is able to generate a topographical map in its internal layer. The map significantly differs from the conventional Kohonen's SOM, in that it preserves the topological characteristics in relevance to the context, for example the labels, of the data. This map is useful if we are interested in visualizing the underlying characteristics of the classifiability of the data that traditionally cannot be visualized with the standard SOM. In this paper, we expand our network into a multilayered structure that allows us visualize and thus better understand on how the neural network perceives the given data in the light of classification task.

Keywords: Self-Organizing Map, Supervised Learning, Hierarchical Representation.

1 Introduction

In our previous study [1], we introduced a model of a hierarchical supervised neural network based on Radial Basis Function (RBF) Network [2], which we named Restricted Radial Basis Function (rRBF) Network. This network internally generates, through its learning process, a topographical map that is similar but differs from the traditional Self-Organizing Map (SOM) [3]. The primary difference between the topographical map in our proposed network and the traditional SOM is that our map preserves not only the topological characteristics of the data but also the underlying relation between the data and their context (for example, labels). We therefore call this map Context Relevant Self-Organizing Map (CRSOM). Some of the mathematical difference between CRSOM and SOM are discussed in [1]. In the previous study, through many experiments, we showed that our proposed network is able to organize an internal representation that enables the network to relate the input data with their context. In contrast to the conventional SOM and many of its variants [4–6] that attempt to capture the topological nature of high dimensional data and visualize it in low dimensional space independent of the context of the data, the topographical arrangement in CRSOM is highly dependent on the context of the data. Therefore, the same data will be ordered differently with each different context . This is interesting because there are many cases where data should be interpreted based on their context, for example in classification problems. Being able to visualize data in this light will give us understanding not only on the structure of the data but also the underlying characteristics of the classification problem. The other

S. Wermter et al. (Eds.): ICANN 2014, LNCS 8681, pp. 339–346, 2014.

difference is that unlike SOM, CRSOM is optimal with regard to a well-defined energy function.

In the previous study, we investigated a single-hidden layered CRSOM. However, recent studies on the deep structure network [7–9] show that many problems benefit from multilayer representation. We think that the visualization features of CRSOM are potentially important in helping us to understand the underlying mapping characteristics of deep structure networks. Hence, in this study we expand the single hidden layer rRBF into a multilayered structure network with the focus on elaborating the hierarchical learning process and visualizing the hierarchical representation of the network.

2   Multilayerd Restricted Radial Basis Function Network

In this study, we expand the rRBF, proposed in the previous study, into a multilayered structure shown in Fig. 1. This rRBF constitutes an input layer, N hidden layers and an output layer. Each hidden layer is composed from many neurons that are arranged in two dimensional grid where each neuron is associated with a reference vector as in the conventional SOM. The running and learning processes of the proposed multilayered rRBF are as follows. Receiving an input vector $X(t)$ in the input layer at time t, the rRBF selects a winner, win^1 among the neurons in the first hidden layer as

$$win^1 = \arg\min_i \|X(t) - W_i^1(t)\|^2 \tag{1}$$

In Eq. 1, W_i^1 denotes the reference vector associated with the i-th neuron in the first hidden layer.

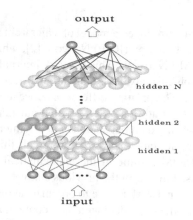

output

hidden N

hidden 2

hidden 1

input

Fig. 1. Multilayer Restricted Radial Basis Function Network

After the winner is decided, the output of the i-th neuron in the first hidden layer, O_i^1, is calculated as

$$O_i^1(t) = e^{-I_i^1(t)}\sigma(win^1, i, t) \tag{2}$$
$$I_i^1(t) = \|X(t) - W_i^1(t)\|^2.$$

Here, $\sigma()$ is the neighborhood function that is a decreasing function with regards to the distance between the winner, win^1, and the i th neuron in the the first hidden layer, at time t. Similarly, the winner in the k-th hidden layer is calculated as

$$win^k = \arg\min_m \|O^{k-1}(t) - W_m^k(t)\|^2 \ (k > 1), \tag{3}$$

where O^{k-1} is the output vector of the $(k-1)$-th hidden layer that becomes the input to the k-th hidden layer, and W_m^k is the the reference vector associated with the m-th neuron in the k-th hidden layer. The output of the m-th neuron in the k-th hidden layer is then computed as

$$O_m^k(t) = e^{-I_m^k(t)}\sigma(win^k, m, t) \tag{4}$$
$$I_m^k(t) = \|O^{k-1}(t) - W_m^k(t)\|^2$$

For an rRBF with N hidden layers, the value of the l-th output neuron, O_l^{out}, is calculated as follows,

$$O_l^{out}(t) = f(I_l^{out}(t)) \tag{5}$$
$$I_l^{out}(t) = \sum_n v_{nl}(t)O_n^N(t) - \theta_l(t),$$

where v_{nl} is the connection weight leading from the n-th neuron in the last hidden layer to the l-th output neuron, and θ_l is the threshold value of the l-th output neuron. For an output receiving a teacher signal, $\mathbf{T}$, the evaluation function, E is chosen as

$$E(t) = \sum_l (O_l^{out}(t) - T_l(t))^2. \tag{6}$$

To minimize the error function in Eq. 6, the connection weights between the N-th hidden layer and the output layer can be modified using gradient descend,

$$v_{nl}(t+1) = v_{nl}(t) - \eta_o \frac{\partial E(t)}{\partial v_{nl}(t)} \tag{7}$$

$$\frac{\partial E(t)}{\partial v_{nl}(t)} = \delta_l^{out}(t)O_n^N(t) \tag{8}$$
$$\delta_l^{out}(t) = (O_l^{out}(t) - T_l(t))O_l^{out}(t)(1 - O_l^{out}(t))$$

Similarly, the reference vectors in the N-th hidden layer can be modified as follows.

$$W_{ij}^N(t+1) = W_{ij}^N(t) - \eta_h \frac{\partial E(t)}{\partial W_{ij}^N(t)} \tag{9}$$

$$\frac{\partial E(t)}{\partial W_{ij}^N(t)} = \delta_j^N(t)\sigma(win^N, j, t)(O_i^{N-1}(t) - W_{ij}^N(t)) \tag{10}$$

In Equation 10, δ_j^N is as follows.

$$\delta_j^N(t) = -4(\sum_l v_{jl}(t)\delta_l^{out}(t))e^{-I_j^N(t)}. \tag{11}$$

The reference vector is then corrected as

$$W_{ij}^N(t+1) = W_{ij}^N(t) + \eta_h \delta_j^N \sigma(win^N, j, t)(O_i^{N-1}(t) - W_{ij}^N(t)) \qquad (12)$$

Here, W_{ij}^N denotes the i-th component of the j-th reference vector in the N-th hidden layer, while O_j^{N-1} is the output of the j-th neuron in the $(N-1)$-th hidden layer. Because its closeness to the output layer, naturally the N-th hidden layer is the first one to benefit from the supervised error signal received in the output layer. In Eq. 11, δ_j^N is the error signal backpropagated to the j-th neuron on the N-th hidden layer, which is the product of the weighted sum of error signals of the output neurons with the excitation level $e^{-I_j^N}$. Only neurons with large excitation levels contribute to the overall error, and hence benefit from the learning process. This error backpropagation characteristics is similar to that of Delta Rule in Multilayered Perceptron [10]. However, neuron activation in rRBF ensures that the learning process in the hidden layers is locally constrained and sparse. The locality and sparsity of the learning process allow the rRBF to generate a topographical internal representation that differs from that of SOM.

From Eq. 12 it is clear that the reference vector modification is regulated by δ^N. If $\delta^N = 1$ then the modification is the same as in the learning process of SOM. However, here the regulatory signal δ^N depends on how well the network approximate the given teacher signal, thus the context of the input, where δ^N can either be positive or negative. When $\delta^N > 0$, the reference vector is corrected in the direction of O^{N-1}, the output vector of from the previous layer, while when $\delta^N < 0$ the reference vector is repelled from the output vector, thus executing a kind of repelling SOM. It is important to notice that although our learning procedure differs in principal with the Willshaw-Von der Malsburg SOM [11], the regulatory signal δ^N enables an inhibitory learning as in this model, a characteristic that is missing from Kohonen's SOM.

Similarly, for the lower layers, for $(0 < \alpha < N)$, the weight modification can be written as follows.

$$W_{ij}^{N-\alpha}(t+1) = W_{ij}^{N-\alpha}(t) + \eta_h \delta_j^{N-\alpha}(t)\sigma(win^{N-\alpha}, j, t)(O_i^{N-(\alpha+1)}(t) - W_{ij}^{N-\alpha}(t))$$
$$\alpha \in \{1, 2, 3, \cdots\} \qquad (13)$$

Here,

$$\delta_j^{N-\alpha}(t) = (-2)^{\alpha+2}(\sum_l \delta_l^{N-\alpha+1}(t)(O_j^{N-\alpha}(t) - W_{jl}^{N-\alpha+1}(t)))e^{-I_j^{N-\alpha}(t)} \qquad (14)$$

$$O_i^0 = X_i \qquad (15)$$

The reference vectors modifications in the hidden layers described in Eq. 13 and Eq. 14 minimize the learning error in Eq. 6, hence each layer is organized to enable the neural network to correctly output the context of the given input. The learning process indicates that CRSOM is an optimum internal representation for the rRBF, thus we can argue that the visualization of the internal layers offers us information not only on the underlying topological characteristics of the data but more importantly on the hierarchical information processing process executed by the classifier.

3 Experiments

In the first experiment, we apply two-layered rRBF into two dimensional artificial data with a class distribution as shown in Fig. 2, where the two classes are represented with two different colors. This problem can be considered as a continous XOR problem. The CRSOMs of two-layered rRBF are shown in Fig. 4. The left-hand side of the figure shows the first hidden layer's CRSOM, while the right-hand side shows the second hidden layer's CRSOM which is close to the output layer.

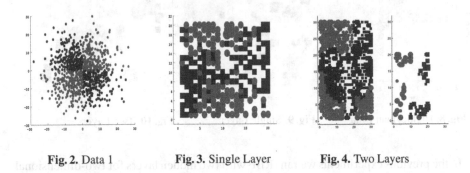

Fig. 2. Data 1   Fig. 3. Single Layer   Fig. 4. Two Layers

Figure 3 shows that the single layer rRBF generates an internal representation that is similar to the class distribution of the original data, while Fig. 4 depicts a more hierarchically structured representation. In the first hidden layer, the rRBF formed a representation with distinctive clusters of classes, while in the second hidden layer it formed a sparser and more organized representation in the light of the class-separability of the original data. Interestingly, while this is a non-linear problem, in the second layer this problem is basically liniarized.

The next problem, which is also an artificial two dimensional two-class problem, is shown in Fig. 5. The internal representation of single-layered rRBF, which is quite complicated and not very structured is shown in Fig. 6. The layered representation in Fig. 7 shows a gradual formation of a structured representation, in which although there is no emergence of a linear structure, the separability of the data is obvious.

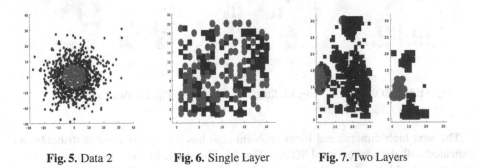

Fig. 5. Data 2   Fig. 6. Single Layer   Fig. 7. Two Layers

The next problem is two dimensional two-class Highleyman problem [12], shown in Fig. 8. The representation of a single hidden layered rRBF is shown in Fig. 9, while the two hidden layered representation is shown in Fig. 10. From Fig. 10 it is clear that rRBF captured the classification characteristics of this problem, where there is an overlapping region that will produce classification errors.

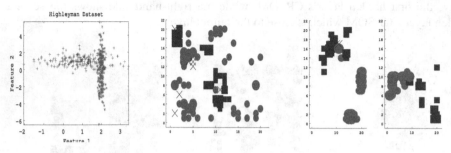

Fig. 8. Highleyman Data   **Fig. 9.** Single Layer   **Fig. 10.** Two Layers

In the previous experiments we ran rRBF with two hidden layers for two-dimensional problems. The next experiments consider rRBF with two hidden layers for higher multi-dimensional problems. The first problem is the Iris classification problem, a four dimensional three-class problem. As this is a four-dimensional problem, the class distribution is shown using conventional SOM in Fig. 11. The single layer representation in Fig. 12 indicates that the three classes are well clustered, hence likely to be nicely separable. However, the layered representation shown in Fig. 13 nicely captured the well-known characteristics of this problem, where one of the classes is linearly separable with the other two, while those two are not linearly separable. In those figures, $\times$ depicts a neuron that is activated for inputs belonging to different classes.

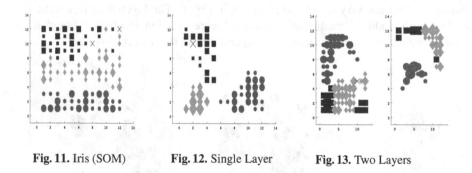

Fig. 11. Iris (SOM)   **Fig. 12.** Single Layer   **Fig. 13.** Two Layers

The next high dimensional Pima problem also has a complex class distribution as indicated with the conventional SOM in Fig. 14. The single hidden layer representation shown in Fig. 15 also formed a disperse class representation, while the visualization of the second hidden layer shown Fig. 16 illustrates that this problem can be linearized

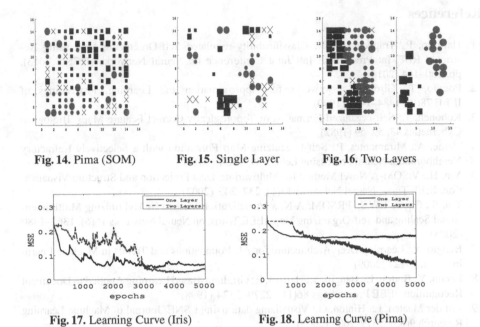

Fig. 14. Pima (SOM)   **Fig. 15.** Single Layer   **Fig. 16.** Two Layers

Fig. 17. Learning Curve (Iris)   **Fig. 18.** Learning Curve (Pima)

with the two hidden layered rRBF. The learning curves for the last two problems are shown in Fig. 17 and Fig. 18.

In all of the experiments above, the learning rates were set so that $\eta_o = 0.003$ and $\eta_h = 0.015$, while the size of each map is $\lfloor \sqrt{N} \rfloor \times \lfloor \sqrt{N} \rfloor$, where N is the size of the data. Before the learning process, the connection weights and the preference vectors were randomly initialized.

4 Conclusions and Future Works

In this paper we expand our previously proposed rRBF into a multilayered structure and illustrate its learning characteristics. Through the experiments we show that the multilayered rRBF is able to generate a hierarchical representation that reflects its ability to recreate the context of the given input. We also argue that the topographical representations in rRBF is different from that of the conventional SOM. When the conventional SOM visualizes the topological characteristics of the raw data independent of their context, our proposed rRBF visualizes how the network perceives the data in the light of their context. The CRSOMs as the internal representation of the rRBF may help us in understanding how the network makes a decision. Our immediate future works includes the application of rRBF into semisupervised learning, context drift learning and visualization of big data.

References

1. Hartono, P., Trappenberg, T.: Classificability-regulated Self-Organizing Map using Restricted RBF. In: Proc. IEEE Int. Joint Conference on Neural Networks (IJCNN 2013), pp. 160–164 (2013)
2. Poggio, T., Girosi, F.: Networks for Approximation and Learning. Proceedings of IEEE 78(9), 1484–1487 (1990)
3. Kohonen, T.: Self-organized Formation of Topologically Correct Feature Maps. Biological Cybernetics 43, 59–69 (1982)
4. Neme, A., Miramontes, P.: Self-Organizing Map Formation with a Selectively Refractory Neighborhood. Neural Processing Letters 39, 1–24 (2014)
5. Yin, H.: ViSOM-A Novel Method for Multivariate Data Projection and Structure Visualization. IEEE Trans. Neural Networks 13(1), 237–243 (2002)
6. Wu, S., Chow, T.W.S.: PRSOM: A New Visualization Method by Hybridizing Multidimensional Scaling and Self-Organizing Map. IEEE Trans. on Neural Networks 16(6), 1362–1380 (2005)
7. Bengio, Y.: Learning Deep Architecture for AI. Foundations and Trends in Machine Learning 2(1), 1–127 (2009)
8. Lecun, Y., Bottou, L., Bengio, Y., Haffner, P.: Gradient-Based Learning Applied to Document Recognition. IEEE Proceedings 86(11), 2279–2324 (1998)
9. van der Maaten, L., Hinton, G.: Visualizing data using t-SNE. Journal of Machine Learning Research 9(85), 2579–2605 (2008)
10. Rumelhart, D., McClelland, J.: Learning Internal Representation by Error Propagation. Parallel Distributed Processing, vol. 1, pp. 318–362. MIT Press (1984)
11. Willshaw, D.J., Von Der Malsburg, C.: How patterned neural connections can be set up by self-organization. Proc. Royal Society of London 194(1117), 431–445 (1976)
12. Duin, R.P.W., et al.: PRTools4, A Matlab Toolbox for Pattern Recognition. Delft University of Technology (2007)

Contingent Features for Reinforcement Learning

Nathan Sprague

Department of Computer Science,
James Madison University,
Harrisonburg, VA 22807, USA
spragunr@jmu.edu

Abstract. Applying reinforcement learning algorithms in real-world domains is challenging because relevant state information is often embedded in a stream of high-dimensional sensor data. This paper describes a novel algorithm for learning task-relevant features through interactions with the environment. The key idea is that a feature is likely to be useful to the degree that its dynamics can be controlled by the actions of the agent. We describe an algorithm that can find such features and we demonstrate its effectiveness in an artificial domain.

1 Introduction

A longstanding challenge in the area of reinforcement learning is scaling up to handle problems with high-dimensional and continuous state spaces. Even in cases where the intrinsic dimensionality of a task may be relatively low, the relevant state information is often embedded in a high-dimensional stream of sensor data.

There has been progress over the last few years in developing feature learning algorithms that extract task-relevant state information. Some approaches explicitly search for features that improve value function estimation [10,11,8,3], while others examine the dynamics of state transitions in order to discover low-dimensional features based on the temporal structure of the task [9,12,7].

Each of these general approaches has drawbacks. Approaches based on value function estimation are dependent on the quality of the reward signal. Where reward is infrequent or absent, little learning can occur. On the other hand, unsupervised approaches based on state dynamics may waste representational power on aspects of the state that are not relevant to reaching the agent's goals.

The idea explored in this paper is that features are likely to be useful to the degree that their dynamics can be controlled by the actions of the agent. Aspects of the environment that are outside of the agent's control are less likely to be task-relevant.

The contingent feature analysis algorithm (CFA) described in this paper quantifies this notion of action contingency by searching for features that have lower variance in their temporal derivative when the agent chooses *not* to act than when it chooses to act. We refer to these as contingent features because their values are contingent upon the agent's actions.

S. Wermter et al. (Eds.): ICANN 2014, LNCS 8681, pp. 347–354, 2014.

The remainder of this paper will describe the contingent feature optimization problem, describe an algorithm for minimizing the objective, and illustrate the effectiveness of the algorithm in an artificial environment.

2 Contingent Feature Analysis

The following description of the contingent feature analysis algorithm builds on the notation and structure introduced by Wiskott and Sejnowski [14] in describing slow feature analysis (SFA). Slow feature analysis discovers slowly varying features overall: features that have a small temporal derivative. In contrast, CFA searches for features with temporal derivatives that have higher variance when actions are taken than when they are not taken. While the two algorithms have a similar structure, the quantities being minimized, and the resulting features, are entirely different.

The CFA algorithm handles signal, action pairs of the form $(\boldsymbol{x}(t), a(t))$, where t indicates time, the $\boldsymbol{x}$ values are are potentially high-dimensional signal vectors, and the action values are drawn from a discrete set of actions $\mathcal{A}$. We will assume that $\mathcal{A}$ contains a designated "No Operation" (NOP) action: an action that the agent may choose in order to avoid driving a state transition.

2.1 The CFA Objective

The optimization problem is to find a vector-valued feature function $\boldsymbol{g}(\boldsymbol{x})$ such that the output signals $y_j := g_j(\boldsymbol{x})$ minimize the objective

$$\langle (\dot{y}_j - \langle \dot{y}_j \rangle)^2 \rangle_{a(t)=NOP} \qquad \text{(variance of derivative after } NOP \text{ actions)} \tag{1}$$

Subject to the following three constraints:

$$\langle y_j \rangle = 0 \quad \text{(zero mean)}, \tag{2}$$

$$\langle (\dot{y}_j - \langle \dot{y}_j \rangle)^2 \rangle = 1 \quad \text{(unit variance of derivative overall)}, \tag{3}$$

$$\forall i < j, \quad \langle \dot{y}_i, \dot{y}_j \rangle - \langle \dot{y}_i \rangle \langle \dot{y}_j \rangle = 0 \quad \text{(decorrelated derivative)}, \tag{4}$$

Where $\langle \cdot \rangle$ indicates temporal averaging, and $\dot{y}$ is the derivative of y with respect to time. We assume that signal values are sampled at discrete time intervals, and that temporal derivatives are approximated by finite differences.

Given constraint 3, the objective in 1 is minimal for features that have low variance in their temporal derivative after NOP actions relative to the overall variance of their temporal derivative. In other words, contingent features change more when actions are taken than when they are not taken. Constraint 4 ensures that different features carry different information, and it imposes an ordering on the features: y_1 is the most contingent feature, y_2 is less contingent since it must obey an additional constraint, etc. Constraint 2 prevents the solution from being under-constrained.

In this paper we will only consider the linear case where $g_j(x) = w_j^T x$ for some weight vectors w_j. It would be straightforward to extend this to the non-linear case by expanding x using a fixed set of non-linear functions, and then searching for appropriate weight vectors in the expanded space.

2.2   The CFA Algorithm

The CFA objective may be minimized as described below. Raw training signals will be indicated with a tilde, test data with a hat, and symbols with neither a tilde nor a hat will refer to normalized training data.

1. Calculate the time derivative of the raw signal: $\dot{\tilde{x}}(t)$.
2. Center and whiten the resulting derivatives:

$$\dot{x}(t) = S(\dot{\tilde{x}}(t) - \langle \dot{\tilde{x}} \rangle) \tag{5}$$

   Here S is a whitening matrix that rescales the derivatives so that they have an identity covariance matrix. The matrix S can be found using principal components analysis. This step ensures that the final features will satisfy constraint 3.
3. Separate out the whitened signal derivatives that correspond to NOP actions:

$$\dot{n}(t) := \{\dot{x}(t) \mid a(t) = NOP\} \tag{6}$$

4. Perform PCA on the $\dot{n}(t)$ values. The contingent features are determined by the eigenvectors with the smallest eigenvalues. For example:

$$y_1(t) = p_1^T S(\dot{\tilde{x}}(t) - \langle \tilde{x} \rangle)$$
$$= w_1^T (\dot{\tilde{x}}(t) - \langle \tilde{x} \rangle) \tag{7}$$

   Where p_1 is the principal component with the smallest corresponding eigenvalue. The magnitude of each eigenvalue provides a measurement of the contingency of the corresponding feature.
5. The contingent features of test data may then be calculated by subtracting the training mean from the test signal, and multiplying the result by the appropriate weight vector:

$$\hat{y}_i(t) = w_i^T (\hat{x}(t) - \langle \tilde{x} \rangle) \tag{8}$$

It may seem odd that the sphering matrix and principal components are calculated based on the time derivatives of the signal data, while the features themselves are calculated directly from the signal values. The resulting features do satisfy constraints 3 and 4. Since the derivative values are approximated by taking the difference between subsequent signal vectors, $\dot{x}(t) \approx x(t+1) - x(t)$, multiplying the signal vectors by the weight vectors has the desired effect on the derivative as well.

The overall time complexity of this algorithm is the same as slow feature analysis: $O(NI^2 + I^3)$, where N is the number of samples, and I is the dimensionality of the input signal [2].

Fig. 1. a. The grid navigation task b. *top*: Weight vectors discovered by slow feature analysis *bottom*: Feature activations at each grid position. The bottom row corresponds to the data from Figure 1 of [7].

2.3   Experiment

In order to illustrate the CFA algorithm we will apply it to a variant of a task introduced by Lange and Riedmiller [6]. The task involves an agent moving in a 6×6 grid world containing an L-shaped wall. The agent's sensory input takes the form of a 30×30 image of the environment showing the position of the agent as a small square. Each pixel is corrupted with noise drawn from the distribution $\mathcal{N}(0, .01)$ and then clipped so that all values remain in the range [0,1]. There are four possible actions that each move the agent by exactly one grid square in one of the cardinal directions. Actions that would result in a collision with the wall or with a boundary have no effect. Figure 1a illustrates the task. This is an intrinsically low-dimensional task embedded in a high-dimensional sensor space.

Luciw and Schmidhuber used this same task as a test-bed for their incremental slow feature analysis algorithm [7]. It has been shown that slow feature analysis is a function approximation of Laplacian Eigenmaps, which provide the basis vectors for proto-value function reinforcement learning [13]. This suggests that slow feature analysis could be a useful approach to feature learning in high-dimensional RL tasks. Indeed, Luciw and Schmidhuber show that a linear reinforcement learning agent can reach near-optimal performance on this task using the four slowest features as a basis. Figure 1b shows the four slowest weight vectors discovered by (non-incremental) slow feature analysis for the environment described above. These features were learned from a sequence of 40,000 randomly generated actions[1].

Figure 2a illustrates a modified version of this task that will be used to demonstrate the CFA algorithm. In this version of the task there are three moving squares. The agent is represented by the small red square, while the green and blue squares are distractors that are not under the control of the agent. The agent's sensor data takes the form of $30 \times 30 \times 3$ color images. There are now five possible actions: the original four plus a *NOP* action which does not result in a movement. Movements that would result in a collision with a wall or another agent have no effect. A reward of 1.0 is received when the agent enters a designated goal location in the upper-right region of the grid. All other actions result in zero reward.

---

[1] Slow feature analysis was performed using the MDP library [15].

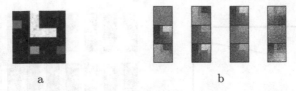

Fig. 2. a. Modified task, with distractors b. Weight vectors discovered by slow feature analysis

In order to gather training data for the following experiments, actions are chosen uniformly at random over the course of 40,000 time steps. The green and blue squares move according to the same logic as the red square, but their movements will have no relationship to the actions chosen by the agent.

In this domain the sensor data associated with each square is segregated into a distinct color channel. This should make it possible to discover a set of features that encode the position of the red square while filtering out the positions of the distractors. This also makes it possible to assess the success of the algorithm by visually inspecting the feature weights. Since the dynamics of the green and blue squares are not under the control of the agent, there should be no structure in the corresponding feature weights.

Figure 2b illustrates the top four features discovered by slow feature analysis on this task. Each column represents a single weight vector, with the top box representing the red channel and the next two boxes representing the green and blue channels respectively. Not surprisingly, these features show no preference for any of the three color channels. Each feature represents a mixture of information from multiple channels. If the goal is to find a feature space that will enable the red agent to navigate in this environment, these features are not ideal.

Figure 3 shows the result of running the CFA algorithm on this data. The left side of Figure 3 shows the eigenvalues associated with the first 100 contingent features. It can be seen that there is abrupt transition between the contingent and non-contingent features in this task. The right-hand side of the figure shows the first thirty features, arranged from most to least contingent (or, equivalently, from lowest to highest eigenvalue).

The most notable attribute of these features is that they only carry information that is related to the agent's position: there is no structure in either the green or blue color channels.

It is also notable that the most contingent features in this task are features with high spatial frequency: as the degree of contingency goes down, the spatial frequency of the features goes down as well, with the last few features showing similarities to the weights discovered by slow feature analysis.

For this task, features with high spatial frequency will also have a large time derivative. The CFA algorithm does not explicitly optimize for features with large derivatives. Instead, the ordering of the features here is likely explained by the fact that the image noise causes background noise in the derivatives in every direction. When the derivative data is whitened, that noise will become proportionally larger in directions that had a low temporal derivative to start

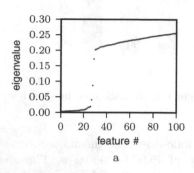 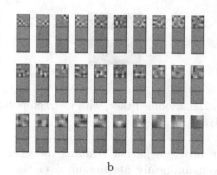

a   b

Fig. 3. a: Eigenvalues associated with the first 100 contingent features b: Weight vectors discovered by contingent feature analysis

with. After the PCA step, those dimensions will then have proportionally larger eigenvalues since the same noise exists regardless of which actions are taken.

In algorithms such as PCA and SFA, it is common to extract the top two or three features and discard the rest. Figure 3 suggests that CFA shouldn't be used in that way. There is a clear demarcation between contingent and non-contingent features, but it appears that there are informative features at the lower end of the range of contingency values. This suggests a two-pass approach where CFA is used to extract a set of contingent features, while a second dimensionality reduction algorithm is applied in the resulting feature space.

Figure 4a shows the result of performing slow feature analysis in the space defined by the 30 contingent features from Figure 3. The red channel here is strikingly similar to the single-agent slow features from Figure 1.

Figure 4b compares several feature types in terms of their effectiveness for reinforcement learning. Each data point represents the average reward received by a policy learned using the indicated number of features. Each policy is evaluated over the course of 1000 trials. Individual trials are terminated after 50 steps or when the agent reaches the goal location. Policies are learned using Least-Squares Policy Iteration (LSPI) applied to the same 40,000 training samples [5]. A small amount of L2 regularization is used to ensure convergence [4].

As expected, contingent feature analysis followed by slow feature analysis appears to produce useful features for this task. The agent is also able to learn the task using pure SFA or CFA features, but in each case it requires more than twice as many features to reach a similar level of performance.

3   Discussion

It should be noted that the contingent features for a domain will not necessarily be sufficient for task learning. As a simple example, imagine a version of the three-square domain above in which the goal is to move the red square so that it comes into contact with the green square. The features from Figures 3 and 4a would clearly be inadequate for that task since they provide no information about the location of the green square.

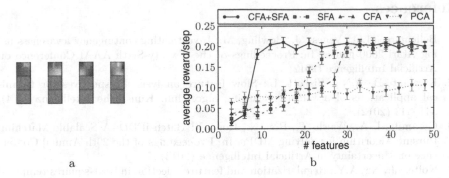

Fig. 4. a. Weight vectors discovered by performing slow feature analysis on the top-30 contingent features. b. Average reward values for different feature types on the example task. Error bars represent 95% confidence intervals.

The contingent features may be useful as part of a larger pool of features, even in cases where they are not themselves sufficient for task learning. Bellemare et. al. have illustrated that learned features based on contingency can significantly improve performance on a learning task that involves playing Atari 2600 games [1]. They explore a different notion of contingency that involves predicting regions of an image that will be changed by the actions of an agent. Those locations are then incorporated into a set of hand-designed features that are used for learning.

In the form described above, the CFA algorithm is only applicable in domains that have a natural notion of not acting. The algorithm could be extended to other domains by sequentially treating each action as the NOP action and executing the CFA algorithm $|\mathcal{A}|$ times. Depending on the application, this version of the algorithm may provide more useful information than the single-NOP version, since it provides a different set of contingent features for each action. Each contingent feature will be tied to the action that governs its dynamics.

4 Conclusions

Feature discovery for reinforcement learning presents a chicken and egg problem. We want features that enable accurate value function estimation, but until we have a value function estimate we lack the supervisory signal that could drive feature learning. Purely unsupervised approaches ignore potentially valuable information about how the agent's actions drive the dynamics of the environment. The CFA algorithm described in this paper addresses these challenges by including information about the agent's action choices in the feature discovery process. The results above illustrate the effectiveness of the approach. We are able to discover relevant features even though the sensor data includes distractor information with exactly the same structure and dynamics as the information related to the agent.

References

1. Bellemare, M.G., Veness, J., Bowling, M.: Investigating contingency awareness using Atari 2600 games. In: Proceedings of the Twenty-Sixth AAAI Conference on Artificial Intelligence (2012)
2. Escalante-B, A.N., Wiskott, L.: Slow feature analysis: Perspectives for technical applications of a versatile learning algorithm. Künstliche Intelligenz 26(4), 341–348 (2012)
3. Geramifard, A., Walsh, T., Roy, N., How, J.: Batch iFDD: A Scalable Matching Pursuit Algorithm for Solving MDPs. In: Proceedings of the 29th Annual Conference on Uncertainty in Artificial Intelligence (2013)
4. Kolter, J., Ng, A.Y.: Regularization and feature selection in least-squares temporal difference learning. In: Proceedings of the 26th Annual International Conference on Machine Learning, pp. 521–528. ACM (2009)
5. Lagoudakis, M.G., Parr, R.: Least-squares policy iteration. The Journal of Machine Learning Research 4, 1107–1149 (2003)
6. Lange, S., Riedmiller, M.: Deep auto-encoder neural networks in reinforcement learning. In: Proceedings of the 2010 International Joint Conference on Neural Networks, pp. 1–8. IEEE (2010)
7. Luciw, M., Schmidhuber, J.: Low complexity proto-value function learning from sensory observations with incremental slow feature analysis. In: Villa, A.E.P., Duch, W., Érdi, P., Masulli, F., Palm, G. (eds.) ICANN 2012, Part II. LNCS, vol. 7553, pp. 279–287. Springer, Heidelberg (2012)
8. Mahadevan, S., Giguere, S., Jacek, N.: Basis adaptation for sparse nonlinear reinforcement learning (2013)
9. Mahadevan, S., Maggioni, M.: Proto-value functions: A laplacian framework for learning representation and control in markov decision processes. Journal of Machine Learning Research 8(16), 2169–2231 (2007)
10. Parr, R., Painter-Wakefield, C., Li, L., Littman, M.: Analyzing feature generation for value-function approximation. In: Proceedings of the 24th International Conference on Machine Learning (2007)
11. Sprague, N.: Basis iteration for reward based dimensionality reduction. In: Proceedings of the 6th IEEE International Conference on Development and Learning (2007)
12. Sprague, N.: Predictive projections. In: Proceedings of the Twenty-First International Joint Conference on Artificial Intelligence (2009)
13. Sprekeler, H.: On the relation of slow feature analysis and laplacian eigenmaps. Neural Computation 23(12), 3287–3302 (2011)
14. Wiskott, L., Sejnowski, T.J.: Slow feature analysis: Unsupervised learning of invariances. Neural Computation 14(4), 715–770 (2002)
15. Zito, T., Wilbert, N., Wiskott, L., Berkes, P.: Modular toolkit for data processing (MDP): a Python data processing frame work. Front. Neuroinform. 2(8) (2008)

A Non-stationary Infinite Partially-Observable Markov Decision Process

Sotirios P. Chatzis[1] and Dimitrios Kosmopoulos[2]

[1] Department of Electrical Eng., Computer Eng., and Informatics
Cyprus University of Technology, Cyprus
[2] Department of Informatics Engineering, TEI Crete, Greece

Abstract. Partially Observable Markov Decision Processes (POMDPs) have been met with great success in planning domains where agents must balance actions that provide knowledge and actions that provide reward. Recently, nonparametric Bayesian methods have been successfully applied to POMDPs to obviate the need of a priori knowledge of the size of the state space, allowing to assume that the number of visited states may grow as the agent explores its environment. These approaches rely on the assumption that the agent's environment remains stationary; however, in real-world scenarios the environment may change over time. In this work, we aim to address this inadequacy by introducing a dynamic nonparametric Bayesian POMDP model that both allows for automatic inference of the (distributional) representations of POMDP states, and for capturing non-stationarity in the modeled environments. Formulation of our method is based on imposition of a suitable dynamic hierarchical Dirichlet process (dHDP) prior over state transitions. We derive efficient algorithms for model inference and action planning and evaluate it on several benchmark tasks.

1 Introduction

Reinforcement learning in partially observable domains is a challenging and attractive research area in machine learning. One of the most common representations used for partially-observable reinforcement learning is the partially observable Markov decision process (POMDP) [13]. POMDPs are statistical models postulating that emission of the observation o_t that an agent receives from the environment at time t follows a distribution $\Omega(o_t|s_t, a_t)$ that depends on the value of some latent (hidden) world-state s_t, and the agent's most recent action a_t. In addition, each action a_t of the agent results in a reward $R(s_t, a_t)$ emitted from the environment, the value of which also depends on the current state s_t, and induces a change in the latent state of the environment, which transitions to a new state s_{t+1}, drawn from a transition distribution $T(s_{t+1}|s_t, a_t)$.

A significant drawback of POMDPs is the large number of parameters entailed from the postulated emission distribution models $\Omega(o|s, a)$, state transition distribution models $T(s'|s, a)$, and reward models $R(s, a)$. These parameters must be learned using data obtained through interaction of the agent with its environment, in an online fashion. However, the combination of the typically limited

S. Wermter et al. (Eds.): ICANN 2014, LNCS 8681, pp. 355–362, 2014.

availability of training data with the large number of parameters may result in uncertain trained models, where planning becomes extremely computationally cumbersome, and the generated policies rather unreliable. Bayesian reinforcement learning approaches [9,7,10] resolve these issues by accounting for both uncertainty in the agent's model of the environment, and uncertainty within the environment itself. This is effected by maintaining distributions over both the parameters of the POMDP and the latent states of the world s.

Most approaches require *a priori* provision of the number of model states: even if the size of the state-space is actually known (which is seldom the case), training a large number of model parameters from the beginning of the learning process (when no data is actually available) might result in poor model estimates and overfitting. Recently, [3] proposed leveraging the strengths of Bayesian nonparametrics, specifically hierarchical Dirichlet process (HDP) priors [15], to resolve these issues. The so-obtained infinite POMDP (iPOMDP) postulates an infinite number of states, conceived as abstract entities whose sole function is to render the dynamics of the system Markovian, instead of actual physical aspects of the system. Note though that, despite the assumption of infinite model states, only a small number of (actually visited) effective states need to be instantiated with parameters at each iteration of the learning algorithm, rendering the model computationally efficient.

Despite these advances, a significant drawback of existing nonparametric Bayesian formulations of POMDPs consists in their lack of appropriate mechanisms allowing for capturing non-stationarity in the modeled environments, expressed in the form of time-adaptive underlying state transition distributions. Indeed, the problem of capturing time-varying underlying distributions in conventional POMDP model formulations has been considered by various researchers in the recent literature (e.g., [16,5]). In this work, we address this inadequacy by introducing a non-stationary variant of the iPOMDP. Formulation of our model is based on imposition of the dynamic hierarchical Dirichlet process (dHDP) prior [8] over the postulated state transitions in the context of our model. We derive efficient model inference and action planning algorithms.

The remainder of this paper is organized as follows: In Section 2, we introduce our proposed model, and derive its learning and action selection algorithms. In Section 3, we provide the experimental evaluation of our approach, and compare it to state-of-the-art alternatives. Finally, in the last section we summarize our results and conclude this paper.

2   Proposed Approach

2.1   Motivation

The iPOMDP model is based on utilization of an HDP prior to describe the state transition dynamics in the modeled environments. The HDP is a model that allows for linking a set of group-specific Dirichlet processes, learning the model components jointly across multiple groups. Specifically, let us assume C latent model states, and A possible actions; let us consider that each possible state-action pair (s, a) defines a different scenario in the environment. The iPOMDP model, being an HDP-based model, postulates that the new state of the environment (after an action is taken) is drawn from a distribution with different parameters $\boldsymbol{\theta}^{sa}$, which are in turn drawn from a scenario-specific Dirichlet process. In addition, the base distribution of the scenario-specific Dirichlet processes is taken as a common underlying Dirichlet process. Under this construction, the following generative model is obtained

$$s'|s, a \sim T(\boldsymbol{\theta}^{s,a}) \tag{1}$$

$$\boldsymbol{\theta}^{s,a} \sim G_{s,a} \tag{2}$$

$$G_{s,a} \sim \mathrm{DP}(\alpha, G_0) \tag{3}$$

$$G_0 \sim \mathrm{DP}(\gamma, H) \tag{4}$$

As we observe, in the context of the HDP, different state transitions that refer to the same state-action pair (scenario) share the same parameters (atoms) that comprise $G_{s,a}$. In addition, transitions might also share parameters (atoms) across different state-action pairs, probably with different mixing probabilities for each $G_{s,a}$; this is a consequence of the fact that the Dirichlet processes $G_{s,a}$ pertaining to all the modeled state-action pairs share a common base measure G_0, which is also a discrete distribution.

Although the HDP introduces a dependency structure over the modeled scenarios, it does not account for the fact that, when it comes to modeling of sequential data, especially data the distribution of which changes over time, sharing of underlying atoms from the Dirichlet processes is more probable in proximal time points. Recently, [8] developed a dynamic variant of the HDP that allows for such a modeling capacity, namely the dynamic HDP (dHDP). Therefore, utilization of this prior emerges as a promising solution for us to effect our goals.

2.2 Model Formulation

To introduce our model, we have to provide our prior assumptions regarding the state transition distributions, observation emission distributions, and reward emission distributions of our model. Let us begin with the state transition distributions of our model. As we have already discussed, to capture non-stationarity, we model state transitions using the dHDP prior [8].

Let us introduce the notation $\boldsymbol{\pi}_\tau^{s,a} = (\pi_{\tau l}^{s,a})_{l=1}^\infty$. $\pi_{\tau l}^{s,a}$ denotes the (prior) probability of transitioning at some time point t to state l from state s by taking action a, given that the distributions of the various state transitions at that time point are the same as they were at time $\tau = \phi_t$. In other words, the employed dHDP assumes that the dynamics of state transition may change over time, with different time points sharing common transition dynamics patterns. Specifically, following [8], we have

$$s_{t+1} = k|s_t = s, a_t = a \sim \mathrm{Mult}(\boldsymbol{\pi}_{\phi_t}^{s,a}) \tag{5}$$

$$\pi_\tau^{s,a} \sim \mathrm{DP}(\alpha, G_0) \tag{6}$$

and

$$G_0 \sim \mathrm{DP}(\gamma, H) \tag{7}$$

whence

$$\pi_{tl}^{s,a} = \tilde{\pi}_{tl}^{s,a} \prod_{h=1}^{l-1} (1 - \tilde{\pi}_{th}^{s,a}) \tag{8}$$

$$\tilde{\pi}_{tl}^{s,a} \sim \mathrm{Beta}(\alpha_t \beta_l, \alpha_t(1 - \sum_{m=1}^{l} \beta_m)) \tag{9}$$

$$\beta_k = \varpi_k \prod_{q=1}^{k-1} (1 - \varpi_q) \tag{10}$$

and

$$\varpi_k \sim \mathrm{Beta}(1, \gamma) \tag{11}$$

In the above equations, the latent variables ϕ_t are indicators of state-transition distribution sharing over time. Following [8], their prior distributions take the form

$$\phi_t | \tilde{\boldsymbol{w}} \sim \mathrm{Mult}(\boldsymbol{w}_t) \tag{12}$$

with $\boldsymbol{w}_t = (w_{tl})_{l=1}^t$, and

$$w_{tl} = \tilde{w}_{l-1} \prod_{m=l}^{t-1} (1 - \tilde{w}_m), \; l = 1, \ldots, t \tag{13}$$

while $\tilde{w}_0 = 1$, and

$$\tilde{w}_t | a_t, b_t \sim \mathrm{Beta}(\tilde{w}_t | a_t, b_t), \; t \geq 1 \tag{14}$$

As observed from (13), this construction induces a proximity-inclined transition dynamics sharing scheme; that is, $w_{t1} < w_{t2} < \cdots < w_{tt}$. In other words, it favors sharing the same dynamics between proximal time points, thus enforcing our assumptions of transition dynamics evolving over time in a coherent fashion.

Finally, our observation emission distributions are taken in the form $\Omega(\boldsymbol{o}|s, a) \sim H$, and our reward emission distributions yield $R(r|s, a) \sim H_R$. The distributions H and H_R can have any form, with the choice depending on the application at hand. In this paper, we shall be considering discrete reward and action distributions; as such, a suitable conjugate selection for the priors over their parameters is the Dirichlet distribution.

This concludes the formulation of our model. We dub our model the infinite dynamic POMDP (iDPOMDP) model. Our model is a completely non-stationary POMDP model, formulated under the assumption of an infinite space of latent POMDP states, and treated under the Bayesian inference paradigm. Note also that limiting the generative non-stationarity assumptions to the transition functions of our model does not limit non-stationarity *per se* to state transitions.

Indeed, the non-identifiability of the postulated model latent states results in the assumed generative non-stationarity of the transition functions being implicitly extended to the observation and reward functions of our model.

2.3   Inference Algorithm

To efficiently perform inference for our model, we combine alternative application of a variant of the block Gibbs sampler of [4], and importance sampling [14], in a fashion similar to the iPOMDP model [3]. Our block Gibbs sampler allows for drawing samples from the true posterior. However, we limit ourselves to using our block Gibbs sampler only on a periodical basis, and not at each time point. In the meanwhile, we use instead an importance sampling algorithm, which merely reweighs the already drawn samples so as to reflect the current posterior as closely as possible. This way, we obtain a significant speedup of our inference algorithm, without compromising model accuracy, since the actual model posterior is not expected to undergo large changes over short time windows.

Block Gibbs Sampler. To make inference tractable, we use a truncated expression of the stick-breaking representation of the underlying shared Dirichlet process of our model, G_0 [12]. In other words, we set a truncation threshold C, and consider $\pi_t^{s,a} = (\pi_{tl}^{s,a})_{l=1}^{C}$, $\forall t, s, a$ [4]. A large value of C allows for obtaining a good approximation of the infinite underlying process, since in practice the $\pi_{tl}^{s,a}$ are expected to diminish quickly with increasing l, $\forall t$ [4]. Note also that, as discussed in [8], drawing one sample from the dHDP model by means of the block Gibbs sampler takes similar time as drawing one sample from HDP.

Let us consider a time horizon T steps long. We have

$$p(\tilde{w}_t | \dots) = \text{Beta}(\tilde{w}_t | a + \sum_{j=t+1}^{T} n_{j,t+1}, b + \sum_{j=t+1}^{T} \sum_{h=1}^{t} n_{jh}) \qquad (15)$$

where n_{th} is the number of time points such that $\phi_t = h$. Similar,

$$p(\tilde{\pi}_{tl}^{s,a} | \dots) = \text{Beta}\Big(\tilde{\pi}_{tl}^{s,a} | \alpha_t \beta_l + \sum_{j=1}^{T} \mathbb{I}(n_{jt} \neq 0) \mathbb{I}(\nu_{jl}^{s,a} \neq 0),$$

$$\alpha_t (1 - \sum_{m=1}^{l} \beta_m) + \sum_{k=l+1}^{C} \sum_{j=1}^{T} \mathbb{I}(n_{jt} \neq 0) \mathbb{I}(\nu_{jk}^{s,a} \neq 0) \Big) \qquad (16)$$

where $\nu_{tk}^{s,a}$ is the number of training episodes where we had a transition from state s to state k, by taking action a at time t.

The updates of the set of indicator variables ϕ_t can be obtained by generating samples from multinomial distributions with entries of the form

$$p(\phi_t = \tau | s_{t-1} = s, a_{t-1} = a; \ldots) \propto \tilde{w}_{\tau-1} \prod_{m=\tau}^{t-1} (1 - \tilde{w}_m) \tilde{\pi}_{\tau s_t}^{s,a} \prod_{q=1}^{s_t-1} (1 - \tilde{\pi}_{\tau q}^{s,a})$$

$$\times p(o_{t+1}|s_t, a_t)\, p(r_{t+1}|s_t, a_t), \quad \tau = 1, \ldots, t$$

$$(17)$$

Further, the posterior distribution over the latent model states yields

$$p(s_t = k | s_{t-1} = s, a_{t-1} = a; \ldots) \propto \tilde{\pi}_{\phi_t k}^{s,a} \prod_{q=1}^{k-1} (1 - \tilde{\pi}_{\phi_t q}^{s,a}) p(o_{t+1}|s_t, a_t)\, p(r_{t+1}|s_t, a_t)$$

$$(18)$$

As we observe, this expression entails Markovian dynamics. Thus, to sample from it, we have to resort to some method suitable for distributions with temporal interdependencies. In our work, we employ the forward filtering-backward sampling (FFBS) algorithm [1]; this way, we can efficiently obtain samples of the underlying latent state sequences.

Finally, the observation and reward distribution parameters of our model are sampled in a manner similar to the original iPOMDP model [3].

Importance Sampling. At time points when we substitute block Gibbs sampling from the true posterior with importance sampling, we essentially reweigh the samples previously drawn from the true posterior. Initially, all samples have equal weight as they are drawn from the true posterior; this changes when we apply importance sampling, so as to capture small changes in the actual posterior in a computationally efficient manner (possible within short time-windows).

Let us denote as μ a sample of our model with weight $w_t(\mu)$ at time t (all samples have initial weights equal to one). Similar to the iPOMDP model, the weight update at time $t + 1$ yields [3]

$$w_{t+1}(\mu) \propto w_t(\mu) \sum_{\forall s_t} \Omega(o_{t+1}|s_t, a_t) b_\mu(s_t) \tag{19}$$

where $b_\mu(s)$ is the belief (posterior probability) for state s, as determined in the sample μ of the model.

2.4   Action Selection

Once we have obtained a set of samples from the posterior distribution of our model, we can use them to perform action selection. For this purpose, in this work we apply *stochastic forward search in the model-space*, as proposed in [3]. The main concept of forward search is to use a forward-looking tree to compute action-values [11]. Starting from the current posterior (belief) over the model parameters of the agent, the tree branches on each action the agent might take and each observation the agent might see. At each action node, the agent computes the (posterior) expectation of the immediate reward, given the drawn samples, in a standard Monte Carlo-type fashion.

3   Experimental Evaluation

We evaluate our method in several benchmark scenarios and compare its performance to related alternatives, namely Medusa [5] and iPOMDP. Medusa is provided with the true number of states, while iPOMDP determines it automatically, similar to our approach. The first benchmark scenario considered here, namely Tiger-3, is adopted from [3]; it comprises an environment that changes over time, thus allowing for us to evaluate the capacity of our model to adapt to new situations. The rest of our considered benchmarks are well-known problems in the POMDP literature, namely, Tiger [6], Shuttle [2], Network [6], and Gridworld [6].

In our experiments, tests had 200 episodes of learning, which interleaved acting and resampling models, and 100 episodes of testing with the models fixed. Our results are provided in Table 1. As we observe, our approach is capable of inferring a smaller number of states than the true count, only retaining states for which adequate information can be derived from the accrued experiences (training episodes); this is attained without any compromises in the yielded accumulated rewards in all scenarios. Given the fact that, as discussed in Section 2.3, drawing one sample from the dHDP by means of the block Gibbs sampler takes similar time as drawing one sample from the HDP, we deduce that our approach allows for obtaining improved total reward compared to the iPOMDP for decreased model complexity and resulting computational costs. Note also that the obtained performance improvement is more prominent in the case of the Tiger-3 problem, where the environment changes over time, thus posing greater learning challenges to the postulated agents. This finding vouches for the capacity of our model to capture non-stationarities in the modeled environments, which is the ultimate goal of this work.

Table 1. Experimental Evaluation: Number of inferred states and total obtained reward

	#States			Total Reward		
Problem	Actual	iPOMDP	iDPOMDP	Medusa	iPOMDP	iDPOMDP
Tiger-3	4	4.1	3.8	-40.26	-42.07	-35.19
Tiger	2	2.1	2.1	0.83	4.06	4.64
Shuttle	8	2.1	2.1	10	10	10
Network	7	4.36	4.07	6671	6508	6749
Gridworld	26	7.36	6.82	-49	-13	-12

4   Conclusions

In this paper, we proposed a nonparametric Bayesian formulation of POMDPs that addressed the problem of capturing non-stationarities in the modeled environments. Formulation of our model was based on the imposition of a suitable dynamic prior over the state transitions of our model, namely the dHDP prior.

We devised efficient learning and planning algorithms for our model, based on a combination of block Gibbs sampling and importance sampling. We showed that our method outperforms related alternatives, namely Medusa and iPOMDP, in several benchmark tasks, combining increased reward performance with shorter model sizes, and, hence, better computational complexity.

Acknowledgments. This work was implemented under the Operational Program "Education and Lifelong Learning" action Archimedes III, co-financed by the European Union (European Social Fund) and Greek national funds (National Strategic Reference Framework 2007 - 2013).

References

1. Carter, C.K., Kohn, R.: On Gibbs sampling for state space models. Biometrika 81, 541–553 (1994)
2. Chrisman, L.: Reinforcement learning with perceptual aliasing: The perceptual distinctions approach. In: Proc. AAAI, pp. 183–188 (1992)
3. Doshi-Velez, F.: The infinite partially observable Markov decision process. In: Proc. NIPS (2009)
4. Ishwaran, H., James, L.F.: Gibbs sampling methods for stick-breaking priors. Journal of the American Statistical Association 96, 161–173 (2001)
5. Jaulmes, R., Pineau, J., Precup, D.: Learning in non-stationary Partially Observable Markov Decision Processes. In: ECML Workshop on Reinforcement Learning in Non-Stationary Environments (2005)
6. Littman, M.L., Cassandra, A.R., Kaelbling, L.P.: Learning policies for partially observable environments: scaling up. In: Proc. ICML (1995)
7. Poupart, P., Vlassis, N., Hoey, J., Regan, K.: An analytic solution to discrete Bayesian reinforcement learning. In: Proc. ICML, pp. 697–704 (2006)
8. Ren, L., Carin, L., Dunson, D.B.: The dynamic hierarchical Dirichlet process. In: Proc. International Conference on Machine Learning (ICML) (2008)
9. Ross, S., Chaib-draa, B., Pineau, J.: Bayes-adaptive POMDPs. In: Proc. NIPS (2008)
10. Ross, S., Chaib-draa, B., Pineau, J.: Bayesian reinforcement learning in continuous POMDPs with application to robot navigation. In: Proc. ICRA (2008)
11. Ross, S., Pineau, J., Paquet, S., Chaib-Draa, B.: Online planning algorithms for pomdps. Journal of Artificial Intelligence Research 32, 663–704 (2008)
12. Sethuraman, J.: A constructive definition of the Dirichlet prior. Statistica Sinica 2, 639–650 (1994)
13. Shani, G., Pineau, J., Kaplow, R.: A survey of point-based POMDP solvers. Auton. Agent Multi-Agent Syst. 27(1), 1–51 (2012)
14. Siegmund, D.: Importance sampling in the Monte Carlo study of sequential tests. The Annals of Statistics 4, 673–684 (1976)
15. Teh, Y.W., Jordan, M.I., Beal, M.J., Blei, D.M.: Hierarchical Dirichlet processes. Journal of the American Statistical Association 101, 1566–1581 (2006)
16. Theocharous, G., Kaelbling, L.P.: Approximate planning in POMDPs with macro-actions. In: Proc. NIPS (2003)

Tool-Body Assimilation Model Based on Body Babbling and a Neuro-Dynamical System for Motion Generation

Kuniyuki Takahashi[1], Tetsuya Ogata[2], Hadi Tjandra[1],
Shingo Murata[1], Hiroaki Arie[2], and Shigeki Sugano[1]

[1] Waseda University, School of Creative Science and Engineering, Tokyo, Japan
[2] Waseda University, School of Fundamental Science and Engineering, Tokyo, Japan

Abstract. We propose a model for robots to use tools without pre-determined parameters based on a human cognitive model. Almost all existing studies of robot using tool require predetermined motions and tool features, so the motion patterns are limited and the robots cannot use new tools. Other studies use a full search for new tools; however, this entails an enormous number of calculations. We built a model for tool use based on the phenomenon of tool-body assimilation using the following approach: We used a humanoid robot model to generate random motion, based on human body babbling. These rich motion experiences were then used to train a recurrent neural network for modeling a body image. Tool features were self-organized in the parametric bias modulating the body image according to the used tool. Finally, we designed the neural network for the robot to generate motion only from the target image.

Keywords: tool-body assimilation, multiple time-scales recurrent neural network.

1 Introduction

Robots that can use tools will be useful for human society. One approach to help develop such robots is modeling human cognitive development [1]. In recent years, tool-body assimilation has gained increasing attention in the field of physiology [2]. Tool-body assimilation is a phenomenon whereby humans recognize tools that they use as an extension of their own bodies. Bias is applied to one's own body model and the tool is treated as an extension of one's body. If the body model can be learned, it becomes easy to learn how to use tools. Therefore, we use the concept of tool-body assimilation to learn tool function effectively.

Attempts to model tool-body assimilation for robot tool use have been made in the field of robotics. Stoytchev showed that robots are capable of acquiring tool function by associating the movement of the tool and the target objects [3]. However, because the robot in this research can only move with predetermined motions, there is the potential problem that not all tool functions could

S. Wermter et al. (Eds.): ICANN 2014, LNCS 8681, pp. 363–370, 2014.

be explored with the available motions. In addition, the robot identified the tool by the tool's color; therefore, it was incapable of using a completely new tool. Nabeshima et al. built a tool-body assimilation model based on the fields of physiology and robotics with computational methods [4]. In this work, they developed a method to have the robot determine tool inertia parameters through dynamic touch. However, predetermined tool features, i.e., the inertial parameters, make it difficult to adapt this method for general tools, and the robot requires dynamic touch for every new tool. Nishide et al. modeled the task of object manipulation with tools without designing tool features in advance by using a tool-body assimilation model with a neural network [5]. This model used dynamic touch to recognize the tools being used. However, there is a need to search for all possible movements for motion generation, and this leads to an enormous number of calculations and long training time. In summary, three issues have to be addressed in tool-body assimilation models: predetermined motion patterns, predetermined tool features and models, and searching from every learned motion.

To address these three issues, we develop the model proposed by Nishide et al. and apply the following approach: (1) Body babbling using a humanoid robot model, (2) Neuro-dynamical system modeled based on human recognition mechanism, and (3) Generation of movement with a final state that has minimum error with the final target. We aim to make a robot acquire tool function and motions using this approach and a tool-body assimilation model.

2   Overview of Tool-Body Assimilation Process

In this section, we present an overview of the tool-body assimilation process. This process consists of three phases: (1) Learning of body model based on body babbling using a humanoid robot, (2) Learning of tool dynamic feature, and (3) Generation of motion from goal image. Fig. 1 shows the overview of the model. First, body babbling is performed, producing motor data and camera images. The camera image features are then extracted with Self-Organizing Map (SOM). Next, the Multiple Time-scales Recurrent Neural Network (MTRNN) is trained by using these motor data and image features. Upon training, the MTRNN then learns the body model of the robot. Also, by training only the Parametric Bias (PB) nodes with different tool images, it is possible for the robot to learn the tool features without changing the body model. PB nodes are smaller than the nodes needed for the body model. Therefore, the time to learn the PB nodes is shorter than that needed for the body model.

2.1   Learn Body Model Based on Body Babbling

In this phase, the robot performs body babbling by a humanoid robot model with a target object without a tool. Body babbling is a behavior consisting of random movements observed in infants. Therefore, by using the concept of babbling, predetermined parameters are not required in the field of robotics [6].

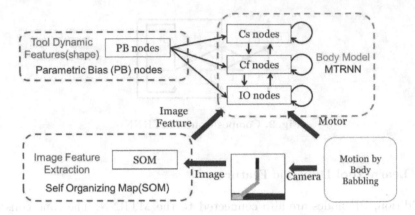

Fig. 1. Overview of the tool-body assimilation model

Body babbling entails numerous movements. Because it is difficult to perform so many trials with real robots, simulated experiments are effective. During babbling, sequential images and motor data are acquired. The features from the images are then extracted by image feature extraction module.

To adapt to unknown situations, the robot should need to have the ability to extract and make sense of image features by itself. To achieve this, we propose the use of SOM for image feature extraction. SOM has proven to be high compatibility with MTRNN [7]. SOM is an unsupervised learning neural network proposed by Kohonen [8]. It is composed of input and output neurons, and is capable of learning without any external help. The neurons in the output layers are two-dimensionally arranged and possess weight vectors w. The weight vectors are set to have the same dimensions (I) as the input vector v. The image features are defined by the formula,

$$p_i = \frac{\exp\left\{-\frac{\|w_i - v\|^2}{\sigma}\right\}}{\sum_{j \in N} \exp\left\{-\frac{\|w_j - v\|^2}{\sigma}\right\}}, \tag{1}$$

where N is the dimension of the SOM and where $i \in I$.

In this research, the input vector consists of the raw image pixels from the robot model's camera. For the robot's body model, we implement the MTRNN proposed by Yamashita et al. [9], as RNN is capable of dealing with time warping by structuring temporal information. In addition, MTRNN is capable of learning multiple sequential data as dynamics and predicting the next state when given a current state. It is composed of three types of neurons: fast context (C_f) nodes, slow context (C_s) nodes, and input-output (IO) nodes. Each type of node has a different time constant. The faster (C_f) nodes learn the primitives of the data, whereas the slower (C_s) nodes learn the sequence of the data. The structure of the MTRNN proposed in this research is shown in Fig. 2. During the learning of the MTRNN, the Back Propagation Through Time (BPTT) algorithm [10] is applied. Details of the learning process are omitted owing to space limitations.

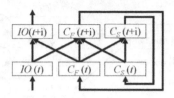

Fig. 2. Composition of MTRNN

2.2 Learn Tool Dynamic Feature

In addition, PB nodes are also connected to the MTRNN. The time constant of PB nodes is set to infinity; therefore, the values of the PB nodes do not change during the full length of each sequence. During training, the weight of the MTRNN and $C_s(0)$ are fixed, and only the weights and values of the PB nodes are trained. After training, PB nodes are able to learn the visual changes resulting from differences in tool types, forming PB space. In other words, the PB space formed represents the tool dynamic features. The PB node then applies bias to the body model according to the tool dynamic features that it learns, changing the body model's dynamics accordingly. This means that there is no need to retrain the robot's body model when a new tool is introduced. The value of the PB node is calculated by using the same method as for $C_s(0)$, and the weights from the PB nodes to other nodes are updated in the same manner as for other weights of the MTRNN.

2.3 Motion Generation

In this phase, a target image is shown to the robot. During this time, the weights of the MTRNN and PB nodes are fixed. The $C_s(0)$ and PB values are recognized using the BPTT algorithms so that the error of the image features between the associated image from the MTRNN and the target image is minimized. Using the PB and $C_s(0)$ values calculated with the algorithm, the MTRNN generates motor sequence data. In Nishide et al.'s research, it is necessary to apply dynamic touch for tool type recognition. However, in this research, it is possible to recognize tool from image of grasped tool.

3 Experimental Setup

3.1 Robot Model in Simulation

To evaluate the tool-body assimilation model, we built a model in the robotics simulator OpenHRP3. The model's size and degrees of freedom (DOF) were based on the humanoid robot ACTROID [11].

3.2   Evaluation Experiment Task

In this experiment, we used an object-pulling task with a bare hand and a T-shaped tool to evaluate the model. This task is commonly used in the study of robotic tool use and tool-body assimilation [3,4,5,12]. The robot performed body babbling in the presence of a target object (a cylinder) on a table for 6 s using its hand and a tool (Fig. 3).

Fig. 3. Experiment settings

3.3   Motion by Body Babbling

To evaluate the effectiveness of this approach, the movement of the robot was confined to the plane of the desk (two-dimensional movements). In doing this, out of the seven DOF of the robot's arm, only three DOF were used. The robot's arm had two initial positions: to the left and to the right of the target object. For each initial position, the robot executed 75 sets of body babbling. The motions were generated by connecting the initial position, the second position, and the third position. The second and third positions are decided by generating random angles within the movable range of each joint. During the body babbling, the robot obtained the data that were used as teaching signal during training for the body model. The acquired data consisted of motor and image sequential data. The motor data of the movable three DOF were recorded for 30 steps during the 6 s of random motion, i.e., 5.0 steps/s. Image data constituted a gray-scale image of 32 × 24 pixels captured by a visual sensor on the robot. Twenty-five dimensions of the image features extracted by using a SOM from the image data and the three dimensions of the joint angles were used for the input data to train the MTRNN. These data were then normalized to [0.0, 1.0] to be used as the teaching signal of the MTRNN. Table 1 shows the construction of the MTRNN.

4   Experimental Results

4.1   Self-organized Tool Function from PB Values

The principal component analysis (PCA) results of the PB values of the tool-body assimilation model are shown in Fig. 4 to evaluate whether the robot was able to differentiate between its bare hand and the T-shaped tool. The PB values in both panels are clustered based on the used tool during motion generation,

Table 1. Construction of MTRNN

Node Name	No. of Node	Time Constant
Motor Input Nodes	3	2
Image Feature Input Nodes	25	2
Fast Context Nodes	30	5
Slow Context Nodes	3	70
Slow Context Nodes (Fixed)	12	70
Parametric Bias Nodes	5	∞

i.e., bare hand or T-shaped tool. The graph on the left of Fig. 4 shows the clustering of the PB values after training of the model; that on the right shows the clustering of the PB values after recognition of the target image using the trained model. Tool features are represented in PC1 and PC2, and of bare hand and T-shaped tool are clustered respectively. Therefore, the robot was able to distinguish the tool from the bare hand.

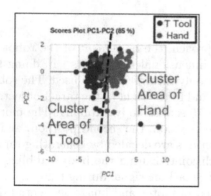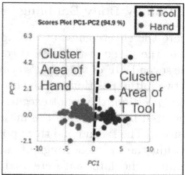

Fig. 4. PCA of PB nodes after training (*left*) and after recognition (*right*)

4.2 Generated Motion

Examples of the motions generated by the robot when shown target images are shown in Fig. 5. It can be observed that the robot was capable of generating motions with final states similar to the target images. In some of the generated motions, the last state of the motion was similar to the target image, but the courses of the motions do not match. In such cases, we suspect that the robot acquired the function of the tool and generated the motion by using the function of the tool.

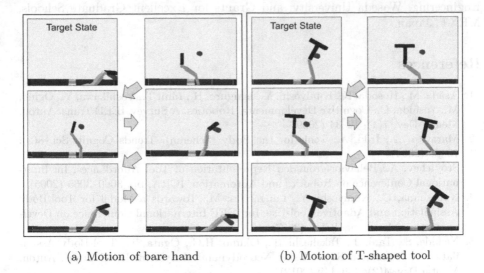

(a) Motion of bare hand   (b) Motion of T-shaped tool

Fig. 5. Motion generation

5   Conclusions

In this paper, we proposed a novel model for robot tool use that does not need predetermined parameters. The model is built based on tool-body assimilation. Previous studies related to robot tool handling required either predetermined motions and tool features or full searches. To overcome these issues, we proposed the following approach: (1) We used a humanoid robot model to generate random motion based on human body babbling. (2) These rich motion experiences were then used to train a recurrent neural network for modeling a body image. Tool features were self-organized in the PB values. (3) We designed a neural network for the robot to be able to generate motion only from the goal image of the tool and target object. Experiments on object manipulation were conducted using the OpenHRP3 simulator, in which the robot's bare hand and a T-shaped tool were used. As a result of the experiment, the robot successfully performed pulling motions when given target images.

As the next step, to make the tool-body assimilation model applicable in real-life situations, it is important to verify that the model is capable of learning other tools.

Acknowledgments. This work has been supported by JST PRESTO "Information Environment and Humans"; MEXT Grant-in-Aid for Scientific Research on Innovative Areas "Constructive Developmental Science" (24119003); JSPS Grant-in-Aid for Scientific Research (S) (2522005); "Fundamental Study for Intelligent Machine to Coexist with Nature" Research Institute for Science and

Engineering, Waseda University; and Grants for Excellent Graduate Schools, MEXT, Japan.

References

1. Asada, M., Hosoda, K., Kuniyoshi, Y., Ishiguro, H., Inui, T., Yoshikawa, Y., Ogino, M., Yoshida, C.: Cognitive Developmental Robotics: A Survey. IEEE Trans. Auton. Mental Dev. 1(1), 12–34 (2009)
2. Maravita, A., Iriki, A.: Tools for the Body (Schema). Trends Cognit. Sci. 8(2), 79–86 (2004)
3. Stoytchev, A.: Behavior-grounded Representation of Tool Affordances. In: International Conference on Robotics and Automation, ICRA, pp. 3060–3065 (2005)
4. Nabeshima, C., Kuniyoshi, Y., Lungarella, M.: Towards a Model for Tool-Body Assimilation and Adaptive Tool-Use. In: IEEE International Conference on Development and Learning–ICDL (2007)
5. Nishide, S., Tani, J., Takahashi, T., Okuno, H.G., Ogata, T.: Tool-Body Assimilation of Humanoid Robot Using Neurodynamical System. IEEE Trans. Auton. Mental Dev. 4(2), 139–149 (2012)
6. Mochizuki, K., Nishide, S., Okuno, H.G., Ogata, T.: Developmental Human-Robot Imitation Learning of Drawing with a Neuro Dynamical System. In: 2013 IEEE International Conference on Systems, Man, and Cybernetics, pp. 2337–2341 (2013)
7. Arie, H., Endo, T., Arakaki, T., Sugano, S., Tani, J.: Creating Novel Goal-directed Actions at Criticality: A Neuro-robotic Experiment. New Math. Nat. Comput. 5, 307–334 (2009)
8. Kohonen, T.: Self-Organization and Associative Memory, 2nd edn. Springer, New York (1988)
9. Yamashita, Y., Tani, J.: Emergence of Functional Hierarchy in a Multiple Timescales Recurrent Neural Network Model: A Humanoid Robot Experiment. PLoS Comput. Biol. 4(11) (2008)
10. Rumelhart, D., Hinton, G., Williams, R.: Learning Internal Representation by Error Propagation. In: Rumelhart, D.E., McLelland, J.L. (eds.) Parallel Distributed Processing. MIT Press, Cambridge (1986)
11. Kokoro: Custom-made robot: ACTROID (2014), http://www.kokoro-dreams.co.jp/rt_tokutyu/actroid.html
12. Hikita, M., Fuke, S., Ogino, M., Asada, M.: Crossmodal Body Representation Based on Visual Attention by Saliency. In: Proc. IROS, pp. 2041–2046 (2008)

A Gaussian Process Reinforcement Learning Algorithm with Adaptability and Minimal Tuning Requirements

Jonathan Strahl[1,*], Timo Honkela[1,2,**], and Paul Wagner[1]

[1] Department of Information and Computer Science
P.O. Box 15400, Aalto University, 00076 Aalto, Finland
[2] Department of Modern Languages, P.O. Box 24
00014 University of Helsinki, Helsinki, Finland

Abstract. We present a novel Bayesian reinforcement learning algorithm that addresses model bias and exploration overhead issues. The algorithm combines different aspects of several state-of-the-art reinforcement learning methods that use Gaussian Processes model-based approaches to increase the use of the online data samples. The algorithm uses a smooth reward function requiring the reward value to be derived from the environment state. It works with continuous states and actions in a coherent way with a minimized need for expert knowledge in parameter tuning. We analyse and discuss the practical benefits of the selected approach in comparison to more traditional methodological choices, and illustrate the use of the algorithm in a motor control problem involving a two-link simulated arm.

Keywords: Non-parametric reinforcement learning, Gaussian processes, batch reinforcement learning, Bayesian reinforcement learning, minimal domain-expert knowledge.

1 Introduction

Reinforcement learning (RL) is maturing and increasingly finding important real world applications [1–3]. However, RL typically requires relatively more domain knowledge and expert knowledge in parameter tuning than supervised learning to prepare the model for a particular task. This may partly explain why the popularity of RL may be considered to be lower than it could be, taking into account the usefulness of this machine learning paradigm. One solution is to combine RL with unsupervised learning (see, e.g., [4–6]).

In this paper, we show how reinforcement learning can be applied with little expert knowledge of the target domain. This is the main focus of the reported

---

* This work has been financially supported by the Foundation of Nokia Corporation and Academy of Finland.
** At its latest stages, this work has been financially supported by the EU Commission through its European Regional Development Fund, and the program "Leverage from the EU 2007-2013".

S. Wermter et al. (Eds.): ICANN 2014, LNCS 8681, pp. 371–378, 2014.

developments. At the same time, the online performance can be comparable or even better than when traditional parametric methods are used. Comparing online performance is valid for when there is a cost and/or risk to running the policy online, e.g. a mechanical robotic arm that is costly to run for many online steps, or controlling a remote control helicopter that cannot afford to crash in order to learn that this is not a good action.

1.1   Reinforcement Learning

The aim of RL is to find an optimal action for any given environment state. This best state to action mapping is an optimal policy π^*. No prior knowledge is used for learning only past experience except in some specialized cases, e.g., using demonstration. An RL learner (or agent) has a feedback loop with the environment. At each state in the state space $s \in S$ (or environment) an action that is possible from that state is chosen $a \in A(s)$, immediately a scalar reward is returned r as a simple representation of a consequence of that action and the agent moves into the next state $s' \in S$. Typically this feedback loop is represented as a Markov decision process (MDP) that is a tuple $\langle S, A, P, R, \gamma \rangle$, where S is the state space and A is the action space. P are the transition dynamics, these are the probability distributions of moving to the next state s' when an action a is undertaken while in a current state s. R is a scalar value representing an immediate reward or cost for making the transition and γ is a discount factor controlling the influence of future rewards on the current state [7].

1.2   SARSA and PILCO

SARSA (state-action-reward-state-action) is an example of a classic temporal difference (TD) RL algorithm that combines dynamic programming (DP) and Monte Carlo (MC) approaches to RL [8, 7].

$$Q(s,a) \leftarrow Q(s,a) + \alpha[r_{t+1} + \gamma Q(s_{t+1}, a_{t+1}) - Q(s_t, a_t)] \,, \tag{1}$$

where $Q(s, a)$ is the action-value function and $\alpha \in [0, 1]$ is the learning rate. As TD learning, like the example above, for a large continuous state and action space becomes intractable, there are parametric methods to reduce the problem space. One effective method is to discretize the space to a finite-MDP. This manual tuning typically requires expert domain knowledge.

Probabilistic inference for learning control (PILCO) for efficient RL [9] uses a non-parametric Gaussian process (GP) to model the environment. A probability distribution is modelled by a GP over the transition function, such that each state prediction is returned as a normal distribution:

$$p(s_t|s_{t-1}, a_{t-1}) = \mathcal{N}(s_t|\mu_t, \sigma_t^2) \,. \tag{2}$$

In a similar approach [10] to manage exploration, a smooth reward function is used:

$$r(s) = 1 - exp(-\frac{b^2}{2}d(s, s_{target})^2) \,, \tag{3}$$

where $r(s)$ is the reward of state s, and $d(s, s_{target})$ is a distance measure from current state s to target state s_{target}. When estimating the state value $\hat{V}^\pi(s_0)$, the variance of the predicted distance to the target $\sigma_s[r(s_t)]$ is incorporated:

$$\hat{V}^\pi(s_0) = \sum_{t=0}^{T} \mathbb{E}_s[r(s_t)] + \lambda\sigma_s[r(s_t)] . \tag{4}$$

The parameter λ controls the amount of exploration. The combination of the prediction variance $\sigma_s[r(s_t)]$ and the expected value of the reward $\mathbb{E}_s[r(s_t)]$ resembles the cost function for human reasoning [11]. Areas of low confidence that are expected to have a high reward are good candidates for exploration.

In PILCO, using direct policy search a value function is not required, as an analytical solution of the transition function directly updates the parametric function approximator for the policy. Gaussian processes are however also successfully used for value function approximation [12, 13]. Approximation of the Q-value using GP has been successfully used for learning. Creating a distribution over a number of forward rewards could be a further development in this area.

2   A Gaussian Process Reinforcement Learning Algorithm

Considerable earlier work has been conducted on the use of non-parametric models in RL [9, 14, 10, 15, 16, 13, 12, 17, 18]. Our Gaussian process RL algorithm uses a non-parametric approach to avoid the need of parametrizing the state and action space. The general idea is to iterate sampling MDP steps from the environment and use these offline to model the environment. The offline policy iteration finds the best policy for the given samples. Each time the policy is improved offline, the policy is run online, whereby additional samples are gathered, this approach is a growing batch update, which maximizes the use of the state-transition observations. This iterative process continues until a stopping criterion is met.

The main motivation of this approach is in minimal domain-specific manual tuning requirements while taking from state-of-the-art reinforcement learning methods. By taking continuous state values as inputs, using continuous action values as outputs, and using non-parametric approximation functions, the need to parameterise the state and action spaces is avoided. Tuning requirements are moved to the GP hyper-parameters, to choosing a finite number of actions to explore offline, and to choosing the reward function parameters (9).

2.1   Gaussian Process Q-Value Function Approximation

During each online episode, a finite set T of state transitions F are accumalated:

$$F_t = \{(s_t, a_t, r_t, s_{t+1})|t = 0, ..., T - 1\}, s_{t=0} = s_{t=1}, a_{t=0} = a_{t=1}. \tag{5}$$

After each online episode, the action-values for the set of known transitions are approximated with a GP model, $\hat{Q}$, trained using all the state transitions (5) aquired so far:

$$\hat{Q}^\pi(s_t, a_t) = \begin{cases} r(s_t) + \sum_{k=t+1}^{T-1} \gamma^{k-t} r(s_k), & \text{if } t = 1 \\ r(s_t) + \sum_{k=t+1}^{T-1} \gamma^{k-t} r(s_k) + \gamma^{T-t+1} \hat{Q}^\pi, & \text{if } t > 1. \end{cases} \quad (6)$$

2.2 Gaussian Process Probabilistic Transition Dynamics Model

This set of sample transitions are used to train a Gaussian process model:

$$p(s_{t+1}|s_t, a_t) \sim \mathcal{GP}(m, K). \quad (7)$$

To gather the initial set of samples, a random policy is used. For each subsequent online episode, the optimized policy π^+ is used. During offline simulation, each sample state's next state is predicted using this GP transition model (2). Using probabilistic predictions for the state transitions, and including the confidence of the predictions in the reward function (9) addresses an often-mentioned weakness of offline modeling, model bias.

2.3 Policy Function, Reward Function and Action-Selection

Online the algorithm uses the optimized policy, initialized with random values.

$$\pi^+(s) = \arg\max_a \hat{Q}(s, a). \quad (8)$$

The combination of the probabilistic transition dynamics model output and the reward function manages exploration. The reward function is based on [10], combining Equations 3 and 4, considering the confidence:

$$r(s_t) = 1 - \exp\left(\frac{-b^2}{2} \mathbb{E}[d] + \lambda \log(\sigma_P^2)\right), \quad (9)$$

$$\sigma_P^2 = \prod_{i=1}^{M} \sigma^2[s_t^i], \quad (10)$$

where M are the number of state dimensions. The input of the reward function is the normalized value of the predicted distance between the current state and the target state, $\mathbb{E}[d]$, where $d = distance(s_t, s_{target})$ and the factor of the variance for each dimension of the state prediction, which gives an overall confidence of the predicted next state, σ_P^2. When using the reward function online $\sigma_P^2 = 0$. The distance from a given state to a target state can be any measure which can be represented as a scalar value (directly or through a function), e.g. the Euclidean distance of two points, or a function of the differences of a set of angles from the target angles.

Figure 1 shows how the reward function manages exploration. As the exploration parameter λ increases, predictions with overall lower confidence (10) are

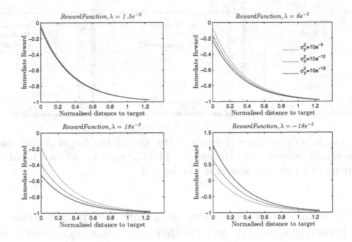

Fig. 1. Smooth reward function (9) encouraging exploration as the confidence factor λ increases from 0, and encouraging exploitation as it decreases from 0. $\lambda = 1.5e^{-3}$: Small λ makes no adjustment to the predicted result, this leads to model bias. $\lambda = 6e^{-3}$: Positive λ gives some preference to low confidence areas. $\lambda = 18e^{-3}$: Higher value of λ gives much larger values to low confidence areas with a lot of exploration. $\lambda = -18e^{-3}$: Negative λ penalises low confident areas and is highly exploitative.

given a higher reward. The reward function is similar to human-like reasoning encouraging exploration in areas of low confidence and potentially higher return.

Tuning the reward function can be done with the visualizations in Figure 1 without domain-expert knowledge. The range of the variance for Figure 1 was gathered during a trial run.

2.4   Offline Policy Iteration

The Gaussian processes RL algorithm uses the Q-value function approximator (6)(11), the probabilistic state transition dynamics function (7), and the reward function (9) during offline policy iteration:

$$\hat{Q}(s_t, a_{t,u}) = r(s_{t+1}) + \sum_{k=1}^{n} \gamma^k r(s_{t+k+1}) + \gamma^{n+1}\hat{Q}^{\pi}(s_{t+n+2}, a_{t+n+2}) \,. \quad (11)$$

For every samples state s_t from the finite set of samples F (5), a finite set of uniformly sampled actions $a_u \in \mathcal{A}(s_t)$ are explored. The summation is over n-step on-policy predictions using the GP model of the transition dynamics. One hundred action samples per state were used for evaluation; this value can be decreased for efficiency or increased for more accuracy. Once every state has been explored, the policy is updated with the optimal action values. The Q-value function approximator is retrained after each iteration, taking the values predicted by the transition model into account. Two techniques are used to

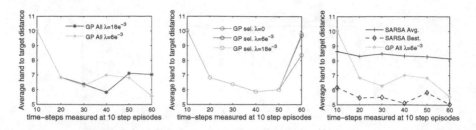

Fig. 2. The y-axis is the average distance of the arm to the target during each 10 step episode. The x-axis values are the time-steps. The GP models use $\gamma=0.1$ and n-steps=2, and the confidence factor λ is shown in the legend.

retrain the Q-value approximator: One uses only the optimal action found for each state $(\max_a(\hat{Q}(s_t, a_{t,u})))$, and another uses all action value samples $a_{t,u}$ explored for each state s_t. The former is less heavy computationally, but the latter is shown to learn more accurately in Figure 2. A requirement for this algorithm is that the reward can be derived from the predicted state.

3   Empirical Illustration

To evaluate the Gaussian processes RL algorithm a simulation, in Blender 3d[1] of an anthropomorphic arm motor-control problem, with two degrees of freedom is used. The angles of each arm, the angular velocities, and the Euclidean distance between the hand and the target comprise the state, and the torque motor controls for each joint are the actions. The goal is to quickly reach up to a target point, located above and forward from the 'shoulder' joint, from a resting-downward position, and hold the arm in that location. The distance function is a Euclidean distance of the hand to the target. The results of the comparisons are shown in Figure 2. Only the number of online time steps are measured, the time duration for the offline policy iteration is not compared. The SARSA model used ϵ-greedy exploration and each arm angle was discretised into 8 equal parts, and the angular velocity was discretised into fast and slow in each direction and still. The action space was simplified to fully on in either direction or no power.

The results are an average over ten repetitions, each with new random seed initialization values. Each repetition was broken down into six ten-step episodes with resets. Additionally, the SARSA's best performing single run of the ten repetitions is plotted to show the effects of the initial values. The left-most graph in Figure 2 shows the performance of using all action values to train the Q-value approximator for each offline policy iteration. The best result was attained setting the exploration parameter to $6e^{-3}$, the results show the average distance decreased to the smallest average distance overall. The center graph shows the results of only using the best action values found for each state in the finite set for each policy iteration, the arm distance decreased on average but

---

[1] http://www.blender.org/

then began to overshoot the target, as the arm moved toward the target and shot past. The right-most graph plots the best performing GP average result against the SARSA average result, and the single best performing SARSA run from the ten repetitions. 'GP All' refers to the use of all the predicted action values for training the Q-value function for each policy iteration. 'GP sel.' refers to using only the selection of the best predicted action per state.

4 Conclusions and Discussion

Using a non-parametric model approach to RL can outperform, on average, a traditional TD method comparing online time steps, and requires much less domain-specific manual tuning (i.e. the continuous state and action spaces were used directly in the algorithm, only the model parameters and the action-space sampling were required, which are not as specific to each environment as parameterising the state and action spaces. This comparison is only useful when there is a cost or risk for running online episodes. The SARSA performance of the basic method depended strongly on the randomly chosen initial Q-values, and there was little improvement from the initial Q-values over the 60 time steps. Also the variance in the results was high. The proposed new algorithm managed consistently in improving the learning results regardless of whether the algorithm had good initial values or not. Moreover, the variance was much lower and the algorithm improved at a much higher rate comparing online time steps. The use of all the data gave a large improvement in the learning compared to the use of only a subset of the data, c.f. Figure 2.

In summary, for a continuous-valued state and action space, where domain-specific knowledge is either not attainable or costly, and where online time steps are not free of cost (e.g. a real robotic arm), and there are only a small number of available samples, the proposed algorithm can be very useful. The experimental results shown in this paper are not conclusive which, on the other hand, is not highly relevant as the main contribution is in decreasing the need for manual tuning. Moreover, the proposed algorithm is theoretically well justified, based on aspects of several state-of-the-art algorithms.

References

1. Abbeel, P., Coates, A., Quigley, M., Ng, A.: An application of reinforcement learning to aerobatic helicopter flight. In: Advances in Neural Information Processing Systems, vol. 19, pp. 1–8 (2007)
2. Głowacka, D., Ruotsalo, T., Konuyshkova, K., Kaski, S., Jacucci, G.: Directing exploratory search: Reinforcement learning from user interactions with keywords. In: Proceedings of the 2013 International Conference on Intelligent User Interfaces, pp. 117–128. ACM (2013)
3. Kober, J., Peters, J.: Reinforcement learning in robotics: A survey. In: Wiering, M., van Otterlo, M. (eds.) Reinforcement Learning. ALO, vol. 12, pp. 569–600. Springer, Heidelberg (2012)

4. Arleo, A., Smeraldi, F., Gerstner, W.: Cognitive navigation based on nonuniform gabor space sampling, unsupervised growing networks, and reinforcement learning. IEEE Transactions on Neural Networks 15(3), 639–652 (2004)
5. Montazeri, H., Moradi, S., Safabakhsh, R.: Continuous state/action reinforcement learning: A growing self-organizing map approach. Neurocomputing 74(7), 1069–1082 (2011)
6. Graziano, V., Koutník, J., Schmidhuber, J.: Unsupervised modeling of partially observable environments. In: Gunopulos, D., Hofmann, T., Malerba, D., Vazirgiannis, M. (eds.) ECML PKDD 2011, Part I. LNCS (LNAI), vol. 6911, pp. 503–515. Springer, Heidelberg (2011)
7. Sutton, R.S., Barto, A.G.: Reinforcement learning: An introduction. Cambridge Univ. Press (1998)
8. Rummery, G.A., Niranjan, M.: On-line Q-learning using connectionist systems. Technical report, Cambridge University Engineering Dept. (1994)
9. Deisenroth, M.P., Rasmussen, C.E.: PILCO: A model-based and data-efficient approach to policy search. In: Proceedings of the International Conference on Machine Learning (2011)
10. Deisenroth, M.P., Rasmussen, C.E.: Efficient reinforcement learning for motor control. In: Proceedings of the 10th International PhD Workshop on Systems and Control, Hlubok nad Vltavou, Czech Republic (2009)
11. Körding, K.P., Wolpert, D.M.: The loss function of sensorimotor learning. Proceedings of the National Academy of Sciences of the United States of America 101(26), 9839–9842 (2004)
12. Rasmussen, C.E., Kuss, M.: Gaussian processes in reinforcement learning. In: Advances in Neural Information Processing Systems 16, pp. 751–759. MIT Press (2004)
13. Jakab, H., Csató, L.: Improving Gaussian process value function approximation in policy gradient algorithms. In: Honkela, T. (ed.) ICANN 2011, Part II. LNCS, vol. 6792, pp. 221–228. Springer, Heidelberg (2011)
14. Englert, P., Paraschos, A., Peters, J., Deisenroth, M.P.: Model-based imitation learning by probabilistic trajectory matching. In: Proceedings of 2013 IEEE International Conference on Robotics and Automation (ICRA) (2013)
15. Ko, J., Klein, D.J.: Gaussian processes and reinforcement learning for identification and control of an autonomous blimp. In: IEEE Intl. Conf. on Robotics and Automation (ICRA) (2007)
16. Ghavamzadeh, M., Engel, Y.: Bayesian actor-critic algorithms. In: Proceedings of the 24th International Conference on Machine Learning, ICML 2007, pp. 297–304. ACM, New York (2007)
17. Sugiyama, M., Hachiya, H., Towell, C., Vijayakumar, S.: Geodesic Gaussian kernels for value function approximation. Auton. Robots 25(3), 287–304 (2008)
18. Engel, Y., Mannor, S., Meir, R.: Reinforcement learning with Gaussian processes. In: Proceedings of the 22nd International Conference on Machine Learning, ICML 2005, pp. 201–208. ACM, New York (2005)

Sensorimotor Control Learning Using a New Adaptive Spiking Neuro-Fuzzy Machine, Spike-IDS and STDP

Mohsen Firouzi[1,2,3], Saeed Bagheri Shouraki[4], and Jörg Conradt[1,2,3]

[1] Neuroscientific System Theory-Technische Universität München, Germany
[2] Bernstein Center for Computational Neuroscience, München, Germany
[3] Graduate School of Systemic Neurosciences-Ludwig-Maximilians-Universität, München, Germany
[4] Research Group of Brain Simulation and Cognitive Science, ACL, Sharif University of Technology, Tehran, Iran
{mohsen.firouzi,conradt}@tum.de, shouraki-s@sharif.edu

Abstract. Human mind from system perspective deals with high dimensional complex world as an adaptive Multi-Input Multi-Output complex system. This view is theorized by reductionism theory in philosophy of mind, where the world is represented as logical combination of simpler sub-systems for human so that operate with less energy. On the other hand, Human usually uses linguistic rules to describe and manipulate his expert knowledge about the world; the way that is well modeled by Fuzzy Logic. But how such a symbolic form of knowledge can be encoded and stored in plausible neural circuitry? Based on mentioned postulates, we have proposed an adaptive Neuro-Fuzzy machine in order to model a rule-based MIMO system as logical combination of spatially distributed Single-Input Single-Output sub-systems. Each SISO systems as sensory and processing layer of the inference system, construct a single rule and learning process is handled by a Hebbian-like Spike-Time Dependent Plasticity. To shape a concrete knowledge about the whole system, extracted features of SISO neural systems (or equivalently the rules associated with SISO systems) are combined. To exhibit the system applicability, a single link cart-pole balancer as a sensory-motor learning task, has been simulated. The system is provided by reinforcement feedback from environment and is able to learn how to get expert and achieve a successful policy to perform motor control.

Keywords: Sensorimotor Control Learning, Spiking Neural Networks, Neuro-Fuzzy, Spike Time Dependent Plasticity, Cart-Pole balancing.

1   Introduction

In order to exploit human intelligence, brain has always been looked through two general outlooks [1]. The Micro-Level studies which leads to connectionism paradigms in AI, e.g. ANNs; and Macro-Level studies, e.g. clinical researches leads to Symbolism in AI where machines model real world by creating formal symbols trying to acquire knowledge by manipulating them and discovering their relations. Expert Systems and Fuzzy Rule Base are good examples of symbolism. One open question

S. Wermter et al. (Eds.): ICANN 2014, LNCS 8681, pp. 379–386, 2014.
© Springer International Publishing Switzerland 2014

as main motivation of this work is how symbolic form of knowledge and rules can be emerged by a biologically realistic and connectionist style of information processing like brain? Hybrid systems in Machine Learning address this question [1].

In this paper we have proposed a new Adaptive Spiking Neuro-Fuzzy Inference System called Spike-IDS evaluated for sensorimotor learning. The architecture of Spike-IDS is motivated by a recursive Fuzzy algorithm called ALM [2]. The main underlying inspiration of proposed system in terms of architecture is Brain functionally distributed structure. Also data is encoded by delay coding through topographically arranged first-order Spike-Response-Model neurons [4]. From system viewpoint, Spike-IDS and ALM is motivated by reductionism in philosophy of mind, by which real world is internalized by human mind as combination of partial knowledge (rules) or emerged by combination of distributed modules [3]. Using this architecture and breaking down a MIMO system into set of SISO subsystems, information is fetched just from part of the whole system during learning and evaluation process without any recursion. It is shown that this style of information processing is faster than neural classifiers and even ANFIS [5]. To construct and modify the rules through synaptic distribution, Hebbian-like STDP learning is provided. In fact each SISO system provides a single rule and captures two important features of sensorimotor sub-space through synaptic distribution: a) input-output characteristic or equally rule consequent part; and b) its degree of contribution in whole MIMO system which is inversely related to output standard deviation around consequent and slope of input-output surface. Finally a Fuzzy rule base consolidates sub-systems (rules) to shape a concrete form of sensory-motor transformation. As a practical application, a cart-pole sensorimotor learning task is evaluated. The results shows system can learn to balance the stick by sensory-motor experiences without external supervisor like actor-critic reinforcement learning in which actor acts as a high level model of action selection in primary motor cortex and critic estimates cost of the action like Basal Ganglia [6]. In the next section, Spike-IDS is described. In section 3 an adaptive sensorimotor learning task has been investigated, and finally in section 4 some remarks is presented.

2   Spiking Neuro-Fuzzy Inference System, Spike-IDS

As is shown in Fig.1 Sensory space (x_1 and x_2) has been partitioned into fuzzy sets and Spike-IDS consists of three general layers. Input layer or Sensory layer, where single input (x_1 or x_2) would activate corresponding SISO systems hereafter Spike-IDS units, according to Fuzzy membership value of inputs. For instance in double-Input-single-output system of Fig.1-left, if each input domain is segmented into two intervals (big and small), there are overall four Spike-IDS units capturing projected SISO points of sensory-motor sub-spaces as follows: $X_{11} = \{(x_1,y)|x_2 \in [0,0.5]\}$, $X_{12} = \{(x_1,y)|x_2 \in [0.5,1]\}$, $X_{21} = \{(x_2,y)|x_1 \in [0,0.5]\}$ and $X_{22} = \{(x_2,y)|x_1 \in [0.5,1]\}$. Second layer or processing layer of the algorithm extracts SISO system characteristic trajectory, hereafter Narrow path (ψ_{ij} in Fig.1) and its effectiveness in entire system or Spread value (σ_{ij} in Fig.1). Spread indicates the deviation of motor output and derivative of sensory-motor surface around extracted Narrow path and shows how much the subsystem contributes in overall decision process. Eventually extracted partial features of sensory space (Narrow, Spread and fuzzy membership values) should be combined by

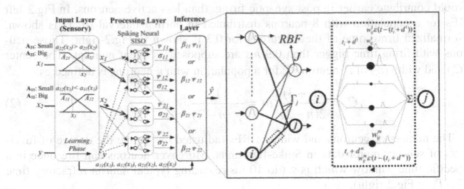

Fig. 1. Left: General Architecture of *Spike-IDS* for 2-Input, 1-output System; **Right**: Structure of RBF-like Spiking Neural Network model for single *Spike-IDS unit* (processing layer)

Inference Layer to achieve a unified form of decision (motor output). Consequent part of single rule is determined by corresponding Spike-IDS unit characteristic or equivalently Narrow path. During on-line learning phase, new sensory-motor experience accompanied with its costs of action (see section 3), result in a local adaptation of SISO characteristic function or equally consequent part of associated Fuzzy rule. In this section network architecture, data coding, learning algorithm of each units and inference layer will be discussed in detail.

2.1   Structure of Spike-IDS Units, SISO Sub-systems

As is depicted in Fig.1-right, each Spike-IDS unit is constructed as a single layer feed-forward Network of SRM neurons with multiple delayed synaptic terminals and overlapping Gaussian Receptive Fields [4]. Each sub-synapse has a constant delay (d^k) and a plastic synaptic weight $(W^k_{i,j})$. Membrane potential for post-synaptic neuron j with m sub-synaptic connection can be expressed as (1):

$$x_j(t) = \sum_{i \in \Gamma_j} \sum_{k=1}^{m} w_{i,j}^k \varepsilon(t - t_i - d^k), \ \varepsilon(t) = \frac{t}{\tau} e^{(1-\frac{t}{\tau})} \tag{1}$$

Where ε is simplified model of Post-Synaptic Potential [7]; t_i is firing time of ith Pre-Synaptic neuron, d^k is fixed delay for k^{th} sub-synapse which is arranged from zero to m-1, ($d^k = \{0, 1,..., m-1\}$); and $W^k_{i,j}$ is k^{th} sub-synaptic weight between i, j neurons. Also Γj is the set of pre-synaptic neurons which are connected to post-synaptic neuron j. When internal state variable, x_j exceeds threshold voltage ϑ, neuron j will fire.

2.2   Sensor Encoding

The input-output of Spike-IDS units are encoded using spatially arranged populations of SRM neurons with overlapping Gaussian Receptive Fields. The coding we have used is population delay coding in which more active neuron would fire earlier and would contribute earlier in post-synaptic firing, than less active neurons. In Fig.2-left RFs for a population with 8 neurons distributed in normal interval [0, 1] is shown. Normalized firing time of these neurons for 0.3 is shown in Fig.2-right. Those neurons with firing time bigger than 0.9 ms are supposed as silent neurons. The center (C_i) and width (ω_i) of ith neuron RF for a population with n neurons is defined as:

$$C_i = \frac{2(i-3)}{2(n-2)}, \omega_i = \frac{1}{\gamma_i(n-2)} \tag{2}$$

The number of neurons and width of RFs (adjusted by γ) tune the degree of fuzziness of sensory-motor data in Spike-IDS units. Moreover neurons can fire once in a specific time window which is set to 10 ms regarding typical neuron refractory time [7] (T_w in Fig.2-right).

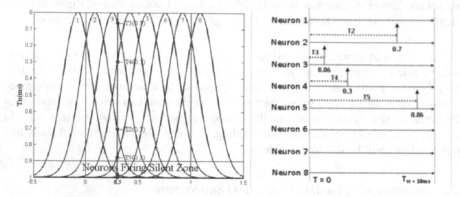

Fig. 2. Left: Gaussian receptive fields for 8 neurons encoding 0.3 as input; **Right**: General scheme of neurons spike time delay for 0.3 as input.

2.3   Hebbian-Like Spike Time Dependent Plasticity

The learning algorithm in Spike-IDS networks is reinforcement Hebbian STDP [7]; by which the pre-synaptic neurons that contribute earlier in firing of post-synaptic neuron should be rewarded and silent neurons should be penalized. Therefore a learning window $L(\Delta t)$ which determines the way of weight modification as function of firing time delay between postsynaptic and presynaptic neurons is defined as following equations ($\Delta t_{ij}^{k} = t_i - t_j + d^k$):

$$\Delta w_{ij}^{k} = \eta L(\Delta t_{ij}^{k}), w_{init} = 0, \ 0 < w < 3 \tag{3}$$

$$L(\Delta t) = (1+b)e^{\frac{(\Delta t - \delta)^2}{2(\kappa-1)}} - b, \ \ \kappa = 1 - \frac{\upsilon^2}{2\ln(b/b+1)} \tag{4}$$

This function potentiates synapses between neurons i, j with rate η if $\Delta t_{i,j}^{k} < \upsilon$ and depress synaptic weights if $\Delta t_{i,j}^{k} > \upsilon$ (Fig.3-left). Due to exponential model of EPSP with time constant τ (1), the firing of neuron i contribute in firing of neuron j not exactly after spike initiation. Therefore learning window should be shifted slightly to take it into consideration (δ in Fig.3-left sets to $-\tau$). Also in (4), parameter v and b indicates reward neighborhood and penalty depth respectively. Besides rewarding contributing neurons, silent neurons should be strongly penalized. So Δw_{ij} for sub-synaptic weights between silent input neurons and fired output neuron has set to $-\eta$.

It is worth to mention that if Spike-IDS is provided by reinforcement signal during learning (see section 3 and Fig.3-right), and if initiated control command was destructive according to sensory inputs and controller policy, Δw_{ij} in (3) should be negative to erase the effect of wrong sensory-motor mapping in current internal model.

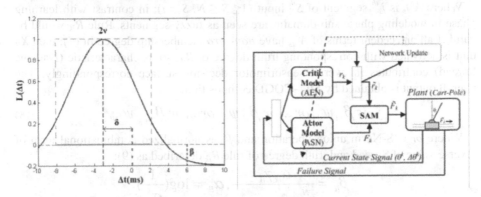

Fig. 3. Left: STDP learning window of Spike-IDS units; **Right.** Block diagram of sensorimotor learning controller using Spike-IDS for cart-pole task

2.4   Sensorimotor Characteristics, Narrow and Spread Decoding

In evaluation phase the Narrow and Spread values in response to sensory input x_{in}, should be decoded from activity of output population. Firing time of output neurons indicates Fuzzy-like activation degree of topographically arranged neurons. So simply by Center of Mass decoding over firing time of each neuron Narrow could be calculated. Similarly difference between first and last fired neuron RF, is a simple and efficient way of Spread decoding:

$$\psi(x_{in}) = \frac{\sum_{j=1}^{m_o} T_j C_j}{\sum_{j=1}^{m_o} T_j}, \quad \sigma(x_{in}) = C_{last} - C_{first}$$

(5)

Where ψ and σ are extracted Narrow and Spread for x_{in}, m_o is number of output neurons, T_j is firing time of output neuron j and C_j is center of jth neuron RFs. C_{last} and C_{first} are centers of receptive fields for last and first fired neurons.

2.5   Inference Layer

Inference layer of the algorithm including constructed rules uses Narrow and Spread values to realize entire system characteristic. In the case of N-sensory inputs with m_i partitions for single i^{th} sensory space (x_i), the number of rules and associated Spike-IDS units for i^{th} input is denoted by l_i and total number of rules, L is as bellow:

$$L = \sum_{i=1}^{N} l_i = \sum_{i=1}^{N} \prod_{k=1,k\neq i}^{N} m_k, \quad l_i = \prod_{k=1,k\neq i}^{N} m_k \tag{6}$$

Also the kth rule of the ith input variable, R_{ik} ($k = 1, 2\ldots l_i$) can be described as bellow:

$$R_{ik} : if x_1 \in A_{j_1}^{1} \wedge x_2 \in A_{j_2}^{2} \wedge \ldots \wedge x_{i-1} \in A_{j_{i-1}}^{i-1} \wedge$$
$$x_{i+1} \in A_{j_{i+1}}^{i+1} \wedge \ldots \wedge x_N \in A_{j_N}^{N} \text{ then } Y = \psi_{ik}(x_i) \tag{7}$$

Where A_{Js}^{S} is j_s^{th} segment of Sth input ($1\leq S \leq N$, $S \neq i$); in contrast with learning phase in modeling phase sub-domains are seen as fuzzy segments. Rule R_{ik} would be valid if all antecedent terms of A_{Js}^{S} have *non-zero* membership degree in (7); then X_{ik} unit is activated with corresponding truth degree of R_{ik}; so its characteristic (Narrow, Spread) contributes in overall sensorimotor decision surface correspondingly. The overall output is obtained by Min–COGD composition:

$$\hat{y} \text{ is } \beta_{11}\psi_{11} or \ldots or \beta_{ik}\psi_{ik} or \ldots or \beta_{Nl_N}\psi_{Nl_N} \tag{8}$$

Where *or* is S-Norm union operation and β_{ik} is normalized combinational term of reverse value of Spread and truth degree of rule R_{ik} described as (9):

$$\beta_{ik} = \frac{\alpha_{ik}\gamma_{ik}}{\sum_{p=1}^{N}\sum_{q=1}^{l_p}\alpha_{pq}\gamma_{pq}}, \alpha_{ik} = \log(\frac{1}{\sigma_{ik}}) \tag{9}$$

In (9), α_{ik} is normalized reverse value of Spread for Spike-IDS unit X_{ik} and γ_{ik} is R_{ik} truth degree. The logarithmic function applies to make smooth the sharpness of Spread reverse value, leading to smoother general decision surface [5].

3   Sensorimotor Learning, Single Cart-Pole Balancer

To show how proposed Adaptive Neuro-Fuzzy machine works in a real world sensorimotor learning scenario, a single link inverted pendulum task as a famous benchmark for sensorimotor learning has been investigated. The general architecture of the controller has been shown in Fig.3-right. The Action Selection Network would realize internal model of sensorimotor function and Action Evaluation Network would generate costs and rewards associated with generated commands as Basal Ganglia does in brain for motor control [6]. In fact ASN suggests an appropriate action (force signal, F_k) in accordance with current state (θ_k, $d\theta_k$). Correspondingly AEN model the reward value (r_k) and shows how much valuable or costly the action is (according to control policy: $\theta=0$; $d\theta=0$). If the cost was too big, Stochastic Action Modifier (SAM) regenerates a new uniform random action ($\tilde{F}_k$) with mean F_k; see (10). Eventually the output of SAM would be applied to the plant. The variance of SAM is a function of $\hat{r}_k$ so that if critic validates suggested action as a low cost action ($\hat{r}_k$ near to 1), it has been changed with less deviation around ASN and vice versa:

$$\tilde{F}_k = F_k + \tilde{N}^{F}(e^{-\hat{r}_k\alpha} - e^{-\alpha}) \tag{10}$$

Where $\bar{N}_F$ is a uniform random value between upper and lower boundary of F, α is constant parameter and $\hat{f}_k$ is normalized value of r_k. The modified action alters state of the plan followed by feedback signals for the evaluation. Then the score of previous action is updated in AEN as (11):

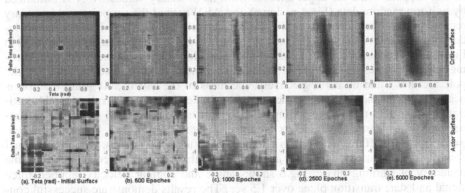

Fig. 4. Up: Critic surfaces, AEN evolution through learning iteration, **Down**: Actor surfaces, ASN evolution through learning iteration

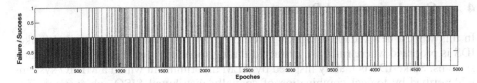

Fig. 5. Failure and success through learning iteration

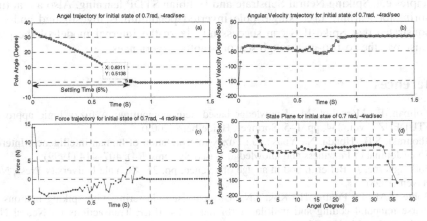

Fig. 6. (a): Angle response trajectory, (b): angular velocity, (c): force trajectory, (d): state transition plane over time; initial state: ($\theta = 0.7$ radian, $d\theta = -4$ radian/sec)

$$r_k^{new} = \frac{(\Delta + \hat{r}_k + 0.5)}{1.5}, \quad \Delta = \lambda(\hat{r}_{k+1} - \hat{r}_k) \tag{11}$$

So the action which generates a good state transition into low cost score (r_k near 1) should be rewarded and bad actions have to be penalized. Since it is more desirable to achieve successful transitions in contrast with failure, so λ for rewards has been set near to 1 and greater than λ for penalty. The failure signal that indicates unrecoverable falling happens when the angel exceeds from its boundary values. ASN is initialized by uniform random data (Fig.4 a, down) and AEN around the set point and boundary regions has been initialized as 1 and -0.5 respectively (Fig.4 a, up). In Fig.4 the evolution of ASN and AEN through learning iterations has been shown. As is depicted in Fig.5 early experiences result in more failure and less success whereas through learning iteration success rate increases. In this experiment, the mass and the length of the pole are 200 g and 60 cm respectively, the mass of the cart is 500 g and fraction is neglected. ASN and AEN are implemented as Spike-IDS with 121 rules (11×11 partitions), Spike-IDS units have 15 input, 25 output neurons with 12 sub-synaptic connections. Also learning parameters are experimentally set to: $\tau=3$, b=0.2, $\delta=-3$, $\nu=5$, $\gamma=1.4$, $\eta=0.3$, $\vartheta=10$mv with epoch number 15. After 3000 epochs, response of final controller is evaluated by initial angle and angular velocity twice bigger than the boundary of learning phase. Fig.6 shows angle and angular velocity, applied force signal and state transition plane over 1.5 sec. The results demonstrate successful control task without any overshoot and undershoot and set-point settling time of 0.83 s.

4   Conclusions and Remarks

In this work a new Adaptive Spiking Neuro-Fuzzy Inference machine called Spike-IDS is proposed where rules are extracted through spatially distributed Spiking neural systems. Spike-IDS is mainly inspired by ALM algorithms in which a MIMO systems is described by logical combination of spatially distributed SISO sub-systems. The sensory and processing layer of this algorithm is implemented by biologically realistic principles e.g. Spiking Neural Substrate and Hebbian STDP learning. Also a real time sensorimotor learning task, single pole inverted pendulum is investigated and it is demonstrated that Spike-IDS can successfully learn the internal model of the plant and discover the cost-to-go through sensory-motor experiences.

References

1. Kolman, E., Margaliot, M.: Knowledge-based neurocomputing: A fuzzy logic approach. STUDFUZZ, vol. 234, pp. 1–5. Springer, Heidelberg (2009)
2. Shouraki, S.B., Honda, N., Yuasa, G.: Fuzzy interpretation of human intelligence. International Journal of Fuzziness and knowledge-Based Systems 7(4), 407–414 (1999)
3. Polkinghorne, J.: Belief in god in an age of science, pp. 25–48. Yale University Press, New Haven (1998)
4. Bohte, S.M., La Poutre, H., Kok, J.N.: Unsupervised clustering with spiking neurons by sparse temporal coding and multilayer rbf networks. IEEE Transactions on Neural Networks 13(2), 426–435 (2002)
5. Firouzi, M., Shouraki, S.B., Afrakuti, I.E.P.: Pattern Analysis by Active Learning Method Classifier. Journal of Intelligent & Fuzzy Systems 26(1), 49–62 (2014)
6. Shadmehr, R., Smith, M.A., Krakauer, J.W.: A computional neuroanatomy for motor control. Exp. Brain. Res. 185(3), 359–381 (2008)
7. Gerstner, W., Kistler, W.M.: Spiking Neuron Models, 1st edn. The Cambridge University Press, Cambridge (2002)

Model-Based Identification of EEG Markers for Learning Opportunities in an Associative Learning Task with Delayed Feedback

Felix Putze[1,*], Daniel V. Holt[2], Tanja Schultz[1], and Joachim Funke[2]

[1] Karlsruhe Institute of Technology, Institute of Anthropomatics and Robotics,
Karlsruhe, Germany
[2] University of Heidelberg, Institute of Psychology, Heidelberg, Germany
{felix.putze,tanja.schultz}@kit.edu,
{daniel.holt,funke}@psychologie.uni-heidelberg.de

Abstract. This paper combines a reinforcement learning (RL) model and EEG data analysis to identify learning situations in a associative learning task with delayed feedback. We investigated neural correlates in occipital alpha and prefrontal theta band power of learning opportunities, identified by the RL model. We show that those parameters can also be used to differentiate between learning opportunities which lead to correct learning and those which do not. Finally, we show that learning situations can also be identified on a single trial basis.

Keywords: Reinforcement Learning, learning situations, EEG, Frequency Analysis.

1 Introduction

Reinforcement learning (RL) is a fundamental mechanism of adaptive behavior in humans. It is often implicitly involved in Human-Computer Interaction (e.g. when users learn to operate a new software) but can also be explicitly employed as part of a predictive user model for adaptive systems. The underlying models of the learning progress are usually individually calibrated through behavioral data (e.g., response probabilities). In recent years biosignals generated by neural activity (as measured by EEG or fMRI methods) have become another relevant source of information for real-time user modeling. The practical utility of this combined approach was illustrated by [1], who showed how the prediction of mental user states in an intelligent tutoring system for an algebra-isomorph can be substantially improved by blending predictions of a cognitive task model with neurally derived information. However, in order to successfully apply this approach, neural markers need to be identified that can be integrated into user

---

* This project was partially funded by the Heidelberg Karlsruhe Research Partnership (HEiKA), a co-operation between the Ruprecht-Karls-University of Heidelberg and the Karlsruhe Institute of Technology.

S. Wermter et al. (Eds.): ICANN 2014, LNCS 8681, pp. 387–394, 2014.

models in a principled manner. In this paper, we employ a simple reinforcement learning model to establish EEG markers for learning opportunities in an associative learning task with delayed feedback.

2   Related Work

In RL organisms learn to select sequences of actions that maximize their subjective reward over time based on the reward signals (feedback) associated with different outcomes. This can be achieved through temporal difference learning (TD), which assigns credit based on the temporal proximity of actions to outcomes. The authors of [4] demonstrated how a TD-based RL model can predict learning performance by TD-based reward propagation in a complex associative learning task with delayed feedback. One neurophysiological approach for studying RL is to analyze the Feedback Related Negativity (FRN). The FRN is a frontocentral neural response appearing 200-300ms after the presentation of feedback indicating prediction errors (i.e., a mismatch between mental model and observation). [15] documents that prediction error can be used in a task with delayed feedback to predict the occurrence of FRN for task states immediately followed by feedback as well as intermediate states. The authors present this effect as evidence for credit assignment to intermediate states from future rewards. [2] moves from time domain analysis to frequency analysis and links prefrontal theta synchronization to adaption effects in a probabilistic reinforcement learning task. A Q-Learning model was used to estimate prediction errors, which indicated whether a situation reflects a learning opportunity. While the work mentioned above explicitly addresses the processing of prediction errors, there are other cognitive processes and corresponding neurological markers related to learning events, for example working memory activity [3]. Early work on the relation of EEG synchronization/de-synchronization and memory processes has identified theta synchronization and alpha desynchronization during supposed memory processes [7,5,16,10]. Regarding alpha oscillations, following research has also identified "paradoxial" alpha synchronization during cognitive activity, which in subsequent work [6,11,9,14] was reinterpreted as a possible inhibition of task irrelevant cortical processes or conscious inhibition of cognitive processes impeding the task.

In this paper, we establish neurological markers of learning opportunities in a complex associative learning task, particularly considering memory encoding and feedback processing. We selected a complex learning task where a sequence of interdependent decisions is required to achieve a desired outcome. Tasks of this type that do not not involve probabilistic outcomes have so far not been considered in EEG studies of RL. However, learning such action sequences is both common and important in human-computer interaction, for example when trying to achieve a particular result with an unfamiliar software.

3   Methods

The behavioral task employed is an modified version of the task used in [4]. Formally, it is an abstract tree-search which requires three binary decisions to move from the root node to a leaf node. Feedback about the success of a decision sequence is provided when reaching a leaf node. When reaching a non-target leaf node (failure), participants are moved back to the last node where they were still on path to the target. When reaching the target leaf node node (success) one learning trial is complete and the participant is returned to the root node for the next trial. Semantically, the task is framed as a "strange machine", which has four buttons (red, yellow, green, blue) and a display showing its current state in a "unknown language" (a pronounceable German non-word such as "Tarfe"). See Figure 1 for a summary of the internal structure and the display of a node. In each state two of the buttons are active to move the machine into the next state. After three button presses, the machine either reaches the target state or a failure state and is reset as described above. The task goal is to learn to reach the target state as consistently as possible without failures. To increase learning load, each state node has three possible labels associated with different response options. At each visit of a node one of these sets is randomly selected and displayed to the participant.

The procedure consisted of brief instructions followed by 15 practice trials and a main learning phase with 100 trials[1]. If participants completed the main learning phase in less than 45 minutes, a second learning phase with a differently labeled version of the machine was conducted.

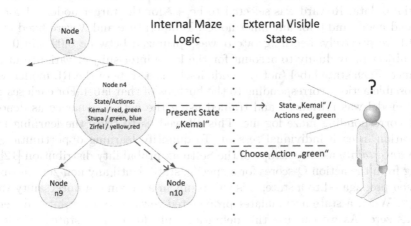

Fig. 1. Internal structure and external view of the "strange machine" task

---

[1] For the first 8 participants the main learning phase lasted 120 or 160 trials, which due to ceiling effects was subsequently reduced to 100.

Data were collected from 34 university students (23 female, mean age 23.1 years). Participants gave written consent and were paid for their participation. 18 participants completed two machines, 16 completed only one.

EEG was recorded from 29 scalp electrodes placed according to the international 10-20 system using actiCAP active electrodes and actiCHamp amplifiers (Brain Products, Germany) at a sampling rate of 500 Hz with Cz as recording reference. The EEG data were re-referenced to a common average reference and segmented into windows of 400ms length starting 100ms after a new state is displayed. Data segments containing ocular artifacts were identified and removed by testing for correlation of electrodes Fp1 and Fp2 above a threshold of 0.97 within the regarded time frame. This procedure rejects approximately 4.5% of all trials. This means each window contains data from processing the feedback (either a new state of direct feedback at a leaf node) following a decision step. Each window was normalized by subtracting the mean from 250-150ms before stimulus. For band power analysis, we used the Thomson's multitaper power spectral density (PSD) estimate [13]. The relevant (sub-)bands for analysis were estimated on an individual basis following the method of [8]. The averaged PSD was then z-normalized for each subject.

Similar to [4], we used a Reinforcement Learning approach to model human learning behavior. We employed the Naive Q-Learning (NQL) algorithm, a variant of Watkin's $Q(\lambda)$ [12] to model the participants' learning progress. NQL is a Temporal Difference (TD) method with eligibility traces. The work of [15] demonstrates that TD methods are capable of reproducing human learning behavior and predict the generation of propagated FRNs. This work also demonstrated the benefit of eligibility traces for the purpose of closely fitting human behavioral data. Reward was selected to be $+7$ for the target node, -1 for the dead-end nodes and 0 for any inner nodes. Temperature and λ were fixed at 1.0 and 0.1, respectively. Learning rate α was optimized between 0.02 and 0.3 for each subject individually to account for the large inter-subject variance in performance. Each state label (not the node itself) is a state of the RL model, with two possible actions corresponding to the buttons of that label. For each session, a new model was initialized and trained using the action sequence as denoted in the corresponding maze log file. This allowed us to trace the learning from observation in each individual session. To quantify learning opportunities, we define *uncertainty* as the entropy of the Softmax probability distribution [12] resulting from the action Q-scores for a specific state. Until any non-zero feedback has been propagated to a state, this will result in a maximum uncertainty value of $\log 2$. When a state accumulates propagated rewards, uncertainty converges towards zero. As we can use this definition only for correct states, we define certain incorrect nodes to have a negative Q-score $< -\epsilon$ for both actions. The benefit of the notion of uncertainty compared to the classic notion of prediction error - which is defined as the update delta of the Q-score of the outgoing state for a certain step (see for example [15]) - is that it is defined in terms of states and not in terms of steps. Therefore, it can help a tutoring system to identify states which are not yet sufficiently well learned.

4   Analysis

We now investigate the relation between the prediction of computational RL model and empirical EEG data to identify situations in which learning occurs. We do this in two main steps: First, we use the RL model to predict learning opportunities and look at neurological correlates in the EEG data. Second, we differentiate learning opportunities between successful and unsuccessful learning attempts. This second step shows how EEG markers and computational model interact to identify learning situations better than each of them can individually.

For the analysis of EEG synchronization and desynchronization, we concentrate on two effects that are related to feeback processing and memory encoding: Theta synchronization in the prefrontal cortex and alpha synchronization in the occipital cortex. We average PSD across electrodes O1 and O2 to represent occipital activity and average PSD across electrode positions Fz, Fc1, Fc2 to represent prefrontal activity.

We assume that memory encoding occurs systematically when new information on the task is learned from the feedback at the end of certain steps. We therefore have to identify those situations which allow learning. To sort the steps into classes, we use the RL model and apply two thresholds to dichotomize uncertainty: A strict threshold t_s (selected to characterize 80% of all values as 'high uncertainty') and a tolerant t_t threshold (selected to characterize 30% of all values as 'high uncertainty'). We use t_s to label outgoing states as (un)certain and t_t to label incoming states. This choice minimizes the number of missed learning opportunities. The left half of Figure 2 summarizes the class definition: Class LEARN denotes a learning opportunity, class NO-INFO denotes absence of a learning opportunity due to missing information and class SATURATED denotes absence of a learning opportunity due to an already saturated knowledge. We expect to see pronounced differences between the first and the latter two classes. We expect the latter two classes to be similar. To avoid class imbalance, we only include the first five occurrences of each state in each class in our analysis. Statistics are calculated on the normalized averaged PSD distributions for the respective classes as a two-sided paired t-test. To rule out that low-frequency ocular artifacts confound the results, we checked that there was no significant difference in eye blink frequency between the different classes during preprocessing.

Figure 3 shows average occipital alpha power and average prefrontal theta power calculated for the three classes separately. We see a increase in alpha power from the NO-INFO class to the LEARN class in the occipital cortex, while there is no significant difference between NO-INFO and SATURATED. Analogously, we see a difference between NO-INFO class to the LEARN and SATURATED classes in the theta band for the prefrontal cortex. However, those differences in the regarded bands marginally miss statistical significance: $t(36) = 1.48$, $p = 0.07$ for occipital alpha and $t(36) = 1.62$, $p = 0.057$ for prefrontal theta. One reason for this observation is that learning opportunities denote the potential for learning, but do not always lead to memory encoding as the subject overlooks the opportunity or is not able to correctly memorize the new information.

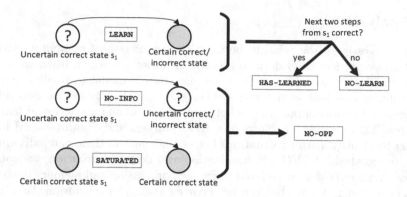

Fig. 2. Definition of learning opportunities (left) and learning situations (right) as derived from the RL model to form the classes for evaluation of classes

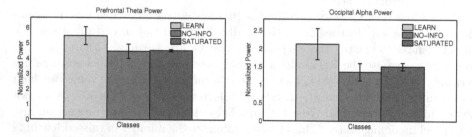

Fig. 3. Theta power at the prefrontal cortex (left) and alpha power at the occipital cortex (right) for the classes LEARN, SATURATED and NO-INFO for learning opportunities. Whiskers indicate standard error.

The criteria we defined in the RL model yield a reasonable prediction whether a learning situation occurs during a specific step. In the previous analysis, we assumed the definition of a learning situation as a given ground truth to investigate neurological markers for learning. However, we concluded that the computational model can only yield a noisy prediction of a successfully learning event. To quantify this predictive power, we introduce the term of a *learned state*. A learned state is a correct state s for which the next two steps starting in s stay on the correct path. 38% of all steps labeled as learning situations do not result in a learned state[2]. In the following, we combine this prediction by the computational RL model with the information of EEG to detect those missed learning opportunities. We propose that the observed alpha and theta synchronization effects are caused by cognitive processes of learning situations. This implies that when sorting learning opportunities in learned and not-learned outgoing states, we should observe a similar difference in PSD: Learned outgoing states show a level of alpha and theta synchronization which is not present for missed learning

---

[2] This number depends of course on the threshold applied to the uncertainty level of the outgoing step. A lower threshold leads to fewer false alarms but also increases the number of missed learning opportunities.

opportunities. To investigate this hypothesis, we sort the steps from the LEARN class of the positive and negative learning opportunities by this criterion, forming the HAS-LEARNED and the NOT-LEARNED classes. Steps which are not categorized as learning opportunities form the NO-OPP class, see the right half of Figure 2. On average, the LEARN class contains 26.1 steps, while the LEARN class contains 16.6 steps. Figure 4 shows the band power for the three different classes, now resulting in a significant ($t(35) = 2.74$, $p < 0.005$) increase in individual alpha power from the non-learned to the learned steps, as well as a significant difference in theta power ($t(35) = 1.76$, $p < 0.05$) in the prefrontal cortex. The steps in the NOT-LEARNED class are not significantly different from steps in NO-OPP for both brain regions.

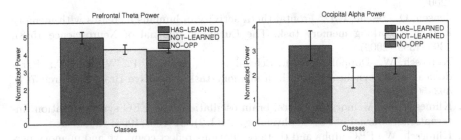

Fig. 4. Theta power at the prefrontal cortex (left) and alpha power at the occipital cortex (right) for the classes HAS-LEARNED, NOT-LEARNED and NO-OPP for learning situations. Whiskers indicate standard error.

To make this significant difference accessible for a tutoring system, we need to provide prediction of learning situations on a single trial basis. For this purpose, we train a Naive Bayes classifier to separate the HAS-LEARNED and the NOT-LEARNED class. As features, we use individual occipital alpha power and prefrontal theta power. We evaluate this classifier in a participant-dependent leave-one-out crossvalidation. To exclude cases where one class receives too few training samples, we remove the most imbalanced sessions where the majority class contains more than 70% of all samples from the analysis. The resulting classifier yields an average recognition accuracy of 71.0% which is significantly better ($t(25) = 2.49$, $p = 0.01$) than the baseline accuracy of 59.6%, as determined by a one-sided paired t-test of classification accuracy vs. size of majority class for each subject. The average improvement over the baseline is 19.7% relative.

To conclude, our results show that we can use the RL model to identify learning opportunities in an associative learning task, despite delayed feedback. We showed this by providing neural evidence for learning. We further showed that we can combine the model with such EEG markers to predict learning success. This is also feasible on a single trial basis. Future work will concentrate on reducing label noise by using a more sophisticated cognitive model (e.g. explicitly representing working memory) implemented in a cognitive architecture.

References

1. Anderson, J.R., Betts, S., Ferris, J.L., Fincham, J.M.: Neural imaging to track mental states while using an intelligent tutoring system. Proceedings of the National Academy of Sciences 107(15), 7018–7023 (2010)
2. Cavanagh, J.F., Frank, M.J., Klein, T.J., Allen, J.J.B.: Frontal theta links prediction errors to behavioral adaptation in reinforcement learning. NeuroImage 49(4), 3198–3209 (2010)
3. Collins, A.G.E., Frank, M.J.: How much of reinforcement learning is working memory, not reinforcement learning? a behavioral, computational, and neurogenetic analysis. European Journal of Neuroscience 35(7), 1024–1035 (2012)
4. Fu, W.-T., Anderson, J.R.: From recurrent choice to skill learning: A reinforcement-learning model. Journal of Experimental Psychology: General 135(2), 184–206 (2006)
5. Jensen, O., Tesche, C.D.: Frontal theta activity in humans increases with memory load in a working memory task. The European Journal of Neuroscience 15(8), 1395–1399 (2002)
6. Klimesch, W., Doppelmayr, M., Schwaiger, J., Auinger, P., Winkler, T.: 'Paradoxical' alpha synchronization in a memory task. Cognitive Brain Research 7(4), 493–501 (1999)
7. Klimesch, W.: Memory processes, brain oscillations and EEG synchronization. International Journal of Psychophysiology 24(1-2), 61–100 (1996)
8. Klimesch, W.: EEG alpha and theta oscillations reflect cognitive and memory performance: a review and analysis. Brain Research Reviews 29(2-3), 169–195 (1999)
9. Klimesch, W., Sauseng, P., Hanslmayr, S.: EEG alpha oscillations: The inhibition-timing hypothesis. Brain Research Reviews 53(1), 63–88 (2007)
10. Osipova, D., Takashima, A., Oostenveld, R., Fernández, G., Maris, E., Jensen, O.: Theta and gamma oscillations predict encoding and retrieval of declarative memory. The Journal of Neuroscience 26(28), 7523–7531 (2006); PMID: 16837600
11. Sauseng, P., Klimesch, W., Doppelmayr, M., Pecherstorfer, T., Freunberger, R., Hanslmayr, S.: EEG alpha synchronization and functional coupling during top-down processing in a working memory task. Human Brain Mapping 26(2), 148–155 (2005)
12. Sutton, R.S., Barto, A.G.: Introduction to Reinforcement Learning, 1st edn. MIT Press, Cambridge (1998)
13. Thomson, D.J.: Spectrum estimation and harmonic analysis. Proceedings of the IEEE 70(9), 1055–1096 (1982)
14. Tuladhar, A.M., ter Huurne, N., Schoffelen, J.-M., Maris, E., Oostenveld, R., Jensen, O.: Parieto-occipital sources account for the increase in alpha activity with working memory load. Human Brain Mapping 28(8), 785–792 (2007)
15. Walsh, M.M., Anderson, J.R.: Learning from delayed feedback: neural responses in temporal credit assignment. Cognitive, Affective, & Behavioral Neuroscience 11(2), 131–143 (2011)
16. Weiss, S., Müller, H.M., Rappelsberger, P.: Theta synchronization predicts efficient memory encoding of concrete and abstract nouns. Neuroreport 11(11), 2357–2361 (2000)

Structured Prediction for Object Detection in Deep Neural Networks

Hannes Schulz and Sven Behnke

Rheinische Friedrich-Wilhelms-Universität Bonn, Institut für Informatik VI,
Friedrich-Ebert-Allee 144, Bonn, Germany
{schulz,behnke}@ais.uni-bonn.de

Abstract. Deep convolutional neural networks are currently applied to computer vision tasks, especially object detection. Due to the large dimensionality of the output space, four dimensions per bounding box of an object, classification techniques do not apply easily. We propose to adapt a structured loss function for neural network training which directly maximizes overlap of the prediction with ground truth bounding boxes. We show how this structured loss can be implemented efficiently, and demonstrate bounding box prediction on two of the Pascal VOC 2007 classes.

Keywords: deep learning, neural networks, object detection.

1 Introduction

After great success in image classification, neural network research has recently turned to detecting instances of object categories in images. Here, the task is to predict a bounding box $y \in \mathbb{R}^4$ for every object of a given class. Object detection differs from image classification in one main aspect—the solution space is huge. In fact, it contains any number of bounding boxes with position, size, and aspect ratio. Correctness is typically defined by measuring overlap with the ground truth, such that more than one correct solution exists. Under these conditions, simply scaling the multinomial logistic loss, which worked for classification of the 1000-class ImageNet dataset, is not an option. Instead, a number of competing approaches have been proposed.

In this paper, we shortly review recently published methods for object detection with deep neural networks and emphasize that they, successfully, optimize heuristic surrogate loss functions. These surrogate loss functions are related to the overlap criterion via an accompanying post-processing step, which is not part of the training algorithm.

We then suggest an alternative method based on structured prediction, which optimizes the overlap criterion directly. We show how to determine bounding boxes efficiently while training and how to translate them into gradients. We evaluate our proposed method on two selected classes of the Pascal VOC 2007 dataset.

S. Wermter et al. (Eds.): ICANN 2014, LNCS 8681, pp. 395–402, 2014.

2   Related Work

Deep neural networks are increasingly applied to computer vision tasks such as image classification [1] or object-class segmentation [2]. Recent advances leading to success in the ImageNet challenge stem from *dropout* to prevent overfitting [3], rectifying linear units for improved convergence, backpropagation through max-pooling [4] and GPU implementations for speed, all of which are also used in this work.

Neural networks trained for an easy task can be adapted to more complex, but related tasks [5, 6]. Consequently, neural net-based object detection methods start with networks trained for classification [7, 8], or learn classification at the same time as detection [9].

Girshick et al. [8] use a pipeline for detection with selective search region proposals [10], which are warped and classified by a deep neural network. The learned features are then used as input to a support vector machine and outputs are ranked. In contrast to our method, this practice relies heavily on the potentially slow pre-segmentation to find object candidates. Sermanet et al. [9] regress on bounding box coordinates and classification confidence from a low-resolution output map. The network is run on six scales and produces many bounding box candidates, which are then merged by a heuristic merging operation for prediction. Here, we directly optimize bounding box overlap and associate predicted bounding boxes and ground truth objects while learning. Erhan et al. [11] produce a fixed set of bounding boxes during training, which are associated to the ground truth bounding boxes to determine the gradient. This method is closest to ours. However, we do not explicitly regress on bounding box coordinates and instead keep the direct correspondence between image and bounding box by using output maps. Our method also does not output a fixed set of bounding box candidates per image, since we infer their number from the network output. Finally, Szegedy et al. [7] construct targets for low-resolution output-maps, which encode the bounding box and its object quadrants. A heuristic function combines the outputs to produce the final bounding boxes. This approach requires one network per class and five times as many output maps as classes, which poses a potential scaling problem. Also, it is not clear whether the network can or should spend effort on refining a regression, when the desired output is a bounding box. Our proposed loss vanishes when the correct bounding box output is produced.

3   Structured Prediction for Object Detection

We start with a deep convolutional neural network, without fully-connected layers. The number of maps in the output layer is equal to the number of detectable object-classes in the dataset. Our goal will be to produce values in the output map from which the bounding boxes in the image can be inferred. For inference, which is also part of our learning procedure, we make use of the fact that the space of bounding boxes is *structured,* i.e. can be searched efficiently. In the following description, we draw heavily on Lampert et al. [13, 12], and adapt their formalism to neural networks.

We are given a training set of tuples $(x^i, Y^i)_{i=1,\ldots,n} \subset \mathcal{X} \times \mathbb{P}(\mathcal{Y})$, where x is an image, Y is a set of bounding boxes, $\mathcal{Y}$ contains all possible bounding boxes in x, and $\mathbb{P}(\mathcal{Y})$ is the powerset of $\mathcal{Y}$. The prediction function $g(x) : \mathcal{X} \mapsto \mathbb{P}(\mathcal{Y})$ should minimize the empirical loss over the training set

$$\mathbb{E}_{x,Y}\left[\Delta(g(x), Y)\right], \tag{1}$$

where $g(x) =: \hat{\mathcal{Y}}$ is the inference function. The evaluation criterion for detection is typically given as a 50% threshold on the Jaccard index of the prediction and a ground truth object,

$$A(\bar{y}, y) = \begin{cases} 0 & \text{if } \frac{\text{area}(\bar{y} \cap y)}{\text{area}(\bar{y} \cup y)} > \frac{1}{2} \\ 1 & \text{otherwise.} \end{cases} \tag{2}$$

We also penalize the case where not all objects in an image have been identified, or more objects were returned than present in the ground truth Y. This is formalized in the set loss $\Delta : \mathbb{P}(\mathcal{Y}) \times \mathbb{P}(\mathcal{Y}) \mapsto \mathbb{R}$. Lampert [13] suggests to use the max loss,

$$\Delta(Y, \hat{Y}) = \max_{y \in Y \ominus \hat{Y}} \lambda(Y, y), \tag{3}$$

where $Y \ominus \hat{Y}$ is the symmetric set difference and

$$\lambda(Y, y) = \begin{cases} 1 & \text{if } y \in Y \\ \min_{\bar{y} \in Y} A(\bar{y}, y) & \text{else.} \end{cases} \tag{4}$$

Expanding the symmetric set difference and simplifying slightly, we get

$$\Delta(Y, \hat{Y}) = \max\left(\min\left(1, \left|Y \setminus \hat{Y}\right|\right), \max_{y \in \hat{Y} \setminus Y} \min_{\bar{y} \in Y} A(\bar{y}, y)\right). \tag{5}$$

The first term accounts for objects in the ground truth for which no corresponding detection $\hat{y} \in \hat{Y}$ exists. The second term penalizes predictions which are not corresponding to ground truth objects. One possible problem here is that we could find one object as many times as there are objects in the image, using slightly different $\hat{y}$ that all overlap with one y. To prevent multile detection, we require that elements of $\hat{Y}$ have a maximum Jaccard index of 0.2, which can be enforced by greedily rejecting non-matching bounding boxes in the sequential inference procedure.

Next, we define a compatibility function f between a neural network output map $N(x)$ and the bounding boxes $y \in Y$ over pixels i, j. A bounding box is a mask y on $N(x)$, where the rectangular part corresponding to the bounding box was set to 1, and all other values to 0:

$$f(x, Y, \theta) = \sum_{y \in Y} \sum_{ij} N_{ij}(x, \theta) \cdot y_{ij}. \tag{6}$$

For learning, we would like to find parameters θ s.t.

$$g(x) = \arg\max_{\hat{Y} \in \mathbb{P}(\mathcal{Y})} f(x, \hat{Y}, \theta) \approx y. \tag{7}$$

For a given training tuple (x^i, Y^i), we can bound the loss using a hinge loss upper bound, as in Taskar et al. [14], obtaining

$$\Delta(g(x^i), Y^i) = \Delta \left(\arg\max_{Y \in \mathbb{P}(\mathcal{Y})} f(x^i, Y, \theta), Y^i \right) \tag{8}$$

$$\leq \max_{\hat{Y} \in \mathbb{P}(\mathcal{Y})} \left[\Delta(\hat{Y}, Y^i) - f(x, Y^i, \theta) + f(x, \hat{Y}, \theta) \right] \tag{9}$$

$$= \max_{\hat{Y} \in \mathbb{P}(\mathcal{Y})} \underbrace{\left[\Delta(\hat{Y}, Y^i) + f(x, \hat{Y}, \theta) \right]}_{H(N(x^i), \hat{Y}, Y^i)} - f(x, Y^i, \theta). \tag{10}$$

The role of the loss term is to ensure that the bounding boxes selected tend to have a bad detection measure, thereby forcing the network in $f(\cdot, \cdot, \cdot)$ to increase its margin over them.

The maximization in Eq. (10) can be performed as described in Lampert et al. [12], using branch-and-bound on $\mathcal{Y}$. Branch-and-bound recursively splits $\mathcal{Y}$ into subsets, which are described by two rectangles; $o_\cup$ describes the maximum extents of all bounding boxes in the set, whereas $o_\cap$ describes the minimum extents. For a given tuple $(o_\cup, o_\cap)$, we construct an upper bound $\overline{\Delta H}$ on the change in Δ caused by adding $\hat{y} \in (o_\cup, o_\cap)$ to $\hat{Y}$,

$$\max_{\hat{y} \in (o_\cup, o_\cap) \subset \mathcal{Y}} \left[H(N(x), \hat{Y} \cup \{\hat{y}\}, Y) - H(N(x), \hat{Y}, Y) \right] \leq \overline{\Delta H}(o_\cup, o_\cap, N(x), \hat{Y}, Y) \tag{11}$$

$$= F^+(N(x), o_\cup) - F^-(N(x), o_\cap)$$
$$+ \max \left(\min(1, \max_{\bar{y} \in (o_\cup, o_\cap)} |Y \setminus (\hat{Y} \cup \{\bar{y}\})|), \min_{\bar{y} \in Y} \bar{A}(\bar{y}, o_\cap, o_\cup) \right) \tag{12}$$

where

$$\bar{A}(y, o_\cap, o_\cup) = \begin{cases} 0 & \text{if } \frac{y \cap o_\cup}{y \cup o_\cap} > \frac{1}{2} \\ 1 & \text{else,} \end{cases} \tag{13}$$

$$F^+(N(x), o_\cup) = \sum_{ij} \max(0, N_{ij}(x)) o_{\cup ij}, \text{ and} \tag{14}$$

$$F^-(N(x), o_\cap) = \sum_{ij} \min(0, N_{ij}(x)) o_{\cap ij}. \tag{15}$$

Table 1. Network Architecture for learning two classes

Layer	Output Size	Filter Size	Channels	Groups	Stride	Padding	Pool Size	Pool Stride
Input	224×224	–	3	–	–	–	–	–
Conv1	108×108	7	96	1	2	0	3	2
Conv2	49×49	5	256	6	1	0	3	2
Conv3	24×24	3	512	8	1	1	–	–
Conv4	24×24	3	512	16	1	1	–	–
Conv5	24×24	3	64	16	1	1	–	–
Conv6	22×22	3	2	1	1	0	–	–

Fig. 1. Sample first-layer features of the classification network trained to discriminate between *cow* and *horse* images

The rectangle sums $F^{\pm}(\cdot,\cdot)$ can be efficiently evaluated by pre-computing one integral image for each. A queue ensures that the search in $\mathcal{Y}$ is efficient.

Intuitively, learning proceeds by minimizing sums in the rectangles which are found by branch-and-bound on an output map $N(\cdot)$ and maximizing the sum of ground truth bounding boxes. Since bounding boxes overlapping with ground truth are given a disadvantage in Eq. (10), we focus on likely false detections (c.f. hard negatives) during optimization. Note that in contrast to Szegedy et al. [7], we do not need to specify on a per-pixel basis which value the output map should have, we only require the sums of regions to be higher or lower. The gradient consists of (differences of) rendered bounding boxes. For non-loss-augmented inference, the loss term is dropped from Eq. (10).

Multi-Class Training with Weak Labelings. In principle, all classes can be handled separately. Labels are typically weak, however, since not all objects are annotated. As commonly done, we only treat images I as negative for class c when no object of class c is annotated in I. Additionally, if a ground truth bounding box y is matched by $\hat{y}$ with a Jaccard index greater 0.5, we render the "negative" bounding box for $\hat{y}$ to refine the position found and eliminate the gradient in the overlap region. Since we intend to increase the margin of ground truth bounding boxes over others in $\mathcal{Y}$, we train only on images or parts of images which contain at least one annotated object.

4 Experiments

We present experiments on two difficult and easily confusable object classes, *cow* and *horse*. Our network architecture is shown in Table 1. It is roughly inspired

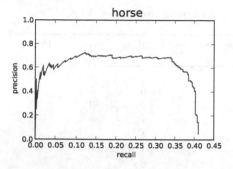
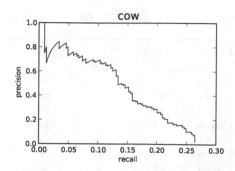

Fig. 2. Precision and recall curves for the two detected object classes *horse* and *cow* on the VOC 2007 test set, with average precision of 0.295 and 0.149, respectively

by Krizhevsky et al. [1][1], but optimized for larger output maps. It also lacks the fully connected layers, which significantly reduces its capacity.

We pre-train the model with binary classification between the two classes we want to detect, using 8193 images from the Pascal10X database [15]. For this purpose, we add two fully connected layers with 1024 hidden neurons and MaxOut non-linearity [16], each. The network is trained using ADAGRAD [17] to adapt the learning rates. The input images are scaled such that their shortest dimension is 256, then we extract a random crop of size 224×224. The images are flipped horizontally with a probability of 0.5. We perform this preprocessing in parallel on CPU, while the network runs on GPU. The network does not overfit on a held-out validation set (4466 images), but reduces the training error to zero. Figure 1 shows a subset of the learned first-layer features.

In a second step, we train the network to detect objects on the same split of Pascal10X, using the methods described in Section 3. Again, we use ADAGRAD for learning rate adaptation, and a learning rate of 0.01. The bounding boxes in the dataset are scaled down by a factor of two before supplying them to the network to aid discrimination between neighboring objects. During loss-augmented inference, we find up to four bounding boxes with a Jaccard index of at most 0.2. The time required for loss-augmented inference amounts to approximately 1/7 of the network evaluation time (forward and backward pass) when performed on CPU without any parallelization. As input we use (possibly flipped) images from three different scales in steps of 1/2 octaves. The largest scale is chosen such that the original image corners are in the center of the receptive field of the corner output neurons. For this purpose, we add margin by mirroring parts of the image. Objects have to be at least two pixels wide when transformed to the output map, otherwise we do not use them as training examples on a given scale.

After convergence, we evaluate the network on the test set of the 2007 version of the Pascal Visual Object Classes Challenge [18] (402 images containing either a horse or a cow). Here, we use a sliding window on all three scales and combine the outputs within one scale by a max($\cdot, \cdot$) operation. We scale all maps to the same

---

[1] We would like to thank Alex Krizhevsky for making his code publicly available.

Fig. 3. Sample object detections. The figure shows the output map activations for the respective class. There are three scales, the lower two are processed with sliding window and merged using $\max(\cdot, \cdot)$. The bottom row shows the input image with detected bounding boxes.

size. Following Szegedy et al. [7], we use k-means clustering on the bounding boxes in the training set and determine 10 reference bounding boxes, which we then scale by factors of $\{0.1, 0.2, \ldots, 0.9\}$. We slide all 90 bounding boxes over every scale and determine local maxima. Finally, we reduce the predicted set by removing bounding boxes which overlap with higher scoring ones by more than 20%. Figure 2 shows precision/recall curves for the two learned classes, and Figure 3 shows sample detections. The average precision for the *horse* class is comparable to Szegedy et al. [7] and Erhan et al. [11], however, both of these works trained on a complete VOC 2012 dataset.

5   Conclusion

Following success on ImageNet classification, there is much attention on adopting deep convolutional neural networks to perform more complex computer vision tasks, especially object detection. Multiple formulations have been proposed so far, to which we added our own. In contrast to previous work, we do not regress surrogate loss functions. Instead, we infer bounding boxes during training and minimize the overlap criterion directly, drawing heavily on previous work on structured prediction in the context of support vector machines.

We evaluate our model on two difficult classes of the VOC 2007 dataset, *cow* and *horse*, pretrained by classification, and show that with our formulation, a deep neural network can learn to localize instances of the two classes well. While results on two classes are not conclusive, we believe that this proof-of-concept shows that learning bounding boxes with structured prediction is feasible in deep neural networks. A more general pre-training on a larger dataset and wider architecture, as well as more network capacity and explicit handling of close-by objects is likely to improve the results significantly.

References

1. Krizhevsky, A., Sutskever, I., Hinton, G.: Imagenet classification with deep convolutional neural networks. In: Adv. In Neural Information Processing Systems (2012)
2. Schulz, H., Behnke, S.: Learning object-class segmentation with convolutional neural networks. In: Eur. Symp. on Art. Neural Networks (2012)
3. Hinton, G.E., Srivastava, N., Krizhevsky, A., Sutskever, I., Salakhutdinov, R.R.: Improving neural networks by preventing co-adaptation of feature detectors. arXiv: 1207.0580 (2012)
4. Scherer, D., Müller, A., Behnke, S.: Evaluation of pooling operations in convolutional architectures for object recognition. In: Diamantaras, K., Duch, W., Iliadis, L.S. (eds.) ICANN 2010, Part III. LNCS, vol. 6354, pp. 92–101. Springer, Heidelberg (2010)
5. Hinton, G.E., Salakhutdinov, R.R.: Reducing the dimensionality of data with neural networks. Science 313(5786) (2006)
6. Bengio, Y., Lamblin, P., Popovici, D., Larochelle, H., et al.: Greedy layer-wise training of deep networks. In: Adv. in Neural Information Processing Systems 19 (2007)
7. Szegedy, C., Toshev, A., Erhan, D.: Deep Neural Networks for Object Detection. In: Adv. in Neural Information Processing Systems (2013)
8. Girshick, R., Donahue, J., Darrell, T., Malik, J.: Rich feature hierarchies for accurate object detection and semantic segmentation. arXiv: 1311.2524 (2013)
9. Sermanet, P., Eigen, D., Zhang, X., Mathieu, M., Fergus, R., LeCun, Y.: Over-Feat: Integrated Recognition, Localization and Detection using Convolutional Networks, arXiv: 1312.6229 (2013)
10. Uijlings, J., van de Sande, K., Gevers, T., Smeulders, A.: Selective search for object recognition. Int. Journal of Computer Vision 104(2) (2013)
11. Erhan, D., Szegedy, C., Toshev, A., Anguelov, D.: Scalable Object Detection using Deep Neural Networks. arXiv: 1312.2249 (2013)
12. Lampert, C.H., Blaschko, M.B., Hofmann, T.: Efficient subwindow search: A branch and bound framework for object localization. IEEE Transactions on Pattern Analysis and Machine Intelligence 31(12) (2009)
13. Lampert, C.H.: Maximum Margin Multi-Label Structured Prediction. In: Adv. in Neural Information Processing Systems, vol. 11 (2011)
14. Taskar, B., Chatalbashev, V., Koller, D., Guestrin, C.: Learning structured prediction models: A large margin approach. In: Int. Conf. on Machine Learning (2005)
15. Zhu, X., Vondrick, C., Ramanan, D., Fowlkes, C.: Do We Need More Training Data or Better Models for Object Detection? In: British Machine Vision Conference (2012)
16. Goodfellow, I.J., Warde-Farley, D., Mirza, M., Courville, A., Bengio, Y.: Maxout networks. In: Int. Conf. on Machine Learning (2013)
17. Duchi, J., Hazan, E., Singer, Y.: Adaptive subgradient methods for online learning and stochastic optimization. The Journal of Machine Learning Research 12 (2011)
18. Everingham, M., Van Gool, L., Williams, C.K., Winn, J., Zisserman, A.: The pascal visual object classes (VOC) challenge. Int. Journal of Computer Vision 88(2) (2010)

A Multichannel Convolutional Neural Network for Hand Posture Recognition

Pablo Barros, Sven Magg, Cornelius Weber, and Stefan Wermter

University of Hamburg, Department of Computer Science,
Vogt-Koelln-Strasse 30, 22527 Hamburg, Germany
{barros,magg,weber,wermter}@informatik.uni-hamburg.de
http://www.informatik.uni-hamburg.de/WTM/

Abstract. Natural communication between humans involves hand gestures, which has an impact on research in human-robot interaction. In a real-world scenario, understanding human gestures by a robot is hard due to several challenges like hand segmentation. To recognize hand postures this paper proposes a novel convolutional implementation. The model is able to recognize hand postures recorded by a robot camera in real-time, in a real-world application scenario. The proposed model was also evaluated with a benchmark database and showed better results than the ones reported in the benchmark paper.

Keywords: Hand Postures, Convolution Neural Networks, Deep Learning.

1 Introduction

Gestures are recognized as crucial for human-human communication [12] and have inspired research for human-robot interaction [1] [4]. Hand gestures are widely used compared to other body parts [6], and thus are the main focus of most of the research in this field.

The most common approach for gesture recognition, as shown in the survey of Rautaray et al. [10] is the application of feature extraction techniques to represent postures. A popular feature extraction solution is to represent the hand by matching it to a template [4]. A problem with the template match approach is that a high variety of gestures executed by different kinds of people cannot be matched. Most of the feature extraction solutions need to segment the hand from the background of the image which can be done using a color scheme. Jmaa et al. [5] use an YCbCr color space model to separate the color information from the image luminance and obtain hand segmentation. This approach is not reliable if using a large variation in skin colors and luminance. Most of the applications using feature extraction use domain-based models and thus provide very specialized solutions [1].

Deep learning models for image classification have been studied in a vast number of experiments in the past few years [3]. Among deep learning techniques, Convolutional Neural Networks [7] have shown good results in the classification

S. Wermter et al. (Eds.): ICANN 2014, LNCS 8681, pp. 403–410, 2014.
© Springer International Publishing Switzerland 2014

of static images [8]. The use of convolutional models focuses on how the human brain enhances and extracts features of an image in an implicit way using a set of local and global features.

This research describes a CNN, called Multichannel Convolutional Neural Network (MCNN), which allows the recognition of hand postures with implicit feature extraction. This novel architecture uses a cubic kernel concept and a multichannel flow of information, which allows it to recognize images even if they have a small size. The proposed architecture uses a similar concept of feature representation found in the research of Wallis et al. [14] and Wiskott et al. [15]. In their research, they create invariant responses of individual units to multiple instances of the same class. In the proposed model, this is possible with the implementation of a cubic kernel in the first convolutional layer. The research of [2] et al. uses convolutional layers stacked together to classify static images. In their research, several independent stacks of convolutional layers are put side-by-side and their results averaged to produce an improved classification rate. In their research, each stack receives the same image preprocessed with different algorithms. In our model, the channels are connected in the deep layers and trained together.

The model is evaluated in two different databases with static hand postures. One contains images taken by a robot in a home-like laboratory, simulating a real world scenario. There are four hand postures that are presented in different positions in each image. The other database is a benchmark database that contains ten different hand postures, three different backgrounds and has the hand always centered in the image.

2   Multichannel Convolutional Neural Network

A Convolutional Neural Network (CNN) is a set of pairs of convolution and max-pooling layers that enable the model to extract and enhance implicit features of an image. When stacked together, the first layers act like an edge enhancement and allow to extract local features which are passed to deeper layers which act like global feature extractors.

Each convolutional layer contains a set of feature maps, or filters, that extract features from a region of units using a convolution. Then an additive bias is applied and the result is passed through a sigmoid function. The value of a unit v_{nc}^{xy} in the position (x,y) at the nth feature map in the cth layer is given by

$$v_{nc}^{xy} = tanh\left(b_{cn} + \sum_{m}\sum_{h=0}^{H_{i-1}}\sum_{w=0}^{W_{i-1}} w_{ijm}^{hw} v_{(i-1)m}^{(x+h)(y+w)}\right), \tag{1}$$

where tanh is the hyperbolic tangent function, b_{cn} is the bias for the nth feature map of the cth layer, m indexes over the set of features maps in the $(i$-$1)$ layer connected to the current layer c. In the equation, w_{nck} is the weight of the connection between the unit (h,w) within a region, or kernel, connected to the previous layer. H_i and W_i are the height and width of the kernel.

In the max-pooling layers, a region of the previous layer is connected to a unit in the current layer, reducing the dimension of the feature maps. For each layer, only the maximum value is passed. This enhances invariance to scale and distortions of the input [2]. The parameters of a CNN could be learned either by a supervised approach tuning the filters in a training database [3], or an unsupervised approach [9]. The proposed model uses the supervised approach.

2.1   Concept of a Cubic Kernel

In a CNN the convolution layers are applied on 2D feature maps to compute spatial features. To improve the feature enhancement the concept of a cubic kernel is applied. A cubic kernel is applied in a stack of images, simulating a 3D filter. The value of a unit (x,y,z) at the nth feature map in the cth layer is defined by

$$v_{nc}^{xyz} = tanh\left(b_{cn} + \sum_{m}\sum_{h=0}^{H_i-1}\sum_{w=0}^{W_i-1}\sum_{r=0}^{R_1-1} w_{ijm}^{pqr} v_{(i-1)m}^{(x+p)(y+q)(z+r)}\right), \qquad (2)$$

where z indexes the image in the image stack, R_i is the amount of pictures stacked together representing the new dimension of the kernel. In the proposed architecture the cubic kernel is applied to a stack of different images that belong to the same class, i.e. with the same hand posture in each image. This way the model can use the variance of images belonging to the same class to improve the tuning of the filters. To minimize the computational effort for the operation, a max operator is applied to the filter. The mean of the pixel intensities is calculated for each region and the pixel that presents the largest distance from the mean is used. This decreases the amount of connections and weights to be updated.

The same unit is connected to a different set of images but always to the same region in each image which makes the model create an average of the received regions. This gives the model the capacity to highlight pixel intensity variance for the class representation in the data, and allows the unit to learn faster than by using only one image. The tuning is improved by the fact that the connection is not shared between images, but each region in each image has its own weighted connection with the unit. This operation enhances the invariant responses within the same class, presenting the model with different pixel intensities in the same region of different images. The weights are tuned to learn this invariant response. This behavior can be found in the research of Wiskott et al. [15] and Wallis et al. [14]. The cubic kernel is applied only in the first convolutional layer, connected directly with the input images. For the recognition task, a set containing the same image is presented to the model instead of different images presented in the training task.

2.2   Multichannel Implementation

To improve the tuning of the filters, a multichannel architecture is implemented in the proposed model. The idea behind this is to make use of existing knowledge,

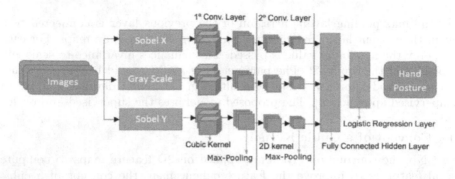

Fig. 1. Proposed architecture for a Multichannel Convolutional Neural Network using 3 channels. In this example, the MCNN has 2 layers and uses a logistic regression to recognize the gestures.

here represented in the edge enhancement by the Sobel operators, to diversify the input. Three channels are used: the first one receiving the raw image, the second and third one receiving the images resulting after applying a Sobel filter in both, horizontal and vertical directions, respectively. In the 3-channel CNN, each channel contains the same number of convolutional layers and the same parameters, but with independent weights. The three channels are connected with a fully-connected hidden layer that produces the output for a logistic regression classifier.

Each channel has its own weight update, but the final error is obtained with the output of the three layers, so that all the three layers act like a bias for each other. This produces a specialized filter tuning based on the edge enhancement of the Sobel filter in both directions. Figure 1 shows the architecture of the model which was used in the experiments.

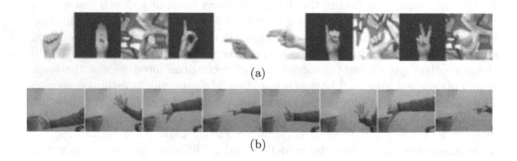

Fig. 2. (a) Examples of hand postures on the JTD. (b) Examples of hand postures recorded with the NCD.

3   Experiments

To evaluate the model an experiment was performed using the Jochen Triesch Database (JTD) [13]. This database contains 10 hand postures, executed by 24 persons in front of 3 different backgrounds, a light, a dark and a complex one. All images are of size 128x128 and have the hand posture centered. Figure 2(a) shows examples of this database.

To evaluate the model in a realistic human-robot interaction scenario, a database using the camera of a small, 58cm tall, robot NAO[1] with four commands was recorded, called NAO Camera hand posture Database (NCD). Figure 2(b) shows example images. Each image has a resolution of 128x128 pixels, and the dataset has a large variance of executions, containing a total of 400-500 examples per hand posture. In each image, the hand was is present in different positions, not always in the centralized, and sometimes with occlusion of some fingers.

To evaluate how the proposed model works in different conditions and how the implementation of the cubic kernel and the three channels affect the final classification, a series of experimental setups was implemented. First, for each experiment, the images were presented in two ways: with the original size and with a reduced size of 28x28 pixels. Second, the experiments were realized with and without the cubic kernel. To evaluate the three channels, the experiments were compared with the utilization of a one-channel, two-channel and three-channel architecture. The network parameters, i.e. the number of convolutional layers, the dimension of the kernel and the max-pooling operation region were based on the research of [11]. The numbers of filters in each layer were found by evaluating the results for a range of numbers. Table 1 shows the parameters for each experimental setup. The parameters for the experiments without the cubic kernel were the same, but excluding the 3rd dimension of the kernel size.

4   Results and Discussion

Each experiment was executed 30 times and the mean of the F1-score for 1000 epochs was calculated. The database was divided into training, test and validation. For all the experiments, the selection was random and it used 60% of the database for training, 20% for validation and 20% for testing. All the experiments were implemented in Python using the library Theano[2] and were executed in a machine with an Intel Core 5i 2.67 Ghz processor, with 8GB of RAM.

The experiment results with the JTD and the cubic kernel, using all the backgrounds (light, dark and complex), are shown at Figure 3(a). The results show that the utilization of the specialized tuning with the three channels produces classification. The advantage of multiple channels is in particular striking for the small 28x28 images: when not using the Sobel operators, the architecture cannot extract or enhance any kind of efficient features, and it recognizes all the

---

[1] http://www.aldebaran-robotics.com/
[2] http://deeplearning.net/software/theano/

Table 1. Parameters for all the experiments evaluated in this paper

Image		128x128			28x28		
		NCD	JTD			NCD	JTD
Layer 1	Filters	30	40	Filters		20	40
	Kernel Size	5x5x5	5x5x5	Kernel Size		5x5x5	5x5x5
	Subsampling Size	5x5	5x5	Subsampling Size		5x5	5x5
Layer 2	Filters	50	60	Filters		30	60
	Kernel Size	4x4	4x4	Kernel Size		2x2	2x2
	Subsampling Size	4x4	4x4	Subsampling Size		2x2	2x2
Layer 3	Filters	70	80	Filters		-	-
	Kernel Size	2x2	2x2	Kernel Size		-	-
	Subsampling Size	2x2	2x2	Subsampling Size		-	-

hand postures as posture 1. When we using only the Sobel filters, illustrated at Figure 3(a) by the columns Sy and Sx, the results show that the architecture still cannot extract an optimal set of features. Only when put together, the Sobel operator acts like a specialization for the original image, giving the model a bias for the edge enhancement, and produces better results.

There are no horizontal connections in the channels, making each channel independent. This makes the filters of each channel act only on the channel's own input. The weight update is guided by the three channels' results, but each filter must act differently for each kind of information it receives, otherwise the information specialization of each filter would be lost.

As expected, the recognition rates for the original image are larger than with the reduced image, but the difference is not so expressive when all the channels are combined. One point to be noted is the training and recognition time for the original image. In the original image, the mean time for recognition with the three-channel architecture is 0.125s. For the reduced image the recognition time is 0.0035s which is small enough to be used in real-time applications. The training time for the reduced image is also smaller, being 200.32s, and 1180.0s for the original image.

In the research of [13], they used an elastic graph matching to find the hand postures in the JTD. Taking together all images in all backgrounds, they obtained a 91% recognition rate. Our model obtained an F-1 score of 92% for the smaller images and 94% for the ones with original size. The model applied by [13] used a template-based match, which restricted the use of their solution in their own database. The nature of the MCNN allows it to be used in different databases without any specialized kind of preprocessing in the images.

The results on the NCD with and without the cubic kernel are shown in Figure 3(b). This experiment shows that with a large amount of data, the F1-scores obtained are very good. It shows also that the utilization of the cubic kernel and the three channels does not improve the results much more when there is a large amount of data, but still allows the model to recognize smaller images, which make the recognition and training tasks faster.

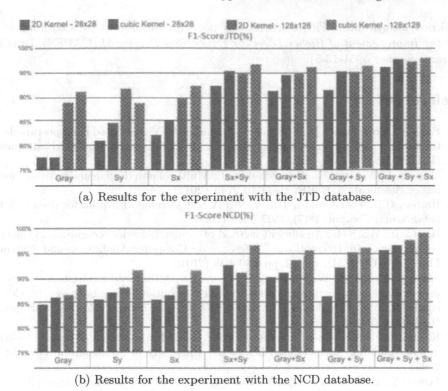

(a) Results for the experiment with the JTD database.

(b) Results for the experiment with the NCD database.

Fig. 3. F1-score for all experiments with all the combinations of architectures on (a) JTD and (b)NCD databases

5 Conclusion

We developed a Multichannel Convolutional Neural Network for hand posture recognition. The model uses a cubic kernel to enhance the features for the classification and uses a multichannel architecture to specialize the tuning of the filters based on the Sobel operators. Each channel receives one kind of information that is used to represent efficient features for the presented database.

The proposed model was evaluated using two different databases: the Jochen Triesch hand posture database and a database recorded with the video camera of a NAO robot. The experiments in both databases show that the proposed model could recognize hand postures using a size-reduced image. The image reduction allowed the use of this deep learning model in recognition of hand postures in real time. For future research, it will be interesting to extend the proposed model to recognize dynamic gestures or multi-modal applications, with the addition of facial expression and audio data.

Acknowledgments. This research was partially supported by *Coordination for the Improvement of Higher Level -or Education- Personnel* (CAPES), Brazil (Grant number 5951-13-5).

References

1. Bilal, S., Akmeliawati, R., El Salami, M., Shafie, A.: Vision-based hand posture detection and recognition for sign language. In: 4th International Conf. Mechatronics (ICOM), pp. 1–6 (May 2011)
2. Ciresan, D.C., Meier, U., Schmidhuber, J.: Multi-column deep neural networks for image classification. CoRR, abs/1202.2745 (2012)
3. Hinton, G.E., Osindero, S., Teh, Y.-W.: A fast learning algorithm for deep belief nets. Neural Comput. 18(7), 1527–1554 (2006)
4. Hu, C.-H., Wo, S.-L.: An efficient method of human behavior recognition in smart environments. In: International Conference on Computer Application and System Modeling (ICCASM), vol. 12, pp. 690–693 (2010)
5. Jmaa, A.B., Mahdi, W., Jemaa, Y.B., Hamadou, A.B.: Hand localization and fingers features extraction: Application to digit recognition in sign language. In: Corchado, E., Yin, H. (eds.) IDEAL 2009. LNCS, vol. 5788, pp. 151–159. Springer, Heidelberg (2009)
6. Karam, M.: PhD Thesis: A framework for research and design of gesture-based human-computer interactions. PhD thesis, University of Southampton (October 2006)
7. Lecun, Y., Bottou, L., Bengio, Y., Haffner, P.: Gradient-based learning applied to document recognition. Proceedings of the IEEE, 2278–2324 (1998)
8. Nagi, J., Ducatelle, F., Di Caro, G., Ciresan, D., Meier, U., Giusti, A., Nagi, F., Schmidhuber, J., Gambardella, L.: Max-pooling convolutional neural networks for vision-based hand gesture recognition. In: IEEE International Conference on Signal and Image Processing Applications (ICSIPA), pp. 342–347 (2011)
9. Ranzato, M., Huang, F.J., Boureau, Y.-L., LeCun, Y.: Unsupervised learning of invariant feature hierarchies with applications to object recognition. In: IEEE Conference on Computer Vision and Pattern Recognition(CVPR), pp. 1–8 (June 2007)
10. Rautaray, S., Agrawal, A.: Vision based hand gesture recognition for human computer interaction: a survey. Artificial Intelligence Review, 1–54 (November 2012)
11. Simard, P., Steinkraus, D., Platt, J.C.: Best practices for convolutional neural networks applied to visual document analysis. In: International Conference on Document Analysis and Recognition, pp. 958–963 (August 2003)
12. Singer, M.A., Goldin-Meadow, S.: Children learn when their teachers' gestures and speech differ. Psychological Science 16(2), 85–89 (2005)
13. Triesch, J., Malsburg, C.V.D.: Robust classification of hand postures against complex backgrounds. In: Interational Conference on Automatic Face and Gesture Recognition, pp. 170–175 (1996)
14. Wallis, G., Rolls, E., Földiák, P.: Learning invariant responses to the natural transformations of objects. In: International Joint Conference on Neural Networks, pp. 1087–1090 (1993)
15. Wiskott, L., Sejnowski, T.J.: Slow feature analysis: Unsupervised learning of invariances. Neural Comput. 14(4), 715–770 (2002)

A Two-Stage Classifier Architecture for Detecting Objects under Real-World Occlusion Patterns

Marvin Struwe[1], Stephan Hasler[2], and Ute Bauer-Wersing[1]

[1] University of Applied Sciences Frankfurt am Main, Germany
[2] Honda Research Institute Europe GmbH, Offenbach, Germany
{mstruwe,ubauer}@fb2.fh-frankfurt.de,
stephan.hasler@honda-ri.de

Abstract. Despite extensive efforts, state-of-the-art detection approaches show a strong degradation of performance with increasing level of occlusion. In this paper we investigate a strategy to improve the detection of occluded objects based on the analytic feature framework from [11] and compare the results in a car detection task. Motivated by an analysis of annotated traffic scenes we focus on a general concept to handle vertical occlusion patterns. For this we describe a two stage classifier architecture that detects vertical car parts in the first stage and combines the local responses in the second. As an extension we provide depth information for the individual car parts helping the classifier in the second stage to reason about typical occlusion patterns.

Keywords: Object detection, Occlusion handling, Supervised learning.

1 Introduction

Despite extensive research visual detection of objects in natural scenes is still not robustly solved. The reason for this is the large appearance variation in which objects or classes occur. A very challenging variation is occlusion which is caused by the constellation of objects in a scene. Occlusion reduces the number of visible features of an object but also causes accidental features. Current object representations show acceptable results during a low to medium level of occlusion but fail for stronger occlusions. Methods like [1,11] train a holistic object template in a discriminative manner and focus resources on differences between classes. This strong specialization on the training problem results in a stronger decrease of performance for occluded objects when trained on unoccluded views. In contrast to this parts-based methods like [8,9] accumulate local features in a voting manner. Also when trained with unoccluded views, these methods can handle arbitrary occlusion patterns, but require that sufficiently many features can still be detected. However, in general the voting methods perform worse than the discriminative ones, whenever test and training set do not show such systematic differences, as discussed in [16] and confirmed by the detection results

S. Wermter et al. (Eds.): ICANN 2014, LNCS 8681, pp. 411–418, 2014.

in [2]. In this paper we investigate a strategy to improve the performance of a holistic discriminative method under stronger occlusion.

Other methods make use of context to explicitly deal with occlusion information, i.e. to exploit knowledge about the possible constellation of objects. In [4,15] Markov-Random-Fields are used to infer if neighboring features are consistent with a single detected instance of an object or have to be assigned to different ones. This allows both approaches to reason about relative depth of objects and to produce a coarse segmentation. However, the process over the whole input image leads to a time consuming iteration. Besides instance-instance relations, also knowledge about general occlusion patterns can be used. In [14] the authors handle vertical occlusion generated by the image border, whereas we try to find a more general concept to handle structured occlusion in a traffic scene.

Occlusion is related to the 3D relation of objects. A general cue of 3D information is depth which can be used to check the physical plausibility of an object's position and size [6] or to segment and put attention to individual scene elements [12]. In [12] temporal differences between RGB-D(epth) views are used to discover movable parts for action representation. Here we integrate depth into the architecture for vertical occlusion to reason about visibility of features.

Other strategies make use of 3D annotated data of car views. A common strategy is the use of the deformable part model (DPM) [3]. In [10] the 3D annotated data of the KITTI dataset [5] is used to generate bounding boxes of the occluder, the occluding object, and their union and for each of the three types a separate DPM is trained. In contrast to this we want to build a system that does not need any labeled information of the occluder. In [17] the authors used hand-annotated 3D CAD models and generated part models additionally to the full car view. A single component DPM detector is trained for each part configuration. To handle occlusion 288 occluder masks are generated for the training data. The approach does not work in real-time and can handle only occlusion cases which match somehow with the generated occlusion masks. Our idea is to make use of the occlusion pattern in real world scenes without generating artificial masks.

In Sec. 2 we shortly describe our basic holistic discriminative detection framework and show how it is influenced by occlusion in a car detection task. In Sec. 3 a two stage architecture for vertical occlusion handling is motivated where the responses of discriminative vertical part detectors are integrated in a second stage. Finally, in Sec. 4 we show how to exploit depth information in the 2-stage architecture, before drawing the conclusion in Sec. 5.

2   Analytic Feature Framework

Holistic discriminative approaches usually extract unspecific features and apply a powerful classifier directly on top. So the popular method proposed in [1] uses Histograms of Oriented Gradients (HOG) with a Support Vector Machine (SVM) and was shown to yield state-of-the-art performance in various detection tasks. In [11] we proposed the analytic feature framework (Fig. 1a) that puts effort in learning a more problem-specific feature representation and uses a simple clas-

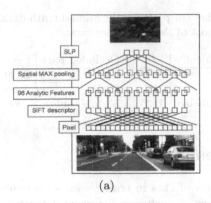
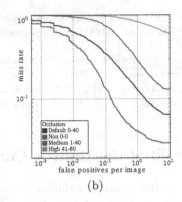

(a)   (b)

Fig. 1. (a) Analytic feature hierarchy. SIFT descriptors are computed on a regular grid and matched to 96 analytic features. After a local maximum filter per feature the SLP templates are used in a convolutional step. Maxima in the final response map denote possible car locations. (b) Receiver Operating Characteristics (ROC) of C_{Std} for car detection scenario. The performance decreases strongly with the percentage of the cars' occlusion.

sifier on top for discrimination. We could show that it provides competitive detection performance. For an input image first Scale Invariant Feature Transform (SIFT) descriptors are computed on a regular grid and then matched to a set of 96 analytic features. The analytic features are the result of a supervised selection process described in [7]. Next, a local maximum filter is performed per feature to enhance robustness against small translations. Finally, the car template, which was trained with a Single Layer Perceptron (SLP), is shifted over the feature representation. The local maxima in the resulting response map denote possible car locations. To deal with cars at different distances we apply the framework on successively reduced image resolutions. For a pedestrian benchmark in [11] we could prove highly competitive performance of the analytic feature framework approach.

In [11] we used the framework for detecting front and back views of cars in real world traffic scenes. These image streams were taken under different weather conditions (sunny, rainy, overcast) and in different scene types (city, rural, industry, highway) and contained cars under all levels of occlusion. The final SLP car template was trained on unoccluded views only. We will refer to this reference system as C_{Std} throughout the paper.

The results of C_{Std} (Fig. 1b) reveal a strong dependency of the performance on the percentage of the cars' occlusion. For a false positive per image rate of 0.1 we get 70% of the cars with an occlusion between 0-40%. This pure detection performance is usually sufficient for a system that applies temporal integration (tracking). However for stronger occlusion the recall drops severely, which can no longer be compensated at system level.

Table 1. Counts of car occluders and occluded car parts for the ground truth data. In total 8796 out of 15514 cars are occluded, most of them by other cars.

Occluding object	#	Occluding object	#	Occluded part	#
Another car	7061	Pedestrian	70	Left	3730
Image border	2137	Traffic sign	31	Right	3124
Motor bike	82	Other/non-labeled	1125	Middle (only)	90

3   Split of the Holistic Car Template

To get a better understanding of occlusion of cars in traffic scenes we counted the number of typical occluders and types of occlusion for ground truth data. The result in Tab. 1 show that most cars are occluded by other cars. Such object-object relations are used in [13] for the detection of small office objects by predicting their spatial position relative to larger and more easily detectable objects. Inspired by this concept we exploited in [11] the fact of car-car occlusion and trained an additional classifier C_{Occ} on occluded cars and applied it only in the vicinity of cars already detected by C_{Std}. The used segment dataset in [11] was simple in the way that the position and size of the occluded car was normalized, whereas in a real scene a strong variance can be expected relative to the position and size of the unoccluded car. Because the concept focused on car-car occlusion it neglected general occluders. Thus we propose other new strategies to deal with a variation of occluder types in the following.

Tab. 1 illustrates that most cars are either occluded on the right or left side. This vertical occlusion is caused by other cars, unlabeled walls, or the image border and results in a mismatch of the holistic car template used in C_{Std}. To improve the detection for this type of occlusion we used following strategy: We subdivided the holistic classifier into three vertical parts and trained each part-classifier with unoccluded car views. So each classifier is forced to make a more local decision about the presence of the car and is later not affected by occlusion of a different part. To integrate the responses of the part-classifiers we use their confidence values as input for an additional SLP which is trained with cars with occlusion rate 0-80%. The resulting two stage architecture is shown in Fig. 2b and will be referred to as C_{3Split}. The structure is equivalent to an MLP but instead of Backprop learning we use for each stage a different training set. In this way the second stage is forced to deal with occlusion in a more symbolic way.

The comparison of C_{Std} and C_{3Split} in Fig. 3a shows an improvement for occlusion rates of 1-40%, while there is no gain for occlusion rates of 41-80%. A possible reason for the strong gain for unoccluded cars, might be that each vertical part template of C_{3Split} is forced to make better use of its local information and thus finds a more general car concept. An analysis of the weights learned by the holistic SLP C_{Std} shows a rather sparse contribution of a small set of analytic features at specific locations, while each part-classifier of C_{3Split} integrates all features at all positions in a much broader manner.

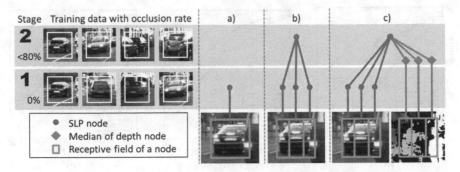

Fig. 2. Different detection architectures. (a) Architecture of C_{Std}. A holistic SLP template is trained on non-occluded car views. (b) Architecture of C_{3Split}. The three vertically subdivided SLP templates are trained on the same examples as (a). In the second stage, a separate SLP learns to combine the three confidence values of the first stage using non-occluded and occluded car views. (c) Architecture of $C_{3SplitDepth}$. The SLP on the second stage uses the median depth for each vertical car part as additional input.

Because of the improved detection performance of C_{3Split} we splitted each vertical part further into two horizontal regions. However, this C_{6Split} showed a much worse performance compared to C_{3Split} in a similar range as C_{Std}. So the pure vertical split seems to better reflect the occlusion constellations in our data.

Besides an adapted classifier architecture C_{3Split} also differs to C_{Std} at training by using additional occluded training examples in the second stage. To demonstrate that the improved performance of C_{3Split} is not simply caused by using different training data we trained a holistic detector similar to C_{Std} but using the training data of the second stage of C_{3Split} with occlusion of 0-80% . We refer to this classifier as C_{AllOcc}. The worse performance of C_{AllOcc} (Fig. 3b) for unoccluded cars indicates that the additional variation in the occluded training examples confuses the representation of unoccluded views. However, for 41-80% occlusion C_{AllOcc} outperforms C_{3Split} and C_{Std}, so the holistic approach can better make use of the remaining information in case of strong occlusion, maybe by directly representing the effect of the occlusion edge.

4 Additional Use of Depth Information

C_{3Split} shows an improvement in detection performance for cars with an occlusion rate of 0-40%. For cars with an occlusion rate of 41-80% the performance is nearly the same as C_{Std}. The confidence values of the sub-segments seem to be insufficient information for the SLP in the second stage.

An analysis of the results revealed that very low confidence values in two of three sub-segments can result in a low confidence value at the top regardless of how good the confidence value of the third sub-segment is. We noticed two

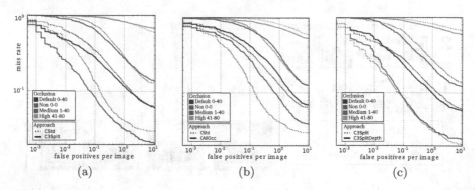

(a)   (b)   (c)

Fig. 3. (a) Performance of C_{3Split}. C_{3Split} generally dominates C_{Std} at occlusion rates up to 40%, with an unexpected, strong gain for unoccluded views. (b) Performance of C_{AllOcc}. For unoccluded views the performance is worse than C_{Std}. But C_{AllOcc} outperforms C_{Std} on strongly occluded cars. (c) Performance of $C_{3SplitDepth}$. $C_{3SplitDepth}$ shows a significant gain for occluded views compared to C_{3Split}.

different scenarios where this constellation occurs. First, some non-car objects accidentally generate a high confidence value in one sub-segment. This potentially happens quite often. Second, a strongly occluded car is only visible in one of three sub-segments. Unfortunately, it is not possible to distinguish both patterns by using only the confidence values. Therefore additional context cues, e.g. stereo disparity, are needed to overcome this limitation. So the fact that the occluded part of a car will be closer to the camera than the visible part could be exploited.

Our idea is to calculate the median depth of each sub-segment and provided as additional input to the SLP at the second stage. We divided the depth values by 100 to scale them to a similar range as the confidences. The resulting architecture is shown in Fig. 2c and referred to as $C_{3SplitDepth}$. The three depth values show a wide range of variation, what might be to difficult to handle with an SLP. We can assume that only the relative distance between the car and a possible occluding object contains the significant information. Therefore, we simply subtracted the largest depth value from all the depth values per segment.

To get a better understanding of the data in the resulting feature space, we plotted the difference between left and right depth over the difference between left and right confidence. Fig. 4a shows that their is no way to separate the two object types linearly. Therefore we extended the input-dimensionality by building all quadratic combinations of the six features (three confidence and three relative depth values). Finally the SLP on the second stage of $C_{3SplitDepth}$ is trained on the resulting 21 dimensional feature space.

The results in Fig. 3c show a significant gain compared to C_{3Split} for all occluded car views, so the detector can exploit the additional information. Only for non-occluded car views $C_{3SplitDepth}$ shows some loss in detection at high or low false positives rates per image, but is at least still better then C_{Std}. To get a better estimation which feature combinations are exploited by the SLP we

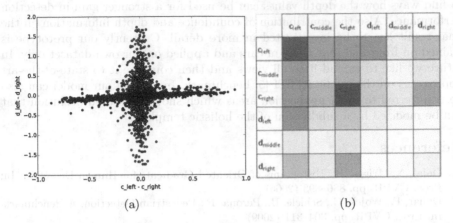

(a)   (b)

Fig. 4. (a) Visualization of confidence and depth values: Blue dots denote car segments and red dots clutter. (b)Visualization of the SLP's weights: Blue denotes positive weights, while red denotes negative ones. The absolute value of the weights is shown by the colors' intensity.

visualized the learned weights in Fig. 4b. In general the SLP seems to use the confidence values more than the depth values. The weights for c_{left}^2 and c_{right}^2 show the highest positive values, that means a high activation in one of this sub-segments can generate a high confidence. In contrast to this the weight for the combination of $c_{left} * c_{right}$ shows a high negative value, so the classifier tries to limit the confidence if c_{left} and c_{right} are activated strongly together. To further quantify the contribution of the individual features more experiments have to be conducted in future.

5   Conclusion

In this paper we presented a two stage architecture to improve the detection of occluded objects. To deal with vertical occlusion, in the first stage we proposed a vertical split of the holistic car template into three parts which were trained on unoccluded views. In the second stage the typical combinations of these part responses where learned on occluded examples. This is in contrast to a Multi Layer Perceptron where each stage is trained with the same data and it helps our architecture to deal with occlusion on a more symbolic level. Our prototype outperformed the reference system for different levels of occlusion. However, there was no gain for strongly occluded cars. We argued that based on a high confidence in only one sub-segment the classifier cannot distinguish car and clutter. Therefore we integrated depth information into the vertical occlusion prototype to give the classifier an independent cue to reason about typical occlusion patterns. We showed that the additional information improves the detection performance for occluded car views. In future more evaluation is needed to find ways how the depth values can be used for a stronger gain in detection performance. Also the contribution of confidence and depth information on the final result has to be investigated in more detail. Currently our prototype is trained on front and rear views of cars and applied on our own dataset only. In future we like to extend it to all views and then compare it to state-of-the-art approaches on the public KITTI [5] benchmark. In general our model can also be transferred to other application areas which show structured occlusion that can be modeled by a subdivision of the holistic template.

References

1. Dalal, N., Triggs, B.: Histograms of Oriented Gradients for Human Detection. In: Proc. CVPR, pp. 886–893 (2005)
2. Dollar, P., Wojek, C., Schiele, B., Perona, P.: Pedestrian Detection: A Benchmark. In: Proc. CVPR, pp. 304–311 (2009)
3. Felzenszwalb, P.F., Girshick, R., McAllester, D., Ramanan, D.: Object Detection with Discriminatively Trained Part Based Models. Proc. PAMI, 1627–1645 (2010)
4. Gao, T., Packer, B., Koller, D.: A Segmentation-aware Object Detection Model with Occlusion Handling. In: Proc. CVPR, pp. 1361–1368 (2011)
5. Geiger, A., Lenz, P., Urtasun, R.: Are we ready for Autonomous Driving? The KITTI Vision Benchmark Suite. In: Proc. CVPR, pp. 3354–3361 (2012)
6. Gould, S., Baumstarck, P., Quigley, M., Ng, A.Y., Koller, D.: Integrating Visual and Range Data for Robotic Object Detection. In: ECCV Workshop M2SF2 (2008)
7. Hasler, S., Wersing, H., Kirstein, S., Körner, E.: Large-scale Real-time Object Identification Based on Analytic Features. In: Alippi, C., Polycarpou, M., Panayiotou, C., Ellinas, G. (eds.) ICANN 2009, Part II. LNCS, vol. 5769, pp. 663–672. Springer, Heidelberg (2009)
8. Leibe, B., Schiele, B.: Interleaved Object Categorization and Segmentation. In: Proc. BMVC, pp. 759–768 (2003)
9. Lowe, D.G.: Distinctive Image Features from Scale-invariant Keypoints. IJCV 60(2), 91–110 (2004)
10. Pepik, B., Stark, M., Gehler, P., Schiele, B.: Occlusion Patterns for Object Class Detection. In: Proc. CVPR, pp. 3286–3293 (2013)
11. Struwe, M., Hasler, S., Bauer-Wersing, U.: Using the Analytic Feature Framework for the Detection of Occluded Objects. In: Mladenov, V., Koprinkova-Hristova, P., Palm, G., Villa, A.E.P., Appollini, B., Kasabov, N. (eds.) ICANN 2013. LNCS, vol. 8131, pp. 603–610. Springer, Heidelberg (2013)
12. Stückler, J., Behnke, S.: Hierarchical Object Discovery and Dense Modelling From Motion Cues in RGB-D Video. In: Proc. IJCAI, pp. 2502–2509 (2013)
13. Torralba, A., Murphy, K.P., Freeman, W.T.: Contextual Models for Object Detection Using Boosted Random Fields. In: Proc. ICIP, pp. 653–656 (2011)
14. Vedaldi, A., Zisserman, A.: Structured Output Regression for Detection with Partial Truncation. In: Proc. NIPS, pp. 1928–1936 (2009)
15. Winn, J., Shotton, J.D.J.: The Layout Consistent Random Field for Recognizing and Segmenting Partially Occluded Objects. In: Proc. CVPR, pp. 37–44 (2006)
16. Yi-Hsin, L., Tz-Huan, H., Tsai, A., Wen-Kai, L., Jui-Yang, T., Yung-Yu, C.: Pedestrian Detection in Images by Integrating Heterogeneous Detectors. In: IEEE Computer Symposium (ICS), pp. 252–257 (2010)
17. Zia, M.Z., Stark, M., Schindler, K.: Explicit Occlusion Modeling for 3D Object Class Representations. In: Proc. CVPR, pp. 3326–3333 (2013)

Towards Sparsity and Selectivity: Bayesian Learning of Restricted Boltzmann Machine for Early Visual Features*

Hanchen Xiong, Sandor Szedmak,
Antonio Rodríguez-Sánchez, and Justus Piater

Institute of Computer Science, University of Innsbruck, Austria
{hanchen.xiong,sandor.szedmak,antonio.rodriguez-sanchez,
justus.piater}@uibk.ac.at

Abstract. This paper exploits how Bayesian learning of restricted Boltzmann machine (RBM) can discover more biologically-resembled early visual features. The study is mainly motivated by the sparsity and selectivity of visual neurons' activations in V1 area. Most previous work of computational modeling emphasize selectivity and sparsity independently, which neglects the underlying connections between them. In this paper, a prior on parameters is defined to simultaneously enhance these two properties, and a Bayesian learning framework of RBM is introduced to infer the maximum posterior of the parameters. The proposed prior performs as the lateral inhibition between neurons. According to our empirical results, the visual features learned from the proposed Bayesian framework yield better discriminative and generalization capability than the ones learned with maximum likelihood, or other state-of-the-art training strategies.

1 Introduction

Over the past decades, there have been a large volume of literature dedicated to model the statistics of natural images in biologically plausible ways. Especially, the primary visual cortex (V1) has been intensively studied and various computational models were proposed to reproduce its functionalities [10,6,12]. It has been well documented that mainly V1 simple cells perform an early stage processing of the visual input signal from the retina and the lateral geniculate nucleus (LGN). One important property of V1 simple cells is that their receptive fields are selective in terms of locations, orientations and frequencies, which can be modelled as Gabor filters. Another characteristic on V1 simple cells is that their activations are sparse. To be more clear, selectivity means that one neuron

---

* The authors would like to thank Dr. George Azzopardi for his helpful comments. The research leading to these results has received funding from the European Community's Seventh Framework Programme FP7/2007-2013 (Specific Programme Cooperation, Theme 3, Information and Communication Technologies) under grant agreement no. 270273, Xperience.

S. Wermter et al. (Eds.): ICANN 2014, LNCS 8681, pp. 419–426, 2014.

only strongly responds to a small number types of stimuli while rarely responding to other types. Sparsity means that the population size of activated neurons should be small given a stimulus, i.e. only a tiny fraction of neurons are activated by a stimulus. Since selectivity and sparsity are interpreted as rareness in lifetime and population domain, sometimes they are also called "lifetime sparseness" and "population sparseness" respectively [12]. It has been hypothesized that the selective and sparse responses of visual neurons are due to certain redundancy reduction mechanism, with which the visual cortex is evolved to encode visual information as efficiently as possible [1]. Based on this hypothesis, a sparse coding strategy was proposed to enhance the coding efficiency, and has led to Gabor-like representations [10]. Although sparse coding has shown success in producing receptive fields similar to those of simple cells, yet it was pointed out that selectivity does not have to be correlated with sparseness in practice [12]. Moreover, it was even suspected that sparse activations of simple cells is only an epiphenomenon or side effect of selectivity [2]. (see section 3 for a detailed analysis). Recently, as another stream of feature learning, restricted Boltzmann machines (RBMs) have attracted increasingly more attention thanks to its success in many application domains [7]. However, the capability of RBMs is rather limited when learning receptive fields of V1 simple cells. To make inference and learning easier, there is no connection between hidden units in RBMs. Consequently, given visible data, all hidden units are conditionally independent to each other (see section 2). It can be easily envisioned that when RBMs are trained on natural images, many learned features will be rather distributed, unlocalized and repeated, which is far from the (selective and sparse) nature of the learning task.

Prior work have exploited different strategies to adapt RBMs towards learning selective and/or sparsely activated neurons [8,9,5] on visual input. However, most of them focus only on one property and does not ensure sparsity and selectivity simultaneously in reproduced neurons. Usually, these strategies are to impose certain regularization to bias learning. To overcome this deficiency, in this paper, we propose to encode an inductive bias about the task as prior probability on parameters. Then, the parameter estimation can be done within a consistent Bayesian learning framework, i.e. maximum a posterior (MAP). In particular, the prior probability on parameters encourages the diversity of neurons' receptive fields, which performs equivalently to the lateral inhibition between neurons. The MAP learning is achieved via a Markov chain Monte Carlo (MCMC)-based simulated annealing. In addition, due to the fact that the parameter space is high-dimensional and multi-modal, annealing importance sampling (AIS) and parallel tempering are employed in subroutines to avoid local maxima (see section 4). In section 5, we verify our Bayesian learning of RBMs on a benchmark database of natural images, comparing to maximum likelihood learning and other state-of-the-art learning strategies. Our empirical results demonstrate that neurons in our model display better sparsity and selectivity than in others; in addition, the features encoded by our neurons via Bayesian learning show better generalization capabilities than the ones from other learning methods.

2   Restricted Boltzmann Machine

The restricted Boltzmann machine (RBM) is a two-layer, bipartite neural network, it is a "restricted version" of the Boltzmann machine with only interconnections between hidden layers and visible layers. Input data is binary and N_v dimensional, they are fed into N_v units in the visible layer $\mathbf{v}$, N_h units in the hidden layer $\mathbf{h}$ are stochastic binary variables, *i.e.* $\mathbf{v} \in \{0,1\}^{N_v}$, $\mathbf{h} \in \{0,1\}^{N_h}$, the joint probability of $\{\mathbf{v}, \mathbf{h}\}$ is[1]:

$$p(\mathbf{v}, \mathbf{h}) = \frac{1}{Z} \exp(-E(\mathbf{v}, \mathbf{h})) \qquad E(\mathbf{v}, \mathbf{h}) = -\mathbf{v}^\top \mathbf{W} \mathbf{h} \qquad (1)$$

where $\mathbf{W} \in \mathbb{R}^{N_v \times N_h}$ is the matrix of symmetry weights, $\mathbf{Z} = \sum_{\mathbf{v},\mathbf{h}} \exp(-E(\mathbf{v}, \mathbf{h}))$ is the partition function for normalization. Because of the restricted connections in RBMs, hidden units h_j are independent of each other conditioned on the visible data $\mathbf{v}$, and similarly, visible units v_i are conditionally independent of each other given $\mathbf{h}$. Given training data $\mathcal{D} = \{\mathbf{v}^{(l)}\}_{l=1}^L$, RBM can be learned by maximizing the average log-likelihood of $\mathcal{D}$:

$$\mathbf{W}^* = \arg \max_{\mathbf{W}} \mathcal{L}(\mathcal{D}) = \arg \max_{\mathbf{W}} \frac{1}{L} \sum_{l=1}^{L} \left(\log \sum_{\mathbf{h}} p(\mathbf{v}^l, \mathbf{h}) \right) \qquad (2)$$

based on(1), the gradient of $\mathcal{L}(\mathcal{D})$ is computed as:

$$\nabla \mathcal{L}(\mathcal{D}) = \frac{1}{L} \sum_{l=1}^{L} [\mathbb{E}_{\mathbf{v}^{(l)} \in \mathbf{V}, \mathbf{h} \sim p(\mathbf{h}|\mathbf{v}^{(l)})}(\mathbf{v}^{(l)} \mathbf{h}^\top) - \mathbb{E}_{\mathbf{v}, \mathbf{h} \sim p(\mathbf{v}, \mathbf{h})}(\mathbf{v} \mathbf{h}^\top)] \qquad (3)$$

where $\mathbb{E}_p(\cdot)$ denotes the expected values with respect to p. Obviously, the sampling $\mathbf{v}, \mathbf{h} \sim p(\mathbf{v}, \mathbf{h})$ makes learning practically infeasible because it requires a large number of Markov chain Monte Carlo (MCMC) iterations to reach equilibrium. Fortunately, we can compute an efficient approximation to the exact gradient: contrastive divergence (CD), which works well in practice [7]. By using CD_k, only a small number k steps are run in block Gibbs sampling (usually $k = 1$), and (3) can be approximated as:

$$\nabla \hat{\mathcal{L}}(\mathcal{D}) = \frac{1}{L} \sum_{l=1}^{L} [\mathbf{v}^{(l)} p(\mathbf{h}^{(l)+}|\mathbf{v}^{(l)})^\top - p(\mathbf{v}^{(l)-}|\mathbf{h}^{(l)+}) p(\mathbf{h}^{(l)-}|\mathbf{v}^{(l)-})^\top] \qquad (4)$$

3   Bias Learning with Selectivity and Sparsity

Simple cells in V1 area are well known to be selective to locations, orientations and frequencies, and their activations are sparse [10] to visual stimuli. The concepts of selectivity and sparsity are illustrated in Figure 1(a), where each row (red) represent how one neuron selectively respond to different visual stimuli while each column (blue) describes how many neurons are activated by one stimulus. Although selectivity and sparsity are related at their average values,

---

[1] Bias vectors on visible and hidden units are omitted them for notation simplicity, but we would like to note that we use such biases in our experiments.

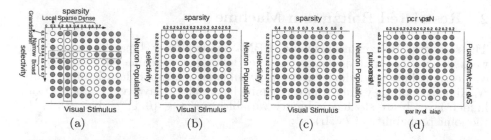

Fig. 1. Understanding sparsity and selectivity: white circles mean activations while gray circles denote inactivations. See text for more description.

they are not necessarily correlated [12]. Selective neurons cannot ensure sparse neuron coding (Figure 1(c)); sparsely activated neurons can also be not narrowly selective (Figure 1(d)).

Sparse group restricted Boltzmann machine (SGRBM) [9] is a RBM trained with the CD algorithm plus a $l1/l2$ norm regularization on the activations of neuron population. Although $l1/l2$ norm regularization can ensure sparsity, yet it can also lead to many "dead" (never respond) and "potential over-tolerant" (always respond) neurons (see Figure 1(d) and section 5). On the other hand, a selectivity-induced regularization was used in [8] by suppressing the average activation probability of each neuron to all training data. One limitation of this strategy, as argued in [5], is that decreasing average activation probabilities can not guarantee selectivity, instead, it will result in many similar neurons with uniformly low activation probabilities to all types of visual stimuli, which prone to be "dead" as well (see section 5). One closely related work to ours is proposed in [5], of which the essence is to tune the activation matrix (Figure 1) towards a target one that is both selective and sparse while maximizing likelihood.

Based on the analysis above, we can see that the motivation of sparsity is to better differentiate neurons while the goal of selectivity is to avoid "over-tolerant" neurons. Assume that there exist N types of visual stimuli and K neurons, and usually $N \gg K$. Obviously, the ideal selectivity rates of neurons is N/K. At the same time, for sparsity, we also want to prevent the existence of any duplicate or similar activations in the neuron population. The best scenario is that there is no overlap among the activations of different neurons (rows in Figure 1), *i.e.* K neurons respond to non-overlapping N/K types of visual stimuli respectively. In the RBM case, the weights W, to some extent, can represent the activation matrix. For so, a natural choice of biasing parameters is to diversify the columns of $\mathbf{W}$ as much as possible. Here we approach diversification by minimizing absolute cosine similarities among columns of $\mathbf{W}$:

$$\arg\min_{\mathbf{W}} \sum_{j=1}^{N_h} \sum_{k \neq j}^{N_h} \left| \frac{\mathbf{W}_{\cdot,j}^{\top}\mathbf{W}_{\cdot,k}}{||\mathbf{W}_{\cdot,j}||\,||\mathbf{W}_{\cdot,k}||} \right| \tag{5}$$

where $\mathbf{W}_{\cdot j}$ denotes the jth column of $\mathbf{W}$. Note that the denominator in (5) is necessary, because eliminating it will generate many "dead" or *principal component analysis* (PCA)-like neurons. An extreme case is that the activation probabilities of neurons are exclusive to each other. Despite selectivity is not so obvious in (5), it can be imagined that it can be better minimized when $|W_{\cdot,j:\forall j \in N_h}|$ are small. Therefore, sparsity and selectivity are enhanced simultaneously by using diversity-induced bias (5) (Figure 1(b)).

4   Bayesian Learning of Restricted Boltzmann Machines

In contrast to the incremental updates composed of CD approximation and regularization-based gradients [8,9,5], we propose to train RBMs in a consistent Bayesian framework. Based on the discussion in the previous section, we can define the prior probability on parameters $p(\mathbf{W})$ as:

$$p(\mathbf{W}) \propto \exp(-\lambda \cdot \sum_{j=1}^{N_h} \sum_{k \neq j}^{N_h} \left| \frac{\mathbf{W}_{\cdot,j}^\top \mathbf{W}_{\cdot,k}}{||\mathbf{W}_{\cdot,j}|| ||\mathbf{W}_{\cdot,k}||} \right|) \tag{6}$$

then the parameters can be estimated via maximum a posterior (MAP):

$$\mathbf{W}^* = \arg\max_{\mathbf{W}} p(\mathbf{W}|\mathcal{D}) = \arg\max_{\mathbf{W}} p(\mathbf{W}) \prod_{l=1}^{L} \sum_{\mathbf{h}} p(\mathbf{v}^{(l)}, \mathbf{h}|\mathbf{W}) \tag{7}$$

Since the derivative of (7) *w.r.t.* $\mathbf{W}$ can not be analytically computed, and (7) in general is not concave, here a Markov chain Monte Carlo (MCMC)-based simulated annealing is employed to find the optimal solution. In the basic Metropolis algorithm, a sample $\mathbf{W}'$ is accepted with probability $\min(1, p(\mathbf{W}'|\mathcal{D})/p(\mathbf{W}|\mathcal{D}))$ where:

$$\frac{p(\mathbf{W}'|\mathcal{D})}{p(\mathbf{W}|\mathcal{D})} = \frac{p(\mathbf{W}')}{p(\mathbf{W})} \frac{p(\mathcal{D}|\mathbf{W}')}{p(\mathcal{D}|\mathbf{W})} = \frac{p(\mathbf{W}')}{p(\mathbf{W})} \frac{\prod_{l=1}^{L} \sum_{\mathbf{h}} p(\mathbf{v}^{(l)}, \mathbf{h}|\mathbf{W}')}{\prod_{l=1}^{L} \sum_{\mathbf{h}} p(\mathbf{v}^{(l)}, \mathbf{h}|\mathbf{W})} \tag{8}$$

Because of the special structure of RBM, the term $\sum_{\mathbf{h}} p(\mathbf{v}, \mathbf{h}|\mathbf{W})$ can be written in a polynomial form as:

$$p(\mathbf{v}|\mathbf{W}) = \sum_{\mathbf{h}} p(\mathbf{v}, \mathbf{h}|\mathbf{W}) = \frac{1}{Z(\mathbf{W})} \prod_{j=1}^{N_h} \exp(1 + \mathbf{v}^\top \mathbf{W}_{\cdot,j}) \tag{9}$$

Consequently, (8) can be further expanded as:

$$\frac{p(\mathbf{W}'|\mathcal{D})}{p(\mathbf{W}|\mathcal{D})} = \frac{p(\mathbf{W}')}{p(\mathbf{W})} \left(\frac{Z(\mathbf{W})}{Z(\mathbf{W}')}\right)^N \exp\left\{ \sum_{l=1}^{L} \sum_{j=1}^{N_h} \mathbf{v}^{(l)\top} (\mathbf{W}'_{\cdot,j} - \mathbf{W}_{\cdot,j}) \right\} \tag{10}$$

Since (10) is invariant to different scales of $\mathbf{W}$, without loss of generality, we constraint $\forall w_{ij} \in \mathbf{W}, w_{i,j} \in [-1, +1]$. One difficulty in computing (10) is the ratio of normalization terms $\frac{Z(\mathbf{W})}{Z(\mathbf{W}')}$. Instead of computing it analytically, we use a tractable approximation of it via *annealing importance sampling* (AIS) [11]. Basically, importance sampling can be used for estimating the ratio:

$$\frac{Z(\mathbf{W})}{Z(\mathbf{W}')} = \frac{\sum_{\mathbf{v}} p(\mathbf{v}|\mathbf{W})}{\sum_{\mathbf{v}} p(\mathbf{v}|\mathbf{W}')} = \sum_{\mathbf{v}} \frac{p(\mathbf{v}|\mathbf{W})}{p(\mathbf{v}|\mathbf{W}')} \frac{p(\mathbf{v}|\mathbf{W}')}{\sum_{\mathbf{v}} p(\mathbf{v}|\mathbf{W}')} = \mathbb{E}_{p(\mathbf{v}|\mathbf{W}')}\left(\frac{p(\mathbf{v}|\mathbf{W})}{p(\mathbf{v}|\mathbf{W}')}\right) \tag{11}$$

However, the estimation will be poor if $\mathbf{W}$ and $\mathbf{W}'$ are not close. By contrast, AIS constructs many intermediary distributions between $p(\mathbf{v}|\mathbf{W}')$ and $p(\mathbf{v}|\mathbf{W})$ as: $p_s(\mathbf{v}) \propto p(\mathbf{v}|\mathbf{W}')^{1-\alpha_s} p(\mathbf{v}|\mathbf{W})^{\alpha_s}$ with $0 < \alpha_0 < \alpha_1 < \cdots < \alpha_s < \cdots < \alpha_S = 1$. Then one AIS run is as follows:

1.Initialize $\mathbf{v}_0^{(m)} \sim p_0(\mathbf{v})$

2.for $s = 1 \to S$, sample $\mathbf{v}_s^{(m)}$ give $\mathbf{v}_{s-1}^{(m)}$ with one Gibbs sampling *w.r.t.* $p_s(\mathbf{v})$;

3.$w^{(m)} = \frac{p_1(\mathbf{v}_1^{(m)})}{p_0(\mathbf{v}_1^{(m)})} \frac{p_2(\mathbf{v}_2^{(m)})}{p_1(\mathbf{v}_2^{(m)})} \cdots \frac{p_S(\mathbf{v}_S^{(m)})}{p_{S-1}(\mathbf{v}_S^{(m)})}$.

When M runs of AIS are implemented, the ratio can be estimated as:

$$\frac{\mathbf{Z}(\mathbf{W})}{\mathbf{Z}(\mathbf{W}')} \approx \frac{1}{M} \sum_{m=1}^{M} w^{(m)} \tag{12}$$

In addition, to avoid being trapped in local maxima, we construct the state transition of a Markov chain as a mixture of a local Metropolis kernel (10) and an independent Metropolis-Hasting kernel. To better explore the sampling space, the uniform distribution $\mathcal{U}$ on $\mathbf{W}$ is set as the Metropolis-Hasting kernel. Therefore, the whole sampling is a weighted combination of local exploitation and global exploration, and here we use the mixture weight $\eta = 0.5$. At iteration n, the invariant distribution which the Markov chain is subject to is $p(\mathbf{W}|\mathcal{D})^{1/T_n}$, where T_n is a decreasing temperature schedule. When $T_n \to 0$, the Markov chain can hardly move and the still state will be used as the maximum. Usually $\mathbf{W}$ is high-dimensional (with large number of neurons and high-dimensional visual input), so the parameter space can be rather complicated, *e.g.* sharp with many isolated modes, and simulated annealing based on one single Markov chain is unreliable. One simple way is to run multiple Markov chains in parallel, and pick the states of one chain which lead to the best result. However, a better strategy is *parallel tempering* [3]. $R+1$ Markov chains are constructed under different initial temperatures $\{p_r(\mathbf{W}|\mathcal{D}) \propto p(\mathbf{W}|\mathcal{D})^{\beta_r}\}_{r=0}^{R}$, $0 \le \beta_R < \cdots \beta_r < \cdots \beta_0 = 1$, β_0 is referred to the base distribution, and others correspond to more flat distributions smoothed with different temperatures. As the simulated annealing on differently tempered Markov chains progress, the states of neighbouring chains $\mathbf{W}^r$, $\mathbf{W}^{r+1}$ can be swapped with probability:

$$\min(1, \frac{p_r(\mathbf{W}^{r+1}|\mathcal{D})p_{r+1}(\mathbf{W}^r|\mathcal{D})}{p_{r+1}(\mathbf{W}^{r+1}|\mathcal{D})p(\mathbf{W}^r|\mathcal{D})}) = \min(1, \exp\{\sum_{l=1}^{L}\sum_{j=1}^{N_h}(\beta_r - \beta_{r+1})\mathbf{v}^{(l)\top}(\mathbf{W}_{\cdot,j}^{r+1} - \mathbf{W}_{\cdot,j}^r)\})$$

$$\tag{13}$$

5   Experiments

To evaluate the proposed learning strategy, a benchmark database [10] was used for training. 100000 small patches (size 14×14) were extracted from random positions of ten whitened images. A sigmoid function was applied on the pixel

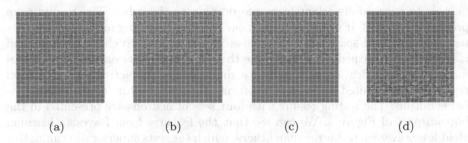

(a)   (b)   (c)   (d)

Fig. 2. The receptive fields of neurons learned from (a) CD algorithm, (b) sparse CD, (c) selective CD and (d)our Bayesian strategy. See text for more description.

	CD	Sparse CD [9]	Selective CD[8]	Bayesian Learning
# Dead Neurons	**0**	68	88	**0**
Ave. Selectivity	0.4582	0.3552	0.4090	**0.3221**
Ave. Sparsity	0.3749	0.1883	0.1939	**0.1671**
Error rate on MNIST[%]	27.21	17.54	19.32	**14.21**

Fig. 3. Performance of different learning methods

intensities to fit their values in the range $[0, 1]$; in addition, the patches with variances smaller than 0.1 were filtered out to accelerate training. For comparison, three additional RBMs were trained by using the CD algorithm, the CD algorithm with sparse regularization (sparse CD) [9] and the CD algorithm with selectivity regularization (selective CD) [8]. For each RBM, 200 hidden neurons were learned and their receptive fields are presented in Figure 2. We can see that many neurons' receptive fields learned from the CD algorithm (Figure 2(a)) are very vague and unlocalized, compared to which, the neurons' receptive fields learned from sparse CD and selective CD (Figure 2(b) and 2(c)) look "clearer" and "sharper". However, both sparse CD and selective CD led to many useless, "dead" neurons. The neurons obtained from our Bayesian learning strategy display rather diverse receptive fields and there seems no "dead" neuron (Figure 2(d)). We roughly obtained the number of "dead" neurons by counting the number of neurons whose maximal activation probabilities to all training visual stimuli is smaller than 0.1, and the results are in the first row of Figure 3.

Selectivity and sparsity are usually measured using activity ratio [4]. For a neuron, its selectivity is computed across all L input visual stimuli: $selectivity = \left(\sum_{l=1}^{L} r_l/L\right)^2 / \left(\sum_{l=1}^{L} r_l^2/L\right)$ where r_l is the activation rate of the neuron given the lth stimulus. The sparsity of activations by one stimulus is computed across all N_h neurons: $sparsity = \left(\sum_{j=1}^{N_h} r_j/N_h\right)^2 / \left(\sum_{j=1}^{N_h} r_j^2/N_h\right)$. We computed the selectivity and sparsity of 4 RBMs on the MNIST patch dataset[2], which contains digit images. Although natural images and digit images are two absolutely different visual domains, we believe that early features encoded in neurons should

---

[2] Available on http://yann.lecun.com/exdb/mnist.

be able to successfully adapt from one domain to the other. The results were presented Figure 3. It can be seen that our Bayesian learning method yields better selectivity and sparsity to other cases. Furthermore, to check the practical effectiveness of learned neurons, we use them as basis filters on the digit images for a multi-classification task. Given a digit image, the activations of hidden neurons are computed as input of a softmax function, and its corresponding label is output. The testing results with four sets of neurons are presented in the bottom part of Figure 3. We can see that the features from Bayesian learning yield lower average test error than others, which suggests superior discriminative and generalization capability.

6   Conclusion

A Bayesian learning framework for RBM was put forward based on many state-of-the-art approximation techniques. To mimic V1 simple cells, a diversity-induced prior was introduced on RBMs' parameters, and maximum a posterior learning yields better results than other learning strategies. In particular, the features encoded in learned neurons display nice discriminative and generalization property for domain adaption. As a possible future work direction, we are studying more sophisticated priors to approach other simple neurons' properties.

References

1. Barlow, H.B.: Unsupervised learning. Neural Computation 1, 295–311 (1989)
2. Berkes, P., White, B., Fiser, J.: No evidence for active sparsification in the visual cortex. In: NIPS. pp. 108–116 (2009)
3. Earl, D.J., Deem, M.W.: Parallel tempering: Theory, applications, and new perspectives. Phys. Chem. Chem. Phys. 7, 3910–3916 (2005)
4. Franco, L., Rolls, E.T., Aggelopoulos, N.C., Jerez, J.M.: Neuronal selectivity, population sparseness, and ergodicity in the inferior temporal visual cortex. Biological Cybernetics 96(6), 547–560 (2007)
5. Goh, H., Thome, N., Cord, M.: Biasing restricted Boltzmann machines to manipulate latent selectivity and sparsity. In: NIPS Workshop on Deep Learning and Unsupervised Feature Learning (2010)
6. van Hateren, J.H., van der Schaaf, A.: Independent component filters of natural images compared with simple cells in primary visual cortex. Proceedings of the Royal Society B: Biological Sciences 265(1394), 359C366 (1998), pMC1688904
7. Hinton, G.E., Salakhutdinov, R.R.: Reducing the dimensionality of data with neural networks. Science 313(5786), 504–507 (Jul 2006)
8. Lee, H., Ekanadham, C., Ng, A.Y.: Sparse deep belief net model for visual area v2. In: NIPS (2007)
9. Luo, H., Shen, R., Niu, C., Ullrich, C.: Sparse group restricted boltzmann machines. In: AAAI (2011)
10. Olshausen, B., Field, D.: Emergence of simple-cell receptive field properties by learning a sparse code for natural images. Nature 381, 607–609 (1996)
11. Salakhutdinov, R., Murray, I.: On the quantitative analysis of deep belief networks. In: ICML (2008)
12. Willmore, B., Tolhurst, D.: Characterising the sparseness of neural codes. Network:Comput.Neural Syst. 12, 255–270 (2001)

Online Learning of Invariant Object Recognition in a Hierarchical Neural Network

Markus Leßmann and Rolf P. Würtz

Institut für Neuroinformatik, Ruhr-Universität, Bochum, Germany
{markus.lessmann,rolf.wuertz}@ini.rub.de

Abstract. We propose the *Temporal Correlation Net (TCN)* as an object recognition system implementing three basic principles: forming temporal groups of features, learning in a hierarchical structure, and using feedback to predict future input. It is a further development of the Temporal Correlation Graph [1] and shows improved performance on standard datasets like ETH80, COIL100, and ALOI. In contrast to its predecessor it can be trained online on all levels rather than in a level per level batch mode. Training images are presented in temporal order showing objects undergoing specific transformations under viewing conditions the system is supposed to learn invariance under. Computation time and memory demands are low because of sparse learned connectivity and efficient handling of neural activities.

1 Introduction

Visual processing is one of the brain functions most mimicked in artificial systems. The aims of different modeling approaches range from theories about the brain's computational processes during cognition to practical applications like surveillance, driver assistance, or control of industrial production processes. These purposes used to be pursued using very different techniques, but the last 10 years have brought several systems that respect important properties of biological neurons and the neural architecture in the brain and properties of biological neurons, and, thanks to computational power, become applicable to large standard test databases and hence interesting for practical applications. Examples include HMAX [2], HTM [3], and VisNetL [4]. Three basic are fruitful in this respect:

1. Learning of temporal sequences to create invariance to transformations contained in the training data.
2. Learning in a hierarchical structure, such that invariance increases gradually from level to level. Additionally lower level knowledge can be reused in higher level contexts and thereby makes memory usage efficient.
3. Prediction of future signals by feedback to disambiguate noisy input.

Here we present a novel system for invariant object recognition implementing these basic ideas. The layout is the following: In the next chapter we present

S. Wermter et al. (Eds.): ICANN 2014, LNCS 8681, pp. 427–434, 2014.

our system in detail. Chapter 3 describes how learning works in the network. Experimental results are presented in chapter 4, and chapter 5 closes the article with an outlook on future work.

2   Our System

The system presented here is called *Temporal Correlation Net (TCN)* and is an further development of the *Temporal Correlation Graph (TCG)* from [1]. Using the same architecture and handling and computation of neural activities the new system learns using biologically plausible learning rules, namely a normal associative Hebbian learning rule for training of neurons representing spatial patterns and the trace rule (as used in VisNet) for learning of temporal groups of features. This permits to train the network online rather than with batches of all objects and on all levels at the same time (in contrast to TCG, VisNet, HMAX, and HTM). Thus, the TCN can be taught new object categories at any time.

The system is a multilayer neural network consisting of three different levels each made up of two sublayers of so called spatial and temporal neurons, respectively, the general structure is shown in figure 1. On the lowest level spatial neurons represent *parquet graphs* [5], visual features containing Gabor wavelet responses. A codebook of those features found in the training set is learned using vector quantization. Each codebook entry gets associated with one spatial neuron. The spatial neurons on higher levels represent configurations of temporal groups simultaneously active at adjacent positions in the preceding sublayer. Temporal neurons represent groups, in which spatial input patterns at the same position of the network appear often close in time. This is important for creating invariance under transformations in viewing conditions. To learn, e.g., invariance under rotation in depth the system is presented different images of a rotating object. At one image position the same object part might be observed from different viewing angles (for example left profile, front view and right profile of a head). A neuron tuned to a group of the corresponding visual patterns will respond to any of these views, and will hence represent the object part at least partly invariant to the viewing angle. This scheme is repeated on all levels of the hierarchy. First spatial patterns of adjacent lower level temporal patterns are learned and then the resulting patterns are temporally grouped. Thus, the partly invariant representation of the object part may be combined with a (partly) invariant representation of other parts. Learning of connection weights to spatial and temporal neurons is unsupervised using neural learning rules (see 3.2). Top level temporal neurons emerge as representatives of complete object categories. Learning associations between top level temporal activities and object categories is supervised by associating vectors of activities averaged over training images of the same category with a category name. The recognized category can then be read out using dot product decoding.

The system has to handle a very large number of neurons (potentially 10^5 or even 10^6 on some levels). For keeping computations tractable TCG and TCN,

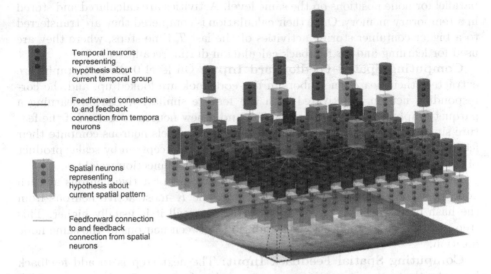

Temporal neurons representing hypothesis about current temporal group

Feedforward connection to and feedback connection from tempora neurons

Spatial neurons representing hypothesis about current spatial pattern

Feedforward connection to and feedback connection from spatial neurons

Fig. 1. Visualization of the network architecture. Connections of nodes represent possible synaptic connections between all neurons in one node and all in the other.

in contrast to other systems, store only non-zero weights and initialize weights of newly created neurons very sparsely. Additionally, they simulate neurons dynamically by just storing an index and a real activity value in specially designed containers called *nodes*. Neurons can be addressed fast via their index using hashing techniques. In addition, neurons can be sorted according to activity and those with weak activation can be pruned. On the lowest level 9×9 nodes are placed in a regular grid on the input image (in both sublayers). On higher levels convergence takes place with a common factor C of 3, i.e., a higher level spatial node receives input from 3×3 adjacent temporal nodes of the preceding layer. Between two sublayers the mapping is one to one, each spatial node yields input to one temporal node of the same level. This scheme leads to 3×3 nodes in the (sublayers of the) middle level and 1 at the top level.

3   Inference and Learning

Learning and inference are not independent since training requires inference on all network levels already containing neurons.

3.1   Inference

Inference is done by computing activities of all neurons for a given input image and then reading out the activities of temporal neurons at the top level, which identify the recognized object category. Calculation of activities is done from bottom to top level for one node position after another and can be done in parallel for node positions on the same level. Activities are calculated and stored in a temporary memory. Once their calculation is completed they are transferred to a bigger container storing activities of the last T time steps, where they are used for learning and for feedback calculation during recall.

Computing Spatial Feedforward Input: On level 0 parquet graphs are extracted, their nearest neighbors in the codebook are looked up, and the corresponding neuron is activated with the feature similarity. During learning a parquet graph is added to the codebook and a new neuron is created if the feature similarity is below a threshold ϑ_Q. On higher levels neurons compute their feedforward activation like neurons in a multilayer perceptron by scalar product of the activity of input neurons and corresponding connection weights.

Inhibiting Spatial Neurons: Next the amount of active neurons at each node position is reduced by deleting all but the K most active neurons from the hash map. During learning K is 1, during recall it is usually higher. This step can be seen as application of inhibition between neurons at the same node position.

Computing Spatial Feedback Input: The next step is to add feedback input to the remaining active neurons coming from temporal neurons which have been active on the T previous images.

Application of the Activation Function: The neuron activities are processed by a tanh nonlinearity. This activation function provides (besides inhibition) the second nonlinearity in the system enabling it to robust classification. Additionally it prevents activity values from growing to infinity, which could happen because of feedback connections. For using more of its nonlinear regime neuron activities (which are between 0 and 1 because of weight normalization) are multiplied with π before.

Transfer into Activity Stack: Then activities are pushed onto an activity stack of the last T images. The current activities are written to position 0, the older ones are shifted by one position, and the last entry gets deleted. In the learning phase, the stack is emptied when a new object category is presented to prevent the system from learning transitions between different categories.

Computations for Temporal Neurons: Now the same kind of calculations are done for neurons representing temporal groups. At first temporal neurons collect their feedforward input, then inhibition is applied and feedback is given to remaining temporal neurons (this time only from higher level spatial neurons active on the preceding image). Finally, the activation function is applied and activities are pushed onto the activity stack.

3.2 Learning

After inference learning is done for each training image on all levels and sublayers at once. It is executed globally on each level meaning that neurons, which can be added during learning, can become active independently at each node position of a level and their connection weights can be trained on any node position.

On level 0 the codebook and spatial neurons are learned using vector quantization. On each other sublayer (on level l) a new neuron is created if the current maximal activity at a node position is below a threshold ϑ_S^l for spatial or ϑ_T^l for temporal neurons, respectively. Incoming weights of new neurons are tuned to current activity of input neurons thus that they would have been maximally active with the current input. They are connected to higher level neurons active on recent time steps using random initial weights. All incoming weights of a temporal neuron are normalized to a Euclidean norm of 1.0. For spatial neurons all incoming weights from the same input node are normalized to a squared euclidian norm of $1/C$. Weights whose absolute value falls below a threshold ϑ_L times the biggest incoming weight of the respective neuron get deleted. The relative threshold makes sure that least one input connection remains.

Spatial neurons need to learn which temporal neurons at adjacent input positions are active at the same time. This is an associative learning task, which is performed by a Hebbian learning rule:

$$\Delta W_{i,j}^{l,\mathrm{t};l+1,\mathrm{s}}(v) = \alpha \cdot \mathbf{n}_i^{l,t}(v) \cdot \mathbf{n}_j^{l+1,s}, \tag{1}$$

where α is a learning factor, $\mathbf{n}_i^{l,t}$ is the activity of temporal neuron i on level l at the currently considered input position v, $\mathbf{n}_j^{l+1,s}$ that of spatial neuron j on level $l+1$ and $W_{i,j}^{l,\mathrm{t};l+1,\mathrm{s}}$ the connection between both of them. Temporal neurons learn temporal groupings of spatial input patterns using the trace rule, an associative Hebbian learning rule based on the trace of a temporal neuron's activity at time τ:

$$\overline{\mathbf{n}}_j^{l,t^\tau} = (1 - \eta) \cdot \mathbf{n}_j^{l,t^\tau} + \eta \cdot \overline{\mathbf{n}}_j^{l,t^{\tau-1}}. \tag{2}$$

It provides a memory of the neurons' past activities and is high if the neuron was activated strongly on the current and on preceding images. η determines the weighting between current and past input. The trace value enables the learning rule to adjust connection weights thus that spatial neurons activated frequently on consecutive time steps all excite the same temporal neuron. The trace rule itself reads as:

$$\Delta W_{i,j}^{l,\mathrm{s};l,\mathrm{t}} = \alpha \cdot \overline{\mathbf{n}}_j^{l,t^\tau} \cdot \mathbf{n}_i^{l,s^\tau}. \tag{3}$$

Here, $\mathbf{n}_i^{l,s^\tau}$ is the activity of spatial neuron i on level l, $\overline{\mathbf{n}}_j^{l,t^\tau}$ the already introduced trace value and $W_{i,j}^{l,\mathrm{s};l,\mathrm{t}}$ the weight between the considered neurons.

4   Experiments

The system was tested on the ETH80 [6] (in the "cropped close perimg" version) containing images of 8 different categories and the COIL100 [7], consisting of images of 100 different objects, each being its own category. In both databases a black background was used instead of additional segmentation information. All tests used one-fold cross validation, the number of views per object was split into two sets, the first was used for training, the rest for testing. All images had

Table 1. Tests for generalization over viewing angle. Given are the percentages of images of each dataset the system was asked to use for training, the number of images that were actually used and the recognition rates of both systems reached on the remaining images. For both TCN and TCG performance on the training set was always 100%. Left: results for ETH80 on the basic category level (apple, car, cow, etc.). Right: results for COIL100 on the name level.

% requ.	# obt.	TCN	TCG	# obt.	TCN	TCG
		ETH80			COIL100	
2.50	160	**63.65**	27.44	200	**61.06**	58.00
5.00	240	**68.32**	25.95	400	**76.57**	74.91
10.00	400	**85.69**	31.70	800	**93.95**	88.89
20.00	720	**98.16**	87.89	1500	**97.56**	97.46
30.00	1040	**99.06**	90.98	2200	**99.58**	99.18
40.00	1360	**99.11**	98.12	2900	**99.81**	99.63
50.00	1680	**99.69**	99.06	3600	99.94	**100.00**
60.00	2000	**99.53**	99.30	4300	**100.00**	99.93
70.00	2320	**99.79**	99.17	5100	**99.95**	99.86
80.00	2640	**99.53**	95.47	5800	**100.00**	99.93
90.00	2960	**100.00**	96.25	6500	**100.00**	99.71

a size of 128×128 pixels. A 3-level network was used as shown in figure 1. Nodes on the lowest level were placed on the input images with a spacing of 14 pixels and an offset of 7 for covering images evenly. Since the network learns temporal groups the training images had to be in a meaningful order. Therefore, views were sorted according to their great-circle distance on the viewing hemisphere. For fifty-fifty-partitioning every other view of the order was taken for training and the rest for testing, for other split-ups every third or fourth, etc.

The relevant parameters are listed for a better overview:

K determines how many neurons are kept active in each node for further computations.

η determines how strong past activities are considered for temporal traces.

α is the learning rate of the neural learning rules.

$T_{tr/te}$ determines for how many past images activities are kept in memory for neuron creation during learning and feedback calculation during recognition.

T_R determines for how many past time steps trace values are kept in memory for neuron creation during learning.

ϑ_Q is the threshold used during learning of the codebook using vector quantization,

ϑ_S^l the threshold for creation of spatial neurons, and

ϑ_T^l the threshold for creation of temporal neurons,

ϑ_L the threshold for deletion of small weights.

N_E is the number of training epochs before adaptation of neuron numbers.

Preliminary parameter tests on ETH80 resulted in the following optimal values: $\vartheta_Q = 0.92$, $T_{tr} = 65$, $T_R = 50$, $\eta = 0.3$, $\alpha = 0.00175$, $\vartheta_S^l = 0.9$, $\vartheta_T^l = 0.0$,

Table 2. Tests for generalization over viewpoints on COIL100 on the name level

viewpoint diff.	TCN	TCG	Westphal	Linde/Lindeberg
10°	99.94	**100.00**	99.68	**100.00**
20°	99.02	98.91	97.97	**99.96**
30°	97.08	95.87	92.93	**100.00**
40°	**96.63**	93.05	88.45	—
45°	91.39	88.61	—	**99.37**
50°	93.95	**88.89**	83.20	—
60°	80.98	79.02	76.61	**99.00**
70°	**83.33**	81.44	75.79	—
80°	**81.10**	77.28	72.39	—
90°	72.16	70.38	65.63	**97.13**

$N_E = 3$ and $\vartheta_L = 10^{-5}$. These gave a recognition rate of 99.69%. For COIL100 most parameters were kept except T_{tr} and T_R which were set to 25, ϑ_Q to 1.00 and ϑ_S^l to 0.95, yielding a recognition rate of 99.94%. T_{te} and K were optimized for each single test.

The following test shows the generalization capabilities of the system for ETH80 and COIL100. The system was trained on different percentages of all images in the database and recognition on the remaining images was done using the two optimal parameter sets.

The results in table 1 demonstrate that on the ETH80 dataset the new system outperforms the old one considerably. Even for 2.50% of training data recognition rates over 63.00% are reached. The TCN shows no decrease in recognition rates at more than 50.00% training data as the TCG does due to parameter optimization. For COIL100 some improvements could be reached in most of the tests although they are not as remarkable as those on ETH80.

Table 2 gives more results on COIL100. The first column shows the distance in viewing angle of two consecutive images in the training set. The other columns show the obtained recognition rates on the test set, on the training set they were 100.00% for both TCN and TCG. We compare the TCN with TCG, the system by Westphal [5] (which uses the same features) and Linde and Lindberg [8,9], who have the best results in the literature. They create a high-dimensional histogram for each image and classify these using SVMs.

The results show that the TCN performs better than TCG for most training sets. In total both systems outperform the approach by Westphal but cannot compete with the system of Linde/Lindeberg for very sparse training sets. They achieve recognition rates of over 97% for 90° distance between training images, where the TCN drops to 78.15%. However, it needs to be considered that they include color information, which is not used in our systems.

Further tests were conducted on the ALOI1000 [10] to show the capability to handle large databases. All images were rescaled to 128 × 128 pixel, and a fifty-fifty-partitioning test was performed on both the viewing angle subset and the subset with varying illumination directions. Recognition rates (test/train) were 99.59%/99.88% and 99.91%/99.97%, respectively, which is very good and shows that the TCN can handle such a large number of object categories. By the conference deadline, not all parameter tests were completed on that database, so these results are expected to improve. Computation times depend strongly on parameters, the major burden being initial vector quantization. For 1680 training images of ETH80, typical learning times are 4 hours on an Intel i7 with 8 cores, 2.93GHz, and 8GB of RAM. Evaluation by the trained network takes about 2 seconds per image.

5   Conclusion

We have presented a powerful object recognition system that improves in several ways on its predecessor. It generalizes very well over different views of the same object on standard datasets and is capable of online learning. In the future we want to test if it can be trained with different categories incrementally.

Acknowledgments. The authors gratefully acknowledge funding from the DFG in the priority program "Organic Computing" (WU 314/5-3) and from the land of Northrhine-Westphalia in the project *MoGES*, which is co-financed by the EFRE program from the European Commission.

References

1. Lessmann, M., Würtz, R.P.: Learning of invariant object recognition in a hierarchical network. Neural Networks 54, 70–84 (2014)
2. Riesenhuber, M., Poggio, T.: Hierarchical models of object recognition in cortex. Nature Neuroscience 2(11), 1019–1025 (1999)
3. George, D.: How the brain might work: a hierarchical and temporal model for learning and recognition. PhD thesis, Stanford University (2008)
4. Rolls, E.T.: Invariant visual object and face recognition: Neural and computational bases, and a model, VisNet. Frontiers in Computational Neuroscience 6(35) (2012)
5. Westphal, G., Würtz, R.P.: Combining feature- and correspondence-based methods for visual object recognition. Neural Computation 21(7), 1952–1989 (2009)
6. Leibe, B., Schiele, B.: Analyzing appearance and contour based methods for object categorization. In: Proc. CVPR., vol. 2, pp. 409–415 (2003)
7. Nene, S., Nayar, S., Murase, H.: Columbia Object Image Library (COIL-100). Technical Report CUCS-006-96, Columbia University (1996)
8. Linde, O., Lindeberg, T.: Object recognition using composed receptive field histograms of higher dimensionality. In: Proc. ICPR, pp. 1–6 (2004)
9. Linde, O., Lindeberg, T.: Composed complex-cue histograms: An investigation of the information content in receptive field based image descriptors for object recognition. CVIU 116(4), 538–560 (2012)
10. Geusebroek, J., Burghouts, G., Smeulders, A.: The Amsterdam Library of Object Images. International Journal of Computer Vision 61, 103–112 (2005)

Incorporating Scale Invariance
into the Cellular Associative Neural Network

Nathan Burles, Simon O'Keefe, and James Austin

Department of Computer Science,
University of York,
York, YO10 5GH, UK
{nburles,sok,austin}@cs.york.ac.uk
http://www.cs.york.ac.uk

Abstract. This paper describes an improvement to the Cellular Associative Neural Network, an architecture based on the distributed model of a cellular automaton, allowing it to perform scale invariant pattern matching. The use of tensor products and superposition of patterns allows the system to recall patterns at multiple resolutions simultaneously. Our experimental results show that the architecture is capable of scale invariant pattern matching, but that further investigation is needed to reduce the distortion introduced by image scaling.

Keywords: pattern recognition, scale invariance, associative memory, correlation matrix memory, distributed computation, cellular automata.

1 Introduction

Cellular automata are formed by connecting simple processing units, known as cells, into a grid or array. Although each individual cell may be simple, exchanging information with their neighbours to update their state can lead to complex or emergent behaviour from the cellular automata. Due to this ability, they are well suited to use for parallel and distributed processing [1].

Architectures based on cellular automata have been used successfully to solve low and medium level problems in computer vision [2]. They have also been extended to incorporate features from neural networks, with similar applications, using weight matrices and continuous time dynamics to replace the simple automaton rules [3]. Orovas introduced an alternative architecture which uses simple correlation matrix memories in each cell, in order to provide fast and efficient processing. The Cellular Associative Neural Network (CANN) was shown to be capable of distributed symbolic processing and pattern recognition with position invariance, but without scale invariance [4].

Apart from the most basic brute force technique—trying to match a pattern at numerous different scales—there are various ways in which scale invariance has been achieved in pattern recognition, using the detection of edges and interest points. These include the Generalised Hough Transform [5], graph matching [6], geometric hashing [7], or curvature scale space [8]. These use a range of analytical

S. Wermter et al. (Eds.): ICANN 2014, LNCS 8681, pp. 435–442, 2014.
© Springer International Publishing Switzerland 2014

techniques, such as statistical and probabilistic models, and Gaussian filtering. None of these methods are suitable, however, for the distributed network of the CANN. Instead we will introduce a novel adaptation of the brute force technique, designed to minimise the performance penalty usually associated with it.

1.1   Correlation Matrix Memories (CMMs)

CMMs are simple, fully connected, associative neural networks consisting of a single layer of weights. Despite this simplicity they are still an active area of research and have been incorporated in a number of complex architectures, including the Associative Rule Chaining Architecture [9] and the Cellular Associative Neural Network. In this work we use binary CMMs, a sub-class of CMMs where the inputs, outputs, and weights are restricted to binary values [10].

Binary CMMs use simple Hebbian learning [11]. Associating pairs of binary vectors, and storing these associations within a CMM, is thus an efficient operation that requires only local updates to the CMM. Equation 1 formalises this learning, where $\mathbf{M}$ is the resulting CMM (or matrix of binary weights), $\mathbf{x}$ is the set of input vectors, $\mathbf{y}$ is the set of output vectors, n is the number of training pairs, and $\vee$ indicates the logical OR of binary vectors.

$$\mathbf{M} = \bigvee_{i=1}^{n} \mathbf{x}_i \mathbf{y}_i{}^T \tag{1}$$

To retrieve information from a CMM, a recall operation is performed as shown in Equation 2. A matrix multiplication between the transposed input vector $\mathbf{x}^T$ and the CMM $\mathbf{M}$ results in a non-binary output vector. A threshold function f must then be applied to this, in order to produce the final binary output vector.

$$\mathbf{y} = f(\mathbf{x}^T \mathbf{M}) \tag{2}$$

There are a number of functions which may be used as the threshold during a recall, although the choice of function may be limited by the application and the data representation used. In this application we use Willshaw's method of thresholding. We know the number of bits set to one in the input vectors during training. On recall, any output element with a value at least this large is set to one. Other output elements are set to zero [10]. This threshold function allows CMMs to operate correctly when superimposed vectors are presented for recall. Relaxation and partial matching is also simple to achieve, by reducing the threshold value.

2   The Cellular Associative Neural Network (CANN)

The CANN is an array of cells—known as associative processors—each of which contains a number of modules. The modules use CMMs to store rules that symbolically describe an object. Each module contains one or more CMMs, configured as an arity network,[1] in order that the number of antecedents to a rule can be variable [12].

---

[1] Arity networks use a number of CMMs, one for each possible arity, to store rules in order that a recall can be performed without unwanted partial matching

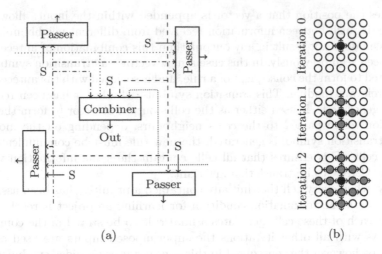

Fig. 1. (a) The "Corner Turning 2" CANN module configuration, where S is the cell state (the output of the combiner module) after each iteration and (b) information flow of this configuration over two iterations [13]

Learning and recognition of an object's structure uses a hierarchical approach, and cells exchange symbolic information with their four direct neighbours during each iteration. This means that after n iterations, each cell is made aware of the state of all cells up to a Manhattan distance of n from it. Various module configurations for the 2D CANN have been investigated, in order to optimise this message passing.

Brewer [13] showed that the "Corner Turning 2" configuration shown in Figure 1a provides the best performance of those tested—allowing information to travel between any two cells, while requiring fewer total rules than alternative suitable configurations. The data flow of this configuration is shown in Figure 1b, where the black cell is the origin of a piece of information, grey cells are those to which the information has been passed, and white cells are those which are not yet aware of the information.

2.1 Learning

Before learning an object's structure, a number of "primitives" are first recognised in the image—vertical and horizontal lines, and the four types of corner: |, —, ⌐, ⌐, ∟, ⌐. Each of these primitives is then represented by a vector, and forms the initial input to each cell. During an iteration, information is received from each of a cell's neighbours' passer modules to form the antecedents of a rule. For each module, an input vector is created by appending the information received from neighbouring cells to the cells' input, according to the module configuration. This vector is then used to recall a new cell state from the combiner module, or a new information vector from a passer module. The module configuration determines the position that a vector is appended within the input, allowing a cell to distinguish between information received from different neighbours.

If a recall does not result in any output then this combination of antecedents has not been seen previously. In this case a new vector—a "transition symbol"—is generated to form the consequent of a rule, and associated with the antecedents into the relevant module. This transition symbol—whether it has been recalled or newly generated—is used either as the cell's output state or to form the new information to be passed to the cell's neighbours, depending on the module. When a transition symbol is generated, the new rule must be communicated to all other cells. This ensures that all cells contain the same information which allows the CANN to be translation invariant.

Finally, when every cell that initially contained a primitive has been assigned a unique state, the termination condition for learning an object is reached. At this point each of these cells generates a final rule to be stored in the combiner module. As with all other iterations the superimposed inputs are used as the antecedents, however the consequent in this case is a user provided symbol which denotes the learnt object.

Appending vectors in order to create a module input, rather than superimposing them, is suitable because each module has a fixed number of inputs n_i. This means that the module has a fixed input length of $n_i \times l$, where l is the vector length used in the system. If one of the cell's neighbours does not have any information to pass, then an empty vector will be transferred and hence included in the input to one or more modules, leading to the requirement of an arity network. For example, in Figure 1a, the "combiner" module has a total of 5 inputs—all four neighbours, and the state of the cell itself (the output of the combiner module). If a vector weight of 4 is chosen, then when all the inputs contain information the total weight is $5 \times 4 = 20$—this is used as the value for Willshaw's threshold. If one of the cell's neighbours does not pass any information, however, then the total weight will only be $4 \times 4 = 16$. If this were to be recalled from a CMM with a threshold value of 20, then it could never result in an output. As such, it is stored in a separate CMM with a threshold value of 16. A recall operation can then present the input vector to the correct CMM in this arity network, using the relevant threshold value.

2.2   Recall

When a pattern is presented for recall, the operation of the CANN is similar to that of a cellular automaton. The rules which govern state transitions are stored in the various modules—with each cell containing exactly the same rules, to allow a pattern to be recognised by any group of cells. To begin a recall, the primitives are extracted from the pattern and used as the input to each cell. As with the learning process, a recall happens iteratively; during each iteration information is received from each of a cell's neighbours and appended to its input, before recall from each of the modules.

If the pattern is recognisable, then after a number of iterations it is labelled with a symbol representing the object. It is unrealistic to expect a perfect recall to happen in every case, however, due to factors such as noisy inputs, distortion, and occlusion. In these cases, the system is able to generalise by taking advantage of a CMM's ability to perform partial matching. If, at any stage, a consequent is not successfully recalled from a module, then relaxation can be employed—that is to say that the threshold value will be reduced in order that an incomplete match may be attempted. This also allows the CANN to recognise inputs which are similar to patterns which have been previously trained [13].

3   Incorporating Scale Invariance

There are two obvious but impractical methods which may be used in order to incorporate scale invariance into the CANN in a neural and distributed manner, both a variant of the brute force method. The first requires training the CANN on multiple versions of the same pattern, presented at numerous different scales (within a predetermined range). This will increase the time required to initially train the network, but allow a recall to be performed quickly. Notably, however, it will significantly increase the number of rules generated—and hence the memory required to store these rules.

The second method trains only a single version of a pattern, presented at its original scale. A pattern must now be presented for recall at numerous different scales (within a predetermined range), in order that the CANN may find a match with the originally trained pattern. This minimises the number of rules generated and the memory required, however potentially imposes a great penalty on every recall performed.

We propose a novel third method which requires only a single version of each pattern to be trained, while minimising the performance penalty imposed by individually recalling a pattern at numerous different scales. Smolensky introduced the concept of a tensor product as a structure which stores bindings between variables and their values [14], and they have been widely investigated, e.g. [15]. Previously we showed that tensor products formed between input data and unique, randomly-generated, binary vectors may be superimposed and successfully recalled from a CMM [16]. Using this technique, we can improve upon the second method by presenting a pattern for recall at numerous different scales simultaneously.

When recalling a pattern, the whole image is first scaled to each of the desired sizes—each of these images is assigned a unique binding vector. Primitives are extracted from each of the images in turn, and a tensor product is formed for each cell by binding this primitive to the image's binding vector. All the tensor products for a given cell are then superimposed, and recall continues in the original fashion—in this case recalling each column of the tensor product in turn. If a pattern is recognised, it is possible to determine the scale at which it was found. Vectors remain in a tensor product throughout the operation of the system, which means that any assigned object labels are also in a tensor product. If this final tensor product is treated as a CMM, and the object label is presented as an input, then the output vector is the binding vector that was originally assigned to the scaled input pattern.

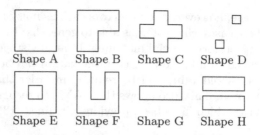

Fig. 2. The 8 patterns trained into the scale invariant CANN [13]

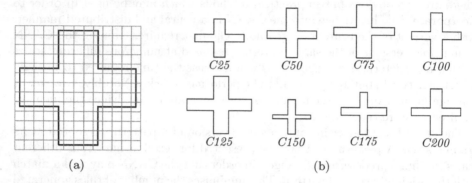

Fig. 3. (a) Cellular grid used when extracting primitives from Shape C and (b) the input image closest to 100% of the original size of Shape C, for each resized version from *C25* to *C200*

3.1   Results

In order to test the recall success of the scale invariant CANN we trained the 8 patterns used in Brewer's previous work [13], shown in Figure 2, into a CANN using the original method. Each pattern was symbolically encoded by overlaying a grid, as shown for Shape C in Figure 3a, and extracting the primitive features to be used as the input for each cell.

Each of the symbolically encoded shapes was then presented for recall at a range of different sizes—every 25% between 25% and 200% of the original size. We then selected a range of scales to use when recalling, such that the scale invariant mechanism would not simply return the images to the original size and result in a perfect recall. Each input shape (e.g. *C25*) was scaled to a range of sizes—every 50% between 50% and 400% of its new size (e.g. *C75* would have been rescaled such that the superimposed recall input ranged from 37.5% to 300% of the original size of Shape C, in steps of 37.5%). As the shapes were already in symbolic form before resizing, the primitive features are immediately available to be bound to their respective binding vectors.

Figure 3b shows the input image closest to 100% of the original size of Shape C, for each resized version from *C25* to *C200*. Resizing the shapes when in symbolic form, rather than as images, has introduced significant variation and

Table 1. Error rates of the scale invariant CANN, when recalling Shapes A–H presented at scales ranging from 25% to 200%. Each result consists of the label(s) applied to the shape after recall, as well as the percentage of incorrectly labelled symbols.

Shape	Scale of image presented for recall							
	25%	50%	75%	100%	125%	150%	175%	200%
A	A 0.00	A 0.00	A 0.00	A 0.00	A 0.00	A 0.00	A 0.00	A 0.00
B	B 6.38	B 0.00	AB 44.83	B 0.00	AB 43.55	AB 27.78	B 0.00	B 0.00
C	C 0.00	C 7.69	C 43.33	C 0.00	100.00	C 10.53	C 0.00	C 0.00
D	D 0.00	D 0.00	D 0.00	D 0.00	D 0.00	D 0.00	D 0.00	D 0.00
E	E 3.45	E 0.00	E 61.11	E 0.00	E 43.59	E 22.73	E 3.57	E 0.00
F	F 0.00	F 0.00	AF 62.86	F 0.00	AF 60.81	F 13.64	F 0.00	F 0.00
G	G 0.00	A 80.00	A 80.95	G 0.00	A 82.61	G 0.00	G 12.50	G 0.00
H	H 0.00	H 0.00	AH 52.38	H 0.00	AH 56.52	H 0.00	H 6.25	H 0.00

distortion. In future work using the scale invariant CANN, in order to achieve the best results, images should be scaled before the primitive features are extracted. For this work, however, the variation serves as an important test of the CANN's ability to recognise distorted shapes.

Table 1 shows the results obtained when presenting the eight shapes for recall at each of the eight scales. Each result shows firstly the label or labels applied to the shape after recall, and then the percentage of the input shape which was incorrectly labelled. In the majority of cases, the shape was correctly labelled, however there are a number of errors that warrant further examination.

A number of recalled shapes, namely various scales of B, F, and H, were labelled as both A and the correct label. Similarly, three of the scales of Shape G were incorrectly labelled as Shape A. Given the similarities between these shapes, and the relaxation ability of the CANN, this is to be expected. This relaxation allows the CANN to recognise distorted and similar shapes, but can lead to incorrect recognition if two similar shapes are both initially trained into the CANN.

Presenting Shape C at a scale of 125% failed to result in any labels being applied. As can be seen in Figure 3b, the *C125* shape is the most distorted— being larger than at any other scale, as well as having different length arms. As mentioned earlier, this distortion could be reduced by scaling images before extracting the primitives.

4   Conclusions and Further Work

This paper has described an improvement to the CANN, to allow it to perform scale invariant pattern matching. Experimental results have shown that the architecture is capable of performing this task effectively, but that further work is needed to reduce the effect of the distortion introduced by image scaling.

The choice of which resolutions to use during a recall is very important, as this will affect how close to the original size a pattern may be scaled. The number of resolutions used may be increased, as the recall process happens simultaneously, however this may not be necessary if the distortion can be reduced by scaling images before extracting primitives. Further work is therefore required to determine the effect of this scaling, before attempting to determine whether there is an optimal set of resolutions to use (within a given range).

Finally, the CANN has largely been applied to synthetic patterns, although it has been shown to be able to operate successfully on simple photographic images [13]. Future work will further examine the application of the CANN to real objects in images.

References

1. Preston, K., Duff, M. (eds.): Modern Cellular Automata: Theory and Applications. Plenum Press (1984)
2. de Saint-Pierre, T., Milgram, M.: New and Efficient Cellular Algorithms for Image Processing. CVGIP: Image Understanding 55(3), 261–274 (1992)
3. Chua, L.O., Yang, L.: Cellular Neural Networks: Theory. IEEE Trans. on Circuits and Systems 35(10), 1257–1272 (1988)
4. Orovas, C., Austin, J.: Cellular Associative Neural Networks for Image Interpretation. In: Int. Conf. on Image Processing and its Appl., pp. 665–669. IET (1997)
5. Ballard, D.H.: Generalizing the Hough Transform to Detect Arbitrary Shapes. Pattern Recognition 13(2), 111–122 (1981)
6. Leung, T.K., Burl, M.C., Perona, P.: Finding Faces in Cluttered Scenes Using Random Labeled Graph Matching. In: Int. Conf. on Comput. Vis., pp. 637–644. IEEE (1995)
7. Wolfson, H.J., Rigoutsos, I.: Geometric Hashing: An Overview. Comput. Sci. & Eng. 4(4), 10–21 (1997)
8. Mokhtarian, F., Mackworth, A.K.: A Theory of Multiscale, Curvature-Based Shape Representation for Planar Curves. IEEE Trans. on Pattern Anal. and Mach. Intell. 14(8), 789–805 (1992)
9. Burles, N., O'Keefe, S., Austin, J.: Improving the Associative Rule Chaining Architecture. In: Mladenov, V., Koprinkova-Hristova, P., Palm, G., Villa, A.E.P., Appollini, B., Kasabov, N. (eds.) ICANN 2013. LNCS, vol. 8131, pp. 98–105. Springer, Heidelberg (2013)
10. Willshaw, D.J., Buneman, O.P., Longuet-Higgins, H.C.: Non-holographic Associative Memory. Nature 222, 960–962 (1969)
11. Ritter, H., Martinetz, T., Schulten, K.: Neural Computation and Self-Organizing Maps: An Introduction. Addison-Wesley, Redwood City (1992)
12. Burles, N., Austin, J., O'Keefe, S.: Extending the Associative Rule Chaining Architecture for Multiple Arity Rules. In: Neural-Symb. Learn. and Reason., Beijing, pp. 47–51 (2013)
13. Brewer, G.: Spiking Cellular Associative Neural Networks for Pattern Recognition. PhD Thesis, Univ. of York (2008)
14. Smolensky, P.: Tensor Product Variable Binding and the Representation of Symbolic Structures in Connectionist Systems. Artif. Intell. 46(1), 159–216 (1990)
15. Stewart, T., Eliasmith, C.: Compositionality and Biologically Plausible Models. In: Werning, M., Hinzen, W., Machery, E. (eds.) The Oxf. Handb. of Compositionality. Oxford University Press, Oxford (2012)
16. Austin, J., Hobson, S., Burles, N., O'Keefe, S.: A Rule Chaining Architecture Using a Correlation Matrix Memory. In: Villa, A.E.P., Duch, W., Érdi, P., Masulli, F., Palm, G. (eds.) ICANN 2012, Part I. LNCS, vol. 7552, pp. 49–56. Springer, Heidelberg (2012)

Shape from Shading by Model Inclusive Learning with Simultaneously Estimating Reflection Parameters

Yasuaki Kuroe[1] and Hajimu Kawakami[2]

[1] Department of Information Science, Kyoto Institute of Technology
Matsugasaki, Sakyo-ku, Kyoto 606-8585, Japan
kuroe@kit.ac.jp
[2] Department of Electronics and Informatics, Ryukoku University
1-5, Yokotani, Ohe-cho, Seta, Ohtsu 520-2194, Japan
kawakami@rins.ryukoku.ac.jp

Abstract. Recovering shape from shading is an important problem in computer vision and robotics and many studies have been done. We have already proposed a versatile method of solving the problem by model inclusive learning of neural networks. The method is versatile in the sense that it can solve the problem in various circumstances. Almost all of the methods of recovering shape from shading proposed so far assume that surface reflection properties of a target object are known a priori. It is, however, very difficult to obtain those properties exactly. In this paper we propose a method to resolve this problem by extending our previous method. The proposed method makes it possible to recover shape with simultaneously estimating reflection parameters of an object.

Keywords: shape from shading, neural network, image-formation model, model inclusive learning.

1 Introduction

The problem of surface-shape recovery of an object from an intensity image is important in computer vision and robotics. The problem was first formulated in the general setting by B.K.P. Horn and many studies have been done based on the formulation [1,2]. It is an ill-posed problem [3] and reduced to a nonlinear-function approximation problem.

There have been increasing research interests of artificial neural networks and many efforts have been made on applications of neural networks to various fields. The most significant features of artificial neural networks are the extreme flexibility due to the learning ability, capability of nonlinear function approximation and the generalization ability. It is expected, therefore, that neural networks make it possible to easily solve the problem of shape from shading by their learning and generalization ability [4].

We have already proposed a neural-network method for solving the problem [5]. The method is versatile in the sense that it can solve the problem in various

S. Wermter et al. (Eds.): ICANN 2014, LNCS 8681, pp. 443–450, 2014.

circumstances. In order to realize the versatility, we introduced the concept of model inclusive learning of neural networks [6,7]. In the model inclusive learning a priori knowledge and inherent property of a target are incorporated into the formulation of learning problem, which can regularize an ill-posed problem and can improve learning and generalization ability of neural networks.

Almost all of the methods of recovering shape from shading proposed so far assume that surface reflection properties of a target object are known a priori. It is, however, very difficult to obtain those properties exactly. In this paper we propose a method to resolve this problem by extending the method in [5]. The proposed method makes it possible to recover shape with simultaneously estimating reflection parameters of an object.

2   Model Inclusive Learning for Shape from Shading

In this section we explain the basic idea and concept of the proposed model inclusive learning for the shape from shading. Its schematic diagram is shown in Fig. 1. An image of a three-dimensional object taken by a camera in an imaging condition depends on its geometric structure (shape), its reflectance property, and the imaging conditions (the distribution of light sources etc.), and the image formation process is illustrated as shown in the upper part of Fig. 1. The process can be regarded as a mapping from the geometric structure of the surface to the image. We call the mathematical model of the mapping 'image-formation model'. Note that the image-formation model, denoted by $\hat{F}$, depends on the reflectance properties and the imaging conditions. We assume that, in the image-formation model $\hat{F}$, the mathematical models of reflectance properties and the imaging conditions are known a priori, while the reflection parameters which are included in the reflectance properties are unknown. This problem of recovering shape from shading can be solved by the model inclusive learning of neural networks as follows. Let $G(x, y)$ denote the brightness at a position (x, y) on the image. The learning problem of a neural network is formulated in such a way that it recovers the geometric structure of the surface of the object as its input and output relation and it is trained with including the image-formation model $\hat{F}$ as follows. As shown in Fig. 1, we input an position (x, y) on the image to the neural network, and we also input the corresponding output of the neural network to the image-formation model $\hat{F}$ together with the reflection properties and the imaging conditions. If the neural network is successfully trained and the geometric structure of the surface of the object is realized as its input and output relation, the output of the image-formation model $\hat{F}$ becomes equal to the brightness data $G(x, y)$ which are taken from the object.

Therefore, training the neural network so as to reduce the error between the output of the image-formation model $\hat{F}$ and the brightness $G(x, y)$ over all data points to zero would make it exhibit the geometric structure of the surface as its input and output relation. Noting that we assume that the reflection parameters are unknown, we adjust not only values of the neural network parameters but also those of the reflection parameters, as shown in Fig. 1, so as to minimize

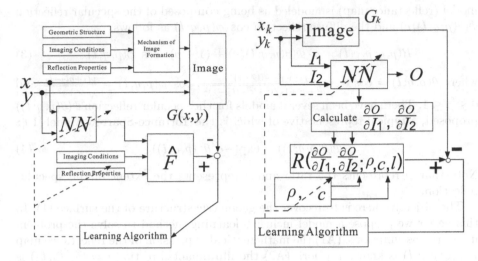

Fig. 1. Shape from shading by model inclusive learning of a neural network

Fig. 2. Proposed model inclusive learning method for shape from shading

the error. If the error can be reduced enough small by the adjustments of the parameters, the surface recovery and the estimation of the unknown reflection parameters are achieved simultaneously.

3   Problem Statement and Proposed Learning Method

3.1   Problem Statement

Suppose that the surface of an object is represented by

$$z = f(x, y) \tag{1}$$

in a camera coordinate system x - y - z, with the x - y plane coinciding with the image plane, and z axis coinciding with the optical axis of the camera. It is known that, assuming that orthographic projection and uniform reflectance property of the object, the brightness at position (x, y) on the image plane can be described as

$$G\left(x,y\right) \;=\; R\left(p,q \;;\; \rho,c,l\right), \qquad p = \frac{\partial f}{\partial x}, q = \frac{\partial f}{\partial y} \tag{2}$$

where p and q are the surface gradient at (x, y), $l = (\ell_1, \ell_2, \ell_3)$ is the illuminant direction, and ρ and c are the reflection parameters. Equation (2) is called image irradiance equation. $R\left(p, q \;;\; \rho, c, l\right)$ is called the reflectance map and represents reflection properties. Note that the image irradiance equation (2) is corresponding to the image-formation model $\hat{F}$. In general the image formation model (reflectance map) is modeled as being composed of the specular reflection $\Phi(\theta(p, q; l), c)$ and the diffuse reflection $\cos \phi(p, q; l)$ as follows.

$$R(p, q; \rho, c, l) = \rho \cdot \Phi(\theta(p, q; l), c) + (1 - \rho) \cdot \cos \phi(p, q; l) \tag{3}$$

where $\theta(p, q; l) = \cos^{-1} \frac{pl_1 + ql_2 - (l_3 - 1)}{\sqrt{p^2 + q^2 + 1}\sqrt{l_1^2 + l_2^2 + (l_3 - 1)^2}}$, $\cos \phi(p, q; l) = \frac{pl_1 + ql_2 - l_3}{\sqrt{p^2 + q^2 + 1}}$ and $0 \le \rho \le 1$. There have been several models for the specular reflection $\Phi(\theta(p, q; l))$ proposed, a typical representative of whici is the Torrance-Sparrow Model [10]:

$$\Phi(\theta(p, q; l)) = \exp(-c^2 \theta^2(p, q; l)) \tag{4}$$

Note that ρ represents the ratio and c represents the extent of the specular reflection.

The objective here is to recover the geometric structure of the surface (1). In this paper we propose a model inclusive learning method to solve the problem under the assumptions: (A1) the mathematical expression of the reflectance map $R(p, q; \rho, c, l)$ is known a priori, (A2) the illuminant direction $l = (\ell_1, \ell_2, \ell_3)$ is known, and (A3) the reflection parameters ρ ($0 \le \rho \le 1$) and c are not known.

3.2   Solution of the Shape from Shading Problem by Model Inclusive Learning

Figure 2 shows the schematic diagram of the proposed model inclusive learning method of neural networks. Let G^k denote the brightness which is observed at a position (x_k, y_k) from an image taken from an object surface. We prepare a neural network (NN) with two inputs denoted by $I = [I_1, I_2]^T$ and one output denoted by O and consider that the input $I = [I_1, I_2]^T$ and the output O correspond to the position (x, y) on the images and the depth z of the surface, respectively. For an observed brightness G^k, we give its position (x_k, y_k) on the the image to the input $I = [I_1, I_2]^T$ of the neural network and derive the derivatives of the output of the neural network with respect to the input, and obtain the values of the derivatives at $[I_1, I_2]^T = (x_k, y_k)^T$:

$$\left.\frac{\partial O}{\partial I}\right|_{I=(x_k,y_k)} = \left(\left.\frac{\partial O}{\partial I_1}\right|_{I=(x_k,y_k)}, \left.\frac{\partial O}{\partial I_2}\right|_{I=(x_k,y_k)} \right). \tag{5}$$

Note that those derivatives becomes equal to the surface gradients p and q at the position (x_k, y_k) if the input and output relation of the neural network exhibits the geometric structure (1) of the object. We substitute the values of the derivatives (5) into the surface gradient p and q of the image-formation model $R(\cdot, \cdot ; \rho, c, l)$. The obtained value of $R(\partial O/\partial I_1, \partial O/\partial I_2; \rho, c, l)$ corresponds to the outputs of the image formation model in Fig. 1 and is to be coincided with the brightness G^k. Accordingly, training the neural network so as to reduce the error between the brightness data G^k and $R(\partial O/\partial I_1, \partial O/\partial I_2; \rho, c, l)$ over the all data points to zero, we can obtain the geometric structure of the surface as the input and output relation of the neural network. Noting that the reflection parameters ρ and c are not known, we adjust not only values of the neural network

Fig. 3. Venus statue made up of curved surfaces

Fig. 4. Target image of the right eye of the Venus statue

parameters but also those of the reflection parameters ρ and c, as shown in Fig. 2. Note also that, since the the reflectance map $R(p, q; \rho, c, l)$ contains unknown reflection parameters ρ and c, in the calculation of $R(\partial O/\partial I_1, \partial O/\partial I_2; \rho, c, l)$ we use the current estimated values of ρ and c.

Define the performance index by

$$J = \frac{1}{2} \sum_{(x_k, y_k) \in D_G} \left\{ R \left(\frac{\partial O}{\partial I_1} \bigg|_{I=(x_k, y_k)}, \frac{\partial O}{\partial I_2} \bigg|_{I=(x_k, y_k)}; \rho, c, l \right) - G^k \right\}^2 \quad (6)$$

where D_G is a set of data points (x_k, y_k) at which the brightness data G^k are observed from the image. The problem is now reduced to finding values of parameters of the neural network and also the reflection parameters ρ and c that minimize the performance index J, which could simultaneously achieve recovering shape and estimating the reflection parameters of an object.

In order to search values of the network parameters and the reflection parameters which minimize J, the gradient based methods can be used. The main problem associated with these algorithms is the computation of the gradients of J with respect to the parameters of the neural network and the reflection parameters ρ and c. Efficient algorithms to calculate these gradients can be derived by introducing adjoint models of the neural network [8]. The derivation is omitted due to the limitation of the space.

4   Experiments

In the experiments a four-layer feedforward neural network with 15 hidden units is used. We utilize the quasi-Newton method with the Davidon-Fletcher-Powell algorithm as a gradient based method. As surface-reflection model we use the Torrance-Sparrow Model given by (4).

In the first experiments the image we used is a Venus statue which is made up of curved surfaces shown in Fig. 3. The experiment was performed by using the image of size 71×51 shown in Fig. 4 which is the right eye of the Venus statue in Fig. 3. The illuminant direction l was set to be $l = (-0.232, -0.082, -0.969)$

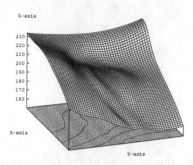

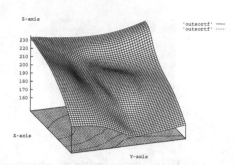

Fig. 5. Recovered eye-surface obtained by the proposed method

Fig. 6. Recovered eye-surface obtained by the method without estimating the reflection parameters ρ and c

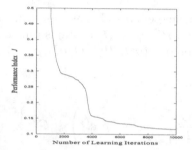

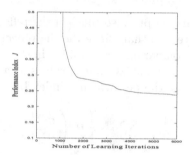

Fig. 7. Convergence behavior of J obtained by the proposed method

Fig. 8. Convergence behavior of J obtained by the method without the estimation

and the initial guess of reflection parameters ρ and c, which are to be estimated, was set to be $\rho = 0.460$, $c = 0.408$. Those values were obtained by preparatory calibration experiments. Figure 5 shows the recovery surface obtained by the proposed method. Figure 6 shows the recovery surface obtained by the proposed method without estimating the reflection parameters ρ and c, which corresponds the method in [5]. The parameters ρ and c were fixed to the values of their initial guess. It is observed by comparing those figures that the result of Fig. 5 can capture the fine structure of the target much more than that of Fig. 6, which reveals the effectiveness of the estimation of the reflection parameters. Figure 7 shows the convergence behavior of the proposed learning method in which the result in Fig. 5 is obtained, and Figure 8 shows that in which the result in Fig. 6 is obtained. In those figures the variations of the performance index J versus the number of the learning iterations are plotted. It can be seen that the value of J in Fig 7 converges to the value much smaller than that in Fig. 8, which also reveals the effectiveness of the estimation. Figures 9 and 10 show the convergence behavior of the estimation of the reflection parameters ρ and c.

The second experiment was performed by using the image of size 56×56 shown in Fig. 12 which are the nose of the Venus statue in Fig. 11. Note that the target surface is made up of plane surfaces and has discontinuous surface gradients, which implies that the surface recovery is much more difficult. The

Fig. 9. Convergence behavior of ρ

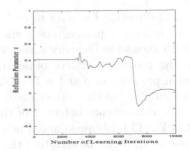

Fig. 10. Convergence behavior of c

Fig. 11. Venus statue made up of plane surfaces

Fig. 12. Target image of the nose of the Venus statue

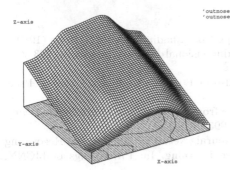

Fig. 13. Recovered nose-surface obtained by the proposed method

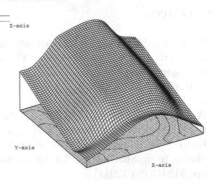

Fig. 14. Recovered nose-surface obtained by the method without estimating the reflection parameters ρ and c

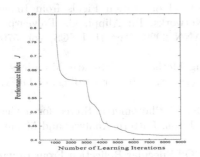

Fig. 15. Convergence behavior of J obtained by the proposed method

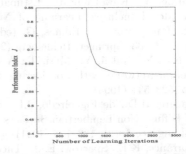

Fig. 16. Convergence behavior of J iteration obtained by the method without estimation

illuminant direction l was set to be $l = (-0.232, -0.082, -0.969)$ and the initial guess of reflection parameters ρ and c was set to be $\rho = 0.460$, $c = 0.408$. Figure 13 shows the recovery surfaces obtained by the proposed method. Fig.14 shows the recovery surfaces obtained by the method without estimating the reflection parameters ρ and c. It is observed that the result of Fig. 13 captures the discontinuity of the surface gradients better than that of Fig. 14. Figure 15 shows the convergence behavior of the proposed learning method in which the result in Fig 13 is obtained and, Figure 16 shows that in which the result in Fig. 14 is obtained. It can be seen that the value of J in Fig 15 converges to the value much smaller than that in Fig. 16.

5   Conclusion

In the problem of recovering shape from shading, almost all of the methods proposed so far assume that surface reflection properties for a target object are known a priori. It is, however, very difficult to obtain those properties exactly. In this paper we have proposed a method to resolve the above problem. The proposed method is a model inclusive learning of neural networks which can recover shape with simultaneously estimating reflection parameters of an object.

References

1. Horn, B.K.P., Brooks, M.J.: edited: Shape from Shading. The MIT Press (1989)
2. Klette, R., et al.: Computer Vision: Three-dimensional data from images, pp. 263–345. Springer (1998)
3. Bertero, M., Poggio, T., Torre, V.: Ill-posed problems in early vision. Proc. IEEE 76, 869–889 (1988)
4. Wei, G.Q., Hirzinger, G.: Learning Shape from Shading by a Multilayer Network. IEEE Trans. Neural Networks 7(4), 985–995 (1996)
5. Kuroe, Y., Kawakami, H.: Versatile Neural Network Method for Recovering Shape from Shading by Model Inclusive Learning. In: Proceedings of IJCNN, pp. 3194–3199 (2011)
6. Kuroe, Y., Kawakami, H.: Vector Field Approximation by Model Inclusive Learning of Neural Networks. In: de Sá, J.M., Alexandre, L.A., Duch, W., Mandic, D.P. (eds.) ICANN 2007. LNCS, vol. 4668, pp. 717–726. Springer, Heidelberg (2007)
7. Kuroe, Y., Kawakami, H.: Estimation Method of Motion Fields from Images by Model Inclusive Learning of Neural Networks. In: Alippi, C., Polycarpou, M., Panayiotou, C., Ellinas, G. (eds.) ICANN 2009, Part II. LNCS, vol. 5769, pp. 673–683. Springer, Heidelberg (2009)
8. Kuroe, Y., Nakai, Y., Mori, T.: A Learning Method of Nonlinear Mappings by Neural Networks with Considering Their Derivatives. In: Proceedings of IJCNN, pp. 528–531 (1993)
9. Tagare, H.D., de Figueiredo, J.P.: A Theory of Photometric Stereo for a Class of Diffuse Non-Lambertian Surfaces. IEEE Trans. Pattern Analysis and Machine Intelligence 13(2), 133–138 (1991)
10. Torrance, K.E., Sparrow, E.M.: Theory for Off-Specular Reflection From Roughened Surfaces. Journal of the Optical Society of America 57(9), 1105–1114 (1967)

Instance-Based Object Recognition with Simultaneous Pose Estimation Using Keypoint Maps and Neural Dynamics

Oliver Lomp[1], Kasim Terzić[2], Christian Faubel[1], J.M.H. du Buf[2], and Gregor Schöner[1]

[1] Institut für Neuroinformatik, Ruhr-Universität, Bochum, Germany
{oliver.lomp,christian.faubel,gregor.schoener}@ini.ruhr-uni-bochum.de
[2] Vision Laboratory (LARSyS), University of the Algarve, Faro, Portugal
{kterzic,dubuf}@ualg.pt

Abstract. We present a method for biologically-inspired object recognition with one-shot learning of object appearance. We use a computationally efficient model of V1 keypoints to select object parts with the highest information content and model their surroundings using simple colour features. This map-like representation is fed into a dynamical neural network which performs pose, scale and translation estimation of the object given a set of previously observed object views. We demonstrate the feasibility of our algorithm for cognitive robotic scenarios and evaluate classification performance on a dataset of household items.

Keywords: Neural Dynamics, Biologically Inspired Keypoints, Vision, Object Recognition, Pose Estimation.

1 Introduction

Object recognition is one of the central problems in vision and remains the focus of much research in Computer Vision, Artificial Intelligence and Computational Neuroscience. Vision for cognitive robotics poses additional constraints: (1) real-time performance is desired in order to support timely interaction with the environment; (2) processing power is often limited, requiring careful data selection and extensive optimisation; (3) fast and online learning in interactive scenarios is preferable to long training times.

In contrast to many computational architectures for cognitive robotics, we propose a neural architecture which uses dynamic neural fields for simultaneous object recognition and scale, translation and rotation estimation. It is capable of one-shot learning of object appearance based on single images and it can learn new objects online. We do not explore the real-time feasibility in the present work. However, the neural principles used throughout the paper lend themselves to parallel and thus fast implementation.

S. Wermter et al. (Eds.): ICANN 2014, LNCS 8681, pp. 451–458, 2014.

1.1 Related Work

Computationally efficient methods have been developed for a number of vision tasks in robotics, including pose-invariant object detection. Typically, invariant features are detected [1–4] and these are matched to stored templates using approximate methods such as RANSAC.

A number of biologically inspired methods have been proposed for object detection and recognition. Some of them expand the Neocognitron architecture [5], originally developed for character recognition, to recognise more general objects such as faces [6]. The HMAX model and its derivatives [7] are based on a simplified alternation of layers of simple and complex cells in order to extract features of increasing complexity, but they require an external classifier (usually an SVM) for final classification. Recently, deep convolutional networks have demonstrated excellent performance on a number of classification tasks, but at a considerable cost in terms of complexity and learning time [8]. All of these state-of-the-art approaches can deal with translation and scale change, but they do not address variation in pose, such as rotation and perspective effects. There is ample evidence that biological vision systems can recognise objects with unfamiliar poses, but that this process is considerably slower, hinting at a separate recurrent neural process [9]. We present a neural framework which addresses this problem.

Our work is based on map-seeking circuits of Arathorn [10], which were applied to object detection by Faubel and Schöner [11]. Instead of using global histograms as in [11], we apply biological keypoints for data selection and extract a set of localised colour features at keypoint locations. Keypoints play an important role in early attention. They indicate areas with large local complexity and exhibit excellent repeatability [4], which makes them useful for pose estimation. We reformulate the original algorithm from [11] so that it uses a consistent neural dynamic approach throughout. This reformulation makes it suitable for localised features, thus removing some ad-hoc parts of the original, global algorithm.

2 Method

2.1 Localised Colour Features Based on V1 Keypoints

We start by extracting multi-scale keypoints using the BIMP algorithm [4]. The image is first processed by a bank of complex Gabor filters representing cortical simple cells. The moduli of simple cell responses are used to model responses of complex cells. Another layer of cells computes spatial derivatives of the complex cell responses, which are combined with two inhibition schemes to obtain responses of end-stopped cells for detecting keypoints. The algorithm is applied at multiple scales by varying the wavelength of the Gabor filters which model simple cells. For a more detailed description of the algorithm we refer to [4].

At each keypoint location, we extract a colour histogram which represents a local neighbourhood with size proportional to filter scale. Each pixel in the neighbourhood is assigned the most similar of ten basic colours in the Lab colour space. Then a Gaussian-weighted sum for each basic colour is computed over the local neighbourhood for each keypoint. The sum for each colour is stored in a 2D map at the keypoint location and then spatially smoothed with an isotropic Gaussian kernel. With ten basic colours, this gives a stack of ten 2D feature maps $I(x, y, c) \mapsto \mathbb{R}$, where x and y are subsampled image coordinates and c represents one of the basic colours. This process is applied at each keypoint scale s, resulting in a 4-dimensional feature vector $K(x, y, c, s) \mapsto \mathbb{R}$.

Localised colour histograms are fast and rotation-invariant, but relatively weak features. We use them here to highlight the importance of spatial configuration and our pose estimation algorithm. We plan to replace them by more powerful features, such as responses of HMAX-based C-cells [7].

2.2   Pose Estimation and Object Recognition

The main idea of map-seeking circuits [10] is that the pose and identity of an object in an input image can be estimated simultaneously by using a recurrent process. This process starts by assuming that all poses and identities are equally likely (although in principle, it is possible to bias certain classes based on domain priors or scene context). In each iteration, estimates are updated by a competitive process which adapts the relative weights of poses by estimating how well they match the current input given the estimates before the update. Over time, the weights converge to a state where only the correct pose and identity have non-zero weights. A version of this approach using dynamic neural fields provides good control over the convergence and enables coupling to online visual input [11].

We expand this earlier work in an architecture, shown in Fig. 1a, that consists of a pose estimation module and an object recognition module. Pose estimation entails a cascade of two-dimensional translation (shift), rotation, and scale that is processed concurrently. Pose is represented in dynamic neural fields (DNFs) and label information in a discrete variant, dynamic neural nodes. DNFs are patterns of activation, $u(\mathbf{x}, t)$, defined over a pose parameter or feature dimension, $\mathbf{x}$, that evolve as a dynamical system according to [12]

$$\tau \dot{u}(\mathbf{x}, t) = -u(\mathbf{x}, t) + h + s(\mathbf{x}, t) + \int (w(\mathbf{x} - \mathbf{x}') - \gamma) f(u(\mathbf{x}', t)) d\mathbf{x}' + \eta. \quad (1)$$

Here, τ is the time scale of the dynamics, $h < 0$ the resting level, $s(\mathbf{x}, t)$ external input; $w(\mathbf{x} - \mathbf{x}')$ the kernel of local excitatory interaction within the DNF, while $\gamma \geq 0$ represents the strength of global inhibitory interaction. The function $f(\cdot)$ is a sigmoid. Noise, η is added because the dynamics goes through instabilities and must escape reliably from unstable solutions. At appropriate values of γ the dynamics is selective, allowing only a single connected and bounded region of the DNF to become active at any given time.

Pose estimation happens in two cascaded DNFs. The first layer, $u_1(\mathbf{x}, t)$, forms an initial hypothesis, driven by the current pose estimate as input with weak global inhibitory interaction. The second layer evolves more slowly with strong inhibitory interaction, and makes the final decision on the pose estimate. It receives input from the first layer, $s_2(\mathbf{x}, t) = \theta(g(u_1(\mathbf{x}, t)))$, where $\theta(u) = u$ for $u > 0$ and zero elsewhere. g is a spatial Gaussian filter. The current pose estimate $p(\mathbf{x}, t)$ is

$$p(\mathbf{x}, t) = c_{\text{mix}}(t) \cdot \theta(u_1(\mathbf{x}, t)) + (1 - c_{\text{mix}}(t)) \cdot f(u_2(\mathbf{x}, t)) , \qquad (2)$$

where $c_{\text{mix}}(t) \in [0, 1]$ is the output of an additional, dimensionless DNF which is activated when $\int f(u_2(\mathbf{x}, t))d\mathbf{x}$ exceeds a threshold.

Object Identity is represented by associating labels with each object. In analogy with the pose representation, there are two layers of dynamic neural nodes, $u_{l,i}(t)$ $(i \in \{1, 2\})$ for each label l, governed by dynamics analogous to Eqn 1. Similar to self-excitation and global inhibition in the DNF, each node excites itself and inhibits all others. The current label estimate, $w_l(t)$, is calculated analogously to Eqn 2.

Matching Pose and Identity for Shifts. We first describe the method for a single scale and for the shift estimate only. Inputs are three-dimensional functions $I(x, y, c) \mapsto \mathbb{R}$, where x, y are image coordinates and c is an additional feature dimension such as colour. $I(x, y, c)$ simply specifies how much of a colour c is perceived at a given location. For matching inputs to the stored views, we first apply the *inverse* of the current pose estimate $p(\delta_x, \delta_y, t)$, where $(\delta_x, \delta_y) = \mathbf{x}$. This is calculated as

$$I'(x, y, c) = \iint p(\delta_x, \delta_y, c) \cdot I(x + \delta_x, y + \delta_y, c)d\delta_x d\delta_y , \qquad (3)$$

i.e., the cross-correlation of the current input and the current pose estimate. The matching value m_l with each memorised pattern $W_l(x, y, c)$ is also calculated using correlation, now taking all colours c into account:

$$m_l(t) = \iiint \hat{I}'(x, y, c) \cdot \hat{W}_l(x, y, c)dxdydc , \qquad (4)$$

where $\hat{I}'$ and $\hat{W}_l$ are zero-mean and normalised versions of I' and W_l. For determining the current shift estimate, we calculate the superposition of the memorised patterns

$$W'(x, y, c) = \sum_l w_l(t) \cdot W_l(x, y, c) \qquad (5)$$

given the current label estimates $w_l(t)$. Analogously to Eqn 4, we can then compute

$$s_1(\delta_x, \delta_y) = \iiint \hat{W}'(x, y, c) \cdot \hat{I}(x + \delta_x, y + \delta_y, c)dxdydc . \qquad (6)$$

This is fed into Eqn 1 as input, forming a closed recurrent loop.

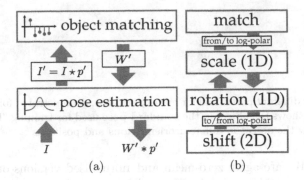

Fig. 1. (a) Interfaces between the *pose estimation* and *object matching* modules. Please refer to the text for an explanation of the symbols. (b) Log-polar transformations between pose estimation modules allow us to estimate scale and rotation.

Scale and Rotation can be estimated by cascading several transformation modules (see Fig. 1). To estimate rotation and scaling, the output of the shift estimation module is transformed to log-polar space, so that rotation and scaling are again shift operations (Fig. 1b).

Pattern Learning is supervised. During learning, Gaussian-shaped inputs are fed into the pose-DNFs. These inputs are centred around the correct pose parameters. The correct label is activated by a strong, localised input to the corresponding label node.

The weights of the pattern memory (W_l) are adapted by a linear dynamical system. This system is chosen so that at the fixed point, $W_l(x, y, c) = T(x, y, c)$, where T is the image used for training, but inversely transformed by the pose parameters in the DNFs.

2.3 Keypoint Scales

The feed-forward stream of the architecture contains keypoints on different scales. So far, we considered input from a single scale of the keypoint-stream. We can also control the scale of keypoints through a matching approach similar to the one presented above. Let $K(x, y, c, s) \mapsto \mathbb{R}$ be the maps of localised histograms for colour c at keypoint scales s.

We need to obtain a measure of the match for each scale. This can be determined analogously to how memory patterns are matched to the currently processed input pattern. Let $W'(x, y, c)$ be the superposition of memories, transformed according to the current pose estimates. Then the match value for scale s can be calculated by

$$m(s) = \iiint \hat{K}(x, y, c, s) \cdot \hat{W}'(x, y, c) dx dy dc \,, \tag{7}$$

Fig. 2. The four different poses used for our experiment, demonstrated for *Cookies*. The left-most image shows the object in the standard pose used for training. The remaining three views show the object in different orientations and positions.

where $\hat{K}$ and $\hat{W}'$ are again zero-mean and normalised versions of K and W'. Note that this matching value is a second input to the scale estimation field rather than having its own estimation process. In order to get the input pattern I for the recognition system, we again form a superposition of the different scales, weighted by the current scale estimate. The system then naturally converges to the keypoint scale that is most appropriate for classifying the given object.

3   Evaluation

We implemented the architecture using *cedar*, a software framework for neural dynamics [13]. For the evaluation, we use a subset (only the 120 images recorded in the center region out of the total of 300) of the images that were used to evaluate its predecessor [11,14]. These images of 30 everyday objects have been recorded with a robotic scenario in mind. The camera looks at somewhat distant objects on a white tabletop. Of the nine different poses in the previous dataset, we chose the four located in the centre region of the image (see Fig. 2). As in the previous experiments, we cut out a subregion (a rectangle of 360×360 pixels in the centre of the image) of the original images (640×480 RGB).

3.1   Performance Evaluation

During the training phase, weights are learned by presenting each training image together with the pose information for a fixed duration. Images are presented only once. In the testing phase, the test images are presented to the system for recognition. The neural dynamics we use are stochastic. This may randomly lead to different outcomes on separate trials, thus we repeat the testing phase three times.

In both phases, the system is reset by lowering the resting level of the DNFs between the presentation of two images. This reset phase is considered complete when the difference between the minimal and maximal activation of the nodes in the second label layer falls below a fixed threshold. This removes residual information from previous trials without restarting the process.

The recognition is considered completed when the $f(u_{l,2})$ exceeds a certain threshold during the recognition phase and the change in $u_{l,1}$ falls below a threshold. A short grace period is given to account for possible changes in the decision.

Table 1. Performance measurements. Refer to the text for an explanation.

System	Correct (%)	Pose Parameter	Average Error
Proposed	68.0	Position (px)	23.8
LNBNN + SIFT	42.2	Rotation (°)	69.3
LNBNN + CH27	10.0	Scale* (factor)	0.22
LNBNN + SIFTP10	40.0	* Only evaluated on scaled images.	

(a) Comparison of recognition perfor-   (b) Evaluation of pose estimation.
mance.

After this period, the recognised label and pose are given by the location of the maximum activation in the layer two activation values. The recognised pose is read out in the same way. A reset is triggered and, once it is completed, a new recognition trial begins.

For comparison, we classified the original dataset using the state of the art LNBNN classifier [15] with three different kinds of features. The first approach uses a full range of SIFT features. The second approach (CH27) uses the same localised colour histograms we use for our approach, but with 27 colour bins. The third approach (SIFTP10) uses a randomly-selected set of ten SIFT prototypes and uses the Euclidean distance to each of them as a 10-dimensional feature vector.

3.2 Results

Results are shown in Table 1. Pose errors are reported as Euclidean distances between the recognised and the annotated pose.

As Table 2a shows, even with relatively weak features, we already obtain good recognition rates. Failures occur for objects with similar feature values. For example, *glue*, an object dominated by red and blue colours, was often confused with *blue_boxcutter*, *blue_tape* and *red_screwdriver*. Objects with low local complexity, such as *yellow_stapler* presented the biggest difficulty for our system.

4 Conclusions

We have presented a neurally-inspired model for object recognition with simultaneous pose estimation based on single views. We expanded and revised previous work that employed global features and non-neural processing steps such as histogram rotations. Our approach is entirely based on neural concepts, from neurally plausible local features to the neural-field-based shift, scale, and rotation estimation. Tests on 30 household items demonstrate the ability of our method to reliably recognise objects learned from single views.

Our implementation does not currently achieve speeds required for real-time processing. The current bottleneck is the calculation of the four-dimensional feature maps.

While our approach outperformed a state-of-the-art approach on our dataset, we only consider this a preliminary result. In future work, we aim to test our approach with stronger features on an established database.

We are currently working on stronger invariant features and integration with a scene representation system. We expect that stronger top-down guidance, which can be easily added to our framework, can significantly improve detection speed and results.

Acknowledgements. This work was supported by the EU under the grant ICT-2009.2.1-270247 *NeuralDynamics* and the Portuguese FCT under the grant PEst-OE/EEI/LA0009/2011.

References

1. Lowe, D.G.: Distinctive image features from scale-invariant keypoints. IJCV 60, 91–110 (2004)
2. Bay, H., Ess, A., Tuytelaars, T., Van Gool, L.: Speeded-up robust features (SURF). CVIU 110, 346–359 (2008)
3. Rublee, E., Rabaud, V., Konolige, K., Bradski, G.: ORB: An efficient alternative to SIFT or SURF. In: ICCV, Barcelona, pp. 2564–2571 (2011)
4. Terzić, K., Rodrigues, J., du Buf, J.: Fast cortical keypoints for real-time object recognition. In: ICIP, Melbourne, pp. 3372–3376 (2013)
5. Fukushima, K.: Neocognitron for handwritten digit recognition. Neurocomputing 51, 161–180 (2003)
6. Do Huu, N., Paquier, W., Chatila, R.: Combining structural descriptions and image-based representations for image, object, and scene recognition. In: IJCAI, pp. 1452–1457 (2005)
7. Serre, T., Wolf, L., Bileschi, S., Riesenhuber, M., Poggio, T.: Object recognition with cortex-like mechanisms. IEEE T-PAMI 29, 411–426 (2007)
8. Schmidhuber, J.: Multi-column deep neural networks for image classification. In: Proceedings of the 2012 IEEE Conference on Computer Vision and Pattern Recognition (CVPR), pp. 3642–3649 (2012)
9. Ullman, S.: High-Level Vision: Object Recognition and Visual Cognition. The MIT Press (1996)
10. Arathorn, D.: Computation in the higher visual cortices: Map-seeking circuit theory and application to machine vision. In: AIPR, pp. 73–78 (2004)
11. Faubel, C., Schöner, G.: A neuro-dynamic architecture for one shot learning of objects that uses both bottom-up recognition and top-down prediction. In: IROS. IEEE Press (2009)
12. Amari, S.: Dynamics of pattern formation in lateral-inhibition type neural fields. Biological Cybernetics 27, 77–87 (1977)
13. Lomp, O., Zibner, S.K.U., Richter, M., Rañó, I., Schöner, G.: A Software Framework for Cognition, Embodiment, Dynamics, and Autonomy in Robotics: Cedar. In: Mladenov, V., Koprinkova-Hristova, P., Palm, G., Villa, A.E.P., Appollini, B., Kasabov, N. (eds.) ICANN 2013. LNCS, vol. 8131, pp. 475–482. Springer, Heidelberg (2013)
14. Faubel, C., Schöner, G.: Learning to recognize objects on the fly: a neurally based dynamic field approach. Neural Networks 21, 562–576 (2008)
15. McCann, S., Lowe, D.: Local naive bayes nearest neighbor for image classification. In: CVPR, Providence, pp. 3650–3656 (2012)

How Visual Attention and Suppression Facilitate Object Recognition?

Frederik Beuth, Amirhossein Jamalian, and Fred H. Hamker

Chemnitz University of Technology, Artificial Intelligence,
Strasse der Nationen 62, 09111 Chemnitz, Germany
beuth@cs.tu-chemnitz.de

Abstract. Visual attention can support object recognition by selecting the relevant target information in the huge amount of sensory data, especially important in scenes composed of multiple objects. Here we demonstrate how attention in a biologically plausible and neuro-computational model of visual perception facilitates object recognition in a robotic real world scenario. We will point out that it is not only important to select the target information, but rather to explicitly suppress the distracting sensory data. We found that suppressing the features of each distractor is not sufficient to achieve robust recognition. Instead, we also have to suppress the location of each distractor. To demonstrate the effect of this spatial suppression, we disable this property and show that the recognition accuracy drops. By this, we show the interplay between attention and suppression in a real world object recognition task.

Keywords: Object Recognition, Neurorobotics, Real World, Computational Neuroscience, Visual Attention, Suppression.

1 Introduction

Object recognition in real world scenarios is a very challenging task. Usually, it involves problems like cluttered scenes analysis, existence of many distracting objects, different scaling, spatial positions, rotations of the objects and etc. The concept of attention can deal with the first two problems, as it can be used to select the relevant target information among the huge amount of sensory data. A vast volume of literature could be found in the field of attention-based object recognition in real-world scenarios or robotics. Many of them are based on bottom-up approaches and assume that the objects of interest are sufficiently salient by themselves. For example Miau et al. [8] combined an attentional front-end with the well-known object recognition system HMAX [12] to recognize either real-world scenes or simple artificial objects like circles and rectangles. Other remarkable real-world applications are the object recognition systems of Walter and Koch [18] and Frintrop and Jensfelt [3]. Since non-salient objects are not detected in bottom-up approaches, other researches used combinations of top-down and bottom-up methods like Hamker [4], Mitri and Frintrop [9], Rasolzadeh and Björkman [10], and Wischnewski et al. [19] (all are real world applications). In this paper, based on terms and concepts of visual attention

S. Wermter et al. (Eds.): ICANN 2014, LNCS 8681, pp. 459–466, 2014.

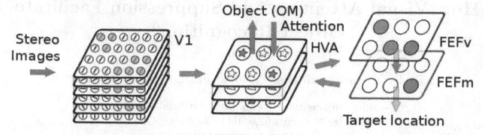

Fig. 1. The object recognition architecture that simulates the brain's visual cortex

mentioned in [2,5,4], we demonstrate the impact of spatial suppression on the robustness of attention-based object recognition. The proposed object recognition system and the learning of invariant object representations are summarized in section 2. Then, section 3 explains the interplay of visual attention with suppression and shows how a new task-specific spatial suppression can be modelled. The accuracy of recognition and localization of the proposed system in presence and absence of the new spatial suppression mechanism is compared in section 4 and finally section 5 concludes the work.

2   Object Recognition System

The object recognition system (Fig. 1) has been developed for a humanoid robot within the European project "Eyeshots" [1]. The goal was to develop a cognitive and biologically plausible object recognition module, so a previously published anatomically and physiologically motivated model of attention was scaled up to allow the processing of real world scenes. Biological background can be found there [5] whereby implementation details reside in [1]. To facilitate reading, its functionality will be explained in the following:

Real world stereo images are fed into the first stage *V1* (primary visual cortex) which encodes simple visual features like the orientation of edges, local contrast differences and retinal disparity [13]. The neurons are organized feature-wise in planes and each plane has the same spatial arrangement as an image (retinotopic organization). Therefore, a particular V1 neuron will be activated if the preferred feature is located at the retinal locations of both eyes underlying its receptive field. The next stage *HVA* (High Visual Area) encodes features representing a single view of an object, similar to cells in the brain areas V4 and IT [7]. HVA is again organized plane-wise and retinotopic. Each view is encoded by the connection weights between V1 and HVA, so each HVA neuron reacts for a specific pattern of V1 neurons (Fig. 2b). These weights were determined in an off-line training phase using unsupervised learning. As this learning should lead to largely depth and scale invariant representation of an object view, our method relies on temporal continuity [16]. The idea is that on the short time scale of stimuli presentations, the visual input is more likely to originate from the same object under the same view, rather than from different objects or views.

Spatial information is encoded in the Frontal Eye Field (*FEF*), simulated by two maps: *FEFv* indicates all possible retinal locations of the searched object (green dots in Fig. 1) whereby *FEFm* indicates only the final location (single green dot in FEFm in Fig. 1). The FEFv is computed by taking the maximum activity over all the features in HVA. The FEFm is calculated from FEFv by applying a Gaussian filter to reinforce adjacent locations and use competition to suppress others. The resulting target signal is projected back to HVA to select the target location in HVA, too. Over time, a single area of activation emerges in FEFm. If this activity reaches a threshold, a saccade will be triggered towards this target location. Physiologically, FEFv and FEFm represent the visual and movement cell types of the FEF [4,14].

Visual attention is used to search for a particular object. The objects are encoded in a separate stage, the object memory (*OM*), like in the prefrontal cortex [5]. The bidirectional binding of HVA neurons to an object neuron was manually designed. In general, attention is defined as selecting a certain feature or object over the whole scene (*feature-based attention*) or attending a certain location (*spatial attention*). At neuronal level, this process enhances the firing rates multiplicatively by the amount of received feedback (called gain control [2,4,5]). For searching an object, the signal OM→HVA is used to implement feature-based attention, i.e. to enhance all HVA neurons that encode a view of the target object, and to implement feature-based suppression, i.e. to suppress distractors (section 3). Additionally, spatial attention is used to localize the target and to segment it from the background. It is implemented by the feedback projection from FEFm to HVA which enhances all HVA neurons at a certain location and suppresses all other locations.

This processing searches an object by its object-identifying features and segment it at the same time. It is executed in parallel via the loop HVA→FEFv→ FEFm→HVA to avoid the chicken-egg problem of segmentation and localization, i.e. that object segmentation depends on localization, which, in turn, requires the segmentation itself.

3   Visual Attention and Suppression

3.1   Interplay of Attention and Suppression

Attending a certain object means to select a set of object-related features or its location. At the neural level, selection usually involves the enhancement of some neurons and the suppression of others. For the latter, it is crucial to accompany visual attention with a suppression mechanism, typically either through an inhibitory network structure [5] or via a generic suppressive drive [11]. We propose to achieve selection via four modulation mechanisms, similar as in other attention models [2,4,5,11]:

- *Feature-based attention* which enhances the neuronal activity of certain features in HVA over the whole scene. This is used to select the target objects via their visual features. In previous work [2,5] and this model, it is implemented via top-down connections to HVA (Fig. 3, signal 1a).
- *Feature-based suppression* to suppress distractors over the whole scene (next section).

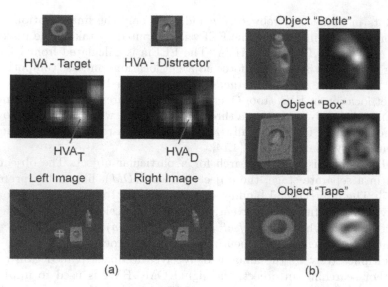

Fig. 2. a) Misclassified example without spatial suppression (C2): the tape (target, green cross) was incorrectly recognized as the box (red cross). b) HVA encodes views of objects. For each object (left), the weights V1→HVA (right) of one exemplary HVA neuron are illustrated.

- *Spatial attention* which enhances the neuronal activity of all features present at a certain location. This mechanism is used to focus attention to a single target location. In previous work [2,5] and this model, it is implemented via the HVA-FEF loop (signals 1a, 2a, 3a and 4 in Fig. 3).
- *Spatial suppression* which decreases the neuronal activity at certain locations. This mechanism is used to move attention away from the location of distractors (next section).

Despite its function in object recognition, this concept of visual attention together with suppression is justified by neurobiological theories such as biased-competition [17]. According to the biased-competition framework, competition takes place when two different stimuli are presented inside a receptive field of a neuron. In the unattended condition, both stimuli suppress each other slightly which can be measured as recorded neurons fire less in comparison with a condition where only a single stimulus is shown. However, if attention is directed to one of the stimuli, the neuron encoding the preferred object fires more strongly whereby a neuron preferring the other stimulus is strongly suppressed.

3.2   New Task-Specific Spatial Suppression

Here we propose an additional mechanism, which actively suppresses the location of distractors. We found that the existing suppression mechanism in models of visual attention [5,11] were not sufficient to suppress distractors under all conditions in a real world scenario. A closer examination of the misclassified cases (Fig. 2a)

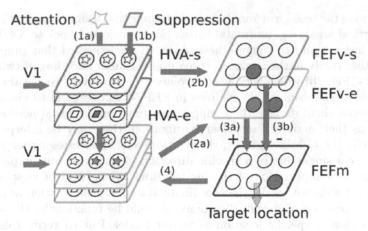

Fig. 3. Object recognition system. It consists of an excitatory component (orange, HVA-e, FEF-e) and a suppressive component (blue, HVA-s, FEF-s).

reveals that a distractor was incorrectly recognized as the target under the condition that some parts of the distractor are visually similar to some parts of the target, i.e., when the feedforward weights (V1→HVA) of two view neurons, belonging to different objects, contain a similar pattern. In our setup, the box and the tape share the inner ring as such a similar pattern (red circle in Fig. 2b). At the distractor location, obviously HVA neurons encoding the distractor view (denoted HVA_D, Fig. 2a) will react strongly, but also the neurons encoding the target view (denoted HVA_T, Fig. 2a) will respond. This HVA_T response is problematic as it will induce an incorrect FEFm activity indicating the wrong target location (red cross in Fig. 2a) instead of the correct one (green cross).

Therefore, a new mechanism was necessary to suppress the HVA_T response at the distractor location. We modeled a task specific *spatial suppression* in which at first, each distractor is seperately to the targets encoded in HVA and FEFv. Secondly, this information is projected inhibitory to FEFm to suppress the distractor location. Thus, HVA and FEFv are split in an excitatory part ($HVA-e$, $FEFv-e$, orange components in Fig. 3) representing targets, as described in section 2, and a suppressive part ($HVA-s$, $FEFv-s$, blue components in Fig. 3) representing distractors. As targets and distractors are typically defined within a specific task, there exists an excitatory feedback projection from higher cortical areas to HVA-s providing task-specificity. This signal serves as *feature-based suppression* (Fig. 3, signal 1b) which enhances the firing rates of the distractors in HVA-s. This information is subsequently projected (Fig. 3, signal 2b) to a separate suppressive FEFv layer ($FEFv-s$, blue) encoding the locations of distractors. Hence, the system can suppress them in FEFm via inhibitory connections (Fig. 3, signal 3b). The FEFm now contains only the location of the target object and projects this back (Fig. 3, signal 4) to HVA-e. In Fig. 3, the spatial suppression effect is visible on the location of the distractor "trapezoid" (single green dot in FEFv-s): it is incorrectly encoded in FEFv-e (lower middle green dot), but is successfully filtered out in FEFm (white circle).

Concerning the biological foundation, we assume that a signal originating from higher cortical areas, e.g. prefrontal cortex [5], is projected back to V4/IT representing instruction like "ignore these objects". We expected that suppression occurs rather rarely in the cortex as it requires a similar encoding of two different objects (Fig. 2b) which is typically avoided [15]. However, we use always the suppression mechanism. As the neurons in FEFv-s will respond to visual stimuli, we denote them despite their suppressive function as visual neurons [14]. However, as their activity can preserve a fixation, they may be interpreted as fixation cells [14]. Physiologically, the fixation cells suppresses either globally a saccade or a single one in a specific direction [6], whereby our implementation results in a suppression of specific locations in the field of view. On the other hand, we do not model the coordinate system transformation in the cortex, so a suppression of specific directions [6] could be functionally the same as the suppression of specific location as in our model. But to verify this, more physiological data is required. Concerning the relation to the standard attention paradigm, e.g. biased-competition, tuning-curve modulation and surrounds suppression [11], the new mechanism shares with them the task-specificity, but serves as a really different function. Hence, it is beyond the scope of this paper to investigate this relation more closely.

In summary, the task-specific spatial suppression facilitates object selection especially if the objects are very similar and challenging to discriminate.

4 Experimental Results

The system was tested under two different conditions (C1 and C2) to evaluate the effect of the new task specific spatial and feature-based suppression:

C1 The system was used with its full capabilities. This is the reference condition.
C2 Spatial suppression was disabled to investigate its influence by cutting the connection from FEFv-s to FEFm (Fig. 3, signal 3b). As this effectively disables both spatial and feature-based suppression, both mechanisms are evaluated together.

The discriminative ability of the object recognition was evaluated on a test set consisting of 27 real world scenes. Each scene was captured as a grayscale, stereo image by the robotic cameras (Fig. 2a shows one example). This test data was separately recorded from the trainings data[1]. Each test scene contains three objects and each object was recognized separately, resulting in 81 object discrimination and localization tests. The system's object discrimination rate drops from 100% in condition C1 to 95% in condition 2 (see Tab. 1 left) illustrating the effect of the proposed spatial suppression. The perfect discriminative accuracy in condition C1 is likely due to the fact that we benchmarked three objects, only. As the focus of the original project [1] was on the overall interplay of the modules, and not on the development of a novel object recognition approach, the number of recognizable objects was kept low. Nevertheless, the system is able to represent other views or objects due to its temporal continuity learning and thus, the approach can successfully be used with a larger number of objects [2].

Table 1. Left) The discrimination abilities (in %) are illustrated by a confusion matrix for each of the conditions C1 and C2. The ordinate denotes the target object and the abcise the detected object. In comparison to C1, the new spatial suppression was disabled in C2. Right) Localization rates in % and maximal mislocalizations in pixel are denoted for each object under the same conditions C1 and C2.

Object	C1: Full			C2: Disabled				Object	C1: Full		C2: Disabled	
	Box	Bot.	Tape	Box	Bot.	Tape			Rate	Mis.	Rate	Mis.
Box	100	0	0	100	0	0		Box	96	7	96	8
Bot.	0	100	0	0	96	4		Bottle	96	20	92	16
Tape	0	0	100	11	0	89		Tape	96	6	96	3

The mislocalization of the target was measured to evaluate the spatial precision of the system. Localization was rated as correct if the saccadic target point was located within an object border. The amount was measured as the Euclidian distance from the saccadic target point to the closest object border. As this evaluation should ignore recognition errors and should only measure spatially inaccurate target coordinates, the distance is always measured to the closest object, even if it was an incorrectly selected one. The localization rate was around 96% in condition C1 and 94% in C2 (see Tab. 1 right). Therefore, disabling the spatial suppression has only little influence on the localization accuracy. That result is not surprising as the spatial precision of the FEF depends mostly on the spatial arrangement of the scene which is identical in both conditions. Therefore, the evaluations shows that this task specific spatial suppression reduces false recognition in the case of similar views belonging to different objects and so improve the overall performance.

5   Conclusion

Visual attention can facilitate object recognition by selecting the relevant target information in the huge amount of sensory data. As such a selection process requires the enhancement of some part of the data and the suppression of the rest, it is always crucial to combine the enhancement effect of attention with an appropriate suppression mechanism.

We proposed a new and biological plausible spatial distractor suppression for existing models of visual attention and showed that this mechanism improves object recognition, especially if parts of the target and the distractor are visually similar. This induces an increase of the recognition rate from 95% to 100%. The increase of only 5% arises from achieving perfect performance on a benchmark setup containing only three objects. The low number of objects was requiered by the orginal project [1], but as the object recognition system is able to learn invariant representations of arbitrary objects, it can be used in setups with a greater number of objects [2]. In such a case, it is more likely that views will contain visually similar parts, so we expect that the new spatial distractor suppression will become more important in such scenes.

Acknowledgments. This work has been supported by the EC Project FP7-ICT "Eyeshots: Heterogeneous 3-D Perception across Visual Fragments" (no. 217077) and in part by the EC Project FP7-NBIS "Spatial Cognition" (no. 600785).

References

1. Antonelli, M., Gibaldi, A., Beuth, F., Duran, A.J., Canessa, A., Chessa, M., Hamker, F., Chinellato, E., Sabatini, S.P.: A hierarchical system for a distributed representation of the peripersonal space of a humanoid robot. Accepted for IEEE Trans. Auton. Mental Develop., 1–15 (2014)
2. Beuth, F., Wiltschut, J., Hamker, F.: Attentive Stereoscopic Object Recognition. In: Villmann, T., Schleif, F.-M. (eds.) Workshop NCNC 2010, p. 41 (2010)
3. Frintrop, S., Nuchter, A.: Saliency-based object recognition in 3D data. In: IROS 2004, pp. 2167–2172 (2004)
4. Hamker, F.H.: The emergence of attention by population-based inference and its role in distributed processing and cognitive control of vision. J. Comput. Vis. Image Underst. 100, 64–106 (2005)
5. Hamker, F.H.: The reentry hypothesis: the putative interaction of the frontal eye field, ventrolateral prefrontal cortex, and areas V4, IT for attention and eye movement. Cerebral Cortex 15(4), 431–447 (2005)
6. Hasegawa, R.P., Peterson, B.W., Goldberg, M.E.: Prefrontal neurons coding suppression of specific saccades. Neuron 43(3), 415–425 (2004)
7. Logothetis, N., Pauls, J., Poggio, T.: Spatial Reference Frames for Object Recognition. Tuning for Rotations in Depth (1995)
8. Miau, F., Papageorgiou, C., Itti, L.: Neuromorphic algorithms for computer vision and attention. In: ISOST 2001, vol. 4479, pp. 12–23 (2001)
9. Mitri, S., Frintrop, S.: Robust object detection at regions of interest with an application in ball recognition. In: ICRA 2005, pp. 126–131 (April 2005)
10. Rasolzadeh, B., Bjorkman, M., Huebner, K., Kragic, D.: An Active Vision System for Detecting, Fixating and Manipulating Objects in the Real World. Int. J. Robot. Res. 29(2-3), 133–154 (2009)
11. Reynolds, J.H., Heeger, D.J.: The normalization model of attention. Neuron 61(2), 168–185 (2009)
12. Riesenhuber, M., Poggio, T.: Hierarchical models of object recognition in cortex. Nat. Neurosci. 2, 1019–1025 (1999)
13. Sabatini, S.P., Gastaldi, G., Solari, F., Pauwels, K., Van Hulle, M.M., Diaz, J., Ros, E., Pugeault, N., Krüger, N.: A compact harmonic code for early vision based on anisotropic frequency channels. J. Comput. Vis. and Image Underst. 114(6), 681–699 (2010)
14. Schall, J.D.: Neuronal activity related to visually guided saccades in the frontal eye fields of rhesus monkeys: comparison with supplementary eye fields. J. Neurophysiol. 66(2), 559–579 (1991)
15. Sigala, N., Gabbiani, F., Logothetis, N.K.: Visual categorization and object representation in monkeys and humans. J. Cognitive Neurosci. 14(2), 187–198 (2002)
16. Teichmann, M., Wiltschut, J., Hamker, F.H.: Learning invariance from natural images inspired by observations in the primary visual cortex. Neural Computation 24(5), 1271–1296 (2012)
17. Treue, S., Trujillo, J.: Feature-based attention influences motion processing gain in macaque visual cortex. Nature 399(6736), 575–579 (1999)
18. Walther, D., Koch, C.: Modeling attention to salient proto-objects. Neural Networks 19(9), 1395–1407 (2006)
19. Wischnewski, M., Belardinelli, A., Schneider, W.X., Steil, J.J.: Where to Look Next? Combining Static and Dynamic Proto-objects in a TVA-based Model of Visual Attention. Cognitive Computation 2(4), 326–343 (2010)

Analysis of Neural Circuit for Visual Attention Using Lognormally Distributed Input

Yoshihiro Nagano[1], Norifumi Watanabe[2], and Atsushi Aoyama[1]

[1] Faculty of Environment and Information Studies,
Keio University, 5322 Endo, Fujisawa-shi, Kanagawa, 252-0882 Japan
[2] School of Computer Science, Tokyo University of Technology
1404-1 Katakura-cho, Hachioji-shi, Tokyo, 192-0982 Japan

Abstract. Visual attention has recently been reported to modulate neural activity of narrow spiking and broad spiking neurons in V4, with increased firing rate and less inter-trial variations. We simulated these physiological phenomena using a neural network model based on spontaneous activity, assuming that the visual attention modulation could be achieved by a change in variance of input firing rate distributed with a lognormal distribution. Consistent with the physiological studies, an increase in firing rate and a decrease in inter-trial variance was simultaneously obtained in the simulation by increasing variance of input firing rate distribution. These results indicate that visual attention forms strong sparse and weak dense input or a 'winner-take-all' state, to improve the signal-to-noise ratio of the target information.

Keywords: Visual Attention, Neural Network Model, Spontaneous Activity, Lognormal Distribution.

1 Introduction

Recent physiological studies have revealed that visual attention modulates neural activity depending on the cell types in V4 [1–4]. Specifically, narrow spiking (NS) neurons and broad spiking (BS) neurons, which are classified according to the spiking waveforms, have been both reported to exhibit increased firing rate and decreased Fano factor for attention [5]. Fano factor is the ratio of spike count variance to mean spike count and decreases when a certain part of cortex receives input [6], especially during attention [5, 7, 8]. NS and BS neurons have been reported to correspond to inhibitory interneurons and excitatory pyramidal neurons, respectively [9–11]. They reported that the increase in the firing rate of NS neurons have been globally observed much larger than that of BS neurons during a visual attention task, and some BS neurons exhibit decreased firing rate by analyzing individual neuronal behaviors. Because both increased and decreased types of BS neurons exist to a similar extent, no clear attention modulation can be totally seen in appearance.

Despite such physiological phenomena, the mechanism of how these phenomena are achieved in the neural circuit have not been formulated. In this study,

S. Wermter et al. (Eds.): ICANN 2014, LNCS 8681, pp. 467–474, 2014.

we simulated the NS and BS neural activity for visual attention using the strong sparse and weak dense (SSWD) model by Teramae et al. [12]. We assumed that the visual attention modulation could be achieved by the change in variance of input firing rate distributed with a lognormal distribution. Under this assumption, the simulated neural activity for the input was evaluated by the firing rate and Fano factor. Moreover, we evaluated neural activity by attention index that were used in Mitchell et al. [5]. The attention index enables us to analyze the effect of visual attention modulation to individual neurons. Using these indices, we tested the relationship between lognormally distributed input and its output during visual attention at the neural circuit level.

2   Neural Activity Simulation

2.1   Original Physiological Experiment

We simulated neural activity during a visual attention task, according to a physiological study achieved by Mitchell et al. [5]. This task was comprised of five periods: CUE, SHUFFLE, PAUSE, SHUFFLE, and SACCADE. Four identical Gabor patterns were presented to the macaque monkeys. In CUE, two patterns were flashed so that the monkeys could mentally track the patterns. The locations of these targets and the other two distracters were randomly shuffled in the first SHUFFLE. Then, all the stimuli stopped for 1 s (PAUSE), with one of the stimuli placed within the visual receptive field (RF). The locations were shuffled again in the second SHUFFLE. Finally, behavioral performance was evaluated in SACCADE by checking if they moved their eyes toward appropriate stimuli.

The neural activities in PAUSE were mainly analyzed. They regarded the condition where the target stimulus was placed within the RF as the attended condition, and the other as the unattended condition. Fig.1 A and C show the averaged activities of the 109 visually responsive BS neurons for the attended (dark blue) and unattended (light blue) stimuli, and Fig.1 B and D show those of the 43 NS neurons for the attended (dark red) and unattended (light red) stimuli. BS and NS neurons showed increased firing rate when a stimulus was placed within the RF. In addition, the firing rates became much larger when the stimulus within the RF was a target as compared with a distracter. Besides, the Fano factor was fluctuated in inverse proportion to the firing rate.

Fig.1 E and F show the individual neural activity by attention index (AI). AI is expressed as $(A - U)/(A + U)$, where A is an attended value and U is an unattended value calculated by averaging either firing rate or Fano factor over 1-s PAUSE. The individual Fano factors for NS and BS neurons were low in the attended condition. Although most of NS and BS neurons showed high firing rates, some BS neurons were significantly low in the attended condition. They thus claimed that NS neurons are much more important for visual attention.

2.2   Neural Network Model

Irregular spontaneous neuronal firing of cerebral cortex (< 10 Hz, typically $1-2$ Hz) reflects various cognitive functions [13]. Because spontaneous firing in V4

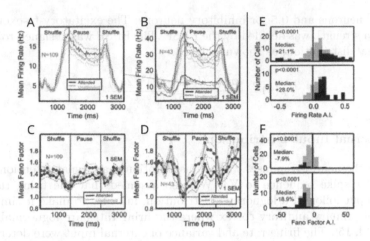

Fig. 1. Comparison of attention-dependent modulation of rate and Fano factor in BS and NS neurons, adapted from Mitchell et al. [5]. A and B: average firing rate of BS (blue) and NS (red) neurons for attended (dark color) and unattended (light color) conditions. C and D: average Fano factor for attended and unattended conditions. E: distribution of attention index for a firing rate. F: attention index for a Fano factor. Significant modulation are indicated in black.

was reported to fluctuate with visual attention [1] and evaluation of neuronal variability is crucial for this study, we used the SSWD recurrent network model proposed by Teramae et al. [12]. The model is obtained by modifying the leaky integrate and fire neuron model using synapse transmission delay d_j. Only the first trigger input exhibits asynchronous spontaneous spiking activity. Dynamics of the membrane potential v and synapse conductance g can be expressed as Eqs. 1 and 2.

$$\frac{dv}{dt} = -\frac{1}{\tau_{mX}}(v - V_L) - g_E(v - V_E) - g_I(v - V_I) \tag{1}$$

$$\frac{dg_X}{dt} = -\frac{g_X}{\tau_S} + \sum_j G_{X,j} \sum_{s_j} \delta(t - s_j - d_j), \qquad (X = E, I) \tag{2}$$

V_L, V_E, and V_I in Eq. 1 are reversal potentials of leak, excitatory, and inhibitory postsynaptic currents, respectively. τ_{mX} is a membrane time constant. s_j in Eq. 2 is a spike timing of synaptic input from the j-th neuron. The value of $\delta(t - s_j - d_j)$ is 1 only when the sum of the j-th neuron's spike timing and its delay equals to the time t. The spike modulates conductance of the post synaptic neuron in proportion to the connection strength G_{XX}. All the parameters in Eqs. 1 and 2 were set to be the same values in [12] except G_{II}. Originally, $G_{II} = 0.0025$, but we set $G_{II} = 0.0027$ to adjust the firing rates of excitatory and inhibitory neurons.

We implemented a random network in which 10000 excitatory and 2000 inhibitory neurons were connected directly, with conjunctive probabilities of 0.1 for excitatory neurons and 0.5 for inhibitory neurons. The excitatory-to-excitatory connection strength was decided by the EPSP. The EPSP was designed to follow a lognormal distribution, as shown in Eq. 3.

$$p(x) = \frac{exp(-(logx - \mu)^2/2\sigma^2)}{\sqrt{2\pi}\sigma x} \tag{3}$$

2.3 External Input Distribution

We tested the neural responses with an assumption that visual attention modulates input spike sequence to V4. We also assumed that the firing rates of external input followed a lognormal distribution, in order to make it similar to the case of primary auditory cortex where the firing rates are lognormally distributed [14, 15]. The firing rate and variance of external input were determined depending on the attended condition or unattended condition, and then input spike sequences were generated according to the Poisson process in each trial. We call the input explained above as external input distribution.

2.4 Simulation

In order to trigger spontaneous neural activity, we set noisy input at the first 0.1 s of simulation. A confirmation period followed for 2.4 s to confirm spontaneous activity. In the first SHUFFLE from 2.5 to 3.0 s, weak external input distribution was generated, and then, the ordinary external input distribution was set from 3.0 to 4.0 s as PAUSE. Again, external input distribution became weak from 4.0 to 4.5 s in the second SHUFFLE. Here, we set firing rate and variance of the external input distribution during PAUSE to be (10.0 Hz, 10.0) in the unattended condition and (10.0 Hz, 140.0) in the attended condition. In SHUFFLE, the firing rate and Fano factor of the input were set to be (1.0 Hz, 1.0). PAUSE and two SHUFFLE periods were used for analysis.

3 Results

3.1 Firing Rate and Fano Factor

Fig.2 shows the simulated neural responses under the assumption that the variance of external input distribution increases for the attended condition relative to the unattended one. Because most of the BS and NS neurons anatomically correspond to excitatory pyramidal neurons and inhibitory interneurons, respectively [9–11], excitatory and inhibitory neurons were used in the simulation, and eventually both showed increased firing rates by the input. The firing rates became much larger in the attended condition than the unattended condition (Fig.2 A and B), and the Fano factor became lower in the attended condition than the unattended condition (Fig.2 C and D).

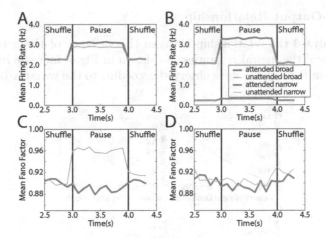

Fig. 2. Simulated neural responses for the external input distribution. A and B: averaged firing rates of BS (blue) and NS (red) neurons for the attended (dark red, dark blue) and unattended (light red, light blue) conditions. C and D: averaged Fano factors of BS and NS neurons for the attended and unattended conditions.

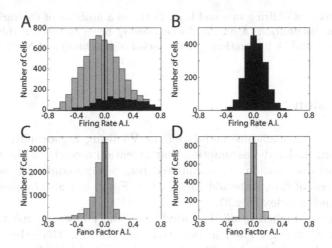

Fig. 3. Distribution of attention index for BS (blue) and NS (red) neurons. A and B: attention index for firing rate. C and D: attention index for Fano factor. Significantly modulated neurons are indicated in black.

3.2 Attention Index

We analyzed the firing rate and the Fano factor of individual neurons during PAUSE using AI. Firing rate AI of the excitatory neurons had larger variance than those of the inhibitory neurons, and Fano factor AI was lower in the attended condition than the unattended condition (Fig.3). Similar to Fig.1 E and F, significantly modulated neurons were observed for the firing rate AI.

3.3 Input-Output Relationship

We then analyzed the relationship between the variance of the external input distribution and the neural responses. As shown in Fig.4, increase in firing rate and decrease in Fano factor were observed according to the variance of the input.

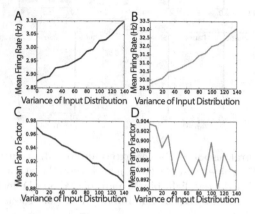

Fig. 4. Fluctuations of firing rate and Fano factor as a function of the variance of the external input distribution. A and B: fluctuations of firing rate of BS (blue) and NS (red) neurons. C and D: fluctuations of Fano factor of BS (blue) and NS (red) neurons.

4   Discussion

We simulated the attention modulation in V4 using lognormally distributed external input, under the assumption that attention modulates the variance of external input distribution. The simulated results were confirmed not only by the global trend of firing rate and Fano factor (Fig.2) but also by the individual trend of attention index (Fig.3).

According to Mitchell et al. [5], individual Fano factors for most of the NS and BS neurons became lower in the attended condition than the unattended condition, as shown in Fig.1 F. Therefore, the averaged Fano factor showed the same trend (Fig.1 C and D). Consistent with Mitchell et al., the simulation results showed that the Fano factor and the Fano factor AI became lower in the attended condition than the unattended condition (Fig.2 C and D, Fig.3 C and D, respectively). Moreover, in Mitchell et al., while individual firing rates of NS and some BS neurons became larger in the attended condition, those of particular BS neurons became significantly lower even in the attended condition (Fig.1 E). In this study, the firing rates became larger in the attended condition than the unattended condition (Fig.2 A and B), and the firing rate AI of the excitatory neurons had larger variance than those of the inhibitory neurons (Fig.3 A and B), which are also consistent with Mitchell et al. Significantly modulated neurons in firing rate AI confirm that the attention modulation variability in excitatory neurons was not caused by noise. Consequently, we succeeded to reproduce the physiological phenomena occurred in V4 for visual attention in the neural circuit.

We observed increase in firing rate and decrease in Fano factor according to the variance of the input. This relationship indicates that the variance change in the external input distribution can be one reasonable explanation for visual attention modulation in V4. If the variance of lognormal distribution increases, most of that input's firing rates become low, and a few input's firing rates become high. From the result about the increase in the firing rates of some neurons and the decrease in Fano factor in the attended condition, we have one possibility that a computation of these neurons in the pre-network might improve signal-to-noise(S/N) ratio. In recent attention study, it is focused on not only firing rate or Fano factor, but also noise correlation that is the pair-wise correlation between two neuron's spike count. It is revealed that noise correlation is significantly modulated by attention [16, 17], and the performance of orientation change detection task improved when noise correlation was low [17]. Moreover, about 80 percent of the stimulus discriminability could be explained by the noise correlation in the simulation study based on physiological data [17]. Noise correlation can be treated as the reciprocal of the independence of neuronal activity, because it is a pair-wise correlation. For these reasons, it is plausible that the computation of S/N ratio to the stimulus is modulated by attention. However, specific hardware which can computes the S/N ratio to arbitrary feature or objects has not been cleared yet. Further studies are needed to the topic.

5   Conclusion

We simulated the attention modulation in V4 using lognormally distributed external input delivered to the spontaneously spiking neural model. Under the assumption that the visual attention is achieved by an increase in variance of external input distribution, both increase in firing rate and decrease in Fano factor were observed, consistent with a physiological report. These results suggest that we succeeded to computationally reproduce the attention modulation in V4 and that the modulation is caused by improved signal-to-noise ratio for a target stimulus. In the future, we are planning to analyze the relationship between the neural network structure and the signal-to-noise ratio of activity, in order to clarify how the signal-to-noise ratio is related to visual attention.

References

1. Luck, S.J., Chelazzi, L., Hillyard, S.A., Desimone, R.: Neural mechanisms of spatial selective attention in areas V1, V2, and V4 of macaque visual cortex. Journal of Neurophysiology 77(1), 24–42 (1997)
2. Fries, P., Reynolds, J.H., Rorie, A.E., Desimone, R.: Modulation of Oscillatory Neuronal Synchronization by Selective Visual Attention. Science 291(5508), 1560–1563 (2001)

3. Weerd, P.D., Peralta, M.R., Desimone, R., Ungerleider, L.G.: Loss of attentional stimulus selection after extrastriate cortical lesions in macaques. Nature Neuroscience 3(4), 409 (2000)
4. Reynolds, J.H., Heeger, D.J.: The normalization model of attention. Neuron 61(2), 168–185 (2009)
5. Mitchell, J.F., Sundberg, K.A., Reynolds, J.H.: Differential attention-dependent response modulation across cell classes in macaque visual area V4. Neuron 55(1), 131–141 (2007)
6. Churchland, M.M., Yu, B.M., Cunningham, J.P., Sugrue, L.P., Cohen, M.R., Corrado, G.S., Newsome, W.T., Clark, A.M., Hosseini, P., Scott, B.B., Bradley, D.C., Smith, M.A., Kohn, A., Movshon, J.A., Armstrong, K.M., Moore, T., Chang, S.W., Snyder, L.H., Lisberger, S.G., Priebe, N.J., Finn, I.M., Ferster, D., Ryu, S.I., Santhanam, G., Sahani, M., Shenoy, K.V.: Stimulus onset quenches neural variability: a widespread cortical phenomenon. Nature Neuroscience 13(3), 369–378 (2010)
7. Tolhurst, D.J., Movshon, J.A., Dean, F.: The statistical reliability of signals in single neurons in cat and monkey visual cortex. Vision Research 23(8), 775–785 (1982)
8. McAdams, C.J., Maunsell, J.H.: Effects of attention on the reliability of individual neurons in monkey visual cortex. Neuron 23(4), 765–773 (1999)
9. Brumberg, J.C., Nowak, L.G., McCormick, D.A.: Ionic mechanisms underlying repetitive high-frequency burst firing in supragranular cortical neurons. The Journal of Neuroscience: the Official Journal of the Society for Neuroscience 20(13), 4829–4843 (2000)
10. Nowak, L.G., Azouz, R., Sanchez-Vives, M.V., Gray, C.M., McCormick, D.A.: Electrophysiological classes of cat primary visual cortical neurons in vivo as revealed by quantitative analyses. Journal of Neurophysiology 89(3), 1541–1566 (2003)
11. Vigneswaran, G., Kraskov, A., Lemon, R.N.: Large identified pyramidal cells in macaque motor and premotor cortex exhibit "thin spikes": implications for cell type classification. The Journal of Neuroscience: the Official Journal of the Society for Neuroscience 31(40), 14235–14242 (2011)
12. Teramae, J., Tsubo, Y., Fukai, T.: Optimal spike-based communication in excitable networks with strong-sparse and weak-dense links. Scientific Reports 2, 485 (2012)
13. Berkes, P., Orbn, G., Lengyel, M., Fiser, J.: Spontaneous cortical activity reveals hallmarks of an optimal internal model of the environment. Science 331(1), 83–87 (2011)
14. Hromádka, T., DeWeese, M., Zador, A.: Sparse representation of sounds in the unanesthetized auditory cortex. PLoS Biology 6(1), e16 (2008)
15. Koulakov, A.A., Hromádka, T., Zador, A.M.: Correlated connectivity and the distribution of firing rates in the neocortex. The Journal of Neuroscience: the Official Journal of the Society for Neuroscience 29(12), 3685–3694 (2009)
16. Mitchell, J.F., Sundberg, K.A., Reynolds, J.H.: Spatial attention decorrelates intrinsic activity fluctuations in macaque area V4. Neuron 63(6), 879–888 (2009)
17. Cohen, M.R., Maunsell, J.H.R.: Attention improves performance primarily by reducing interneuronal correlations. Nature Neuroscience 12(12), 1594–1600 (2009)

Dynamic Ensemble Selection and Instantaneous Pruning for Regression Used in Signal Calibration

Kaushala Dias and Terry Windeatt

Centre for Vision, Speech and Signal Processing (CVSSP), University of Surrey,
Guildford, Surrey, GU2 7XH, UK
{k.dias,t.windeatt}@surrey.ac.uk

Abstract. A dynamic method of selecting a pruned ensemble of predictors for regression problems is described. The proposed method enhances the prediction accuracy and generalization ability of pruning methods that change the order in which ensemble members are combined. Ordering heuristics attempt to combine accurate yet complementary regressors. The proposed method enhances the performance by modifying the order of aggregation through distributing the regressor selection over the entire dataset. This paper compares four static ensemble pruning approaches with the proposed dynamic method. The experimental comparison is made using MLP regressors on benchmark datasets and on an industrial application of radio frequency source calibration.

Keywords: Ensemble Pruning, Dynamic Ensemble Selection, Ensemble Methods, Calibration.

1 Introduction

In the context of ensemble methods, it is recognized that the combined outputs of several regressors generally give improved accuracy compared to a single predictor [1]. It has also been shown that ensemble members that are complementary can be selected to further improve the performance [1]. The selection, also called pruning, has the potential advantage of both reduced ensemble size as well as improved accuracy. However the selection of classifiers, rather than regressors, has previously received more attention and given rise to many different approaches to pruning [3]. A categorization of different pruning methods for classifiers, including ranking-based, clustering-based and optimization based can be found in [1]. Some of these methods have been adapted to the regression problem [4]. The purpose of the research described in this paper is to propose a dynamic method [5], [9] that can improve the performance of ranking-based methods. By dynamic, we mean that the subset of predictors is chosen differently depending on the test sample and its relationship to the training set.

In general, an ensemble of regressors is constructed in two phases. First the component members of the ensemble are trained and secondly the predictions are combined. In the training of ensembles two approaches are widely used, namely Bagging

S. Wermter et al. (Eds.): ICANN 2014, LNCS 8681, pp. 475–482, 2014.

and Boosting. Both use re-sampling, but Bagging is a simpler method and introduces randomness into the training process by sampling with replacement. Bagging is chosen here due to its robustness, its ability to perform well on noisy data and its generalization ability [4].

In this paper a novel method of dynamic selection of pruned ensembles for regression is presented. Initially ordering using Reduced Error method without back fitting [3] is performed on the pool of regressors, generated by Bagging. This ordering is thus based on randomized bootstraps over the full training set and performed on every instance of the training set. This information is then archived for later retrieval for test instances where the ensemble order relating to the closest training instance is retrieved. The output for the test sample is generated by combining the output of the selected ensemble in the order specified.

2   Related Research

The main objective of using ensemble methods in regression problems is to harness the complementarity of individual ensemble member predictions [1]. In [2] ordered aggregation pruning using Walsh coefficients has been suggested. In Negative Correlation Learning, diversity of the predictors is introduced by simultaneously training a collection of predictors using a cost function that includes a correlation penalty term [4]; thereby collectively enhancing the performance of the entire ensemble. By weighting the outputs of the ensemble members before aggregating, an optimal set of weights is obtained in [10] by minimizing a function that estimates the generalization error of the ensemble: this optimization being achieved using genetic algorithms. With this approach, predictors with weights below a certain level are removed from the ensemble. In [4] genetic algorithms have been utilized to extract sub-ensemble from larger ensembles. In Stacked Generalization a meta-learner is trained with the outputs of each predictor to produce the final output [1]. Empirical evidence shows that this approach tends to over-fit, but with regularization techniques for pruning ensembles over-fitting is eliminated. Ensemble pruning by Semi-definite Programming has been used to find a sub-optimal ensemble in [4]. A dynamic ensemble selection approach in which many ensembles that perform well on an optimization set or a validation set are searched from a pool of over-produced ensembles and from this the best ensemble is selected using a selection function for computing the final output for the test sample [5]. Similarly a dynamic multistage organizational method based on contextual information of the training data is used to select the best ensemble for classification in [6]. A dynamically weighted technique that determines the ensemble member weights based on the prediction accuracy of the training data set is described in [11]. Here a Generalized Regression Neural Network is used for predicting the weights dynamically for the test instance. Recursive Feature Elimination has been used in [8] as method of pruning ensembles. Here the weights of a trained combiner are evaluated to determine the least performing predictor that is removed from the ensemble.

2.1   Calibration Using Neural Networks

Calibration is essential for a machine's operation. With the help of learning algorithms such as Neural Networks calibration can be automated by means of learning sensor linearization characteristics in measuring machines [13]. Neural Networks in calibration have been used to establish the relationship between inputs and outputs [13], between geometric parameters [12], between functional models [14, 15]. In [15] the neural network has learnt the functional difference between an actual test bed and its abstract model that has enabled fast simulation of a problem while maintaining accuracy. Prediction accuracy of Neural Network models thus require to be very high and reliable and this is demonstrated in the application described in this paper.

Like most radar threat detectors the input sensors as well as the threat detection algorithms of the radar system requires testing. Due to the complex nature of the radio frequency (RF) signal modulation methods and the changes these RF signals undergo during reflection off stationary as well as moving surfaces a simulator that can produce these variations to the RF signal is employed in the testing process. With complex circuitry these signals are generated as well as measured in the simulator. Paths where RF energy travels within the simulator requires calibration to a very high degree of accuracy in order to simulate the physical parameters of the changing RF signal.

The novel method of pruning ensembles described this paper has been used in the calibration process of the signal levels in the RF paths. In this application Reduced Error pruning without back fitting method (RE) [8], modified for regression, is used to establish the order of regressors in the ensemble that produces a minimum in the ensemble training error. In RE, starting with the regressor that produces the lowest training error, the remaining regressors are subsequently incorporated one at a time into the ensemble to achieve a minimum ensemble error.

3   Method

In contrast to static ensemble selection, Dynamic Ensemble Selection with Instantaneous Pruning (DESIP) provides an ensemble tailored to the specific test instance based on the information of the training set. The proposed method described here is for a regression problem where the regressors are ordered for every individual training instance based on the method of RE. Therefore each ensemble selection for every training instance contains the same regressors as constituent members but aggregated in a different order. However, potentially this dynamic method can be implemented with any pruning technique.

The implementation of DESIP consists of two stages. First the base regressors M are trained on bootstrap samples of the training dataset and the regressor order is found for every instance in the training set. As shown in the pseudo-code in figure 1, this is achieved by building a series of nested ensembles, per training instance, in which the ensemble of size u contains the ensemble of size u-1. Taking a single instance of the training set, the method starts with an empty ensemble S, in step 2, and builds the ensemble order, in steps 6 to 15, by evaluating the training error of each regressor in M. The regressor that increases the ensemble training error least is iteratively added to S. This is achieved by minimizing z in step 9. Therefore each regressor in M takes a unique position in S as S grows. This order is archived in a two dimensional matrix A with regressor order in rows and training instance in columns.

Training data $D = (x_n, y_n)$, where $n = (1, 2,.., N)$ and f_m is a regressor, where $m = (1, 2,.., M)$. The Archive Matrix $A = (a_n)$ where a_n is a column vector with max index of m. S is also a vector with max index of m.

1. **For** $n = 1....N$
2. $S \leftarrow$ empty vector
3.   **For** $m = 1...M$
4.   Evaluate $C_m = f_m(x_n) - y_n$
5.   **End for**
6.   **For** $u = 1...M$
7.   min $\leftarrow +\infty$
8.   **For** k in $(1,..., M)\backslash\{S_1, S_2,..., S_u\}$
9.   Evaluate $z = u^{-1}\left(\sum_{i=1}^{u-1} C_{S_i} + C_k\right)$
10.   **If** $z <$ min
11. $S_u \quad \leftarrow k$
12.   min $\leftarrow z$
13.   **End if**
14.   **End for**
15.   **End for**
16. $a_n \leftarrow S$
17. **End for**

Fig. 1. Pseudo-code implementing the archive matrix with ordered ensemble per training data

In the second stage, the regressor order that is associated with the training instance closest to the test instance is retrieved from matrix A. Here the closeness is determined by calculating the L1 Norm of the distance measure between the test instance and the training set. This is performed in steps 1 to 6 in figure 2. All input features of the training set are considered to identify the closest training instance, using the K-Nearest Neighbors method [7], where K = 1. The resulting vector g_n, where n is the index of the training instance, is searched for the minimum value and is identified as the closest training instance to be retrieved from A. The selected ensemble has the order of regressors determined by the training instance.

Test and train instance $x_{f,test}$, $x_{f,n,train}$ where $f = (1, 2,.., F)$ features.
From figure 1 Archive Matrix $A = (a_n)$ where a_n is the column vector containing the order of regressors, $n = 1, 2,.., N$.
e_f is a vector with max index of F and g_n is a vector with max index of N.
1.   **For** n = 1....N
2.   **For** f = 1....F
3.   Evaluate $e_f = |x_{f,n,train} - x_{f,test}|$
4.   **End for**
5.
6.   **End for**
7.   Search for the minimum values in g_n and note n
8. a_n is the ensemble selection for the test instance.

Fig. 2. Pseudo-code implementing the identification of the nearest training instance to the test instance

For the comparison of DESIP with static methods, four static pruning methods were implemented with DESIP. They are Ordered Aggregation (OA) as described in [4] for regression, Recursive Feature Elimination (RFE) in [8], ensemble optimization using Genetic Algorithm (GA) [4] and Reduced Error Pruning without back fitting (RE)[3].

4   Experimental Results

In this section the results of the four ensemble selection methods applied to benchmark datasets are presented. An MLP architecture with 5 nodes in the hidden layer has been selected in this experiment to train the ensemble of base regressors. The training/test data split is 70/30 percent, and bootstrap samples for 32 base regressors are trained. The Mean Squared Error (MSE) is used as the performance indicator for both training set and test set, and an average is obtained over 100 iterations.

Figure 3 shows train and test MSE versus sub-ensemble size. It can be observed from figure 3 that the MSE of the dynamic method for the training set is significantly lower than the static methods, indicating that the individual ensembles selected based on the training set have been optimized. In the graphs of the MSE of the test set in figure 3, the apparent optimal solution of the problem has been achieved by the proposed dynamic method. It is also observed that the minimum occurs at a lower ensemble size with the dynamic selection method than the static methods.

Table 1 shows the MSE performance of the four static methods with and without DESIP. In table 1, grayed results indicate the minimum MSE over the eight methods. It is observed that the majority of the lowest MSE values have been achieved by DESIP.

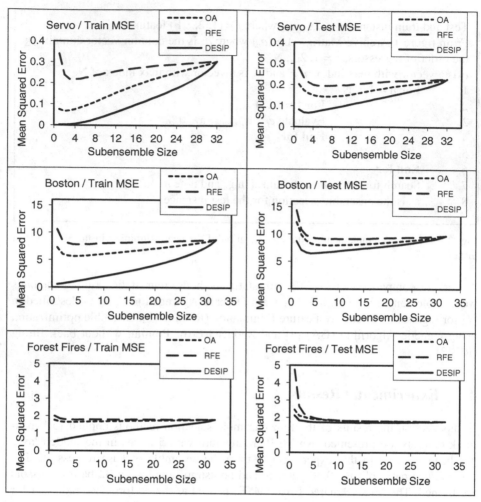

Fig. 3. Comparison of the MSE plots of the training set and the test set for OA, RFE and DESIP using RE

Table 1. Averaged MSE of Ensemble Pruning Methods: Static / DESIP with static adopted

Dataset	Multiplier	OA	RFE	GA	RE
Servo	10^{-1}	1.43 / 0.66	1.94 / 1.46	2.37 / 1.35	1.42 / 0.66
Boston Housing	10^{0}	7.94 / 6.47	9.12 / 8.70	9.91 / 8.06	7.97 / 6.47
Forest Fires	10^{0}	1.78 / 1.72	1.78 / 1.76	1.81 / 1.79	1.78 / 1.72
Wisconsin	10^{1}	2.54 / 2.27	2.55 / 2.29	2.58 / 2.18	2.53 / 2.27
Concrete Slump	10^{1}	3.02 / 3.09	3.54 / 3.16	3.66 / 3.14	2.89 / 3.09
Auto93	10^{1}	5.50 / 5.85	6.37 / 6.35	6.52 / 6.51	5.58 / 5.85
Auto Price	10^{6}	3.81 / 3.88	5.04 / 5.16	6.09 / 5.85	3.88 / 3.88
Body Fat	10^{-1}	6.91 / 6.12	6.80 / 6.17	8.44 / 5.96	5.99 / 6.12
Bolts	10^{1}	7.70 / 7.44	10.50 / 7.42	10.95 / 7.33	7.81 / 7.44
Pollution	10^{3}	2.28 / 2.15	2.47 / 2.30	2.54 / 2.35	2.26 / 2.15
Sensory	10^{-1}	8.70 / 5.48	6.10 / 5.85	6.29 / 6.11	5.73 / 5.48

5   Signal Calibration Application

In this application the output of a Radio Frequency Source device used in a military environment is calibrated to give out a signal with a variable amplitude level, where the amplitude level is specified by the user of the device. A learning based system is trained with measurements taken from the un-calibrated device, which is then used to predict values for the intermediate levels. These predicted values are then used as correction values in the calibration process. Here the accuracy of the predictions is important in order to meet tight specification requirements, since a large error in the prediction would produce undesirable behavior by the device, rendering the device unsuitable for its intended use. Therefore in the real world this learning based application would be required to operate with its own tight specification requirements.

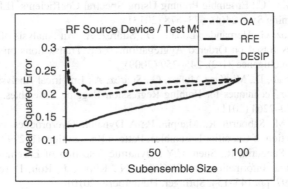

Fig. 4. Calibration application MSE performance of OA, FRE and DESIP using RE

For this application a neural network with 10 hidden layer nodes was used. The data set consisted of 660 training instances and 630 test instances. Here the static ensemble methods OA, RFE and DESIP with RE adopted have been applied to obtain the performance differences and the results follow a similar trend to the performance on the benchmark data. This is shown in figure 4 and the minimum MSE is shown in table 2.

Table 2. Average MSE with standard deviation for 10 iterations

OA	RFE	DESIP/RE
0.2±0.07	0.21±0.05	0.13±0.03

6   Discussion

Dynamic ensemble pruning utilizes a distributed approach to ensemble selection and is an active area of research for both classification and regression problems. In this paper, a novel method of dynamic pruning of regression ensembles is proposed. Experimental results as well the calibration application show that test error has been reduced by modifying the pruning based on the closest training instance. On a few datasets the proposed method has not improved performance, and will be investigated further along with different distance measures, varying K for K-NN and relevant feature selection. Bias/Variance and time complexity analysis should also help to understand the performance relative to other static and dynamic pruning methods with similar complexity.

References

1. Tsoumakas, G., Partalas, I., Vlahavas, I.: An Ensemble Pruning Primer. In: Okun, O., Valentini, G. (eds.) Applications of Supervised and Unsupervised Ensemble Methods. SCI, vol. 245, pp. 1–13. Springer, Heidelberg (2009)
2. Windeatt, T., Zor, C.: Ensemble Pruning Using Spectral Coefficients. IEEE Trans. Neural Network. Learning Syst. 24(4), 673–678 (2013)
3. Martínez-Muñoz, G., Hernández-Lobato, D., Suárez, A.: An Analysis of Ensemble Pruning Techniques Based on Ordered Aggregation. IEEE Transactions on Pattern Analysis and Machine Intelligence 31(2), 245–259 (2009)
4. Hernández-Lobato, D., Martínez-Muñoz, G., Suárez, A.: Empirical Analysis and Evaluation of Approximate Techniques for Pruning Regression Bagging Ensembles. Neurocomputing 74(12-13), 2250–2264 (2011)
5. Dos Santos, E.M., Sabourin, R., Maupin, P.: A Dynamic Overproduce-and-choose Strategy for the selection of Classifier Ensembles. Pattern Recognition 41, 2993–3009 (2008)
6. Cavalin, P.R., Sabourin, R., Suen, C.Y.: Dynamic Selection of Ensembles of Classifiers Using Contextual Information. In: El Gayar, N., Kittler, J., Roli, F. (eds.) MCS 2010. LNCS, vol. 5997, pp. 145–154. Springer, Heidelberg (2010)
7. Dubey, H., Pudi, V.: CLUEKR: Clustering Based Efficient K-NN Regression. In: Pei, J., Tseng, V.S., Cao, L., Motoda, H., Xu, G. (eds.) PAKDD 2013, Part I. LNCS, vol. 7818, pp. 450–458. Springer, Heidelberg (2013)
8. Windeatt, T., Dias, K.: Feature Ranking Ensembles for Facial Action Unit Classification. In: Prevost, L., Marinai, S., Schwenker, F. (eds.) ANNPR 2008. LNCS (LNAI), vol. 5064, pp. 267–279. Springer, Heidelberg (2008)
9. Cavalin, P.R., Sabourin, R., Suen, C.Y.: Dynamic Selection Approaches for Multiple Classifier Systems. In: Formal Aspects of Cognitive Processes. LNCS, vol. 22 (3-4), pp. 673–688. Springer (2013)
10. Zhau, Z.-H., Wu, J., Tang, W.: Ensembling Neural Networks: many could be better than all. Artificial Intelligence 137, 239–263 (2002)
11. Shen, Z.-Q., Kong, F.-S.: Dynamically Weighted Ensemble Neural Networks for Regression Problems. Machine Learning and Cybernetics, 3492–3496 (2004)
12. Mendonca, M., Da Silva, I.N., Castanho, J.E.C.: Camera Calibration Using Neural Networks. Journal of WSCG 10(1-3), POS61–POS68 (2002)
13. Khan, S.A., Shahani, D.T., Agarwala, A.K.: Sensor calibration and compensation using artificial neural network. ISA Transactions 43(3) (2003)
14. Wang, D.-S., Liu, X.-G., Xu, X.-H.: Calibration of Arc-Welding Robot by Neural Network. Fourth International Conference on Machine Learning and Cybernetics, Guangzhou (2005)
15. Liu, E., Cuthbert, L., Schormans, J., Stoneley, G.: Neural Network in Fast Simulation Modelling. IEEE-INNS-ENNS International Joint Conference on Neural Networks 6, 109–113 (2000)

Global and Local Rejection Option in Multi–classification Task

Marcin Luckner

Warsaw University of Technology,
Faculty of Mathematics and Information Science,
Koszykowa 75, 00–662 Warszawa, Poland
mluckner@mini.pw.edu.pl
http://www.mini.pw.edu.pl/~lucknerm/en/

Abstract. This work presents two rejection options. The global rejection option separates the foreign observations – not defined in the classification task – from the normal observations. The local rejection option works after the classification process and separates observations individually for each class. We present implementation of both methods for binary classifiers grouped in a graph structure (tree or directed acyclic graph). Next, we prove that the quality of rejection is identical for both options and depends only on the quality of binary classifiers. The methods are compared on the handwritten digits recognition task. The local rejection option works better for the most part.

Keywords: Rejection Option, Support Vector Machines, Graph Ensemble, Pattern Recognition.

1 Introduction

Pattern recognition tasks very often omit the aspect of rejection of foreign observations. The foreign observations do not belong to the normal classes, where the normal classes are defined by the classification task.

The examples of foreign elements in the recognition of printed texts are: blots, fragments of damaged symbols, or symbols omitted in the definition of the classification task.

The multi–classification task is described by the classification function

$$\phi_\alpha(x, \bigcup_{i=1}^{n} L_i) = i, \tag{1}$$

where i is decision that classifies the observation x to one of the n normal classes C_i described by the learning sets L_i using a classification method defined by the coefficient α.

Theoretically, the rejection option can be implemented by extending the classification function by an additional class. However, we have an intuition that the class of foreign observations may be significantly different from the normal classes.

S. Wermter et al. (Eds.): ICANN 2014, LNCS 8681, pp. 483–490, 2014.

We proposed two rejection options to eliminate foreign observations. The theoretical description is presented using a graph G as an ensemble of binary classifiers. The vertices of the graph $V(G)$ are connected with the recognised classes (leaves) or classifiers (the rest of vertices). The edges $E(G)$ define the decision path. The good examples of such structures are decision trees and directed acyclic graphs.

The first approach – the global rejection option – assumes that the foreign observations are significantly different from the rest of classes and eliminates them in the first classification step. The second approach – the local rejection option – focuses on the elimination of the foreign observations from the classified observations and is implemented in the last classification step.

The idea of the rejection option was presented in [2] as the tradeoff between classes. The multi–class solution was proposed in [4]. However, that work is limited to misclassifications among the normal classes. Also in newer theoretical works on the rejection option the issue is defined in a domain of the normal classes and foreign observations stay out of the focus of research (for example [7,3]).

The rest of this work is structured as follows. The global rejection option is presented in section 2. In section 3, the local rejection option is presented. Both options are compared in section 4. The tests of the rejection options are given in section 5. Conclusions and directions of further research are presented in section 6.

2   Global Rejection Option

The global rejection option is an alternative classification task with the additional class C_0. All observations that are classified to this class are rejected.

For the given learning set L_0 of the class C_0, a new classification function ϕ'_α has the form:

$$\phi'_\alpha(x, \bigcup_{i=0}^{n} L_i) = i, \tag{2}$$

The observation is rejected when the function ϕ'_α returns zero.

The additional condition assumes that not rejected observations belong to the same class as in the previous classification task

$$(\forall i)\,(\phi_\alpha(x) = i) \Rightarrow ((\phi'_\alpha(x) = i) \vee (\phi'_\alpha(x) = 0))\,. \tag{3}$$

2.1   Graph Structure

When the classification function is defined by the graph ensemble $G = (V, E)$ with the specified root, then the rejection class C_0 can be connected to the graph by an additional binary classifier that splits the data space between normal and

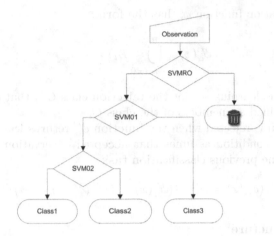

Fig. 1. The SVM tree with the global rejection option. The classifier SVMR0 rejects foreign observations.

foreign observations. The modification of the graph structure is done by the following operations:

$$V(G) = V(G) \cup v_n, \tag{4}$$
$$V(G) = V(G) \cup v_{C_0},$$
$$E(G) = E(G) \cup (v_n, v_{C_0}),$$
$$E(G) = E(G) \cup (v_n, v_0).$$

The old root v_0 is replaced by a new one v_n that connects v_0 and the vertex assigned to the rejection class v_{C_0}. Figure 1 presents the obtained tree. The tree fulfils condition (3).

We may assume that the global rejection option will work fine when foreign observations are disparate from normal observations. In other cases, the classification error for the SVMR0 classifier will be significant and influence the classification results.

3 Local Rejection Option

The local rejection option applies the same technique as the global rejection option – creates an additional class for rejected objects – although separately for each recognised class.

The local rejection option is an alternative classification task with the additional classes C_{-i}. For each class the learning set L_{-i} is defined as a set of foreign observations that are classified as members of the class C_i by a classifier without a rejection option

$$C_{-i} = \{x \in X : \phi_\alpha(x) = i \land x \notin C_i\}. \tag{5}$$

A new classification function ϕ'_α has the form:

$$\phi'_\alpha(x, \bigcup_{i=-n,i\neq 0}^{n} L_i) = i, \tag{6}$$

where L_{-i} is the learning set for the rejection class C_{-i} that collects foreign observations classified as members of the class C_i.

The observation is rejected when the function ϕ'_α returns less than zero.

The additional condition assumes that accepted observations belong to the same class as in the previous classification task

$$(\forall i)\,(\phi_\alpha(x) = i) \Rightarrow ((\phi'_\alpha(x) = i) \vee (\phi'_\alpha(x) = -i)), \tag{7}$$

3.1 Graph Structure

In a graph ensemble, the rejection classes C_{-i} are connected by additional binary classifiers that replace leaves. Each such classifier splits the data space between normal and foreign observations for the given class. The modification of the graph structure is done by the following operations:

$$V(G) = V(G) \cup v_{C_i|C_{-i}}, \tag{8}$$
$$V(G) = V(G) \cup v_{C_{-i}},$$
$$E(G) = E(G) \setminus (v, v_{C_i}) \quad \forall_v (v, v_{C_i}) \in E(G),$$
$$E(G) = E(G) \cup (v, v_{C_i|C_{-i}}),$$
$$E(G) = E(G) \cup (v_{C_i|C_{-i}}, v_{C_i}),$$
$$E(G) = E(G) \cup (v_{C_i|C_{-i}}, v_{C_{-i}}).$$

For each class, the leaf v_{C_i} is replaced in the graph by the vertex $v_{C_i|C_{-i}}$ that contains an SVM classifier. The new vertex connects the leaf v_{C_i} and the vertex assigned to the rejection class $v_{C_{-i}}$. Figure 2 presents the obtained tree. The tree fulfils condition (7).

Unlike the global rejection option misclassifications of the additional classifiers are not propagate. However, they may reject normal observations from the local classes. Comparison of both methods is given in the next section.

4   Comparison of Rejection Options

The decision graph is a collection of binary classifiers. Each classifier can be described by the probability of misclassification q_i or the probability of correct classification $p_i = (1 - q_i)$. The total probability of misclassification is given by the probability of at least one misclassification on the decision path

$$E_k = q_1 + p_1 q_2 + \ldots + p_1 * \ldots * p_{n-1} q_n. \tag{9}$$

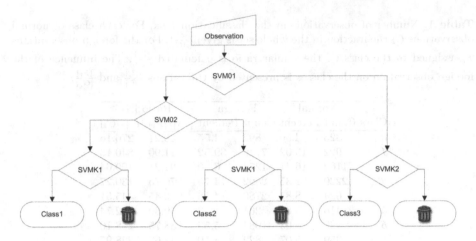

Fig. 2. The SVM tree with the local rejection option. The classifiers SVMKi separate foreign observations from normal observations.

In the case of the global rejection method, an additional classifier with the probability of misclassification q_o is added as the first classifier on the path. The probability of misclassification for the global rejection option equals

$$E_G = q_0 + p_0 E_k, \qquad (10)$$

In the case of the local rejection method, an additional classifier with the probability of misclassification q_{n+1} is added as the last classifier on the path. The probability of misclassification for the local rejection option equals

$$E_L = E_k + p_1 * \ldots * p_n q_{n+1}. \qquad (11)$$

Let us compare both probabilities of misclassification. We assume that the probability of misclassification for the additional binary classifier is the same in both cases $q_0 = q_{n+1}$.

We can present E_G as

$$E_G = q_0 + (1 - q_0)E_k = E_k - (1 - E_k) * q_0. \qquad (12)$$

We will prove that E_L equals E_G. Let us compare both values

$$E_k + p_1 * \ldots * p_n q_{n+1} = E_k - (1 - E_k) * q_0. \qquad (13)$$

For $q_0 = q_{n+1} = 0$ expression (13) is true. In other case we must prove that

$$p_1 * \ldots * p_n = 1 - E_k. \qquad (14)$$

From the right side of the equation (14) we have

$$R = 1 - E_k = (1 - q_1) - p_1 q_2 - \ldots - p_1 * \ldots * p_{n-1} q_n \qquad (15)$$
$$= p_1((1 - q_2) - p_2 q_3 - \ldots - p_2 * \ldots * p_{n-1} q_n)$$
$$= p_1 * \ldots * p_n = L.$$

Table 1. Number of observations in the classification task. For each class of normal observations C_i the fraction in the whole set is given $\frac{|C_i|}{|C|}$. For the foreign observations F_i assigned to the class C_i the similar ratio is calculated $\frac{|F_i|}{|F|}$. The influence of the foreign observation on the classes is presented by the rations $\frac{|C_i|}{|F_i|}$ and $\frac{|F_i|}{|C_i|}$.

	Normal		Foreign		Ratio [%]	
Class	Count	Percent	Count	Percent	$|C_i|/|F_i|$	$|F_i|/|C_i|$
0	323	4.56	892	4.55	36.21	276.16
1	922	13.02	7746	39.52	11.90	840.13
2	1162	16.41	1274	6.50	91.21	109.64
3	2220	31.35	2892	14.75	76.76	130.27
4	624	8.81	2780	14.18	22.45	445.51
5	416	5.87	261	1.33	159.39	62.74
6	420	5.93	1084	5.53	38.75	258.10
7	359	5.07	822	4.19	43.67	228.97
8	293	4.14	835	4.26	35.09	284.98
9	342	4.83	1015	5.18	33.69	296.78

Therefore, for a single classification path, the misclassification risk is the same for both rejection options. For the whole classification graph, the misclassification risk is the same if the classification accuracy of the binary classifier in the global rejection option equals the average accuracy of the binary classifiers in the local rejection option.

The practice shows that binary classification solving for separate classes brings better results that for meta–classes [1]. One versus One strategy usually gives better results than One versus All [6]. Therefore, we may expect that the local rejection option is better than the global rejection option.

5   Tests

Public repositories lack data sets with observations outside the recognised classes. Therefore, we collected 7,081 digits form hand–drawn geodetics maps. Among them 5,291 observations (approximately 75 percent) were taken as the learning set and 1,790 observations were taken as the testing set.

From the same map sheets we collected 19,601 observations that are not digits but have similar sizes and densities (black to white pixels ratio). Among them 14,711 observations were taken as the learning set and 4890 observations were taken as the testing set. Table 1 shows details.

To evaluate both rejection options we treated correct detections of foreign observations as *true positive* and correct detections of normal observations as *true negative*. Additionally we calculated sensitivity and specificity. Sensitivity is the fraction of correctly recognised foreign observations among all foreign observations and specificity is the fraction of detected normal observations among all normal observations.

Table 2. Classification with the global rejection option. Results are given for normal classes *0-9* and the rejection class *R*.

Class	Count	Correct	Wrong	Correct [%]	Wrong [%]
R	4890	4533	357	92.70	7.30
0	87	64	23	73.56	26.44
1	234	112	122	47.86	52.14
2	312	270	42	86.54	13.46
3	535	490	45	91.59	8.41
4	172	86	86	50.00	50.00
5	102	91	11	89.22	10.78
6	93	73	20	78.49	21.51
7	86	69	17	80.23	19.77
8	82	62	20	75.61	24.39
9	87	63	24	72.41	27.59
Summary	**6680**	**5913**	**767**	**88.52**	**11.48**

Table 3. Classification with the local rejection option. Results are given for normal classes *0-9* and the rejection class *R*.

Class	Count	Correct	Wrong	Correct [%]	Wrong [%]
R	4890	4696	194	96.03	3.97
0	87	72	15	82.76	17.24
1	234	154	80	65.81	34.19
2	312	281	31	90.06	9.94
3	535	494	41	92.34	7.66
4	172	147	25	85.47	14.53
5	102	91	11	89.22	10.78
6	93	82	11	88.17	11.83
7	86	78	8	90.70	9.30
8	82	67	15	81.71	18.29
9	87	56	31	64.37	35.63
Summary	**6680**	**6218**	**462**	**93.08**	**6.92**

The observations were described by 197 features. The tree classifier consisted of binary SVM classifiers with linear kernels. The linear kernel was chosen to reduce the number of parameter. The cost coefficient C was set to 10.

Table 2 shows results for the global rejection option. The sensitivity and specificity calculated for these results equals 0.92 and 0.79 respectively. The results for the local rejection option – presented in Table 3 – are better. The sensitivity and specificity calculated for these results equals 0.95 and 0.99 respectively.

In both cases, the specificity is lower than the sensitivity. In the result, the foreign observations are better recognised than the normal observations. It can be explained by the difference in the sizes of both sets.

Both rejection options expand the same classification function. Therefore, all differences in the results arise due to the rejection option. For the global rejection options nearly half of the observations in the classes *1* and *4* were rejected. The local rejection option improved the results for these classes, but obtained the worse results for the class *9*.

We omitted comparison of the rejection options with a pure classification function. Such comparison is important, because presents an influence of the rejection option on the classification result. However, new evaluation methods should be introduced to compare them (for example [5]) and we lack in space for that.

6   Conclusions

We proposed two rejection options. The global rejection option separates the foreign observations from the normal observations in the first classification step. The local rejection option separates observations individually for each recognised class. The first method needs the learning set that collects all foreign observations. For the second method, the foreign observations must be assigned to the most similar recognised classes. We tested the method on the handwritten digits recognition task with the additional foreign observations. The test showed that the local rejection option works better, although not for all classes.

In the future, we plan to test the rejection options on wider range of data sets and try to create a solution that combines both rejection options in a single method.

Acknowledgments. The research is supported by the National Science Center, grant No 2012/07/B/ST6/01501, decision no UMO–2012/07/B/ST6/01501.

References

1. Abe, S.: Support Vector Machines for Pattern Classification (Advances in Pattern Recognition). Springer-Verlag New York, Inc. (2005)
2. Chow, C.: On optimum recognition error and reject tradeoff. IEEE Transactions on Information Theory 16(1), 41–46 (1970)
3. Fumera, G., Roli, F.: Support Vector Machines with Embedded Reject Option. In: Lee, S.-W., Verri, A. (eds.) SVM 2002. LNCS, vol. 2388, pp. 68–82. Springer, Heidelberg (2002)
4. Ha, T.: Optimum Tradeoff between Class-selective Rejection Error and Average Number of Classes. Engineering Applications of Artificial Intelligence 10(6), 525–529 (1997)
5. Homenda, W., Luckner, M., Pedrycz, W.: Classification with rejection: concepts and formal evaluations. In: Proceedings of KICSS 2013, Cracow, pp. 161–172 (2013)
6. Hsu, C., Lin, C.: A comparison of methods for multiclass support vector machines. IEEE Transactions on Neural Networks 13(2), 415–425 (2002)
7. Sundararajan, R., Pal, A.K.: Learning with an Embedded Reject Option. In: Rutkowski, L., Siekmann, J.H., Tadeusiewicz, R., Zadeh, L.A. (eds.) ICAISC 2004. LNCS (LNAI), vol. 3070, pp. 664–669. Springer, Heidelberg (2004)

Comparative Study of Accuracies on the Family of the Recursive-Rule Extraction Algorithm

Yoichi Hayashi, Yuki Tanaka, Shota Fujisawa, and Tomoki Izawa

Dept. of Computer Science, Meiji University,
Tama-ku, Kawasaki, Kanagawa 214-8571, Japan
hayashiy@cs.meiji.ac.jp, {yuuuuuki.t.124,hoiminn627}@gmail.com,
0hs7681738f2c3j@ezweb.ne.jp

Abstract. In this paper, we first compare the accuracies of the Recursive-Rule Extraction algorithm family, i.e., the Re-RX algorithm, its variant and the "Three-MLP Ensemble by the Re-RX algorithm" (shortened to "Three-MLP Ensemble") using the Re-RX algorithm as a core part for six kinds of two-class mixed (i.e., discrete and continuous attributes) datasets. Two-class mixed datasets are commonly used for credit scoring and generally in financial domains. In this paper, we compare the accuracy by only the Re-RX algorithm family because of recent comparison reviews and benchmarking study results, obtained by complicated statistics, support vector machines, neuro-fuzzy hybrid classifications, and similar techniques. The Three-MLP Ensemble algorithm cascades standard backpropagation (BP) to train a three neural-network ensemble, where each neural network is a Multi-Layer Perceptron (MLP). Thus, strictly speaking, three neural networks do not need to be trained simultaneously. In addition, the Three-MLP Ensemble is a simple and new concept of rule extraction from neural network ensembles and can avoid previous complicated neural network ensemble structures and the difficulties of rule extraction algorithms. The extremely high accuracy of the Three-MLP Ensemble algorithm generally outperformed the Re-RX algorithm and the variant. The results confirm that the output from the network ensemble can be expressed in the form of rules, and thus opens the "black box" of trained neural network ensembles.

Keywords: Re-RX Algorithm, Rule Extraction, Neural Network Ensemble, Two-Class Mixed Dataset, Ensemble Concept.

1 Introduction

Many rule extraction algorithms have been designed to generate classification rules from neural networks (NNs) that have been trained to distinguish data samples from different classes. These algorithms frequently assume that the input data attributes are discrete in order to make the rule extraction process more manageable.

Real-world classification problems usually involve both discrete and continuous input attributes. All the continuous attributes must be discretized. The drawback of discretizing the continuous attributes is that the accuracy of the networks, and hence the accuracy of the rules extracted from the networks, may decrease. This is because discretization leads to a division of the input space into hyper rectangular regions.

S. Wermter et al. (Eds.): ICANN 2014, LNCS 8681, pp. 491–498, 2014.
© Springer International Publishing Switzerland 2014

Setiono et al. [1] proposed a recursive algorithm for rule extraction from a neural network that has been trained for solving a classification problem having mixed discrete and continuous input data attributes. This algorithm shares some similarities with other existing rule extraction algorithms.

Bologna [5] proposed the Discretized Interpretable Multi-Layer Perceptron (DIMLP) model with generated rules from neural network ensembles. The DIMLP is a "special" neural network model for which symbolic rules are generated to clarify the knowledge embedded within connections and activation neurons.

Zhou et al. [7] proposed the Rule Extraction From Network Ensemble (REFNE) approach to extract symbolic rules from trained neural network ensembles that perform classification tasks.

In 2012, Hara and Hayashi [6] first proposed the Two-MLP ensembles by using the Recursive-Rule eXtraction (Re-RX) algorithm for data with mixed attributes. The accuracy of the proposed algorithm outperformed that of almost all previous algorithms.

In 2013, Hayashi et al. [8] presented the Three-MLP Ensemble by the Re-RX algorithm with an extremely high performance result for the German Credit dataset, which is a two-class mixed dataset.

In this paper, we conduct a comparative study of accuracies on the Recursive-Rule Extraction algorithm family. In this ensemble family, each neural network is an MLP. The Re-RX algorithm is an effective rule extraction algorithm for datasets that comprise both discrete and continuous attributes, and so it is a core part of the Two- or Three-MLP Ensemble by the Re-RX algorithm.

We treat the Three-MLP Ensemble as a "virtual" ensemble system. From an overall viewpoint, this algorithm cascades BP to train the three neural-network ensemble. Thus, strictly speaking, the three neural networks do not need to be trained simultaneously. In addition, this simple and new concept of rule extraction from the neural network ensemble can avoid previous complicated neural network ensemble structures and the difficulties of rule extraction algorithms. The extracted rules maintain the high learning capabilities of neural networks while expressing highly comprehensible rules.

2   Recursive Rule Extraction Algorithm: Re-RX Algorithm

The Re-RX algorithm [1] is designed to generate classification rules from datasets that have both discrete and continuous attributes. The algorithm is recursive in nature and generates hierarchical rules. The rule conditions for discrete attributes are disjointed from those for continuous attributes. The continuous attributes only appear in the conditions of the rules lowest in the hierarchy. The outline of the algorithm is as follows.

Algorithm Re-RX(S, D, C)

Input: A set of data samples S having discrete attributes D and continuous attributes C.

Output: A set of classification rules.

1. Train and prune a neural network using the dataset S and all its D and C attributes.
2. Let D' and C' be the sets of discrete and continuous attributes, respectively, still present in the network, and let S' be the set of data samples correctly classified by the pruned network.

3. If D' = φ, then generate a hyperplane to split the samples in S' according to the values of the continuous attributes C', and stop.

Otherwise, by using only the discrete attributes D', generate the set of classification rules R for dataset S'.

4. For each rule Ri generated:

If support(R_i)>δ_1 and error(R_i)>δ_2, then

- Let S_i be the set of data samples that satisfy the condition of rule R_i and let D_i be the set of discrete attributes that do not appear in rule condition R_i.

- If $D_i =$ φ, then generate a hyperplane to split the samples in S_i according to the values of their continuous attributes C_i, and stop.

- Otherwise, call Re-RX(S_i, D_i, C_i).

The support of a rule is the percentage of samples that are covered by that rule. The support and the corresponding error rate of each rule are checked in step 4. If the error exceeds the threshold δ_2 and the support meets the maximum threshold δ_1, then the subspace of this rule is further subdivided by either recursively calling Re-RX when discrete attributes are still not present in the conditions of the rule or by generating a separating hyperplane involving only the continuous attributes of the data.

3   Three-MLP Ensemble by the Re-RX Algorithm

We have recently extended the Two-MLP Ensemble by the Re-RX algorithm to the Three-MLP Ensemble [8, 9] to achieve extremely high accuracy. The Three-MLP Ensemble is shown as follows.

Three-MLP Ensemble by the Re-RX algorithm

Inputs: Learning datasets LD', LDf', LDff'

Outputs: Primary rule set, secondary rule set, and tertiary rule set.

1. Randomly extract a dataset of an arbitrary proportion from learning dataset LD, and name the set of extracted data as LD'.
2. Train and prune [10] the first neural network using LD'.
3. Apply the Re-RX algorithm to the output of step 2, and output the primary rule set.
4. Based on these primary rules, create a dataset LDf from a dataset (LD) that is not correctly classified by the rules.
5. Randomly extract the dataset of an arbitrary proportion from learning dataset LDf, and name the set of extracted data as LDf'.
6. Train and prune [10] the two ensemble neural networks by using LDf'.
7. Apply the Re-RX algorithm to the output of step 6, and output the secondary rule set.
8. Integrate the primary rule set and the secondary rule set.
9. Based on the rules integrated in step 8, create a dataset LDff from a dataset (LD) that is not correctly classified by the rules.

10. Randomly extract data samples of an arbitrary proportion from learning dataset LDff, and name the set of extracted data as LDff'.
11. Train and prune [10] the ensemble of three neural networks by using LDff'.
12. Apply the Re-RX algorithm to the output of step 11, and output the tertiary rule set.
13. Integrate the primary rule set, the secondary rule set, and the tertiary rule set.

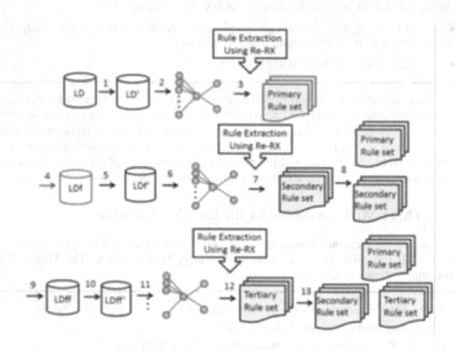

Fig. 1. Schematic diagram of Three-MLP Ensemble by the Re-RX algorithm

4   Datasets and Experimental Setup

One of the key actions necessary for financial institutions is to decide whether to grant a loan or credit card to a customer. This decision is typically made by a credit scoring approach that uses a mathematical decision model to accurately distinguish good customers (likely to repay) from bad ones (likely to default) based on a set of customer characteristics (e.g., age, income, and years at current address). It is also important that the models are interpretable to the financial expert. Hence, having a "white-box", transparent credit scoring model plays a pivotal role in credit-risk evaluations, as the evaluator may be required to justify why a certain credit application is approved or rejected.

4.1   CARD Credit Datasets

A credit card approval dataset is available from the University of California Irvine Machine Learning Repository [4]. It consists of a total of 690 data samples, each of which is described by 6 continuous attributes and 9 discrete (nominal, categorical) attributes. The discrete attributes were coded by a binary representation. As a result, the dataset has a total of 51 input attributes and two outputs.

Three permutations of the CARD dataset (CARD1, CARD2, CARD3) were used for splitting the training and testing observations.

4.2   German Credit Dataset

The German credit dataset [4] contains a total of 1000 samples with 20 attributes. The class attribute describes people as having credit that is either good (approximately 700 observations) or bad (approximately 300 observations). Other attributes include 20 items. In this paper, the dataset was randomly split. The first 70% was put in the training set and the second 30% in the test set.

4.3   Bene1 and Bene2 Credit Datasets

The Bene1 and Bene2 datasets [12] were obtained from major financial institutions in Benelux countries (Belgium, the Netherlands, and Luxembourg). These datasets contain the application characteristics of customers who applied for credit scores. In accordance with common banking practices and regulations, a bad customer in these datasets was defined as someone who had been in payment arrears for more than 90 days at some point in the observed loan history.

Table 1. Characteristics of Datasets

	Dataset Size	Input Total	Input Continuous	Input Discrete
CARD1	690	51	6	45
CARD2	690	51	6	45
CARD3	690	51	6	45
German	1000	20	7	13
Bene1	3123	27	13	14
Bene2	7190	28	18	10

5   Experimental Results

We trained six kinds of two-class mixed datasets by the Re-RX algorithm family and obtained the accuracies and the number of extracted rules for each test dataset as follows. In tables [2]-[4], the bold numbers are the highest test accuracies than the accuracies reported in previous papers. Some cells in the tables are empty, e.g., Three-MLP Ensemble of CARD1. This means that the proposed Three-MLP Ensemble by the Re-RX algorithm did not provide meaningful rules, because the LDff' was too small to provide tertiary rules. In this case, the final accuracy for the test dataset by the Two-MLP Ensemble by the Re-RX algorithm was the highest for each dataset.

Table 2. Performance of training datasets and test datasets for CARD1 and CARD2

	CARD1 Training (%)	Test (%)	No. Rules	CARD2 Training (%)	Test (%)	No. Rules
Re-RX only	87.26	83.14	5	88.99	84.93	6
2-MLP Ensemble	95.37	**93.02**	7	97.10	**94.78**	9
3-MLP Ensemble						

Table 3. Performance of training datasets and test datasets for CARD3 and German

	CARD3 Training (%)	Test	No. Rules	German Training (%)	Test	No. Rules
Re-RX only	86.67	80.57	7	73.00	74.40	13
2-MLP Ensemble	90.43	85.80	11	78.80	**81.80**	19
3-MLP Ensemble						

Table 4. Performance of training datasets and test datasets for Bene1 and Bene2

	Bene1 Training (%)	Test	No. Rules	Bene2 Training (%)	Test	No. Rules
Re-RX only	73.02	72.07	27	72.38	72.93	42
2-MLP Ensemble	96.61	96.99	34	73.32	73.91	45
3-MLP Ensemble	97.63	**98.14**	36	81.36	**81.56**	54

The highest recent accuracies by using the Re-RX algorithm and the variant of the Re-RX algorithm stated by Setiono et al. in peer-reviewed journals are listed in Table 5. In each reference [1, 2, 11] of this table, the bold number for the accuracy of only CARD3 is slightly higher accuracy than our test accuracy of CARD3 as of Feb. 17, 2014.

Table 5. Highest recent accuracies by using the Re-RX algorithm and the variant of the Re-RX algorithm, appearing in peer-reviewed journals

	Test accuracy (%)	Author	Ref. No.	Year
CARD1	89.53	Setiono et al.	[2]	2011
CARD2	87.21	Setiono et al.	[2]	2011
CARD3	**88.95**	Setiono et al.	[11]	2009
German	78.74	Setiono et al.	[2]	2011
Bene1	73.68	Setiono et al.	[1]	2008
Bene2	75.26	Setiono et al.	[1]	2008

6   Discussion

We focus on only the highlights of the experimental results. The accuracy for the test data of rules extracted from CARD1 and CARD2 by the proposed algorithm outperforms the accuracies of others' previous work. We believe the approximately 10% increase in accuracies from the Re-RX only (raw Re-RX), compared to the Two-MLP Ensemble in CARD1 and CARD2, occurred for the following two reasons:

(1) After the integration of primary rules and secondary rules, we had two new rules in the CARD1 dataset. Then we conducted a sensitivity analysis of the contribution of each extracted rule for the entire test dataset. We summed the values of the two rules and obtained 93.02%. This is identical to the actual experimental value. For the CARD2 dataset, we obtained the same results.

(2) Originally, we need the micro-analysis of the decision trees. Consequently, we explain only the important points for the 10% boost of the accuracies. A typical search by decision trees such as C4.5 [3] and J4.8 is executed many times in the Re-RX algorithm. However, the Three-MLPs Ensemble by the Re-RX algorithm has a chance to execute a decision tree search much more times. Thus, if the decision tree search overlooks some classification rules in the Re-RX only (raw Re-RX), the search in the Two-MLP Ensemble or the search in the Three-MLPs Ensemble can possibly find much more effective classification rules.

The accuracy for the CARD3 test dataset by Setiono et al. [11] is slightly higher than the 85.80% reported in our study.

For the Bene1 test dataset, our algorithm obtained 98.14%. The accuracy by the raw Re-RX algorithm was 73.68 % [1]. Thus, our algorithm greatly outperformed the raw Re-RX algorithm in accuracy for the Bene1 test dataset. After the sensitivity analysis of the contribution of each extracted rule for the entire test dataset, we summed the values of 9 rules and obtained 98.14%. This is identical to the actual experimental value. We believe that the reason for this value is the same as that for the CARD1 and CARD2 datasets.

For the Bene2 dataset, our algorithm obtained 81.56% for the test dataset. The number of rules extracted was 54. Setiono et al. reported a 75.26% accuracy for the Bene2 test dataset and 67 rules extracted by the raw Re-RX algorithm for the Bene2 test dataset [1].

Clearly, our algorithm showed considerably better accuracy and a much more concise form than that of Setiono et al [1]. Since we used large test datasets, such as Bene1 and Bene2, our number of rules extracted also becomes large (36 rules and 54 rules for Bene1 and Bene2, respectively).

7   Conclusion

In this paper, we focused on the Re-RX algorithm family and compared the accuracy within the family. The "Three-MLP Ensemble by the Re-RX algorithm" is capable of extracting classification rules from neural network ensembles using datasets of both trained discrete and trained continuous mixed attributes. The novel characteristic of the algorithm lies in its extremely high accuracy for two-class mixed attribute datasets.

Furthermore, since the Re-RX algorithm is a core part of the proposed algorithm, the excellent characteristics of the Re-RX algorithm contribute to the success of the proposed algorithm.

Finally we will try to clarify the relationships between a raw Re-RX algorithm [1] and our multiple-MLPs ensemble. As we used an example of Three-MLPs ensemble algorithm stated in the Section 3, the most important principle in the design of our algorithm is an "attrition" system for the dataset from the learning dataset that is not correctly classified by the extracted rules. Thus, the size of datasets for the rule extraction will be monotonically decreasing so that our algorithm has well designed so as to finally output extracted rules to be included, which uses minimum necessary number of multiple-MLPs ensemble and terminated automatically.

This situation can be interpreted as a kind of "saturated situation". Depending on the characteristics of datasets, we may see the case of the saturation by only Two-MLPs ensemble. In the other cases, our algorithm may proceed to Five-MLPs ensemble with increasing accuracies. Thus, we need not set the number of multiple-MLPs ensemble in advance but our algorithm will terminate at the saturated situation with the minimum necessary numbers of multiple-MLPs ensemble where our algorithm does not output anymore new extracted rules.

Almost all datasets used in benchmarking or experimental comparative studies are not so huge, so called, a big data so that actually we will not be confronted with difficulties in the saturated situation.

All of the family of the Re-RX use C4.5 (J4.8) to generate discrete rules so that the C4.5 (J4.8) algorithm will generate the decision tree based on amount of information in datasets. Thus, the branches of decision trees will not be generated in the case of low information gain. Therefore, we believe that extracted rules in smaller numbers of multiple-MLPs ensemble can reflect the characteristics of entire learning datasets. Accordingly, since the increase rate of accuracies will decrease with increase of multiple-MPLs ensemble, there is a strong possibility that the final accuracy will gradually become saturated.

References

1. Setiono, R., et al.: Recursive neural network rule extraction for data with mixed attributes. IEEE Trans. Neural Netw. 19(2), 299–307 (2008)
2. Setiono, R., et al.: Rule extraction from minimal neural networks for credit card screening. Inter. J. of Neural Systems. 21(4), 265–276 (2011)
3. Quinlan, R.: C4.5: Programming for Machine Learning. Morgan Kaufman, San Mateo (1993)
4. Univ. of California, Irvine Learning Repository, http://archive.ics.uci.edu/m/
5. Bologna, G.: Is it worth generating rules from neural network ensemble? J. of Applied Logic 2, 325–348 (2004)
6. Hara, A., Hayashi, Y.: Ensemble neural network rule extraction using Re-RX algorithm. In: Proc. WCCI (IJCNN 2012), Brisbane, Australia, June 10-15, pp. 604–609 (2012)
7. Zhou, Z.-H.: Extracting symbolic rules from trained neural network ensembles. AI Communications 16, 3–15 (2003)
8. Hayashi, Y., et al.: A New approach to Three Ensemble neural network rule extraction using Recursive-Rule eXtraction algorithm. In: Int. Joint Conf. Neural Networks (IJCNN 2013), Dal-las, August 4-9, pp. 835–841 (2013)
9. Hayashi, Y.: Neural network rule extraction by a new ensemble concept and its theoretical and historical background: A review. Int. J. of Computational Intelligence and Applications 12(4), 1340006-1–1340006-22 (2013)
10. Setiono, R., et al.: A penalty-function approach for pruning feedforward neural networks. Neural Comp. 9(1), 185–204 (1997)
11. Setiono, R., et al.: A note on knowledge discovery using neural networks and its application to credit card screening. European J. Operational Research 192, 326–332 (2009)
12. Baesens, B., et al.: Using neural network rule extraction and decision tables for credit-risk evaluation. Management Science 49(3), 312–329 (2004)

Improving the Convergence Property of Soft Committee Machines by Replacing Derivative with Truncated Gaussian Function

Kazuyuki Hara[1] and Kentaro Katahira[2]

[1] College of Industrial Technology, Nihon University,
1-2-1 Izumi-cho, Narashino-shi, Chiba, 275-8575 Japan
[2] Graduate School of Environmental Studies, Nagoya University
Furo-cho, Chikusa-ku, Nagoya, 464-8601 Japan

Abstract. In online gradient descent learning, the local property of the derivative of the output function can cause slow convergence. This phenomenon, called a *plateau*, occurs in the learning process of a multilayer network. Improving the derivative term, we propose a simple method replacing the derivative term with a truncated Gaussian function that greatly increases the convergence speed. We then analyze a soft committee machine trained by proposed method, and show how proposed method breaks a plateau. Results showed that the proposed method eventually led to break the symmetry between hidden units.

Keywords: truncated Gaussian function, derivative, residual error, soft committee machine

1 Introduction

Learning in neural networks can be formulated as the optimization of an objective function that quantifies the system's performance. An important property of feed-forward networks is their ability to learn a rule from examples. Statistical mechanics has been successfully used to study this property [1,2]. A compact description of learning dynamics can be obtained by using statistical mechanics, which feature a large input dimension N and provide an accurate model of mean behavior for a realistic N [1,2].

Several previous studies have investigated ways to accelerate the learning process [3,4]. One problem is that slow convergence due to *plateaus* occurs in learning processes that use a gradient descent algorithm [4]. In gradient descent algorithm, the weight vector is updated in the direction of the steepest descent of the objective function and the derivative of the output is taken into account.

In this work, we replace a derivative of a gradient descent algorithm with a truncated Gaussian function to train a soft committee machine and show how the proposed method solves breaking a plateau. We formulate the learning settings similar to those of statistical mechanics because we will build a theory for the proposed method for a future study. We investigated the behavior of the proposed

S. Wermter et al. (Eds.): ICANN 2014, LNCS 8681, pp. 499–506, 2014.

method in a plateau by using the inner products of teacher and student hidden weight vectors R_k and the squared norms of student hidden weight vector Q_{kk}^2. We demonstrate the validity of the proposed method by computer simulation and then compare its performance with that of the conventional method.

2　Model

In this work, we employ a teacher-student formulation and assume the existence of a teacher network that produces the desired output for the student network. By introducing teacher network, we can directly measure the similarity of the student weight vector to that of the teacher. First we formulate a teacher network and a student network and then we introduce the gradient descent algorithm.

Teacher and student are a soft committee machine with N input units, hidden units, and an output, as shown in Fig. 1. The teacher consists of K hidden units and the student consists of K' hidden units. Each hidden unit is a perceptron. The kth hidden weight vector of teacher is $\boldsymbol{B}_k = (B_{k1}, \ldots, B_{kN})$ and the k'th hidden weight vector of student is $\boldsymbol{J}_{k'}^{(m)} = (J_{k'1}^{(m)}, \ldots, J_{k'N}^{(m)})$, where m denotes learning iterations. In the soft committee machine, all the hidden-to-output weights are fixed to be $+1$ [2]. This network calculates the majority vote of hidden outputs.

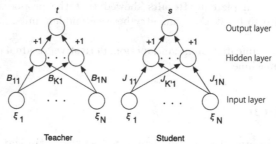

Fig. 1. Network structures of teacher and student

We assume that both the teacher and the student receive N-dimensional input $\boldsymbol{\xi}^{(m)} = (\xi_1^m, \ldots, \xi_N^{(m)})$, that the teacher outputs $t^{(m)} = \sum_{k=1}^{K} t_k^{(m)} = \sum_{k=1}^{K} g(d_k^{(m)})$, and that the student outputs $s^{(m)} = \sum_{k'=1}^{K'} s_{k'}^{(m)} = \sum_{k'=1}^{K'} g(y_{k'}^{(m)})$. Here, $g(\cdot)$ is the output function of hidden unit, $d_k^{(m)}$ is the inner potential of the kth hidden unit of the teacher calculated using $d_k^{(m)} = \sum_{i=1}^{N} B_{ki}\xi_i^{(m)}$, and $y_{k'}^{(m)}$ is the inner potential of the k'th hidden unit of the student calculated using $y_{k'}^{(m)} = \sum_{i=1}^{N} J_{k'i}^{(m)}\xi_i^{(m)}$.

We assume that the elements $\xi_i^{(m)}$ of the independently drawn input $\boldsymbol{\xi}^{(m)}$ are uncorrelated random variables with zero mean and unit variance; that is, that the ith element of the input is drawn from a probability distribution $\mathrm{P}(\xi_i)$. The thermodynamic limit of $N \to \infty$ is also assumed. The statistics of the inputs in the thermodynamic limit are $\left\langle \xi_i^{(m)} \right\rangle = 0$, $\left\langle (\xi_i^{(m)})^2 \right\rangle \equiv \sigma_\xi^2 = 1$, and $\langle \|\boldsymbol{\xi}^{(m)}\| \rangle =$

$\sqrt{N}$, where $\langle \cdots \rangle$ denotes the average and $\| \cdot \|$ denotes the norm of a vector. Each element B_{ki}, $k = 1 \sim K$ is drawn from a probability distribution with zero mean and $1/N$ variance. With the assumption of the thermodynamic limit, the statistics of the teacher weight vector are $\langle B_{ki} \rangle = 0, \langle (B_{ki})^2 \rangle \equiv \sigma_B^2 = 1/N$, and $\langle \| \boldsymbol{B_k} \| \rangle = 1$. This means that any combination of $\boldsymbol{B_l} \cdot \boldsymbol{B_{l'}} = 0$. The distribution of inner potential $d^{(m)}$ follows a Gaussian distribution with zero mean and unit variance in the thermodynamic limit.

$$\langle d_k \rangle = \sum_i \langle B_{ki} \rangle \langle \xi_i \rangle = 0, \langle d_k^2 \rangle \equiv \sigma_d^2 = \left\langle \left(\sum_i B_{ki} \xi_i \right)^2 \right\rangle = N \sigma_B^2 \sigma_\xi^2 = 1 \quad (1)$$

For the sake of analysis, we assume that each element of $J_{k'i}^{(0)}$, which is the initial value of the student vector $\boldsymbol{J_{k'}^{(0)}}$, is drawn from a probability distribution with zero mean and $1/N$ variance. The statistics of the k'th hidden weight vector of the student are $\left\langle J_{k'i}^{(0)} \right\rangle = 0, \left\langle (J_{k'i}^{(0)})^2 \right\rangle \equiv \sigma_J^2 = 1/N$, and $\left\langle \| \boldsymbol{J_{k'}^{(0)}} \| \right\rangle = 1$ in the thermodynamic limit. This means that any combination of $\boldsymbol{J_l^{(0)}} \cdot \boldsymbol{J_{l'}^{(0)}} = 0$. The output function of the hidden units of the student $g(\cdot)$ is the same as that of the teacher. The statistics of the student weight vector at mth iteration are $\left\langle J_{k'i}^{(m)} \right\rangle = 0, \left\langle (J_{k'i}^{(m)})^2 \right\rangle = (Q_{k'k'}^{(m)})^2/N$, and $\left\langle \| \boldsymbol{J_{k'}^{(m)}} \| \right\rangle = Q_{k'k'}^{(m)}$. Here, $(Q_{k'k'}^{(m)})^2 = \boldsymbol{J_{k'}^m} \cdot \boldsymbol{J_{k'}^m}$. By similar calculation to eq. (1), the distribution of the inner potential $y_{k'}^{(m)}$ follows a Gaussian distribution with zero mean and $(Q_{k'k'}^{(m)})^2$ variance in the thermodynamic limit.

Next, we introduce the gradient descent algorithm for the soft committee machine. For the possible inputs $\{ \boldsymbol{\xi} \}$, we want to train the student network to produce the desired outputs $t = s$. The generalization error is defined as the error ε averaged over possible inputs:

$$\varepsilon_g^{(m)} = \left\langle \varepsilon^{(m)} \right\rangle = \frac{1}{2} \left\langle (t^{(m)} - s^{(m)})^2 \right\rangle = \frac{1}{2} \left\langle \left(\sum_{k=1}^{K} g(d_k^{(m)}) - \sum_{k'=1}^{K'} g(y_{k'}^{(m)}) \right)^2 \right\rangle,$$
$$(2)$$

At each learning step m, a new uncorrelated input $\boldsymbol{\xi}^{(m)}$ is presented, and the current hidden weight vector of student $\boldsymbol{J_{k'}^{(m)}}$ is updated using

$$\boldsymbol{J_{k'}^{(m+1)}} = \boldsymbol{J_{k'}^{(m)}} + \frac{\eta}{N} \left(\sum_{l=1}^{K} g(d_l^{(m)}) - \sum_{l'=1}^{K'} g(y_{l'}^{(m)}) \right) g'(y_{k'}^{(m)}) \boldsymbol{\xi}^{(m)}, \quad (3)$$

where η is the learning step size and $g'(x)$ is the derivative of the output function of the hidden unit $g(x)$. We refer to this method as the conventional method in this paper.

3 Proposed Method

In this section, we discuss how to improve the residual error of the soft committee machine. The soft committee machine is a kind of multi-layer perceptron, so plateaus can appear in the learning process for any inputs [4]. A plateau is a phenomenon in which the error stays at the same value for an extended period. We assume $g(y_{k'}) = \mathrm{erf}(y_{k'}/\sqrt{2})$ in the following. $\mathrm{erf}(x)$ is the error function (similar to sigmoidal function) defined as $2/\sqrt{\pi}\int_0^x \exp(-t^2)dt$. Figure 2 shows an example of typical plateau behavior, including the effect of the derivative. Horizontal axis shows time $t = m/N$ and vertical axis shows the mean square error. Computer simulation results are shown, where $N = 1000$ and $\eta = 0.1$. The number of hidden units is $K = K' = 2$. Figure 2(a) shows the time course of inner product R_{11}, R_{12} and the mean square error ε of the conventional method. Inner prodct of $\boldsymbol{B}_k$ and $\boldsymbol{J}_{k'}$ are defined as $R_{kk'} = \boldsymbol{B}_k \cdot \boldsymbol{J}_{k'}$. R_{11} and R_{12} were different values at the beginning of the learning (left end of the figure), but as learning proceeded, they become the same value (roughly at the middle of the learning). Finally, R_{11} and R_{12} again separated from each other and converged into $R_{12} = 1$ and $R_{11} = 0$. This shows how the plateau was broken after a long time interval. Figure 2(b) show the plateaus of the soft committee machine whose derivative ($g'(y_k)$ in Eq. (3)) is replaced by a constant [7]. Because of this replacement, the learning equation relates only to common error $\sum_{l=1}^{K} g(d_l^{(m)}) - \sum_{l'=1}^{K'} g(y_{l'}^{(m)})$ —i.e., it does not relate to y_k —so all the weight vectors of the hidden units are updated in the same way. R_{11} and R_{12} always have the same value, and the plateau does not break. This means a larger residual error remains. The networkfs inability to break the plateau is what causes the large residual error, as shown in Fig. 2(b). To improve the error, we have to break the plateau.

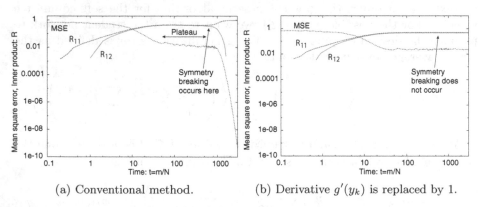

(a) Conventional method.   (b) Derivative $g'(y_k)$ is replaced by 1.

Fig. 2. Time course of mean square error and inner product. Learning step size is set to $\eta = 0.1$.

Here, let us give a more detailed explanation of what causes plateaus. In a soft committee machine, there are more than two hidden units. The error is calculated at the output layer and all the hidden-to-output weights are fixed to be +1, so the same error is given to all hidden units. The same input is given to all the hidden units, too, and so the updates of all the hidden units tend to be the same and they become trapped in a saddle point. At the saddle point, all the hidden units output the same values. We can break the plateau if we break the symmetry of the hidden unit outputs by exploiting the small difference between the hidden unit outputs. To break the plateau, each hidden unit outputs a different value. This mean that the derivative must relate to hidden unit output $y_{k'}$ as shown in eq. (3). Keeping this in mind, we employ a truncated Gaussian function $u(y_{k'})$ as follows:

$$J_{k'}^{(m+1)} = J_{k'}^{(m)} + \frac{\eta}{N} \left(\sum_{l=1}^{K} g(d_l^{(m)}) - \sum_{l'=1}^{K'} g(y_{l'}^{(m)}) \right) u(y_{k'}^{(m)}) \xi^{(m)}. \qquad (4)$$

Here, $u(y_{k'}) = \sqrt{2/\pi} \exp(-y_{k'}^2/2)$ when $|y_{k'}| < a$ and is 0 otherwise. As we will show later, the size of a is related to the standard deviation of the teacher hidden unit output d_k. Figure 3 shows the Gaussian function of zero mean and the unit variance (broken line) and the truncated Gaussian function (solid line). "a=1" is used.

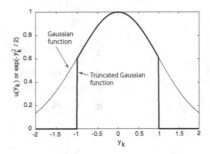

Fig. 3. Gaussian function and truncated Gaussian function

Let us give a brief intuitive explanation of why using a truncated Gaussian function breaks the plateau faster than the conventional method. When lth hidden unit outputs $|y_l| < a$ and l'th hidden unit outputs $|y_{l'}| > a$, the lth hidden weight vector is updated and the l'th hidden unit is not. The symmetry within the hidden units is then broken and the student breaks the plateau.

Figure 4 shows the time course of the mean square error of the original and proposed methods. The same setting as Fig. 2 is used. $a = 0.5, 0.8, 1, \sqrt{2}$, or 2. Horizontal axis is time $t = m/N$ and the vertical line is the mean square error. Each plot is the average of 20 trials. As shown, the proposed method using $a = 1$ converges the fastest between all settings include the conventional method.

Next, we show the dynamic behavior of the proposed method in a plateau. The inner product $R_{kk'}$ shows similarity of $\boldsymbol{B}_k$ and $\boldsymbol{J}_{k'}$. The squared norm of the student weight vector $Q_{k'k'}^2$ shows the length of the vector $\boldsymbol{J}_{k'}$. The inner product of the student weight vector Q_{12}^2 shows similarity of $\boldsymbol{J}_1$ and $\boldsymbol{J}_2$. Then, the behavior of the weight vectors in the plateau can be described by using $R_{kk'}$, $Q_{k'k'}^2$, and Q_{12}^2. Figure 5 shows results. The same setting as Fig. 4 is used. Horizontal axis is Q_{11}^2 or Q_{22}^2 and vertical axis is R_{11}, R_{12}, R_{21}, or R_{22}. Figure 5 (a) shows the dynamic behavior of the conventional method and from

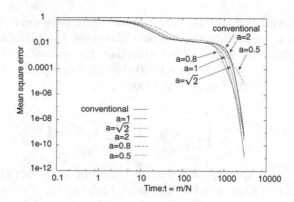

Fig. 4. Learning dynamics of conventional and proposed methods

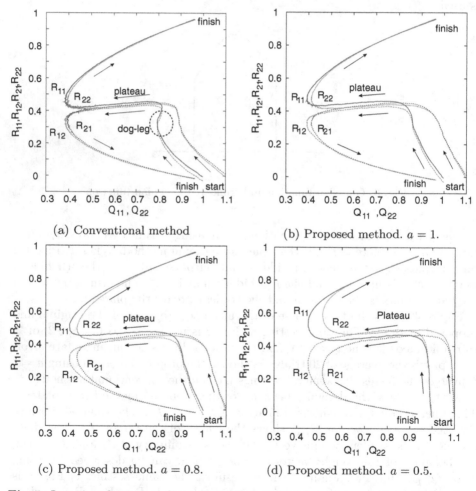

(a) Conventional method

(b) Proposed method. $a = 1$.

(c) Proposed method. $a = 0.8$.

(d) Proposed method. $a = 0.5$.

Fig. 5. Learning dynamics of conventional method (a) and proposed methods using different coefficients((b) $\sim$ (d))

Fig. 5(b) to (d) show that of the proposed methods. Initial conditions were $R_{11}^{(0)} = R_{12}^{(0)} = R_{21}^{(0)} = R_{22}^{(0)} = 0$, and $(Q_{11}^{(0)})^2 = (Q_{22}^{(0)})^2 = 1$ for both cases.

In the conventional method, which starts from the bottom right (as shown by 'start') of Fig. 5 (a), $R_{11} \sim R_{22}$ become gradually larger after the dog-leg (as shown by dashed circle), finally settling at $R_{11} \sim R_{22}$ are about 0.4. At the same time, Q_{11}^2 and Q_{12}^2 become shorter until Q_{11}^2 and Q_{12}^2 are about 0.4. After that, R_{12} and R_{21} converge into $Q_{11}^2 = 1.0$ and $R_{12} = R_{21} = 1.0$ (as shown by 'final'). R_{11} and R_{22} pass the other way and converge into $R_{11} = R_{22} = 0.0$, and $Q_{11}^2 = Q_{22}^2 = 1.0$ (as shown by 'final'). From the figure, $R_{11} \sim R_{22}$ are almost the same value when Q_{11}^2 and Q_{22}^2 are from 0.8 to 0.4. This interval constitutes the plateau. The plateau breaks around $R_{11} = R_{12} = R_{21} = R_{22} = 0.4$, and $Q_{11}^2 = Q_{22}^2 = 0.4$.

In contrast, in the proposed method, which starts from the bottom right of Fig. 5 (b) (as shown by 'start'), $R_{11} \sim R_{22}$ gradually become larger without the dog-leg. They stay near $R_{11} \sim R_{22}$ are about 0.4, but vary widely compared with the conventional method. This tendency becomes significant in Fig. 5 (c) and (d). This difference is what eventually breaks the plateau. Note that in Fig. 5 (c) and (d), Q_{11}^2 and Q_{22}^2 at converged point (as shown by 'final') are smaller than 1.0. So, convergence property of these settings become worse.

Next, we examine the effect of constant a in the truncated Gaussian function. When we changed the variance of element of the teacher weight vector to $\sigma_B^2 = 2/N$ (Figure 6), then, the variance of teacher output is changed to $\sigma_d^2 = N\sigma_B^2\sigma_\xi^2 = 2$ (See eq. (1)). Figure 6 shows the time course of mean square error when $a = 1, \sqrt{2}$, or 2 is used. The conventional method is also used. From the figure, $a = \sqrt{2}$ breaks plateau fastest and remarks best convergence property between other settings. These results show that setting constant $a = \sigma_d$ will realize the fast breaking plateau and the smallest residual error.

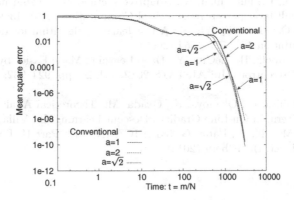

Fig. 6. Time course of mean square error when the variance of element of teacher weights is $2.0/N$

4   Conclusion

In this paper, we proposed a learning method that replaces the derivative with a truncated Gaussian function in a soft committee machine. First we explained how plateaus occur and then we described how they can be overcome by introducing a truncated Gaussian function in a soft committee machine. The effectiveness of the proposed method was apparent when we compared the time course of its mean square error with that of the conventional method. We also investigated the dynamic properties of the proposed method in plateau via $Q - R$ curve. Results showed that the proposed method can break the plateau by breaking the balance of updating the weight vectors of hidden units. Recently, the deep learning [5] becomes popular in machine learning, however, it has convergence problem. The natural gradient may solve this problem, but it requires heavy computation. So, many improvements of deep learning have proposed [6]. Improvement of the deep learning by using the proposed method is our future study.

Acknowledgments. The authors thank Professor Masato Okada for insightful discussions.

References

1. Biehl, M., Schwarze, H.: Learning by on-line gradient descent. Journal of Physics A: Mathematical and General Physics 28, 643–656 (1995)
2. Saad, D., Solla, S.A.: On-line learning in soft-committee machines. Physical Review E 52, 4225–4243 (1995)
3. Rattray, M., Saad, D.: Incorporating Curvature Information into On-line learning. In: Saad, D. (ed.) On-line Learning in Neural Networks, pp. 183–207. Cambridge University Press, Cambridge (1998)
4. Amari, S., Park, H., Fukumizu, K.: Adaptive method of realizing natural gradient learning for multilayer perceptrons. Neural Computation 12(6), 1399–1409 (2000)
5. Hinton, G.E., Osindero, S., Teh, Y.: A fast learning algorithm for deep belief nets. Neural Computation 18, 1527–1554 (2006)
6. Vatanen, T., Valpola, H., LeCun, Y.: Deep Learning Made Easier by Linear Transformation in Perceptrons. In: AISTATS 2012, vol. 22, pp. 924–932. JMLR W&CP (2012)
7. Hara, K., Katahira, K., Okanoya, K., Okada, M.: Theoretical Analysis of Function of Derivative Term in On-Line Gradient Descent Learning. In: Villa, A.E.P., Duch, W., Érdi, P., Masulli, F., Palm, G. (eds.) ICANN 2012, Part II. LNCS, vol. 7553, pp. 9–16. Springer, Heidelberg (2012)

Fast Sensitivity-Based Training of BP-Networks

Iveta Mrázová and Zuzana Petříčková

Faculty of Mathematics and Physics, Charles University in Prague,
Malostranské nám. 25, 118 00 Prague, Czech Republic
iveta.mrazova@mff.cuni.cz, zuzana.reitermanova@matfyz.cz

Abstract. Sensitivity analysis became an acknowledged tool used to study the performance of artificial neural networks. Sensitivity analysis allows to assess the influence, e.g., of each neuron or weight on the final network output. In particular various feature selection and pruning strategies are based on this capability. In this paper, we will present a new approximative sensitivity-based training algorithm yielding robust neural networks with generalization capabilities comparable to its exact analytical counterpart, yet much faster.

Keywords: neural networks, back-propagation, internal representation, sensitivity analysis, feature selection, pruning, generalization.

1 Introduction

In the area of artificial neural networks, sensitivity analysis represents already an established means to assess the significance of each respective parameter for the final system output. In particular various feature selection and pruning strategies make use of this capability when searching for redundant neurons characterized by a low sensitivity that could be removed from the network. On the other hand, reliable neural networks are expected to provide also adequate generalization capabilities accompanied with a low sensitivity to noise in the processed data and a transparent network structure.

For neural networks of the back-propagation type (BP-networks), we developed in [4] and [5] a technique capable of enforcing low network sensitivities already during training – the Sensitivity-based SCG-training algorithm (SCGS). Despite of a high robustness, the trained networks also developed a network structure, that was very easy to prune by the following structure optimizing heuristics. Yet as the proposed SCGS method is computationally extremely demanding, our goal will be to derive a faster approximative sensitivity based training algorithm that preserves, however, the advantages of SCGS.

2 Related Works

The following notation will be used in the paper: the training set T is a finite set of P ordered pairs of input/output patterns: $T = \{[\boldsymbol{x}_1, \boldsymbol{d}_1], \ldots, [\boldsymbol{x}_P, \boldsymbol{d}_P]\}$.

S. Wermter et al. (Eds.): ICANN 2014, LNCS 8681, pp. 507–514, 2014.

A neuron with the weights $(w_1, \ldots, w_n)$, the threshold ϑ and the input vector $z = (z_1, \ldots, z_n)$, computes its potential value as $\xi = \sum_{i=0}^{n} z_i w_i$, where $w_0 = \vartheta$ and $z_0 = 1$. The output neurons have a linear transfer function $y = f(\xi) = \xi$ with the derivative $f'(\xi) = 1$ and the hidden neurons:

$$y = f(\xi) = \frac{1 - e^{-2\xi}}{1 + e^{-2\xi}} \text{ , with the derivative } f'(\xi) \text{ equal to: } f'(\xi) = 1 - y^2 \quad (1)$$

The behavior of standard BP-networks is evaluated by the objective function $E = (1/2) \sum_p \sum_v (y_{v,p} - d_{v,p})^2$, where p indexes the training patterns, v the output neurons, y is their actual and d their desired output value. To clarify the role of hidden neurons in BP-networks, we want to group the outputs of hidden neurons around three possible values: $+1$ (active states), -1 (passive states) and 0 (silent states). Such a kind of internal knowledge representation is called condensed [6] and allows for a clear understanding of the role of each respective neuron in the network.

The criterion for developing a condensed internal representation can be formulated as: $F = \sum_p \sum_{lay} \sum_{h_{lay}} (1 + y_{h_{lay},p})^s (1 - y_{h_{lay},p})^s y_{h_{lay},p}^2$, where p indexes the training patterns and h_{lay} the hidden neurons from the hidden layer lay. y represents their actual output value. s tunes the shape of the representation error function F (a recommended value is $s = 4$). When considering both goals, E and F, during training, the objective function $\hat{H}$ corresponds to: $\hat{H} = E + c_F F$, where c_F reflects the trade-off between the influence of E and F in $\hat{H}$. The negative partial derivatives of E and F with respect to each weight w_{ij} correspond to $-\partial E / \partial w_{ij} = \delta_j y_i$ and $-\partial F / \partial w_{ij} = \varrho_j y_i$:

$$\delta_j = \begin{cases} d_j - y_j & \text{for output neurons} \\ (1 - y_j^2) \sum_k \delta_k w_{jk} & \text{for hidden neurons} \end{cases} \quad (2)$$

$$\varrho_j = \begin{cases} 0 & \text{for output neurons} \\ 2\left[(s+1)y_j^2 - 1\right]\left[(1 - y_j^2)\right]^s y_j & \\ & \text{for neurons in the last hidden layer} \\ (1 - y_j^2) \sum_k \varrho_k w_{jk} + 2\left[(s+1)y_j^2 - 1\right]\left[(1 - y_j^2)\right]^s y_j & \\ & \text{for other hidden neurons} \end{cases} \quad (3)$$

w stands for the weights. i and k index neurons in the layers below and above the neuron j, respectively. y_j is the actual output value of the neuron j and s tunes the shape of the representation error function. In [4], internal representations were enforced in the form of an enhancement of the fast scaled conjugate gradients (SCG) training algorithm [3].

2.1 Feature Selection and Sensitivity Analysis

Very often, practical implementations of neural networks face a serious problem of an excessive task dimensionality. Ideally, the system should learn to ignore redundant and irrelevant inputs by itself. But in practice, superfluous inputs may lead to worse generalization and should be therefore omitted.

A strategy capable of detecting non-linear dependencies among the data [8] measures the influence of network inputs by means of sensitivity coefficients S_{ij} corresponding to the derivatives of the j-th network output y_j with respect to its i-th input x_i: $S_{ij} = \partial y_j / \partial x_i$. Input neurons with sensitivity coefficients close to 0 are considered to be less important and can be pruned from the network. To measure also the curvature, both the first- and second-order partial derivatives of the output variables with respect to the input variables can be used.

The concept of network sensitivities can be, however, applied also during training. [1] uses the sensitivity terms in single-hidden-layer BP-networks to adjust the estimated "desired" output values for the hidden neurons. [9] employs the output sensitivity of a binary feedforward neural network to its parameter variation. The neuron with the highest sensitivity (to the output) will be selected for training, because in this way, the output can be altered the most.

In [4],[5], we proposed a general framework capable of (analytical) sensitivity control in BP-networks with an arbitrary number of hidden layers. The introduced SCGS-method was likely to find an adequate network structure automatically during training. At the same time, the formed network generalized well and supported an easy interpretation of the extracted knowledge, e.g. by means of the formed internal representations. The sensitivity of network output towards its input was controlled by means of the function G:

$$ G = \frac{1}{2} \sum_p \sum_u \sum_v S_{uv,p}^2 = \frac{1}{2} \sum_p \sum_u \sum_v \left(\frac{\partial y_{v,p}}{\partial x_{u,p}} \right)^2 \qquad (4) $$

where p indexes the training patterns, v the output neurons and u the input neurons. y denotes the actual output values while x corresponds to the considered element of the presented input pattern. $S_{uv,p}$ stands for the sensitivity of the output $y_{v,p}$ to the u-th element of the input. The entire objective function H used during SCGIR training had then the form of: $H(\boldsymbol{w}) = E(\boldsymbol{w}) + c_F F(\boldsymbol{w}) + c_G G(\boldsymbol{w})$. E represents the standard BP-error function, F stands for the above-defined representation error function and G corresponds to the network sensitivity criterion to be minimized during training. c_F and c_G reflect the influence of E, F and G in H. Excessive computational demands tied to recursive sensitivity computations within the network pose, however, a significant challenge for this otherwise powerful method.

3 Approximative Sensitivity-Based SCG-Training

In order to avoid the huge complexity of the analytical method, the function G will be replaced in the introduced SCGSA algorithm by an alternative (approximative) expression for the overall network sensitivity. The sensitivity terms

$S_{uv,p} = \partial y_{v,p}/\partial x_{u,p}$ from Equation (4) could be approximated by $(\Delta y_{v,p}/\Delta x_{u,p})$ with $\Delta x_{u,p} = x_{u,p} - x_{u,p}^*$ and $\Delta y_{v,p} = y_{v,p} - y_{v,p}^*$. $x_{u,p}^*$ denotes then the value of $x_{u,p}$ corrupted by a small amount of random noise (within the range of 0.1-1%) and $y_{v,p}^*$ corresponds to the actual network output v determined for the noise-corrupted input pattern x_p^*. In such a case, however, all the denominators $\Delta x_{u,p}$ should be different from zero. To avoid serious rounding problems during training, we chose to minimize for the training patterns rather the ratio between the squared (Euclidean) distances of the outputs, $\sum_v \Delta^2 y_{v,p}$, and the squared (Euclidean) distances of the inputs, $\sum_u \Delta^2 x_{u,p}$, by means of G^A:

$$G^A = \frac{1}{2} \sum_p \frac{\sum_v \Delta^2 y_{v,p}}{\sum_u \Delta^2 x_{u,p}} \tag{5}$$

where p indexes the training patterns, v the output neurons and u the input neurons. y denotes the actual output value of the respective neuron while x corresponds to the considered element of the presented input pattern. For the SCGSA-algorithm, we will thus use the following objective function $H(\boldsymbol{w}) = E(\boldsymbol{w}) + c_F F(\boldsymbol{w}) + c_G G^A(\boldsymbol{w})$ with

$$-\frac{\partial H(\boldsymbol{w})}{\partial w_{ij}} = -\frac{\partial E(\boldsymbol{w})}{\partial w_{ij}} - c_F \frac{\partial F(\boldsymbol{w})}{\partial w_{ij}} - c_G \frac{\partial G^A(\boldsymbol{w})}{\partial w_{ij}} . \tag{6}$$

E represents here the standard BP-error function, F stands for the representation error function and G^A corresponds to the new-proposed network criterion minimized during training. The coefficients c_F and c_G reflect the trade-off between the influence of E, F and G^A in H. The negative partial derivatives $-\partial E/\partial w_{ij}$ and $-\partial F/\partial w_{ij}$ were already stated in Eq. (2)–(3). To inhibit also the sensitivity of the network, we have to determine the term $-\partial G^A/\partial w_{ij}$ as well. By omitting the pattern index p, we obtain:

$$-\partial G^A/\partial w_{ij} = -\left(\sigma_j y_i - \sigma_j^* y_i^*\right), \tag{7}$$

where for an output neuron j: $\sigma_j = \sigma_j^* = \left(\frac{1}{\sum_u \Delta^2 x_u}\right)(y_j - y_j^*)$, while for a hidden neuron j: $\sigma_j = (\sum_k \sigma_k w_{jk})(1 - y_j^2)$ and $\sigma_j^* = (\sum_k \sigma_k^* w_{jk})(1 - y_j^{*2})$. In (7), i indexes neurons connected with the neuron j via the weight w_{ij}. y_j is the actual output value of the neuron j and for i from the input layer, $y_i = x_i$. u denotes the input neurons, x_u is the u-th element of the input. k indexes the neurons from the layer above the neuron j.

4   Supporting Experiments

During testing, the new SCGSA-method was compared with pure scaled conjugate gradients (SCG, $c_F = c_G = 0$), SCG with enforced condensed internal representation (SCGIR, $c_G = 0$) and SCG with the analytical sensitivity control (SCGS). SCG and SCGIR were further tested on extended noisy training data as this might positively influence the network's robustness and generalization capabilities (SCG*, SCGIR*). The extended training set contained for each original training pattern also its copy corrupted by noise (0.1-1% of the original input values), the outputs remained the same. The chosen level of noise kept the input alterations within the same range like SCGSA. In the case of test sets, however, larger amounts of added noise had been involved.

The tested training strategies were enhanced with the following pruning mechanism comprising two repetitive phases: a) training with early stopping (stop, if the error on the validation set has grown for 5 consecutive runs; though for real data affected by a lot of noise other strategies might yield even better results [2]), b) prune the network in the same way like [4] (either according to the developed internal representation that prunes, e.g., neurons yielding always the same output like another neuron from the same hidden layer, or based on low sensitivities that identify limited influence of the network output).

The tests involved 2 types of data: binary and continuous. The Binary Addition data consists of 320 examples with 18 bipolar input features and 4 bipolar output features (the training set contains 192 of them, the validation set 64 and the test set 64). The first 6 input features stand for two three-bit binary numbers and the 4 bits of the output indicate their sum. Each of the 64 possible training patterns is present 3-times in the training set and once in the other two subsets. The other 12 input features are bipolar bits generated randomly with a uniform distribution to examine whether the methods will be able to prune them as irrelevant. All the trained networks had the topology 18-12-4. The Binary Multiplication data has a similar form, however, with 6 bipolar output features. For this task, all the trained networks had the initial topology 18-12-12-6.

The continuous data provided by the World Bank [7] consists of 956 examples with 25 numerical input features encoding the WDI-indicators of 162 different countries from the years 2001-2006. The desired output labels the five classes of the so-called Income Groups. The other 10 input features were generated randomly with a uniform distribution. The results were obtained by a 10-times repeated 10-fold cross-validation. The initial topologies were 35-50-4 and 35-15-15-4. The results obtained for the binary addition and multiplication are stated in Table 1. Table 2 contains the results for the World Bank data.

All the training algorithms and their parameter settings were applied to the same set of 100 different networks randomly initialized for the respective data (with the weights from the interval $[-1, 1]$). The stability test was performed in two steps: first, the networks were trained with SCGS or SCGSA and an experimentally chosen value for $c_G = a * 10^b$. Afterwards, training was repeated with altered values of c_G with the exponent being randomly chosen from the interval $[b - 1, b + 1]$ with a uniform distribution. The tests were run on a 2.8 GHz quad core processor, 12 GB RAM under Matlab 7.0.1.

In the tables, *epochs* denotes the number of training epochs, $t(s)$ is the elapsed training time in seconds and S_t the average (analytical) sensitivity of the network on the test data. Mean squared error on the test and noisy test set (random normally distributed noise within the range of 5%) will be denoted by MSE_t

Table 1. Performance of the SCG, SCGIR, SCGSA and SCGS methods (with pruning) on the Binary addition data (using the 18-12-4 network architecture) and on the Binary multiplication data (using the 18-12-12-6 network architecture). The stated values correspond to the mean and variance over 100 random network initiations.

Binary addition data									
method	c_F	c_G	n_A c_R c_A	MSE_t	$MSE(noise_t)$	imp	S_t	epochs	t(s)
SCG	–	–	20 14 3	0.003 ± 0.017	0.035 ± 0.028	1.0	0.09 ± 0.12	1413.7	5.9
SCG*	–	–	23 25 13	0.001 ± 0.008	0.031 ± 0.035	1.1	0.09 ± 0.09	1312.9	7.1
SCGIR	10^{-6}	–	25 39 18	0.003 ± 0.015	0.036 ± 0.036	1.0	0.08 ± 0.11	1429.2	11.2
SCGIR*	10^{-6}	–	24 29 11	0.001 ± 0.005	0.031 ± 0.036	1.1	0.08 ± 0.08	1384.3	15.6
SCGSA	–	10^{-5}	22 29 12	0.002 ± 0.009	0.028 ± 0.020	**1.2**	0.09 ± 0.09	1308.6	**8.4**
SCGSA	–	$10^{[-6,-4]}$	21 32 13	0.001 ± 0.008	0.029 ± 0.022	**1.2**	0.09 ± 0.07	1292.5	**10.2**
SCGSA	10^{-6}	10^{-5}	19 31 10	0.003 ± 0.015	0.029 ± 0.022	1.2	0.08 ± 0.08	1378.3	13.5
SCGSA	10^{-6}	$10^{[-6,-4]}$	22 27 11	0.003 ± 0.015	0.029 ± 0.024	1.2	0.09 ± 0.07	1395.5	16.7
SCGS	–	$5 \cdot 10^{-7}$	22 33 11	0.002 ± 0.012	0.028 ± 0.022	1.3	0.07 ± 0.07	1636.3	420.5
SCGS	–	$5 \cdot 10^{[-8,-6]}$	25 35 14	0.003 ± 0.014	0.029 ± 0.026	1.2	0.08 ± 0.06	1662.3	431.9
SCGS	10^{-6}	$5 \cdot 10^{-7}$	21 *39* 11	0.002 ± 0.011	0.027 ± 0.020	*1.3*	0.07 ± 0.06	1625.7	*420.1*
SCGS	10^{-6}	$5 \cdot 10^{[-8,-6]}$	24 *38* 14	0.001 ± 0.007	0.027 ± 0.021	*1.3*	0.07 ± 0.06	1750.7	*473.9*
Binary multiplication data									
method	c_F	c_G	n_I c c_n	MSE_t	$MSE(noise_t)$	imp	S_t	epochs	t(s)
SCG	–	–	33 51 0	0.045 ± 0.060	0.297 ± 0.189	1.0	0.28 ± 0.22	601.0	6.1
SCG*	–	–	38 49 0	0.044 ± 0.050	0.300 ± 0.210	1.0	0.26 ± 0.22	601.0	10.4
SCGIR	10^{-6}	–	35 50 0	0.045 ± 0.063	0.301 ± 0.191	1.0	0.28 ± 0.23	601.0	10.5
SCGIR*	10^{-6}	–	33 51 0	0.041 ± 0.055	0.263 ± 0.145	1.1	0.27 ± 0.23	601.0	22.0
SCGSA	–	$5 \cdot 10^{-5}$	30 38 19	0.053 ± 0.061	0.085 ± 0.064	3.5	0.11 ± 0.06	601.0	8.3
SCGSA	–	$5 \cdot 10^{[-6,-4]}$	34 32 4	0.060 ± 0.066	0.101 ± 0.073	2.9	0.11 ± 0.09	600.1	9.1
SCGSA	10^{-6}	$5 \cdot 10^{-5}$	27 42 16	0.047 ± 0.049	0.079 ± 0.053	**3.8**	0.10 ± 0.06	600.8	**13.3**
SCGSA	10^{-6}	$5 \cdot 10^{[-6,-4]}$	38 37 7	0.059 ± 0.062	0.097 ± 0.064	**3.1**	0.11 ± 0.08	599.1	**13.0**
SCGS	–	$5 \cdot 10^{-7}$	34 55 11	0.038 ± 0.048	0.098 ± 0.057	3.0	0.14 ± 0.09	601.0	3733.8
SCGS	–	$5 \cdot 10^{[-8,-6]}$	38 53 9	0.039 ± 0.046	0.110 ± 0.073	2.7	0.15 ± 0.11	601.0	3688.1
SCGS	10^{-6}	$5 \cdot 10^{-7}$	31 53 10	0.038 ± 0.050	0.097 ± 0.060	3.0	0.14 ± 0.09	601.0	3620.7
SCGS	10^{-6}	$5 \cdot 10^{[-8,-6]}$	32 56 8	0.040 ± 0.053	0.110 ± 0.084	2.7	0.16 ± 0.12	601.0	3723.8

and $MSE(noise_t)$, respectively. *imp* is the improvement of the error when compared to the *SCG* method. c and c_n stand for the number of networks with no error on the test and noisy test set, resp. c_R is the number of networks with a well-formed condensed internal representation and no error on the training and test set. c_A is the number of networks with a well-formed condensed internal representation and an optimum number of hidden and input neurons, no errors on the training, validation and test sets. n_I and n_A are the numbers of networks with the optimum number of input / both hidden and input neurons. Based on the results, we can summarize the properties of SCGSA trained networks.

1. set of experiments – on the performance of the networks: Experiments performed so far confirmed that both SCGS and SCGSA techniques significantly improve generalization capabilities of trained networks (indicated by the values of MSE_t, $MSE(noise_t)$ and *imp* in Tables 1 and 2). For *Binary Multiplication*, the SCGSA method even outperformed the SCGS method. Convergence rates (*epochs*) were comparable for all the tests. The time required for SCGSA is comparable with SCG and about 2-3 orders of magnitude lower than for SCGS depending on the network size and character of the data.

2. set of experiments – on the structure of the networks: On average, the finally developed architecture was similar for all the tested methods. In the case of the

Table 2. Performance of the SCG, SCGIR, SCGSA and SCGS methods (with pruning) on the World bank data. The stated values correspond to the mean and variance over 100 random network initiations.

method	c_F	c_G	MSE_t	$MSE(noise_t)$	imp	S_t	epochs	t(s)
Using the 35-50-5 network architecture								
SCG	–	–	0.058 ± 0.017	0.063 ± 0.017	1.00	0.09 ± 0.03	969.0	23.6
SCG*	–	–	0.057 ± 0.017	0.062 ± 0.017	1.02	0.09 ± 0.03	974.5	32.0
SCGIR	10^{-6}	–	0.058 ± 0.017	0.063 ± 0.017	1.00	0.09 ± 0.03	968.0	48.5
SCGIR*	10^{-6}	–	0.057 ± 0.017	0.062 ± 0.018	1.01	0.08 ± 0.03	967.6	78.2
SCGSA	–	$2 \cdot 10^{-4}$	0.050 ± 0.016	0.054 ± 0.015	1.17	0.06 ± 0.03	978.2	35.2
SCGSA	–	$2 \cdot 10^{[-5,-3]}$	0.054 ± 0.018	0.057 ± 0.018	1.10	0.06 ± 0.03	962.3	35.1
SCGSA	10^{-6}	$2 \cdot 10^{-4}$	0.051 ± 0.017	0.055 ± 0.017	**1.14**	0.06 ± 0.02	945.4	**59.0**
SCGSA	10^{-6}	$2 \cdot 10^{[-5,-3]}$	0.053 ± 0.016	0.056 ± 0.016	**1.12**	0.06 ± 0.03	965.2	**58.0**
SCGS	–	10^{-5}	0.048 ± 0.015	0.051 ± 0.016	1.23	0.05 ± 0.02	964.0	2036.0
SCGS	–	$10^{[-6,-4]}$	0.052 ± 0.015	0.054 ± 0.015	1.16	0.05 ± 0.02	955.3	2050.3
SCGS	10^{-6}	10^{-5}	0.048 ± 0.015	0.050 ± 0.016	*1.25*	0.05 ± 0.02	968.4	*1984.2*
SCGS	10^{-6}	$10^{[-6,-4]}$	0.051 ± 0.016	0.054 ± 0.016	*1.17*	0.05 ± 0.02	952.0	*1951.3*
Using the 35-15-15-5 network architecture								
SCG	–	–	0.061 ± 0.037	0.064 ± 0.038	1.00	0.05 ± 0.02	305.1	15.6
SCG*	–	–	0.055 ± 0.019	0.057 ± 0.025	1.11	0.04 ± 0.02	305.9	18.5
SCGIR	10^{-6}	–	0.061 ± 0.037	0.064 ± 0.037	0.99	0.05 ± 0.02	304.5	24.2
SCGIR*	10^{-6}	–	0.060 ± 0.028	0.062 ± 0.029	1.03	0.04 ± 0.02	301.9	33.8
SCGSA	–	10^{-4}	0.050 ± 0.017	0.052 ± 0.022	**1.23**	0.04 ± 0.01	303.4	**19.8**
SCGSA	–	$10^{[-5,-3]}$	0.053 ± 0.028	0.055 ± 0.029	**1.15**	0.04 ± 0.02	304.6	**19.3**
SCGSA	10^{-6}	10^{-4}	0.052 ± 0.023	0.054 ± 0.025	1.19	0.04 ± 0.02	304.1	28.5
SCGSA	10^{-6}	$10^{[-5,-3]}$	0.056 ± 0.033	0.058 ± 0.031	1.11	0.04 ± 0.02	304.7	27.6
SCGS	–	10^{-5}	0.050 ± 0.015	0.050 ± 0.021	*1.26*	0.03 ± 0.01	302.7	*53188.0*
SCGS	–	$10^{[-6,-4]}$	0.060 ± 0.037	0.049 ± 0.034	*1.30*	0.03 ± 0.01	304.4	*54040.0*

Fig. 1. Average values of $MSE(noise_t)$ for various noise levels and the SCG, SCGIR, SCGS, SCGSA, SCG* and SCGIR* methods enhanced with pruning on the Binary addition, Binary multiplication and World Bank data (involving one hidden layer)

World Bank data, even a few more hidden neurons could be pruned when trained with sensitivity control resulting to the architecture of 23-23-5 for one hidden layer and to 21-12-8-5 for two hidden layers, resp. For *Binary Addition*, sensitivity control increases also the chance to form an optimum network structure.

3. set of experiments – on the stability of the networks: Both the SCGS and SCGSA methods are quite stable with respect to the choice of the parameter c_G. For all the experiments, when changing the suboptimal value of c_G even 10-times, we were still able to achieve outstanding results. At the same time, both sensitivity inhibiting techniques confirmed a remarkable stability when tested on data corrupted by various amounts of noise – see Figure 1.

5   Conclusions

The proposed approximative sensitivity-based training algorithm SCGSA proved to develop a transparent network structure and improve generalization similarly to the more precise analytical approach introduced in [4], [5]. Both sensitivity inhibiting techniques (SCGSA and SCGS) outperformed training with noise-corrupted data used traditionally to improve network's generalization. The entire training process required for both cases about the same number of iterations. Anyway, their complexity was much lower for the approximative technique and required about twice the time spent by SCG to train the network.

The actual behavior of the new-proposed method, however, seems to depend on the character of the processed data and on the architecture of the trained network. Based on the experiments performed so far, a higher improvement might be achieved for binary / discrete data and for networks with more hidden layers. SCGSA exhibits, however, a quite stable behavior with regard to the actual choice of training parameters and to noise.

Acknowledgments. This research was partially supported by the Czech Science Foundation under Grant-No P103/10/0783.

References

1. Castillo, E., Guijarro-Berdiñas, B., Fontenla-Romero, O., Alonso-Betanzos, A.: A very fast learning method for neural networks based on sensitivity analysis. Journal of Machine Learning Research 7, 1159–1182 (2006)
2. Dias, F.M., Antunes, A.: Test error versus training error in artificial neural networks for systems affected by noise. Int. J. of Systems Engineering, Applications and Development 2(3), 83–90 (2008)
3. Møller, M.: A scaled conjugate gradient algorithm for fast supervised learning. Neural Networks 6, 525–533 (1993)
4. Mrázová, I., Reitermanová, Z.: A new sensitivity-based pruning technique for feedforward neural networks that improves generalization. In: IJCNN 2011, pp. 2143–2150. IEEE, New York (2011)
5. Mrázová, I., Reitermanová, Z.: Sensitivity-based SCG-training of BP-networks. Procedia Computer Science 6, 177–182 (2011)
6. Mrázová, I., Wang, D.: Improved generalization of neural classifiers with enforced internal representation. Neurocomputing 70(16-18), 2940–2952 (2007)
7. The World Bank Group: World development report 2007/2008. Washington (2008)
8. Yeh, I.C., Cheng, W.L.: First and second order sensitivity analysis of MLP. Neurocomputing 73, 2225–2233 (2010)
9. Zhong, A., Zeng, X., Wu, S., Han, L.: Sensitivity-based adaptive learning rules for binary feedforward neural networks. IEEE Transactions on Neural Networks and Learning Systems 23(3), 480–491 (2012)

Learning Anisotropic RBF Kernels

Fabio Aiolli and Michele Donini

University of Padova, Department of Mathematics
Via Trieste, 63, 35121 Padova, Italy
{aiolli,mdonini}@math.unipd.it

Abstract. We present an approach for learning an anisotropic RBF kernel in a game theoretical setting where the value of the game is the degree of separation between positive and negative training examples. The method extends a previously proposed method (KOMD) to perform feature re-weighting and distance metric learning in a kernel-based classification setting. Experiments on several benchmark datasets demonstrate that our method generally outperforms state-of-the-art distance metric learning methods, including the Large Margin Nearest Neighbor Classification family of methods.

1 Introduction

Kernel machines have gained great popularity in the last decades. Their fortune is greatly due to the possibility to plug general kernels into them. The kernel function represents a priori knowledge about similarities between pairs of examples in a domain.

The most popular kernel is undoubtedly the RBF kernel, which is a general purpose kernel that is based on the Euclidean distance between examples. Similarly to the Euclidean distance, the RBF kernel gives an equal weight to different features and the strength of this weight depends on a single external parameter that needs to be tuned against validation data. However, it is well known that different features typically have unequal impact and importance in solving a given classification task.

This issue has motivated several feature selection methods to select or weight different features in different ways. While feature selection is generally very difficult to perform with nonlinear kernels, one can learn the metric directly from data more easily. This task is known as distance metric learning (DML). For example, many researchers (see [1], [2], [3], [4]) have proposed a number of algorithms for the optimization of the Mahalanobis distance. Specifically, they replace the common Euclidean metric with the more powerful distance $(\mathbf{x}_i - \mathbf{x}_j)^\top \mathbf{M}(\mathbf{x}_i - \mathbf{x}_j)$ and try to learn the combination matrix $\mathbf{M}$. The learned distance in DML is typically optimized for (and used in) a nearest neighbors setting. Given the high number of free parameters to learn together with the fact that these methods are used with nearest neighbors, these approaches can be prone to overfitting, in particular when the training sample is small.

Recently, there have been also attempts to learn the kernel directly from data. In this setting, called kernel learning (KL), one looks for a kernel matrix which maximizes a measure of agreement between training labels and the similarity induced by the learned kernel matrix. This has been done either by optimizing with respect to the notion of

S. Wermter et al. (Eds.): ICANN 2014, LNCS 8681, pp. 515–522, 2014.

alignment ([5],[6]) or minimizing the value of the dual of the objective function of the SVM constructed on the kernel itself ([7]).

In this paper, we propose to combine ideas from DML and KL. Specifically, we focus on the family of anisotropic RBF kernels, that is kernels in the form $K(\mathbf{x}_i, \mathbf{x}_j) = \exp(-(\mathbf{x}_i - \mathbf{x}_j)^T \mathbf{M}(\mathbf{x}_i - \mathbf{x}_j))$ where $\mathbf{M} = \mathbf{diag}(\beta)$ is the diagonal matrix created using the vector $\beta \in \mathbb{R}^m$ of parameters (one value for each feature) to learn. This form generalizes the RBF kernel for which we have $\beta = \beta_0 \mathbf{1}$ being β_0 the external RBF shape parameter and $\mathbf{1}$ the vector with all entries equal to 1. The method proposed extends a recent kernel based algorithm, namely the Kernel Optimization of Margin Distribution (KOMD) method, to learn an *anisotropic RBF* from data. We maintain the same game theoretical setting where two players compete and the value of the game consists of the separation between positive and negative training data.

Definitions and Notation. We consider a classification problem with training examples $\{(\mathbf{x}_1, y_i), \ldots, (\mathbf{x}_l, y_l)\}$, and test examples $\{(\mathbf{x}_{l+1}, y_{l+1}), \ldots, (\mathbf{x}_L, y_L)\}$, $\mathbf{x}_i \in \mathbb{R}^m$, $y_i \in \{-1, +1\}$. We use $\mathbf{X} \in \mathbb{R}^{L \times m}$ to denote the matrix where examples are arranged in rows and $\mathbf{y} \in \mathbb{R}^L$ is the vector of labels. The matrix $\mathbf{K} \in \mathbb{R}^{L \times L}$ denotes the complete kernel matrix containing the kernel values of each data pair. Further, we indicate with an hat, like for example $\hat{\mathbf{X}} \in \mathbb{R}^{l \times m}$, $\hat{\mathbf{y}} \in \mathbb{R}^l$, and $\hat{\mathbf{K}} \in \mathbb{R}^{l \times l}$, the submatrices (or subvectors) obtained considering training examples only. We let $\mathbb{R}_+$ the set of non-negative real numbers. Given a training set, we consider the domain Γ of probability distributions $\gamma \in \mathbb{R}_+^l$ defined over the sets of positive and negative examples. More formally, $\Gamma = \{\gamma \in \mathbb{R}_+^l \mid \sum_{i \in \oplus} \gamma^{(i)} = 1, \sum_{i \in \ominus} \gamma^{(i)} = 1\}$, where $\oplus$ and $\ominus$ are the sets of the indices of positive and negative examples respectively. Finally, we define the submatrix of positive (negative) examples of the matrix $\hat{\mathbf{X}}$ as $\hat{\mathbf{X}}^+$ ($\hat{\mathbf{X}}^-$).

2 Distance Metric Learning

Distance metric learning (DML) methods try to learn the best metric for a specific input space and dataset. The performance of a learning algorithm (nearest-neighbors classifiers, kernel algorithms etc.) mostly depends on the metric used. Many DML algorithms have been proposed. All of them try to find a positive semi-definite (PSD) matrix $\mathbf{M} \in \mathbb{R}^{m \times m}$ such that the induced metric $d_{\mathbf{M}}(\mathbf{x}_i, \mathbf{x}_j) = (\mathbf{x}_i - \mathbf{x}_j)^T \mathbf{M}(\mathbf{x}_i - \mathbf{x}_j)$ is optimal for the task at hand. For example, the Euclidian distance is a special case where $\mathbf{M} = \mathbf{I}$. There are three principal families of DML algorithms [8]: *eigenvector methods*, *convex optimization* and *neighborhood component analysis*.

In the eigenvector methods, the matrix $\mathbf{M}$ is parameterized by the product of a real valued matrix with its transposed, namely $\mathbf{M} = \mathbf{L}^\top \mathbf{L}$, in order to maintain the matrix positive semi-definite. In this case, the matrix $\mathbf{M}$ is called *Mahalanobis metric*. These methods use the covariance matrix to optimize the linear transformation $\mathbf{x}_i \rightarrow \mathbf{L}\mathbf{x}_i$ that projects the training inputs. Finding the optimal projection is the task of eigenvector methods with a constraint that defines $\mathbf{L}$ as a projection matrix: $\mathbf{L}\mathbf{L}^\top = \mathbf{I}$. These algorithms don't use the training labels and then they are totally unsupervised.

Convex optimization algorithms represent another family of DML algorithms. It is possible to formulate a DML as a convex optimization problem over the cone of correct matrices $\mathbf{M}$. This cone is the cone of positive semi-definite matrices, namely $\mathfrak{M} = \{\mathbf{M} \in \mathbb{R}^{m \times m} : \forall \tau \in eig(\mathbf{M}), \tau \geq 0\}$. Algorithms in this family are supervised and optimal positive semi-definite matrix $\mathbf{M}$ is obtained optimizing the square root of the *Mahalanobis metric* and enforcing the SDP constraint $\mathbf{M} \succeq 0$. There are also online versions of convex optimization algorithms for DML, like *POLA* [3] for example.

Another family of algorithms for DML is called neighborhood component analysis. In [2], for example, the authors try to learn a *Mahalanobis metric* from the expected leave-one-out classification error. In this case they use a stochastic variant of k-nearest neighbor with *Mahalanobis metric*. This algorithm has an objective function that is not convex and can suffer from local minima. Metric Learning by Collapsing Classes (MLCC) [1] is an evolution of the above mentioned method that can be formulated by a convex problem but with the hypothesis that the examples in each class have only one mode. Another important algorithm in this family is the Large Margin Nearest Neighbor Classification (LMNNC) [8] that learns a *Mahalanobis distance metric* with a k-nearest neighbor by semi-definite programming and also in this case we have the semi-positive constraint for $\mathbf{M}$ in the optimization problem. Finally, a generalization of the LMNNC is the Gradient Boosted LMNNC (GB-LMNNC) [9] that learns a non-linear transformation directly in the function space. Specifically, it extends the *Mahalanobis metric* between two examples (e.g.: $\|\mathbf{L}\mathbf{x}_i - \mathbf{L}\mathbf{x}_j\|_2$) by using a non linear transformation ϕ to define the new Euclidian distance $\|\phi(\mathbf{x}_i) - \phi(\mathbf{x}_j)\|_2$. Given the non linearity of ϕ, GB-LMNNC uses the gradient boosted regression tree in order to change the metric (GBRT) [10]. So, the algorithm learns and combines an ensemble of multivariate regression trees (that are weak learners) using gradient boosting that minimizes the original LMNN objective function in the function space.

3   The KOMD Algorithm

The KOMD [11] algorithm is a kernel machine that optimizes the margin distribution in a game theoretic setting allowing the user to specify a trade-off between the minimal and the average value of the margin over the training set. Specifically, the classification task is posed as a two-player zero-sum game. The classification task requires to learn a unitary norm vector $\mathbf{w}$ such that $\mathbf{w}^\top (\phi(\mathbf{x}_p) - \phi(\mathbf{x}_n)) > 0$ for most of positive-negative instance pairs in the training data. The scenario of the game consists of one player that choose the vector of unitary norm $\mathbf{w}$ and the other that picks pairs of positive-negative examples according to distributions γ^+ and γ^- over the positive and negative examples, respectively. The value of the game is the expected margin obtained, that is $\mathbf{w}^\top (\phi(\mathbf{x}_p) - \phi(\mathbf{x}_n))$, $\mathbf{x}_p \sim \gamma^+$, $\mathbf{x}_n \sim \gamma^-$. The first player wants to maximize this value while the second one wants to minimize it. This setting generalizes the hard SVM and can be solved efficiently by optimizing a simple regularized and linearly constrained convex function defined on variables γ, namely,

$$\min_{\gamma \in \Gamma} (1 - \lambda) \underbrace{\gamma^\top \mathbf{Y} \hat{\mathbf{K}} \mathbf{Y} \gamma}_{\mathcal{Q}(\gamma)} + \lambda \underbrace{\gamma^\top \gamma}_{\mathcal{R}(\gamma)}.$$

with $\mathbf{Y} = \mathbf{diag}(\hat{\mathbf{y}})$. The regularization parameter λ has two critical points: $\lambda = 0$ and $\lambda = 1$. When $\lambda = 0$, the solution is the hard SVM. In fact, let $\gamma^* \in \Gamma$ the vector that minimizes $\mathcal{Q}(\gamma)$, value of $\mathcal{Q}(\gamma^*)$ in this case is the squared distance between the convex hull enclosing positive points $\phi(\mathbf{x}_p), \mathbf{x}_p \in \hat{\mathbf{X}}^+$, and the convex hull enclosing negative points $\phi(\mathbf{x}_n), \mathbf{x}_n \in \hat{\mathbf{X}}^-$, in the features space induced by the kernel $\mathbf{K}$. When $\lambda = 1$ the optimal solution is analytically defined by the vector of uniform distributions over positive and negative examples, that is, $\gamma_{unif}^{(i)} = 1/|\hat{\mathbf{X}}^+|$ when $y_i = +1$, and $\gamma_{unif}^{(i)} = 1/|\hat{\mathbf{X}}^-|$ when $y_i = -1$. In this case, the optimal objective value is the squared distance from the positive and negative centroids in feature space. The external parameter $\lambda \in (0,1)$ allows to select the correct trade-off between the two extreme cases above. Clearly, a correct selection of this parameter is fundamental if we are interested in finding the best performance for a classification task and this is usually made by validating on training data. In Figure 1 an example of the solutions found by the above algorithm for a toy problem varying the value of λ is depicted.

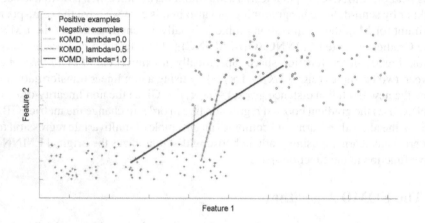

Fig. 1. KOMD solutions found using different λ in a simple toy classification problem

4   Extending the Game to Features

In this paper, we propose to extend the game illustrated in Section 3 by considering an additional player which selects the kernel matrix $\mathbf{K}$ from the family of anisotropic *(Gaussian) Radial Basis Function* kernel (RBF). The RBF kernel is defined by

$$K(\mathbf{x}_i, \mathbf{x}_j) = \exp(-\beta_0 \|\mathbf{x}_i - \mathbf{x}_j\|_2^2) = \exp(-(\mathbf{x}_i - \mathbf{x}_j)^\top \beta_0 \mathbf{I}(\mathbf{x}_i - \mathbf{x}_j))$$

where $\beta_0 \in \mathbb{R}_+$ is an external parameter. The RBF kernel can also be seen as using the trivial metric $\mathbf{M} = \beta_0 \mathbf{I} = \mathbf{diag}(\beta_0, ..., \beta_0)$. In the anisotropic RBF we have a generalized metric $\mathbf{M} = \mathbf{diag}(\beta^{(1)}, ..., \beta^{(m)})$ and we can write the anisotropic RBF as:

$$K_\beta(\mathbf{x}_i, \mathbf{x}_j) = \prod_{r=1}^{m} \exp(-\beta^{(r)}(\mathbf{x}_i^{(r)} - \mathbf{x}_j^{(r)})^2), \quad \boldsymbol{\beta} \in \mathbb{R}_+^m$$

where $\mathbf{x}_i^{(r)}$ is the rth feature of the ith example and $\beta^{(r)} \in \mathbb{R}_+$.

This new formulation has a greater number of degrees of freedom than the classical RBF kernel. A useful observation is that $K_\beta(\cdot, \cdot)$ can be seen as a element-wise product of kernels evaluated on a single feature. More formally:

$$K_\beta = \bigotimes_{r=1}^{m} K_{\beta^{(r)}}$$

with $K_{\beta^{(r)}}$ the RBF kernel defined on the rth feature only with parameter $\beta^{(r)}$. From this point of view, finding the best parameters for an *anisotropic* RBF is a DML problem and we need to optimize the kernel representation by finding a trade-off between the components of β.

We are now interested in an extension of the game presented in a previous section. For this, we define an additional player that sets the parameters of the anisotropic RBF. This player will prefer uncorrelated features so to avoid redundancies. For this reason we define a redundancy (or correlation matrix) $\mathbf{C}$ among the features $f_1, ..., f_m$, defined using an RBF kernel with parameter τ and normalized with respect to the number of features. Basically, each feature is considered as an example in order to generate the correlation matrix $\mathbf{C} \in \mathbb{R}_+^{m \times m}$ such that:

$$\mathbf{C}_{ij} = \exp(-\frac{\tau}{m}\|f_i - f_j\|_2^2) \ \forall i, j = 1, ..., m.$$

Finally, we propose to use the following regularized optimization problem as objective for the player β:

$$\max_{\beta \in \mathbb{R}_+^m} \ \mathcal{Q}(\beta, \gamma) - \mu\mathcal{C}(\beta) \tag{1}$$

where $\mathcal{Q}(\beta, \gamma) = \gamma^\top \mathbf{Y}\mathbf{K}(\beta)\mathbf{Y}\gamma$ and $\mathcal{C}(\beta) = \frac{1}{2}\beta^t \mathbf{C}\beta$.

Note that, the proposed type of regularizer differs significantly from the usual trace regularizer used in kernel learning. In our opinion, the trace regularizer does not fit the notion of complexity in terms of the space of functions that can be generated using a kernel. For example, all RBF kernels have the same trace independently from the RBF parameter weighting the distance between examples, while the complexity of the resulting kernels can be dramatically different. On the other side, the correlation of the features on the parameters β that we propose, well fits the idea that good features are more useful if they represent different points of view of the examples.

Summarizing, the extended game we propose has value $\mathcal{Q}(\beta, \gamma)$ and the two players individually aim at optimizing their strategies according to the following optimization problems:

$$\mathbf{P}_\gamma : \min_{\gamma \in \Gamma} \ (1 - \lambda)\mathcal{Q}(\beta, \gamma) + \lambda\|\gamma\|^2 \tag{2}$$

$$\mathbf{P}_\beta : \max_{\beta \in \mathbb{R}_+^d} \ \mathcal{Q}(\beta, \gamma) - \mu\mathcal{C}(\beta) \tag{3}$$

In the following, we give the simple alternating algorithm we used to solve the multi-objective problem given above.

(0) Find the best β_0 and λ with KOMD validation;

for $t=1,...,T$ **do**

> (1) Set $\beta = \beta_{t-1}$ and generate a solution γ_t optimizing the problem described in Eq. 2;
>
> (2) Set $\gamma = \gamma_t$ and generate a solution β_t optimizing the problem described in Eq. 3;

end

Algorithm 1. ARBF algorithm

4.1 Gradient Based Optimization for P_β

The function $\mathcal{Q}(\beta)$ in Eq. 3 has the rth component of the gradient equal to:

$$\frac{\partial \mathcal{Q}(\beta)}{\partial \beta^{(r)}} = -\sum_{i,j} y_i y_j \gamma^{(i)} \gamma^{(j)} K_\beta(\mathbf{x}_i, \mathbf{x}_j)(\mathbf{x}_i^{(r)} - \mathbf{x}_j^{(r)})^2 = -\gamma^\top \mathbf{Y}(\mathbf{D}_r \otimes \mathbf{K}_\beta)\mathbf{Y}\gamma$$

where $\mathbf{D}_r \in \mathbb{R}^{n \times n}$ is the simmetric matrix of pairwise squared differences of the rth feature, that is, $\mathbf{D}_r(i,j) = (\mathbf{x}_i^{(r)} - \mathbf{x}_j^{(r)})^2$. Then, the partial derivative of Eq. 3 with respect to $\beta^{(r)}$ will be:

$$\frac{\partial \mathcal{Q}(\beta)}{\partial \beta^{(r)}} - \mu \mathbf{C}_r \beta,$$

where $\mathbf{C}_r$ is the rth row of $\mathbf{C}$.

4.2 Reducing the Problem P_β to an Unconstrained Optimization Problem

It is well known that solving a constrained optimization problem with gradient based optimization techniques is particularly difficult. For this, we reduced the problem to an unconstrained one by performing a simple change of variables, that is $\beta^{(r)} = e^{-\alpha^{(r)}}$. Computing the gradient with respect to variables $\alpha^{(r)}$ we obtain

$$\frac{\partial \mathcal{Q}(\alpha)}{\partial \alpha^{(r)}} = \frac{\partial \mathcal{Q}(\beta)}{\partial \beta^{(r)}} \frac{\partial \beta^{(r)}(\alpha)}{\partial \alpha^{(r)}} = (\gamma^\top \mathbf{Y}(\mathbf{D}_r \otimes \mathbf{K}_\beta)\mathbf{Y}\gamma)e^{-\alpha^{(r)}}$$

$$\frac{\partial \mathcal{C}(\alpha)}{\partial \alpha^{(r)}} = \frac{\partial \mathcal{C}(\beta)}{\partial \beta^{(r)}} \frac{\partial \beta^{(r)}(\alpha)}{\partial \alpha^{(r)}} = \mathbf{C}_r \beta e^{-\alpha^{(r)}}$$

which leads to the following update

$$\beta^{(r)} \leftarrow e^{-\alpha^{(r)} - \mu(\frac{\partial \mathcal{Q}(\alpha)}{\partial \alpha^{(r)}} - \frac{\partial \mathcal{C}(\alpha)}{\partial \alpha^{(r)}})} = \beta^{(r)} \Delta_{\beta^{(r)}}$$

where we set $\Delta_{\beta^{(r)}} = e^{-\mu(\frac{\partial \mathcal{Q}(\alpha)}{\partial \alpha^{(r)}} - \frac{\partial \mathcal{C}(\alpha)}{\partial \alpha^{(r)}})}$.

The simple update above leads to an easy update for the kernel as in the following,

$$\mathbf{K}_\beta \leftarrow \mathbf{K}_\beta \otimes \exp((1 - \Delta_{\beta^{(r)}})\mathbf{D}_r)$$

where $\exp(\mathbf{M})$ denotes the element-wise exponential of a matrix $\mathbf{M}$.

5   Experiments and Results

We have performed the evaluation of our algorithm against six benchmark datasets of varying size, typology and complexity, and we have compared our performances with the same experiments performed using other techniques. The datasets used are *splice, ionosphere,* and *diabet* from UCI; *german, australian* and *heart* from Statlog (obtained from LIBSVM website[1]). The datasets have all the features scaled to the interval $[-1, 1]$. For each dataset, we constructed several splits containing 70% of the examples for the training set, 10% of the examples for the validation set and used the remaining 20% of the examples as the test set.

We compared our algorithm **ARBF** at different number of steps T, against the following baselines and state-of-the-art techniques:

- **KOMD**: in this case, model selection has been used to find the best parameters $\lambda \in \{0, 0.1, 0.5, 0.9\}$ and $\beta_0 \in \{0.01, 0.1, 0.5, 1.0\}$. A KOMD with standard RBF (shape parameter β_0) has been trained.
- **K-Raw**: this is kNN without learning any new metric, with validation and model selection to find the best k.
- **K-LMNN** and **K-GB-LMNN**: we used the implementation made by the authors[2] and we performed a model selection in order to find the best k for kNN.

Concerning our method, KOMD validation has been used to obtain the initial parameters (β_0 and λ, see Algorithm 1). The parameters $\mu \in \{1, 10, 100\}$ and $\tau \in \{1, 10, 100, 1000\}$ as been selected by model selection. For each technique a ranking over the examples in the test set is obtained (a function from the test set to $\mathbb{R}$). The Area Under Curve (AUC) metric is used to measure the performance of such a ranking function. AUC represents an estimation of the probability that a rank of a positive example is bigger than a rank of a negative one (both picked randomly). We evaluated AUC metric for each data set with different techniques and we have obtained the results in Table 1 (using $T = 20$ and $T = 50$, called respectively **ARBF**$_{20}$ and **ARBF**$_{50}$) and the convergence curves in Figure 2 with the AUC values for each iteration of our algorithm up to $T = 150$.

Table 1. AUC % (average$_{\pm std}$) obtained against 6 datasets with N_e examples and N_f features

Data set	(N_e, N_f)	KOMD	K-Raw	K-LMNN	K-GB-LMNN	ARBF$_{20}$	ARBF$_{50}$
australian	(690,14)	93.2$_{\pm1.5}$	79.2$_{\pm4.8}$	79.1$_{\pm5.3}$	92.4$_{\pm9.2}$	93.8$_{\pm2.1}$	**94.1**$_{\pm1.6}$
german	(1000,24)	79.5$_{\pm2.2}$	66.3$_{\pm2.6}$	65.5$_{\pm3.0}$	78.9$_{\pm5.6}$	80.5$_{\pm4.1}$	**80.7**$_{\pm2.5}$
splice	(1000,60)	93.7$_{\pm1.5}$	68.1$_{\pm4.7}$	79.7$_{\pm3.5}$	**95.1**$_{\pm2.8}$	94.2$_{\pm1.5}$	**95.1**$_{\pm1.4}$
heart	(270,13)	90.6$_{\pm3.4}$	76.6$_{\pm9.5}$	74.1$_{\pm11.2}$	92.6$_{\pm7.5}$	91.1$_{\pm6.0}$	**93.8**$_{\pm3.7}$
diabet	(768,8)	84.0$_{\pm1.9}$	72.0$_{\pm5.5}$	70.9$_{\pm5.8}$	86.3$_{\pm4.6}$	86.9$_{\pm3.2}$	**87.1**$_{\pm3.1}$
ionosphere	(351,34)	97.5$_{\pm1.4}$	88.4$_{\pm3.8}$	89.3$_{\pm4.3}$	97.3$_{\pm3.8}$	97.7$_{\pm3.5}$	**98.0**$_{\pm3.5}$

According to these results, our method obtains the best performance in all the six datasets and significantly improve on the baseline (KOMD) and other state-of-the-art techniques.

[1] http://www.csie.ntu.edu.tw/~cjlin/libsvmtools/datasets/
[2] http://www.cse.wustl.edu/~kilian/code/code

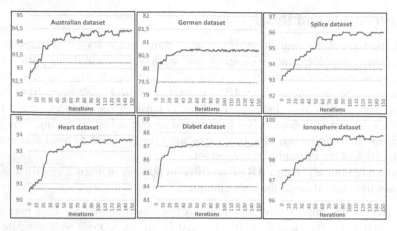

Fig. 2. AUC % values for each iteration of ARBF compared to the KOMD baseline (red dots)

6 Conclusions

We have presented a principled method to learn the parameters of a Anisotropic RBF kernel. We extended an existing kernel based method, namely KOMD, following the same game theoretical ideas used for learning the classifier to learn the kernel. The obtained results seems very promising as most of the times our methods improve the performance of the baseline significantly.

References

1. Globerson, A., Roweis, S.T.: Metric learning by collapsing classes. In: NIPS (2005)
2. Goldberger, J., Roweis, S.T., Hinton, G.E., Salakhutdinov, R.: Neighbourhood components analysis. In: NIPS (2004)
3. Shalev-Shwartz, S., Singer, Y., Ng, A.Y.: Online and batch learning of pseudo-metrics. In: ICML (2004)
4. Domeniconi, C., Gunopulos, D.: Adaptive nearest neighbor classification using support vector machines. In: NIPS, pp. 665–672 (2001)
5. Cristianini, N., Shawe-Taylor, J., Elisseeff, A., Kandola, J.S.: On kernel-target alignment. In: NIPS, pp. 367–373 (2001)
6. Shawe-Taylor, J., Cristianini, N.: Kernel Methods for Pattern Analysis. Cambridge University Press (2004)
7. Lanckriet, G.R.G., Cristianini, N., Bartlett, P.L., El Ghaoui, L., Jordan, M.I.: Learning the kernel matrix with semidefinite programming. Journal of Machine Learning Research 5, 27–72 (2004)
8. Weinberger, K.Q., Saul, L.K.: Distance metric learning for large margin nearest neighbor classification. Journal of Machine Learning Research 10, 207–244 (2009)
9. Kedem, D., Tyree, S., Weinberger, K., Sha, F., Lanckriet, G.: Non-linear metric learning. In: Bartlett, P., Pereira, F.C.N., Burges, C.J.C., Bottou, L., Weinberger, K.Q. (eds.) Advances in Neural Information Processing Systems 25, pp. 2582–2590 (2012)
10. Friedman, J.H.: Greedy function approximation: A gradient boosting machine. Annals of Statistics 29, 1189–1232 (2000)
11. Aiolli, F., Da San Martino, G., Sperduti, A.: A kernel method for the optimization of the margin distribution. In: Kůrková, V., Neruda, R., Koutník, J. (eds.) ICANN 2008, Part I. LNCS, vol. 5163, pp. 305–314. Springer, Heidelberg (2008)

Empowering Imbalanced Data in Supervised Learning: A Semi-supervised Learning Approach

Bassam A. Almogahed and Ioannis A. Kakadiaris

Computational Biomedicine Lab, Dept. of Computer Science, Univ. of Houston, USA

Abstract. We present a framework to address the imbalanced data problem using semi-supervised learning. Specifically, from a supervised problem, we create a semi-supervised problem and then use a semi-supervised learning method to identify the most relevant instances to establish a well-defined training set. We present extensive experimental results, which demonstrate that the proposed framework significantly outperforms all other sampling algorithms in 67% of the cases across three different classifiers and ranks second best for the remaining 33% of the cases.

1 Introduction

The class imbalance problem occurs when samples from one class in a dataset significantly outnumber samples from another. Most learning systems are greatly biased when applied to imbalanced datasets [1]. Specifically, models trained from imbalanced datasets strongly favor the majority class, while largely ignoring the minority class [2].

Several approaches offer solutions at both the algorithmic and data levels [1]. Typical algorithmic methods adjust how the existing algorithm operates to make the classifier more conducive to the classification of the minority class [3, 4].

The main drawback of this category of approaches is that they require special knowledge of both the application domain and the corresponding classifier. Conversely, data-preprocessing methods can be grouped into two categories: over-sampling (OS) [5, 6] and under-sampling (US) [7, 8, 9]. The data-preprocessing approach has garnered more investigation since it is classifier-independent and can be easily implemented for any problem [9]. The main problem of data-preprocessing solutions is that they artificially alter the original class distribution. US may exclude potentially useful data [10], which could be important for the model training process, and engender low performance of the classifier. OS, on the other hand, expands the size of the training set, consequently increasing the time required to build models, and potentially causing an over-fitting problem. However, the disadvantages of these two approaches can be countered by using more intelligent sampling strategies.

The simplest strategy to broaden the minority class is random OS (ROS) [8]. Although efficacious, the main drawback of this method is that it increases the likelihood of over-fitting. The most commonly used over-sampling method is

S. Wermter et al. (Eds.): ICANN 2014, LNCS 8681, pp. 523–530, 2014.

Synthetic Minority Over-sampling Technique (SMOTE) [2]. SMOTE synthesizes new minority class examples using several neighboring minority examples, rather than simply duplicating them as is done in ROS [11]. SMOTE is highly effective, but may cause an over-generalization problem due to its creation of synthetic data, resulting in increased overlap between the two classes [12]. To overcome this challenge, recent literature has proposed several ameliorations, including the Borderline SMOTE (B-SMOTE) algorithm [7], and adaptive synthetic (ADASYN) [13]. Conversely, US techniques aim to balance a dataset by removing instances that will not cause the classifier to miss important concepts pertaining to the majority class. Some of the classic US methods for balancing class distribution are: Random Under-Sampling (RUS), One-Sided Selection (OSS) [5], Class Purity Maximization (CPM) [14], NearMiss-2 [15], and Under-Sampling Based on Clustering (SBC) [16].

A successful US technique retains all minority examples and prunes only unreliable majority examples which: (i) suffer from the class-label noise, (ii) are *redundant*, such that their part can be taken over by other examples, (iii) are *borderline* (i.e., close to the boundary between the minority and majority regions), and (iv) borderline examples from the majority class in the *overlapping* regions between classes (in particular for non-linear decision boundaries). This latter category can also plague synthetic examples created by the OS techniques mentioned above. Categories (i) through (iii) above are not as harmful to classifier performance as category (iv); they can be easily detected and eliminated by the *Tomek links* concept [17]. Any performance degradation is caused mainly by the overlap between the imbalanced classes. More recent experiments on artificial data with different degrees of overlapping have demonstrated that overlapping is more important than the overall imbalance ratio [18].

This paper sets forth a new framework which addresses these issues while making no prior assumptions. Our approach is to create a semi-supervised learning problem from an unbalanced supervised problem and then solve it to further remove the overlapping instances from the critical areas, thus establishing a more balanced and well-defined dataset. Our approach can be integrated into both OS and US techniques, regardless of their varied settings. Due to space limitations, we will only demonstrate the integration of the US technique with semi-supervised learning (SSL). We will present the integration of over-sampling in a longer version of the paper.

2   Methodology

Overview: Traditionally, SSL is of interest when a dataset has both labeled and unlabeled data. It can potentially utilize both labeled and unlabeled data to achieve better performance than supervised learning. The key to SSL is that it allows for exploitation into the geometric structure of the data distribution. Close data points should belong to the same class and decision boundaries should lie in regions of low data density [19].

The targeted datasets are all initially labeled, but they are yet imbalanced. With under-sampling, we create unlabeled data by stripping the labels from the

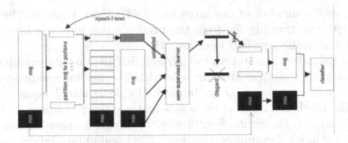

Fig. 1. Illustration of the US-SSL algorithm

majority class instances. As such, the problem is transformed from supervised to semi-supervised. It is then solved to identify and remove borderline instances, especially those which overlap largely with the minority instances (Fig. 1).

US and SSL can each be viewed as possessing the common goal of drastically compressing data without losing the underlying information. All learning strategies must therefore be based on a belief in the hidden inherent simplicity of relationships $P(A|B)$. Our method will take advantage of this concept to undersample the data using SSL. We will refer to this technique as US-SSL. In this method, removing overlapping examples establishes well-defined class clusters in the training set, which leads to well-defined classification rules.

SSL: We will extend three algorithms from the existing paradigms to demonstrate the effectiveness of our approach: Local and Global Consistency (LGC) [19], Yet Another Two-Stage Idea (YATSI) [20], and Semi-Supervised Learning via Random Forests (SSLRF) [21].

(i) LGC: A graph-based approach where the graph G is fully connected, with no self-loop. The edges of G are weighted with a positive and symmetric function w which represents a pairwise relationship between the vertices. The key point of the method is to let every point iteratively spread its label information to its neighbors until a global state is reached. The weights are scaled by a parameter σ for propagation. During each iteration, each point receives the information from its neighbor and also retains its initial information. A parameter α allows for adjustment of the relative amount of information provided by the neighbors and the initial point. When convergence is reached, each unlabeled point is assigned the label of the class it has received the most information for during the iteration process [19].

(ii) YATSI: An algorithm that uses one classifier for labeling the test data after training on the training set. In the initializing step, all instances from the test set have a weight of 0. In each subsequent step, they get a weight of *current step / number of steps*. This implies that all provided classifiers need to be able to handle weighted instances [20].

(iii) SSLRF: A collective classifier which uses Random Trees to build predictions on the test set. It divides the test set into folds and successively adds the test instances with the best predictions to the training set. The first iteration trains solely on the training set and determines the distributions for all the instances in the test set. From these predictions the best are chosen (this number

is the same as the number of instances in a fold). From then on, the classifier is trained with the training file from the previous run plus the best instances determined during the previous iteration [21].

US-SSL: Consider the dataset D which contains all minority examples and all remaining majority examples after the redundant, borderline and noisy examples are removed. All examples in D are labeled. Divide D into k equal sets of size $1/k$. Strip the labels from one of these sets and use the remaining $k - 1$ sets to relabel it via an SSL algorithm. Specifically, we have k datasets of size X where $X = (X_l, X_u)$ of labeled examples $X_l = \{x_1, ..., x_l\}$ and unlabeled examples $X_u = \{x_{l+1}, ..., x_n\}$, along with the corresponding class labels $\{y_1, ..., y_l\}$, where y_i in our settings has two possible classes: either positive (minority) or negative (majority). After a semi-supervised method is applied in each dataset X_1 to X_k, all examples in D are then labeled. The safe negative examples are more likely to keep their labels. The examples in the overlapping regions between classes, and those located farther from the decision boundary, will be relabeled as positive examples if they are closer to the minority examples or lie in regions in decision boundaries of low minority density. These mislabeled majority examples are removed from D. The resulting set T is used as the training set for the corresponding imbalance problem (Fig. 1). If further under-sampling is desired to achieve a specific balance ratio, RUS is then used to remove additional majority examples. To better observe the effect of US-SSL, we provide an example of a training dataset (vehicle1) with 677 majority examples and 137 minority examples (Fig. 2). The blue circles represent the majority group, and the red squares represent the minority group. (a) is the original dataset, (b) - (f) are the top 5 algorithms in terms of performance (not ordered). The proposed US-SSL variations - (d), (e) and (f) - always perform in the top three among all classifiers tested.

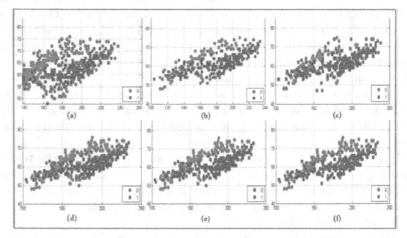

Fig. 2. Comparison of different US mechanisms (the blue circles represent the majority group and the red squares represent the minority group): (a) original imbalanced data distribution, (b) data distribution after OSS method, (c) data distribution after RUS method, (d) data distribution after US-LGC method, (e) data distribution after US-SSLRF method, and (f) data distribution after US-YATSI method

US-SSL Implementation Details:

1. Let S be the original training set.
2. Remove redundant examples and all negative examples participating in Tomek links (this removes those negative examples that are believed to be borderline and/or noisy). The resulting set D will have the remaining negative examples and all positive examples.
3. Divide D into k equal-sized sets.
4. Iteratively strip the labels of $1/k$ set and create a dataset X, where $k - 1$ sets are labeled and one set is unlabeled.
5. Apply a semi-supervised algorithm to relabel the stripped label set.
6. Remove all majority examples that were relabeled as minority, and generate a new training set T which will be used to build the prediction model for the imbalance problem.

3   Results

Experimental Setup: We obtained the fourteen datasets used in our empirical study from the UCI repository [22]. All original multi-class datasets were first transformed into two-class problems. If the original dataset had multiple classes, we combined all classes except one, which became the minority class. The data from the rest of the classes are considered the majority. Table 1 summarizes the characteristics of the datasets, where (A) is the number of samples, (B) is the number of minority samples, (C) is the imbalance ratio, and (D) is the number of attributes.

Three different well-known classifiers were used: C4.5, Random Forest (RF) and SVM [23]. We used the Waikato Environment for Knowledge Analysis (WEKA) implementation for the three algorithms [23]. These different classification algorithms allowed us to compare our approach to other methods which are able to handle misclassification costs directly. We have adopted a five-fold cross validation technique to estimate the AUC measure. Each fold is divided into $k = 20$ equal sets of size $1/20$ for the relabeling step via the SSL algorithm. Each classifier has been applied to the original (imbalanced) training datasets and also to the preprocessed datasets using state-of-the-art US techniques. We integrated the three SSL algorithms described earlier into our framework to demonstrate the effectiveness of our approach. All

Table 1. Imbalanced datasets

Dataset	A	B	C	D
Glass-0	214	4	2.06	9
Ecoli-1	336	11	3.36	7
LetterA	20,000	789	3.95	17
Thyroid-2	215	10	4.92	5
PC1	1,109	77	6.94	21
Glass-3	214	17	7.94	10
Yeast-3	1,484	120	8.11	8
Ecoli-3	336	27	8.19	7
Page-blocks	5,472	479	8.77	10
Satimage-4	6,435	626	9.73	37
CM1	498	49	9.83	22
Vehicle1	846	181	21.30	18
ILPD	583	167	28.60	10
Liver Disorder	345	144	41.70	7

Table 2. Average AUC values

	C4.5	RF	SVM
Imbalanced	0.720	0.764	0.600
CPM	0.678	0.732	0.596
NearMiss-2	0.669	0.671	0.672
OSS	0.772	0.790	0.721
RUS	0.788	**0.808**	**0.745**
SBC	0.581	0.591	0.552
US-LGC	0.738	0.770	0.698
US-SSLRF	**0.791**	**0.808**	0.732
US-YATSI	0.772	0.791	0.736

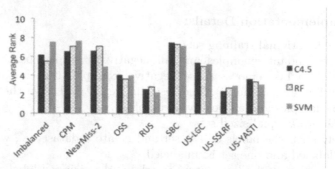

Fig. 3. Friedman's average ranks for the three classifiers

Table 3. US-SSL results obtained from the Wilcoxon signed-rank test

Algorithm	z	p value (10^3)	Algorithm	z	p value (10^3)	Algorithm	z	p value (10^3)
C4.5 (US-SSLRF is the control method)			RF (US-SSLRF is the control method)			SVM (US-SSLRF is the control method)		
Imbalanced	-3.849	0	Imbalanced	-6.380	0	Imbalanced	-5.958	0
CPM	-6.721	0	CPM	-6.172	0	CPM	-5.480	0
NearMiss-2	-5.761	0	NearMiss-2	-6.702	0	RUS	-4.820	0
SBC	-6.902	0	OSS	-5.189	0	SBC	-5.170	0
US-LCG	-4.778	0	SBC	-6.006	0	OSS	-2.451	14
OSS**	-1.553	121	US-LCG	-6.730	0	US-LCG**	-1.699	89
US-YATSI**	-1.520	129	RUS	-3.735	2	US-YATSI**	-1.615	105
RUS**	-0.154	881	US-YATSI**	-1.427	153	NearMiss-2**	-0.859	390

techniques have been applied to the datasets so that they are balanced to the 50% distribution, where we remove majority instances until the two class distributions are approximately equal. In our analysis, we use the AUC measure as an evaluation criterion (Table 2).

We applied Friedman's ranking of the algorithms for each dataset independently, according to the AUC results, to evaluate how well our algorithms ranked compared to the other algorithms (Fig. 3). Next, to support our findings, we used the non-parametric statistical test - Wilcoxon's paired signed rank test with a 95% confidence level - to asses the statistically significant differences between each pair of the US algorithms (Table 3).

Discussion: Table 2 presents the average AUC values across all datasets obtained with the three classifiers using different sampling approaches. US-SSLRF significantly outperformed other US algorithms for C4.5 and Random Forest classifier, followed by RUS and US-YATSI. In the case of SVM, the US-SSLRF and US-YATSI algorithms ranked second and third after RUS, respectively LGC did not perform as well as the SSLRF and YATSI semi-supervised algorithms, due to its sensitivity to the initial labels and label class imbalance [19].

The Friedman's average ranks for the three classifiers are depicted in Fig. 3. This serves as further confirmation of the findings with regard to the AUC. Among the US algorithms, US-SSLRF has the best overall ranking, followed by RUS and US-YATSI. Imbalanced datasets produced the highest average ranks (worst performance) with all classifiers.

For the non-parametric Wilcoxon signed-rank test, Table 3 reports the z-values and the p-values obtained, where the symbol "**" indicates that the null-hypothesis of equivalence with the control algorithm is not rejected at a significance level of $\alpha = 0.05$ (no significant difference between the two methods).

The Wilcoxon test results reveal the higher performance of US-SSLRF and US-YATSI over all other US approaches with Random Forest. With C4.5, US-SSLRF performs significantly better than all other algorithms, except RUS, US-YATSI and OSS, which behave equally well. For SVM, the presented three SSL algorithms and NearMiss-2 outperform all other techniques.

As a general framework, US-SSL improves the classification performance for imbalanced datasets. Two of the three semi-supervised learners proposed outperformed all other algorithms (or performed equally well). No one algorithm performed the best in all given datasets. Generally, given an imbalanced dataset, it is difficult to determine which sampling technique should to be used. This proposed framework has great potential to solve this problem. By knowing the underlying structure of the dataset, we can choose the most suitable semi-supervised learner based on which category of learner has already been established as performing well for the given structure.

4   Conclusion

We presented a novel framework which integrates semi-supervised learning and US techniques to improve classification performance for imbalanced datasets. Specifically, SSL is used to identify the most relevant instances in the majority. By removing overlapping examples, we establish a well-defined training set. The results support our analysis and indicate that the frameworks we have proposed provide statistically significant improvements. Aside from extending the algorithm to multi-class imbalanced classification problems, further significant enhancements and expansions to the current algorithm could include determining which imbalanced datasets are most likely to take advantage of this approach and the corresponding SSL method that should be used.

Acknowledgments. This research was funded in part by the US Department of Education (P200A070377 and P200A100119) with cost sharing provided by the University of Houston (UH) and the UH Hugh Roy and Lillie Cranz Cullen Endowment Fund.

References

[1] He, H., Garcia, E.A.: Learning from imbalanced data. IEEE Transactions on Knowledge and Data Engineering 21(9), 1263–1284 (2009)

[2] Chawla, N., Bowyer, K.W., Hall, L.O., Kegelmeyer, W.P.: SMOTE: Synthetic minority over-sampling technique. Journal of Artificial Intelligence Research 16, 321–357 (2002)

[3] Oh, S.: Error back-propagation algorithm for classification of imbalanced data. Neurocomputing 74(6), 1058–1061 (2011)

[4] Elkan, C.: The foundations of cost-sensitive learning. In: Proc. International Joint Conference on Artificial Intelligence, Seattle, WA, vol. 17, pp. 973–978 (August 2001)

[5] Kubat, M., Matwin, S.: Addressing the curse of imbalanced training sets: One-sided selection. In: Proc. 14th International Conference on Machine Learning, Nashville, TN, USA, July 8-12, pp. 179–186 (1997)

[6] Yen, S., Lee, Y., Lin, C., Ying, J.: Investigating the effect of sampling methods for imbalanced data distributions. In: Proc. IEEE International Conference on Systems, Man and Cybernetics, Taipei, vol. 5, pp. 4163–4168 (October 2006)

[7] Han, H., Wang, W.-Y., Mao, B.-H.: Borderline-SMOTE: A new over-sampling method in imbalanced data sets learning. In: Huang, D.-S., Zhang, X.-P., Huang, G.-B. (eds.) ICIC 2005. LNCS, vol. 3644, pp. 878–887. Springer, Heidelberg (2005)

[8] Batista, G., Prati, R., Monard, M.C.: A study of the behavior of several methods for balancing machine learning training data. ACM SIGKDD Explorations Newsletter 6(1), 20–29 (2004)

[9] García, V., Sánchez, J.S., Mollineda, R.A.: On the effectiveness of preprocessing methods when dealing with different levels of class imbalance. Knowledge-Based Systems 25(1), 13–21 (2012)

[10] Weiss, G.M.: Mining with rarity: A unifying framework. ACM SIGKDD Explorations Newsletter 6(1), 7–19 (2004)

[11] Holte, R.C., Acker, L.E., Porter, B.W.: Concept learning and the problem of small disjuncts. In: Proc. 11th International Joint Conference on Artificial Intelligence, Detroit, vol. 1 (August 1989)

[12] Wang, B.X., Japkowicz, N.: Imbalanced data set learning with synthetic samples. In: Proc. IRIS Machine Learning Workshop, Canada (June 2004)

[13] He, H., Bai, Y., Garcia, E.A., Li, S.: ADASYN: adaptive synthetic sampling approach for imbalanced learning. In: Proc. IEEE International Joint Conference on Neural Networks, Hong Kong, pp. 1322–1328 (June 2008)

[14] Yoon, K., Kwek, S.: An unsupervised learning approach to resolving the data imbalanced issue in supervised learning problems in functional genomics. In: Proc. Hybrid Intelligent Systems, p. 6. Rio de Janeiro, Brazil (2005)

[15] Mani, I., Zhang, I.: Knn approach to unbalanced data distributions: A case study involving information extraction. In: Proc. Proceedings of Workshop on Learning from Imbalanced Datasets, Washington DC (January 2003)

[16] Yen, S., Lee, Y.: Under-sampling approaches for improving prediction of the minority class in an imbalanced dataset. In: Huang, D.-S., Li, K., Irwin, G.W. (eds.) ICIC 2006. LNCIS, vol. 344, pp. 731–740. Springer, Heidelberg (2006)

[17] Tomek, I.: Two modifications of CNN. IEEE Trans. Syst. Man Cybern. 6, 769–772 (1976)

[18] Ramanna, S., Jain, L.C., Howlett, R.J.: Emerging paradigms in machine learning. Springer Publishing Company, Incorporated (2012)

[19] Zhou, D., Bousquet, O., Navin Lal, T., Scholkopf, B.: Learning with local and global consistency. Advances in Neural Information Processing Systems 16(16), 321–328 (2004)

[20] Driessens, K., Reutemann, P., Pfahringer, B., Leschi, C.: Using weighted nearest neighbor to benefit from unlabeled data. In: Ng, W.-K., Kitsuregawa, M., Li, J., Chang, K. (eds.) PAKDD 2006. LNCS (LNAI), vol. 3918, pp. 60–69. Springer, Heidelberg (2006)

[21] Leistner, C., Saffari, A., Bischof, H.: Semi-supervised random forests. In: Proc. 12th International Conference on Computer Vision, Kyoto, Japan, pp. 506–513 (October 2009)

[22] Murphy, P.M., Aha, D.W.: UCI repository of machine learning databases. Machine-readable repository. University of California, Department of Information and Computer Science, Irvine (1992)

[23] Hall, M., Frank, E., Holmes, G., Pfahringer, B., Reutemann, P., Witten, H.: WEKA data mining software. ACM SIGKDD Explorations Newsletter 11(1), 10–18 (2009)

A Geometrical Approach for Parameter Selection of Radial Basis Functions Networks

Luiz C.B. Torres, André P. Lemos, Cristiano L. Castro, and Antônio P. Braga

Federal University of Minas Gerais, Department of Electronics Engineering
Av. Antonio Carlos, 6627, Pampulha 30161-970, Belo Horizonte, MG, Brazil
{luizlitc,crislcastro}@gmail.com, andrepl@cpdee.ufmg.br,
apbraga@ufmg.br

Abstract. The RBF network is commonly used for classification and function approximation. The center and radius of the activation function of neurons is an important parameter to be found before the network training. This paper presents a method based on computational geometry to find these coefficients without any parameters provided by the user. The method is compared with a SVM and experimental results showed that our approach is promising.

Keywords: machine learning, classification, RBF neural network, gabriel graph.

1 Introduction

Radial Basis Function (RBF) neural networks performs data mapping from the input space $\mathbb{R}^n$ to a high dimensionality feature space $\mathbb{R}^m$ (usually $m >> n$). In the feature space, the problem may become linearly separable according to Cover's Theorem [7]. This is also the basic principle of Support Vector Machines (SVM) [6] which uses kernels in order to induce a nonlinear mapping followed by the estimation of a maximum margin separating hyperplane.

In contrast to Multilayer Perceptron (MLP) neural networks, which can be designed with more than one hidden layer, RBFs are typically formulated with only a single hidden layer (Fig. 1 shows an example). In order to construct an RBF, it is first necessary to specify the number of hidden neurons or basis functions $\varphi(\cdot)$. Usually, $\varphi(\cdot)$ is described as a Gaussian function $\varphi(\mathbf{x}) = \exp\left(-\frac{\|\mathbf{x}-c_i\|^2}{2\sigma_i^2}\right)$, so that its parameters, represented by the centers c_i and the radius σ_i, should be specified.

Earlier studies in the literature for determining c_i are typically based on clustering algorithms like K-Means and its variations [11], such as Fuzzy C-means (FCM), Self-Organizing Maps (SOM) network [4] and Winner-Takes-All (WTA). However, it is worth noticing that the use of such methods is dependent on the specification of at least one parameter a priori: the number of centers k. The radius σ_i, in turn, is usually determined empirically or based on the relative distances among centers. Another methodology which has been commonly used to obtain the parameters c_i and σ_i is cross-validation [10].

S. Wermter et al. (Eds.): ICANN 2014, LNCS 8681, pp. 531–538, 2014.

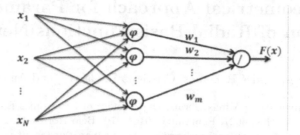

Fig. 1. Topology of the RBF network

In order to overcome the difficulties in determining the parameters of RBFs, this paper presents a new strategy aimed at classification problems. The optimum values of c_i and σ_i are found without the need of specifying any priori information. By using Computational Geometry principles [8], our method aims at searching for patterns that are in the separation region between the classes, and to assign them as centers of the RBF basis functions $\varphi(\cdot)$. Besides not needing additional parameters for obtaining the centers, our approach uses the geometric coordinates of each margin sample in order to obtain the corresponding σ_i for each neuron. A preliminary experimental study with known benchmarks from the literature, show that the proposed method is promising. The results obtained are compared with SVMs.

This paper is organized as follows. Section 2 presents the new methodology proposed in this paper to find the parameters of RBFs. In Section 3 is described the methodology adopted in conducting the experiments and the results obtained from the application of the new method. Finally, the main conclusions are provided in Section 4.

2   Proposed Methodology

SVM's approach ensures maximum margin for a given parameter setting. However, most often it is necessary user experience and exhaustive search, such as cross-validation, to set parameters. From the geometrical perspective, support vectors (SV) yielded by SVM's training are the set of closest examples of the decision boundary [3], [9]. The methodology proposed in this paper searches for the samples in the separation margin between classes. The corresponding "support vectors" obtained geometrically, and named here as Geometric Vectors (GV), are used to find the parameters of RBF network without user interference or exhaustive search. This algorithm can be formulated according to the following steps:

1. The data set is transformed into a graph called Gabriel Graph (G_G), as shown in Fig. 2(a). Let the vertex set V be composed of all input patterns $V = \{\mathbf{x}_i \mid i = 1 \ldots N\}$, and the set of edges E that satisfy the condition

$$(v_i, v_j) \in E \leftrightarrow \delta^2(v_i, v_j) \leq \left[\delta^2(v_i, z) + \delta^2(v_j, z)\right] \; \forall \, z \in V, v_i, v_j \neq z \quad (1)$$

where $\delta(\cdot)$ is the Euclidean distance between the vertices.

2. This step of algorithm is responsible for detecting and removing the noise from the data. For all $\mathbf{x}_i \in V$, analyze the subgraph induced by the vertex $\mathbf{x}_i$, i.e, the subgraph formed by the edges that have $\mathbf{x}_i$ as one of the ends. If most of the neighbors (adjacent vertices $\mathbf{x}_i$) has different label of $\mathbf{y}_i$, then $\mathbf{x}_i$ is considered as noise and eliminated of V. This step should be repeated until there are no more exclusion.

3. The geometric vectors (GV) are found as follows: let $\mathbf{x}_i \in V$ and $\forall \, \mathbf{x}_j \in V$ with $j \neq i$, if the edge $(\mathbf{x}_i, \mathbf{x}_j)$ is formed by distinct classes of vertices (with different labels), then it is included in the set GV.

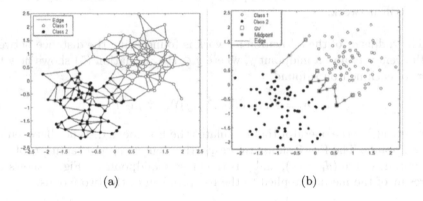

(a)   (b)

Fig. 2. (a) Set of input patterns modeled with the Gabriel graph. (b) Midpoints and Geometric Vectors (GV).

4. In this step, the algorithm calculates the midpoints between the vertices of the set GV. For all edges $(\mathbf{x}_i, \mathbf{x}_j)$ belonging to the set GV, the midpoint between the vertices $\mathbf{x}_i$ e $\mathbf{x}_j$ is calculated according the following expression,

$$\bar{\mathbf{x}}_{ij} = \sum_{t=1}^{n} \mu(\mathbf{x}_i(t), \mathbf{x}_j(t)) \quad (2)$$

where n is the number of attributes of the input patterns and $\mu(\cdot)$ is the operator that computes the average to t^{th} attribute. After calculating the midpoints for all edges GV, the algorithm obtains a set of midpoints (P_M) concerning the edges of the classes, as shown in Fig. 2(b).

5. Let V be the set resulting from step 2, the Equations (3) and (4) below provide the data input and output for training the RBF network,

$$X = [V \cup P_M], \ V \cap P_M = \emptyset \tag{3}$$

$$Y = \begin{cases} -1 & \text{if } \mathbf{x}_i \in V \ e \ \mathbf{y}_i = -1 \\ 1 & \text{if } \mathbf{x}_i \in V \ e \ \mathbf{y}_i = 1 \\ 0 & \text{if } \mathbf{x}_i \in P_M \end{cases} \tag{4}$$

where X is the union of all samples of V and P_M, Y is the set of labels, where $\mathbf{y}_i \in Y$ and $\mathbf{y}_i = 0$ if $\mathbf{x}_i \in X$ is a midpoint.

6. Each element of the set GV is used as the center of activation function of the neurons of the RBF network, i.e, each example that belongs to the edge is a center $c_i \in GV$ for activation function φ_i of a neuron network. The number of samples in the set (GV) is equal to the number m of hidden layer neurons of RBF network.

7. The radius σ_i of the ith neuron network is found using the distance between the center c_i and a midpoint j, where $j \in P_M$. Equation (5) shows how the σ_i of each neuron is found.

$$\sigma_i = 2(\min \delta(c_i, P_M(j))), \ \forall j \in P_M \tag{5}$$

where $\delta(.)$ is the operator that calculates the Euclidean distance between the two points. The Fig. 3 shows the respective centers c_i and radius σ_i of each neuron, where $(d_i = \sigma_i)$, and j is the closest midpoint c_i. Fig. 4 shows the result of the method applied to the toy problem of the two moons.

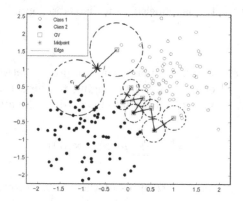

Fig. 3. Centers and radius of the activation functions of neurons in the hidden layer

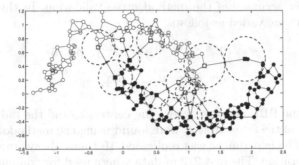

Fig. 4. Proposed methodology applied to the toy problem of two moons

3   Results

Most of the databases where obtained at the public UCI benchmark repository
[2]. The database "Appendicitis data set" was obtained from the Keel Data Set
Repository [1]. These databases are referenced in many papers in the literature, which makes them a good benchmark for this work. All databases used in
the work are binary, they are: Stalog Australian Credit (acr), Bupa liver dis-
orders (bld), The Statlog Heart Disease (hea), The Johns Hopkins University
ionosphere (ion), The Pima Indians Diabetes (pid), The Wisonsin Breast cancer (wbc) and Appendicitis data set (adc). All bases were preprocessed. The
examples containing missing attributes were removed and the remaining data
were normalized with mean $\overline{x}_j = 0$ and standard deviation equal to 1. Table
1 shows the characteristics of the databases, where the number of numerical
and categorical attributes are denoted by n_{num} and n_{cat}, respectively, and N is
the total number of samples. Our methodology was compared with the classifier
Support Vector Machine (SVM). The implementation of the SVM method used
was the LIBSVM. [5]. With this implementation, Equation (6) is minimized as
follows:

$$\min_{\mathbf{w},b,\xi} \quad \frac{1}{2}\mathbf{w}^T\mathbf{w} + \lambda\sum_{i=1}^{N}\xi_i \tag{6}$$

$$S.t. \quad g(x) \leq 0$$

$$y_i(\mathbf{w}^T\vartheta(\mathbf{x_i}) + b) \geq 1 - \xi_i, \quad \xi_i \geq 0$$

where

$$\vartheta(\mathbf{x_i}, \mathbf{x_j}) = \exp(-\gamma\|\mathbf{x_i} - \mathbf{x_j}\|), \quad \gamma > 0. \tag{7}$$

The grid-search and 10-fold cross-validation methods were used to find the co-
efficients γ e λ. The purpose of this methodology is to find the pair (γ, λ) which

results in higher accuracy of the method cross-validation. In this experiment, the parameters were varied as follows

$$\gamma = \{2^{-n}, 2^{-(n-2)}, \cdots, 2^{15}\}, \ n = 5$$

$$\lambda = \{2^{-n}, 2^{-(n-2)}, \cdots, 2^{2}\}, \ n = 15.$$

In contrast to the RBF network, where the centers c_i and the radius σ_i of activation function of the ith neuron φ_i were found using the methodology proposed in this paper. The experiment was replicated 10 times always randomizing the data in each iteration. The first 2/3 of data where used for training, and the remaining 1/3 for testing. Table 2 presents the results of our proposal (GV-RBF) and SVM. The average accuracy and standard deviation of test set are shown respectively.

Table 1. Characteristic of Databases

Base	n_{num}	n_{cat}	n	N
acr	6	8	14	690
bld	6	0	6	345
hea	7	6	13	270
ion	33	0	33	351
pid	8	0	8	768
snr	60	0	60	208
wbc	9	0	9	683
adc	7	0	7	106

Table 2. Results: average accuracy and standard deviation

Base	GV-RBF	SVM
acr	0.8586 (0.0214)	0.8551 (0.0094)
bld	0.6672 (0.0334)	0.6920 (0.0166)
hea	0.8280 (0.0259)	0.8427 (0.0295)
ion	0.9270 (0.0206)	0.9270 (0.0236)
pid	0.7494 (0.0196)	0.7545 (0.0161)
snr	0.7588 (0.0629)	0.8485 (0.0326)
wbc	0.9627 (0.0084)	0.9680 (0.0104)
adc	0.6058 (0.0566)	0.6044 (0.0477)

We have also performed a statistical analysis of the results presented in Table 2. Wilcoxon signed rank test [12] was applied in order to test the difference between GV-RBF and SVM. The hypothesis for the Wilcoxon test were formulated as follows:

- H_0: The two classifiers are identical. (Null hypothesis)
- H_1: The classifiers are different. (Alternative hypothesis)

The Wilcoxon test yielded a p-value of 0.078125. which is bigger than the significance level of 0.05. Thus, we can conclude with a significance level of 5% that the null hypothesis H_0 cannot be neglected. In other words, for the datasets of Table 1, the method proposed in this paper is statistically equivalent to SVM,

4   Conclusions

This paper presented preliminary results of a new approach to design RBF neural networks. Classifiers based on Support Vectors Machines (SVM) and regularization networks usually are designed using exhaustive methods and cross-validation to obtain their parameters, demanding too much time and user experience. The method proposed in this article, in turn, is not sensitive to initial settings. All required parameters for the design of the classifier are obtained geometrically and directly from the database, without needing to provide any prior information. In the particular case of this work, we assume that the " optimal" parameters are found within the margin of class separation and input vectors generated from them yield valuable information to the problem. The results showed that for problems with multi-dimensional databases, our method is statistically equivalent to SVM, without parameter or settings selection from the user.

References

1. Alcalá-Fdez, J., Fernández, A., Luengo, J., Derrac, J., García, S., Sánchez, L., Herrera, F.: Keel data-mining software tool: Data set repository, integration of algorithms and experimental analysis framework. Journal of Multiple-Valued Logic & Soft Computing 17 (2011)
2. Bache, K., Lichman, M.: UCI machine learning repository (2013), http://archive.ics.uci.edu/ml
3. Boser, B.E., Guyon, I.M., Vapnik, V.N.: A training algorithm for optimal margin classifiers. In: Proceedings of the Fifth Annual Workshop on Computational Learning Theory, pp. 144–152. ACM (1992)
4. Bouchired, S., Ibnkahla, M., Roviras, D., Castanie, F.: Equalization of satellite mobile communication channels using combined self-organizing maps and rbf networks. In: Proceedings of the 1998 IEEE International Conference on Acoustics, Speech and Signal Processing, 1998, vol. 6, pp. 3377–3379. IEEE (1998)
5. Chang, C.C., Lin, C.J.: LIBSVM: A library for support vector machines. ACM Transactions on Intelligent Systems and Technology 2, 27:1–27:27 (2011), available at http://www.csie.ntu.edu.tw/~cjlin/libsvm

6. Cortes, C., Vapnik, V.: Support-vector networks. Machine Learning 20(3), 273–297 (1995)
7. Cover, T.M.: Geometrical and statistical properties of systems of linear inequalities with applications in pattern recognition. IEEE Transactions on Electronic Computers (3), 326–334 (1965)
8. De Berg, M., Van Kreveld, M., Overmars, M., Schwarzkopf, O.C.: Computational Geometry: Algorithms and Applications, 2nd edn. Springer (2000)
9. Guyon, I., Boser, B., Vapnik, V.: Automatic capacity tuning of very large vc-dimension classifiers. Advances in Neural Information Processing Systems, 147 (1993)
10. Kohavi, R., et al.: A study of cross-validation and bootstrap for accuracy estimation and model selection. In: International Joint Conference on Artificial Intelligence, pp. 1137–1145. Lawrence Erlbaum Associates Ltd (1995)
11. Sing, J.K., Basu, D.K., Nasipuri, M., Kundu, M.: Improved k-means algorithm in the design of rbf neural networks. In: TENCON 2003. Conference on Convergent Technologies for Asia-Pacific Region, vol. 2, pp. 841–845. IEEE (2003)
12. Wilcoxon, F.: Individual comparisons by ranking methods. Biometrics Bulletin 1(6), 80–83 (1945)

Sampling Hidden Parameters
from Oracle Distribution

Sho Sonoda and Noboru Murata

Schools of Advanced Science and Engineering, Waseda University
3-4-1 Ohkubo, Shinjuku-ku, Tokyo, 169-8555, Japan
s.sonoda0110@toki.waseda.jp
noboru.murata@eb.waseda.ac.jp

Abstract. A new sampling learning method for neural networks is proposed. Derived from an integral representation of neural networks, an *oracle* probability distribution of hidden parameters is introduced. In general rigorous sampling from the oracle distribution holds numerical difficulty, a linear-time sampling algorithm is also developed. Numerical experiments showed that when hidden parameters were initialized by the oracle distribution, following backpropagation converged faster to better parameters than when parameters were initialized by a normal distribution.

Keywords: Integral representation, neural networks, sampling learning, oracle distribution, backpropagation, weight initialization.

1 Introduction

In the backpropagation (BP) training of a neural network, the initial weight parameters are crucial to its final estimates. Since hidden parameters are put inside nonlinear activation functions, simultaneous training of all parameters by BP is accompanied by a non-convex optimization problem. When the machine starts from an initial point far from the goal, the learning curve easily gets stuck in local minima or lost in plateaus, and it fails to provide good performance.

In this paper, we introduce a new sampling learning technique which can avoid the difficulty of BP. The key concept is the probability distribution of hidden parameters derived from Murata's integral representation of neural networks [8]. Based on the analytical background, this *oracle* distribution can give a direction where efficient hidden parameters exist. Sampling parameters from the oracle distribution, we can start BP advantageously than just initializing by ordinary normal/uniform distributions. In particular, for relatively simple or low dimensional problems, oracle sampling of hidden parameters and linear regression of output parameters can attain high accuracy without BP.

1.1 Related Works

For ordinary random initialization, some authors have suggested to preset parameters in the *linear region*, where an activation function behaves linearly,

S. Wermter et al. (Eds.): ICANN 2014, LNCS 8681, pp. 539-546, 2014.

since parameters outside there have small gradients. For instance LeCun et al.
[6] have proposed to draw initial parameters from a distribution with mean zero
and standard deviation $\sigma = m^{-1/2}$, where m is the dimensionality of input vectors. Other authors have suggested to preset parameters to *respond selectively*
to representative input vectors (e.g., Denoeux and Lengellé [2]). Although these
suggestions are practical guidelines, they lack theoretical perspective that how
whole parameters should be distributed.

The integral representation of neural networks is one way to gain such a
perspective. In fact, most studies have exclusively focused on theoretical analysis.
For example Kůrková [4] established a general theory, including Murata's work.
Few studies have implemented the integral representations. For example Sprecher
[9] have proposed a deterministic *polynomial-time* algorithm.

Deep Neural Networks (DNNs) are said to learn good data *representations* [1].
The oracle distribution can also provide data with a good integral representation.
While DNNs obtain the representations by unsupervised learning, ours does by
supervised learning.

De Freitas et al. [3] also have investigated sampling learning based on Sequential Monte Carlo. They also construct a distribution of parameters in an
iterative manner, we have an advantage in that the oracle distribution can be
obtained without iterations.

2   Preliminary

2.1   Framework of Sampling Learning

Let $g : \mathbb{R}^m \to \mathbb{R}$ be a neural network with a single hidden layer expressed as

$$g(\mathbf{x}) = \sum_{j=1}^{J} w_j \phi \left(\mathbf{a}_j \cdot \mathbf{x} - b_j \right) + w_0 \,, \tag{1}$$

where the map ϕ is called the *activation function*; $\mathbf{a}_j$ and b_j are called *hidden
parameters*, and w_j are *output parameters*. With an ordinary *sigmoid function*
$\sigma(z) := \frac{1}{1+\exp(-z)}$, the activation function ϕ is supposed to be the *sigmoid pair*
in the form

$$\phi(z) := \frac{1}{H} \left\{ \sigma(z + h) - \sigma(z - h) \right\}, \quad (h > 0) \,, \tag{2}$$

where $H := \sigma(h) - \sigma(-h)$ normalizes the maximum value of ϕ to be one.

We consider an *oracle* distribution $p(\mathbf{a}, b)$ of hidden parameters. By sampling
from $p(\mathbf{a}, b)$, we expect to avoid the difficulty in BP training. Once hidden parameters are determined, the rest output parameters can be fixed by ordinary
linear regression. Candidates of $p(\mathbf{a}, b)$ would be some generic distributions such
as the normal distribution. In the following sections we derive a data dependent
distribution from an integral representation of neural networks.

2.2   Murata's Integral Representation of Neural Networks

Consider approximating a map $f : \mathbb{R}^m \to \mathbb{R}$ with a neural network. Murata [8] defined an integral transform T of f with respect to a *decomposing kernel* ϕ_d as

$$T(\mathbf{a}, b) := \frac{1}{C} \int_{\mathbb{R}^m} \phi_d^*(\mathbf{a} \cdot \mathbf{x} - b) f(\mathbf{x}) d\mathbf{x} , \tag{3}$$

where C is a normalizing constant, $\cdot^*$ denotes the complex conjugate. He also showed that given the decomposing kernel ϕ_d, there exists the associating *composing kernel* ϕ_c such that for any $f \in C_0^{(m+1)}(\mathbb{R}^m)$, the inversion formula

$$f(\mathbf{x}) = \int_{\mathbb{R}^{m+1}} \phi_c(\mathbf{a} \cdot \mathbf{x} - b) T(\mathbf{a}, b) d\mathbf{a} db , \tag{4}$$

holds (Th. 1, Cor. 2 in [8]).

In particular one can set a composing kernel ϕ_c as a sigmoid pair ϕ given in Eq. 2 and the associating decomposing kernel as:

$$\phi_d(z) = \begin{cases} \rho^{(m)}(z) & \text{if } m \text{ is even} \\ \rho^{(m+1)}(z) & \text{otherwise} \end{cases} , \tag{5}$$

where ρ is a nonnegative C^∞-smooth function whose support is in the interval $[-1, 1]$. The *standard mollifier* $\rho(z) = \exp \frac{1}{z^2-1}$ is a well-known example. Hereafter we assume ϕ_c is a sigmoid pair and ϕ_d is the corresponding derivative of the standard mollifier.

Let $\tau(\mathbf{a}, b)$ be a probability distribution function over $\mathbb{R}^{m+1}$ which is proportional to $|T(\mathbf{a}, b)|$, and $c(\mathbf{a}, b)$ be satisfying $c(\mathbf{a}, b)\tau(\mathbf{a}, b) = T(\mathbf{a}, b)$ for all $(\mathbf{a}, b) \in \mathbb{R}^{m+1}$. With this notations, the inversion formula is rewritten as the expectation form with respect to $\tau(\mathbf{a}, b)$, that is,

$$f(\mathbf{x}) = \int_{\mathbb{R}^{m+1}} c(\mathbf{a}, b)\phi_c(\mathbf{a} \cdot \mathbf{x} - b)\tau(\mathbf{a}, b) d\mathbf{a} db . \tag{6}$$

The expression implies the finite sum

$$g_J(\mathbf{x}) := \frac{1}{J} \sum_{j=1}^{J} c(\mathbf{a}_j, b_j)\phi_c(\mathbf{a}_j \cdot \mathbf{x} - b_j), \quad (\mathbf{a}_j, b_j) \overset{i.i.d.}{\sim} \tau(\mathbf{a}, b) , \tag{7}$$

converges to f in mean square as $J \to \infty$, i.e. $\mathbb{E}[g_J] = f$ and $\text{Var}[g_J] < \infty$ for any J (Th.2 in [8]). Here g_J is a neural network with $2J$ hidden units, therefore we can regard the inversion formula as an *integral representation* of neural networks, and $\tau(\mathbf{a}, b)$ as the *oracle distribution*.

3   Method

3.1   Practical Calculation of the Integral Representation

Given a data set $\{(\mathbf{x}_n, y_n)\}_{n=1}^{N} \subset \mathbb{R}^m \times \mathbb{R}$, $T(\mathbf{a}, b)$ is approximated as

$$T(\mathbf{a}, b) \approx \frac{1}{Z} \sum_{n=1}^{N} \phi_d(\mathbf{a} \cdot \mathbf{x}_n - b) y_n , \tag{8}$$

with some constant $Z > 0$ which can be omitted in sampling. In the next section, the following upper bound, which we call the *mixture approximation* of $p(\mathbf{a}, b)$,

$$p(\mathbf{a}, b) \propto |T(\mathbf{a}, b)| \approx \frac{1}{Z} \left| \sum_{n=1}^{N} y_n \phi_d(\mathbf{a} \cdot \mathbf{x}_n - b) \right| ,$$

$$\leq \frac{1}{Z} \sum_{n=1}^{N} |y_n| |\phi_d(\mathbf{a} \cdot \mathbf{x}_n - b)| \propto \sum_{n=1}^{N} \eta_n p_n(\mathbf{a}, b) , \qquad (9)$$

helps where $\eta_n \propto |y_n|$ and $p_n(\mathbf{a}, b) \propto |\phi_d(\mathbf{a} \cdot \mathbf{x}_n - b)|$.

As a decomposing kernel ϕ_d, we employed the kth derivative of the standard mollifier $\rho(z) = \exp \frac{1}{z^2-1}$ defined on the interval $I = [-1, 1]$, where $k = m$ if m is even and $k = m + 1$ otherwise. In general $\rho^{(k)}(z)$ takes the form

$$\rho^{(k)}(z) = \frac{P_k(z)}{(z^2 - 1)^{2k}} \rho(z) \quad (k = 0, 1, 2, \cdots) , \qquad (10)$$

where $P_k(z)$ is a polynomial of z calculated by the following recurrence formula:

$$P_0(z) \equiv 1 \text{ (const.)} , \qquad (11)$$

$$P_{k+1}(z) = P_k'(z)(z^4 - 2z^2 + 1) + P_k(z) \left\{ -4kz^3 + 2(2k - 1)z \right\} . \qquad (12)$$

When k gets higher, $\rho^{(k)}$ comes to oscillate more rapidly at the both ends of I.

3.2   Sampling from Mixture Annealed Distribution

Rigorous sampling from $p(\mathbf{a}, b)$ can be conducted by acceptance-rejection sampling. In higher dimensional cases, the high dimensional sampling gets inefficient, and the high order differentiation causes numerical instability.

In order to overcome the high dimensional sampling difficulty, we employed the mixture distribution $p(\mathbf{a}, b) \approx \sum_{n=1}^{N} \eta_n p_n(\mathbf{a}, b)$ described in Eq. 9 and conducted two-step sampling: first choose one component distribution $p_n(\mathbf{a}, b)$ according to the mixing probability η_n, second draw a sample $(\mathbf{a}, b)$ from $p_n(\mathbf{a}, b)$.

Sampling from $p_n(\mathbf{a}, b)$ still holds the difficulty of high order differentiation. In general, $\rho^{(k)}(z)(= \phi_d(z))$ has its almost all *mass* around both ends of its domain I and almost no mass in the center. Hence we approximated, or *annealed*, $\rho^{(k)}(z)$ by a beta distribution, which could model the extreme skewness of $\rho^{(k)}(z)$ (e.g., Beta$(z; 100, 3)$). In this way sampling from $p_n(\mathbf{a}, b)$ is reduced to: first sampling z from a beta distribution, then sampling $(\mathbf{a}, b)$ under the restriction $z = \mathbf{a} \cdot \mathbf{x}_n - b$.

Obviously the last restriction is loose and gives rise to the virtual freedom in $(\mathbf{a}, b)$. We introduced two additional assumptions. First, $\mathbf{a}$ is parallel to given $\mathbf{x}_n$. Since $\mathbf{a}$ always appears in the form $\mathbf{a} \cdot \mathbf{x}_n$, only the parallel component of $\mathbf{a}$ could have any effect (on one particular $\mathbf{x}_n$). Hence we eliminated the extra freedom in the orthogonal component. Second, the inverse of the norm $a := \|\mathbf{a}\|$ has similar scale to the distances $\|\mathbf{x}_n - \mathbf{x}_m\|$ between input vectors. Because $1/a$ determines how broad part of the input space the unit covers, or which input vectors the unit selectively respond to. Therefore, too small $1/a$ cause the unit to respond to only one input vector. In order to avoid such an isolated case, we assumed $1/a$ is no smaller than the distance between input vectors. In this procedure, we set $1/a$ as a distance $\|\mathbf{x}_n - \mathbf{x}_m\|$ of randomly selected two input examples $\mathbf{x}_n$ and $\mathbf{x}_m$. We denote this procedure simply by $1/a \sim p(\|\mathbf{x} - \mathbf{x}'\|)$. Once $\mathbf{a}$ is fixed, b is determined as $b = \mathbf{a} \cdot \mathbf{x}_n - z$.

Given shape parameters α, β of the beta distribution, one cycle of sampling is summarized as Alg. 1. This method consists of no more expensive steps. It scales linearly with the dimensionality of the input space and the number of required sample parameters respectively. Moreover, it does not depend on the size of the training data.

Algorithm 1 Sampling from mixture annealed distribution $\sum_{n=1}^{N} \eta_n p_n(\mathbf{a}, b)$

---

choose a suffix n of $\mathbf{x}_n$ according to the mixing probability η_n
draw $\zeta \sim \text{Beta}(\zeta; \alpha, \beta)$ and $\gamma \sim \text{Bernoulli}(\gamma; p = 0.5)$
$z \leftarrow (-1)^\gamma \zeta$
draw $1/a \sim p(\|\mathbf{x} - \mathbf{x}'\|)$
$\mathbf{a} \leftarrow a\mathbf{x}_n/\|\mathbf{x}_n\|$
$b \leftarrow \mathbf{a} \cdot \mathbf{x}_n - z$
return $(\mathbf{a}, b)$

---

4   Experimental Results

We conducted both artificial and real world data tasks comparing three methods:

SR Hidden parameters are initialized by $\underline{S}$ampling from $p(\mathbf{a}, b)$; the rest output parameters are fit by linear $\underline{R}$egression. (Additional BP training was conducted in the second task.)

SBP Hidden and output parameters are initialized by $\underline{S}$ampling from $p(\mathbf{a}, b)$ and a normal distribution, respectively, then whole parameters are trained by $\underline{BP}$.

BP Whole parameters are initialized by sampling from a normal distribution, and trained by $\underline{BP}$.

4.1   Artificial Data Regression — Topologist's Sine Curve $\sin \frac{2\pi}{x}$

First, we performed one-dimensional curve regression. The objective function is *topologist's sine curve* (TSC) $f(x) := \sin \frac{2\pi}{x}$ defined on the interval $[-1, 1]$ with $f(0) = 0$. TSC is such a complicated curve whose spatial frequency gets arbitrary high as x tends to zero. For training, 201 points were sampled from the domain $[-1, 1]$ in equidistant manner. The number of hidden parameters was fixed to 100 in each case. Note that relatively redundant quantity of parameters are needed for our sampling learning to obtain good parameters. The output function was set to linear and the batch learning was performed by BFGS quasi-Newton method.

Random initialization parameters for BP and SBP were drawn from $\mathcal{N}(0, 1)$. Sampling from $p(\mathbf{a}, b)$ was performed by acceptance-rejection sampling.

Figure 1 summarizes the training result of three methods. It is remarkable that SR, without BP training, attained the highest accuracy and learned a smooth curve. SBP also followed relatively high frequency, with noise. In this experiment, we examined the flexibility of our method by fitting a complicated curve. The experimental result supports that the oracle distribution gave advantageous directions.

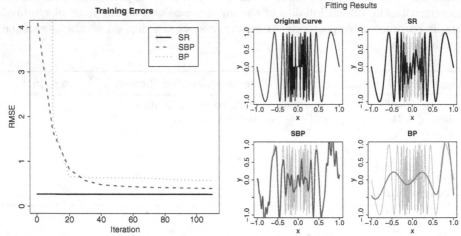

Fig. 1. Training results of three methods for fitting $\sin \frac{2\pi}{x}$. **Left**: SR by itself achieved the highest accuracy without BP. SBP converged to lower RMSE than BP does. **Right**: Original curve has numerical instability around the origin, which makes fitting difficult. SR fit smoothly except around the origin. SBP also approximated the curve with noise. BP only fit moderate part of the curve.

4.2   Real World Data Classification — MNIST

Second, we performed a real world data classification task using the MNIST data set [7], which consists of 60,000 training examples and 10,000 test examples. Each input vector is a 256-level gray-scaled $(28 \times 28 =)784$-pixel image of a handwritten digit. The corresponding label is one of 10 digits. We implemented these labels as 10-dimensional binary vectors whose components are chosen randomly with equivalent probability for one and zero. We used randomly sampled 15,000 training examples for training and whole 10,000 testing examples for testing. The number of hidden units was fixed to 300, which is the same size as used in the previous report of LeCun et al. [5], which marked the error rate 4.7%. Although they used more tricky initial parameters, this setting is the most comparable to our experiment. Note that J sigmoid pairs corresponds to $2J$ sigmoid units, therefore we used 150 sigmoid pairs for SR and SBP, and 300 sigmoid units for BP. The output function was set to sigmoid and the loss function was set to cross-entropy. In accordance with LeCun et al. [5], input vectors were normalized and randomly initialized parameters for BP and SBP were drawn from a normal distribution with mean zero and standard deviation $784^{-1/2} \approx 0.0357$.

Sampling from the oracle distribution was conducted by the mixture annealed sampling technique. Linear regression for SR was solved by singular value decomposition. BP training was conducted by stochastic gradient descent (SGD) with adaptive learning rates and diagonal approximated Hessian [6]. The experiment was performed in R on a Xeon X5660 2.8GHz with 50GB memory.

Figure 2 depicts the classification error rates for the test examples. Since SR by itself could not attain good accuracy, SR was also conducted by BP training. While SBP decreased the fastest of the three and attained the lowest error rate, SR did not monotonically decrease. It appears that SR got stuck in a local minimum. Table 1 lists the training times. It is remarkable that sampling from $p(\mathbf{a}, b)$ for SR and SBP was as fast as sampling from a normal distribution for BP. The regression step cost much more time than the sampling step did. The BP step also cost, however one iteration cost just around 0.05 seconds, it would be shorten if the initial parameters had better accuracy.

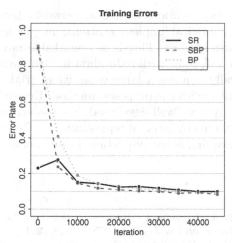

Fig. 2. Classification error rates for 10, 000 test examples. SR marked 23.0% at the beginning, which is the lowest of the three at that time, and finished 9.94%. SBP reduced the steepest in the first 5, 000 iterations and finished 8.30%, which is the lowest of the three at that time. BP declined the slowest and finished 8.77%.

Table 1. Training Times for MNIST

Method	Sampling [s]	Regression [s]	BP training [s]
SR	1.15×10^{-2}	2.60	2.00×10^{3}
SBP	1.14×10^{-2}	-	2.31×10^{3}
BP	1.15×10^{-2}	-	2.67×10^{3}

In this experiment, we confirmed that our method worked for a real world data. Although SR showed an overfitting aspects, the fastest convergence of SBP supported that the oracle distribution could give meaningful parameters, and the annealed sampling technique could draw meaningful samples.

5 Conclusion

In this paper, we introduced sampling learning methods for neural networks. Based on Murata's [8] integral representation of neural networks, we constructed the oracle distribution $p(\mathbf{a}, b)$ in a data dependent way. Since sampling from $p(\mathbf{a}, b)$ has numerical difficulty, in particular in high dimensional settings, we also developed a linear-time sampling technique: the mixture annealed sampling.

In the experiments we compared three methods: SR, SBP and BP (control). Both SR and SBP achieved better accuracy than BP did, which supports that both the oracle distribution and the sampling technique worked. For TSC regression task SR attained the best accuracy, while SBP showed overfitting aspect. For the MNIST classification task SR got stuck in a local minimum, while SBP showed the fastest error reduction. These results indicate that users should select SR as long as it attains enough accuracy without BP training, and otherwise select SBP.

Although integral representations of neural networks have been well investigated theoretically, numerical implementations, in particular sampling approaches have been merely done. This is a remarkable novelty of this study. Sampling learning methods come with redundant hidden parameters since drawing good samples usually requires a large quantity of trial. Therefore pruning algorithms are compatible with the proposed method. Recently, neural networks with deep structure have been well developed. We conjecture that these structures can also be interpreted by integral representation. Extending our sampling framework into deep learning is our important future work.

References

1. Bengio, Y., Courville, A., Vincent, P.: Representation learning: A review and new perspectives. IEEE Trans. on PAMI 35(8), 1798–1828 (2013)
2. Denoeux, T., Lengellé, R.: Initializing back propagation networks with prototypes. Neural Networks 6(3), 351–363 (1993)
3. De Freitas, J.F.G., Niranjan, M., Gee, A.H., Doucet, A.: Sequential Monte Carlo methods to train neural network models. Neural Computation 12(4), 955–993 (2000)
4. Kůrková, V.: Complexity estimates based on integral transforms induced by computational units. Neural Networks 33, 160–167 (2012)
5. LeCun, Y., Bottou, L., Bengio, Y., Haffner, P.: Gradient-based learning applied to document recognition. Proceedings of the IEEE 11, 2278–2324 (1998)
6. LeCun, Y.A., Bottou, L., Orr, G.B., Müller, K.-R.: Efficient Backprop. In: Montavon, G., Orr, G.B., Müller, K.-R. (eds.) NN: Tricks of the Trade, 2nd edn. LNCS, vol. 7700, pp. 9–48. Springer, Heidelberg (2012)
7. LeCun, Y., Cortes, C.: The MNIST database of handwritten digits, http://yann.lecun.com/exdb/mnist/
8. Murata, N.: An integral representation of functions using three-layered networks and their approximation bounds. Neural Networks 9(6), 947–956 (1996)
9. Sprecher, D.A.: A numerical implementation of Kolmogorov's superpositions. Neural Networks 9(5), 765–772 (1996)

Incremental Input Variable Selection
by Block Addition and Block Deletion

Shigeo Abe

Kobe University
Rokkodai, Nada, Kobe, Japan
abe@kobe-u.ac.jp
http://www2.kobe-u.ac.jp/~abe

Abstract. In selecting input variables by block addition and block deletion (BABD), multiple input variables are added and then deleted, keeping the cross-validation error below that using all the input variables.
The major problem of this method is that selection time becomes large
as the number of input variables increases. To alleviate this problem, in
this paper, we propose incremental block addition and block deletion of
input variables. In this method, for an initial subset of input variables we
select input variables by BABD. Then in the incremental step, we add
some input variables that are not added before to the current selected input variables and iterate BABD. To guarantee that the cross-validation
error decreases monotonically by incremental BABD, we undo incremental BABD if the obtained cross-validation error rate is worse than that
at the previous incremental step. We evaluate incremental BABD using
some benchmark data sets and show that by incremental BABD, input
variable selection is speeded up with the approximation error comparable
to that by batch BABD.

1 Introduction

Input variable selection for regression is to select a set of input variables deleting
irrelevant or redundant input variables from an original set of input variables.
This is an important step in realizing a regressor with high generalization ability.
In the following, we simply say variables instead of input variables, if there is no
confusion. Because variable selection methods are usually applicable to feature
selection in pattern recognition, variables and features are used interchangeably.

According to the selection criterion, the variable selection methods are classified into wrapper methods, which use an approximation error by regressors
and filter methods, which use other selection criteria. Since the introduction of
support vector machines (SVMs) [1–3], imbedded methods [4] are proposed, in
which the variable selection criterion is included in the objective function of
SVMs.

In wrapper or filter methods, variables are selected by forward selection, in
which informative variables are added step by step, or by backward selection, in
which unnecessary variables are deleted step by step. As their variant, forward
selection and backward selection are combined [5–7].

S. Wermter et al. (Eds.): ICANN 2014, LNCS 8681, pp. 547–554, 2014.

To speed up variable selection, incremental selection has been proposed [8–11]. In [8], for the randomly selected set of training samples, feature selection is performed. Then if the inconsistency occurs in the remaining training data, in that the features of samples of different classes match, these samples are added to the randomly selected samples and repeat feature selection until no inconsistency is found. In [9], the L_0 feature selection criterion is added to the objective function. Starting from a small set of selected features, at each iteration, the feature that is estimated to improve the objective function value most is added to the selected feature set, and the objective function excluding the feature selection criterion is improved by the steepest descent method. In [10], initially all the features are ranked, and then sequential forward selection is performed using the ranked features. In [12], to speed-up wrapper methods, multiple variables are added by forward selection (block addition), then multiple variables are deleted by backward selection (block deletion).

To speed up BABD, in this paper, we propose incremental BABD. Initially, we calculate the approximation error by cross-validation using the subset of the initial variable set and set it as the threshold of variable selection. Then, we select variables from the subset by BABD. If the approximation error lower than the threshold is obtained, we update the threshold. We add subset of variables to the set of selected variables and do variable selection by BABD. But if the obtained threshold is worse than that at the previous step, we undo the variable selection. We iterate the above procedure, until all the variables are processed. We evaluate this incremental BABD using some benchmark data sets.

In Section 2, we discuss the idea of incremental BABD and its algorithm and in Section 3, we show the results of computer experiments using benchmark data sets.

2   Incremental BABD

2.1   Idea

In selecting a set of variables from a large number of variables, forward selection is more efficient than backward selection. But variables are selected only considering the relation among selected variables and the candidate variable. While by backward selection, the variable that does not deteriorate the selection criterion the least among the remaining variables is deleted. Therefore, forward selection is less stable than backward selection. To alleviate such a problem, we have proposed BABD. In BA, multiple variables are added according to the ranked variables until the selected set realizes the approximation error smaller than or equal to that for the set of original variables. Then by BD, multiple variables are deleted that do not increase the approximation error.

In BA, variables are ranked according to the approximation errors, which are calculated by temporarily adding one variable to the selected set of variables. Therefore, if the number of variables is large, the ranking procedure takes time. To alleviate the computation of ranking, we consider incremental variable selection. Initially, we start with a subset of original variables, and select variables by BABD for the subset. Then we add remaining variables to the set and iterate the BABD until all the variables are processed. If we replace BABD with BD in the above procedure, incremental BD is also possible.

2.2 Algorithm

Now we explain incremental BABD more in detail. (Please see [12] for details of BABD.)

Let $I^m = \{1, \ldots, m\}$ be the set of variables, where m is the number of variables. We select the subset of I^m, I^j, as the initial set of variables, where j is the number of initial variables. We calculate the approximation error for I^j, E^j, by cross-validation and set the threshold of variable selection, T^j:

$$T^j = E^j. \tag{1}$$

By BA, we first rank variables whose indices are in I^j in the ascending order of approximation errors, which are evaluated by adding a variable to the set of selected variables temporarily, and add multiple variables to the selected set from the top ranked variables that decrease the approximation error most. For the variables in I^j that are not selected, we iterate the above procedure until

$$E^{j'} \leq T^j. \tag{2}$$

Is satisfied, where $I^{j'}$ is the selected set of variable indices, j' is the number of selected variables, $j' \leq j$, and $I^{j'} \subseteq I^j$. Then we set the threshold by

$$T^{j'} = E^{j'}. \tag{3}$$

Further by BD first we rank variables whose indices are in $I^{j'}$, according to the approximation errors, which are calculated by deleting a variable temporarily. And we delete multiple variables that decrease the approximation error the most. We iterate the above variable ranking and deletion until no further variables are deleted. Let the resulting set of variable indices be I^k, where k is the number of selected variables. The approximation error E^k for I^k satisfies

$$E^k \leq T^{j'}. \tag{4}$$

Then we update the threshold by $T^k = E^k$.

According to the above procedure, the approximation error for the selected variables is not larger than that for I^j, i.e., $E^k \leq E^j$.

Now we add i_{Inc} indices from $I^m - I^j$ to I^k, where i_{Inc} is the number of variables that are added at the incremental step. The resulting set of indices be $I^{k+i_{\text{Inc}}}$. The approximation error for $I^{k+i_{\text{Inc}}}$ is $E^{k+i_{\text{Inc}}}$ and we set the threshold $T^{k+i_{\text{Inc}}}$ by $T^{k+i_{\text{Inc}}} = E^{k+i_{\text{Inc}}}$. We must notice that

$$T^{k+i_{\text{Inc}}} \leq T^k. \tag{5}$$

is not always satisfied.

We iterate the above BABD for $I^{k+i_{\text{Inc}}}$. Let the resulting set of indices be I^o, where $o \leq k + i_{\text{Inc}}$ and

$$E^o \leq T^{k+i_{\text{Inc}}} \tag{6}$$

is satisfied. But there is no guarantee that the following inequality is satisfied:

$$E^o \leq T^k \tag{7}$$

If (7) is satisfied, we repeat BABD adding the variables not processed. If it is not satisfied, we consider that the BABD for this step failed and undo the variable selection at this step; namely, we restart BABD with threshold T^k and I^k, and add remaining indices of variables to I^k.

We repeat the BABD until all the variables are processed. This is a one-pass incremental variable selection. To reduce the approximation error further, we may repeat the above procedure until the selected variable set does not change. But it will increase the computation time. Therefore, in the following we only consider one-pass incremental BABD.

3   Performance Evaluation

Because BABD has been compared with other methods in [12, 13], and shown to be comparable to or better than other methods, in this section, we compare incremental BABD with batch BABD.

3.1   Evaluation Conditions

In performance evaluation we used the mean absolute error (MAE) for the validation data set evaluated by cross-validation using least squares support vector regressors (LS SVRs). We used a personal computer (3GHz, 2GB memory, Windows XP operating system) in measuring variable selection time.

The primal problem of the LS SVR is given by

$$\text{minimize} \quad \frac{1}{2}\mathbf{w}^\top \mathbf{w} + \frac{C}{2}\sum_{i=1}^{M} \xi_i^2 \tag{8}$$

$$\text{subject to} \quad y_i = \mathbf{w}^\top \phi(\boldsymbol{x}_i) + b + \xi_i \quad \text{for} \quad i = 1, \ldots, M, \tag{9}$$

Where $\mathbf{w}$ is the coefficient vector of the hyperplane, C is the margin parameter, $\phi(\mathbf{x})$ is the mapping function that maps $\mathbf{x}$ into the feature space, and M is the number of training data. In training the LS SVR, we solve the set of linear equations that is derived by transforming the primal problem into the dual problem. As a kernel function, we use linear kernels: $K(\mathbf{x}, \mathbf{x}') = \mathbf{x}^\top \mathbf{x}'$ or RBF kernels: $K(\mathbf{x}, \mathbf{x}') = \exp(-\gamma \|\mathbf{x} - \mathbf{x}'\|^2 / m)$, where $K(\mathbf{x}, \mathbf{x}') = \phi^T(\mathbf{x})\,\phi(\mathbf{x}')$, γ is a parameter for determining the spread of the radius, and m is the number of variables.

We determined the initial MAE by fivefold cross-validation changing $\gamma = \{0.001, 0.01, 0.5, 1.0, 5.0, 10, 15, 20, 50, 100\}$ and $C = \{1, 10, 50, 100, 500, 1000,$

2000}. To reduce the computational cost of training the LS SVR during variable selection, fixing the kernel parameter value, we optimize the margin parameter value by cross-validation. To reduce the computation cost further, we can fix the margin parameter value.

To determine whether we should change the C value during variable selection, we carried out variable selection for the orange juice data [16] using RBF kernels. Figure 1 shows the result. For the validation data set, the MAEs by the fixed C value (FC) was higher than those by the variable C value (VC) for the change of number of added variables. In some cases, the MAEs were larger than initial MAE using all the variables (see Fig. (a)).

For the test data set, depending on the number of added variables, MAEs by VC were not always lower than those by FC (see Fig. (b)) but variable selection time by VC was much longer than by FC (Fig. (c)). The numbers of selected variables did not vary much between the two but as the number of added variables was increased, the number of selected variables was also increased (see Fig. (d)). According to the above results, because VC did not always give better results than FC, we used FC in the following study.

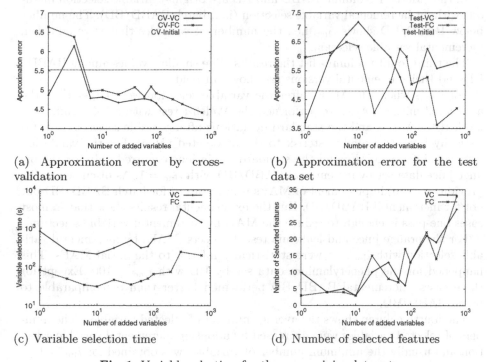

(a) Approximation error by cross-validation

(b) Approximation error for the test data set

(c) Variable selection time

(d) Number of selected features

Fig. 1. Variable selection for the orange juice data set

3.2   Experimental Results

We evaluated Incremental BABD using the six benchmark data sets listed in Table 1. The first column shows the benchmark data sets with the numbers of variables, training data, and test data. If the data set was not divided into training and test data sets, the corresponding number of test data is shown in "−." For the first three data sets, we randomly divided the set into training and test data sets with the ratio of 3 to 2 and generated 20 files for triazines and pyrimidines data sets and 40 files for phenetylamines data set. For the orange juice, breast cancer, and leukemia data sets, we combined the training and test data sets, and randomly generated 100 training and test data sets, each with the numbers of training and test data equal to the original numbers. The breast cancer and leukemia data sets are classification problems but we treated them as function approximation problems considering the $+1/-1$ labels as target values. For these data sets we used linear kernels with $C = 1$ because overfitting occurs for the C value larger than 1. For the other data sets, we used RBF kernels.

We calculated MAEs for the original variables, those after variable selection, and measured the feature selection time. In the first column of the table, the MAEs with the standard deviations for the test data sets using the original variables are shown. In the parentheses those for the validation data sets are shown.

In the "Method" column, BABD and BD are original variable selection methods without incremental variable selection (i.e., batch BABD/BD). The number below BABD/BD shows i_{Inc}, i.e., the number of variables that were added in incremental variable selection.

The third to fifth columns list the results. The smallest values among BABD/BD and their incremental versions are shown in bold.

For cases where the MAEs after the variable selection were larger than the associated initial MAEs, we performed the Welch t-test with a 5% significance level. If the MAEs and the standard deviations after variable selection are statistically inferior, we add asterisk to the associated values. For the validation data set, inferior MAEs and the standard deviations occurred only for the orange juice data set by incremental BABD/BD with $i_{\text{Inc}} = 1$. As discussed in the previous section, improvement of MAEs is guaranteed for batch BABD/BD but not for incremental BABD/BD. But the experimental results show that in most cases one-pass is enough to reduce the MAE by incremental variable selection.

For the orange juice and leukemia test data sets, MAEs by incremental variable selection with $i_{\text{Inc}} = 1$ were statistically inferior to the initial MAEs. This happened for the phenetylamines data set by BD with $i_{\text{Inc}} = 100$. Except for these cases, incremental BABD/BD performed better than or comparable to batch BABD/BD.

The fourth column shows the average number of selected variables. The numbers of selected variables were decreased by adopting incremental variable selection and usually the minimum number of variables was obtained for $i_{\text{Inc}} = 1$.

The final column shows the variable selection time. For the first three data sets, there is not much difference in selection time because the number of features and/or the number of data is small. But for the remaining three data sets, incremental training was faster except for some cases with $i_{\text{Inc}} = 1$.

Table 1. Performance comparison of incremental BABD and batch BABD

Data	Method	Average Error	Selected	Time [s]
Triazines (60/186/—) [14]	BABD	0.0036±0.0039(0.0019±0.0011)	4.5±2.3	**2.30**±0.84
0.0052±0.0036(0.0070±0.0023)	10	**0.0032**±0.0030(0.0018±0.0011)	3.9±1.6	3.30±0.64
	1	**0.0032**±0.0024(**0.0015**±0.0010)	**3.0**±1.0	6.60±0.86
	BD	0.0034±0.0033(**0.0016**±0.0010)	5.7±3.2	**2.05**±0.59
	10	**0.0025**±0.0020(0.0018±0.0010)	4.2±2.0	2.35±0.57
	1	0.0033±0.0020(**0.0016**±0.0013)	**3.1**±0.9	4.25±0.77
Pyrimidines (27/74/—) [14]	BABD	0.0191± 0.0112(**0.0112**±0.0089)	2.3±1.3	0.25±0.43
0.0309±0.0093(0.037±0.012)	10	0.0193±0.0110(0.0120±0.0091)	2.2±1.2	**0.20**±0.40
	1	**0.0183**±0.0110(0.0124±0.0097)	**2.0**±0.9	0.35±0.48
	BD	0.0228±0.0124(0.0130±0.0100)	3.3±3.6	0.20±0.40
	10	0.0195±0.0104(**0.0123**±0.0088)	3.0±2.1	**0.15**±0.36
	1	**0.0177**±0.0114(0.0124±0.0095)	**2.1**±1.0	0.20±0.40
Phenetylamines (628/22/—) [15]	BABD	0.2589*±0.1206*(0.0520±0.0289)	12.1±4.6	0.85±0.42
0.2092±0.0586(0.1875±0.0502)	100	**0.2227**±0.0861*(**0.0435**±0.0240)	10.7±5.9	**0.60**±0.49
	1	0.2488±0.1390*(0.0562±0.0300)	**6.3**±2.1	1.70±0.87
	BD	**0.2282**±0.0659(**0.0428**±0.0268)	21.2±11.0	1.12±0.51
	100	0.2718*±0.1652*(0.0452±0.0245)	8.6±3.4	**0.37**±0.48
	1	0.2593±0.1710*(0.0623±0.0263)	**5.9**±1.6	0.90±0.58
Orange Juice (700/150/68) [16]	BABD	5.6395±0.9222(**4.2132**±0.7461)	26.0±16.3	173.21±320.08
5.8184±0.8649(5.3375±0.6187)	200	**5.6357**±1.0307(4.2676±0.6672)	15.4±8.1	**59.02**±46.72
	1	6.8030*±1.0408(5.8087*±0.8223*)	**4.3**±2.1	91.99±29.51
	BD	5.4824±0.8409(**4.1034**±0.6046)	33.7±35.6	108.06±89.13
	200	**5.4578**±0.9275(4.2464±0.6297)	17.5±13.3	**46.51**±27.20
	1	6.5802*±0.9712(5.8136*±0.8226*)	**5.3**±2.5	56.19±22.33
B. Cancer (3226/14/8) [17]	BABD	**0.2891**±0.0585(**0.0424**±0.0055)	42.4±9.5	7.13±2.41
0.4076±0.1544(0.3107±0.0355)	200	0.3036±0.1156(0.0443±0.0051)	37.8±6.0	**3.00**±0.55
	1	0.3305±0.1954(0.0486±0.0058)	**31.2**±4.3	17.56±3.58
	BD	0.3260±0.1349(**0.0477**±0.0125)	105.0±86.1	28.64±10.22
	200	0.3260±0.1453(0.0562±0.0078)	34.8±10.4	**2.40**±0.63
	1	**0.3155**±0.1013(0.0511±0.0077)	31.9±4.1	13.60±2.63
Leukemia (7129/38/34) [18]	BABD	**0.1984**±0.0431(**0.0447**±0.0065)	62.2±15.9	134.00±53.09
0.2220±0.0208(0.2433±0.0196)	200	0.2072±0.0313(0.0452±0.0061)	57.4±8.8	**71.18**±6.86
	1	0.2414*±0.0344*(0.0601±0.0089)	**48.8**±6.0	536.08±110.09
	BD	**0.2037**±0.0250(**0.0388**±0.0106)	271.9±205.7	1350.17±672.78
	200	0.2278±0.0309*(0.0598±0.0075)	**40.0**±6.7	**34.62**±2.88
	1	0.2497*±0.0383*(0.0634±0.0094)	51.4±5.5	438.99±79.46

4   Conclusions

In this paper we extended batch block addition and block deletion (BABD) to incremental BABD. For a given subset of variables we select variables by BABD and add remaining variables to the selected variable set. We iterate BABD for the augmented set and if the obtained approximation error is smaller than that of the previous step, we iterate the above procedure adding remaining variables to the set of selected variables. If not, we undo the variable selection of the current step and iterate the above procedure. By computer experiments using six benchmark data sets, the approximation errors of the incremental BABD were comparable to or better than batch BABD and the selection time of incremental BABD was shortened for large numbers of variables when an appropriate number of data were added.

Acknowledgment. This work was supported by JSPS KAKENHI Grant Number 25420438.

References

1. Vapnik, V.N.: Statistical Learning Theory. John Wiley & Sons (1998)
2. Suykens, J.A.K.: Least squares support vector machines for classification and non-linear modeling. Neural Network World 10(1–2), 29–47 (2000)
3. Abe, S.: Support Vector Machines for Pattern Classification. Springer (2005)
4. Fung, G.M., Mangasarian, O.L.: A feature selection Newton method for support vector machine classification. Computational Optimization and Applications 28(2), 185–202 (2004)
5. Stearns, S.D.: On selecting features for pattern classifiers. In: Proc. Third International Conference on Pattern Recognition, pp. 71–75 (1976)
6. Pudil, P., Novovičová, J., Kittler, J.: Floating search methods in feature selection. Pattern Recognition Letters 15(11), 1119–1125 (1994)
7. Zhang, T.: Adaptive forward-backward greedy algorithm for sparse learning with linear models. In: Proc. NIPS 1921, pp. 1921–1928. MIT Press (2009)
8. Liu, H., Setiono, R.: Incremental feature selection. Applied Intelligence 9(3), 217–230 (1998)
9. Perkins, S., Lacker, K., Theiler, J.: Grafting: Fast, incremental feature selection by gradient descent in function space. Journal of Machine Learning Research 3, 1333–1356 (2003)
10. Ruiz, R., Riquelme, J.C., Aguilar-Ruiz, J.S.: Incremental wrapper-based gene selection from microarray data for cancer classification. Pattern Recognition 39(12), 2383–2392 (2006)
11. Bermejo, P., Gamez, J.A., Puerta, J.M.: Speeding up incremental wrapper feature subset selection with naive Bayes classifier. Knowledge-Based Systems 55, 140–147 (2014)
12. Nagatani, T., Ozawa, S., Abe, S.: Fast variable selection by block addition and block deletion. Journal of Intelligent Learning Systems and Applications 2(4), 200–211 (2010)
13. Nagatani, T., Abe, S.: Feature selection by block addition and block deletion. In: Mana, N., Schwenker, F., Trentin, E. (eds.) ANNPR 2012. LNCS (LNAI), vol. 7477, pp. 48–59. Springer, Heidelberg (2012)
14. Asuncion, A., Newman, D.J.: UCI machine learning repository (2007), http://www.ics.uci.edu/~mlearn/MLRepository.html
15. Milano Chemometrics and QSAR Research Group, http://michem.disat.unimib.it/chm/download/download.htm
16. UCL Machine Learning Group, http://mlg.info.ucl.ac.be/index.php?page=DataBases
17. Hedenfalk, I., et al.: Gene-expression profiles in hereditary breast cancer. The New England Journal of Medicine 344(8), 539–548 (2001)
18. Golub, T.R., et al.: Molecular classification of cancer: Class discovery and class prediction by gene expression monitoring. Science 286, 531–537 (1999)

A CFS-Based Feature Weighting Approach to Naive Bayes Text Classifiers

Shasha Wang[1], Liangxiao Jiang[1,*], and Chaoqun Li[2]

[1] Department of Computer Science, China University of Geosciences
Wuhan, Hubei, China 430074
ljiang@cug.edu.cn
[2] Department of Mathematics, China University of Geosciences
Wuhan, Hubei, China 430074

Abstract. Recent work in supervised learning has shown that naive Bayes text classifiers with strong assumptions of independence among features, such as multinomial naive Bayes (MNB), complement naive Bayes (CNB) and the one-versus-all-but-one model (OVA), have achieved remarkable classification performance. This fact raises the question of whether a naive Bayes text classifier with less restrictive assumptions can perform even better. Responding to this question, we firstly evaluate the correlation-based feature selection (CFS) approach in this paper and find that it performs even worse than the original versions. Then, we propose a CFS-based feature weighting approach to these naive Bayes text classifiers. We call our feature weighted versions FWMNB, FWCNB and FWOVA respectively. Our proposed approach weakens the strong assumptions of independence among features by weighting the correlated features. The experimental results on a large suite of benchmark datasets show that our feature weighted versions significantly outperform the original versions in terms of classification accuracy.

Keywords: Text classification, feature selection, feature weighting, multinomial naive Bayes, complement naive Bayes, the one-versus-all-but-one model.

1 Introduction and Related Work

In recent years, the exponential growth of the text documents on the Internet, digital libraries or other fields [1] has attracted the attention of many scholars. The task of automatic text classification is to assign text documents to pre-specified classes, which has been an important task in information retrieval [2]. Text classification presents unique challenges due to large number of features, large number of documents and strong dependencies among features [3,4].

To tackle text classification tasks, documents are characterized by the words that appear in them. Thus, one of the simplest way to apply machine learning to text classification is to treat each word as a boolean variable. This is the

---

* Corresponding author.

S. Wermter et al. (Eds.): ICANN 2014, LNCS 8681, pp. 555–562, 2014.

first statistical language model called multi-variate Bernoulli naive Bayes model (BNB) [5]. BNB assumes that a document is represented by a vector of binary feature variables indicating which words occur or not in the document. When calculating the class membership probability $P(c|d)$ that a document d belongs to the class c, one multiplies the probability of all of the feature values, including the probability of non-occurrence for words that do not occur in the document. BNB is more traditional in the field of Bayesian networks, and is appropriate for text classification tasks that have a fixed number of attributes [6]. However, the main shortcoming with it is that the information of the number of times a word occurs in a document is not captured.

To overcome the shortcoming confronting the multi-variate Bernoulli model, the multinomial model is proposed by capturing the information of the number of times a word occurs in a document. This multinomial model is widely called multinomial naive Bayes (MNB). According to the experimental results by [6], MNB provides on average a 27% reduction in error rate over the multi-variate Bernoulli model at any vocabulary size. However, one systemic problem confronting MNB is that when one class has more training documents than the others, MNB selects poor weights for the decision boundary. This is due to an under-studied bias effect that shrinks weights for classes with few training documents. To balance the amount of training documents used per estimate and to deal with skewed training data, a complement class version of MNB, called complement naive Bayes (CNB) is proposed [7]. The one-versus-all-but-one model (commonly misnamed one-versus-all, simply denoted by OVA) is a direct combination of MNB and CNB. The references [8] and [9] found that OVA performs much better than MNB. Rennie et al. [7] attributed the improvement with OVA to the use of the complement weights.

Although recent work in supervised learning has shown that these naive Bayes text classifiers, such as MNB, CNB and OVA, have achieved remarkable classification performance, all of them assume that all features are independent given the class. However, it is obvious that the conditional independence assumption in them is rarely true in reality, which would harms their performance in the real-world text classification applications with complex dependencies among features. In order to weaken their assumptions of independence among features, Jiang et al. propose a discriminative instance weighting approach [10] and a locally weighted learning approach [11]. Li et al. [12] focus their attentions on the feature weighting approach and propose a χ^2 statistic-based feature weighting approach, denoted by $R_{w,c}$. The $R_{w,c}$ approach can measure positive term-class dependency accurately and thus can improves the classification performance of the basic naive Bayes classifier in most cases.

In this paper, we firstly evaluate the correlation-based feature selection (CFS) [13] approach and find that it performs even worse than the original versions. Then, we propose a CFS-based feature weighting approach to these naive Bayes text classifiers. We call our feature weighted versions FWMNB, FWCNB and FWOVA respectively. Our proposed approach weakens the strong assumptions of independence among features by weighting the correlated features. For detail, our proposed approach firstly conducts a correlation-based feature selection process to select the best feature subset from the whole space of features and then assigns larger weights to the features in the selected feature subset and smaller weights to others. The extensive empirical study on a large suite of benchmark datasets validate the effectiveness of our proposed approach.

The rest of the paper is organized as follows. In Section 2, we propose our feature weighted naive Bayes text classifiers including FWMNB, FWCNB and FWOVA. In Section 3, we describe the experiment setup and results. In Section 4, we draw conclusions.

2   Feature Weighted Naive Bayes Text Classifiers

Given a test document d, represented by a word vector $< w_1, w_2, \cdots, w_m >$, FWMNB uses Equation 1 to classify the document d.

$$c(d) = \arg \max_{c \in C} [log P(c) + \sum_{i=1}^{m} W_i f_i log P(w_i|c)], \qquad (1)$$

where m is the number of words, w_i $(i = 1, 2, \cdots, m)$ is the ith word in the document d, W_i is the weight of the word w_i, f_i is the frequency count of word w_i, the prior probability $P(c)$ and the conditional probability $P(w_i|c)$ can be estimated by Equation 2 and Equation 3 respectively.

$$P(c) = \frac{\sum_{j=1}^{n} \delta(c_j, c) + 1}{n + l}, \qquad (2)$$

$$P(w_i|c) = \frac{\sum_{j=1}^{n} W_i f_{ji} \delta(c_j, c) + 1}{\sum_{i=1}^{m} \sum_{j=1}^{n} W_i f_{ji} \delta(c_j, c) + m}, \qquad (3)$$

where n is the number of training documents, l is the number of classes, c_j is the class label of the jth training document, f_{ji} is the frequency count of word w_i in the jth training document, and $\delta(\bullet)$ is a binary function, which is one if its two parameters are identical and zero otherwise.

FWCNB uses Equation 4 to classify the document d.

$$c(d) = \arg \max_{c \in C} [-log P(\bar{c}) - \sum_{i=1}^{m} W_i f_i log P(w_i|\bar{c})], \qquad (4)$$

where $\bar{c}$ is the complement classes of the class c (all classes except the class c), the prior probability $P(\bar{c})$ and the conditional probability $P(w_i|\bar{c})$ can be estimated by Equation 5 and Equation 6 respectively.

$$P(\bar{c}) = \frac{\sum_{j=1}^{n} \delta(c_j, \bar{c}) + 1}{n + l}, \qquad (5)$$

$$P(w_i|\bar{c}) = \frac{\sum_{j=1}^{n} W_i f_{ji} \delta(c_j, \bar{c}) + 1}{\sum_{i=1}^{m} \sum_{j=1}^{n} W_i f_{ji} \delta(c_j, \bar{c}) + m}. \qquad (6)$$

FWOVA is a direct combination of FWMNB and FWCNB, which uses Equation 7 to classify the document d.

$$c(d) = \arg\max_{c \in C}[(logP(c) - logP(\bar{c})) + \sum_{i=1}^{m} W_i f_i(logP(w_i|c) - logP(w_i|\bar{c}))], \quad (7)$$

where the probabilities $P(c)$, $P(w_i|c)$, $P(\bar{c})$, and $P(w_i|\bar{c})$ are computed by Equations 2, 3, 5 and 6 respectively.

Obviously, how to learn the weight of each feature W_i $(i = 1, 2, \cdots, m)$ is crucial in constructing feature weighted naive Bayes text classifiers. In order to learn the weights of features, we propose a CFS-based feature weighting approach. Therefore, our research starts from our revisiting to CFS [13].

CFS is a correlation-based filter algorithm for feature selection. The central hypothesis of it is that good feature subsets contain features that are highly correlated with the class variable, yet uncorrelated with each other. CFS uses the best first strategy to search the feature subset space and uses Equation 8 to evaluate the merit of a feature subset S containing k features.

$$Merit_s = \frac{k\overline{r_{cf}}}{\sqrt{k + k(k-1)\overline{r_{ff}}}}, \quad (8)$$

where $\overline{r_{cf}}$ is the average feature-class correlation, and $\overline{r_{ff}}$ is the average feature-feature inter-correlation. Obviously, the heuristic merit tries to search a feature subset with bigger $\overline{r_{cf}}$ by removing irrelevant features and smaller $\overline{r_{ff}}$ by removing redundant features.

Intuitively, removing the redundant and/or uncorrelated features can scale up the performance of text classifiers to some extent, especially when it comes to the high-dimensional text datasets. However, our experimental results in Section 3 show that CFS performs even worse than the original versions when it is applied to some state-of-the-art naive Bayes text classifiers such as MNB.

Inspired by this phenomenon, we propose a CFS-based feature weighting approach. Our approach firstly employs CFS to select the best feature subset from the whole space of features and then assigns larger weights to the features in the selected feature subset and smaller weights to others. For simplicity, in our current version we simply set the weights of the selected features to 2 and 1 to others. In our experiments, we also observed the performance of our proposed approach using different weights of the selected attributes and found that the weight of 2 is almost the best. Due to the limit of space, we have not presented the detailed experimental results here. Now, let us give the detailed description of our algorithm as follows.

Algorithm : A CFS-based Feature Weighting Approach (**D**)
Input : the original training data **D**
Output : the weight of each feature W_i $(i = 1, 2, \cdots, m)$
    1. Employ CFS to select the best feature subset S.
    2. For each feature w_i $(i = 1, 2, \cdots, m)$ from D.
        (a) If w_i is in S, then set the weight W_i to 2.

(b) Otherwise, set the weight W_i to 1.

3. Return the weight of each feature W_i $(i = 1, 2, \cdots, m)$.

Please note that, our approach just increases the weights of the selected features and does not completely eliminate the unselected features, which is different from CFS. Also note that, different from the existing feature weighting approaches, our approach incorporates the learned weights of features not only into the classification equations such as Equations 1, 4 and 7, but also into the conditional probabilities $P(w_i|\bar{c})$ and $P(w_i|\bar{c})$ by Equations 3 and 6 respectively.

3   Experiments and Results

The purpose of this section is to validate the classification performance (accuracy) of our proposed algorithms. We implement our proposed FWMNB, FWCNB, FWOVA and other competitors CFS-MNB and $R_{w,c}$-MNB in WEKA platform [14]. We ran our experiments on 16 widely used text classification benchmark datasets published on the main web site of WEKA platform [14], which represent a wide range of domains and data characteristics. The detailed description of these 16 datasets is shown in Table 1. Please note that, for saving the time and memory in running experiments, we don't include three very large datasets: "la1s", "la2s", and "new3s" in our experiments. We carefully observe these three datasets and find that there exist a mass of too sparse words in them.

Table 1. Datasets used in our experiments

Dataset	Documents number	Words number	Classes number
fbis	2463	2000	17
oh0	1003	3182	10
oh10	1050	3238	10
oh15	913	3100	10
oh5	918	3012	10
ohscal	11162	11465	10
re0	1657	3758	25
re1	1504	2886	13
tr11	414	6429	9
tr12	313	5804	8
tr21	336	7902	6
tr23	204	5832	6
tr31	927	10128	7
tr41	878	7454	10
tr45	690	8261	10
wap	1560	8460	20

In our experiments, we design six groups of experiments to compare six pairs of algorithms: MNB versus FWMNB, CNB versus FWCNB, OVA versus FWOVA, MNB versus CFS-MNB, MNB versus $R_{w,c}$-MNB, and $R_{w,c}$-MNB

Table 2. Classification accuracy comparisons for MNB versus FWMNB, CNB versus FWCNB, and OVA versus FWOVA

Algorithms	MNB vs FWMNB			CNB vs FWCNB			OVA vs FWOVA		
Datasets	MNB	FWMNB		CNB	FWCNB		OVA	FWOVA	
fbis	77.11	78.69	○	76.78	77.17		80.33	81.36	○
oh0	89.55	91.47	○	92.31	93.62	○	91.46	92.84	○
oh10	80.6	82.25	○	81.76	83.26	○	82.1	83.6	○
oh15	83.6	85.63	○	84.38	86.1	○	84.5	86.25	○
oh5	86.63	89.32	○	90.58	92.15	○	89.38	90.96	○
ohscal	74.7	76.31	○	76.5	78.17	○	75.96	77.63	○
re0	80.02	80.93		82.37	83.47	○	81.5	82.45	
re1	83.31	85.38	○	84.99	84.82		85.03	85.99	○
tr11	85.21	86.83		82.64	83.27		84.6	86.31	○
tr12	80.99	82.62	○	86.32	87.88		84.18	86.32	○
tr21	61.9	65.12	○	85.94	87.67		79.4	82.71	○
tr23	71.15	73.4	○	70.59	77.06	○	71.45	76.3	○
tr31	94.6	95.54	○	94.67	96.02	○	94.91	96.12	○
tr41	94.65	95.61	○	94.23	94.91		94.89	95.73	○
tr45	83.64	86.59	○	87.2	89.07	○	87.51	89.81	○
wap	81.22	82.53	○	77.53	78.41	○	80.58	81.79	○
Average	81.81	83.64		84.3	85.82		84.23	86.01	
$W/T/L$	14/2/0			10/6/0			15/1/0		

○, ● statistically significant improvement or degradation

Table 3. Classification accuracy comparisons for MNB versus CFS-MNB, MNB versus $R_{w,c}$-MNB, and $R_{w,c}$-MNB versus FWMNB

Algorithms	MNB vs CFS-MNB			MNB vs $R_{w,c}$-MNB			$R_{w,c}$-MNB vs FWMNB		
Datasets	MNB	CFS-MNB		MNB	$R_{w,c}$-MNB		$R_{w,c}$-MNB	FWMNB	
fbis	77.11	74.8	●	77.11	79.87	○	79.87	78.69	●
oh0	89.55	80.52	●	89.55	89.05		89.05	91.47	○
oh10	80.6	71.96	●	80.6	80.41		80.41	82.25	○
oh15	83.6	76.33	●	83.6	83.61		83.61	85.63	○
oh5	86.63	77.43	●	86.63	86.46		86.46	89.32	○
ohscal	74.7	67.21	●	74.7	74.18	●	74.18	76.31	○
re0	80.02	75.54	●	80.02	77.07	●	77.07	80.93	○
re1	83.31	77.39	●	83.31	82.72		82.72	85.38	○
tr11	85.21	85.93		85.21	85.44		85.44	86.83	
tr12	80.99	78.75		80.99	84.76	○	84.76	82.62	
tr21	61.9	90.46	○	61.9	69.63	○	69.63	65.12	●
tr23	71.15	90.53	○	71.15	73.82		73.82	73.4	
tr31	94.6	96.51	○	94.6	94.2		94.2	95.54	○
tr41	94.65	94.33		94.65	93.05	●	93.05	95.61	○
tr45	83.64	89.32	○	83.64	88.88	○	88.88	86.59	●
wap	81.22	75.49	●	81.22	76.33	●	76.33	82.53	○
Average	81.81	81.41		81.81	82.47		82.47	83.64	
$W/T/L$	4/3/9			4/8/4			10/3/3		

○, ● statistically significant improvement or degradation

versus FWMNB. The classification accuracy of each algorithm on each dataset are obtained via 10 runs of 10-fold cross-validation. Runs with the various algorithms are carried out on the same training sets and evaluated on the same test sets. In particular, the cross-validation folds are the same for all the experiments on each data set. The detailed experimental results are presented in Tables 2 and 3. The symbols ∘ and • in tables respectively denote statistically significant improvement or degradation over the competitors with a 95% confidence level [15]. Besides, the averages and the $W/T/L$ values are summarized at the bottom of the tables. Each entry $W/T/L$ in tables means that the improved algorithms win on W datasets, tie on T datasets, and lose on L datasets, compared to their competitors. From our experimental results, we can see that:

(1) The existing correlation-based feature selection (CFS) approach can not be directly used to improve naive Bayes text classifiers such as MNB and performs even worse than the original versions. Seen from Table 3, CFS-MNB is a little worse than MNB with 4 wins and 9 losses.

(2) The recently published χ^2 statistic-based feature weighting approach ($R_{w,c}$) almost ties the original naive Bayes text classifiers such as MNB. Seen from Table 3, the $W/T/L$ value between MNB and $R_{w,c}$-MNB is 4/8/4.

(3) Our CFS-based feature weighting approach can significantly scale up the classification performance of the naive Bayes text classifiers. Seen from Table 2, our feature weighted versions FWMNB, FWCNB and FWOVA are much better than the original versions MNB, CNB and OVA with 14, 10, and 15 wins respectively and surprisingly 0 losses.

(4) Our CFS-based feature weighting approach is also much better than the recently published χ^2 statistic-based feature weighting approach. Seen from Table 3, FWMNB significantly outperforms $R_{w,c}$-MNB on 10 datasets and only loses on 3 datasets. With regards to CNB and OVA, we can almost get the same conclusions. Due to the limit of space, we have not presented the detailed experimental results here.

4 Conclusion

Of numerous proposals to address the text classification issues, multinomial naive Bayes (MNB), complement naive Bayes (CNB) and the one-versus-all-but-one model (OVA), have demonstrated remarkable classification performance. However, all of them assume that all features are independent given the class. In this paper, we propose a CFS-based feature weighting approach to weakening the strong assumptions of independence among features by weighting the correlated features. The extensive empirical study on a large suite of benchmark datasets shows that our feature weighted versions FWMNB, FWCNB and FWOVA significantly outperform the original versions MNB, CNB and OVA in terms of classification accuracy.

Acknowledgements. This work was partially supported by the National Natural Science Foundation of China (61203287), the Program for New Century Excellent Talents in University (NCET-12-0953), the Provincial Natural Science Foundation of Hubei (2011CDA103), and the Fundamental Research Funds for the Central Universities (CUG130504, CUG130414).

References

1. Yan, J., Gao, X.: Detection and recognition of text superimposed in images base on layered method. Neurocomputing 134, 3–14 (2014)
2. Losada, D.E., Azzopardi, L.: Assessing multivariate Bernoulli models for information retrieval. ACM Transactions on Information Systems (TOIS) 26(3), Article No. 17 (2008)
3. Han, E.-H., Karypis, G.: Centroid-based document classification: Analysis and experimental results. In: Zighed, D.A., Komorowski, J., Żytkow, J.M. (eds.) PKDD 2000. LNCS (LNAI), vol. 1910, pp. 424–431. Springer, Heidelberg (2000)
4. Han, E.-H(S.), Karypis, G., Kumar, V.: Text Categorization Using Weight Adjusted K-Nearest Neighbor Classification. In: Cheung, D., Williams, G.J., Li, Q. (eds.) PAKDD 2001. LNCS (LNAI), vol. 2035, pp. 53–65. Springer, Heidelberg (2001)
5. Ponte, J.M., Croft, W.B.: A language modeling approach to information retrieval. In: Proceedings of the 21st Annual International ACM SIGIR Conference on Research and Development in Information Retrieval, pp. 275–281. ACM (1998)
6. McCallum, A., Nigam, K.: A comparison of event models for naive bayes text classification. In: Working Notes of the 1998 AAAI/ICML Workshop on Learning for Text, pp. 41–48. AAAI Press (1998)
7. Rennie, J.D., Shih, L., Teevan, J., Karger, D.R.: Tackling the poor assumptions of naive bayes text classifiers. In: Proceedings of the Twentieth International Conference on Machine Learning, pp. 616–623. Morgan Kaufmann (2003)
8. Berger, A.: Error-correcting output coding for text classification. In: IJCAI 1999: Workshop on Machine Learning for Information Filtering (1999)
9. Zhang, T., Oles, F.J.: Text categorization based on regularized linear classification methods. Information Retrieval, 5–31 (2001)
10. Jiang, L., Wang, D., Cai, Z.: Discriminatively Weighted Naive Bayes and its Application in Text Classification. International Journal on Artificial Intelligence Tools 21(01), 1250007, 19 (2012)
11. Jiang, L., Cai, Z., Zhang, H., Wang, D.: Naive Bayes Text Classifiers: A Locally Weighted Learning Approach. Journal of Experimental & Theoretical Artificial Intelligence 25(2), 273–286 (2013)
12. Li, Y., Luo, C., Chung, S.M.: Weighted Naive Bayes for Text Classification Using positive Term-Class Dependency. International Journal on Artificial Intelligence Tools 21(01), 1250008, 16 (2012)
13. Hall, M.: Correlation-based feature selection for discrete and numeric class machine learning. In: Proceedings of the 17th International Conference on Machine Learning, pp. 359–366 (2000)
14. Witten, I.H., Frank, E., Hall, M.A.: Data Mining: Practical Machine Learning Tools and Techniques, 3rd edn., p. 978. Morgan Kaufmann (January 2011) ISBN 978-0-12-374856-0
15. Nadeau, C., Bengio, Y.: Inference for the generalization error. Machine Learning 52(3), 239–281 (2003)

Local Rejection Strategies
for Learning Vector Quantization

Lydia Fischer[1,2], Barbara Hammer[2], and Heiko Wersing[1]

[1] HONDA Research Institute Europe GmbH,
Carl-Legien-Str. 30, 63065 Offenbach, Germany
[2] Bielefeld University, Universitätsstr. 25, 33615 Bielefeld, Germany

Abstract. Classification with rejection is well understood for classifiers which provide explicit class probabilities. The situation is more complicated for popular deterministic classifiers such as learning vector quantisation schemes: albeit reject options using simple distance-based geometric measures were proposed [4], their local scaling behaviour is unclear for complex problems. Here, we propose a local threshold selection strategy which automatically adjusts suitable threshold values for reject options in prototype-based classifiers from given data. We compare this local threshold strategy to a global choice on artificial and benchmark data sets; we show that local thresholds enhance the classification results in comparison to global ones, and they better approximate optimal Bayesian rejection in cases where the latter is available.

Keywords: Prototype-based reject, classification, local thresholds.

1   Motivation

Learning vector quantisation (LVQ) [9] constitutes a powerful and efficient method for multi-class classification tasks which, due to its representation of models in terms of prototypes, is particularly suited for on-line scenarios or lifelong learning [8]. While classical LVQ models have been introduced on heuristic grounds, modern variants are based on cost-function models like generalized LVQ (GLVQ) [12], or robust soft LVQ (RSLVQ) [15] with guarantees on generalization performance and learning dynamics [2,13]. One particular success story links LVQ classifiers to simultaneous metric learners which enrich the classifier with interpretable feature weighting terms or a direct classifier visualisation [13,14]. Still, LVQ classifiers face the problem that real world data do not necessarily allow an unambiguous classification: overlap in the data, outliers, noise, or similar effects can be observed frequently where wrong classifications are unavoidable. A wrong classification can be more costly than postponing a decision and gathering new evidence like in medical diagnostics. Mathematically, such settings can be modelled by introducing a reject option for a classifier: instead of a decision, rejecting is possible for cases with low certainty. This setting has formally been analysed by Chow [3], deriving an optimum decision rule depending on the costs of a reject in comparison to a wrong classification. While this early approach

S. Wermter et al. (Eds.): ICANN 2014, LNCS 8681, pp. 563–570, 2014.

addresses the setting that reliable class probabilities are available, the approach [7] extends this optimum decision by plug-in rules which rely on empirical estimations of class probabilities only, providing guarantees of the quality in case of a reliable estimator and a suitably low density of data at the reject thresholds.

Still, these schemes rely on the assumption that conditional class probabilities or reliable estimations thereof are available. Albeit there exist few approaches which model LVQ classifiers by means of class probabilities such as RSLVQ [15], it is unclear whether such discriminative models converge to the correct underlying class distributions, and most popular LVQ schemes are based on deterministic decision models only instead of a reference to class probabilities [5,12,17]. Recently [4,5] it has been analysed if alternative real-valued outputs correlated to the deterministic classification model can take the role of a certainty value for a reject option: examples include the distance of a data vector to the closest decision boundary, prototype. Interestingly, using simple thresholds, these measures offer classification schemes with a reject option with the quality close to optimum Bayesian decisions in simple model cases [4,5].

One drawback of these techniques is that they are based on one global threshold for a reject option, thus relying on the assumption that the considered measures scale independently of the data region. This is usually not the case: measures such as distances, unlike a certainty, are not normalized and scaling varies within a given data set. Hence reject options with a global threshold are restricted to simple models only. In cases where the classes or parts of classes have not the same compactness or where the scaling of the values is unclear, this approach is limited, and it can be an advantage to use local thresholds [6,17].

For prototype-based classification there exists an intuitive strategy to define regions for the local thresholds: Use the Voronoi-tessellation of the input space provided by the prototypes. Here we present a greedy optimization method to adaptively determine local thresholds for an LVQ classifier based on given data. We compare the resulting local rejection strategies to the global counterparts as proposed in [4,5] using several benchmarks and one artificial data set. We show that local thresholds outperform their global counterpart, approximating the optimal reject option of Chow [3] in cases where the latter is available.

2   Learning Vector Quantization

Assume N training samples $x \in \mathbb{R}^n$ with attached class labels $y \in \{1, \ldots, L\}$, if L classes are considered. An LVQ classifier is represented by a set of prototypes $W = \{w_i \in \mathbb{R}^n\}_{i=1}^k$ which are equipped with class labels $c(w) \in \{1, \ldots, L\}$. Classification takes place by a winner takes all scheme: A data vector x is mapped to the class label $c(x) = c(w_i)$ of the closest prototype w_i according to a distance measure d. Here, we use the squared Euclidean distance $d(x, w) = \|x - w\|^2$.

For a GLVQ model [12], the position of the prototypes W are determined by a stochastic gradient decent on the following cost function:

$$E = \sum_i \Phi((d^+(x_i) - d^-(x_i))/(d^+(x_i) + d^-(x_i))) . \tag{1}$$

$\Phi(\cdot)$ is a monotonic increasing function, e.g. the identity. The distances of a data vector x to the closest prototypes with the same/different label are denoted as d^+/d^-. Replacing the distance measure by a general quadratic form $(x - w_i)^T \Lambda (x - w_i)$ with positive semi-definite matrix Λ results in a generalization of GLVQ, generalised matrix LVQ (GMLVQ) [13] whereby matrix parameters can be adapted coevally to the prototypes according to the given data.

The cost E (1) correlates with the classification error because a data vector is classified correctly iff the nominator of (1) is below zero. The nominator can be connected to the hypothesis margin of the classifier which relates to its generalisation ability [13]. Note that the argument of $\Phi(\cdot)$ ranges in $[-1, 1]$. A value near -1 indicates a high certainty of the classification because $d^+ \ll d^-$.

3   Reject Option

The aim of a reject option is to identify outliers and data vectors with low certainty of classification [17]. A *rejection measure* refers to a real-valued function $r : \mathbb{R}^n \to \mathbb{R}^+, x \mapsto r(x)$ indicating the certainty of the classification. We assume that high values indicate a more certain classification. A vector is rejected iff $r(x) < \theta$, where $\theta \geq 0$ is a threshold. We refer to such strategies as *global* rejection strategies if one global threshold θ is chosen for all inputs $x \in \mathbb{R}^n$.

A *local threshold strategy* where the input space is partitioned into single regions enables a finer control of rejection [17]. Following the suggestion in [17], we use the natural decomposition of the input space into the Voronoi-cells

$$V_j = \{x_i | d(x_i, w_j) \leq d(x_i, w_k), \forall k \neq j\} ; \tag{2}$$

as induced by the prototypes of an LVQ classifier. For a local threshold strategy based on Voronoi-cells (2) a separate threshold $\theta_j \geq 0$ is chosen for every cell, and the reject strategy is given by a threshold vector of the dimension $|W|$ equal to the number of V_j. A vector x is rejected iff $r(x) < \theta_j$ for $x \in V_j$. In the case of one prototype per class, local thresholds realise a class-wise reject option.

After defining local and global threshold strategies, we need to specify the rejection measure and a method for finding suitable local θ_j.

Choice of the Rejection Measure: In our experiments we use the relative similarity (RelSim) as proposed in [4] as rejection measure:

$$\mathrm{RelSim}(x) = \frac{d^-(x) - d^+(x)}{d^-(x) + d^+(x)} . \tag{3}$$

This measure can be applied for new data vectors after defining their class label with the winner takes all scheme. RelSim is inspired by the cost function of GLVQ (1) [12]. Its values are normalised to $[0, 1]$ and 1 indicates a high certainty of the classification with respect to the trained prototypes. It can efficiently be calculated and it combines a reject option for outliers and ambiguous data vectors due to its design (Fig. 1, left). As baseline for an artificial data set the maximum of the class probabilities $\max_y p(y|x)$ of the Bayes classifier with known densities [3] is used for rejection (Fig. 1, right).

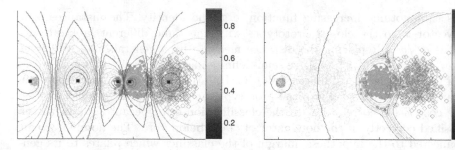

Fig. 1. Level curves of RelSim (3) (left) and Bayes (right) for an artificial five-class problem. The black squares are prototypes. A critical region for a global threshold is between the third and fourth cluster from left. The third cluster needs a high threshold because the data vectors are very compact. Applying the same threshold for the fourth cluster would lead to rejection of the most vectors in this cluster which is undesired.

Adaptation of Local Thresholds: The baseline case with no rejection is given when all local thresholds are set to $\theta_j = 0$. We propose the following greedy strategy: For rejection increase those θ_j, where most wrongly classified vectors can be rejected while accepting a constant number of rejected correct vectors. We associate the rejection of a correct vector with a constant cost of 1. Starting from 0, the global cost is increased in steps of 1, and the θ_j are adapted accordingly.

We assume that the vectors $\boldsymbol{x}_i \in V_j$ are sorted according to their (RelSim) certainty value $r(\boldsymbol{x}_i)$. Let $\mathbf{q}_j$ denote the vector of classification results for the vectors in V_j with $q_j(\boldsymbol{x}_i) = 1\,(+)$ for correct and $q_j(\boldsymbol{x}_i) = -1\,(-)$ for wrong classification (cp. Fig. 2). Voronoi-cells V_j without errors can be neglected (i. e. $\theta_j = 0$), because they cannot contribute reasonably to rejec-

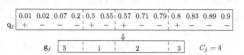

Fig. 2. V_j with 13 vectors. First row implies the sorted $r(\boldsymbol{x}_i)$ values, the second codes if a vector is correct $(+)$/wrong $(-)$ classified. The third row implies the coding of the gain g_j of rejection steps during the algorithm.

tion. Let $C_j = \sum_{i|q_j(\boldsymbol{x}_i)=1} 1$ be the number of correct vectors in V_j and let $E_j = \sum_{i|q_j(\boldsymbol{x}_i)=-1} 1$ be the number of errors in V_j. The aim of the algorithm 3.1 is to return an accuracy reject curve which consists of two vectors $\mathbf{t}_c$ and $\mathbf{t}_a$. For an iteration step s a single point $(t_c(s), t_a(s))$ reports the relative size $t_c(s)$ of the set of accepted vectors X_θ in comparison to $|X|$ and the accuracy on X_θ which is $t_a(s)$. The original model without rejection initialises these vectors with $t_c(0)=1$ and $t_a(0)=\sum_j C_j/|X|$. Respectively we define E_R and C_R as counter for rejected errors and rejected correct classified vectors. If $\boldsymbol{x}_i$ with $\max_{\boldsymbol{x}_i \in V_j} r(\boldsymbol{x}_i)$ is correct classified then $\mathbf{a}$ denotes the indexes of the correct classified vectors in V_j. Otherwise the first C_j entries of $\mathbf{a}$ contains indexes of the correct classified vectors and the last entry is given with $|V_j|+1$ ($\mathbf{a} = (1, 5, 7, 10, 14)$ for example in Fig. 2). If $a_j(1) > 1$ there exist errors in V_j which can be rejected with zero cost. We code the wrongly classified vectors for constant costs in the gain vector $\boldsymbol{g}_j$ and the accumulated gains $\hat{\boldsymbol{g}}_j$ as follows:

$$g_j(k) = a_j(k+1) - a_j(k) - 1, \quad \hat{g}_j(k) = \sum_{l=1}^{k} g_j(l), \quad k = 1, \ldots, C_j \quad (4)$$

$g_j(k)$ is the local gain for rejecting the next correct vector (cf. Fig. 2) and $\hat{g}_j(k)$ states the accumulated gains for costs of k in V_j. An example for $\boldsymbol{g}_j$ and $\hat{\boldsymbol{g}}_j$ with three Voronoi-cells is given in table 1.

Algorithm 3.1: GREEDY OPTIMIZATON$(\boldsymbol{a}_j, \boldsymbol{g}_j, \hat{\boldsymbol{g}}_j \forall j)$

$C_R := 1;\ E_R := \sum_j (a_j(1) - 1)$ //errors whose rejection is gratis
$t_c(1) := 1 - E_R/|X|;\ t_a(1) := \sum_j C_j/(|X| - E_R)$
$s := 2;\ k_j := 0\ \forall j$
while $E_R \neq \sum_j E_j$

do $\begin{cases} m := \operatorname{argmax}_j\{g_j(k_j + 1)\} \quad \text{//index: most improvement locally} \\ \hat{m} := \operatorname{argmax}_j\{\hat{g}_j(C_R)\} \quad \text{//index: most improvement globally} \\ \textbf{if } \max_j\{\hat{g}_j(C_R)\} > \max_j\{g_j(k_j + 1)\} \\ \quad \textbf{then } \begin{cases} k_j := 0,\ \forall j;\ k_{\hat{m}} := C_R \quad \text{//discard whole solution} \\ C_R := C_R + 1;\ E_R := \hat{g}_{\hat{m}} \end{cases} \\ \textbf{else } \begin{cases} \textbf{if } \exists!\max_j\{g_j(k_j + 1)\} \\ \quad \textbf{then } \begin{cases} k_m := k_m + 1;\ C_R := C_R + 1 \\ E_R := E_R + g_m(k_m) \end{cases} \\ \quad \textbf{else } \begin{cases} o := 1 \quad \text{//allows increasing} > 1 \text{ for } C_R \\ \textbf{while } \neg(\exists!\max_j\{g_j(k_j + 1)\}) \\ \quad \textbf{do } \{o := o + 1;\ m := \operatorname{argmax}_j\{g_j(k_j + o)\} \\ C_R := C_R + o;\ k_m := k_m + o \\ E_R := E_R + \sum_{l=1}^{o} g_m(k_m + l) \end{cases} \end{cases} \\ t_c(s) := 1 - (C_R + E_R)/|X| \\ t_a(s) := (\sum_j C_j - C_R)/(|X| - (C_R + E_R)) \\ s := s + 1 \end{cases}$

return $(\boldsymbol{t}_c, \boldsymbol{t}_a)$

The greedy algorithm for the local threshold adaptation (Alg. 3.1) operates mainly on $\boldsymbol{g}_j$ and $\hat{\boldsymbol{g}}_j$. Using the example (Tab. 1) one obtains the steps in table 2. First the algorithm checks if errors can be rejected with no cost, then checks for the cell with highest gain. E.g. the gains $g_1(1) = 3$, $g_2(1) = 2$, $g_3(1)=1$ are possible and the algorithm picks $g_1(1)=3$ which results in $k_1 = 1$ ($\hat{g}_j(1) = g_j(1), \forall j$). Then $g_1(2) = 1$, $g_2(2) = 2$, $g_3(1) = 1$ are possible and it

Table 1. Examples for $\boldsymbol{g}_j$, $\hat{\boldsymbol{g}}_j$ for three V_j

# (+)	1	2	3	4	1	2	3	4
	$\boldsymbol{g}_j$				$\hat{\boldsymbol{g}}_j$			
V_1	3	1	2	3	3	4	6	9
V_2	2	1	3	-	2	3	6	-
V_3	1	1	8	10	1	2	10	20

picks $g_2(1)=2$, raising θ_j in this cell because $\max_j\{\hat{g}_j(C_R)\}$ is lower. Now we have 2 correct data vectors and 5 errors rejected. In the next step, $g_1(2) = 1$, $g_2(2) = 1$, $g_3(1) = 1$ are possible and we choose a gain of 1 and 3 correct data vectors would be rejected. The overall gain of this solution is $3 + 2 + 1 = 6$. Checking table. 1 we see for 3 correct data vectors the gains $\hat{g}_1(3)=6$, $\hat{g}_2(3)=6$, $\hat{g}_3(3)=10$. Then it is better to discard the previous solution and reject only in

V_3 because of a gain of 10 instead of 6. An exception rule comes into operation when there are more than one optima in the gains and discarding the whole solution is no option. This means there is no single maximum in g_j and $\hat{g}$. In this case the algorithm increases the costs till one local optimum remains.

4   Experiments

We evaluate the benefit of a local threshold strategy as compared to the global counterpart in a variety of experiments. Thereby, we train all models using GLVQ and GMLVQ with one prototype per class. Evaluations are obtained as results of a repeated 10-fold cross-validation with ten repetitions. For one artificial data set, an optimum Bayesian reject option based on the quantity $\max_y p(y|x)$ can be evaluated

Table 2. Iterations of the algorithm. Shows how the costs are split to V_j

costs	1	2	3	4	5	6	8	9	10
$V_1 : k_1$	1	1	0	0	1	1	1	2	3
$V_2 : k_2$	0	1	0	0	0	1	3	3	3
$V_3 : k_3$	0	0	3	4	4	4	4	4	4

as proposed in [3]. We will use this ground truth as baseline where it is possible. The data sets which we will consider include the following:

- *Pearl necklace*: This data set consists of five artificially generated Gaussian clusters in two dimensions with overlap. (parameters: $\mu_{y_i} = 3 \ \forall i, \mu_x = (2, 44, 85, 100, 136), \sigma_x = (1, 20, 0.5, 7, 11), \sigma_x = \sigma_y$)
- *Image Segmentation*: The image segmentation data set consists of 2310 data vectors which contain 19 real-valued image descriptors. The data vectors represent small patches from outdoor images with 7 different classes with equal distribution such as grass, cement, etc. [1].
- *Tecator data*: The Tecator data set [16] consists of 215 spectra of meat probes. The 100 spectral bands ranging from 850 nm to 1050 nm. The task is to predict the fat content (high/low) of the probes, which is turned into a two class classification problem. Both classes have the same size.
- *Haberman*: The Haberman survival data set includes 306 instances from two classes indicating being alive for more than 5 years after breast cancer surgery [1]. One instance is represented by three attributes linked to the age, the year, and the number of positive axillary nodes detected.
- *Coil*: The Columbia Object Image Database Library (COIL-20) contains gray scaled images of twenty objects [11]. Each object is rotated in 5° steps, resulting in 72 images per object. The data set contains 1440 vectors with a dimension of 16384. We reduce the dimensionality to 30 with PCA.

Figure 3 displays the classification accuracy obtained by local and global reject options for these data sets and the GLVQ and GMLVQ classifier on the set of classified vectors versus the percentage of vectors which are not rejected for a given threshold [10]. More precisely, assume X_θ denotes the set of data vectors which are not rejected using the respective threshold strategy. Then the graphs display the relative size $|X_\theta|/|X|$ against the classification accuracy on X_θ. The local thresholds are determined with algorithm 3.1 on the train sets and then applied on the test sets. Figure 3 shows that local thresholds are slightly better than a global threshold in almost all cases. The local thresholds seem to be more efficient for GLVQ than for GM-LVQ (Image Segmentation, Coil). The biggest improvement of the local strategy can be seen for the pearl necklace data set which was designed to show its advantage. Because of the huge differences in the standard deviations of the single classes/clusters one global threshold would be very ineffective. For low standard deviations a higher threshold than for a cluster with a huge standard deviation is needed. In most cases it is obvious that one needs a very high threshold for the global strategy to reject all errors. For the local strategy all errors can be rejected without rejecting all correctly classified data vectors in some cases (both

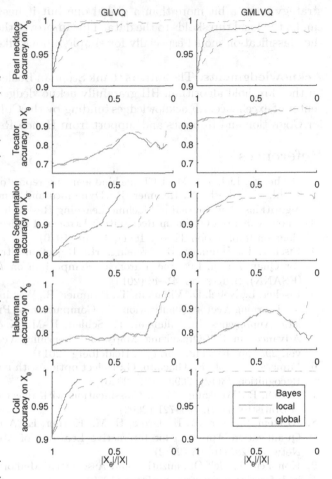

Fig. 3. Results of the global and local reject option with RelSim when applied to G(M)LVQ models trained for different data sets (test sets). We report accuracy reject curves [10]. The averaged curve is plotted, where at least 80 % of the single runs deliver a value.

models GLVQ and GMLVQ: Pearl necklace, Image Segmentation).

5   Conclusion

We analysed the performance of a global and a local threshold strategy of a reject option. The results of artificial and benchmark data sets show that the local strategy delivers better accuracy values than the global counterpart in most cases. We showed a way of evaluating the local threshold strategy for different rejection rates obtaining also the local thresholds. Applying a local threshold strategy costs a bit more than a global one but it has the advantage that one can fit the local thresholds to the data. This improves the accuracy and enhances the classification model especially for simple models like GLVQ.

Acknowledgments. The authors thank Stephan Hasler for very helpful debates on the threshold algorithm. BH gratefully acknowledges funding by the CITEC center of excellence. LF acknowledges funding by the CoR-Lab Research Institute for Cognition and Robotics and support from Honda Research Institute Europe.

References

1. Bache, K., Lichman, M.: UCI machine learning repository (2013)
2. Biehl, M., Ghosh, A., Hammer, B.: Dynamics and generalization ability of LVQ algorithms. The Journal of Machine Learning Research 8, 323–360 (2007)
3. Chow, C.K.: On Optimum Recognition Error and Reject Tradeoff. IEEE Transactions on Information Theory 16(1), 41–46 (1970)
4. Fischer, L., Hammer, B., Wersing, H.: Rejection Strategies for Learning Vector Quantization. In: Proc. European Symposium on Artificial Neural Networks (ESANN), Bruges, pp. 41–46 (2014)
5. Fischer, L., Nebel, D., Villmann, T., Hammer, B., Wersing, H.: Rejection Strategies for Learning Vector Quantization – a Comparison of Probabilistic and Deterministic Approaches. In: Villmann, T., Schleif, F.-M., Kaden, M., Lange, M. (eds.) Advances in Self-Organizing Maps and Learning Vector Quantization. AISC, vol. 295, pp. 109–118. Springer, Heidelberg (2014)
6. Fumera, G., Roli, F., Giacinto, G.: Reject option with multiple thresholds. Pattern Recognition 33(12), 2099–2101 (2000)
7. Herbei, R., Wegkamp, M.H.: Classification with reject option. Canadian Journal of Statistics 34(4), 709–721 (2006)
8. Kirstein, S., Wersing, H., Gross, H.-M., Körner, E.: A Life-Long Learning Vector Quantization Approach for Interactive Learning of Multiple Categories. Neural Networks 28, 90–105 (2012)
9. Kohonen, T.: Self-Organization and Associative Memory, 3rd edn. Springer Series in Information Sciences. Springer (1989)
10. Nadeem, M.S.A., Zucker, J.-D., Hanczar, B.: Accuracy-Rejection Curves (ARCs) for Comparing Classification Methods with a Reject Option. In: International Workshop on Machine Learning in Systems Biology, pp. 65–81 (2010)
11. Nene, S.A., Nayar, S.K., Murase, H.: Columbia Object Image Library (COIL-20). Technical Report CUCS-005-96 (February 1996)
12. Sato, A., Yamada, K.: Generalized Learning Vector Quantization. In: Advances in Neural Information Processing Systems, vol. 7, pp. 423–429 (1995)
13. Schneider, P., Biehl, M., Hammer, B.: Adaptive Relevance Matrices in Learning Vector Quantization. Neural Computation 21(12), 3532–3561 (2009)
14. Schneider, P., Bunte, K., Stiekema, H., Hammer, B., Villmann, T., Biehl, M.: Regularization in matrix relevance learning. IEEE Transactions on Neural Networks 21(5), 831–840 (2010)
15. Seo, S., Obermayer, K.: Soft Learning Lector Quantization. Neural Computation 15(7), 1589–1604 (2003)
16. Thodberg, H.H.: Tecator data set, contained in StatLib Datasets Archive (1995)
17. Vailaya, A., Jain, A.K.: Reject Option for VQ-Based Bayesian Classification. In: International Conference on Pattern Recognition (ICPR), pp. 2048–2051 (2000)

Efficient Adaptation of Structure Metrics in Prototype-Based Classification

Bassam Mokbel, Benjamin Paassen, and Barbara Hammer*

CITEC centre of excellence, Bielefeld University, Germany

Abstract. More complex data formats and dedicated structure metrics have spurred the development of intuitive machine learning techniques which directly deal with dissimilarity data, such as relational learning vector quantization (RLVQ). The adjustment of metric parameters like relevance weights for basic structural elements constitutes a crucial issue therein, and first methods to automatically learn metric parameters from given data were proposed recently. In this contribution, we investigate a robust learning scheme to adapt metric parameters such as the scoring matrix in sequence alignment in conjunction with prototype learning, and we investigate the suitability of efficient approximations thereof.

1 Introduction

An ever increasing availability of problem-specific data formats and a rapidly growing data complexity raises the issue that data are often no longer vectorial, rather data structures such as sequences, trees, graphs, or similar have to be dealt with [3]. One prominent approach which enables machine learning for structures is based on a dissimilarity representation [13]: data are described by pairwise dissimilarities given by some problem-specific dissimilarity measure such as sequence alignment, structure alignment, graph or tree kernels. Then any machine learning technique which is capable of processing proximity data can be applied.

Facing such data, one particular problem with classical learning techniques is the inherent discrete nature of structured data, hence smooth model updates become difficult. For dissimilarity data we can rely on an implicit embedding of data in an underlying pseudo-Euclidean vector space or more general Krein space [13]. Mimicking the popular kernel trick, it is possible to extend many vectorial, distance-based methods to such an embedding, resulting in so-called *relational* methods. Popular examples include unsupervised models such as *relational self-organising maps* and *relational generative topographic mapping*, or supervised counterparts such as *learning vector quantization* (LVQ) based schemes. [7,4,6]. Here we will exemplarily address prototype-based LVQ.

Specifically, we will consider *relational generalized LVQ* (RGLVQ) as an extension of *generalized LVQ* (GLVQ) to dissimilarity data [7]. GLVQ constitutes a popular and mathematically well-founded LVQ scheme with successful applications ranging from bioinformatics to robotics [14,10,15]. One interesting extension is its combination with metric learning, which not only enhances the

* Funding by the DFG under grant number HA 2719/6-1 and by the CITEC centre of excellence is gratefully acknowledged.

S. Wermter et al. (Eds.): ICANN 2014, LNCS 8681, pp. 571–578, 2014.
© Springer International Publishing Switzerland 2014

representational power but also facilitates model interpretability [15]. While relational variants also yield a robust prototype-based model, their metric parameters are usually fixed, failing in situations where these parameters are unsuitable. We address the challenge to adapt metric parameters in RGLVQ, extending upon a well-proven concept of smooth metric learning in vectorial GLVQ [15].

More specifically, we consider symbolic sequences and sequence alignment as one relevant type of structured representation. Alignment heavily depends on the underlying scoring matrix which assigns scores to local symbolic comparisons and gaps. In bioinformatics, these can be inferred from evolutionary models, but in general their choice is based on a-priori assumptions about the domain or data space [16]. A few promising approaches how to infer scores from exemplary alignments have been proposed [5,17,1,2]. One approach proposes to adapt scores for a discriminative classification task in conjunction with RGLVQ training, leading to first promising results [12]. The goal of this contribution is to extend this approach to a more robust adaptation suitable for realistic problems, and to test how it can be approximated to increase computational efficiency.

2   Learning Vector Quantization for Sequence Alignments

LVQ models represent vectorial data $\boldsymbol{a}^i$ by prototypes $\boldsymbol{w}^j$ with labels $c(\boldsymbol{w}^j)$ [15]. Classification uses a winner-takes-all rule: a data point is classified according to its closest prototype. Given labeled data $(\boldsymbol{a}^i, c(\boldsymbol{a}^i))$, GLVQ minimizes the cost

$$\sum_{i=1}^{N} \Phi \left(\frac{d^+(\boldsymbol{a}^i) - d^-(\boldsymbol{a}^i)}{d^+(\boldsymbol{a}^i) + d^-(\boldsymbol{a}^i)} \right)$$

where Φ is a monotonic function, d^+ is the distance of $\boldsymbol{a}^i$ to the closest prototype with a matching label, d^- refers to a non-matching label [15].

For dissimilarity data described by a symmetric matrix D with entries d_{ij}, an extension to *relational LVQ* is possible [13,7]: a pseudo-Euclidean space and vectors $\boldsymbol{a}^i$ exist which induce d_{ij} [13]. Prototypes are given as convex combinations $\boldsymbol{w}^j = \sum_i \alpha_i^j \boldsymbol{a}^i$ with $\sum_i \alpha_i^j = 1$ inducing $d(\boldsymbol{a}^i, \boldsymbol{w}^j) = \sum_l \alpha_l^j d_{il} - 0.5 \sum_{ll'} \alpha_l^j \alpha_{l'}^j d_{ll'}$. This can be computed based on the coefficients $\boldsymbol{\alpha}^j$ and dissimilarities D only, without explicitly referring to vectors $\boldsymbol{a}^i$ or their counterparts of actual data entities (e.g. string sequences), see [7]. We can adapt the coefficients $\boldsymbol{\alpha}^+$ or $\boldsymbol{\alpha}^-$ of the closest correct or incorrect prototype, by a stochastic gradient descent.

For sequence data, we can choose dissimilarities D according to pairwise alignments. We denote sequences over an alphabet Σ as $\bar{a} = (a_1, \ldots, a_I, \ldots, a_{|\bar{a}|})$ with $a_i \in \Sigma$ and length $|\bar{a}|$. Assume a symmetric dissimilarity measure $d_\lambda(a_i, a_j) = \lambda_{ij}$ is fixed on $(\Sigma \cup \{-\})^2$ with $d_\lambda(a_i, a_i) = 0$ and $d_\lambda(a_i, b_j) \geq 0$ for $a_i \neq b_j \in \Sigma \cup \{-\}$. A (global) *alignment* of sequences $\bar{a}$ and $\bar{b}$ consists of extensions $(\bar{a}^*, \bar{b}^*) \in ((\Sigma \cup \{-\})^*)^2$ by gaps such that $|\bar{a}^*| = |\bar{b}^*|$. *Alignment costs* are

$$d^*(\bar{a}, \bar{b}) = \min \left\{ \sum_{i=1}^{|\bar{a}^*|} d_\lambda(a_i^*, b_i^*) \mid (\bar{a}^*, \bar{b}^*) \text{ is alignment of } (\bar{a}, \bar{b}) \right\} .$$

Setting $\bar{a}(I) = (a_1, \ldots, a_I)$ and $\bar{b}(J) = (b_1, \ldots, b_J)$, alignment costs can be computed by dynamic programming (DP) using the recursion

$$d^*(\bar{a}(0), \bar{b}(0)) = 0, \quad d^*(\bar{a}(0), \bar{b}(J)) = \sum_{j \leq J} d_\lambda(-, b_j),$$
$$d^*(\bar{a}(I), \bar{b}(0)) = \sum_{i \leq I} d_\lambda(a_i, -),$$
$$d^*(\bar{a}(I+1), \bar{b}(J+1)) = \min\{ \ A_1 := d^*(\bar{a}(I), \bar{b}(J)) + d_\lambda(a_{I+1}, b_{J+1}),$$
$$A_2 := d^*(\bar{a}(I+1), \bar{b}(J)) + d_\lambda(-, b_{J+1}),$$
$$A_3 := d^*(\bar{a}(I), \bar{b}(J+1)) + d_\lambda(a_{I+1}, -) \ \} \ .$$

3   Adaptive Scoring for Alignments

Sequence alignment crucially depends on the scores λ of d_λ. Similar to [12], we propose an adaptation of λ based on the RGLVQ costs. Derivatives of the summand corresponding to a sequence $\bar{a}^i$ with respect to λ_{km} yield

$$\Phi' \cdot \frac{2d^-(\bar{a}^i)}{(d^+(\bar{a}^i) + d^-(\bar{a}^i))^2} \cdot \frac{\partial d^+(\bar{a}^i)}{\partial \lambda_{km}} - \Phi' \cdot \frac{2d^+(\bar{a}^i)}{(d^+(\bar{a}^i) + d^-(\bar{a}^i))^2} \cdot \frac{\partial d^-(\bar{a}^i)}{\partial \lambda_{km}}$$

with $\partial d(\bar{a}^i, \bar{w}^j)/\partial \lambda_{km} = \sum_l \alpha_l^j \partial d_{il}^* / \partial \lambda_{km} - 0.5 \sum_{ll'} \alpha_l^j \alpha_{l'}^j \partial d_{ll'}^* / \partial \lambda_{km}$ where d_{il}^* refers to the alignment of sequences i and l. Alignment $d^*(\bar{a}, \bar{b})$ is not differentiable, but an approximation is, substituting min by
$\text{softmin}(x_1, \ldots, x_n) = \sum_i x_i \cdot \exp(-\beta x_i)/\sum_j \exp(-\beta x_j)$ with the derivative
$\text{softmin}'(x_i) = (1 - \beta \cdot (x_i - \text{softmin})) \cdot \exp(-\beta x_i)/\sum_j \exp(-\beta x_j)$. The derivative
$\partial d^*(\bar{a}, \bar{b})/\partial \lambda_{km}$ can be computed in a DP scheme analog to the alignment:

$$\frac{\partial d^*(\bar{a}(I+1), \bar{b}(J+1))}{\partial \lambda_{km}} = \text{softmin}'(A_1) \cdot \left(\frac{\partial d^*(\bar{a}(I), \bar{b}(J))}{\partial \lambda_{km}} + \delta_k(a_{I+1})\delta_m(b_{J+1}) \right)$$
$$+ \text{softmin}'(A_2) \cdot \left(\frac{\partial d^*(\bar{a}(I+1), \bar{b}(J))}{\partial \lambda_{km}} + \delta_k(-)\delta_m(b_{J+1}) \right)$$
$$+ \text{softmin}'(A_3) \cdot \left(\frac{\partial d^*(\bar{a}(I), \bar{b}(J+1))}{\partial \lambda_{km}} + \delta_k(a_{I+1})\delta_m(-) \right)$$

where $\delta_k(a_i)$ tests whether the symbol a_i is element k in Σ.

We will investigate the role of the parameter β and efficient approximations of the computation in the experiments. For $\beta \to \infty$ the derivative $\partial d^*(\bar{a}, \bar{b})/\partial \lambda_{km}$ converges to the number of times symbols number k and m are paired in the alignment $(\bar{a}, \bar{b})$. For $\beta \to 0$, all three possible choices A_1, A_2, and A_3 are taken into account and no alignment paths stand out for the adaptation, resulting in homogeneous values λ_{km}. It is expected that optimal choices lie in between these extremes, corresponding to a good balance of exploitation of optimal alignment paths and exploration of competing alignment paths with similar quality. The latter is particularly relevant at the beginning of training and for large $|\Sigma|$. Because of the computational complexity, experiments have been reduced to the crisp case $\beta \to \infty$ only in [12]. Here, we will investigate different choices β, and will rely on the following two approximations for efficiency:

Approximation of Prototypes by Closest Exemplars: $\partial d(\bar{a}^i, \bar{w}^j)/\partial \lambda_{km}$ refers to two sums with all coefficients α_l^j of $\bar{w}^j$. We use a k-approximation of the prototype which restricts to the closest k exemplars [7]. For the particularly interesting case k = 1, the derivative becomes $\partial d_{il}/\partial \lambda_{km}$, where $\bar{a}^l$ is the closest exemplar.
Dropping alignment paths with small contribution: In the limit $\beta \to \infty$, contributions restrict to the best alignment path, hence derivatives $\partial d^*(\bar{a}, \bar{b})/\partial \lambda_{km}$ for all λ_{km} can be computed in time $\mathcal{O}(|\bar{a}| + |\bar{b}|)$ based on the alignment matrix.

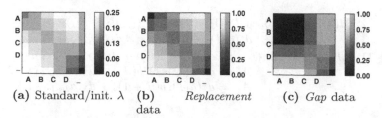

(a) Standard/init. λ (b)   *Replacement* data   (c) *Gap* data

Fig. 1. Visualizations of the scoring matrix λ, where color/intensity encodes the values. On the left is a standard choice of λ which also serves as the initial state for the training, the middle and right show the final state of λ after adaptation.

In general, derivatives are weighted sums corresponding to alignments of the symbols m and l at some position (I, J) of the matrix. Weighting takes into account all possible paths which include this pair according to the path eligibility measured by $\text{softmin}'(A_i)$ for actions A_i on the path; the worst case complexity is $\mathcal{O}(|\bar{a}| \cdot |\bar{b}| \cdot |\Sigma|^2)$ using backtracing in the alignment matrix. We propose an approximation based on the observation that a small $\text{softmin}'(A_i)$ leads to a small weight of paths including A_i. Hence, we store the 3 terms A_1, A_2, A_3 together with the distances $\text{softmin}(A_1, A_2, A_3)$ in the matrix, and we cut all values $\text{softmin}'(A_i) < \theta$ for fixed $\theta \geq 0$. Backtracing depends on the nonzero values only, so that a speed-up to linear complexity is possible in the best case.

4   Experiments

We investigate the performance characteristics of RGLVQ using a fixed scoring matrix λ in comparison to adaptive scores λ based on the proposed approximations. First, we discuss the influence of the 'crispness' parameter β, and thereafter, the applicability and efficiency regarding real-world classification scenarios.

4.1   Artificial Data

Replacement Data: In this data set, all strings have 12 symbols randomly generated from the alphabet $\Sigma = \{A, B, C, D\}$ according to the regular expressions: $(A|B)^5 (A|B) (C|D) (C|D)^5$ for the first class, and $(A|B)^5 (C|D) (A|B) (C|D)^5$ for the second. Hence, replacements of A or B by C or D are discriminative, while replacements A with B, and C with D are not. After the training of λ, we expect high costs for discriminative replacements, while other replacement costs are close to zero. Also, we expect positive gap costs, since gaps could otherwise circumvent the alignment of the discriminative middle parts.

Gap Data: The second data set focuses on gap scoring. Strings in the first class are random sequences $\bar{a}^i \in \Sigma^{10}$ of length 10, whereas strings $\bar{a}^l \in \Sigma^{12}$ in the second class are longer by 2 symbols. Therefore, replacements of letters are not discriminative, while the introduction of any gaps discriminates classes. Thus, gap costs should be high, while any symbol replacements should cost less.

Evaluation: For each data set, we created $N = 100$ sequences and evaluated the average classifier performance in a 5-fold cross-validation with 5 repeats. RGLVQ was trained using one prototype per class for 10 epochs. The learning

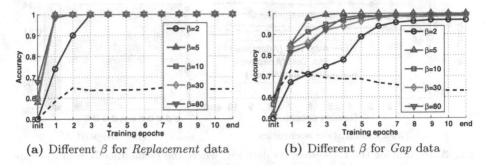

(a) Different β for *Replacement* data   **(b)** Different β for *Gap* data

Fig. 2. The figures show how the crispness β affects the adaptation of λ and convergence of RGLVQ training. For different β, the mean test accuracy over all cross-validation runs is given in every learning epoch. The dashed black line represents RGLVQ training without adapting λ and serves as a baseline.

rate for the adaptation of λ_{km} was set to $\eta = 1/N$ for replacement as well as gap scores. As initialization, we use a standard choice of $\lambda_{km} = 1/|\Sigma| \, \forall \, (k, m) \in (\Sigma \cup \{-\})^2$, $k \neq m$, and add small random noise to break ties in the initial alignments. All self-replacement scores remain fixed $\lambda_{kk} = 0$. During the adaptation, small or negative values $\lambda_{km} < \epsilon = 0.005$ are reset to ϵ in order to keep D non-negative.

The experimental results in Fig. 2 show the increased accuracy when adapting λ, e.g. for $\beta = 5$ a test accuracy of 100% (with 0 deviation) was achieved after the 4th epoch. Respectively, the adapted λ represent ideal scoring matrices for both data sets, which exactly fulfill our previously described expectations, see Fig. 1. In contrast, training RGLVQ with a fixed standard scoring λ remained close to a random guess throughout the learning epochs, see the baseline in Fig. 2.

We further evaluated how the 'crispness' parameter β influences the classifier and the training progress. In Fig. 2, we can see how a lower crispness (e.g. for $\beta = 2$) generally slows down the adaptation, while higher values seem to facilitate a faster convergence, sometimes at the expense of robustness (see $\beta = 80$ in Fig. 2b). Generally, we can observe that β directly affects the convergence characteristics, with an optimal value lying in a medium range.

4.2 Applicability and Efficiency for Real-World Data Sets

Chromosomes Data: The sequences in this set represent band patterns from the Copenhagen Chromosomes database [11]. Every sequence encodes the differential succession of density levels observed in gray-scale images of a human chromosome. Since 7 levels of density are distinguished, a 13-letter alphabet $\Sigma = \{f, \ldots, a, =, A, \ldots, F\}$ represents a difference coding of successive positions, where upper and lower case letters mark positive and negative changes respectively, and "=" means no change[1]. From the database, we use a common benchmark set for binary classification, containing class 17 and 18, with 200 sequences each ($N = 400$). To handle the full 22-class data set, a local scoring matrix λ^j for every prototype w^j would be necessary, which is ongoing work, see Sec. 5.

---

[1] For details, see http://algoval.essex.ac.uk/data/sequence/copchrom/

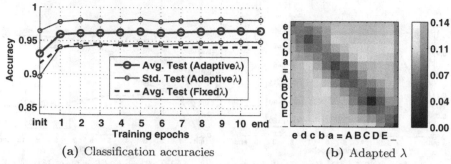

(a) Classification accuracies   (b) Adapted λ

Fig. 3. Results for the *Chromosomes* data set, where the (semantically sound) adaptation of λ (right) yields an improvement of 3% in test accuracy (left)

The initial setup of λ was analog to the previous experiment, and one prototype per class was trained in a 5-fold cross-validation with 5 repeats. Crispness $\beta = 35$ was chosen, and $\eta_{Rep} = 0.6 \cdot (1/N)$ was set for learning replacement costs λ_{km} and $\eta_{Gap} = 0.4 \cdot (1/N)$ for gaps λ_{k-}. The results in Fig. 3 show an improvement of the average test accuracy by 3% after adaptation of λ. The ratio of mean intra-class distance to mean inter-class distance dropped from 0.94 to 0.91 in the adapted metric. Interestingly, λ shows a semantically meaningful pattern, with rather low values in the 1st and 2nd off-diagonals, which resembles the fact that density differences on neighboring scales are exchangeable within classes. (Note, that symbols f, F did not occur in the data and were thus not considered.)

Protein Data: The sequences in this set are taken from a subset of the *SwissProt* database (release 37), which originally consists of 10,988 protein sequences in 32 classes. This subset was previously used in the context of RGLVQ classification, see [8]. For efficient testing of binary classification, we restrict here to the two classes with the lowest mean sequence lengths, using 617 sequences in total (class 4FE4S_FERREDOXIN with 289 sequences, and ADH_SHORT with 323). RGLVQ training with 3 prototypes per class and distances based on the fixed standard scoring λ resulted in a test accuracy of 92%. Although the adaptation of λ lead to a slightly decreased 90% accuracy, it also produced a rather sparse scoring model: many values in λ are close to ϵ and only a smaller portion of the parameters influence the alignment with significant positive costs, namely $|\{(k, m) \mid \lambda_{km} > \epsilon + 0.01\}| = 488$ out of $650 = |(\Sigma \cup \{-\})^2|$ possible pairs. Looking at low-dimensional embeddings of the standard vs. the adapted distances (embedded by the t-SNE technique [18], see Fig. 4), we can observe that the main clusters of each class become more clearly distinguished by the adaptation. This is substantiated by the fact that the ratio of mean intra-class distance to mean inter-class distance decreases from 1.02 to 0.88. A detailed investigation about the semantic value of the sparse scoring model and increased class-separation is ongoing work.

Table 1. Runtimes (in minutes) to calculate the alignment derivative for all pairs of random strings $\bar{a}^i \in \Sigma^L$, $i \in \{1 \ldots 10\}$, using different thresholds θ and $\beta = 10$

Sequence length L	100	150	200	250
Runtime ($\theta = 0$)	0.12	0.41	1.46	7.10
Runtime ($\theta = 0.15$)	0.07	0.22	0.53	1.64
Runtime ($\theta = 0.2$)	0.03	0.11	0.23	0.45
Runtime ($\theta = 0.25$)	0.02	0.06	0.12	0.22

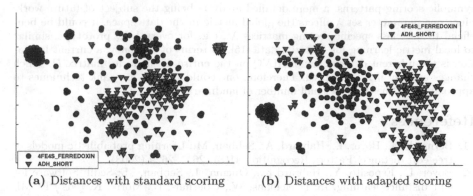

(a) Distances with standard scoring   (b) Distances with adapted scoring

Fig. 4. t-SNE visualizations of pairwise distances from the *Protein* data set: the adapted scoring (right) yields more class separation than standard scoring (left)

Approximated Alignment Derivative for Computational Speedup: Since the calculation speed of derivatives $\partial d^*(\bar{a}, \bar{b})/\partial \lambda_{km}$ severely affects the overall runtime, we empirically evaluate the speedup by the approximation proposed in the end of Section 3. The threshold θ determines that values $\text{softmin}'(A_i) < \theta$ are ignored in the backtracing of alignment paths. Since the impact of θ depends on the alphabet size and sequence length, it should be tuned according to good classification results for the given data set. Typical values are $\theta \in (0.01, 0.2)$. As a simple test scenario, we created several sets of random sequences, each consisting of 10 sequences $\bar{a}^i \in \Sigma^L$ with $\Sigma = \{A, B, C, D\}$, for different choices of length L. For different thresholds θ, we tracked the runtime of calculating alignment derivatives for all 100 sequence pairs on a standard laptop computer with an *Intel Core i7* processor (4 cores, and calculations done in parallel). The results in Tab. 1 clearly show how increasing θ drastically reduces the computational effort, especially for longer sequences. At the same time, approximation to a certain extent does not reduce classifier performance: average test accuracy on the *Chromosomes* data remained at 97% for $\theta = 0.02$, decreasing the mean runtime by 7%.

5   Discussion

We presented a technique to integrate the supervised adaptation of metric parameters (in this case the scoring pattern for sequence alignments) into a LVQ-based classifier framework. Specifically, we utilized RGLVQ as an overarching learning regime, which is able to process (dis)similarity data [7]. The goal is to facilitate class discrimination in the adapted dissimilarities, while the training of prototypes yields a sparse classification model for the data. Unlike in [9], we do not assume differentiability of the dissimilarity measure with respect to the data structures itself, but differentiability with respect to the metric parameters only. Therefore, our approach could serve as a generic foundation for metric adaptation schemes using dissimilarity measures for discrete structures such as sequences or, as a generalization, trees or graph structures. In addition to an improved class separation in adapted distances, the learned scoring could highlight the importance of structural replacement operations, and thus give further insight into the classification model. In the experiments, we demonstrated the viability of our method, and evaluated the influence of the crispness β, along with the computational speedup by an approximation technique. The adaptation of λ revealed semantically interesting symbolic scoring patterns, a more detailed analysis being the subject of future work. Since one parameter set λ affects the global metric in the data space, it could be beneficial to use class-specific scoring matrices λ^j, e.g. for every LVQ prototype, similar to local metric learning for vectorial data [15]. In terms of efficiency, a current limitation is the inherent dependency of RLVQ on the entire dissimilarity matrix D, which changes entirely if λ is adapted. Therefore, one could refer to low-rank techniques to approximate D based on a small number of landmark sequences.

References

1. Bernard, M., Boyer, L., Habrard, A., Sebban, M.: Learning probabilistic models of tree edit distance. Pattern Recognition 41(8), 2611–2629 (2008)
2. Boyer, L., Esposito, Y., Habrard, A., Oncina, J., Sebban, M.: Sedil: Software for edit distance learning. In: Daelemans, W., Goethals, B., Morik, K. (eds.) ECML PKDD 2008, Part II. LNCS (LNAI), vol. 5212, pp. 672–677. Springer, Heidelberg (2008)
3. Gärtner, T., Garriga, G., Meinl, T. (eds.): Proc. of The Workshop on Mining and Learning with Graphs (2006)
4. Gisbrecht, A., Mokbel, B., Hammer, B.: Relational generative topographic mapping. Neurocomputing 74(9), 1359–1371 (2011)
5. Habrard, A., Iñesta, J.M., Rizo, D., Sebban, M.: Melody recognition with learned edit distances. In: da Vitoria Lobo, N., Kasparis, T., Roli, F., Kwok, J.T., Georgiopoulos, M., Anagnostopoulos, G.C., Loog, M. (eds.) SSPR&SPR 2008. LNCS, vol. 5342, pp. 86–96. Springer, Heidelberg (2008)
6. Hammer, B., Hasenfuss, A.: Topographic mapping of large dissimilarity data sets. Neural Computation 22(9), 2229–2284 (2010)
7. Hammer, B., Hofmann, D., Schleif, F.-M., Zhu, X.: Learning vector quantization for (dis-)similarities. Neurocomputing (2013) (in Press)
8. Hammer, B., Mokbel, B., Schleif, F.-M., Zhu, X.: White box classification of dissimilarity data. In: Corchado, E., Snášel, V., Abraham, A., Woźniak, M., Graña, M., Cho, S.-B. (eds.) HAIS 2012, Part I. LNCS, vol. 7208, pp. 309–321. Springer, Heidelberg (2012)
9. Kästner, M., Nebel, D., Riedel, M., Biehl, M., Villmann, T.: Differentiable kernels in generalized matrix learning vector quantization. In: ICMLA, pp. 132–137 (2012)
10. Kirstein, S., Denecke, A., Hasler, S., Wersing, H., Gross, H.-M., Körner, E.: A vision architecture for unconstrained and incremental learning of multiple categories. Memetic Computing 1(4), 291–304 (2009)
11. Lundsteen, C., Phillip, J., Granum, E.: Quantitative analysis of 6985 digitized trypsin G-banded human metaphase chromosomes. Clin. Genet. 18, 355–370 (1980)
12. Mokbel, B., Paassen, B., Hammer, B.: Adaptive distance measures for sequential data. In: Verleysen, M. (ed.) ESANN, pp. 265–270 (2014), i6doc.com
13. Pekalska, E., Duin, B.: The Dissimilarity Representation for Pattern Recognition. Foundations and Applications. World Scientific (2005)
14. Schleif, F.-M., Hammer, B., Kostrzewa, M., Villmann, T.: Exploration of mass-spectrometric data in clinical proteomics using learning vector quantization methods. Briefings in Bioinformatics 9(2), 129–143 (2008)
15. Schneider, P., Biehl, M., Hammer, B.: Adaptive relevance matrices in learning vector quantization. Neural Computation 21(12), 3532–3561 (2009)
16. Sperschneider, V.: Bioinformatics. Springer (2008)
17. Takasu, A., Fukagawa, D., Akutsu, T.: Statistical learning algorithm for tree similarity. In: IEEE Int. Conf. on Data Mining, ICDM, pp. 667–672 (2007)
18. van der Maaten, L., Hinton, G.: Visualizing high-dimensional data using t-sne. Journal of Machine Learning Research 9, 2579–2605 (2008)

Improved Adaline Networks
for Robust Pattern Classification

César Lincoln C. Mattos[1], José Daniel Alencar Santos[2],
and Guilherme A. Barreto[1]

[1] Federal University of Ceará (UFC), Department of Teleinformatics Engineering,
Center of Technology, Campus of Pici, Fortaleza, Ceará, Brazil
cesarlincoln@terra.com.br, gbarreto@ufc.br
[2] Federal Institute of Education, Science and Technology of Ceará (IFCE)
Department of Industry, Maracanaú, Ceará, Brazil
jdaniel@ifce.edu.br

Abstract. The Adaline network [1] is a classic neural architecture whose
learning rule is the famous least mean squares (LMS) algorithm (a.k.a.
delta rule or Widrow-Hoff rule). It has been demonstrated that the LMS
algorithm is optimal in H_∞ sense since it tolerates *small* (in energy) disturbances, such as measurement noise, parameter drifting and modelling
errors [2,3]. Such optimality of the LMS algorithm, however, has been
demonstrated for regression-like problems only, not for pattern classification. Bearing this in mind, we firstly show that the performances of
the LMS algorithm and variants of it (including the recent Kernel LMS
algorithm) in pattern classification tasks deteriorates considerably in the
presence of labelling errors, and then introduce robust extensions of the
Adaline network that can deal efficiently with such errors. Comprehensive computer simulations show that the proposed extension consistently
outperforms the original version.

Keywords: Adaptive linear classifiers, least mean squares, labelling errors, outliers, M-estimation, robust pattern recognition.

1 Introduction

Linear neural network architectures, such as the *ADAptive LINear Element*
(Adaline) network [1], have been used either as a standalone device that forms
itself the core of the designed intelligent system, or as a fundamental building
block of more advanced multilayer nonlinear neural networks, such as the multilayer perceptron (MLP), the radial basis functions networks (RBFN) [4], the
No-Propagation (No-Prop) network [5] and the echo-state network (ESN) [6].

Weights in the Adaline are updated using the well-known least mean squares[1]
(LMS) algorithm, which minimizes the mean squared error (MSE) by updating
the weight vector in the negative direction of the instantaneous gradient of the
MSE with respect to the weight vector. It has been demonstrated that the LMS
algorithm is optimal in H_∞ sense since it tolerates *small* disturbances, such as

---

[1] Also known as delta rule or the Widrow-Hoff rule.

S. Wermter et al. (Eds.): ICANN 2014, LNCS 8681, pp. 579–586, 2014.

measurement noise, parameter drifting and modelling errors [2,3]. However, when the disturbances are not small (e.g. presence of impulsive noise) the performance of the LMS algorithm deteriorates considerably [7].

It is important to highlight that the aforementioned studies on the robustness of the LMS algorithm have been ascertained for regression-like tasks, typically found in the signal processing domain, such as channel equalization and time series prediction. In this paper, however, we are interested in evaluating the performance of the Adaline classifier trained by means of the LMS algorithm and variants in pattern classification tasks contaminated with outliers, in particular those resulting from labelling errors[2]. It is important to emphasize that the online behavior of the Adaline/LMS algorithm is desirable in scenarios where the full dataset is not initially available.

In order to handle labelling errors efficiently, we evaluate the performance of the Adaline network as a pattern classifier for different variants of the LMS algorithm, such as the Kernel LMS (KLMS) [8] and the least mean M-estimate (LMM) [7] algorithms, in order to devise an improved robust variant for that classifier. For the sake of completeness, performance comparison of the Adaline classifier with an SVM classifier trained with the kernel Adatron algorithm [9] is also carried out.

The remainder of the paper is organized as follows. Section 2 describes all the LMS-based algorithms that will be applied. Section 3 presents the experimental results with both artificial and real data within a robust classification context. Finally, Section 4 concludes the paper.

2   The Basics of the LMS Algorithm and Variants

Given a sequence of input-output pairs $\{(\boldsymbol{x}_i, y_i)\}_i^N \in \mathbb{R}^D \times \mathbb{R}$, the corresponding output of the Adaline classifier[3] is estimated as

$$\hat{y}_i = \boldsymbol{w}_i^T \boldsymbol{x}_i, \qquad i \in \{1, \dots, N\} \tag{1}$$

where N is the total number of available inputs, $\boldsymbol{w}_i \in \mathbb{R}^D$ is the weight vector and $\hat{y}_i \in \mathbb{R}$ is the estimated output provided by the linear model. The problem of training an Adaline classifier corresponds to the process of recursively updating the weight vector $\boldsymbol{w}_i$ for each input vector. In the following paragraphs we briefly describe the LMS and some variants of it that will be evaluated in this paper. Before proceeding, however, it is worth mentioning that the LMS variants to be described next were introduced in the context of signal processing applications and have not been evaluated before in the robust classification scenario.

---

[2] This type of outlier may result either from mistakes during labelling the data points (e.g. misjudgment of a specialist) or from typing errors during creation of data storage files (e.g. by striking an incorrect key on a keyboard).

[3] In this paper we discuss only binary classification problems. Thus, we need only one output neuron. Generalization of the presented concepts to multiclass problems is straightforward.

The LMS can be seen as a search algorithm in which a steepest-descent-based approach is applied to obtain a solution that minimizes the MSE:

$$J_{\mathrm{MSE}}(\boldsymbol{w}_i) = \sum_{i=1}^{N} \mathbb{E}\{e_i^2\} = \sum_{i=1}^{N} \mathbb{E}\{(y_i - \boldsymbol{w}_i^T \boldsymbol{x}_i)^2\}, \tag{2}$$

where $\mathbb{E}\{\cdot\}$ is the expectation operator and $e_i = y_i - \boldsymbol{w}_i^T \boldsymbol{x}_i$ is the error for the i-th iteration. Minimization of the Eq. (2) is obtained by taking its gradient with respect to the weights: $\frac{\partial J_{\mathrm{MSE}}(\boldsymbol{w}_i)}{\partial \boldsymbol{w}_i} = -2\mathbb{E}\{e_i \boldsymbol{x}_i\}$. The recursive algorithm is calculated updating $\boldsymbol{w}_i$ at each iteration in the negative direction of this gradient, which involves approximating $\mathbb{E}\{e_i \boldsymbol{x}_i\}$ by its instantaneous value $e_i \boldsymbol{x}_i$:

$$\boldsymbol{w}_{i+1} = \boldsymbol{w}_i - \mu \frac{\partial J_{\mathrm{MSE}}(\boldsymbol{w}_i)}{\partial \boldsymbol{w}_i} = \boldsymbol{w}_i + \mu e_i \boldsymbol{x}_i, \tag{3}$$

where μ is a learning step which controls the convergence rate. The choice of the μ is problem dependent and can reduce the efficiency of the method. One possible alternative arises when a variable step size is applied. In the normalized LMS (NLMS) algorithm, the learning step is divided by the squared L_2-norm of the input as follows:

$$\boldsymbol{w}_{i+1} = \boldsymbol{w}_i + \frac{\mu}{\epsilon + \|\boldsymbol{x}\|^2} e_i \boldsymbol{x}_i, \tag{4}$$

where ϵ is a very small positive constant needed to avoid division by zero.

The second algorithm to be described is the LMM algorithm [10,7] which borrows concepts from robust statistics and the M-estimation framework introduced by Huber [11]. The goal of robust statistics is to devise parameter estimation algorithms that provides faithful estimates in modelling scenarios where the assumption of Gaussianity for estimation errors does not hold. In this regard, the LMM algorithm derives from a more general objective function than the MSE:

$$J_{\mathrm{LMM}}(\boldsymbol{w}_i) = \sum_{i=1}^{N} \mathbb{E}\{\rho(e_i)\} = \sum_{i=1}^{N} \mathbb{E}\{\rho(y_i - \boldsymbol{w}_i^T \boldsymbol{x}_i)\}, \tag{5}$$

where $\rho(\cdot)$ is the M-estimate function [11]. The function $\rho(\cdot)$ computes the contribution of each error e_i to the objective function $J_{\mathrm{LMM}}(\boldsymbol{w}_i)$. Note that when $\rho(u) = u^2$, the function $J_{\mathrm{LMM}}(\boldsymbol{w}_i)$ reduces to the MSE function $J_{\mathrm{MSE}}(\boldsymbol{w}_i)$.

Weight updating in LMM follows the same logic of the LMS algorithm:

$$\boldsymbol{w}_{i+1} = \boldsymbol{w}_i - \mu \frac{\partial J_{\mathrm{LMM}}(\boldsymbol{w}_i)}{\partial \boldsymbol{w}_i} = \boldsymbol{w}_i + \mu q(e_i) e_i \boldsymbol{x}_i, \tag{6}$$

where $q(e_i) = \frac{1}{e_i} \frac{\partial J_{\mathrm{LMM}}(\boldsymbol{w}_i)}{\partial \boldsymbol{w}_i}$ is the weighting function. Note that, if $\rho(e_i) = e_i^2$, then $q(e_i) = 1$, and Eq. (6) becomes equal to Eq. (3). In the present paper the modified Huber M-estimate function will be considered [7]:

$$\rho(e_i) = \begin{cases} e_i^2/2, & 0 \leq |e_i| < \xi \\ \xi^2/2, & \text{otherwise} \end{cases}, \qquad q(e_i) = \begin{cases} e_i, & 0 \leq |e_i| < \xi \\ 0, & \text{otherwise} \end{cases}, \tag{7}$$

where ξ is a threshold parameter which avoids the influence of inputs with large errors. Smaller values of ξ produce more resistance to outliers, but at the expense of lower efficiency when the errors are normally distributed.

If we divide the step size of the LMM algorithm by the squared L_2-norm of the input vector, we get the Normalized LMM (NLMM) algorithm [7]:

$$\boldsymbol{w}_{i+1} = \boldsymbol{w}_i + \frac{\mu q(e_i) e_i \boldsymbol{x}_i}{\epsilon + \boldsymbol{x}_i^T \boldsymbol{x}_i}, \tag{8}$$

where ϵ has the same meaning as in Eq. (4).

The third LMS-like algorithm to be described is the KLMS algorithm, which works as the LMS algorithm but now operating on the feature space obtained by applying a mapping $\Phi(\cdot)$ to the inputs, generating a new sequence of input-output pairs $\{(\Phi(\boldsymbol{x}_i), y_i)\}_{i=1}^N$ [8]. Weight updating is similar to the Eq. (3), i.e.

$$\boldsymbol{w}_{i+1} = \boldsymbol{w} + \mu e_i \Phi(\boldsymbol{x}_i). \tag{9}$$

Considering $\boldsymbol{w}_0 = \boldsymbol{0}$, where $\boldsymbol{0}$ is the null-vector, after N iterations we get

$$\boldsymbol{w}_N = \mu \sum_{i=1}^{N-1} e_i \Phi(\boldsymbol{x}_i), \qquad \hat{y}_N = \boldsymbol{w}_N^T \Phi(\boldsymbol{x}_N) = \mu \sum_{i=1}^{N-1} e_i \kappa(\boldsymbol{x}_i, \boldsymbol{x}_N), \tag{10}$$

where $\kappa(\boldsymbol{x}_i, \boldsymbol{x}_j) = \Phi(\boldsymbol{x}_i)^T \Phi(\boldsymbol{x}_j)$ is a positive-definite kernel function. It should be noted that only Eq. (10) is needed both for training and testing. Although the values of the weight vector do not need to be computed, the *a priori* errors $e_i, i \in \{1, \cdots N\}$, and the training inputs $\boldsymbol{x}_i, i \in \{1, \cdots N\}$, must be maintained for prediction. In [12] a normalized version of the KLMS algorithm, named NKLMS, was proposed by modifying Eq. (10) as follows

$$\hat{y}_N = \mu \sum_{i=1}^{N-1} e_i \frac{\kappa(\boldsymbol{x}_i, \boldsymbol{x}_N)}{\kappa(\boldsymbol{x}_i, \boldsymbol{x}_i)}. \tag{11}$$

Since we are going to evaluate the performance of the Adaline classifier, when experimenting with KLMS and NKLMS algorithms we used their linear versions, choosing the linear kernel $\kappa(\boldsymbol{x}_i, \boldsymbol{x}_j) = \boldsymbol{x}_i^T \boldsymbol{x}_j + C$, where C is a constant.

The last estimation algorithm to be described, the Kernel Adatron (KAdatron) [9], is an on-line algorithm for training linear perceptron-like classifiers by providing a procedure that emulates Support Vector Machines without resorting to any quadratic programming toolboxes. By writing the KAdatron algorithm in the data-dependent representation $\{(\boldsymbol{x}_i, y_i)\}_{i=1}^N$, we obtain the following steps:

1. Initialize $\alpha_i = 0$ (Lagrange multipliers).
2. Calculate $z_i = \sum_{j=1}^N \alpha_j y_j \kappa(\boldsymbol{x}_i, \boldsymbol{x}_j)$.
3. Calculate $\gamma_i = y_i z_i$.
4. Let $\delta \alpha_i = \mu(1 - \gamma_i)$ be the proposed change to α_i;
   - If $(\delta \alpha_i + \alpha_i) \leq 0$ then $\alpha_i = 0$.
   - If $(\delta \alpha_i + \alpha_i) > 0$ then $\alpha_i = \alpha_i + \delta \alpha_i$.

5. If a maximum number of presentations of the training set has been exceeded then stop, otherwise return to Step 2.

The estimation for a new input $\boldsymbol{x}_*$ can be written as:

$$\hat{y}_* = \sum_{i \in SV} y_i \alpha_i^o \kappa(\boldsymbol{x}_*, \boldsymbol{x}_i), \tag{12}$$

where α_i^o is the solution of KAdatron algorithm and SV represents the index set of support vectors. As with KLMS and NKLMS cases, we will also use a linear kernel for experiments with KAdatron.

3   Experimental Results and Discussion

The experimental results were separated in two groups: one with artificial 2-dimensional data for the sake of visualization of the decision regions obtained by each classifier; and other with two real-world datasets (Iris and Vertebral Column)[4], for analyzing classifiers' performance due to the presence of outliers.

The first group of experiments involved a 120 2-dimensional samples from two classes (red and blue), which are linearly separable. All data samples are used for training the classifiers, since the goal is to visualize the final position of the decision line and not to compute recognition rates. A number of outliers from the red class was gradually added at each experiment, close to the region associated to the blue class. The obtained decision lines for each version of the Adaline classifier is shown in Figure 1. The learning step μ was set to 0.01 and the number of training epochs was set to 100 for all experiments.

One may notice that with the addition of 10 and 15 outliers, the Adaline/LMM, Adaline/NLMM and Adaline/NKLMS were less sensitive to the presence of outliers than the other classifiers. With the addition of 30 outliers, all the classifiers were strongly affected, except the Adaline/NKLMS. A remark is then required here. It is commonsense that the very nature of outliers demand that they should appear in a small number. When this number is too high, perhaps they should not be considered as outliers anymore, but as usual data samples of the class. In this situation, we recommend a more powerful classifier (e.g. the ELM or the MLP) to be used, since it can produce a nonlinear decision curve.

In the second group of experiments, the Iris dataset was prepared in the following way: the Virginica and Versicolor classes were labeled +1 and −1, respectively. From those two classes, 80% was used for training and 20% for testing. During training step, some samples from Setosa class were added with the label +1, being considered as outliers from the Virginica class. The number of generated outliers were 0%, 5%, 10%, 20% and 30% of the original number of Virginica samples in the training set.

The results obtained after 100 training-testing cycles are summarized in Table 1. It can be noticed that in the experiment without outliers, aside from Adaline/KLMS and Adaline/NKLMS, all methods achieved similar results. From

---

[4] Freely available at [13].

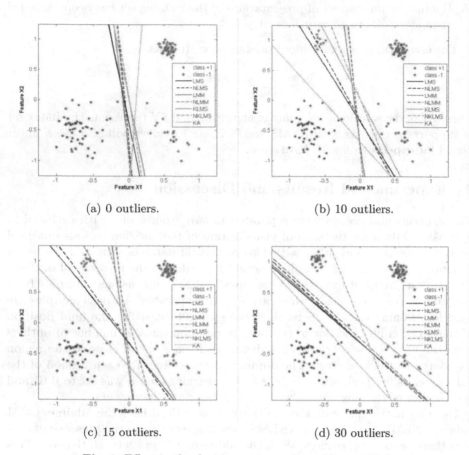

(a) 0 outliers.

(b) 10 outliers.

(c) 15 outliers.

(d) 30 outliers.

Fig. 1. Effect in the decision regions after adding outliers

5% to 10%, Adaline/LMM and Adaline/NLMM practically did not change their performances, while all the others methods suffered with the inclusion of outliers. With 20% of outliers, Adaline/LMM is also penalized, but Adaline/NLMM maintains high accuracy rates. With 30%, all algorithms obtain lower accuracy values. For this last case we again emphasize that those samples cannot actually be considered *outliers* anymore, but normal training samples.

The Vertebral Column dataset was configured as a 2-class problem since we removed the samples from the Disk Hernia class and considered only the ones from Normal and Spondylolisthesis classes. The same 80% − 20% partitioning was used. The addition of outliers was done by mislabeling some patterns on purpose: a portion (0%, 5%, 10%, 20% and 30%) of training samples from the Spondylolisthesis class had their labels changed to the Normal class. The results averaged after 100 repetitions are presented in Table 1.

Table 1. Results for Iris and Vertebral Column classification without and with outliers

	0%	5%	10%	20%	30%
Iris dataset					
Adaline/LMS	96.25 ± 3.72	88.95 ± 6.68	83.85 ± 7.81	75.10 ± 10.02	68.95 ± 10.88
Adaline/NLMS	96.15 ± 3.75	93.50 ± 4.58	91.90 ± 6.02	83.75 ± 8.11	77.30 ± 9.86
Adaline/LMM	95.85 ± 4.02	94.95 ± 4.17	94.90 ± 4.44	75.10 ± 9.61	69.05 ± 10.84
Adaline/NLMM	95.70 ± 3.63	94.90 ± 4.38	94.80 ± 4.76	95.10 ± 4.14	77.10 ± 9.83
Adaline/KLMS	92.15 ± 6.08	87.35 ± 8.12	85.50 ± 8.48	76.45 ± 10.08	69.15 ± 10.28
Adaline/NKLMS	91.15 ± 6.66	87.85 ± 7.73	86.50 ± 8.42	84.05 ± 8.75	79.75 ± 8.94
KAdatron	95.20 ± 5.27	86.55 ± 7.27	76.20 ± 11.17	71.60 ± 9.92	68.00 ± 9.97
Vertebral Column dataset					
Adaline/LMS	90.06 ± 4.85	89.52 ± 3.93	89.32 ± 4.32	84.22 ± 4.99	76.60 ± 7.14
Adaline/NLMS	91.10 ± 3.86	90.90 ± 3.88	90.88 ± 3.85	85.92 ± 4.41	78.52 ± 5.93
Adaline/LMM	91.90 ± 3.66	92.18 ± 3.27	92.16 ± 3.61	90.54 ± 3.61	82.02 ± 7.36
Adaline/NLMM	91.32 ± 3.63	91.36 ± 3.65	92.02 ± 3.76	88.74 ± 3.98	80.32 ± 6.32
Adaline/KLMS	85.32 ± 4.97	85.22 ± 5.17	83.78 ± 5.30	79.00 ± 5.37	68.52 ± 6.75
Adaline/NKLMS	81.02 ± 5.13	81.78 ± 5.28	83.08 ± 5.03	80.30 ± 5.77	68.24 ± 6.88
KAdatron	95.80 ± 2.66	92.98 ± 4.91	91.12 ± 5.59	85.06 ± 9.00	77.24 ± 9.55

In this case, only from 20% of outliers the Adaline/LMS, Adaline/NLMS and KAdatron algorithms suffered from performance degradation. The Adaline/NLMM classifier and mainly the Adaline/LMM classifier suffered less reduction in the mean accuracy rate when compared to the other classifiers. Similar behavior was observed for 30% of outliers. Once again the Adaline/KLMS and the Adaline/NKLMS classifiers did not achieve good overall results.

Concerning the results achieved by the Adaline/KLMS and Adaline/NKLMS classifiers when compared with Adaline/LMM, Adaline/NLMM, KAdatron and even with Adaline/LMS and Adaline/NLMS, they did not achieved good results. One possible explanation might be our choice of a linear kernel, as those methods were originally proposed mainly for non-linear applications with Gaussian and polynomial kernels [8,12]. It is also interesting to notice that although the KAdatron classifier algorithm obtained good results in the scenarios without outliers (for the Column dataset it was the best method), its results were strongly affected when for the scenarios with outliers.

4 Conclusion

In the present paper we evaluated several variants of the LMS learning rule to obtain different Adaline-like classifiers. The methods were evaluated for binary classification with outliers added during training, to check their robustness. After the experiments, the performances of Adaline/LMM and Adaline/NLMM classifiers exceeded the other techniques as the number of outliers was increased. The obtained results indicate the feasibility of the application in robust pattern recognition of algorithms usually related to filtering and regression problems. For instance, to the best of our knowledge, this is the first time the LMM, NLMM,

KLMS and NKLMS learning rules are applied to classification in the presence of outliers. Currently we are applying the concepts presented in this paper to add robustness to nonlinear classifiers, such as the Extreme Learning Machine.

Acknowledgments. The authors would like to thank FUNCAP (Fundação Cearense de Apoio ao Desenvolvimento Científico e Tecnológico) and NUTEC (Fundação Núcleo de Tecnologia Industrial do Ceará) for their financial support.

References

1. Widrow, B.: Thinking about thinking: The discovery of the LMS algorithm. IEEE Signal Processing Magazine 22(1), 100–106 (2005)
2. Hassibi, B., Sayed, A.H., Kailath, T.: H_∞ optimality of the LMS algorithm algorithm. IEEE Transactions on Signal Processing 44(2), 267–280 (1996)
3. Bolzern, P., Colaneri, P., De Nicolao, G.: H_∞-robustness of adaptive filters against measurement noise and parameter drift. Automatica 35(9), 1509–1520 (1999)
4. Poggio, T., Girosi, F.: Networks for approximation and learning. Proceedings of the IEEE 78(9), 1481–1497 (1990)
5. Widrow, B., Greenblatt, A., Kim, Y., Park, D.: The No-Prop algorithm: A new learning algorithm for multilayer neural networks. Neural Networks 37, 182–188 (2013)
6. Jaege, H.: Optimization and applications of echo state networks with leaky-integrator neurons. Neural Networks 20(3), 335–352 (2007)
7. Chan, S.C., Zhou, Y.: On the performance analysis of the least mean M-estimate and normalized least mean M-estimate algorithms with gaussian inputs and additive gaussian and contaminated gaussian noises. Journal of Signal Processing Systems 80(1), 81–103 (2010)
8. Liu, W., Pokharel, P., Principe, J.: The kernel least-mean-square algorithm. IEEE Transactions on Signal Processing 56(2), 543–554 (2008)
9. Friess, T.T., Cristianini, N., Campbell, C.: The kernel Adatron algorithm: A fast and simple learning procedure for support vector machines. In: Proceedings of the 15th International Conference of Machine Learning (ICML 1998), pp. 188–196 (1998)
10. Zou, Y., Chan, S.C., Ng, T.S.: Least mean M-estimate algorithms for robust adaptive filtering in impulsive noise. IEEE Transactions on Circuits and Systems II 47(12), 1564–1569 (2000)
11. Huber, P.J.: Robust estimation of a location parameter. Annals of Mathematical Statistics 35(1), 73–101 (1964)
12. Modaghegh, H., Khosravi, R., Manesh, S.A., Yazdi, H.S.: A new modeling algorithm-normalized kernel least mean square. In: Proceedings of the International Conference on Innovations in Information Technology (IIT 2009), pp. 120–124 (2009)
13. Bache, K., Lichman, M.: UCI machine learning repository (2014), http://archive.ics.uci.edu/ml

Learning under Concept Drift
with Support Vector Machines

Omar Ayad

Université de Reims Champagne-Ardenne, Centre de recherché en STIC (URCA-CReSTIC)
Moulin de la Housse, BP 1039, 51687 Reims Cedex, France
omar.ayad@univ-reims.fr

Abstract. Support Vector Machines (SVMs) have been recognized as one of the most successful classification methods for many applications in static environment. However in dynamic environment, data characteristics may evolve over time. This leads to deteriorate dramatically the performance of SVMs over time. This is because of the use of data which is no more consistent with the characteristics of new incoming one. Thus in this paper, we propose an approach to recognize and handle concept changes with support vector machine. This approach integrates a mechanism to use only the recent and most representative patterns to update the SVMs without a catastrophic forgetting.

Keywords: dynamic learning, concept drift, support vector machine, classification.

1   Introduction

A considerable body of research has been devoted to the design of classifiers whose operating environments are supposed to be static [1]. The classes' descriptions in static environments are learned from data distribution assumed to be fixe over time. Therefore, there is no need to adjust the classifier parameters in order to preserve the classification accuracy. However, in most real word applications data distribution evolves over time [4]. The ideal classification scenario in this case is to detect the changes when they come and to update the classifier parameters automatically.

In the literature, environment change was presented by two concepts [7]. The first concept is *concept-drift* [5]. In this concept, the underlying data distribution changes gradually over time. The second concept is *concept-evolution* [4]. In this concept, a sudden change in the underlying data distribution can manifest. In both cases, the classifier parameters and structure must be updated using the recent and useful patterns in order to preserve classifier performance over time. Recently a lot of the machine learning research has focused, on developing a variety of algorithms that that can track such changes and update the classifier parameters accordingly.

The most popular approach is to use a sliding window on incoming data, and retrain a classifier with the latest data that fall within the window [3]. These methods can monitor the performance indicators of a learner, the estimators of data distributions or the learner's structure and parameters. Other approaches treat the concept drift as a prediction problem and use an adaptive neural network that can adjust its

S. Wermter et al. (Eds.): ICANN 2014, LNCS 8681, pp. 587–594, 2014.

parameters according to the environment [6]. Recently a new group of algorithms used for nonstationary learning is the ensemble of classifiers, or multiple classifier systems (MCS) based approaches [8]. These algorithms use more than one classifier to track the changing environment.

In this paper, we propose a method for learning with Support Vector Machines under concept drift. It updates regularly SVMs according to the changes in its environment conditions. The changes in the classifier environment are detected by observing the conditional PDF of each class during a temporal sliding window. Following the evolution of the classes conditional PDF, if a serious change is detected and when this change exceeds a certain predefined threshold, SVMs parameters are updated. To achieve this end, in the first time, we ignore all aged data which became obsolete, and in the second time, the SVMs are retrained using only the recent and the most representative patterns. The main idea behind the adaptation in the absence of the obsolete data is to avoid a catastrophic degradation in the classification performances.

The remainder of this paper is organized as follows. In section 2, we present the proposed approach. In section 3, this approach is evaluated using both real and artificial examples. The last section concludes the paper.

2   Proposed Approach

In this section, we describe the proposed approach to learn with SVMs in a dynamic environment. This approach comprises three steps (fig 1): decision functions generation, monitoring and updating steps. In the first step, SVMs are trained using the learning data set and it is used to predict the class of each new pattern. In the second step, a mechanism to detect any significant changes in the classes' characteristics' is engaged. It is based on the observation of the change in the conditional   Probability Density Function (PDF) of each class y_i during a growing time window. In the third step, if the dissimilarity between the conditional PDF of the class y_i before and after the classification of new patterns x_i confirm the presence of drift, the updating of y_i becomes necessary to prevent a significant decrease of the SVMs performances. The proposed alternative to update y_i is to treat the no more representative patterns as noise patterns and ignore them. Finally, we re-train SVMs using only the recent patterns as good prototypes of y_i to any further classification.

2.1   SVMs Decision Function Generation

This step aims at building the SVMs decision to separate the different classes [8]. In the first phase, all labeled patterns of known classes are learned by SVMs. This one implement a complex decision rules by using a kernel function to map training points to a high dimensional feature space where the labeled points are separable. Thus, a separating hyperplane which maximizes the distance between itself and the nearest training points (this distance is called the margin) is established. In the next we give a brief description of SVMs.

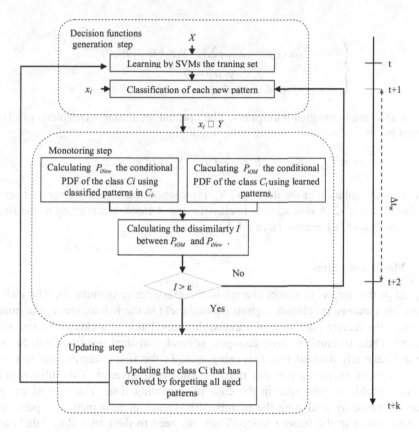

Fig. 1. General architecture of the proposed approach to learn with SVMs in changing environments

In their basic form, for classification about the training data

$$T = \{(x_1, y_1), ..., (x_l, y_l)\} \in (R^n \times Y)^l \qquad (1)$$

where $x_i \in R^n, y_i \in Y = \{+1, -1\}, i = 1 ... l$. SVMs linear decision rule is to solve the following primal QPP.

$$\begin{cases} V(w, b, \gamma) = \frac{1}{2}\|w\|^2 + C\sum_{i=1}^n \gamma_i \\ \forall_{i=1}^n: y_i(w.x_i + b) \geq 1 - \gamma_i \\ \forall_{i=1}^n: \gamma_i \geq 0, \ i = 1, 2, ..., l \end{cases} \qquad (2)$$

where C is a penalty parameter and γ_i are the slack variables. The goal is to find an is to find an optimal separating hyperplane

$$w^T x + b = 0 \qquad (3)$$

where $x \in R^n$. The Wolfe dual of (2) can be expressed as

$$\begin{cases} \max_{\alpha} \sum_{j=1}^{l} \alpha_j - \frac{1}{2}\sum_{i=1}^{l} \sum_{j=1}^{l} y_i y_j (x_i.x_j)\alpha_i\alpha_j \\ \qquad \sum_{i=1}^{l} y_i \alpha_i = 0, \\ \qquad 0 \leq \alpha_i \leq C, i = 1,...,l \end{cases} \qquad (4)$$

where $\alpha \in R^l$ are lagrangian multipliers. The optimal separating hyperplane of (3) can be given by

$$w = \sum_{i=1}^{l} \alpha_i^* y_i x_i, \quad b = \frac{1}{N_{sv}}(y_j - \sum_{i=1}^{N_{sv}} \alpha_i^* y_i(x_i.x_j)) \qquad (5)$$

where α^* is the solution of the dual (4), N_{sv} representes the number of support vectors such that $0 < \alpha < C$. A new sample is classified as $+1$ or -1 according to the finally decision function $f(x) = sgn((w.x) + b)$.

2.2   Monitoring Step

The goal of this step is to detect change in the classifier environments. The changes can lead to a change in: classes regions (boundaries) in the feature space, the number of classes, the feature relevance of a class, the prevalence of a class, it's conditional PDF, etc. Thus, to monitor these changes, several statistical measures can be used. They are generally divided into two categories. In the first category, the true class label of the new incoming patterns must be known in advance. This information is often unavailable in particular in the case of streaming data. The second category detects a change by analyzing the membership values of new incoming patterns or their distribution in the feature space. Thus, no need to their true class labels to be known a priori. For this reason, we have selected a statistical measure belonging to the second category. This measure is the change in the class conditional PDF.

The conditional PDF of each class represents patterns distribution in this class. Thus, conditional PDF describes a certain structure of the data in a class. If the class distribution, obtained after classification of new patterns in the current time window, differs from the one of previous time windows, this may indicate a change in the underlying class structure.

Let $P_{iold}(X_i, Y_i)$ be the conditional PDF of a class Y_i learned using the patterns of the previous time window. Let P_{iNew} be the conditional PDF of the class Y_i using only the new assigned patterns in Y_i. There are various measures that are used to compare two PDFs [2]. They measure the geometric distance between two PDFs. We have selected the following distance measure, based on the use of SØrensen distance, to measure the change in conditional PDF of the class Y_i:

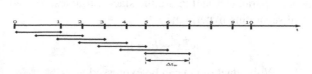

Fig. 2. Moving time windows of constant length to measure each class conditional PDF

$$I = max_{j \in \{1,..,d\}} \left(\frac{\sum_{i=1}^{d} |P_{iOld} - P_{iNew}|}{\sum_{i=1}^{d} |P_{iOld} + P_{iNew}|} \right), 0 \leq I \leq 1 \tag{6}$$

The reason of this choice is to take into account with equal weights all the differences between the bins of the tow PDFs. If I is equal to zero, then the new patterns do not carry any change to the class to which they are assigned. While I equal to 1 indicates a complete change (class shift) in the class PDF carried by the new assigned patterns.

2.3   Updating Step

The updating step aims at reacting to the changes detected by the monitoring step. It uses a mechanism to update the SVMs classifier according to the detected changes in order to preserve its performance over time.

Two types of changes exist: slight and abrupt changes. The slight change may represent a drift. However, in order to distinguish between a drift and a natural variation, because of noises or other stochastic perturbations, the slight changes are accumulated until they reach a predefined threshold $I \geq \varepsilon, 0 \leq I \leq 1$. All the patterns contributing to theses accumulated changes are used to relearn SVMs parameters. The drift ends when the new patterns do not carry any new information, i.e., they have the same characteristics as the ones of the evolving set. Thus, when the new incoming patterns do not any more change one of the conditional PDF measure, this means that the drift is ended.

3   Experimental Evaluation

3.1   Synthetic Data Set

In the following experiment, we test the performances of the proposed approach on synthetic drifting data, for this end tow class's y_1 and y_2 in non-stationary environment as flows:

- $t = 0$: two classes of 100 samples each have been generated from two Gaussian distribution. In the Fig.3.(a), these classes are pictured in black color.
- $t = 1$: 1600 new incoming patterns occur in the class y_1 and y_2, the accumulation of this patterns which causes a drift in y_1 and y_2, in Fig.3.(a) the point pictured in gray show a drift of these classes in the course of time.

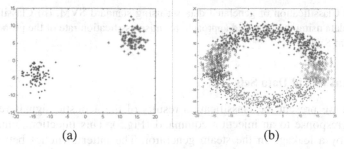

(a)   (b)

Fig. 3. (a) Data set, blue points correspond to y_1, red asterisk correspond to y_2 before evolution. (b) The green and maroon points show the evolution of the class's.

All the patterns created at $t=0$ (black points for y_1 and black asterisks for y_2) are used to learn SVMs. This one calculates the optimal hyperplane with a maximal margin.

From $t=1$ SVMs classify each new incoming pattern, at the same time we observe the change in the conditional PDF measure for each class during a growing time window (see table 1). If this change exceed the predefined threshold $\varepsilon=0.3$, we stop the classification to update the classes that have evolved.

Table 1. Class's conditional PDF change measure

WINDOW	PDF CHANGE MEASURE FOR CLASS 1	PDF CHANGE MEASURE FOR CLASS 2	UPDATING
1	0.53	0.35	CLASS 1 AND 2
2	0.54	0.79	CLASS 1 AND 2
3	0.27	0.68	CLASS 2
4	0.95	0.96	CLASS 1 AND 2
5	0.47	0.46	CLASS 1 AND 2
6	0.35	0.26	CLASS 1
7	0.64	0.66	CLASS 1 AND 2
8	0.86	0.49	CLASS 1 AND 2

Table 1 shows the PDF change measure for both classes (C_1 and C_2) in the course of time. We can observe that this measure justifies the classifier update.

Fig.4 shows the adaption of the SVMs parameters and classification with static SVMs. We can observe that the dynamic classifier has a better misclassification rate thanks to its parameters updating. This classifier updating leads to forget the patterns becoming useless and this to increase the separability between classes.

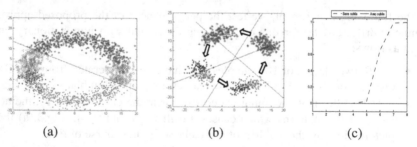

(a)   (b)   (c)

Fig. 4. (a) Classification of generated data set using standard SVM, (b) Classification of the generated data using the proposed approach, (c) misclassification rate of the proposed approach and standard SVMs

3.2   Real World Data Sets

Hereafter, we present the classification results of the acoustic signals recorded by a sensor in response to an injection command (Fig.5). This injection simulates a fault occurred by a leakage in the steam generator. The latter switches between the two functioning modes (normal: non-injection and faulty: injection) in several time instants as it is shown in Fig. 5. The signal is sampled at the frequency 2048 Hz.

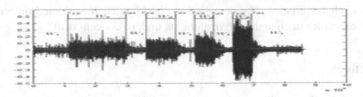

Fig. 5. Acoustic signal in response to injection command

In order to capture this change, features are calculated during a sliding time window. We have tested several sizes of time window. We have selected the one which maximizes the discrimination power between the different modes in the feature space, i.e. obtaining compact and separated classes. This experimentation leads to select a sliding window with an initial length = 8192 data points and a shift length equal to 2048 data points. Therefore, to define a pattern in the feature space, a time window containing 8192 data points is required.

Table 2 shows the PDF change measure for both class's non-injection and injection. We can observe that this measure justifies the classifier update. Table 3 shows the misclassification rate in the case of using a standard SVMs classifier and the proposed dynamic one. We can observe that the dynamic classifier has a better misclassification rate thanks to its parameters updating. This classifier updating leads to forget the patterns becoming useless and thus to increase the separability between classes.

Table 2. PDF change measure in response to the successive argon injections

Argon injection number	PDF change measure for class 1	PDF change measure for class 1	Updating
2nd	1	0.28	Class 1
3rd	1	0.8	Classes 1 and 2
4th	0.93	0.96	Classes 1 and 2

Table 3. Misclassification rate calculated for standard SVMs and our approach

Argon injection number	Misclassification ERROR	
	Standard SVMs	Proposed approach
2nd	1	0.28
3rd	1	0.38
4th	0.93	0.56

4   Conclusion

In this paper, an approach to learn and to update SVMs parameters according to the changes in its environment conditions is proposed. This method uses a monitoring measure to observe a change in the classes' conditional probability distributions during a growing time window. When this change becomes serious (greater than a predefined threshold), the classifier adapts its parameters using the recent and useful patterns. The threshold is used to distinguish between a drift and normal fluctuations of classes' characteristics. The proposed method has been evaluated on both real and artificial examples in changing environments under "concept drift".

References

1. Ripley, B.D.: Pattern Recognition and Neural Networks. Cambridge University Press, Cambridge (1996)
2. Cha, S.H.: Comprehensive survey on distance/similarity measures between probability density functions. International Journal of Mathematical Models and Methods in Applied Sciences 4, 300–307 (2007)
3. Medasani, S., Zliobaite, K., Kuncheva, L.I.: Theoretical window size for classification in the presence of sudden concept drift. Technical Report # BCS-TR-001-2010. Bangor University, UK (2010)
4. Sobhani, P., Beigy, H.: New drift detection method for data streams. In: Bouchachia, A. (ed.) ICAIS 2011. LNCS, vol. 6943, pp. 88–97. Springer, Heidelberg (2011)
5. Rutkowski, L.: Adaptive probabilistic neural networks for pattern classification in time-varying environment. IEEE Transactions on Neural Networks 15(4), 811–827 (2004)
6. Lughofer, E., Angelov, P.: Handling drifts and shifts in on-line data streams with evolving fuzzy systems. Applied Soft Computing 11, 2057–2068 (2011)
7. Kuncheva, L.I.: Classifier ensembles for changing environments. In: Roli, F., Kittler, J., Windeatt, T. (eds.) MCS 2004. LNCS, vol. 3077, pp. 1–15. Springer, Heidelberg (2004)
8. Burges, C.J.C.: A Tutorial on support vector machines for pattern recognition. International Journal of Data Mining and Knowledge Discovery 2, 121–167 (1998)

Two Subspace-Based Kernel Local Discriminant Embedding*

Fadi Dornaika[1,2] and Alireza Bosaghzadeh[1]

[1] University of the Basque Country EHU/UPV, San Sebastian, Spain
[2] IKERBASQUE, Basque Foundation for Science, Bilbao, Spain

Abstract. We propose Two Subspace-based Kernel Local Discriminant Embedding (TSKLDE) for feature extraction and recognition. The procedure of TSKLDE is divided into two stages. The first stage applies the Kernel Principal Component Analysis (KPCA) to the raw data. Based on the output of KPCA, the second stage seeks two kinds of discriminant information, regular and irregular. These are based on transforms derived from the within-class locality preserving scatter. The resulting framework retain the advantages of supervised global and local techniques. Besides, it is an inductive nonlinear technique in the sense that novel examples or images can be directly mapped. The proposed algorithm was tested and evaluated using three public face databases. The experimental results show that the proposed TSKLDE outperforms other Kernel based algorithms.

Keywords: Manifold learning, Kernel embedding methods, Kernel LDA, Local Discriminant Embedding.

1 Introduction

Feature extraction with dimensionality reduction is an important step and essential process in embedding data analysis[1–3]. The classical linear embedding methods (e.g., Principal Component Analysis (PCA), Linear Discriminant Analysis (LDA), Maximum Margin Criterion (MMC)[4]) and Locally LDA [5] are demonstrated to be computationally efficient and suitable for practical applications, such as pattern classification and visual recognition. The use of Kernels in the frameworks of machine learning [6, 7] and linear embedding techniques was first introduced in the 90's. Kernel PCA (KPCA) was originally developed by Schölkopf in 1998 [8], while Kernel Fisher Discriminant Analysis (KFD) (a Kernelized version of the classical LDA) was first proposed by Mika et al. in 1999 [9]. Subsequent research saw the development of a series of KFD algorithms. Baudat et al. [10] extends the original KFD to deal with a multi-class classification problem. Lu et al. [11] generalized Direct LDA (DLDA) [12] using the idea of kernels and presented kernel direct discriminant analysis (KDDA). Their method was demonstrated effective for face recognition, but, as a nonlinear version of DLDA, KDDA unavoidably suffers the weakness of DLDA in the sense

---

* This work was supported by the projects EHU13/40 and TIN2010-18856.

S. Wermter et al. (Eds.): ICANN 2014, LNCS 8681, pp. 595–602, 2014.

that it overlooked the regular information provided by the non-null space of the within-class scatter matrix [12] whenever the SSS problem occurs. Yang et al. [13] proposed a Complete Kernel Fisher Discriminant method. The implemented method was intended to perform discriminant analysis in double discriminant subspaces: regular and irregular associated with the within-class scatter matrix after KPCA projection.

The Kernelized versions can give better results than the linear discriminant methods. Most of the Kernelized methods are build on the classic LDA framework, which means that the resulting framework still inherits the global nature of LDA in the sense that it ignores the local structures of data. Thus, the performance of KFD and its variants may not be optimal. This paper proposes Two Subspace-based Kernel Local Discriminant Embedding (TSKLDE) for feature extraction and recognition. The procedure of TSKLDE is divided into two stages, i.e., one is to apply the Kernel Principal Component Analysis (KPCA), and the second is to seek the optimal projection matrices for dimensionality reduction in two subspaces. In the second stage, two kinds of discriminant information, regular and irregular, are retrieved from the within-class locality preserving scatter. The paper is structured as follows: in Section 2, we provide a review of the Local Discriminant Embedding (LDE) method as well as of its kernelized version. In Section 3, we describe our proposed two subspace based Kernel LDE. The experimental results are presented in Section 4.

2   LDE and Its Kernelized Version

LDE is intrinsically a supervised manifold learning algorithm. In the neighbor searching step, LDE searches the K_1 same-class and K_2 different-class nearest neighbors for each sample via the Euclidean metric. Then in the local geometry modeling step, LDE builds two affinity matrices, an intrinsic matrix $\mathbf{W}_w$ and a penalty matrix $\mathbf{W}_b$, to record the geometrical information for each type of neighbors, respectively; the entries of these two matrices can be defined by any similarity measure such as the cosine and the Gaussian kernel. Finally in the embedding computation step, LDE seeks the linear matrix transform $\mathbf{A}$ that simultaneously optimizes the two criteria:

$$\min_{\mathbf{A}} \frac{1}{2} \sum_{i,j} \|\mathbf{A}^T (\mathbf{x}_i - \mathbf{x}_j)\|^2 W_{w,ij} = \min_{\mathbf{A}} trace \left(\mathbf{A}^T \mathbf{X} \mathbf{L}_w \mathbf{X}^T \mathbf{A} \right) \quad (1)$$

$$\max_{\mathbf{A}} \frac{1}{2} \sum_{i,j} \|\mathbf{A}^T (\mathbf{x}_i - \mathbf{x}_j)\|^2 W_{b,ij} = \max_{\mathbf{A}} trace \left(\mathbf{A}^T \mathbf{X} \mathbf{L}_b \mathbf{X}^T \mathbf{A} \right) \quad (2)$$

where $\mathbf{X}$ denotes the data matrix, and $\mathbf{L}_b$ and $\mathbf{L}_w$ are the Laplacian matrices associated with penalty and intrisic affinity matrices, that is, $\mathbf{L}_b = \mathbf{D}_b - \mathbf{W}_b$ and $\mathbf{L}_w = \mathbf{D}_w - \mathbf{W}_w$ with $\mathbf{D}_b = Diag(\mathbf{W}_b \mathbf{1})$ and $\mathbf{D}_w = Diag(\mathbf{W}_w \mathbf{1})$. LDE method computes a linear transform, $\mathbf{A}$, that simultaneously maximizes the local margins between heterogenous samples and pushes the homogeneous samples closer to each other (after the transformation). LDE maximizes:

$$J = \frac{trace\left(\mathbf{A}^T \mathbf{X} \mathbf{L}_b \mathbf{X}^T \mathbf{A}\right)}{trace\left(\mathbf{A}^T \mathbf{X} \mathbf{L}_w \mathbf{X}^T \mathbf{A}\right)} = \frac{trace\left(\mathbf{A}^T \widetilde{\mathbf{S}}_b \mathbf{A}\right)}{trace\left(\mathbf{A}^T \widetilde{\mathbf{S}}_w \mathbf{A}\right)} \tag{3}$$

where the symmetric matrix $\widetilde{\mathbf{S}}_b = \mathbf{X} \mathbf{L}_b \mathbf{X}^T$ denotes the locality preserving between class scatter matrix, and the symmetric matrix $\widetilde{\mathbf{S}}_w = \mathbf{X} \mathbf{L}_w \mathbf{X}^T$ denotes the locality preserving within class scatter matrix. The columns of the sought matrix $\mathbf{A}$ are given by the generalized eigenvectors associated with the largest eigenvalues of the following equation:

$$\widetilde{\mathbf{S}}_b \mathbf{a} = \lambda \widetilde{\mathbf{S}}_w \mathbf{a} \tag{4}$$

Kernelized LDE. LDE is a linear algorithm. It may fail to discover the intrinsic geometry when the data manifold is highly nonlinear. Suppose $\mathbf{X}$ is the data matrix associated with N training samples. The corresponding symmetric Kernel matrix, in Reproducing Kernel Hilbert Space (RKHS), is given by $\mathbf{K}$ where $K(i, j)$ encodes the similarity between the samples $\mathbf{x}_i$ and $\mathbf{x}_j$. Kernel LDE solves for a set of vectors $\boldsymbol{\alpha}$ using the following eigenvector problem:

$$\mathbf{K} \mathbf{L}_b \mathbf{K} \boldsymbol{\alpha} = \lambda \mathbf{K} \mathbf{L}_w \mathbf{K} \boldsymbol{\alpha} \tag{5}$$

For a test datum $\mathbf{x}$, its kth projection coordinate is given by $\sum_{i=1}^{N} \alpha_i^k K(\mathbf{x}_i, \mathbf{x})$ where α_i^k is the ith of the vector $\boldsymbol{\alpha}^k$.

3   Proposed Two Subspace Kernel LDE

Suppose there are C known pattern classes. The between-class and within-class locality preserving scatter matrices are given by $\widetilde{\mathbf{S}}_b^{\phi} = \boldsymbol{\Phi} \mathbf{L}_b \boldsymbol{\Phi}^T$ and $\widetilde{\mathbf{S}}_w^{\phi} = \boldsymbol{\Phi} \mathbf{L}_w \boldsymbol{\Phi}^T$, respectively (where $\boldsymbol{\Phi}$ is the data representation in Hilbert space). Thus, in Hilbert space, the LDE criterion function can be defined by $J(\mathbf{a}) = \frac{\mathbf{a}^T \widetilde{\mathbf{S}}_b^{\phi} \mathbf{a}}{\mathbf{a}^T \widetilde{\mathbf{S}}_w^{\phi} \mathbf{a}}$.

If the within-class locality preserving scatter matrix $\widetilde{\mathbf{S}}_w^{\phi}$ is invertible, $\mathbf{a}^T \widetilde{\mathbf{S}}_w^{\phi} \mathbf{a} > 0$ always holds for every nonzero vector $\mathbf{a}$. In such a case the LDE criterion can be directly employed to extract a set of optimal discriminant vectors (projection axes) using the standard LDE algorithm [14].

However, in a high-dimensional (even infinite-dimensional) feature space, it is almost impossible to make $\widetilde{\mathbf{S}}_w^{\phi}$ invertible because of the limited amount of training samples in real-world applications. That is, there always exist vectors satisfying $\mathbf{a}^T \widetilde{\mathbf{S}}_w^{\phi} \mathbf{a} = 0$ (actually, these vectors are from the null space of $\widetilde{\mathbf{S}}_w^{\phi}$). These vectors turn out to be very effective if they satisfy $\mathbf{a}^T \widetilde{\mathbf{S}}_b^{\phi} \mathbf{a} > 0$ at the same time. This is because the positive between-class scatter makes the data become well separable when the within-class scatter is zero. In such a case, the LDE criterion degenerates into the following between-class scatter criterion:

$$J_b(\mathbf{a}) = \mathbf{a}^T \widetilde{\mathbf{S}}_b^\phi \, \mathbf{a} \tag{6}$$

As a special case of the LDE criterion, the criterion given in (6) is very intuitive since it is reasonable to use the between-class locality preserving scatter to measure the discriminatory ability of a projection axis when the within-class scatter is zero. Our work inspires from the work of [13] and [15] that used two kinds of discriminant features for performing the embedding of data. In [13], the authors introduced a variant of the Kernelized Linear Discriminant Analysis. In [15], the authors introduce an imporved scheme that can enhance the performance of the Locality Preserving Projections (LPP). We propose to expand the idea of using two sets of discriminant features to the Kernelized LDE. Thus, the advantages of our proposed work are: (i) our proposed method can handle the locality of data better than the discriminant features obtained by [13] since the latter relies on LDA which is a global method, (ii) the number of discriminant features in [13] is bounded by $2(C-1)$ where C is the number of classes, whereas the number of discriminant features in our framework is limited by the number of samples which is usually greater than $2(C-1)$, and (iii) our method is supervised and a Kernel-based whereas the scheme introduced in [15] was to handle the unsupervised LPP technique without any Kernalization

We will use the between-class scatter criterion defined in (6) to derive the irregular discriminant vectors from the null space of $\widetilde{\mathbf{S}}_w^\phi$, while using the standard LDE criterion to derive the regular discriminant vectors from the complementary set. The basic idea is to apply KPCA to the raw data as a pre-processing step. Then, based on the within-class locality preserving scatter in KPCA space, we retrieve two subspaces using the classic LDE and criterion (6). Despite the fact that KPCA can remove the singularity of the within-class locality preserving scatter, we will show that separating large eigenvalues (regular discriminant information) from its small eigenvalues (irregular discriminant information) can enhance the classification performance. The proposed algorithm is as follows.

3.1   Two Subspace KLDE Algorithm

Step1. Use KPCA to transform the input space $\mathbb{R}^n$ into an m-dimensional space, where m is the rank of the total covariance matrix in Hilbert space (high dimensional space). Datum $\mathbf{x}$ in $\mathbb{R}^n$ is transformed to be KPCA-based feature vector $\mathbf{y}$ in $\mathbb{R}^m$.

Step2. In $\mathbb{R}^m$, construct the between-class and within-class locality preserving matrices $\widetilde{\mathbf{S}}_b$ and $\widetilde{\mathbf{S}}_w$. Calculate $\widetilde{\mathbf{S}}_w$'s orthonormal eigenvectors, $(\boldsymbol{\beta}_1, \ldots, \boldsymbol{\beta}_m)$, assuming the first q (q is the rank of $\widetilde{\mathbf{S}}_w$) ones are corresponding to positive eigenvalues.

Step3. Extract the regular discriminant features: Let $\mathbf{P}_1 = (\boldsymbol{\beta}_1, \ldots, \boldsymbol{\beta}_q)$. Define $\hat{\widetilde{\mathbf{S}}}_w = \mathbf{P}_1^T \widetilde{\mathbf{S}}_w \, \mathbf{P}_1$ and $\hat{\widetilde{\mathbf{S}}}_b = \mathbf{P}_1^T \widetilde{\mathbf{S}}_b \, \mathbf{P}_1$ and calculate the generalized eigenvectors

$\mathbf{u}_1, \ldots, \mathbf{u}_d$ $(d < m)$ of $\hat{\tilde{\mathbf{S}}}_b \mathbf{u} = \lambda \hat{\tilde{\mathbf{S}}}_w \mathbf{u}$ (i.e., using the LDE framework). Let $\mathbf{U} = (\mathbf{u}_1, \ldots, \mathbf{u}_d)$. The regular discriminant feature vector is $\mathbf{z}^1 = \mathbf{U}^T \mathbf{P}_1^T \mathbf{y}$.

Step4. Extract the irregular discriminant features: Let $\mathbf{P}_2 = (\boldsymbol{\beta}_{q+1}, \ldots, \boldsymbol{\beta}_m)$. Define $\hat{\tilde{\mathbf{S}}}_b = \mathbf{P}_2^T \tilde{\mathbf{S}}_b \mathbf{P}_2$. Calculate $\hat{\tilde{\mathbf{S}}}_b$'s orthonormal eigenvectors $\mathbf{w}_1, \ldots, \mathbf{w}_{d'}$ corresponding to the d' $(d' < m)$ largest eigenvalues of $\hat{\tilde{\mathbf{S}}}_b \mathbf{u} = \lambda \mathbf{u}$. Let $\mathbf{W} = (\mathbf{w}_1, \ldots, \mathbf{w}_{d'})$. The irregular discriminant feature vector is $\mathbf{z}^2 = \mathbf{W}^T \mathbf{P}_2^T \mathbf{y}$.

Step5. Fuse the regular and irregular discriminant features for classification.

For numerical robustness, in Step 2 of the algorithm, q could be selected as a number that is properly less than the real rank of $\tilde{\mathbf{S}}_w$ in practical applications. We adopted the following heuristic. We choose q as the number of eigenvalues that are less than $\frac{\lambda_{max}}{2000}$ where λ_{max} is the biggest eigenvalue of $\tilde{\mathbf{S}}_w$. Usually the real rank of $\tilde{\mathbf{S}}_w$ is greater than $\frac{\lambda_{max}}{2000}$. Once the linear embedding is computed, every datum $\mathbf{x}$ will be mapped to two subspaces, that is, the sample $\mathbf{x}$, will have a projection $\mathbf{z}$ containing two vectors, regular $\mathbf{z}^1$ and irregular $\mathbf{z}^2$, so $\mathbf{z} = [\mathbf{z}^1; \mathbf{z}^2]$.

4 Experimental Results

The proposed method is used in a face recognition scenario on three public face databases: **Extended Yale** (28 subjects, 1774 images), **PIE** (68 subjects, subset of 1926 images) and **PF01** (101 subjects, 1819 images). Two kinds of experiments were conducted in order to compare our proposed method with the following Kernel methods: Kernel PCA (KPCA) [8], Regularized Kernel LDA (RKDA) [16, 17], Complete Kernel Fisher Discriminant (CKFD) [13] and Kernel Local Discriminant Embedding (KLDE) [14].

In the first kind of experiments, cropped face images were used in the task of face recognition. The kernel used was Gaussian. Each test image was projected to the embedding space which is provided by the mentioned methods and then classification was carried out in the new space by Nearest Neighbor classifier. For each database, l images were selected for training and the rest of data were used for test, this process was repeated for 10 different random splits of the whole data set. The recognition rate was calculated for different dimensions in the embedded space and then averaged over 10 splits. The average is a curve depicting the rate as a function of dimensions. The maximum value of that average curve was picked as the Maximum Average Recognition Rate (MARR) and reported. For each database we chose three different l values and for each one the recognition rates were calculated and reported.

Table 1 shows the obtained MARR for Extended Yale, PF01 and PIE datasets. The values in the parenthesis show the dimensionality in which the maximum recognition rate occurred.

In the second kind of experiments, the training data were the same as in the previous experiment. Three different types of noise (Uniform, Gaussian and Salt & Pepper) were added to the test images. Figure 1 illustrates the effect of adding each kind of noise to three images. We quantified the recognition rate as

Table 1. Maximum Average Recognition rate (%) over 10 random splits on three face datasets. Each column corresponds to a fixed number of train samples. Numbers in the parenthesis correspond to the dimensionality at which the recognition rate has been reported.

Method\ExtYALE	10	15	20
KPCA	71.1(140)	77.1(14)	80.6(140)
RKDA	74.8(25)	82.0(25)	87.1(25)
CKFD	86.3(25)	91.6(25)	94.8(20)
KLDE	88.7(135)	93.3(130)	95.8(120)
TSKLDE	**91.5**(100)	**94.8**(135)	**96.4**(140)
Method\PF01	6	9	12
KPCA	53.8(140)	61.7(140)	63.5(140)
RKDA	65.5(25)	77.4(35)	81.8(50)
CKFD	81.0(30)	84.4(20)	86.5(20)
KLDE	82.4(135)	88.9(115)	91.8(140)
TSKLDE	**83.4**(110)	**91.1**(135)	**93.9**(130)
Method\PIE	10	15	20
KPCA	47.8(140)	56.1(140)	59.6(140)
RKDA	73.8(30)	83.5(30)	87.8(35)
CKFD	82.9(25)	86.9(20)	88.7(20)
KLDE	82.2(135)	87.0(125)	88.9(135)
TSKLDE	**83.6**(65)	**88.6**(65)	**91.0**(55)

Fig. 1. First column: Original images. Second column: Uniform noise added. Third column: Gaussian noise added. Fourth column: Salt & Pepper noise added.

a function of the noise level (Uniform noise), its standard deviation (Gaussian noise), or its density percentage (Salt & Pepper noise). For each such level, we report the recognition rate (i.e., Maximum Average Recognition Rate) over ten different random splits. In this experiment, the number of train images for Extended Yale database and PF01 is 15. For each such level, we report the recognition rate (i.e., Maximum Average Recognition Rate) over ten different random splits. Figure 2 shows the Maximum Average Recognition Rate when test images are affected by three types of Noise. The First row corresponds to Extended Yale dataset and the second row to PF01 dataset. In each plot,

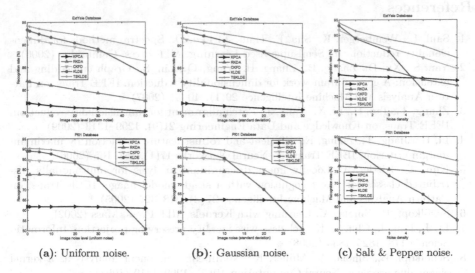

(a): Uniform noise. (b): Gaussian noise. (c) Salt & Pepper noise.

Fig. 2. Maximum Average Recognition Rate when test images are affected by three types of Noise. **First row**: Extended Yale dataset. **Second row**: PF01 dataset.

the horizontal axis illustrates the noise level (Uniform), the standard deviation (Gaussian), and density percentage (Salt and Pepper). The images used have 256 gray levels. We note that for CKFD and the proposed TSKLDE, the regular and irregular vectors are jointly used, the maximum dimensionality is limited to the minimum length of regular or irregular vectors.

We now highlight some observations about the two kinds of conducted experiments: (1) Since the core of RKDA and CKFD is LDA, the final dimensionality of these methods can not be more than the number of classes minus one. (2) The proposed TSKLDE method in all evaluations was able to outperform other Kernel methods. (3) For noisy images, the proposed method shows good results. More importantly, in the presence of noise, the performance of the proposed two subspace KLDE downgrades less than the KLDE.

5   Conclusion

We proposed a two Subspace-based Kernel Local Discriminant Embedding (TSKLDE) for feature extraction and recognition. Two-subspaces were introduced and used for final embedding. The resulting embedding is inductive (applied to unseen images). The experimental results on three public face databases, Extended Yale, PIE and PF01 show that the proposed TSKLDE which is a Two subspace-based, nonlinear, supervised local technique, has better performance than some state of art methods like CKFD. The experiments showed that the introduced framework is more robust with respect to noise than the competing Kernel methods.

References

1. Saul, L., Weinberger, K., Sha, F., Ham, J., Lee, D.: Spectral methods for dimensionality reduction. In: Semisupervised Learning. MIT Press, Cambridge (2006)
2. Yan, S., Xu, D., Zhang, B., Zhang, H., Yang, Q., Lin, S.: Graph embedding and extension: A general framework for dimensionality reduction. IEEE Trans. on Pattern Analysis and Machine Intelligence 29(1), 40–51 (2007)
3. Zhang, T., Tao, D., Li, X., Yang, J.: Patch alignment for dimensionality reduction. IEEE Trans. on Knowledge and Data Engineering 21(9), 1299–1313 (2009)
4. Li, H., Jiang, T., Zhang, K.: Efficient and robust feature extraction by maximum margin criterion. IEEE Trans. on Neural Networks 17(1), 157–165 (2006)
5. Kim, T., Kittler, J.: Locally linear discriminant analysis for multimodally distributed classes for face recognition with a single model image. IEEE Trans. on Pattern Analysis and Machine Intelligence 27(3), 318–327 (2005)
6. Schölkopf, B., Smola, A.: Learning with Kernels. MIT Press, Mass (2002)
7. Li, J., Pan, J., Chu, S.: Kernel class-wise locality preserving projection. Informatio Science 178, 1825–1835 (2008)
8. Schölkopf, B., Smola, A., Müller, K.: Nonlinear component analysis as a kernel eigenvalue problem. Neural Computation 10(5), 1299–1319 (1998)
9. Mika, S., Rätsch, G., Schölkopf, B., Smola, A., Weston, J., Müller, K.: Invariant feature extraction and classification in kernel spaces. In: NIPS (1999)
10. Baudat, G., Anouar, F.: Generalized discriminant analysis using a kernel approach. Neural Computation 12(10), 2385–2404 (2000)
11. Lu, J., Plataniotis, K., Venetsanopoulos, A.: Face recognition using kernel direct discriminant analysis algorithms. IEEE Trans. Neural Networks 14(1), 117–126 (2003)
12. Chen, L., Liao, H., Lin, J., Kao, M., Yu, G.: A new LDA-based face recognition system which can solve the small sample size problem. Pattern Recognition 33(10), 1713–1726 (2000)
13. Yang, J., Frangi, A.F., Yang, J.Y., Zhang, D., Jin, Z.: KPCA plus LDA: A complete kernel fisher discriminant framework for feature extraction and recognition. IEEE Trans. on Pattern Analysis Machine Intelligence 27(2), 230–244 (2005)
14. Chen, H., Chang, H., Liu, T.: Local discriminant embedding and its variants. In: IEEE International Conference on Computer Vision and Pattern Recognition (2005)
15. Xu, Y., Zhong, A., Yang, J., Zhang, D.: LPP solution schemes for use with face recognition. Pattern Recognition 43, 4165–4176 (2010)
16. Cai, D., He, X., Han, J.: Efficient kernel discriminant analysis via spectral regression. In: International Conference on Data Mining (2007)
17. Cai, D., He, X., Han, J.: Speed up kernel discriminant analysis. The International Journal on Very Large Data Bases 20(1), 21–33 (2011)

Coupling Gaussian Process Dynamical Models with Product-of-Experts Kernels

Dmytro Velychko[1,2], Dominik Endres[1,2,*], Nick Taubert[1],
and Martin A. Giese[1,*]

[1] Section Computational Sensomotorics, Department of Cognitive Neurology,
University Clinic Tübingen, CIN, HIH and University of Tübingen,
Otfried-Müller-Str. 25, 72076 Tübingen, Germany
[2] Theoretical Neuroscience, Dept. of Psychology, Philipps-University Marburg
Gutenbergstr. 18, 35032 Marburg, Germany
{dmytro.velychko,dominik.endres}@gmail.com
{nick.taubert,martin.giese}@uni-tuebingen.de

Abstract. We describe a new probabilistic model for learning of coupled dynamical systems in latent state spaces. The coupling is achieved by combining predictions from several Gaussian process dynamical models in a product-of-experts fashion. Our approach facilitates modulation of coupling strengths without the need for computationally expensive re-learning of the dynamical models. We demonstrate the effectiveness of the new coupling model on synthetic toy examples and on high-dimensional human walking motion capture data.

Keywords: Gaussian Process, Products of Experts, Computer Graphics.

1 Introduction

Mathematical models of dynamical systems are used in many fields of science. For example, coordinated motor patterns have been accounted for by networks of coupled dynamic movement primitives or 'central pattern generators' [7]. We are primarily concerned with the modeling of human motion data for experiments in psychophysics and neuroscience, but our approach lends itself naturally to applications in computer graphics and robotics.

While whole-body human motion data is high-dimensional, the intrinsic dimensionality is usually much smaller. Applying dynamical models to such data directly often results in poor generalization abilities, e.g. when one wants to vary parameters affecting the dynamical coupling strength between body parts. Therefore, a dimensionality reduction component is usually part of such a model. Lawrence [12] introduced a new probabilistic, non-linear dimensionality reduction method, the Gaussian process latent variable model (GPLVM), which is based on Gaussian processes (GP). A GP can be obtained from a neural network with a particular prior on the weights and biases in the limit of infinitely

---

* Equal contribution.

S. Wermter et al. (Eds.): ICANN 2014, LNCS 8681, pp. 603–610, 2014.

many hidden units [17]. The GPLVM was extended by a latent dynamics in [24] resulting in the Gaussian process dynamical model (GPDM). Due to its probabilistic nature, it is well equipped to handle the variability of natural motion data. It is possible to model full-body human motion with just one GPDM [21, 22, 24]. However, such 'monolithic' motion models do not allow for modulation of parts of the dynamics (e.g. different motion styles of body parts for movement design in computer graphics) or for recombining previously learned component dynamics for complex coordinated movements. Such a recombination would allow us to construct a rich repertoire of full-body movements from a much smaller set of dynamical primitives. We therefore present an approach to coupling GPDMs based on a product-of-experts (PoE) [9] construction. PoE results in less uncertain overall predictions than any of its parts, which is conducive to stability. Furthermore, we can then modulate the coupling strengths after learning, *without* costly re-training of the components.

We briefly review related work in section 2, and introduce the model's building blocks in section 3. The main theoretical development of this paper, the product-of-experts kernel is derived in section 4. Section 5 presents results on illustrative toy examples, and on human locomotion data.

2   Related Work

There are, broadly speaking, two approaches for learning of dynamical systems: as a deterministic system of differential equations (see e.g. [5, 10]), and statistical approaches, where the evolution of a system is described in terms of a probabilistic mapping from the previous state to the next, for example [3, 4, 8, 23]. Both approaches may be augmented with deep hierarchies.

Deterministic systems based on differential equations have to be carefully designed and tuned. Even though the theory of learning of complex dynamical systems for motion synthesis is in active development, and some sophisticated applications of it for robotics, computer graphics and neuroscience exist [1, 10, 13], the nature of nonlinear dynamical systems makes it hard to design and train such models. One approach for their design is contraction theory [15], which allows for the construction of dynamically stable systems from stable components [1, 16].

On the other hand, probabilistic approaches promise to capture the variability of human motion and its styles [8, 21, 23]. Ease of learning and manipulation of the parameters are crucial advantages for such applications as psychophysical experiments in emotion perception [21], computer graphics [14] and human locomotion modeling [22]. However, a stability analysis of these models is non-trivial, and has not been accomplished to date.

3   Model Components

Gaussian Process Latent Variable Model (GPLVM). A GPLVM comprises a prior on mappings $f_Y(X)$ from a a (possibly vector-valued) latent variable X onto observable variables Y [12]. The $f_Y(X)$ is drawn from a Gaussian

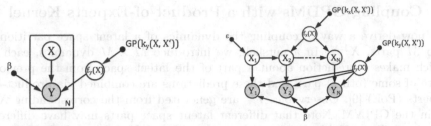

Fig. 1. Left: Graphical model representation of a GPLVM, which is a prior on functions from a (low-dimensional) latent space X to a (high-dimensional, observed) space Y [12]. **Right**: in a GPDM, a Markov chain in the latent space X models the dynamics of the observed data Y [24]. For details, see text.

Process (GP) prior, parametrized by a mean function (constant zero in this paper) and kernel (covariance function) $k_Y(X, X')$. Furthermore Y may be corrupted by additive Gaussian noise with standard deviation β, see Fig. 1, left. The prior on X is typically an isotropic Gaussian, too, but may be replaced by predictions from a higher level model in a hierarchical architecture [21].

Assume $D = \dim(Y)$, $q = \dim(X)$ and that we had observed N instances $\mathbf{y}_i$ of Y. We index component d of instance i as $y_{d,i}$. We also use slice notation for arrays, e.g. $\tilde{\mathbf{y}} = y_{d,:}$ denotes the vector comprised of all instances of component d, whereas $\mathbf{y}_i = y_{:,i}$. We write $p(\mathbf{y})$ as a short-hand for $p(Y = \mathbf{y})$. Like in [12], we learn the GPLVM by maximizing the joint posterior density of the corresponding $\mathbf{x}_:$. Since all finite-dimensional marginals of a GP are multivariate Gaussian with density $\mathcal{N}(\mathbf{y}|\mu, \Sigma)$, and the components of a vector-valued GP are independent, it follows that the likelihood of $y_{:,d}$ is given by

$$p(y_{d,:}|k_Y(X, X'), \beta, \mathbf{x}_:) = \mathcal{N}(y_{d,:}|\mathbf{0}_N, \mathbf{K}_Y + \beta^2 \mathbf{1}_{N,N}) \tag{1}$$

where $\mathbf{K}_Y$ is the kernel matrix, with $(\mathbf{K}_Y)_{i,j} = k_Y(\mathbf{x}_i, \mathbf{x}_j)$ and $\mathbf{1}_{N,N}$ is the N-dimensional identity matrix. Thus, the total posterior of the latent variables is proportional to

$$p(\mathbf{x}_:|\mathbf{y}_:, k(X, X')) \propto \prod_d p(y_{d,:}|, k_Y(X, X'), \beta, \mathbf{x}_:) \prod_i p(\mathbf{x}_i) \tag{2}$$

which can be optimized by standard non-linear methods; we use [20].

Gaussian Process Dynamical Model (GPDM). Wang [24] extended the GPLVM with a dynamical auto-regressive prior on the latent X_i, where the data point index i now denotes discrete time. The evolution function $f_X(X)$ of this dynamics is drawn from a GP with kernel $k_X(X, X')$ and $\mathbf{x}_{i+1} = f_X(\mathbf{x}_i) + \eta$; $\eta \sim \mathcal{N}(\mathbf{0}_q, \xi^2 \mathbf{1}_{q \times q})$. This approach leads to a non-linear, continuous generalization of a hidden Markov model. For a first-order dynamics, one obtains (cf. Fig. 1, right):

$$p(\mathbf{x}_:|k_X(X, X'), \xi, \epsilon) = p(\mathbf{x}_1|\epsilon) \prod_{i=2}^{N} p(\mathbf{x}_i|\mathbf{x}_{i-1}, f_X(X), \xi) \tag{3}$$

$$p(\mathbf{x}_i|\mathbf{x}_{i-1}, f(X), \xi) = \mathcal{N}(\mathbf{x}_i|f(\mathbf{x}_{i-1}), \xi^2 \mathbf{1}_{q \times q}) \tag{4}$$

$$p(\mathbf{x}_1|\epsilon) = \mathcal{N}(\mathbf{x}_1|\mathbf{0}_q, \epsilon^2 \mathbf{1}_{q \times q}) \ , \ f(X) \sim GP(k_X(X, X')) \tag{5}$$

The GPDM is easily extensible to higher-order dynamics. The mapping onto observable variables Y is done in the same fashion as for the GPLVM.

4   Coupling GPDMs with a Product-of-Experts Kernel

We now derive a way of coupling the dynamics of a latent space partitioned into M parts, $X^{1:M}$. In a nutshell, we introduce $M \times M$ dynamics, each of which makes a prediction about a part of the latent space from the previous state of some (other) part, and these predictions are combined via product-of-experts (PoE) [9]. Observables Y^m are generated from the corresponding X^m as in the GPLVM. Note that different latent space parts may have different dimensionalities. Unlike [11], we do not create a new kernel by computing some inner product between two probability distributions. Rather, we multiply M probability distributions, each described by a kernel, and renormalize the result.

More specifically, let X^m_{i-1} be the latent state of part m at (discrete) time $i-1$. We introduce $M \times M$ evolution functions $f_{m,r}(X^m)$ generating the prediction $X^{m,r}_i$ which the latent state of part m makes about the latent state of part r at time i, see Fig. 2, left, for an example with $M = 2$. The $f_{m,r}(X^m)$ are drawn from GPs with kernels $k_{m,r}(X^m, X^{m\prime})$. Observables Y^m have been omitted to keep graphical model less cluttered . The $X^{m,r}_i$ are the means of Gaussian 'experts' with isotropic coupling variances $\sigma^2_{m,r}$. Denoting the total predictive PoE variance of part r by

$$\sigma^2_r = \left(\sum_m \sigma^{-2}_{m,r} \right)^{-1} \tag{6}$$

We find, by multiplying the parts' densities together and renormalizing:

$$p(\mathbf{x}^r_i | \mathbf{x}^{:,r}_i, \sigma_{:,r}) \propto \prod_m \mathcal{N}\left(\mathbf{x}^r_i | \mathbf{x}^{m,r}_i, \sigma^2_{m,r}\right)$$

$$\Rightarrow p(\mathbf{x}^r_i | \mathbf{x}^{:,r}_i, \sigma_r) = \frac{\exp\left[-\frac{1}{2\sigma^2_r}\left(\mathbf{x}^r_i - \sigma^2_r \sum_m \frac{\mathbf{x}^{m,r}_i}{\sigma^2_{m,r}}\right)^2\right]}{(2\pi\sigma^2_r)^{\frac{\dim(X^r)}{2}}} \tag{7}$$

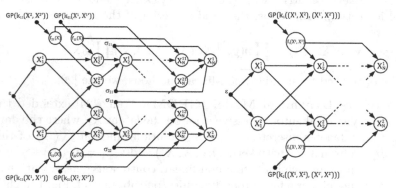

Fig. 2. Coupled latent space dynamics with two parts, observables Y^m omitted for clarity. **Left**: full model. Every part m of the latent X^m_{i-1} at time step $i-1$ generates a prediction $X^{m,r}_i$ about every part r at time step i via an evolution function $f_{m,r}(X^m)$. These individual predictions are combined through a Product-of-Experts approach. **Right**: after the (closed-form) marginalization of the $X^{m,r}_i$ and the $f_{m,r}(X^m)$, the model can be equivalently written as having only one evolution function $f_m(X^1, \ldots, X^M)$ per part m. For details, see text.

Note that the total PoE variance (eqn. 6) is smaller than any of the individual coupling variances.

Next, we marginalize the part predictions $X_i^{m,r}$ and the evolution functions $f_{m,r}(X^m)$, to obtain the joint density of the X_i^m. To this end, we make use of conditional independence properties of the model, which can be read off the graphical model (Fig. 2, left) using the D-separation rules [18]. In the following, assume the $X_i^{\cdot}$ were fixed. Then, the tail-to-tail paths from $X_i^{m,r}$ to any $X_i^{m,q}$ with $r \neq q$ are blocked. Also, the head-to-tail paths from $X_i^{m,r}$ to any $X_j^{q,p}$ for $j \neq i$ are blocked, because there is (at least one) fixed node between them. There are no other open paths from $X_i^{m,r}$ to any $X_j^{q,p}$ for $r \neq p$, hence the part predictions about part r are independent from those about p across all time steps. On the other hand, fixing X_i^r opens head-to-head paths between the $X_i^{\cdot,r}$. Finally, observe that there is an open tail-to-tail path from $X_i^{m,r}$ and $X_j^{m,r}$ for all i, j through the function node $f_{r,m}(X^m)$, which induces a dependency between predictions about the same part across time steps. Hence, we can marginalize the $X_i^{m,r}$ separately for each r, but we need to do so jointly across all m and i.

The dependency between the $X_i^{\cdot,r}$ through fixed X_i^r is multivariate Gaussian for every i, see eqn. 7. The dependency induced by the unobserved evolution functions is multivariate Gaussian in time, because these functions are drawn from GPs. Since the priors on X_1^m are Gaussian, the joint density of the X_i^m must be a multivariate Gaussian as well. Hence, the marginalization boils down to a multivariate Gaussian integral, which we carry out using the following

Lemma 1. *Let* $\mathbf{v}$ *and* $\mathbf{w}$ *be multivariate Gaussian random variates. Assume* $p(\mathbf{v}|\mathbf{w}) = \mathcal{N}(\mathbf{v}|\mathbf{Pw}, \boldsymbol{\Sigma})$ *and* $p(\mathbf{w}) = \mathcal{N}(\mathbf{w}|\boldsymbol{\mu}, \mathbf{K})$, *where* $\mathbf{P}$ *is a* $dim(\mathbf{v}) \times dim(\mathbf{w})$ *projection matrix, and both* $\boldsymbol{\Sigma}$ *and* $\mathbf{K}$ *are positive definite. Then* $p(\mathbf{v}) = \mathcal{N}(\mathbf{P}\boldsymbol{\mu}, \boldsymbol{\Sigma} + \mathbf{PKP}^T)$. **Proof:** *marginalize* $\mathbf{w}$ *using standard matrix algebra results [19].*

To use this lemma, let $\mathbf{v} = x_{d,2:N}^r$ for some part r and component d. Construct the $M(N-1)$-dimensional vector $\mathbf{w}$ by stacking the $x_{d,2:N}^{m,r}$ for all m. Then, by virtue of eqn. 7, $\boldsymbol{\Sigma} = \sigma_r^2 \mathbf{1}_{(N-1)\times(N-1)}$ and $\mathbf{P} = \sigma_r^2(\sigma_{1,r}^{-2}, \dots, \sigma_{M,r}^{-2}) \otimes \mathbf{1}_{(N-1),(N-1)}$ ($\otimes$ denotes the Kronecker product). $\mathbf{K}$ is a block-diagonal matrix, with M blocks K^m, where the entries of these kernel matrices are computed from the kernel functions $k_{m,r}(X^m, X^{m\prime})$ (cf. Fig. 2) as $\mathbf{K}_{i,j}^m = k_{m,r}(x_{:,i}^m, x_{:,j}^m)$ with $i, j = 2, \dots, N$. Since all GPs in our model have zero mean, $\boldsymbol{\mu} = \mathbf{0}_{M(N-1)}$. Thus, the mean of $\mathbf{v} = \mathbf{P}\boldsymbol{\mu} = \mathbf{0}_{N-1}$. The covariance matrix of $\mathbf{v}$ is given by

$$\boldsymbol{\Sigma} + \mathbf{PKP}^T = \sigma_r^2 \mathbf{1}_{(N-1)\times(N-1)} + \sigma_r^4 \sum_{m=1}^{M} \frac{\mathbf{K}^m}{\sigma_{m,r}^4} \qquad (8)$$

Since this holds for any choice of $x_{:,i}^m$, the Kolmogorov extension theorem guarantees the existence of a GP with constant zero mean function and a kernel function k_r generating these covariance matrices:

$$k_r(X^{\cdot}, X^{\cdot\prime}) = \sigma_r^2 \delta(X^{\cdot}, X^{\cdot\prime}) + \sigma_r^4 \sum_{m=1}^{M} \frac{k_{m,r}(X^m, X^{m\prime})}{\sigma_{m,r}^4} \qquad (9)$$

where $X^{\cdot}$ denotes the tuple $(X^1, \dots, X^M)$ and $\delta(X, Y)$ is the Dirac delta function. We can therefore rewrite the graphical model of the coupled dynamical systems as depicted in Fig. 2, right: for every part r, there is one evolution function that generates the current X_i^r from all previous X_{i-1}^m. This function is drawn from a GP prior with zero mean and a kernel as in eqn. 9. Note that we could in principle choose different kernel parts $k_{m,r}(X^m, X^{m\prime})$ for every m, r. That eqn. 9 is a valid kernel also follows from standard 'kernel engineering' rules [2], its maximum-a-posteriori parameters are learned with [20].

5   Results

We tested the model on simple synthetic data sets first, see Fig. 3. The data (black lines with squares, visible in the pdf when zoomed) were created by sampling sine waves at 100 time steps with amplitudes 1, 2, 3, and adding $\approx 5\%$ high-frequency distortions. All three curves in one panel have the same frequency but different phase. We learned a coupled 2nd order GPDM with three parts and an RBF+linear dynamics kernel for the parts. The latent space had 2 dimensions, latent points formed a circle after learning. The coupling matrices in Fig. 3 show the learned values of the relative coupling variances $\sigma_{r,r}^2 / \sigma_{m,r}^2$, which are the higher the stronger the coupling is, and thus measure coupling strength. After learning, we generated the gray data by running the GPDMs in generative mode to show that they can reproduce and continue the training data. In the data on the left side of Fig. 3 (panels A-C), all generating frequencies were different between panels. Consequently, the CGPDM learns that there should be no strong coupling between the parts (small off-diagonal values). In contrast, on the right side of of Fig. 3, the sine waves of panels E and F have the same frequency, but shifted phases. Here, the coupling from part E to parts E and F is strong. Hence, part E can be used to drive both parts E and F, and vice versa.

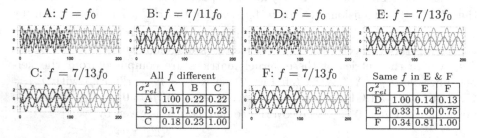

Fig. 3. Toy example. Data for three parts (panels A-C and D-F) were synthesized from sine waves with different or same frequencies f and phases, distorted by high-frequency sines, Gaussian noise was added (black lines). The learned model could reproduce and continue the data (gray lines). Matrices show relative coupling variances $\sigma_{rel}^2 = \sigma_{r,r}^2 / \sigma_{m,r}^2$ from part m (row) to r (column) averaged on 100 runs with different noise sampling, large values indicate strong coupling (cf. eqn. 7). For details, see text.

Human Walking Data. To illustrate the power of the CGPDM on real-world data, we learned a two-part model on human walking data recorded with a Vicon motion capture system. The latent space of each part was three-dimensional, we used a RBF+linear+isotropic noise kernel for each coupling, and second order dynamics. The raw data were converted into exponential map format [6], which is suitable for learning with GPs since it represents a joint rotation as a 3 dimensional real vector with unconstrained component values. The data were divided into upper body (thorax, arms and head) and lower body (legs and pelvis). After learning, we found that the relative coupling variances were ≈ 1 for both upper-to-lower and lower-to-upper coupling, indicating strong coupling between upper and lower body in natural walking motion. We then synthesized walking motions by running the CGPDM generatively. **Panel a)** of the supplemental movie available at `http://www.compsens.uni-tuebingen.de/icannCoupledDynamics.html` shows a generated walk with the learned coupling variances. It looks quite natural, including variability between steps, but a rigorous psychophysical test of this observation has yet to be conducted. In **panels b) & c)**, the upper and lower body were started with a phase-shift of 20 frames, and coupled strongly (b) or weakly (c, small relative coupling variances). The difference in synchronization speed is clearly visible. Note that this kind of coupling manipulation is impossible with a monolithic GPDM model. **Panels d) & e)** show the result of driving one body part completely by the other: using the lower body as the driver leads to a smooth walking motion, whereas unnatural variability in the legs appears when the upper part drives the lower. Finally, **panel f)** demonstrates that the body parts will not synchronize when completely decoupled.

6 Conclusion

We have derived a coupled GPDM from a product-of-experts principle, and demonstrated its ability to learn complex full-body human motion. Natural variability in the data is preserved. The coupling strengths can be modulated without needing to re-train the individual dynamics. Future work will focus on establishing dynamical stability conditions for the coupling kernel, possibly employing contraction theory [15]. We will also design experimental paradigms for a quantitative comparison to other models and causality detection.

Acknowledgments. This work was supported by EU projects TANGO FP7-249858-TP3, AMARSi- EC FP7-ICT-248311; DFG GI 305/4-1, DFG GZ: KA 1258/15-1; BMBF, FKZ: 01GQ1002A, FP7-PEOPLE-2011-ITN(Marie Curie): ABC PITN-GA-011-290011, HBP FP7-ICT-2013-FET-F/ 604102; Koroibot FP7-ICT-2013-10/ 611909, DFG GRK 1901 'The Brain in Action'.

References

1. Ajallooeian, M., van den Kieboom, J., Mukovskiy, A., Giese, M.A., Ijspeert, A.: A general family of morphed nonlinear phase oscillators with arbitrary limit cycle shape. Physica D: Nonlinear Phenomena 263, 41–56 (2013), `http://www.sciencedirect.com/science/article/pii/S0167278913002339`
2. Bishop, C.M.: Pattern Recognition and Machine Learning. Springer (2006)

3. Brand, M., Hertzmann, A.: Style machines. In: Proc. SIGGRAPH 2000, pp. 183–192 (2000)
4. Chai, J., Hodgins, J.K.: Performance animation from low-dimensional control signals. ACM Trans. Graph. 24(3), 686–696 (2005)
5. Giese, M.A., Mukovskiy, A., Park, A.-N., Omlor, L., Slotine, J.-J.E.: Real-Time Synthesis of Body Movements Based on Learned Primitives. In: Cremers, D., Rosenhahn, B., Yuille, A.L., Schmidt, F.R. (eds.) Visual Motion Analysis. LNCS, vol. 5604, pp. 107–127. Springer, Heidelberg (2009)
6. Grassia, F.S.: Practical parameterization of rotations using the exponential map. J. Graph. Tools 3(3), 29–48 (1998), http://dx.doi.org/10.1080/10867651.1998.10487493
7. Grillner, S., Wallen, P.: Central pattern generators for locomotion, with special reference to vertebrates. Ann. Rev. Neurosci. 8(1), 233–261 (1985)
8. Grochow, K., Martin, S.L., Hertzmann, A., Popovic, Z.: Style-based inverse kinematics. ACM Trans. Graph. 23(3), 522–531 (2004)
9. Hinton, G.E.: Products of experts. In: Proc. ICANN 1999, vol. 1, pp. 1–6 (1999)
10. Ijspeert, A.J., Nakanishi, J., Hoffmann, H., Pastor, P., Schaal, S.: Dynamical movement primitives: Learning attractor models for motor behaviors. Neu. Comp. 25(2), 328–373 (2013)
11. Jebara, T., Kondor, R., Howard, A.: Probability product kernels. J. Mach. Learn. Res. 5, 819–844 (2004)
12. Lawrence, N.D.: Gaussian process latent variable models for visualisation of high dimensional data. In: NIPS 2003 (2003)
13. Lee, S.H., Sifakis, E., Terzopoulos, D.: Comprehensive biomechanical modeling and simulation of the upper body. ACM Trans. Graph. 99, 99 (2009)
14. Levine, S., Wang, J.M., Haraux, A., Popović, Z., Koltun, V.: Continuous character control with low-dimensional embeddings. ACM Trans. Graph. 28, 28 (2012)
15. Lohmiller, W., Slotine, J.J.E.: On contraction analysis for non-linear systems. Automatica 34(6), 683–696 (1998)
16. Mukovskiy, A., Slotine, J.J., Giese, M.: Design of the dynamic stability properties of the collective behavior of articulated bipeds. In: 10th IEEE-RAS Intl. Conf. Humanoid Robots, pp. 66–73 (2010)
17. Neal, R.: Bayesian Learning for Neural Networks. Ph.D. thesis, Dept. of Computer Science, University of Toronto (1994)
18. Pearl, J.: Probabilistic Reasoning in Intelligent Systems. Morgan Kaufmann (1997)
19. Petersen, K.B., Pedersen, M.S.: The matrix cookbook (2012), version 20121115
20. Rasmussen, C.E.: minimize.m (2006), http://learning.eng.cam.ac.uk/carl/code/minimize/
21. Taubert, N., Endres, D., Christensen, A., Giese, M.A.: Shaking hands in latent space. In: Bach, J., Edelkamp, S. (eds.) KI 2011. LNCS (LNAI), vol. 7006, pp. 330–334. Springer, Heidelberg (2011)
22. Urtasun, R., Fleet, D.J., Lawrence, N.D.: Modeling human locomotion with topologically constrained latent variable models. In: Elgammal, A., Rosenhahn, B., Klette, R. (eds.) Human Motion 2007. LNCS, vol. 4814, pp. 104–118. Springer, Heidelberg (2007)
23. Wang, J.M., Fleet, D.J., Hertzmann, A.: Multifactor gaussian process models for style-content separation. In: ICML, pp. 975–982 (2007)
24. Wang, J.M., Fleet, D.J., Hertzmann, A.: Gaussian process dynamical models for human motion. IEEE Trans. Pattern Anal. Mach. Intell. 30(2), 283–298 (2008)

A Deep Dynamic Binary Neural Network and Its Application to Matrix Converters

Jungo Moriyasu and Toshimichi Saito*

Hosei University, Koganei, Tokyo, 184-8584 Japan
tsaito@hosei.ac.jp

Abstract. This paper studies the deep dynamic binary neural network that is characterized by the signum activation function, ternary weighting parameters and integer threshold parameters. In order to store a desired binary periodic orbit, we present a simple learning method based on the correlation learning. The method is applied to a teacher signal that corresponds to control signal of the matrix converter in power electronics. Performing numerical experiments, we investigate storage of the teacher signal and its stability as the depth of the network varies.

Keywords: Binary neural networks, Deep learning, Matrix converters.

1 Introduction

This paper presents the deep dynamic binary neural network (DDBN) and considers its application to power electronics. The DDBN is constructed by applying time delay to multi-layer feed-forward binary neural networks [1]-[6]. The DDBN is characterized by the signum activation function, ternary weighting parameters and integer threshold parameters. The number of layers m is a variable that controls the "depth" of the DDBN. Each layer shares the output of the DDBN. Depending on parameters and initial value, the DDBN can exhibit various binary periodic orbits (BPOs). The DDBN can be regarded as an example of digital dynamical systems represented by the cellular automata with various engineering applications [7]-[9]. Analysis and synthesis of the DDBN are important from both basic and application viewpoints.

Since discussion of general learning methods is hard in the DDBN, this paper considers basic problems: storage of one BPO, stability of the stored BPO and an engineering application. In order to store a desired BPO, we present a simple learning method based on the correlation learning (CL, [1] [10] [11]). The CL-based learning can determine the parameters uniquely and can guarantee storage of a class of BPOs. This learning method is much simpler than the genetic algorithm based learning for two- and three-layer dynamic binary neural networks in our previous papers [1]-[3]. We then consider an application to the matrix converter that is a typical ac/ac converter in power electronics [12]-[14]. In this application, the teacher signal BPO corresponds to control signal of the

* This work is supported in part by JSPS KAKENHI#24500284

S. Wermter et al. (Eds.): ICANN 2014, LNCS 8681, pp. 611–618, 2014.
© Springer International Publishing Switzerland 2014

converter and the BPO is derived from a desired switching pattern. Stability of the BPO is basic to realize robust and reliable circuit operation. Performing basic numerical experiments, we have clarified that the BPO can be stored for $m \geq 2$. Stability of the stored BPO is reinforced as m increases. Note that the teacher signal does not include any information of stability and the stored BPO is stabilized automatically.

Since the DDBN can realize various stable BPOs that correspond to various switching signals, our results may be developed into reconfigurable and robust control circuits of various switching converters. The results also may be developed into systematic analysis and synthesis methods of the DDBN. This is the first paper that considers the depth of the dynamic binary neural networks.

2   Deep Dynamic Binary Neural Network

Dynamics of the DDBN is described by

1st layer: $x_i^{t+1} = \text{sgn}\left(\sum_{j=1}^N w_{ij}^1 x_j^t - \theta_i^1\right)$ ab. $\boldsymbol{x}^{t+1} = F_1(\boldsymbol{x}^t)$

2nd layer: $x_i^{t+2} = \text{sgn}\left(\sum_{j=1}^N w_{ij}^2 x_j^{t+1} - \theta_i^2\right)$ ab. $\boldsymbol{x}^{t+2} = F_2(\boldsymbol{x}^{t+1})$

$\vdots$

m-th layer: $x_i^{t+m} = \text{sgn}\left(\sum_{j=1}^N w_{ij}^m x_j^{t+m-1} - \theta_i^m\right)$ ab. $\boldsymbol{x}^{t+m} = F_m(\boldsymbol{x}^{t+m-1})$

$$\text{sgn}(x) = \begin{cases} +1 \text{ for } x \geq 0 \\ -1 \text{ for } x < 0 \end{cases} \quad i = 1 \sim N, \ t = 1, 1+m, 1+2m, \cdots$$

$$\tag{1}$$

where $\boldsymbol{x}^t \equiv (x_1^t, \cdots, x_N^t)$, $x_i^t \in \{-1, 1\} \equiv B$, is a binary state vector at discrete time t. The signum activation function realizes the binarization. The weighting parameters are ternary and the threshold parameters are integer:

$$w_{ij}^l \in \{-1, 0, 1\}, \ \theta_i^l \in \mathbf{Z}, \ i = 1 \sim N, \ j = 1 \sim N, \ l = 1 \sim m \tag{2}$$

The DDBN has m layers and we refer to m as the order of DDBN hereafter. As an initial state vector $\boldsymbol{x}^1$ is given, the first layer outputs $\boldsymbol{x}^2$, the second layer outputs $\boldsymbol{x}^3$ and the m-th layer outputs $\boldsymbol{x}^{m+1}$. The $\boldsymbol{x}^{m+1}$ is fed back to the first layer. Repeating in this manner, the DDBN can generate various binary sequences. The fundamental case $m = 1$ corresponds to two-layer dynamic binary neural networks (2DBN) discussed in [1]. The DDBN can be regarded as a composition of 2DBNs with different parameters:

$$\boldsymbol{x}^{t+m} = F_m \circ \cdots \circ F_1(\boldsymbol{x}^t) \equiv F_D(\boldsymbol{x}^t), \ F_D : B^N \to B^N$$

where F_l, $l = 1 \sim m$, correspond to the 2DBNs. In this iteration, the DDBN can output a variety of BPOs. Note that the second to $(m-1)$-th layers correspond to hidden layers in the multi-layer perceptrons (MLPs). Although the hidden-layer of the MLP does not give an explicit output, the l-th layer of DDBN gives

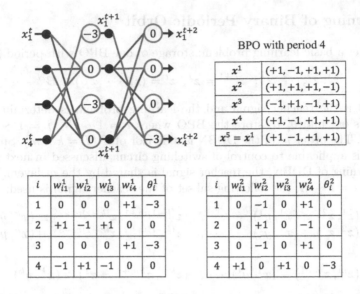

Fig. 1. A simple example of the deep dynamic binary neural networks (DDBN) for $m = 2$, $N = 4$. Red and blue segments represent $w_{ij} = +1$ and $w_{ij} = -1$, respectively. $w_{ij} = 0$ means no connection. The threshold parameters θ_i are shown in the circles.

the explicit output. Also, the input layer of MLP is different from the first layer of the DDBN and is the "0-th layer" of the DDBN. Since the number of lattice points in the domain of F_D is 2^N, memory of all the outputs of F_D becomes impossible as N increases. However, in the DDBN, the number of parameters is $m(N^2 + N)$ and memory of all the parameters is possible as N increases.

Since the domain of F_D consists of a finite number of lattice points, the steady state of the DDBN is a BPO. The DDBN cannot exhibit non-periodic steady state. A BPO with period T is defined by

$$F_D^k(x^1) = x^{T+1} = x^1; \; x^1, \cdots, x^T \text{ are all different} \qquad (3)$$

where m is a divisor of T ($T = k \times m$) and is the order of DDBN. Figure 1 shows an example of DDBN for $m = 2$ and $N = 4$. This DDBN is described by

$$x_i^{t+1} = \text{sgn}\left(\sum_{j=1}^4 w_{ij}^1 x_j^t - \theta_i^1\right) \qquad \text{ab. } x^{t+1} = F_1(x^t)$$
$$x_i^{t+2} = \text{sgn}\left(\sum_{j=1}^4 w_{ij}^2 x_j^{t+1} - \theta_i^2\right) \qquad \text{ab. } x^{t+2} = F_2(x^{t+1}) \qquad (4)$$

where $i = 1 \sim 4$ and $t = 1, 3, 5, 7 \cdots$. The ternary weighing parameters can be expressed by color ($+1$=red, -1=blue and 0=no connection) as shown in Fig. 1. The dynamics is governed by the iteration $x^{t+2} = F_D(x^t)$. This DDBN can output a BPO with period $T = 4$ as shown in the figure:

$$F_1(x^1) = x^2, \; F_2(x^2) = x^3, \; F_3(x^3) = x^4, \; F_4(x^4) = x^5 = x^1$$

3   Learning of Binary Periodic Orbit

We consider a basic learning problem: storage of one BPO with period T:

$$z^1, z^2, \cdots, z^T; \quad z^{T+1} = z^1; \quad z^t = (z_1^t, \cdots, z_N^t) \in B^N \tag{5}$$

This BPO is the teacher signal and the learning problem is determination of parameters w_{ij}^l and θ_i^l to store the BPO where $i = 1 \sim N$, $j = 1 \sim N$ and $l = 1 \sim m$. The order m of the DDBN is a divisor of T ($T = k \times m$). Storage of one BPO is applicable to control of switching circuit discussed in next section. In the learning of DDBN, the teacher signal is shared by the m layers. For the l-th layer, $l = 1 \sim m$, the following subset of the teacher signal is used:

$$
\begin{aligned}
l = 1:&\ (z^1, z^2) \equiv (x^1, y^1), & \cdots, &\ (z^{(k-1)m+1}, z^{lk-1)m+2}) \equiv (x^k, y^k) \\
l = 2:&\ (z^2, z^3) \equiv (x^1, y^1), & \cdots, &\ (z^{(k-1)m+2}, z^{lk-1)m+3}) \equiv (x^k, y^k) \\
&\ \ \vdots & & \ \ \vdots \\
l = m:&\ (z^m, z^{m+1}) \equiv (x^1, y^1), & \cdots, &\ (z^{km}, z^{km+1} = z^1) \equiv (x^k, y^k)
\end{aligned}
\tag{6}
$$

We define the CL-based learning that can determine the parameters uniquely:

$$w_{ij}^l = \begin{cases} +1 & \text{for } c_{ij} > 0 \\ 0 & \text{for } c_{ij} = 0 \\ -1 & \text{for } c_{ij} < 0 \end{cases}, \ c_{ij} = \sum_{\tau=1}^{k} y_i^\tau x_j^\tau, \ \theta_i^l = \frac{R_i + L_i}{2} \tag{7}$$

$$R_i = \min_\tau \sum_{j=1}^{N} w_{ij} x_j^\tau \text{ for } y_i^\tau = +1, \quad L_i = \max_\tau \sum_{j=1}^{N} w_{ij} x_j^\tau \text{ for } y_i^\tau = -1$$

The weighting parameters w_{ij}^l are given by ternarising the correlation matrix elements c_{ij} which are based on the Hebb rule [11]. After w_{ij}^l are given, the threshold parameters θ_i^l are determined by the quantities R_i and L_i. Note that R_i exists if $y_i^\tau = +1$ for some τ and that L_i exists if $y_i^\tau = -1$ for some τ. If $y_i^\tau = -1$ for all τ then R_i does not exist and let $\theta_i^l = k + 1$. If $y_i^\tau = +1$ for all τ then L_i does not exist and let $\theta_i^l = -k - 1$. If a teacher signal BPO satisfies the following condition, then the storage of the BPO is guaranteed.

$$R_i > L_i \text{ for } i \text{ such that both } R_i \text{ and } L_i \text{ exist} \tag{8}$$

As an example of the teacher signal, we consider the BPO with period 4 in Fig. 1 ($N = 4$, $T = 4$). If we try to store the BPO into the DDBN ($m = 2$), the teacher signal is shared: (x^1, x^2) and (x^3, x^4) for the first layer F_1; (x^2, x^3) and $(x^4, x^5 = x^1)$ for the second layer F_2. Applying the CL-based learning, we obtain the parameters as shown in the figure and the BPO can be stored.

4   Application to the Matrix Converter

Although there exist various examples of BPOs as application objects, we consider the case where a BPO corresponds to a control signal of the switching circuits as illustrated in Fig. 2 (a). An input u is transformed into an output y

via a switching circuit consisting of N switches. The switch=on and =off can be symbolized by 1 and -1, respectively. If operation of the switching is periodic, the control signal of the circuit is represented by a BPO. If the BPO is stable, it is suitable for robust and reliable operation of the circuit. Although examples of such switching circuits are many, we consider the matrix converter as shown in Fig. 2 (b). The matrix converter is a basic ac-ac converter in the power electronics. (there exists four kinds of power converters: dc-dc, dc-ac, ac-dc and ac-ac converters [12]). The matrix converter converts a three-phase ac input into some three-phase ac output with different period via nine switches. Figure 2 shows 3 switching signals for the first output voltage V_U. The switching signal can be described by binary values. Considering all the nine switches, we obtain the teacher signal BPO with period 12 as shown in Table 1: $z^t = (z_1^t, \cdots .z_9^t)$ and $z^{t+12} = z^t$. This BPO controls the nine switches such that $z_i^t = +1$ and $z_i^t = -1$ correspond to Switch = on and off, respectively. Using this switching signal, the 3-phase ac input (V_R, V_S, V_T) with period $T = 12$ is converted into the 3-phase ac output (V_U, V_V, V_W) with period $T/2$ (In Fig. 2, 360° corresponds to T).

Applying the CL-based learning method, the teacher signal BPO can be stored into the DDBN for $m \geq 2$. The cases of $m = 2$ and $m = 3$ are shown in Fig. 3

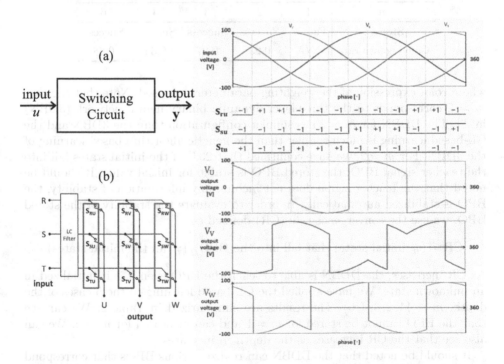

Fig. 2. Basic matrix converter and switching signal. (a) Switching circuit, (b) matrix converter. The 9 elements ($z_1, \cdots .z_9$) correspond to the 9 switches ($S_{RU}, S_{SU}, S_{TU}, S_{RV}, S_{SV}, S_{TV}, S_{RW}, S_{SW}, S_{TW}$).

Table 1. Teacher signal BPO with period 12 ($z^{t+12} = z^t$)

z^1	$(-1,-1,+1,-1,+1,-1,-1,-1,+1)$
z^2	$(+1,-1,-1,-1,+1,-1,-1,+1,-1)$
z^3	$(+1,-1,-1,+1,-1,-1,-1,+1,-1)$
z^4	$(-1,-1,+1,+1,-1,-1,-1,-1,+1)$
z^5	$(-1,-1,+1,+1,-1,-1,+1,-1,-1)$
z^6	$(-1,-1,+1,-1,-1,+1,-1,+1,-1)$
z^7	$(-1,+1,-1,-1,-1,+1,-1,+1,-1)$
z^8	$(-1,+1,-1,+1,-1,-1,+1,-1,-1)$
z^9	$(-1,+1,-1,-1,+1,-1,+1,-1,-1)$
z^{10}	$(+1,-1,-1,-1,-1,+1,+1,-1,-1)$
z^{11}	$(+1,-1,-1,-1,-1,+1,-1,-1,+1)$
z^{12}	$(-1,+1,-1,-1,+1,-1,-1,-1,+1)$

Table 2. Results of the learning. The convergence rate is the proportion of initial states that fall into the BPO.

m	1	2	3	4	6
Storage	Failure	Success	Success	Success	Success
Convergence rate	N/A	0.23	0.27	0.34	0.68

where color expression of the weighting parameters are used. Note that the case $m = 2$ corresponds to the three-layer dynamic binary neural network (3DBN) in [2]. The DDBN for $m = 2$ has simpler configuration than the 3DBN and the CL-based learning is much simpler than the genetic algorithm based learning of the 3DBN. For $m = 2$, we have confirmed that 23% of the initial states fall into the teacher signal BPO: the stored BPO is stable for initial value. It should be noted that the teacher signal does not include any information of stability, the BPO is stabilized automatically. In order to evaluate the stability of the stored BPO, we use the convergence rate (CR) defined as

CR = (# initial states that fall into the BPO)/(# all the initial states)

As CR increases, the DDBN is able to reach the BPO even if it is initialized in an unknown state. We have applied the CL-based learning to the 5 cases of the depth: $m \in \{1, 2, 3, 4, 6\}$. The results are summarized in Table 2. We can see that the BPO cannot be stored for $m = 1$ and can be stored for $m \geq 2$. We can also see that the CR increases as the depth m increases.

It should be noted that the DDBN can realize various BPOs that correspond to control signal of various switching converters. For example, Kouzuki and Saito [1] shows a two-layer dynamic binary neural network that realizes stable control signal of a dc/ac inverter. Although this paper considers one example of the

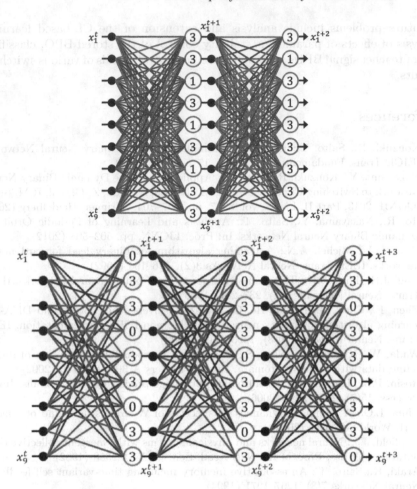

Fig. 3. Deep dynamic binary neural network after the learning for $m = 2$ and $m = 3$

control signals, the DDBN can be developed into reconfigurable control circuits for various switching power converters with robust and reliable operation.

5   Conclusions

The DDBN and its learning method have been studied in this paper. The DDBN has m layers (except for the input layer). Each layer shares the output and DDBN can output a variety of BPOs. In order to store a desired BPO, we present a simple CL-based learning method that can guarantee storage of a class of BPOs. We then apply the learning method to a BPO that corresponds to control signal of the matrix converters. The BPO can be stored successfully into the DDBN for $m \geq 2$ and stability of the BPO reinforced as m increases.

Future problems include analysis and extension of the CL-based learning, analysis of effects of parameters, stability control of the stored BPO, classification of teacher signal BPOs and application to control signals of various switching circuits.

References

1. Kouzuki, R., Saito, T.: Learning of Simple Dynamic Binary Neural Networks. IEICE Trans. Fundamentals E96-A(8), 1775–1782 (2013)
2. Nakayama, Y., Kouzuki, R., Saito, T.: Application of the Dynamic Binary Neural Network to Switching Circuits. In: Lee, M., Hirose, A., Hou, Z.-G., Kil, R.M. (eds.) ICONIP 2013, Part II. LNCS, vol. 8227, pp. 697–704. Springer, Heidelberg (2013)
3. Ito, R., Nakayama, Y., Saito, T.: Analysis and Learning of Periodic Orbits in Dynamic Binary Neural Networks. In: Proc. IJCNN, pp. 502–508 (2012)
4. Gray, D.L., Michel, A.N.: A training algorithm for binary feed forward neural networks. IEEE Trans. Neural Networks 3(2), 176–194 (1992)
5. Kim, J.H., Park, S.K.: The geometrical learning of binary neural networks. IEEE Trans. Neural Networks 6(1), 237–247 (1995)
6. Chen, F., Chen, G., He, Q., He, G., Xu, X.: Universal perceptron and DNA-like learning algorithm for binary neural networks: non-LSBF implementation. IEEE Trans. Neural Networks 20(8), 1293–1301 (2009)
7. Wada, W., Kuroiwa, J., Nara, S.: Completely reproducible description of digital sound data with cellular automata. Physics Letters A 306, 110–115 (2002)
8. Rosin, P.L.: Training cellular automata for image processing. IEEE Trans. Image Process. 15(7), 2076–2087 (2006)
9. Chua, L.O.: A nonlinear dynamics perspective of Wolfram's new kind of science, I, II. World Scientific (2005)
10. Hopfield, J.J.: Neural networks and physical systems with emergent collective computation abilities. Proc. of the Nat. Acad. Sci. 79, 2554–2558 (1982)
11. Araki, K., Saito, T.: An associative memory including time-variant self-feedback. Neural Networks 7(8), 1267–1271 (1994)
12. Vithayathil, J.: Power Electronics. McGraw-Hill (1992)
13. Bose, B.K.: Neural network applications in power electronics and motor drives - an introduction and perspective. IEEE Trans. Ind. Electron. 54(1), 14–33 (2007)
14. Rodriguez, J., Rivera, M., Kolar, J.W., Wheeler, P.W.: A Review of Control and Modulation Methods for Matrix Converters. IEEE Trans. Ind. Electron. 59(1), 58–70 (2012)

Improving Humanoid Robot Speech Recognition with Sound Source Localisation

Jorge Dávila-Chacón[1], Johannes Twiefel[1], Jindong Liu[2], and Stefan Wermter[1]

[1] University of Hamburg, Department of Informatics, Knowledge Technology Group
Vogt-Kölln-Straße 30, 22527 Hamburg, Germany
davila@informatik.uni-hamburg.de
[2] Imperial College London, Department of Computing
Huxley Building, South Kensington Campus, London, SW7 2AZ, UK
http://www.informatik.uni-hamburg.de/WTM/

Abstract. In this paper we propose an embodied approach to automatic speech recognition, where a humanoid robot adjusts its orientation to the angle that increases the signal-to-noise ratio of speech. In other words, the robot turns its face to 'hear' the speaker better, similar to what people with auditory deficiencies do. The robot tracks a speaker with a binaural sound source localisation system (SSL) that uses spiking neural networks to model relevant areas in the mammalian auditory pathway for SSL. The accuracy of speech recognition is doubled when the robot orients towards the speaker in an optimal angle and listens only through one ear instead of averaging the input from both ears.

Keywords: Human-robot interaction, robot speech recognition, binaural sound source localisation.

1 Introduction

Perception is a complex cognitive task that allows us to represent our environment and find meaning in it. In the case of auditory perception, our brain is capable of extracting information from diverse cues encoded in sound. Low-level sound cues help us to localise sound sources in space and track their motion, which in turn, allows us to segregate sound sources from noisy backgrounds and to understand natural language. Recent work in automatic speech recognition (ASR) use robotic platforms to replicate such processing pipeline. Some robotic approaches use arrays of several microphones to locate speech sources in space. Afterwards they use this knowledge to separate the speech signals from a noisy background [1,9]. However, they require prior knowledge about the presence of sound sources and their number. Other robotic approaches make use of binaural platforms [5,8]. In these systems sound source localisation (SSL) only makes use of spatial cues in sound's low frequencies, and speech segregation can only be done when speech comes from the set of trained angles.

In this paper we explore the possibility of improving robotic ASR with a neural SSL system. Our SSL approach is inspired by the neural processing of sound in the mammalian auditory pathway, which makes use of sound cues in low

S. Wermter et al. (Eds.): ICANN 2014, LNCS 8681, pp. 619–626, 2014.

and high frequency components, and it is not constrained to specific angles [14]. For speech segregation we take a behavioural approach, where the robot orients optimally to the speaker.

1.1 Neural Correlates of Acoustic Localisation

Sound waves approaching a human are firstly affected by the absorption and diffraction from the torso, head and pinnae. The first stage for the neural encoding of information in sound waves occurs in the cochlea, where the organ of Corti transduces mechanical vibrations from the basilar membrane into neural spikes. These spikes are then delivered through the auditory nerve to the cochlear nucleus, a relay station that forwards information to the medial superior olive (MSO) and the lateral superior olive (LSO). The MSO and LSO are of our particular interest, as they are in charge of extracting interaural time differences (ITD) and interaural level differences (ILD).

The MSO encodes more efficiently ITDs from low-frequencies in sound [14]. Such delay mechanisms can be achieved by different axon lengths -or different thicknesses of myelin-sheaths on the axon- of excitatory neurons from the ipsilateral and contralateral cochlear nucleus. The LSO encodes more efficiently ILDs from high-frequencies in sound [14]. In the case of the LSO, the mechanism underlying the extraction of level differences is less clear. However, it is known that LSO neurons receive excitatory input from the ipsilateral ear and inhibitory input from the contralateral ear, and they show a characteristic change in their spiking rate for sound sources located at specific angles on the azimuthal plane. Finally, the output from the MSO and the LSO is integrated in the inferior colliculus (IC), where a more coherent spatial representation is formed across the frequency spectrum [14]. This combination of both cues can be seen as a multimodal integration case, where ITDs and ILDs represent the different modalities to be merged in order to improve the SSL performance of a natural system.

2   Experimental Setup and Basis Methodologies

2.1   Virtual Reality Setup

Our experiments were carried in a virtual reality (VR) setup designed for testing multimodal integration architectures. This experimental setup allows to control the temporal and spatial presentation of images and sounds to robotic and human subjects. When experiments are run, the subject is located at the radial center of a projection screen shaped as half cylinder. As seen in figure 1, behind the screen there are 13 speakers evenly distributed on the azimuth plane at angles $\theta_{lspk} \in \{0°, 15°, \dots, 180°\}$. A detailed description of this setup –and the principles behind its design– can be found in [2].

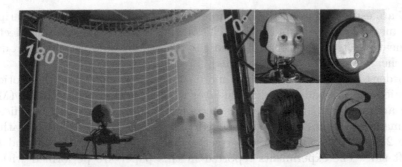

Fig. 1. On the left is shown the audio-visual VR experimental setup. The grid shows the curvature of the projection screen surrounding the iCub humanoid head and the dots represent the location of sound sources behind the screen. On the right can be seen the humanoid heads used during our experiments. The robot ears consist of microphones perpendicular to the sagittal plane surrounded by pinnae.

2.2   Humanoid Robotic Platforms

The humanoid platforms used in our experiments are the iCub robotic head [3] and the Soundman wooden head[1] modified by our group to rotate on the azimuth plane. The iCub is a humanoid robot designed for research in cognitive developmental robotics. The Soundman head is a commercial product designed for the production of binaural recordings that maximize the perception of spatial effects. Our intention is to find out if the resonance of the iCub head, from the skull and interior components, significantly reduces the performance of ASR. Both platforms offer the possibility of extracting spatial cues from binaural sound, as such cues are produced by the geometric and material properties of the humanoid heads. A lateral view of both platforms can be seen in figure 1.

2.3   Biomimetic Sound Source Localisation

As a first step in our SSL architecture, a filter bank modelling the cochlear frequency decomposition [15] is used to reproduce the phase-locking mechanism of the organ of Corti. Signals reaching the ears are decomposed in several frequency components $f \in \{1, 2, \ldots, F\}$. In healthy young people, f's are logarithmically separated and respond to frequencies between $\sim$20 Hz and $\sim$20000 Hz [14]. As we are mainly interested in the localisation of speech signals, we constrain the set of f's to frequencies between 200 Hz and 4000 Hz. The MSO is modelled as a Jeffress coincidence detector, where ITDs are represented spatially by different neurons that fire at specific time delays [12]. The LSO model represent ILDs spatially as $\log(I_f/C_f)$, where I_f and C_f are sound pressure levels at the ipsilateral and contralateral microphones for a given f [12].

The following layer in the architecture models the IC, where the output from the MSO and the LSO is integrated. The MSO and LSO connection weights to

---

[1] http://www.soundman.de/en/dummy-head/

the IC are estimated using Bayesian inference [12]. A more detailed description of the method can be found in [6]. The output of the IC layer can reflect the non-linear effects of reverberation and the intense levels of ego-noise produced by the head's cooling system (∼60 dB).

In order to classify the IC output more robustly for controlling the motion of a robotic head, we add an additional layer with a multilayer perceptron (MLP) to the architecture [7]. This layer is necessary for improving the classification performance and does not model a particular region in the auditory pathway. Figure 2 shows the SSL system correctly classifying an incoming sound from the left side. The experiments reported in this paper are performed with the robot heads static. However, the performance of our neural SSL architecture is documented in [7] and compared with other statistical approaches.

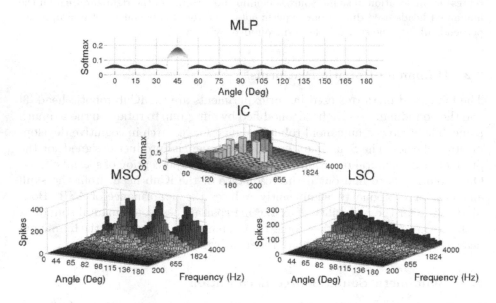

Fig. 2. Output of different layers in the SSL system for white noise presented at 45° on the azimuth. Even though many of the IC frequency components disagree on the sound source angle, the MLP is able to cope with these non-linearities and correctly classifies the IC output. Detailed results for static SSL using the iCub are given in [7]

2.4   Architecture for Automatic Speech Recognition

We selected the Google ASR engine [13] based on deep neural networks, as it was more robust against the ego-noise produced by the iCub than other popular ASR engines we tested. The speech corpus used in our experiments is the TIMIT core-test-set (CTS) [10], as it includes all the existing phoneme components in the English language. The CTS is formed by 192 sentences spoken by 24 different speakers: 16 male and 8 female pronouncing 8 sentences each. We map the output of Google ASR to the best matching sentence from the CTS. However, this mapping does not impede generalization from our experimental results as we are only interested in measuring the performance of ASR with and without the support from an SSL system. Whenever a sound file is sent to the Google ASR engine, a list with the 10 most plausible sentences (G10) is returned. The post-processing consists of transforming the G10 and the CTS from *grapheme* to *phoneme* representation [4] and then computing the Levenshtein distance [11] between each of the generated phoneme sequences from the G10 and the CTS. Finally, the sentence in the CTS with the smallest distance to any of the sentences in the G10 is considered the winning result and it is considered a correct recognition when it is equal to the ground truth. We refer to this domain-specific ASR architecture as the DASR system.

In general, the Levenshtein distance $\mathcal{L}(\mathbf{A}, \mathbf{B})$ refers to the minimum number of *deletions*, *insertions* and *substitutions* required to convert string $\mathbf{A} = a_1 \ldots a_m$ into string $\mathbf{B} = b_1 \ldots b_n$. Formally, the distance $\mathcal{L}(\mathbf{A}, \mathbf{B}) = \mathbf{D}(m, n)$, where

$$\mathbf{D}(i,j) = \begin{cases} i & \text{for} \quad 0 \leq i \leq m \ \text{and} \quad j = 0, \\ j & \text{for} \quad 0 \leq j \leq n \ \text{and} \quad i = 0, \\ \min \begin{cases} \mathbf{D}(i-1,j)+1 \\ \mathbf{D}(i,j-1)+1 \\ \mathbf{D}(i-1,j-1)+\kappa \end{cases} & \text{for} \quad 1 \leq i \leq m \ \text{and} \quad 1 \leq j \leq n. \end{cases}$$

Where $\kappa = 0$ if $a_i = b_j$ and $\kappa = 1$ if $a_i \neq b_j$.

3   Experimental Results and Discussion

In the following experiments we measure the performance of the DASR system when the speech is presented around the robotic heads from the loudspeakers at angles θ_{lspk} at ~1.6 m from the robot. Let θ_{neck} be the angle faced by the robot at any given time, and δ_{diff} be the angular difference between θ_{lspk} and θ_{neck}. We hypothesise that there is an angle -or set of angles- δ_{best} for which the signal-to-noise ratio (SNR) is highest and hence, for which the DASR system performs better. For this purpose we measure the performance of the DASR system after reproducing 10 times the CTS utterances from the loudspeaker at angle θ_{lspk}. The performance is measured as the average success rate at the sentence-level for the entire CTS corpus over the 10 trials. We refer to success rate as to what *sentence accuracy* is in the ASR domain, the ratio of correct recognitions over the total number of recognitions. It is also desirable to visualize the results of this binary evaluation in a continuous domain. Such transformation is made by measuring the average Levenshtein distance between the output of the DASR system and the ground truth sentences.

It is important to remember that the sounds recorded through the robotic heads contain 2 channels, i.e. the audio waves from the left and right microphones. As the DASR system requires monaural files as input, there are 3 possible reduction procedures: Using the sound wave from the left channel only (LCh), using the sound wave from the right channel only (RCh) or averaging the sound waves from both channels (LRCh). The average success rates of the 3 reduction procedures on the recordings obtained with both heads are shown in figure 3 and the average Levenshtein distances in figure 4. It is clear that the performance curves obtained from the recordings of both robotic heads follow the same patterns. Notice that the performance of the DASR system improves with the Soundman head on the most favourable angles δ_{best}. However, the difference is not large enough to conclude that the resonance of the iCub head reduces the performance of the DASR system.

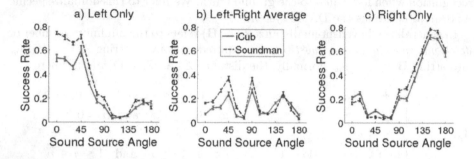

Fig. 3. Average success rates of the DASR system. Results obtained with both robotic heads for the frontal 180° on the azimuth plane.

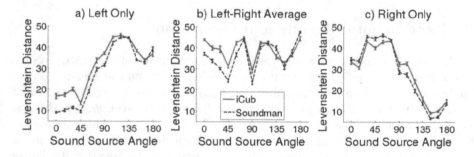

Fig. 4. Average Levenshtein distances between the DASR output and the ground truth. Results obtained with the both robotic heads for the frontal 180° on the azimuth plane.

Even though the volume of each loudspeaker was measured to output the same intensity level ($\sim$75 dB), the smoothness of the performance curves is affected by the difference in fidelity from each of the loudspeakers. Nevertheless, the graphs clearly show a set of angles δ_{best} where the DASR system considerably improves its performance. For all reduction procedures with both robotic heads performance is best near $\delta_{best} \in \{45°, 150°\}$, where the robotic heads reduce minimally the SNR of incoming speech.

In the LRCh reduction, most sound source angles θ_{lspk} produce recordings where one channel has higher SNR than the other. Therefore, when both signals are averaged the speech SNR will be reduced. The exceptions are sound sources at 90°, 45° and 150°. This can be explained by considering the moderate SNR both channels have in the case of 90°, and by considering the high and low SNR in the ipsilateral and contralateral signals in the case of 45° and 150°. It is also important to notice the magnitude of this effect, as the highest success rates from the LCh and RCh reductions are twice larger than the highest success rates from the LRCh reduction. This difference can be related to the strong shadowing from the geometry and material of the humanoid heads. The same effect can be seen in the LCh and RCh reductions alone. It is commonly assumed that speech SNR will increase when the sound source is in the front or parallel to the interaural axis, and when the input to an ASR system comes only from the channel closest to the sound source. However, the angles found to be optimal for our DASR system are counter intuitive, and the difference between the lowest and highest values in the LCh and RCh reductions is unexpectedly large.

The periodical shape in the LCh and RCh plots can be understood by considering the effect of the round shape of the heads and the position of the microphones. The pinnae are placed slightly behind the coronal plane. Therefore, the distance travelled by the sound waves from the sound source to the contralateral ear is maximal at approximately 45° and 135° instead of 0° and 180°. This explains the increase in performance before 135° for LCh and after 45° for RCh. On the other hand, the decrease in performance before 45° for LCh and after 135° for RCh can be produced by the shadowing of the pinnae and reverberation from the metal structure on the sides of the the VR setup.

4 Conclusion and Future Work

It became clear from the experimental results that robotic ASR systems can improve considerably their performance when supported by a parallel SSL system. Any humanoid robotic platform can be tested -or learn autonomously- to find the optimal angles for increasing the SNR of incoming signals. Such process can teach the robot to face a speaker in the optimal direction, in the same way people with auditory deficiencies do.

A natural extension of this work is to make the robot focus its attention in a single source of information from a possible multitude of concurrent stimuli. It is in this extended scenario where the input from other sensory modalities comes into play. Vision can be used to disambiguate the location of an addressing speaker between a crowd by observing the orientation of the torso, gaze and lips movement of each individual detected. Afterwards, this information can be used to perform auditory grouping in time and frequency domains in order to perform speech segregation in noisy environments [16]. This is the scope of current research by the authors towards multimodal speech recognition.

Acknowledgements. This work was supported by the DFG German Research Foundation (grant #1247) - International Research Training Group CINACS (Cross-modal Interaction in Natural and Artificial Cognitive Systems).

References

1. Asano, F., Goto, M., Itou, K., Asoh, H.: Real-time sound source localization and separation system and its application to automatic speech recognition. In: INTERSPEECH, pp. 1013–1016 (2001)
2. Bauer, J., Davila-Chacon, J., Strahl, E., Wermter, S.: Smoke and mirrors — Virtual realities for sensor fusion experiments in biomimetic robotics. In: Intl. Conf. on Multisensor Fusion and Integration, MFI, pp. 114–119. IEEE (2012)
3. Beira, R., Lopes, M., Praga, M., Santos-Victor, J., Bernardino, A., Metta, G., Becchi, F., Saltarén, R.: Design of the robot-cub (iCub) head. In: Intl. Conf. on Robotics and Automation, ICRA, pp. 94–100. IEEE (2006)
4. Bisani, M., Ney, H.: Joint-sequence models for grapheme-to-phoneme conversion. Speech Communication 50(5), 434–451 (2008)
5. Cong-qing, L., Fang, W., Shi-jie, D., Li-xin, S., He, H., Li-ying, S.: A novel method of binaural sound localization based on dominant frequency separation. In: Intl. Cong. on Image and Signal Processing, CISP, pp. 1–4. IEEE (2009)
6. Davila-Chacon, J., Heinrich, S., Liu, J., Wermter, S.: Biomimetic binaural sound source localisation with ego-noise cancellation. In: Villa, A.E.P., Duch, W., Érdi, P., Masulli, F., Palm, G. (eds.) ICANN 2012, Part I. LNCS, vol. 7552, pp. 239–246. Springer, Heidelberg (2012)
7. Davila-Chacon, J., Magg, S., Liu, J., Wermter, S.: Neural and statistical processing of spatial cues for sound source localisation. In: Intl. Joint Conf. on Neural Networks, IJCNN. IEEE (2013)
8. Deleforge, A., Horaud, R.: The cocktail party robot: Sound source separation and localisation with an active binaural head. In: Proceedings of the International Conference on Human-Robot Interaction, pp. 431–438. ACM/IEEE (2012)
9. Fréchette, M., Létourneau, D., Valin, J., Michaud, F.: Integration of sound source localization and separation to improve dialogue management on a robot. In: Intl. Conf. on Intelligent Robots and Systems, IROS, pp. 2358–2363. IEEE (2012)
10. Garofolo, J.S., Lamel, L.F., Fisher, W.M., Fiscus, J.G., Pallett, D.S.: Darpa timit acoustic-phonetic continuous speech corpus cd-rom. nist speech disc 1-1.1. NASA STI/Recon Technical Report N 93, 27403 (1993)
11. Levenshtein, V.I.: Binary codes capable of correcting deletions, insertions and reversals. In: Soviet Physics Doklady, vol. 10, pp. 707–710 (1966)
12. Liu, J., Perez-Gonzalez, D., Rees, A., Erwin, H., Wermter, S.: A biologically inspired spiking neural network model of the auditory midbrain for sound source localisation. Neurocomputing 74(1-3), 129–139 (2010)
13. Schalkwyk, J., Beeferman, D., Beaufays, F., Byrne, B., Chelba, C., Cohen, M., Kamvar, M., Strope, B.: Your word is my command: Google search by voice: A case study. In: Advances in Speech Recognition, pp. 61–90. Springer (2010)
14. Schnupp, J., Nelken, I., King, A.: Auditory neuroscience: Making sense of sound. The MIT Press (2011)
15. Slaney, M.: An efficient implementation of the Patterson-Holdsworth auditory filter bank. Tech. rep. Apple Computer, Perception Group (1993)
16. Zion-Golumbic, E., Schroeder, C.E.: Mechanisms underlying selective neuronal tracking of attended speech at a "cocktail party". Neuron 77(5), 980–991 (2013)

Control of UPOs of Unknown Chaotic Systems via ANN

Amine M. Khelifa and Abdelkrim Boukabou

Department of Electronics, Faculty of Sciences and Technology,
Jijel University, 98 Ouled Aissa, Jijel 18000, Algeria

Abstract. In this paper an artificial neural network (ANN) is developed for modeling and controlling unknown chaotic systems to unstable periodic orbits (UPOs). In the modeling phase, the ANN is trained on the unknown chaotic systems using the input-output data obtained from the unknown (or uncertain) underlying chaotic systems, and a specific computational algorithm is employed for the parameter optimization. In the controlling phase, the L_2-stability criterion is used, which forms the basis of the main design principle. Some simulation results on the chaotic Henon and Duffing systems are given, for both modeling and controlling phases, to illustrate the effectiveness of the proposed chaos control scheme and the proposed neural network.

Keywords: Chaos control, artificial neural network, L_2-stability, unstable periodic orbits.

1 Introduction

With fast advances in nonlinear dynamic study, especially the study of chaotic phenomenon, many successful methods and techniques for controlling chaos have been proposed and evaluated in recent years. Since the presentation of chaos control known as the OGY method [1], the research in chaos control has been developed greatly. Many control methods are the improvement or the generalization of the OGY method. Some works gave a systematic explanation and generalization of the OGY method by the delay feedback method [2], the evolutionary algorithms [3], the high order perturbations [4], the sliding mode concept [5]. These methods have the same spirit. First, an identification of the chaotic dynamic about the unstable fixed point or unstable periodic orbit is made. On the second step, by eliminating the error on the unstable direction, the desired target (unstable fixed point or unstable periodic orbit) is stabilized.

On the other hand, the prediction of chaos is another topic which has been developed for many years. Due to the nonlinearity of chaotic systems, linear approximation methods are inadequate for chaos prediction. And there is a general understanding, that local approximation can usually give better predictions than global approximation. ANN does not need any priory knowledge of the actual physical processes and given that there is an exact relationship between the input and the output data, the ANN can be trained to learn that relationship. So the ANN is a promising method in chaos prediction especially when the

S. Wermter et al. (Eds.): ICANN 2014, LNCS 8681, pp. 627–634, 2014.

chaotic system model is unknown or uncertain. Many chaos prediction methods have been proposed based on different neural networks, such as recurrent predictor neural networks [8], wavelet networks [9], functional networks [10] and time delay dynamic neural networks [11]. But the methods above have the same limitations. Because the chaos dynamic is identified only around the fixed point, the control input is active only around this point. The shape of the whole orbit is uncontrollable. Shen et al. proposed in [12] a neural network which can be divided into two parts. The first part performs the classification of the input and the second part comprises a series of sub neural networks which will be switched on according to the classification result. By this scheme, the control input can eliminate the errors not only on the unstable direction but also on the stable direction. The own problem is how to build the classification part. Lin et al. [13] proposed an effective control method of uncertain chaotic systems using dynamic fuzzy neural networks modeling and adaptive backstepping tracking control approach. The proposed method is very useful for controlling uncertain chaotic systems around only desired targets.

Inspired by the prediction-based feedback control, we are looking into the possibility of developing a simple neural network model that can be used to predict unknown or uncertain chaotic system model and to control it to its unstable periodic orbits, using only input-output data.

2   ANN Modeling of Unknown Chaotic Systems

For a neural network with $(x(i), y(i))$ input output data pairs, $i = 1, 2, ..., n$ number of iterations and one hidden layer of $j = 1, 2, ..., m$ neurons. For a such network, the input to j^{th} unit of the hidden layer denoted by I_j is the weighed sum of all the inputs added to the bias

$$I_j = \sum_{i=1}^{n} w_{ji} x(i) + b_{ji}, \tag{1}$$

where w_{ji} are the interconnection weights from the jth function and the ith input to the output and the b_{ji} biases. The input I_j is then passed through an activation function to produce an output O_j. There are many ways to define the activation function. One that is often used in neural networks is the sigmoid function which is used in this network,

$$O_j(x(i)) = \frac{1}{1 + \exp(-b_{ji} - w_{ji}x(i))}. \tag{2}$$

The network output $y^{NN}(i)$ is obtained in a similar fashion as a weighted sum of outputs,

$$y^{NN}(i) = F(x(i)) = \sum_{j=1}^{m} w_o O_j(x(i)) + b_o. \tag{3}$$

The neural network has to be trained such that it can perform both prediction and control tasks. Initially, the network weights w_{ji} and biases b_{ji} of the hidden layer and the weight w_o and bias b_o of the output layer are assigned randomly. The output $y^{NN}(i)$ is calculated for each associated input $x(i)$.

In order to obtain the ANN model, we have to determine the network weights w_{ji} and bias b_{ji} of the hidden layer and the weight w_o and bias b_o of the output layer. For that, and for a given unknown chaotic system represented by measured input and output data pairs, we seek to minimize a quadratic function e which quantifies the error between the current output data y and the ANN model output y^{NN} for all input-output data pairs.

$$e(i) = \frac{1}{2} \sum_{i=1}^{n} \left(y(i) - y^{NN}(i) \right)^2 . \tag{4}$$

This is done by adjusting the different parameters of the ANN model. If we denote the Jacobian for each of the parameters w_{ji}, b_{ji}, w_o and b_o by

$$J_{w_{ji}} = \frac{\partial O_j(x(i))}{\partial w_{ji}}, \ J_{b_{ji}} = \frac{\partial O_j(x(i))}{\partial b_{ji}}, \ J_{w_o} = \frac{\partial F(x(i))}{\partial w_o}, \ J_{b_o} = \frac{\partial F(x(i))}{\partial b_o}, \tag{5}$$

Then, the weights and biases can be trained using the Levenberg-Marquardt algorithm [15] as follows

$$w_{ji}(i+1) = w_{ji}(i) - \left(\lambda I + J_{w_{ji}}^T J_{w_{ji}} \right)^{-1} J_{w_{ji}}^T e(i), \tag{6}$$

$$b_{ji}(i+1) = b_{ji}(i) - \left(\lambda I + J_{b_{ji}}^T J_{b_{ji}} \right)^{-1} J_{b_{ji}}^T e(i), \tag{7}$$

$$w_o(i+1) = w_o(i) - \left(\lambda I + J_{w_o}^T J_{w_o} \right)^{-1} J_{w_o}^T e(i), \tag{8}$$

$$b_o(i+1) = b_o(i) - \left(\lambda I + J_{b_o}^T J_{b_o} \right)^{-1} J_{b_o}^T e(i), \tag{9}$$

where the parameter λ will help to keep the updates moving in the right direction and I represents the identity matrix.

The weights are adjusted to minimize the error function by using Levenberg-Marquardt optimization algorithm. This very efficient optimization algorithm has the capability to converge to the optimum of any quadratic nonlinear function with a good approximation. The adjustments in the weights should result in a decrease in the error. The Levenberg-Marquardt optimization algorithm runs until the error quadratic function e is minimized, so the algorithm has found a minimum and it can be terminated; however, parameters w_{ji}, b_{ji}, w_o and b_o are reinitialized.

The proposed algorithm could be run many reprises to train the neural network system to much data pairs very well. The algorithm runs until all of the parameters stop moving or change very little over a series of update steps. This indicates that the value of the error is minimized, so the algorithm has found a minimum and it can be terminated. However, parameters are reinitialized if the time taken is over the allowable limit.

3   ANN Based Controller Design

The control objective is to stabilize chaos on UPO, that is, to drive the unknown chaotic system from a chaotic regime to a regular motion. We use ANN model (3) to perform the control. Thus, the controlled ANN model will be given by

$$y^{NN}(i) = F(x(i)) + u(i) = \sum_{j=1}^{m} w_o O_j(x(i)) + b_o + u(i). \tag{10}$$

Hence, and based on the ANN model, it is possible to predict the future state of the uncontrolled ANN model as follows

$$F(x(i+1)) = \sum_{j=1}^{m} w_o O_j(x(i+1)) + b_o. \tag{11}$$

We formulate the unstable periodic orbit neural control as an input-output L_2-stability problem of a linear periodic feedback system, which allows employ predictive criteria in the L_2-setting, to determine stability bounds of the periodic orbit.

Given an input-output relation $(r_0, v_0) \in L_2 \times L_2$ of a dynamical system Σ, we now recall the definitions of input-output L_2-stability [14]:

Definition 1. *The solution v_0 of system Σ is L_2-stable if there exits a constant γ such that*

$$\|v - v_0\|_2 < \gamma \|r - r_0\|_2 \tag{12}$$

for all r with $(r - r_0) \in L_2$.

Definition 2. *The solution v_0 of system Σ is locally L_2-stable if there exit positive constants M_v and M_r such that*

$$\|v - v_0\|_2 < M_v, \tag{13}$$

for all signals r satisfying

$$\|r - r_0\|_2 < M_r. \tag{14}$$

Our objective is to design a controller that stabilizes the family of the periodic solutions corresponding to the original unstable periodic orbits embedded in the unknown chaotic systems.

Let us consider (x_d, y_d) to be the states of the desired UPO to be stabilized. From definitions of input-output L_2-stability criterion [14], $u(i)$ stabilizes the UPO of the unknown chaotic system if there exists a constant γ such that

$$\|x(i+1) - y_d\|_2 \leq \gamma \|x(i) - x_d\|_2. \tag{15}$$

The condition (15) ensures local input-output L_2-stability of system (3) only if the system trajectory is in the vicinity of the unstable periodic orbit states (x_d, y_d).

The control input $u(i)$ is then formed by the information of the desired UPO and the ANN model of the unknown chaotic system. In this case, the controller $u(i)$ is determined by

$$u(i) = -F(x(i+1)) + F(x_d) = -\sum_{j=1}^{m} w_o O_j(x(i+1)) - b_o + \sum_{j=1}^{m} w_o O_j(x_d) + b_o,$$

$$= \sum_{j=1}^{m} w_o \left[O_j(x_d) - O_j(x(i+1))\right], \tag{16}$$

which will be applied in a short vicinity of the UPO. The ANN based controller thus becomes

$$u(k) = \begin{cases} \sum_{j=1}^{m} w_o \left[O_j(x_d) - O_j(x(i+1))\right], & \text{if } \|x(i+1) - y_d\|_2 \leq \gamma \|x(i) - x_d\|_2, \\ 0, & \text{otherwise,} \end{cases}$$

$$\tag{17}$$

for small positive real number γ.

Remark 1. We note that the stabilization of chaotic systems on the original UPO is a standard procedure [1–3]. Likewise, such systems with additive feedback control can also be stabilized on the other periods (4, 8, ...) or even unstable fixed points, where the parameters of the ANN based controller are modified such that they guarantee the stability requirement.

4   Numerical Simulations

In this section, numerical simulations of the Henon and Duffing systems are used to verify the effectiveness of the proposed chaos prediction and control method performed by ANN. The input-output data pairs were generated using the underlying systems and then used to establish the ANN models of the unknown chaotic systems. In example one and two, we consider that the unknown chaotic systems are represented by $N = 200$ and $N = 600$ input-output data pairs, respectively. We let $\lambda = 0.01$ for the Levenberg-Marquardt algorithm and $\gamma = 0.05$ for the L_2-stability condition. In other hand, it is necessary to determine the maximum size of the attractive region given in (11) such that the controlled ANN models converge toward the desired unstable periodic orbits. From different testes, stability is guaranteed for $|x(i) - x_d| \leq 0.01$ providing the local input-output L_2-stability of the ANN controlled models.

4.1   Henon System

In this simulation, the input-output data pairs are generated from the following Henon system

$$y(i) = a - x^2(i) + bx(i-1) + u(i), \tag{18}$$

where $a = 1.4$ and $b = 0.3$ and for $u = 0$ the standard Henon system is obtained.

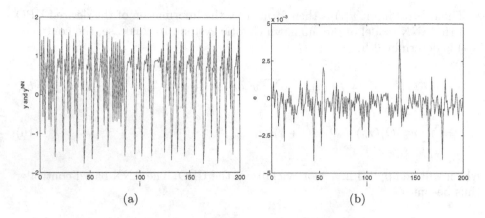

(a)   (b)

Fig. 1. The ANN model of the Henon system

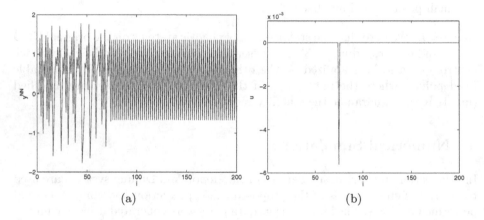

(a)   (b)

Fig. 2. (a) The controlled ANN model of the Henon system. (b) The control input.

Again it is assumed that the mathematical model of the Henon system is unknown and using the proposed ANN prediction method, the simulation result of the predicted ANN model is shown in Fig. 1.

In order to construct the attractive domain that corresponds to the particular unstable periodic orbit, it is necessary to determine the maximum size of the attractive region given in (15). By varying the width $(x(i) - x_d)$, it is possible to change the size of the attractive domain with respect to the particular unstable periodic orbit. From different testes, stability is guaranteed for $|x(i) - x_d| \leq 0.01$ providing the local input-output L_2-stability of the ANN controlled system. In other hand, unstable periodic orbit of the system of difference equation (18) is satisfied, resulting original unstable periodic orbit. Once the system states reach to the attractive domain, ANN controller will drive the Henon system toward the unstable periodic orbit. Fig. 2 illustrates the ANN controller using the proposed concept.

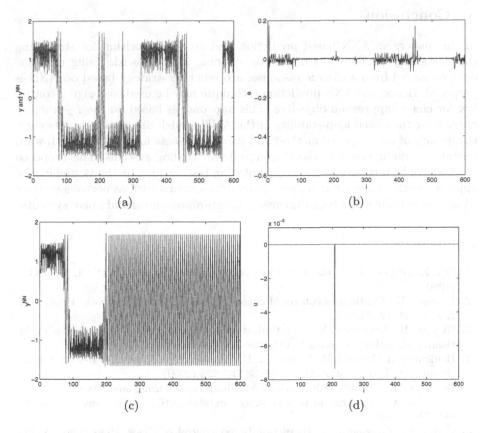

Fig. 3. (a) The ANN model of the Duffing system. (b) The ANN prediction error. (c) The controlled ANN model of the Duffing system. (d) The control input.

4.2 Duffing System

We consider the unknown chaotic system generated by the chaotic Duffing system with following modified equation used for simulation

$$y(i) = ax(i) + bx^3(i) + cx(i-1) + u(i), \tag{19}$$

where u is the control action and for $u = 0$ the standard Duffing system is obtained. For $a = 2.75$, $b = -1$ and $c = -0.2$, the uncontrolled Duffing system shows chaotic behavior.

To implement the proposed ANN chaos based prediction and control method, it is assumed that the mathematical model of the Duffing system is unknown and represented by only input-output data pairs. The control action has the form of Eq. (13). The plot of the ANN model and the controlled ANN model of the Duffing system are depicted in Figs. 3 (a)–(d). Once the system states reach to the attractive domain, ANN controller will drive the system toward the unstable periodic orbit.

5   Conclusion

In this paper, an ANN based prediction and control algorithm for stabilizing the unstable periodic orbits of chaotic systems is introduced. Using only the data measured from a chaotic response, a prediction strategy based on ANN is proposed. Hence, the ANN prediction technique may be used to design a control law for chaos suppression objective. This approach is based on the L_2-stability criteria for the closed loop-stability of the ANN model. Simulation results show the quality of the proposed method and its effectiveness in chaos control toward unstable periodic orbits of the Henon and the Duffing systems. The proposed method can be further improved by employing fast learning methods, and can be applied to other complex nonlinear dynamical systems such as nervous systems which are considered as high-dimensional, non-autonomous and noisy systems.

References

1. Ott, E., Grebogi, C., Yorke, J.A.: Controlling chaos. Phys. Rev. Lett. 64, 1196–1199 (1990)
2. Pyragas, K.: Continuous control of chaos by self-controlling feedback. Phys. Lett. A 170, 421–428 (1992)
3. Richter, H., Reinschke, K.J.: Optimization of local control of chaos by an evolutionary algorithms. Physica D 144, 309–334 (2000)
4. Boukabou, A., Sayoud, B., Boumaiza, H., Mansouri, N.: Control of n-scroll Chua's circuit. Int. J. Bifurcation Chaos 19, 3813–3822 (2009)
5. Bessa, W.M., de Paula, A.S., Savi, M.A.: Chaos control using adaptive sliding mode controller with application to a nonlinear pendulum. Chaos Solitons Fractals 42, 784–791 (2009)
6. Ushio, T., Yamamoto, S.: Prediction-based control of chaos. Phys. Lett. A 264, 30–35 (1999)
7. Boukabou, A., Chebbah, A., Mansouri, N.: Predictive control of continuous chaotic systems. Int. J. Bifurcat. Chaos 18, 587–592 (2008)
8. Han, M., Xi, J., Xu, S., Yin, F.: Prediction of chaotic time series based on the recurrent predictor neural network. IEEE Trans. Signal Proc. 52, 3409–3416 (2004)
9. Cao, L., Hong, Y., Fang, H., He, G.: Predicting chaotic time series with wavelet networks. Physica D 85, 225–238 (1995)
10. Leung, H., Lo, T., Wang, S.: Prediction of noisy chaotic time series using an optimal radial basis function neural network. IEEE Trans. Neural Networks 12, 1163–1172 (2001)
11. Becerikli, Y., Oysal, Y.: Modeling and prediction with a class of time delay dynamic neural networks. Appl. Soft Comput. 7, 1164–1169 (2007)
12. Shen, L., Wang, M., Liu, W., Sun, G.: Prediction based chaos control via a new neural network. Phys. Lett. A 372, 6916–6921 (2008)
13. Lin, D., Wang, X., Nian, F., Zhang, Y.: Dynamic fuzzy neural networks modeling and adaptive backstepping tracking control of uncertain chaotic systems. Neurocomputing 73, 2873–2881 (2010)
14. Sastry, S.: Nonlinear systems: Analysis, stability, and control. Springer, Berlin (1999)
15. Nocedal, J., Wright, S.J.: Numerical optimization, 2nd edn. Springer, NY (2006)

Event-Based Visual Data Sets
for Prediction Tasks in Spiking Neural Networks

Tingting (Amy) Gibson, Scott Heath, Robert P. Quinn, Alexia H. Lee,
Joshua T. Arnold, Tharun S. Sonti, Andrew Whalley, George P. Shannon,
Brian T. Song, James A. Henderson, and Janet Wiles

The University of Queensland, Australia
{t.ng1,j.wiles}@uq.edu.au

Abstract. For spiking networks to perform computational tasks,
benchmark data sets are required for model design, refinement and
testing. Classic machine learning benchmark data sets use classification
as the dominant paradigm, however the temporal characteristics of
spiking neural networks mean they are likely to be more useful for
problems involving sequence data. To support these paradigms, we
provide data sets of 11 moving scenes, each with multiple variations,
recorded from a dynamic vision sensor (DVS128), comprising high
dimensional (16k pixels) and low latency (15 microsecond) events. We
also present a novel long range prediction task based on the DVS128
data, and introduce a pilot study of a spiking neural network learning
to predict thousands of events into the future.

Keywords: Event-based data sets, predictions, spiking neural networks.

1 Introduction

For artificial spiking neural networks (SNNs) to move out of the laboratory and
into the real world, they need to be able to process real world data, deal with real
world noise, and solve real world tasks. We are interested in developing SNNs for
embodied robots that face a range of tasks such as sensorimotor coordination,
navigation and social interaction at the hundred millisecond time scale.

Real world robot studies are time and energy consuming, and benchmark
data can facilitate the design process. While there are many data sets for
testing sensory processing algorithms, computer vision in particular, they are
not inherently spike based and need to be pre-processed into spikes before
using with an SNN. SNNs are well suited for processing asynchronous spiking
inputs with high temporal resolution, but the majority of data sets are
frame-based with coarse temporal precision. In addition, despite the
importance of prediction to robot cognition, the dominant paradigms within
currently available data sets are those of classification, tracking and mapping.

Traditional frame-based video data contains a huge amount of redundant
information, compared to biological sensory data which only signals new
information. Sensory inputs are better represented by event streams—sequences

S. Wermter et al. (Eds.): ICANN 2014, LNCS 8681, pp. 635–642, 2014.

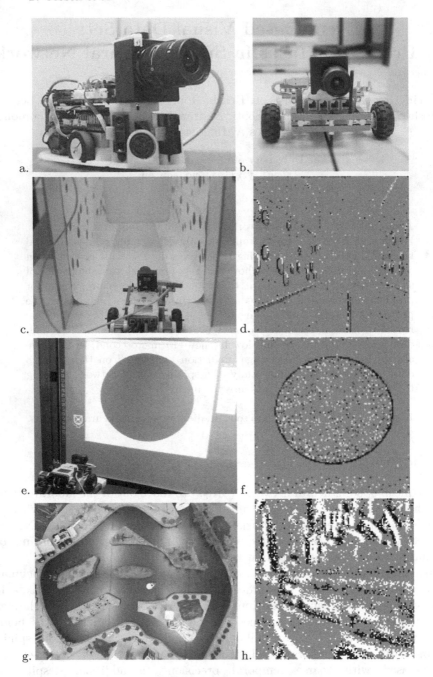

Fig. 1. Experimental setup. The DVS128 mounted on the iRat (a), and the Lego NXT robot (b). Collecting data from self-motion on a linear track (c), and its corresponding data (d). Recording from a static camera facing a projector (e), and its corresponding data (f). Overhead view of a 3x3m Australia maze to collect locomotion data (g), and a scene from the maze recorded by the DVS128 (h) .

of events each indicating a change in state in the environment [1]. The temporal intervals between events in the real world vary, making event streams inherently multi-scale.

High temporal precision event streams can be recorded by event-based neuromorphic sensory devices, such as the silicon retina Dynamic Vision Sensor (DVS) [2] and the silicon cochlea [3]. Such devices require low bandwidth and power, making them ideal for robot embodiment. The DVS has been used for classification tasks including recognising hand gestures [4], classifying the DVS version of the MNIST postcode data set [5] and extracting pulsed laser line for terrain reconstruction [6]. DVS data have also been used in tracking tasks, such as tracking people [7], particles [8], optic flow [9], ball and car trajectories [10, 11] and LED markers with the camera mounted on a robot [12]. Object depth has also been calculated using two DVS cameras for stereo visual inputs [13, 14]. DVS data have been fed to modified simultaneous localization and mapping (SLAM) algorithms for robot self-localisation [15, 16]; and to control robot motors [17, 18]. Most of the studies conducted with the DVS cameras are for classification, tracking and mapping tasks. There is a lack of studies that utilise the event-based nature of the DVS to investigate long range prediction.

This paper presents a novel set of benchmark data sets based on event data, and introduces a new SNN prediction paradigm with learnable time delays in both the dendrites and axons to demonstrate how the event data can be used to learn long range prediction.

2   Methods

2.1   Experimental Setup

The DVS128 [2] is a neuromorphic camera that contains a 128x128 array of light sensors, with each emitting a spike asynchronously at a time resolution of 15 microseconds if a change in luminosity is detected. Spikes are encoded using a 32 bit AER (Address Event Representation) containing an *(x, y)* coordinate, a time-stamp, a change in intensity (+1 or -1) and additional synchronising bits to allow multiple cameras to be used together.

Two robot platforms were used for collecting data—UQ's iRat robot [19] and a LEGO NXT (Fig. 1 a and b). The iRat is a small rat animat which has the computational power of a PC on wheels. The iRat has IR sensors and wheel encoders which allow it to maintain distances from walls, making it suitable for recording navigation data. The LEGO robot is the equivalent of adding motors to the DVS camera. It requires a wired connection so it is more limited in its applications. However, it provides more options when mounting the camera. A data projector and a custom track were also used. A python program was written to generate feature rich patterns which were then displayed on the projector or printed out and used as the walls of the track. The general purpose event-stream viewer jAER (Java tools for AER) [20] and the embedded system based cAER (C tools for AER) [21] were used to collect all the data sets in this paper.

2.2   Data Set Collection: Event-Based Visual Data

The task of interest is to learn from the high dimensional features presented in the event-based data and predict future sequences of events. A robust prediction paradigm requires diverse data sets to test its abilities. We created a wide range of data sets including 11 moving scenes, each with 1-180 variations, and 5-10 instances per variation (see Table 1). These data sets were collected using a static camera and embodied autonomous robots, focusing on self-motion (M1-M4) and object flow (M1, M3, S1a, S1c, S2-S7). The data sets contain single (M2, S1, S2, S4, S6, S7) or multiple (M1, M3, S2-S5) objects; some scenes are simple with few primitive shapes (M2a, S1a, S1c, S2, S4, S6, S7b) while the others are complex with irregular or dense objects (M1, M3, S1b, S3, S5, S7a); and a special data set for environment navigation (M4). Note that most SLAM data sets (eg. [22]) contain a single instance, here we are interested in sensory prediction, and hence we have provided multiple instances of each motion trajectory. Details of the data sets are listed in Table 1 (full data sets are available from www.itee.uq.edu.au/cis), which shows examples of the collection sources (left column) and the DVS128 data accumulated over a short period (right column):

1. Ego-motion (M1-M4)—perspective of stationary scenes from a moving agent:
   (a) The LEGO robot was moving along a straight track in which patterns of dots and shapes were attached to the walls of the track.
   (b) The LEGO robot was facing a large screen displayed with patterns of dots and shapes. The robot was moving towards and away from the projected images to collect data generated by ego-motion.
   (c) The iRat mounted with the DVS128 was navigating through the UQ Australia maze to collect data of complex scenery change.
2. Static camera (S1-S7)—perspective on object motion from a static agent:
   (a) The stationary DVS128 was facing a projector screen displaying a wide range of transforming patterns, vary from simple to complex trajectories.
   (b) The stationary DVS128 facing real moving objects.

2.3   Performance Measurement of Sensory Data Stream Prediction

To evaluate the prediction paradigms, their performance needs to be measured and assessed. An advantage of tasks that predict the future of sensory data streams is that the "ground truth" is self-contained within the data. Performance measurement of a prediction paradigm depends on the representation of the event streams. If these events are treated as spikes and the predicting model is also outputting spikes, binned spike count differences, iterative closest point (ICP) [23] or any distance metric (Euclidean, Hamming, mean squared error) could be used to compare the predictions to the data. If the events are represented as probability densities (as used in Section 3 or [7]) the accuracy of the predicted densities can be compared to the actual event densities by using a range of divergences including chi-squared divergence or Kullback-Liebler divergence [24].

Table 1. The benchmark data sets (www.itee.uq.edu.au/cis)

Self-motion datasets	Trials	Sources Data
M1. Moving forward and backward on a track		
M1a Variable dots, 4 spacings x 3 speeds	12x10=120	
M1b Various shapes, 3 spacings x 3 speeds	9x10=90	
M2. Facing objects, moving forward and backward		
M2a Smooth ball, 3 speeds	3x10=30	
M2b Spiky ball, 3 speeds	3x10=30	
M3. Facing projector, moving forward and backward		
M3a Same sized dots, 2 sizes x 3 speeds	6x10=60	
M3b Variable dots, 3 variations x 3 speeds	9x10=90	
M3c Variable sized shapes, 3 speeds	3x10=30	
M4. iRat navigating Australia maze	1x5=5	(see Fig. 1 g & h)
Static camera data sets		
S1. Shape transformations		
S1a Circle expanding and contracting	1x10=10	
S1b Spinning spirals	1x10=10	
S1c Disc moving 1 in circle & 1 in spiral	2x10=10	
S2. Uniform circles moving in trajectories		
S2a 1-4 circles x 3 sizes x 3 speeds x 5 paths	180x10=1800	
S2b Variable sizes & speeds, 1-4 circles x 5 paths	20x10=200	
S3. Various shapes moving in trajectories		
S3a 2-5 shapes x 3 sizes x 3 speeds x 5 paths	180x10=1800	
S3b Variable sizes & speeds, 2-5 shapes x 5 paths	20x10=200	
S4. Circles radiating out		
S4a 1-5 circles x 2 sizes x 3 speeds x 5 paths	150x10=1500	
S4b Variable sizes & speeds, 1-5 circles x 5 paths	25x10=250	
S5. Various shapes radiating out		
S5a 2-4 shapes x 2 sizes x 3 speeds x 5 paths	90x10=900	
S5b Variable sizes & speeds, 2-4 shapes x 5 paths	15x10=150	
S6. LED pointer drawing		
S6a Circles; S6b Figure 8; S6c Sideway movement; S6d Inward spirals; S6e Squares; S6f Stars	6x10 = 60	
S7. Real objects		
S7a Remote car moving, 4 directions	4x5 = 20	
S7b Ball rolling	1x5 = 5	

3   Spiking Neural Network Prediction of DVS128 Data

We have developed a novel spiking neuron model, in which a spike can be viewed as a link between a past temporal pattern recorded by the neuron's dendritic arbour and a future pattern effected by the neuron's axonal arbour [25]. A network of such prediction neurons trained on data set M2a (Table 1) predicted the motion trajectory of the object into the far future (Fig. 2). The input event stream was first approximated as self-scaling Gaussian distributions, and the network captured the temporal relationship of these events using learnable temporal delays at both dendrites and axons (Fig. 2-left). The dendrites (blue and magenta lines) learnt from inputs of both positive (blue contour lines) and negative (magenta contour lines) event distributions and the axons (black and red lines) predicted into the future a sequence of both positive (black contour lines) and negative (red contour lines) event distributions; see [25] for details of the delays and learning mechanism. After training the network with 43.13s of the data, the network was tested with an unseen section (0.66s) of the data (blue contour lines in Fig. 2-right are the Gaussian representations of the input data) and it predicted the future trajectory (for 14.13s) of the moving object (predicted positive events distributions in black and that of the negative events in red).

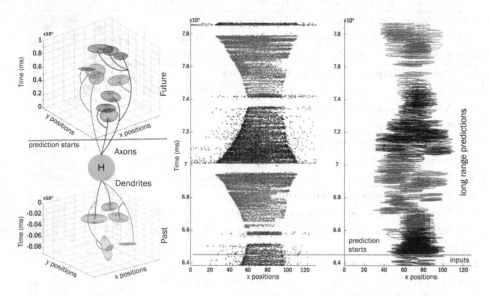

Fig. 2. The SNN prediction paradigm, with contour lines indicating the Gaussian representation of the data. Left: A prediction spiking neuron with dendrites that sample the past (blue: positive; magenta: negative) and axonal branches which predict into the future (black: positive; red: negative). Middle: The raw data in spikes of data set M2a (black dots: positive events; red dots: negative events). Right: The network's prediction of the future events in the form of Gaussians (blue: positive input; black: predicted positive; red: predicted negative).

4   Summary

The DVS128 data sets were developed as an SNN community resource, to facilitate the work of our group's bio-inspired research and to provide easily accessible data for other modellers. Key design features include (i) ego-motion (resulting in whole field dynamics; sets M1-4) and object motion (local field dynamics; sets S1-7); (ii) trajectories suitable for prediction tasks based on episodic memory (rather than categorisation tasks); (iii) event-based encoding which does not require uniform time sampling or video frames, comparable to the clock-free processes of biological neurons; (iv) real-world recordings (rather than simulated data); (v) a range of simple and complex trajectories. The main challenge for collecting the data was creating untethered ego-motion, which was addressed by mounting the DVS128 on the UQ iRat robot and using cAER for direct data capture. Practical challenges result from the size of DVS data. For model development, we have used self-scaling Gaussians to estimate space-time densities, which enables rapid prototyping, with a view to increasing fidelity with more computational power.

Current projects using this data include an event-based SNN to predict future motion trajectories (see Section 3 and [25]); an SNN with a deep learning architecture designed to abstract different levels of features from the temporal flow; and vector flow analysis for prediction of motion trajectories.

Acknowledgments. This work was supported by an APA to TG, AOARD Grant FA2386-12-1-4050 and UQ summer scholarships. The authors are grateful to David Tingley for his support and Tobi Delbrück for his valuable advice and for the jAER software infrastructure.

References

1. Chandy, K.M.: Event-driven applications: Costs, benefits and design approaches. Presented at the Gartner Application Integration and Web Services Summit, San Diego, CA (2006)
2. Lichtsteiner, P., et al.: A 128x128 120 db 15 s latency asynchronous temporal contrast vision sensor. IEEE Journal of Solid-State Circuits 43(2), 566–576 (2008)
3. Liu, S.-C., et al.: Event-based 64-channel binaural silicon cochlea with q enhancement mechanisms. In: Proceedings of 2010 IEEE International Symposium on Circuits and Systems (ISCAS), pp. 2027–2030 (2010)
4. Ahn, E.Y., et al.: Dynamic vision sensor camera based bare hand gesture recognition. In: 2011 IEEE Symposium on Computational Intelligence for Multimedia, Signal and Vision Processing (CIMSIVP), pp. 52–59 (April 2011)
5. O'Connor, P., et al.: Real-time classification and sensor fusion with a spiking deep belief network. Frontiers in Neuroscience 7(178) (2013)
6. Brandli, C., et al.: Adaptive pulsed laser line extraction for terrain reconstruction using a dynamic vision sensor. Frontiers in Neuroscience 7(275) (2014)
7. Piatkowska, E., et al.: Spatiotemporal multiple persons tracking using dynamic vision sensor. In: 2012 IEEE Computer Society Conference on Computer Vision and Pattern Recognition Workshops (CVPRW), pp. 35–40. IEEE (2012)

8. Drazen, D., et al.: Toward real-time particle tracking using an event-based dynamic vision sensor. Experiments in Fluids 51(5), 1465–1469 (2011)

9. Koeth, F., et al.: Self-organisation of motion features with a temporal asynchronous dynamic vision sensor. Biologically Inspired Cognitive Architectures 6(0), 8–11 (2013)

10. Bichler, O., et al.: Extraction of temporally correlated features from dynamic vision sensors with spike-timing-dependent plasticity. Neural Networks 32, 339–348 (2012)

11. Gomez-Rodriguez, F., et al.: Real time multiple objects tracking based on a bio-inspired processing cascade architecture. In: Proceedings of 2010 IEEE International Symposium on Circuits and Systems (ISCAS), pp. 1399–1402 (May 2010)

12. Censi, A., et al.: Low-latency localization by active led markers tracking using a dynamic vision sensor. In: 2013 IEEE/RSJ International Conference on Intelligent Robots and Systems (IROS), pp. 891–898. IEEE (2013)

13. Rogister, P., et al.: Asynchronous event-based binocular stereo matching. IEEE Transactions on Neural Networks and Learning Systems 23(2), 347–353 (2012)

14. Pikatkowska, E., Belbachir, A.N.: Asynchronous stereo vision for event-driven dynamic stereo sensor using an adaptive cooperative approach. In: 2013 IEEE International Conference on Computer Vision (ICCV) Workshops, pp. 45–50 (2013)

15. Weikersdorfer, D., Hoffmann, R., Conradt, J.: Simultaneous localization and mapping for event-based vision systems. In: Chen, M., Leibe, B., Neumann, B., et al. (eds.) ICVS 2013. LNCS, vol. 7963, pp. 133–142. Springer, Heidelberg (2013)

16. Weikersdorfer, D., Conradt, J.: Event-based particle filtering for robot self-localization. In: 2012 IEEE International Conference on Robotics and Biomimetics (ROBIO), pp. 866–870. IEEE (2012)

17. Perez-Peña, F., et al.: Neuro-inspired spike-based motion: From dynamic vision sensor to robot motor open-loop control through spike-vite. Sensors 13(11), 15, 805–15, 832 (2013)

18. Delbrück, T., Lang, M.: Robotic goalie with 3ms reaction time at 4% cpu load using event-based dynamic vision sensor. Frontiers in Neuroscience 7(223) (2013)

19. Ball, D., et al.: Irat: Intelligent rat animat technology. In: Proceedings of the 2010 Australasian Conference on Robotics and Automation, pp. 1–3 (2010)

20. Delbrück, T.: Jaer open source project (2007), http://jaer.wiki.sourceforge.net

21. Delbrück, T.: Caer (2013), http://sourceforge.net/projects/jaer/files/cAER/

22. Ball, D., et al.: Openratslam: An open source brain-based slam system. Autonomous Robots 34(3), 149–176 (2013)

23. Besl, P., McKay, N.D.: A method for registration of 3-d shapes. IEEE Transactions on Pattern Analysis and Machine Intelligence 14(2), 239–256 (1992)

24. Kullback, S., Leibler, R.A.: On information and sufficiency. In: The Annals of Mathematical Statistics, pp. 79–86 (1951)

25. Gibson, T., et al.: Predicting temporal sequences using an event-based spiking neural network incorporating learnable delays. In: The International Joint Conference on Neural Networks, IJCNN (in press 2014)

Modeling of Chaotic Time Series
by Interval Type-2 NEO-Fuzzy Neural Network

Yancho Todorov[1] and Margarita Terziyska[2]

[1] Institute of Information and Communication Technologies,
Bulgarian Academy of Sciences,
Acad. G. Bontchev st., bl. 2, 1113, Sofia, Bulgaria
yancho.todorov@iit.bas.bg
[2] Technical University-Sofia, Branch Plovdiv,
25, Tsanko Dustabanov St., 4000, Plovdiv, Bulgaria
terzyiska@gmail.com

Abstract. This paper describes the development of Interval Type-2 NEO-Fuzzy Neural Network for modeling of complex dynamics. The proposed network represents a parallel set of multiple zero order Sugeno type approximations, related only to their own input argument. The induced gradient based learning procedure, adjusts solely the consequent network parameters. To improve the robustness of the network and the possibilities for handling uncertainties, Type-2 Gaussian fuzzy sets are introduced into the network topology. The potentials of the proposed approach in modeling of Mackey-Glass and Rossler Chaotic time series are studied.

Keywords: neo-fuzzy neuron, neural networks, type-2 fuzzy set, dynamic modeling, chaotic time-series prediction.

1   Introduction

Neural Networks (NN's) [1] and Fuzzy Logic systems (FL's) [2] are well known as universal approximators and they are successfully used for modeling and identification of nonlinear dynamics. Hybrid Neuro-Fuzzy Networks emerged as a synergism of these two major directions in computational intelligence. They possess the learning capabilities similar to those of neural networks, and provide the interpretability and "transparency" of results, inherent to the fuzzy approach. Recently, many applications to solve a wide range of problems such as data mining and processing of complex dynamic signals of different nature under *a priori* uncertainty have been reported [3].

During the last years, many Neuro-Fuzzy Networks have been adopted in the practice as: ANFIS [4], DENFIS [5], NEFCON [6] and e.t.c. The main advantage of these modeling concepts relies on their flexibility to employ data from the process and to adapt quickly the parameters of the network to changing nonlinear process behavior by using fairly standard optimization procedures. A serious drawback for their on-line application for dynamical modeling purposes is the number of parameters under adaptation at each sampling period, since it grows exponentially with the increasing level

S. Wermter et al. (Eds.): ICANN 2014, LNCS 8681, pp. 643–650, 2014.

of nonlinearity. Another disadvantage of the classical neuro-fuzzy systems, especially when they operate in on-line mode is the slow convergence of the conventional gradient-based learning procedures and the computational complexity of second-order ones [7]. As well, such classical structures cannot handle major process uncertainties in many complex situations.

To overcome such deficiencies of the classical Neuro-Fuzzy networks, it has been introduced the idea for Neo-Fuzzy Network (NFN), as special tool for modeling of complex dynamical behavior. Usually, the concept of the Neo-Fuzzy Neuron relies on the quite close to the conventional n-inputs artificial neuron. However, instead of usual synaptic weights, it contains the so-called nonlinear synapses. When an input of an NFN is fed by a vector signal, its output is defined by both the input membership functions and the tunable synaptic weights [7]. It is proved that among the most important advantages of the NFN are: the learning rate, the high approximation properties, the computational simplicity and the possibility of finding the global minimum of the learning criterion in real time [8].

During the recent years, many NFN architectures are reported in literature. In [9] are presented different NFN topologies, while in [10,11] are reported respective learning approaches. Applications of modified neo-fuzzy neuron-based approach for economic and environmental optimal power dispatch and approach for bottom parameters estimation in oil wells, are also reported in [12,13]. In [14] authors propose an applied idea for Neo-Fuzzy Neuron model for seasonal rainfall forecast and cascade NFN in the problem of forecasting at the Stock Exchange [15].

Due to its potentials, the NFN approach seems to be a promising solution for modeling of complex dynamical systems, but its application in purpose of process modeling under uncertainties, are not yet well studied.

This paper describes a modified approach for designing of a Neo-Fuzzy Network. The network topology comprises a number of cascade connected Neo-Fuzzy Neurons, whose inputs are fuzzified in terms of Gaussian Type-2 Interval Fuzzy sets with uncertain variance in order to improve the ability of the network for handling occurring uncertainties. As learning procedure for the proposed network structure, a supervised learning scheme, minimizing an error cost term is adopted. The capabilities of the proposed Neo-Fuzzy structure in modeling of different Chaotic Time Series, Mackey-Glass and Rossler are evaluated.

2   Neo-Fuzzy Neural Network Design

The Neo-Fuzzy Network is a nonlinear multi-input, single-output system which can be described in general as:

$$\hat{y}(k) = f(x(k)) \tag{1}$$

where $\mathbf{x(k)}$ is an input vector of the states in terms of different time instants. Each Neo-Fuzzy Neuron comprises a simple fuzzy inference which produces reasoning to singleton weighting consequents:

$$R^{(i)} : if \ x_i \ is \ \tilde{A}_i \ then \ f_i(x_i) \tag{2}$$

Each element of the input vector is being fuzzified using Type-2 Interval Fuzzy set:

$$\mu_{ij}(x_i) = -\exp\left(\frac{x_i - c_{ij}}{2\sigma_{ij}}\right)^2 = \begin{cases} \bar{\mu}_{ij} \ as \ \sigma_{ij} = \bar{\sigma}_{ij} \\ \underline{\mu}_{ij} \ as \ \sigma_{ij} = \underline{\sigma}_{ij} \end{cases} \tag{3}$$

where μ is the membership degree defined by a Gaussian membership function with uncertain variance and c and σ represent the center (mean) and the width (standard deviation) depending on the defined footprint of uncertainty. Graphically the fuzzification procedure is demonstrated on Fig. 1.

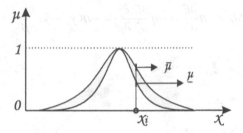

Fig. 1. Gaussian Membership Function with uncertain upper and lower membership functions

The fuzzy inference should match the output of the fuzzifier with fuzzy logic rules performing fuzzy implication and approximation reasoning in the following way:

$$\mu_{ij}* = \begin{cases} \bar{\mu}_{ij}* = \prod_{i=1}^{n} \bar{\mu}_{ij} \\ \underline{\mu}_{ij}* = \prod_{i=1}^{n} \underline{\mu}_{ij} \end{cases} \tag{4}$$

The output of the network is produced by implementing consequence matching, type reduction and linear combination as follows:

$$\hat{y}(k) = \frac{1}{2}\sum_{j=1}^{l}(\bar{\mu}_{ij}* + \underline{\mu}_{ij}*)f_i(x_i) = \frac{1}{2}\sum_{i=1}^{l}(\bar{\mu}_{ij}* + \underline{\mu}_{ij}*)w_{ij} \tag{5}$$

which in fact represents a weighted product composition of the ith input to j^{th} synaptic weight, as presented in Fig. 2.

2.1   Learning Algorithm for the Proposed Neo-Fuzzy Neural Network

To train the proposed modeling structure a supervised learning scheme has been used. For that purpose, a defined error cost term is being minimized at each sampling period in order to update the weights in the consequent part of the fuzzy rules:

$$E = \varepsilon^2\!\!\Big/\!2 \text{ and } \varepsilon(k) = y_d(k) - \hat{y}(k) \tag{6}$$

where y_d is the reference output measured form the process and $\hat{y}$ is the output being estimated by the model. As learning approach is used the well known back propagation approach:

$$\beta(k+1) = \beta(k) + \Delta\beta = \beta(k) + \eta\left(\frac{\partial E(k)}{\partial \beta(k)}\right) \tag{7}$$

where η is the learning rate and β is a vector of the trained parameters: the synaptic links in the consequent part of the rules. Form (6) and (7) it can be derived using the chain rule notation:

$$\Delta\beta = -\eta\frac{\partial E}{\partial \beta} = -\eta\frac{\partial E}{\partial \hat{y}}\frac{\partial \hat{y}}{\partial \beta} = -\eta(y_d - \hat{y})\frac{\partial \hat{y}}{\partial \beta} \tag{8}$$

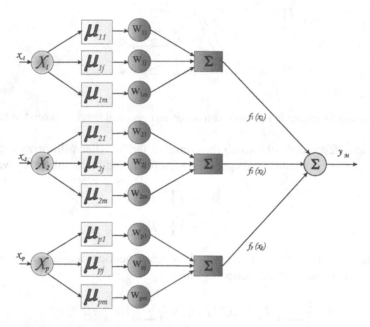

Fig. 2. Structure of the proposed Neo-Fuzzy Neural Network

3   Results and Discussion

Chaos is a common dynamical phenomenon in various fields [16] and different definitions as series representations exist. Chaotic time series are inherently nonlinear, sensitive to initial conditions and difficult to be predicted. Therefore, the chaotic time series prediction based on measurement is a practical technique for studying characteristics of complicated dynamics [17] and evaluation of the accuracy of different types of nonlinear models. In this section the proposed interval Type-2 NEO-Fuzzy Network is tested to model two chaotic time series - Mackey-Glass [18] and Rossler [19] for 200 time steps. The Mackey-Glass chaotic series is defined by the following parameters: a=0.2; b=0.1; C=10; initial conditions x(0)=0.1 and s= 17s. and on Fig. 3 is demonstrated performance of the proposed network using η=0.05. For greater clarity, the results are given in linear and logarithmic scales. As it can be seen, the proposed model structure estimate accurately the generated time series, with minimum MSE and RMSE and fast transient response of the RMSE, reaching values closer to zero.

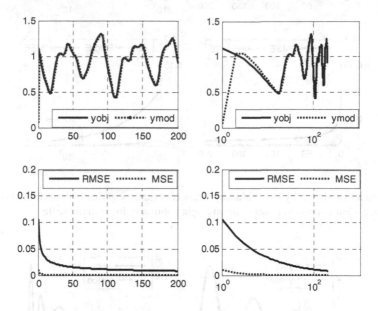

Fig. 3. Model validation by using Mackey-Glass chaotic time series – left column in linear scale and right column in logarithmic scale

On Fig.4 is presented the same case when is added uniformly distributed disturbance to the Mackey-Glass chaotic system of about 10% of the nominal input signal. The aim is to investigate the model behavior when an uncertain condition occurs. It can be seen that the interval Type-2 Neo-Fuzzy network model follows again the Mackey-Glass signal with minimum error and a slight increase of the RMSE.

Another test of the proposed model is made with Rossler chaotic time series with the following conditions: a=0.2; b=0.4; c=5.7; initial conditions x0=0.1; y0=0.1; z0=0.1. The results with the above presented cases are given respectively on Fig.5 and Fig.6. As it can be seen the model behavior is similar to the studied above. An increased value of the RMSE is observed again in the case of additive uniformly distributed disturbance, but the model performance is still stable.

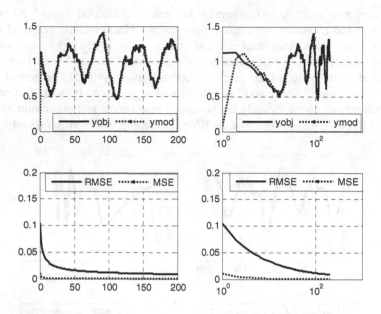

Fig. 4. Model validation by using Mackey-Glass chaotic time series with uniformly distributed disturbance – left column in linear scale and right column in logarithmic scale

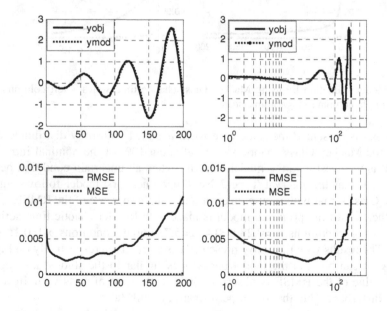

Fig. 5. Model validation by using Rossler chaotic time series – left column in linear scale and right column in logarithmic scale

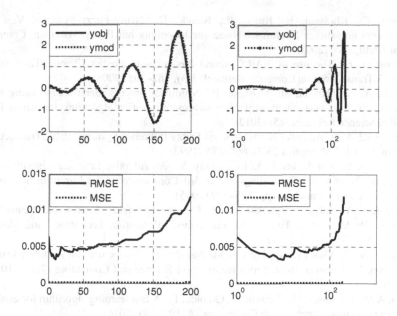

Fig. 6. Model validation by using Rossler chaotic time series – left column in linear scale and right column in logarithmic scale

Conclusions: It was presented in this paper an approach for designing a Neural Network, using the concept of NFN. For each input neuron is defined an Interval Type-2 Gaussian Fuzzy set in order to improve the ability of the network to handle uncertainties. The model output is produced by simple consequence matching, type reduction and linear combination. The achieved results in modeling of two common benchmark chaotic time series: Rossler and Mackey-Glass, have shown a stable model performance and slight error increase in the case of occurring uniformly distributed disturbance. A major benefit of the proposed approach is the relatively simple model structure with less number of parameters under adaptation and fuzzy mechanism dealing with input uncertainties. This opens new horizons to be studied in the future the potentials of the proposed approach in purpose of model based control strategies, where the computational accuracy of the model is crucial issue.

Aknowlegment. The research work reported in the paper is partly supported by the project *AComIn* "Advanced Computing for Innovation", grant 316087, funded by the FP7 Capacity Programme (Research Potential of Convergence Regions).

References

1. Jang, J.-S.R., Sun, C.-T., Mizutani, E.: Neuro-Fuzzy and Soft Computing – A Computational Approach to Learning and Machine Intelligence. Prentice Hall (1997)
2. Jin, Y.: Advanced Fuzzy Systems Design and Applications. Physica (2003)

3. Borgelt, C., Klawonn, F., Kruse, R., Nauck, D.: Neuro-Fuzzy-Systeme. Von den Grundlagen künstlicher Neuronaler Netze zur Kopplung mit Fuzzy-Systemen. Computational Intelligence (2003)
4. Diaconescu, E.: The use of NARX Neural Networks to predict Chaotic Time Series. WSEAS Transactions on Computer Research 3(3), 182–191 (2008)
5. Esmaili, A., Shahbazian, M., Moslemi, B.: Nonlinear process identification using fuzzy wavelet neural network based on particle swarmoptimization algorithm. Journal of Basic Applied Science Research 3(5) (2013)
6. Jang, J.S.R.: Anfs: Adaptive Network based Fuzzy Inference Systems. IEEE Transactions, System, Man & Cybernetics 23(3), 665–685 (1993)
7. Bodyanskiy, Y., Kokshenev, I., Kolodyazhniy, V.: An Adaptive Learning Algorithm for a Neo-Fuzzy Neuron. In: Proceedings of the 3rd Conference of the European Society for Fuzzy Logic and Technology, pp. 375–379 (2005)
8. Bodyanskiy, Y., Pliss, I., Vynokurova, O.: Flexible Neo-fuzzy Neuron and Neuro-fuzzy Network for Monitoring Time Series Properties. Information Technology and Management Science 16, 47–52 (2013)
9. Bodyanskiy, Y., Viktorov, Y.: The cascade Neo-Fuzzy architecture and its online learning algorithm. International Book Series Information Science and Computing 17(1), 110–116 (2010)
10. Silva, A.M., Caminhas, W., Lemos, A., Gomide, F.: A fast learning algorithm for evolving Neo-Fuzzy neuron. Applied Soft Computing 14, 194–209 (2014)
11. Kim, H.D.: Optimal Learning of Neo-Fuzzy Structure Using Bacteria Foraging Optimization. In: Proceedings of the ICCA 2005 (2005)
12. Chaturvedi, K.T., Pandit, M., Srivastava, L.: Modified Neo-Fuzzy neuron-based approach for economic and environmental optimal power dispatch. Applied Soft Computing 8, 1428–1438 (2008)
13. Camargo, E., Aguilar, J., Rios, A., Rivas, F., Aguilarmartin, J.: A Neo-Fuzzy Approach for Bottom Parameters Estimation in Oil Wells. WSEAS Transactions on Systems and Control 9(4), 445–454 (2009)
14. De Castro, T.N., Souza, F., Alves, J., Pontes, R., Dos Reis, L., Daher, S.: Neo-fuzzy neuron model for seasonal rainfall forecast: A case study of Ceara's eight homogenous regions. Journal of Intelligent & Fuzzy Systems 25, 389–394 (2013)
15. Zaychenko, Y., Gasanov, A.: Investigations of Cascade Neo-Fuzzy Neural Networks in the Problem of Forecasting at the Stock Exchange. In: Proc. of the IVth IEEE International Conference "Problems of Cybernetics and Informatics" (PCI 2012), pp. 227–229 (2012)
16. Yao, J., Mao, J., Zhang, W.: Application of Fuzzy Tree on Chaotic Time Series Prediction. In: IEEE Proc. of Int. Conf. on Aut. and Logistics, pp. 326–330 (2008)
17. Lai, Y.: Recent developments in chaotic time series analysis. International Journal of Bifurcation and Chaos 13(6), 1383–1422 (2003)
18. Diaconescu, E.: The use of NARX Neural Networks to predict Chaotic Time Series. WSEAS Transactions on Ccomputer Rresearch 3(3), 182–191 (2008)
19. Archana, R., Unnikrishnan, A., Gopikakumari, R.: Bifurcation Analysis of Chaotic Systems using a Model Built on Artificial Neural Networks. In: Proc. of Int. Conf. on Comp. Tech. and Artificial Intelligence, pp. 198–202 (2013)

Excitation/Inhibition Patterns in a System of Coupled Cortical Columns

Daniel Malagarriga[1,2], Alessandro E.P. Villa[2],
Jordi García-Ojalvo[3], and Antonio J. Pons[1]

[1] Departament de Física i Enginyeria Nuclear, Universitat Politècnica de Catalunya,
Edifici Gaia, Rambla Sant Nebridi 22, 08222 Terrassa, Spain
[2] Neuroheuristic Research Group, Faculty of Business and Economics, University of
Lausanne, CH-1015 Lausanne, Switzerland
[3] Department of Experimental and Health Sciences, Universitat Pompeu Fabra,
Barcelona Biomedical Research Park (PRBB), Dr. Aiguader 88,
08003 Barcelona, Spain

Abstract. We study how excitation and inhibition are distributed meso-
scopically in small brain regions, by means of a computational model of
coupled cortical columns described by neural mass models. Two cortical
columns coupled bidirectionally through both excitatory and inhibitory
connections can spontaneously organize in a regime in which one of the
columns is purely excitatory and the other is purely inhibitory, provided
the excitatory and inhibitory coupling strengths are adequately tuned.
We also study the case of three columns in different coupling configurations (linear array and all-to-all coupling), finding abrupt transitions
between heterogeneous and homogeneous excitatory/inhibitory patterns
and strong multistability in their distribution.

1 Introduction

The synchronization of regular and irregular dynamics in the brain has revealed
the key role played by the excitatory/inhibitory balance at various levels of observation of brain activity [1–8]. In order to establish how this excitation/inhibition
balance plays out at the level of large neuronal populations, we need to use mesoscopic models that combine computational efficiency and biological plausibility.
One such type of description is the neural mass model, which represents the average interactions of three neuronal populations: pyramidal excitatory projecting
neurons, excitatory interneurons and inhibitory interneurons. This model does
not consider the precise anatomical substructures present in cortical columns
(mini columns or subnetworks [9]), but gathers its main dynamical features
present at the mesoscopic scale. Lopes da Silva and Zetterberg [10, 11] and
later Jansen and coauthors [12] introduced and popularized such type of model,
respectively. This model is considered to provide a descriptive dynamics of a single cortical column displaying a whole repertoire of dynamical states, depending
on the external excitatory input acting on the pyramidal population. The neural mass model evolves at a slow scale, and the average activities of the neural

S. Wermter et al. (Eds.): ICANN 2014, LNCS 8681, pp. 651–658, 2014.
© Springer International Publishing Switzerland 2014

populations are mainly characterized by their tendency to develop synchronized activity. Here we use small networks of two and three cortical columns, coupled by both excitatory and inhibitory connections, to assess how excitation and inhibition is distributed at the mesoscopic level.

2   Dynamical Model and Methods

Model

The dynamical evolution of the three populations of neurons considered by the neural mass (NM) model (i.e., the excitatory and inhibitory interneurons and the pyramidal cells) is introduced considering two different transformations [12]. Each population transforms the total average density of action potentials reaching their synapses from different origins, $\sum_q p_q(t)$, into an average postsynaptic excitatory or inhibitory membrane potential $y_n(t)$. This transformation, which inputs into the population, can be introduced into the model using the differential operator $L(y_n(t); a)$:

$$L(y_n(t); a) = \frac{d^2 y_n(t)}{dt^2} + 2a \frac{dy_n(t)}{dt} + a^2 y_n(t) = Aa \left[\sum_q p_q(t) \right], \qquad (1)$$

for the excitatory postsynaptic potential and, similarly, $L(y_n(t); b)$ for the inhibitory postsynaptic potential. A and B are related with the maximum height of the excitatory and inhibitory postsynaptic potential (EPSP and IPSP, respectively), while a and b represent the inverse of the membrane time constants and the dendritic delays. Here $A = 3.25\ mV$, $a = 100\ Hz$, $B = 22\ mV$ and $b = 50\ Hz$, which sets the system in an oscillatory regime of frequency $10.8\ Hz$.

The second dynamical transformation considered to build the model is the conversion of the net average membrane potential into an average density of spikes. This conversion is done at the somas of the neurons which form the population and is described mathematically by a sigmoidal function defined as:

$$S(m_q(t)) = \frac{2e_0}{1 + e^{r(\nu_0 - m_q(t))}}. \qquad (2)$$

Here, $e_0 = 2.5\ Hz$ determines the maximum firing rate of the neural population, $\nu_0 = 0.6\ mV$ sets the net PSP for which a 50% firing rate is achieved, $r = 0.56\ mV^{-1}$ is the steepness of the sigmoidal transformation and $m_q(t)$ corresponds to the net PSP input into the population that produces the specific firing rate, $p_q(t)$, which turns out to be $p_q(t) = C_p\ S(m_q(t))$. C_p weights the contact between the origin population and destination population of the train of spikes. The intra-columnar connectivity constants values which define the model are given by C_p, with $p = 1, ..., 4$, as shown in Jansen et al. [12]. Here $C = 133.5$.

In our model the different cortical columns, which form small networks, interact with each other through both excitatory and inhibitory connections. So, we set pyramidal-pyramidal excitatory couplings and inhibitory interneuron-pyramidal inhibitory couplings mimicking short range inputs from nearby columns. These inter-column interactions correspond to incoming pulse densities $p_e^i(t)$ for excitatory input into the pyramidal population, and $p_i^i(t)$ for inhibitory input into the pyramidal population, respectively:

$$p_e^i(t) = \sum_{\substack{j=1 \\ j \neq i}}^{N_i} \alpha_{ij} S(y_1^j(t) - y_2^j(t)), \tag{3}$$

$$p_i^i(t) = \sum_{\substack{j=1 \\ j \neq i}}^{N_i} \beta_{ij} S(C_3 y_0^j(t)), \tag{4}$$

where i labels the column, N_i is the number of neighbors of column i and j labels the neighbors of column i. We choose this contact arrangement because pyramidal cells are widely regarded as responsible for non local connectivity [13]. In all cases, we consider bidirectional coupling, so $\alpha_{ij} = \alpha_{ji}$ and $\beta_{ij} = \beta_{ji}$. Besides, each pyramidal population receives a constant excitatory density of spikes $\bar{p}^i = 155.0 \ Hz$ from other sources in the brain.

Combining Eqs. (1-4) we obtain the complete model for the network of different NMs:

$$L(y_0^i(t); a) = Aa\{S(y_1^i(t) - y_2^i(t))\} \tag{5}$$
$$L(y_1^i(t); a) = Aa\{\bar{p}^i + p_e^i(t) + C_2 S(C_1 y_0^i(t))\} \tag{6}$$
$$L(y_2^i(t); b) = Bb\{p_i^i(t) + C_4 S(C_3 y_0^i(t))\}. \tag{7}$$

where i labels the column number, $y_0(t)$, is the excitatory postsynaptic potential (EPSP) which inputs into the interneuron populations from the pyramidal population, $y_1(t)$, is the EPSP which inputs into the pyramidal population arriving from the excitatory interneurons of the same column, from the pyramidal populations of external columns and the constant term from other areas of the brain $(\bar{p}^i)$, and, finally, $y_2(t)$, is the IPSP which inputs into the pyramidal population arriving from inhibitory interneurons from the same and external columns.

The dynamical evolution of the cortical columns is traced by means of $y_1^i(t) - y_2^i(t)$, which is the PSP affecting the pyramidal population. For the sake of clarity we will refer to it as $y_{exc}^i(t) - y_{inh}^i(t)$, as it is the difference between the EPSP and the IPSP in node i.

Analysis

A C++ code implementation of Heun's method was used to integrate the model equations [14]. For each run a total simulated time of $t = 50 \ s$ was considered with a time step of 1 ms. The initial period of 25 s was omitted to avoid considering transient dynamics. The random number generator (RNG) to set different initial conditions when performing the statistical analysis of data was provided by the package GSL [15].

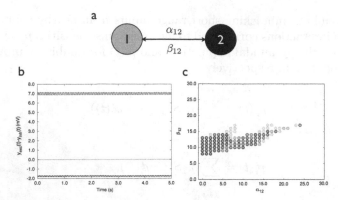

Fig. 1. a Two bidirectionally coupled cortical columns. **b** Time traces of the dynamical evolutions of the two nodes for 10 different sets of initial conditions. Segregation, in terms of $\langle y_{exc}(t) - y_{inh}(t) \rangle$, occurs. **c** Scatter plot of the occurrence of segregation in terms of the coupling constants α_{12} and β_{12}. Gray (black) circles indicate α_{12}, β_{12} values for which segregation occurs. Darker circles indicate higher occurrence of segregation for the 10 different sets of initial conditions. The blue circle indicates the case displayed in panel **b**.

The computation of the excitatory and inhibitory separation (segregation) was performed by calculating the histograms, or probability of occurrence, of the time average of the variable $y_{exc}^i(t) - y_{inh}^i(t)$ in each column. We will symbolize this average by $\langle y_{exc}(t) - y_{inh}(t) \rangle_t$. We computed 10 different realizations for coupling strength exploration (panel **b** in Figs. 2, 3, 4), and 100 different realizations for histograms computation (panel **c** in Figs. 2, 3, 4). All the analysis calculations were performed using the platform Matplotlib provided by Python [16].

3   Results

The interaction between excitatory and inhibitory populations of neurons in Eqs. (5-7) may give rise to oscillatory dynamics emerging at a mesoscopic time scale [12]. Besides, the contacts between neural ensembles form loops that enhance the excitation or inhibition activity of these populations in a feedforward or in a feedback manner. Here, we study how different simple architectures allow a network of bidirectionally coupled cortical columns to *segregate* displaying different excitatory or inhibitory dominated dynamics for the nodes which form the network [8]. We focus on scenarios in which the interaction between the simple topology and the intrinsic dynamics results in the segregation of the columns.

First we consider a simple case (see Fig. 1a) where two columns are coupled bidirectionally. Each node representing a cortical column can be considered as inhibitory if $\langle y_{exc}(t) - y_{inh}(t) \rangle_t < 0$ or excitatory if $\langle y_{exc}(t) - y_{inh}(t) \rangle_t \geq 0$. We have found the ranges for α_{12} and β_{12} where the columns in Fig. 1a segregate into excitation and inhibition dominated dynamics (see Fig. 1c).

Note that the bidirectional coupling sets a symmetry in the inter-column contacts that, nevertheless, allows an asymmetry in the settlement of $y_{exc}(t) -$

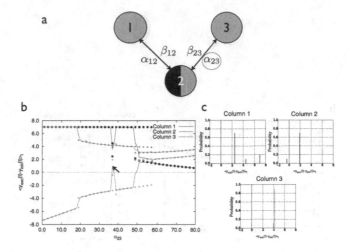

Fig. 2. a Three bidirectionally coupled cortical columns forming a chain. **b** Variation of the coupling strength α_{23} while keeping all other coupling strengths fixed ($\alpha_{12} = 6.0$, $\beta_{12} = \beta_{23} = 13.0$). Points represent the values obtained for the different realizations and the continuous line the average of these values. The system shows multistability in the regions where α_{23} is between 30.0 and 40.0 and where is between 40.0 and 50.0. We can see that column 1 remains excitatory through the different realizations, column 2 switches from inhibitory to excitatory dynamics and column 3 remains excitatory for all realizations. **c** Histogram of $\langle y_{exc}(t) - y_{inh}(t) \rangle$ for the three columns for the situation indicated with an arrow in panel **b** ($\alpha_{23} = 36.0$).

$y_{inh}(t)$ for the two columns. In the different realizations of the dynamics the first (second) node may become excitatory (inhibitory) and in other realizations it may become inhibitory (excitatory). The excitatory/inhibitory character of the two nodes is dictated by the initial conditions of the two columns.

In Fig. 2 we have studied the dynamics of 3 columns coupled bidirectionally forming a chain. The central column is connected to the other two, and so it is influenced by the coupling terms with them (see Fig. 2a). In this configuration we have set, on the one hand, α_{12} and β_{12} to force the node 1 and the central node to segregate (as shown in Fig. 2) and, on the other hand, we have fixed the same inhibitory coupling strength on the other link and we have scanned the excitatory coupling α_{23} afterwards. The variation of α_{23} results in the identification of regions with monostable or multistable excitatory/inhibitory dynamics (see Fig. 2b).

Column 1 remains excitatory through this range of α_{23} but, in general, decreases when the parameter increases. $\langle y_{exc}(t) - y_{inh}(t) \rangle$ for Column 3 decreases in general but seems to start increasing for the highest values of α_{23}. Finally, the central Column starts being inhibitory but becomes excitatory for $\alpha_{23} \approx 60$. So in this configuration, the excitatory unbalance between the two branches fixes the segregation of the central column. In particular, when α_{23} is small, the central node is inhibitory dominated but as α_{23} increases the excitation becomes

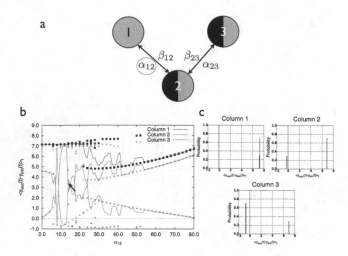

Fig. 3. a Three bidirectionally coupled cortical columns forming a chain. **b** Variation of the coupling strength α_{12} while keeping all other coupling strength fixed ($\alpha_{23} = 12.0$, $\beta_{12} = 2.1, \beta_{23} = 21.5$). Points represent the values obtained for the different realizations and the continuous line the average of these values. The arrow indicates a situation in which column 2 and column 3 switch their characteristic excitatory/inhibitory behavior due to the influence of coupling strength α_{12}. The system is strongly multistable for α_{12} between 10.0 and 55.0. **c** Histogram of $\langle y_{exc}(t) - y_{inh}(t) \rangle$ for the three columns for the situation indicated with an arrow in panel **b** ($\alpha_{12} = 15.0$) .

dominant in all nodes. One interesting result is the multistability observed for extended ranges of α_{23}. In Fig. 2c we have analyzed the case of multistable dynamics indicated by the arrow in Fig. 2b by computing the histograms of $\langle y_{exc}(t) - y_{inh}(t) \rangle_t$ for the different columns. As it can be seen some realizations in Column 2 are excitatory dominated and others are inhibitory dominated, whereas columns 1 and 2 remain excitatory.

Still using the same topology, we have explored coupling values that allow multistable excitatory/inhibitory dynamics in two of the columns. Fig. 3b shows the behavior of $\langle y_{exc}(t) - y_{inh}(t) \rangle_t$ for each column and for increasing coupling strength α_{12}, keeping all other coupling strengths fixed (see caption in Fig. 3). In this case the inhibitory coupling strengths are not equal (i.e. $\beta_{12} \neq \beta_{23}$), but, alongside with α_{12}, they force the columns 2 and 3 to *segregate* and switch between excitation and inhibition (see dots indicating $\langle y_{exc}(t) - y_{inh}(t) \rangle_t$ values). Similarly as shown in Fig. 2, column 1 remains excitatory but suffers from abrupt changes in $\langle y_{exc}(t) - y_{inh}(t) \rangle_t$ from very low α_{12} values up to $\alpha_{12} \approx 55.0$. Columns 2 and 3 can switch between excitatory or inhibitory dynamics between $\alpha_{12} \approx 5.0$ and $\alpha_{12} \approx 25.0$ (see blue circles and gray triangles in Fig. 3b). The histograms in Fig. 3 show the probability of columns 2 and 3 to be either excitatory or inhibitory while column 1 remains excitatory for the case indicated with an arrow in Fig. 3b. Again, there exist extended regions of multistability in terms of α_{12}.

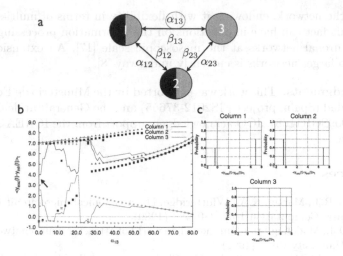

Fig. 4. a Three bidirectionally coupled cortical columns forming a closed circuit. **b** Variation of the coupling strength α_{13} while keeping all other coupling strength fixed ($\alpha_{12} = \alpha_{23} = 1.0, \beta_{12} = 8.0, \beta_{13} = \beta_{23} = 1.0$). Points represent the values obtained for the different realizations and the continuous line shows the average of these values. The arrow indicates a situation in which column 2 and column 3 switch their characteristic excitatory/inhibitory behavior due to the influence of coupling strength α_{13}. The system is strongly multistable for small values of α_{13} up to $\alpha_{13} \approx 50.0$. **c** Histogram of $\langle y_{exc}(t) - y_{inh}(t) \rangle_t$ for the three columns for the situation indicated with an arrow in panel **b** ($\alpha_{13} = 1.0$).

Dynamical features displayed in Fig. 3 can also be found in Fig. 4 for closed circuit architecture and setting the coupling values to allow for segregated dynamics. The unbalance between inhibitory couplings in the circuit (see caption in Fig. 4) allows bistable dynamics to appear in columns 1 and 2 for low values of coupling strengths (see Fig. 4b). The three columns suffer steep changes in $\langle y_{exc}(t) - y_{inh}(t) \rangle_t$ as α_{13} increases. Once more, there exist extended regions of multistability in terms of α_{13}. Finally, the multistable excitatory/inhibitory dynamics in columns 1 and 2 for the case indicated with an arrow in Fig. 4b can be seen in the histograms of Fig. 4c, showing that this behavior is not exclusive of chain-like architectures.

4   Conclusions

Our computational analysis of a small number of coupled cortical columns shows that excitation and inhibition are distributed in a non-trivial manner at the mesoscopic level. This behavior requires the cortical columns to be coupled via both excitatory and inhibitory connections, which is a reasonable assumption if the columns are in close proximity. Our observations indicate that depending on the coupling architecture each column acquires a well-defined excitatory or inhibitory character, although multiple patterns of excitation and inhibition can coexist in the network, endowing it with flexibility in terms of multi-stable dynamics. This fact can have implications on the information processing capacity of large neuronal networks at the mesoscopic scale [17]. An extension of this behavior to larger networks is currently underway [8].

Acknowledgments. This work was supported by the Ministerio de Economia y Competividad (Spain, project FIS2012-37655) and the Generalitat de Catalunya (project 2009SGR1168). JGO acknowledges support from the ICREA Academia programme.

References

1. Douglas, R.J., Martin, K.A., Whitteridge, D.: A canonical microcircuit for neocortex. Neural Computation 1(4), 480–488 (1989)
2. Amit, D.J.: Modeling brain function: The world of attractor neural networks. Cambridge University Press (1992)
3. van Vreeswijk, C., Sompolinsky, H.: Chaos in neuronal networks with balanced excitatory and inhibitory activity. Science 274(5293), 1724–1726 (1996)
4. Hill, S., Villa, A.E.P.: Dynamic transitions in global network activity influenced by the balance of excitation and inhibtion. Network: Computational Neural Networks 8, 165–184 (1997)
5. Iglesias, J., García-Ojalvo, J., Villa, A.E.P.: Effect of feedback strength in coupled spiking neural networks. In: Kůrková, V., Neruda, R., Koutník, J. (eds.) ICANN 2008, Part II. LNCS, vol. 5164, pp. 646–654. Springer, Heidelberg (2008)
6. van Vreeswijk, C., Sompolinsky, H.: Chaotic balanced state in a model of cortical circuits. Neural Comput. 10(6), 1321–1371 (1998)
7. Singer, W.: Neuronal synchrony: A versatile code for the definition of relations? Neuron 24(1), 49–65 (1999)
8. Malagarriga, D., Villa, A.E.P., García-Ojalvo, J., Pons, A.J.: Spontaneous segregation of excitation and inhibition in a system of coupled cortical columns (to be submitted)
9. Yoshimura, Y., Dantzker, J.L.M., Callaway, E.M.: Excitatory cortical neurons form fine-scale functional networks. Nature 433(7028), 868–873 (2005)
10. Lopes da Silva, F.H., Hoeks, A., Smits, H., Zetterberg, L.H.: Model of brain rhythmic activity. the alpha-rhythm of the thalamus. Kybernetik 15(1), 27–37 (1974)
11. Zetterberg, L.H., Kristiansson, L., Mossberg, K.: Performance of a model for a local neuron population. Biol. Cybern. 31(1), 15–26 (1978)
12. Jansen, B.H., Rit, V.G.: Electroencephalogram and visual evoked potential generation in a mathematical model of coupled cortical columns. Biol. Cybern. 73(4), 357–366 (1995)
13. Blackstad, T.W., Osen, K.K., Mugnaini, E.: Pyramidal neurones of the dorsal cochlear nucleus: A golgi and computer reconstruction study in cat. Neuroscience 13, 827–854 (1984)
14. García-Ojalvo, J., Sancho, J.M.: Noise in spatially extended systems (1999)
15. Galassi, M., et al.: Gnu scientific library reference manual. 3rd edn. (January 1, 2009)
16. Hunter, J.D.: Matplotlib: A 2d graphics environment. Computing In Science & Engineering 9(3), 90–95 (2007)
17. Mariño, J., Schummers, J., Lyon, D.C., Schwabe, L., Beck, O., Wiesing, P., Obermayer, K., Sur, M.: Invariant computations in local cortical networks with balanced excitation and inhibition. Nature Neuroscience 8(2), 194–201 (2005)

Self-generated Off-line Memory Reprocessing Strongly Improves Generalization in a Hierarchical Recurrent Neural Network

Jenia Jitsev[1]

Functional Neural Circuits Group, Institute of Neuroscience and Medicine (INM-6) & Institute for Advanced Simulation (IAS-6), Forschungszentrum Juelich, 52425 Juelich, Germany
j.jitsev@fz-juelich.de

Abstract. Strong experimental evidence suggests that cortical memory traces are consolidated during off-line memory reprocessing that occurs in the off-line states of sleep or waking rest. It is unclear, what plasticity mechanisms are involved in this process and what changes are induced in the network in the off-line regime. Here, we examine a hierarchical recurrent neural network that performs unsupervised learning on natural face images of different persons. The proposed network is able to self-generate memory replay while it is decoupled from external stimuli. Remarkably, the recognition performance is tremendously boosted after this off-line regime specifically for the novel face views that were not shown during the initial learning. This effect is independent of synapse-specific plasticity, relying completely on homeostatic regulation of intrinsic excitability. Comparing a purely feed-forward network configuration with the full version reveals a substantially stronger boost in recognition performance for the fully recurrent network architecture after the off-line regime.

Keywords: Unsupervised learning, off-line memory reprocessing, plasticity of intrinsic excitability, hierarchical recurrent neural network.

1 Introduction

The reprocessing of memory network during brain off-line states like sleep, where brain is decoupled from external sensory input and is not performing any particular task, constitutes an essential part of the learning process as hinted at by experimental evidence. Still, modeling studies on plasticity and learning in neural networks often focus on the on-line regime of learning only, where the external input is continuously impinging on the network, ignoring the possibility of function improvement in absense of external stimulation. In this work, we present a hierarchical recurrent neural network that spontaneously generates activity even in absence of external stimuli due to its inherently self-excitable dynamics. The network is able to perform off-line memory reprocessing if it is decoupled from external input after on-line unsupervised learning from natural face images. Remarkably, this off-line regime turns out to boost recognition performance strongly, and specifically on the novel face views that were not shown to the network before.

S. Wermter et al. (Eds.): ICANN 2014, LNCS 8681, pp. 659–666, 2014.

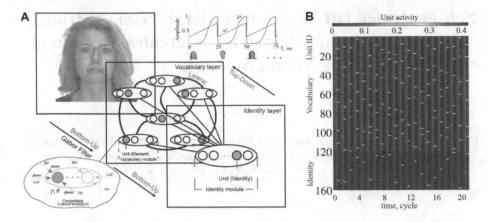

Fig. 1. Hierarchical memory network. (**A**) Two recurrently interconnected layers to store and represent faces in combinatorial, parts-based fashion. During on-line learning, the face images were presented incrementally showing one image per cycle, defined by excitatory and inhibitory gamma rhythms ω and ν ($T = 25ms$) (**B**) Activity patterns over 20 successive cycles generated by the network during off-line regime being decoupled from image input.

Surprisingly, this positive effect turns out to be completely independent of synapse-specific plasticity, as synaptic plasticity can be disabled during off-line regime without affecting the performance boost observed afterwards. The positive effect is entirely mediated by a local synapse-unspecific activity regulation mechanism that homeostatically regulates excitability of the network units. Furthermore, off-line reprocessing provides a dramatically stronger boost for fully recurrent network architecture than for its reduced purely feed-forward version as revealed by comparision of their performance before and after the off-line regime. The observed beneficial effect of synapse-unspecific, homeostatic regulation of intrinsic excitability during the off-line regime on the network performance afterwards provides an explanation how similar mechanisms that might act during sleep states and wakeful resting could lead to subsequent functional improvement in the brain following off-line memory reprocessing.

2   Model

Fast Neural Dynamics with Winner-take-all-like Behavior. We use a hierarchical recurrent neural network architecture as introduced in [1]. Briefly, the network consists of two consecutive, reciprocally interconnected layers of distributed cortical modules, or simply *modules* (Fig. 1 (**A**)). We denote the lower network layer as *vocabulary* layer and the higher layer as *identity* layer, applying the same terminology to the layer-specific modules. Each module is identified with a localized cortical cluster of fine-scale excitatory subnetworks. A single module contains a number of subunits or simply units, receiving common excitatory afferents and being bounded by common lateral inhibition. This model has its roots in previous work done by Lücke, where an abstract formulation of a cortical column (termed here *module*) was derived from considerations about dynamics of coupled populations of simplified spiking neurons [2]. Module's dynamics used here is described by a set of n stochastic differential equations that define evolution of a population activity variable p for each unit:

$$\tau \frac{dp}{dt} = \underbrace{\omega(t)\,(1 + I^{LAT} + I^{TD})}_{\text{Lateral and top-down input}} \underbrace{p^2(1-p)}_{\text{self-excitation}} - \underbrace{p^3}_{\text{self-inhibition}} - \underbrace{2\,\omega(t)\nu(t)(\max(\mathbf{p}_t) - p)p}_{\text{lateral inhibition}}$$
$$+ \underbrace{I^{BU}p^2}_{\text{Bottom-up input}} + \underbrace{\theta p}_{\text{intrinsic excitability}} + \underbrace{\sigma\eta_t p}_{\text{threshold noise}} + \underbrace{\omega(t)\epsilon}_{\text{unspecific excitation}}$$

(1)

where $\tau = 0.02\,ms$ is the time constant, $\max(\mathbf{p}_t)$ is the activity of the strongest unit in the module, I^{BU}, I^{LAT}, I^{TD} are bottom-up, lateral and top-down inputs, time-varying parameters ω and ν define ongoing excitatory and inhibitory gamma rhythms ($T = 25ms$), θ is the adaptive intrinsic excitability of the unit, $\sigma = 0.001$ parameterizes the multiplicative Gaussian white noise η_t, and ϵ is an unspecific excitatory drive which depends on the number n of units in the module.

The network operates in discrete successive fragments termed *decision cycles* or *gamma cycles* that are defined by frames of the ongoing excitatory and inhibitory rhythms ω and ν (Fig. 1 **(A)**), identifiable with fast cortical gamma rhythms ($40 - 100Hz$) [3]. A frame of a gamma cycle serves as a reference window for executing the WTA computation. The cycles are synchronized across distributed modules, modulating lateral inhibition and thus the competition strength simultaneously within each module from low at the beginning of a cycle to high at its end. This produces highly sparse activity during course of a cycle, selecting and amplifying only few winner units in the network. Importantly, due to self-excitatory nature of unit's dynamics, winner units become active even in absence of external afferent input ([4], Chap. 2.1), so that the network is able to generate spontaneous sparse activity without being driven from outside (Fig. 1 **(B)**).

Homeostatic Regulation of Intrinsic Excitability. The network modification during on-line learning is governed by two adaptive mechanisms, a bidirectional synaptic plasticity and a non-synaptic plasticity of unit intrinsic excitability [1, 4]. We focus on the latter mechanism, as synaptic plasticity turns out to be not relevant for the phenomenon studied here. Synapse-unspecific intrinsic plasticity is modeled as a homeostatic activity regulation mechanism that tunes unit excitability θ (see Eq. 1) on a time scale much slower (six orders of magnitude) than neural dynamics, using the history of previous unit activation :

$$\frac{d\theta}{dt} = \tau_\theta^{-1}(p_{aim} - \langle p \rangle),$$

(2)

where $\langle p \rangle = \frac{1}{T}\int_t^{t+T} p(t)dt$ is the average unit activity measured over the period T of a gamma cycle, p_{aim} specifies the target activity level and $\tau_\theta^{-1} = 10^{-4}ms^{-1}$ is the inverse time constant. The target activity level p_{aim} is a simple function of the number of units n in a module, $p_{aim} = \frac{1}{n}$. The initial value of the intrinsic excitability is $\theta(0) = 0$.

Given the strong competitive character of the neuronal dynamics, the regulation of the intrinsic excitability θ changes the *a priori* probability of a unit to be the winner

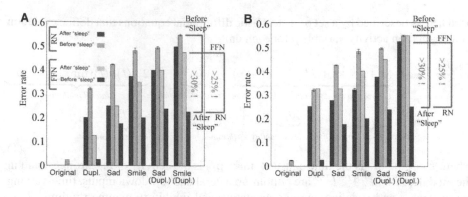

Fig. 2. Comparison of recognition performance before and after the off-line memory reprocessing on the original and alternative face views. Synaptic plasticity was disabled during the off-line regime, while unit excitability regulation was still active. Two network configurations, fully recurrent (RN) and purely feed-forward (FFN), were tested (see text). Identity error rate for the higher identity **(A)** and the lower vocabulary layer **(B)** is shown.

in a gamma cycle. By tuning less active units more and overactive units less excitable and thus imposing uniform winning probability, the mechanism enforces a uniform usage load across the network units, assuring their equal participation in memory trace formation during the on-line learning phase [1, 4].

On-line Training Procedure, Off-line Mode and Performance Evaluation. Before learning, the initial network is in state of undifferentiated, intermodular all-to-all connectivity within and across the layers, all excitatory synapses - bottom-up, lateral and top-down - being plastic (Fig. 1 (**A**)). The network is trained in an incremental, unsupervised fashion on natural face images from the AR database [5], which contains different alternative views for 40 persons. The training set comprised only images with neutral facial expression. Each training image was picked randomly and presented at the begin of a gamma cycle as a collection of local Gabor filter banks extracted from specified landmarks (6 landmarks in total, Fig. 1 (**A**)). Each module on the lower memory layer subserves one landmark and contains $n = 20$ units. The identity module on the higher layer contains $m = 40$ units (Fig. 1 (**A**)). As the learning procedure is *open-ended*, the system runs until reaching a stable mature connectivity state and no significant changes can be registered neither in the synaptic connectivity nor in the training error (after approximately $4 \cdot 10^5$ gamma cycles). Both adaptive mechanisms, bidirectional synaptic plasticity and homeostatic activity regulation, are active during on-line learning.

The memory network which emerges during the on-line learning is able to self-generate activity without external stimuli, so that we can stop presenting images and put it in an off-line regime [6]. Back in on-line regime, we test the person identity recognition performance for both layers on the original views from the training data set and on the alternative face views not shown before. We can then compare the performance after the off-line memory reprocessing with the performance the system showed before going into the off-line regime. During the test, both synaptic plasticity and homeostatic activity regulation are disabled, so that it is reassured that no further changes in the network organization can occur. To define a recognition error during the test phase, we use previous history of network responses to face images observed during unsupervised learning. Network response can be then interpreted as a guess for a face identity on the input that can be either right or wrong.

3   Results

Strong and Rapid Improvement via Self-generated off-line Reprocessing.   Following the simulation setup described above, we put the trained network after a prolonged period of on-line learning (ca. $4 \cdot 10^5$ gamma cycles) into the off-line regime by removing image input. Due to the self-excitatory, but competitive unit dynamics, the network continues to run autonomously, generating patterned sparse activity similar to that observed during on-line learning (Fig. 1 (**B**)). For each gamma cycle spent in off-line regime, one such a sparse pattern is produced, containing an assembly of winner units. Some of the patterns are replay of memory traces for face identities stored in the memory. Other patterns can be arbitrary combinations of vocabulary and identity units that may be interpreted as "phantasized" faces never experienced during on-line learning.

The network runs in the off-line regime until no substantial changes in the network organization (synaptic weights and units' intrinsic excitabilities) can be observed. The network is then again exposed to face images in the test mode, where both synaptic and intrinsic plasticity are disabled, to compare its recognition performance to the performance shown before entering the off-line regime. After the off-line mode, the network shows a substantial boost in recognition performance across all face views, the original and the alternative ones not shown before, on both layers (Fig. 2). Surprisingly, this boost remains unaffected even if synaptic plasticity is disabled during the off-line regime. This means that the observed improvement in network function is independent of synaptic connectivity modifications and can be completely explained by changes induced by synapse-unspecific, homeostatic regulation of unit excitability during the off-line regime.

Furthermore, the improvement is hardly seen on original face views used during the training, while the boost is tremendous for the alternative views not shown before. The drop in the error rate for face identity observed on the both network layers after off-line reprocessing amounts up to 30% on alternative views (Fig. 2). Thus, the off-line memory reprocessing improves particularly the ability of the network to generalize over new, previously unexperienced data. Interestingly, already short time spent in the off-line regime is sufficient to achieve the positive effect. Spending few thousands (ca. $3 - 6 \cdot 10^3$) cycles in the off-line regime turns out to be enough to boost the network performance (compared to about $4 \cdot 10^5$ cycles needed to create mature network organization during on-line learning).

Excitability Equalization Is Responsible for the Strong Performance Boost.   As synaptic connectivity modification can be ruled out from being responsible for the performance boost observed after the off-line regime, we take a look at changes of excitability that is homeostatically regulated across the network units in the off-line mode.

Examining the simulation data, a striking trend towards layerwise equalization of initially different unit excitability levels is revealed. Excitability levels move closer

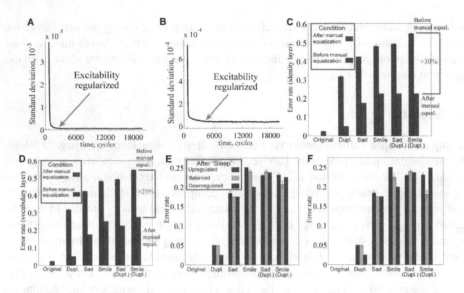

Fig. 3. Excitability equalization during the off-line regime on the lower vocabulary layer (**A**) and higher identity layer (**B**). Excitability levels become equalized as indicated by shrinkage of their within-layer standard deviation. (**C**), (**D**) Excitability equalization done manually by hand produces the same positive effect. The positive effect is further independent of regulation direction. Identity error for the identity layer (**E**) and for the vocabulary layer (**F**) is shown following downregulation, upregulation or no change of the average layerwise excitability.

together, approaching a common value already after a short time spend in the off-line regime (around $3 \cdot 10^3$ cycles). This equalization, or regularization, of intrinsic excitability constitutes the main effect exerted on network organization by the off-line reprocessing. To test whether this equalization is indeed the cause of observed improvement, we simply set excitability levels of the original network equal by hand, surpassing the reprocessing in the off-line regime. The very same positive effect is then observed when comparing the recognition performance of the equalized network against the non-equalized one (Fig. 3 (**C**)). Hereby, the excitabilities can be set to the minimum, the average or the maximum layerwise value, without a significant difference in the produced improvement (the value can also be computed for each module). This indicates that the positive effect is independent of particular direction of excitability regulation.

The same observation is made if employing different off-line regimes that lead either to downregulated, upregulated, or balanced average equalized excitability in the network (Fig. 3 (**D**), (**E**)). The performance improvement turns out to be again largely independent of the regulation direction. Taken together, these findings confirms that the main cause of the positive effect is the equalization of the excitability levels within the network layers, performed by homeostatic activity regulation during the off-line regime in absence of external stimulation.

Only Weak Off-line Performance Boost for Purely Feed-forward Network Architecture. Having obtained these results, we asked how a purely feed-forward version (FFN) of the original network architecture would benefit from off-line reprocessing and how it would compare to the fully recurrent network (RN) employed so far. We trained a network that utilized only bottom-up synaptic connectivity during on-line learning, being otherwise identical to the original fully recurrent network. The training procedure, the off-line regime and test phase afterwards remained the same.

We looked at recognition performance of the both network configurations, comparing them in the state before and after the off-line reprocessing (Fig. 2). From the comparison, it becomes apparent that the FFN gains only slight improvement after the off-line regime for the higher layer, for the lower layer the recognition performance even decreases. Remarkably, before entering off-line regime the comparison of recognition performance slightly favors the FFN. This situation changes dramatically after off-line reprocessing. There, the RN strongly outperforms the FFN for both layers. The advantage of the RN over its purely feed-forward version is particularly strong for the alternative face views not shown to the networks during on-line learning. Apparently, the organization of the fully recurrent network is by far more susceptible to the positive effect of off-line reprocessing than the organization of its purely feed-forward version.

4   Discussion

The studied network model highlights an intriguing possibility that network function can be strongly improved without ever changing the organization of synaptic connectivity. This is different from most modeling work on learning in neural networks, where synaptic plasticity is the main force behind network reorganization. It is natural then to speculate about why excitability equalization causes this improvement. As the positive effect is particularly strong for novel data, it is tempting to think that excitability equalization removes an overfitting effect that is imposed onto the network as a result of exposure to the limited training data observed during on-line learning. In this case, overfitting affects network unit excitability levels, which then get equalized without intervening external stimuli during off-line reprocessing. This equalization, which may be seen as a regularization procedure, restores then network capability to generalize over novel data when back in the on-line regime.

Interestingly, there is strong evidence that memory reprocessing during brain off-line states may enhance learning, improving declarative and non-declarative memory formation [7, 8]. Following our findings, homeostatic excitability regulation [9, 10] becomes a promising candidate mechanism that can be made responsible for the functional improvements observed in behavioral experiments. It could induce the improvement without relying on synapse-specific plasticity and without altering the network connectivity organization, and it could do it fast, providing explanation for behavioral improvement observed even after ultra-short naps [11, 12]. A related hypothesis is provided by Tononi and Cirelli, stressing the importance of local synaptic strength homeostasis and renormalization for the maintenance of ongoing plasticity [13, 14, 15]. This is different and not mutually exclusive from synapse-unspecific regulation of neuronal excitability that reorganizes globally network memory traces as proposed here.

The model presented here can be further extended to a full wake-sleep learning cycle containing off-line states where synaptic plasticity is active, resembling REM-sleep and waking rest. In those states, off-line replay may lead to a different quality of structural network reorganization, including memory trace stabilization and amplification and reduction of interference between competing traces that overlap substantially [16, 17]. Considerung full wake-sleep cycle advocates the view of memory formation and maintenance as a constantly evolving dynamic multi-stage learning process that utilizes different modes during both stimulus coupled and stimulus decoupled states. The ultimate aim of such a process is of course to optimize memory function, delivering an evolutionary explanation for the different regimes of sleep being manifest in the nervous system of most living organisms [18].

References

1. Jitsev, J., von der Malsburg, C.: Experience-driven formation of parts-based representations in a model of layered visual memory. Front. Comput. Neurosci. 3, 15 (2009)
2. Lücke, J.: Receptive field self-organization in a model of the fine structure in V1 cortical columns. Neural Comput. 21(10), 2805–2845 (2009)
3. Fries, P., Nikolić, D., Singer, W.: The gamma cycle. Trends Neurosci. 30(7), 309–316 (2007)
4. Jitsev, J.: On the self-organization of a hierarchical memory for compositional object representation in the visual cortex. PhD thesis, Goethe University Frankfurt, Frankfurt Institute for Advanced Studies (November 2010)
5. Martinez, A.M., Benavente, R.: The AR face database. Technical Report 24, CVC Technical Report 24 (June 1998)
6. Jitsev, J., von der Malsburg, C.: Off-line memory reprocessing following on-line unsupervised learning strongly improves recognition performance in a hierarchical visual memory. In: International Joint Conference on Neural Networks (IJCNN), pp. 3123–3130. IEEE (July 2010)
7. Rasch, B., Born, J.: Maintaining memories by reactivation. Curr. Opin. Neurobiol. 17(6), 698–703 (2007)
8. Diekelmann, S., Born, J.: The memory function of sleep. Nat. Rev. Neurosci. 11(2), 114–126 (2010)
9. Zhang, W., Linden, D.J.: The other side of the engram: experience-driven changes in neuronal intrinsic excitability. Nat. Rev. Neurosci. 4(11), 885–900 (2003)
10. Karmarkar, U.R., Buonomano, D.V.: Different forms of homeostatic plasticity are engaged with distinct temporal profiles. Eur. J. Neurosci. 23(6), 1575–1584 (2006)
11. Axmacher, N., Haupt, S., Fernández, G., Elger, C.E., Fell, J.: The role of sleep in declarative memory consolidation–direct evidence by intracranial EEG. Cereb. Cortex 18(3), 500–507 (2008)
12. Lahl, O., Wispel, C., Willigens, B., Pietrowsky, R.: An ultra short episode of sleep is sufficient to promote declarative memory performance. J. Sleep Res. 17, 3–10 (2008)
13. Tononi, G., Cirelli, C.: Sleep and synaptic homeostasis: A hypothesis. Brain Res. Bull. 62(2), 143–150 (2003)
14. Olcese, U., Esser, S.K., Tononi, G.: Sleep and synaptic renormalization: A computational study. J. Neurophysiol. 104(6), 3476–3493 (2010)
15. Tononi, G., Cirelli, C.: Sleep and the price of plasticity: from synaptic and cellular homeostasis to memory consolidation and integration. Neuron 81(1), 12–34 (2014)
16. Crick, F., Mitchison, G.: The function of dream sleep. Nature 304(5922), 111–114 (1983)
17. Baran, B., Wilson, J., Spencer, R.C.: REM-dependent repair of competitive memory suppression. Exp. Brain Res. 203(2), 471–477 (2010)
18. Cirelli, C., Tononi, G.: Is sleep essential? PLoS Biol. 6(8), e216 (2008)

Lateral Inhibition Pyramidal Neural Networks Designed by Particle Swarm Optimization

Alessandra M. Soares, Bruno J.T. Fernandes, and Carmelo J.A. Bastos-Filho

Polytechnic School of Pernambuco, University of Pernambuco, Brazil
{ams3,bjtf,carmelofilho}@ecomp.poli.br

Abstract. LIPNet is a pyramidal neural network with lateral inhibition developed for pattern recognition, inspired in the concept of receptive and inhibitory fields from the human visual system. Although this network can implicitly extract features and use these features to properly classify patterns in images, many parameters must be defined prior to the network training and operation. Besides, these parameters have a huge impact on the recognition performance. This paper proposes an encoding scheme aiming at optimizing the LIPNet structure using Particle Swarm Optimization. Preliminary results for a face detection problem using a well known benchmark set showed that our approach achieved better classification rates when compared to the original LIPNet.

Keywords: LIPNet, Neural Networks, Pattern Recognition, Machine Learning, Particle Swarm Optimization, Swarm Intelligence.

1 Introduction

Computer vision applications have attracted a lot of attention in the last years, specially for face detection [1], optical character identification [2] and writing recognition [3]. Alongside, many Artificial Neural Networks (*ANN*) architectures have been developed to tackle many tough problems, such as data clustering, data compression, function regression and pattern recognition [4]. For the case of pattern recognition, some *ANN* architectures have been proposed to enable implicit feature extraction [4]. In principle, this is a desired characteristic for a recognition system, since the *ANN* designer does not need to pre-define shapes or geometric relationships between the elements to be recognized.

Aiming to include the implicit feature extraction capability in the *ANN*s for image processing, Phung and Bouzerdoum [5] proposed the *PyraNet*, which was inspired in the receptive fields of the human visual system. According to Mao and Massaquoi [6], the use of inhibitory fields can increase the stability and efficiency of *ANN*s. Based on this, Fernandes *et al* [7] proposed to include a lateral inhibition mechanism in *PyraNet*, resulting in a novel *ANN*, called *LIPNet* (Lateral Inhibition Pyramidal Neural Network). *LIPNet* presented promising results when compared to other state-of-the-art *ANN*s [7].

Particle Swarm Optimization (*PSO*) [8] is an optimization algorithm suitable to tackle hyper dimensional problems with continuous variables. Teixeira *et al* [9]

S. Wermter et al. (Eds.): ICANN 2014, LNCS 8681, pp. 667–674, 2014.

and Santos *et al* [10] showed that *PSO* can be used successfully for training One-dimensional *ANN*s. Since the definition of the *LIPNet* parameters results in a high impact on the recognition rates, our hypothesis is that better results can be obtained if the *LIPNet* parameters are optimized.

In this paper we propose to use the *PSO* algorithm in order to optimize the *LIPNet* parameters aiming at improving the recognition rates. The remainder of the paper is organized as follows: Section 2 presents the theoretical background, highlighting the basic concepts related to the *LIPNet*, and the encoding scheme deployed for the *PSO* optimization. In Section 3, simulations are detailed and their respective results are presented. Finally, Section 4 summarizes the main contributions and suggests some future work.

2   LIPNet Designed by Particle Swarm Optimization

In the human eye, photoreceptor cells are located in a region called retina and are responsible for generating electrical impulses when stimulated by light. Sensory neurons are connected to a specific region of the retina and an appropriate stimulus in this region leads to a response of these neurons. This region is called the receptive field [11]. After that, the impulses are driven by the optic nerve to the brain from neurons located in a lower-layer to neurons in an upper-layer.

Rizzolati and Camarda [12] perceived that the application of another simultaneous stimulus within the same receptive field can affect the neuron response. In this case, this lateral stimulus acts as a neural inhibitory effect: an active neuron is able to negatively interfere in the output of its neighbouring neurons. This effect was incorporated in the *PyraNet* to generate the *LIPNet* model.

The *LIPNet* architecture is depicted in Fig. 1a. There are two types of layer: Two-dimensional layers, which enable the extraction of implicit patterns and allows dimensionality reduction; and One-dimensional layers, which are responsible for image classification based on the features extracted in the previous layer. As shown in Fig. 1a, the first 2D layer receives an image as input and each neuron (located at an immediately upper-layer) is associated with a region of neurons in the previous layer, the receptive field (dashed square), generating a pyramidal topology. The One-dimensional layers are shown in the right side of Fig. 1a. The interface between the two types of layer is performed by mapping the neurons from a matrix (2D) to a vector (1D). In general, the number of neurons in the output layer of the *LIPNet* is equal to the number of training classes. In this case, the output of each neuron in this layer gives the probability of an image to belong to its respective class.

Still in Fig. 1a, the relation between the 2D layer neurons is highlighted. A neuron at position (u, v) of layer l binds to neurons belonging to their receptive field in layer $l-1$. The receptive fields size is denoted by $r \times r$. The superposition between adjacent receptive fields can occur and is denoted by the overlap o. The lateral inhibition is emphasized in Fig. 1a by filled arrows, in which the output of a neuron in the origin of each arrow interferes negatively in the neuron pointed by the arrow in the same layer. The force with which the neighbors influence the

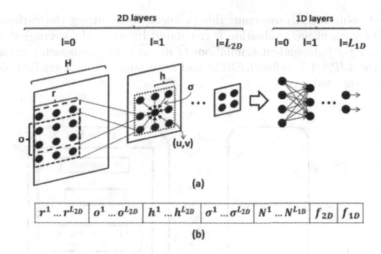

Fig. 1. LIPNet Architecture: (a) overview of the network topology illustrating the inhibitory process in the 2D-layer number 1, and (b) encoding scheme for the particle

output of a neuron depends on the inhibitory weight σ. This effect only occurs between neurons in the same layer, within an inhibitory field (dotted square) radius h. L_{2D} and L_{1D} are, respectively, the quantity of 2D and 1D layers.

As mentioned in the previous Section, *PSO* is used to define the *LIPNet* parameters. Fig. 1b illustrates the structure of the particle for the optimization process. As can be observed, many parameters are to be optimized for both types of layers. For each 2D layer l, the variables are: the width of each receptive field (r^l), the overlap in each layer (o^l), the radius of the inhibitory field in each layer (h^l), the lateral inhibition weight in each layer (σ^l) and the activation function used in the 2D layers (f_{2D}). For each 1D layer, the variables are: the number of neurons in each layer (N^l) and the activation function deployed in the One-dimensional layers (f_{1D}). One can observe that the number of layers L_{2D} and L_{1D} must be defined in advance. We considered that the 2D layers, receptive and inhibitory fields are squared. The size H of the 2D layer l is given by (1), and H^0 equals the input image size, since the first 2D layer corresponds to a one-to-one mapping of input image.

$$H^l = \left\lfloor \frac{H^{l-1} - o^l}{r^l - o^l} \right\rfloor. \tag{1}$$

Fig. 2 summarizes the optimization scheme, illustrating the relationship between inputs and outputs. First, the optimization algorithm receives the quantity of 2D layers (L_{2D}) and 1D layers (L_{1D}) as inputs. In order to evaluate the fitness of each particle, a *LIPNet* is built based on the current values for the parameters contained in the particle. Then, the initialization, training and testing procedures of the *LIPNet* are executed and the obtained fitness is returned. Since we assumed that the *LIPNet* weights are randomly initialized for the training phase, then two or more evaluations with the exact same parameters may result in distinct solutions. To overcome this problem, by reducing the variability of the results, each fitness evaluation is calculated by using the average value obtained from q_{fit} independent simulations ($\overline{Fitness}$). The approach proposed for training the *LIPNet* is called *RPROP* and is an adaptation of gradient descent for two dimensional layers [7].

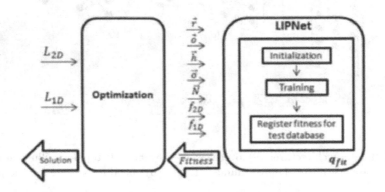

Fig. 2. Optimization scheme

Each group of variables of the particle has different characteristics and generates different constraints. Because of this, it is necessary to treat each groups of variables separately. In addition, some dependency relationships must be taken into account. As an example, the overlap must necessarily be smaller than the receptive field. Thus, the update of velocities and positions must obey an order of precedence. For the result provided by a particle to be valid, the premise $H^l \geq H^l_{min}$ must be obeyed, so the quantity of 2D layers (L_{2D}) is constant for any particle in the swarm. Since H^l is calculated from r and o (see Eq. 1), then, necessarily, there is at least one combination of receptive field r and overlap o which eases the premise and the minimum size of the receptive field $r_{min} = 2$ simultaneously. Otherwise, if $r > r_{max}$ or $o < o_{min}$, it is impossible to obtain L_{2D} layers. Hence, H^l_{min} is given by (2).

$$H^l_{min} = (r_{min})^{L_{2D}-l}. \tag{2}$$

Table 1 highlights the precedence and the maximum and minimum boundaries assumed by each dimension of the particle. The assumed range is [minimun, maximum), in order to consider the truncation of discrete variables.

If L_{2D} and L_{1D} are not treated as constants in the optimization process, they would cause loss of information when reducing or increasing the amount of layers. A possible consequence if this rule is not obeyed is, particles which were previously valid, could become invalid. All variables of the particle, except the inhibitory weights, are truncated by the *PSO* for the assessment of the *LIPNet*.

Table 1. Precedence and boundaries for the encoded variables

Element	Precedence	Minimum	Maximum
r^l	-	r_{min}	$r_{max} = H^{l-1} - H^l_{min} + 2$
o^l	r^l	$o_{min} = \left\lceil \frac{H^l_{min} r^l - H^{l-1}}{H^l_{min} - 1} \right\rceil$	$o_{max} = r^l$
h^l	o^l	$h_{min} = 0$	$h_{max} = (H^l - 1)/2 + 1$

3 Experimental Results

We selected the face detection problem in order to validate our proposal and compare with previous results [7]. Images were extracted from the database of faces of the Center for Biological and Computational Learning (CBCL) [13]. CBCL is divided into two groups: training and testing. The training base is composed by 2429 training faces and 4548 non-faces. The group for test has 472 faces and 23573 non-faces. All images are in grayscale and their size is 19×19. For all images, we applied the global histogram equalization. The training and validation benches used in experiments were extracted from the training base of the CBCL, whereas we used the complete test database for the testing phase.

Fitness evaluation is based on ROC curves which relates True Positive classification rates and False Positive error rates. The accuracy is assessed using the Area Under the Curve (AUC) [14], which is bounded by the interval [0, 1]. AUC values closer to 1 means better performance.

We considered two possible activation functions: logistic sigmoid and hyperbolic tangent. For all simulations, we considered $r_{min} = 2$, $\sigma_{min} = 0.1$ and $\sigma_{max} = 30$. The initialization ranges for the variables of the particles are depicted in Table 2, in which $\Delta x = x_{max} - x_{min}$ and x is a generalization for r, o, h and σ. These boundaries are based on the equations outlined in Table 1.

Five different runs were performed for the optimization process, in which we used 10 particles, $q_{fit} = 10$ and a maximum of 30 iterations for each *PSO* run. In order to allow the comparison with the results obtained in [7], the same number of layers was used ($L_{1D} = 1$ and $L_{2D} = 2$). The stop criterion for the *LIPNet* training is given by cross validation: when the maximum of 500 iterations is achieved, or the evaluation of bank validation stagnate for 30 seasons, or when the validation error grows for 30 iterations consecutively. In this case, when the training phase is finished, the network weights are updated according to the weights of the season in which the lowest validation error is found.

Regarding positive training bench, we randomly selected 100 faces among the first 1000 of the base. The same procedure was adopted for the negative training bench. For the validation bench, we considered the first 500 images not belonging to the training bench for both positive and negative databases. Once the training and the validation databases are generated, they are kept constant for all particles and all fitness evaluations.

Table 2. Range for initialization of particles

Elemento	r^l	o^l	h^l	σ^l
Min	$r_{min} + 0,25\Delta r$	$o_{min} + 0,5\Delta o$	$h_{min} + 0,5\Delta h$	σ_{min}
Max	$r_{max} - 0,25\Delta r$	o_{max}	h_{max}	$\sigma_{max} - 0,8\Delta\sigma$

3.1   Results

After five *LIPNet-PSO* runs, we obtained a maximum AUC equal to 0.89 and a minimum AUC equal to 0.865. The average value for the AUC was 0.875, which is a little bit lower than 0.878, which is the value obtained in [7]. Nevertheless, this difference is irrelevant compared to the effort required to adjust the network parameters empirically. Analysing from other point of view, after five trials, the *LIPNet-PSO* found superior configurations when compared to the original set of parameters defined for the *LIPNet* in [7]. In rode to assess the quality of the configuration provided by the *PSO*, we performed 10 LIPNet training trials using the best set of parameters returned by the *PSO* (*LIPNet-PSO*) and 10 LIPNet training trials using the configuration proposed in [7]. Fig. 3 presents the AUC for both cases applied to test data. The AUC values for the *LIPNet-PSO* are in average higher than the AUC values found by using the configuration proposed in [7]. We performed the Wilcoxon non parametrical test with 5% significance, and confirmed that the solution found by *LIPNet-PSO* is statistically better.

Furthermore, the maximum classification rate achieved is in agreement with the result obtained in [7], where the best result is a solution with non-zero inhibitory fields. However, we observed that the *PSO* is susceptible to be trapped

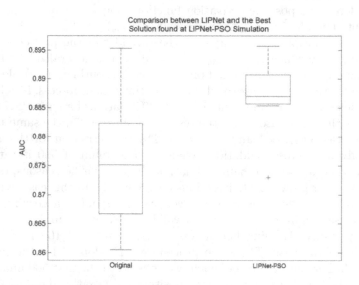

Fig. 3. Boxplot of the AUC values obtained for the original *LIPNet* [7] and for our proposal *LIPNet-PSO*

Table 3. Comparison between classifiers

Classifier	PyraNet	SVM	LIPNet	LIPNet-PSO
Average AUC	0.86	0.886	0.878	0.89

in local minima, since the worst value of AUC found for *LIPNet-PSO* is lower than the AUC average value found by the configuration proposed in [7]. This suggests that the proposed optimization process is not able to identify the best solution in some cases. This probably happened because *PSO* is originally designed to handle continuous variables and most of the variables are discrete, causing a convergence to local minima.

Table 3 shows a comparison between the average AUC value found for different classifiers that perform implicit feature extraction and applied to test data. As one can observe, our proposal achieved the best results. Specifically, the Support Vector Machine (*SVM*) used is nonlinear with polynomial kernel based on the results of Makine and Raisamo [15] for face detection.

The best configuration obtained by LIPNet-PSO is ($r^1 = 7$, $o^1 = 4$, $h^1 = 2$, $\sigma^1 = 5.56$), ($r^2 = 4$,$o^2 = 2$, $h^2 = 0$), f_{2D} and f_{1D} are the logistic sigmoid.

4   Conclusions

We proposed to apply *PSO* in order to define automatically the *LIPNet* parameters, such as the size of receptive and inhibitory fields. The results showed that the *PSO* is able to find configurations that present better rates than those found in [7]. Furthermore, the classification rate confirmed the result obtained in [7], where the best result obtained is a solution with non-zero inhibitory fields. However, the proposal is still not robust to avoid local minima in every case. Then, for future work, we aim to test evolutionary techniques in order to reduce this susceptibility. Furthermore, the training algorithms based on gradient descent are susceptible to be trapped on local minima [16] [17] and depending on the dimensionality of the search space, many local minima can be found in the search space for large *ANN*s. Therefore, we aim to apply a meta-heuristic for defining the synaptic weights.

References

1. Rowley, H.A., Baluja, S., Kanade, T.: Neural network-based face detection. IEEE Transactions on Pattern Analysis and Machine Inteligence 20(1), 23–38 (1998)
2. Ganis, M.D., Wilson, C.L., Blue, J.L.: Neural network-based systems for handprint OCR applications. IEEE Transactions Image Processing 7(8), 1097–1112 (1998)
3. LeCun, Y., Bottou, L., Bengio, Y., Haffner, P.: Gradient-based learning applied to document recognition. Proceedings of IEEE 86(11), 2278–2324 (1998)
4. Fukushima, K., Miyake, S., Ito, T.: Neocognitron: A neural network model for a mechanism of visual pattern recognition. IEEE Transactions on Systems, man and Cybernetics, SMC 13(5), 826–834 (1983)

5. Phung, S.L., Bouzerdoum, A.: A pyramidal neural network for visual pattern recognition. IEEE Transactions on Neural Networks 18(2), 329–343 (2007)
6. Mao, Z.-H., Massaquoi, S.G.: Dynamics of winner-take-all competition in recurrent neural networks with lateral inhibition. IEEE Transactions on Neural Networks 18(1), 55–69 (2007)
7. Fernandes, B.J.T., Cavalcanti, G.D.C., Ren, T.I.: Lateral inhibition pyramidal neural network for image classification. IEEE Transactions on Cybernetics 43, 2082–2092 (2013)
8. Bratton, D., Kennedy, J.: Defining a Standard for Particle Swarm Optimization. In: IEEE Swarm Intelligence Symposium, SIS, pp. 120–127 (2007)
9. Teixeira, L.A., Toledo, F.S.R., Oliveira, A.L.I., Bastos-Filho, C.J.A.: Adjusting weights and architecture of neural networks through pso with time-varying parameters and early stopping. In: SBRN 2008 (the 10th Brazilian Symposium on Neural Networks), pp. 33–38 (2008)
10. Santos, S.M., Valença, M.J.S., Bastos-Filho, C.J.A.: Comparing particle swarm optimization approaches for training multi-layer perceptron neural networks for forecasting. In: Yin, H., Costa, J.A.F., Barreto, G. (eds.) IDEAL 2012. LNCS, vol. 7435, pp. 344–351. Springer, Heidelberg (2012)
11. Levine, M., Shefner, J.: Fundamentals of sensation and perception. Oxford Univ. Press (2000)
12. Rizzolati, G., Camarda, R.: Inhibition of visual responses of single units in the cat visual area of the lateral suprasylvian gyrus (Clare-Bishop area) by the introduction of a second visual stimulus. Brain Research 88(2), 357–361 (1975)
13. Heisele, B., Poggio, T., Pontil, M.: Face detection in still gray images. Technical report. Center for Biological and Computational Learning. MIT (2000)
14. Bradley, A.P.: The use of the area under the roc curve in the evaluation of machine learning algorithms. Pattern Recognition 30(7), 1145–1159 (1997)
15. Makinen, E., Raisamo, R.: Evaluation of gender classifications methods with automatically detected and aligned faces. IEEE Transactions on Pattern Analysis and Machine Intelligence 30(3), 541–547 (2008)
16. Riedmiller, M., Braun, H.: A direct adaptive method for faster backpropagation learning: The rprop algorithm. In: Proc. IEEE Int. Conf. Neural Networks, pp. 586–591 (1993)
17. Wang, X., Wang, H., Dai, G., Tang, Z.: A reliable resilient backpropagation method with gradient ascent. In: Huang, D.-S., Li, K., Irwin, G.W. (eds.) ICIC 2006. LNCS (LNAI), vol. 4114, pp. 236–244. Springer, Heidelberg (2006)

Bio-mimetic Path Integration
Using a Self Organizing Population of Grid Cells

Ankur Sinha and Jack Jianguo Wang*

Faculty of Engineering and Information Technology
The University of Technology
Sydney, Australia
ankur.sinha@student.uts.edu.au,
jianguo.wang@uts.edu.au

Abstract. Grid cells in the dorsocaudal medial entorhinal cortex (dMEC) of the rat provide a metric representation of the animal's local environment. The collective firing patterns in a network of grid cells forms a triangular mesh that accurately tracks the location of the animal. The activity of a grid cell network, similar to head direction cells, displays path integration characteristics. Classical robotics use path integrators in the form of inertial navigation systems to track spatial information of an agent as well. In this paper, we describe an implementation of a network of grid cells as a dead reckoning system for the PR2 robot.

1 Introduction

Navigation is a capability any animal must possess to survive. It is also a capability that must be implemented in a mobile robotic system capable of carrying out any meaningful tasks. It is known that even smaller mammals, such as rats, have sufficiently well developed navigation systems that enable them to carry out tasks necessary for their survival, such as foraging for food or finding shelter. It is, therefore, of great interest to study these biological navigation systems and attempt to implement bio-mimetic navigation systems on robots.

Discoveries of neurons that provide information on the agent's spatial parameters, such as head direction cells[9,15], place cells[12] and grid cells[6], have lead to the formation of a cognitive map theory[10,8,18,13,11] of biological navigation. This theory states that via a combination of neurons with specific behaviours, animals maintain a "cognitive map" of their environment.

The collective firing of grid cells gives rise to a regular triangular lattice representation of the location of the animal. These neurons, similar to head direction cells, have path integrator components that integrate velocity signals, like an INS[1].

In section 1.1 , we briefly introduce grid cells and their computational modelling. We then detail our model in section 2. In section 3, we present our results and briefly discuss challenges and our future work plans in section 4. Finally, we summarize and conclude in section 5.

* We're most grateful to Dr. Xun Wang at the "Magic" Lab, The University of Technology, for his inputs and assistance with the PR2 robot.

S. Wermter et al. (Eds.): ICANN 2014, LNCS 8681, pp. 675–682, 2014.
© Springer International Publishing Switzerland 2014

1.1 Grid Cells

Grid cells in the dorsocaudal medial entorhinal cortex of rats were observed by Hafting and colleagues[6] when they were looking for spatial information upstream from the hippocampus that could project on to place cells. They observed neurons with multiple discreet fields of similar amplitude in the dMEC and recorded spike activity in the region to ascertain the presence of a map like organization. On observing the autocorrelogram, neurons considered as central peaks were observed to be surrounded by six nearly equidistant neurons at angular separations of 60°, forming a regular triangular grid. The number of activity nodes increased with the size of the environment, suggesting a structure with infinite size. Unlike head direction and place cells where no topographical structure is observed, grid cells exhibit a precise topographical organization. Also unlike neurons in the hippocampus where neuron sets vary per environment, the grid structure appears common across environments.

As with head direction and place cells, various computational models have been proposed that attempt to model the grid like firing patterns exhibited by grid cells. In their recent review[5], Giocomo and colleagues have classified these models into two categories: oscillatory-interference models which use changes in membrane potential oscillator frequencies to encode speed and direction information into grid patterns; attractor based networks which use specific activity of a local set of neurons to generate grid patterns. Our model belongs to the latter category since we use Hebbian style learning rules to set up local excitation between neurons to produce the required grid attractor network.

We humbly refer the reader to recent reviews for further information on the properties of grid cells[2] and their computational modelling[5].

2 Methods: The Model

The model detailed here is a modified version of the self organizing two dimensional attractor network model Stringer et al. proposed for place cells[17]. In the original model, Stringer and colleagues detailed how their one dimensional attractor model for a head direction cell system[16] could be extended to two dimensions to produce place fields. The model successfully set up a two dimensional attractor network using Hebbian style learning rules and displayed spatial firing patterns consistent with biological observations of place cell networks. While using similar Hebbian style learning rules, we make modifications to the structure of the network required for the formation of a triangular lattice of neurons, rather than a traditional co-ordinate map. We also modify the organization process to ensure that the lattice forms a toroid of grid cells, rather than a flat map to work around edge effects.

2.1 Structure

Figure 1a shows a schematic of the neuron sets implemented in the model. The model consists of two fully connected attractors, one for the head direction cell set and another for the grid cell set. The head direction cell set has also been implemented on the ROS platform and is detailed in another, unpublished work[1]. Each head direction cell, HD_i is connected to every other head direction cell HD_j via recurrent synapses w_{ij}^{HD}. Similarly, every grid cell, G_k is connected to every other grid cell G_l via recurrent synapses w_{kl}^G. In this way, each synapse possesses a pre-synaptic and post-synaptic neuron necessary for our Hebbian learning based organization rule. The head direction cell set takes input from a set of rotation cells, ROT_m, which project angular velocity information on to them via synapses, $w_{ijm}^{HD\text{-}ROT}$. Similarly, a set of velocity cells, VEL_n, project speed information on to the grid cell set via synapses $w_{kln}^{G\text{-}VEL}$. It is noteworthy that these synapses are *effective synapses* in that they represent the synaptic weight between a pre-synaptic head/grid cell, the rotation/velocity cell, and the post-synaptic head/grid cell. A set of visual feature cells, VIS_o projects on to both the head direction and grid cell sets via synapses $w_{io}^{HD\text{-}VIS}$ and $w_{ko}^{G\text{-}VIS}$ respectively. The visual feature cells are used for initial training of the synapses only in this model and represent an abstraction of the visual processing system.

2.2 Dynamics

We employ a model similar to the one proposed by Stringer et al. for place cells[17]. The activation of each grid cell, G_k is given by:

$$
\tau \frac{\mathrm{d}h_k^G(t)}{\mathrm{d}t} = -h_k^G(t) + \frac{\phi_0}{C^G} \sum_l (w_{kl}^G - w^{INH})r_l^G(t)
$$

$$
+ \frac{\phi_1}{C^{G \times HD \times VEL}} \sum_{ljn} (w_{kjn}^{G\text{-}VEL} r_l^G(t) r_j^{HD}(t) r_n^{VEL}(t)) \tag{1}
$$

$$
+ \frac{\phi_2}{C^{G \times VIS}} \sum_o (w_{ko}^{G\text{-}VIS} r_o^{VIS}(t))
$$

Here, τ is the time constant while ϕ_0, ϕ_1, ϕ_2, C^G, $C^{G \times HD \times VEL}$, $C^{G \times VIS}$ and w^{INH} are tunable parameters. These parameters control the effect the respective inputs have on the grid cell attractor. w^{INH} represents global inhibition that the GABAergic interneurons exert on the system. The combination of local excitation of grid cells and the global inhibition gives the system continuous attractor characteristics.

The firing rate of each grid neuron is a sigmoid function of its activation:

$$
r_k^G(t) = f(h_k^G(t)) = \frac{1}{1 + e^{-2\beta(h_k^G(t) - \alpha)}} \tag{2}
$$

where α and β are constants. Figure 3a shows the firing rate profile exhibited by the grid cell lattice after stabilization during a test run . Due to the regular

---

[1] Paper submitted to IJCNN 2014 for consideration.

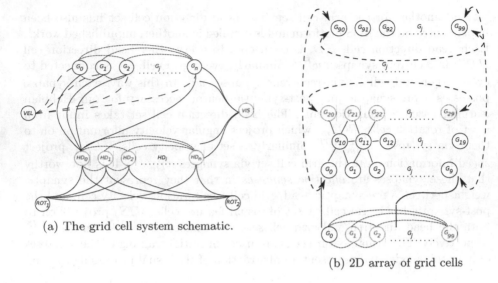

(a) The grid cell system schematic.

(b) 2D array of grid cells

Fig. 1. The grid cell model

learning employed in this implementation, the firing rates of all grid cells are similar. This isn't the case in biology, where the firing rates of grid cells vary from one another and from layer to layer.

The synapses between all neuron sets are set up using Hebbian learning:

$$\Delta w = k.(r^{post} * r^{pre}) \tag{3}$$

Here, Δw is the change in synaptic weight. k is the *learning rate* of the synapse. r^{pre} and r^{post} are the firing rates of the pre-synaptic and post-synaptic neurons respectively. This learning rule does not, however, include synaptic depression, or bounding of synaptic weights. We use a competition based normalization rule to bound our synapses:

$$\hat{w} = \frac{w}{|w|} \tag{4}$$

Here $|w|$ is the norm of the w matrix and $\hat{w}$ is the normalized synaptic weight. It is worth noting that the above normalization departs from the Hebbian learning requirement of *locality*[4],i.e., the synapse between two neurons should only be modified by their behaviour. Various formulations of Hebbian learning have been proposed to overcome this shortcoming[3]. However, we use the normalization rule for sake of simplicity.

3   Experimental Procedure and Results

We implemented the model based on the ROS(Robot operating system)[14] platform which provides support for a number of robots, including the PR2. For development and testing, we collected data bags from the IMU sensors of the PR2

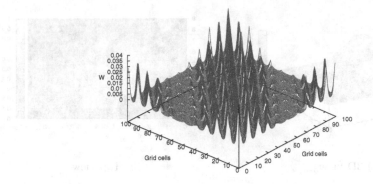

Fig. 2. Recurrent synaptic weight in grid cells

robot to run our simulations. We extended our earlier work on head direction cells to also include grid cells. We used a hundred grid cells to form a 10×10 mesh, and a hundred head direction cells to cover the 360°direction space. We used two rotation cells, one each for clockwise and anti clockwise rotation, a single speed cell, and a single visual cell (Figure 1a).

The grid cell lattice merits some discussion. Conforming to biological observations, we designed a regular triangular lattice as shown in Figure 1b. Each cell is assigned a *preferred location* such that it coincides with the vertices of the equilateral triangles of the lattice. The distance between any two adjacent neurons is, therefore, one unit. Figure 1b shows how our implementation expands out to a two dimensional lattice.

The system runs in three phases:

3.1   Setting Up of Synaptic Weights to Appropriate Values

During this phase, we set up the synaptic weights in the network to their appropriate values. The network is initialized with all synaptic weights as zero, implying that no learning or association has taken place between the sets of neurons. In order to set up both the internal grid cell synapses w_{kl}^{G} and the effective velocity synapses $w_{kjn}^{G\text{-}VEL}$, we simulate movement in the system in the four major directions: forward, backward, left and right; neuron by neuron by projections from the visual feature cell. The firing rate of a grid cell is calculated as a function of the distance between it's preferred location and the preferred direction for the respective training iteration, ΔS:

$$r_l^G = exp(-\frac{1 + \Delta S^2}{2\sigma^{G2}}) \tag{5}$$

where ΔS is given by:

$$\Delta S = \sqrt{(min(|x|, |10 - x|))^2 + (min(|y|, |(10 * (\sqrt{3}/2)) - y|))^2} \tag{6}$$

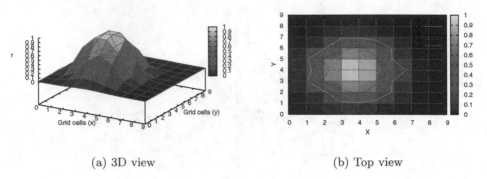

(a) 3D view   (b) Top view

Fig. 3. Stabilized activity packet

where, for each neuron G_k with preferred location $x_k^{preferred}$, $y_k^{preferred}$ for a location X, Y

$$(x, y) = (X, Y) - (x_k^{preferred}, y_k^{preferred}) \tag{7}$$

σ^G controls the width of the Gaussian profile. The above formulation of ΔS ensures the formation of a regular toroidal continuous attractor neural network.

In order to calibrate the synapses of the network, we simulate activity in the input neuron sets: visual feature cell, velocity cell and head direction cells. Projections from the visual feature cell force a firing profile in the grid cell network which acts as the post synaptic neuron set. Since the velocity and head direction cells are simultaneously simulated to fire in accordance, they function as pre-synaptic neurons in our Hebbian style learning rule.

Figure 2 shows the recurrent synaptic weights of the grid cell network, w_{kl}^G. As expected, the synaptic weights are maximum for neurons with similar preferred directions and decrease as the difference in preferred directions increase.

3.2 Initializing the Network with an Initial Packet of Activity

Once the synapses are trained, the network is initialized with a packet of activity which is the initial location or reference location of the system. An initial packet of activity is forced on to the grid cell attractor via projections from the visual cell and permitted to stabilize in the absence of input. Figure 3a shows the two dimensional attractor with a packet of activity after initialization. Note that in order for the packet of activity to be stable in the absence of input, as is the characteristic of an attractor network, both the recurrent synaptic weights between the grid cells and the constants, ϕ_0 and w^{INH}, that control the behaviour of the network must be set up correctly. (If this is not the case, the packet of activity will not be maintained in the absence of inputs and will instead *flatten out*.)

3.3   Running the System with Velocity Information

The firing rate of the rotation cells and the velocity cell are linear functions of the angular velocity and forward velocity respectively. The angular velocity is first integrated in the head direction cell attractor which in turn projects on to the grid cell set attractor. The rate at which the activity packet translates depends on the strength of projections on to the network: projections from the velocity set and the head direction cell set.

4   Discussion

A combination of head direction cells, border cells and grid cells can be thought to provide a complete path integrator system in biology. In spite of successful modelling of head direction and grid cells, our system is not yet complete enough for deployment as a bio-mimetic system.

The first issue to be tackled is the calibration of constants in the system that map movement in world co-ordinates. A method based on evolutionary algorithms has been employed by Kyriacou for a one dimensional head direction attractor network[7] that could be extended to our two dimensional attractor. Even when the system has been calibrated to exhibit considerable accuracy, it still suffers from the issue of drift, like any other path integrator. In order to correct drift, these neuron sets anchor to visual landmarks in biology. Implementing such a visual feature system that will project on to our attractors is a task we consider important for progress towards a complete bio-mimetic navigation system. In order to complete the bio-mimetic navigation system which the robot could use to navigate to goal locations safely, the implementation of other neuron sets such as place cells, border cells, and a reward system are also required. We set these as our future work.

5   Conclusion

In this paper, we detail the implementation of a grid cell network for bio-mimetic navigation. Our system uses self organized Hebbian synapses to train a two dimensional attractor network, the activity packet in which responds to angular velocity and speed inputs from head direction and velocity cells to encode the location of the agent. The navigation stack in the ROS platform is based on classical robotic techniques due to the robustness of such systems, which has been tested and improved over time. On the other hand, computational modelling with bio-mimetic navigation as a goal is still a field in its infancy. The aim of our work is to bridge the gap between robotics and bio-mimetic navigation at a lower, neural level, rather than just at a high, behavioural one. In the process, we hope to contribute to both neuroscience and robotics with our interdisciplinary research.

References

1. Barshan, B., Durrant-Whyte, H.F.: Inertial navigation systems for mobile robots. IEEE Transactions on Robotics and Automation 11(3), 328–342 (1995)
2. Derdikman, D., Moser, E.I.: A manifold of spatial maps in the brain. Trends in Cognitive Sciences 14(12), 561–569 (2010)
3. Gerstner, W., Kistler, W.M.: Mathematical formulations of hebbian learning. Biological Cybernetics 87(5-6), 404–415 (2002)
4. Gerstner, W., Kistler, W.M.: Spiking neuron models: Single neurons, populations, plasticity. Cambridge University Press (2002)
5. Giocomo, L.M., Moser, M.B., Moser, E.I.: Computational models of grid cells. Neuron 71(4), 589–603 (2011)
6. Hafting, T., Fyhn, M., Molden, S., Moser, M.B., Moser, E.I.: Microstructure of a spatial map in the entorhinal cortex. Nature 436(7052), 801–806 (2005)
7. Kyriacou, T.: Using an evolutionary algorithm to determine the parameters of a biologically inspired model of head direction cells. Journal of Computational Neuroscience 32(2), 281–295 (2012)
8. McNaughton, B.L., Battaglia, F.P., Jensen, O., Moser, E.I., Moser, M.B.: Path integration and the neural basis of the 'cognitive map'. Nature Reviews Neuroscience 7(8), 663–678 (2006)
9. Muller, R.U., Ranck, J.B., Taube, J.S.: Head direction cells: properties and functional significance. Current Opinion in Neurobiology 6(2), 196–206 (1996)
10. Muller, R.U., Stead, M., Pach, J.: The hippocampus as a cognitive graph. The Journal of General Physiology 107(6), 663–694 (1996)
11. Nadel, L., MacDonald, L.: Hippocampus: Cognitive map or working memory? Behavioral and Neural Biology 29(3), 405–409 (1980)
12. O'Keefe, J.: Place units in the hippocampus of the freely moving rat. Experimental Neurology 51(1), 78–109 (1976)
13. O'Keefe, J.: The hippocampal cognitive map and navigational strategies (1991)
14. Quigley, M., Conley, K., Gerkey, B., Faust, J., Foote, T., Leibs, J., Wheeler, R., Ng, A.Y.: Ros: an open-source robot operating system. In: ICRA Workshop on Open Source Software, vol. 3 (2009)
15. Ranck Jr., J.: Head direction cells in the deep cell layer of dorsal presubiculum in freely moving rats. In: Society for Neuroscience Abstracts, vol. 10 (1984)
16. Stringer, S., Rolls, E., Trappenberg, T., De Araujo, I.: Self-organizing continuous attractor networks and path integration: two-dimensional models of place cells. Network: Computation in Neural Systems 13(4), 429–446 (2002)
17. Stringer, S., Trappenberg, T., Rolls, E., Araujo, I.E.T.: Self-organizing continuous attractor networks and path integration: one-dimensional models of head direction cells. Network: Computation in Neural Systems 13(2), 217–242 (2002)
18. Trullier, O., Meyer, J.A.: Animat navigation using a cognitive graph. Biological Cybernetics 83(3), 271–285 (2000)

Learning Spatial Transformations
Using Structured Gain-Field Networks

Jan Kneissler and Martin V. Butz

Cognitive Modeling, Department of Computer Science,
Eberhard Karls University of Tübingen, Tübingen, Germany
{jan.kneissler,martin.butz}@uni-tuebingen.de

Abstract. Brains experience sensory information grounded in sensor-relative frames of reference. To compare sensory information from different sensor sources, such as vision and touch, this information needs to be mapped onto each other. To do so, the brain needs to learn suitable spatial transformations and the literature suggests that gain fields accomplish such transformations. However, when transforming three dimensional spaces or even six dimensional configuration spaces then simple gain fields do not scale to such a dimensionality. We are investigating how this curse of dimensionality can be overcome. Based on neural population-encoded, component-wise spatial representations, we show that a hierarchy of gain fields can accomplish higher-dimensional transformations and that its weights can be learned effectively by means of standard backpropagation.

Keywords: Population Code, Gain Field, Multilayer Network, Back-Propagation, Hierarchical Decomposition, Function Approximation.

1 Introduction

Particularly in the parietal cortex, where sensory information from multiple sensory sources including proprioception and touch as well as auditory and visual information are combined [1,2], the brain integrates information sources, which are encoded in strongly differing frames of reference. While visual information, for example, is encoded retinotopic, tactile information is encoded skin-relative. To map these two information sources onto each other, a kinematic model about the own body and estimates about the current body posture are necessary.

Evidence continues to accumulate that suggest that the parietal cortex accomplishes to map different information sources onto each other by employing gain-field encodings [3,4]. Also velocity information appears to be mapped in a similar manner [5]. Moreover, a strong behavioral relevance has been postulated for such encodings [6,7,4]. Even causal relations and mirror neuron structures appear to depend on gain field encodings [8]. However, learning gain fields was typically restricted to one or two dimensional spaces, if learning was applied at all [6]. Here we investigate how gain fields can be learned in higher dimensions.

We assume spatial representations based on neural population codes [9]. In doing so, we mimic typical receptive field properties of primary sensory neurons.

S. Wermter et al. (Eds.): ICANN 2014, LNCS 8681, pp. 683–690, 2014.

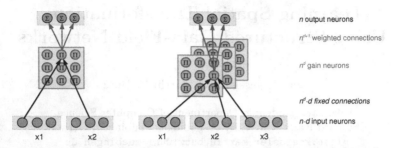

Fig. 1. A gain field network for modeling an arbitrary multidimensional mapping: the function arguments and the output are supposed to be encoded in d populations, consisting of n input neurons each. The intermediate layer of gain neurons has n^d multiplicative units, corresponding to all possible ways of selecting single neurons in the input populations. Thus each gain neuron has d inputs (not weighted), exactly one per input population. The gain neurons are fully connected to the n output neurons. The activities of an output neuron are given by the weighted sum of all gain neurons' outputs. Shown are the cases $n = 3$, $d = 2$ (left) and $n = 3$, $d = 3$ (right), omitting all connections except those of the gain neuron $(1, 2)$ and $(2, 3, 1)$, respectively.

Moreover, such representations allow the representation of multimodal distributions and enable flexible Bayesian information processing [10]. Nonetheless, the encoded spaces should not be larger than three dimensional, as otherwise the encodings become too coarse-grained.

For example, when representing kinematic chains with more than two degrees of freedom (dofs) – such as the seven dofs of a human arm – such a space is hardly representable in a sufficiently fine-grained resolution with a seven-dimensional population code. Modularization is required. A highly modularized, neural model of a human arm is available, in which each population code is maximally three dimensional [11]. This model represents arm limbs and joints in separate but interactive modules, continuously integrating sensory information in each module and respective frame of reference and exchanging information across frames of reference to maintain an overall consistent arm state estimate. Despite the model's modularity, the involved spatial transformations are still rather elaborate and limited in their scalability.

Combining the gain field motivation, the challenge of mapping multiple sensory information sources onto each other, and the aim to represent a complete human body effectively (ultimately for realizing highly flexible behavior control), we investigate how higher-dimensional spatial transformations can be learned effectively using population encodings and gain-field structures.

2   Methods

2.1   Function Approximation by Gain Fields

We utilize gain field networks to represent multidimensional functions of the form $f : \mathbb{R}^d \to \mathbb{R}$, $(x_1, \ldots, x_d) \mapsto f(x_1, \ldots, x_d)$. We assume that only a bounded sub-range $[a, b]^d$ of the input space is relevant and that input and output values are encoded by means of a population code. The structure of a gain field is shown in Fig. 1: The internal multiplicative gain units are arranged in the form of a d-dimensional hypercube, where each unit is connected to the d input neurons corresponding to its coordinates. We assume that input neurons' activities follow a narrow Gaussian centered at the value of the corresponding input coordinate. Since the gain units multiply the activities of their inputs, only a few gain neurons close to the place of the current d dimensional input vector (mapped into the hypercube) show significant activity. Thus, the hypercube directly encodes the relevant part of the input space.

By adjusting the connection weights from each gain unit to the output population, one obtains a network effectively reproducing the desired transformation specified in the target function f.

2.2 Representing Decomposable Functions as Binary Trees

In addition to the usual requirement that f is smooth, we assume that f can be constructed using a set of component functions (f_i), each of which having exactly two arguments. For example, the inner product function in $3D$ space (which has 6 arguments, thus $d = 6$) can be composed out of two component functions $f_1(a, b) = a + b$ and $f_2(a, b) = a \cdot b$ in the following way:

$$x_1 \cdot y_1 + x_2 \cdot y_2 + x_3 \cdot y_3 = f_1\Big(f_1\big(f_2(x_1, y_1), f_2(x_2, y_2)\big), f_2(x_3, y_3)\Big)$$

Formally, we define that a function f with d arguments shall be called *decomposable* if $f(x_1, \dots, x_d) = g\big(h_1(x_{i_1}, \dots, x_{i_k}), h_2(x_{j_1}, \dots, x_{j_m})\big)$, where h_1 and h_2 are decomposable and $k, m < d$. The identity function $id(x) = x$ shall also be considered *decomposable*.

The computation of any decomposable function f can be arranged in form of an oriented graph whose internal vertices all have exactly two incoming edges. If the value computed at each node is represented in a population code, and the two incoming edges are combined via a gain field, we obtain a *gain field network* that computes f using gain fields of dimension no higher than $d = 2$.

Due to our interest in mappings between different coordinate systems, we restrict ourselves to the special case that the subsets of indices $\{i_1, \dots, i_k\}$ and $\{j_1, \dots, j_m\}$ are disjoint, which means that each variable is at most only once in the computation. In this case the graph always takes the form of a binary tree. We asked the question if such binary gain field trees can be learned effectively by backpropagation.

2.3 Supervised Learning in Gain Field Networks

Clearly, in the case of a single-layer network, when the number of observed samples exceeds n^d, the weights can be optimally estimated by means of linear regression. We are however more interested in online-capable learning paradigms and thus analyze the performance of the well established back-propagation algorithm (that can be extended in a straightforward way to networks with multiplicative units): Inputs are applied to the lowest layer, activities are propagated towards the outputs where the deviation with the target is calculated and propagated backwards through the network to lead to updates of the weights $\mathbf{w}$ that follow the negative gradient of the sum of squared errors E. We use a normalized version of the weight update: $\Delta \mathbf{w} = -\eta \frac{E}{\|\nabla_{\mathbf{w}} E\|^2} \nabla_{\mathbf{w}} E$. This has the advantage that the dynamic range of the optimal learning rate η becomes comparable for different setups (typically between 0.1 and 1.0). We apply a learning momentum to reduce the effect of random fluctuations.

2.4 General-Purpose Multilayer Gain-Field Networks

The binary gain field trees require an explicit knowledge of the structure of the function to be learned. We propose using a general purpose multilayer gain field architecture, which can represent any decomposable function. To do so, all we have to do is to provide a layered feed-forward network with

- sufficiently many layers ($\geq$ the nesting depth of the decomposition),
- sufficiently many neurons per layer (to act as neural populations required at that nesting level),
- a gain unit for each pair of neurons in the same layer (connecting these two neurons to all neurons of the next layer).

Note that any binary gain field graph (not only trees) can be emulated in this architecture, simply by disabling the gain units that are not needed, by setting the weights of all outgoing connections to 0.

2.5 Complexity Analysis

The classical (single layered) gain field of Sec. 2.1 modeling a function of dimension d with n neurons per population requires n^d gain units and n^{d+1} adjustable weight values (see Fig. 1). Representing a decomposable function by a binary gain tree network requires $n^2(d-1)$ gain units and $n(d-2)$ internal neurons and has to learn $n^3(d-1)$ weight values. The general-purpose network that connects a layer of p neurons with the next layer of q neurons has $\frac{1}{2}p(p-1)$ gain units and $\frac{1}{2}p(p-1)q$ weighted connections. Assuming that the number of neurons is decreasing by at least a factor of 2 from one layer to the next (i.e. $q \leq \frac{1}{2}p$) throughout the network and starting with an initial input layer size of $p = nd$, the network size is bounded by $\frac{2}{3}n^2d^2$ gain units, nd internal units, and $\frac{2}{7}n^3d^3$ weighted connections.

This analysis shows that the use of networks of gain fields is beneficial for $d \geq 3$ and effectively circumvents exponential network size growth. In the next section we evaluate if such structures can be indeed learned effectively by means of backpropagation.

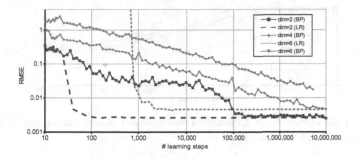

Fig. 2. Curse of dimensionality: Learning the inner product functions. Learning curves for $n = 5$, produced by online back-propagation (solid lines labeled "BP") and linear regression (dashed lines, labeled "LR").

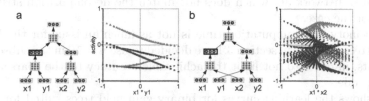

Fig. 3. Examples of binary gain-field trees for $d = 4$ together with activity profiles of intermediate neurons (box with thick border) dependent on the product of the two used inputs. The activity was evaluated for all 441 pairs of inputs $\in \{-1, -0.9, \ldots, 0.9, 1\}$ and is shown in different symbol and color for each neuron of the population ($n = 5$). **a:** Tree according to the decomposition of the inner product mapping $x_1 \cdot y_1 + x_2 \cdot y_2$. **b:** Tree not suitable for representing the inner product mapping.

3 Results

3.1 Single Gain Field Layer

Using a single, exponentially growing gain field layer, the target function can be learned sufficiently well, albeit at a cost of increasingly high learning times, as the dimensionality of the problem rises (Fig. 2). Roughly speaking, for $d = 6$ the number of iterations required to reach a certain performance (e.g. 0.1) is multiplied by a factor of 1000 compared to $d = 2$. The back-propagation algorithm is able to eventually reach the optimal performance (determined by linear regression, see dashed lines), but only after a huge number of learning steps: 10^5 for $d = 2$, 10^7 for $d = 4$.

3.2 Binary Gain-Field Trees

First we tested, for the simplest case $d = 2$, our intuition that a decomposition of the mapping would be automatically realized when a gain-field network with a suited topology is utilized. We trained the two networks Fig. 3, with 5 neurons

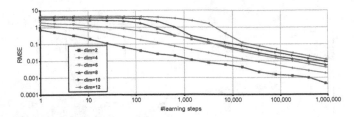

Fig. 4. Learning curves using gain-field trees tailored to the target function (inner product) for $d = 2, 4, 6, 8, 10, 12$ ($n = 10$)

per population, until the error had become sufficiently small. In network 3a, which matches the decomposition of the target function, the neurons in the intermediate populations encoded the product of the two respective input values. In the control network 3b, which does not match the decomposition structure, this was not the case.

Since memory and computation time is not as much an issue for the binary gain-field trees as it was in section 3.1, we decided to use $n = 10$ in the subsequent experiments, in order to not limit the achievable accuracy by the coarseness of the neural code.

Fig. 4 shows the learning curves for binary gain field trees suited for calculating the target function for $d = 2, \ldots, 12$. At some point, the slopes become independent of the dimension and the offset increases with d. However, unlike Fig. 2, the factor in learning time from one dimension to the next, now appears to decrease with dimensionality and much higher dimensions can be learned.

Apparently, the curse of dimensionality is not only broken with respect to computational effort, but also with respect to learning times.

3.3   General-Purpose Multilayer Gain-Fields

Fig. 5c illustrates, for $d = 6$, that the proposed multilayer gain-field network performs almost as good as the tree specifically adapted to the structure of the target function. Fig. 5d shows that also the higher dimensional general purpose networks can be learned quite well, with an approximate offset factor of roughly 2 per additional input dimension.

4   Future Work

The connection matrices produced in all but the last layer are usually densely populated. In order to take the dramatic complexity gain derived in Sec. 2 one step further (to $O(n^2 d^2)$ parameters instead of $O(n^3 d^3)$), it would be necessary to force the learning to establish and maintain sparsity. In principle, an almost perfect approximation that uses only a few outgoing connections per gain unit is possible. However, the space of solutions of equal accuracy is large and the current learning algorithm does not necessarily find the desirable sparse solution.

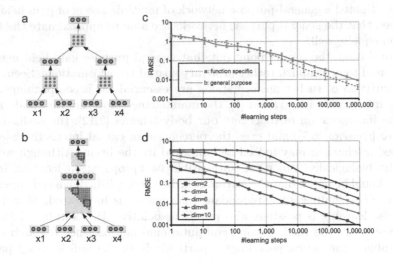

Fig. 5. Learning an unstructured multi-layer gain field network. *a:* Function-specific topology for $d = 4$. *b:* Unspecific topology for $d = 4$ with same number of internal (additive) neurons. The gain units enclosed in the squares are the ones that are used when emulating the topology of the network of panel a. *c:* Comparison of learning performance ($d = 6$, $n = 10$). *d:* Learning curves for $n = 10$ and $d = 2, 4, 6, 8, 10$.

Thus, we are currently working on adding sparsity-enforcing learning mechanisms to the architecture to generate more compact spatial transformations.

Furthermore, we are investigating if the requirement of representing the input spaces in form of orthogonal coordinate systems is necessary. It is unlikely that an Euclidean coordinate system is established in the brain before spatial transformations are learned. Rather, we may assume that some arbitrary local coordinate functions are represented in the input population codes and that the set of coordinate functions is redundant (there are more populations than the dimensionality of the problem requires). It is in our opinion highly relevant to verify if our findings generalize to this biologically even more plausible setting.

5 Summary

We have shown that gain-field trees can suffer much less from the curse of dimensionality when trying to acquire multidimensional, structured mappings. In the case of the inner product, which is relevant to mappings arising in transformations between redundant body representations, we have seen that the cost factor in computational resources and learning time observed in the transition from $1D$ to $3D$ body models for the classical gain field approach is drastically reduced when using a gain field tree that is tailored specifically to the target function's structure.

As it is very questionable that the function structure can be presumed in the architecture of the neural network (in the brain fixed by evolution), we also investigated a general-purpose network of multiple layers of gain fields. We have seen that the general-purpose networks are able to approximate the target function equally well.

In conclusion, the results point-out that general purpose gain-field networks can be used to accomplish rather arbitrary spatial transformations. Seeing that the calculation of such transformations are essential for accomplishing multi-sensory information integration [1], the maintenance of an internal body model [11], the incorporation of tools into our body schema [2,12], the realization of adaptive behavior [6,7], and even the perception of causal interactions [8], the proposed mechanism may indeed be employed by the brain. Although we have used the biologically somewhat implausible backpropagation learning in this case, it should be noted that the learning can be accomplished in a self-supervised manner, when multisensory, redundant information is integrated. Moreover, if stage-wise learning is possible, also purely associative, Hebbian-based learning mechanisms may be used. Future, computational neuroscience research should thus evaluate the neural encodings – particularly in the multisensory parietal areas – further to reveal in which way general purpose, multilayer gain fields may be actually implemented by the brain.

References

1. Calvert, G.A., Spence, C., Stein, B.E. (eds.): The Handbook of Multisensory Processes. MIT Press, Cambridge (2004)
2. Holmes, N.P., Spence, C.: The body schema and multisensory representation(s) of peripersonal space. Cognitive Processing 5, 94–105 (2004)
3. Andersen, R.A., Essick, G.K., Siegel, R.M.: Encoding of spatial location by posterior parietal neurons. Science 230(4724), 456–458 (1985)
4. Salinas, E., Sejnowski, T.J.: Correlated neuronal activity and the flow of neural information. Nature Reviews Neuroscience 2, 539–550 (2001)
5. Hwang, E.J., Donchin, O., Smith, M.A., Shadmer, R.: A gain-field encoding of limb position and velocity in the internal model of arm dynamics. PLoS Biology 1, e25 (2003)
6. Baraduc, P., Guigon, E., Burnod, Y.: Recoding arm position to learn visuomotor transformation. Cerebral Cortex 11, 906–917 (2001)
7. Chang, S.W.C., Papadimitriou, C., Snyder, L.H.: Using a compound gain field to compute a reach plan. Neuron 64, 744–755 (2009)
8. Fleischer, F., Christensen, A., Caggiano, V., Thier, P., Giese, M.: Neural theory for the perception of causal actions. Psychological Research 76(4), 476–493 (2012)
9. Pouget, A., Dyan, T., Zemel, R.: Information processing with population codes. Nature Reviews Neuroscience 1, 125–132 (2000)
10. Doya, K., Ishii, S., Pouget, A., Rao, R.P.N.: Bayesian brain: Probabilistic approaches to neural coding. The MIT Press (2007)
11. Ehrenfeld, S., Herbort, O., Butz, M.V.: Modular neuron-based body estimation: Maintaining consistency over different limbs, modalities, and frames of reference. Frontiers in Computational Neuroscience 7(148) (2013)
12. Maravita, A., Driver, J.: Cross-modal integration and spatial attention in relation to tool use and mirror use: Representing and extending multisensory space near the hand. In: Calvert, G.A., Spence, C., Stein, B.E. (eds.) The Handbook of Multisensory Processes, pp. 819–835. MIT Press, Cambridge (2004)

Flexible Cue Integration by Line Attraction Dynamics and Divisive Normalization

Mohsen Firouzi[1,2,3], Stefan Glasauer[2,3,4], and Jörg Conradt[1,2,3]

[1] Neuroscientific System Theory, Technische Universität München, München, Germany
[2] Bernstein Center for Computational Neuroscience, München, Germany
[3] Graduate School of Systemic Neurosciences, Ludwig-Maximilians-Universität, München, Germany
[4] Center for Sensorimotor Research, Ludwig-Maximilians-Universität München, Germany
{mohsen.firouzi,conradt}@tum.de, sglasauer@lmu.de

Abstract. One of the key computations performed in human brain is multisensory cue integration, through which humans are able to estimate the current state of the world to discover relative reliabilities and relations between observed cues. Mammalian cortex consists of highly distributed and interconnected populations of neurons, each providing a specific type of information about the state of the world. Connections between areas seemingly realize functional relationships amongst them and computation occurs by each area trying to be consistent with the areas it is connected to. In this paper using line-attraction dynamics and divisive normalization, we present a computational framework which is able to learn arbitrary non-linear relations between multiple cues using a simple Hebbian Learning principle. After learning, the network dynamics converges to the stable state so to satisfy the relation between connected populations. This network can perform several principle computational tasks such as inference, de-noising and cue-integration. By applying a real world multisensory integrating scenario, we demonstrate that the network can encode relative reliabilities of cues in different areas of the state space, over distributed population vectors. This reliability based encoding biases the network's dynamics in favor of more reliable cues and realizes a near optimal sensory integration mechanism. Additional important features of the network are its scalability to cases with higher order of modalities and its flexibility to learn smooth functions of relations which is necessary for a system to operate in a dynamic environment.

Keywords: Multi-sensory Cue Integration, Line Attraction Dynamics, Divisive Normalization, Associative Hebbian Learning, Heading estimation.

1 Introduction

A key requirement for any system, including biological or man-made systems is their capability to estimate physical properties of the real world through partially reliable observations to interact properly with their environment. For instance, to reach an object by hand, one must configure the arm joints with respect to the visual location

S. Wermter et al. (Eds.): ICANN 2014, LNCS 8681, pp. 691–698, 2014.
© Springer International Publishing Switzerland 2014

of the object and proprioceptive cues [1]. Apart from intrinsic variability of neural activity in the brain, accessible sensory cues are often uncertain and ambiguous. The human brain can combine these noisy and partially reliable pieces of information to optimally estimate the state of the world and consequently handle cognitive tasks efficiently [2].

Despite decades of research the underlying cortical processing that enables us to optimally operate in ambiguous environments is not well understood yet; what the processing consists of, or even how the processed data is represented [3]. Some computational frameworks using probabilistic population code with hand-crafted connectivity have shown how de-noising, inference (estimation) and sensor perception can possibly be performed by cortical and sub-cortical circuits [1][4]. Recently an unsupervised framework of relation learning between two interacting populations of neurons has been proposed, which allows the network to learn arbitrary relations between two encoded variables [5]. However, a flexible computational framework which could learn relationships between cues rather than using fixed networks is still addressed as a challenge, especially in the presence of higher order modalities [5].

Another issue in multi-sensory integration which is less investigated is how to encode and learn reliability of cues into spatially registered form of neural activity. In fact sensory cues do not have equal distribution of reliability over sensory space. For instance, the location of visual stimuli near fovea is more reliable and identifiable than periphery ones [6].

In this work, we suggest a recurrent attractor network capable of learning arbitrary relations between one of the encoded sensory variables as a function of other variables using biologically realistic algorithms like Hebbian Learning and Divisive Normalization. In another point of view the attraction surface of the network's dynamics is the same surface (hyper-surface) of the relation function through which the network realizes a relation satisfaction mechanism. We demonstrate that after constructing plastic weights, the network is able to perform inference and reasoning, de-noising, reliability based cue-integration and decision making. This framework is well scalable for scenarios with higher order of modalities and with acceptable flexibility to wide range of smooth functions. Another important feature of the network is the possibility of spatially distributed reliability representation in form of neural encoding. In fact we can strengthen encoded activity of the stimuli according to their relative reliability so that network converges to the point on the relation surface which is closer to initial point of more reliable cue. In better word network dynamics would change more reliable cue slower than the others.

In next section we elaborate the general architecture, encoding, dynamics and learning in the network. In Section 3 some computational abilities of the network e.g. estimation, de-nosing, cue integration and decision making are shown for a linear and a non-linear relation function. In section 4 we demonstrate a practical heading estimation robotic application using a distributed dual-modal version of the proposed network. And finally section 5 summarizes and concludes the paper.

2   Attractor Network Model

2.1   General Architecture and Input Encoding

General architecture of the attractor network for a tri-modal cue integration scenario is shown in Fig.1-left. The network consists of three encoded populations (R^n) and an intermediate layer (A_{lm}). As is shown in Fig.1-right, cues are encoded by activity of the spatially distributed population of neurons with overlapping wrap-around Gaussian tuning curves. Since intrinsic neural activity in brain is governed by Poisson variability, the initial activity or equivalently selectivity of a single neuron r_i (*number of spikes per second*), is drawn from a Poisson distribution with mean firing rate of neuron tuning curves, $\Phi(\kappa, x)$; see equations below where κ and σ are constant showing activity strength and width of neurons tuning curve respectively, x^c_i is preferred value of ith neuron, ν is spontaneous activity which is set to 0.1, and finally x is input stimulus.

$$P(r_i|x) = \frac{[\Phi_i(\kappa,x)]^{r_i}}{(r_i)!} e^{-\Phi_i(\kappa,x)} \tag{1}$$

$$\Phi_i(\kappa,x) = \kappa e^{-\frac{|x-x^c_i|}{2\sigma^2}} + \nu \tag{2}$$

All neurons are linear threshold neurons and input neurons are reciprocally connected to intermediate layer A_{lm} ($W^n_{RA} = W^n_{AR}$). To keep input stimuli into topographically arranged spatial registers and to copy the cues into a common frame of reference, R^1 and R^2 populations (population vectors of x_1, x_2) are projected to the intermediate layer using a fixed *von-Mises* weighting distribution as following equation [4]:

$$W^1_{ilm} = e^{\frac{(i-l)\left(\cos[\frac{2\pi}{N}]\right)-1}{(\sigma_1)^2}}, \; W^2_{jlm} = e^{\frac{(j-m)\left(\cos[\frac{2\pi}{N}]\right)-1}{(\sigma_2)^2}} \tag{3}$$

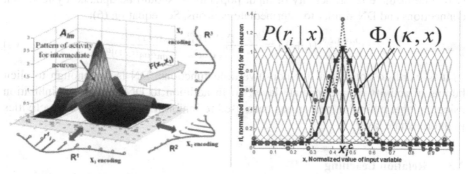

Fig. 1. Left: Network connectivity for three variables encoded by probabilistic population code, R^1 and R^2 are projected to intermediate neurons by *Von-Mises* weight pattern. The connection of third variable "x_3" is plastic so as to realize relation function $F(x_1,x_2)$.
Right: red diagram shows selectivity or the activity of the ith neuron (r_i) in response to normalized stimuli x, governed by *Poisson* variability; Blue: i^{th} neuron tuning curve or equally expected activity (Φ_i), centered at x^c_i as preferred value.

Where W^n_{ilm} is the synaptic weight between i^{th} neuron of nth input population (r_i^n) and lm^{th} intermediate neuron (a_{lm}), N is the number of neurons in each population and σ_n tunes width of projection. Synaptic connectivity between R^3 neurons and intermediate layer, W^3_{klm} (*yellow arrow in Fig.1-left*) is modifiable so as to construct the relation F by means of associative Hebbian Learning. In order to perform integration over more than three spatial cues, intermediate layer can be simply organized as a cubic or hyper-cubic topographically arranged population of neurons. Furthermore the way of encoding and line-attraction dynamics of the network, enable us to initialize input cues, based on their relative reliabilities.

2.2   Network Dynamics

Through dynamics of the network, population activities or equivalently encoded cues would be shifted so to satisfy relation function. In other word during the network's dynamics, input cues follow a trajectory to be converged toward surface of attraction in steady-state. In each time step the activity of single intermediate neuron is weighted sum of momentary activity of connected input neuron which is normalized by Divisive Normalization to keep single bumps of activities and eliminate the effect of ridge-like pattern of activities (see Fig.1-left). Equations (4)-(5) represent the dynamics of intermediate neurons:

$$A_{lm}(t+1) = \frac{(d_{lm}(t))^\alpha}{\beta + s \sum_p \sum_q (d_{pq}(t))^\alpha} \tag{4}$$

$$d_{lm}(t) = \sum_{k=1}^N W^1_{klm} r^1_k(t) + \sum_{k=1}^N W^2_{klm} r^2_k(t) + \sum_{k=1}^N W^3_{klm} r^3_k(t) \tag{5}$$

Where α is divisive power which tunes the sharpness of normalization, β is a constant bias to prevent division by zero and W^n_{klm} synaptic weight between k^{th} input neuron of nth input population and $l_{lm}{}^{th}$ intermediate neuron. After updating the activity of intermediate layer, activity of input populations should be updated by feedback connections and DN similar to intermediate neurons. See equation (6):

$$r_i^{n\{=1,2,3\}}(t+1) = \frac{[\sum_l \sum_m W^n_{ilm} A_{lm}(t+1)]^\alpha}{\beta + s \sum_{k=1}^N [\sum_l \sum_m W^n_{klm} A_{lm}(t+1)]^\alpha} \tag{6}$$

It is worth to notice that for non-invertible functions, DN is not enough to elicit bumps of activity in intermediate layer, so in addition to DN an additive inhibition using a global inhibition neuron has been used to inhibit irrelevant pattern of activities in intermediate layer.

2.3   Relation Learning

As is mentioned in previous section, to construct an arbitrary relation function $F(x_1,x_2)$ between input cues, synaptic connection of third input population with intermediate layer, W^3_{klm} can be modified by a simple associative Hebbian learning. In learning phase, after projection of R^1 and R^2 into intermediate layer followed by DN and additive inhibition, a single bump of activity would emerge, and then plastic connections would be modified as following equation (δ is learning rate):

$$W_{klm}^3(t+1) = W_{klm}^3(t) + \delta\, r_k^3\, A_{lm} \tag{7}$$

In each learning epoch, synaptic weights are normalized to maintain relative strength of connections and regulate overall synaptic drive received by a single neuron similar to Synaptic Scaling in biological neurons [7].

3   De-noising, Inference and Cue-Integration

In this section we will validate attractor network in some computational principles. The network is first trained to learn a simple linear relation function: $x_3 = x_2 + x_1$. After learning, network is initialized by noisy patterns of activity as is depicted in Fig.2a. Also R^1 has been initialized by two peaks of activity or equivalently two different stimuli located in different position in uni-sensory state space; one which is totally inconsistent with other cues according to relation and another is more consistent with other cues but not perfectly satisfies the relation. In the equilibrium state of the network's dynamics (after 10 epochs), activity of intermediate neurons will converge to a single bump of activity (Fig.3c). This bump would generate final stabilized population vectors (Fig.2b). As is shown in Fig.2b the network is able to remove internal noise perfectly. More interestingly the stimulus which is not consistent with the other stimuli has been totally removed, and the more consistent stimulus (more spatially correlated) has been strengthened (R^1 or square-red dash curve in Fig.2a & b). The hills of activities (or equally encoded variables) are moving towards being in equilibrium point where three encoded variables perfectly satisfy the relation (Fig.2c). In this network N is set to 40, $\beta = 0.1$, $s = 0.001$, $\alpha = 2$ and $\sigma = 0.45$.

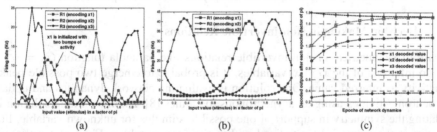

(a)   (b)   (c)

Fig. 2. (a) Initial population, (b) Population vectors after 10 epochs, (c) Decoded values in each epoch

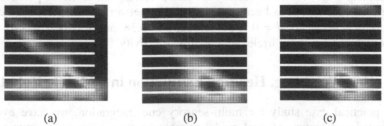

(a)   (b)   (c)

Fig. 3. Momentary transient activity of intermediate neurons emerged as a single bump of activity in stable state of network dynamic, (a) epoch=1, (b) epoch=5, c) epoch=10

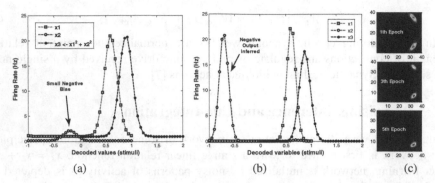

Fig. 4. (a) Initial populations, (b) Final populations, (c) Intermediate activity in 5-epochs

By initializing one of the population vectors with zero (shutting all neurons), the network can infer and retrieve the value for unknown variable that is consistent with the other initialized variables (consistency in terms of relation). Another important feature of the network is demonstrated in Fig.2c; the less reliable cue (x_1) tends to move faster (steeper trajectory) compared to the other cues. Similarly if one of the modalities is encoded by a smaller peak of activity (smaller κ in (2)) compared with the others, the attractor dynamics weights that cue as less confident cue and it would be changed faster toward being coherent with other cues with respect to relation (weighted cue integration). In section 4 by showing a realistic scenario, we will show if we perform weighted encoding or equivalently weighted projection to intermediate layer, according to relative reliability of cues (e.g. reverse of Gaussian noise power in each sensory modality), the network can simply follow a near optimal cue integration.

3.1   Decision Making in Non-invertible Relations

In case of symmetrical or non-invertible relations like parabola function ($x_3 = x_1^2 + x_2^2$), to infer one of the x_1 or x_2 variables, it is probable to emerge two possible peaks of activity as inferred value. One solution is evaluating network dynamics and updating neuron activities using an asynchronous dynamics [8]. Another simple solution is violating the symmetry in support of one possible stimulus for unknown variable. For instance if the network is initialized with a tiny negative bias (Fig.4 a) for the unknown cue, this negative bias helps the network to retrieve the negative peak for hidden variable (Fig.4 b). Consequently the bump corresponding to the positive value in the intermediate layer has been removed during network dynamics (Fig.4 c). In this network N is set to 40, $\beta = 0.1$, $s = 0.002$, $\sigma = 0.38$, and finally $\alpha = 3$ to achieve a sharper DN inhibition for irrelevant patterns of activity.

4   Cue Weighting, Heading Estimation in a Mobile Robot

As a practical case study for multi-sensory cue integration, we have evaluated a distributed architecture of dual-modal attractor networks for head estimation in an Omni-direction mobile robot [9]. The robot is equipped with an IMU unit including on board Gyroscope and Compass sensor. The robot exploring the space through a closed trajectory and an efferent copy of motor command driving wheels (*odometry*) is provided to estimate angle of heading [9]. Consequently we have three sensory readings; each is supposed to estimate the angle of heading of the robot with respect to room coordinates. We have assumed that external noise has Gaussian distribution, so simply using EM algorithm variance of noise process for a single sensor can recursively be estimated and updated by exploring around the space (from $0°$ to $360°$). Since we want to evaluate how possibly optimal, Line Attractor Network can operate in noisy environment, we have compared the network's outcome with Maximum Likelihood Estimator as a statistically optimal estimator [2]. Let's assume sensory measurements are statistically independent, so MLE optimally combines uni-sensory estimates $\{x_k\}$ by a simple weighted average computation in which weights are reversely related to noise power (variance). See equation bellow (σ_k^2 is noise power of kth sensor):

$$x_{MLE} = \frac{1}{\sum \frac{1}{\sigma_k^2}} \sum \frac{1}{\sigma_k^2} x_k \qquad (8)$$

We have evaluated two way of cue weighting in LAN network. First way which does not need any information about noise process is voting-based method [9] [10]. Simplified underlying idea of this method is that the most reliable cue is the one which is closest to Center of Gravity of all sensory estimates. In better word the best sensor is the one which is more coherent with the others. The second method is weighting the initial peak of population activities (κ in (2)) with a normalized value similar to gain filed tuning in cortical circuits and in accordance with relative reliability [11]. The normalized weight is proportional to reverse of sensory variance over exploring space. In Fig.5-down this reliability map has been shown for 1780 sample points of the state space from $0°$ to $360°$. It is clear that Compass sensor is much noisier and less reliable than Gyro and odometry. It is worth to mention that in this scenario a dual-modal version of the network with three input populations is used.

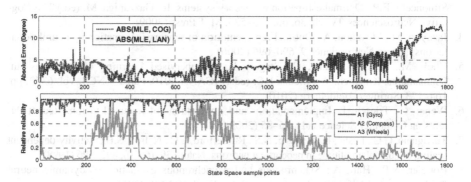

Fig. 5. Upper: Absolute error of MLE and COG voting integration algorithm, and LAN network. **Lower**: normalized relative reliability of cues calculated using recursive EM algorithm.

In Fig.5-up absolute error between MLE as an optimal estimator, and both methods are depicted and it is illustrated that the outcome of LAN network with normalized relative reliability map which is shown in Fig.5-down, is near optimal and close to MLE. Despite of simplicity of COG based weighted encoding, since it does not take into account the noise variability it is less noise robust.

5   Conclusion and Remarks

The idea of retrieving information from perturbed patterns using association networks is not new in machine learning. But the architecture of these networks is a promising and inspiring framework to understanding how cortical circuits can possibly represent, preserve and combine information to establish a coherent and robust representation of the world. On the other hand, seemingly distributed cortical areas implement functional relation between each other through mutual connectivity and correlated neural activity. In this work we have investigated how a simple recurrent attractor network can come up with relation learning amongst multiple sensory cues and how possibly to combine them in an optimal fashion. The network provides a computational framework for relation satisfaction using attraction dynamics and is able to represent cues reliabilities in a distributed form of neural activity.

Results exhibit the capability of the network to perform de-noising, cue integration and inference even for non-invertible and smooth nonlinear functions. A real world sensory integration scenario for heading estimation is investigated and it is observed that by proper encoding of the reliability, based on uni-sensory variability, the network is capable of performing weighted integration in near optimal fashion.

Acknowledgment. This work was supported by the German Federal Ministry of Education and Research, Grant 01GQ0440 (BCCN).

References

1. Pouget, A., Sejnowsky, T.J.: Spatial Transformation in the Parietal Cortex Using Basis Functions. Journal of Cognitive Neuroscience 9(2), 222–237 (1997)
2. Ernst, M.O., Bülthoff, H.H.: Merging the senses into a robust percept. Trends on Cognitive Science 8, 162–168 (2004)
3. Simoncelli, E.P.: Optimal estimation in sensory systems. In: Gazzaniga, M. (ed.) The Cognitive Neurosciences, IV, ch. 36, pp. 525–535. MIT Press (2009)
4. Jazayeri, M., Movshon, A.: Optimal representation of sensory information by neural populations. Nature Neuroscience 9, 690–696 (2006)
5. Cook, M., Jug, F., Krautz, C., Steger, A.: Unsupervised Learning of Relations. In: Diamantaras, K., Duch, W., Iliadis, L.S. (eds.) ICANN 2010, Part I. LNCS, vol. 6352, pp. 164–173. Springer, Heidelberg (2010)
6. Weber, C., Triesch, J.: Implementations and implications of foveated vision. Recent Patents on Computer Science 2(1), 75–85 (2009)
7. Turrigiano, G.G., Leslie, K.R., Desai, N.S., Rutherford, L.C., Nelson, S.B.: Activity-dependent scaling of quantal amplitude in neocortical neurons. Nature 391(6670), 892–896 (1998)
8. Rougier, N.P., Hutt, A.: Synchronous and asynchronous evaluation of dynamic neural fields. Journal of Difference Equations and Applications 17(8) (2011)
9. Axenie, C., Conradt, J.: Cortically Inspired Sensor Fusion Network for Mobile Robot Heading Estimation. In: Mladenov, V., Koprinkova-Hristova, P., Palm, G., Villa, A.E.P., Appollini, B., Kasabov, N. (eds.) ICANN 2013. LNCS, vol. 8131, pp. 240–247. Springer, Heidelberg (2013)
10. Trische, J., Von der Malsburg, C.: Democratic Integration: Self-Organized Integration of Adaptive Cues. Neural Computation 13(9), 2049–2207 (2001)
11. Brostek, L., Büttner, U., Mustari, M.J., Glasauer, S.: Eye Velocity Gain Fields in MSTd during Optokinetic Stimulation. Cerebral Cortex (in press February 20, 2014)

Learning to Look: A Dynamic Neural Fields Architecture for Gaze Shift Generation

Christian Bell, Tobias Storck, and Yulia Sandamirskaya

Institut für Neuroinformatik, Ruhr-Universität Bochum
Universitättstr. 150, 44780 Bochum, Germany
{yulia.sandamirskaya,christian.bell,tobias.storck}@ini.rub.de

Abstract. Looking is one of the most basic and fundamental goal-directed behaviors. The neural circuitry that generates gaze shifts towards target objects is adaptive and compensates for changes in the sensorimotor plant. Here, we present a neural-dynamic architecture, which enables an embodied agent to direct its gaze towards salient objects in its environment. The sensorimotor mapping, which is needed to accurately plan the gaze shifts, is initially learned and is constantly updated by a gain adaptation mechanism. We implemented the architecture in a simulated robotic agent and demonstrated autonomous map learning and adaptation in an embodied setting.

Keywords: Dynamic Neural Fields, looking, adaptation.

1 Introduction

The ability to direct gaze towards interesting objects in the surrounding environment is one of the most basic goal-directed behaviours of an embodied agent. Bringing the interesting object into the foveal (central) region of the retina not only puts the object's image into the receptive fields of a larger number of photoreceptors, but also aligns the motor system of the agent with the outside world and allows to calibrate motor plans of other motor actions directed at objects, such as reaching, pointing, or walking towards them [12]. The neural system, responsible for the looking behaviour has been studied experimentally since the beginning of the last century. The neural circuits, involved in generating the goal-directed eye movements, have been identified [4,11] and include the cerebellum, basal ganglia, superior colliculus, and the frontal eye field.

A prominent property of eye movements is their adaptability. Indeed, the saccadic eye movements[1] are too fast for the visual feedback to influence their accuracy. Thus, gaze shifts have to be planned based on the location of the visual

---

[1] Here, we don't distinguish between saccades, i.e. goal-directed eye movements with restrained head, and saccadic gaze shifts, which include both eye and head movement. See [16] for a discussion of the relation of the neural mechanisms, revealed for saccadic eye movements, and the gaze shifts. In our experiments, the robotic head was moved, which corresponds to a gaze shift.

S. Wermter et al. (Eds.): ICANN 2014, LNCS 8681, pp. 699–706, 2014.
© Springer International Publishing Switzerland 2014

stimulus on the retina. However, the pathway from the retina to the representation of the motor plan and further to muscles is subject to noise and trial-to-trial as well as developmental variations. Consequently, the amplitude of the planned gaze shift towards the object, detected on the retina, needs to be constantly updated. Indeed, the experiments on saccadic adaptation [19,17,10] reveal pervasive adaptation capacity of the eye movement circuitry in humans and primates. In these experiments, the saccadic target is shifted during the saccade, when this shift cannot be perceived by the subject. Over several trials, the amplitude of saccades to the given target changes to compensate for the error, perceived after the manipulated saccades. Neural models of this adaptation process include cerebellum and superior colliculus [6,15,2,8,3], as well as the parietal cortex [9]. Learning mechanisms based on internal feedback and the visual error after a saccade [19] have been proposed to act in this adaptive circuitry. The models of gaze shift generation, mentioned above, focus on identifying neuronal structures involved in saccades generation and adaptation. These models typically do not demonstrate autonomous processing of visual inputs in this system and actual generation and adaptation of eye movements.

Here, we present a model for saccadic gaze shifts, which includes all stages of sensorimotor processing from acquiring visual input from a simulated camera, selecting the target, generating motor command, to actually executing the motor act with simple motor dynamics and updating the sensorimotor gains when a gaze-shift error is detected. This 'wholistic' and embodied approach demonstrates how the mechanistic level of a neural architecture may be bridged with the behavioural level of an embodied agent, using the framework of Dynamic Neural Fields.

In this paper, we focus on the learning and adaptation mechanisms, which update the map of gains between the retinal representation of targets and the amplitude of the motor command, which brings the target into the fovea. The actual implementation of the model in a simulated robotic agent revealed nonlinearities in this mapping and dependence of the mapping on both the location of the target on the retina and the motor state of the system prior to the saccade. The gain map is updated based on the error after a saccade; the region of adaptation is selected autonomously based on the perceptual and motor state of the agent before the movement. Our neural-dynamic architecture may be related to the neuronal structures, involved in generation and updating of saccadic eye movements, but the focus of this work is not on neuronal modelling, but on demonstrating the adaptivity of looking behaviour and of the underlying sensorimotor circuits in an artificial system, inspired by the equivalent neuronal system.

2   Methods

2.1   Dynamic Neural Fields: Choice of the Mathematical Framework

Dynamic Neural Fields (DNFs) are continuous in time and in the underlying behavioural space descriptions of activity of neuronal populations [1,5]. DNFs are the basis of the Dynamic Field Theory [14], which aims to extend the neural-dynamic modelling approach to account for cognitive behaviour in an embodied and situated agent [13]. DNFs, which form the basis for our architecture, follow the Amari equation, Eq. 1:

$$\tau \dot{u}(x,t) = -u(x,t) + h + S(x,t) + \int f(u(x',t))\, w(x-x')\, dx', \qquad (1)$$

where $\dot{u}(x,t)$ is the rate of change of the activation function, $u(x,t)$, defined over a behaviourally relevant space x (e.g., color, location, or motor command). τ is the time constant and $h < 0$ is a negative resting level, which ensures that the DNF is silent (below activation threshold) in an inactivated state. $S(x,t)$ is input to the DNF, which may come from the sensory system or other DNFs. The last term formalizes the lateral neural interactions in the DNF, which are shaped by the interaction kernel, $w(x-x')$. The lateral connectivity is homogeneous within DNFs, with nearby sites exciting each other and far-off sites inhibiting each other. $f(\cdot)$ is a sigmoidal non-linearity, which defines the output of the DNF. This non-linearity and the lateral interactions in the field result in a special form of solution of the DNF equation – a localised activity peak, which is the unit of representation of DFT and a bridge between the continuous in time and in space dynamics of the activation function (which may be directly linked to the sensory input coming from a physical sensor) and discrete, categorical states of the cognitive system. DNFs were previously used to detect, select, and stabilise the representation of target objects, as well as to account for timing of gaze-shift generation in early models for looking behaviour [7,18,20].

2.2   The DNF Architecture for Looking

The complete DNF architecture for looking has four components, shown in Fig. 1. Adaptation of the saccadic gains happens in the gaze-shift generation system. The fixation system tracks the target during fixation and drives the memory formation processes when the target is foveated. The memory formation system

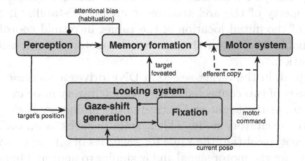

Fig. 1. The DNF architecture for looking. Shaded regions mark four components of the architecture. Arrows show direction of activation flow between different subsystems, lines with circles denote inhibitory couplings.

combines the features of the currently attended object with the motor state of the camera head when the object is fixated, creating a body-centred representation of the visual scene.

Fig. 2 shows the gaze-shift generating circuitry, which is the focus of this work. A *perceptual DNF* is defined over the retinotopic space and the visual feature (color, the third dimension, not shown in the figure). Activity peaks over salient objects in the visual field are induced in this DNF by the visual input.

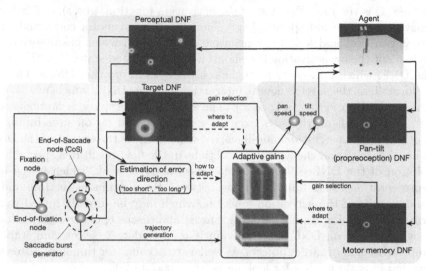

Fig. 2. The gaze-shift generation system. Shaded regions and arrows have the same meaning as in Fig. 1. Dashed lines show couplings involved in adaptation.

The perceptual DNF provides input to the *target DNF*, also defined over the retinotopic space. A single peak evolves in the target DNF over the location of the most salient object. In our architecture, the activity peak in the target DNF is stabilised by very strong lateral interactions, such that this peak is self-sustained. Once initiated, the peak conserves its location even if the initial input from the perceptual system moves (e.g., due to the initiated eye movement). This is a critical property of the architecture: it creates a stabilised, self-sustained representation of the initial location of the target in retinal coordinates, which is critical to enable learning of the gain to the motor system, associated with this retinal location.

An activity peak in the target selection DNF drives a *saccadic burst generator*, which consists of two connected nodes: the excitatory node eventually drives the motor system of the agent and activates the inhibitory node, which, in its turn, inhibits the excitatory node. This system behaves as an oscillator, which generates a stereotypical (i.e. the same for saccades of all directions and amplitudes) trajectory for the motor signal and is similar to neuronal burst generators, involved in saccades generation.

Before arriving in the motor system, the oscillatory signal is scaled with an *adaptive gain*, which depends on the location of the target object on the retina (represented by the activity peak in the target selection DNF) and the gaze direction of the agent before the saccade (represented in the *motor memory DNF*, driven by the proprioceptive inputs). These dependences are marked with "gain selection" labels in Fig. 2. The latter input is required in our robotic agent, because the mapping from the retinal locations of targets to the respective motor commands (in terms of the amplitude of pan and tilt joints' movements) is non-linear because of the geometry of the robot. In the human looking system, non-linearities come from the non-linearities of the neuromascular plant. The motor signal eventually drives the motor system, setting velocities of the two motor joints, which control the camera head in our experiments.

After a gaze shift, an *end-of-saccade node* (condition-of-satisfaction) is activated by the saccadic burst generator, which has finished its single oscillation. The end-of-saccade node activates the fixation system (see Fig. 1), which stabilises the target in the central portion of the visual field and enables memory formation for the gaze-centred representation of the foveated object. A detailed description of the fixation system, as well as memory formation are outside the scope of this paper.

The end-of-saccade node also excites an *error-estimation circuit*, which compares the location relative to the fovea of the activity peaks in the perceptual DNF (after the saccade) and in the target DNF (holding the memory for the target location before the saccade) and represents the decision whether the saccade was too short or too long along the horizontal and the vertical directions in the image plane. This error-sign signal defines whether the gain, specified by the target location and the initial motor state ("where to adapt" labels in Fig. 2), will be increased or decreased ("how to adapt" label in the figure). Next, we describe this adaptation mechanism in more detail.

2.3 Learning and Adaptation of the Sensorimotor Gain Maps

Here, we describe the learning process, which initially learns and constantly updates the gain maps if a saccadic error is detected. Initially, the gains are set to small random values and are updated according to the following learning rule:

$$\tau_l \dot{G}^{h,v}(x, y, m, t) = \epsilon^{h,v}(t) f(u_{EoS}(t)) f(u_m(m, t)) f(u(x, y, t)). \tag{2}$$

Here, $G^{h,v}(x, y, m, t)$ are two sets of gain maps (for the horizontal and vertical components of movement). Each of the m gain maps in the two sets is defined over the dimensions of the target DNF, $u(x, y, t)$. The sets span m different initial motor states (the tilt joint angle in our setup). The gains change in the map(s), which are selected by the output of the motor DNF, $f(u_m(m, t))$, at the locations, which are set by the activity peak in the target DNF. $f(u_{EoS}(t))$ is the output of the end-of-saccade node, which is required to be positive (saccade finished) for learning to become active. $\epsilon^{h,v}(t)$ is the error in each of the movement components, τ_l is the learning rate. Using this rule, the whole gain map may be learned in a learning session, where the whole visual-motor space is sampled. The map is updated locally over a few gaze-shifts if an unexpected change in the sensorimotor plant happens.

3   Results

In our learning experiments we used a simulated robot CoRa, which may be seen in the upper right corner of Fig. 2. The implementation allows to transfer the architecture onto a real robot, but this was not the focus of our work here. In this paper, we report two sets of experiments.

3.1   Learned Gain Maps

In the first experiment, we investigated how the whole gain-map may be learned by the agent based on a coarse prestructure that associates horizontal movements on the retina with the pan joint of the camera head, and vertical movements with the tilt joint, which is not correct for all initial joint configurations. The objects were placed systematically (on a virtual 16x15 grid in the image, projected on the table) in front of the simulated robot to sample the whole visual space. The initial camera head pose was also varied systematically to sample the whole space of initial motor states (we used only five different initial poses).

Fig. 3 shows the learned gain maps for five slices along the tilt motor dimension. It took 6000 saccades to learn these maps (i.e. approx. five saccades per location and initial tilt). In our experiments, the pan angle of the initial pose of the robot did not affect the gain maps, because of the geometry of the robot. The dependence on the initial tilt angle was successfully learned by the agent and calibrated the sensorimotor mapping, needed to direct actions at the visually perceived objects.

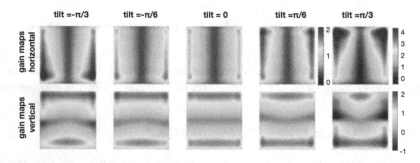

Fig. 3. Gain maps: each map is defined over retinotopic (image-based) coordinates. Maps are arranged according to the initial state (tilt angle) of the camera head. Note that the gain maps change with the initial tilt angle.

3.2   Adaptation Experiments

In the second set of experiments, we simulated a gaze adaptation session, in which the target object was displaced during the saccade. This shift is not perceived by the system, since the activity peak in the target DNF is self-sustained

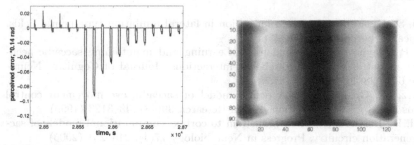

(a) Gaze shift error. Blue: horizontal, (b) The adapted horizontal gain map.
red: vertical.

Fig. 4. Results of an adaptation experiment

and thus 'decoupled' from the perceptual system. Fig. 4 shows results for an experiment with the initial pose fixed at [0, 0] (the robot looks straight ahead). The robot performs horizontal saccades, during which the target is shifted against the saccade direction.

Fig. 4a shows the time-course of the gaze error. The gaze error is estimated only in the periods when the end-of-saccade node is active and is zero otherwise (see the plot). First six saccades demonstrate a low error, since the system has already learned the gain map. Starting with the seventh saccade, the target is shifted (during each gaze shift) against the saccade direction horizontally. Over a few saccades, the error is decreased again; the agent performs shorter saccades to the manipulated target. Fig. 4b shows a slice of the adapted gain map, which corresponds to the initial pose of the robot in the adaptation session. Note the slightly decreased amplitude of the gains around the adapted location ([25, 55] in image coordinates), where the target was perceived.

4   Discussion

In this paper, we presented the neural-dynamic architecture for generation of saccadic gaze shifts and their adaptation, which may be coupled to sensory inputs and drive a physical motor system. On the one hand, the architecture offers a neural-dynamic framework, in which various aspects of saccades and gaze shift generation, as well as their adaptation, may be studied. On the other hand, the system allows to study sensorimotor learning in an adaptive artificial cognitive agent.

Acknowledgement. The project was funded by the DFG SPP "Autonomous learning" within the Priority program 1527.

References

1. Amari, S.: Dynamics of pattern formation in lateral-inhibition type neural fields. Biological Cybernetics 27, 77–87 (1977)
2. Dean, P., Mayhew, J.E., Langdon, P.: Learning and maintaining saccadic accuracy: A model of brainstem-cerebellar interactions. Journal of Cognitive Neuroscience 6(2), 38–117 (1994)
3. Gancarz, G., Grossberg, S.: A neural model of saccadic eye movement control explains task-specific adaptation. Vision Research 39(18), 43–3123 (1999)
4. Girard, B., Berthoz, A.: From brainstem to cortex: computational models of saccade generation circuitry. Progress in Neurobiology 77(4), 215–251 (2005)
5. Grossberg, S.: Nonlinear neural networks: Principles, mechanisms, and architectures. Neural Networks 1, 17–61 (1988)
6. Hopp, J.J., Fuchs, A.F.: The characteristics and neuronal substrate of saccadic eye movement plasticity. Progress in Neurobiology 72(1), 27–53 (2004)
7. Kopecz, K., Schöner, G.: Saccadic motor planning by integrating visual information and pre-information on neural dynamic fields. Biological Cybernetics 60, 49–60 (1995)
8. Optican, L.M., Quaia, C.: Distributed model of collicular and cerebellar function during saccades. Annals of the New York Academy of Sciences 956(1), 164–177 (2002)
9. Panouillères, M., Habchi, O., Gerardin, P., Salemme, R., Urquizar, C., Farne, A., Pélisson, D.: A Role for the Parietal Cortex in Sensorimotor Adaptation of Saccades. Cerebral Cortex (2012)
10. Pélisson, D., Alahyane, N., Panouillères, M., Tilikete, C.: Sensorimotor adaptation of saccadic eye movements. Neurosci. Biobehav. Rev. 34(8), 1103–1120 (2010)
11. Quaia, C., Lefèvre, P., Optican, L.M.: Model of the control of saccades by superior colliculus and cerebellum. Journal of Neurophysiology 82(2), 999–1018 (1999)
12. Reuschel, J., Rösler, F., Henriques, D.Y.P., Fiehler, K.: Spatial updating depends on gaze direction even after loss of vision. The Journal of Neuroscience: The Official Journal of the Society for Neuroscience 32(7), 9–2422 (2012)
13. Sandamirskaya, Y., Zibner, S.K.U., Schneegans, S., Schöner, G.: Using Dynamic Field Theory to extend the embodiment stance toward higher cognition. New Ideas in Psychology 31(3), 322–339 (2013)
14. Schöner, G.: Dynamical Systems Approaches to Cognition. Dynamical Systems (2008)
15. Schweighofer, N., Arbib, M.A., Dominey, P.F.: A model of the cerebellum in adaptive control of saccadic gain. Biological Cybernetics 75(1), 19–28 (1996)
16. Sparks, D.L.: Conceptual issues related to the role of the superior colliculus in the control of gaze. Current Opinion in Neurobiology 9(6), 698–707 (1999)
17. Srimal, R., Diedrichsen, J., Ryklin, E.B., Curtis, C.E.: Obligatory adaptation of saccade gains. Journal of Neurophysiology 99(3), 8–1554 (2008)
18. Trappenberg, T.P., Dorris, M.C., Munoz, D.P., Klein, R.M.: A model of saccade initiation based on the competitive integration of exogenous and endogenous signals in the superior colliculus. Journal of Cognitive Neuroscience 13(2), 71–256 (2001)
19. Wallman, J., Fuchs, A.F.: Saccadic gain modification: Visual error drives motor adaptation. Journal of Neurophysiology 80(5), 2405–2416 (1998)
20. Wilimzig, C., Schneider, S., Schöner, G.: The time course of saccadic decision making: dynamic field theory. Neural networks: The official Journal of the International Neural Network Society 19(8), 74–1059 (2006)

Skeleton Model for the Neurodynamics
of Visual Action Representations

Martin A. Giese

Section Computational Sensomotorics, Dept. of Cognitive Neurology
CIN & HIH, University Clinic Tübingen
Otfried-Müller-Str. 25, 72076 Tübingen, Germany
Martin.giese@uni-tuebingen.de

Abstract. The visual recognition of body motion in the primate brain requires the temporal integration of information over complex patterns, potentially exploiting recurrent neural networks consisting of shape- and optic-flow-selective neurons. The paper presents a mathematically simple neurodynamical model that approximates the mean-field dynamics of such networks. It is based on a two-dimensional neural field with appropriate lateral interaction kernel and an adaptation process for the individual neurons. The model accounts for a number of, so far not modeled, observations in the recognition of body motion, including perceptual multi-stability and the weakness of repetition suppression, as observed in single-cell recordings for the repeated presentation of action stimuli. In addition, the model predicts novel effects in the perceptual organization of action stimuli.

Keywords: Action recognition, biological motion, neural field, adaptation, superior temporal sulcus, premotor cortex.

1 Introduction

Body motion recognition is a central visual function with high importance for social communication and the learning of movements by imitation [1]. The cortical core circuit of visual action recognition might be based on a competitive network of neurons that are selective for motion and optic flow patterns, and which detect such patterns in a sequence-selective manner [2]. Consistent with this hypothesis is the observation of neurons in the superior temporal sulcus (STS) that respond selectively to snapshots of action movies [3-5], and which often show temporal sequence selectivity, i.e. they respond differently for action movies shown in normal and inverted temporal order [3]. Neurons with very similar properties were found in higher action-selective areas, such as area F5 in monkey premotor cortex [Pomper et al., SFN, 2011, abstract 914.02/QQ7]. Another interesting property of such visual action-selective neurons is that they often show view-dependence, i.e. they respond preferentially to one particular view, but much less to other views of the same action [3, 5, 6]. These observations constrain a simple neurodynamical model that accounts for the joint neural encoding of the view and the time structure of action stimuli.

S. Wermter et al. (Eds.): ICANN 2014, LNCS 8681, pp. 707–714, 2014.

On the behavioral side, body motion perception has interesting dynamic properties which so far have not been studied very much by theoreticians. Firstly, body motion perception can show multi-stability. This has been first demonstrated by Vanrie and collaborators [7], who showed that the same two-dimensional point-light body motion stimuli can be interpreted as locomoting in two different directions, e.g. towards or away from the observer. This ambiguous percept shows spontaneous perceptual switching between the two possible perceptual interpretations, in a similar manner as this is known for other multi-stable displays, such as the Necker cube or binocular rivalry [8]. This observation suggests the existence of an underlying multi-stable neural dynamics that gives rise to these perceptual switching, and to decisions between the two alternative perceptual interpretations.

Secondly, many perceptual processes, including object recognition, are characterized by adaptation when the same stimulus is presented repeatedly. This fact is fundamental for repetition suppression paradigms in fMRI experiments, which have been extensively applied in the field of visual object recognition [9]. For action stimuli, however, the results on fMRI repetition suppression have been ambiguous, and electrophysiological experiments have either failed to show substantial adaptation effects in action-selective areas, such as area F5 in single units [10], or they have reported only very week adaptation effects after a large number of stimulus repetitions [11]. This raises the question how adaptation interacts with the perceptual organization of body motion stimuli, and why adaptation effects are so much weaker in action recognition areas than in object recognition in the inferotemporal cortex (IT) [12].

We present in the following a relatively simple mathematical neurodynamical model that provides an account for these phenomena, and which offers a possible explanationation why adaptation effects for action stimuli might be much weaker than the ones found in experiments with static shape stimuli. In addition, the model provides a possibility to coarsely estimate the importance of noise and internal fluctuations (or top-down effects) in the causation of perceptual switches for ambiguous body motion stimuli.

The paper is structured as follows: We first review some related theoretical approaches. Then the model will be briefly described. In the subsequent section discusses the simulation results and relates them to the experimental literature, followed by some conclusions.

2   Related Theoretical Work

The experimental literature on body motion perception and perceptual multi-stability is vast, and space allows here only to review a few related theoretical models. While initial models for body motion perception have been purely computational (e.g. [13]), more recently a number of neural models have been developed. Our model is based on the dynamical core circuit of a physiologically-inspired hierarchical recognition model that integrates form and motion features [2]. More recently it has been shown that architectures of this type can be made computationally sufficiently powerful to compete with state-of-the-art algorithms for action detection (e.g. [14]). Many neural models exist for the perceptual multistability of static stimuli, e.g. the Necker cube, or ambiguous coherent or apparent motion displays (e.g. [15-17]). Typically, such models are based on competitive dynamic neural networks. More recently, perceptual multi-stability for such phenomena has been analyzed using probabilistic approaches for the analysis of the activity of competing neural ensembles [18]. While we acknowledge that some phenomena, such as synchronized oscillations, might necessitate the use of spiking neuron models, we reside to a mean-field approximation for this paper because it results in a model that is in principle mathematically tractable, and permits a qualitative understanding of the underlying dynamical phenomena.

3   Model Architecture

The model is based on a two-dimensional neural field [19], that represents the view and the keyframe (time point) of body shapes within an action sequence. The model represents a two-dimensional extension of the dynamic layer of a model in [2], which did not represent views in a continuous manner. The input of this neural field is given by the responses of shape-selective neurons that are selective for particular body postures and views arising during action stimuli. The selectivity of such neurons can be established by learning [2]. For the simulations presented in this paper we assumed an idealized input signal, where we replaced the real input by moving peaks in the input distribution. However, the same model has also been tested also while embedded in the hierarchical visual recognition architecture from [2], using real stimuli as input. In the following we focus on the neural encoding of periodic body motions, such as walking. In this case, the neural field is periodic in the view as well as in the direction of the stimulus frame.

The proposed model is defined by two dynamic equations. The first defines an activation dynamics, which is modeled by a two-dimensional neural field, where the first dimension ϕ specifies the stimulus view, and where the second dimension θ defines the frame or snapshot (e.g. within the gait cycle) that is represented by corresponding neuron (or point within the neural field). The second equation specifies a 'point-wise' simple linear adaptation dynamics that is associated with each neuron (point) in the field. More specifically, the model is defined by the equations:

$$\tau_u \dot{u}(\phi,\theta,t) = -u(\phi,\theta,t) + w(\phi,\theta)*1(u(\phi,\theta,t)) + s(\phi,\theta,t) - h$$
$$- \alpha a(\phi,\theta,t) + \xi(\phi,\theta,t) \tag{1}$$

$$\tau_a \dot{a}(\phi,\theta,t) = -a(\phi,\theta,t) + 1(u(\phi,\theta,t)) \tag{2}$$

In equation (1) the variable u specifies the (average) membrane potential for a neuron ensemble representing view ϕ and snapshot (body configuration) θ. The constant h specifies the resting potential. The recurrent interaction kernel w specifies the interaction between different points in the field. It is symmetric with respect to the origin in the ϕ-direction (view), and asymmetric in the θ-direction (snapshot), with an additional strong inhibitory component. Its functional form is given by equations $w(\phi,\theta) = w_\phi(\phi)w_\theta(\theta) - w_0$, with the functions $w_\phi(\phi) = \exp((\cos\phi - 1)/\sigma_\phi)$ and $w_\theta(\theta) = \exp((\cos(\theta - \eta) - 1)/\sigma_\theta)$ and the global inhibition $w_0 > 0$. The parameters σ_ϕ and σ_θ specify the tuning width, and the parameter η specify the asymmetry of the kernel in θ-direction. It has been shown elsewhere that such asymmetric kernels, if designed appropriately, result in temporal sequence selectivity and a well-defined speed tuning curve of the neurons in the field with respect to this direction [20]. The symbol * signifies a spatial convolution, which is periodic since the field is periodic in both directions. The step threshold function $1(u)$ takes the value 1 for $u > 0$, and zero otherwise.

The stimulus input signal s models an (idealized) activity distribution over shape-selective neurons. The value $s(\theta,\phi,t)$ defines the average input activity of shape-selective neurons (neuron ensembles) that respond maximally to the body configuration appearing at (normalized) time θ of the gait / action cycle, and with the view angle ϕ. The stimulus input was modeled in an idealized manner, assuming peaks of activity with amplitude s_0 that propagate in the θ-direction with speed v. More specifically, these peaks were specified by the equation: $s(\theta,\phi,t) = s_0 \exp((\cos(\theta - \theta_c(t)) - 1)/\sigma_s)\exp((\cos(\phi - \phi_c) - 1)/\sigma_s)$, where the peak center θ_c in θ-direction was moving with speed v, and where the ϕ_c corresponds to the view angle of the body in the corresponding frame. The parameters σ_s defines the width of the idealized input peak. For ambiguous action stimuli that simultaneously activate two different competing views [7], we added a second peak with view angle the $-\phi_c$ to the input signal distribution. The noise distribution ξ is defined by a Gaussian process whose kernel function is the product of a spatial kernel function that was fitted in order to reproduce coarsely the correlation statistics, dependent on the tuning similarity of the neurons [21], and a delta function with respect to time.

The dynamic neural field define by equation (1) stabilizes a stimulus-locked travelling peak solution in θ-direction, i.e. an activation peak that follows the stimulus peak, if the frames of an action stimulus appear in the correct temporal order, and if the speed of the input peak falls in the range of preferred speeds that is determined by the parameters of the neural field. If the frames of an action movie are shown in the wrong temporal order, or if the speed of the presentation of the movie deviates very strongly from the natural speed of the action (that matches the preferred speed of the field) the activation in the neural field remains relatively small [2]. In addition, the lateral interactions in (view) ϕ-direction result in a winner-takes-all competition along this dimension, resulting in a decision for one stimulus view for stimuli that are ambiguous and activate simultaneously interpretations corresponding to multiple views.

Equation (2) specifies a simple adaptation process, independently for each point in the neural field. The adaptation variable $a(\phi,\theta)$ feeds back negatively in the activation field with a strength that is determined by the positive parameter α. It is driven by the output activity of the corresponding point in the neural field. The time scales of the activation and the adaptation dynamics were given by positive parameters $\tau_u = 120$ ms and $\tau_a = 2.4$ s.

4   Simulation Results

I) Multi-stability: The proposed neural model defines a multi-stable dynamics. For ambiguous stimuli activating the views $\pm\phi_c$ that deviate sufficiently from the side view ($\phi_c = 0$) of a walker, the field has two alternative stable travelling pulse solutions, moving together with the stimulus peaks in the θ-direction with speed v. One of these solutions is depicted in the first three panels of Fig. 1A, where the selected view is the one corresponding to the view angle ($\phi_c = -72$ deg). Strong noise can induce a spontaneous switch to the other stable travelling pulse solution, corresponding to ($\phi_c = 72$ deg). Such a spontaneous switch is taking place in panels 3 and 4 of Fig. 1A. After the switch the activity peak propagates with speed v along a horizontal line that correspond to the view angle 72 deg.

This behavior is confirmed by an analysis of the sum of the activity in the field. Fig 1B shows the sums of the thresholded activity over all values of θ, and the regions with positive respectively negative values of the variable ϕ. Due to the noise, these sum activity show strong fluctuations. A spontaneous transition to the other stable solution occurs within time interval close to $t = 8$ s, corresponding to a perceptual switch between the two alternative views that are compatible with the stimulus.,

In addition, the model predicts an interesting bifurcation (see Fig. 1C): For view angle differences below ± 21 deg the bistability disappears, and only a single stable traveling pulse solutions exists that follows the average of the compatible stimulus views $\pm\phi_c$. Initial psychophysical observations seem to confirm this bifurcation.

II) Adaptation: The adaptation dynamics was fitted using data from single cell recordings in inferotemporal (IT) cortex [12]. To account for the recognition of static stimuli, the interaction kernel was made symmetrical (choosing $\eta = 0$), and a static stimulus distribution s was used. The time course and the maximum rate of adaptation in these experiments were coarsely matched (Fig. 2A). The adaptation results in a flattening of the tuning curve, not just in a multiplicative rescaling (Fig. 2B), consistent with the data [12]. Applying the same adaptation mechanisms to the original model in absence of internal noise ($\xi \equiv 0$) was insufficient to account for spontaneous switches, suggesting that these perceptual switches are not adaptation-induced.

The repetition of a single action stimulus (one gait or action cycle), following the procedure in fMRI studies and in [10], results in a very small adaptation effect that is difficult to detect in presence of noise (red curve, Fig 2C). (The noise level here was far below the one required for inducing perceptual switches.) Using a special stimulus that repeats a fragment from an action movie with a duration of about 200 ms very quickly, but keeping the total stimulus time (3 s) constant, results in a much stronger adaptation effect. The model thus predicts that such stimuli might be more efficient adaptors than the repetition of whole actions.

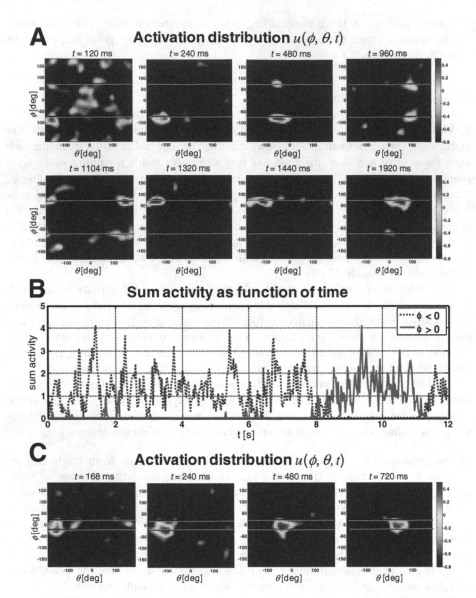

Fig. 1. Multi-stability **of the neural field dynamics. A** For an ambiguous body motion stimulus that equally activates two view directions ($\phi_c = \pm72$ deg relative to the side view; indicated
by the pink lines) the solution peak first propagates along with the stimulus peak at $\phi = -72$ deg.
A spontaneous transition to the other stable travelling pulse solution, centered at the view angle
$\phi = 72$ deg occurs after some time (panel 4)). **B** The sum activity over frames and over positive,
respectively negative view angles shows strong random fluctuations, resulting in a spontaneous
switching between the two stable solutions for t around 8 s. **C** For view angles ϕ_c that deviate
less form the side view than ±21 deg the bistability disappears (bifurcation). Only a single
stable travelling peak solution exists that follows the midpoint of the two peaks of the input
signal distribution in ϕ direction (which are indicated by the pink lines).

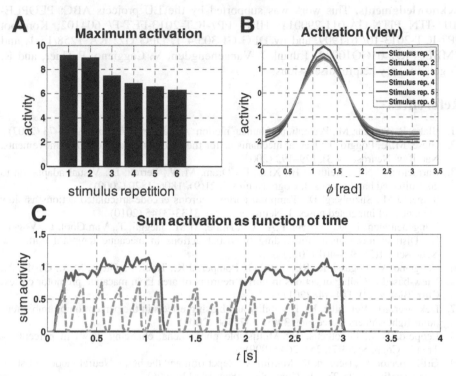

Fig. 2. Activation-dependent **adaptation. A** Simulating adaptation effects in area IT [12], using static stimuli and a field with symmetric interaction kernel ($v = 0$), the repeated presentation of static patterns results in a maximum adaptation of the neuron activity of about 30 %. **B** The adaptation results in a widening of the tuning curve, consistent with the experimental data from area IT. **C** Using the same adaptation dynamics, only very weak adaptation is found for repetition of action stimuli (red curve: sum activity for one stimulus repetition). A different stimulus with fast repetition of the same short action fragment (duration of about 200 ms) results in much stronger adaptation for the same total stimulus duration.

5   Conclusions

This paper proposed a neurodynamical model that captures several aspects of the perceptual dynamics in body motion perception. It provides a unifying explanation for several phenomena: i) multi-stability in the perception of views of body motion; ii) a possible cause for the difficulty to demonstrate adaptation effects for the stimulus repetition of action stimuli. In addition, the model makes a number of predictions: a) It predicts a bifurcation of the dynamics in dependence of the deviation of the stimulus views from the side view. b) It suggests a new action stimulus that might result in stronger adaptation effects than simple stimulus repetition. Furthermore, the proposed model is mathematically quite simple and thus accessible for mathematical analysis. Experimental testing of these predictions and such a mathematical analysis are the topics of ongoing work.

Acknowledgments. This work was supported by the EU projects ABC: PEOPLE-2011-ITN PITN-GA-011-290011; HBP: FP7-ICT-2013-FET-F/ 604102; Koroibot FP7-ICT-2013-10/ 611909, and by DFG GI 305/4-1, DFG GZ: KA 1258/15-1, and BMBF, FKZ: 01GQ1002A. I thank J. Vangeneugden, V. Caggiano, P Thier, and R. Vogels for very helpful discussions.

References

1. Blake, R., Shiffrar, M.: Perception of human motion. Annu. Rev. Psychol. 58, 47–73 (2007)
2. Giese, M.A., Poggio, T.: Neural mechanisms for the recognition of biological movements. Nat. Rev. Neurosci. 4(3), 179–192 (2003)
3. Barraclough, N.E., Keith, R.H., Xiao, D., Oram, M.W., Perrett, D.: Visual adaptation to goal-directed hand actions. J. Cogn. Neurosci. 21(9), 1806–1820 (2009)
4. Singer, J.M., Sheinberg, D.: Temporal cortex neurons encode articulated actions as slow sequences of integrated poses. J. Neurosci. 30(8), 3133–3145 (2010)
5. Vangeneugden, J., De Mazière, P.A., Van Hulle, M.M., Jaeggli, T., Van Gool, L., Vogels, R.: Distinct mechanisms for coding of visual actions in macaque temporal cortex. J. Neurosci. 31(2), 385–401 (2011)
6. Caggiano, V., Fogassi, L., Rizzolatti, G., Pomper, J.K., Thier, P., Giese, M.A., Casile, A.: View-based encoding of actions in mirror neurons of area f5 in macaque premotor cortex. Curr. Biol. 21(2), 144–148 (2011)
7. Dekeyser, M., Verfaillie, K.: Bistability and biasing effects in the perception of ambiguous point-light walkers. Perception 33(5), 547–560 (2004)
8. Leopold, D.A., Logothetis, N.: Multistable phenomena: changing views in perception. Trends. Cogn. Sci. 3(7), 254–264 (1999)
9. Grill-Spector, K., Henson, R., Martin, A.: Repetition and the brain: Neural models of stimulus-specific effects. Trends. Cogn. Sci. 10(1), 14–23 (2006)
10. Caggiano, V., Pomper, J.K., Fleischer, F., Fogassi, L., Giese, M., Thier, P.: Mirror neurons in monkey area F5 do not adapt to the observation of repeated actions. Nat. Commun. 4, 1433 (2013)
11. Kilner, J.M., Kraskov, A., Lemon, R.: Do monkey F5 mirror neurons show changes in firing rate during repeated observation of natural actions? J. Neurophysiol. 111(6), 1214–1226 (2013)
12. De Baene, W., Vogels, R.: Effects of adaptation on the stimulus selectivity of macaque inferior temporal spiking activity and local field potentials. Cereb. Cortex. 20(9), 2145–2165 (2010)
13. Marr, D., Vaina, L.: Representation and recognition of the movements of shapes. Proc. R. Soc. Lond. B Biol. Sci. 214(1197), 501–524 (1982)
14. Jhuang, H., Garrote, E., Mutch, J., Yu, X., Khilnani, V., Poggio, T., Steele, A.D., Serre, T.: Automated home-cage behavioural phenotyping of mice. Nat. Commun. 1, 68 (2010)
15. Kawamoto, A.H., Anderson, J.A.: A neural network model of multi-stable perception. Acta. Psy. 59, 35–65 (1985)
16. Kelso, J.A.S.: Dynamic Patterns. MIT Press, Cambridge (1995)
17. Giese, M.A.: Dynamic Neural Field Theory for Motion Perception. Kluwer Academic Publishers, Dordrecht (1998)
18. Gigante, G., Mattia, M., Braun, J., Del Giudice, P.: Bistable perception modeled as competing stochastic integrations at two levels. Comput. Biol. 5(7), e1000430 (2009)
19. Amari, S.: Dynamics of pattern formation in lateral-inhibition type neural fields. Biol. Cybern. 27(2), 77–87 (1977)
20. Xie, X., Giese, M.: Nonlinear dynamics of direction-selective recurrent neural media. Phys. Rev. E. Stat. Nonlin. Soft. Matter. Phys. 65(5 Pt 1), 51904 (2002)
21. Cohen, M.R., Kohn, A.: Measuring and interpreting neuronal correlations. Nat. Neurosci. 14(7), 811–819 (2011)

Latency-Based Probabilistic Information Processing in Recurrent Neural Hierarchies

Alexander Gepperth and Mathieu Lefort

ENSTA ParisTech, 828 Blvd des Marechaux, 91762 Palaiseau, France
firstname.lastname@ensta-paristech.fr
and INRIA FLOWERS, 100 avenue de la Liberation, 44801 Talence, France

Abstract. In this article, we present an original neural space/latency code, integrated in a multi-layered neural hierarchy, that offers a new perspective on probabilistic inference operations. Our work is based on the dynamic neural field paradigm that leads to the emergence of activity bumps, based on recurrent lateral interactions, thus providing a spatial coding of information. We propose that lateral connections represent a data model, i.e., the conditional probability of a "true" stimulus given a noisy input. We propose furthermore that the resulting attractor state encodes the most likely "true" stimulus given the data model, and that its latency expresses the confidence in this interpretation. Thus, the main feature of this network is its ability to represent, transmit and integrate probabilistic information at multiple levels so that to take near-optimal decisions when inputs are contradictory, noisy or missing. We illustrate these properties on a three-layered neural hierarchy receiving inputs from a simplified robotic object recognition task. We also compare the network dynamics to an explicit probabilistic model of the task, to verify that it indeed reproduces all relevant properties of probabilistic processing.

1 Introduction

With the advent of Bayesian inference accounts of biological information processing [1], a large body of literature [2–6] focuses on probabilistic aspects of neural coding. Most authors explicitly assume that neural population activity is related to probability distributions. Such an assumption faces two major problems trying to give account of neural processing. First, such a coding, which needs multiplication of probabilistic values, collides with summation based neural computation. To overcome this conflict, a very influential idea posits that single-neuron activity is related to log-probability [4, 5], which would allow to perform multiplications by summation. An alternative approach [3] is to consider firing rates as the realizations of Poisson-like random variables. Under certain conditions, sums of such variables come from a distribution whose mean corresponds to the product of individual means, thus realizing a multiplication by summation. Second, probabilistic approaches generally work on the single-neuron level without reference to other neurons in the same population [2–5]. However, biological processing makes heavy use of lateral connections.

S. Wermter et al. (Eds.): ICANN 2014, LNCS 8681, pp. 715–722, 2014.

We aim to overcome these limitations by taking another way: we propose to process probabilistic information in population based processing using the latency of attractor states. There is converging evidence from both physiological [7–10] and behavioral [11, 12] investigations that latency plays a role in the neural encoding of information. Neurons in the striate cortex, for example, encode stimulus contrast into response latency [8], whereas decision making processes typically take longer depending on the number of conflicting alternatives [11], conceivably reflecting increased response latency on the neural level. Similar effects have also been observed in language processing [12].

Our work is based on the dynamic neural field paradigm [13–15] of recurrent interactions through lateral connections. We posit that lateral connections implement a data model expressing the conditional probability $p(M|S)$ of an underlying "true" stimulus M given the noisy/mixed/corrupted input S. The competitive neural field dynamics will converge to an attractor state maximally compatible with the input and the data model, see [16]. Furthermore, it is a well-documented effect [17, 13] that latency of this process varies depending on inputs, and we posit that it encodes the match of input to data model. In this combined space/latency code[18], the position of the emergent activity represents the most likely "true" stimulus $M^* = \arg\max p(M|S)$ and the latency expresses its probability under the data model, $p(M^*|S)$, which we term "confidence". Thus, neural populations are not viewed as representing full probability distributions as sub-leading interpretations are suppressed by competition.

While in a previous publication [18] we demonstrated that such a combined space/latency neural code can implement Bayes-optimal decision making in a simple setting, this article is dedicated to the study of this coding in a deeper hierarchy with more complex inputs inspired by works on a simple robotic object recognition task [17]. In particular, we wish to analyze the effects of model violations (which we will often denote by "uncertainty"), focusing on the encoding of uncertainty into response latency, the transport and accumulation of latency across hierarchy levels, and the decoding of latency into optimal local decisions. Analogies to an exact probabilistic model will be discussed as well.

2   Model

2.1   Architecture

We use a three-layered multimodal architecture (see Fig. 1), in which feedforward connections between maps are plastic and each map evolves according to very general competitive dynamics, so our results should apply to wide range of spiking/non-spiking models.

2.2   Model Equations

Activity computation The field activity L ($L \in \{H_1, H_2, H_3, M_1, M_2, M_3, D\}$) at position x and time t is equal to $f[u^L(x,t)]$ with the quantity u^L that represents the membrane potential of the field which evolves according to a slightly modified version of dynamic neural field proposed in [14]:

$$\tau \dot{u}^L(x,t) = -u^L(x,t) + \alpha g^L[S^L(x,t)] + \beta \left(w(x-x') * f[u(x',t)]\right) + \gamma \Sigma(x,t) + h$$

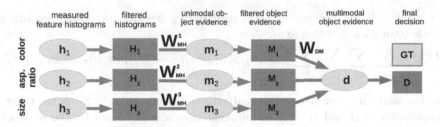

Fig. 1. Neural hierarchy which is the basis for all investigations in this article. Each orange box corresponds a neural field and each oval represents the corresponding neural field input which is basically a weighted sum of the neural activity of the previous layer or input from the environment (see section 2.2 for details). *GT* is the ground truth that describes the current object corresponding to input features h_1, h_2 and h_3.

with w the fixed lateral interaction kernel, $f[u]$ the point-wise applied transfer function given by $f[u] = \left(1 + \exp(\frac{-2(u-\theta)}{\nu})\right)^{-1}$, Σ normally distributed white noise, h the resting potential and τ the time scale of field evolution. S^L is the afferent input:

$$S^L = \begin{cases} \mathbf{h_i} \text{ if } L = H_i \\ \mathbf{m_i} = \sigma\left(\mathbf{W_{MH}^i} \cdot \mathbf{u^{H_i}}\right) \text{ if } L = M_i \\ \mathbf{d} = \sigma\left(\sum_i \mathbf{W_{DM}^i} \cdot \mathbf{u^{M_i}}\right) \text{ if } L = D \end{cases}$$

with σ a logistic transfer function (refer to figure 1 for other notations). We use an input transfer function $g^L[S]$ so that inputs can excite the field effectively:

$$g^L[S^L] = \begin{cases} k^L S^L \text{ if } k^L S^L \leq 1 \\ 1 \qquad \text{else} \end{cases} \qquad (1)$$

with a suitably chosen constant k^L that depends on average input strength. The coefficients α, β and γ respectively determine the contribution of afferent input, lateral recurrent interactions and noise. The interaction kernel w is usually chosen to be symmetric: $w(dx) = a_0 G_{\mu=0,\sigma=\sigma_{on}}(dx) - b_0 G_{\mu=0,\sigma=\sigma_{off}}(dx) - c_0$, where $G_{\mu,\sigma}$ denotes a Gaussian with mean μ and standard deviation σ, and $\sigma_{on} < \sigma_{off}$. The constants a_0, b_0, c_0 are chosen suitably to achieve the desired level of local excitation/inhibition (a_0, b_0) as well as global inhibition (c_0). To ensure numerical stability, we clip the neural field potentials u whenever they exceed the range defined by $[u_{min}, u_{max}]$. Please notice that all model parameters are identical for each field of the model except for g^L function that needs to be tuned for each field so that input is sufficiently high to trigger an activity.

Weights Learning. All feed-forward weights between fields are trained by online logistic regression [19] with logistic transfer function σ, using a step size λ_{LR}, where the learning target is always the population-encoded object identity GT.

Probabilistic Model. Using the notation of Fig. 1, we introduce the following shorthand: $\mathfrak{M} \equiv \{M_i\}$, $\mathfrak{m} \equiv \{m_i\}$, $\mathfrak{H} \equiv \{H_i\}$ and $\mathfrak{h} \equiv \{h_i\}$. The probability for the presence of a certain object as a function of the inputs is thus expressed as as $p(\boldsymbol{D}|\mathfrak{h})$. Using the law of total probability, we can introduce the other network quantities into this expression:

$$p(\boldsymbol{D}|\mathfrak{h}) = \sum_{\{d_j\}} \sum_{\{\mathfrak{M}_k\}} \sum_{\{\mathfrak{m}_l\}} \sum_{\{\mathfrak{H}_m\}} p(\boldsymbol{D}|d_j)p(d_j|\mathfrak{M}_k)p(\mathfrak{M}_k|\mathfrak{m}_l)p(\mathfrak{m}_l|\mathfrak{H}_m)p(\mathfrak{H}_m|\mathfrak{h}) \quad (2)$$

where the sums run over all possible realizations of each variable. Since the transformations $\mathfrak{M} \to \boldsymbol{d}$ and $\mathfrak{H} \to \mathfrak{m}$ are deterministically governed by the network weights W^i_{MH} and W^i_{DM} (see Fig. 1), the corresponding distributions $p(\boldsymbol{d}|\mathfrak{M})$ and $p(\mathfrak{m}|\mathfrak{H})$ are delta-like and the sums over these variables thus vanish. Due to the splitting of the hierarchy into independent modal flows (see Fig. 1), the expressions $p(\mathfrak{H}_m|\mathfrak{h})$ and $p(\mathfrak{M}_k|W_{MH}\mathfrak{H})$ factorize into products of the unimodal probabilities. In order to better approximate the network dynamics, we suppose that the sums over conditional probabilities are approximated by their maxima $\mathfrak{M}^*_k \equiv \arg\max p(\mathfrak{M}_k|W_{MH}\mathfrak{H})$ and $\mathfrak{H}^*_k \equiv \arg\max p(\mathfrak{H}_k|\mathfrak{h})$. Thus:

$$p(\boldsymbol{D}|\mathfrak{h}) = \sum_{\{\mathfrak{M}_k\}} \sum_{\{\mathfrak{H}_m\}} p(\boldsymbol{D}|W_{DM}\mathfrak{M}_\ell)p(\mathfrak{M}_k|W_{MH}\mathfrak{H}_m)p(\mathfrak{H}_m|\mathfrak{h}) \approx$$
$$\approx p(\boldsymbol{D}|W_{DM}\mathfrak{M}^*)p(\mathfrak{M}^*|W_{MH}\mathfrak{H}^*)p(\mathfrak{H}^*|\mathfrak{h}) \equiv$$
$$\equiv \mathrm{conf}(\boldsymbol{D})\Pi_i\mathrm{conf}(\boldsymbol{M}_i)\Pi_j\mathrm{conf}(\boldsymbol{H}_j). \quad (3)$$

As each of the terms in eqn.(3) represents a confidence tied to a specific neural field, it is very natural to associate them with response latencies. Please note that, in the highest layer $\boldsymbol{D}$, decisions and confidences are effectively dissociated as the same decision can be reached for many confidence combinations. Each confidence contributes equally to the final expression, independently of its hierarchical position. The functional form of confidences will depend generally on the problem, in our case it would punish deviations from a unimodal distribution.

3   Experiments

3.1   Temporal Organization of a Single Input Presentation

Feature histograms h_i are presented to the lowest hierarchy levels H_i of the network at time $t_0 + 1$ and maintained for a total of T simulation steps. Directly before this happens, at time t_0, all field potentials in the hierarchy are reset to the resting potential h, see Sec. 2.2. Subsequently, field potentials and weights evolve freely according to the dynamic models described in Sec. 2.2

3.2   Input Stimuli

We mimic a robotic object recognition task containing the objects "red screwdriver", "yellow voltmeter" and "blue tape" (see Fig. 2). We generate fixed "measurements" in the modalities of color, aspect ratio and size for a random succession of these three objects drawn from an uniform distribution. Following [17], measurements are modeled as one-dimensional histograms over different modalities. These histograms contain a single Gaussian peak of amplitude

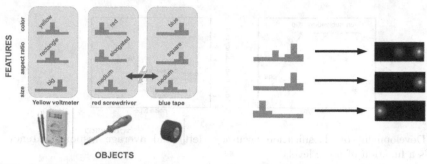

Fig. 2. Simplified synthetic object recognition task. Left: objects and their visual properties (expressed as feature histograms) in the three modalities color, aspect ratio and size. Please note the overlap in the "size" modality between screwdriver and tape, leading to potential ambiguities in feedforward processing. Right: population-encoding of these one-dimensional histograms input.

$A_S = 1.0$, at a position determined by object identity as shown in Fig. 2. To serve as inputs, these one-dimensional histograms are encoded along one axis (the other axis coes not carry any meaning) of a two-dimensional image of dimensions $(60, 10)^T$ using the convolution coding technique with a Gaussian basis function of standard deviation of 3 pixels, see Fig. 2 (right). The layers H_i, M_i and D are connected as indicated in Fig. 1. The length of a single input presentation is set to $T = 200$, the learning rate for all connections is $\lambda_{LR} = \frac{0.05}{60 \cdot 100}$. New inputs, as shown in Fig. 2 arrive every T iterations, draw from a uniform object distribution. In the beginning there is a learning phase of 12000 iterations corresponding to 20 presentations per object, after which learning is disabled for performing experiments. We choose a uniform parametrization of neural field layers of size 60x10 (see Sec. 2.2): $\tau = 15$, $\theta = 0$, $\nu = 2.5$, $\alpha = 1$, $\beta = 4$, $\gamma = 0.11$, $\sigma_{on} = 3$, $\sigma_{off} = 6$, $a_0 = b_0 = 1$, $c_0 = 0.55$, $h = -1$. Zero-padding boundary conditions are used for all lateral interactions. The input transfer function constant k_I is set to 1 for the fields H_i, to 1.8 for the fields M_i and to 1.3 for the field D. Response latency is defined as the time until an activity ≥ 0.9 is observed.

3.3 Classification Performance

We measure the ability of the network to recognize the currently "presented" object when various levels of noise are applied, which can be of the types "clean" (no noise), "sub-leading noise" (small peak of strength 0.5 introduced at a random position in all h_i), "flip" (peak in the "color" modality is flipped to a wrong position) and "chaos" (peaks in the color and aspect ratio modalities are randomly switched to a wrong position). This decision is expressed by the position of maximal activity in the field D, where object identity is encoded into one of three possible Gaussian peak positions, just as in GT.

Fig .3 shows the corresponding classification rates and average response latencies for these four cases. It is clearly visible that latencies increase in the "sub-leading noise" case and even more for the case "flip", even though classification accuracies stay at 100%. This very nicely reflects the probabilistic nature

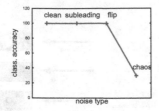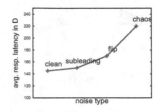

Fig. 3. Development of classification accuracy (left) and average response latency (right) as a function of noise levels

of processing, as the network can signal something was wrong, and to what degree, even though it delivers perfect performance. For the "chaos" case, evidently no above-chance classification is possible as two-thirds of the modalities are corrupted, which is again reflected in the strongly increased latencies for this case.

3.4 Case Studies

Using the "clean" condition described in the previous section, we investigate the reaction of the hierarchy to an inherent ambiguity which stems from the fact the size "medium" votes for both "blue tape" and "red screwdriver" in the mid-level of the hierarchy. Instead of one peak of amplitude 1.0, there will now be two peaks of amplitude 0.5 in m_3. As seen in Fig. 4, activity will still appear in M_3 since the input transfer function of that field scales inputs to a sufficient strength. However, as a consequence of competition, the response will be delayed, reflecting its lower confidence (i.e., probability under the data model). This in turn will delay activity buildup in the highest layer D, expressing that the top-level decision is not as certain as it could be. Indeed, the vote of M_3 is not really taken into account in defining the response of D as it comes too late, demonstrating the basic principle of probabilistic information processing in this architecture: later-coming inputs have less influence in attractor formation in recurrent layers. Going beyond the "sub-leading noise" and "flip" conditions, we now investigate what happens when the feature histogram in a single modality is ambiguous and also incorrect: for presentations of the "yellow voltmeter" object, we put a Gaussian of strength 1.0 at the (incorrect) position "red", as well as a Gaussian of strength 0.8 at the (correct) position "yellow" in the color histogram input h_1, simulating a measurement ambiguity leading to a locally wrong conclusion, see Fig. 4 (right). This wrong conclusion is propagated forward to M_1 where it activates the "screwdriver" population. As the other modalities $M_i, i \neq 1$ vote for the correct object (yellow voltmeter), a correct high-level decision will still be taken in D.

4 Discussion and Outlook

Comparison to probabilistic model This article is based on a novel probabilistic interpretation of neural activities making use of biologically plausible neural

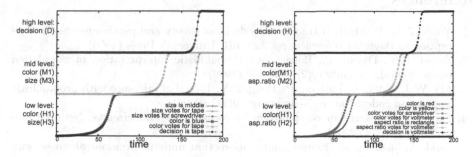

Fig. 4. Selected demonstrations of latency effects. Graphs are organized in three rows corresponding to the temporal development of activity in different hierarchy levels. Left: reaction to the ambiguous "blue tape" object. The unambiguous fields H_1 (color) and H_3 (size) have exactly the same latency. Middle row: unimodal object field M_1 (color) and M_3 (size), the latter having a strongly increased latency due to the ambiguity in object definitions. The lacking input strongly delays activity buildup in the top-level decision field D, which nevertheless occurs since the other modalities are unambiguous. Right: presenting the "yellow voltmeter" object with corrupted histogram input in the color modality. Activity in layers H_1 (color) and H_2 (aspect ratio) differs in latency as color is corrupted. Activity in unimodal object layers M_1 (color) and M_2 (aspect ratio) retains the low-level latency difference as no ambiguity is present at this level. Top row: final decision of the network, expressed by delayed activity in layer D.

dynamics. As it is the case with the probabilistic model of eqn.(3), model violations/uncertainty may, with equal influence, originate at any place in the hierarchy as observed in Fig. 4 where uncertainty arising on the lowest or middle layers is transported to the top. This also shows that confidence from any layer is propagated to the top without change if other layers do not add to it, which is another corollary of eqn.(3). We furthermore observe that not only the fact but also the strength of model violations is transported to the top-level regardless of their origin, although the mapping from conditional probability values to latency is not linear. In addition, the development of response latencies depending on noise, see Sec. 3.3, directly show that decisions and confidences are dissociated as in the model of eqn.(3), thus forming two independent coding dimensions. Lastly, it may be stated that the approximation (and thus the information loss) accepted in eqn.(3), as well as in neural field dynamics, is one that will not usually have negative effects unless a significant part of hierarchy inputs is corrupted.

Outlook. We intend to limit information loss in our model by "re-activating" suppressed inputs by feedback when high-level decisions are consistent with what was suppressed. Another focus will be the application of this model to more difficult and realistic tasks, the automatic tuning of the various coupling constants by homeostatic processes, and the learning of data models.

References

1. Yuille, A.L., Bulthoff, H.H.: Bayesian decision theory and psychophysics. In: Perception as Bayesian Inference, pp. 123–161. University Press (1996)
2. Zemel, R.S., Dayan, P., Pouget, A.: Probabilistic interpretation of population codes. Neural Comput. 10(2), 403–430 (1998)
3. Ma, W.J., Beck, J., Latham, P., Pouget, A.: Bayesian inference with probabilistic population codes. Nature Neuroscience 9(11) (2006)
4. Rao, R.P.N.: Bayesian computation in recurrent neural circuits. Neural Comput. 16(1), 1–38 (2004)
5. Gold, J., Shadlen, M.: Neural computations that underlie decisions about sensory stimuli. Trends Cogn. Sci. 5(1), 10–16 (2001)
6. Knill, D.C., Pouget, A.: The bayesian brain: The role of uncertainty in neural coding and computation. Trends Neurosci. 27(12), 712–719 (2004)
7. Oram, M.W., Xiao, D., Dritschel, B., Payne, K.R.: The temporal resolution of neural codes: Does response latency have a unique role? Philos. Trans. R. Soc. Lond. B Biol. Sci. 357(1424), 987–1001 (2002)
8. Reich, D.S., Mechler, F., Victor, J.D.: Temporal coding of contrast in primary visual cortex: when, what, and why. J. Neurophysiol. 85(3), 1039–1050 (2001)
9. Kiani, R., Esteky, H., Tanaka, K.: Differences in onset latency of macaque inferotemporal neural responses to primate and non-primate faces. J. Neurophysiol. 94(2), 1587–1596 (2005)
10. Michelet, T., Duncan, G.H., Cisek, P.: Response competition in the primary motor cortex: Corticospinal excitability reflects response replacement during simple decisions. Journal of Neurophysiology 104(1) (2010)
11. Hazeltine, E., Poldrack, R.A., Gabrieli, J.D.E.: Neural activation during response competition. Journal of Cognitive Neuroscience, 118–129 (2000)
12. Borowsky, R., Masson, M.E.J.: Semantic ambiguity effects in word identification. J. Exp.Psych: Learning, Memory, and Cognition 22(1), 63 (1996)
13. Erlhagen, W., Schöner, G.: Dynamic field theory of movement preparation. Psychological Review 109(3), 545 (2002)
14. Amari, S.-I.: Mathematical foundations of neurocomputing. Proceedings of the IEEE 78(9), 1441–1463 (1990)
15. Cisek, P.: Integrated neural processes for defining potential actions and deciding between them: A computational model. J. Neurosci. 26(38), 9761–9770 (2006)
16. Kubota, S., Aihara, K.: Anayzing global dynamics of a neural field model. Neural Processing Letters 21 (2005)
17. Faubel, C., Schöner, G.: Learning to recognize objects on the fly: A neurally based dynamic field approach. Neural Networks 21(4), 562–576 (2008)
18. Gepperth, A.: Processing and transmission of confidence in recurrent neural hierarchies. Neural Processing Letters (2013)
19. Bishop, C.M.: Pattern recognition and machine learning. Springer, New York (2006)

Factors Influencing Polychronous Group Sustainability as a Model of Working Memory

Panagiotis Ioannou[1], Matthew Casey[2], and André Grüning[1]

[1] Department of Computing, University of Surrey, Guildford, Surrey, GU2 7XH, UK
[2] Pervasive Intelligence Ltd, Stoneleigh, Frimley Road,
Ash Vale, Surrey, GU12 5PN, UK

Abstract. Several computational models have been designed to help our understanding of the conditions under which persistent activity can be sustained in cortical circuits during working memory tasks. Here we focus on one such model that has shown promise, that uses polychronization and short term synaptic dynamics to achieve this reverberation, and explore it with respect to different physiological parameters in the brain, including size of the network, number of synaptic connections, small-world connectivity, maximum axonal conduction delays, and type of cells (excitatory or inhibitory). We show that excitation and axonal conduction delays greatly affect the sustainability of spatio-temporal patterns of spikes called polychronous groups.

Keywords: Spiking neural networks, polychronization, working memory.

1 Introduction

The elevated, sustained and selective firing activity of neurons during working memory (WM) tasks has been observed in a number of *in vivo* electrophysiological experiments [1,2,3]. A number of models have been suggested to explain this elevated firing frequency of neurons, mainly in the form of recurrent neural networks based on NMDA receptor-mediated synaptic dynamics [4,5,6]. The main shortcoming of these models is that memories are represented by specific non-overlapping groups of spiking neurons. The extension of the memory content in such networks increases the overlap between the memory representations and subsequently, the activation of one representation spreads to others, resulting in an uncontrolable excitation. This limitation can be overcome by a model that accounts for the precise spike-timing patterns of firing of individual neurons. In [7], memories are represented by extensively overlapping groups of neurons that exhibit stereotypical time-locked spatiotemporal spike-timing patterns, called polychronous groups (PNGs). The synapses forming such PNGs are subject to associative synaptic plasticity in the form of both long-term and short-term spike-timing dependent plasticity (STDP). While long-term potentiation is essential in PNG formation, it was shown that short-term plasticity can temporarily strengthen the synapses of selected PNGs and lead to an increase

S. Wermter et al. (Eds.): ICANN 2014, LNCS 8681, pp. 723–731, 2014.

in the spontaneous reactivation rate of these PNGs, which is consistent with the in vivo recordings of individual neurons during working WM tasks. These short term changes were simulated through associative short-term synaptic plasticity via STDP, where synaptic changes — that decay to baseline within a few seconds — are induced by the classical STDP protocol.

The short-term mechanism selectively affects synapses according to the relative spike timing of pre- and post-synaptic neurons. This differs from the short-term synaptic strengthening used in previous WM models mentioned above, which are not associative, and hence non-selectively affect all synapses belonging to the same presynaptic neuron [7]. By selectively activating a PNG, the short term mechanism strengthens the synapses of their constituent neurons, and in conjuction with the stochastic synaptic noise, their reactivation rate increases and is persistent for a few seconds, resulting in activity similar to that observed in vivo during working memory tasks [7].

During WM tasks a variety of brain areas are being activated, which exhibit structural, physiological and functional differences. Here we test the effect of network size, number of connections, axonal delays, small-world connectivity, and ratio of excitatory to inhibitory neurons. The work presented here focuses on how the *quality* of PNGs changes if various network parameters are changed and continues our work from [8] which focused on how the *quantity* of PNGs changed when network parameters were changed. We show that the maximum axonal conduction delays and number of excitatory neurons have a significant contribution to the PNG sustainability.

2   Method

We need to find a way to measure the quality of a PNG when interpreted as an item in WM. Unfortunately, literature is not very clear on how to measure aspects of WM [9] such as sustainability, item retention, delay interval and the decay of memory traces etc. Here we therefore measure PNG quality in two ways: 1. by their *strength*, and by 2. their *duration*.

We understand as the strength of a PNG the activation of the neurons that belong to the PNG for the duration of the simulation as a percentage of neurons activated over total number of neurons in a PNG, where PNG membership is determined as in [10]. Here we calculate strength as the area under curve of a PNG activation rate plot (Fig. 1). We assume that the greater the strength and activation rate of the memory trace, the greater will be the objective amount of information remembered, representing for example the amount of accurately remembered details connected to a memory item.

We define the duration of a PNG as the time interval between the onset of the stimulation where the activation frequency increases until it drops back down to a baseline (Fig. 1), representing the duration of the sustained activation rate in the context of confidence on remembering the substance or general meaning of a scene or memory or just the existence of a memory trace. For us this duration represents the duration of the memory. To bring sustainability strength and duration in context, if we have big values in both strength and duration, then the memory of an item or a scene will be remembered accurately with a lot of detail (strength) and for a long time (duration). Or in another example, if you have a small sustainability strength value but with a big sustainability duration value, that could represent a memory that is remebered for a long period of time however without a lot of detail.

We follow the methodology used in [7], in which the original network consists of 1000 neurons, 800 excitatory (regular spiking pyramidal neurons), 200 inhibitory (GABAergic fast spiking interneurons) representing standard neocortical parameters. Excitatory synaptic connections have random delays up to 20ms. Inhibitory connections have 1ms delays. The connectivity probability is 0.1. We use the simple model of spiking neurons (eqs 1, 2), as proposed by Izhikevich [11]. Variable v represents the membrane potential of the neuron; u represents the so-called recovery variable, and provides negative feedback to v; and I represents synaptic or injected currents. The parameter a describes the time scale of the recovery variable u. Smaller values result in slower recovery. The parameter b describes the sensitivity of the recovery variable u to the subthreshold fluctuations of the membrane potential v. The parameter c describes the after-spike reset value of the membrane potential v. The parameter d describes after-spike reset of the recovery variable u.

$$v' = 0.04v^2 + 5v + 140 - u + I \tag{1}$$

$$u' = a(bv - u) \text{ with reset conditions, if } v \geq +30 \text{ mV, then } \begin{cases} v \leftarrow c \\ u \leftarrow u + d \end{cases} \tag{2}$$

Excitatory to inhibitory and all inhibitory connections are non-plastic. Excitatory synaptic strengths change according to the STDP rule [12]. That is, the magnitude of change of synaptic strength between a pre- and a postsynaptic neuron depends on the timing of spikes: The synapse gets potentiated if the presynaptic spike arrives at the postsynaptic neuron before the postsynaptic neuron fires; whereas the synapse gets depressed if the presynaptic spike arrives at the postsynaptic neuron after that fired. The magnitude of change for potentiation equals $A_+ e^{-\frac{\Delta t}{\tau}}$; and for synaptic depression is $A_- e^{-\frac{\Delta t}{\tau}}$, where Δt is the inter-spike interval between the arrival of the presynaptic spike and the postsynaptic spike, $\tau = 20$ms, $A_+ = 0.1$, and $A_- = 0.12$. The synaptic strengths are bound within the interval $[0 \ldots 8]$mV, which implies that the simultaneous arrival of at least three pre-synaptic spikes is needed to reliably elicit a post-synaptic response. About $10 - 20$ optimal pre-then-post spike pairs are needed to increase the synaptic strength of a weak synapse to the maximum value.

The efficacy of synaptic transmission for synapses connecting excitatory neurons are also scaled up or down, relative to a baseline, on a short timescale. With short-term STDP, input to neuron i at time t, $I_i(t)$, equals $\sum_{j \in J} s_{ij}(1 + sd_{ij})$, where s_{ij} is synaptic weight for the synapse between neuron j and i; and J is the set of presynaptic neurons whose spike arrived at neuron i at time t. The effect of a presynaptic spike is scaled up or down by the factor sd, where this

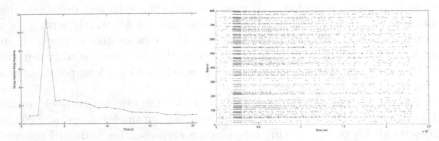

Fig. 1. Left: Firing frequency of a PNG. At the 3rd second, in which we stimulate the group 10 times, its firing frequency increases 10 fold. Then it decays back to a baseline, here 23 seconds after the stimulation. We measure sustainability in two ways: By strength, represented by the area under the curve, and duration, represented by the time the groups' firing frequency drops down to 2Hz. Right: Firing plot of a PNG for the duration of the simulation.

variable is different for each synapse, follows the classical STDP rule with the parameters A_+, A_- as above and in the absence of synaptic activity it decays back to 0 with a time constant 5 seconds. Therefore in the absence of synaptic activity the synaptic efficacy does not change, pre-then-post spikes temporarily increase the synaptic efficacy, and post-then-pre spikes temporarily decrease the synaptic efficacy.

We run the simulations for a period of time to find emerging PNGs as described in [10]. To achieve persistent 'reverberation', we select one PNG, and we stimulate the intra-PNG neurons sequentially with the corresponding polychronous pattern at 100ms intervals during a one second interval to temporarily increase the intra-PNG synaptic efficacy (see Fig. 1). To explore sustainability we run different simulations and we vary each time: the network size, the number of neuronal synaptic connections, the maximum axonal conduction delays between neurons, the connectivity pattern, and then we vary the percentage of excitatory towards inhibitory neurons in the network. We run 10 simulations for each experiment to check consistency of our results.

3   Experiments and Evaluation

3.1   Network Size

Here we use the model as described in the method section, however we vary the network size: 800, 850, 900, 950 and 1000 neurons, keeping the ratio excitatory to inhibitory 4:1. We keep the PNG size towards the rest of the network constant (10%).

There is a slight increase at the duration on networks consisting of 950 and 1000 neurons respectively, however there is a great variance and very small difference between the means of each set of experiments to suggest significant changes (see Fig. 2). This can also be quantified with an analysis of variance (ANOVA) resulting

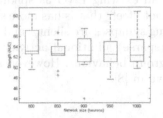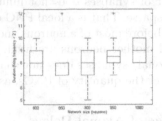

Fig. 2. Sustainability of polychronous groups of various network sizes. The network size does not affect sustainability strength, but slightly increases the duration on networks consisting of 950 and 1000 neurons respectively. Boxplots denote the median, the 25th and 75th percentiles, extreme points and outliers (+).

in a very large p value for strength ($p = 0.7833$) and duration ($p = 0.3563$), indicating that the differences between column means are not significant. The relative insensitivity of the quality of PNGs to global size of the network can be explained because a PNG is a local motif in a network – and this local motif does not change if the global size is varied. The number of PNGs, i.e. their *quantity* however does depend on the global size of the network [8]. This could suggest that memory decay per se is not a key factor in WM capacity, but is a result of the ability to represent larger memory content with larger networks [8].

3.2   Number of Synaptic Connections

Synaptogenesis explodes synaptic numbers, while synaptic pruning reduces the number of neurons and synapses. Here we varied the number of synapses from 80 to 100 in scale of 5 to explore how sustainability is affected keeping all other parameters fixed.

The large variances suggest that the number of connections is not an important parameter in the quality of a PNG (see Fig. 3). This is also evident after an ANOVA showing large p values for strength ($p = 0.3631$) and duration ($p = 0.3563$). The relative insensitivity of the quality of PNGs to changes in

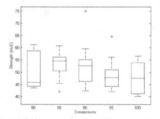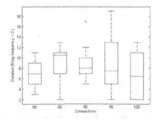

Fig. 3. Sustainability of polychronous groups when we vary the number of synaptic connections per neuron. There is an optimal mean value for strength and duration for 85 connections per neuron, increased from 80 connections per neuron and gradually decreases for 90, 95, and 100 connections per neuron.

the number of synapses does not influence an existing PNG as spiking in the network is sparse. That is a local PNG does not "feel" that is has more synapses, because as before most of a neurons' incomimg synapses are silent – and once the anchor and mother neurons are fired, the (sparse) additional activity through the (additional) synapses does not change group behaviour. However, synapses greatly affect the quantity of PNGs, as shown in [8].

3.3   Range of Axonal Delays

Evidence suggests that conduction time in the mammalian brain can reach from a few ms up to over 50ms [13]. In our experiment, we set the upper limit to 50ms. This parameter can be interpreted in the brain as populations with short synapses, or areas with high density.

We get small values for strength and duration for up to $10ms$ delays with very small variance, and increasingly much bigger values for 20, 30, 40 and 50ms delays (see Fig. 4). The big mean differences and the very small variance between our results indicate how crucial the maximum range of axonal conduction delays in the network is to PNG sustainability. This can also be indicated by the very small p values after an ANOVA both for strength ($p = 0.0006$) and duration ($p = 0.033$). Axonal delays, influence the PNG locals, as it determines the "spread" of spike times locally. There may be a maximum of quality: If the spread is too narrow there are no PNGs, because all need to fire more or less at once. If the spread is too big, the likelihood decreases of arrival of several spikes within the membrane time constant at a target neuron, so no PNGs either.

3.4   Small World Connectivity

Next we apply a small world connectivity pattern in the network using a variation of the Watts–Strogatz algorithm [14] that produces graphs with small-world properties: We construct a regular lattice (here a neural network), a graph with N nodes (neurons) each connected to K neighbours, K/2 on each side. For every node $n_i = n_0,\ldots, n_{N-1}$ we take every edge (synapse) n_i, n_j with $i < j$ and

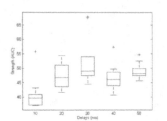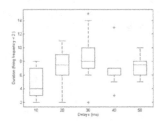

Fig. 4. Sustainability of polychronous groups when we vary the maximum length of the axonal conduction delays, or the time required for an action potential to travel from a pre- to a postsynaptic neuron. We get very small values for strength and duration for up to 10ms delays, with very small variance especially for 10ms delays, and much bigger values for 20, 30, 40 and 50ms delays.

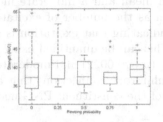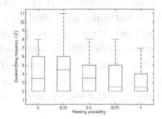

Fig. 5. Sustainability of PNGs when we vary the rewiring probability of a neighbouring synaptic connection to move from a local connectivity network ($\beta = 0$) to a random connectivity network ($\beta = 1$). There is an optimum mean value for $\beta = 0.25$, however with a big variance in all results, especially in the sustainability duration (right).

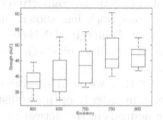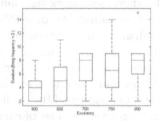

Fig. 6. Sustainability of polychronous groups when we vary the number of excitatory neurons in the model, keeping the total number of neurons at 1000. There is an increase to the strength and duration as the excitatory neurons increase.

rewire it with probability β. Rewiring is done by replacing (n_i, n_j) with (n_i, n_k) where k is chosen with uniform probability from all possible values. We vary the rewiring probability of a neighbouring synaptic connection to move from a local connectivity network ($\beta = 0$) to a random connectivity network ($\beta = 1$). In addition, we assign the delays according to the relevant distance between pre- and postsynaptic neurons.

There appears to be an optimum sustainability mean value for $\beta = 0.25$ (see Fig. 5), however there is a big variance in all the results, especially in the sustainability duration (right) indicating that the differences between column means are not significant. This is also quantified after an ANOVA with which we get high p values both for strength ($p = 0.5432$) and duration ($p = 0.7811$). Connectivity does not influence quality of PNG, as it does not matter for a group where the neurons that are part of as long as they have enough connections to the anchor neurons. So while the global connectivity looks different for a different network topology, the algorithm selects on those motifs that fit into the PNG pattern anyway, it explicitly affects a certain connectivity structure.

3.5 Excitation versus Inhibition

Here we explore how sustainability strength and duration of PNGs is affected when we vary the number of excitatory neurons in the model, keeping the total number of neurons to 1000.

There is a large increase to the strength mean and a moderate increase in duration (large variance for duration) mean as the number of excitatory neurons in the network increase (see Fig. 6), indicating that excitation is a crucial parameter for sustainability in the model. This can be quantified using ANOVA resulting to very small p values for strength ($p = 0.0022$) and moderate for duration ($p = 0.1284$). The large number of inhibitory connections that a neuron receives can supress the synaptic dynamics of the constituent PNG neurons.

4 Conclusion

We explored how different parameters affect the sustainability of a PNG. The range of axonal conduction delays and excitatory neurons affect sustainability in the network, whereas network size, number of connections, connectivity pattern do not impact sustainability of a PNG. Previous work has shown that these parameters can affect memory content as quantity of emerging PNGs [8], however here they do not affect the intrinsic properties (quality) of PNGs due to the associative nature of the synaptic dynamics.

Axonal delays and excitation results suggest that we need specific values of parameters as a percentage of the whole network in order to optimise sustainability. Here the bigger the number of excitatory neurons in the network the bigger sustainability follows. This could suggest that there is a bigger sustainability efficiency in brain areas where we have a big percentage of excitatory neurons i.e. in the hippocampus as opposed to smaller percentage in cortical areas [15]. This could also relate to the fMRI data results revealing that activation in left ventral lateral prefrontal cortex and temporoparietal junction predicted subsequent confidence ratings and in contrast, parahippocampal and hippocampal activity predicted the number of details remembered [9].

Acknowledgements. AG is supported by the Human Brain Project (HBP).

References

1. Fuster, J.M., Alexander, G.E., et al.: Neuron activity related to short-term memory. Science 173(3997), 652–654 (1971)
2. Miyashita, Y.: Neuronal correlate of visual associative long-term memory in the primate temporal cortex. Nature 335(6193), 817–820 (1988)
3. Funahashi, S., Bruce, C.J., Goldman-Rakic, P.S.: Mnemonic coding of visual space in the monkey's dorsolateral prefrontal cortex. Journal of Neurophysiology 61(2), 331–349 (1989)
4. Wang, X.J.: Synaptic basis of cortical persistent activity: the importance of nmda receptors to working memory. The Journal of Neuroscience 19(21), 9587–9603 (1999)
5. Machens, C.K., Romo, R., Brody, C.D.: Flexible control of mutual inhibition: a neural model of two-interval discrimination. Science 307(5712), 1121–1124 (2005)
6. Mongillo, G., Barak, O., Tsodyks, M.: Synaptic theory of working memory. Science 319(5869), 1543–1546 (2008)

7. Szatmáry, B., Izhikevich, E.M.: Spike-timing theory of working memory. PLoS Computational Biology 6(8), e1000879 (2010)
8. Ioannou, P., Casey, M., Grüning, A.: Evaluating the effect of spiking network parameters on polychronization. In: Villa, A.E.P., Duch, W., Érdi, P., Masulli, F., Palm, G. (eds.) ICANN 2012, Part I. LNCS, vol. 7552, pp. 255–263. Springer, Heidelberg (2012)
9. Qin, S., van Marle, H.J., Hermans, E.J., Fernández, G.: Subjective sense of memory strength and the objective amount of information accurately remembered are related to distinct neural correlates at encoding. The Journal of Neuroscience 31(24), 8920–8927 (2011)
10. Izhikevich, E.M.: Polychronization: computation with spikes. Neural Computation 18(2), 245–282 (2006)
11. Izhikevich, E.M., et al.: Simple model of spiking neurons. IEEE Transactions on Neural Networks 14(6), 1569–1572 (2003)
12. Sjöström, J., Gerstner, W.: Spike-timing dependent plasticity. Scholarpedia 5(2), 1362 (2010)
13. Swadlow, H.A., Waxman, S.G.: Axonal conduction delays. Scholarpedia 7(6), 1451 (2012)
14. Watts, D.J., Strogatz, S.H.: Collective dynamics of 'small-world' networks. Nature 393(6684), 440–442 (1998)
15. Shepherd, G.M.: The Organization of the Brain. Oxford University Press (2004)

Pre- and Postsynaptic Properties Regulate Synaptic Competition through Spike-Timing-Dependent Plasticity

Hana Ito and Katsunori Kitano

Department of Human and Computer Intelligence, Ritsumeikan University,
1-1-1 Nojihigashi, Kusatsu, Shiga 5258577, Japan
hana@cns.ci.ritsumei.ac.jp, kitano@ci.ritsumei.ac.jp

Abstract. Brain functions such as learning and memory rely on synaptic plasticity. Many studies have shown that synaptic plasticity can be driven by the timings between pre- and postsynaptic spikes, also known as spike-timing-dependent plasticity (STDP). In most of the modeling studies exploring STDP functions, presynaptic spikes have been postulated to be Poisson (random) spikes and postsynaptic neurons have been described using an integrate-and-fire model, for simplicity. However, experimental data suggest this is not necessarily true. In this study, we investigated how STDP worked in synaptic competition if more neurophysiologically realistic properties for pre- and postsynaptic dynamics were incorporated; presynaptic (input) spikes obeyed a gamma process and the postsynaptic neuron was a multi-timescale adaptive threshold model. Our results showed that STDP strengthened specific combinations of pre- and postsynaptic properties; regular spiking neurons favored regular input spikes whereas random spiking neurons did random ones, suggesting neural information coding utilizes both the properties.

Keywords: Synaptic plasticity, synaptic competition, interspike intervals, adaptive spike threshold.

1 Introduction

Synaptic plasticity is a physical change in synapses that embeds learning and memories in neural circuits. A significant neural activity encoding such a cognitive function is transformed into a configuration of synaptic strengths, suggesting that the activity patterns strengthening synapses should be the method by which neural information is coded. Many experimental studies have reported that synapses undergo changes depending on the relative timings between pre- and postsynaptic spikes, which is called spike-timing-dependent plasticity (STDP) [1, 2]. To understand the functional roles of STDP, many computational models have been proposed thus far [3, 4]. According to those studies, STDP regulates the firing rate of postsynaptic neurons, bringing about competition between synapses, and detecting coherent neural activities. Most of those studies, however, have hypothesised that input spikes mediated by STDP synapses were Poisson (random) spikes and that the spike generation mechanism is well described

S. Wermter et al. (Eds.): ICANN 2014, LNCS 8681, pp. 733–740, 2014.

by the simple leaky integrate-and-fire (LIF) model. However, experimental and theoretical studies have shown that these hypotheses do not necessarily explain the mechanism [5–8]. Considering the significance of pre- and postsynaptic spike timings in STDP, an important issue is to investigate its functional roles in the case of more realistic temporal structures of synaptic inputs and spike generation mechanisms.

To address this issue, we incorporated more neurophysiologically realistic features into a computational model for synaptic competition by STDP [3]. In our model, interspike intervals (ISIs) of presynaptic spikes obey gamma distributions with various values of shape parameter. This implementation enables us to generate a wide spectrum of spike trains, from Poisson to periodic by changing the shape parameter. In addition, we adapted a multi-timescale adaptive threshold (MAT) model, not merely an LIF model, as the postsynaptic neuron because the MAT model is capable of mimicking the spiking activity of a real cortical neuron much more precisely than any other neuron model [9]. We investigated how the interplay between the pre- and postsynaptic features affects synaptic competition through STDP and what the most effective combination of these features to strengthen synapses is, which could act as the method of encoding for various cognitive functions.

2   Methods

In our model, a single postsynaptic neuron received synaptic inputs from 1,000 excitatory synapses and 200 inhibitory ones. We here focused on synaptic competition among only excitatory synapses and therefore fixed strengths (conductances) of the inhibitory synapses and the firing rate of inhibitory inputs.

2.1   Postsynaptic Neuron Model

The dynamics of the postsynaptic neuron was modeled by the MAT model [9] that was proven to most precisely reproduce the spiking activity of a cortical neuron. The membrane potential V of the MAT model obeyed the following linear differential equation:

$$\tau_{\mathrm{m}} \frac{dV}{dt} = -(V - E_{\mathrm{rest}}) + I_{\mathrm{syn}}, \tag{1}$$

where τ_{m} and E_{rest} are the membrane time constant and the resting membrane potential, respectively. I_{syn} is the sum of synaptic currents mentioned below. When the membrane potential V reached the time-varying threshold $\theta(t)$, the neuron is supposed to emit a neuronal spike without the resetting used in an LIF model. The time course of $\theta(t)$ was described by

$$\theta(t) = \theta_{\infty} + \sum_{t_i^{\mathrm{spk}} < t} \left(\alpha_1 e^{-(t - t_i^{\mathrm{spk}})/\tau_1} + \alpha_2 e^{-(t - t_i^{\mathrm{spk}})/\tau_2} \right), \tag{2}$$

where θ_∞, α_n and τ_n ($\tau_1 < \tau_2$) are the constant component, amplitudes of time-varying components, and the time constant, respectively. Each time-varying component of $\theta(t)$ increased instantaneously at every spike timing t_i^{spk} by α_n and then exponentially decayed. As the MAT neuron evoked spikes faster than the time-varying components decayed, the adaptive spike threshold was gradually increased and then its neuronal spiking slowed down. In particular, the time-varying component with the time constant of 100 to 200 ms was responsible for this spike frequency adaptation seen in a 'regular-spiking' neuron, the majority of excitatory cortical neurons.

2.2 Synaptic Currents

The synaptic inputs consisted of both excitatory and inhibitory inputs

$$I_{\mathrm{syn}} = \sum_{j=1}^{1000} g_j^{\mathrm{ex}}(E_{\mathrm{ex}} - V) + \sum_{k=1}^{200} g_k^{\mathrm{in}}(E_{\mathrm{in}} - V), \tag{3}$$

where g_j^{ex}, g_k^{in}, E_{ex} and E_{in} are the conductance of the j-th excitatory synapse, the conductance of the k-th inhibitory synapse, the reversal potential of excitatory synapses, and reversal potential of inhibitory synapses, respectively. Changes in g_j^{ex} and g_k^{in} obeyed the simple first-order kinetics; they instantaneously increased at a presynaptic spike timing and then decayed exponentially. The peak conductance of g_j^{ex} engaged in the spike-timing-dependent plasticity defined by pre- and postsynaptic spike pairs and the additive rule [3].

2.3 Presynaptic Spike Trains

The $(i + 1)$-th spike timing t_{i+1} is generated by adding an ISI, T_i, to the previous timing t_i, namely, $t_{i+1} = t_i + T_i$. The ISI T_i was drawn from the gamma distribution

$$T_i \sim p(t; k, \lambda) = \frac{\lambda^k t^{k-1} e^{-\lambda t}}{\Gamma(k)}, \tag{4}$$

where k, λ and $\Gamma(k)$ are a shape parameter, a rate parameter, and a gamma function, respectively. The mean of ISIs, $\bar{T}$, is $\bar{T} = \frac{k}{\lambda}$. The shape parameter k defines the shape of the distribution. If $k = 1$, the $p(t; 1, \lambda)$ is equivalent to the exponential distribution with a rate parameter λ. For a larger k, the distribution takes a symmetric shape, like a normal distribution, and consequently such a spike train exhibits nearly periodic firing. A spike train was generated by the ISI distribution independently of other spike trains.

2.4 Numerical Simulations

In order to examine how synaptic competition is affected by the interplay between the features of input spikes and postsynaptic dynamics, we compared different combinations of the pre- and postsynaptic features. Typically, the input spikes were generated by the gamma distribution with $k = 1$ or with $k = 2$ whereas the LIF or the MAT model were implemented as the postsynaptic neuron. In the last investigation, 1,000 excitatory synapses were divided into 10 subgroups (100 synapses per a subgroup). Synapses in a subgroup delivered spike trains generated by the gamma distribution with an identical shape parameter; the parameter for the i-th group was set to $k = i$.

The parameters of the MAT model were: $\tau_m = 20$ms, $\theta_\infty = -58$mV, $\tau_1 = 20$ms, $\tau_2 = 200$ms, $\alpha_1 = 20$mV, and $\alpha_2 = 3$mV. The other parameters were the same as those in a previous study [3].

3   Results

For various input firing rates, we conducted numerical simulations using our computational model until the distribution of synaptic strengths reached a stationary state. We here focused on this stationary distribution of synaptic strengths and the firing characteristics of the postsynaptic neuron in the stationary state.

3.1   Dependence on Postsynaptic Dynamics

First, we examined the synaptic competition mediated by the MAT model. Figure 1 shows the stationary distributions of synaptic strengths for various input firing rates and the spike statistics of the postsynaptic neuron in the stationary state. As shown in Fig. 1a–d, all the distributions exhibited bimodal shapes in which there existed a population of strengthened synapses (around 1) and that of weakened synapses (around 0). As the input firing rate was increased, the population of strengthened synapses became smaller, whereas that of the weakened ones became larger. Fig. 1e indicates that the postsynaptic firing rate was smaller than the case of an LIF model (10–15Hz) and that coefficients of variation (Cv) of postsynaptic ISIs were also much smaller than the previous ones (~ 0.9) [3]. The obtained spike statistics looked different from those of an LIF model, which can be attributed to the spike generation mechanism of the MAT model. However, we found that synapses competed with each other in a manner similar to that found in a previous study [3].

3.2   Dependence on Temporal Structures of Input Spike Trains

Next, to see how synaptic competition was affected by spike trains obeying a gamma process, such spike trains were fed into the LIF and MAT neuron models. Spike trains were generated by the gamma distribution with $k = 2$. The rate parameter was adjusted so that the means of ISIs were kept to the inverse of a preset input firing rate. Moreover, in this case, stationary distributions of synaptic strengths exhibited bimodal shapes similar to Fig. 1a–d (not shown). As shown in Fig. 2a and b, the firing rates of both models saturated with an increase in the input firing rate. The Cv of the LIF neuron decreased in comparison with

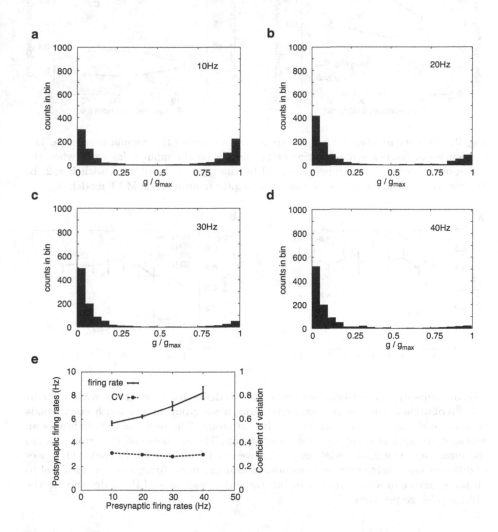

Fig. 1. Synaptic competition and activity regulation when the MAT model received Poisson spike trains ($k = 1$). **a.** Stationary distributions of synaptic strengths for the input firing rate of 10 spikes/s. The abscissa axis indicates the normalised synaptic conductance. **b, c,** and **d** are similar to **a**, but for 20 spikes/s, 30 spikes/s and 40 spikes/s, respectively. **e.** Dependencies of postsynaptic firing rates and coefficients of variation (Cv) on input firing rates.

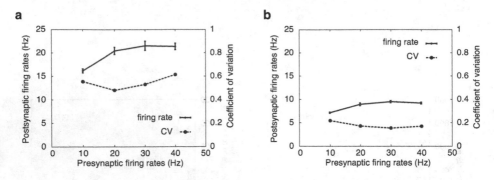

Fig. 2. Activity regulation for input spike trains obeying the gamma process. **a.** Dependencies of the postsynaptic firing rates and Cv on the input firing rates when the LIF model received spike trains generated by the gamma distribution with $k = 2$. **b.** Similar to **a**, but in the case that the postsynaptic neuron is the MAT model.

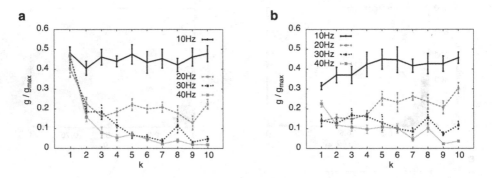

Fig. 3. Synaptic competition between synapses delivering spike trains with different ISI distributions. The abscissa axis represents a subgroup index, which corresponds to a value of the shape parameter for the subgroup. The ordinate axis indicates an averaged strength of synapses within a subgroup. The symbols and the error bars are the means and standard deviations of the averaged strengths for 10 trials. The cases of different input firing rates were examined, but the input firing rate was identical to all the synapses in a trial. **a.** and **b.** illustrate the case for an LIF model and for the MAT model, respectively.

that in the case of Poisson spike trains (~ 0.9) [3]. Similarly, the Cv of the MAT model became smaller than that shown in Fig. 1e. Irrespective of neuron models, spike trains could alter the spike statistics of the postsynaptic neuron, but not its synaptic competition.

3.3 Extracted Combinations of Pre- and Postsynaptic Features

Finally, we investigated whether each of the neuron models showed a preferred or favourite type of spike trains. In this simulation, the postsynaptic neuron

(LIF or MAT) received different types of spike trains from different subgroups of synapses; synapses in the i-th subgroup fed spikes generated by the gamma distribution with $k = i$ into the postsynaptic neuron. Figure 3 shows the synaptic strengths averaged over synapses in each subgroup for various input firing rates. For the LIF model (Fig. 3a), synapse strength in all the subgroups changed equally when the input firing rate was 10 Hz. In the case of higher input firing rates (20–40Hz), however, subgroups with the larger ks tended to be depressed, compared with the subgroup of $k = 1$. In contrast, the tendency was quite different for the MAT model (Fig. 3b). For the lower input firing rates (10 and 20Hz), synapses in subgroups with larger ks were strengthened. However, for the larger input firing rate (40Hz), those subgroups were more depressed. Thus, we found that the favoured spike trains depended on the neuron models and the input firing rates.

4 Discussion

Most of previous computational studies have assumed that spikes were randomly generated so that ISIs obeyed an exponential distribution. However, ISI distributions of experimentally recorded spike trains exhibit asymmetric unimodal shapes like Gamma distributions rather than exponential distributions. As for a computational neuron model, although an LIF model has been frequently used for simplicity, the model does not reproduce spiking activity of a real cortical neuron, for example, a regular spiking neuron that show spike frequency adaptation. These properties would have a considerable impact on many aspects of neuronal dynamics including activity-dependent neural network formation. Therefore, we studied synaptic competition brought about by STDP when we incorporated the more realistic properties of pre- and postsynaptic dynamics.

According to our results, as long as all synapses delivered spike trains with an identical feature (an ISI distribution), synapses competed similarly to how they did in a previous study [3] and stationary distributions of synaptic strengths were bimodal, irrespective of the choice of postsynaptic neuron model, or ISI distributions of input spikes. The bimodal shape emerged from the nature of the pairwise additive STDP rule that makes an unstable point at an intermediate strength [10], whereas the spike statistics of the postsynaptic neurons were influenced by the neuronal dynamics and the input ISI structures. For the case of a mixture of differently structured spike trains (with different k), strengthened synapses relied on combinations of the postsynaptic neuron models and the input ISI structures. Considering that spike trains mediated by strengthened synapses evoked postsynaptic spikes more effectively, we could determine which types of spike trains were favoured by the postsynaptic neuron by observing which synapses were strengthened. The LIF neuron favoured random spike trains for any input firing rate. In contrast, the MAT neuron favoured more regular spike trains (with a large k) for a lower input firing rate, but more random spike trains (with a small k) for a higher input firing rate. Taken together, the method of neural information encoding, by a configuration of synaptic strengths, is determined not only by presynaptic spike structures but also by postsynaptic neuronal dynamics.

Previous studies have revealed that cortical neurons can be classified into several neuron types from the viewpoints of the shapes of their ISI distributions, and that the neuron-type distributions differ between cortical areas [5]. For example, in motor-related areas, neurons exhibiting regular spike trains were dominant over those exhibiting random spike trains, but the opposite was observed in the prefrontal areas. From our results, the MAT model, which exhibited low Cv spiking, favoured regular spike trains whereas the LIF, which exhibited high Cv spiking, favoured random spike trains. This suggests that our results are consistent with the previous analysis reported in [5]. Furthermore, this implies that different functions processed in different cortical areas should utilise different methods of neural information coding.

Here we assumed a stationary process for input spike trains, which might limit the biological plausibility of our results, for example, the obtained Cv values (Fig.2b) were much smaller than those of experimental spike data. Implementing non-stationary inputs would improve them. Furthermore, if a cognitive function is represented by a transient neural activity, it is necessary to take into account such non-stationary dynamics. Even in that case, however, our results would serve as the basis for related future studies.

References

1. Markram, H., Lubke, J., Frotscher, M., Sakmann, B.: Regulation of Synaptic Efficacy by Coincidence of Postsynaptic APs and EPSPs. Science 275, 213–215 (1997)
2. Bi, G.-Q., Poo, M.-M.: Synaptic Modifications in Cultured Hippocampal Neurons: Dependence on Spike Timing, Synaptic Strength, and Postsynaptic Cell Type. J. Neurosci. 18, 10464–10472 (1998)
3. Song, S., Miller, K.D., Abbott, L.F.: Competitive Hebbian Learning Through Spike-Timing-Dependent Synaptic Plasticity. Nat. Neurosci. 3, 919–926 (2000)
4. Izhikevich, E.M., Gally, J.A., Edelman, G.M.: Spike-Timing Dynamics of Neuronal Groups. Cereb. Cortex. 14, 933–944 (2004)
5. Shinomoto, S., Miyazaki, Y., Tamura, H., Fujita, I.: Regional and Laminar Differences in In Vivo Firing Patterns of Primate Cortical Neurons. J. Neurophysiol. 94, 567–575 (2005)
6. Shinomoto, S., Miura, K., Koyama, S.: A Measure of Local Variation of Inter-spike Intervals. Biosystems 79, 67–72 (2005)
7. Brette, R., Gerstner, W.: Adaptive Exponential Integrate-and-Fire Model as an Effective Description of Neuronal Activity. J. Neurophysiol. 94, 3637–3642 (2005)
8. Izhikevich, E.M.: Which Model to Use for Cortical Spiking Neurons? IEEE Trans. Neural Netw. 15, 1063–1070 (2004)
9. Kobayashi, R., Tsubo, Y., Shinomoto, S.: Made-to-order Spiking Neuron Model Equipped with a Multi-Timescale Adaptive Threshold. Front. Comput. Neurosci. 3, 9 (2009)
10. Cateau, H., Fukai, T.: A Stochastic Method to Predict the Consequence of Arbitrary Forms of Spike-Timing-Dependent Plasticity. Neural Comput. 15, 597–620 (2003)

Location-Dependent Dendritic Computation in a Modeled Striatal Projection Neuron

Youwei Zheng[1,2], Lars Schwabe[2], and Joshua L. Plotkin[1]

[1] Feinberg School of Medicine, Department of Physiology,
Northwestern University, USA
[2] Faculty of Computer Science and Electrical Engineering,
University of Rostock, Germany

Abstract. The striatum comprises part of a feedback loop between the cerebral cortex, thalamus and other nuclei of the basal ganglia, ultimately guiding action selection and motor learning. Much of this is facilitated by striatal projection neurons, which receive and process highly convergent cortical and thalamic excitatory inputs. All of the glutamatergic inputs to projection neurons synapse on dendrites, many directly on spine heads. The distal, but not proximal, dendrites of projection neurons are capable of supporting synaptically driven regenerative events, which are transfered to the soma as depolarized upstates from which action potentials can occur. In this study we present a modified NEURON model of a striatal projection neuron, and use it to examine the location-dependence of upstate generation and action potential gating. Specifically, simulations show that the small diameter of distal SPN dendrites can support plateau potentials by increasing the cooperativity among neighboring spines. Furthermore, such distally evoked plateaus can boost the somatic response to stimulation of proximal dendritic spines, facilitating action potential generation. The implications these results have for action selection are discussed.

Keywords: Computational neuroscience, striatum, dendrite, upstate, association-based information processing.

1 Introduction

As the major input nucleus of the basal ganglia, the striatum integrates diverse cortical and thalamic inputs. Striatal spiny projection neurons (SPNs), the principal cells in the striatum, relay this processed information to output nuclei of the basal ganglia as action potentials. *In vivo* SPNs only fire action potentials from depolarized "up states", which represent the spatial and temporal convergence of multiple excitatory inputs [5,6]. Such synaptically driven state transitions are therefore believed to endow SPNs with the capacity to associate cortical and thalamic contextual, sensory and motor cues to control striatal output.

It was proposed that the generation of such state transitions may require highly coordinated spiking from hundreds of cortical neurons. However, the model of how upstates are produced has been recently revised. Rapid activation of tens, not hundreds, of neighboring spines on a distal dendrite is sufficient to induce a state transition that can last hundreds of milliseconds [5].

S. Wermter et al. (Eds.): ICANN 2014, LNCS 8681, pp. 741–748, 2014.

We proposed in a previous study that one functional and computational role of such distally evoked upstates is to associate proximally driven inputs such that the neuron could act as a classifier to distinguish between contextually appropriate action cues and irrelevant background action noises [7]. However, the integrative properties of proximal inputs in conjunction with distal ones remain unclear.

In the present work, we present an active multicompartmental model of a SPN that replicates both distal upstate generation and somatic spiking behavior. We then use the model to explore another factor, dendritic anatomy, that was implicated in governing the upstate generation process and its restriction to distal (but not proximal) dendrites. Finally, we propose a computational model by which, proximal-distal integration carried out by a SPN can realize associative information processing.

2   A Brief Description of NEURON Modeling

A SPN model was programmed using NEURON version 7.2 [3]. The stylized multicompartmental cylindrical model of the cell was adapted from [5], containing 6 primary, 12 secondary and 24 tertiary dendrites, with each branch bifurcating twice. 349 spines were added only to 2 tertiary dendrites and the others were modeled by compensating for the additional membrane area attributable to the spines. The model was updated to include voltage-gated sodium channels in the soma and dendrites, enabling the generation of realistic somatic spiking. Spines were explicitly modeled with spine heads connected to spine necks attached to their parent dendritic shafts. The spine necks were passive but spine heads were endowed with fast-activating AMPA and NMDA receptors, and various voltage-dependent ion channels, such as T-type and R-type calcium channels and Kir2 potassium channels.

3   Results

3.1   5-step Model Verification

In Fig.1A we illustrate a part of the SPN model, showing a soma, one complete dendritic branch and spine locations that receive proximal and distal inputs. Various protocols were conducted to match the model to reported somatic electrophysiological recordings.

For the first step of model verification, the somatic response was examined in current-clamp conditions. One signature characteristic of a SPN is an extended depolarizing ramp in response to somatic current injection before firing the first spike. This behavior was manifest in the model in response to suprathreshold current injection (Fig.1B, red). Larger amplitude current injection led to repetitive firing (Fig.1B, black), consistent with previously published data [1].

Second, experimental uncaging of glutamate has shown that somatically measured EPSP amplitude evoked by activating glutamate receptors on a single spine is independent of its location (see Supplementary Fig.3 in [5]). We confirmed this observation in the presented model by synaptically activating one proximal and one distal spine, each with an identical glutamate receptor composition. The resulting somatically measured EPSPs had similar amplitudes whether triggered by stimulation of distal or proximal spines (Fig.1C).

Third, SPN state transitions can be evoked experimentally by spatially and temporally coordinated activation of about a dozen distal dendritic spines. We reproduced this in our model by activating 12 spines in rapid succession (500 HZ) on a distal dendrite ($> 120 \, \mu m$ from soma). The resulting membrane potential trajectory at the soma demonstrated at least 3 features of an experimentally observed distal upstate: 1) it peaked tens of milliseconds after the termination of the stimulus; 2) depolarization was sustained as a plateau and, 3) depolarization decayed to the baseline exponentially after the plateau (Fig.1D, solid red).

Fourth, unlike distal dendrites, proximal dendrites are not capable of sustaining regenerative events [5]. Consistent with this observation, activating 12 proximal spines ($> 60 \, \mu m$ from soma) in rapid succession (500 Hz) produced a somatic response that reached the same peak as the distally-evoked response but decayed almost immediately after the protocol ended (Fig.1D, solid black).

Fifth, dendritically-evoked upstates require NMDA receptor (NMDAR) and voltage-gated calcium channels (VGCCs). We confirmed the contribution of these channels to EPSPs evoked by rapid activation of 12 distal or proximal spines. Removal of these conductances reduced both the amplitude and duration of distally-evoked EPSPs (dashed red), but had little effect on proximally-evoked responses (Fig.1D, dashed black). These results confirmed our previous demonstration that not only do NMDAR and VGCCs contribute to dendritic plateau potentials, but they are more efficiently engaged in distal dendrites.

Taken together, the above model verification demonstrates that our presented model is able to faithfully replicate a number of hallmark SPN characteristics.

3.2   Anatomical Constraints of Upstate Generation

Plateau potentials in distal SPN dendrites require current flow through NMDAR and VGCCs, and are subject to the effects of neuromodulators [5]. Our previous work suggested that the ability of distal, but not proximal, SPN dendrites to support regenerative events is a consequence of a distance-dependent increase in input resistance caused by dendritic tapering.

Here we examine the role of dendritic tapering in the origin of plateau potentials and distance-dependent responses to synaptic stimulation. We hypothesized that if dendritic shaft tapering enhances distal synaptic responses by increasing input resistance and restricting ion flow away from the site of stimulation, then local dendritic depolarization induced by a single synaptic stimulus should be greater in distal dendritic shafts (see also Discussion in [5]). To test this hypothesis, single spines were activated at proximal and distal locations within the tertiary dendritic segment. Although the local peak EPSP amplitude in spine heads was independent of the distance from the soma, the local EPSP amplitude in distal dendritic shafts was 2-fold larger than their proximal counterparts

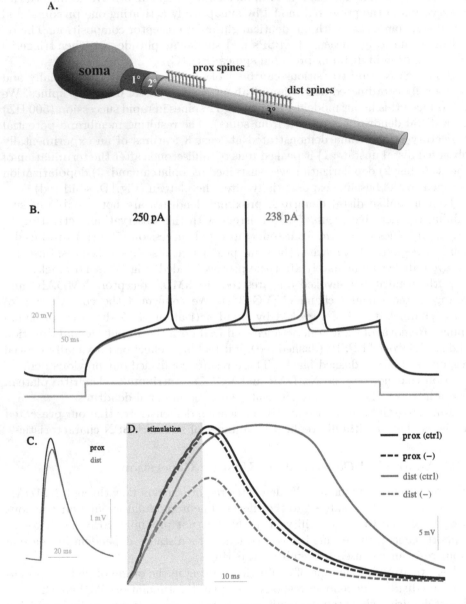

Fig. 1. 5-step model verification. A: Schematic representation of the modeled SPN showing a soma (green) and one primary (blue), one secondary (cyan) and one tertiary (purple) dendrite. Proximal and distal spines are represented using matchsticks as labeled. **B:** Somatic membrane potential traces in response to depolarizing current injections. **C:** Somatic EPSPs evoked by stimulating either a proximal (prox) or distal (dist) spine. **D:** Somatic voltage traces in response to stimulation of 12 proximal (black, solid) or distal (red, solid) dendritic spines at 500 Hz. Dashed traces are in a modeled SPN lacking NMDAR and VGCCs in spine heads.

(Fig.2A, CTRL). When NMDAR and VGCCs were removed from spine heads, we again observed no significant distance-dependence of peak EPSP amplitude in spines (Fig.2A, -NMDAR & VGCCs). The distance dependence of peak EPSP amplitude in dendritic shafts, however, was now greatly attenuated (+NMDAR & VGCCs: dist/prox=2; -NMDAR & VGCCs: dist/prox=1.2).

These results can be interpreted with the aid of previously published spine-shaft models [2,4]. The total spine input impedance (R_{sp}) is assumed to be the summed impedance of spine neck (R_n) and parent dendritic shaft (R_{sh}):

$$R_{sp} = R_n + R_{sh} \tag{1}$$

we can express the amplitude of the EPSP evoked at the dendritic shaft as:

$$V_{sh} = g_{head}E_{head}\frac{R_{sh}}{1 + g_{head}R_{sp}} \tag{2}$$

where g_{head} is the total input conductance of ion channels at the spine head and E_{head} is the reversal potential. Given that in our model g_{head} is much smaller than R_{sp}, we can simplify (2) to (3):

$$V_{sh} \approx g_{head}E_{head}R_{sh} \tag{3}$$

From Eqn.3, we see that as the reversal potential is always constant, V_{sh} depends on two variables: g_{head} and R_{sh}. Impedance calculation of R_{sh}^{prox} and R_{sh}^{dist} was performed using the compute function provided by NEURON Impedance class (data not shown). In control conditions, tapering of the tertiary dendrite produced a static R_{sh} that was twice as high distally vs proximally ($R_{sh}^{dist} = 2*R_{sh}^{prox}$). The attenuated distance-dependence of dendritic shaft EPSP amplitude in the absence of NMDAR and VGCCs likely reflects a reduction in absolute shaft depolarization due to a decrease in g_{head}.

As activation of a single spine depolarized distal dendritic shafts more robustly than proximal ones, it stands to reason that rapid activation of multiple neighboring spines will induce a larger depolarization in distal shafts, supporting their ability to sustain regenerative events. Indeed, sequential activation of 12 neighboring spines induced summating depolarization of both distal and proximal parent dendritic shafts (Fig.2B, solid red lines), but the amplitude was twice as high in distal dendrites (Fig.2B, vertical double arrows). Such ample distal dendritic depolarization in turn boosted the activation of NMDAR and VGCCs in the stimulated spines. Although this boost only modestly enhanced the peak EPSP amplitude at individual distal spines, it sustained the membrane potential of distal spine heads at a high voltage (above -30 mV) well after the stimulus, in contrast to the fast decay in proximal spines (Fig.2B). The resulting plateau potential generated in distal dendrites then transfered, via cable properties of the dendrite to the soma where it was expressed as a long-lasting upstate (Fig.2B, dashed green lines). These simulations expand our previous work to offer a model by which dendritic tapering slows the decay of synaptically-induced dendritic depolarizations by amplifying interspine cooperativity, consistent with studies in pyramidal neurons [2].

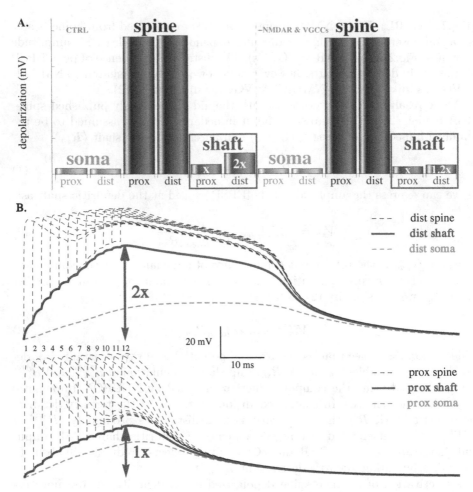

Fig. 2. Small diameter distal dendrite can support state transition by amplifying depolarization. A: Peak EPSP amplitudes in both control conditions (CTRL) and in the absence of NMDAR and VGCCs (-NMDAR & VGCCs). The red rectangles highlight the ratio of distal to proximal shaft depolarization. **B:** Membrane potential traces from soma (green), shaft (red) and spine heads (blue) of the modeled SPN in response to stimulation of 12 neighboring distal (top) or proximal (bottom) spines.

3.3   Association-Based Dendritic Computation

Active dendrites are able to generate regenerative events and therefore serve as elementary computational units of information processing in the brain. Our previous work suggested that even in a passive Rall model, associative dendritic computation can be implemented. Specifically, when the model was endowed with the capacity to generate plateau potentials in distal dendrites, synaptic stimulation of passive proximal dendrites immediately after the distally generated plateau potential produced larger amplitude EPSPs that drove the soma close to the action potential threshold [7].

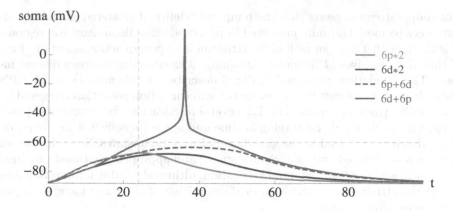

Fig. 3. Synaptically driven distal plateau potential facilitates the generation of action potentials by proximal inputs. Somatic responses evoked by stimulating: 6 neighboring proximal spines twice each (green); 6 neighboring distal spines twice each (blue); 6 proximal spines followed by 6 distal spines (dashed red); 6 distal spines followed by 6 proximal spines (solid red). All spines are stimulated at 500 Hz.

Here we conceptualized our active SPN model as an association-based information processing unit capable of integrating distally-encoded regenerative events with temporally restricted proximally encoded cues. To begin testing this, the dendritic length stimulated to evoke a plateau potential was reduced by half (from 12 to 6 spines, stimulated twice each, maintaining 12 total stimuli), sharpening the spatial parameter. Just as in Fig.1, this modification induced robust plateau potentials when delivered distally but not proximally (Fig.3, blue vs. green). Neither stimulation pattern induced a somatic action potential. Integration of distal and proximal cues was then examined by distributing the 12 stimuli among distal and proximal spines. Stimulation of 6 neighboring proximal spines immediately followed by stimulation of 6 neighboring distal spines produced a long somatic plateau potential (Fig.3, dashed red). Stimulation of 6 distal spines before 6 proximal spines, however, induced a plateau potential and initiated a somatic action potential (Fig.3, solid red). These simulations raise the possibility that SPNs can associate discrete clusters of excitatory inputs based on the timed innervation of specific portions of their dendritic tree.

4   Discussion

We have previously shown that the highly tapered distal dendrites of SPNs can support local regenerative events while the larger diameter proximal dendrites can not [5]. The present simulations expand upon this, suggesting that the small diameter of distal dendrites only modestly affects the peak EPSP amplitude of stimulated spines, but robustly increases the amount of time neighboring stimulated spines reside above a possible "threshold" depolarization. The nature of this cooperativity suggests that the temporal fidelity of clustered excitatory inputs may be more faithfully preserved in proximal than distal dendritic regions. It is thought that a major task of the striatum is to govern action selection. Part of this likely involves SPNs making meaningful associations between diverse inputs. The simulations presented in Fig. 3 describe a mechanism by which SPN distal dendrites may gate the generation of somatic action potentials triggered by proximally-synapsing inputs. This has several implications for striatal computations. First, only inputs converging in time and space (in sufficient numbers) on distal dendrites will lead to the generation of somatic upstates. Second, once an upstate is established, only sufficiently strong and appropriately timed proximal inputs will lead to action potential generation, ultimately gating information flow out of the striatum and inhibition or disinhibition of the basal ganglia output nuclei controlling action.

References

1. Gertler, T.S., Chan, C.S., Surmeier, D.J.: Dichotomous anatomical properties of adult striatal medium spiny neurons. The Journal of Neuroscience 28(43), 10814–10824 (2008)
2. Harnett, M.T., Makara, J.K., Spruston, N., Kath, W.L., Magee, J.C.: Synaptic amplification by dendritic spines enhances input cooperativity. Nature 491(7425), 599–602 (2012)
3. Hines, M.L., Carnevale, N.T.: The neuron simulation environment. Neural Comput. 9, 1179–1209 (1997)
4. Koch, C., Anthony, Z.: The function of dendritic spines: devices subserving biochemical rather than electrical compartmentalization. The Journal of Neuroscience 13(2), 413–422 (1993)
5. Plotkin, J.L., Day, M., Surmeier, D.J.: Synaptically driven state transitions in distal dendrites of striatal spiny neurons. Nat. Neurosci. 14(7), 881–888 (2011)
6. Wilson, C.J., Kawaguchi, Y.: The origins of two-state spontaneous membrane potential fluctuations of neostriatal spiny neurons. The Journal of Neuroscience 16(7), 2397–2410 (1996)
7. Zheng, Y., Schwabe, L.: Dendritic computations in a rall model with strong distal stimulation. In: Mladenov, V., Koprinkova-Hristova, P., Palm, G., Villa, A.E.P., Appollini, B., Kasabov, N. (eds.) ICANN 2013. LNCS, vol. 8131, pp. 304–311. Springer, Heidelberg (2013)

Classifying Spike Patterns
by Reward-Modulated STDP

Brian Gardner, Ioana Sporea, and André Grüning

Department of Computing, University of Surrey,
Guildford, Surrey, GU2 7XH, UK
{b.gardner,i.sporea,a.gruning}@surrey.ac.uk

Abstract. Reward-modulated learning rules for spiking neural networks
have emerged, that have been demonstrated to solve a wide range of reinforcement learning tasks. Despite this, little work has aimed to classify
spike patterns by the timing of output spikes. Here, we apply a reward-
maximising learning rule to teach a spiking neural network to classify
input patterns by the latency of output spikes. Furthermore, we compare
the performance of two escape rate functions that drive output spiking
activity: the Arrhenius & Current (A&C) model and Exponential (EXP)
model. We find A&C consistently outperforms EXP, and especially in
terms of the time taken to converge in learning. We also show that jittering input patterns with a low noise amplitude leads to an improvement
in learning, by reducing the variation in the performance.

Keywords: Neuronal Plasticity, Stochastic Neuron, Spiking Neural
Network, Latency Encoding.

1 Introduction

There is increasing interest in Reward-modulated Spike-Timing-Dependent Plasticity (R-STDP) as a biologically plausible rule for modelling learning in the
brain, where candidate weight changes triggered by STDP only become effective
by the presence of an external reward signal [4,12,13]. However, whilst there has
been significant progress in applying R-STDP to solving many reinforcement
learning problems [19,6,7], there still remains a lack of work that has aimed to
apply R-STDP to classifying spike patterns by the timing of output spikes.

In the literature, two main forms of reward-modulated learning for a Spiking
Neural Network (SNN) have been identified: an empirically formulated R-STDP
rule, and a theoretically derived Reward-maximising (R-max) rule [12,14,5]. Both
approaches rely on three factors for learning to succeed: 1. presynaptic activity
as the stimulus, 2. postsynaptic activity as the response, and 3. the feedback of a
success signal to allow synaptic changes. The approaches differ by the lack of an
unsupervised learning bias with R-max, as opposed to R-STDP. In general, an
unsupervised component hinders reward-modulated learning, as R-STDP was
found to have decreased performance in comparison with R-max when learning
several target spike trains [5].

S. Wermter et al. (Eds.): ICANN 2014, LNCS 8681, pp. 749–756, 2014.

Therefore, we aim to investigate the efficacy of an SNN that uses the R-max rule in learning to classify input spike patterns by the timing of output spikes, where we also compare the performance of two escape rate functions that drive output spiking activity. This paper generalises our method presented in [8], where previously only a single fixed input pattern was mapped to a target spike train.

2   Method

2.1   Single Neuron Model

A single readout neuron receives input from m presynaptic neurons, where the spike train due to the jth input, $1 \leq j \leq m$, is given as a sum of δ-functions: $X_j(t) = \sum_f \delta(t - t_j^f)$. In response to an input pattern $\mathbf{X} = \{X_j\}$, the membrane potential of the readout neuron at time t, given a last spike time $\hat{t}$, is defined by the Spike Response Model [10,5]:

$$u(t|\mathbf{X}, \hat{t}) := U_{rest} + \sum_j w_j \int_{\hat{t}}^t \epsilon(t - t') X_j(t') \, dt' + \kappa(t - \hat{t}) , \qquad (1)$$

where $U_{rest} = -70$ mV is the resting membrane potential and w_j the jth afferent synaptic weight. The Postsynaptic Potential (PSP) kernel is taken as $\epsilon(s) = \frac{\epsilon_0}{\tau_m - \tau_s}(e^{-s/\tau_m} - e^{-s/\tau_s})$, where $\epsilon_0 = 20$ mV·ms is a scaling constant, $\tau_m = 10$ ms the membrane time constant and $\tau_s = 2$ ms the synaptic rise time. The reset kernel is $\kappa(s) = \kappa_0 e^{-s/\tau_m}$, with $\kappa_0 = -5$ mV. Both kernels are set to 0 for $s < 0$. Output spike times are distributed according to an instantaneous firing rate or escape rate $\rho(t) = \rho(u(t))$ [10], where the probability for a spike being generated at time t over a small interval δt is given as $\rho(t) \, \delta t$. Throughout our simulations we take $\delta t = 1$ ms, being the simulation time step.

In our simulations we consider two different functional forms for the escape rate, the first being the Arrhenius & Current (A&C) model [10]:

$$\rho^{A\&C}(u, \dot{u}) = 2 \left(\frac{c_1}{\tau_m} + \frac{c_2}{\sigma}[\dot{u}]_+ \right) \frac{\exp\left\{ - \frac{[u - \vartheta]^2}{\sigma^2} \right\}}{1 + \operatorname{erf}\left\{ - \frac{u - \vartheta}{\sigma} \right\}} , \qquad (2)$$

where u is the time-dependent, noise-free trajectory of the neuron's membrane potential and $\dot{u} = du/dt$ its time derivative. We set the firing threshold as $\vartheta = -55$ mV. The noise amplitude is set as $\sigma = 5$ mV, that corresponds to the variation in u due to background noise. The parameters c_1 and c_2 are set to 0.72 and $\frac{1}{\sqrt{\pi}}$ respectively [15]. The term $[\dot{u}]_+$ indicates that only positive gradients in the membrane potential contribute to the firing intensity, defined as $[\dot{u}]_+ = (|\dot{u}| + \dot{u})/2$. The error function erf is included to ensure a linear increase in the firing rate for $u > \vartheta$ [11].

The second simpler escape rate, the Exponential (EXP) model, is more commonly used [10]:

$$\rho^{EXP}(u) = \rho_0 \exp\left(\frac{u - \vartheta}{\Delta u} \right) , \qquad (3)$$

where $\rho_0 = 0.1$ ms^{-1} is the firing rate at threshold and $\Delta u = 3$ mV determines the degree of noise about the threshold. For both the A&C and EXP escape rate models, the stochasticity parameters were selected such that for $u < \vartheta$: $\rho^{\mathrm{EXP}}(u) \approx \rho^{\mathrm{A\&C}}(u, \dot{u} = 0)$, giving comparable levels of noise between the two models.

2.2   Learning Algorithm

Learning takes place on an episodic basis, where each episode corresponds to the presentation of an input pattern lasting duration $T = 500$ ms. Feedback to the network is given in the form of a success signal $S(R)$, where S is a monotonic function of the reward R. The delivery of reward to the network is delayed until the end of each episode, therefore it is necessary to introduce an eligibility trace $\tilde{e}_j$ that determines candidate changes in the weights w_j [1]. More specifically, weights are updated at the end of each episode according to [5,12]:

$$\tau_e \frac{\mathrm{d}\tilde{e}_j}{\mathrm{d}t} = -\tilde{e}_j + \eta\, e_j(t) \tag{4}$$

$$\Delta w_j = S(R)\,\tilde{e}_j(T)\,, \tag{5}$$

where the time constant $\tau_e = 500$ ms is matched to the duration of each episode, η is the learning rate and $e_j(t)$ the synaptic eligibility. We use the R-max learning rule in our simulations, where the eligibility is given as [4,14]:

$$e_j(t) = \frac{\rho'(u)}{\rho(u)}\,[\mathcal{Y}(t) - \rho(u)] \int_{\hat{t}}^{t} \epsilon(t - t')\, X_j(t')\, \mathrm{d}t'\,, \tag{6}$$

where $\rho'(u) = \frac{\mathrm{d}\rho(u)}{\mathrm{d}u}$ and $\mathcal{Y}(t) = \sum_f \delta(t - t^f)$ is the output spike train.

In [8], we originally determined the eligibility for the A&C model, given here as:

$$e_j^{\mathrm{A\&C}}(t) = \mathcal{A}(u)\,[\mathcal{Y}(t) - \rho^{\mathrm{A\&C}}(u, \dot{u})] \int_{\hat{t}}^{t} \epsilon(t - t')\, X_j(t')\, \mathrm{d}t' \qquad \text{with} \tag{7}$$

$$\mathcal{A}(u) = \frac{2}{\sigma} \left(\frac{1}{\sqrt{\pi}} \frac{\exp\left\{ -\frac{[u - \vartheta]^2}{\sigma^2} \right\}}{1 + \mathrm{erf}\left\{ -\frac{u - \vartheta}{\sigma} \right\}} - \frac{u - \vartheta}{\sigma} \right)\,. \tag{8}$$

For the EXP model, the eligibility is:

$$e_j^{\mathrm{EXP}}(t) = \frac{1}{\Delta u}\,[\mathcal{Y}(t) - \rho^{\mathrm{EXP}}(u)] \int_{\hat{t}}^{t} \epsilon(t - t')\, X_j(t')\, \mathrm{d}t'\,. \tag{9}$$

2.3   Learning a Target Spike Train

To teach the network to map an input pattern to a target spike train, we follow the same approach as [8]. Specifically, at the end of each learning episode, the van Rossum Distance (vRD) [16] is used to measure the (dis)similarity between the output/target spike trains, giving the metric $\mathcal{D}$, with the coincidence time constant set as $\tau_c = 15$ ms. $\mathcal{D} \in [0, \infty)$ is then mapped to a reward value $R \in (0, 1]$ as $R = \exp(-\alpha \mathcal{D})$, where we set $\alpha = 2$ such that reward becomes negligible for large $\mathcal{D}$. Furthermore, we set $\mathcal{R} = 0$ for no output spikes, since reinforcing a lack of firing activity would negatively impact on learning. Finally, we define the success signal as $S(R) = R - \bar{R}$, with $\bar{R}$ being a moving average of the reward: $\bar{R} \leftarrow \bar{R} + (\bar{R} - R)/\tau_R$ with each episode, where the time constant is set to $\tau_R = 5p$ for p input patterns. Taking a moving average has been shown to reduce the impact of noise on learning [5], that allows for a larger learning rate.

2.4 Plasticity Rules

During learning, weights are 'hard bound' to the range $[w_{\min}, w_{\max}]$, where we set $w_{\min} = -10$ and $w_{\max} = 10$ as the minimum and maximum allowable values. Weights are additionally subject to synaptic scaling [18], where weights are additively modified by the following scaling rule:

$$\Delta w_j = \gamma |w_j| \left[N^{\text{ref}} - N^{\text{out}} \right] , \tag{10}$$

where $\gamma = 1 \times 10^{-3}$ is the scaling strength, $N^{\text{ref}} = 1$ the number of target spikes and N^{out} the number of output spikes over each episode. As found in [17,2], synaptic scaling decreases the sensitivity of the network to its initial state, and is essential to prevent extremes in the firing rate of the readout neuron whilst learning target spike trains.

2.5 Network Setup and Pattern Statistics

We implemented a fully-connected feedforward network, with 500 input neurons and a single readout neuron. Either the A&C or the EXP escape rate defined the spiking activity of the readout neuron. Input patterns consisted of Poisson-distributed spike trains, independently generated at each input neuron, with a mean firing rate of 6 Hz. Synaptic weights were initialized by independently selecting each value from a Gaussian distribution, with the mean and standard deviation both equal to 0.09 and 0.06 for A&C and EXP respectively. This gave an initial distribution of weights where $\sim 16\%$ had negative values, and drove the initial firing rate of the readout neuron to ~ 2 Hz. Depending on the learning task, jitter was added to input pattern presentations for increased realism, where each input spike time was randomly selected from a normalised Gaussian distribution centered around its reference time with an amplitude ς.

3 Results

The network was tasked with learning to classify $p = 10$ input patterns into $c = 10$ classes by the latency of output spikes, where each input pattern was assigned to a unique class. The target output for each class $k \in \{1, ..., c\}$ consisted

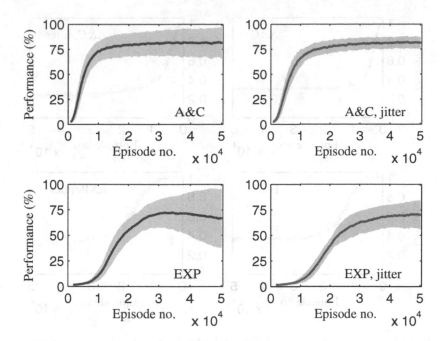

Fig. 1. Performance $\tilde{P}$ as a function of the episode number when learning to classify 10 input patterns by the latency of output spikes, with an accuracy of at least 10 ms between an actual output spike time and target spike time. (Left) No input jitter. (Right) Input jitter with amplitude $\varsigma = 5$ ms. (Top) The A&C escape rate. (Bottom) The EXP escape rate. Each data point was averaged over 24 different realizations, each with a random network initialization. The shaded region around each curve shows the standard deviation.

of a single spike at $k\,T/(c+1)$ [3]. In all cases, we set the number of learning episodes to $5000p$, where input patterns were randomly selected to be presented to the network on each episode. For the learning rate we set $\eta = 20$ for both A&C and EXP, that gave the best performance for each escape rate.

An input pattern was considered to be correctly classified if the fired output spike was within 10 ms of its target. On each episode, a correct classification gave the performance $P = 100\%$ and $P = 0$ otherwise. Since we implemented a stochastic neuron model in our simulations, it was necessary to take a moving average of the performance with each episode: $\tilde{P} \leftarrow (1 - \lambda)\tilde{P} + \lambda P$, where we set the timing parameter $\lambda = 2/(1 + 100p)$.

Figure 1 shows the progression in learning of the network, where either the A&C or EXP escape rate defined the readout neuron. In our simulations, we also considered the effect of input noise on learning by jittering input spike times with an amplitude $\varsigma = 5$ ms, corresponding to a mean timing displacement of $\Delta t \approx 4$ ms. It was found that A&C converged in learning much more rapidly than EXP, with an increased convergent peformance, for both noiseless and jittered inputs. The increased performance of A&C over EXP was most pronounced for noiseless

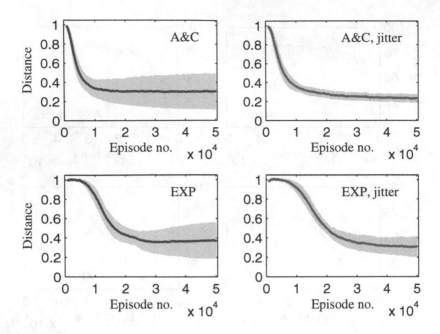

Fig. 2. Distance $\tilde{\mathcal{D}}$ between actual output and target spike times as a function of the episode number, when classifying 10 input spike patterns. (Left) No input jitter. (Right) Input jitter with amplitude $\varsigma = 5$ ms. (Top) The A&C escape rate. (Bottom) The EXP escape rate. These results correspond to those shown in figure 1, with 24 averages per data point and the shaded region showing the standard deviation.

inputs, with a convergent performance $\tilde{P} = 81 \pm 3\%$ and $\tilde{P} = 67 \pm 6\%$ for A&C and EXP respectively (errors given as standard error of mean). Both escape rate models benefited from input jitter, in terms of having a reduced variation in the performance. However, only EXP found an improvement in the convergent performance, with final values $\tilde{P} = 81 \pm 1\%$ and $\tilde{P} = 70 \pm 3\%$ for A&C and EXP respectively.

To measure the accuracy of output spike times with respect to target spike times, we used the vRD measure $\mathcal{D}$. To give a perspective of this measure, for a single actual output spike, values for $\mathcal{D} < 1/2$ correspond to an output timing that lies within 10 ms its target. A value $\mathcal{D} = 0$ corresponds to an exact match. Similarly as before, it was necessary to take a moving average of $\mathcal{D}$ with each episode: $\tilde{\mathcal{D}} \leftarrow (1 - \lambda)\tilde{\mathcal{D}} + \lambda\mathcal{D}$.

Figure 2 shows the distance between the actual output and target spike times of the network with each episode. As before, results were obtained for both noiseless and jittered input patterns, with the same input noise amplitude $\varsigma = 5$ ms. A&C was found to be somewhat more accurate than EXP, and converged much more rapidly during learning. The increased accuracy of A&C over EXP held for both noiseless and jittered input patterns. In the case of no input noise, the final distances were found to be $\tilde{\mathcal{D}} = 0.31 \pm 0.04$ and $\tilde{\mathcal{D}} = 0.37 \pm 0.04$

for A&C and EXP respectively, and for jittered inputs the final distances were $\tilde{\mathcal{D}} = 0.235 \pm 0.009$ and $\tilde{\mathcal{D}} = 0.31 \pm 0.02$ for A&C and EXP respectively (errors given as standard error of mean). It was found that adding input jitter led to a dramatic reduction in the variation of the network responses, and especially for A&C, where the variation was reduced by a factor of at least four.

4   Discussion

This paper applied a reward-maximising learning rule to teach an SNN to classify input spike patterns by the latency of output spikes. We also compared the performance of two escape rate functions that define neuronal spike-timing: A&C and EXP, both for noiseless and jittered input patterns.

We found A&C consistently outperformed EXP when learning to classify 10 input spike patterns by the timing of output spikes: both in terms of the convergent performance, and especially the time taken to converge in learning. A&C also demonstrated greater reliability over EXP during learning, with a smaller variance for both noiseless and jittered inputs. These results further support the advantages of implementing A&C over EXP on a reward-modulated learning task, that was first indicated in [8]. The gradient term $[\dot{u}]_+$ in the A&C model is likely to be responsible for its enhanced performance, since this has the effect of increasing the precision of output spike times in response to input spike times.

Interestingly, adding jitter to input spike times increased the performance of the network, and in particular by reducing the variation in the performance. For noiseless input patterns, a large variation in the performance was associated with trials where the network failed to learn target responses, that was caused by a lack of stochastic exploration during learning. By adding a small amount of input jitter, the timing of output spikes initially became more random, thereby facilitating the learning of target output spikes by the network. However, adding excessive input jitter led to decreased performance by the network, indicating an intermediate level of background noise that was optimal for learning. Such an effect has also been observed in [13] when learning a target spike train by delayed reinforcement.

With our setup we only considered single output spikes. Teaching the network to classify input spike patterns by multiple-spike target trains would increase the complexity of the task significantly, since reward delivery is delayed and the network would have to stochastically explore a wider range of possible output spike trains for learning to succeed. In a previous paper [9], we have explored the classification performance of an SNN that uses multiple output spikes to classify input spike patterns by supervised learning. However, future work could aim to further quantify the performance of an SNN that learns to classify a wider range of input patterns by R-STDP.

Acknowledgements. BG was fully supported by EPSRC grant EP/J500562/1. AG and IS were fully supported by the Human Brain Project (HBP).

References

1. Barto, A., Sutton, R.: Reinforcement learning: An introduction. MIT Press, Cambridge (1998)
2. Farries, M., Fairhall, A.: Reinforcement learning with modulated spike timing dependent synaptic plasticity. Journal of Neurophysiology 98(6), 3648–3665 (2007)
3. Florian, R.V.: The chronotron: A neuron that learns to fire temporally precise spike patterns. PloS One 7(8), e40233 (2012)
4. Florian, R.: Reinforcement learning through modulation of spike-timing-dependent synaptic plasticity. Neural Computation 19(6), 1468–1502 (2007)
5. Frémaux, N., Sprekeler, H., Gerstner, W.: Functional requirements for reward-modulated spike-timing-dependent plasticity. The Journal of Neuroscience 30(40), 13326–13337 (2010)
6. Frémaux, N., Sprekeler, H., Gerstner, W.: Reinforcement learning using a continuous time actor-critic framework with spiking neurons. PLoS Computational Biology 9(4), e1003024 (2013)
7. Friedrich, J., Urbanczik, R., Senn, W.: Spatio-temporal credit assignment in neuronal population learning. PLoS Computational Biology 7(6), e1002092 (2011)
8. Gardner, B., Grüning, A.: Learning temporally precise spiking patterns through reward modulated spike-timing-dependent plasticity. In: Mladenov, V., Koprinkova-Hristova, P., Palm, G., Villa, A.E.P., Appollini, B., Kasabov, N. (eds.) ICANN 2013. LNCS, vol. 8131, pp. 256–263. Springer, Heidelberg (2013)
9. Gardner, B., Grüning, A.: Classifying patterns in a spiking neural network. In: Proceedings of the 22nd European Symposium on Artificial Neural Networks (ESANN 2014) (2014)
10. Gerstner, W., Kistler, W.: Spiking neuron models: Single neurons, populations, plasticity. Cambridge University Press, Cambridge (2002)
11. Herrmann, A., Gerstner, W.: Noise and the psth response to current transients: I. general theory and application to the integrate-and-fire neuron. Journal of Computational Neuroscience 11(2), 135–151 (2001)
12. Izhikevich, E.: Solving the distal reward problem through linkage of stdp and dopamine signaling. Cerebral Cortex 17(10), 2443–2452 (2007)
13. Legenstein, R., Pecevski, D., Maass, W.: A learning theory for reward-modulated spike-timing-dependent plasticity with application to biofeedback. PLoS Computational Biology 4(10), e1000180 (2008)
14. Pfister, J., Toyoizumi, T., Barber, D., Gerstner, W.: Optimal spike-timing-dependent plasticity for precise action potential firing in supervised learning. Neural Computation 18(6), 1318–1348 (2006)
15. Plesser, H., Gerstner, W.: Noise in integrate-and-fire neurons: from stochastic input to escape rates. Neural Computation 12(2), 367–384 (2000)
16. Rossum, M.: A novel spike distance. Neural Computation 13(4), 751–763 (2001)
17. Sporea, I., Grüning, A.: Supervised learning in multilayer spiking neural networks. Neural Computation 25(2), 473–509 (2013)
18. Van Rossum, M., Bi, G., Turrigiano, G.: Stable hebbian learning from spike timing-dependent plasticity. The Journal of Neuroscience 20(23), 8812–8821 (2000)
19. Vasilaki, E., Frémaux, N., Urbanczik, R., Senn, W., Gerstner, W.: Spike-based reinforcement learning in continuous state and action space: when policy gradient methods fail. PLoS Computational Biology 5(12), e1000586 (2009)

Quantifying the Effect of Meaning Variation in Survey Analysis

Henri Sintonen[1], Juha Raitio[1], and Timo Honkela[2,1]

[1] Aalto University School of Science,
Department of Information and Computer Science, Finland
[2] University of Helsinki,
Department of Modern Languages, Helsinki, Finland

Abstract. Surveys are widely conducted as a means to obtain information on thoughts, opinions and feelings of people. The representativeness
of a sample is a major concern in using surveys. In this article, we consider meaning variation which is another potentially remarkable but less
studied source of problems. We use Grounded Intersubjective Concept
Analysis (GICA) method to quantify meaning variation and demonstrate
the effect on survey analysis through a case study in which food prices
and food concepts are considered.

Keywords: Survey analysis, questionnaire data, computational episte-
mology, conceptual spaces, meaning variation.

1 Introduction

Survey research is commonly used to find out what kinds of thoughts, opinions, and feelings people have on some matter. Different individuals, cultures,
and subcultures can interpret words and phrases in a questionnaire in different
ways [1]. For instance, it is obvious that two persons may not have a common
conceptions related to words like "important", "democratic", or "scientific".

Traditionally, the means for handling meaning variation have been close to
non-existing. To quantify meaning variation, a method called Grounded Intersubjective Concept Analysis (GICA) has recently been developed [2]. In this paper, we develop further the underlying theoretical framework and demonstrate
the use of the GICA method in survey research. The contribution is multi-
disciplinary including aspects from computational modeling, cognitive science,
cognitive linguistics and social sciences.

2 Theory and Methods

Next we present a theoretical formulation and methodological background for
the work.

S. Wermter et al. (Eds.): ICANN 2014, LNCS 8681, pp. 757–764, 2014.

2.1   Vector Space Models of Cognitive Conceptual Systems

According to the theory of conceptual spaces [3], conceptual representations are constructed from quality dimensions. Each dimension D_i has a geometric form and the concept space C is defined as a set of quality dimensions $\{D_1, ..., D_N\}$. Similarity between concepts is seen as the degree of correlation between sets of quality dimensions. In essence, the concept space is a vector space model regarding which a lot of research within, for instance, information retrieval area has been conducted [4,5].

A concept is a convex area in the concept space. This ensures that the transitional quality dimension configurations – or points in the concept space – between any two points in the convex area belong to the same concept. Thus any concept can have multiple, slightly different values of the quality dimensions [3].

The role of the concept space can be seen when communication between agents is formalized as an improvement of an earlier formulation [6]. Each agent has a concept space C^a, which is made up of quality dimensions $D_i^a, i = 1...N^a$, where N^a is the agent specific number of quality dimensions. Agents also have a symbol space S^a, which contains symbols of communication such as words. Function ξ^a maps the symbols $s^a \in S^a$ to the concept space C^a.

To communicate a point c^a from concept space, the agent chooses a symbol s^* so that the difference between the chosen point and the point that the symbol s^* maps to is minimized. That is to say, the agent optimizes

$$s^* = \arg \min_{s \in S^a} \omega(c^a, \xi^a(s)), \tag{1}$$

where ω is a function that calculates the distance between two points in a concept space. Equation 1 assumes that the agent has no information about the concept space of the listener.

2.2   Modeling Meaning Negotiation

According to Grice, people follow the cooperation principle in communication, which states that people try to work together to advance the discussion [7]. Part of the principle is the maxim of quantity, according to which people give just the right amount of information. It would require people to be aware how much of the information is shared between them. This is part of the definition of common ground, which also includes beliefs and assumptions [8]. On the other hand, according to egocentric heuristic, listeners interpret what they hear solely on the basis of their own perspective, because maintaining the common ground is cognitively too demanding [9]. Common ground is used only afterwards to solve problems in communication.

It might be that both strategies are used depending on the current constraints on cognitive processing [10, p. 391]. In light of this, equation 1 can be seen as the egocentric situation. When agents are trying to reach the common ground, they try to optimize the symbol selection by estimating the concept space of the listeners. This can be written as

$$s^* = \arg \min_{s \in S^a} \lambda(c^a, \tilde{\xi}^a(s)), \tag{2}$$

where λ is a function that calculates the distance between two points in separate concept spaces and $\tilde{\xi}$ maps to the estimated concept space of the listener.

For the full symbol optimization problem faced by the agent, the equations 1 and 2 have to be combined. Here the original notation [6] is expanded with a gamma function that weights the equations 1 and 2 based on, for example, cognitive processing constraints and pragmatic factors like context and the goals of the speaker. Now the optimization can be written as

$$s^* = \arg \min_{s \in S^a} \gamma(\omega(c^a, \xi^a(s)), \lambda(c^a, \tilde{\xi}^a(s))) \tag{3}$$

The listener, who has another individual knowledge base, receives the message and maps the received symbols in the message with corresponding inverse functions to their concept space. Variance sensitivity is divided into different levels. Variance in pragmatics is on the level of the gamma function, as the agent may choose a slightly different point from the concept space compared to what the intended meaning would require. Variance in the concepts themselves would be on the level of the concept space, as the quality dimension configurations of the agent might be slightly different for each concept compared to other agents.

This theoretical formulation serves to highlight what it is that we are trying to quantify. We assume that properties of the conceptual space can be inferred by carefully analyzing the behavior, including verbal behavior, of agents.

2.3   Survey Analysis

Sources of unreliability or error in survey answers can be classified as memory related (forgetting or misremembering information), motivation related (awareness of the consequences of the answers), communication related (misunderstanding the question), and as the lack of required knowledge to answer the questions [11, p. 30]. Properties of language and its interpretation are related both to communication and memory [12].

2.4   GICA: Grounded Intersubjective Concept Analysis

Research on statistical natural language processing has clearly shown that meaningful relationships between words and their features can be found automatically based on co-occurrence data (see, e.g., [5,13]). The basic idea in such an analysis is to collect data such as a term-document matrix in which the statistics of words occurring in different contexts is collected. In essence, understanding the role of an *object* (like a word or phrase) in relation to other objects is obtained by examining the pattern of *contexts* in which it appears.

Traditionally, the statistical analysis of the context information has taken place without consideration of the person who has created or is assessing the object-context relationship. In other words, it has been assumed that any piece of text or other relevant data can do without consideration of subjective variation. In the Grounded Intersubjective Concept Analysis (GICA) method [2], the idea of considering objects in their contexts is taken a step further. In order to capture the epistemological subjectivity, a third dimension is added to the analysis. Namely, the set of observations, objects × contexts, is extended into subjects × objects × contexts, i.e. one additionally considers what is the contribution of each subject in the context analysis [2]. Adopting the notation used by Kolda and Bader [14], the *order of a tensor* is the number of the array dimensions, also known as ways or *modes*. As a GICA data set is observed under varied conditions of the three modes, these form the ways of the order-three tensor $\mathcal{X} \in \mathcal{R}^{S \times O \times C}$, where S, O, C are the number of values (levels) in ranges $\{s_1, s_2, \ldots, s_S\}$, $\{o_1, o_2, \ldots, o_O\}$, and $\{c_1, c_2, \ldots, c_C\}$ of the categorical variables subject **s**, object **o**, and context **c**, respectively. An element of the tensor, $x_{ijk} \in \mathcal{R}$, is the individual observation under certain levels (s_i, o_j, c_k). $\mathcal{R}$ is the range of the observed variable [2].

3   Case Study

The goal of the case study was to find out whether meaning variance affects questionnaire answers and to determine whether the GICA method is a viable tool to uncover such effects. The data set was gathered via a two-part online questionnaire. In the first part the test, subjects were asked to consider the following twelve grocery objects:

milk (1 l)	rye bread (500 g)	tomatoes (1 kg)
ice cream (1 l)	pizza (regular)	minced meat (500 g)
eggs (12 pcs)	salmon fillet (1 kg)	butter (500 g)
margarine (400 g)	potatoes (1 kg)	beef tenderloin steak (150 g)

Subjects gave two prices in euros for each object. The first price was the highest price they still considered as cheap for the product and the second was the lowest price they considered to be expensive. The prices were constrained between 0 and 20 euros and given in ten cent intervals using a slider.

In the second part of the questionnaire, the test subjects were asked to evaluate how well the following nine contexts suit each grocery product: ETHICAL, ECOLOGICAL, FILLING, LIGHT, TASTY, HEALTHY, NUTRITIOUS, AESTHETIC, and DISGUSTING. The contexts were intended to be well-known and opinion dividing quality dimensions. The degree of suitability of the context on the products was determined on a 1-5 Likert scale.

The contexts and objects have been translated here to English from Finnish. The prices where a test subject set the first price higher than the second price were removed from the data set. The Tensor Toolbox for MATLAB [15] and the self-organizing map (SOM) algorithm [16] were used in the data analysis.

The tensor of the answers was flattened to a matrix so that rows correspond to subjects ($S = 67$) and objects ($O = 12$) and columns correspond to contexts ($C = 9$). The resulting 804 × 9 matrix, where each row is a 9 dimensional data vector representing a subject-object pair, was used as an input to generate an SOM [16]. The distribution of each context on the map can be seen on Figure 1.

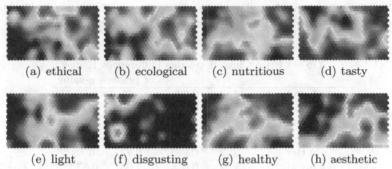

(a) ethical   (b) ecological   (c) nutritious   (d) tasty

(e) light   (f) disgusting   (g) healthy   (h) aesthetic

Fig. 1. Eight context components of the self-organizing map based on the food item data. Dark red means a high degree of suitability between the context and the objects (answer closer to a value of 5) and dark blue refers to a weak suitability (answer closer to 1).

Table 1. For each context, the number of clusters used and the mean number of significantly ($p < 0.05$) differing pairs of clusters from one hundred repetitions.

Context	k_c	Differing pairs	Context	k_c	Differing pairs
ethical	2	0	disgusting	2	0
ecological	2	1.10	healthy	2	3.12
nutritious	3	2.72	filling	3	2.50
tasty	3	4.00	aesthetic	2	2.09
light	3	6.22			

Contexts LIGHT, HEALTHY and NUTRITIOUS have similar basic structure and on the upper right corner of the map they also coincide to a large degree with the contexts ECOLOGICAL and ETHICAL. The high negative correlation between contexts DISGUSTING and TASTY is understandable and clearly visible.

Because of the grouping tendency, the answers of each context were clustered. The number of clusters for each context k_c was determined by running k-means algorithm with different values of k and minimizing the within standard deviation of the clusters and not allowing clusters with less than ten data points. This procedure was repeated one hundred times and the k_c-values of each repetition were averaged and rounded to produce the final k_c-values.

Next the contexts were clustered with the chosen k_c-values without any constraints on the cluster sizes. To see whether the clustering affects the prices subjects determined, within each context the mean prices were calculated for all clusters. Each of the 24 price-product pairs has k_c mean prices. Within each price-product pair, clusters were tested in a pairwise manner using the Mann-Whitney U-test to find the number of times clusters differ in their mean prices in a statistically significant ($p < 0.05$) way.

The procedure was repeated one hundred times and the mean number of significantly differing pairs of clusters was calculated for each context. The results are presented in Table 1 alongside the number of clusters k_c for each context.

Table 2. The results of one clustering in the context LIGHT. The thresholds for Hedges' g-values were 0.2 for small (*), 0.5 for medium (**), and 0.8 for a large (***) effect [17].

Object	Price	Clusters	p-value	Differences of prices	Hedges' g-value
rye bread	1	1, 2	0.022	0.63	0.81 ***
pizza	1	2, 3	0.033	0.79	0.60 **
eggs	1	1, 2	0.010	0.72	0.76 **
salmon fillet	1	1, 2	0.033	2.03	0.66 **
butter	1	2, 3	0.013	0.72	0.78 **
rye bread	2	1, 2	0.015	1.08	0.87 ***
ice cream	2	1, 3	0.048	0.88	0.59 **
eggs	2	1, 2	0.019	1.26	0.70 **
eggs	2	2, 3	0.010	1.26	0.68 **
margarine	2	2, 3	0.049	0.78	0.59 **
minced meat	2	2, 3	0.047	1.09	0.57 **

There were significantly differing pairs in each context except in ETHICAL and DISGUSTING. TASTY and LIGHT had the most significantly differing pairs.

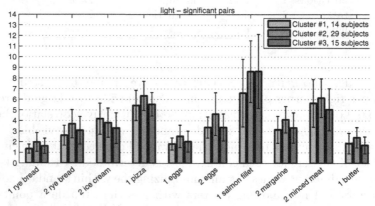

Fig. 2. The price-product pairs that have statistically significant differences in the mean prices of the clusters. The error bars represent the standard deviation. The results are from one clustering of the answer in the context LIGHT.

One clustering in context LIGHT is presented in more detail in Table 2. In 11 out of the 72 comparisons the mean prices were significantly different from one another. Each cluster differed from the others on some price-product pair. The price-product pairs of these comparisons are presented in Figure 2. The rest of the pairs can be seen in Figure 3. These figures also indicate a tendency for the second cluster to accept higher prices as inexpensive when compared to other clusters.

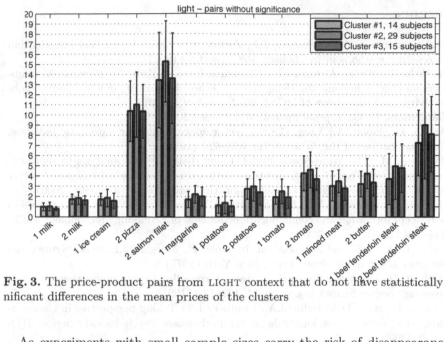

Fig. 3. The price-product pairs from LIGHT context that do not have statistically significant differences in the mean prices of the clusters

As experiments with small sample sizes carry the risk of disappearance of small effects when repeated on a larger sample, the effect size was calculated using Hedges' g-value [18]. Hedges' g-value can be interpreted using the same guidelines originally set for Cohen's d-value. That is, 0.2 implies a small effect, 0.5 a medium one, and 0.8 a large one [17]. The Hedges' g-values can be read from Table 2 and they suggest that the effect the clustering had was either medium or large in size.

4   Conclusions and Discussion

In this paper, we have discussed how meaning variation is an often neglected phenomenon that is of practical importance. We have described a theoretical framework to handle the phenomenon, and shown how to use a practical statistical machine learning method called GICA to evaluate the effect of meaning variation, here in the context of survey research. To best of our knowledge, this kind of exercise has not earlier been conducted.

The results of the experiment show that differences in the answers to a questionnaire can be identified with the GICA method. Subjects were clustered according to the level of association they reported between objects and contexts and this grouping had an effect on the questions regarding the objects. It was shown that the effect can be statistically significant ($p < 0.05$) and be large in size (Hedges' g-value > 0.8). In conclusion, the GIGA method appears to be a viable tool in detecting the effects of meaning variation in survey data.

References

1. Zechmeister, E.B., Shaughnessy, J.J., Zechmeister, J.S.: A practical introduction to research methods in psychology. McGraw-Hill (1992)
2. Honkela, T., Raitio, J., Lagus, K., Nieminen, I.T., Honkela, N., Pantzar, M.: Subjects on objects in contexts: Using GICA method to quantify epistemological subjectivity. In: Proceedings of IJCNN 2012, pp. 1–9 (2012)
3. Gärdenfors, P.: Conceptual Spaces. MIT Press (2000)
4. Salton, G., Wong, A., Yang, C.S.: A vector space model for automatic indexing. Communications of the ACM 18(11), 613–620 (1975)
5. Sahlgren, M.: The Word-Space Model: Using distributional analysis to represent syntagmatic and paradigmatic relations between words in high-dimensional vector spaces. PhD thesis, Computational Linguistics, Stockholm University (2006)
6. Honkela, T., Könönen, V., Lindh-Knuutila, T., Paukkeri, M.: Simulating processes of concept formation and communication. Journal of Economic Methodology 15(3), 245–259 (2008)
7. Grice, H.P.: Logic and conversation. In: Cole, P., Morgan, J.L. (eds.) Syntax and Semantics, vol. 3. Academic Press, New York (1975)
8. Herbert, H.: Clark and Susan E. Brennan. Grounding in communication. Perspectives on Socially Shared Cognition 13, 127–149 (1991)
9. Keysar, B., Barr, D.J., Balin, J.A., Brauner, J.S.: Taking perspective in conversation: The role of mutual knowledge in comprehension. Psychological Science 11(1), 32–38 (2000)
10. Eysenck, M.W., Keane, M.T.: Cognitive Psychology: A Student's Handbook, 6th edn. Taylor & Francis Group (2010)
11. Bradburn, N.M., Sudman, S., Wansink, B.: Asking Questions: The Definitive Guide to Questionnaire Design – For Market Research, Political Polls, and Social and Health Questionnaires. Research Methods for the Social Sciences. Wiley (2004)
12. Loftus, E.F., Palmer, J.C.: Reconstruction of automobile destruction: An example of the interaction between language and memory. Journal of Verbal Learning and Verbal Behavior 13(5), 585–589 (1974)
13. Honkela, T., Hyvärinen, A., Väyrynen, J.J.: WordICA – emergence of linguistic representations for words by independent component analysis. Natural Language Engineering 16, 277–308 (2010)
14. Kolda, T.G., Bader, B.W.: Tensor decompositions and applications. SIAM Review 51(3), 455–500 (2009)
15. Bader, B.W., Kolda, T.G., et al.: Matlab tensor toolbox version 2.5. Available online (January 2012)
16. Kohonen, T.: Self-Organizing Maps. Springer, Heidelberg (2001)
17. Cohen, J.: Statistical power analysis for the behavioral sciences. Routledge Academic (1988)
18. Hedges, L.V.: Distribution theory for Glass's estimator of effect size and related estimators. Journal of Educational and Behavioral Statistics 6(2), 107–128 (1981)

Discovery of Spatio-Temporal Patterns from Foursquare by Diffusion-type Estimation and ICA

Yoshitatsu Matsuda, Kazunori Yamaguchi, and Ken-ichiro Nishioka

Department of General Systems Studies,
Graduate School of Arts and Sciences, The University of Tokyo,
3-8-1, Komaba, Meguro-ku, Tokyo, 153-8902, Japan
{matsuda,yamaguch,nishioka}@graco.c.u-tokyo.ac.jp

Abstract. In this paper, we extract various patterns of the spatio-temporal distribution from Foursquare. Foursquare is a location-based social networking system which has been widely used recently. For extracting patterns, we employ ICA (Independent Component Analysis), which is a useful method in signal processing and feature extraction. Because the Foursquare dataset consists of check-in's of users at some time points and locations, ICA is not directly applicable to it. In order to smooth the dataset, we estimate a continuous spatio-temporal distribution by employing a diffusion-type formula. The experiments on an actual Foursquare dataset showed that the proposed method could extract some plausible and interesting spatio-temporal patterns.

1 Introduction

Recently, many geosocial networks such as Foursquare[1], Facebook Places[2], and Waze[3] have emerged. From such data, various information such as point of interests [13], traffic patterns [2], patterns across different temporal scales [8], and personal behavior patterns [5] were extracted. In addition, the extracted information was used in some applications, for example, for improving road safety [7]. One of the important patterns in such data is the spatio-temporal distribution of users. They show the overall behaviors of users and provide the basis for further analysis. For example, in [7], PCA (Principal Component Analysis) was applied to the time vs. situation (work/home/no signal/else/off of mobiles) matrix. Then, typical patterns in terms of times and situations were found out. However, no sophisticated extraction method such as ICA (Independent Component Analysis) has been applied to the data from geosocial networks yet as far as we know.

In this paper, we extract patterns from the spatio-temporal distribution of users in a Foursquare dataset. For extracting patterns, we employ ICA, which

---

[1] https://foursquare.com/

[2] https://www.facebook.com/about/location

[3] http://www.waze.com/

S. Wermter et al. (Eds.): ICANN 2014, LNCS 8681, pp. 765–772, 2014.
© Springer International Publishing Switzerland 2014

is a widely-used method in signal processing and feature extraction [10,3]. ICA extracts statistically-independent patterns from given datasets and has been applied to extracting spatial-temporal patterns from many real datasets such as fMRI [11], EEG [4], and weather data [1]. It has been known in many cases that ICA is useful even if the statistical independence does not hold rigorously. Because a Foursquare dataset consists of check-in's at some time points and locations, ICA is not directly applicable to it. To smooth the dataset, we employ a two-dimensional diffusion-type formula $(2\pi t)^{-1} e^{-\left(\frac{|x-y|^2}{2t}\right)}$. A similar diffusion-type formula was used in quantum mechanics [6] and seismology [14] and it gives a simple and natural model for estimating the movement of users when the location information between the check-in's is not available. In summary, we applied ICA to the Foursquare dataset with the diffusion-type estimation in this paper. This paper is organized as follows. In Sect. 2, a formula for the diffusion-type distribution estimation and the covariance among distributions at different time points are introduced. In Sect. 3, the results extracted by ICA are explained and discussed. Sect. 4 concludes this paper.

2 Method

Each check-in from Foursquare indicates only a specific location and a time point. In order to smooth such data, a method using a diffusion-type formula is introduced here. We denote a location x at a time point t as xt (called a "check-in" in this paper) and a user's check-in sequence as $(x_1t_1, x_2t_2, \cdots, x_nt_n)$. Rigorously, a location x is a point in the three dimensional space on the surface of the earth. However, we assume that each location is in a two-dimensional flat surface for simplicity. Because there is no information among the check-in's, we assume that each user moves as a free particle, which moves from a check-in xt to a check-in yu with the probability $P_{\text{diff}}(y|xt, u)$ in the following equation (a two-dimensional diffusion-type formula):

$$P_{\text{diff}}(y|xt, u) = \frac{\beta}{2\pi(u-t)} \exp\left(-\frac{\beta(x-y)^2}{2(u-t)}\right) \tag{1}$$

where β is the scale parameter on the time. Note that the time point u is regarded as a given variable in the conditional distribution. P_{diff} in Eq. (1) has the following preferable property. Let zv be a candidate check-in on a path from xt to yu. We also assume that $P(y|zv, u)$ and $P(z|xt, v)$ are given by P_{diff}. Then, $P(y|xt, u)$ is given as the following marginalized form w.r.t. z and v:

$$P(y|xt, u) = \int P_{\text{diff}}(y|zv, u) P_{\text{diff}}(z|xt, v) P(v) \, dz dv.$$

$$= \int P_{\text{diff}}(y|xt, u) P(v) \, dv = P_{\text{diff}}(y|xt, u), \tag{2}$$

where $P(v)$ is any distribution of the candidate time point v which does not affect the final equation. This shows that Eq. (1) gives a consistent framework.

Now, we estimate $P\left(\boldsymbol{x}|\boldsymbol{x}_i t_i, \boldsymbol{x}_{i+1}t_{i+1}, t\right)$ for $t_i \leq t < t_{i+1}$. We assume the 1-Markov property of check-in's by $P\left(\boldsymbol{x}_{i+1}|\boldsymbol{x}t, \boldsymbol{x}_i t_i, t_{i+1}\right) = P_{\text{diff}}\left(\boldsymbol{x}_{i+1}|\boldsymbol{x}t, t_{i+1}\right)$. Then, $P\left(\boldsymbol{x}|\boldsymbol{x}_i t_i, \boldsymbol{x}_{i+1}t_{i+1}, t\right)$ is given as

$$
P\left(\boldsymbol{x}|\boldsymbol{x}_i t_i, \boldsymbol{x}_{i+1}t_{i+1}, t\right) = \frac{P\left(\boldsymbol{x}, \boldsymbol{x}_{i+1}|\boldsymbol{x}_i t_i, t_{i+1}, t\right)}{P\left(\boldsymbol{x}_{i+1}|\boldsymbol{x}_i t_i, t_{i+1}\right)}
$$

$$
= \frac{P_{\text{diff}}\left(\boldsymbol{x}_{i+1}|\boldsymbol{x}t, t_{i+1}\right) P_{\text{diff}}\left(\boldsymbol{x}|\boldsymbol{x}_i t_i, t\right)}{P_{\text{diff}}\left(\boldsymbol{x}_{i+1}|\boldsymbol{x}_i t_i, t_{i+1}\right)} = \mathcal{N}_x\left(\boldsymbol{\mu}_{\text{dist}}, \sigma^2_{\text{dist}}\right) \tag{3}
$$

where $\mathcal{N}_x\left(\boldsymbol{\mu}, \sigma^2\right)$ is a two-dimensional circular Gaussian function defined as

$$
\mathcal{N}_x\left(\boldsymbol{\mu}, \sigma^2\right) = \frac{1}{2\pi\sigma^2} \exp\left(-\frac{(\boldsymbol{x} - \boldsymbol{\mu})^2}{2\sigma^2}\right). \tag{4}
$$

$\boldsymbol{\mu}_{\text{dist}}$ and σ^2_{dist} are given as

$$
\boldsymbol{\mu}_{\text{dist}} = \frac{(t - t_i)\,\boldsymbol{x}_{i+1} + (t_{i+1} - t)\,\boldsymbol{x}_i}{t_{i+1} - t_i} \tag{5}
$$

and

$$
\sigma^2_{\text{dist}} = \frac{(t - t_i)\,(t_{i+1} - t)}{\beta\,(t_{i+1} - t_i)}, \tag{6}
$$

respectively. The mean $\boldsymbol{\mu}_{\text{dist}}$ is the location linearly interpolating $\boldsymbol{x}_i$ and $\boldsymbol{x}_{i+1}$ with the ratio of t in $[t_i, t_{i+1}]$. The variance σ^2_{dist} takes the maximum at the middle of t_i and t_{i+1}, and it takes the minimum 0 at $t = t_i$ or $t = t_{i+1}$. So, $P\left(\boldsymbol{x}t|\boldsymbol{x}_i t_i, \boldsymbol{x}_{i+1}t_{i+1}\right)$ distributes widely at the middle of t_i and t_{i+1}, and it sharply (as the Dirac delta function) converges to $\boldsymbol{x}_i$ at t_i and $\boldsymbol{x}_{i+1}$ at t_{i+1}.

Regarding the multiple users, a sequence of check-in's of a user ω is denoted as $(\boldsymbol{x}_1^\omega t_1^\omega, \boldsymbol{x}_2^\omega t_2^\omega, \cdots, \boldsymbol{x}_n^\omega t_n^\omega)$. If the dataset consists of N users, we use the average of Eq. (3) over all users. Thus, $P(\boldsymbol{x}|t)$ for all users is given as

$$
P\left(\boldsymbol{x}|t\right) = \frac{1}{N} \sum_\omega P\left(\boldsymbol{x}|\boldsymbol{x}_i^\omega t_i^\omega, \boldsymbol{x}_{i+1}^\omega t_{i+1}^\omega, t\right),
$$

where i is such that $t_i^\omega \leq t \leq t_{i+1}^\omega$. \tag{7}

From Eq. (7), we can calculate the covariance among the spatial distributions at any time point t and at another time point t' as

$$
\int P\left(\boldsymbol{x}|t\right) P\left(\boldsymbol{x}|t'\right) \mathrm{d}\boldsymbol{x} = \frac{1}{N^2} \sum_{\omega,\omega'} \frac{1}{2\pi\sigma^2_{\text{cov}}[\omega, \omega']} \exp\left(-\frac{(\boldsymbol{\mu}_{\text{cov}}[\omega, \omega'])^2}{2\sigma^2_{\text{cov}}[\omega, \omega']}\right) \tag{8}
$$

where $\boldsymbol{\mu}_{\text{cov}}$ and σ^2_{cov} are given by

$$
\boldsymbol{\mu}_{\text{cov}}[\omega, \omega'] = \frac{(t - t_i^\omega)\,\boldsymbol{x}_{i+1}^\omega + \left(t_{i+1}^\omega - t\right)\,\boldsymbol{x}_i^\omega}{t_{i+1}^\omega - t_i^\omega} - \frac{\left(t' - t_{i'}^{\omega'}\right)\,\boldsymbol{x}_{i'+1}^{\omega'} + \left(t_{i'+1}^{\omega'} - t'\right)\,\boldsymbol{x}_{i'}^{\omega'}}{t_{i'+1}^{\omega'} - t_{i'}^{\omega'}}
$$

$$\tag{9}$$

and

$$\sigma^2_{\text{cov}}[\omega, \omega'] = \frac{(t - t_i^\omega)(t_{i+1}^\omega - t)}{\beta(t_{i+1}^\omega - t_i^\omega)} + \frac{(t' - t_{i'}^{\omega'})(t_{i'+1}^{\omega'} - t')}{\beta(t_{i'+1}^{\omega'} - t_{i'}^{\omega'})}. \tag{10}$$

In order to estimate the scale parameter β in Eq. (3), the maximum log-likelihood estimation is employed. In a check-in sequence $(x_1 t_1, x_2 t_2, \cdots, x_n t_n)$, $x_i t_i$ is between $x_{i-1} t_{i-1}$ and $x_{i+1} t_{i+1}$. So, the estimated probability of x_i at t_i from $x_{i-1} t_{i-1}$ and $x_{i+1} t_{i+1}$ is given by $P(x_i | x_{i-1} t_{i-1}, x_{i+1} t_{i+1}, t_i)$ in Eq. (3). Then, the log-likelihood over all the triples $(x_{i-1}^\omega t_{i-1}^\omega, x_i^\omega t_i^\omega, x_{i+1}^\omega t_{i+1}^\omega)$ in check-in sequences of all the users is given by

$$L(\beta) = \sum_{i,\omega} \log P\left(x_i^\omega | x_{i-1}^\omega t_{i-1}^\omega, x_{i+1}^\omega t_{i+1}^\omega, t_i^\omega\right) = \sum_{i,\omega} \left(\log \beta + \log C_i^\omega - \beta q_i^\omega\right) \tag{11}$$

where

$$q_i^\omega = \frac{\left(x_i^\omega - \frac{(t_i^\omega - t_{i-1}^\omega)x_{i+1}^\omega + (t_{i+1}^\omega - t_i^\omega)x_{i-1}^\omega}{t_{i+1}^\omega - t_{i-1}^\omega}\right)^2}{2\frac{(t_i^\omega - t_{i-1}^\omega)(t_{i+1}^\omega - t_i^\omega)}{t_{i+1}^\omega - t_{i-1}^\omega}} \tag{12}$$

and C_i^ω is a constant independent of β. By solving the equation of the derivative of Eq. (11) being 0, we get the optimal $\hat{\beta} = \frac{\sum_\omega n_\omega}{\sum_{i,\omega} q_i^\omega}$ where n_ω is the number of triples for each ω.

3 Results

3.1 Data Collection

Foursquare provides an API[4] to get check-in information. However, the number of API accesses per day is limited and not enough for our analysis. Therefore we collected check-in information from Twitter[5] in a similar way as used in [12]. Foursquare enables the users to share their check-in's if they choose to share them. Each shared check-in is available as a tweet for anyone if its twitter feed is public. Each tweet contains the unique URL from which anyone can get the detailed check-in information such as time, location (name, latitude, and longitude), and tags. For collecting the data, we crawled check-in tweets by the Twitter streaming API with the search keyword '4sq' from Feb. 28 to Mar. 31 in 2012. Then, we got about ten millions of tweets. In this paper, we focused on the Japanese area. So, we selected the users who set their language Japanese. In addition, we selected only the users with at least 50 check-in's during the period. Consequently, we got 843194 check-in tweets from 7710 users. Only 100 users were randomly sampled in order to reduce the computational costs.

---

[4] https://developer.foursquare.com/
[5] https://twitter.com/

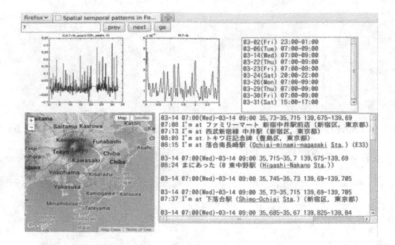

Fig. 1. An interface system displaying extracted spatial and temporal patterns

3.2 Analysis Method by ICA

Because the estimated spatial distribution at each time point may include approximate delta functions and is often unstable, ICA is applied to only the estimated covariance matrix defined by Eq. (8). First, some principal components are extracted from the covariance matrix by the standard PCA. Next, ICA rotates the principal components by an orthogonal transformation so that they are as independent of each other as possible. The Fast ICA algorithm with kurtosis [9] is employed here. Then, the spatial and temporal patterns for each independent components are extracted.

3.3 Implementation

The diffusion-type estimation of the Foursquare dataset was implemented in C++ with multi-threading on 60 cores. Eq. (3) goes to infinity at $t = t_i$ or $t = t_{i+1}$ because of $\sigma^2_{\text{dist}} \to 0$. In order to avoid this divergence, we used a very small lower bound (set to 8.64 seconds in this paper) on the σ^2_{dist}. If σ^2_{dist} is smaller than the bound, the bound replaces it. In order to alleviate the effects of outliers in the estimation of the scale parameter $\hat{\beta}$, we eliminated some large $q_i^{[\omega]}$'s of Eq. (12) (ten times larger than the average of them). The data processing and the extraction of patterns by ICA were implemented in Ruby and MATLAB, respectively. The extracted spatial and temporal patterns were displayed in a browser-based interface with Javascript. Fig. 1 is a snapshot of the system, where the temporal patterns in the time and frequency domains (the upper-left and upper-middle boxes), the time points in the peaks of the temporal pattern in the time domain (upper-right), the spatial patterns on the map (lower-left), and the tweets at the peaks of the spatial and temporal patterns (lower-right) are shown. The spatial pattern on the map is displayed by Google Maps API.

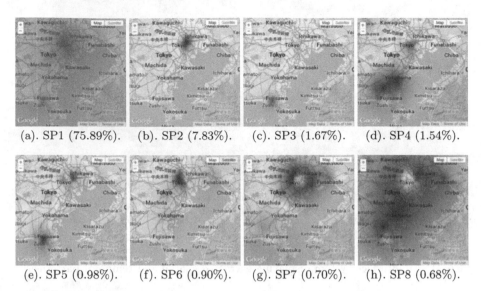

(a). SP1 (75.89%).   (b). SP2 (7.83%).   (c). SP3 (1.67%).   (d). SP4 (1.54%).

(e). SP5 (0.98%).   (f). SP6 (0.90%).   (g). SP7 (0.70%).   (h). SP8 (0.68%).

Fig. 2. Extracted spatial patterns on the map referred by SP1-SP8 with the dominance percentages: The map is limited to Tokyo metropolitan area and its outskirts. The color strength of red and blue means more crowded and less crowded, respectively. The intensity of the colors corresponds to the degree of crowdedness.

3.4   Extraction of Patterns from Foursquare

The Foursquare dataset described in Sect. 3.1 was utilized in order to estimate the spatial distributions by Eq. (7) and their covariance by Eq. (8). Eight independent components were extracted from the covariance by ICA. The total dominance of the eight components was 90.19%.

The extracted eight spatial patterns are shown in Fig. 2. They show that the proposed method could extract various spatial patterns from small samples (100 users). Some of them are global patterns over the map (e.g. SP1, SP7, and SP8) and some are local patterns concentrating on small areas (e.g. SP2 and SP3). SP2 is the pattern related to the central area of Tokyo. SP3 is the pattern related to Kamakura, which is relatively smaller than other cities on the outskirts of Tokyo. The result suggests that the distribution of the users in Kamakura is independent of that in the global metropolitan area. It may be because Kamakura is a famous ancient city which has been visited by many tourists.

Regarding the temporal patterns, we focused on the three patterns for SP1, SP2, and SP7. The temporal patterns in the time and frequency domains for SP1 and SP2 are shown in Figs. 3-(a) and 3-(b). Note that the flat temporal patterns around days 20-22 in the time domain in these figures correspond to the period when the users could not check in Foursquare probably because of a major fault. Fig. 2-(a) and Fig. 3-(a) show that the spatial pattern is distributed globally over the metropolitan area and the most part of the temporal pattern for SP1

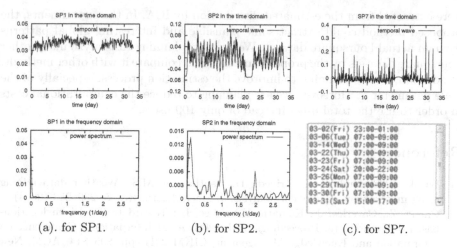

(a). for SP1.   (b). for SP2.   (c). for SP7.

Fig. 3. Temporal patterns in the time and frequency domains for SP1 (left), SP2 (middle) and SP7 (right): In the upper figures, the patterns are shown in the time domain. The lower ones correspond to the patterns in the frequency domain (for SP1 (a) and SP2 (b)) or the list of time points at the peaks (for SP7 (c)).

is stationary. So, SP1 can be regarded as the stationary distribution of users in Tokyo. Fig. 3-(b) shows that SP2 is quite periodic and the length of the period is one day or a half day. Because Fig. 2-(b) shows that SP2 corresponds to the central area in Tokyo, the results probably correspond to the concentration and dispersion of the population over the central area in each day and each half day. On the other hand, Fig. 3-(c) shows the temporal pattern for SP7 and the list of the extracted time points at the peaks of the temporal pattern. Although the temporal pattern in Fig. 3-(c) is not strictly periodic, the peaks seem to have a regular pattern. Most of the peaks are in the weekday morning (7:00-9:00) and a few of them are in the night. In addition, Fig. 2-(g) shows that only the central area (corresponding to SP2) and the outskirts are more crowded than usual and the other metropolitan area is less crowded. It suggests a hypothesis that SP7 may be a pattern of traffic jam which often occurs in rush hours, where some users are left in the outskirts.

In summary, SP1 and SP2 can explain the global stationary distribution of users and the periodic behaviors at the central area, respectively. They are plausible and consistent with our intuition. On the other hand, some new knowledge was discovered in SP3 (the specificity of Kamakura) and SP7 (the traffic jam hypothesis). So, these results verify that the proposed method is useful in the data analysis of the Foursquare dataset.

4   Conclusion

In this paper, a diffusion-type formula is applied to the estimation of the spatio-temporal distribution of the users in Foursquare. In addition, global patterns were extracted from the estimated distribution by ICA. In the experiments, the proposed method could extract some plausible and interesting global patterns from an actual Foursquare dataset. We are now planning to analyze many other Foursquare datasets by the proposed method and compare it with other methods. In addition, we are planning to improve the estimation process, especially of the scale parameter β. Moreover, we are planning to reduce the computational costs in order to use the total users instead of only 100 users.

References

1. Basak, J., Sudarshan, A., Trivedi, D., Santhanam, M.S.: Weather data mining using independent component analysis. J. Mach. Learn. Res. 5, 239–253 (2004)
2. Cheng, Z., Caverlee, J., Kamath, K.Y., Lee, K.: Toward traffic-driven location-based web search. In: Proceedings of the 20th ACM International Conference on Information and Knowledge Management, CIKM 2011, pp. 805–814. ACM, New York (2011)
3. Cichocki, A., Amari, S.: Adaptive Blind Signal and Image Processing: Learning Algorithms and Applications. Wiley (2002)
4. Delorme, A., Makeig, S.: EEGLAB: an open source toolbox for analysis of single-trial eeg dynamics including independent component analysis. Journal of Neuroscience Methods 134(1), 9–21 (2004)
5. Eagle, N., Pentland, A.S.: Eigenbehaviors: identifying structure in routine. Behavioral Ecology and Sociobiology 63(11), 1057–1066 (2009)
6. Feynman, R., Hibbs, A.: Quantum mechanics and path integrals. International series in pure and applied physics, McGraw-Hill (1965)
7. Fire, M., Kagan, D., Puzis, R., Rokach, L., Elovici, Y.: Data mining opportunities in geosocial networks for improving road safety. In: 2012 IEEE 27th Convention of Electrical Electronics Engineers in Israel (IEEEI), pp. 1–4 (2012)
8. Huang, C.M., Jia-Chin Ying, J., Tseng, V.: Mining users behavior and environment for semantic place prediction. In: Nokia Mobile Data Challenge 2012 Workshop. Dedicated task (2012)
9. Hyvärinen, A.: Fast and robust fixed-point algorithms for independent component analysis. IEEE Transactions on Neural Networks 10(3), 626–634 (1999)
10. Hyvärinen, A., Karhunen, J., Oja, E.: Independent Component Analysis. Wiley (2001)
11. McKeown, M.J., Makeig, S., Brown, G., Jung, T.P., Kindermann, S.S., Bell, A., Sejnowski, T.: Analysis of fMRI data by decomposition into independent spatial components. Human Brain Mapping 6(3), 160–188 (1998)
12. Noulas, A., Scellato, S., Mascolo, C., Pontil, M.: An empirical study of geographic user activity patterns in foursquare. In: ICWSM 2011, pp. 70–573 (2011)
13. Rae, A., Murdock, V., Popescu, A., Bouchard, H.: Mining the web for points of interest. In: Proceedings of the 35th International ACM SIGIR Conference on Research and Development in Information Retrieval, SIGIR 2012, pp. 711–720. ACM, New York (2012)
14. Schoenberg, F.P., Brillinger, D.R., Guttorp, P.: Point Processes, Spatial-Temporal, pp. 1573–1577. John Wiley & Sons, Ltd. (2006)

Content-Boosted Restricted Boltzmann Machine for Recommendation

Yongqi Liu[1], Qiuli Tong[2], Zhao Du[2], and Lantao Hu[1]

[1] Tsinghua National Laboratory
for Information Science and Technology(TNList) Department of Computer Science
and Technology, Tsinghua University, Beijing, China
{tianjinbaodier,hulantao}@gmail.com
[2] Information Technology Center, Tsinghua University, Beijing, China
{tql,duzhao}@tsinghua.edu.cn

Abstract. Collaborative filtering and Content-based filtering methods are two famous methods used by recommender systems. Restricted Boltzmann Machine(RBM) model rivals the best collaborative filtering methods, but it focuses on modeling the correlation between item ratings. In this paper, we extend RBM model by incorporating content-based features such as user demograohic information, items categorization and other features. We use Naive Bayes classifier to approximate the missing entries in the user-item rating matrix, and then apply the modified UI-RBM on the denser rating matrix. We present expermental results that show how our approach, Content-boosted Restricted Boltzmann Machine(CB-RBM), performs better than a pure RBM model and other content-boosted collaborative filtering methods.

Keywords: Recommendation Systems, Restricted Boltzmann Machine, Content-Based Filtering.

1 Introduction

Most recommender systems nowadays are based on two approaches: Collaborative Filtering (CF) and Content-based (CB) recommending, or the combination of them. Collaborative Filtering approach has the advantage of not requiring machine analyzable content, but suffers from ?cold start? problem [1]. Content-based filtering can be used to solve this problem. So in order to improve the accuracy of the algorithm, we can use hybrid collaborative filtering techniques.

In this paper, we describe and experiment with a simple algorithm for incorporating content information into a modified UI-RBM [2]. We use naive bayes as content classifier and fill in some of the missing ratings in the rating matrix to form a pseudo rating matrix. We modify the original UI-RBM in some directions. Unlike the noise-free reconstruction in the negative phase, we normalize the visible layer and use sigmoid activation function instead. Applying the modified UI-RBM on the pseudo rating matrix, we achieve great improvement in the accuracy of prediction.

S. Wermter et al. (Eds.): ICANN 2014, LNCS 8681, pp. 773–780, 2014.

2   Related Work

RBMs were first introduced to Collaborate Filtering by Salakhutdinov et al. in 2007 [6]. Because of the non-linearity, RBMs are superior compared to other CF algorithms such as SVD, AFM. Georgiev et al. proposed a non-IID framework for collaborate filtering with RBM, which is called UI-RBM [2]. They model both user-user and item-item correlations in a unified hybrid non-IID framework. It is reported that UI-RBM rivals the best previously-proposed approaches.

Content-based filtering algorithms rely on features of users and items for predictions. They are often used together with Collaborative Filtering, which form Hybrid Collaborative Filtering techniques. The Fab system [4] generates user profiles from Web page ratings and uses CF techniques to identify profiles with similar tastes. Condiffet et al. [5] propose a Bayesian mixed-effects model which integrates user, user ratings, and item features in a unified framework. Forbes and Zhu [1] incorporate content information directly as a natural linear constraint to the matrix factorization algorithm and achieve better performance.

3   Method

We propose a framework to incorporate content-based features with UI-RBM. There are four main step in this approach, which are given below:

- In the first step, we gather information about items and users. For example, in a movie recommender system, what we concern about are movie title, actors, producers, user gender, age, and occupation.
- In the second step, Naive Bayes Classifier is used to predict rating for a user-item pair. Naive Bayes is suitable for cases with high input dimensions.
- In the third step, we create a pseudo user-item rating matrix. Unlike most hybrid collaborative filtering techniques, we don?t fill in all the missing values of the rating matrix. Instead, we propose a two-stage method to judge which missing value should be filled.
- In the last step, a modified UI-RBM is applied on the pseudo rating matrix to give prediction.

In this section, we will show some detail about step 2 to step 4.

3.1   Naive Bayes Classifier

Naive Bayes classifier is based on Bayes Theorem. The strong (naive) independence assumption assumes that the presence or absence of a particular feature is unrelated to the presence or absence of any other feature, for instance, the age of a user does not depend on the gender of that user. So if a item-user pair has user profiles and item features $F_1, F_2, \ldots, F_n$, then the probability of an item i being rated R_j is calculated as follows:

$$P(R_j|i) = \frac{P(R_j)P(i|R_j)}{P(i)} = \frac{P(R_j)\prod_{k=1}^{n}P(F_k|R_j)}{P(F_1, F_2, \ldots, F_n)} \tag{1}$$

Where $P(R_j|i)$, $P(R_j)$, $P(i|R_j)$ and $P(i)$ are called the posterior, prior, likelihood, and evidence respectively.

To predict a rating, Naive Bayes calculates posteriors for each rating and assigns the rating to that particular R_j that has the greatest $P(R_j|i)$.

3.2 Pseudo Rating Matrix

Most algorithms suffer from the sparsity of rating matrix. To deal with this problem, Melville et al. proposed a method in [7], they created a full pseudo rating matrix and applied a modified item-based CF on the pseudo rating matrix. Entry in a pseudo rating matrix is defined as

$$p_{ui} = \begin{cases} r_{ui} & \text{if user u has rated item i} \\ c_{ui} & \text{otherwise} \end{cases} \tag{2}$$

p_{ui} is an element in the pseudo rating matrix, r_{ui} denotes the actual rating provided by user u for item i, while c_{ui} stands for the rating predicted by some content-based filtering algorithm, such as Naive Bayes Classifier.

However, this method has some shortcomings. First, the accuracy of this algorithm depends sensitively on the accuracy of the content-based method used in creating the pseudo rating matrix. On the other hand, a full matrix increases the computational complexity greatly for the following CF algorithm. We came up with a two-step method to solve these problems. First, we determine the confidence in the Naive Bayes?s prediction. Then we find a threshold α to ignore some predicted ratings which we have little confident in.

Let $p_{ui}(j)$ be the posterior probability of rating j predicted by the Naive Bayes classifier for an user-item pair (u, i), $d_{ui}(m, n)$ be the absolute difference between two rating probabilities:

$$d_{ui}(m, n) = |p_{ui}(m) - p_{ui}(n)|, \quad where \ m \neq n \tag{3}$$

We define the confidence of a prediction to be equation 4, where S represents the class label with highest posterior probability, while T with second-highest posterior probability.

$$Conf(u, i) = d_{ui}(S, T) \tag{4}$$

We only fill in the missing ratings whose prediction confidence is larger than a threshold α . α is learned from training set. We use Naive Bayes classifier to predict ratings of user-item pairs in the training set and calculate their confidence. After that, we sort the confidence in descending order and measure the accuracy of N predicted ratings with the highest confidence. N is changed from 1 to the size of the training set. The common style is that the Mean Absolute Error(MAE) increases with the increase of N, which means that predictions with low confidence are not as accurate as those with high confidence. Thus, there is a trade off between the sparsity and accuracy of the pseudo rating matrix. Through observing the relationship between N and MAE, we should find the proper N that not only corresponds to low MAE but also brings in enough predicted ratings. The threshold α is the Nth largest confidence in all the predictions.

3.3 Modified UI-RBM

UI-RBM. UI-RBM is a combination of User-RBM (also known as U-RBM) and Item-RBM (also known as I-RBM) [2], their relationship is shown in Fig. 1. User-RBM and Item-RBM are similar, here we take User-RBM as an example. Suppose we have N users and M items and the ratings are integers between 1 and K, or 0 if not rated. An RBM has a linear visible layer V with M real-valued units and a binary hidden layer H with F binary units. The visible layer and the hidden layer are fully connected and there are no connections within each layer. Each unit has a bias, for the visible unit v_i is a_i, while for the hidden unit h_j is b_j. The probability of a hidden unit given the visible units is shown in equation 5 while the value of a visible unit is shown in equation 6 [1].

$$p(h_j = 1|\boldsymbol{v}) = \sigma(b_j + \Sigma_{i=1}^{M} w_{ij} v_i) \tag{5}$$

$$v_i = a_i + \Sigma_{j=1}^{N} w_{ij} h_j \tag{6}$$

Where $\sigma(x) = 1/(1 + e^{-x})$. We can use Contrastive Divergence (CD) [8] for the learning process of User-RBM and Item-RBM.

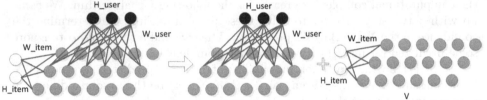

Fig. 1. UI-RBM (the left one) is a combination of User-RBM (the middle one) and Item-RBM (the right one)

In order to train a UI-RBM, we train User-RBM and Item-RBM with rating matrix V seprately. After the negtive phase of CD, each RBM generate a new prediction matrix according to its current state. Then we substitute V with the average sum of these two prediction matrixs, according to equation 7.

$$v_{ij} = \frac{1}{2} \left[a_i^U + \Sigma_{p=1}^{F^U} w_{ip}^U h_{ip}^U + a_j^I + \Sigma_{q=1}^{F^I} w_{jq}^I h_{jq}^I \right] \tag{7}$$

Modification. We made some modification in the training of UI-RBM to achieve better performance. First, according to Georgiev et al. [2], the value of visible units is between 0 and K. A more common way for training is to normalize the visible units and regard the real-valued activities of the visible units in the RBM as the activation probabilities of the hidden units, just as what

---

[1] RBM can also model real-valued data using Gaussian visible units: $p(v_i|h) = \mathcal{N}(a_i + \Sigma_{j=1}^{F} w_{ij} h_j, \sigma_i^2)$ [6]

Hinton et al. did in [9]. Second, in our experiments, we found that instead of noise-free reconstruction we can use logistic function in the negative phase of CD to achieve the better result, just as the following equation :

$$v_{ij} = \frac{1}{2} \left[\sigma \left(a_i^U + \Sigma_{p=1}^{F^U} w_{ip}^U h_{ip}^U \right) + \sigma \left(a_j^I + \Sigma_{q=1}^{F^I} w_{jq}^I h_{jq}^I \right) \right] \tag{8}$$

4 Experiments and Evaluation

4.1 Dataset and Evaluation Measure

We evaluate CB-RBM model on Movielens 100k dataset[2]. It consists of 100,000 ratings for 1682 movies and 943 users. Each rating is an interger between 1 (worst) and 5 (best). The dataset contains simple demographic info for the users (age, gender, occupation and zip code) and items (movie title, release date, video release date, IMDb URL and categories). We perform 5-fold cross-validation to evaluate the algorithm.

We use the Mean Absolute Error (MAE) to measure the deviation of the predicted ratings from their true values.

4.2 Experimental Setup

For the Naive Bayes classifier, we use user profile and movie information to create a 23-dimension feature vector for each user-item pair and use the actual rating as its classification label. The features include user age, gender, occupatio, movie release date, genre(including Action | Adventure | Animation . . .). We calculated posteriors for each rating and assigned the rating to that particular R_j that has the greatest $p(R_j|i)$.

We use a the two-stage selection method to create the pseudo rating matrix. We trained the threshold α through the training set and got the relationship between the amount of predictions N and MAE, as shown in Fig. 2.

We can see that $N = 20\% * (size\ of\ training\ set)$ is a good choice. MAE is small when $N < 20\% * (size\ of\ training\ set)$ while it increases fast when N is larger. $N = 20\% * (size\ of\ training\ set)$ means that we can only fill in 20% of the missing ratings in the rating matrix. The percentage is low because our experiment did not have enough content-based feature. For comparison with other works on Movielens dataset, we only used the feature given by MovieLens dataset. After we have found N, we can get the threshold α, which is the Nth largest confidence in all prediction. Only predicted rating that has a confidence larger than α is used in creating the pseudo matrix.

The training process is almost the same as UI-RBM in [2]. For each update of weight and bias, we used a learning rate of 0.15/training-size, momentum of 0.9, and a weight decay of 0.002. The weights were initialized with small random values sampled from a zero-mean normal distribution with standard deviation 0.1. $T = 1$ is used for the CD learning during training, which reduced training time considerably.

---

[2] http://www.grouplens.org/node/73

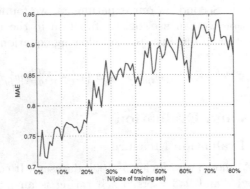

Fig. 2. Determining the optimal value of N for MovieLens

4.3   Results

We report results on Movielens 100k dataset and compare CB-RBM with 1) pure CF models 2) other previously-published content-boosted methods.

Fig. 3 shows the comparison between CB-RBM and other RBM-based models. In order to achieve optimal performance of each model, we used different hidden numbers. We can see that I-RBM (F=50) performs a bit worse than U-RBM(F=50) when trained for less than 200 epochs but then outperforms U-RBM. UI-RBM(F^U =40,F^I =40) works better than I-RBM obviously at the beginning but not much in the end. CB-RBM(F^U=50, F^I=50) significantly outperforms other models. CB-RBM has the best prediction accuracy and converges quickly. CB-RBM(full matrix) is CB-RBM without the two-stage selection method and all predictions by Naive Bayes classifier are used in creating the pseudo rating matrix. CB-RBM(full matrix) achieves bad performance, which improve the effect of our two-stage predicted rating selection method.

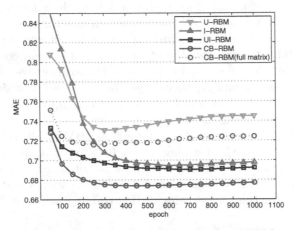

Fig. 3. Comparision between CB-RBM and other RBM-based models

Table 1. Comparision between CB-RBM and pure CF

Algorithm	MAE
SVD [10]	0.733
Item-based CF [3]	0.726
Iter PCA + Kmeans [16]	0.712
I-RBM [2]	0.695
UI-RBM [2]	0.690
Latent CF [11]	0.685
CB-RBM	0.674

Table 2. Comparision between CB-RBM and content-boosted CF

Algorithm	MAE
CBCF [7]	0.726
KMR^{Var}_{Hybrid}[13]	0.711
SMCF [12]	0.706
Rec_{NBCF} [14]	0.696
Rec_{SVMCF} [14]	0.685
IBCF + NBM [15]	0.685
CB-RBM	0.674

Table 1 shows the comparision of the prediction quality between some other CF models and our CB-RBM model, we can see that CB-RBM performs better than SVD, item-based CF, Latent CF[11], Iterative PCA[16] and other RBM based algorithm.

Table 2 shows the comparison of the prediction quality of some content-boosted method in collaborate filtering. The percentage improvement, in case of CB-RBM, over the traditional Content-boosted Collaborate Filtering (CBCF) is 7.2% for MovieLens. CB-RBM works much better than other method.

5   Conclusion

In this paper, we extend RBM model by incorporating content-based features. We use Naive Bayes classifier to approximate the missing entries in the user-item rating matrix, and then use a novel two-stage predicted rating selection method to create pseudo rating matrix. Finally we apply a modified UI-RBM model on the denser rating matrix. Evaluation on the MovieLens 100k dataset has shown that our Content-boosted Restricted Boltamann Machine(CB-RBM), rivals the prediction quality of the best previously proposed CF algorithms, including both pure CF models and other content-boosted collaborative filtering models.

In future work, we would like to enhance the content-based classifier to achieve more accurate prediction, so we can create a more denser pseudo rating matrix. Another possibility for extension is to incorporate content information directly into the structure of RBM. In CB-RBM, content information and RBM are still seperated. Although the performance of CB-RBM has already been so good, we are willing to know if it would help to build a unified model.

References

1. Forbes, P., Zhu, M.: Content-boosted matrix factorization for recommender systems: experiments with recipe recommendation. In: Proceedings of the Fifth ACM Conference on Recommender Systems, pp. 261–264. ACM (2011)
2. Georgiev, K., Nakov, P.: A non-iid framework for collaborative filtering with restricted Boltzmann machines. In: Proceedings of the 30th International Conference on Machine Learning, pp. 1148–1156 (2013)

3. Sarwar, B., Karypis, G., Konstan, J., et al.: Item-based collaborative filtering recommendation algorithms. In: Proceedings of the 10th International Conference on World Wide Web, pp. 285–295. ACM (2001)
4. Balabanovi, M., Shoham, Y.: Fab: content-based, collaborative recommendation. Communications of the ACM 40(3), 66–72 (1997)
5. Condliff, M.K., Lewis, D.D., Madigan, D., et al.: Bayesian mixed-effects models for recommender systems. ACM SIGIR 99, 23–30 (1999)
6. Salakhutdinov, R., Mnih, A., Hinton, G.: Restricted Boltzmann machines for collaborative filtering. In: Proceedings of the 24th International Conference on Machine Learning, pp. 791–798. ACM (2007)
7. Melville, P., Mooney, R.J., Nagarajan, R.: Content-boosted collaborative filtering for improved recommendations. In: AAAI/IAAI, pp. 187–192 (2002)
8. Hinton, G.E.: Training products of experts by minimizing contrastive divergence. Neural Computation 14(8), 1771–1800 (2002)
9. Hinton, G.E., Osindero, S., Teh, Y.W.: A fast learning algorithm for deep belief nets. Neural Computation 18(7), 1527–1554 (2006)
10. Vozalis, M.G., Markos, A., Margaritis, K.G.: Collaborative filtering through SVD-based and hierarchical nonlinear PCA. In: Diamantaras, K., Duch, W., Iliadis, L.S. (eds.) ICANN 2010, Part I. LNCS, vol. 6352, pp. 395–400. Springer, Heidelberg (2010)
11. Langseth, H., Nielsen, T.D.: A latent model for collaborative filtering. International Journal of Approximate Reasoning 53(4), 447–466 (2012)
12. Su, X., Greiner, R., Khoshgoftaar, T.M., et al.: Hybrid collaborative filtering algorithms using a mixture of experts. In: Proceedings of the IEEE/WIC/ACM International Conference on Web Intelligence, pp. 645–649. IEEE Computer Society (2007)
13. Ghazanfar, M.A., Prügel-Bennett, A., Szedmak, S.: Kernel-mapping recommender system algorithms. Information Sciences 208, 81–104 (2012)
14. Ghazanfar, M., Prugel-Bennett, A.: Building switching hybrid recommender system using machine learning classifiers and collaborative filtering. IAENG International Journal of Computer Science 37(3) (2010)
15. Su, X., Khoshgoftaar, T.M., Greiner, R.: A Mixture Imputation-Boosted Collaborative Filter. In: FLAIRS Conference, pp. 312–316 (2008)
16. Kim, D., Yum, B.J.: Collaborative filtering based on iterative principal component analysis. Expert Systems with Applications 28(4), 823–830 (2005)

Financial Self-Organizing Maps

Marina Resta

DIEC, via Vivaldi 5, 16126
University of Genova, Italy
resta@economia.unige.it

Abstract. This paper introduces Financial Self–Organizing Maps (Fin–SOM) as a SOM sub–class where the mapping of inputs on the neural space takes place using functions with economic soundness, that makes them particularly well–suited to analyze financial data. The visualization capabilities as well as the explicative power of both the standard SOM and the FinSOM variants is tested on data from the German Stock Exchange. The results suggest that, dealing with financial data, the FinSOM seem to offer superior representation capabilities of the observed phenomena.

Keywords: Self–Organizing Maps, Value at Risk, Granger Causality.

1 Introduction

The 2008 great crisis dramatically highlighted the poor forecasting performance of existing Earling Warning Systems (EWS) i.e. those automatic systems that looking at proper combinations of macroeconomic variables would have alerted both policy makers and investors, hence stemming most dramatic aspects of the flooding financial wave. From the perspective of automatic systems design, this experience suggested the importance to develop new systems that are able to offer more readable and intuitive results, to facilitate the task of monitoring and regulating the overall level of risk. This rationale has recently inspired the development of EWS based on the paradigm of Kohonen maps [5]: an EWS based on Self–Organizing Maps (SOM) was suggested in [8] to measure the economic vulnerability of countries, and to estimate the probability of future crises; [13] and [14] discussed a fuzzified version of SOM, particularly well suited to apply on macroeconomic variables and to pickup alerting signal for upcoming financial shocks; [9] and later [10] analyzed a hybrid structure joining SOM to graphs in order to enhance clusters visualization capabilites of Kohonen maps, and used it to analyze the topological structure of various financial markets. A common aspect of the cited works is that in substance they leave unchanged the backbone of the original Kohonen's algorithm. However, a not negligible issue concerns the way SOM perform the mapping task. Obviously, depending on the metric in use, results can consistently vary: [6], for instance, discovered that hyperbolic space is ideally suited to embed large hierarchical structures, as later proved by the Hyperbolic Self-Organizing Map [12]. Moreover [1] show that in high dimensional

S. Wermter et al. (Eds.): ICANN 2014, LNCS 8681, pp. 781–788, 2014.

space, the concept of proximity, distance or nearest neighbor may not even be qualitatively meaningful.

The main point, however, is that despite of the importance of information retrieval from financial markets, there is a lack of metrics specifically thought to manage financial data.

Moving from this point, in this paper we discuss an alternative approach, replacing the similarity measure which represents the core of the SOM algorithm by way of alternative functions with greater financial soundness, thus originating Financial Self Organizing Maps (FinSOM). FinSOM would allow to make the SOM algorithm most suitable to analyze financial data and to capture relevant information. In our view rather than a single algorithmic procedure FinSOM must be intended as a family of different SOM, whose members are characterized depending on the function used to manage the similarity between inputs and neurons in the topological grid. In this respect, we hereafter discuss two SOM variants obtained incorporating into the learning procedure, respectively, Value at Risk (VaR–SOM), and Linear Granger Causality (LGC–SOM). The structure of the paper is therefore as follows. Section 2 is divided into two subsections, to provide the reader with basic understanding of the proposed algorithms. Section 3 discusses an application on financial data, while Section 4 concludes.

2   The FinSOM Framework

As widely known, Self Organizing Maps [5] (SOM) assume to order a set of neurons, often (but not exclusively) arranged either in a mono–dimensional or in a 2–D rectangular/hexagonal grid, to form a discrete topological mapping of an input space $X \subset \mathbb{R}^n$.

Assuming for sake of simplicity a map made by M nodes, if we denote by $\boldsymbol{w}_i \in \mathbb{R}^n$ $(i = 1, \ldots, M)$ the weight vector associated to neuron r_i, the algorithm works as shown in the Box 1.

Algorithm 1. The basic SOM algorithm explained.

Assume T as the size of input space X.
Set M as the map size.
At $t = 0$ initialize the weights at random.
for $1 \leq t \leq T$ **do**
  (i) Present an input $\boldsymbol{x}(t) \in X$
  (ii) Select the winner: $\nu(t) = \arg\min_i \|\boldsymbol{x}(t) - \boldsymbol{w}_i(t)\|$
  (iii) Update the weights of the winner and its neighbors: $\Delta \boldsymbol{w}_i(t) = h(t)\eta(\nu, i, t)(\boldsymbol{x}(t) - \boldsymbol{w}_\nu)$.
end for

Here $\| \cdot \|$ denotes a distance (usually the Euclidean distance or, more generally, a function in the family of either Minkowsky or Riemann norms), while

$\eta(\nu, i, t) = \exp\left(-\frac{\|r_\nu - r_i\|^2}{2s^2}\right)$ is the neighborhood function among the leader node r_ν and all the grid neurons r_i $(i = 1, \ldots, M)$, s is the effective range of the neighborhood; finally $h(t)$ is the so called learning rate, that is a scalar–valued function, decreasing monotonically, and satisfying: $(i)\, 0 < h(t) < 1$; $(ii)\lim\limits_{t \to 0} h(t) \to +\infty; (iii)\lim\limits_{t \to \infty} h(t) \to 0$ [5,11].

Next paragraphs are devoted to provide insights on how to modify the standard SOM backbone, thus making it more suitable to deal with financial and economic data.

2.1 The Value at Risk SOM

The Value at Risk SOM (VaR–SOM) is a SOM based on the key concept of Value at Risk.

In a quite informal way, assuming the level of confidence α, $VaR_{1-\alpha}$ is a smallest value such that probability that loss exceeds or equals to this value is bigger than or equals to α:

$$VaR_{1-\alpha} = -x_\alpha \tag{1}$$

where x_α is the left–tail α percentile of a normal distribution: $N(\mu, \sigma^2)$ with mean μ and variance σ^2; x_α is described in the expression: $P[R < x_\alpha] = \alpha$, where R is the expected return. Using a standard normal distribution enables to replace x_α by z_α through the following permutation: $z_\alpha = (x_\alpha - \mu)/\sigma$, which yields: $x_\alpha = \mu + z_\alpha \cdot \sigma$, being z_α the left-tail α percentile of a standard normal distribution. Consequently, it is possible to re-write (1) as:

$$VaR_{1-\alpha} = -(\mu + z_\alpha \cdot \sigma) \tag{2}$$

In order for VaR to be meaningful, the confidence level is generally set equal to 95% or 99%: the higher the confidence level, the higher the VaR, as it travels downwards along the tail of the distribution (further left on the x-axis).

Incorporating VaR into the SOM algorithm means to pair any input to a node in the map having similar behavior in the left hand side of the sampled distribution; in the case of financial data this means to match patterns sharing similar losses profile.

In Box 2 some pseudo–code is provided, explaining how the Kohonen's algorithm is modified to take the VaR information into account. Note that $VaR_{1-\alpha}$ $(z(t))$ and $Var_{1-\alpha}(w_i(t))$, $(i = 1, \ldots, M)$ indicate the Value at Risk associated to the normalized input $z(t)$ and the normalized map nodes, respectively at the level $(1 - \alpha)\%$. As VaR is generally negative (it represents a loss!), here we considered its absolute value.

2.2 The Linear Granger Causality SOM

The Linear Granger Causality [3] (LGC) is a statistical measure of causality based on forecast power. Given two stationary time–series A and B, (for sim-

---

Algorithm 2. The VaR–SOM algorithm.

Assume T as the size of input space X.

Set M as the map size.

Set the confidence level α.

At $t = 0$ initialize the weights at random.

for $1 \leq t \leq T$ **do**

    (i) Convert the input $\boldsymbol{x}(t) \in X$ into $\boldsymbol{z}(t)$

    (ii) Select the winner: $\nu(t) = \arg\min_{i} ||VaR_{1-\alpha}(\boldsymbol{z}(t))| - |VaR_{1-\alpha}(\boldsymbol{w}_i(t))||$

    (iii) Update the weights of the winner and its neighbors: $\Delta\boldsymbol{w}_i(t) =$
$h(t)\eta(\nu, i, t)\,(\boldsymbol{z}(t) - \boldsymbol{w}_\nu)$.

end for

---

plicity assume that they have zero mean), we can represent their linear inter-relationships with the following model:

$$
\begin{aligned}
A_t &= \sum_{j=1}^{p} a_j A_{t-j} + \sum_{j=1}^{q} b_j B_{t-j} + \varepsilon_t \\
B_t &= \sum_{j=1}^{p} c_j B_{t-j} + \sum_{j=1}^{q} d_j A_{t-j} + \theta_t
\end{aligned}
\tag{3}
$$

where ε_t and θ_t are two uncorrelated white noise processes; p, q are the maximum lags considered; a_j, b_j, c_j and d_j are the real valued model coefficients. The definition of causality implies that B causes A when b_j is different from zero; likewise, A causes B when d_j is different from zero. The causality is based on the F–test [7] of the null hypothesis that coefficients b_j or d_j are equal to zero according to the direction of the Granger causality.

Incorporating Granger causality into the SOM algorithm, means testing whether some causality is present or not among the input patterns and the map nodes. Under the F–test the following situations can therefore occur: (i) the causality is not significant; (ii) the causality is significant towards one direction (either from X to M or from M to X); (iii) the causality is significant towards both direction. Clearly, the most desiderable situations are either (ii), in the direction from M to X, or (iii). In both cases, in fact, the nodes behavior should increase the prediction (and hence the knowledge) of input patterns.

Box 3 shows how to build a SOM incorporating such information.

Note that selecting the winner implies now to choose either the node for which the causality is highest, if the F–score is significant, or the neuron whose non–causality is lowest, if the null hypothesis cannot be rejected. Clearly the results are conditioned by the choice of the lags amplitude p and q. A way to stem this issue is to run a bunch of LGC–SOM varying the couple $\{p, q\}$, and hence selecting the map that assures the best performance under the Akaike Information Criterion [2].

Algorithm 3. The LGC–SOM algorithm.

Assume T as the size of input space X.

Set M as the map size.

Set p, q as the lag amplitudes.

At $t = 0$ initialize the weights at random with zero mean.

for $1 \leq t \leq T$ **do**

  Present an input $\boldsymbol{x}(t) \in X$

  for $1 \leq i \leq M$ **do**

    (*i*) $\boldsymbol{x}(t) \to A_t$

    (*ii*) $\boldsymbol{w}_i(t) \to B_t$

    (*iii*) Apply (3)

    (*iv*) Run the F–test $\to F_i$

  end for

  Select the winner: $\nu(t)$ as the node having the best F test score F_ν.

  Update the weights of the winner and its neighbors: $\Delta \boldsymbol{w}_i(t) = h(t)\eta(\nu, i, t)\left(\boldsymbol{x}(t) - \boldsymbol{w}_\nu\right).$

end for

3 Case study

The FinSOM class has been tested on a data sample made up by daily quotations of 207 German companies, in the period: October 2012-December 2013. for an overall number of 301 observations for each stock. The resulting 207×301 input matrix of price levels $\ell(t)$ at time t has been then turned in the correspondent 207×300 matrix of log-returns X, where the log-return at time t for the i–th stock is given by:

$$lr_i(t) = \log \ell(t) - \log \ell(t-1), \, t = 2, \dots 301 \tag{4}$$

We then launched both SOM and FinSOM procedures: in order to choose optimal map dimensions we run extensive simulations, and motivated by the robustness of the results, we are now going to discuss the results obtained by way of equally sized maps composed by 96 neurons, arranged into a 8×12 grid. VaR computations have been made at both 95% and 99% levels of confidence, while LGC–SOM assumed: $p = 5 = q$, as to say, we assumed that causality can affect log–returns on a five days basis. This *magic* number corresponds to the value of the fractal dimension estimated on data by way of the False Nearest Neighbor (FNN) method [4]. The final maps are shown in Figure 1.

Clearly there is no room enough for a deeper investigation of the results, however, from a visual perspective, it is possible to observe that the number of maps clusters is quite different: six in the case of SOM, nine for VaR–SOM with $\alpha = 99\%$, and five for both VaR–SOM with $\alpha = 95\%$ and LGC–SOM.

Furthermore, it should be noted that in the case of standard SOM the nodes coloring has been made uniquely by referring to the unified distance matrix (UMatrix), while VaR–SOM nodes were colored by considering also the losses profile associated to each neuron. Finally, color shades in the LGC–SOM take also the causality significance of each node into account.

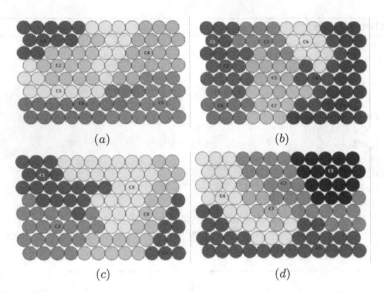

(a)   (b)

(c)   (d)

Fig. 1. From left to right and from top to bottom: SOM (*a*), VaR–SOM with $\alpha = 99\%$ (*b*), VaR–SOM with $\alpha = 95\%$ (*c*), and LGC–SOM (*d*), trained on data in the range October 2012–December 2013

The groups highlighted in the standard SOM (Fig.1*a*), are strongly connoted by sectors: C1 mainly embodies Banking and Finance stocks, C2 groups Heavy Industry companies, C3 contains High–Tech firms, while Health–Care and Energy Commodities are equally shared between C4 and C5.

In the case of VaR–SOM, nodes (and hence firms) with similar probability of losses exposition are highlighted. In particular, when $\alpha = 99\%$ (Fig.1*b*), lowest VaR is associated to clusters C1 to C4, where we can find stocks of companies that operating mainly at international rather than at national level have had greater opportunities to hedge from local crisis effect. On the other hand, the clusters C7 to C9 gather stocks/companies more sensitive to possible defaults and characterized by highest volatility levels, as well as by higher VaR values. Clusters C5 and C6, are of dubious interpretation, and refers to borderline situations with respect to those highlighted for both the groups C1 to C4, and C7 to C9. For what is concerning the VaR–SOM with $\alpha = 95\%$ (Fig.1*c*), the lower number of clusters probably depends on the variation in the confidence level. Now clusters C1 and C2 enclose German firms mainly projected at the international level and with lower VaR values, cluster C3 and C4 contain German stocks with middle–high levels of exposure, while C5 groups stocks with highest loss probability.

Moving to LGC–SOM, the visual inspection of the map needs to be coupled to the analysis of the regression coefficients that the procedure associates to every pair (node, stock), and *a fortiori* to the values of the related F–statistics. In this case, the analysis reveals that in three clusters of five (C1, C2 and C3) the nodes exhibit Linear Granger Causality (LGC) towards the input space;

in the remaining clusters the LGC assumption has been either weakly (C4) or hardly (C5) rejected. From an economical perspective, the former information is quite important, because it can be read in a forecasting key, that is the patterns associated to the map nodes can be helpful to forecast the behaviour of related stocks in the input space. However, it is difficult to get an interpretation key for the results corresponding to nodes in clusters C4 and C5.

4 Conclusion

In this work we discussed an enhancement of Self Organizing Maps (SOM), thought to improve the capability of the original algorithm to exploit meaningful patterns from financial data. The main issue, in fact, is that similarity measures do not take enough into account the intrinsic complexity of this kind of data.

According to this rationale, we introduced Financial SOM (FinSOM) as a family of SOM whose members modify the original SOM algorithm by evaluating the similarity (and hence the proximity) among inputs and neurons by way of functions with more economic soundness. In particular, we introduced a risk–oriented SOM based on Value at Risk (VaR–SOM), and a SOM based on Linear Granger Causality (LGC–SOM).

Financial SOM have been compared to standard SOM in an application on stocks data from the German market, observed in the period: October 2012-December 2013. By comparison to the classical SOM, FinSOM seem to provide more meaningful economic taxonomies. This seems particularly true in the case of VaR–SOM, that offer a quite intuitive intepretation of the generated clusters.

Clearly the results are sensitive to the parameters in use, and this can be a not negligible issue. Despite our general impression that FinSOM can be effective tools to inspect financial data, and to exploit significant patterns, future research must be oriented in search of further improvements of the technique. Towards this direction we think there is great room for improvements, due to the wide basin from which functions to replace standard metrics can be drawn.

References

1. Aggarwal, C.C., Hinneburg, A., Keim, D.A.: On the surprising behavior of distance metrics in high dimensional spaces. In: Van den Bussche, J., Vianu, V. (eds.) ICDT 2001. LNCS, vol. 1973, pp. 420–434. Springer, Heidelberg (2000)
2. Akaike, H.: A new look at the statistical model identification. IEEE Transactions on Automatic Control 19(6), 716–723 (1974)
3. Granger, C.W.J.: Investigating Causal Relations by Econometric Models and Cross-spectral Methods. Econometrica 37(3), 424–438 (1969)
4. Kennel, M.B., Brown, R., Abarbanel, H.D.I.: Determining embedding dimension for phase-space reconstruction using a geometrical construction. Phys. Rev. A 45, 3403 (1992)
5. Kohonen, T.: Self-Organizing Maps. Springer, Heidelberg (2002)
6. Lamping, J., Rao, R.: Laying out and visualizing large trees using a hyperbolic space. In: ACM Symposium on User Interface Software and Technology, pp. 13–14 (1994)

7. Lomax, R.G., Hahs-Vaughn, D.L.: Statistical Concepts: A Second Course. Routledge/Taylor & Francis (2007)
8. Resta, M.: Early Warning Systems: An Approach via Self Organizing Maps with Applications to Emergent Markets. In: Apolloni, B., Bassis, S., Marinaro, M. (eds.) Proceedings of the 2009 Conference on New Directions in Neural Networks: 18th Italian Workshop on Neural Networks, WIRN 2008, pp. 176–184. IOS Press, Amsterdam (2009)
9. Resta, M.: The Shape of Crisis. Lessons from Self Organizing Maps. In: Kahraman, C. (ed.) Computational Intelligence Systems in Industrial Engineering. Springer Atlantis series in Computational Intelligence Systems, vol. 6, pp. 535–555 (2012)
10. Resta, M.: On a Data Mining Framework for the Identification of Frequent Pattern Trends. In: Perna, C., Sibillo, M. (eds.) To appear in Mathematical and Statistical Methods for Actuarial Sciences and Finance (2014), doi:10.1007/978-3-319-05014-0_39
11. Ritter, H., Schulten, K.: Convergence properties of Kohonen's topology conserving maps: fluctuations, stability, and dimension selection. Biological Cybernetics 60, 59–71 (1988)
12. Ritter, H.: Self–organizing maps in non–euclidian spaces. In: Oja, E., Kaski, S. (eds.) Kohonen Maps, pp. 97–110. Elsevier (1999)
13. Sarlin, P., Eklund, T.: Fuzzy Clustering of the Self-Organizing Map: Some Applications on Financial Time Series. In: Laaksonen, J., Honkela, T. (eds.) WSOM 2011. LNCS, vol. 6731, pp. 40–50. Springer, Heidelberg (2011)
14. Sarlin, P.: Visual tracking of the millennium development goals with a fuzzifieed self–organizing neural network. International Journal of Machine Learning and Cybernetics 3, 233–245 (2012)

RatSLAM on Humanoids - A Bio-Inspired SLAM Model Adapted to a Humanoid Robot

Stefan Müller, Cornelius Weber, and Stefan Wermter

University of Hamburg, Department of Computer Science,
Vogt-Koelln-Strasse 30, 22527 Hamburg, Germany
{3smuelle,weber,wermter}@informatik.uni-hamburg.de
http://www.informatik.uni-hamburg.de/WTM/

Abstract. Mapping, localization and navigation are major topics and challenges for mobile robotics. To perform tasks and to interact efficiently in the environment, a robot needs knowledge about its surroundings. Many robots today are capable of performing simultaneous mapping and localization to generate own world representations. Most assume an array of highly sophisticated artificial sensors to track landmarks placed in the environment. Recently, there has been significant interest in research approaches inspired by nature and RatSLAM is one of them. It has been introduced and tested on wheeled robots with good results. To examine how RatSLAM behaves on humanoid robots, we adapt this model for the first time to this platform by adjusting the given constraints. Furthermore, we introduce a multiple hypotheses mapping technique which improves mapping robustness in open spaces with features visible from several distant locations.

Keywords: SLAM, visual SLAM, RatSLAM, Humanoid robot, Mapping, Localization.

1 Introduction

For successful and efficient interaction with the environment, world knowledge is needed. The challenge to gain this information can be addressed by the tasks of mapping, localization and navigation. Basic world interaction approaches rely on a-priori generated maps of static environments and perform localization with (noisy) odometric data and pre-defined landmarks. The main disadvantage of these approaches is the inability to deal with changes in dynamic environments, since geometry is not reliable to determine landmarks with single sensors [11] or arrays of different sensors [4].

During the last decades, many approaches tried to overcome this problem by creating an internal world representation for the robots themselves. The most successful ones form an entire group of methods that can perform Simultaneous Localization and Mapping (SLAM). Many combine multiple sensors, resulting in a multiplicity of sensor data that needs to be processed. Recently, SLAM has been used more frequently with humanoid robots to form probabilistic robot pose

S. Wermter et al. (Eds.): ICANN 2014, LNCS 8681, pp. 789–796, 2014.

estimates in complex 3D environments (SE3) supported by laser rangefinders and idiothetic on-board sensors [6] or to create accurate grid maps in SE2 [13].

An alternative to these approaches with high demand on processing power can be found in nature itself: Most animals do not have precise sensors like laser rangefinders to measure distances with an accuracy of millimeters for large ranges. Nevertheless, they perform successful mapping, localization and navigation tasks. Plenty of approaches try to adapt biological mechanisms and sensor usage to computational models. Most research in this area is focused on understanding the function of the brain and to develop exact biological models, tested only regarding their biological plausibility [1,5]. Only few models, like from Arleo et al. [2] or Weiller et al. [14], have been tested regarding practical mapping, localization and performance on real robots. However, they have only been shown to work under many constraints in relatively small worlds.

In 2004, Milford et al. developed RatSLAM [10], a biological SLAM approach based on mapping and localization mechanisms in the rodent's hippocampus. In contrast to other models, biological validity and correctness was not as important as to create a reliable SLAM system with low computational complexity, usable on robots with low computing power. RatSLAM had been developed with and for wheeled robots. However, the physical characteristics and constraints of this type of robot differ from those of humanoids. Hence, applied to a humanoid, we encountered several problems related to robot instability, sensors and movement characteristics during evaluation. These issues led to false localizations and false positive loop closures in the topological map. To address these challenges, we developed an improved extended approach, called *Multi-hypotheses Experience Maps* (multi-EMs). This approach tracks multiple spatial robot position hypotheses at the same time and weights their plausibility, achieving more robust, less fault-prone mapping.

1.1   RatSLAM - A Bio-Inspired SLAM Solution

RatSLAM is a vision-based, biologically inspired model, able to achieve competitive SLAM results in real-world environments with a camera sensor and optionally sensors that gather odometric data [8,9,12]. Commonly used sensors like laser, ultrasonic or depth sensors are not used. It is a rough computational model of the part of the rodent's hippocampus that maintains its believed location in the world. RatSLAM uses techniques of landmark sensing in combination with odometric information to form a *Competitive Attractor Network* (CAN). This CAN forms a topological representation of adjacent world locations, which mostly includes Cartesian properties. RatSLAM consists of several processing units which are introduced here in short in the order they perform sensor data processing (fig. 1).

Local View (LV): The *local view* (LV) is a collection of simple neural units that store image templates. Templates are generated from a down-sampled 8bit-greyscale part (*Region of Interest*, ROI) of the current raw camera image. Templates are used to determine the robot location in space via scanline intensity profile matching. Whenever a new camera image is received, the ROI is processed to a template and compared to all previously stored templates. If the new template sufficiently matches a stored one, the robot is deemed at a familiar location and the new template is not added to the network. Otherwise, if no sufficient match was found, the actual template is added to the LV cells for recognition.

Visual Odometry (VO): Odometric data is necessary to maintain an approximate robot location hypothesis if no visual cue is available. Usually, it is measured with sensors like rotary encoders [8,9,12]. Apart from that, RatSLAM is able to use visual methods to determine translational and rotational robot movement. In addition to the ROI for the LV, other ROIs are defined in the image: Forward movement and orientation changes are determined based on the rate of filtered average absolute intensity difference between consecutive scanline intensity profiles.

Pose Cell (PC) Network: The *Pose Cell network* is the core of RatSLAM and it forms three-dimensional localization and orientation hypotheses (x', y', θ') for the robot's pose within the real environment (x, y, θ). This network consists of a three-dimensional CAN of inter-connected neural units (PCs) with wrap-around connections. Each PC represents a location and orientation in the environment and is linked to LV cells by Hebbian learning links. The robot's current pose belief is represented by an activity level of the PCs. Cell activity can change due to injected energy whenever a familiar visual template is recognized. Multiple LV templates can match the same template and lead to a conformity level that is larger than a given threshold for multiple LV cells. All these LV cells inject energy into the PC network via the weighted Hebbian links. This can result in multiple activity packets being active at the same time. The total amount of energy, however, is kept constant by internal CAN attractor dynamics. The packet with the highest amount of energy is the strongest believed robot position. Another factor influencing the activity of PCs is path integration: The activity is shifted relative to odometry to nearby PCs while the robot moves in order to maintain consistency between real world and the internal map. Over time, the energy of packets can increase or decrease, new packets can appear, existing disappear or they can unite. For this reason, the robot's position cannot be determined for sure, and pose estimation is threated probabilistically.

Experience Map (EM): Experiments on the PC map showed that, especially in large environments, the PC representation is not topologically correct and only partially Cartesian [9,12]. Reasons for this are path integration, from increasing odometric drift and particularly ever increasing numbers of re-localization ("loop closure") based on LV cells, linked to multiple world locations ("(hash) collision") and vice versa ("discontinuity"). Therefore, Milford et al. extended RatSLAM with a topological Cartesian world representation called *Experience Map* (EM) [8]. This map represents each world location by a unique experience $e_i = (P_i, L_i, \mathbf{p}_i)$ at an independent spatial position $\mathbf{p}_i = (x, y)$. The experience is linked to an individual PC $P_i(x', y', \theta')$ and exactly one LV cell L_i and gets activated whenever the linked PC and the corresponding LV cell are active. Consecutive experiences are connected relative to each other by transitions which span a traversable graph that, in combination with information about the relative pose of involved experiences, movement behavior and movement duration for inter-experience traveling, can be used for path planning and navigation. A map correction algorithm inside the EM maintains Cartesian consistency at all time by relative location correction of experiences to each other to eliminate inconsistencies, which becomes obvious in loop closure events.

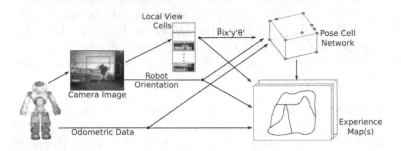

Fig. 1. The complete system consists of several processing units which in the end form a topological world representation inside the experience map

2   Approach: RatSLAM on Humanoids

RatSLAM is available in an open source implementation called OpenRatSLAM [3] which has been used as basis for this adaption to humanoid robots. In the following, we will describe how RatSLAM is adapted to this type of robot. Thereafter, an extension is introduced to enhance the EM's overall accuracy.

2.1   Adapting RatSLAM to a Humanoid

RatSLAM was developed for wheeled robots. Hence, constraints have been made regarding the possible actions the robot can perform. Humanoid robots, however, have a different physical structure and come along with other constraints. These have to be integrated into the RatSLAM model while old constraints can be dismissed. To enable functionalities not implemented for wheeled robots, like forward, backward and sideways walking or turning on a spot, sensor data processing has been adapted: For our approach, the algorithm uses camera images for template generation and rotation detection only. Translational movements are obtained by a translational motion controller.

Humanoids in comparison to wheeled robots, move quite slowly while most of the image movement comes from the shaking of the robot during walking. Hence, exploration with humanoids takes much more time. To enhance exploration and the overall map quality, we integrated an autonomous exploration approach, based on touch-and-turn techniques to create a spatial and comprehensive map. Over time, this exploration behavior spans a graph of trajectories over the complete environment that can be used for later navigation tasks. From time to time, the robot pauses and looks around on the spot, to create *anchor-points* which represent locations in the environment with independent view templates for plenty of different orientations. These locations extend the robot's narrow field of view (FOV) and improve re-localization capabilities immensely. We did not extend RatSLAM to account for the fact that humanoids can climb stairs and thereby may have access to 3D Euclidean space (SE3).

2.2   Multi-Hypotheses Experience Maps

One major issue while using RatSLAM is the affection to false positive loop closures during exploration (*"perceptual aliasing"*). False positive matches and snaps introduce inconsistency and irremediable failures to the map and have to be avoided. Generally, false positives are more serious than false negatives, as false negatives only reduce the overall recall rate but in the end have negligible impact on the total map precision [7]. This difficulty is caused by two reasons:

1. Robot instability during movement: A relatively high center of mass in combination with a comparatively high-mounted camera on the robot's forehead results in swaying movements whenever the robot moves. VO based on image differences does not work under these conditions;
2. Image quality: Due to the low image resolution, the LV algorithm is unable to distinguish locations with almost identical orientations but different distances to the same environmental feature and assumes an identical position.

Although multiple pose hypotheses in the PC network and threshold adaption for image classification introduce stability, false positive loop closures appear frequently. Further increased thresholds would lead to many missing (false negative) loop closures.

In our approach, we introduce multiple EMs with multiple robot pose hypotheses at once to increase the overall accuracy and to repair hastily loop closures (fig. 1). Independent loop closures for each EM create different hypotheses for traveled paths and the current robot pose. All EMs get ranked in comparison to an artificial map of arithmetic means $\overline{em}$ for all experiences e_i in all EMs k (with $k \geq 2$) linked to the same PC pc_i:

$$\bar{x}_i = \frac{1}{n} \sum_{k=1}^{n} x_{i_k} \qquad \bar{y}_i = \frac{1}{n} \sum_{k=1}^{n} y_{i_k} \tag{1}$$

The rating is done for the last n experiences. Regarding figure 2, the distance d_i of two experiences $\overline{em}_i$ and e_i is calculated by

$$d_i(\bar{e}_i, e_i) = \sqrt{(\bar{x}_i - e_{i,x})^2 + (\bar{y}_i - e_{i,y})^2} \ = \sqrt{(\Delta x + \Delta y)^2}. \tag{2}$$

Experiences existing for some time have already adjusted their pose by the path integration algorithm. Their position is more reliable than recently created experiences. Hence, to strengthen already modified positions, each distance d_i is weighted dependent on the time the experience exists.

The overall aberration $\Delta(\overline{em}, em_k)$ of EMs em_k and $\overline{em}$ considering the last n experiences with $n \leq |em_k|$ is computed by

$$\Delta(\overline{em}, em_k) = \frac{1}{n} \sum_{i=|em_k|-n}^{|em_k|} (|em_k| - i)\sqrt{(\Delta x_i + \Delta y_i)^2} \tag{3}$$

Periodically, based on $\Delta(\overline{em}, em_k)$, the EM with the highest accumulated x- and y-distance values is rated worst. If one map was rated worst for four times, it is replaced by a copy of the best ranked EM. The more frequent this replacement is performed, the more the system does rely on its odometry in place of re-localizations.

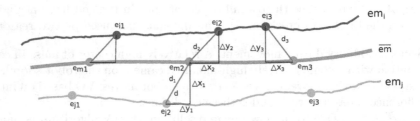

Fig. 2. The distance d_i for an experience to a calculated experience e_{m_i} is based on the x, y-offset. Adjusted weights for d_i refer to the age of the experience.

3   Experiments

The modified RatSLAM system has been tested on a NAO[1] robot. This 58cm tall humanoid is equipped with cameras with narrow Field-of-Views (FOVs, HOR: 60.9°, VER: 47.6°) located in its head. 14 joint motors offer 25 DOFs for flexible movements. RatSLAM and the NAO were linked through a *Robot Operating System*[2] (ROS) wrapper[3] to make the robot's API accessible with ROS.

SLAM was performed in a domestic environment with daylight from a window. RatSLAM was confronted with ambiguous situations that, normally, lead to false re-localizations and loop closures. Anchor-points (yellow spots in fig. 3), created during exploration, represent locations with visual templates for different orientations. All paths were planned in a way that locations near these points are traversed more than once and map ranking was triggered every two seconds.

---

[1] http://www.aldebaran-robotics.com/
[2] http://www.ros.org/
[3] http://wiki.ros.org/Robots/Nao

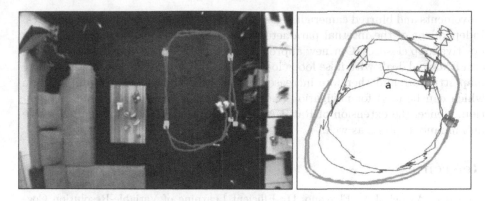

Fig. 3. The robot walked the red path of $2m \times 4m$ with yellow anchor-points twice. The internal map for one EM is drawn in thin blue (a defect resulting from false snapping is marked by "a"), the mean-map based on 4 EMs in bold lime-green color.

4 Results and Discussion

We evaluated the mapping and localization abilities of RatSLAM on the NAO robot, especially for the crucial task of loop closure. The integration of anchor-points enhances the recognition rate of familiar locations. Although it cannot achieve the accuracy of a bi-directional path exploration, it is a benefit for mapping tasks on humanoids with slow movement speeds and limited horizontal FOV. The focus of this work is on the enhancement of the system to Multi-Experience-Maps to reduce false positive loop closures and to strengthen the map's accuracy. To generate comparable results, we tested the system's original implementation as well as the modified version with multiple EMs on identical data sets. Fig. 3 displays the walked trajectory (red) as automatically recorded by a ceiling camera with anchor-points (yellow), the internal map based on the original RatSLAM approach (blue) and based on a map of means $\overline{em}$ (green).

Results show that this extension reduces technical drawbacks of the humanoid architecture. As can be seen in figure 3, it interpolates the jagged trajectory by correcting the location of experiences. Together with the replacement of the worst rated EM, $\overline{em}$ prevents the whole system from hasty false loop closures in ambivalent situations (like at "a") and, over time, leads to a more accurate world representation without false connections between distant experiences.

5 Conclusion

So far, RatSLAM has only been used in combination with wheeled and aerial robots. Our approach adapted RatSLAM to humanoids. The different physical architecture of this type of robot led to different robot characteristics and constraints and, hence, did not allow using the model without adjustments and new constraints. This led to problems that differ a lot from the ones on previous implementations. Therefore, the used NAO robot responded with swaying movements and blurred camera images with lost details and washed-out features. Independent of the internal parameters of RatSLAM this led to multiple false positive loop closures. Our new approach creates multiple pose estimates in several EMs and deals with false loop closures. This improves the overall topological map structure and therefore increases the accuracy of the map representation which can be used for navigation and many further tasks that include navigation. Hence, the extension of RatSLAM with multi-EMs is now a model usable on humanoid robots as well.

References

1. Arleo, A., del, J.A., Floreano, D.: Efficient Learning of Variable-Resolution Cognitive Maps for Autonomous Indoor Navigation. IEEE Trans. Robot. Automat., 990–1000 (1999)
2. Arleo, A., Gerstner, W.: Spatial cognition and neuro-mimetic navigation: a model of hippocampal place cell activity. Biological Cybernetics 83(3), 287–299 (2000)
3. Ball, D., Heath, S., Wiles, J., Wyeth, G., Corke, P., Milford, M.: OpenRatSLAM: an open source brain-based SLAM System 34(3), 149–176 (2013)
4. Castellanos, J.A., Neira, J., Tardos, J.D.: Multisensor fusion for simultaneous localization and map building. IEEE Trans. on Rob. and Autom. 17(6), 908–914 (2001)
5. Franz, M., Mallot, H.A.: Biomimetic Robot Navigation. Robotics and Autonomous Systems, 133–153 (2000)
6. Hornung, A., Wurm, K.M., Bennewitz, M.: Humanoid robot localization in complex indoor environments. In: 2010 IEEE/RSJ Int. Conf. on Intelligent Robots and Systems (IROS), pp. 1690–1695. IEEE (October 2010)
7. Magnusson, M., Andreasson, H., Nüchter, A., Lilienthal, A.J.: Automatic appearance-based loop detection from three-dimensional laser data using the normal distributions transform. Journal of Field Robotics 26(11-12), 892–914 (2009)
8. Milford, M., Prasser, D., Wyeth, G.: Experience mapping: producing spatially continuous environment representations using RatSLAM. In: Conf. on Rob. and Autom. (2005)
9. Milford, M., Wyeth, G., Prasser, D.: Efficient Goal Directed Navigation using RatSLAM. In: Proc. of the 2005 IEEE Int. Conf. on Rob. and Autom. (ICRA), pp. 1097–1102. IEEE (April 2005)
10. Milford, M.J., Wyeth, G.F., Prasser, D.: RatSLAM: A hippocampal model for simultaneous localization and mapping. In: Proc. of the IEEE Int. Conf. on Rob. and Autom. (ICRA), vol. 1, pp. 403–408. IEEE (April 2004)
11. Nuske, S., Roberts, J., Wyeth, G.: Robust Outdoor Visual Localization Using a Three-Dimensional-Edge Map (2009)
12. Prasser, D., Wyeth, G., Milford, M.: Experiments in outdoor operation of ratslam. In: Proc. of Australasian Conf. on Rob. and Autom. (2004)
13. Stachniss, C., Bennewitz, M., Grisetti, G., Behnke, S., Burgard, W.: How to learn accurate grid maps with a humanoid. In: IEEE Int. Conf. on Rob. and Autom. (ICRA), pp. 3194–3199. IEEE (May 2008)
14. Weiller, D., Läer, L., Engel, A.K., König, P.: Unsupervised learning of reflexive and action-based affordances to model adaptive navigational behavior. Frontiers in Neurorobotics 4 (2010)

Precise Wind Power Prediction with SVM Ensemble Regression

Justin Heinermann and Oliver Kramer

Department of Computing Science,
University of Oldenburg, 26111 Oldenburg, Germany
{justin.philipp.heinermann,oliver.kramer}@uni-oldenburg.de

Abstract. In this work, we propose the use of support vector regression ensembles for wind power prediction. Ensemble methods often yield better classification and regression accuracy than classical machine learning algorithms and reduce the computational cost. In the field of wind power generation, the integration into the smart grid is only possible with a precise forecast computed in a reasonable time. Our support vector regression ensemble approach uses bootstrap aggregating (bagging), which can easily be parallelized. A set of weak predictors is trained and then combined to an ensemble by aggregating the predictions. We investigate how to choose and train the individual predictors and how to weight them best in the prediction ensemble. In a comprehensive experimental analysis, we show that our SVR ensemble approach renders significantly better forecast results than state-of-the-art predictors.

Keywords: Support Vector Regression, SVR Ensemble, Wind Power Prediction, Bagging, Weighting, Parallelization.

1 Introduction

The successful integration of wind energy into the grid depends on precise predictions of the amount of energy produced. It has been shown that good forecast results can be achieved using support vector regression (SVR) [11]. The main problem of the SVR algorithm is the huge computational cost. In particular, when doing parameter studies and investigating the prediction performance on large data sets, the optimization process becomes impractically slow. The training time required for an acceptable forecast can easily become thousands of seconds. Therefore, often a worse prediction performance has to be accepted.

In this work, we propose an SVR ensemble method for wind power prediction in order to ameliorate the forecast quality and spend less computation time. Instead of using one single support vector regressor, we train a number of regressors, called *weak predictors*, which together form an ensemble. Each of them is trained on a smaller subset sample of the training set. The prediction is computed by a weighted average of the regression results of the weak predictors. This paper is structured as follows. Our ensemble method is described in Section 2. The experimental results, presented in Section 3, show that a random parameter

S. Wermter et al. (Eds.): ICANN 2014, LNCS 8681, pp. 797–804, 2014.

choice and an mean squared error (MSE) based weighting renders the best computation time as well as prediction performance. Compared to state-of-the-art algorithms, our approach yields a better forecast performance in a reasonable computation time. Our conclusions and future work can be found in Section 4.

1.1 Related Work

A comprehensive overview and empirical analysis for ensemble classification is given by Bauer and Kohavi [1]. Another, more up-to-date review paper was written by Rokach [8]. The most important ensemble techniques are bagging and boosting. *Bagging*, which stands for bootstrap aggregating, was introduced by Breiman [2] and is a relatively simple algorithm. The main idea is to build independent predictors using samples of the training set and average the output of these predictors. In contrast, *Boosting* approaches like AdaBoost [4], make use of predictors trained a consecutive manner with continuous adaptation of the ensemble weights.

Kim *et al.* [6] build up classifiers using support vector machine (SVM) ensembles using both bagging and boosting. The single SVMs are aggregated by using majority voting, an LSE-based weighting, or combined in an hierarchical manner. Important in SVM ensemble construction is "that each individual SVM becomes different with another SVM as much as possible" [6]. This aspect was also investigated by Tsang, Kocsor and Kwok [12] by introducing orthogonality constraints for the weak SVM predictors in order to diversify them. Due to the lack of space, we refer to Schölkopf and Smola [9] for an introduction to support vector machines.

In the field of wind power prediction, ensembles were used for postprocessing numerical weather forecasts [5,10]. For solar power output prediction, Chakraborty *et al.* [3] built up an ensemble of a weather forecast-driven model and machine learning predictors.

2 Support Vector Regression Ensemble with Weighted Bagging

Our research goal is to answer the question, if SVR ensembles can be used to improve the prediction accuracy in the field of wind power forecasts while reducing the computation time. The basic idea of the resulting training algorithm is depicted in Algorithm 1. Let $P = \{p_i | i = 1, \ldots, k\}$ be the set of predictors and $W = \{w_i \in \mathbb{R} | i = 1, \ldots, k\}$ the set of the corresponding weights. Each weight belongs to the predictor with the same index. For computing the final prediction value for an unknown instance $\mathbf{x}$, the results of the weak predictors $p_i \in P$ are combined using the weights $w_i \in W$:

$$\hat{y} = \Sigma_{i=1}^{k} w_i \cdot p_i(\mathbf{x})$$

As the design goal is to find a balance between a good regression performance and a feasible computational cost, we decided to implement a relatively simple bagging approach, which can easily be parallelized: Every iteration of the for-loop in line 4 is independent from its preceding run, so the loop can be replaced by a map-Operation and then executed on distributed computing systems or on multicore processors. The same holds for the prediction step. In contrast to our bagging approach, iterative algorithms like AdaBoost were too expensive because of interdependent steps of the training algorithm.

Algorithm 1. Training of the SVR Ensemble Predictor

1: **Inputs:**
$T = \{(\mathbf{x}_1, y_1), \ldots, (\mathbf{x}_n, y_n)\} \subset \mathbb{R}^d \times \mathbb{R}$ (training set),
s (sample size),
k (number of weak predictors)
2: **Returns:**
$P = \{p_i | i = 1, \ldots, k\}$ (weak predictors),
$W = \{w_i \in \mathbb{R} | i = 1, \ldots, k\}$ (ensemble weights)
3: **Initialize:**
$w_i \leftarrow 1, \; i = 1, \ldots, k$
4: **for** i = 1 **to** k **do**
5: $\quad T_i \leftarrow sample(T, s)$
6: $\quad T_{val,i} \leftarrow T - T_i$
7: $\quad C, \gamma = ChooseParameters(SVR, T_i)$
8: $\quad p_i = FitSVR(T_i, C, \gamma)$
9: $\quad w_i = 1/RegressionPerformance(p_i, T_{val,i})$
10: **end for**

2.1 Training the Weak Predictors

When training the weak predictors, one must consider which samples are used for the design of the training set and which settings are the best for the particular machine learning algorithm. Like Kim *et al.* [6], we build training sets T_i of the weak predictors by randomly sampling s instances from the global training set T. Hence, the single sets T_i are non-disjoint and one single training instance $(\mathbf{x}_i, y_i)$ can occur multiple times or not at all. In future work, one could also test disjoint sets or even introduce orthogonality constraints like Tsang, Kocsor, and Kwok [12], but randomly chosen sampling turned out to be a good choice.

An important research aspect is the parameter tuning implemented in the ChooseParameters method. In our case, we considered the regularization parameter C and the RBF (radial basis function) kernel bandwidth γ the most important ones[1] and only varied these two parameters. We tested three different variants of parameter choice:

Global Optimization Each weak predictor's regression performance is given by the mean square error on the whole $T_{val,i}$ validation set, which is the

---

[1] We are using the *Scikit-learn* implementation [7] of ϵ-support vector regression, which uses γ instead of σ.

global training data set T without the training data sample T_i. Thus, all weak predictors are optimized for the training data set via grid search.

Local Optimization The weak predictors regression performance is optimized by a grid search using a cross-validation on the belonging training data sample T_i.

Random Choice The parameters are randomly chosen. No optimization will be performed.

Obviously, both the global and local optimization are inherent expensive, because of the need to call the SVR training algorithm multiple times[2]. Thus, one would prefer the random method if the prediction quality is not worse. Our experiments show that a random choice of parameters can result in a better prediction performance.

2.2 Ensemble Prediction and Learning Weights

Many different methods of combining the weak predictors to a reasonable prediction output are possible. We decided to test uniform ranking with $w_i = 1$ and different weighting methods using a prediction error E on a validation data set $T_{val,i}$ interpreted as importance of each weak predictor p_i:

$$w_i = \frac{1}{E(p_i, T_{val,i})}$$

For E we tested the mean square error (MSE), the square of the MSE, the inverse of the least square error (LSE), or the biggest square error (BSE).

Besides the SVR and kernel parameters, and the ensemble weights, the two most important factors of the algorithm's success are the sample size s and the number of weak predictors k. As shown in Section 3, it turns out to be the best choice to balance both sizes.

2.3 Runtime of the Approach

Because of the runtime bound $\mathcal{O}(N^3)$ of the usual SVR training algorithm with a training set of size N, it is often much cheaper to train many SVR predictors on small training data sets than one single SVR predictor on a large training data set. For the case of partitioning of the training data set into partitions of size $n < N$, the runtime bound of our approach is given by:

$$\frac{N}{n} \cdot n^3 = N \cdot n^2 < N^3 \text{ for } n < N \tag{1}$$

In our case, we do not necessarily divide the whole training data set in partitions but rather sample k subsets of the size n. Therefore, our runtime and space complexity does not longer depend on the training set size and the runtime boundary is given by

$$\mathcal{O}(k \cdot n^3) = k \cdot \mathcal{O}(n^3) \tag{2}$$

---

[2] Also when using other optimization techniques like evolutionary algorithms, the SVR training has to be called multiple times, which induces a long computation time.

3   Experimental Results

In our experiments, we analyze the prediction performance of our ensemble regression approach. The first thing we have to do is finding the settings that achieve the best prediction performance and the lowest computation time needed. Given the best results that can be reached with our approach, we can compare the algorithm to the commonly used techniques k Nearest Neighbors (kNN) and SVR. The experiments were run on an Intel Core i5 ($4 \times 3.10 GHz$) with $8 GiB$ of RAM using the kNN and SVR implementations of *Scikit-learn* [7].

3.1   Wind Power Prediction with Machine Learning

In contrast to numerical weather forecast models, we are using statistical learning methods for wind power prediction. The prediction task is formulated as regression problem on observed wind speed or power output time series. The forecast problem for a given target turbine is to predict the measurement with a forecast horizon λ. As input features for the regression algorithm, we use a feature window μ, determining how much past measurements to consider for the forecast. For both parameters μ and λ, we use 30 minutes. It has been shown that involving the measurements of neighboring turbines within a radius of a few kilometers can be helpful to ameliorate the forecast accuracy [11]. Let $p_i(t)$ be the measurement of a turbine i at a time t, and $1 \leq i \leq n$ the indices of the n neighboring turbines. Then, for a target turbine with the index j we define a pattern-label-pair $(\mathbf{x}, y)$ for a given time t_0 as

$$
\begin{pmatrix}
p_1(t_0 - \mu) & p_1(t_0 - \mu + 1) & \dots & p_1(t_0) \\
p_2(t_0 - \mu) & p_2(t_0 - \mu + 1) & \dots & p_2(t_0) \\
\dots & \dots & \dots & \dots \\
p_n(t_0 - \mu) & p_n(t_0 - \mu + 1) & \dots & p_n(t_0)
\end{pmatrix}
\rightarrow p_j(t_0 + \lambda)
\tag{3}
$$

In our experiments, we use the *NREL western wind resources dataset*[3], which contains the simulated power output of 32,043 wind power stations in the US. Each grid point has a maximum power output of $30 MW$ and 10-minute data is given for the years 2004 - 2006. Therefore, for every station there are $157,680$ wind speed and power output measurements available. In our experiments, we use the power output data of five wind parks[4] that consist of the wind turbine the power output shall be predicted for, and the turbines in a radius of 3 kilometers. As training data set, the whole time series for the year 2004 is used and the data of the year 2005 serves as test data set.

3.2   Experiment 1: Optimization and Weighting of the Weak Predictors

In our first experiment, we analyze the use of the different parameter optimization variants for the weak predictors. For C, the possible values used are

---

[3] http://wind.nrel.gov/
[4] The IDs of the turbines in the NREL dataset are: Cheyenne=17423, Lancaster=2473, Palmsprings=1175, Vantage=28981, Yucca Valley=1539.

Table 1. Comparison of parameter choice methods and ensemble weighting methods ($k = 32, n = 1,000$). For the locally optimized, globally optimized, and random chosen parameters, the mean squared prediction error is evaluated for five turbines (repeated ten times). For the weighting of the ensemble members, 1, $\frac{1}{MSE}$ and $\frac{1}{MSE^2}$ are tested. Furthermore, the runtime for training is given. The least error reached for each turbine is printed in bold, the least runtime is printed in italic.

Parameters	Locally Optimized			Globally Optimized			Random		
Value	Error		Time	Error		Time	Error		Time
Weights	1	M^{-1} M^{-2}		1	M^{-1} M^{-2}		1	M^{-1} M^{-2}	
Cheyenne	7.84	7.84 7.84	175.93s	7.87	7.87 7.86	607.56s	12.38	8.14 **7.69**	*45.77s*
Lancaster	8.89	8.89 8.89	161.37s	9.04	9.04 9.03	513.66s	13.85	9.52 **8.81**	*36.80s*
Palm Springs	6.12	6.12 6.11	221.60s	6.13	6.12 6.12	476.66s	7.75	6.04 **5.96**	*41.68s*
Vantage	**5.63**	5.63 5.63	151.42s	5.67	5.67 5.67	525.88s	8.41	6.19 5.75	*37.68s*
Yucca Valley	10.29	10.29 10.29	226.89s	10.44	10.43 10.43	614.51s	10.59	10.10 **10.05**	*51.07s*

$\{1; 10; 100; 1,000; 10,000\}$ and γ is taken from $\{1 \cdot 10^e | e \in \{1, \ldots, 5\}\}$. Furthermore, we compare the different weighting methods for each of the three algorithm variants. The results are presented in Table 1. For five wind parks, the prediction error (MSE) is compared for the three parameter choice methods. For the weights, LSE and BSE based weights are not listed because of poor prediction performance. The results show that a random choice of the weak predictors parameters is better in the most cases while providing a much shorter runtime compared to the optimized variants. This behaviour may be surprising at first, but complies with the intuition behind diversification [12] and random forests [2]. Another consideration is the possible overfitting when using the optimized variants. Therefore, we are using the computational cheap random variant with $\frac{1}{MSE^2}$ weighting in the following.

3.3 Experiment 2: Number of Weak Predictors and Samples

Because of the stochastic sampling of the training subsets, the expected prediction performance depends on the number of weak predictors. Furthermore, it is non-deterministic and we have to analyze the properties of our algorithm for varying parameters. Figure 1 (a) shows the behaviour of our algorithm depending on the sample size n for a wind park near Palm Springs using $k \in \{8, 32, 64\}$ weak predictors: When increasing the number n of samples used for each weak predictor, the prediction error decreases. The standard deviation also decreases: E.g., for the case $k = 32$, the standard deviation when using predictors with sample size $n = 100$ is 0.30, and is reduced to 0.07 when using $n = 1,000$. Every prediction error is given by a mean of 25 repeated measures. For the other parks, our approach yields the same behaviour. Figure 1 (b) shows the dependency of the prediction error on the number k of weak predictors used. The results show that a larger number k greatly decreases the prediction error and the standard deviation is reduced, too. E.g., for $k = 5$, the standard deviation is 0.58, it decreases to 0.10 for $k = 100$. Thus, one can only expect reliable results with a sufficient k and sufficient n.

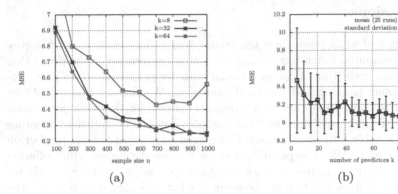

Fig. 1. (a) Prediction error for a wind park near Palm Springs depending on n, (b) Prediction error and standard deviation for a wind park near Lancaster depending on k

3.4 Experiment 3: Comparison with State-Of-The-Art Predictors

Table 2 shows the comparison of our approach to kNN and SVR algorithms, which are state-of-the art prediction algorithms. In order to give a fair comparison to the kNN model, the parameter k was first optimized using a 3-fold cross-validation on the training set. The training times for the cross-validation as well as the training times using the best number k of neighbors are given. The SVR approach is far too expensive in order to justify any cross-validation. Therefore, we only searched for a good parameter guess on 10% of the training data and used the parameters $C = 10,000$ and $\gamma = 1e-5$ in the comparison. Our SVR ensemble approach is using $k = 64$ and $n = 2,000$. In four of five cases, our proposed prediction algorithm outperforms kNN and SVR algorithms. A conclusion cannot be given without considering the runtime needed. The training and testing with our algorithm only needs a few minutes, giving better results than the SVR algorithm in thousands of seconds. However, the kNN algorithm is faster for the given data and would often give a good first guess.

Table 2. Comparison of SVR ensemble regressor (SVRENS, repeated 10 times) using $n = 2,000$ and $k = 64$ with state-of-the-art regressors. For every turbine, the best result is printed in bold

Algorithm	kNN				SVR			SVRENS		
	CV	Train	Test	Error	Train	Test	Error	Train	Test	Error
Cheyenne	319.33	0.21	42.76	7.85	1671.55	154.94	7.70	303.12	146.07	**7.54**
Lancaster	209.24	0.60	26.69	8.97	2067.55	126.43	9.98	266.35	115.30	**8.87**
Palm Springs	122.59	1.54	14.50	**6.06**	1907.32	87.56	7.59	252.69	83.88	6.12
Vantage	307.44	0.73	40.90	5.77	2194.81	164.78	8.33	224.04	122.77	**5.55**
Yucca Valley	147.36	0.08	19.67	10.35	536.80	115.43	10.40	276.51	121.70	**10.20**

4   Conclusions

The integration of wind power into the smart grid is only possible with a precise forecast computed in reasonable time. For an improvement of the prediction performance and reduction of computational cost, we presented an SVR ensemble method using bagging and weighted averaging. We showed that we obtain the best results when using a random parameter choice for the weak predictors. The number of weak predictors and the samples have to be sufficient in order to provide a reliable forecast accuracy. Compared to state-of-the-art prediction methods kNN and SVR, the prediction error can be decreased while offering a reasonable runtime. As future work, we plan to analyze other methods for optimization and diversification of the weak predictors in order to improve the prediction performance.

References

1. Bauer, E., Kohavi, R.: An empirical comparison of voting classification algorithms: Bagging, boosting, and variants. Machine Learning 36(1-2), 105–139 (1999)
2. Breiman, L.: Bagging predictors. Machine Learning 24(2), 123–140 (1996)
3. Chakraborty, P., Marwah, M., Arlitt, M.F., Ramakrishnan, N.: Fine-Grained Photovoltaic Output Prediction Using a Bayesian Ensemble. In: AAAI Conference on Artificial Intelligence (2012)
4. Freund, Y., Schapire, R.E., et al.: Experiments with a new boosting algorithm. In: International Conference on Machine Learning, vol. 96, pp. 148–156 (1996)
5. Gneiting, T., Raftery, A.E., Westveld, A.H., Goldman, T.: Calibrated Probabilistic Forecasting Using Ensemble Model Output Statistics and Minimum CRPS Estimation. Monthly Weather Review 133(5), 1098–1118 (2005)
6. Kim, H.-C., Pang, S., Je, H.-M., Kim, D., Bang, S.Y.: Constructing support vector machine ensemble. Pattern Recognition 36(12), 2757–2767 (2003)
7. Pedregosa, F., Varoquaux, G., Gramfort, A., Michel, V., Thirion, B., Grisel, O., Blondel, M., Prettenhofer, P., Weiss, R., Dubourg, V., Vanderplas, J., Passos, A., Cournapeau, D., Brucher, M., Perrot, M., Duchesnay, E.: Scikit-learn: Machine learning in Python. Journal of Machine Learning Research 12, 2825–2830 (2011)
8. Rokach, L.: Ensemble-based classifiers. Artificial Intelligence Review 33(1-2), 1–39 (2010)
9. Schölkopf, B., Smola, A.: Learning with Kernels: Support Vector Machines, Regularization, Optimization, and Beyond. Adaptive computation and machine learning. MIT Press (2002)
10. Thorarinsdottir, T.L., Gneiting, T.: Probabilistic forecasts of wind speed: ensemble model output statistics by using heteroscedastic censored regression. Journal of the Royal Statistical Society: Series A (Statistics in Society) 173(2), 371–388 (2010)
11. Treiber, N.A., Heinermann, J., Kramer, O.: Aggregation of features for wind energy prediction with support vector regression and nearest neighbors. In: European Conference on Machine Learning, Workshop Data Analytics for Renewable Energy Integration (2013)
12. Tsang, I.W., Kocsor, A., Kwok, J.T.: Diversified SVM ensembles for large data sets. In: Fürnkranz, J., Scheffer, T., Spiliopoulou, M. (eds.) ECML 2006. LNCS (LNAI), vol. 4212, pp. 792–800. Springer, Heidelberg (2006)

Neural Network Approaches
to Solution of the Inverse Problem of Identification
and Determination of Partial Concentrations of Salts
in Multi-component Water Solutions

Sergey Dolenko[1], Sergey Burikov[2], Tatiana Dolenko[2], Alexander Efitorov[1,2],
Kirill Gushchin[2], and Igor Persiantsev[1]

[1] D.V. Skobeltsyn Institute of Nuclear Physics, M.V. Lomonosov Moscow State University,
Moscow, Russia
dolenko@srd.sinp.msu.ru
[2] Physical Department, M.V. Lomonosov State University, Moscow, Russia
{burikov,tdolenko}@lid.phys.msu.ru

Abstract. The studied inverse problem is determination of partial concentrations of inorganic salts in multi-component water solutions by their Raman spectra. The problem is naturally divided into two parts: 1) determination of the component composition of the solution, i.e. which salts are present and which not; 2) determination of the partial concentration of each of the salts present in the solution. Within the first approach, both parts of the problem are solved simultaneously, with a single neural network (perceptron) with several outputs, each of them estimating the concentration of the corresponding salt. The second approach uses data clusterization by Kohonen networks for consequent identification of component composition of the solution by the cluster, which the spectrum of this solution falls into. Both approaches and their results are discussed in this paper.

Keywords: inverse problems, multi-component solutions, component composition, identification, clusterization, Raman spectroscopy.

1   Introduction

The problem of determination of concentrations of substances dissolved in water is very important for oceanology, ecological monitoring and control of mineral, service and waste waters. This problem is required to be solved in non-contact express mode with acceptable precision.

The method of Raman spectroscopy complies with all these requirements. Principle opportunity of using Raman spectra for diagnostics of solutions results from high sensitivity of their characteristics to types and concentrations of salts dissolved in water. In [1,2] it was suggested to use Raman spectra of complex ions (such as bands of NO_3^-, SO_4^{2-}, PO_4^{3-}, CO_3^{2-} anions in the area of 1000 cm^{-1}) to determine types and concentrations of salts in water. Anion type can be determined by the position of the

S. Wermter et al. (Eds.): ICANN 2014, LNCS 8681, pp. 805–812, 2014.
© Springer International Publishing Switzerland 2014

corresponding band, its concentration by its intensity. However, this method can be used only for analysis of substances having proper Raman bands, i.e. for salts with complex ions. The authors of [3,4,5,6] developed the method for determination of concentrations of dissolved salts by water Raman valence band. In [3,4], water Raman valence band was used to determine concentration of the single salt in the solution. In [5,6], a method for determination of partial concentrations of salts in multi-component solutions by water Raman valence band was suggested and elaborated. This was possible due to use of neural networks (NN) to solve this inverse problem (IP).

In this study, a method of identification and determination of partial concentrations of salts having both complex and simple ions is used. The method was first suggested by the authors in [7] and developed in [8,9,10]. Presence of complex ions is determined in the easiest way by presence of their valence bands in low-frequency region of Raman spectrum, and their concentration can be determined by dependence of the intensity of these bands on concentration, taking into account the influence of other salts. Recognition and determination of concentration of simple ions is performed by the change of shape and position of water Raman valence band in presence of all salts dissolved in water. Simultaneous determination of partial concentrations of a number of ions dissolved in water and their identification are provided by use of a NN performing simultaneous analysis of both regions of Raman spectrum (valence and low-frequency). Use of NN is appropriate due to presence of strong non-linear interaction in the solution among ions of different types, what causes distortion of concentration dependences of spectrum shape and does not allow using simple linear methods for determination of concentrations.

The first approach to the solution of the studied IP is training a NN with the number of inputs equal to the number of channels in raw or pre-processed spectra, and the number of outputs equal to the maximum number of salts in the solution. The amplitude at an output of a trained NN is proportional to the concentration of the salt corresponding to this output. Thus, the task of determination of the component composition of the solution and the inverse problem of determination of the salts concentrations are solved simultaneously.

However, this approach was developed for diagnostics of mainly natural waters - seawater, river waters, mineral waters. In contrast to natural water, ionic composition and ion concentrations in technology waters vary within significantly larger ranges. This means that a method that uses an ANN trained to recognize certain ions, may turn ineligible. Such situation causes the necessity of prior determination of ionic composition of the solution, e.g. by solving the problem of clusterization of data array with subsequent correlation of each cluster to a definite ionic composition. In this study, data clusterization was performed by Kohonen neural networks.

Kohonen neural networks and self-organizing maps (SOM) [11] have been successfully used for a long time to solve problems of clusterization and visualization of multi-dimensional data in different domains of human activity [12,13,14]. However, at present time the authors didn't succeed in finding any references to application of Kohonen ANN and SOM to solve the problem of determination of composition of multi-component mixtures. This study is possibly the first one in this direction.

2   Experimental

Excitation of Raman spectra was performed by argon laser (wavelength 488 nm, output power 450 mW). Raman spectra of water solutions of inorganic salts were measured in 90° geometry using monochromator (resolution 2 cm^{-1}) and CCD-camera (Jobin Yvon). The temperature of samples during experiment was stabilized at 22.0±0.2 °C. Spectra were normalized to laser radiation power, to spectrum-channel sensitivity of the detector and to spectrum accumulation time.

Spectra were measured in two regions: 300-2300 cm^{-1} and 2300-4000 cm^{-1} for every sample. Raman spectra of water and water solutions in the region 300-1800 cm^{-1} have lines corresponding to valence vibrations of complex anions. Intensities of the bands depend on concentrations of the corresponding salts. The shape of water Raman valence band (2600 – 4000 cm^{-1}) depends on types of salts and their concentrations. When salt concentration increases, water Raman valence band shifts towards higher frequencies, its halfwidth decreases, the intensity of its high-frequency part rises and the intensity of low-frequency part falls [4].

3   Approach 1: Solution of the Inverse Problem by a Single Perceptron

3.1   Data Preparation

The objects of research were water solutions of salts with significant content in nature waters – NaCl, NH$_4$Br, Li$_2$SO$_4$, KNO$_3$, CsI. Concentration of each salt in the solutions changed in the range from 0 to 2.5 M with concentration step 0.2 – 0.25 M.

Initially, each of the two bands of Raman spectrum was recorded in the range 1024 channels wide, in the frequency range 200...2300 cm^{-1} for the low-frequency band (LFB) and 2300...4000 cm^{-1} for the valence band (VB). For further processing, more narrow informative ranges were extracted: 766 channels in the range 281...1831 cm^{-1} for LFB and 769 channels in the range 2700...3900 cm^{-1} for VB. The procedure of data preparation and pre-processing is described in [7,8]. Due to complexity of the object there is no adequate physical model that would allow numerically obtaining the dependence of water Raman spectrum on concentrations of the dissolved salts. Therefore, in this study, the "experiment-based" approach to IP solution [15] was used.

The obtained data array (1535 features, 9144 samples) was randomly divided into training set (for NN training), test set (used to prevent overtraining), and examination set (for out-of-sample testing) in the ratio of 70:20:10. The results on all the three sets were close, confirming sufficient representativity.

In all computational experiments, the perceptron used to solve the problem had three hidden layers containing 40, 20, and 10 neurons. The transfer function used in the output layer was linear, in the hidden layers – logistic. The following parameters were used: learning rate 0.01; moment 0.5; stop training criterion – 1000 epochs after minimum of the error on test data set. Due to such criterion, the results were not very sensitive to the number of neurons in the hidden layers in a wide range. To ensure statistical robustness, each result was obtained as an average over 5 network training runs with different random sets of initial weights. In several computational experiments, alternative algorithms were also tested – general regression NN and GMDH, but in all cases perceptron with the architecture described above showed the best results. Note that the ratio of initial number of input features (1535) and the number of samples in the training set (9144*70%=6400) was unfavorable. The subject of several preceding studies and of this study was comparative analysis of the methods for reducing the number of input features used, i.e. for input data compression.

3.2   Results

Table 1 presents the best results obtained with various methods of input data compression for identification and determination of concentrations of salts by both bands of Raman spectrum. As benchmark values, one can use the results obtained on initial data with no compression (numerical experiment Exp.1). The results are reported in more detail elsewhere [8,9,10], [16,17].

Table 1. Mean absolute error of determination of concentrations of salts in 5-component solutions in the range up to 2.5 M by both bands of Raman spectrum within the "experiment-based" approach (M, on the examination data set)

Exp. No.	1	2	3	4	5	6
Source	[16]	[10]	[17]	[16]	This study	
Inputs	1535	1134	192	196	192	174
Compression	None	Sel. by CC, CE	Uniform aggregation	Non-uniform aggr. by StD	Non-uniform aggr. by CC	Sel.by CC,CE over un.aggr.
NaCl	0.028	0.028	0.024	0.024	0.024	0.024
NH$_4$Br	0.022	0.022	0.020	0.020	0.019	0.020
Li$_2$SO$_4$	0.019	0.019	0.016	0.013	0.016	0.017
KNO$_3$	0.019	0.018	0.016	0.014	0.016	0.016
CsI	0.023	0.024	0.020	0.020	0.020	0.020

Exp.2 involved feature selection based on the values of cross-correlation (CC) and cross-entropy (CE). The procedure of selection is described in [10]. Comparison of the results of Exp.2 and Exp.1 shows that the errors in general do not decrease. Other types of feature selection also failed to produce a significant error decrease [10], [16].

An alternative chosen to the significant input feature selection was their aggregation, implying creation of new features by summation of intensity values over several adjacent channels of a spectrum. This approach has already proved its efficiency in the solution of the IP of simultaneous determination of water temperature and salinity by water Raman valence band in presence of dissolved organic matter [18].

The values given in Table 1 (Exp.3) were obtained for optimal uniform aggregation by each 12 channels. It can be seen that use of aggregation of input features provided decreasing the error of determination of concentrations of salts on the average by 16%. In particular, this means that to solve the desired problem one can use much less expensive experimental equipment with spectral resolution 12 fold worse than that of the equipment used in this study (i.e., equipment with resolution about 20 cm^{-1} would be sufficient). Use of non-uniform aggregation (with various numbers of channels aggregated into different features – based on the sum of values of standard deviation (StD) in aggregated channels) (Exp.4) resulted in additional reduction of the error of determination of complex salts – down to 0.013-0.014 M. Among other methods of estimation of channel significance, the best results were produced by non-uniform aggregation based on the sum of the values of CC in aggregated channels (Exp.5).

Exp.6 demonstrates the best results obtained by feature selection (by CC and CE) in the space of values produced by uniform aggregation. Note that Exp.5 and Exp.6 failed to result in lower error levels as compared with Exp.3 and Exp.4.

Better results demonstrated for complex salts are obviously connected with presence of characteristic bands for each of these salts in Raman spectrum.

4   Approach 2: Determination of Salt Composition of the Solution by Kohonen Neural Networks

4.1   Data Preparation

The studied object were the water solutions of KI, NH_4F, $NaNO_3$, $MgSO_4$, $AlCl_3$ inorganic salts. The concentration of each salt in the solutions was changed in the range from 0 to 3-4 M, so that the total concentration would not exceed 4 M. The step of concentration change was 0.05 – 0.1 M for all salts.

The experimentally obtained data array consisted of 807 spectra.

In this study, we used the implementation of Kohonen ANN and SOM in the software package Deductor Academic 5.3 – Russian version of Loginom software [19]. The following network parameters were used that turned out to be optimal: the network consisted of 8*8 hexagonal cells with Euclidean distance function; the initial learning rate was 0.5; training continued for 1000 epochs. In this series of computational experiments, full dimensionality data were used (1954 input features). The number of obtained clusters varied from 2 to 40.

4.2   Results

Since in this study the investigated solutions contained from 0 to 5 salts, it was possible to discriminate $2^5=32$ data classes with respect to what combination of salts was present in the solutions belonging to a given class. These 32 classes could be divided into the following groups: 1 class with spectra of distilled water, 5 classes with spectra of single-salt solutions, 10 classes with two- and 10 classes with three-component solutions spectra, 5 classes with spectra of solutions of 4 salts, 1 class with spectra of solutions containing all the 5 salts. In connection with that, one could expect that the most contrast picture would be given by clusterization with the number of clusters close to the following values: 6, 16, 26, 31, 32.

To describe the properties of the obtained clusterizations, let us introduce the following quantitative characteristics.

Let N_i^{max} be the maximum number of samples from class i that fell into one cluster for the given clusterization. Let us call the sum over all classes $\sum_i N_i^{max} / N$, normalized to the total number of samples N and expressed in percent, the *contrast* of clusterization. In the ideal case (if all the samples from each class fall into the same cluster) this index is equal to 100%.

Let us call the ratio of the number of classes, which fell into different clusters by the majority of their samples, to the total number of classes (32), expressed in percent, the *degree of separation*. It is clear that with increasing number of clusters C, the degree of separation grows, tending to 100%, but this growth is non-linear due to existence of unused clusters.

Fig.1 displays the dependences of clusterization contrast (solid line, left axis) and of the degree of separation (dashed line, right axis) on the number of clusters C.

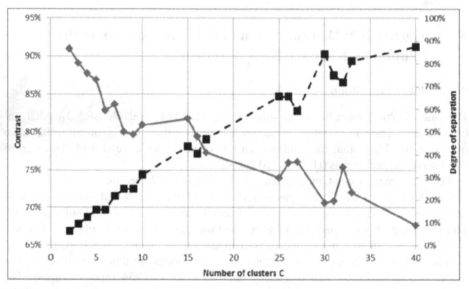

Fig. 1. The dependences of contrast (solid line) and of the degree of separation (dashed line) on the number of clusters in the clusterization

The analysis of clusterizations obtained with different number of clusters allows one to make the following observations and conclusions:

1) Classes corresponding to distilled water, to single-component solutions (solutions of a single salt), and to the solutions of all the five salts, completely fall to a single cluster each nearly in all clusterizations. This means that each of these classes form a compact group in the space of input features.

2) Locally optimal clusterizations corresponding to local maxima on the contrast curve (Fig.1) are observed near the expected values – at C = 7, 15, 26-27, and 32.

3) The formed clusters are non-uniform by their quantitative composition. Thus, samples from the classes corresponding to the solutions containing simultaneously two salts with simple ions (KI and $AlCl_3$), often fall into the same cluster. This may be the manifestation of the fact that changes in the spectrum, introduced by simultaneous

presence of these salts, are substantial, and the influence of other salts is less significant against this background.

4) This series of computational experiments on data clusterization, conducted on the full array of input features (1954), should be considered as a reference point for future studies, in which similar work will be performed on a reduced number of features, obtained as the result of their selection or extraction. Such method was already applied by the authors before [18] while solving the inverse problem described above (Table 1). It is expected that this will improve the quality of clusterization.

5 Conclusion

Complex inverse problem of determination of types and partial concentrations of salts in 5-component water solutions by Raman spectra has been solved within the "experiment-based" approach using two bands of Raman spectrum – low-frequency band $(280-1830 \text{ cm}^{-1})$ and valence band $(2700-3900 \text{ cm}^{-1})$.

Comparative analysis of various methods of input data compression has been performed. It has been shown that best results were achieved using aggregation of input features: mean absolute error of determination of concentrations of salts made from 0.016 to 0.024 M in the concentration range from 0 to 2.5 M using uniform aggregation. At that, it is sufficient to use equipment with low spectral resolution about 20 cm^{-1}. Use of non-uniform aggregation allowed reducing the error down to 0.013-0.014 M for determination of complex salts.

It has been demonstrated that data clusterization with the help of Kohonen neural networks can be used to distinguish groups in the space of intensities in channels of Raman spectra of multi-component solutions of inorganic salts. The obtained clusterization may serve as the base for identification of ions (salts) present in the solution.

The main direction of future studies will be reveal of a feature space of lower dimension, in which clusterization will have optimal properties.

Acknowledgements. This study was supported by RFBR grants no. 12-01-00958-a (Approach 1) and 13-01-00897-a (Approach 2).

References

1. Baldwin, S.F., Brown, C.W.: Detection of Ionic Water Pollutants by Laser Excited Raman Spectroscopy. Water Research 6, 1601–1604 (1972)
2. Rudolph, W.W., Irmer, G.: Raman and Infrared Spectroscopic Investigation on Aqueous Alkali Metal Phosphate Solutions and Density Functional Theory Calculations of Phosphate-Water Clusters. Applied Spectroscopy 61(12), 274A–292A (2007)
3. Furic, K., Ciglenecki, I., Cosovic, B.: Raman Spectroscopic Study of Sodium Chloride Water Solutions. J. Molecular Structure 6, 225–234 (2000)
4. Dolenko, T.A., Churina, I.V., Fadeev, V.V., Glushkov, S.M.: Valence Band of Liquid Water Raman Scattering: Some Peculiarities and Applications in the Diagnostics of Water Media. J. Raman Spectroscopy 31, 863–870 (2000)

5. Burikov, S.A., Dolenko, T.A., Fadeev, V.V., Sugonyaev, A.V.: New Opportunities in the Determination of Inorganic Compounds in Water by the Method of Laser Raman Spectroscopy. Laser Physics 15(8), 1–5 (2005)
6. Burikov, S.A., Dolenko, T.A., Fadeev, V.V., Sugonyaev, A.V.: Identification of Inorganic Salts and Determination of Their Concentrations in Water Solutions from the Raman Valence Band Using Artificial Neural Networks. Pattern Recognition and Image Analysis 17(4), 554–559 (2007)
7. Burikov, S.A., Dolenko, S.A., Dolenko, T.A., Persiantsev, I.G.: Neural network solution of the inverse problem of identification and determination of partial concentrations of inorganic salts in multi-component water solution. In: Neuroinformatics-2010. Proceedings of the XIIth All-Russian Scientific and Technical Conference, part 2, pp. 100–110. MEPhI, Moscow (2010) (in Russian)
8. Burikov, S.A., Dolenko, S.A., Dolenko, T.A., Persiantsev, I.G.: Use of adaptive neural network algorithms to solve problems of identification and determination of concentrations of salts in multi-component water solution by Raman spectra. Neurocomputers: Development, Application (3), 55–69 (2010) (in Russian)
9. Burikov, S.A., Dolenko, S.A., Dolenko, T.A., Persiantsev, I.G.: Application of Artificial Neural Networks to Solve Problems of Identification and Determination of Concentration of Salts in Multi-Component Water Solutions by Raman spectra. Optical Memory and Neural Networks (Information Optics) 19(2), 140–148 (2010)
10. Dolenko, S.A., Burikov, S.A., Dolenko, T.A., Persiantsev, I.G.: Adaptive Methods for Solving Inverse Problems in Laser Raman Spectroscopy of Multi-Component Solutions. Pattern Recognition and Image Analysis 22(4), 551–558 (2012)
11. Kohonen, T.: Self-Organizing Maps, 3rd edn. Springer, Berlin (2001)
12. Deboeck, G., Kohonen, T. (eds.): Visual explorations in finance with self-organizing maps. Springer-Verlag London Limited (1998)
13. Seiffert, U., Jain, L.C. (eds.): Self-Organizing neural networks: recent advances and applications. Physica-Verlag, Heidelberg (2002)
14. Self-Organizing Maps - Applications and Novel Algorithm Design (2011), http://www.intechopen.com/books/self-organizing-maps-applications-and-novel-algorithm-design
15. Gerdova, I.V., Dolenko, S.A., Dolenko, T.A., Persiantsev, I.G., Fadeev, V.V., Churina, I.V.: New opportunity solutions to inverse problems in laser spectroscopy involving artificial neural networks. Izv. AN SSSR. Seriya Fizicheskaya 66(8), 1116–1124 (2002)
16. Dolenko, S., Burikov, S., Dolenko, T., Efitorov, A., Persiantsev, I.: Methods of input data compression in neural network solution of inverse problems of spectroscopy of multi-component solutions. In: 11th International Conference on Pattern Recognition and Image Analysis: New Information Technologies (PRIA-11-2013), September 23-28. Conference Proceedings, vol. II, pp. 541–544. IPSI RAS, Samara (2013)
17. Dolenko, S.A., Burikov, S.A., Dolenko, T.A., Efitorov, A.O., Persiantsev, I.G.: Compression of input data in neural network solution of inverse problems of spectroscopy of multi-component solutions. In: Neuroinformatics-2013. XVth All-Russian Scientific and Technical Conference. Proceedings, part 2, pp. 205–215. MEPhI, Moscow (2013) (in Russian)
18. Dolenko, S., Dolenko, T., Burikov, S., Fadeev, V., Sabirov, A., Persiantsev, I.: Comparison of Input Data Compression Methods in Neural Network Solution of Inverse Problem in Laser Raman Spectroscopy of Natural Waters. In: Villa, A.E.P., Duch, W., Érdi, P., Masulli, F., Palm, G. (eds.) ICANN 2012, Part II. LNCS, vol. 7553, pp. 443–450. Springer, Heidelberg (2012)
19. Loginom – analytical platform, http://loginom.basegroup.ru/

Lateral Inhibition Pyramidal Neural Network for Detection of Optical Defocus (Zernike Z_5)

Bruno J.T. Fernandes and Diego Rativa

Escola Politécnica, Universidade de Pernambuco Recife-PE, Brazil
{bjtf,diego.rativa}@ecomp.poli.br
http://www.ecomp.poli.br

Abstract. Optical distortions of an image are created in astronomical, optical microscopy and communication systems by light propagation throughout a variety of optical components. Usually, optical aberrations are corrected by using an Adaptive Optics system, where a wavefront sensor is used to measure the optical distortion. In this work, we propose to use a Lateral Inhibition Pyramidal Neural Network (LIPNet) in the frequency domain to classify optical defocus (using Zernike polynomials Z_5), such that optical defocus value can be detected directly from the image without the use of wavefront sensing. The results show the potentiality of the method and open new opportunities to explore this kind of neural networks algorithms for wavefront sensing and Adaptive optic systems.

Keywords: Neural network, Defocus image, Blurring.

1 Introduction

Optical aberrations are distortions in the image created by light propagation through an optical system compared to the original [1]. Optical aberrations can be either chromatic (optical dispersion, when using more than one wavelength of light) or monochromatic caused by propagation, reflection and refraction of light.

Monochromatic aberrations can be described mathematically comparing a wavefront reference (theoretical planewave, i.e. e^{kx}) with the wavefront of the light propagated (i.e. $e^{kx+\phi}$), where ϕ is related with the optical distortion [2]. Aberrations negatively impact image quality varying the size and shape of point spread function (PSF), which blurs the image [3]. Distortions created by optical systems with circular pupils can be described by Zernike Polynomial with a name and a wavefront coefficient, such as: Tilt- X (Z_1), Tilt- Y (Z_2), Astigmatism 1st order-45° (Z_4), Defocus (Z_5), Astigmatism 1st order-0° (Z_6), Trifoil 30° (Z_7), Coma Y-direction (Z_8) and higher order aberrations [3]. Taking advantage of the Zernike orthogonality properties, individual aberration contributions to a total wavefront may be isolated and quantified separately. Zernike coefficient values are used to quantify optical aberrations of the human eye, for instance the astigmatism coefficient (Z_6) is related with the inability of the eye to focus

S. Wermter et al. (Eds.): ICANN 2014, LNCS 8681, pp. 813–820, 2014.

a point object into a sharp focused image (Astigmatism), as well as, a positive and a negative Defocus coefficient (Z_5) are proportional to the Myopia and Hyperopia level, respectively [2].

One of the most explored techniques to reduce the effect of wavefront distortions is the Adaptive optics (AO) system [4]. AO is broadly used in astronomical and communication systems to reduce the effect of atmospheric distortions, as well as, in optical microscopy and retinal imaging systems to reduce optical aberrations [5]. Adaptive optics is a closed-loop control system composed by a sensorial and an active part, measuring the wavefront distortion and compensating it (minimizing the Zernike coefficient values) instantaneously with active optical components.

In the AO correction is used a wavefront sensor that explores optical techniques such as diffraction and interference to indirectly reconstruct the wavefront [6], usually it is used a Hartmann-Shack sensor (HS) [4]. The human eye works like an adaptive optics system (eye's acomodation mechanism) [7], where the crystalline changes its shape such that the image at the retina is always at the best possible focused condition which suggests that human visual systems are good at perceiving images blurring, however the mechanism of this processing is not completely understood, disallowing a metric to estimate blur in images [8]. Therefore, the human visual system may characterize a well-focused image without the use of a wavefront sensor.

On other hand, the Neural networks tool has been proposed in astronomy for wavefront reconstruction from the intensity centroid values created by the lenses array of the microlensed structure of a HS sensor [9]. Cancellere and Gai [10] have suggested a neural network to reconstruct aberrations directly from the images using a centre of gravity and the first central moments, describing the aberrations by Seidel polynomials, these methods show the neural networks potentiality for image aberration detection.

A neural network entitled Lateral Inhibition Pyramidal Neural Network (LIP-Net) has been recently proposed by Fernandes et al. [11] to classify an input image without any previous feature extraction method. LIPNet achieved high classification rates in detection tasks with a low computational cost, as well as, it was able to deal with blur variations in the input images on the spatial domain.

In this work, we propose a novel method using the LIPNet on the frequency domain that is able to detect optical defocus directly from the image without the use of a wavefront sensor. The method has been tested with different images blurred with a defocus distortion (implemented using the Franhoufer optical diffraction theory), and using a well-accepted metric to describe the defocus distortion, i.e. Zernike polynomials (adopted by the Optical Society of America, OSA). The results show the potentiality of the method for optical wavefront characterization.

This paper is organized as follows: Section 2 describes the proposed defocus estimation system, Section 3 presents the configuration used in the optical simulations and in Section 4, experimental results defocus estimation are shown. Finally, in Section 5, some concluding remarks are given.

2   Defocus Estimation System

In summary, the Lateral Inhibition Pyramidal Neural Network (LIPNet) [11] is a supervised neural network that receives as input a 2-D image and outputs its classification according to some criteria. It is important to note that LIPNet incorporates in its architecture concepts presented in the human visual system, such as receptive and inhibitory fields. LIPNet architecture is composed of two kinds of layers:

- 2-D: layers located at the basis of the neural network that are responsible for feature extraction and image compression;
- 1-D: layers located at the top of the neural network and are responsible for classify the input image;

Unlike previous works where the LIPNet technique is explored on the spatial domain, LIPNet is implemented on the frequency domain such that the defocus estimation method uses a neural network to evaluate an image in frequency domain where defocus variations are more evident. Thus, after transforming the input image to the frequency domain, no explicit feature extraction operation is necessary to estimate the defocus parameter. The LIPNet is then independent of specialist knowledge to determine the important information regarding the defocus issue.

The entire system architecture for defocus estimation is represented in Figure 1. Initially, the image is transformed to the frequency domain by using a Fast Fourier Transform (FFT) [12], after that the LIPNet technique estimates the *a posteriori* probability of the image is not defocused. Finally, the calculated probability is used to define the parameter applied in the defocus process following the next criterion: a probability of 100% indicates that the image is not defocused at all, $\phi = 0$ and a probability next to 0% indicates that the image is completely defocused, $\phi = 0.8$.

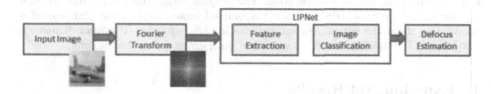

Fig. 1. System architecture for defocus estimation. The image is transformed to the frequency domain by using a Fast Fourier Transform (FFT) where the defocus distortion parameter is estimated exploring the LIPNet method.

A logarithmic scale conversion is used to adjust the balance between frequency components, i.e. emphasizing high frequency variations. Previous experiments performed in this work confirm that LIPNet is able to reach higher accuracy rates with a logarithmic scale than the obtained using a linear scale for the frequency domain.

3   Optical Simulation Configuration

Based on Franhoufer diffraction theory [13], a well-controlled optical defocused blurring effect has been simulated convoluting original images with point spread functions (PSF) of an aberrated circular pupil. A MatLab script has been created to generate a PSF for a wave aberration mode associated with Defocus (Zernike polynomial, Z_5), a wavelength of $\lambda = 633nm$ and a pupil diameter of 8mm.

As shown in Figure 2, the MatLab script represents an optical setup where a telescope (composed by two lenses) propagates the image to a conjugated plane, the solid lines are the wavefront representation where $\Psi(x)$ and $\Psi(x, \phi)$ are the reference and defocus-aberrated wavefront, respectively; dotted lines represent the optical ray propagation of the images. A set of 800 images selected from the airplane class of the Caltech-101 image database [14] resized to 80×80 pixels has been defocused with RMS wavefront errors varying between 0.2 to 0.8 microns generating a set of 3200 images. All images are transformed to the frequency domain by using a FFT, an example of defocused images from the same airplane and their respective frequency domain representation are shown in Figure 3.

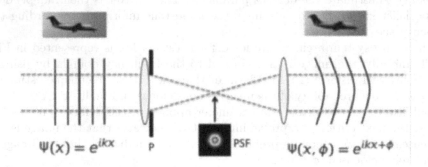

$$\Psi(x) = e^{ikx} \qquad P \qquad PSF \qquad \Psi(x, \phi) = e^{ikx + \phi}$$

Fig. 2. Optical simulation configuration. The original image (left) is convoluted with a point spread function (PSF) creating a blurred image (right), the PSF contains information about the optical characteristic setup, i.e. pupil size (P =8mm diameter), wavelength ($\lambda = 633nm$) and RMS wavefront errors from 0.2 to 0.8 microns.

4   Experimental Results

The proposed system is used in the experiments to determine the defocus parameter applied to an image of an airplane from the Caltech-101 database not seen in the training step of the neural network. The database images are randomly classified in three distinct groups: training, validation and test. The training group is composed by 2450 images, the validation group by 1050 images and the test group by 500 images. The training group is employed to train the LIPNet and adjust the neural network weights, the validation group is used to determine whether the classification accuracy of the neural network is increasing or overfitting. Finally, the test group is going to evaluate the trained neural network.

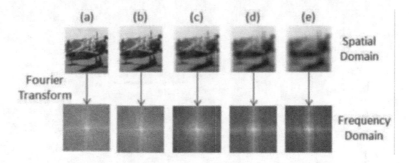

Fig. 3. Original and blurred images of the *Airplane* object, id 0089, from the Caltech database. The images are presented in the spatial and frequency domain, left and right side of the figure, respectively. The original image has been defocused with a RMS wavefront defocus (Z_5) error of (a) 0.0μm, (b) 0.2μm, (c) 0.4μm, (d) 0.6μm and (e) 0.8μm.

This procedure is repeated ten times such that an averaged estimation from all repetitions is obtained. All the experiments in this work were performed in Java 6 using an Intel Core i7 with a 2.2GHz CPU and 8-GB RAM.

As proposed by Fernandes et al. [11], the LIPNet used in the experiments has two 2-D layers and one 1-D layer. Experiments performed with a small subset of the used database indicated the configuration used to estimate the defocus parameter, which is: receptive fields of size 8 and 4 for the first and second 2-D layers, respectively, with an overlap factor of 1 for both 2-D layers and the activation function used for neurons in the 2-D layers is the logistic sigmoid, while neurons in the 1-D layer used the hyperbolic tangent function. The size of 2-D layers are 9×9 and 2×2 neurons, while the 1-D layer has two neurons, one that outputs the defocus parameter, ϕ, and other that outputs $1 - \phi$. Thus, the LIPNet is trained using a cross-entropy optimization function [15], in which the network output estimates the value for ϕ.

As shown in Figure 4, most images are classified correctly in relation to the defocus parameter applied, the relation between the mean estimated parameter defocus and its real parameter used is represented for visualization. The proposed system achieves a classification rate of 91.8% regarding the five possible classifications between the different defocus parameters and when an error happens it is usually lower than 0.2μm.

The estimated parameters values (Defocus aberration coefficient) are summarized in Table 1. The average value of the Defocus parameter estimated by the LIPNet for the real parameters 0.0 and 0.8 microns are shifted by 0.03 microns. That uncertainty can by explained as a limitation of the neural network in representing patterns closer to the upper and lower bounds of the probability interval.

The images corresponding to the best and the worst classification results for each defocus parameter are shown in Figure 5. The amount of detail in an image may give the wrong impression about the defocus, for instance the defocused image shown in Figure 5(g), with a RMS wavefront error of 0.2μm has been

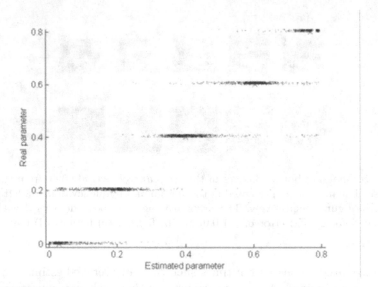

Fig. 4. Defocus estimation. The vertical axis presents the real parameter used in the defocus process, ϕ, and the horizontal axis the defocus parameter estimated with the LIPNet. The red marker × represents the estimated averaged parameter. The vertical and horizontal scales are in micrometers.

classified by the system as an image with a defocus parameter of $0.012\mu m$. For the Figure 5(a) case, the amount of detail helped the classifier to correctly return 0.0 for the defocus parameter. On other hand, both the lack of details as the low contrast may lead to the neural network to classify an image as more defocused than it really is, an example are the Figures 5(e) and 5(f).

It is also important to note that the experiments were performed with small images. Although, the system achieves a good classification rate of 91.8%, the use of bigger images should increase the efficacy of the presented system. The classification process has been realized in a total of 0.3 miliseconds, the high velocitiy of the classification process opens horizon for applications in real-time optical wavefront sensing and adaptive optics systems.

Table 1. Real Defocus parameters in microns (μm) and mean and standard deviation of the estimated parameters for all test images

Real parameter	Estimated parameter ($\bar{x}(s)$)
0.0	0.03±0.01
0.2	0.19 ± 0.04
0.4	0.40 ± 0.03
0.6	0.60 ± 0.03
0.8	0.77 ± 0.02

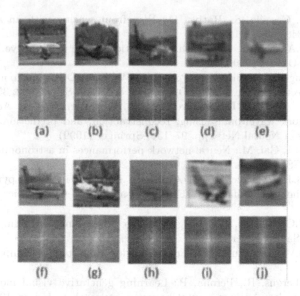

Fig. 5. Best and the worst classification results for each defocus parameter. (a), (b), (c), (d) and (e) were correctly classified and their defocus parameters are 0.0, 0.2, 0.4, 0.6 and 0.8, respectively. On other hand, (f), (g), (h), (i) and (j) have also defocus parameters of 0.0, 0.2, 0.4, 0.6 and 0.8, but were classified as 0.34, 0.01, 0.71, 0.26 and 0.50, respectively.

5   Conclusion

A Lateral Inhibition Pyramidal Neural Network (LIPNet) in the frequency domain has been proposed and proved to classify optical defocus directly from images. The proposed method has achieved a classification rate of 91.8%. However, it is expected that the use of bigger images should increase the efficacy of the presented system. The results show the potentiality of the method and open new opportunities for wavefront sensing and future applications in Adaptive optic systems.

References

1. Born, M., Wolf, E.: Principles of optics: electromagnetic theory of propagation, interference and diffraction of light. CUP Archive (1999)
2. Bass, M., Van Stryland, E.W., Williams, D.R., Wolfe, W.L.: Handbook of optics, vol. 2. McGraw-Hill (2001)
3. Malacara, D.: Optical shop testing, vol. 59. John Wiley & Sons (2007)
4. Platt, B.C.: History and principles of shack-hartmann wavefront sensing. Journal of Refractive Surgery 17, S573–S577 (2001)
5. Vohnsen, B., Rativa, D.: Ultrasmall spot size scanning laser ophthalmoscopy. Biomedical Optics Express 2, 1597–1609 (2011)

6. Vohnsen, B., Castillo, S., Rativa, D.: Wavefront sensing with an axicon. Optics Letters 36, 846–848 (2011)
7. Atchison, D.A., Smith, G., Smith, G.: Optics of the human eye. Butterworth-Heinemann, Oxford (2000)
8. Chen, L., Singer, B., Guirao, A., Porter, J., Williams, D.R.: Image metrics for predicting subjective image quality. Optometry & Vision Science 82, 358–369 (2005)
9. McGuire, P.C., Sandler, D.G., Lloyd-Hart, M., Rhoadarmer, T.A.: Adaptive optics: Neural network wavefront sensing, reconstruction, and prediction. In: Scientific Applications of Neural Nets, pp. 97–138. Springer (1999)
10. Cancelliere, R., Gai, M.: Neural network performances in astronomical image processing. In: ESANN, pp. 515–520. Citeseer (2003)
11. Fernandes, B.J.T., Cavalcanti, G.D.C., Ren, T.I.: Lateral inhibition pyramidal neural network for image classification. IEEE Transactions on Cybernetics 43, 2082–2092 (2013)
12. Gonzalez, R.C., Woods, R.E.: Digital Image Processing, 3rd edn. Prentice-Hall, Inc., Upper Saddle River (2006)
13. Goodman, J.W.: Introduction to Fourier optics. Roberts and Company Publishers (2005)
14. Fei-Fei, L., Fergus, R., Perona, P.: Learning generative visual models from few training examples: An incremental bayesian approach tested on 101 object categories. Computer Vision and Image Understanding 106, 59–70 (2007)
15. Bishop, C.M.: Neural Networks for Pattern Recognition. Clarendon, Oxford (2007)

Development of a Dynamically Extendable SpiNNaker Chip Computing Module

Rui Araújo, Nicolai Waniek, and Jörg Conradt

Technische Universität München, Neuroscientific System Theory,
Karlstraße 45, 80333 München, Germany
{rui.araujo, nicolai.waniek, conradt}@tum.de
http://www.nst.ei.tum.de

Abstract. The SpiNNaker neural computing project has created a hardware architecture capable of scaling up to a system with more than a million embedded cores, in order to simulate more than one billion spiking neurons in biological real time. The heart of this system is the SpiNNaker chip, a multi-processor System-on-Chip with a high level of interconnectivity between its processing units. Here we present a Dynamically Extendable SpiNNaker Chip Computing Module that allows a SpiNNaker machine to be deployed on small mobile robots. A non-neural application, the simulation of the movement of a flock of birds, was developed to demonstrate the general purpose capabilities of this new platform. The developed SpiNNaker machine allows the simulation of up to one million spiking neurons in real time with a single SpiNNaker chip and is scalable up to 256 computing nodes in its current state.

Keywords: Mobile robotics, parallel computing module, spiking neural networks simulations, SpiNNaker.

1 Introduction

Abstract processes carried out in the biological brain are still one of the great challenges for computational neuroscience. Despite an increasing amount of experimental data and knowledge of individual components, we only have an insufficient understanding of the operations of intermediate levels. However, those are believed to be the key elements in constructing thoughts and in processing information [5].

Large-scale neural network simulations will help increasing our knowledge about these intermediate levels. However, the huge amount of neurons in the human brain [6] and their connectivities [2] are difficult if not impossible to simulate. General purpose digital hardware is ill suited to perform these simulations, as they are unable to cope with the massive parallelism carried out in the brain. A possible approach is the usage of neuromorphic systems such as the BrainScales [7] or the Neuro-Grid hardware [3] which *emulate* the neural network with a physical implementation of the individuals neurons.

S. Wermter et al. (Eds.): ICANN 2014, LNCS 8681, pp. 821–828, 2014.

Another possible approach is the SpiNNaker system, which is a massively-parallel computer architecture based on a multi-processor System-on-Chip (MP-SoC) technology that can scale up to a million cores. It is capable of simulating up to a billion spiking neurons in biological real time with realistic levels of interconnectivity between the neurons.

The SpiNNaker system was motivated by the attempt to understand and study biological computing structures. Their high level of parallelism with frugal amounts of energy as opposed to traditional electronics designs, which were mostly driven by serial throughput just until recently. The biological approach to the design of such *many-cores* architecture also brings new concerns in terms of fault-tolerance computation and efficiency. The SpiNNaker chip, the basic building block of a SpiNNaker machine, relies on smaller processors than other machines but in larger numbers, it has 18 highly efficient embedded ARM processors that allow the SpiNNaker system to be competitive according to two metrics, MIPS/mm^2 and MIPS/W.

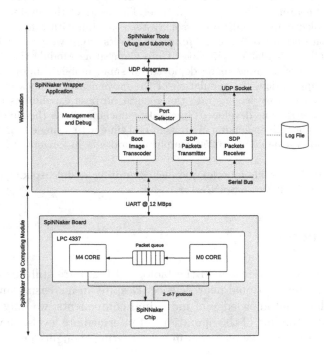

Fig. 1. The SpiNNaker Chip Computing Module Dataflow Architecture

The currently available machines with SpiNNaker chips are relatively large, the minimum size at this moment is 105×95mm, which limits their deployment on systems with limited size as for example, small mobile robots, specially flying ones due to very strict weight and space constraints. Additionally the SpiNNaker systems currently require a workstation, usually a desktop or a laptop, connected through an Ethernet connection to bootstrap the system every time it powers on and to feed the processing data into the system. This requirement seriously limits the independence and deployment capabilities of systems with embedded SpiNNaker chips. At present, it is necessary to add an wireless router in order to have a mobile system with a SpiNNaker machine [4]. The drawbacks from this approach are fairly obvious, such as increased power consumption and space requirements since the typical wireless router consumes around 4 to 5 Watt and even though there are fairly small models available at the market it would still take up some space.

Furthermore the amount of extensibility provided by standard SpiNNaker machines is very limited since it only allows increases of computing power in fixed amounts. The current single board SpiNNaker machines are available in two versions, one with four chips and another with forty eight. These are wildly different amounts of processing capability which make it difficult to create intermediate solutions. It would be interesting to have the capability of selecting how many SpiNNaker chips one needs to deploy without having to design new hardware.

The current requirements of the SpiNNaker architecture are not suitable for a lot of applications where its processing power and capabilities would be helpful. It is then necessary to design a new solution that can overcome the limitations of the present options.

2   SpiNNaker Chip Computing Module

Traditional SpiNNaker systems rely on the host system to provide the input data. This limits the possibilities of interfacing the SpiNNaker chip with the external environment. In order to overcome this restriction, we added a microcontroller which is responsible for communicating with the outside world. Figure 1 presents the general architecture for the developed solution which involves: 1) the design of a PCB with a single SpiNNaker chip and a microcontroller, 2) the software to drive the microcontroller, and 3) an application that runs on the host system to communicate with the board. We strived to keep the hardware as simple and small as possible to achieve one of our main goals: portability. Therefore, our solution consists only of the necessary components.

Several requirements determined the usage of our system. For instance, backwards compatibility with the standard tools used for the bigger SpiNNaker machines, *ybug* and *tubotron*, was an important aspect that lead to the creation of the host system application. Having backwards compatibility allows users of our novel system to simply apply their already established know-how about SpiNNaker and its tools.

Adding the microcontroller had various benefits. We could replace the Ethernet connection with a simpler, albeit slower, universal asynchronous receiver/ transmitter (UART) at a baud rate of 12 MBps, which roughly translates into 1.2 Megabytes/s each way. Additionally, the microcontroller can boot the SpiNNaker chip without a host system as it is capable of storing the previously transmitted image. The microcontroller and the application in the workstation act jointly to pretend they are another SpiNNaker chip which is connected to

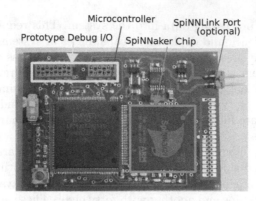

Fig. 2. The SpiNNaker Chip Computing Module

the Ethernet, having their own point to point (P2P) address and position in the grid. SpiNNaker machines are a two dimensional grid of nodes, where a node is a SpiNNaker chip, each with its own P2P address, a 16 bit number.

2.1 Evaluation

We took measurements to characterize our computing module. The main objective was to determine the input and output capacity in terms of SpiNNaker packets since higher level protocols rely on these. Both cores ran at 180 MHz during all tests. The methodology used for these procedures was as follows:

- change the source code to set and clear a GPIO pin around the action to be measured.
- use the switch present in the prototype board to trigger the transmission of a packet.
- using an oscilloscope, measure the time taken between the changes in state of the previously selected GPIO pin.

The results are compiled in Table 1. The first two lines represent the time taken to transmit a packet, including the calculation of the parity bit and consequential addition to the header, while the following two lines represent the time taken only during the symbol transmission. There is no such difference for the input side since it is only reading symbols and placing them at the queue in the correct position.

It is possible to calculate the symbol transmission capacity with these results. Each symbol takes around 90 ns to be transmitted, which translates into a 11 MSymbol transmission rate. The input capacity, around 43 % of the transmission rate, lies at 4.78 MSymbols.

These numbers are fairly small when compared to the capacity on the SpiN-Naker side, which is around 62.4 MSymbols in both directions. This large difference is explained by the fact the microcontroller implementation is entirely software based as opposed to the SpiNNaker which is implemented in dedicated hardware. Furthermore, the difference between the transmission and the reception rate lies in the increased complexity when receiving symbols. Whereas receiving includes a step to identify symbols, no such step is required when transmitting packets. Another analysis showed that the transmission and reception capacity exceeds the UART's 12 MBps by far. This means that this communication channel is currently the bottleneck.

The packet transmission rate resides at 455K packets per second for packets with payload and 770K packets per second for packets without further payload. As for the packet reception rate, 435K packets per second can be received if they do not include a payload, whereas the rate for packets with payload is around 238K packets per second.

Table 1. Performance Measurements for the transmission and reception of SpiNNaker packets

Action	Time taken (μs)
Packet Transmission with payload	2.20
Packet Transmission without payload	1.30
Symbol transmission for packet with payload	1.80
Symbol transmission for packet without payload	1.00
Packet reception with payload	4.20
Packet reception without payload	2.30

3 Boids Model

We developed a case study for the SpiNNaker Chip Computing Module to demonstrate possible applications. SpiNNaker was obviously designed to simulate spiking neural networks. however, we opted for a more general example and simulated the aggregate motion of a flock of birds while using distributed rules for each bird. The implemented model for this simulation is traditionally named the Boids model.

The Boids model is a distributed behavioral model [8] for flocks of flying birds or fish schools. It shares many characteristics with particle systems – large sets of individual items, each with its own behavior – but has several crucial differences. Traditional particle systems are usually employed to model fire, smoke, or water. Each particle is created, ages, and finally dies, and is generally denoted by a point-like structure. In a boids simulation however, individual boids have a geometrical shape and, consequently, describe an orientation. Additionally, typical particles do not interact between themselves as opposed to e.g. a bird which must do so in order to flock appropriately.

Boids models are often referred to as a prime example of Artificial Life [1]. They illustrate a variety of principles which appear in natural systems, such as *emergence* where complex behavior comes from the local interaction of simple rules. Another example is *unpredictability*. Although a bird usually does not behave chaotically in a temporally local context, it is difficult or near impossible to predict its behavior on a larger time scale.

A natural flock has certain behavioral rules that allows it to exist and survive. For instance, birds tend to avoid collisions with other birds but still stay close to the flock in order to protect the whole flock against predators. We impose such possibly contradictory rules on our simulated boids to induce seemingly natural flocking behaviors. The basic rules are:

- Collision Avoidance: avoid collisions with nearby flock members
- Velocity Matching: attempt to match velocity with nearby flock members
- Flock Centering: attempt to stay close to nearby flock members

Each behavior rule produces an *acceleration* which is a contribution to a tunable weighted average. The relative strength of each rule will dictate the general behavior of the flock. For example, if the flock centering behavior has a very low impact then the flock will be very sparse while it will still follow a common direction.

Since the model attempts to simulate the movement of birds, it must be based on a semi-realistic model of flight. It does not need to take in consideration all physical forces like aerodynamic drag or even gravity but it must limit the velocity and instantaneous accelerations to realistic values. These restrictions help modeling creatures with finite amounts of energy.

Fig. 3. A frame of the Boids Visualizer with 2176 birds

3.1 Evaluation

We developed two distinct versions of the simulation. One incorporates the capabilities of our SpiNNaker Chip Computing Module to simulate the boids model which is described above, the other does not and executes the simulation on a standard desktop computer. Both implementations use a desktop computer to visualize the simulation results. The differences between the two simulations can be directly inspected with this approach. A screenshot of the simulation is shown in Figure 3 and video of the simulation can be found online at https://www.youtube.com/watch?v=KiyhVRgxugY. The method used for the evaluation is as follows:

- select a number of birds for the simulation.
- run the simulation on the SpiNNaker Chip Computing Module, and record the frames per second (FPS) of the visualization.
- run the simulation on the computer and, again, record the frames per second.

The results of this benchmark are compiled in Table 2. The central processing unit (CPU) of the computer used for running this simulation was an AMD Phenom II X4 945 running at 3 GHz.

The $O(N^2)$ complexity of the algorithm is clearly visible in the results. The increase of the number of birds leads to an ever increasing reduction of the frame rate. The version that uses the SpiNNaker Chip Computing Module also suffers from a reduction in the frame rate due to the shear number of objects it has to represent. The graphics code was not optimized to handle a large number of birds, but as it is the same code for both versions, the rendering time is negligible. The upper limit of 60 frames per second is due to the monitor's internal refresh rate setting.

Clearly, the SpiNNaker Chip Computing Module is advantageous. The simulation delivers higher frame rates when using the module when compared to the desktop version of the simulation.

Table 2. Frames per second for the simulation with and without the SpiNNaker Chip Computing Module (SCCM)

Number of birds	FPS on SCCM	FPS on Desktop Computer
2176	60	60
4352	59	30
6528	43	15

4   Summary and Conclusions

We developed hardware and software for a novel module consisting of a single SpiNNaker chip and an auxiliary microcontroller. The system can simulate huge neural networks but still has a very low power consumption. In fact, its real-time I/O capabilities with limited power requirements make it highly suitable for mobile power efficient systems. This point is even more emphasized by the module's small size. Furthermore, our module is designed to be easily extendable by other SpiNNaker Chip Computing Modules or by other SpiNNaker systems. We demonstrated the capabilities of one single module using a boids simulation. The evaluation shows that our system is capable of simulating large numbers of distributed items. Hence, the module is ideal to simulate large networks of artificial neurons.

We are currently working on a version which is even further reduced in size. It will thus be able to use the module on tiny robots, in neuroprosthetics, or multiple connected modules to simulate even larger artificial neural networks with only little space consumption.

Acknowledgments. This project would not have been possible without the precious help from Steve Temple, Luis Plana and Francesco Gallupi from the University of Manchester who supplied the SpiNNaker chips and provided essential guidance while studying the SpiNNaker system.

References

1. Bedau, M.A.: Artificial life: organization, adaptation and complexity from the bottom up. Trends in Cognitive Sciences 7(11), 505–512 (2003)
2. Brotherson, S.: Understanding Brain Development in Young Children (April 2009), http://www.ag.ndsu.edu/pubs/yf/famsci/fs609.pdf
3. Choudhary, S., et al.: Silicon neurons that compute. In: Villa, A.E.P., Duch, W., Érdi, P., Masulli, F., Palm, G. (eds.) ICANN 2012, Part I. LNCS, vol. 7552, pp. 121–128. Springer, Heidelberg (2012)
4. Denk, C., Llobet-Blandino, F., Galluppi, F., Plana, L., Furber, S., Conradt, J.: Real-time interface board for closed-loop robotic tasks on the spinnaker neural computing system. In: Mladenov, V., Koprinkova-Hristova, P., Palm, G., Villa, A.E.P., Appollini, B., Kasabov, N. (eds.) ICANN 2013. LNCS, vol. 8131, pp. 467–474. Springer, Heidelberg (2013)
5. Furber, S., Brown, A.: Biologically-inspired massively-parallel architectures - computing beyond a million processors. In: Ninth International Conference on Application of Concurrency to System Design, ACSD 2009, pp. 3–12 (2009)
6. Nguyen, T.: Total number of synapses in the adult human neocortex. Journal of Mathematical Modeling: One + Two 3(1) (2010)
7. Pfeil, T., Grübl, A., Jeltsch, S., Müller, E., Müller, P., Petrovici, M.A., Schmuker, M., Brüderle, D., Schemmel, J., Meier, K.: Six networks on a universal neuromorphic computing substrate. ArXiv e-prints (October 2012)
8. Reynolds, C.W.: Flocks, herds and schools: A distributed behavioral model. SIGGRAPH Comput. Graph. 21(4), 25–34 (1987)

The Importance of Physiological Noise Regression in High Temporal Resolution fMRI

Norman Scheel[1,2], Catie Chang[3], and Amir Madany Mamlouk[1]

[1] University of Lübeck,
Institute for Neuro- and Bioinformatics, Germany
[2] Graduate School for Computing in Medicine and Life Sciences,
Ratzeburger Allee 160, 23562 Lübeck, Germany
[3] National Institutes of Health, Advanced MRI (AMRI),
10 Center Dr., Bethesda, MD 20892-1065, USA
norman.scheel@neuro.uni-luebeck.de,
catie.chang@nih.gov, madany@inb.uni-luebeck.de
http://www.inb.uni-luebeck.de, http://www.amri.ninds.nih.gov,
http://www.gradschool.uni-luebeck.de

Abstract. Recently a new technique called multiband imaging was introduced, it allows extremely low repetition times for functional magnetic resonance imaging (fMRI). As these ultra fast imaging scans can increase the Nyquist rate by an order of magnitude, there are many new effects, that have to be accounted for. As more frequencies can now be sampled directly, we want to analyze especially those that are due to physiological noise, such as cardiac and respiratory signals. Here, we adapted RETROICOR [4] to handle multiband fMRI data. We show the importance of physiological noise regression for standard temporal resolution fMRI and compare it to the high temporal resolution case. Our results show that especially for multiband fMRI scans, it is of the utmost importance to apply physiological noise regression, as residuals of these noises are clearly detectable in non noise independent components if no prior physiological noise has been applied.

Keywords: RETROICOR, ICA, SOCK, multiband fMRI, resting-state, physiological noise.

1 Introduction

During the last years, recordings of brain activity at rest, so called resting-state fMRI [1] has drawn more and more attention, as these experiments are not limited to a predefined task setup. Recently a new technique called multiband imaging was introduced [2]: While enabling imaging at extremely low repetition times (TR) only minor signal quality impairments are the tradeoff. TRs below 1s can easily be reached with a multiband factor of 4, meaning simultaneous recording of four slices. Using ultra fast imaging in fMRI may provide additional power for studying temporal processes that underlie brain function [3]. Here it is of the utmost importance to filter nuisance signals, e.g. heart rate or breathing,

S. Wermter et al. (Eds.): ICANN 2014, LNCS 8681, pp. 829–836, 2014.

as these may lead to false correlations in higher level analyses. This is already important for standard fMRI, as even for slow sampling rates aliasing takes place. With multiband imaging approaching the nyquist rate of these signals, this work emphasizes the importance of physiological noise regression and proposes an extended version of RETROICOR-RVHR [4] that also can be used with multiband data.

2   Materials and Methods

2.1   The Dataset

We used a public dataset, kindly shared by NKI, Orangeburg, NY [5]: The Enhanced Rockland Community Sample. It provides diverse scanning protocols, simultaneous recording of cardiac and respiratory signals and a large number of subjects. Up until now there are four releases of this data set. In the following we will use the third release, it provides data of 46 subjects of which we had to discard 9 subjects, due to incomplete or erroneous recordings, leaving 37 subjects for our analyses (19 female and 18 male). As a community sample, the age span of participants was quiet large: mean age was 38 years with a standard deviation of 15 years. Of all the fMRI sessions provided in the data set of every participant, we focused on the following two resting-state sessions: a session with standard temporal resolution (STR), meaning 120 volumes which were recorded with a TR of 2.5s and one session with high temporal resolution (HTR), meaning 900 volumes which were recorded with multiband factor 4 and a TR of 0.645s. Both sessions were acquired using an isotropic voxel resolution of 3mm.

2.2   Physiological Noise Regression

As a first step, we adapted RETROICOR-RVHR to enable multiband data handling. Exact slice timing is fundamentally important for this regression step and standard implementations of RETROICOR calculate the timing information using slice order and TR. For multiband an interleaved slice order with simultaneous acquired slices needs to be accounted for. As scanning procedures may vary due to different implementations (multiband is not a standard for MRI manufactures yet), we adapted RETROICOR to handle the exact timing information from the scanning protocol, this way the exact slice times do not need to be calculated but can be entered directly for further processing.

2.3   Preprocessing

To compare the effects of RETROICOR, we used the physiological noise regressed data set as well as the raw data set without physiological noise regression and applied the following preprocessing steps on both equally. Prior to every following preprocessing step, we manually reoriented all subject scans and set the origin to the anterior commissure. Then we used FSL-BET [6] for brain extraction, to remove all non-brain tissues. As a following step we applied FSL standard motion correction, a high pass filter at 100s and 4mm smoothing.

Overall, this procedure results in four different base data sets: for the High Temporal Resolution (HTR) session (multiband) once with Physiological Noise Regression (PNR) applied and once without (RAW). The same also applies to the Standard Temporal Resolution (STR). In short: HTR-PNR, HTR-RAW, STR-PNR and STR-RAW.

2.4   ICA and Component Selection

Using the FSL toolbox, we then performed a probabilistic single subject ICA with automatic dimensionality estimation to extract the independent components of the resting-state fMRI signal [6].

In addition, we used a novel method for the automatic identification of artifactual ICs from resting-state fMRI data called "Spatially Organized Component

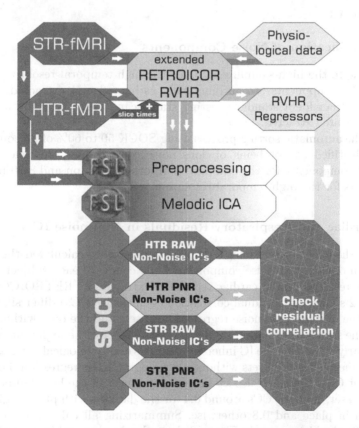

Fig. 1. Processing Pipeline - Standard Temporal Resolution (STR) and High Temporal Resolution (HTR) fMRI with Physiological Noise Regression (PNR) or without (RAW)

Klassifikator"(SOCK). It uses the spatial and temporal information of the extracted independent components to classify them into noise and non-noise categories. It offers high accuracies and very low false positive rates [7].

2.5   Residual Correlations with Physiological Recordings

After the automatic sorting process, we compared the residual correlation of the physiological signals with the time-courses of the non-noise ICs, for all four preprocessing branches. This is done through calculating the correlation of the cardiac and respiratory regressors, extracted via RETROICOR with the time-courses of all non-noise components of each single subject. As RETROICOR regressors are voxel-specific and voxel coordinates are not preserved during preprocessing we used the full subspace of RETROICOR sinusoids to extract residual correlations with the IC time courses.

Figure 1 gives an overview over our complete processing pipeline.

3   Results

3.1   Identification of Noise Components

Mainly due to the high sampling rate, for the high temporal resolution dataset usually 130 components are automatically estimated and extracted, which is a lot more than for a standard resting state scan, where typically around 50 components are extracted.

After the automatic sorting process using SOCK 50 to 60% of all components can be identified as not being obvious noise components. This leads to ~30 non noise components for the standard temporal resolution and ~70 non noise components for the high temporal resolution.

3.2   Cardiac and Respiratory Residuals in Non-noise IC's

To assess the effect of physiological noise regression we calculated the residual correlation of each non-noise components time course of each subject with the individual respiratory and cardiac regressors extracted by RETROICOR.

Figure 2 shows that residual correlation coefficients (CCs) differ significantly between the physiological noise regressed data sets and the ones without. Mean CCs for the standard temporal resolution, as well as for the high temporal resolution clearly show that the IC inherent residuals of physiological noise are significantly higher in the data sets without physiological noise regression. Looking at the highest CCs, there are also significant differences in the high temporal resolution data set, showing CCs around 0.4 for the data set with physiological noise regression in place and 0.8 otherwise. Summarizing all calculated correlation coefficients, the histograms in Figure 2 show clearly, that residuals of physiological noise present in non noise components are significantly higher without prior regression of these signals.

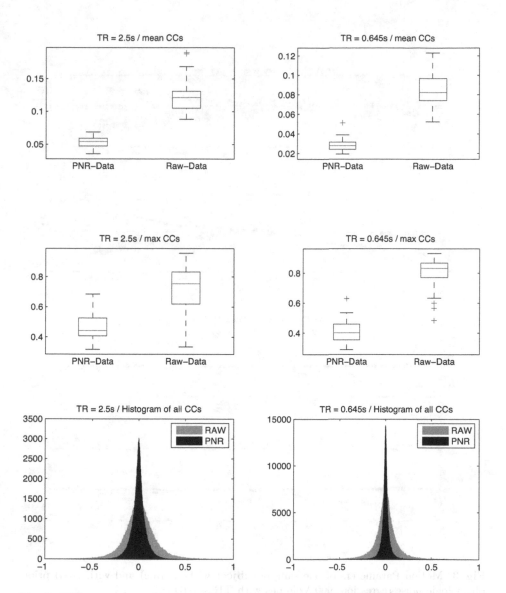

Fig. 2. Differences in residual correlation coefficients (CCs) for the physiological noise regressed data sets and the ones without

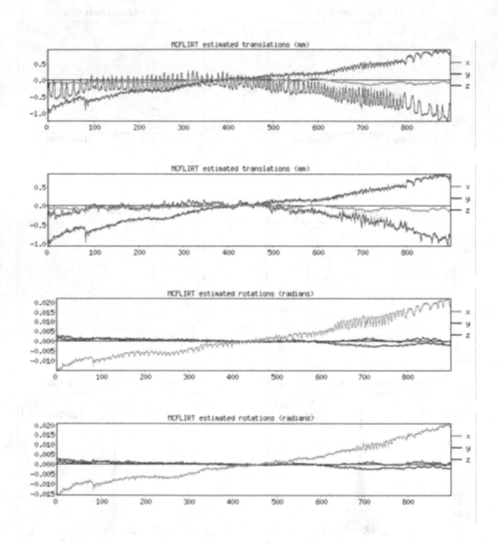

Fig. 3. Motion Parameters of one sample subject without (a,c) and with (b,d) prior physiologic noise regression. 900 Volumes with TR = 0.645s.

3.3   Motion Parameters

When checking motion parameters after realignment for the high temporal resolution data set, we found that physiological noise, esp. respiration has a tremendous effect on the data. Figure 3 illustrates the artifacts for an exemplary subject. It displays that respiration could actually be sampled using motion parameters at this high temporal resolution. The repetitive motion along the Z axis with a frequency of three to four per minute most likely shows in- and exhaling artifacts, which can be filtered out using physiological noise regression.

4   Discussion

As the results show, physiological noise regression is extremely important, for standard temporal resolution fMRI and even more so for high temporal resolution fMRI. Components which are not associated with physiological noise still display residuals of cardiac and respiratory signals. This is very interesting since it is widely accepted that if noise components have been discarded, all noise in the data set has been ruled out. This is clearly not the case and should be kept in mind. It is debatable if motion correction is enough for compensation of respiratory noise in the HTR-fMRI signal, as seen in Figure 3, as motion correction only handles some of the artifact associated with RETROICOR. For STR-fMRI respiratory regressors should definitely be considerd.

Cardiac associated noise, on the other hand, can only be minimized by using some kind of physiological noise regression prior to preprocessing as those artifacts will not be corrected using motion correction. Here we chose RETROICOR-RVHR and adapted it for the multiband recording scenario. The results show that data quality is significantly enhanced with this algorithm. We recommend this step to become a standard procedure in every fMRI preprocessing routine.

References

1. Biswal, B.B.: Resting state fMRI: A personal history. NeuroImage 62(2), 938–944 (2012)
2. Feinberg, D.A., Yacoub, E.: The rapid development of high speed, resolution and precision in fMRI. NeuroImage 62(2), 720–725 (2012)
3. Smith, S.M., Miller, K.L., Moeller, S., Xu, J., Auerbach, E.J., Woolrich, M.W., Beckmann, C.F., Jenkinson, M., Andersson, J., Glasser, M.F., Van Essen, D.C., Feinberg, D.A., Yacoub, E.S., Ugurbil, K.: Temporally-independent functional modes of spontaneous brain activity. Proceedings of the National Academy of Sciences of the United States of America 109(8), 3131–3136 (2012)
4. Chang, C., Cunningham, J.P., Glover, G.H.: Influence of heart rate on the BOLD signal: the cardiac response function. NeuroImage 44(3), 857–869 (2009)

5. Nooner, K.B., Colcombe, S.J., Tobe, R.H., Mennes, M., Benedict, M.M., Moreno, A.L., Panek, L.J., Brown, S., Zavitz, S.T., Li, Q., Sikka, S., Gutman, D., Bangaru, S., Schlachter, R.T., Kamiel, S.M., Anwar, A.R., Hinz, C.M., Kaplan, M.S., Rachlin, A.B., Adelsberg, S., Cheung, B., Khanuja, R., Yan, C., Craddock, C.C., Calhoun, V., Courtney, W., King, M., Wood, D., Cox, C.L., Kelly, A.M.C., Di Martino, A., Petkova, E., Reiss, P.T., Duan, N., Thomsen, D., Biswal, B., Coffey, B., Hoptman, M.J., Javitt, D.C., Pomara, N., Sidtis, J.J., Koplewicz, H.S., Castellanos, F.X., Leventhal, B.L., Milham, M.P.: The NKI-Rockland Sample: A Model for Accelerating the Pace of Discovery Science in Psychiatry. Frontiers in Neuroscience 6, 152 (2012)
6. Jenkinson, M., Beckmann, C.F., Behrens, T.E.J., Woolrich, M.W., Smith, S.M.: Fsl. NeuroImage 62, 782–790 (2011)
7. Bhaganagarapu, K., Jackson, G.D., Abbott, D.F.: An automated method for identifying artifact in independent component analysis of resting-state FMRI. Frontiers in human Neuroscience 7, 343 (2013)

Development of Automated Diagnostic System for Skin Cancer: Performance Analysis of Neural Network Learning Algorithms for Classification

Ammara Masood, Adel Ali Al-Jumaily, and Tariq Adnan

School of Electrical, Mechanical and Mechatronic Engineering,
University of Technology, Sydney, Australia
ammara.masood@student.uts.edu.au, Adel.Ali-Jumaily@uts.edu.au,
engr_tariq_adnan@yahoo.com

Abstract. Melanoma is the most deathly of all skin cancers but early diagnosis can ensure a high degree of survival. Early diagnosis is one of the greatest challenges due to lack of experience of general practitioners (GPs). In this paper we present a clinical decision support system designed for general practitioners, aimed at saving time and resources in the diagnostic process. Segmentation, pattern recognition, and change detection are the important steps in our approach. This paper also investigates the performance of Artificial Neural Network (ANN) learning algorithms for skin cancer diagnosis. The capabilities of three learning algorithms i.e. Levenberg-Marquardt (LM), Resilient Back propagation (RP), Scaled Conjugate Gradient (SCG) algorithms in differentiating melanoma and benign lesions are studied and their performances are compared. The results show that Levenberg-Marquardt algorithm was quick and efficient in figuring out benign lesions with specificity 95.1%, while SCG algorithm gave better results in detecting melanoma at the cost of more number of epochs with sensitivity 92.6%.

Keywords: Neural Network, Diagnostic systems, Segmentation, Feature extraction, Classification.

1 Introduction

Malignant melanoma is rapidly increasing in Europe, North America, and Australia [1]. An estimated 76,250 new cases of invasive melanoma were diagnosed in the US in 2012, with an estimated 9,180 resulting in death. Over 1,890 Australians die from skin cancer each year [2]. Skin cancer treatment is expensive. In 2001, it was estimated the treatment of non-melanoma skin cancer cost $264 million and melanoma $30 million. But early diagnosis can make the situation better as melanoma has near 95% cure rate if diagnosed and treated early. Dermatologist's data indicate that even in specialized centers visual diagnostic accuracy is not high, and they are also overloaded by GP referrals.

S. Wermter et al. (Eds.): ICANN 2014, LNCS 8681, pp. 837–844, 2014.

Computerized diagnostic tools are necessary to be used as a standalone warning tools for helping the GPs in early diagnosis and to provide quantitative information about lesion for experts to be considered during biopsy decision making. Diagnostic tools demand efficient image processing, segmentation and feature extraction and classification algorithms. As discussed in [3] detailed research is necessary to make the best choice and setting benchmarks for diagnostic system development and validation. Our research is intended to come up with a best combination of algorithms which can form a basis of generalized and accurate skin cancer diagnostic system.

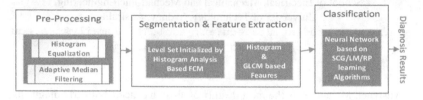

Fig. 1. Computer Aided Diagnostic Support System

The diagnostic model used in this study is shown in Fig. 1.Adaptive median filtering and histogram equalization is done in pre-processing stage to reduce the ill effects in skin images. It is followed by the detection of the lesion by histogram based fuzzy C mean thresholding algorithm that we proposed in [4]. This algorithm provided efficient segmentation results as compared to other segmentation results used in literature [5]. Once the lesion is localized, different intensity and texture based features is quantified using gray level co-occurrence matrix. Finally, artificial neural network is used for classification of cancerous and non-cancerous skin lesions. In this paper, we investigated the performance of three most popular ANN learning algorithms i.e. Levenberg-Marquardt (LM), Resilient Back propagation (RP), Scaled Conjugate Gradient (SCG). These algorithms are compared based on their generalization and prediction performances during training and testing respectively.

This paper is organized as follows: Section 2 describes the computer-aided diagnosing (CAD) which consists of the pre-processing, segmentation, the features extraction and classification. Section 3 presents the experimental set up. Performance Analysis is done in Section 4, and finally section for conclusions and future work.

2   Material and Methods

2.1   Experimental Data Set

A clinical database of color dermoscopic and clinical view lesion images were obtained from varies sources but most images came from the Sydney Melanoma Diagnostic Centre, Royal Prince Alfred Hospital and Hôpital Charles Nicolle CHU Rouen, France. The images have been stored in the RGB color format having different dimensions which were rescaled to a resolution of 150x150 with bit depth 24 and size around 68KB. Since we had no control over the image acquisition and camera calibration, images that had at least one of the following problems were omitted from the study: (i) the lesion that does not fit entirely within the image frame, (ii) presence of too much hair, and (iii) insufficient contrast between the lesion and the background skin. This selectivity was necessary to ensure accurate border detection and reliable feature extraction. A total of 135 images (81 benign, 54 melanoma) free from the above mentioned problems were included in the experimental image set.

2.2   Pre-processing

For skin lesion images, there are certain extraneous artifacts such as skin texture, air bubbles, dermoscopic gel, presence of ruler markings and hair that make border detection a bit difficult. In order to reduce the effect of these artifacts on segmentation results we used adaptive median filtering and histogram equalization. Adaptive median filtering can handle high level of noise that may be present in skin lesion images and it seeks to preserve detail while smoothing non impulse noise.

2.3   Segmentation

We proposed a segmentation algorithm, histogram analysis based fuzzy C mean algorithm for Level Set initialization (H-FCM-LS) refer figure 2. Mathematical details of our proposed segmentation algorithm can be found in our research publication [6]. We found that practical significance of fuzzy clustering for multidimensional feature space is of great importance when it comes to diagnosis. A deterministic misclassification can be very costly and a sophisticated thresholding procedure is required for increasing accuracy of segmentation. In the proposed method, histogram analysis of image was done to see average intensity distribution in images and then hard threshold was selected between classes with dominant intensity value. This method solves the difficulty that may arise in finding effective threshold automatically for different images regardless of intensity variety. This method was further used for initializing complex segmentation method like Level set having spatial information. Segmentation and thresholding results for some of the skin lesion images are shown in figure 2.

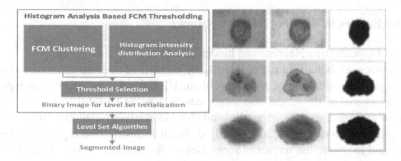

Fig. 2. Block Diagram & Results of Segmentation Algorithm (H-FCM-LS)

2.4   Feature Extraction

When performing analysis of skin lesions it is difficult to obtain a general mathematical model for various textures because of the large variation in their properties. Though texture plays a significant role in image analysis and pattern recognition, only a few architectures implement on board textural feature extraction [7].

In this paper, we used both histogram based features and texture-based features which are consequently used for classification. Histogram based features include; Mean, Variance, Standard deviation, Skewness, Energy and Entropy.

GLCM (Grey Level Co-occurrence Matrix) provides one of the most popular statistical methods in analysis of grey tones in an image [8].The GLCM functions characterize texture of an image by calculating how often pairs of pixel with specific values and in a specified spatial relationship occur in an image, creating a GLCM, and then extracting statistical measures from this matrix [9]. The GLCM features that we have selected for classification stage include Autocorrelation, Contrast, Correlation, Cluster Prominence, Cluster shade, Dissimilarity, Energy, Entropy, Homogeneity, Maximum probability, Difference variance, Difference entropy, Inverse difference normalized, Inverse difference moment normalized, Information measure of correlation and Information measure of correlation. Mathematical details can be found in [8,9,10].

2.5   Classification

There is a large variety of skin lesions with different features that can be indicative of cancer. It is complicated to develop statistical algorithms for diagnosis. In the research review on existing automated skin lesion diagnostic systems [3], it is found that neural network (NN) can perform well for diagnostic systems. Because, neural network have better capability of handling complex relationships between different parameters and making classification based on learning from training data [11]. Good training and validation of NN can lead to better diagnosis. Success in training artificial NN based on type of problem in first step depends on model architecture (the number of neurons of output and input layers, the number of layers and the neurons of hidden layer) and in the second step depends on algorithm for training network.

Effective Factors in Training Neural Networks

Number of Input/output Neurons and hidden neurons

When using ANN in different problems, the number of neurons in input and output layers is generally determined by the problem. High number of neurons in input and output layers makes the model size larger which may be harmful to learning quality and learning time. However, in applications like skin cancer diagnosis where several factors play role in diagnosis, it is usually difficult to restrict the inputs of the neural network and to ignore the impact of some factors for a better network learning. However, learning quality may improve by reducing the number of input variables, for which a choice of minimal number of important input features is necessary.

There are no rigorous rules to guide the choice of number of hidden layers and number of neurons in the hidden layers. However, more layers are not better than few, and it is generally known that a network containing few hidden neurons generalizes better than one with many neurons. Also, the best network among a number of individually trained networks is then selected by trial and error.

Algorithm of training artificial neural network

The learning algorithm for multilayer Perceptron networks is referred to as back-propagation algorithm. This was improved over time and various types of back-propagation algorithm were presented for training the network. When using artificial neural networks, the proper learning algorithm is usually determined based on internal mental medications and via trial and error method [12,13]. The Perceptron neural networks learning algorithms chosen for this study are as follows:

A. LM (Levenberg–Marquardt) algorithm [14] is an approximation to Newton's method that finds a minimum of a function that is expressed as the sum of squares of linear functions. The Newton method approximates the error of the network with a second order expression, which contrasts to the former category which follows a first order expression. LM is popular in the ANN domain, which is a very simple, but robust, method for approximating a function.

B. SCG (scaled-conjugate gradient) algorithm: Scaled conjugate gradient algorithm developed by Moller [15], was designed to avoid the time-consuming line search. The basic idea is to combine the model-trust region approach (used in the LM algorithm), with the conjugate gradient approach. SCG differs from other conjugate gradient algorithms given by Hagan et al. [13] mostly in its use of nonlinear search technique. This makes the computations decreased in a single epoch.

C. Resilient Back Propagation (RP): When sigmoid functions are used as the functions for every activity on the set of hidden layer neurons, the large numbers face problem at the network entrance because they are "squashing" functions. This problem is solved in resilient back propagation algorithm only through employing the sign of derivation to determine the direction of the weight update; the magnitude of the derivative has no effect on the weight update.

This research is mainly aimed at providing performance analysis of these learning algorithms for the case of pattern recognition for skin cancer diagnosis.

3   Experimental Set Up

A two layer feed forward network with sigmoid activation function is designed for experiments. The choice of neurons in hidden layer is made empirically through experimental analysis considering best performance accuracy in diagnosis results. For choosing the number of hidden layers and their neurons properly, we did several experiments. We started with considering proportion of the number of inputs of network. When the network didn't converge to a desired account, the number of neurons was increased. When the network converges to the same number of neurons and achieved potential for extension, then less number of neurons was experimented.

For the training purpose we used the 107 samples, 14 samples for validation and 14 samples for the testing. The training stops when a classifier gives a higher accuracy value with minimum training and testing errors. Neural Networks is implemented using MATLAB software R2013 and simulated by a system with corei5 3.10 GHz processor and 4 GB memory under Windows7 operating system.

4   Performance Analysis

For experimental analysis, several neural networks varying in the number of neurons in the hidden layer as well as different learning algorithms were generated. Measurements of the performance index (Mean Square Error), classification accuracy, and the number of epochs (number of training examples iteration) to achieve a good performance index of these networks is collected. Comparative results for different training algorithms, with respect to changing the number of neurons, in the networks training process are presented in the figures 3 and 4.

The study findings indicated that LM and SCG algorithms had close evaluation in terms of performance index (MSE) and performance accuracy, and they showed higher predictive accuracy than the BP algorithms. SCG showed relatively better accuracy than LM at the cost of more number of epochs. But as high number of epochs to reach a good performance index puts the training application of this algorithm to challenge. So keeping this idea in mind, LM outperformed the other two algorithms which is quite consistent with its performance for different other classification applications.

For analyzing the performance for our specific application of skin cancer diagnosis, it is important to have a look at the confusion matrix. Confusion matrix provides details of performance in terms of sensitivity (accurate classification of cancer), specificity (accurate classification of non-cancerous lesions) & overall accuracy.

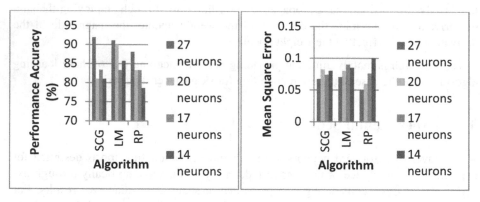

Fig. 3. Diagram of accuracy & respective performance index (MSE) in ANN training process

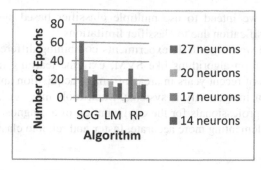

Fig. 4. Diagram of Number of epochs in the networks training process

Figure 5 shows confusion matrix for the best diagnosis performance of each training algorithm. It can be seen that the best overall classification 91.9% was obtained using SCG with sensitivity 92.6% and specificity 91.4%. The overall performance of LM was close to SCG, but it can be seen that although it worked better in detecting benign lesions specificity 95.1% but its classification efficiency for melanoma is lower than SCG (sensitivity 85.2%).While Resilience BP algorithm could acquire accuracy of 88.1%, specificity 95.1% and sensitivity 77.8%.

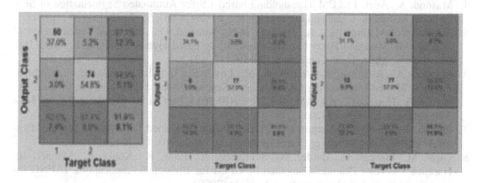

Fig. 5. Confusion Matrix for SCG , LM, RP algorithm (arranged left to right)

5   Conclusion and Future Work

In this study, a methodological approach to classification of skin lesion images is presented. Considering the capabilities of ANN in classification of complex data, performance analysis of most prominent learning algorithms is done for skin cancer diagnosis. Despite the high accuracy that can be achieved by computer aided diagnostic systems employing statistics obtained from low-level features such as the one presented here, at least two issues need to be addressed before these systems can gain greater clinical acceptance. First, higher level features such as atypical pigment networks, globules, and blue-white areas, can increase the diagnostic accuracy of computerized dermoscopy image analysis systems. Second, for developing a more reliable diagnostic system we intend to use multiple classifier based systems to undo the chances of misclassification due to classifier limitations.

For this purpose we intend to do experiments combining different neural networks and other classification algorithms like SVM, extreme learning machine. The technical achievements of recent years in areas of image acquisition and processing allow the improvement of image analysis systems. Such tools may serve as diagnostic adjuncts for medical professionals for the confirmation of a diagnosis, and can give the opportunity of implementing more accurate, faster and reliable classification systems.

References

1. Siegel, R., et al.: Cancer statistics, 2011. CA: A Cancer Journal for Clinicians 61(4), 212–236 (2011)
2. Australian, C.C.: Cancer Council to launch new research/ failure to monitor highlights cancer risk (2010), http://www.cancer.org.au/cancersmartlifestyle/SunSmart/Skincancerfactsandfigures.htm
3. Masood, A., Ali Al-Jumaily, A.: Computer Aided Diagnostic Support System for Skin Cancer: A Review of Techniques and Algorithms. International Journal of Biomedical Imaging 2013, 22 (2013)
4. Masood, A., Adel, J.: FCM Thresholding based LS for Automated Segmentation of Skin Lesions. Journal of Signal and Information Processing 4(3B), 66–71 (2013)
5. Masood, A., Al Jumaily, A.A., Hoshyar, A.N., Masood, O.: Automated segmentation of skin lesions: Modified Fuzzy C mean thresholding based level set method. In: 2013 16th International Multi Topic Conference (INMIC) (2013)
6. Masood, A., Al-Jumaily, A.A., Maali, Y.: Level Set Initialization Based on Modified Fuzzy C Means Thresholding for Automated Segmentation of Skin Lesions. In: Lee, M., Hirose, A., Hou, Z.-G., Kil, R.M. (eds.) ICONIP 2013, Part III. LNCS, vol. 8228, pp. 341–351. Springer, Heidelberg (2013)
7. Parekh, R.: Improving Texture Recognition using Combined GLCM and Wavelet Features. International Journal of Computer Applications 29(10), 41–46 (2011)
8. Gipp, M., Marcus, G., Harder, N., Suratanee, A., Rohr, K., König, R., Männer, R.: Haralick's Texture Features Computed by GPUs for Biological Applications. IAENG International Journal of Computer Science 36(1) (2009)
9. Mohanaiah, P., Sathyanarayana, P., Guru, L.: Image Texture Feature Extraction Using GLCM Approach. International Journal of Scientific and Research Publications (IJSRP) 3(5), 1–5 (2013)
10. Zulpe, N., Pawar, V.: GLCM Textural Features for Brain Tumor Classification. International Journal of Computer Science Issues 9(3), 354–359 (2012)
11. Lau, H.T., Al-Jumaily, A.: Intelligent Automatically Early Detection of Skin Cancer: Study Based on Neural Network Classification. In: International Conference on Soft Computing and Pattern Recognition, SoCPaR 2009 (2009)
12. Dreiseitl, S., et al.: A Comparison of Machine Learning Methods for the Diagnosis of Pigmented Skin Lesions. Journal of Biomedical Informatics 34(1), 28–36 (2001)
13. Hagan, M.T., Demuth, H.B., Beal, M.H.: Neutral network design. PWS, Beston (2003)
14. Ayat, S., Mehdi, H.A.F., Alian, M., Marquardt, D.W.: an algorithm for Least-SquareEstimation of Nonlinear Parameters. SIAM Journal on Applied MAthematics 11(2), 431–441 (1963)
15. Moller, M.F.: A scaled conjugate gradient algorithm for fast supervised learning. Neural Networks 6, 525–533 (1993)

Entrepreneurship Support Based on Mixed Bio-Artificial Neural Network Simulator (ESBBANN)

Eugenio M. Fedriani and Manuel Chaves-Maza

Dpt. Economía, Métodos Cuantitativos e Historia Económica,
Pablo de Olavide University of Seville, Spain
{efedmar,mchaves}@upo.es

Abstract. Based on large global databases of support entities for entrepreneurship and their experienced technical staff, a simulation model has been built to predict the potential level for growth and prospects of success for entrepreneurs and companies that ask for public support, in order to adapt services and technical recommendations, to implant a money-saving policy and improving probabilities of economic and financial sustainability.

Keywords: entrepreneurship, artificial neural network, mixed bio-artificial, support, entrepreneurship policy, big data, entrepreneur, artificial intelligence, survival, success, sponsorship, incubated firms.

1   Introduction

Most entities that support entrepreneurs have the same problem in the normal course of their activity: the lack of a correct identification of potential entrepreneurship and a precise detection of capacities and skills profile. In general, they would like to make their service more user-centric. There is a vast amount of information, but the technical support is never able to make correct use of it. We propose a design of Neural Network (NN) that comprises at least one artificial (informatics engineered) component combined with a biological one: the technical staff of support entities for entrepreneurship. We split this NN into two parts[1]:

- **Artificial.** An objective data set has been used to build an Artificial NN (ANN).
- Entrepreneur and project information: an objective, accurate and reliable piece of information that was collected by some entrepreneurship support entities. We handle up more than 40,000 entrepreneurs and 920 variables from 1999 to 2013.
- Environment: a large database of any possible relevant information is included. Official statistics and other data collections which are relevant for entrepreneurs have been used.

Biological. Based on experience and subjective information that has been collected by technical staff of support entities, a Biological Neural Network (BNN) has been defined and connected with our ANN.

---

[1] See Figure 1.

S. Wermter et al. (Eds.): ICANN 2014, LNCS 8681, pp. 845–846, 2014.

- Technical support information: a subjective piece of data that can be collected by any technical support staff of the entrepreneur or the company. We have designed models based on NNs to explain the relationships between any subjective variable and the other groups of variables (entrepreneur variables, project information and environment aspects).

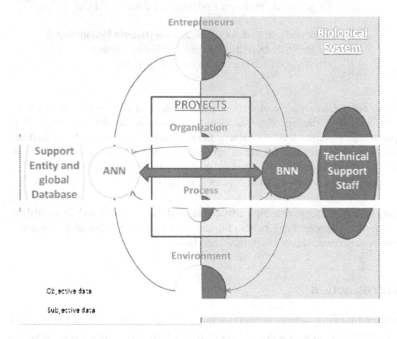

Fig. 1. Operation scheme of entrepreneurship support based on mixed bio-artificial neural network simulator. ANN: Artificial Neural Network. BNN: Biological neural Network.

2   Approach Demonstration

The simulator has been developed by designing an appropriate algorithm and it has been implemented by using the statistical software included into the computational package MATHEMATICA 9. The final results have been adapted to different environments through its Computable Document Format (CDF).

First, different ANN helps us decide the relevant variables, according to their influence over the success for the entrepreneur. Then, another ANN determined the main connections between relevant variables. The final NN integrates all the groups of variables, including them in an algorithm after the corresponding training process.

To authors' knowledge, it is the first time that a mixed neural network model is constructed to predict success for entrepreneurship with more than 95% of accurate predictions. We think this model can be adapted and applied to other situations.

Live Demonstration: Real-Time Motor Rotation Frequency Detection by Spike-Based Visual and Auditory Sensory Fusion on AER and FPGA*

Antonio Rios-Navarro, Angel Jimenez-Fernandez, Elena Cerezuela-Escudero,
Manuel Rivas, Gabriel Jimenez-Moreno, and Alejandro Linares-Barranco

Robotic and Technology of Computers Lab, University of Seville, Spain
arios@atc.us.es

Abstract. Multisensory fusion is commonly used in various areas of robotic and also for the neuromorphic engineering community to collect information from an environment using different and complementary types of sensor. This demonstration shows a scenario where the motor rotation frequency is obtained using a DVS retina chip (Dynamic Vision Sensor) and a binaural auditory system on FPGA that mimics a biological cochlea. Both are spike-based sensors with Address-Event-Representation (AER) output. A new AER monitor hardware interface allows two operation modes: real-time (up to 5 Mevps through USB2.0) and off-line (up to 20Mevps and 33.5Mev stored in DDR RAM).

Keywords: Address-Event-Representation, spike, neuromorphic engineering, vision, DVS, retina, cochlea, sensor fusion.

1 Introduction

Several works about spike-based vision and auditory fusion (1,2) have been published in order to present the advantages of spike-based multisensory fusion. This demonstration consists of the system shown in the scheme (fig 1). A circle of metal with a shape drawn is mounted on a DC motor that will be rotating while DVS and binaural cochlea (3) are capturing information from the scene. The two spike-based sensors information are transmitted on board where both are merged and sent to the controller board. Two operation modes are implemented in this controller board: *real-time*, in which all information received from the sensor is timestamped and sent to the jAER(4) application through USB 2.0 board interface; and *off-line*, where sensor information is stored in DDR2 RAM memory, together with precise temporal information, allowing later processing in a PC by downloading it from DDR2.

The captured sensor information is computed in the jAER application to estimate the motor rotation frequency.

2 Hardware Involved

The components used in this demonstration are: a DC motor with a metal circle; a DVS retina; a binaural auditory system that mimics a cochlea; a merger AER board; and the XEM 6010 Opal Kelly board.

---

* This work has been supported by BIOSENSE (TEC2012-37868-C04-02/01).

S. Wermter et al. (Eds.): ICANN 2014, LNCS 8681, pp. 847–848, 2014.

The CPLD located at merger AER board joins in its output the two AER sensors information, which are differenced by most significant bit of event addresses. The new Datalogger/Player circuit captures this information. It is implemented on the Opal Kelly Spartan 6 FPGA. As discussed above, DataLogger/Player circuit allows two operations mode: *real-time* and *off-line*.

In *real-time* mode, the AER data stream from the AER Merge board is time-stamped and sent to a PC directly through a USB 2.0 interface. The maximum amount of information captured can be up to 5 Mevps. This limitation is due to the bottleneck of the USB 2.0 interface.

In *off-line* mode the maximum amount of information captured by the system is higher (about 20 Mevps) because the events are time-stamped and stored immediately in DDR2 memory where the FPGA-DDR2 interface is faster than USB 2.0 interface. Opal Kelly's DDR2 memory has a capacity for 33.5 Mevents.

For both methods the DataLogger/Player circuit splits retina and cochlea data into two different USB EndPoints. In jAER application the information is read from these EndPoints and the motor rotation frequency is estimated combining results from two sensors. Both visual and auditory information will give in parallel two estimation results. They are fused and combined by taking the average.

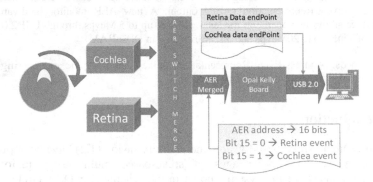

Fig. 1. Complete demonstration scheme in which is shown the information flow. The two yellow rectangles correspond to the two sensor data endpoints.

3   Visitors Experience

Visitors can interact with the system by changing, through a microcontroller, the motor rotation frequency and the DVS and binaural cochlea position, while they are capturing events to estimate the motor frequency.

References

1. O'Connor, P., et al.: Real-time classification and sensor fusion with a spiking deep belief network. Frontiers in Neuroscience 7(178) (2013)
2. Yue-Sek, C.V., et al.: Neuromorphic Audio-Visual Sensor Fusion on a Sound-Localising Robot. Frontiers in Neuroscience 6(21) (2012)
3. Jimenez-Fernandez, A., et al.: On AER Binaural Cochlea for FPGA: design, synthesis and experimental analysis. Sensors, under revision (2014)
4. jAER Open-Source Software Project, http://jaer.wiki.sourceforge.net/

Author Index